2006 | WORLD DEVELOPMENT INDICATORS

Manufactured in the United States of America
First printing April 2006

This volume is a product of the staff of the Development Data Group of the World Bank's Development Economics Vice Presidency, and the judgments herein do not necessarily reflect the views of the World Bank's Board of Executive Directors or the countries they represent.

The World Bank does not guarantee the accuracy of the data included in this publication and accepts no responsibility whatsoever for any consequence of their use. The boundaries, colors, denominations, and other information shown on any map in this volume do not imply on the part of the World Bank any judgment on the legal status of any territory or the endorsement or acceptance of such boundaries. This publication uses the Robinson projection for maps, which represents both area and shape reasonably well for most of the earth's surface. Nevertheless, some distortions of area, shape, distance, and direction remain.

Photo credits: Front cover, from top to bottom, Shaida Badiee/World Bank, Mark Edwards/Still Pictures, World Bank photo library, and Digital Vision.

If you have questions or comments about this product, please contact:

Development Data Center
The World Bank
1818 H Street NW, Room MC2-812, Washington, D.C. 20433 USA
Hotline: 800 590 1906 or 202 473 7824; fax 202 522 1498
Email: data@worldbank.org
Web site: www.worldbank.org or www.worldbank.org/data

ISBN 0-8213-6470-7

2006 WORLD DEVELOPMENT INDICATORS

THE WORLD BANK

FOREWORD

The developing world has made remarkable progress. The number of people living in extreme poverty on less than $1 a day has fallen by about 400 million in the last 25 years. Many more children, particularly girls, are completing primary school. Illiteracy rates have fallen by half in 30 years. And life expectancy is nearly 15 years longer, on average, than it was 40 years ago.

These often spectacular achievements have put many countries securely on track to meet the Millennium Development Goals by 2015. But many others are being left behind, and for them progress in eradicating poverty and improving living standards remains stubbornly slow. In Sub-Saharan Africa the number of people living on less than $1 a day has nearly doubled since 1981. Every day thousands of people, many of them children, still die from preventable diseases. AIDS, malaria, and simple dehydration ravage the developing world.

Reaching the Millennium Development Goals is a challenge that depends on having access to the best information available. In designing policies and targeting resources, we need to know how many people are poor and where they live. We need vital information about them, such as their gender, age, and the nature of their work or, indeed, if they have work. We also need to know whether they have access to health care, schools, and safe water. And because economic growth is essential to poverty reduction, we need to know more about the economy, the business environment, the expected demographic trends, the scale of environmental degradation, and the infrastructure services available, among many other statistics.

Since 1978 *World Development Indicators* has compiled statistics to provide an annual snapshot of progress in the developing world and the challenges that remain. It is the product of intensive collaboration with numerous international organizations, government agencies, and private and nongovernmental organizations. Our collective efforts have greatly improved the coverage and reliability of statistics on poverty and development. But more is needed.

Better statistics are of value to us all. They allow us to assess the scope of the problems we face and measure progress in solving them. They make politicians and policymakers more accountable. They discourage arbitrariness, corruption, and reliance on anecdotal evidence. But they are costly to produce. Improving our knowledge base will require sustained investment, backed by a sustained commitment by national governments and international agencies. To achieve the ambitious targets we have set ourselves, we must scale up our efforts to produce reliable statistics that will inform public policy, guide debate, and strengthen the effectiveness of development efforts.

Paul D. Wolfowitz
President
The World Bank Group

ACKNOWLEDGMENTS

This book and its companion volumes, *Little Data Book* and *The Little Green Data Book*, are prepared by a team led by Eric Swanson and comprising Awatif Abuzeid, Mehdi Akhlaghi, David Cieslikowski, Mahyar Eshragh-Tabary, Richard Fix, Amy Heyman, Masako Hiraga, Raymond Muhula, M. H. Saeed Ordoubadi, Sulekha Patel, Juan Carlos Rodriguez, Changqing Sun, K. M. Vijayalakshmi, and Vivienne Wang, working closely with other teams in the Development Economics Vice Presidency's Development Data Group. The CD-ROM development team included Azita Amjadi, Ramgopal Erabelly, Saurabh Gupta, Reza Farivari, and William Prince. The work was carried out under the management of Shaida Badiee.

The choice of indicators and text content was shaped through close consultation with and substantial contributions from staff in five of the World Bank's thematic networks—Environmentally and Socially Sustainable Development, Human Development, Poverty Reduction and Economic Management, Private Sector Development, and Infrastructure—and staff of the International Finance Corporation and the Multilateral Investment Guarantee Agency. Most important, the team received substantial help, guidance, and data from external partners. For individual acknowledgments of contributions to the book's content, please see *Credits*. For a listing of our key partners, see *Partners*.

Communications Development Incorporated provided overall design direction, editing, and layout, led by Meta de Coquereaumont and Bruce Ross-Larson, with the assistance of Christopher Trott. The editing and production team consisted of Jodi Baxter, Brendon Boyle, Michael Diavolikis, Timothy Walker, and Elaine Wilson. Communications Development's London partner, Grundy & Northedge, provided art direction and design. Staff from External Affairs oversaw publication and dissemination of the book.

PREFACE

In the 10 years that we have been producing the *World Development Indicators*, the world of development statistics has grown larger and deeper. It has also become better integrated. The demand for statistics to measure progress and demonstrate the effectiveness of development programs has stimulated growing interest in the production and dissemination of statistics. And not just in the traditional domains of debt, demographics, and national accounts, but in new areas such as biodiversity, information, communications, technology, and measures of government and business performance. In response *World Development Indicators* has continued to grow and change.

In 1999 members of the statistical community, recognizing that the production of sound statistics for measuring progress is a global responsibility, established the Partnership in Statistics for Development in the Twenty-first Century (PARIS21) to strengthen statistical capacity at all levels. In 2000 the United Nations Millennium Summit called on all countries to work toward a quantified, time-bound set of development targets, which became the Millennium Development Goals.

In the five years since the Millennium Summit, the idea of working toward specific goals has evolved into a general strategy of managing for development results. Countries are reporting on progress toward the Millennium Development Goals and monitoring their own results using a variety of economic and social indicators. Bilateral and multilateral development agencies are incorporating results into their own management planning and evaluation systems and using new indicators to set targets for harmonizing their joint work programs. All of these efforts depend on statistics.

So, what has been done to improve the quality and availability of statistics? A lot. Supported by five donors, the Trust Fund for Statistical Capacity Building has provided $20 million in grants for 86 projects, many to create national statistical development strategies. Several countries, recognizing the need for large-scale investments in their statistical systems, have taken out loans or credits to finance them. PARIS21 has conducted advocacy and training workshops around the world to strengthen national statistical systems. The International Comparison Program has more than 100 countries participating in the largest ever global collection of price data. The Health Metrics Network, sponsored by the World Health Organization and the Bill & Melinda Gates Foundation, is now under way. The United Nations Children's Fund launched a new round of data collection through its Multiple Indicators Cluster Surveys. And the program of Demographic and Health Surveys, funded largely by the United States, continues to operate in many countries.

To accelerate global cooperation in statistical capacity building, the World Bank will provide $7.5 million a year toward implementing the Marrakech Action Plan for Statistics (MAPS), a grant-funded program. In its first year MAPS will fund the International Household Survey Network to harmonize, document, and provide technical support to survey programs everywhere. It is also funding work by the United Nations Statistics Division to prepare for the 2010 round of censuses; work on education by the United Nations Educational, Scientific, and Cultural Organization's Institute for Statistics; a project on migration by the International Labour Organization; and work on measuring slums by the United Nations Human Settlements Programme. And through PARIS21 it is supporting a pilot program to accelerate the production of key development indicators in low-income countries.

National statistical offices and international and regional agencies now find themselves at the center of attention. The challenge is to maintain the momentum in producing more and better quality data. The fruits of today's efforts will be harvested in the years to come. When they are, you will see them here in the tables of *World Development Indicators*.

Shaida Badiee
Director
Development Data Group

TABLE OF CONTENTS

FRONT

1. WORLD VIEW

2. PEOPLE

3. ENVIRONMENT

TABLE OF CONTENTS

4. ECONOMY

5. STATES AND MARKETS

6. GLOBAL LINKS

BACK

PARTNERS

Defining, gathering, and disseminating international statistics is a collective effort of many people and organizations. The indicators presented in *World Development Indicators* are the fruit of decades of work at many levels, from the field workers who administer censuses and household surveys to the committees and working parties of the national and international statistical agencies that develop the nomenclature, classifications, and standards fundamental to an international statistical system. Nongovernmental organizations and the private sector have also made important contributions, both in gathering primary data and in organizing and publishing their results. And academic researchers have played a crucial role in developing statistical methods and carrying on a continuing dialogue about the quality and interpretation of statistical indicators. All these contributors have a strong belief that available, accurate data will improve the quality of public and private decisionmaking.

The organizations listed here have made *World Development Indicators* possible by sharing their data and their expertise with us. More important, their collaboration contributes to the World Bank's efforts, and to those of many others, to improve the quality of life of the world's people. We acknowledge our debt and gratitude to all who have helped to build a base of comprehensive, quantitative information about the world and its people.

For easy reference, Web addresses are included for each listed organization. The addresses shown were active on March 1, 2006. Information about the World Bank is also provided.

International and government agencies

Carbon Dioxide Information Analysis Center

The Carbon Dioxide Information Analysis Center (CDIAC) is the primary global climate change data and information analysis center of the U.S. Department of Energy. The CDIAC's scope includes anything that would potentially be of value to those concerned with the greenhouse effect and global climate change, including concentrations of carbon dioxide and other radiatively active gases in the atmosphere; the role of the terrestrial biosphere and the oceans in the biogeochemical cycles of greenhouse gases; emissions of carbon dioxide to the atmosphere; long-term climate trends; the effects of elevated carbon dioxide on vegetation; and the vulnerability of coastal areas to rising sea levels.

For more information, see http://cdiac.esd.ornl.gov/.

Deutsche Gesellschaft für Technische Zusammenarbeit

The Deutsche Gesellschaft für Technische Zusammenarbeit (GTZ) GmbH is a German government-owned corporation for international cooperation with worldwide operations. GTZ's aim is to positively shape political, economic, ecological, and social development in partner countries, thereby improving people's living conditions and prospects.

For more information, see www.gtz.de/.

Food and Agriculture Organization

The Food and Agriculture Organization, a specialized agency of the United Nations, was founded in October 1945 with a mandate to raise nutrition levels and living standards, to increase agricultural productivity, and to better the condition of rural populations. The organization provides direct development assistance; collects, analyzes, and disseminates information; offers policy and planning advice to governments; and serves as an international forum for debate on food and agricultural issues.

For more information, see www.fao.org/.

International Civil Aviation Organization

The International Civil Aviation Organization (ICAO), a specialized agency of the United Nations, is responsible for establishing international standards and recommended practices and procedures for the technical, economic, and legal aspects of international civil aviation operations. ICAO's strategic objectives include enhancing global aviation safety and security and the efficiency of aviation operations, minimizing the adverse effect of global civil aviation on the environment, maintaining the continuity of aviation operations, and strengthening laws governing international civil aviation.

For more information, see www.icao.int/.

International Labour Organization

The International Labour Organization (ILO), a specialized agency of the United Nations, seeks the promotion of social justice and internationally recognized human and labor rights. As part of its mandate, the ILO maintains an extensive statistical publication program.

For more information, see www.ilo.org/.

International Monetary Fund

The International Monetary Fund (IMF) was established to promote international monetary cooperation, facilitate the expansion and balanced growth of international trade, promote exchange rate stability, help establish a multilateral payments system, make the general resources of the IMF temporarily available to its members under adequate safeguards, and shorten the duration and lessen the degree of disequilibrium in the international balance of payments of members.

For more information, see www.imf.org/.

International Telecommunication Union

The International Telecommunication Union (ITU), a specialized agency of the United Nations, covers all aspects of telecommunication, from setting standards that facilitate seamless interworking of equipment and systems on a global basis to adopting operational procedures for the vast and growing array of wireless services and designing programs to improve telecommunication infrastructure in the developing world. The ITU is also a catalyst for forging development partnerships between government and private industry.

For more information, see www.itu.int/.

National Science Foundation

The National Science Foundation (NSF) is an independent U.S. government agency whose mission is to promote the progress of science; to advance the national health, prosperity, and welfare; and to secure the national defense. It is responsible for promoting science and engineering through almost 20,000 research and education projects. In addition, the NSF fosters the exchange of scientific information among scientists and engineers in the United States and other countries, supports programs to strengthen scientific and engineering research potential, and evaluates the impact of research on industrial development and general welfare.

For more information, see www.nsf.gov/.

Organisation for Economic Co-operation and Development

The Organisation for Economic Co-operation and Development (OECD) includes 30 member countries sharing a commitment to democratic government and the market economy. With active relationships with some 70 other countries, nongovernmental organizations, and civil society, it has a global reach. It is best known for its publications and statistics, which cover economic and social issues from macroeconomics to trade, education, development, and science and innovation.

The Development Assistance Committee (DAC, www.oecd.org/dac/) is one of the principal bodies through which the OECD deals with issues related to cooperation with developing countries. The DAC is a key forum of major bilateral donors, who work together to increase the effectiveness of their common efforts to support sustainable development. The DAC concentrates on two key areas: the contribution of international development to the capacity of developing countries to participate in the global economy and the capacity of people to overcome poverty and participate fully in their societies.

For more information, see www.new.oecd.org/.

Stockholm International Peace Research Institute

The Stockholm International Peace Research Institute (SIPRI) conducts research on questions of conflict and cooperation of importance for international peace and security, with the aim of contributing to an understanding of the conditions for peaceful solutions to international conflicts and for a stable peace. SIPRI's main publication, *SIPRI Yearbook*, is an authoritive and independent source on armaments and arms control and other conflict and security issues.

For more information, see www.sipri.org/.

Understanding Children's Work

As part of broader efforts to develop effective and long-term solutions to child labor, the International Labor Organization, the United Nations Children's Fund (UNICEF), and the World Bank initiated the joint interagency research program "Understanding Children's Work and Its Impact" in December 2000. The Understanding Children's Work (UCW) project was located at UNICEF's Innocenti Research Centre in Florence, Italy, until June 2004, when it moved to the Centre for International Studies on Economic Growth in Rome.

The UCW project addresses the crucial need for more and better data on child labor. UCW's online database contains data by country on child labor and the status of children.

For more information, see www.ucw-project.org/.

United Nations

The United Nations currently has 191 member states. The purposes of the United Nations, as set forth in the Charter, are to maintain international peace and security; to develop friendly relations among nations; to cooperate in solving international economic, social, cultural, and humanitarian problems and in promoting respect for human rights and fundamental freedoms; and to be a center for harmonizing the actions of nations in attaining these ends.

For more information, see www.un.org/.

United Nations Centre for Human Settlements, Global Urban Observatory

The Urban Indicators Programme of the United Nations Human Settlements Programme was established to address the urgent global need to improve the urban knowledge base by helping countries and cities design, collect, and apply policy-oriented indicators related to development at the city level.

With the Urban Indicators and Best Practices programs, the Global Urban Observatory is establishing a worldwide information, assessment, and capacity building network to help governments, local authorities, the private sector, and nongovernmental and other civil society organizations.

For more information, see www.unhabitat.org/.

United Nations Children's Fund

The United Nations Children's Fund works with other UN bodies and with governments and nongovernmental organizations to improve children's lives in more than 140 developing countries through community-based services in primary health care, basic education, and safe water and sanitation.

For more information, see www.unicef.org/.

United Nations Conference on Trade and Development

The United Nations Conference on Trade and Development (UNCTAD) is the principal organ of the United Nations General Assembly in the field of trade and development. Its mandate is to accelerate economic growth and development, particularly in developing countries. UNCTAD discharges its mandate through policy analysis; intergovernmental deliberations, consensus building, and negotiation; monitoring, implementation, and follow-up; and technical cooperation.

For more information, see www.unctad.org/.

United Nations Educational, Scientific, and Cultural Organization, Institute for Statistics

The United Nations Educational, Scientific, and Cultural Organization is a specialized agency of the United Nations that promotes "collaboration among nations through education, science, and culture in order to further universal respect for justice, for the rule of law, and for the human rights and fundamental freedoms . . . for the peoples of the world, without distinction of race, sex, language, or religion."

For more information, see www.uis.unesco.org/.

United Nations Environment Programme

The mandate of the United Nations Environment Programme is to provide leadership and encourage partnership in caring for the environment by inspiring, informing, and enabling nations and people to improve their quality of life without compromising that of future generations.

For more information, see www.unep.org/.

United Nations Industrial Development Organization

The United Nations Industrial Development Organization was established to act as the central coordinating body for industrial activities and to promote industrial development and cooperation at the global, regional, national, and sectoral levels. Its mandate is to help develop scientific and technological plans and programs for industrialization in the public, cooperative, and private sectors.

For more information, see www.unido.org/.

World Bank Group

The World Bank Group is the world's largest source of development assistance. Its mission is to fight poverty and improve the living standards of people in the developing world. It is a development bank, providing loans, policy advice, technical assistance, and knowledge sharing services to low- and middle-income countries to reduce poverty. The Bank promotes growth to create jobs and to empower poor people to take advantage of these opportunities. It uses its financial resources, trained staff, and extensive knowledge base to help each developing country onto a path of stable, sustainable, and equitable growth in the fight against poverty. The World Bank Group has 184 member countries.

For more information, see www.worldbank.org/data/.

World Health Organization

The objective of the World Health Organization (WHO), a specialized agency of the United Nations, is the attainment by all people of the highest possible level of health. The WHO carries out a wide range of functions, including coordinating international health work; helping governments strengthen health services; providing technical assistance and emergency aid; working for the prevention and control of disease; promoting improved nutrition, housing, sanitation, recreation, and economic and working conditions; promoting and coordinating biomedical and health services research; promoting improved standards of teaching and training in health and medical professions; establishing international standards for biological, pharmaceutical, and similar products; and standardizing diagnostic procedures.

For more information, see www.who.int/.

World Intellectual Property Organization

The World Intellectual Property Organization (WIPO) is an international organization dedicated to helping to ensure that the rights of creators and owners of intellectual property are protected worldwide and that inventors and authors are thus recognized and rewarded for their ingenuity. WIPO's main tasks include harmonizing national intellectual property legislation and procedures, providing services for international applications for industrial property rights, exchanging intellectual property information, providing legal and technical assistance to developing and other countries facilitating the resolution of private intellectual property disputes, and marshalling information technology as a tool for storing, accessing, and using valuable intellectual property information. A substantial part of its activities and resources is devoted to development cooperation with developing countries.

For more information, see www.wipo.int/.

World Tourism Organization

The World Tourism Organization is an intergovernmental body entrusted by the United Nations with promoting and developing tourism. It serves as a global forum for tourism policy issues and a source of tourism know-how.

For more information, see www.world-tourism.org/.

World Trade Organization

The World Trade Organization (WTO) is the only international organization dealing with the global rules of trade between nations. Its main function is to ensure that trade flows as smoothly, predictably, and freely as possible. It does this by administering trade agreements, acting as a forum for trade negotiations, settling trade disputes, reviewing national trade policies, assisting developing countries in trade policy issues—through technical assistance and training programs—and cooperating with other international organizations. At the heart of the system—known as the multilateral trading system—are the WTO's agreements, negotiated and signed by a large majority of the world's trading nations and ratified by their parliaments.

For more information, see www.wto.org/.

Private and nongovernmental organizations

Containerisation International

Containerisation International Yearbook is one of the most authoritative reference books on the container industry. The information can be accessed on the Containerisation International Web site, which also provides a comprehensive online daily business news and information service for the container industry.

For more information, see www.ci-online.co.uk/.

International Institute for Strategic Studies

The International Institute for Strategic Studies (IISS) provides information and analysis on strategic trends and facilitates contacts between government leaders, business people, and analysts that could lead to better public policy in international security and international relations. The IISS is a primary source of accurate, objective information on international strategic issues.

For more information, see www.iiss.org/.

International Road Federation

The International Road Federation (IRF) is a nongovernmental, not-for-profit organization with a mission to encourage and promote development and maintenance of better and safer roads and road networks. It helps put in place technological solutions and management practices that provide maximum economic and social returns from national road investments.

The IRF has a major role to play in all aspects of road policy and development worldwide. For governments and financial institutions, the IRF provides a wide base of expertise for planning road development strategy and policy. For its members, the IRF is a business network, a link to external institutions and agencies and a business card of introduction to government officials and decisionmakers. For the community of road professionals, the IRF is a source of support and information for national road associations, advocacy groups, companies, and institutions dedicated to the development of road infrastructure.

For more information, see www.irfnet.org/.

Netcraft

Netcraft's work includes the provision of network security services and research data and analysis of the Internet. It is an authority on the market share of Web servers, operating systems, hosting providers, Internet service providers, encrypted transactions, electronic commerce, scripting languages, and content technologies on the Internet.

For more information, see www.netcraft.com/.

PricewaterhouseCoopers

PricewaterhouseCoopers provides industry-focused assurance, tax, and advisory services for public and private clients in corporate accountability, risk management, structuring and mergers and acquisitions, and performance and process improvement.

For more information, see www.pwcglobal.com/.

Standard & Poor's Emerging Markets Data Base

Standard & Poor's Emerging Markets Data Base (EMDB) is the world's leading source for information and indices on stock markets in developing countries. It currently covers 53 markets and more than 2,600 stocks. Drawing a sample of stocks in each EMDB market, Standard & Poor's calculates indices to serve as benchmarks that are consistent across national boundaries. Standard & Poor's calculates one index, the S&P/IFCG (Global) index, that reflects the perspective of local investors and those interested in broad trends in emerging markets and another, the S&P/IFCI (Investable) index, that provides a broad, neutral, and historically consistent benchmark for the growing emerging market investment community.

For more information, see www.standardandpoors.com/.

STANDARD &POOR'S

World Conservation Monitoring Centre

The World Conservation Monitoring Centre provides information on the conservation and sustainable use of the world's living resources and helps others to develop information systems of their own. It works in close collaboration with a wide range of people and organizations to increase access to the information needed for wise management of the world's living resources.

For more information, see www.unep-wcmc.org/.

WORLD CONSERVATION MONITORING CENTRE

World Information Technology and Services Alliance

The World Information Technology and Services Alliance (WITSA) is the global voice of the information technology industry. It is dedicated to advocating policies that advance the industry's growth and development; facilitating international trade and investment in information technology products and services; strengthening WITSA's national industry associations; and providing members with a broad network of contacts. WITSA also hosts the World Congress on Information Technology and other worldwide events.

For more information, see www.witsa.org/.

World Resources Institute

The World Resources Institute is an independent center for policy research and technical assistance on global environmental and development issues. The institute provides—and helps other institutions provide—objective information and practical proposals for policy and institutional change that will foster environmentally sound, socially equitable development. The institute's current areas of work include trade, forests, energy, economics, technology, biodiversity, human health, climate change, sustainable agriculture, resource and environmental information, and national strategies for environmental and resource management.

For more information, see www.wri.org/.

USERS GUIDE

Tables

The tables are numbered by section and display the identifying icon of the section. Tables 1.1, 1.2, 1.3, and 1.5 are presented by World Bank region, with the economies for each region listed alphabetically within the region. For other tables countries and economies are listed alphabetically (except for Hong Kong, China, which appears after China). Data are shown for 152 economies with populations of more than 1 million, as well as for Taiwan, China, in selected tables. Table 1.6 presents selected indicators for 56 other economies—small economies with populations between 30,000 and 1 million and smaller economies if they are members of the International Bank for Reconstruction and Development (IBRD) or, as it is commonly known, the World Bank. The term *country*, used interchangeably with *economy*, does not imply political independence, but refers to any territory for which authorities report separate social or economic statistics. When available, aggregate measures for income and regional groups appear at the end of each table.

Indicators are shown for the most recent year or period for which data are available and, in most tables, for an earlier year or period (usually 1990 in this edition). Time-series data are available on the *World Development Indicators* CD-ROM and in *WDI Online*.

Known deviations from standard definitions or breaks in comparability over time or across countries are either footnoted in the tables or noted in *About the data*. When available data are deemed to be too weak to provide reliable measures of levels and trends or do not adequately adhere to international standards, the data are not shown.

Aggregate measures for income groups

The aggregate measures for income groups include 208 economies (the economies listed in the main tables plus those in table 1.6) wherever data are available. To maintain consistency in the aggregate measures over time and between tables, missing data are imputed where possible. The aggregates are totals (designated by a *t* if the aggregates include gap-filled estimates for missing data and by an *s*, for simple totals, where they do not), median values (*m*), weighted averages (*w*), or simple averages (*u*). Gap filling of amounts not allocated to countries may result in discrepancies between subgroup aggregates and overall totals. For further discussion of aggregation methods, see *Statistical methods*.

Aggregate measures for regions

The aggregate measures for regions include only low- and middle-income economies (note that these measures include developing economies with populations of less than 1 million, including those listed in table 1.6).

The country composition of regions is based on the World Bank's analytical regions and may differ from common geographic usage. For regional classifications, see the map on the inside back cover and the list on the back cover flap. For further discussion of aggregation methods, see *Statistical methods*.

Statistics

Data are shown for economies as they were constituted in 2004, and historical data are revised to reflect current political arrangements. Exceptions are noted throughout the tables.

Additional information about the data is provided in *Primary data documentation*. That section summarizes national and international efforts to improve basic data collection and gives information on primary sources, census years, fiscal years, and other background. *Statistical methods* provides technical information on some of the general calculations and formulas used throughout the book.

Data consistency and reliability

Considerable effort has been made to standardize the data, but full comparability cannot be assured, and care must be taken in interpreting the indicators. Many factors affect data availability, comparability, and reliability. Statistical systems in many developing economies are still weak; statistical methods, coverage, practices, and definitions differ widely; and cross-country and intertemporal comparisons involve complex technical and conceptual problems that cannot be unequivocally resolved. Data coverage may not be complete because of special circumstances or for economies experiencing problems (such as those stemming from conflicts) affecting the collection and reporting of data. For these reasons, although data are drawn from the sources thought to be most authoritative, they should be construed only as indicating trends and characterizing major differences among economies rather than offering precise quantitative measures of those differences.

Discrepancies in data presented in different editions of *World Development Indicators* reflect updates by countries as well as revisions to historical series and changes in methodology. Thus readers are advised not to compare data series between editions of *World Development Indicators* or between different World Bank publications. Consistent time-series data for 1960–2004 are available on the *World Development Indicators* CD-ROM and in *WDI Online*.

Except where otherwise noted, growth rates are in real terms. (See *Statistical methods* for information on the methods used to calculate growth rates.) Data for some economic indicators for some economies are presented in fiscal years rather than calendar years; see *Primary data documentation*. All dollar figures are current U.S. dollars unless otherwise stated. The methods used for converting national currencies are described in *Statistical methods*.

Country notes

- Unless otherwise noted, data for China do not include data for Hong Kong, China; Macao, China; or Taiwan, China.
- Data for Indonesia include Timor-Leste through 1999 unless otherwise noted.
- External debt data presented for the Russian Federation prior to 1992 are for the former Soviet Union. See *About the data* for table 4.16 for details.

Changes in the System of National Accounts

World Development Indicators uses terminology in line with the 1993 United Nations System of National Accounts (SNA). For example, in the 1993 SNA *gross national income* (GNI) replaces *gross national product* (GNP). See *About the data* for tables 1.1 and 4.8.

Most economies continue to compile their national accounts according to the 1968 SNA, but more and more are adopting the 1993 SNA. Economies that use the 1993 SNA are identified in *Primary data documentation*. A few low-income economies still use concepts from older SNA guidelines, including valuations such as factor cost, in describing major economic aggregates.

Classification of economies

For operational and analytical purposes the World Bank's main criterion for classifying economies is GNI per capita. Each economy is classified as low income, middle income (subdivided into lower middle and upper middle), or high income. For income classifications see the map on the inside front cover and the list on the front cover flap. Low- and middle-income economies are sometimes referred to as developing economies. The use of the term is convenient; it is not intended to imply that all economies in the group are experiencing similar development or that other economies have reached a preferred or final stage of development. Note that classification by income does not necessarily reflect development status.

Because GNI per capita changes over time, the country composition of income groups may change from one edition of *World Development Indicators* to the next. Once the classification is fixed for an edition, based on GNI per capita in the most recent year for which data are available (2004 in this edition), all historical data presented are based on the same country grouping.

Low-income economies are those with a GNI per capita of $825 or less in 2004. Middle-income economies are those with a GNI per capita of more than $825 but less than $10,066. Lower-middle-income and upper-middle-income economies are separated at a GNI per capita of $3,255. High-income economies are those with a GNI per capita of $10,066 or more. The 12 participating member countries of the European Monetary Union (EMU) are presented as a subgroup under high-income economies.

Symbols

..

means that data are not available or that aggregates cannot be calculated because of missing data in the years shown.

0 or 0.0

means zero or less than half the unit shown.

/

in dates, as in 2003/04, means that the period of time, usually 12 months, straddles two calendar years and refers to a crop year, a survey year, an academic year, or a fiscal year.

$

means current U.S. dollars unless otherwise noted.

>

means more than.

<

means less than.

Data presentation conventions

- A blank means not applicable or, for an aggregate, not analytically meaningful.
- A billion is 1,000 million.
- A trillion is 1,000 billion.
- Figures in italics refer to years or periods other than those specified or to growth rates calculated for less than the full period specified.
- Data for years that are more than three years from the range shown are footnoted.

The cutoff date for data is February 1, 2006.

1 WORLD VIEW

The Millennium Development Goals have become the principal global scorecard for development. In September 2005 the United Nations World Summit reaffirmed the principles in the 2000 Millennium Declaration and recognized the need for ambitious national development strategies backed by increased international support.

Financing the needed investments. Financing the investments needed to achieve the Goals remains a challenge for the domestic resources of developing countries and the aid budgets of developed countries. Developing countries need to pursue good governance and sound macroeconomic policies, and rich countries need to increase their support for developing countries able to absorb more aid. Some developed countries have adopted timetables to increase official development assistance to 0.7 percent of gross national income by 2015 and to reach at least 0.5 percent by 2010, while ensuring that at least 0.2 percent goes to the least developed countries. The World Summit also called for increased debt relief or restructuring for countries with unsustainable debt burdens that are not part of the Heavily Indebted Poor Countries Initiative.

The challenge of measurement. Many of these strengthened goals and targets are not easily measured. Reliable, direct measures of the incidence or prevalence of many diseases are unavailable. And because models and data sources are still evolving, estimates may not be comparable over time or across countries. Gaps remain even for the well established measures of poverty, education, mortality, and health care, and major investments in statistical systems will be needed to fill them, by developing countries themselves and international agencies.

Expanding targets to support the goals. The World Summit resolution draws attention to four issues that should receive greater prominence over the next five years:

- *Reproductive health*, integrating reproductive health into strategies for achieving the goals of improving maternal health, reducing child mortality, promoting gender equality, combating HIV/AIDS, and eradicating poverty.
- *Combating disease*, intensifying the fight against HIV/AIDS by "providing sufficient health workers, infrastructure, management systems, and supplies to achieve the health-related [goals] by 2015" and calling for renewed efforts to come "as close as possible to the goal of universal access to HIV treatment by 2010."
- *Employment*, strengthening the focus of the goals on employment by making it "a central objective of our relevant national and international policies as well as our national development strategies. . . ."
- *Environment*, extending the areas of concern in at least three dimensions: biodiversity, development of indigenous people, and protection from natural and human-caused hazards. The resolution calls on all states to "significantly reduce the loss of biodiversity by 2010."

The next five years. When the Millennium Development Goals were promulgated in 2000, the international community reached back a decade to establish a baseline. Nothing could be done to alter the course of those preceding 10 years. In the succeeding five years the world took stock of its commitments and took the first steps to accelerate progress toward the goals. But without measures that accelerate change, many countries may fall short of the targets set for 2015. That is why the next five years are so important. By 2010 we will know whether the goals can be achieved. If by then we have not committed the necessary resources, adopted reforms, and implemented effective new programs, it will be difficult to make further course corrections.

- **Halve, between 1990 and 2015, the proportion of people living on less than $1 a day**
- **Halve, between 1990 and 2015, the proportion of people who suffer from hunger**

Goal 1 Reducing poverty and hunger

Poverty exists everywhere, but there has been progress.

Extreme poverty in developing countries fell from 28 percent in 1990 to 19 percent in 2002. Over the same period the number of people in developing countries grew 20 percent, to more than 5 billion, leaving 1 billion people in extreme poverty. If economic growth rates in developing countries are sustained, global poverty will fall to 10 percent by 2015—a striking success.

But more than 600 million people will still be trapped in poverty in 2015, most of them in Sub-Saharan Africa and South Asia and wherever poor health and lack of education deprive people of productive employment; environmental resources have been depleted or spoiled; and corruption, conflict, and misgovernance waste public resources and discourage private investment.

Even as the first target of the Millennium Development Goals appears in sight, the efforts to eliminate poverty must be renewed.

Poverty rates are falling, but progress has been uneven

Share of people living on less than $1 or $2 a day (%)

In Sub-Saharan Africa the number of poor people has increased by a third, but accelerating growth in India has put South Asia on track to meet the goal

East Asia has experienced a sustained period of economic growth, led by China, while growth and poverty reduction have been slower in Latin America and the Caribbean.

The transition economies of Europe and Central Asia saw poverty rates rise in the 1990s and then fall. There and in the Middle East and North Africa consumption of $2 a day may be a more realistic limit of extreme poverty.

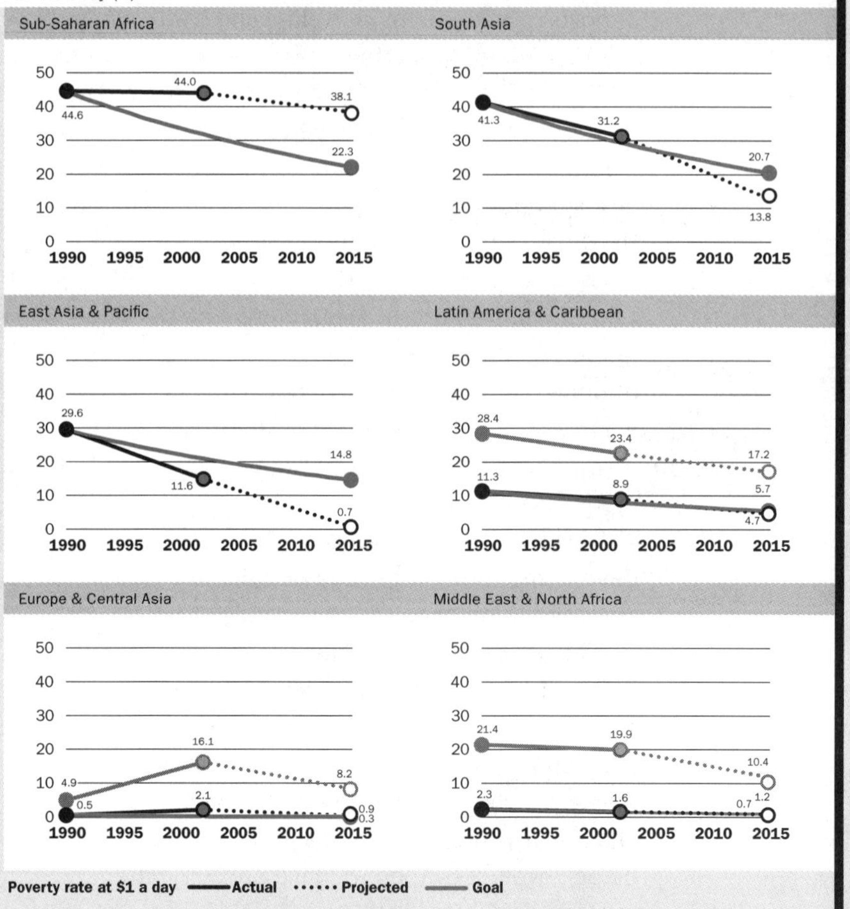

Source: World Bank staff estimates.

Country by country progress on poverty

Share of countries on track to achieve the poverty reduction target (%)

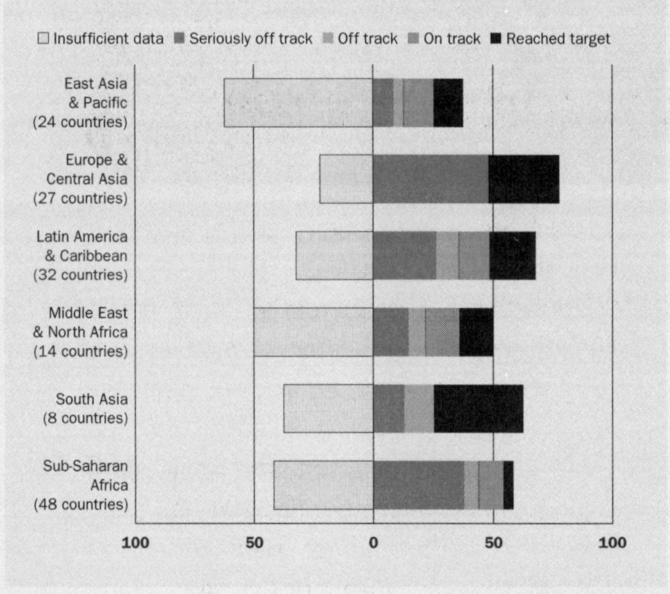

Source: World Bank staff estimates.

The Millennium Development Goals are intended to be met by all countries. This figure shows the share of countries in each region that are on track to achieve the poverty reduction target, based on available survey estimates. Some countries have already achieved the target. Those shown as on track could reach the 2015 target if they maintain their current progress. But those shown as off track or seriously off track are reducing poverty too slowly—or have even seen it increase—to achieve the first of the Millennium Development Goals.

Malnutrition rates are predicted to fall everywhere—except in Sub-Saharan Africa

Prevalence of moderate to severe malnutrition (% of children under age 5)

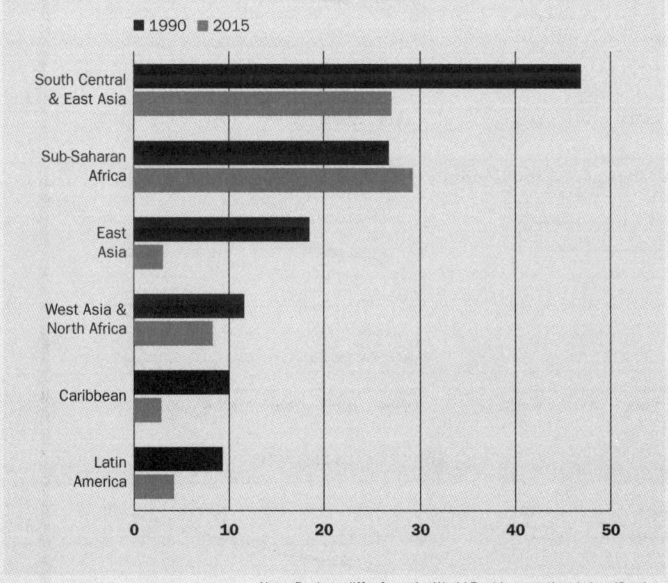

Note: Regions differ from the World Bank's operational classification.
Source: de Onis and others 2004.

Malnutrition in children often begins at birth. Malnourished children develop more slowly, enter school later, and perform less well. The proportion of severely underweight children is falling, but fewer than 40 percent of the 77 countries with adequate data to monitor trends are on track to reach the Millennium Development Goal target. Faster progress is possible. Programs to continue breastfeeding and to improve the diets of pregnant and lactating mothers help. So do appropriate care and feeding of sick children, oral rehydration therapy, control of parasitic diseases, and vitamin A supplementation.

Malnutrition—a persistent problem

Moderately and severely malnourished children (millions under age 5)

In 2020 the number of malnourished children will have fallen everywhere, except in Sub-Saharan Africa, where there are likely to be more than in 1997.

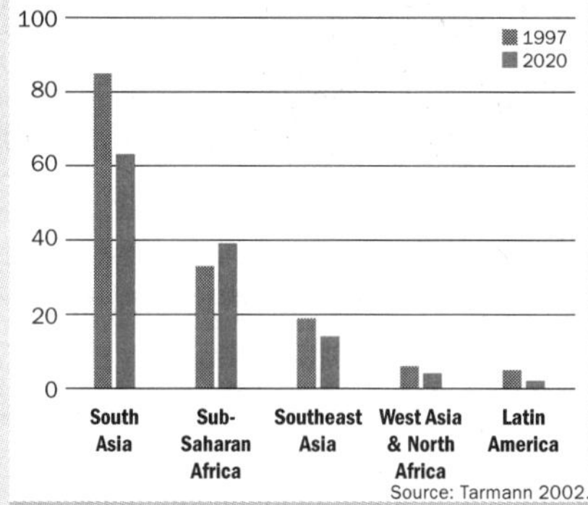

Source: Tarmann 2002.

Sub-Saharan Africa
Share of children under age 5 (%)

Malnutrition rates will fall too slowly in most of Africa to meet the Millennium Development Goal target, and they may rise in eastern Africa.

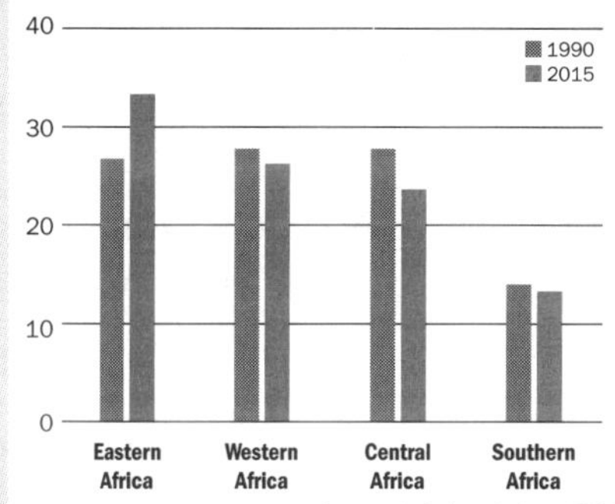

Source: de Onis and others 2004.

Malawi
Share of children under age 5, by wealth quintile (%)

Child malnutrition remained unchanged in Malawi during the 1990s, with improvements in some groups offset by increases in others.

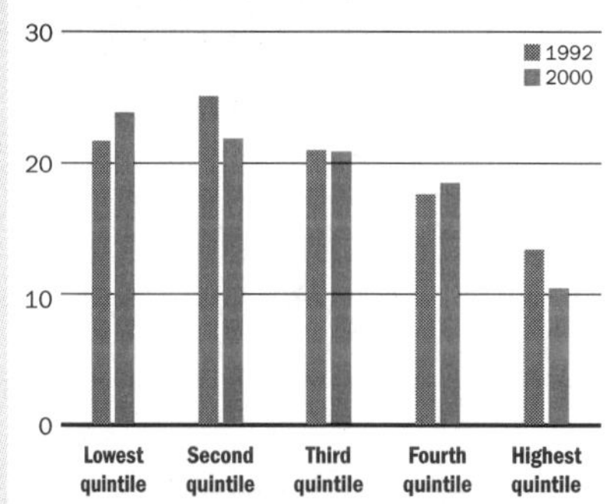

Source: Demographic and Health Surveys.

Mali
Share of children under age 5, by wealth quintile (%)

In Mali average child malnutrition rates fell, but most of the improvement was among the wealthier part of the population.

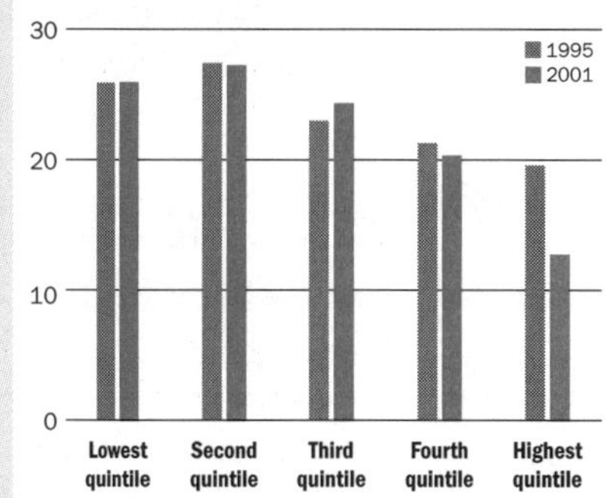

Source: Demographic and Health Surveys.

• **Ensure that by 2015 children everywhere, boys and girls alike, will be able to complete a full course of primary schooling**

GOAL 2 Educating all children

EDUCATION

Since 1990 the world has called for all children to be able to complete primary school. But more than 100 million primary school age children remain out of school.

To reach the target of universal primary education by 2015, school systems with low completion rates will need to start now to train teachers, build classrooms, and improve the quality of education. Most important, they will have to remove such barriers to attendance as fees and lack of transportation, and address parents' concern for the safety of their children.

Education is the foundation of all societies and globally competitive economies. It is the basis for reducing poverty and inequality, improving health, enabling the use of new technologies, and creating and spreading knowledge. In an increasingly complex, knowledge-dependent world, primary education, as the gateway to higher levels of education, must be the first priority.

More children everywhere are completing primary school

Primary completion rate, total (% of relevant age group)

Neither Sub-Saharan Africa nor South Asia are on track to achieve the goal, but in both regions some countries have shown that it can be done.

East Asia and Pacific and Latin America and the Caribbean are close to achieving universal primary education. However, high regional averages disguise some countries that lag behind.

Slow progress in Europe and Central Asia reflects the dislocations of the transition period. In the Middle East and North Africa there has been a decline in completion rates for boys.

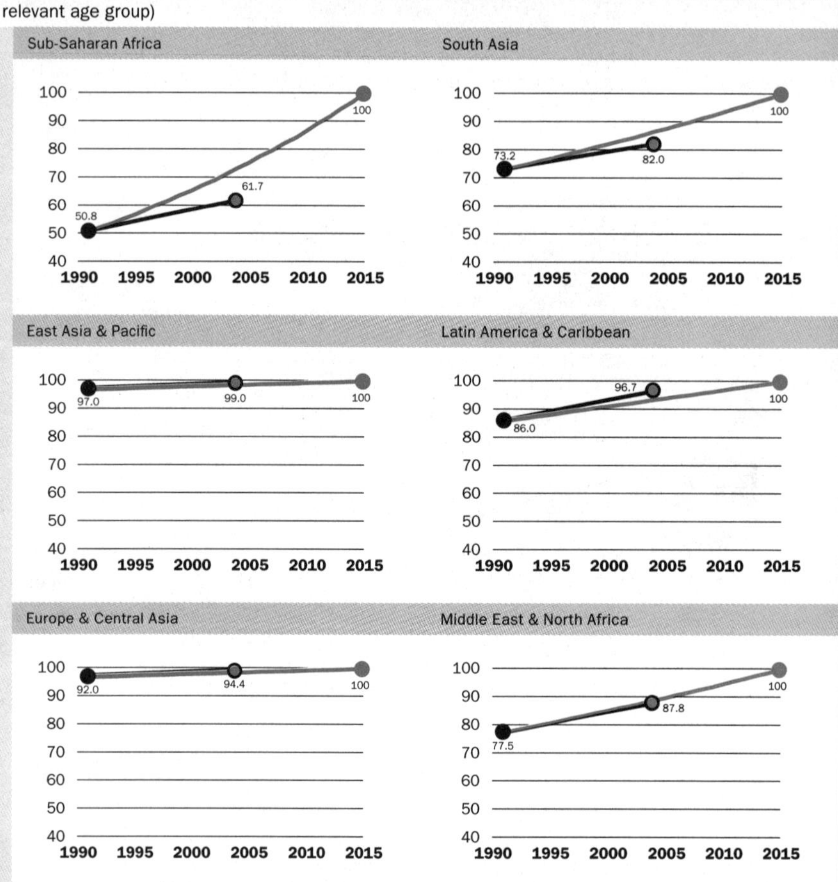

Actual — Goal

Source: World Bank staff estimates.

Country by country progress toward universal primary education

Share of countries on track to achieve the primary education target (%)

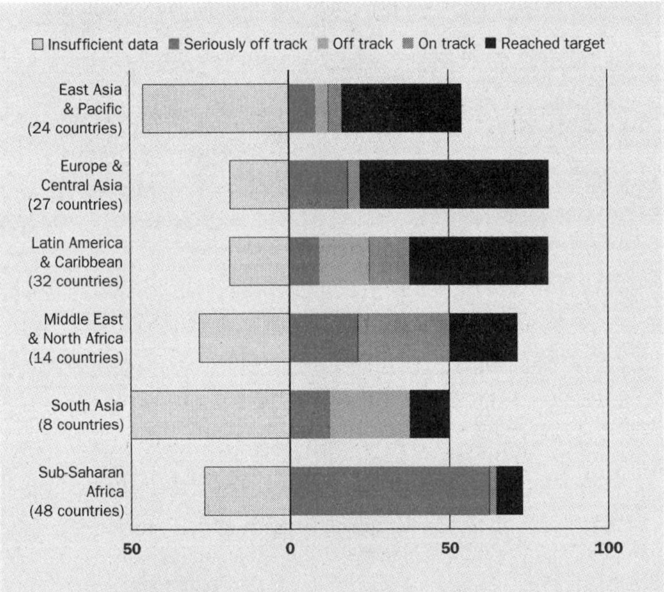

Source: World Bank staff estimates.

In many developing countries children are already able to complete a full course of primary education, but in all regions at least a few countries remain off track and unlikely to reach the target of education for all by 2015. Countries that are off track typically need to raise their completion rates by about 10 percentage points to achieve the target. But those that are seriously off track have much farther to go. Unless they accelerate progress, they will not reach the target before 2040, depriving several more generations of the benefits of education.

A long march to literacy

Youth literacy rate (% of youths ages 15–24)

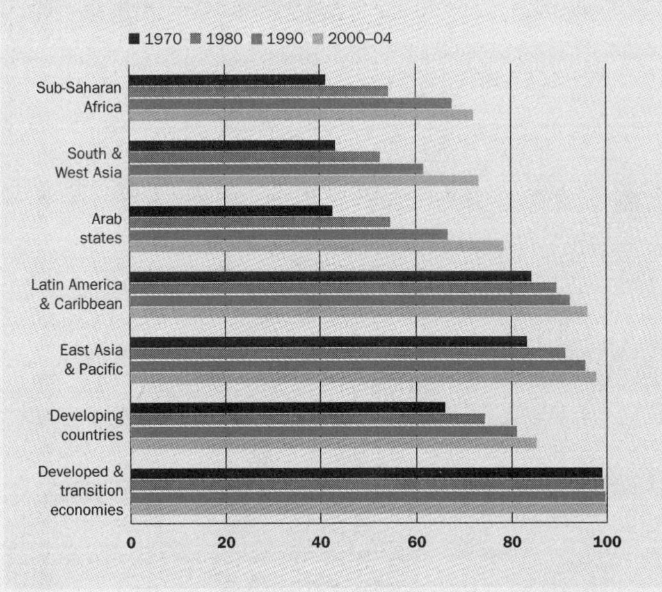

Source: UNESCO 2005.

Literacy rates among young people ages 15–24 are the only widely reported measure of educational outcomes. As more children have entered school and stayed in school longer, the global youth literacy rate has risen from 75 percent in 1970 to 88 percent in 2000–04. Throughout the developing world literacy rates are higher among youth than among adults, a sign of progress. Efforts are under way to develop better measures of literacy and more direct measures of the quality of educational outcomes.

Patterns of school attendance

Share of children ages 6–11 enrolled in primary school, by gender (%)

Gabon, by wealth quintile, 2000

Gabon has high levels of primary school attendance across all income groups, although completion rates are still low.

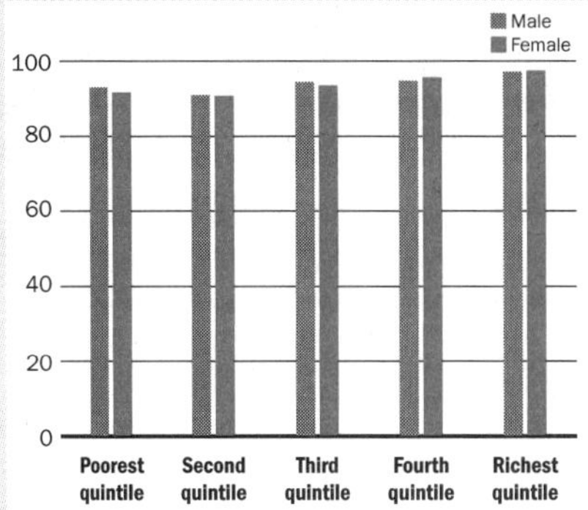

Nigeria, by wealth quintile, 2003

In Nigeria only the wealthiest families are able to provide primary education for all their children.

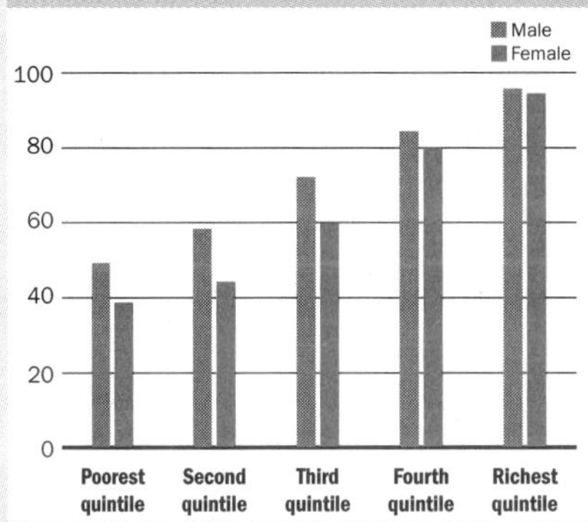

Gabon, by urban and rural area, 2000

In Gabon attendance rates are equally high for boys and girls and in urban and rural settings.

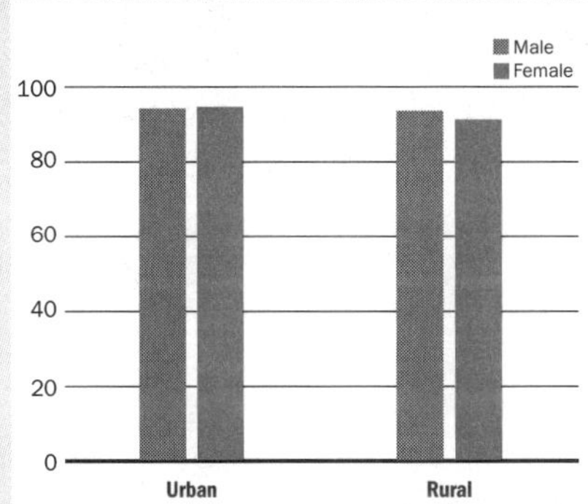

Nigeria, by urban and rural area, 2003

But in Nigeria rural children have fewer opportunities to attend and complete primary school.

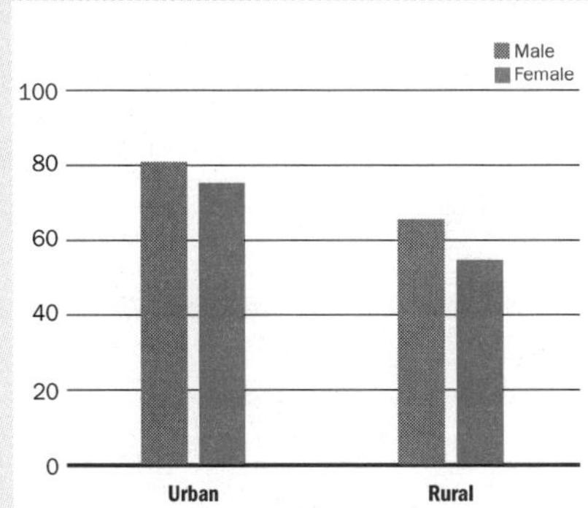

Source: World Bank staff estimates based on Demographic and Helth Surveys.

- **Eliminate gender disparity in primary and secondary education, preferably by 2005, and at all levels by 2015.**

GOAL

3 Empowering women

GENDER EQUALITY

When a country educates its girls, its mortality rates usually fall, fertility rates decline, and the health and education prospects of the next generation improve.

Unequal treatment of women—by the state, in the market, and by their community and family—puts them at a disadvantage throughout their lives and stifles the development prospects of their societies. Illiterate and poorly educated mothers are less able to care for their children. Low education levels and responsibilities for household work prevent women from finding productive employment or participating in public decisionmaking.

What will it take to improve girls' enrollments? Mainly, overcoming the social and economic obstacles that stop parents from sending their daughters to school. For many poor families the economic value of girls' work at home exceeds the perceived returns to schooling. Improving the accessibility of schools and their quality and affordability is a first step.

More girls in school, but many countries have missed the 2005 target

Ratio of girls to boys in primary and secondary education (%)

The differences between boys' and girls' schooling are greatest in regions with the lowest primary school completion rates and the lowest average incomes.

East Asia and Pacific has almost achieved the 2005 target. In some Latin American countries girls' enrollments exceed boys'.

In Europe and Central Asia a strong tradition of educating girls needs to be sustained. In the Middle East and North Africa more girls are overcoming a bias against educating them.

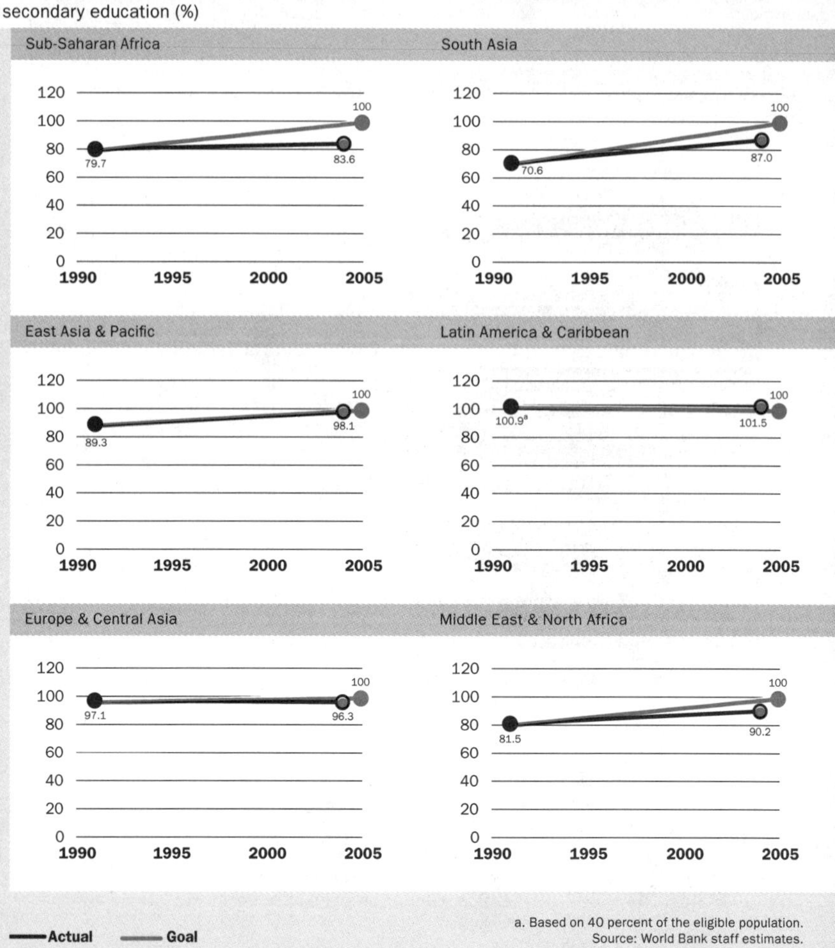

a. Based on 40 percent of the eligible population.
Source: World Bank staff estimates.

Country by country progress toward equal enrollment

Share of countries on track to achieve equal enrollment of girls and boys in primary and secondary school (%)

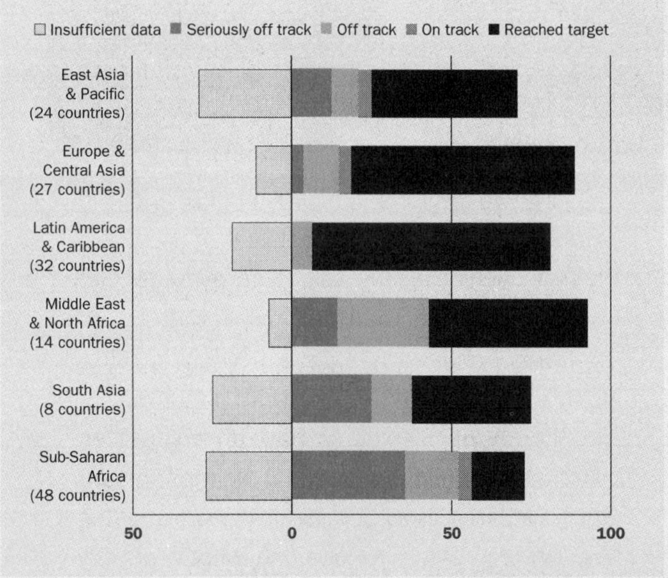

Source: World Bank staff estimates.

The first target of the Millennium Development Goals to fall due calls for enrolling equal numbers of boys and girls in primary and secondary school by 2005, an important stepping stone on the way to full gender equality at all levels of education. But even in regions that have achieved the target on average, such as Europe and Central Asia and Latin American and the Caribbean, some countries still fall short. And in South Asia and Sub-Saharan Africa, where large numbers of children are out of school, girls are at a severe disadvantage.

Degrees of difference

Ratio of girls' to boys' gross enrollment rates (%)

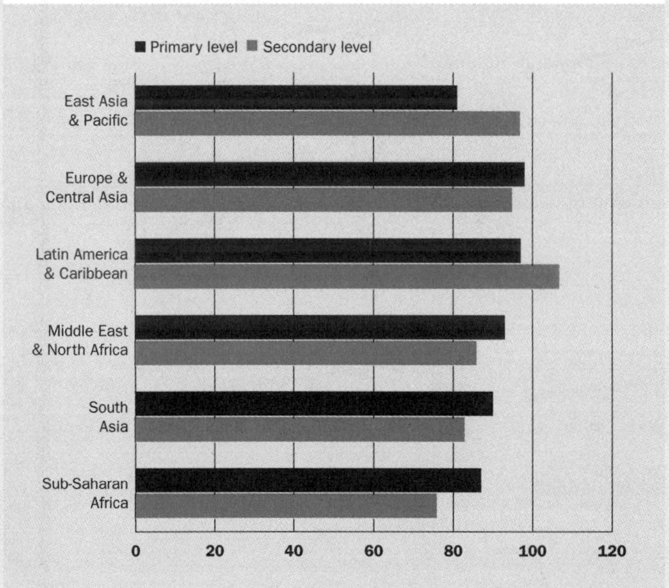

Note: A value of more than 100 means that enrollment rates of girls exceed those of boys.
Source: World Bank staff estimates.

In a competitive world economy both boys and girls need to be educated to higher levels. Girls are underrepresented in primary education in all regions, but in some they are overrepresented at the secondary level. This may happen because boys take longer to complete primary school or drop out of secondary school faster than girls. In other regions the familiar pattern is repeated: fewer girls are enrolled in primary schools and their share falls even farther at higher levels. Whatever the cause, the result is not equitable.

Wealth, gender, and location make a difference

Share of children 15–19 who have completed primary school, by gender (%)

Benin, by wealth quintile, 2002

School attendance rates are low in Benin, except among the rich. Poor children rarely complete school, and even among rich families girls have few opportunities to complete primary education.

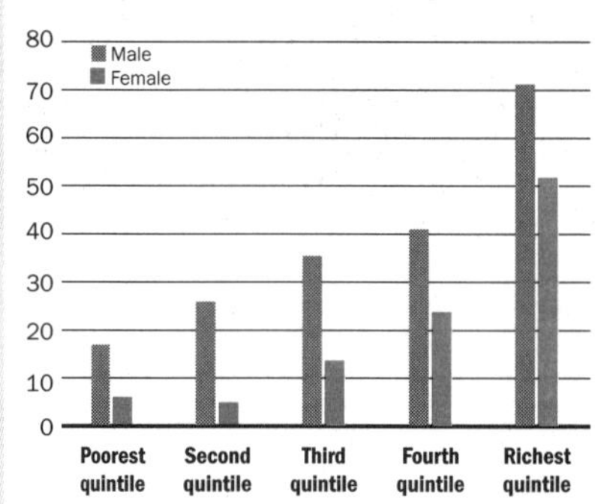

Malawi, by wealth quintile, 2000

A recent survey in Malawi found almost equal completion rates for boys and girls, although children of the poorest families are still less likely to attend school.

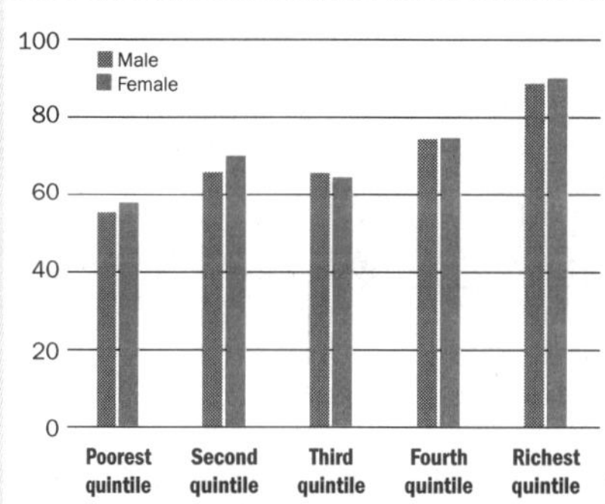

Benin, by urban and rural area, 2002

In Benin efforts to increase girls' attendance will have to improve the accessibility of schools and overcome the reluctance of rural families to send their daughters to school.

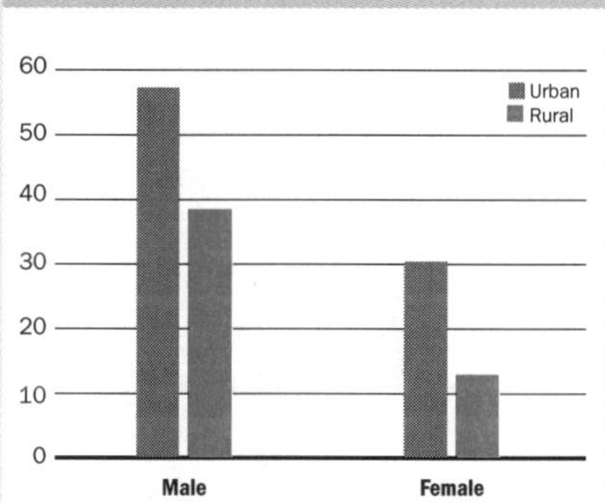

Malawi, by urban and rural area, 2000

In Malawi, where completion rates have risen in recent years, rural areas still lag, but boys and girls are represented equally among those who complete primary school.

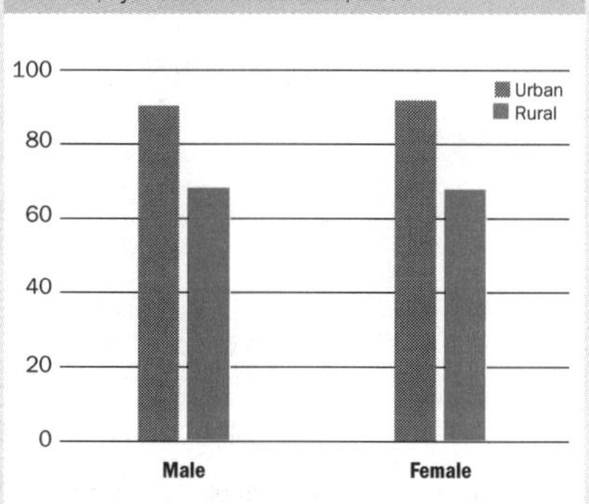

Source: World Bank staff estimates based on Demographic and Health Surveys.

- **Reduce by two thirds, between 1990 and 2015, the under-five mortality rate.**

GOAL 4 Saving children

CHILD MORTALITY

Rapid improvements before 1990 gave hope that mortality rates for infants and children under five could be cut by two-thirds in the following 25 years. But progress slowed almost everywhere in the 1990s.

Every year almost 11 million children in developing countries still die before the age of five. Most die from causes that are readily preventable in rich countries: acute respiratory infections, diarrhea, measles, and malaria.

Only two regions, Latin America and the Caribbean and Europe and Central Asia, are close to achieving the target on average. But even there, more than half the countries are off track. Progress has been particularly slow in Sub-Saharan Africa, where civil disturbances and the HIV/AIDS epidemic have driven up rates of infant and child mortality. By the most recent data available, only 35 countries are making enough progress to reduce under-five mortality rates to one-third of their 1990 level by 2015.

Improving the odds for children

Under-five mortality rate (deaths per 1,000 children)

The gap between goal and reality is greatest in Sub-Saharan Africa, but millions of children are also at risk in populous South Asia.

The pace of mortality reduction in East Asia and Pacific is slowing. The regional average in Latin America and the Caribbean disguises wide variations.

In Europe and Central Asia questions remain about the quality and comparability of data over time. More than half the countries in the Middle East and North Africa are on track to reach the target.

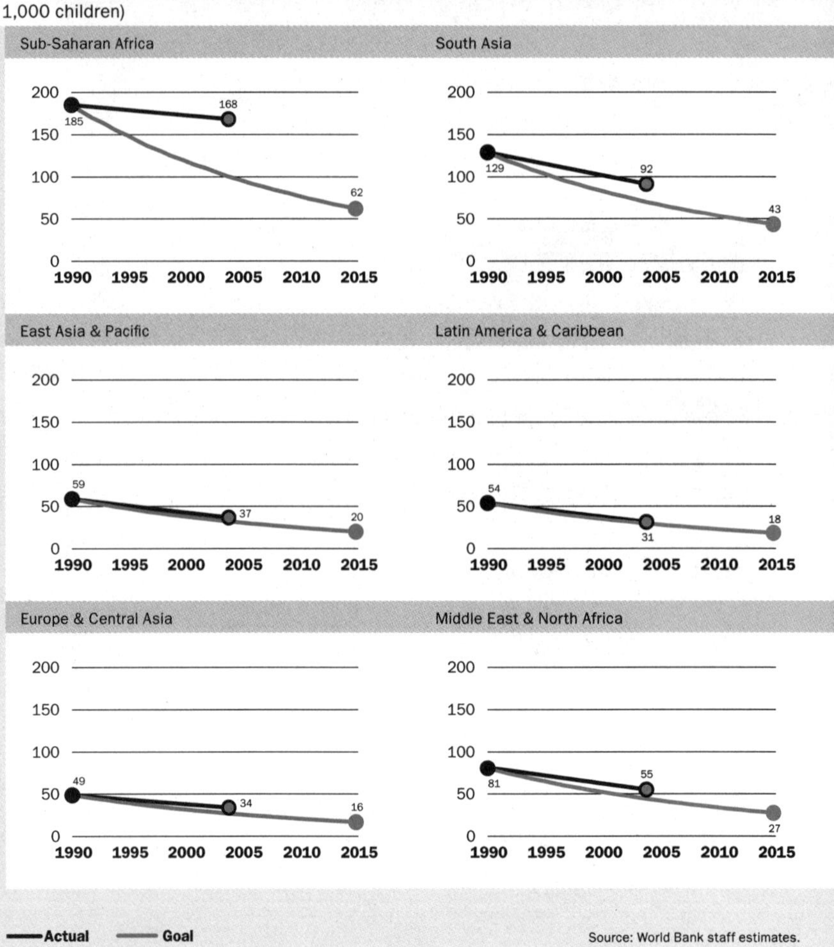

Source: World Bank staff estimates.

Country by country progress toward reduced child mortality

Share of countries on track to achieve the child mortality target (%)

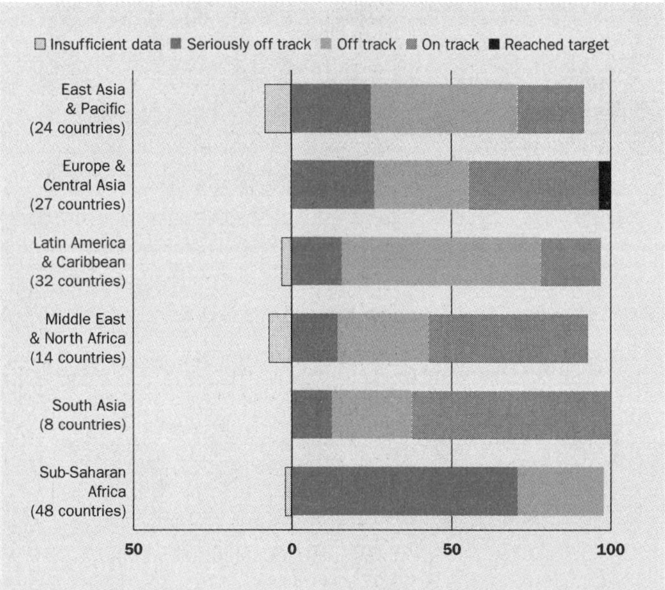

Source: World Bank staff estimates.

A concerted effort to improve the measurement of infant and child mortality has filled many gaps in the international data set, revealing that many countries still fall short of achieving the target, even where regional averages have been improving. Based on estimates through 2004, only 35 countries are on track to achieve a two-thirds reduction in mortality rates. Every country in Sub-Saharan Africa is off track, and in some countries mortality rates have increased since 1990. The good news is that recent surveys have found rapidly falling mortality rates. These could be the first signs of faster progress.

Prevention comes first

Measles immunization rate (% of children ages 12–23 months)

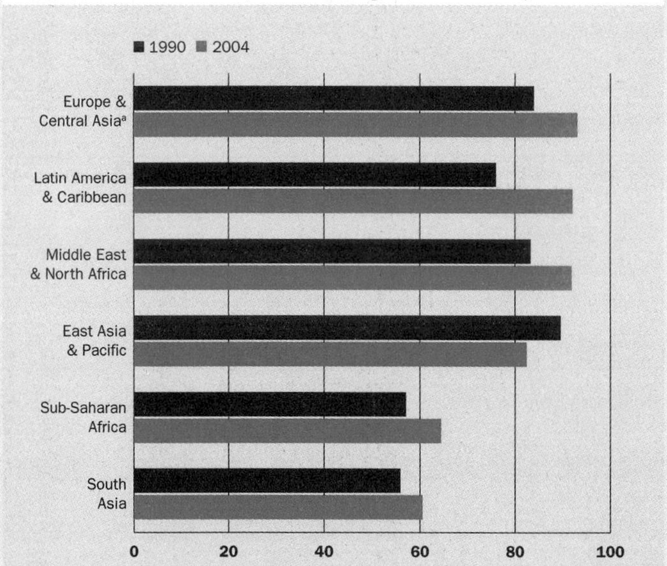

a. Data are for 1992 and 2004.

Source: World Health Organization and United Nations Children's Fund estimates.

Many causes of early childhood deaths are preventable through the basic elements of public health: immunization programs, hand washing, access to safe water and sanitation facilities, and good nutrition. Measles immunization now reaches more infants, and measles deaths are falling. Developing regions with more than 90 percent immunization rates are on par with the high-income economies.

Cruel differences

Under-five mortality and immunization rates by wealth quintiles

Child mortality rates in Mali are high even for comparatively wealthy families.

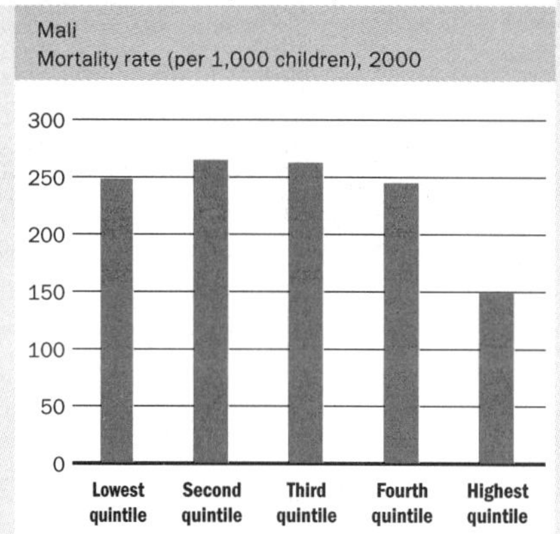

In South Africa the disparity between rich and poor is greater, but the average is much lower than in Mali.

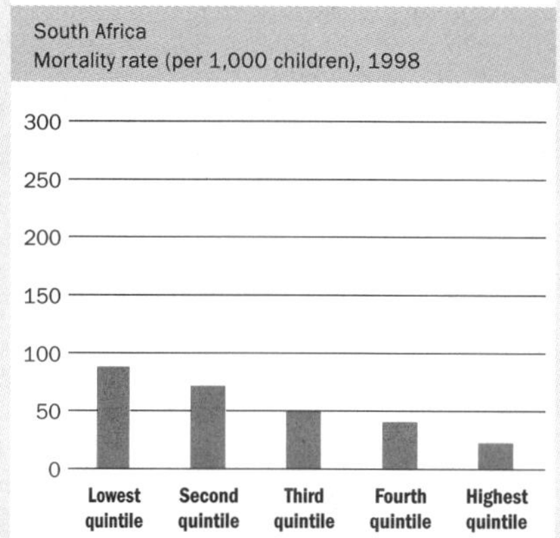

Mali has low immunization rates, especially for its poorest children. Diphtheria, pertussis, and tetanus (DPT) immunization, which is harder to deliver, lags behind measles for all income groups.

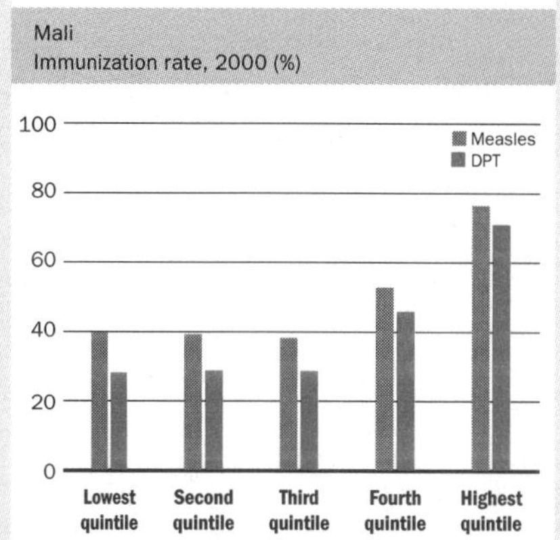

In South Africa immunization programs reach most children in all income groups, and DPT immunization rates are almost equal to those for measles immunization.

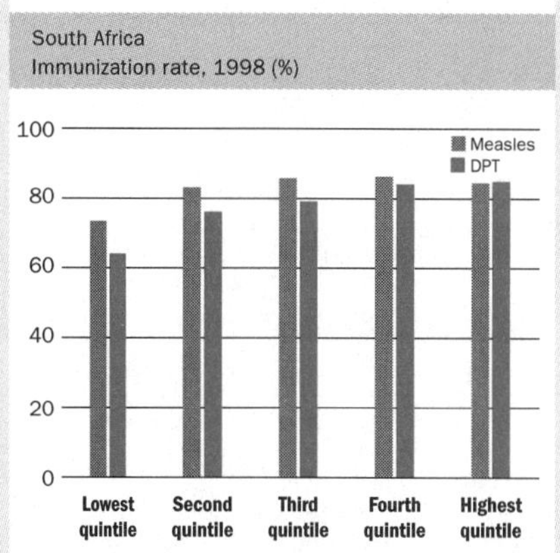

Source: World Bank staff estimates based on Demographic and Health Surveys.

• **Reduce by three-quarters, between 1990 and 2015, the maternal mortality ratio**

GOAL 5 Caring for mothers

MATERNAL MORTALITY

Death in childbirth is a rare event in rich countries, where there are typically fewer than 10 maternal deaths for every 100,000 live births. But in the poorest countries of Africa and Asia the ratio may be 100 times higher. And because women in poor countries have more children, their lifetime risk of maternal death may be more than 200 times greater than for women in Western Europe and North America.

More than 500,000 women die each year in childbirth, most of them in developing countries. What makes maternal mortality such a compelling problem is that it strikes young women experiencing a natural function of life. They die because they are poor. Malnourished. Weakened by disease. Exposed to multiple pregnancies. And they die because they lack access to trained health care workers and modern medical facilities.

Mothers at risk in Africa and South Asia

Left axis (line): total fertility rate (births per woman); right axis (bar): maternal mortality ratio (deaths per 100,000 live births)

Maternal mortality ratios are still unacceptably high in many developing countries as a result of high fertility rates and a high risk of dying each time a woman becomes pregnant.

Some developing countries have substantially improved maternal health through better services in hospitals and increased numbers of trained birth attendants and midwives.

Still others not only improved maternal health, but significantly lowered fertility rates directly through use of contraceptives and indirectly through increased female education.

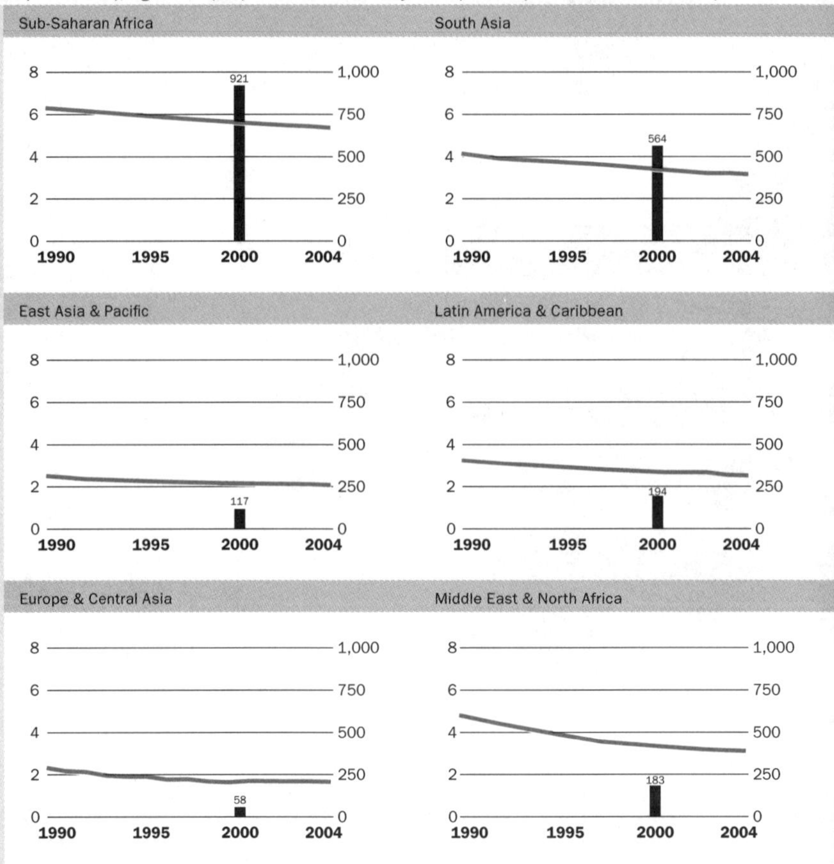

Source: World Bank staff estimates.

Country by country progress in providing skilled care at births

Share of countries on track to achieve adequate coverage of births by skilled health personnel (%)

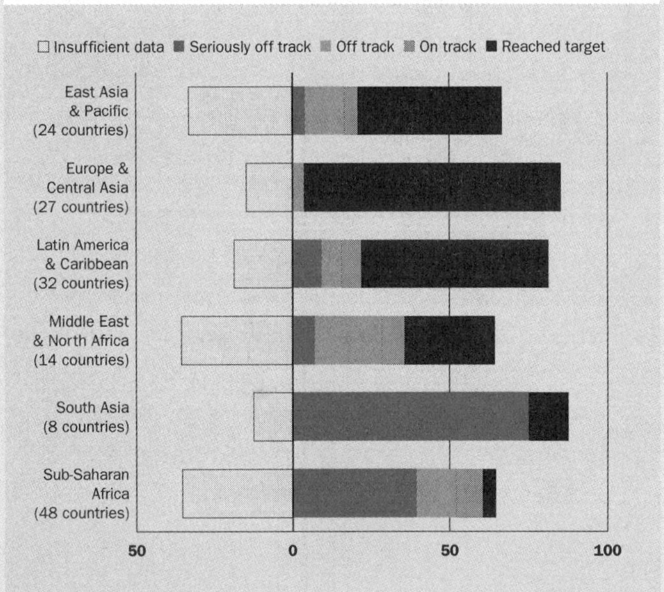

Source: World Bank staff estimates.

Because few countries are able to measure maternal mortality over time, other indicators are often used to measure progress toward this goal. Skilled health personnel and modern medical facilities are needed to deal with the complications of childbirth that can claim mothers' lives. This figure shows the proportion of countries in each region that provide skilled health personnel for 90 percent of births or could do so by 2015 based on current trends. Countries that are off track may be able to achieve 75 percent coverage by 2015, while seriously off-track countries will not reach even that level unless they make rapid progress in the next decade.

Decreasing risk of young motherhood

Adolescent fertility rate (births per 1,000 women ages 15–19)

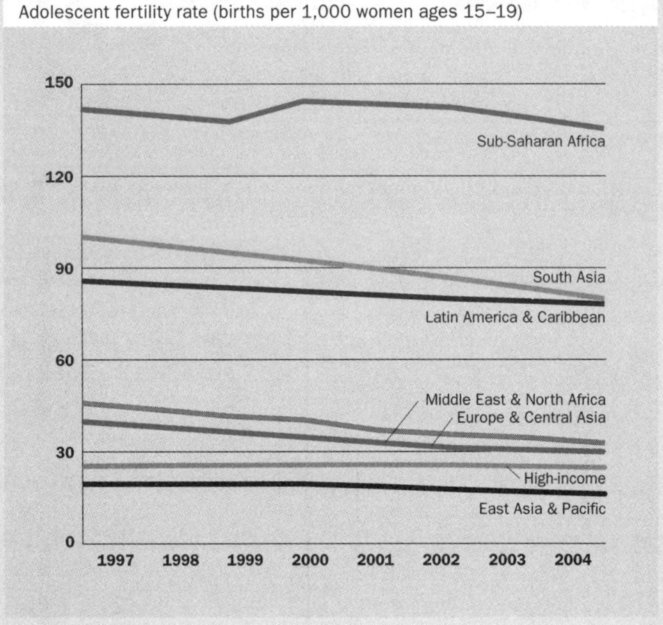

Source: World Bank staff estimates.

Fertility rates among young women have been falling, but they remain high in Sub-Saharan Africa, South Asia, and Latin America and the Caribbean. Young mothers run higher risks of complications in childbirth and lower birthweight babies. They are also likely to have more births over their lifetime, increasing their lifetime risk of maternal death. Education and access to reproductive health services help to lower fertility rates.

Poor women need reproductive health services

Zimbabwe, 1999
Total fertility rate by wealth quintile (births per woman)

In Zimbabwe total fertility rates are high except for women from the highest income group.

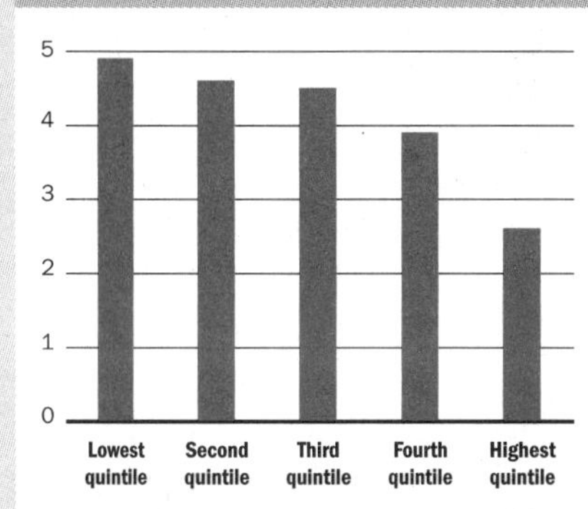

Zimbabwe, 1999
Contraceptive prevalence rate by wealth quintile (%)

Wealthier men and women are more likely to use contraception.

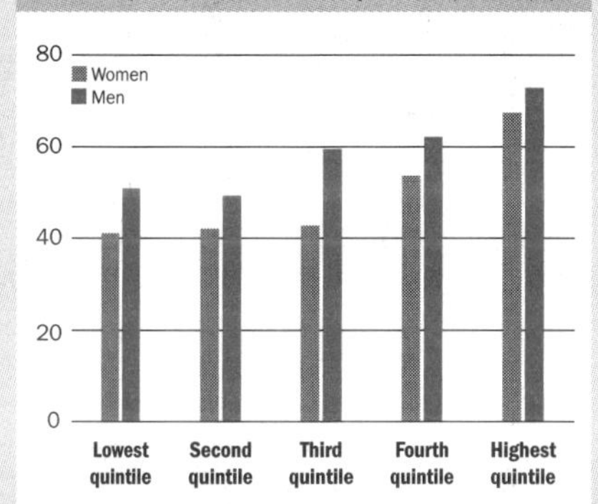

Zimbabwe, 1999
Source of contraception by wealth quintiles (%)

In Zimbabwe both poor and rich rely heavily on public sources for contraception.

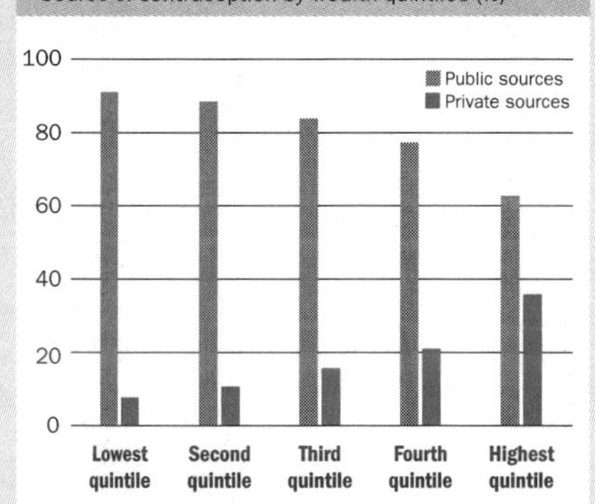

Contraceptive prevalence rates
Share of women in union (%)

Where contraceptive prevalence rates are higher, men and women are more likely to be using modern methods.

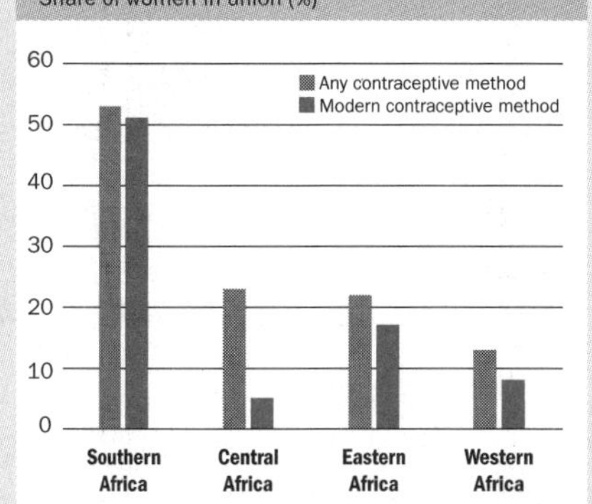

Source: World Bank staff estimates based on Demographic and Health Surveys; UNFPA 2005.

- **Have halted by 2015 and begun to reverse the spread of HIV/AIDS.**
- **Have halted by 2015 and begun to reverse the incidence of malaria and other major diseases.**

GOAL 6 Combating disease

DISEASE

Epidemic diseases exact a huge toll in human suffering and lost opportunities for development. Poverty, armed conflict, and natural disasters contribute to the spread of disease and are worsened by it.

In Africa the spread of HIV/AIDS has reversed decades of improvements in life expectancy and left millions of children orphaned. It is draining the supply of teachers and eroding the quality of education.

There are 300–500 million cases of malaria each year, leading to more than 1 million deaths. Nearly all the cases and more than 95 percent of the deaths occur in Sub-Saharan Africa. Most deaths from malaria are among children younger than five years old.

Tuberculosis kills some 2 million people a year, most of them 15–45 years old. The disease is spreading more rapidly because of the emergence of drug-resistant strains of tuberculosis; the spread of HIV/AIDS, which reduces resistance to tuberculosis; and the growing number of refugees and displaced people.

As the HIV/AIDS epidemic matures, the death toll keeps rising

Left axis: adult (ages 15–49) HIV prevalence rate (%); right axis: number of deaths due to AIDS (millions)

Worldwide, 40 million adults and children are living with HIV/AIDS and almost 5 million new infections occurred in 2005. The adult prevalence rate has stabilized in Sub-Saharan Africa and other developing regions, not because the epidemic has been halted but because the death rate now equals the rate of new infections.

Although prevalence rates are lower outside of Sub-Saharan Africa, the number of people infected is increasing and so is the death rate. There were almost a million new cases in South and East Asia, where more than 7 million people are now living with HIV/AIDS.

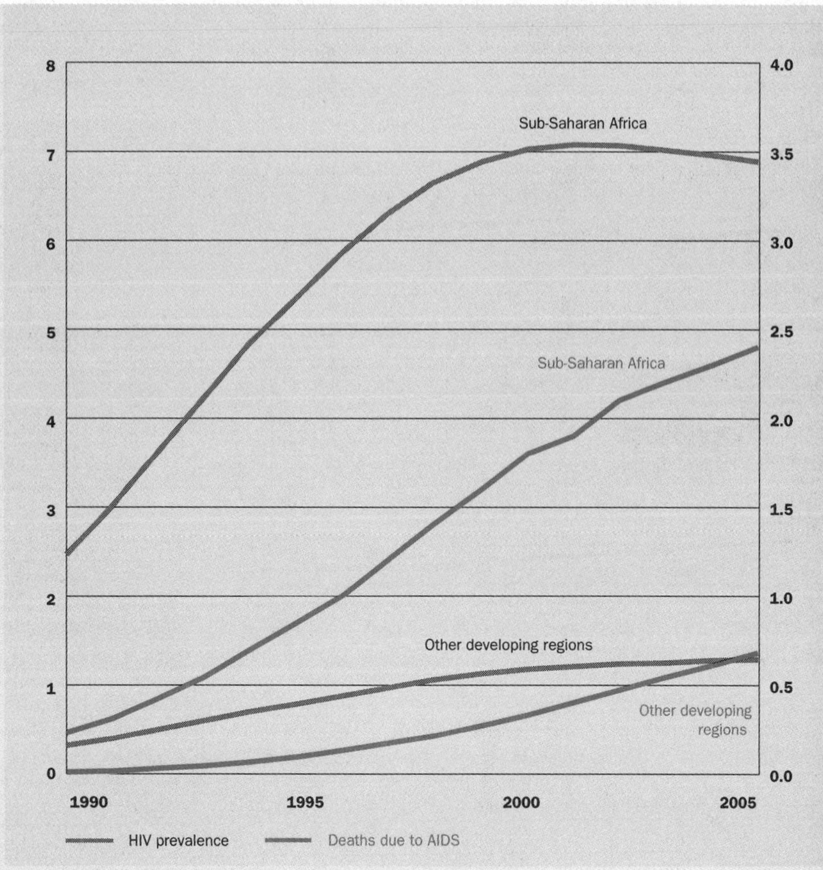

Source: UNAIDS/WHO 2005.

The HIV epidemic can be reversed

Model projections of HIV infections in Sub-Saharan Africa (millions)

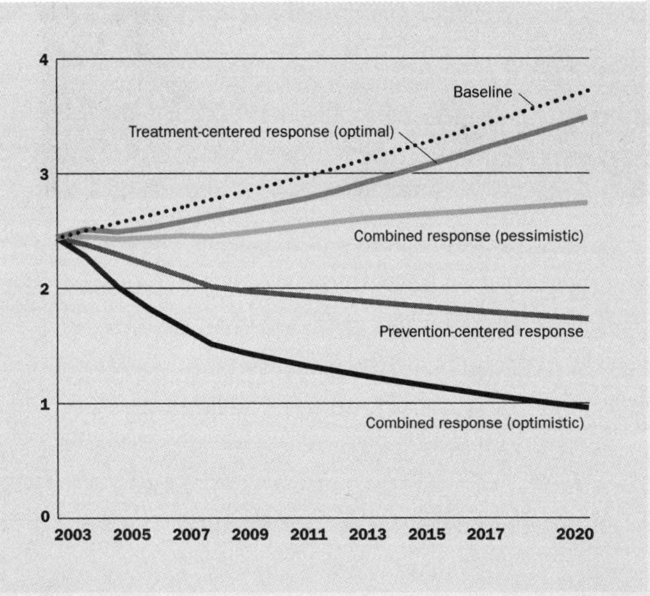

Source: Salomon and others 2005.

What will it take to halt and reverse the HIV epidemic? A combination of effective treatment and prevention programs. Antiretroviral therapy is starting to reach people in poor countries, although not yet at the levels needed, and prevention programs have begun to alter behavior. Computer simulations of the epidemic suggest that a combination of intensive treatment and prevention programs would be most effective in reducing new infections and averting 10 million deaths between now and 2020.

Tuberculosis rates on the rise or falling slowly

Incidence of tuberculosis (per 100,000 people)

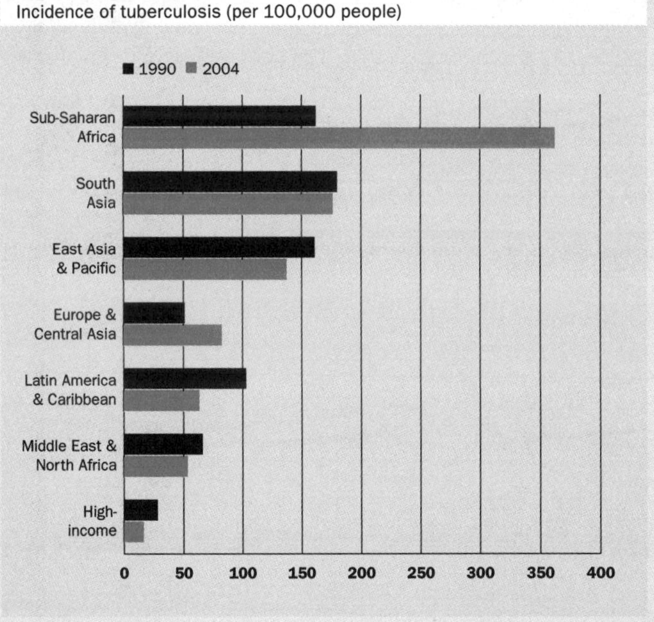

Source: World Bank staff estimates.

Each year there are 8 million new cases of tuberculosis—3 million in South and East Asia, 2 million in Sub-Saharan Africa, and more than a quarter million in countries of the former Soviet Union.

The disease has spread fastest in poor countries with ineffective health systems. Poorly managed tuberculosis programs allow drug-resistant strains to spread. And tuberculosis is often associated with HIV infections, which compromise the body's immune system. Positive diagnosis, effective treatment, and follow-up care can achieve high cure rates, but many cases go undetected.

Malaria is a leading killer in Africa

Malaria deaths (per 100,000 people)

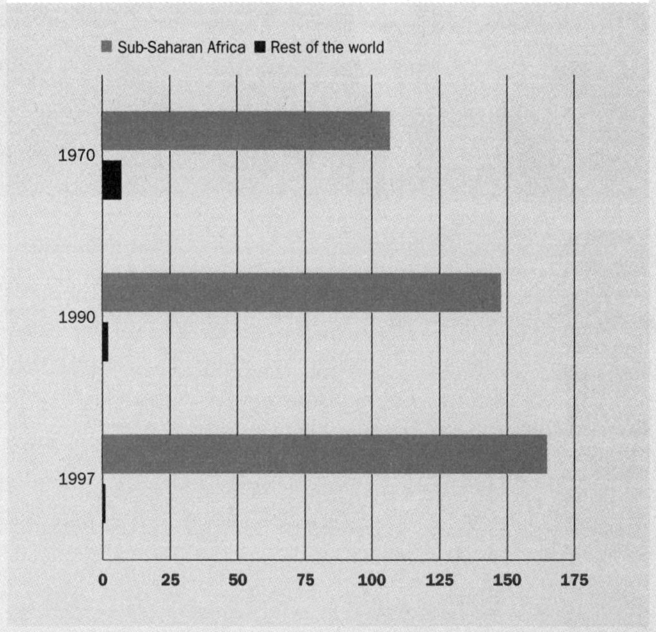

Source: WHO 1999.

Malaria, once widespread, is now largely a disease of the tropics. It takes its greatest toll in Sub-Saharan Africa, where more than 1 million people die each year, most of them children under the age of five. Millions more suffer from repeated infections, leaving them unable to work for weeks at a time. The World Bank estimates that the disease has slowed economic growth in Africa by 1.3 percent a year (World Bank 2001).

Poor children bear the burden of malaria

Children under age 5 receiving antimalarial treatment (%)

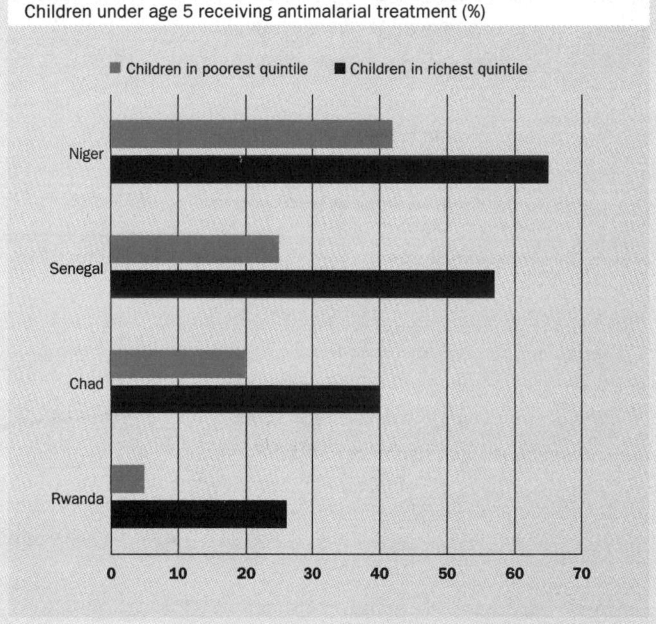

Source: World Bank 2005e.

Malaria is a disease of poverty and a cause of poverty. Although adults may experience repeated bouts of the debilitating disease, children are most likely to die—more than 2,000 children die each day because of malaria in Sub-Saharan Africa. Effective treatment can save lives and reduce the burden of disease, but in many countries children in the poorest families do not receive treatment. Prevention is also important. The use of insecticide-treated bednets has been shown to protect children.

- **Integrate the principles of sustainable development into country policies and programs and reverse the loss of environmental resources.**

- **Reduce by half the proportion of people without sustainable access to safe drinking water.**

- **Achieve significant improvement in the lives of at least 100 million slum dwellers by 2020.**

GOAL 7 Using resources wisely

ENVIRONMENT

Sustainable development can be ensured only by protecting the environment and using its resources wisely. Poor people, often dependent on environmental resources for their livelihood, are the most affected by environmental degradation and natural disasters (fires, storms, earthquakes) whose effects are worsened by environmental mismanagement.

Most countries have adopted principles of sustainable development and agreed to international accords on protecting the environment. But good intentions are not enough. Around the world land is being degraded. Forests are being lost. Fisheries are being overused. Plant and animal species are becoming extinct. And carbon dioxide emissions are driving changes in global climate.

Rich countries are major consumers of products and services from the environment. Thus rich countries and poor countries alike have a stake in using environmental resources wisely.

Water and sanitation—basic services needed by all

Population without access to an improved water source or sanitation facilities (%)

In Sub-Saharan Africa 300 million people lack access to improved water sources and 450 million lack adequate sanitation services. South Asia has made excellent progress in providing water, but progress has been slower in providing sanitation.

In East Asia rapid urbanization is posing a challenge for the provision of water and other public utilities. Latin America and the Caribbean, the most urban developing region, has made slow progress in providing sanitation services.

Many countries in Europe and Central Asia lack reliable benchmarks for the early 1990s. In the Middle East and North Africa, Egypt, Tunisia, and Morocco have made the fastest progress.

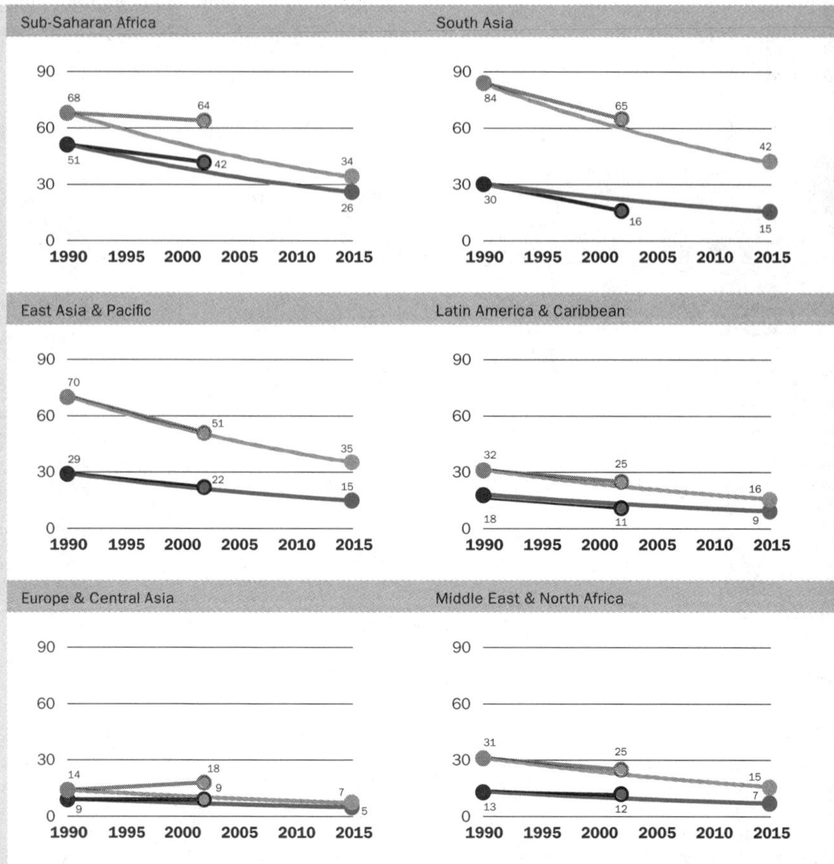

Without access to an improved water source — **Actual** — **Goal**

Without access to improved sanitation facilities — **Actual** — **Goal**

Source: World Bank staff estimates.

Country by country progress toward access to water . . .

Share of countries on track to achieve the target for access to improved water source (%)

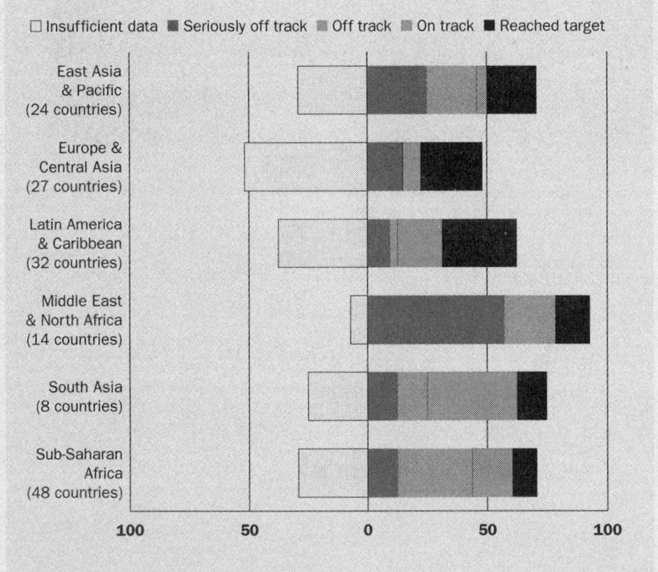

Source: World Bank staff estimates.

Lack of clean water and basic sanitation is the main reason diseases transmitted by feces are so common in developing countries. Water is a daily need that must be met, but in some places people spend many hours to obtain water from sources that are not protected from contamination. Even the modest target of reducing by half the number of people without access to an improved water source will not be met in many countries at the current rate of progress.

. . . and to sanitation

Share of countries on track to achieve the target for access to improved sanitation source (%)

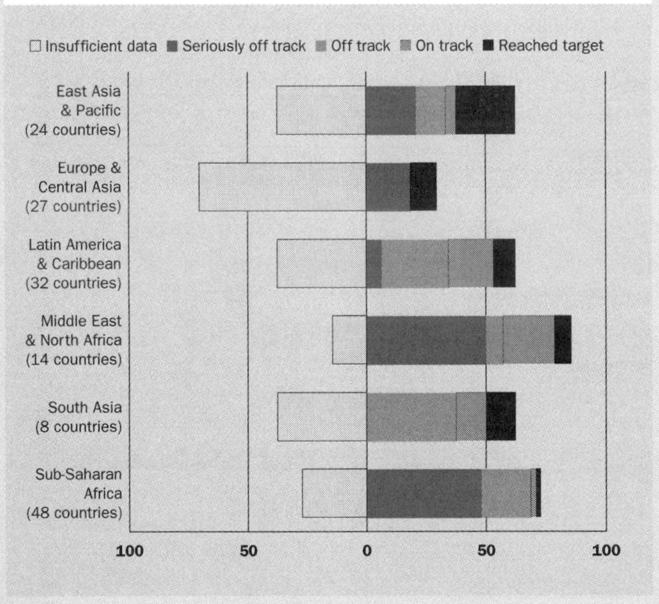

Source: World Bank staff estimates.

An improved sanitation system provides disposal facilities that can effectively prevent human, animal, and insect contact with excreta. It does not, however, ensure treatment of effluents to remove harmful substances before they are released into the environment. Large populations in Africa and Asia still lack adequate sanitation facilities, and few countries are currently on track to reach the target.

Forests falling

Forest area (thousands of square kilometers)

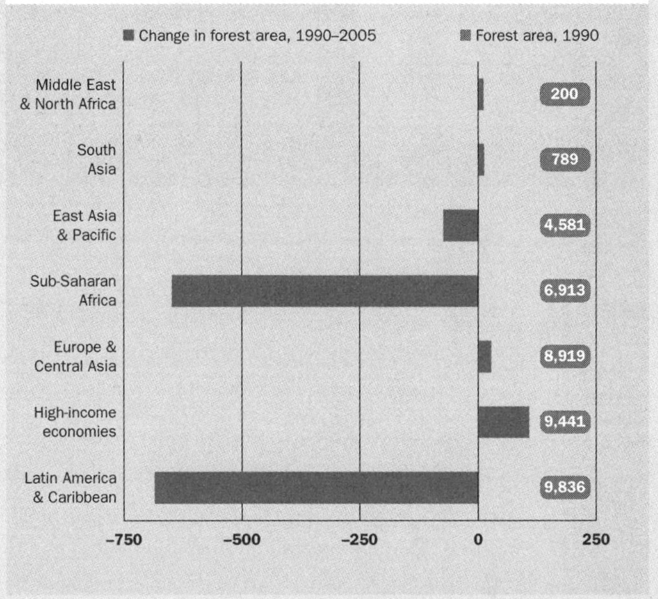

Note: Positive values indicate an increase in forest area.
Source: FAO data and World Bank staff estimates.

Since 1990 the world has lost about 1.3 million square kilometers of forest—almost 100,000 square kilometers each year. The losses have been greatest in the great tropical forests of Sub-Saharan Africa and Latin America and the Caribbean. Forest products, including timber, are important sources of livelihood for people in developing countries, and forests provide habitat for many plant and animal species. To ensure sustainable development, forests must be managed wisely to continue to benefit future generations.

Fuel for climate change—high carbon dioxide emitters

Emissions of carbon dioxide, 2002 (billions of metric tons)

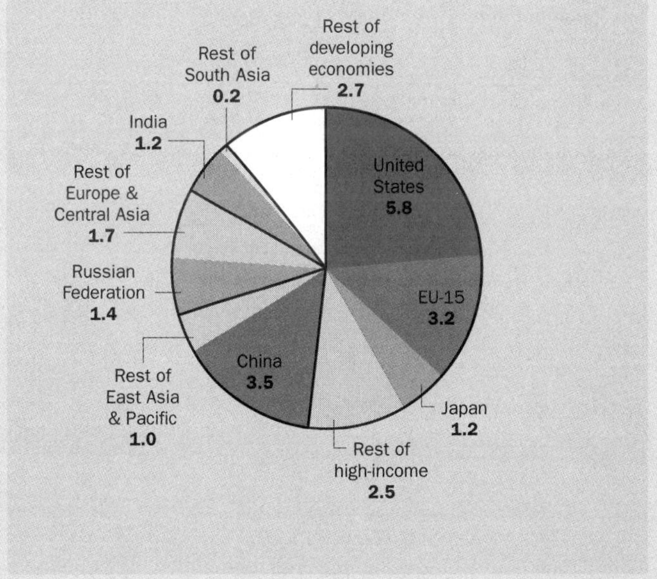

Source: CDIAC data and World Bank staff estimates.

Carbon dioxide, which is produced by burning fossil fuels and manufacturing cement, is a greenhouse gas that contributes to global climate change. Emissions rose by 3 billion metric tons between 1990 and 2002. High-income economies are the largest emitters of carbon dioxide, and their share has increased. However, China is the world's second largest emitter, next to the United States. Emissions by India are also increasing.

- Develop further an open trading and financial system that is rule-based, predictable, and nondiscriminatory.
- Address the special needs of the least developed countries.
- Address the special needs of landlocked and small island developing states.
- Deal comprehensively with developing countries' debt problems to make debt sustainable in the long term.
- Develop decent and productive work for youth.
- Provide access to affordable essential drugs in developing countries.
- Make available the benefits of new technologies—especially information and communications technologies.

GOAL 8 Working together

The eighth and final goal complements the others. In partnership, wealthy countries work with developing countries to create an environment in which rapid, sustainable development is possible. Important steps toward global partnership were taken at international meetings in 2001 in Doha, which launched a new "development round" of trade negotiations, and in 2002 at the International Conference on Financing for Development in Monterrey, Mexico, where high-income and developing countries reached consensus on mutual responsibilities for achieving the Millennium Development Goals. The consensus calls for developing countries to improve governance and policies aimed at increasing economic growth and reducing poverty and for high-income countries to provide more and better aid and greater access to their markets.

Goal 8 also reminds us that the development challenges differ for large countries and small countries. And that developing countries need access to new technologies to increase productivity and improve people's lives.

Many sources and many patterns

Selected net flows, 2004 ($ billions)

Aid plays an important role in development, especially in low-income countries. The extremely poor countries of Sub-Saharan Africa and Asia still need substantial increases in aid to reach their development goals. Countries in all regions borrow from multilateral institutions, such as the World Bank, but some are repaying more than they borrow.

In addition to aid, developing countries meet part of their financing needs through private capital flows. Rapidly growing economies need and attract large flows of direct and portfolio investment, which have been particularly important in East Asia and Pacific.

Export demand can be an important source of growth, and trade surpluses can also provide substantial foreign exchange earnings. Remittances from people living and working abroad are a growing source of income for households in some developing economies.

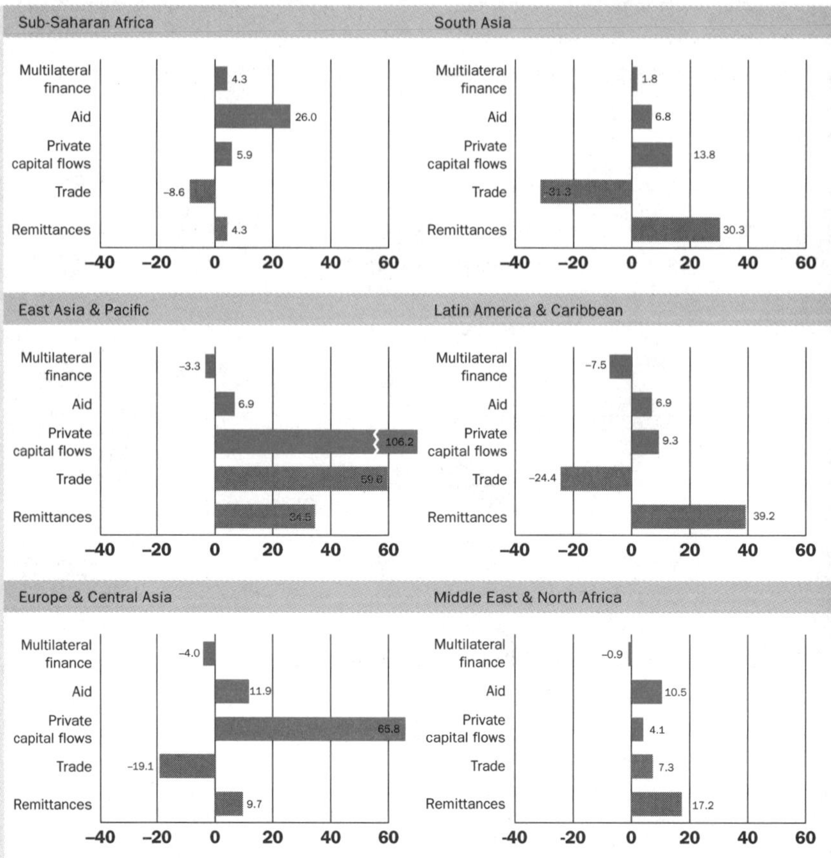

Source: World Bank staff estimates.

Official development assistance is rising, but still too little

Left axis (bars): official development assistance (2003 $ billions);
right axis (line): net disbursements as a share of 2003 donors' GNI (%)

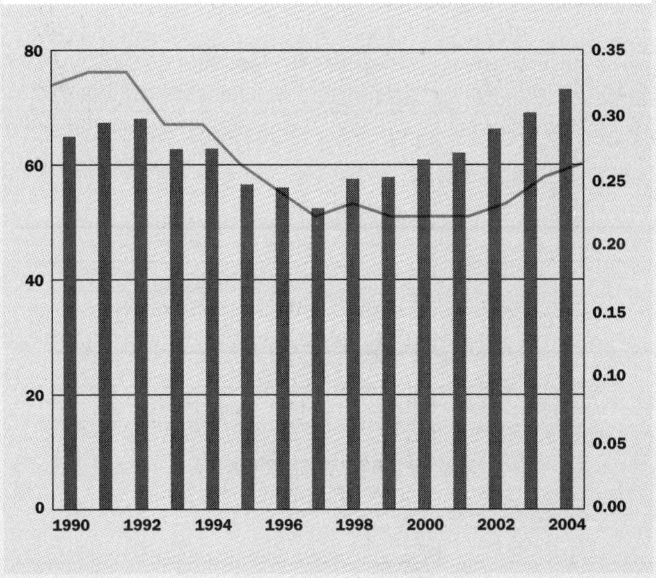

Source: OECD Development Assistance Committee.

Official development assistance (ODA) is the aid provided by the richest countries to the poorest. Through much of the 1990s ODA levels fell while ODA as a proportion of donors' GNI fell even faster. Many donors pledged to provide at least 0.7 percent of GNI, but the average remains below 0.26 percent. Since 2002 donors have pledged to increase aid by $20 billion a year in 2006 and to provide nearly $130 billion a year by 2010. But large increases in aid have, so far, gone to only a few countries such as Iraq, Afghanistan, and the Democratic Republic of Congo.

Debt service is falling, but more relief is needed

Ratio of external debt service to exports of goods and services including workers' remittances (%)

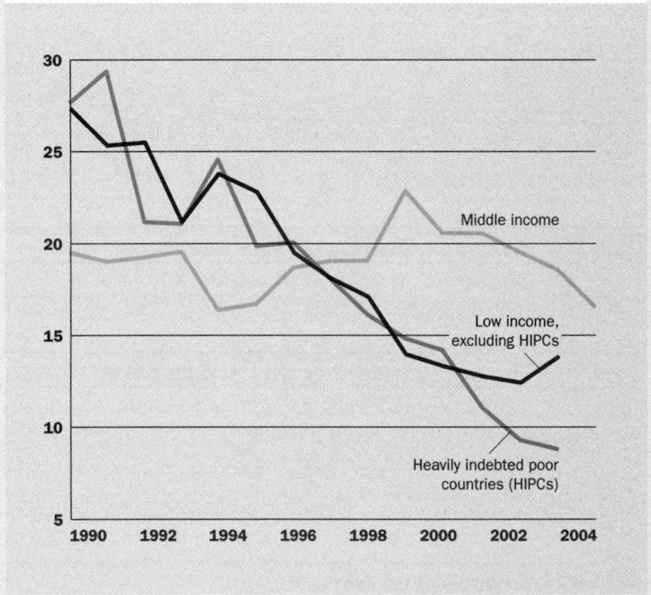

Source: World Bank staff estimates.

Low-income countries paid $26 billion in debt service on public debt in 2004. Middle-income countries paid $173 billion.

Developing country export earnings, needed to acquire the currencies to pay their creditors, have been rising while debt service has grown more slowly, reducing debt burdens for many countries. But for extremely poor countries debt service represents a crucial loss of potential development resources. Since 1998 the Heavily Indebted Poor Countries Initiative has provided $57 billion in debt relief.

Tariffs remain high on poor countries' exports

Average tariffs imposed by developed countries on developing country imports (%)

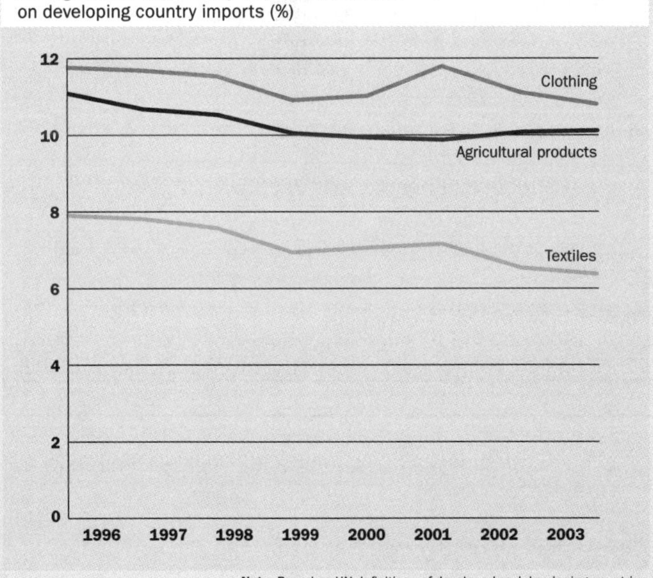

Note: Based on UN definitions of developed and developing countries, which may differ slightly from those of the World Bank.
Source: International Trade Centre, World Trade Organization, and United Nations Conference on Trade and Development.

Creating opportunities for developing countries to sell their products in wealthier markets is an important complement to aid. Many high-income countries allow selected exports of poor countries to enter duty-free. The recent dropping of quotas on textiles has created new opportunities for efficient producers. But high-income countries' tariffs on goods important to developing countries, such as textiles and agricultural products, remain high.

New technologies are spreading quickly

Information and communications technology users in low- and middle-income economies (per 1,000 people)

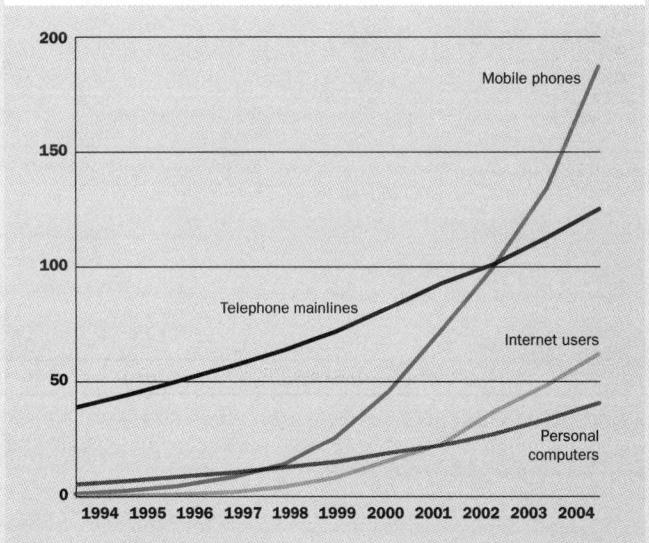

Source: World Bank staff estimates and data from the International Telecommunication Union.

New technologies bring new opportunities to developing countries. Mobile phones help to eliminate the bottlenecks of fixed, mainline phone service. Personal computers are more widely available, and the Internet is expanding rapidly. These are examples of integrating technologies, which reduce barriers of time, space, and culture. Developing countries also need access to new medicines to reduce the terrible burden of disease. Bringing these and other life-saving technologies to poor people will require willing cooperation between the public and private sectors.

Goals, targets, and indicators

Goals and targets from the Millennium Declaration		Indicators for monitoring progress	
Goal 1	**Eradicate extreme poverty and hunger**		
Target 1	Halve, between 1990 and 2015, the proportion of people whose income is less than $1 a day	1	Proportion of population below $1 (PPP) a day [a]
		1a	Poverty headcount ratio (percentage of population below the national poverty line)
		2	Poverty gap ratio [incidence x depth of poverty]
		3	Share of poorest quintile in national consumption
Target 2	Halve, between 1990 and 2015, the proportion of people who suffer from hunger	4	Prevalence of underweight children under five years of age
		5	Proportion of population below minimum level of dietary energy consumption
Goal 2	**Achieve universal primary education**		
Target 3	Ensure that, by 2015, children everywhere, boys and girls alike, will be able to complete a full course of primary schooling	6	Net enrollment ratio in primary education
		7	Proportion of pupils starting grade 1 who reach grade 5 [b]
		8	Literacy rate of 15- to 24-year-olds
Goal 3	**Promote gender equality and empower women**		
Target 4	Eliminate gender disparity in primary and secondary education, preferably by 2005, and in all levels of education no later than 2015	9	Ratios of girls to boys in primary, secondary, and tertiary education
		10	Ratio of literate women to men ages 15–24
		11	Share of women in wage employment in the nonagricultural sector
		12	Proportion of seats held by women in national parliaments
Goal 4	**Reduce child mortality**		
Target 5	Reduce by two-thirds, between 1990 and 2015, the under-five mortality rate	13	Under-five mortality rate
		14	Infant mortality rate
		15	Proportion of one-year-old children immunized against measles
Goal 5	**Improve maternal health**		
Target 6	Reduce by three-quarters, between 1990 and 2015, the maternal mortality ratio	16	Maternal mortality ratio
		17	Proportion of births attended by skilled health personnel
Goal 6	**Combat HIV/AIDS, malaria, and other diseases**		
Target 7	Have halted by 2015 and begun to reverse the spread of HIV/AIDS	18	HIV prevalence among pregnant women ages 15–24
		19	Condom use rate of the contraceptive prevalence rate [c]
		19a	Condom use at last high-risk sex
		19b	Percentage of 15- to 24-year-olds with comprehensive correct knowledge of HIV/AIDS [d]
		19c	Contraceptive prevalence rate
		20	Ratio of school attendance of orphans to school attendance of nonorphans ages 10–14
Target 8	Have halted by 2015 and begun to reverse the incidence of malaria and other major diseases	21	Prevalence and death rates associated with malaria
		22	Proportion of population in malaria-risk areas using effective malaria prevention and treatment measures [e]
		23	Prevalence and death rates associated with tuberculosis
		24	Proportion of tuberculosis cases detected and cured under directly observed treatment, short course (DOTS)
Goal 7	**Ensure environmental sustainability**		
Target 9	Integrate the principles of sustainable development into country policies and programs and reverse the loss of environmental resources	25	Proportion of land area covered by forest
		26	Ratio of area protected to maintain biological diversity to surface area
		27	Energy use (kilograms of oil equivalent) per $1 GDP (PPP)
		28	Carbon dioxide emissions per capita and consumption of ozone-depleting chlorofluorocarbons (ODP tons)
		29	Proportion of population using solid fuels
Target 10	Halve, by 2015, the proportion of people without sustainable access to safe drinking water and basic sanitation	30	Proportion of population with sustainable access to an improved water source, urban and rural
		31	Proportion of population with access to improved sanitation, urban and rural

Goals and targets from the Millennium Declaration		Indicators for monitoring progress
Target 11	By 2020, to have achieved a significant improvement in the lives of at least 100 million slum dwellers	32 Proportion of households with access to secure tenure
Goal 8	**Develop a global partnership for development**	
Target 12	Develop further an open, rule-based, predictable, nondiscriminatory trading and financial system Includes a commitment to good governance, development and poverty reduction—both nationally and internationally	Some of the indicators listed below are monitored separately for the least developed countries (LDCs), Africa, landlocked countries and small island developing states. **Official development assistance (ODA)** 33 Net ODA, total and to the least developed countries, as a percentage of OECD/DAC donors' gross national income 34 Proportion of total bilateral, sector-allocable ODA of OECD/DAC donors to basic social services (basic education, primary health care, nutrition, safe water and sanitation) 35 Proportion of bilateral official development assistance of OECD/DAC donors that is untied 36 ODA received in landlocked countries as a proportion of their gross national incomes 37 ODA received in small island developing states as proportion of their gross national incomes **Market access** 38 Proportion of total developed country imports (by value and excluding arms) from developing countries and from the least developed countries, admitted free of duty 39 Average tariffs imposed by developed countries on agricultural products and textiles and clothing from developing countries 40 Agricultural support estimate for OECD countries as a percentage of their gross domestic product 41 Proportion of ODA provided to help build trade capacity **Debt sustainability** 42 Total number of countries that have reached their HIPC decision points and number that have reached their HIPC completion points (cumulative) 43 Debt relief committed under HIPC Debt Initiative 44 Debt service as a percentage of exports of goods and services
Target 13	Address the special needs of the least developed countries Includes tariff and quota free access for the least developed countries' exports; enhanced programme of debt relief for heavily indebted poor countries (HIPC) and cancellation of official bilateral debt; and more generous ODA for countries committed to poverty reduction	
Target 14	Address the special needs of landlocked countries and small island developing states (through the Programme of Action for the Sustainable Development of Small Island Developing States and the outcome of the 22nd special session of the General Assembly)	
Target 15	Deal comprehensively with the debt problems of developing countries through national and international measures in order to make debt sustainable in the long term	
Target 16	In cooperation with developing countries, develop and implement strategies for decent and productive work for youth	45 Unemployment rate of 15- to 24-year-olds, male and female and total[f]
Target 17	In cooperation with pharmaceutical companies, provide access to affordable essential drugs in developing countries	46 Proportion of population with access to affordable essential drugs on a sustainable basis
Target 18	In cooperation with the private sector, make available the benefits of new technologies, especially information and communications	47 Telephone lines and cellular subscribers per 100 people 48a Personal computers in use per 100 people 48b Internet users per 100 people

Note: Goals, targets, and indicators effective September 8, 2003.

a. For monitoring country poverty trends, indicators based on national poverty lines should be used, where available. b. An alternative indicator under development is "primary completion rate." c. Among contraceptive methods, only condoms are effective in preventing HIV transmission. Since the condom use rate is only measured among women in union, it is supplemented by an indicator on condom use in high-risk situations (indicator 19a) and an indicator on HIV/AIDS knowledge (indicator 19b). Indicator 19c (contraceptive prevalence rate) is also useful in tracking progress in other health, gender, and poverty goals. d. This indicator is defined as the percentage of 15- to 24-year-olds who correctly identify the two major ways of preventing the sexual transmission of HIV (using condoms and limiting sex to one faithful, uninfected partner), who reject the two most common local misconceptions about HIV transmission, and who know that a healthy-looking person can transmit HIV. However, since there are currently not a sufficient number of surveys to be able to calculate the indicator as defined above, UNICEF, in collaboration with UNAIDS and WHO, produced two proxy indicators that represent two components of the actual indicator. They are the percentage of women and men ages 15–24 who know that a person can protect herself from HIV infection by "consistent use of condom," and the percentage of women and men ages 15–24 who know a healthy-looking person can transmit HIV. e. Prevention to be measured by the percentage of children under age five sleeping under insecticide-treated bednets; treatment to be measured by percentage of children under age five who are appropriately treated. f. An improved measure of the target for future years is under development by the International Labour Organization.

1.1 Size of the economy

	Population	Surface area	Population density	Gross national income		Gross national income per capita		PPP gross national income[a]			Gross domestic product	
	millions	thousand sq. km	people per sq. km	$ billions	Rank	$	Rank	$ billions	Per capita $	Rank	% growth	Per capita % growth
	2004	2004	2004	2004[b]	2004	2004[b]	2004	2004	2004	2004	2003–04	2003–04
East Asia & Pacific[c]	**1,870 s**	**16,301 s**	**118 w**	**2,647.2 t**		**1,416 w**		**9,968 t**	**5,332 w**		**9.0 w**	**8.1 w**
Cambodia	14	181	78	4.8	128	350	183	32[d]	2,310[d]	154	7.7	5.6
China	1,296	9,598[e]	139	1,938.0	5	1,500	129	7,634[f]	5,890[f]	108	10.1	9.4
Hong Kong, China	7	..	..	183.5	28	26,660	27	217	31,560	12	8.1	6.9
Indonesia	218	1,905	120	248.0	22	1,140	137	757	3,480	140	5.1	3.7
Korea, Dem. Rep.	22	121	186	..	..	..[g]	..	..	..	..	..	..
Lao PDR	6	237	25	2.3	154	390	180	11	1,880	171	6.3	3.9
Malaysia	25	330	76	112.6	37	4,520	79	242	9,720	78	7.1	5.2
Mongolia	3	1,567	2	1.5	164	600	161	5	2,040	162	10.7	9.2
Myanmar	50	677	76	..	..	..[g]	..	..	..	..	..	..
Papua New Guinea	6	463	13	3.3	*142*	560	164	13[d]	2,280[d]	155	2.5	0.4
Philippines	82	300	274	95.1	41	1,170	136	404	4,950	125	6.1	4.2
Thailand	64	513	125	158.4	31	2,490	104	505	7,930	88	6.2	5.3
Vietnam	82	332	252	44.6	58	540	168	222	2,700	149	7.7	6.6
Europe & Central Asia	**472 s**	**24,238 s**	**20 w**	**1,557.1 t**		**3,295 w**		**3,945 t**	**8,350 w**		**7.2 w**	**7.1 w**
Albania	3	29	114	6.6	114	2,120	120	16	5,070	124	5.9	5.3
Armenia	3	30	107	3.2	143	1,060	139	13	4,160	135	7.0	7.4
Azerbaijan	8	87	101	7.8	105	940	147	32	3,810	137	10.2	9.2
Belarus	10	208	47	21.0	75	2,140	119	68	6,970	97	11.0	11.6
Bosnia and Herzegovina	4	51	76	8.0	104	2,040	122	28	7,230	95	6.2	6.4
Bulgaria	8	111	70	21.3	73	2,750	99	62	7,940	86	5.6	6.4
Croatia	4	57	79	30.3	61	6,820	69	53	11,920	69	3.8	3.8
Czech Republic	10	79	132	93.3	42	9,130	59	188	18,420	51	4.4	4.3
Estonia	1	45	32	9.5	99	7,080	67	18	13,630	62	7.8	8.2
Georgia	5	70	65	4.8	129	1,060	139	13[d]	2,900[d]	146	6.2	7.3
Hungary	10	93	110	84.6	46	8,370	62	160	15,800	57	4.6	4.9
Kazakhstan	15	2,725	6	33.8	60	2,250	114	104	6,930	99	9.4	8.8
Kyrgyz Republic	5	200	27	2.1	155	400	178	9	1,860	172	7.1	5.9
Latvia	2	65	37	12.9	91	5,580	75	27	11,820	70	8.3	8.9
Lithuania	3	65	55	19.7	77	5,740	74	44	12,690	65	6.7	7.2
Macedonia, FYR	2	26	80	4.9	126	2,420	105	13	6,560	102	2.9	2.7
Moldova	4	34	128	2.6[h]	147	720[h]	157	8	1,950	165	7.3	7.6
Poland	38	313	125	232.9	25	6,100	72	486	12,730	64	5.4	5.5
Romania	22	238	94	64.2	51	2,960	98	181	8,330	85	8.3	8.6
Russian Federation	144	17,098	9	488.5	16	3,400	94	1,392	9,680	79	7.1	7.7
Serbia and Montenegro	8	102	80	21.8[i]	72	2,680[i]	101	..	..	106	8.2	8.3
Slovak Republic	5	49	112	34.9	59	6,480	71	78	14,480	59	5.5	5.4
Tajikistan	6	143	46	1.8	162	280	190	7	1,160	186	10.6	9.4
Turkey	72	784	93	269.0	20	3,750	89	554	7,720	90	8.9	7.4
Turkmenistan	5	488	10	..	..	..	..	..	..	..	..	..
Ukraine	47	604	82	60.2	53	1,270	132	300	6,330	104	12.1	13.0
Uzbekistan	26	447	62	11.9	93	450	172	49	1,860	172	7.7	6.1
Latin America & Carib.	**546 s**	**20,418 s**	**27 w**	**1,952.1 t**		**3,576 w**		**4,183 t**	**7,661 w**		**5.9 w**	**4.4 w**
Argentina	38	2,780	14	137.3	35	3,580	93	481	12,530	66	9.0	7.9
Bolivia	9	1,099	8	8.6	101	960	145	23	2,600	151	3.6	1.6
Brazil	184	8,515	22	551.6	13	3,000	97	1,460	7,940	86	4.9	3.5
Chile	16	757	22	84.2	47	5,220	76	171	10,610	77	6.1	4.9
Colombia	45	1,139	43	90.9	43	2,020	123	312[d]	6,940[d]	98	4.1	2.5
Costa Rica	4	51	83	19.0	79	4,470	80	39[d]	9,220[d]	82	4.2	2.3
Cuba	11	111	102	..	..	..[j]	..	..	..	..	*1.1*	*0.8*
Dominican Republic	9	49	181	18.4	81	2,100	121	60[d]	6,860[d]	100	2.0	0.5
Ecuador	13	284	47	28.9	63	2,210	116	49	3,770	138	6.9	5.4
El Salvador	7	21	326	15.7	84	2,320	109	33[d]	4,890[d]	126	1.5	–0.2
Guatemala	12	109	113	26.9	65	2,190	117	52[d]	4,260[d]	130	2.7	0.2
Haiti	8	28	305	*3.3*	140	*400*	175	..	..	166	*0.4*	*–1.0*
Honduras	7	112	63	7.3	109	1,040	141	19[d]	2,760[d]	148	4.6	2.3

Size of the economy

	Population	Surface area	Population density	Gross national income		Gross national income per capita		PPP gross national income[a]			Gross domestic product	
	millions 2004	thousand sq. km 2004	people per sq. km 2004	$ billions 2004[b]	Rank 2004	$ 2004[b]	Rank 2004	$ billions 2004	Per capita $ 2004	Rank 2004	% growth 2003–04	Per capita % growth 2003–04
Jamaica	3	11	244	8.7	100	3,300[k]	96	10	3,950	136	0.9	0.4
Mexico	104	1,958	54	704.9	10	6,790	70	1,001	9,640	80	4.4	2.9
Nicaragua	5	130	44	4.5	132	830[l]	149	19	3,480	140	5.1	3.0
Panama	3	76	43	13.4	89	4,210	83	21[d]	6,730[d]	101	6.2	4.4
Paraguay	6	407	15	6.9	113	1,140	137	29[d]	4,820[d]	127	4.0	1.6
Peru	28	1,285	22	65.0	50	2,360	108	149	5,400	118	4.8	3.3
Trinidad and Tobago	1	5	254	11.4	95	8,730	61	15	11,430	73	6.2	5.9
Uruguay	3	176	20	13.4	88	3,900	88	31	9,030	83	11.9	11.1
Venezuela, RB	26	912	30	105.3	38	4,030	86	152	5,830	110	17.9	15.8
Middle East & N. Africa	**300 s**	**8,984 s**	**34 w**	**592.0 t**		**1,972 w**		**1,722 t**	**5,734 w**		**5.9 w**	**3.8 w**
Algeria	32	2,382	14	73.3	49	2,270	113	204[d]	6,320[d]	105	5.2	3.6
Egypt, Arab Rep.	73	1,001	73	90.6	45	1,250	133	305	4,200	134	4.2	2.2
Iran, Islamic Rep.	67	1,648	41	155.3	32	2,320	109	505	7,530	92	5.6	4.6
Iraq	..	438	..	..	..	..[j]	..	..	..	..	46.5	..
Jordan	5	89	62	11.9	92	2,190	117	26	4,770	128	7.7	5.1
Lebanon	4	10	346	21.3	74	6,010	73	20	5,550	117	6.3	5.2
Libya	6	1,760	3	25.3	68	4,400	81	..	..	84	4.5	2.5
Morocco	30	447	67	46.9	56	1,570	128	127	4,250	131	4.2	0.7
Oman	3	310	8	23.0	*70*	9,070	60	37	14,680	58	3.1	2.2
Syrian Arab Republic	19	185	101	22.8	71	1,230	134	65	3,500	139	2.0	–0.4
Tunisia	10	164	64	26.3	66	2,650	102	74	7,430	94	5.8	4.9
West Bank and Gaza	4	..	..	*3.8*	*135*	*1,120*	135	..	..	142	*–1.7*	*–5.6*
Yemen, Rep.	20	528	39	11.2	96	550	167	16	810	197	2.7	–0.5
South Asia	**1,447 s**	**5,140 s**	**303 w**	**859.0 t**		**594 w**		**4,129 t**	**2,854 w**		**6.7 w**	**5.0 w**
Afghanistan	..	652	..	5.5	..	..[g]	..	..	..	..	7.5	..
Bangladesh	139	144	1,069	61.3	52	440	174	274	1,970	164	6.3	4.3
India	1,080	3,287	363	673.2	11	620	159	3,369[d]	3,120[d]	144	6.9	5.4
Nepal	27	147	186	6.6	115	250	193	39	1,480	178	3.5	1.4
Pakistan	152	796	197	90.7	44	600	161	330	2,170	157	6.4	3.9
Sri Lanka	19	66	300	19.5	78	1,010	143	82	4,210	133	5.4	4.5
Sub-Saharan Africa	**726 s**	**24,265 s**	**31 w**	**436.5 t**		**601 w**		**1,337 t**	**1,842 w**		**4.8 w**	**2.6 w**
Angola	15	1,247	12	14.4	85	930	148	30[d]	1,930[d]	167	11.1	7.9
Benin	8	113	74	3.7	139	450	172	9	1,090	189	2.7	–0.5
Botswana	2	582	3	7.7	106	4,360	82	17	9,580	81	4.9	5.0
Burkina Faso	13	274	47	4.4	133	350	183	15[d]	1,170[d]	184	3.9	0.6
Burundi	7	28	284	0.7	189	90	208	5[d]	660[d]	206	5.5	1.9
Cameroon	16	475	34	13.0	90	810	151	34	2,120	160	4.3	2.4
Central African Republic	4	623	6	1.2	169	310	187	4[d]	1,100[d]	188	1.3	0.0
Chad	9	1,284	8	2.3	152	250	193	13	1,340	182	29.8	25.5
Congo, Dem. Rep.	56	2,345	25	6.4	116	110	206	38[d]	680[d]	203	6.3	3.2
Congo, Rep.	4	342	11	2.9	145	760	152	3	740	201	3.6	0.6
Côte d'Ivoire	18	322	56	13.6	87	760	152	26	1,470	180	1.6	0.1
Eritrea	4	118	42	0.8	180	190	199	4[d]	960[d]	191	1.8	–2.5
Ethiopia	70	1,104	70	7.6	107	110	206	52[d]	750[d]	200	13.1	10.9
Gabon	1	268	5	5.6	119	4,080	85	8	5,700	112	1.4	–0.2
Gambia, The	1	11	148	0.4	192	280	190	3[d]	1,890[d]	170	8.3	5.4
Ghana	22	239	95	8.3	102	380	182	48[d]	2,220[d]	156	5.8	3.6
Guinea	9	246	37	3.8	138	410	177	20	2,160	158	2.6	0.4
Guinea-Bissau	2	36	55	0.3	203	160	201	1[d]	690[d]	202	4.3	1.2
Kenya	33	580	59	16.1	83	480	171	38	1,130	187	4.3	2.0
Lesotho	2	30	59	1.3	166	730	156	6[d]	3,250[d]	143	2.3	2.5
Liberia	3	111	34	0.4	195	120	205	..	..	203	2.4	1.8
Madagascar	18	587	31	5.2	124	290	189	15	840	195	5.2	2.4
Malawi	13	118	134	2.0	156	160	201	8	630	207	6.7	4.4
Mali	13	1,240	11	4.3	134	330	184	12	950	193	2.2	–0.8
Mauritania	3	1,026	3	1.6	163	530	169	6[d]	2,050[d]	161	6.9	3.7

1.1 Size of the economy

	Population	Surface area	Population density	Gross national income		Gross national income per capita		PPP gross national income[a]			Gross domestic product	
	millions	thousand sq. km	people per sq. km	$ billions	Rank	$	Rank	$ billions	Per capita $	Rank	% growth	Per capita % growth
	2004	2004	2004	2004[b]	2004	2004[b]	2004	2004	2004	2004	2003–04	2003–04
Mauritius	1	2	608	5.7	118	4,640	78	15	11,950	68	4.2	3.2
Mozambique	19	802	25	5.3	122	270	192	23[d]	1,170[d]	184	7.2	5.1
Namibia	2	824	2	4.8	130	2,380	107	15[d]	7,520[d]	93	6.0	4.7
Niger	13	1,267	11	2.8	146	210	196	11[d]	780[d]	199	0.9	–2.4
Nigeria	129	924	141	55.3	54	430	175	125[d]	970[d]	190	6.0	3.7
Rwanda	9	26	360	1.9	158	210	196	11	1,240	183	4.0	2.5
Senegal	11	197	59	7.2	110	630	158	19[d]	1,660[d]	176	6.2	3.7
Sierra Leone	5	72	75	1.1	175	210	196	3	550	208	7.4	3.0
Somalia	8	638	13	..	..	..[g]	..	..	..	..	..	..
South Africa	46	1,219	37	165.3	30	3,630	92	499[d]	10,960[d]	75	3.7	4.4
Sudan	36	2,506	15	18.7	80	530	169	64[d]	1,810[d]	174	6.0	4.0
Swaziland	1	17	65	1.9	160	1,660	127	6	5,650	114	2.1	0.8
Tanzania	38	945	43	11.6[m]	94	320[m]	185	25	670	205	6.3	4.3
Togo	6	57	110	1.9	159	310	187	9[d]	1,510[d]	177	3.0	0.4
Uganda	28	241	141	6.9	112	250	193	40[d]	1,450[d]	181	5.7	2.1
Zambia	11	753	15	4.6	131	400	178	10	890	194	4.6	2.9
Zimbabwe	13	391	33	8.0	103	620	159	26	2,040	162	–4.2	–4.7
High income	**1,004 s**	**34,595 s**	**30 w**	**32,245.3 t**		**32,112 w**		**31,138 t**	**31,009 w**		**3.4 w**	**2.6 w**
Australia	20	7,741	3	544.3	14	27,070	25	590	29,340	22	3.0	1.8
Austria	8	84	99	263.9	21	32,280	15	260	31,800	10	2.2	1.5
Belgium	10	33	318	326.0	18	31,280	17	329	31,530	13	2.9	2.5
Canada	32	9,985	4	905.0	9	28,310	21	984	30,760	16	2.9	1.8
Denmark	5	43	127	220.2	26	40,750	6	172	31,770	11	2.4	2.1
Finland	5	338	17	171.9	29	32,880	14	156	29,800	19	3.7	3.4
France	60	552	110	1,888.4[n]	6	30,370[n]	19	1,779	29,460	20	2.3	1.7
Germany	83	357	236	2,532.3	3	30,690	18	2,324	28,170	27	1.6	1.6
Greece	11	132	86	185.0	27	16,730	42	246	22,230	41	4.2	3.9
Ireland	4	70	59	139.6	34	34,310	12	134	32,930	8	4.9	3.0
Israel	7	22	313	118.0	36	17,360	39	162	23,770	37	4.4	2.8
Italy	58	301	196	1,513.1	7	26,280	28	1,613	28,020	28	1.2	1.4
Japan	128	378	351	4,734.3	2	37,050	9	3,809	29,810	18	2.7	2.5
Korea, Rep.	48	99	487	673.1	12	14,000	50	987	20,530	46	4.6	4.1
Kuwait	2	18	138	55.3	55	22,470	33	53[d]	21,610[d]	43	7.2	4.5
Netherlands	16	42	481	523.1	15	32,130	16	511	31,360	15	1.4	1.1
New Zealand	4	271	15	81.2	48	19,990	37	90	22,260	40	4.4	3.1
Norway	5	324	15	237.8	24	51,810	2	178	38,680	4	2.9	2.6
Portugal	11	92	115	149.3	33	14,220	49	202	19,240	49	1.0	0.4
Puerto Rico	4	9	439	..	..	..[o]	..	..	..	..	..	..
Saudi Arabia	24	2,150	11	242.9	23	10,140	55	331[d]	13,810[d]	61	5.2	2.5
Singapore	4	1	6,329	105.0	39	24,760	29	116	27,370	29	8.4	7.0
Slovenia	2	20	99	29.5	62	14,770	47	42	20,830	45	4.6	4.5
Spain	43	505	86	919.1	8	21,530	34	1,057	24,750	33	3.1	1.4
Sweden	9	450	22	322.3	19	35,840	10	269	29,880	17	3.6	3.2
Switzerland	7	41	185	366.5	17	49,600	3	264	35,660	6	2.1	1.4
United Arab Emirates	4	84	52	102.7	40	23,770	31	104	24,090	34	8.5	1.5
United Kingdom	60	244	247	2,013.4	4	33,630	13	1,882	31,430	14	3.1	2.6
United States	294	9,629	32	12,168.5	1	41,440	5	11,693	39,820	3	4.2	3.2
World	**6,365 s**	**133,941 s**	**49 w**	**40,282.3 t**		**6,329 w**		**56,289 t**	**8,844 w**		**4.1 w**	**2.9 w**
Low income	2,343	30,276	80	1,187.7		507		5,291	2,258		6.5	4.6
Middle income	3,018	69,070	45	6,862.7		2,274		20,051	6,644		7.2	6.3
Lower middle income	2,442	39,173	63	4,116.0		1,686		14,233	5,829		7.6	6.6
Upper middle income	576	29,897	20	2,748.2		4,769		5,859	10,168		6.6	6.0
Low & middle income	5,361	99,346	55	8,050.1		1,502		25,334	4,726		7.1	5.8
High income	1,004	34,595	30	32,245.3		32,112		31,138	31,009		3.4	2.6

a. PPP is purchasing power parity. b. Calculated by the *World Bank Atlas* method. c. Hong Kong, China, a high-income economy, is not included in this aggregate. d. Based on regression; others are extrapolated from International Comparison Program benchmark estimates. e. Includes Hong Kong, China; Macao, China; and Taiwan, China. f. Based on a 1986 bilateral comparison of China and the United States (Rouen and Kai 1995) employing a different methodology than that used for other countries. This interim methodology will be revised in the next few years. g. Estimated to be low income. h. Excludes data for Transnistria. i. Excludes data for Kosovo. j. Estimated to be lower middle income. k. Included in the aggregates for lower-middle-income economies based on earlier data. l. Included in the aggregates for low-income economies based on earlier data. m. Data refers to mainland Tanzania only. n. Includes French Guiana, Guadeloupe, Martinique, and Réunion. o. Estimated to be high income.

Size of the economy 1.1

About the data

Population, land area, income, output, and growth in output are basic measures of the size of an economy. They also provide a broad indication of actual and potential resources. Population, land area, income (as measured by gross national income, GNI) and output (as measured by gross domestic product, GDP) are therefore used throughout *World Development Indicators* to normalize other indicators.

Population estimates are generally based on extrapolations from the most recent national census. For further discussion of the measurement of population and population growth, see *About the data* for table 2.1 and *Statistical methods*.

The surface area of an economy includes inland bodies of water and some coastal waterways. Surface area thus differs from land area, which excludes bodies of water, and from gross area, which may include offshore territorial waters. Land area is particularly important for understanding an economy's agricultural capacity and the environmental effects of human activity. (For measures of land area and data on rural population density, land use, and agricultural productivity, see tables 3.1–3.3.) Innovations in satellite mapping and computer databases have resulted in more precise measurements of land and water areas.

GNI measures the total domestic and foreign value added claimed by residents. GNI comprises GDP plus net receipts of primary income (compensation of employees and property income) from nonresident sources. The World Bank uses GNI per capita in U.S. dollars to classify countries for analytical purposes and to determine borrowing eligibility. For definitions of the income groups in *World Development Indicators*, see *Users guide*. For discussion of the usefulness of national income and output as measures of productivity or welfare, see *About the data* for tables 4.1 and 4.2.

When calculating GNI in U.S. dollars from GNI reported in national currencies, the World Bank follows its *Atlas* conversion method, using a three-year average of exchange rates to smooth the effects of transitory fluctuations in exchange rates. (For further discussion of the *Atlas* method, see *Statistical methods*.) GDP and GDP per capita growth rates are calculated from data in constant prices and national currency units.

Because exchange rates do not always reflect differences in price levels between countries, this table also converts GNI and GNI per capita estimates into international dollars using purchasing power parity (PPP) rates. PPP rates provide a standard measure allowing comparison of real levels of expenditure between countries, just as conventional price indexes allow comparison of real values over time. The PPP conversion factors used here are derived from price surveys covering 118 countries conducted by the International Comparison Program. For Organisation for Economic Co-operation and Development (OECD) countries data come from the most recent round of surveys, completed in 2002; the rest are from either the 1996 or the 1993 survey or earlier round and extrapolated to the 1996 benchmark. Estimates for countries not included in the surveys are derived from statistical models using available data.

All economies shown in *World Development Indicators* are ranked by size, including those that appear in table 1.6. The ranks are shown only in table 1.1. No rank is shown for economies for which numerical estimates of GNI per capita are not published. Economies with missing data are included in the ranking at their approximate level, so that the relative order of other economies remains consistent.

Definitions

• **Population** is based on the de facto definition of population, which counts all residents regardless of legal status or citizenship—except for refugees not permanently settled in the country of asylum, who are generally considered part of the population of their country of origin. The values shown are midyear estimates for 2004. See also table 2.1. • **Surface area** is a country's total area, including areas under inland bodies of water and some coastal waterways. • **Population density** is midyear population divided by land area in square kilometers. • **Gross national income** (GNI) is the sum of value added by all resident producers plus any product taxes (less subsidies) not included in the valuation of output plus net receipts of primary income (compensation of employees and property income) from abroad. Data are in current U.S. dollars converted using the *World Bank Atlas* method (see *Statistical methods*). • **GNI per capita** is gross national income divided by midyear population. GNI per capita in U.S. dollars is converted using the *World Bank Atlas* method. • **PPP GNI** is gross national income converted to international dollars using purchasing power parity rates. An international dollar has the same purchasing power over GNI as a U.S. dollar has in the United States. • **Gross domestic product** (GDP) is the sum of value added by all resident producers plus any product taxes (less subsidies) not included in the valuation of output. Growth is calculated from constant price GDP data in local currency. • **GDP per capita** is gross domestic product divided by midyear population.

1.1a

Developing countries produce slightly less than half the world's output

Share of PPP GNI, 2004

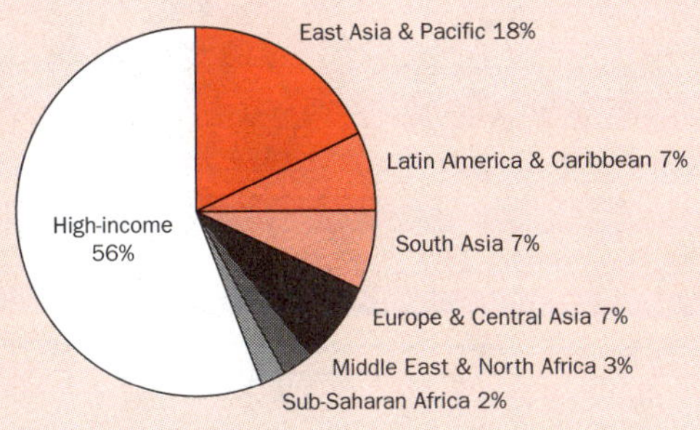

When measured by purchasing power parities (PPPs), which take into account national differences in the cost of living, developing countries produce a large part of the world's output. Much of this is in the form of nontradable goods and services, which are undervalued at market exchange rates. For this reason PPPs are used in international comparisons of well-being such as $1 and $2 a day measures of absolute poverty.

Source: World Bank staff estimates.

Data sources

Population estimates are prepared by World Bank staff from a variety of sources (see *Data sources* for table 2.1). Data on surface and land area are from the Food and Agriculture Organization (see *Data sources* for table 3.1). GNI, GNI per capita, GDP growth, and GDP per capita growth are estimated by World Bank staff based on national accounts data collected by World Bank staff during economic missions or reported by national statistical offices to other international organizations such as the OECD. Purchasing power parity conversion factors are estimates by World Bank staff based on data collected by the International Comparison Program.

1.2 Millennium Development Goals: eradicating poverty and improving lives

	Eradicate extreme poverty and hunger			Achieve universal primary education		Promote gender equality		Reduce child mortality		Improve maternal health		
	Share of poorest quintile in national consumption or income %	Prevalence of child malnutrition Underweight % of children under age 5		Primary completion rate[a] %		Ratio of female to male enrollments in primary and secondary school[a] %		Under-five mortality rate per 1,000 live births		Maternal mortality ratio Modeled estimates per 100,000 live births	Births attended by skilled health staff % of total	
	1992–2004[b,c]	1989–94[b]	2000–04[b]	1991	2004	1991	2004	1990	2004	2000	1989–94[b]	2000–04[b]
East Asia & Pacific[d]		19 w	12 w	97 w	99 w	89 w	*98* w	59 w	37 w	117 w	.. w	86 w
Cambodia	6.9	..	45	..	82	73	*85*	115	141	450	..	32
China	4.7	17	8	103	*99*	87	*98*	49	31	56	..	96
Hong Kong, China	5.3	..	..	102	111	107	104	..	..	..	..	..
Indonesia	8.4	..	28	91	*101*	93	*98*	91	38	230	37	72
Korea, Dem. Rep.	..	..	24	..	..	..	..	55	55	67	..	97
Lao PDR	8.1	40	40	*43*	74	75	84	163	83	650	..	19
Malaysia	4.4	22	11	90	*95*	101	*105*	22	12	41	..	97
Mongolia	5.6	12	13	..	95	109	108	108	52	110	..	99
Myanmar	..	31	32	..	*72*	96	*99*	130	106	360	..	57
Papua New Guinea	4.5	..	..	50	*55*	80	*87*	101	93	300	..	41
Philippines	5.4	30	28	*86*	*98*	100	*102*	62	34	200	53	60
Thailand	6.3	19	..	..	..	95	98	37	21	44	..	99
Vietnam	7.5	45	28	..	*101*	..	94	53	23	130	..	90
Europe & Central Asia		.. w	.. w	92 w	94 w	97 w	*96* w	49 w	34 w	58 w	.. w	94 w
Albania	9.1	..	14	..	*99*	96	*97*	45	19	55	..	98
Armenia	8.5	..	3	*90*	107	..	103	60	32	55	..	97
Azerbaijan	12.2	..	7	..	96	100	97	105	90	94	..	84
Belarus	8.5	..	..	95	101	..	100	17	11	35	..	100
Bosnia and Herzegovina	9.5	..	4	..	..	..	..	22	15	31	97	100
Bulgaria	8.7	..	..	90	*97*	99	*97*	19	15	32	..	99
Croatia	8.3	1	..	*85*	*91*	106	98	12	7	8	..	100
Czech Republic	10.3	1	..	..	*102*	101	*103*	13	4	9	..	100
Estonia	6.7	..	..	*93*	*103*	68	73	16	8	63	..	100
Georgia	5.6	..	..	..	86	99	*99*	47	45	32	..	..
Hungary	9.5	..	..	82	*96*	100	*100*	17	8	16	..	100
Kazakhstan	7.4	..	..	..	110	102	98	63	73	210	..	..
Kyrgyz Republic	8.9	..	7	..	93	..	101	80	68	110	..	99
Latvia	6.6	..	..	..	*98*	100	*99*	18	12	42	..	..
Lithuania	6.8	..	..	*89*	*105*	..	*98*	13	8	13	..	100
Macedonia, FYR	6.1	..	..	*98*	*97*	99	*99*	38	14	23	..	99
Moldova	7.8	..	..	..	83	105	102	40	28	36	..	..
Poland	7.5	..	..	96	*100*	101	*97*	18	8	13	..	100
Romania	8.1	6	3	*96*	*90*	99	*100*	31	20	49	99	99
Russian Federation	6.1	4	6	*93*	..	104	*99*	29	21	67	..	99
Serbia and Montenegro	..	..	2	71	*96*	103	*101*	28	15	11	..	93
Slovak Republic	8.8	..	..	*96*	*101*	..	*100*	14	9	3	..	99
Tajikistan	7.9	..	..	..	92	..	88	119	93	100	..	71
Turkey	5.3	10	4	90	..	81	*85*	82	32	70	76	83
Turkmenistan	6.1	..	12	..	..	..	..	97	103	31	..	97
Ukraine	9.2	..	1	92	*91*	..	99	26	18	35	..	100
Uzbekistan	9.2	..	8	..	*98*	94	*98*	79	69	24	..	96
Latin America & Carib.		.. w	.. w	86 w	97 w	.. w	*102* w	54 w	31 w	194 w	77 w	87 w
Argentina	3.2[e]	2	..	..	*102*	..	*103*	29	18	82	96	99
Bolivia	1.5	15	8	71	100	..	98	125	69	420	47	67
Brazil	2.6	7	..	*93*	*111*	..	*103*	60	34	260	72	96
Chile	3.3	1	1	..	*97*	100	*99*	21	8	31	100	100
Colombia	2.5	10	7	71	94	..	..	36	21	130	82	86
Costa Rica	3.9	2	..	74	92	65	*68*	18	13	43	98	98
Cuba	..	..	4	96	93	98	*101*	13	7	33	100	100
Dominican Republic	3.9	10	5	*61*	91	..	100	65	32	150	93	98
Ecuador	3.3	..	12	*91*	101	81	*94*	57	26	130	..	..
El Salvador	2.7	11	10	41	84	..	73	60	28	150	51	92
Guatemala	2.9	..	23	..	70	46	72	82	45	240	..	41
Haiti	2.4	27	17	27	..	108	..	150	117	680	23	24
Honduras	3.4	18	17	65	79	103	95	59	41	110	45	56

Millennium Development Goals: eradicating poverty and improving lives

	Eradicate extreme poverty and hunger			Achieve universal primary education		Promote gender equality		Reduce child mortality		Improve maternal health		
	Share of poorest quintile in national consumption or income %	Prevalence of child malnutrition Underweight % of children under age 5		Primary completion rate[a] %		Ratio of female to male enrollments in primary and secondary school[a] %		Under-five mortality rate per 1,000 live births		Maternal mortality ratio Modeled estimates per 100,000 live births	Births attended by skilled health staff % of total	
	1992–2004[b,c]	1989–94[b]	2000–04[b]	1991	2004	1991	2004	1990	2004	2000	1989–94[b]	2000–04[b]
Jamaica	6.7	5	4	90	*84*	102	*101*	20	20	87	79	97
Mexico	4.3	17	..	86	*97*	98	*102*	46	28	83	..	95
Nicaragua	5.6	11	10	41	73	109	103	68	38	230	..	67
Panama	2.5	6	..	*86*	97	..	101	34	24	160	86	93
Paraguay	2.2	4	5	65	*89*	99	*98*	41	24	170	67	77
Peru	3.2	11	7	..	*96*	96	*97*	80	29	410	..	59
Trinidad and Tobago	5.5	..	6	100	94	101	101	33	20	160	..	96
Uruguay	5.0[e]	4	..	95	*94*	..	*105*	25	17	27	..	..
Venezuela, RB	4.7	5	4	81	89	105	103	27	19	96	..	94
Middle East & N. Africa		**.. w**	**.. w**	**78 w**	**88 w**	**81 w**	**90 w**	**81 w**	**55 w**	**183 w**	**42 w**	**72 w**
Algeria	7.0	9	10	79	94	83	99	69	40	140	77	96
Egypt, Arab Rep.	8.6	10	9	..	*93*	102	98	104	36	84	41	69
Iran, Islamic Rep.	5.1	..	..	91	95	85	100	72	38	76	..	90
Iraq	..	12	16	*59*	74	78	78	50	..	250	54	72
Jordan	6.7	6	4	101	*97*	101	*101*	40	27	41	87	100
Lebanon	..	..	..	..	94	..	102	37	31	150	..	..
Libya	..	..	..	..	..	..	*103*	41	20	97	..	..
Morocco	6.5	10	10	46	*67*	70	88	89	43	220	31	63
Oman	..	24	..	*74*	91	89	98	32	13	87	..	95
Syrian Arab Republic	..	12	7	89	107	85	94	44	16	160	77	..
Tunisia	6.0	..	4	74	*94*	86	*102*	52	25	120	..	90
West Bank and Gaza	..	..	..	..	98	..	103	..	..	..	..	97
Yemen, Rep.	7.4	39	46	..	62	..	63	142	111	570	16	27
South Asia		**53 w**	**.. w**	**73 w**	**82 w**	**71 w**	***87* w**	**129 w**	**92 w**	**564 w**	**.. w**	**36 w**
Afghanistan	..	..	39	*25*	..	54	34	260	..	1,900	..	14
Bangladesh	9.0	68	48	*49*	*73*	..	*106*	149	77	380	10	13
India	8.9	53	..	..	*84*	70	*88*	123	85	540	34	43
Nepal	6.0	..	48	51	*71*	59	*90*	145	76	740	7	15
Pakistan	9.3	40	38	..	..	..	73	130	101	500	19	23
Sri Lanka	8.3	38	30	94	..	102	*102*	32	14	92	94	96
Sub-Saharan Africa		**.. w**	**.. w**	**51 w**	**62 w**	**80 w**	**84 w**	**185 w**	**168 w**	**921 w**	**41 w**	**42 w**
Angola	..	20	31	35	..	..	..	260	260	1,700	..	45
Benin	7.4	..	23	21	49	49	71	185	152	850	..	66
Botswana	2.2	..	13	79	*92*	109	*102*	58	116	100	..	94
Burkina Faso	6.9	33	38	21	29	62	76	210	192	1,000	42	38
Burundi	5.1	..	45	46	33	82	82	190	190	1,000	..	25
Cameroon	5.6	15	18	56	72	83	87	139	149	730	58	62
Central African Republic	2.0	..	24	27	..	60	..	168	193	1,100	..	44
Chad	..	..	37	18	29	41	58	203	200	1,100	..	14
Congo, Dem. Rep.	..	..	31	46	..	85	*87*	205	205	990	..	61
Congo, Rep.	..	..	..	54	66	101	101	110	108	510	..	..
Côte d'Ivoire	5.2	24	17	43	*43*	102	*101*	157	194	690	45	68
Eritrea	..	41	40	*19*	44	104	*100*	147	82	630	..	28
Ethiopia	9.1	48	47	*21*	51	109	*106*	204	166	850	..	6
Gabon	..	..	12	*58*	*66*	64	*85*	92	91	420	..	86
Gambia, The	4.8	..	17	*44*	..	98	99	154	122	540	44	55
Ghana	5.6	27	22	63	65	99	*101*	122	112	540	44	47
Guinea	6.4	27	33	17	48	..	*65*	240	155	740	31	56
Guinea-Bissau	5.2	..	25	..	*27*	95	..	253	203	1,100	..	35
Kenya	6.0	23	20	..	89	94	94	97	120	1,000	45	42
Lesotho	1.5	21	18	58	71	124	104	104	112	550	50	60
Liberia	..	..	27	..	..	..	..	235	235	760	..	51
Madagascar	4.9	45	42	33	45	98	..	168	123	550	57	51
Malawi	4.9	28	22	31	58	81	98	241	175	1,800	55	61
Mali	4.6	..	33	11	44	59	74	250	219	1,200	..	41
Mauritania	6.2	48	32	33	43	67	96	133	125	1,000	40	57

1.2 Millennium Development Goals: eradicating poverty and improving lives

	Eradicate extreme poverty and hunger			Achieve universal primary education		Promote gender equality		Reduce child mortality		Improve maternal health		
	Share of poorest quintile in national consumption or income %	Prevalence of child malnutrition Underweight % of children under age 5		Primary completion rate[a] %		Ratio of female to male enrollments in primary and secondary school[a] %		Under-five mortality rate per 1,000 live births		Maternal mortality ratio Modeled estimates per 100,000 live births	Births attended by skilled health staff % of total	
	1992–2004[b,c]	1989–94[b]	2000–04[b]	1991	2004	1991	2004	1990	2004	2000	1989–94[b]	2000–04[b]
Mauritius	..	..	..	102	100	102	103	23	15	24	97	99
Mozambique	6.5	..	24	26	29	72	82	235	152	1,000	..	48
Namibia	1.4	26	24	*78*	*81*	108	*105*	86	63	300	68	76
Niger	2.6	43	40	17	25	57	71	320	259	1,600,	15	16
Nigeria	5.0	39	29	..	76	79	84	230	197	800	31	35
Rwanda	..	29	24	47	37	96	100	173	203	1,400	26	31
Senegal	6.4	22	23	*39*	45	69	90	148	137	690	47	58
Sierra Leone	..	29	27	..	..	67	*71*	302	283	2,000	..	42
Somalia	..	..	26	..	..	..	..	225	225	1,100	..	25
South Africa	3.5	..	..	75	*96*	104	*101*	60	67	230	..	..
Sudan	..	34	41	40	49	78	88	120	91	590	86	87
Swaziland	2.7	..	10	62	*61*	98	*96*	110	156	370	56	74
Tanzania	7.3	29	..	61	57	97	..	161	126	1,500	44	46
Togo	..	..	..	35	66	59	73	152	140	570	..	61
Uganda	5.9	23	23	..	57	82	97	160	138	880	38	39
Zambia	6.1	25	23	..	66	..	93	180	182	750	51	43
Zimbabwe	4.6	16	..	91	*80*	92	*96*	80	129	1,100	69	..
High income		.. w	.. w	.. w	.. w	100 w	*101* w	11 w	7 w	14 w	.. w	.. w
Australia	5.9	..	..	..	*100*	101	*98*	10	6	8	100	..
Austria	8.6	..	..	..	..	95	*96*	10	5	4	100	..
Belgium	8.5	..	..	79	..	101	*106*	10	5	10	..	..
Canada	7.2	..	..	..	..	99	*100*	8	6	6	..	98
Denmark	8.3	..	..	98	*103*	..	105	9	5	5	..	..
Finland	9.6	..	..	97	*102*	102	*100*	7	4	6	100	100
France	7.2	..	..	104	..	..	..	9	5	17	99	..
Germany	8.5	..	..	*100*	*97*	79	91	9	5	8	..	..
Greece	6.7	..	..	*99*	..	..	91	11	5	9	..	..
Ireland	7.4	..	..	..	*101*	104	*103*	9	6	5	..	100
Israel	5.7	..	..	..	*101*	105	*99*	12	6	17	..	..
Italy	6.5	..	..	104	*103*	100	*99*	9	5	5	..	..
Japan	10.6	..	..	101	..	101	*100*	6	4	10	100	..
Korea, Rep.	7.9	..	..	98	105	99	100	9	6	20	98	..
Kuwait	..	..	..	*57*	91	97	104	16	12	5	..	..
Netherlands	7.6	..	..	..	*100*	97	*98*	9	6	16	..	..
New Zealand	6.4	..	..	100	..	100	*107*	11	7	7	95	..
Norway	9.6	..	..	100	*103*	102	*101*	9	4	16	..	..
Portugal	5.8	..	..	95	..	103	*102*	14	5	5	98	100
Puerto Rico	..	..	..	..	..	..	..	..	..	25	..	..
Saudi Arabia	..	15	..	56	62	84	92	44	27	23	..	..
Singapore	5.0	..	3	..	..	95	..	8	3	30	..	..
Slovenia	9.1	..	..	*95*	*102*	..	*99*	10	4	17	100	100
Spain	7.0	..	..	..	..	104	*102*	9	5	4	..	..
Sweden	9.1	..	..	96	..	102	*111*	7	4	2	..	..
Switzerland	7.6	..	..	53	*96*	97	*96*	9	5	7	..	..
United Arab Emirates	..	..	..	95	75	104	102	14	8	54	..	..
United Kingdom	6.1	..	..	..	..	98	*116*	10	6	13	..	..
United States	5.4	1	2	..	..	100	*100*	11	8	17	99	..
World		.. w	.. w	.. w	.. w	86 w	*93* w	95 w	79 w	410 w	.. w	60 w
Low income		..	..	66	74	74	*86*	147	122	682	..	40
Middle income		..	11	92	97	91	*98*	57	37	142	..	87
Lower middle income		..	11	93	98	89	*98*	61	40	153	..	86
Upper middle income		..	..	88	96	98	*98*	42	28	92	..	95
Low & middle income		..	..	81	86	84	*92*	103	86	450	..	60
High income		..	..	..	..	100	*101*	11	7	14	..	..

a. Break in series between 1997 and 1998 due to change from International Standard Classification of Education (ISCED) 1976 to ISCED97. b. Data are for the most recent year available. c. See table 2.8 for survey year and whether share is based on income or consumption expenditure. d. Hong Kong, China, is classified as a high-income economy and is not included in the East Asia and Pacific aggregate. e. Urban data.

Millennium Development Goals: eradicating poverty and improving lives 1.2

About the data

This table and the following two present indicators for 17 of the 18 targets specified by the Millennium Development Goals. Each of the eight goals comprises one or more targets, and each target has associated with it several indicators for monitoring progress toward the target. Most of the targets are set as a value of a specific indicator to be attained by a certain date. In some cases the target value is set relative to a level in 1990. In others it is set at an absolute level. Some of the targets for goals 7 and 8 have not yet been quantified

The indicators in this table relate to goals 1–5. Goal 1 has two targets between 1990 and 2015: to reduce by half the proportion of people whose income is less than $1 a day and to reduce by half the proportion of people who suffer from hunger. Estimates of poverty rates can be found in table 2.7. The indicator shown here, the share of the poorest quintile in national consumption, is a distributional measure. Countries with more unequal distributions of consumption (or income) will have a higher rate of poverty for a given average income. No single indicator captures the concept of suffering from hunger. Child malnutrition is a symptom of inadequate food supply, lack of essential nutrients, illnesses that deplete these nutrients, and undernourished mothers who give birth to underweight children.

Progress toward achieving universal primary education is measured by primary school completion rates. Before *World Development Indicators 2003*, progress was measured by net enrollment ratios. But official enrollments sometimes differ significantly from actual attendance, and even school systems with high average enrollment ratios may have poor completion rates. Estimates of primary school completion rates were calculated by World Bank staff using data provided by the United Nations Educational, Scientific, and Cultural Organization Institute of Statistics and national sources.

Eliminating gender disparities in education would help to increase the status and capabilities of women. The ratio of girls' to boys' enrollments in primary and secondary school provides an imperfect measure of the relative accessibility of schooling for girls. With a target date of 2005, this is the first of the goals to fall due.

The targets for reducing under-five and maternal mortality are among the most challenging. Although estimates of under-five mortality rates are available at regular intervals for most countries, maternal mortality is difficult to measure, in part because it is relatively rare.

Most of the 48 indicators relating to the Millennium Development Goals can be found in *World Development Indicators*. Table 1.2a shows where to find the indicators for the first five goals. For more information about data collection methods and limitations, see *About the data* for the tables listed there. For information about the indicators for goals 6, 7, and 8, see *About the data* for tables 1.3 and 1.4.

1.2a

Location of indicators for Millennium Development Goals 1–5

Goal 1. Eradicate extreme poverty and hunger	Table
1. Proportion of population below $1 a day	2.7
2. Poverty gap ratio	2.7
3. Share of poorest quintile in national consumption	1.2, 2.8
4. Prevalence of underweight in children under age five	1.2, 2.17
5. Proportion of population below minimum level of dietary energy consumption	2.17
Goal 2. Achieve universal primary education	
6. Net enrollment ratio	2.11
7. Proportion of pupils starting grade 1 who reach grade 5	2.12
8. Literacy rate of 15- to 24-year-olds	2.13
Goal 3. Promote gender equality and empower women	
9. Ratio of girls to boys in primary, secondary, and tertiary education	1.2*
10. Ratio of literate females to males among 15- to 24-year-olds	2.13*
11. Share of women in wage employment in the nonagricultural sector	1.5, 2.2*
12. Proportion of seats held by women in national parliament	1.5
Goal 4. Reduce child mortality	
13. Under-five mortality rate	1.2, 2.19
14. Infant mortality rate	2.19
15. Proportion of one-year-old children immunized against measles	2.15
Goal 4. Improve maternal health	
16. Maternal mortality ratio	1.2, 2.16
17. Proportion of births attended by skilled health personnel	1.2, 2.16

* Table shows information on related indicators.

Definitions

• **Share of poorest quintile in national consumption or income** is the share of consumption or, in some cases, income that accrues to the poorest 20 percent of the population. • **Prevalence of child malnutrition** is the percentage of children under age five whose weight for age is more than two standard deviations below the median for the international reference population ages 0–59 months. The reference population, adopted by the World Health Organization in 1983, is based on children from the United States, who are assumed to be well nourished. • **Primary completion rate** is the percentage of students completing the last year of primary school. It is calculated as the total number of students in the last grade of primary school, minus the number of repeaters in that grade, divided by the total number of children of official graduation age. • **Ratio of female to male enrollments in primary and secondary school** is the ratio of female to male gross enrollment rate in primary and secondary school. • **Under-five mortality rate** is the probability that a newborn baby will die before reaching age five, if subject to current age-specific mortality rates. The probability is expressed as a rate per 1,000. • **Maternal mortality ratio** is the number of women who die from pregnancy-related causes during pregnancy and childbirth, per 100,000 live births. The data shown here have been collected in various years and adjusted to a common 2000 base year. The values are modeled estimates (see *About the data* for table 2.16). • **Births attended by skilled health staff** are the percentage of deliveries attended by personnel trained to give the necessary supervision, care, and advice to women during pregnancy, labor, and the postpartum period; to conduct deliveries on their own; and to care for newborns.

Data sources

The indicators here and throughout this book have been compiled by World Bank staff from primary and secondary sources. Efforts have been made to harmonize these data series with those published on the United Nations Millennium Development Goals Web site (www.un.org/millenniumgoals), but some differences in timing, sources, and definitions remain.

1.3 Millennium Development Goals: protecting our common environment

	Combat HIV/AIDS and other diseases		Ensure environmental sustainability						Develop a global partnership for development	
	HIV prevalence % of population ages 15–49	Incidence of tuberculosis per 100,000 people	Carbon dioxide emissions per capita metric tons		Access to an improved water source % of population		Access to improved sanitation facilities % of population		Youth unemployment % ages 15–24	Fixed-line and mobile phone subscribers per 1,000 people[a]
	2003	**2004**	**1990**	**2002**	**1990**	**2002**	**1990**	**2002**	**2004**	**2004**
East Asia & Pacific[b]	**0.2 w**	**138 w**	**1.9 w**	**2.4 w**	**71 w**	**78 w**	**30 w**	**49 w**	**.. w**	**435 w**
Cambodia	2.6	510	0.0	0.0	..	34	..	16	..	*40*
China	0.1	101	2.1	2.7	70	77	23	44	..	499
Hong Kong, China	0.1	75	4.6	5.2	..	..	..	..	*15*	1,733
Indonesia	0.1	245	0.9	1.4	71	78	46	52	..	184
Korea, Dem. Rep.	..	178	12.4	6.5	100	100	..	59	..	*41*
Lao PDR	0.1	156	0.1	0.2	..	43	..	24	..	48
Malaysia	0.4	103	3.1	6.3	..	95	96	..	..	766
Mongolia	<0.1	192	4.7	3.4	62	62	..	59	*20*	*184*
Myanmar	1.2	171	0.1	0.2	48	80	21	73	..	10
Papua New Guinea	0.6	233	0.6	0.4	39	39	45	45	..	*14*
Philippines	<0.1	293	0.7	0.9	87	85	54	73	*26*	446
Thailand	1.5	142	1.8	3.7	81	85	80	99	5	537
Vietnam	0.4	176	0.3	0.8	72	73	22	41	5	184
Europe & Central Asia	**0.7 w**	**83 w**	**10.2 w**	**6.7 w**	**.. w**	**91 w**	**86 w**	**82 w**	**.. w**	**536 w**
Albania	..	22	2.2	0.8	97	97	..	89	*36*	*438*
Armenia	0.1	78	*1.1*	1.0	..	92	..	84	..	260
Azerbaijan	<0.1	75	*6.4*	3.4	66	77	..	55	..	333
Belarus	..	60	*9.3*	6.0	100	100	..	..	..	*424*
Bosnia and Herzegovina	<0.1	53	*1.2*	4.7	98	98	..	93	..	*507*
Bulgaria	0.1	36	8.6	5.3	100	100	100	100	*28*	966
Croatia	<0.1	41	*3.8*	4.7	..	..	..	..	*37*	*996*
Czech Republic	0.1	11	*13.1*	11.2	..	..	..	..	20	1,392
Estonia	1.1	46	*16.2*	11.7	..	..	..	..	*21*	1,260
Georgia	0.1	82	*2.8*	0.7	..	76	..	83	*25*	337
Hungary	0.1	26	5.8	5.6	99	99	..	95	16	1,217
Kazakhstan	0.2	151	*15.4*	9.9	86	86	72	72	*15*	351
Kyrgyz Republic	0.1	122	*2.4*	1.0	..	76	..	60	*20*	*106*
Latvia	0.6	68	*4.8*	2.7	..	..	..	..	*19*	937
Lithuania	0.1	63	*5.8*	3.6	..	..	..	..	*25*	1,235
Macedonia, FYR	<0.1	30	*5.5*	5.1	..	..	..	..	*66*	*642*
Moldova	0.2	138	*4.8*	1.6	..	92	..	68	*15*	391
Poland	0.1	29	9.1	7.7	..	..	..	..	41	*777*
Romania	<0.1	146	6.7	4.0	..	57	..	51	*19*	673
Russian Federation	1.1	115	*13.3*	9.8	94	96	87	87	..	*508*
Serbia and Montenegro	0.2	33	..	*3.7*	93	93	87	87	..	*910*
Slovak Republic	<0.1	19	*8.1*	6.8	100	100	100	100	33	1,027
Tajikistan	<0.1	177	*3.7*	0.7	..	58	..	53	..	*46*
Turkey	..	28	2.6	3.0	81	93	84	83	20	751
Turkmenistan	<0.1	65	*7.2*	9.1	..	71	..	62	..	*82*
Ukraine	1.4	101	*11.5*	6.4	..	98	99	99	*17*	545
Uzbekistan	0.1	117	*5.3*	4.8	89	89	58	57	..	*79*
Latin America & Carib.	**0.7 w**	**64 w**	**2.4 w**	**2.4 w**	**82 w**	**89 w**	**68 w**	**75 w**	**14 w**	**499 w**
Argentina	0.7	43	3.4	3.5	94	..	82	..	*34*	579
Bolivia	0.1	217	0.8	1.2	72	85	33	45	..	269
Brazil	0.7	60	1.4	1.8	83	89	70	75	*18*	587
Chile	0.3	16	2.7	3.6	90	95	85	92	*19*	799
Colombia	0.7	50	1.6	1.3	92	92	82	86	..	427
Costa Rica	0.6	14	0.9	1.4	..	97	..	92	*15*	533
Cuba	0.1	10	3.0	2.1	..	91	98	98	..	75
Dominican Republic	1.0[c]	91	1.3	2.5	86	93	48	57	..	396
Ecuador	0.3	131	1.6	2.0	69	86	56	72	*22*	472
El Salvador	0.7	54	0.5	1.0	67	82	51	63	*11*	402
Guatemala	1.1	77	0.6	0.9	77	95	50	61	..	350
Haiti	5.6	306	0.1	0.2	53	71	15	34	..	64
Honduras	1.8	77	0.5	0.9	83	90	49	68	*8*	153

Millennium Development Goals: protecting our common environment 1.3

	Combat HIV/AIDS and other diseases		Ensure environmental sustainability						Develop a global partnership for development	
	HIV prevalence % of population ages 15–49	Incidence of tuberculosis per 100,000 people	Carbon dioxide emissions per capita metric tons		Access to an improved water source % of population		Access to improved sanitation facilities % of population		Youth unemployment % ages 15–24	Fixed-line and mobile phone subscribers per 1,000 people[a]
	2003	2004	1990	2002	1990	2002	1990	2002	2004	2004
Jamaica	1.2	7	3.3	4.1	92	93	75	80	*26*	1,021
Mexico	0.3	32	4.5	3.8	80	91	66	77	6	545
Nicaragua	0.2	63	0.7	0.7	69	81	47	66	*13*	177
Panama	0.9	45	1.3	2.0	..	91	..	72	*29*	388
Paraguay	0.5	71	0.5	0.7	62	83	58	78	*14*	*349*
Peru	0.5	178	1.0	1.0	74	81	52	62	*19*	223
Trinidad and Tobago	3.2	9	13.9	31.8	92	91	100	100	*21*	745
Uruguay	0.3	28	1.3	1.2	..	98	..	94	*38*	465
Venezuela, RB	0.7	42	5.9	4.3	..	83	..	68	*28*	450
Middle East & N. Africa	**0.1 w**	**54 w**	**2.5 w**	**3.2 w**	**87 w**	**88 w**	**69 w**	**75 w**	**.. w**	**219 w**
Algeria	0.1	54	3.0	2.9	95	87	88	92	..	215
Egypt, Arab Rep.	<0.1	27	1.4	2.1	94	98	54	68	*28*	235
Iran, Islamic Rep.	0.1	27	4.0	5.5	91	93	83	84	..	*270*
Iraq	<0.1	132	2.6	..	83	81	81	80	..	57
Jordan	<0.1	5	3.2	3.2	98	91	..	93	..	407
Lebanon	0.1	11	3.3	4.7	100	100	..	98	..	429
Libya	0.3	20	8.7	9.1	71	72	97	97	..	*156*
Morocco	0.1	110	1.0	1.5	75	80	57	61	*17*	357
Oman	0.1	11	6.0	12.1	77	79	83	89	..	413
Syrian Arab Republic	<0.1	41	2.8	2.8	79	79	76	77	*26*	269
Tunisia	<0.1	22	1.6	2.3	77	82	75	80	..	480
West Bank and Gaza	..	23	..	..	..	94	..	76	*43*	380
Yemen, Rep.	0.1	89	0.8	0.7	69	69	21	30	..	92
South Asia	**0.8 w**	**177 w**	**0.7 w**	**1.0 w**	**70 w**	**84 w**	**16 w**	**35 w**	**.. w**	**76 w**
Afghanistan	..	333	0.2	..	..	13	..	8	..	23
Bangladesh	..	229	0.1	0.3	71	75	23	48	..	37
India	0.9	168	0.8	1.2	68	86	12	30	..	85
Nepal	0.5	184	0.0	0.2	69	84	12	27	..	22
Pakistan	0.1	181	0.6	0.7	83	90	38	54	*13*	63
Sri Lanka	<0.1	60	0.2	0.5	68	78	70	91	*27*	165
Sub-Saharan Africa	**7.2 w**	**363 w**	**0.8 w**	**0.7 w**	**49 w**	**58 w**	**32 w**	**36 w**	**.. w**	***65 w***
Angola	3.9	259	0.4	0.5	32	50	30	30	..	*29*
Benin	1.9	87	0.1	0.3	60	68	11	32	..	*38*
Botswana	37.3	670	1.5	2.3	93	95	38	41	*40*	396
Burkina Faso	1.8[d]	191	0.1	0.1	39	51	13	12	..	37
Burundi	6.0	343	0.0	0.0	69	79	44	36	..	*12*
Cameroon	5.5[e]	179	0.1	0.2	50	63	21	48	..	*74*
Central African Republic	13.5	322	0.1	0.1	48	75	23	27	..	18
Chad	4.8	279	0.0	0.0	20	34	6	8	..	14
Congo, Dem. Rep.	4.2	366	0.1	0.0	43	46	18	29	..	*11*
Congo, Rep.	4.9	377	0.5	0.6	..	46	..	9	..	102
Côte d'Ivoire	7.0	393	0.4	0.4	69	84	31	40	..	*86*
Eritrea	2.7	271	*0.0*	0.2	40	57	8	9	..	14
Ethiopia	4.4	353	0.1	0.1	25	22	4	6	..	*8*
Gabon	8.1	280	6.3	2.6	..	87	..	36	..	388
Gambia, The	1.2	233	0.2	0.2	..	82	..	53	..	*99*
Ghana	2.2[d]	206	0.2	0.4	54	79	43	58	..	93
Guinea	3.2	240	0.2	0.1	42	51	17	13	..	*15*
Guinea-Bissau	..	199	0.2	0.2	..	59	..	34	..	*8*
Kenya	6.7[d]	619	0.2	0.2	45	62	42	48	..	85
Lesotho	28.9	696	..	..	..	76	37	37	..	109
Liberia	5.9	310	0.2	0.1	56	62	38	26	..	*3*
Madagascar	1.7	218	0.1	0.1	40	45	12	33	..	*19*
Malawi	14.2	413	0.1	0.1	41	67	36	46	..	25
Mali	1.9	281	0.0	0.0	34	48	36	45	..	36
Mauritania	0.6	287	1.3	1.1	41	56	28	42	..	*135*

1.3 Millennium Development Goals: protecting our common environment

	Combat HIV/AIDS and other diseases		Ensure environmental sustainability						Develop a global partnership for development	
	HIV prevalence % of population ages 15–49	Incidence of tuberculosis per 100,000 people	Carbon dioxide emissions per capita metric tons		Access to an improved water source % of population		Access to improved sanitation facilities % of population		Youth unemployment % ages 15–24	Fixed-line and mobile phone subscribers per 1,000 people[a]
	2003	2004	1990	2002	1990	2002	1990	2002	2004	2004
Mauritius	..	64	1.4	2.6	100	100	99	99	..	700
Mozambique	12.2	460	0.1	0.1	..	42	..	27	..	*27*
Namibia	21.3	717	0.0	1.1	58	80	24	30	*45*	206
Niger	1.2	157	0.1	0.1	40	46	7	12	..	13
Nigeria	5.4	290	0.5	0.4	49	60	39	38	..	79
Rwanda	5.1	371	0.1	0.1	58	73	37	41	..	18
Senegal	0.8	245	0.4	0.4	66	72	35	52	..	*72*
Sierra Leone	..	443	0.1	0.1	..	57	..	39	..	*19*
Somalia	..	411	0.0	..	..	29	..	25	..	88
South Africa	15.6[c]	718	8.1	7.6	83	87	63	67	*60*	*473*
Sudan	2.3	220	0.2	0.3	64	69	33	34	..	58
Swaziland	38.8	1,226	0.6	0.9	..	52	..	52	..	*119*
Tanzania	7.0[e]	347	0.1	0.1	38	73	47	46	..	*32*
Togo	4.1	355	0.2	0.3	49	51	37	34	..	*48*
Uganda	4.1	402	0.0	0.1	44	56	43	41	..	44
Zambia	15.6[f]	680	0.3	0.2	50	55	41	45	..	*29*
Zimbabwe	24.6	674	1.6	1.0	77	83	49	57	*25*	55
High income	**0.4 w**	**17 w**	**11.8 w**	**12.8 w**	**.. w**	**99 w**	**.. w**	**.. w**	**13 w**	**1,306 w**
Australia	0.1	6	16.0	18.1	100	100	100	100	12	1,359
Austria	0.3	14	7.5	7.9	100	100	100	100	10	1,438
Belgium	0.2	13	10.1	8.9	..	..	..	..	18	1,333
Canada	0.3	5	15.0	16.5	100	100	100	100	13	*1,053*
Denmark	0.2	8	9.7	8.8	100	100	..	..	8	1,599
Finland	0.1	9	10.3	12.0	100	100	100	100	21	1,407
France	0.4	12	6.4	6.2	..	..	..	..	23	1,299
Germany	0.1	8	12.3	10.3	100	100	..	..	12	1,525
Greece	0.2	19	7.1	8.5	..	..	..	..	27	1,465
Ireland	0.1	11	8.7	11.0	..	..	..	..	8	1,425
Israel	0.1	9	7.1	10.6	100	100	..	..	*22*	1,499
Italy	0.5	7	6.9	7.5	..	..	..	..	24	1,541
Japan	<0.1	30	8.7	9.4	100	100	100	100	10	1,176
Korea, Rep.	<0.1	90	5.6	9.4	..	92	..	..	10	1,303
Kuwait	..	26	21.3	25.6	..	..	..	..	..	1,015
Netherlands	0.2	8	9.3	9.3	100	100	100	100	*8*	1,393
New Zealand	0.1	11	6.8	8.6	97	..	..	..	9	1,189
Norway	0.1	5	11.1	13.9	100	100	..	..	12	*1,396*
Portugal	0.4	42	4.3	6.0	..	..	..	..	15	1,384
Puerto Rico	..	5	3.3	3.5	..	..	..	..	*24*	974
Saudi Arabia	..	40	11.0	15.0	90	..	..	..	..	537
Singapore	0.2	40	14.8	13.7	..	..	..	..	*8*	1,350
Slovenia	<0.1	15	*6.2*	7.7	..	..	..	..	*15*	*1,278*
Spain	0.7	25	5.5	7.4	..	..	..	..	22	1,321
Sweden	0.1	4	5.8	5.8	100	100	100	100	17	*1,750*
Switzerland	0.4	7	6.4	5.6	100	100	100	100	8	1,560
United Arab Emirates	..	17	34.2	25.0	..	..	100	100	..	1,128
United Kingdom	0.2	12	9.9	9.2	..	..	..	..	11	1,584
United States	0.6	5	19.3	20.2	100	100	100	100	12	1,223
World	**1.1 w**	**139 w**	**4.0 w**	**3.9 w**	**75 w**	**82 w**	**43 w**	**54 w**	**.. w**	**476 w**
Low income	2.1	224	0.8	0.8	64	75	20	36	..	76
Middle income	0.7	114	3.5	3.3	77	83	48	61	..	486
Lower middle income	0.3	114	2.4	2.6	75	81	42	57	..	438
Upper middle income	2.6	112	8.1	6.2	88	93	80	81	..	*564*
Low & middle income	1.2	162	2.4	2.2	71	79	37	50	..	312
High income	0.4	17	11.8	12.8	..	99	..	..	13	1,306

a. Data are from the International Telecommunication Union's (ITU) World Telecommunication Development Report database. Please cite the ITU for third-party use of these data.
b. Hong Kong, China, is classified as a high-income economy and is not included in the East Asia and Pacific aggregate. c. Survey data, 2002. d. Survey data, 2003. e. Survey data, 2004.
f. Survey data, 2001/02.

Millennium Development Goals: protecting our common environment 1.3

About the data

The Millennium Development Goals address issues of common concern to all nations. Diseases and environmental degradation do not respect national boundaries. Epidemic diseases, wherever they persist, pose a threat to people everywhere. And damage to the environment in one location may affect the well-being of plants, animals, and humans far away.

The indicators in the table relate to goals 6 and 7 and the targets of goal 8 that address youth employment and access to new technologies. For the other targets of goal 8, see table 1.4.

Measuring the prevalence or incidence of a disease can be difficult. Much of the developing world lacks reporting systems for monitoring diseases. Estimates are often derived from surveys and reports from sentinel sites that must be extrapolated to the general population. Tracking diseases such as HIV/AIDS, which has a long latency between contraction of the virus and the appearance of symptoms, or malaria, which has periods of dormancy, can be particularly difficult. For some of the most serious illnesses international organizations have formed coalitions such as the Joint United Nations Programme on HIV/AIDS and the Roll Back Malaria campaign to gather information and coordinate global efforts to treat victims and prevent the spread of disease.

The models and data used to estimate HIV prevalence depend on the nature of the epidemic in each country. In early stages infections are usually concentrated in high risk groups for which data are collected from sentinel sites or through targeted surveys. In older, generalized epidemics antenatal clinics are a key site for monitoring HIV and other sexually transmitted diseases. Recently, household surveys have been used to track the disease. The table shows the estimated prevalence among adults ages 15–49. Prevalence rates in the older population can be affected by life-prolonging treatment. The incidence of tuberculosis is based on data on case notifications and estimates of the proportion of cases detected in the population.

Carbon dioxide emissions are the primary source of greenhouse gases, which are believed to contribute to global warming.

Access to reliable supplies of safe drinking water and sanitary disposal of excreta are two of the most important means of improving human health and protecting the environment. There is no widespread program for testing the quality of water. The indicator shown here measures the proportion of households with access to an improved source, such as piped water or protected wells. Improved sanitation facilities prevent human, animal, and insect contact with excreta but do not include treatment to render sewage outflows innocuous.

The eighth goal—to develop a global partnership for development—takes note of the need for decent and productive work for youth. Labor market information, such as unemployment rates, is still generally unavailable for most low- and middle-income economies. Fixed telephone lines and mobile phones are among the telecommunications technologies that are changing the way the global economy works. For more information on goal 8, see table 1.4.

1.3a

Location of indicators for Millennium Development Goals 6–7

	Goal 6. Combat HIV/AIDS, malaria, and other diseases	Table
18.	HIV prevalence among pregnant women ages 15–24	1.3*, 2.18*
19.	Condom use rate of the contraceptive prevalence rate	—
19a.	Condom use at last high-risk sex	—
19b.	Percentage of 15- to 24-year-olds with comprehensive correct knowledge of HIV/AIDS	—
19c.	Contraceptive prevalence rate	2.16
20.	Ratio of school attendance of orphans to school attendance of nonorphans ages 10–14	—
21.	Prevalence and death rates associated with malaria	—
22.	Proportion of population in malaria-risk areas using effective malaria prevention and treatment measures	2.15*
23.	Prevalence and death rates associated with tuberculosis	1.3*, 2.18*
24.	Proportion of tuberculosis cases detected and cured under DOTS	2.15
	Goal 7. Ensure environmental sustainability	
25.	Proportion of land area covered by forest	3.4
26.	Ratio of area protected to maintain biological diversity to surface area	3.4
27.	Energy use (kilograms of oil equivalent) per $1 of GDP (PPP)	3.8
28.	Carbon dioxide emissions per capita and consumption of ozone-depleting chlorofluorocarbons	3.8*
29.	Proportion of population using solid fuels	3.7*
30.	Proportion of population with sustainable access to an improved water source, urban and rural	2.15, 3.5
31.	Proportion of population with access to improved sanitation, urban and rural	2.15, 3.10
32.	Proportion of population with access to secure tenure	3.11

— No data are available in the World Development Indicators database. * Table shows information on related indicators.

Definitions

• **HIV prevalence** is the percentage of people ages 15–49 who are infected with HIV. • **Incidence of tuberculosis** is the estimated number of new tuberculosis cases (pulmonary, smear positive, extrapulmonary). • **Carbon dioxide emissions** are those stemming from the burning of fossil fuels and the manufacture of cement. They include carbon dioxide produced during consumption of solid, liquid, and gas fuels and gas flaring. • **Access to an improved water source** refers to the percentage of the population with reasonable access to an adequate amount of water from an improved source, such as a household connection, public standpipe, borehole, protected well or spring, or rainwater collection. Unimproved sources include vendors, tanker trucks, and unprotected wells and springs. Reasonable access is defined as the availability of at least 20 liters a person a day from a source within 1 kilometer of the dwelling. • **Access to improved sanitation facilities** refers to the percentage of the population with access to at least adequate excreta disposal facilities (private or shared but not public) that can effectively prevent human, animal, and insect contact with excreta. Improved facilities range from simple but protected pit latrines to flush toilets with a sewerage connection. To be effective, facilities must be correctly constructed and properly maintained. • **Youth unemployment** refers to the share of the labor force ages 15–24 without work but available for and seeking employment. Definitions of labor force and unemployment differ by country. • **Fixed-line and mobile phone subscribers** are telephone mainlines connecting a customer's equipment to the public switched telephone network, and users of portable telephones subscribing to an automatic public mobile telephone service using cellular technology that provides access to the public switched telephone network.

Data sources

The indicators here and throughout this book have been compiled by World Bank staff from primary and secondary sources. Efforts have been made to harmonize these data series with those published on the United Nations Millennium Development Goals Web site (www.un.org/millenniumgoals), but some differences in timing, sources, and definitions remain.

1.4 Millennium Development Goals: overcoming obstacles

Development Assistance Committee members

	Official development assistances (ODA) by donor		Least developed countries' access to high-income markets								Support to agriculture
	Net % of donor GNI	For basic social services[a] % of total sector-allocable ODA	Goods (excluding arms) admitted free of tariffs %		Average tariff on exports of least developed countries: Agricultural products %		Textiles %		Clothing %		% of GDP
	2004	2003–04	1997	2004	1997	2004	1997	2004	1997	2004	2004[b]
Australia	0.25	15.8	96.6	97.3	0.2	0.4	10.0	0.9	28.3	0.0	0.3
Canada	0.27	29.0	65.9	98.6	0.5	0.2	11.4	0.3	21.8	1.4	0.7
European Union			97.3	95.9	3.4	2.8	0.0	0.2	0.0	1.0	1.2
Austria	0.23	12.6									
Belgium	0.41	14.7									
Denmark	0.85	23.6									
Finland	0.35	15.3									
France	0.41	10.0									
Germany	0.28	12.7									
Greece	0.23	20.6									
Ireland	0.39	28.9									
Italy	0.15	18.4									
Luxembourg	0.83	20.7									
Netherlands	0.73	18.1									
Portugal	0.63	2.8									
Spain	0.24	13.8									
Sweden	0.78	16.0									
United Kingdom	0.36	31.8									
Japan	0.19	5.4	67.9	37.9	7.4	6.6	3.9	1.7	0.5	0.1	1.3
New Zealand	0.23	19.1									0.4
Norway	0.87	18.0									1.3
Switzerland	0.41	8.4	72.8	99.4	7.2	6.7	0.0	0.0	0.0	0.0	1.7
United States	0.17	19.1	22.5	67.0	4.9	3.5	6.9	5.7	14.6	12.3	0.9

Heavily indebted poor countries (HIPCs)

	HIPC decision point[c]	HIPC completion point[d]	Estimated total nominal debt service relief[e] $ millions		HIPC decision point[c]	HIPC completion point[d]	Estimated total nominal debt service relief[e] $ millions
Benin	Jul. 2000	Mar. 2003	460	Madagascar	Dec. 2000	Oct. 2004	1,900
Bolivia	Feb. 2000	Jun. 2001	2,060	Malawi	Dec. 2000	Floating	1,000
Burkina Faso	Jul. 2000	Apr. 2002	930	Mali	Sep. 2000	Mar. 2003	895
Cameroon	Aug. 2005	Floating	1,472	Mauritania	Feb. 2000	Jun. 2002	1,100
Burundi	Oct. 2000	Floating	2,800	Mozambique	Apr. 2000	Sep. 2001	4,300
Chad	May 2001	Floating	260	Nicaragua	Dec. 2000	Jan. 2004	4,500
Congo, Dem. Republic	Jul. 2003	Floating	10,389	Niger	Dec. 2000	Apr. 2004	1,190
Côte d'Ivoire	Mar. 1998	..	800	Rwanda	Dec. 2000	Apr. 2005	1,400
Ethiopia	Nov. 2001	Apr. 2004	3,275	São Tomé & Principe	Dec. 2000	Floating	200
Gambia, The	Dec. 2000	Floating	90	Senegal	Jun. 2000	Apr. 2004	850
Ghana	Feb. 2002	Jul. 2004	3,500	Sierra Leone	Mar. 2002	Floating	950
Guinea	Dec. 2000	Floating	800	Tanzania	Apr. 2000	Nov. 2001	3,000
Guinea-Bissau	Dec. 2000	Floating	790	Uganda	Feb. 2000	May 2000	1,950
Guyana	Nov. 2000	Dec. 2003	1,353	Zambia	Dec. 2000	Apr. 2005	3,900
Honduras	Jul. 2000	Apr. 2005	1,053				

a. Includes basic health, education, nutrition, and water and sanitation services. b. Preliminary. c. Except for Côte d'Ivoire the date refers to the Enhanced Heavily Indebted Poor Countries (HIPC) Initiative. The following countries also reached their decision point under the original HIPC framework: Bolivia in September 1997, Burkina Faso in September 1997, Côte d'Ivoire in March 1998, Guyana in December 1997, Mali in September 1998, Mozambique in April 1998, and Uganda in April 1997. d. The date refers to the Enhanced HIPC Initiative. The following countries also reached completion points under the original framework: Bolivia in September 1998, Burkina Faso in July 2000, Guyana in May 1999, Mali in September 2000, Mozambique in July 1999, and Uganda in April 1998. e. Includes estimated total nominal debt service relief under original and enhanced HIPC, as well as a topping-up of HIPC debt relief at completion point for Burkina Faso, Ethiopia, and Niger.

Millennium Development Goals: overcoming obstacles 1.4

About the data

Achieving the Millennium Development Goals will require an open, rule-based global economy in which all countries, rich and poor, participate. Many poor countries, lacking the resources to finance their development, burdened by unsustainable levels of debt, and unable to compete in the global marketplace, need assistance from rich countries. For goal 8—develop a global partnership for development—many of the indicators therefore monitor the actions of members of the Development Assistance Committee (DAC) of the Organisation for Economic Co-operation and Development (OECD).

Official development assistance (ODA) has risen in recent years as a share of donor countries' gross national income (GNI), but the poorest countries will need additional assistance to achieve the Millennium Development Goals. Official aid rose to a record high of $79 billion in 2004, and donor countries have pledged to increase ODA by $20 billion by 2006 and to a total of more than $100 billion by 2010. However, this would still fall short of levels considered necessary to achieve the Millennium Development Goals.

One of the most important actions that high-income economies can take to help is to reduce barriers to the exports of low- and middle-income economies. The European Union has launched a program to eliminate tariffs on developing country exports of "everything but arms," and the United States offers special concessions to exports from Sub-Saharan Africa. However, there are still many restrictions built into these programs.

The average tariffs in the table reflect the tariff schedules applied by high-income OECD members to exports of countries designated least developed countries by the United Nations. Agricultural commodities, textiles, and clothing are three of the most important categories of goods exported by developing economies. Although average tariffs have been falling, averages may disguise high tariffs targeted at specific goods (see table 6.7 for estimates of the share of tariff lines with "international peaks" in each country's tariff schedule). The averages in the table include ad valorem duties and ad valorem equivalents of non-ad valorem duties. Subsidies to agricultural producers and exporters in OECD countries are another form of barrier to developing economies' exports. The table shows the value of total support to agriculture as a share of the economy's gross domestic product (GDP). Agricultural subsidies in OECD economies are estimated at $378 billion in 2004.

The Debt Initiative for Heavily Indebted Poor Countries (HIPCs) is the first comprehensive approach to reducing the external debt of the world's poorest, most heavily indebted countries. It represents an important step forward in placing debt relief within an overall framework of poverty reduction. A major review in 1999 led to an enhancement of the original framework. Through the HIPC Initiative nominal debt service relief of more than $56 billion has been approved for 28 countries, reducing the net present value of their external debt by approximately two-thirds. Of these countries, 19 have reached the completion point and have been granted unconditional debt service relief of more than $37 billion.

1.4a

Location of indicators for Millennium Development Goal 8

Goal 8. Develop a global partnership for development		Table
33.	Net ODA as a percentage of DAC donors' gross national income	6.9
34.	Proportion of ODA for basic social services	1.4
35.	Proportion of ODA that is untied	6.9
36.	Proportion of ODA received in landlocked countries as a percentage of GNI	—
37.	Proportion of ODA received in small island developing states as a percentage of GNI	—
38.	Proportion of total developed country imports (by value, excluding arms) from developing countries admitted free of duty	1.4
39.	Average tariffs imposed by developed countries on agricultural products and textiles and clothing from developing countries	1.4, 6.7*
40.	Agricultural support estimate for OECD countries as a percentage of GDP	1.4
41.	Proportion of ODA provided to help build trade capacity	—
42.	Number of countries reaching HIPC decision and completion points	1.4
43.	Debt relief committed under new HIPC initiative	1.4
44.	Debt services as a percentage of exports of goods and services	4.17
45.	Unemployment rate of 15- to 24-year-olds	1.3, 2.9
46.	Proportion of population with access to affordable, essential drugs on a sustainable basis	—
47.	Telephone lines and cellular subscribers per 100 people	1.3, 5.10
48a.	Personal computers in use per 100 people	5.11
48b.	Internet users per 100 people	5.11

— No data are available in the World Development Indicators database.
* Table shows information on related indicators.

Definitions

• **Net official development assistance** (ODA) comprises grants and loans (net of repayments of principal) that meet the DAC definition of ODA and are made to countries and territories on part I of the DAC list of recipient countries. • **ODA for basic social services** is aid reported by DAC donors for basic health, education, nutrition, and water and sanitation services. • **Goods admitted free of tariffs** refer to the value of exports of goods (excluding arms) from least developed countries admitted without tariff, as a share of total exports from least developed countries. • **Average tariff** is the simple mean tariff, the unweighted average of the effectively applied rates for all products subject to tariffs. • **Agricultural products** comprise plant and animal products, including tree crops but excluding timber and fish products. • **Textiles and clothing** include natural and synthetic fibers and fabrics and articles of clothing made from them. • **Support to agriculture** is the annual monetary value of all gross transfers from taxpayers and consumers arising from policy measures that support agriculture, net of the associated budgetary receipts, regardless of their objectives and impacts on farm production and income, or consumption of farm products. • **HIPC decision point** is the date at which a heavily indebted poor country with an established track record of good performance under adjustment programs supported by the International Monetary Fund and the World Bank commits to undertake additional reforms and to develop and implement a poverty reduction strategy. • **HIPC completion point** is the date at which the country successfully completes the key structural reforms agreed on at the decision point, including developing and implementing its poverty reduction strategy. The country then receives the bulk of debt relief under the HIPC Initiative without further policy conditions. • **Estimated total nominal debt service relief** is the amount of debt service relief, calculated at the decision point, that will allow the country to achieve debt sustainability at the completion point.

Data sources

The indicators here, and where they appear throughout the rest of the book, have been compiled by World Bank staff from primary and secondary sources. The World Trade Organization, in collaboration with the UN Conference on Trade and Development and the International Trade Centre, provided the estimates of goods admitted free of tariffs and average tariffs. Subsidies to agriculture are compiled by the OECD. Data on the HIPC Initiative are from the August 2005 "HIPC Status Report."

1.5 Women in development

	Female population	Life expectancy at birth		Pregnant women receiving prenatal care	Teenage mothers	Women in nonagricultural sector	Unpaid family workers		Women in parliaments	
		years					Male	Female		
	% of total	Male	Female	%	% of women ages 15–19	% of total	% of male employment	% of female employment	% of total seats	
	2004	2004	2004	2000–04[a]	1995–2004[a]	2003	2000–04[a]	2000–04[a]	1990	2006
East Asia & Pacific[b]	49.1 w	68 w	72 w			39.7 w	.. w	.. w	19 w	17 w
Cambodia	51.7	53	60	38	8	52.6	31.6	53.3	..	10
China	48.6	70	73	89	..	39.5	..	..	21	20
Hong Kong, China	52.7	79	85	..	..	46.9	0.2	1.4	..	..
Indonesia	50.1	66	69	92	10	30.8	..	..	12	11
Korea, Dem. Rep.	50.0	61	67	..	..	..	..	..	21	20
Lao PDR	50.0	54	57	27	..	..	..	..	6	23
Malaysia	49.2	71	76	74	..	38.0	2.2	9.6	5	9
Mongolia	49.9	62	68	94	..	49.4	18.4	31.7	25	7
Myanmar	50.3	58	64	76	..	..	..	..	..	..
Papua New Guinea	48.4	55	57	..	..	35.4	..	..	0	1
Philippines	49.7	69	73	88	8	41.1	..	..	9	16
Thailand	50.8	67	74	92	..	46.9	16.0	35.2	3	11
Vietnam	50.1	68	73	86	3	51.8	21.9	50.3	18	27
Europe & Central Asia	52.1 w	64 w	73 w			47.3 w	2.9 w	7.3 w	.. w	13 w
Albania	50.4	71	77	91	..	40.3	..	..	29	7
Armenia	53.3	68	75	92	6	47.0	1.1	0.8	36	5
Azerbaijan	51.4	70	75	66	..	48.5	..	..	..	12
Belarus	53.2	63	74	..	..	55.9	..	..	..	29
Bosnia and Herzegovina	51.4	72	77	99	..	..	..	..	..	17
Bulgaria	51.5	69	76	..	..	52.2	1.3	2.6	21	22
Croatia	51.9	72	79	..	..	46.3	1.8	6.3	..	22
Czech Republic	51.3	73	79	..	..	45.8	0.3	1.2	..	17
Estonia	54.0	66	77	..	..	51.5	0.3	0.4	..	19
Georgia	52.7	67	74	..	..	45.2	19.9	38.8	..	9
Hungary	52.4	69	77	..	..	47.1	0.4	0.7	21	9
Kazakhstan	52.0	60	71	..	7	48.7	0.8	1.2	..	10
Kyrgyz Republic	50.8	64	72	..	9	44.0	6.5	15.9	..	0
Latvia	54.2	66	78	..	..	53.4	3.5	3.9	..	21
Lithuania	53.3	66	78	..	..	50.0	2.8	4.3	..	22
Macedonia, FYR	50.1	71	76	81	..	42.2	7.0	18.1	..	19
Moldova	52.2	65	72	..	..	54.6	1.3	3.4	..	22
Poland	51.5	70	79	..	..	47.7	4.0	7.2	14	20
Romania	51.2	68	75	..	..	45.3	7.8	23.4	34	11
Russian Federation	53.6	59	72	..	..	50.1	0.1	0.1	..	10
Serbia and Montenegro	50.3	71	76	..	..	44.9	..	..	..	8
Slovak Republic	51.5	70	78	..	..	52.1	..	..	..	17
Tajikistan	50.3	61	67	71	..	52.3	..	..	..	18
Turkey	49.6	69	71	81	10	20.6	8.2	49.0	1	4
Turkmenistan	50.7	59	67	98	4	..	..	..	26	16
Ukraine	54.1	63	74	..	..	53.6	1.1	2.0	..	5
Uzbekistan	50.3	64	70	97	10	41.5	..	..	..	18
Latin America & Carib.	50.6 w	69 w	75 w			43.7 w	.. w	.. w	8 w	20 w
Argentina	51.1	71	78	98	..	47.6	0.8	1.6	6	35
Bolivia	50.2	62	67	79	16	36.5	5.2	11.1	9	17
Brazil	50.7	67	75	..	18	46.9	..	..	5	9
Chile	50.5	75	81	..	..	37.3	1.4	3.3	..	15
Colombia	50.6	70	76	91	19	48.8	4.3	8.5	5	12
Costa Rica	49.2	76	81	..	..	39.5	2.1	3.6	11	35
Cuba	50.0	75	79	100	..	37.7	..	..	34	36
Dominican Republic	49.5	64	71	99	23	34.9	..	..	8	17
Ecuador	49.8	72	78	..	..	41.1	3.0	8.6	5	16
El Salvador	50.9	68	74	86	..	31.1	8.5	9.0	12	11
Guatemala	51.2	64	71	84	22	38.7	21.3	24.5	7	8
Haiti	50.8	51	53	79	18	..	..	..	..	4
Honduras	49.6	66	70	83	..	50.5	12.9	11.0	10	23

Women in development 1.5

	Female population	Life expectancy at birth		Pregnant women receiving prenatal care	Teenage mothers	Women in nonagricultural sector	Unpaid family workers		Women in parliaments	
		years					Male	Female		
	% of total	Male	Female	%	% of women ages 15–19	% of total	% of male employment	% of female employment	% of total seats	
	2004	2004	2004	2000–04[a]	1995–2004[a]	2003	2000–04[a]	2000–04[a]	1990	2006
Jamaica	50.6	69	73	..	..	48.0	0.7	2.0	5	12
Mexico	51.1	73	78	..	..	37.4	5.5	11.3	12	24
Nicaragua	50.0	68	73	86	25	..	..	..	15	21
Panama	49.5	73	78	..	..	44.0	3.1	4.0	8	17
Paraguay	49.6	69	74	94	..	42.0	..	..	6	10
Peru	49.7	68	73	84	13	37.2	2.0	6.2	6	18
Trinidad and Tobago	50.6	67	73	92	..	41.3	0.5	1.9	17	19
Uruguay	51.5	72	79	..	..	46.3	0.9	2.0	6	11
Venezuela, RB	49.7	71	77	94	..	41.5	1.8	3.3	10	17
Middle East & N. Africa	**49.5 w**	**68 w**	**71 w**			**.. w**	**.. w**	**.. w**	**4 w**	**8 w**
Algeria	49.6	70	73	81	..	15.5	..	..	2	6
Egypt, Arab Rep.	49.8	68	72	69	9	21.6	8.4	19.5	4	2
Iran, Islamic Rep.	49.3	69	72	..	..	..	..	..	2	4
Iraq	..	..	..	77	..	..	..	..	11	26
Jordan	48.0	70	73	99	4	24.9	..	..	0	6
Lebanon	51.0	70	75	..	..	..	..	..	0	5
Libya	48.4	72	77	..	..	..	..	..	..	5
Morocco	50.3	68	72	68	7	26.2	21.6	52.5	0	11
Oman	43.4	73	76	100	..	25.6	..	..	..	2
Syrian Arab Republic	49.7	72	75	71	..	18.2	..	..	9	12
Tunisia	49.6	71	75	92	..	25.3	..	..	4	23
West Bank and Gaza	49.1	71	75	..	..	..	7.0	32.5	..	..
Yemen, Rep.	49.3	60	63	41	16	6.1	..	..	4	0[c]
South Asia	**48.7 w**	**63 w**	**64 w**			**18.1 w**	**.. w**	**.. w**	**6 w**	**14 w**
Afghanistan	..	..	..	16	..	..	..	..	4	..
Bangladesh	48.9	63	64	49	33[d]	24.2	10.1	73.2	10	15
India	48.7	63	64	..	21	17.5	..	..	5	8
Nepal	50.4	62	63	28	21	..	..	..	6	0
Pakistan	48.5	64	66	43	..	8.7	16.4	46.9	10	21
Sri Lanka	49.2	72	77	95	..	43.2	4.2	20.9	5	5
Sub-Saharan Africa	**50.1 w**	**46 w**	**47 w**			**.. w**	**.. w**	**.. w**	**.. w**	**16 w**
Angola	50.7	40	43	66	..	..	..	..	15	15
Benin	49.7	54	55	81	22	..	..	..	3	7
Botswana	50.9	36	35	97	..	47.0	1.4	1.2	5	11
Burkina Faso	49.8	47	49	73	23	15.2	..	..	..	12
Burundi	51.3	43	45	78	..	..	..	..	..	31
Cameroon	50.3	45	47	83	28	..	9.5	27.2	14	9
Central African Republic	51.3	39	40	62	36	..	..	..	4	11
Chad	50.5	43	45	42	39	..	..	..	..	7
Congo, Dem. Rep.	50.4	43	45	68	..	..	..	..	5	12
Congo, Rep.	50.4	51	54	..	..	..	..	..	14	9
Côte d'Ivoire	49.1	45	47	88	31	20.2	..	..	6	9
Eritrea	51.0	53	56	70	14	35.0	..	..	..	22
Ethiopia	50.3	42	43	27	16	..	..	..	..	21
Gabon	50.2	54	55	94	33	..	..	..	13	9
Gambia, The	50.4	55	58	91	..	..	..	..	8	13
Ghana	49.4	57	58	92	14	..	..	..	..	11
Guinea	48.8	54	54	84	37	..	..	..	..	19
Guinea-Bissau	50.6	44	46	62	..	..	..	..	20	14
Kenya	50.0	49	47	88	23	38.5	..	..	1	7
Lesotho	53.5	35	37	85	..	..	..	..	..	12
Liberia	50.1	42	43	85	..	..	..	..	..	13
Madagascar	50.3	54	57	80	34	..	29.7	51.9	7	7
Malawi	50.4	40	40	94	33	12.5	..	..	10	14
Mali	50.2	48	49	57	40	..	..	..	..	10
Mauritania	50.6	52	55	64	16	..	..	..	..	..

1.5 Women in development

	Female population	Life expectancy at birth		Pregnant women receiving prenatal care	Teenage mothers	Women in nonagricultural sector	Unpaid family workers		Women in parliaments	
		years					Male	Female		
	% of total	Male	Female	%	% of women ages 15–19	% of total	% of male employment	% of female employment	% of total seats	
	2004	2004	2004	2000–04[a]	1995–2004[a]	2003	2000–04[a]	2000–04[a]	1990	2006
Mauritius	50.3	69	76	..	..	38.5	..	..	7	17
Mozambique	51.7	41	42	85	41	..	..	..	16	35
Namibia	50.4	47	48	91	18	50.8	12.8	22.0	7	27
Niger	48.9	45	45	41	43	..	..	..	5	12
Nigeria	49.4	43	44	58	25	..	..	..	..	6
Rwanda	51.6	42	46	92	7	..	..	..	17	49
Senegal	50.8	55	57	79	22	..	..	..	13	19
Sierra Leone	50.7	40	43	68	..	..	..	..	..	15
Somalia	50.4	46	48	..	..	..	..	..	4	8
South Africa	50.9	44	45	..	16	..	0.5	1.1	3	33
Sudan	49.7	55	58	60	..	18.9	..	..	..	15
Swaziland	51.9	43	42	90	..	31.3	..	..	4	11
Tanzania	50.3	46	47	94	25	..	3.0	4.6	..	30
Togo	50.6	53	57	85	19	..	..	..	5	7
Uganda	50.0	48	49	92	31	..	10.3	40.5	12	24
Zambia	50.0	39	38	93	32	..	..	..	7	13
Zimbabwe	50.5	38	37	..	21	21.8	10.4	13.6	11	16
High income	50.7 w	76 w	82 w			46.0 w	.. w	3.1 w	8 w	22 w
Australia	50.6	77	83	..	..	48.9	0.3	0.4	6	25
Austria	51.1	76	82	..	..	44.5	1.4	3.0	12	34
Belgium	50.9	76	82	..	..	44.4	..	..	9	35
Canada	50.4	77	83	..	..	49.2	0.2	0.3	13	21
Denmark	50.5	75	80	..	..	48.3	0.3	1.1	31	37
Finland	51.1	75	82	..	..	50.6	0.4	0.4	32	38
France	51.3	77	84	..	..	47.0	..	..	7	12
Germany	51.2	76	81	..	..	46.4	0.5	1.9	..	32
Greece	50.6	77	81	..	..	41.1	3.9	14.2	7	13
Ireland	50.3	76	81	..	..	47.4	0.8	1.3	8	13
Israel	50.5	77	81	..	..	48.9	0.2	0.7	7	15
Italy	51.5	77	83	..	..	41.2	3.1	5.8	13	12
Japan	51.1	78	85	..	..	40.8	1.6	9.2	1	9
Korea, Rep.	49.8	74	81	..	..	41.2	1.3	16.7	2	13
Kuwait	39.8	75	79	..	..	24.1	..	..	..	2
Netherlands	50.4	76	81	..	..	45.7	0.2	1.1	21	37
New Zealand	50.9	77	81	..	..	51.3	0.5	0.9	14	32
Norway	50.4	78	82	..	..	49.1	0.3	0.4	36	38
Portugal	51.7	74	81	..	..	46.9	1.0	2.3	8	21
Puerto Rico	52.0	73	82	..	..	40.1	0.1	1.1	..	..
Saudi Arabia	46.0	70	74	..	..	14.5	..	..	..	0
Singapore	49.7	77	81	..	..	47.8	0.3	1.3	5	16
Slovenia	51.2	73	80	..	..	47.4	3.1	5.6	..	12
Spain	50.9	77	84	..	..	40.7	0.9	2.7	15	36
Sweden	50.4	78	83	..	..	50.9	..	..	38	45
Switzerland	51.5	79	84	..	..	46.9	1.6	3.0	14	25
United Arab Emirates	32.0	77	81	..	..	14.4	..	..	0	0
United Kingdom	51.2	76	81	..	..	49.9	0.6	0.7	6	20
United States	50.8	75	80	..	..	48.8	..	0.1	7	15
World	49.7 w	65 w	69 w			38.1 w	.. w	.. w	11 w	17 w
Low income	49.3	58	60			23.3	..	..	7	16
Middle income	49.8	68	73			40.5	..	..	15	15
Lower middle income	49.4	68	73			39.9	..	..	16	15
Upper middle income	51.4	66	73			44.1	2.8	6.7	..	15
Low & middle income	49.6	63	67			36.1	..	..	12	15
High income	50.7	76	82			46.0	..	3.1	8	22

a. Data are for the most recent year available. b. Hong Kong, China, is classified as a high-income economy and is not included in the East Asia and Pacific aggregate. c. Less than 0.5. d. Refers to women ages 15–49.

About the data

Despite much progress in recent decades, gender inequalities remain pervasive in many dimensions of life—worldwide. But while disparities exist throughout the world, they are most prevalent in poor developing countries. Gender inequalities in the allocation of such resources as education, health care, nutrition, and political voice matter because of the strong association with well-being, productivity, and economic growth. This pattern of inequality begins at an early age, with boys routinely receiving a larger share of education and health spending than do girls, for example.

Because of biological differences girls are expected to experience lower infant and child mortality rates and to have a longer life expectancy than boys. This biological advantage, however, may be overshadowed by gender inequalities in nutrition and medical interventions, and by inadequate care during pregnancy and delivery, so that female rates of illness and death sometimes exceed male rates, particularly during early childhood and the reproductive years. In high-income countries women tend to outlive men by four to eight years on average, while in low-income countries the difference is narrower—about two to three years. The difference in child mortality rates (table 2.19) is another good indicator of female social disadvantage because nutrition and medical interventions are particularly important for the 1–5 age group. Female child mortality rates that are as high as or higher than male child mortality rates might be indicative of discrimination against girls.

Having a child during the teenage years limits girls' opportunities for better education, jobs, and income and increases the likelihood of divorce and separation. Pregnancy is more likely to be unintended during the teenage years, and births are more likely to be premature and are associated with greater risks of complications during delivery and of death. In many countries maternal mortality (tables 1.2 and 2.16) is a leading cause of death among women of reproductive age. Most maternal deaths result from preventable causes—hemorrhage, infection, and complications from unsafe abortions. Prenatal care is essential for recognizing, diagnosing, and promptly treating complications that arise during pregnancy. In high-income countries most women have access to health care during pregnancy, but in developing countries an estimated 8 million women suffer pregnancy-related complications every year, and over half a million die (WHO 2004). This is reflected in the differences in maternal mortality ratios between high- and low-income countries.

Women's wage work is important for economic growth and the well-being of families. But restricted access to education and vocational training, heavy workloads at home and in nonpaid domestic and market activities, and labor market discrimination often limit women's participation in paid economic activities, lower their productivity, and reduce their wages. When women are in salaried employment, they tend to be concentrated in the nonagricultural sector. However, in many developing countries women are a large part of agricultural employment, often as unpaid family workers. Among people who are unsalaried, women are more likely than men to be unpaid family workers, while men are more likely than women to be self-employed or employers. There are several reasons for this.

Few women have access to credit markets, capital, land, training, and education, which may be required to start up a business. Cultural norms may prevent women from working on their own or from supervising other workers. Also, women may face time constraints due to their traditional family responsibilities. Because of biases and misclassification substantial numbers of employed women may be underestimated or reported as unpaid family workers even when they work in association or equally with their husbands in the family enterprise.

Women are vastly underrepresented in decision-making positions in government, although there is some evidence of recent improvement. Gender parity in parliamentary representation is still far from being realized. In 2005 women represented 16 percent of parliamentarians worldwide, compared with 9 percent in 1987. Without representation at this level, it is difficult for women to influence policy.

For information on other aspects of gender, see tables 1.2 (Millennium Development Goals: eradicating poverty and improving lives), 2.3 (employment by economic activity), 2.4 (child labor), 2.5 (unemployment), 2.12 (education efficiency), 2.13 (education completion and outcomes), 2.16 (reproductive health), 2.18 (health risk factors and future challenges), and 2.19 (mortality).

Definitions

• **Female population** is the percentage of the population that is female. • **Life expectancy at birth** is the number of years a newborn infant would live if prevailing patterns of mortality at the time of its birth were to stay the same throughout its life. • **Pregnant women receiving prenatal care** are the percentage of women attended at least once during pregnancy by skilled health personnel for reasons related to pregnancy. • **Teenage mothers** are the percentage of women ages 15–19 who already have children or are currently pregnant. • **Women in nonagricultural sector** refers to women wage employees in the nonagricultural sector as a percentage of total nonagricultural employment. • **Unpaid family workers** are those who work without pay in a market-oriented establishment or activity operated by a related person living in the same household. • **Women in parliaments** are the percentage of parliamentary seats in a single or lower chamber occupied by women.

Data sources

Data on female population and life expectancy are from the World Bank's population database. Data on pregnant women receiving prenatal care are from United Nations Children's Fund's *State of the World's Children 2006*. Data on teenage mothers are from Demographic and Health Surveys by Macro International. Data on labor force and employment are from the ILO's *Key Indicators of the Labour Market*, fourth edition. Data on women in parliaments are from the Inter-Parliamentary Union.

1.6 Key indicators for other economies

	Population	Surface area	Population density	Gross national income				Gross domestic product		Life expectancy at birth	Adult literacy rate	Carbon dioxide emissions
						PPP[a]						
	thousands 2004	thousand sq. km 2004	people per sq. km 2004	$ millions 2004[b]	Per capita $ 2004	$ millions 2004	Per capita $ 2004	% growth 2003–04	Per capita % growth 2003–04	years 2004	% ages 15 and older 2004	thousand metric tons 2002
American Samoa	57	0.2	285	..	..[c]	..	..	..	..	..	..	286
Andorra	66	0.5	140	..	..[d]	..	..	..	..	..	..	..
Antigua and Barbuda	80	0.4	182	759	9,480	889	11,100	4.1	2.9	*75*	..	370
Aruba	99	0.2	521	..	..[d]	..	..	..	..	..	..	1,982
Bahamas, The	319	13.9	32	*4,684*	*15,100*	*5,071*	*16,350*	*0.7*	*–0.7*	70	..	2,081
Bahrain	716	0.7	1,008	10,288	14,370	14,080	19,670	5.4	3.9	75	..	21,292
Barbados	269	0.4	625	2,831[e]	10,530[e]	..	..	..	..	75	100	1,220
Belize	283	23.0	12	1,115	3,940	1,851	6,550	4.2	0.9	72	..	788
Bermuda	64	0.1	1,280	..	..[d]	..	..	..	..	..	..	498
Bhutan	896	47.0	19	677	760	..	..	4.9	2.3	64	..	399
Brunei Darussalam	366	5.8	69	..	..[d]	..	..	..	..	77	..	6,174
Cape Verde	495	4.0	123	852	1,720	2,803[f]	5,660[f]	5.5	3.1	70	76	147
Cayman Islands	44	0.3	169	..	..[d]	..	..	..	..	..	..	289
Channel Islands	149	0.2	745	..	..[d]	..	..	..	..	79	..	..
Comoros	588	2.2	264	328	560	1,135[f]	1,930[f]	1.9	–0.2	63	56	84
Cyprus	826	9.3	89	13,633	16,510	18,360[f]	22,230[f]	3.7	2.5	79	..	6,661
Djibouti	779	23.2	34	739	950	1,675[f]	2,150[f]	3.0	1.1	53	..	359
Dominica	71	0.8	95	262	3,670	378	5,290	2.0	1.6	*77*	..	121
Equatorial Guinea	492	28.1	18	..	..[c]	3,731[f]	7,580[f]	10.0	7.5	43	..	169
Faeroe Islands	48	1.4	34	..	..[d]	..	..	..	..	..	..	652
Fiji	841	18.3	46	2,286	2,720	4,835	5,750	4.1	3.2	68	..	1,352
French Polynesia	253	4.0	69	..	..[d]	..	..	..	..	74	..	700
Greenland	57	410.5	0	..	..[d]	..	..	..	..	*69*	..	564
Grenada	106	0.3	311	397	3,750	746	7,050	–2.8	–3.8	*73*	..	231
Guam	167	0.6	303	..	..[d]	..	..	..	..	75	..	4,089
Guyana	750	215.0	4	765	1,020	3,181[f]	4,240[f]	1.6	1.4	64	..	1,608
Iceland	292	103.0	3	11,077	37,920	9,455	32,370	5.2	4.3	80	..	2,213
Isle of Man	77	0.6	135	*2,138*	*23,750*	..	..	*6.3*	..	..	..	..

About the data

This table shows data for 55 economies—small economies with populations between 30,000 and 1 million and smaller economies if they are members of the World Bank. Where data on gross national income (GNI) per capita are not available, the estimated range is given. For more information on the calculation of GNI (gross national product, or GNP, in the System of National Accounts 1968) and purchasing power parity (PPP) conversion factors, see *About the data* for table 1.1. Since 2000 this table has excluded France's overseas departments—French Guiana, Guadeloupe, Martinique, and Réunion—for which GNI and other economic measures are now included in the French national accounts.

Definitions

• **Population** is based on the de facto definition of population, which counts all residents regardless of legal status or citizenship—except for refugees not permanently settled in the country of asylum, who are generally considered part of the population of their country of origin. The values shown are midyear estimates for 2004. See also table 2.1. • **Surface area** is a country's total area, including areas under inland bodies of water and some coastal waterways. • **Population density** is midyear population divided by land area in square kilometers. • **Gross national income (GNI)** is the sum of value added by all resident producers plus any product taxes (less subsidies) not included in the valuation of output plus net receipts of primary income (compensation of employees and property income) from abroad. Data are in current U.S. dollars converted using the *World Bank Atlas* method (see *Statistical methods*). • **GNI per capita** is gross national income divided by midyear population. GNI per capita in U.S. dollars is converted using the *World Bank Atlas* method. • **PPP GNI** is gross national income converted to international dollars using purchasing power parity rates. An international dollar has the same purchasing power over GNI as a U.S. dollar has in the United States. • **Gross domestic product (GDP)** is the sum of value added by all resident producers plus any product taxes (less subsidies)

Key indicators for other economies

	Population	Surface area	Population density	Gross national income		PPP[a]		Gross domestic product		Life expectancy at birth	Adult literacy rate	Carbon dioxide emissions
	thousands 2004	thousand sq. km 2004	people per sq. km 2004	$ millions 2004[b]	Per capita $ 2004	$ millions 2004	Per capita $ 2004	% growth 2003–04	Per capita % growth 2003–04	years 2004	% ages 15 and older 2004	thousand metric tons 2002
Kiribati	98	0.7	134	95	970	..	..	1.8	0.3	*63*	..	29
Liechtenstein	34	0.2	213	..	..[d]	..	..	..	..	..	..	..
Luxembourg	453	2.6	174	25,559	56,380	27,928	61,610	4.5	3.8	*78*	..	9,427
Macao, China	457	..	..	..	..[d]	..	..	*10.1*	*9.3*	80	..	1,806
Maldives	321	0.3	1,071	773	2,410	..	..	10.8	8.1	67	..	1,030
Malta	401	0.3	1,254	4,834	12,050	7,460	18,590	0.4	−0.2	79	..	2,953
Marshall Islands	61	0.2	340	142	2,320	..	..	1.5	−2.2	..	..	..
Mayotte	172	0.4	430	..	..[c]	..	..	..	..	..	..	..
Micronesia, Fed. Sts.	110	0.7	157	252	2,300	..	..	−3.8	−4.6	68	..	..
Monaco	33	0.0	16,923	..	..[d]	..	..	..	..	..	..	..
Netherlands Antilles	181	0.8	226	..	..[d]	..	..	..	..	76	97	4,928
New Caledonia	230	18.6	13	..	..[d]	..	..	..	..	75	..	1,821
Northern Mariana Islands	77	0.5	161	..	..[c]	..	..	..	..	..	..	..
Palau	20	0.5	43	137	6,870	..	..	2.0	0.5	..	..	234
Qatar	777	11.0	71	..	..[d]	..	..	..	..	74	89	36,391
Samoa	184	2.8	65	338	1,840	1,031[f]	5,610[f]	3.1	2.3	70	99	143
São Tomé and Principe	153	1.0	159	60	390	..	..	4.5	2.1	63	..	92
Seychelles	84	0.5	182	685	8,190	1,328[f]	15,880[f]	−2.0	−3.0	*73*	*92*	535
Solomon Islands	466	28.9	17	263	560	838	1,800	5.5	2.8	63	..	172
San Marino	28	0.1	463	*653*	..[d]	..	..	*2.3*	..	..	..	..
St. Kitts and Nevis	47	0.4	131	*326*	*6,980*	*510*	*10,910*	*2.1*	*2.1*	*71*	..	114
St. Lucia	164	0.6	268	684	4,180	915	5,590	3.5	1.6	73	..	377
St. Vincent & Grenadines	118	0.4	304	403	3,400	714	6,030	6.0	5.4	71	..	183
Suriname	446	163.3	3	997	2,230	..	..	4.6	3.9	69	..	2,250
Timor-Leste	887	14.9	60	506	570	..	..	1.8	−5.0	56	..	..
Tonga	102	0.8	142	190	1,860	801[f]	7,850[f]	4.3	3.9	72	..	106
Vanuatu	207	12.2	17	287	1,390	612[f]	2,950[f]	3.0	1.0	69	..	84
Virgin Islands (U.S.)	113	0.4	323	..	..[d]	..	..	..	..	79	..	10,241

a. PPP is purchasing power parity; see *Definitions*. b. Calculated using the *World Bank Atlas* method. c. Estimated to be upper middle income ($3,256–$10,065). d. Estimated to be high income ($10,066 or more). e. Refers to GDP and GDP per capita at factor cost. f. The estimate is based on regression; others are extrapolated from the latest International Comparison Program benchmark estimates.

not included in the valuation of output. Growth is calculated from constant price GDP data in local currency. • **Life expectancy at birth** is the number of years a newborn infant would live if prevailing patterns of mortality at the time of its birth were to stay the same throughout its life. • **Adult illiteracy rate** is the percentage of adults ages 15 and older who cannot, with understanding, read and write a short, simple statement about their everyday life. • **Carbon dioxide emissions** are those stemming from the burning of fossil fuels and the manufacture of cement. They include carbon dioxide produced during consumption of solid, liquid, and gas fuels and gas flaring.

Data sources

The indicators here and throughout the rest of the book have been compiled by World Bank Group staff from primary and secondary sources. More information about the indicators and their sources can be found in the *About the data*, *Definitions*, and *Data sources* entries that accompany each table in subsequent sections.

2 PEOPLE

The world is in the middle of a major demographic transition. Its population continues to grow every year, but the pace of growth has slowed as fertility rates decline. As population growth slows, the age structure of the population is changing, with the share of the young declining and that of the elderly growing. This changing age structure has important implications for economic and social policies and hence for sustainable development.

But different countries and regions are at varying stages of this transition, depending on their fertility, mortality, and migration trends, creating a "demographic divide" between countries (Kent and Haub 2005). In much of the industrial world increasing life expectancy and aging populations have coincided with income growth, healthier lifestyles, and fertility rates that are below population replacement levels. For these countries there will be little change in future population size in the absence of inmigration. In fact, large increases in inmigration or in the retirement age would be needed to stabilize the labor force and maintain current labor force to population ratios. In developing countries fertility rates have also declined but remain much higher than in industrial countries, and fertility rates vary considerably across regions: high in Sub-Saharan Africa and the Middle East, but low in East Asia. Except in the transition economies of Eastern Europe, where fertility rates are near or below replacement levels, the population in developing countries will continue to grow well into the twenty-first century, and outmigration will only modestly reduce the population growth rate.

Technology, consumption patterns, unequal distribution of wealth, and the choices people and governments make all affect demographic trends. These, in turn, affect social and economic outcomes, and, consequently, what place these countries will take on the world stage in the future. Sub-Saharan African countries are trailing most others in their progress through the demographic transition. And if economic growth continues to lag behind population growth, as was the case in the early 1990s, it will exacerbate poverty in the region.

Rapid population growth in Sub-Saharan Africa

The challenges facing Sub-Saharan Africa as it strives to meet its development objectives are more daunting than those facing other regions. Its efforts to alleviate poverty, empower women, reduce child mortality, and improve maternal health have been undercut by the AIDS epidemic, by conflict, and by human displacement in the wake of natural disasters. In the past three decades its population has grown faster than that of any other region, doubling between 1975 and 2000 and now growing at 2.5 percent a year. Roughly 47 percent of the Sub-Saharan population is between the ages of 5 and 24, indicating that the population will continue to increase well into the twenty-first century. This large cohort will require substantial increases in future spending on health, education, and care for dependents.

Has success bred complacency?

Too little is being said about the challenge of continuing rapid population growth to African development. One possible reason for this may be that the success of fertility reductions in other regions and in some African countries has left the impression that the population problem has been solved (Cleland and Sinding 2005). Fertility rates have declined dramatically in the past 25 years where governments have increased investments in education and in women's reproductive health (table 2a). Globally, contraceptive prevalence increased from 54 percent in 1990 to 59 percent in 1995 and to more than 60 percent in 2003 (box 2b).

The slowdown in population growth (table 2c) can be traced to these fertility declines. In Europe and Central Asia women now have on average only 1.6 births—too few to replace today's population. At the other extreme is Sub-Saharan Africa, with average fertility remaining very high.

Even in Sub-Saharan Africa regional figures mask huge differences across countries (table 2d). In South Africa, Botswana, Zimbabwe, and Lesotho fertility continues to decline as a result of successful family planning programs. Of women ages 15–49, 54 percent were using contraception in Zimbabwe and 48 percent in Botswana, compared with 14 percent in Niger and 8 percent in Chad in the past decade. Even in countries with high fertility, the rates vary by socioeconomic status. In Benin the fertility rate was 7.3 births for women in the lowest asset quintile and 3.8 for women in the richest quintile.

2a

Total fertility rates by region, 1970, 1980, and 2004

Region	1970	1980	2004
East Asia & Pacific	5.4	3.0	2.1
Europe & Central Asia	2.5	2.2	1.6
Latin America & Caribbean	5.3	4.2	2.4
Middle East & North Africa	6.7	6.2	3.1
South Asia	6.0	5.2	3.1
Sub-Saharan Africa	6.8	6.7	5.4
High-income	2.5	1.9	1.7
World	4.8	3.7	2.6

Source: World Bank database.

2b

Family planning and the fertility transition

The use of family planning among married women worldwide rose from 10 percent in 1960 to more than 60 percent in 2003. Due in part to modern contraception, the decline in fertility and the shift to smaller families occurred faster in developing countries—in only a few decades—than had occurred in industrial countries, where the transition to low fertility began in the 1830s. Crude birth rates were about 37 per 1,000 people in pre-Revolutionary France and 42–43 in the 1850s in the United States, before gradually commencing a decline to their current levels of 8 per 1,000 people.

What contributed to smaller families? Organized family planning programs bringing contraceptive supplies and services to the people, along with information campaigns promoting smaller, healthier families. Studies in the 1990s showed that these programs were responsible for about half the fertility decline of developing countries since the 1960s. Even couples in remote rural communities in Bangladesh and Vietnam gained access to modern contraceptives through nationwide family planning programs.

Contraceptive prevalence is a key determinant of declining fertility. Based on the current use of family planning services, contraceptive rates are not expected to increase rapidly because of Africa's widespread poverty, high rates of illiteracy, largely rural populations, and strong traditional preferences for large families. However, there is an emerging preference for spacing and limiting births among married women of reproductive age in African countries, ranging from 10 percent to 35 percent. The increased availability of contraception has reduced the gap between the number of women who want to limit births and those who can in most countries. But in some countries unmet need remains high.

Why is fertility still high?

Sub-Saharan Africa is becoming fragmented in its fertility declines. There are several reasons for this. The logistical and cultural challenge of delivering family planning programs, the often poor quality of health services, ignorance about reproductive health issues, differences in economic status, and continuing gender inequality all contribute to high fertility rates. Desired family size, though decreasing slowly over past decades, remains high—as high as eight children in some

2c

Population growth rates by region (%)

Region	1950–80	1980–90	1990–2004
East Asia & Pacific	2.0	1.6	1.2
Europe & Central Asia	1.3	0.9	0.1
Latin America & Caribbean	2.6	2.0	1.6
Middle East & North Africa	2.6	3.0	2.1
South Asia	2.2	2.2	1.8
Sub-Saharan Africa	2.6	2.9	2.5
High-income	1.1	0.7	0.8
World	1.9	1.7	1.4

Source: World Bank database.

2d

Total fertility rates in selected Sub-Saharan countries, 2004

Country	Fertility rate	Country	Fertility rate
Niger	7.7	Lesotho	3.5
Uganda	7.1	Zimbabwe	3.4
Guinea-Bissau	7.1	Botswana	3.1
Mali	6.9	South Africa	2.7
Burundi	6.8	Mauritius	2.0

Source: World Bank database.

African countries (table 2e). By contrast, the desired family size in South Asia is typically fewer than three children.

High desired family sizes are associated with high infant mortality rates. But when birth rates began to drop in Bangladesh and Nepal in the 1980s their infant mortality rates were higher than those in many western and central African countries (Cleland and Sinding 2005).

Another reason for high fertility rates is that contraceptive prevalence rates remain low. For 9 of 20 African countries that conducted Demographic and Health Surveys between 1999 and 2005, contraceptive use, including traditional methods, was less than 10 percent for women ages 15–49. Compare that with other regions, where on average 40 percent of women were using a method of contraception. In addition to contraceptive use, the method of contraception is also important for sustained fertility declines. In countries with low contraceptive prevalence, fewer women use modern methods, further diluting the effect of low contraceptive use on fertility (table 2f). Of 17 African countries that conducted Demographic and Health Surveys between 2000 and 2004, in 8 of them use of modern methods was estimated at less than 10 percent.

Finally, HIV/AIDS has affected fertility and mortality trends in Sub-Saharan Africa. AIDS-related deaths among working-age adults in the seven worst AIDS-affected countries will produce an age structure not seen before, with large numbers of old and very young and a relatively small working-age population. But recent data indicate that prevalence among pregnant women attending antenatal clinics in Zimbabwe is declining in all age groups. In South Africa, with the largest number of infected people, rates of HIV infection among pregnant women ages 15–24 have stabilized since 2000. HIV prevalence among pregnant women has declined countrywide in Kenya and Uganda (UNAIDS and WHO 2005). But in western and central Africa there is no consistent evidence of declining prevalence among pregnant women in recent years. And overall in Sub-Saharan Africa the prevalence of HIV infections in people ages 15–49 has remained at about 7 percent since 2000. So while life expectancy has fallen in some cases, fertility remains stubbornly high for many Sub-Saharan African countries, and high fertility remains the dominant influence on current and future population growth and size.

In many West African countries, where HIV prevalence has remained lower than in other regions in Africa, more women die from unsafe abortions than as a result of AIDS (Population Action International 2006). If African nations can expand the capacity and quality of family planning sevices, that will bring about much needed declines in fertility rates while strengthening the status of women. Until this happens, continuing high fertility rates and rapid population growth may prove a more serious obstacle to poverty reduction than will AIDS.

2e

Desired family size in selected countries in Sub-Saharan Africa and South Asia, latest year available

Sub-Saharan Africa	Desired number of children	South Asia	Desired number of children
Cameroon (2004)	5.7	Bangladesh (1999/2000)	2.5
Chad (1996/97)	8.3	India (1998/99)	2.6
Eritrea (2002)	5.8	Nepal (2001)	2.6
Niger (1998)	8.2		

Source: Demographic and Health Surveys.

2f

Contraceptive method mix, selected countries, 2000–04

Country	Contraceptive use: Any method	Contraceptive use: Any modern
Kenya	39.3	31.5
Madagascar	27.1	18.3
Benin	18.6	7.2
Burkina Faso	13.8	8.8
Nigeria	12.6	8.2
Bangladesh	58.5	47.6
Haiti	28.1	22.8
Cambodia	23.8	18.8

Source: Demographic and Health Surveys.

What will high fertility mean for Sub-Saharan Africa's future population?

The population of Sub-Saharan Africa has grown from 225 million in 1960 to 733 million in 2004. The World Bank projects a doubling of the population to 1.4 billion by 2050, increasing the region's share of the world population from 13 percent today to 20 percent. Fertility rates will remain over 3.5 births per woman until 2025, producing a youthful age structure, with a large proportion of children under 15 years old. Comparisons with South Asia, another region with high fertility, show that the fertility transition in Sub-Saharan Africa lags one generation behind (figure 2g).

Very rapid population growth is expected to continue in several African countries, with the population likely to triple in Burkina Faso, Burundi, Chad, Democratic Republic of Congo, Republic of Congo, Guinea-Bissau, Liberia, Mali, Niger, and Uganda (United Nations 2005). Among the nine countries expected by the United Nations to account for half the world's projected population increase between 2005 and 2050, four are in Sub-Saharan Africa: Democratic Republic of Congo, Ethiopia, Nigeria, and Uganda.

Although fertility rates have started to decline in many Sub-Saharan countries, the rates of decline are expected to be more modest and to be achieved over a longer period of time. And they will occur at different paces. For several

2g

Sub-Saharan Africa's delayed demographic transition

Share of deaths in each age group (%)

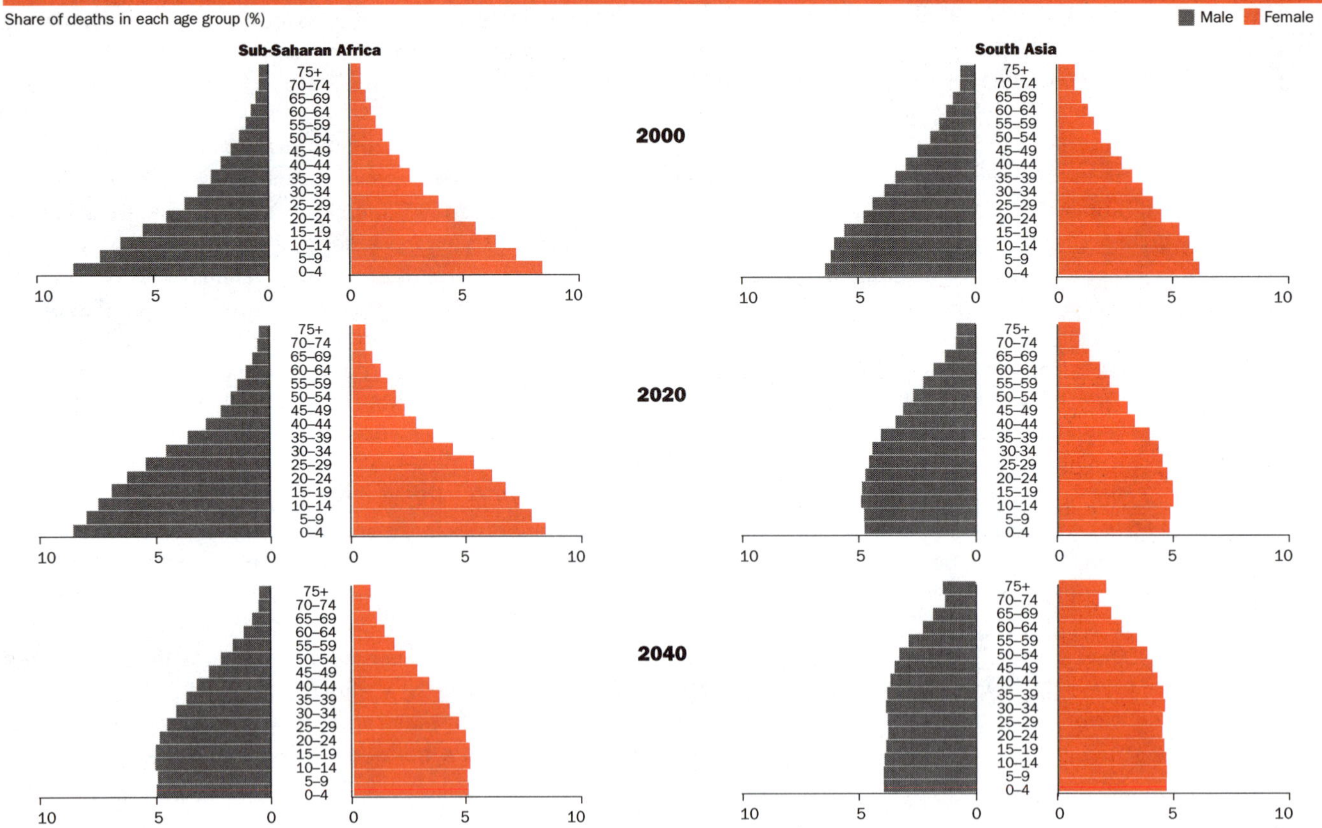

Source: World Bank staff estimates.

2h

Projected fertility rates in selected African regions

Region	2005–10	2010–15	2015–20	2020–25	2025–30	2030–35	2035–40
Western Africa	5.4	4.8	4.4	3.9	3.5	3.2	3.0
Central Africa	6.1	5.8	5.4	5.0	4.5	4.1	3.6
Southern Africa	2.7	2.5	2.4	2.3	2.2	2.1	2.0

Source: United Nations 2005.

decades fertility declines in western and central Africa are expected to lag behind those that have already taken place in southern Africa (table 2h).

What does high fertility mean for Africa's development?

As average population growth slowed globally over the past half century, the range of national and regional demographic experiences widened. Growth rates remained high in many African countries such as Burkina Faso and Chad, while they plummeted in countries in other regions, including Italy, the Republic of Korea, and Thailand. Other countries with moderate growth rates—such as Bangladesh, Brazil, India, and Indonesia, which have had impressive fertility declines—still have considerable momentum for future growth due to a young age structure.

Each demographic situation is associated with its own social, economic, environmental, and political challenge (box 2i). What is of concern about the demographic divide is not the differences in population growth rates, but the disparities in living standards, personal well-being, and future prospects associated with these trends.

People in Japan and Nigeria, with populations of similar size in 2004 but at opposing ends of the divide, have starkly different lives today—and they face very different futures (table 2j). In Japan the elderly dependency ratio is expected to increase dramatically, straining government budgets because of higher spending on pensions, health care, and long-term residential care. Econometric models suggest that the projected decline in the working-age population could result in lower savings and investment rates and slower GDP growth (IMF 2004).

By contrast, in Nigeria, a microcosm of Sub-Saharan Africa, per capita growth could be boosted by the increase in the working-age population. With 36 percent of its population under age 15 in 2025, Nigeria has a considerable momentum for future growth well into the twenty-first century. This growth depends, however, on the country pursuing sound economic and social policies to enable the large wave of potential workers to acquire skills and find productive employment. Its inability to deal with a higher burden of infectious diseases, lower education levels, and limited investment in health infrastructure could result in very different economic outcomes. Without investments in physical stocks and human capital, Nigeria's population growth will exert an unsustainable demand for public-sector-provided health, education, and other services.

2i

Population projections—trends and uncertainty

Future trends in population size, age structure, births, deaths, and other demographic variables are of interest to policymakers, government planners, and industry strategists. The reason: population forecasts can imply a wide range of consequences for society and its environment. Country projections became more accurate over the 1950s and 1960s, as demographic data improved, but since then there have been few significant improvements.

Fertility, mortality, and migration are the components of population growth. While broad trends can be discerned and projected into the future with reasonable confidence, substantial uncertainty is attached to the specific trend for any country or region. Uncertainty arises in part because the present demographic situation in any country is not known perfectly. But the main cause of uncertainty is that future trends in fertility, mortality, and migration are subject to unpredictable influences. Future economic development; societal, cultural, epidemiological, and environmental changes; or progress in science and technology cannot be predicted. Uncertainty also arises from the fact that humans can influence the future through deliberate policy intervention, such as investing heavily in family planning and reproductive services.

Some demographers argue that population forecasts should not go beyond a horizon of 30–35 years, due to the rapid increase in uncertainty beyond this point. Others note, however, that if the forecast carries an appropriate indication of the range of uncertainty, users can decide when the informational content of the forecast ceases to be useful.

Source: NRC 2000.

2j

The demographic divide: Nigeria and Japan

	Nigeria		Japan	
	2004	2025	2004	2025
Population (millions)	137	205	128	120
Total fertility rate per woman	5.6	3.3	1.3	1.8
Population ages 0–14 (percent)	45.1	36.2	14.8	12.5
Population ages 65 and older (percent)	2.7	3.4	16.5	28.1
Life expectancy at birth (years)	45	52	82	84
Infant mortality rate (per 1,000 live births)	98	72	3	3
Adults with HIV/AIDS (percent ages 15–49)	5.4	..	0.1	..
Health expenditure per capita	60	..	2,476	..
GNI per capita	430	..	37,060	..

Source: World Bank database.

2.1 Population dynamics

	Total population			Average annual population growth rate		Population age composition			Dependency ratio		Crude death rate	Crude birth rate
	millions			%		%			dependents as proportion of working-age population		per 1,000 people	per 1,000 people
						Ages 0–14	Ages 15–64	Ages 65+	Young	Old		
	1990	2004	2020	1990–2004	2004–20	2004	2004	2004	2004	2004	2004	2004
Afghanistan	14.6	..	..	..	..	..	..	..	..	..	..	..
Albania	3.3	3.1	3.4	–0.4	0.6	27.6	64.3	8.1	0.4	0.1	6	17
Algeria	25.3	32.4	40.6	1.8	1.4	30.4	65.1	4.5	0.5	0.1	5	21
Angola	10.5	15.5	23.8	2.8	2.7	46.6	51.0	2.5	0.9	0.0[a]	22	48
Argentina	32.6	38.4	44.5	1.2	0.9	26.7	63.1	10.1	0.4	0.2	8	18
Armenia	3.5	3.0	3.0	–1.1	–0.2	21.7	66.4	11.9	0.3	0.2	9	12
Australia	17.1	20.1	23.3	1.2	0.9	20.0	67.5	12.6	0.3	0.2	7	13
Austria	7.7	8.2	8.3	0.4	0.1	15.8	67.8	16.4	0.2	0.2	9	10
Azerbaijan	7.2	8.3	9.4	1.1	0.8	26.8	66.2	6.9	0.4	0.1	6	16
Bangladesh	104.0	139.2	181.2	2.1	1.6	35.9	60.5	3.6	0.6	0.1	8	27
Belarus	10.2	9.8	8.9	–0.3	–0.6	15.8	69.7	14.6	0.2	0.2	15	9
Belgium	10.0	10.4	10.6	0.3	0.1	16.9	65.6	17.5	0.3	0.3	10	11
Benin	5.2	8.2	12.7	3.3	2.8	44.5	52.8	2.7	0.8	0.1	12	41
Bolivia	6.7	9.0	11.6	2.1	1.6	38.5	57.0	4.5	0.7	0.1	8	29
Bosnia and Herzegovina	4.3	3.9	3.8	–0.7	–0.1	16.9	69.6	13.5	0.2	0.2	9	9
Botswana	1.4	1.8	1.7	1.5	–0.4	37.9	58.9	3.2	0.6	0.1	26	26
Brazil	149.4	183.9	219.2	1.5	1.1	28.1	65.9	6.0	0.4	0.1	7	20
Bulgaria	8.7	7.8	6.9	–0.8	–0.8	14.1	69.2	16.8	0.2	0.2	14	9
Burkina Faso	8.5	12.8	20.3	2.9	2.9	47.4	49.8	2.8	1.0	0.1	17	47
Burundi	5.7	7.3	12.3	1.8	3.3	45.5	51.7	2.8	0.9	0.1	18	45
Cambodia	9.7	13.8	18.6	2.5	1.9	37.7	59.0	3.4	0.6	0.1	11	30
Cameroon	11.7	16.0	20.4	2.3	1.5	41.6	54.7	3.7	0.8	0.1	17	35
Canada	27.8	32.0	36.4	1.0	0.8	17.9	69.1	13.0	0.3	0.2	7	10
Central African Republic	3.0	4.0	5.0	2.0	1.4	43.1	52.9	4.0	0.8	0.1	22	37
Chad	6.1	9.4	14.9	3.2	2.8	47.2	49.7	3.1	0.9	0.1	20	48
Chile	13.2	16.1	18.6	1.4	0.9	25.5	66.6	7.9	0.4	0.1	5	16
China	1,135.2	1,296.2	1,423.9	0.9	0.6	22.0	70.5	7.5	0.3	0.1	6	12
Hong Kong, China	5.7	6.9	8.1	1.3	1.0	14.8	73.4	11.8	0.2	0.2	5	7
Colombia	35.0	44.9	55.0	1.8	1.3	31.4	63.6	5.0	0.5	0.1	5	21
Congo, Dem. Rep.	37.8	55.9	90.0	2.8	3.0	47.2	50.1	2.7	0.9	0.1	20	50
Congo, Rep.	2.5	3.9	6.4	3.2	3.1	47.0	50.1	2.9	0.9	0.1	13	44
Costa Rica	3.1	4.3	5.3	2.3	1.3	29.0	65.3	5.7	0.4	0.1	4	17
Côte d'Ivoire	12.7	17.9	23.3	2.5	1.7	42.1	54.6	3.2	0.8	0.1	17	37
Croatia	4.8	4.4	4.4	–0.5	–0.1	15.8	67.2	17.0	0.2	0.3	11	9
Cuba	10.5	11.2	11.4	0.5	0.1	19.5	70.0	10.5	0.3	0.2	7	11
Czech Republic	10.4	10.2	9.9	–0.1	–0.2	15.0	71.0	14.1	0.2	0.2	11	10
Denmark	5.1	5.4	5.6	0.4	0.2	18.8	66.3	14.9	0.3	0.2	10	12
Dominican Republic	7.1	8.8	10.7	1.5	1.2	33.1	62.8	4.1	0.5	0.1	6	24
Ecuador	10.3	13.0	16.0	1.7	1.3	32.8	61.5	5.7	0.5	0.1	5	23
Egypt, Arab Rep.	55.7	72.6	94.8	1.9	1.7	33.9	61.4	4.7	0.6	0.1	6	26
El Salvador	5.1	6.8	8.5	2.0	1.5	34.3	60.4	5.3	0.6	0.1	6	24
Eritrea	3.0	4.2	6.6	2.4	2.8	44.8	52.9	2.3	0.8	0.0[a]	11	39
Estonia	1.6	1.3	1.3	–1.1	–0.4	15.6	68.1	16.3	0.2	0.2	13	10
Ethiopia	51.2	70.0	107.7	2.2	2.7	44.8	52.3	2.9	0.9	0.1	19	40
Finland	5.0	5.2	5.4	0.3	0.2	17.5	66.8	15.7	0.3	0.2	9	11
France	56.7	60.4	63.0	0.4	0.3	18.2	65.2	16.6	0.3	0.3	8	13
Gabon	1.0	1.4	1.7	2.5	1.4	40.5	55.1	4.4	0.7	0.1	13	30
Gambia, The	0.9	1.5	2.1	3.3	2.1	40.3	56.0	3.7	0.7	0.1	12	35
Georgia	5.5	4.5	4.1	–1.4	–0.7	19.5	66.5	14.1	0.3	0.2	11	11
Germany	79.4	82.5	82.3	0.3	0.0[a]	14.6	67.2	18.3	0.2	0.3	10	9
Ghana	15.5	21.7	28.8	2.4	1.8	39.5	56.9	3.6	0.7	0.1	11	31
Greece	10.2	11.1	11.2	0.6	0.1	14.4	67.6	18.0	0.2	0.3	9	9
Guatemala	8.9	12.3	17.5	2.3	2.2	43.5	52.3	4.3	0.8	0.1	6	35
Guinea	6.2	9.2	13.4	2.8	2.3	43.8	52.7	3.5	0.8	0.1	13	41
Guinea-Bissau	1.0	1.5	2.5	3.0	3.0	47.4	49.5	3.1	1.0	0.1	20	50
Haiti	6.9	8.4	10.3	1.4	1.3	38.0	58.1	4.0	0.7	0.1	13	30

Population dynamics 2.1

	Total population			Average annual population growth rate		Population age composition			Dependency ratio		Crude death rate	Crude birth rate
						%			dependents as proportion of working-age population			
	millions			%		Ages 0–14	Ages 15–64	Ages 65+	Young	Old	per 1,000 people	per 1,000 people
	1990	2004	2020	1990–2004	2004–20	2004	2004	2004	2004	2004	2004	2004
Honduras	4.9	7.0	9.5	2.6	1.9	39.7	56.5	3.8	0.7	0.1	6	29
Hungary	10.4	10.1	9.6	−0.2	−0.3	16.0	68.9	15.1	0.2	0.2	13	9
India	849.5	1,079.7	1,332.0	1.7	1.3	32.5	62.3	5.2	0.5	0.1	8	24
Indonesia	178.2	217.6	255.9	1.4	1.0	28.6	66.0	5.4	0.4	0.1	7	20
Iran, Islamic Rep.	54.4	67.0	85.0	1.5	1.5	29.8	65.7	4.5	0.5	0.1	5	19
Iraq	18.5	..	..	..	..	..	..	..	..	..	..	..
Ireland	3.5	4.1	4.9	1.1	1.2	20.3	68.7	10.9	0.3	0.2	7	16
Israel	4.7	6.8	8.3	2.7	1.2	27.9	62.0	10.1	0.4	0.2	6	21
Italy	56.7	57.6	57.1	0.1	0.0[a]	14.1	66.3	19.7	0.2	0.3	9	10
Jamaica	2.4	2.6	2.8	0.7	0.3	31.7	60.8	7.6	0.5	0.1	6	18
Japan	123.5	127.8	126.7	0.2	−0.1	14.1	66.7	19.2	0.2	0.3	9	9
Jordan	3.2	5.4	7.6	3.9	2.1	37.6	59.3	3.1	0.6	0.1	4	27
Kazakhstan	16.3	15.0	14.9	−0.6	0.0[a]	23.9	67.8	8.3	0.4	0.1	10	15
Kenya	23.4	33.5	49.6	2.5	2.5	42.9	54.2	2.8	0.8	0.1	15	39
Korea, Dem. Rep.	19.7	22.4	23.7	0.9	0.4	25.4	68.0	6.5	0.4	0.1	11	16
Korea, Rep.	42.9	48.1	49.4	0.8	0.2	19.1	71.9	9.0	0.3	0.1	5	9
Kuwait	2.1	2.5	3.7	1.0	2.5	24.5	73.8	1.7	0.3	0.0[a]	2	19
Kyrgyz Republic	4.4	5.1	6.1	1.0	1.1	32.1	61.8	6.1	0.5	0.1	7	22
Lao PDR	4.1	5.8	8.0	2.4	2.0	41.2	55.1	3.6	0.7	0.1	12	35
Latvia	2.7	2.3	2.1	−1.0	−0.5	15.2	68.1	16.6	0.2	0.2	14	9
Lebanon	2.7	3.5	4.1	1.8	1.0	29.1	63.6	7.3	0.5	0.1	7	19
Lesotho	1.6	1.8	1.7	0.9	−0.3	39.0	55.8	5.2	0.7	0.1	25	28
Liberia	2.1	3.2	5.0	3.0	2.8	47.0	50.8	2.2	0.9	0.0[a]	21	50
Libya	4.3	5.7	7.5	2.0	1.7	30.4	65.7	4.0	0.5	0.1	4	23
Lithuania	3.7	3.4	3.2	−0.5	−0.4	17.4	67.4	15.2	0.3	0.2	12	9
Macedonia, FYR	1.9	2.0	2.1	0.4	0.1	20.1	69.0	10.9	0.3	0.2	9	12
Madagascar	12.0	18.1	26.6	2.9	2.4	44.2	52.7	3.1	0.8	0.1	12	39
Malawi	9.5	12.6	17.8	2.1	2.2	47.3	49.7	3.0	1.0	0.1	21	43
Malaysia	17.8	24.9	31.5	2.4	1.5	32.8	62.8	4.5	0.5	0.1	5	22
Mali	8.9	13.1	20.9	2.8	2.9	48.3	49.0	2.7	1.0	0.1	17	49
Mauritania	2.0	3.0	4.5	2.7	2.5	43.1	53.5	3.4	0.8	0.1	14	41
Mauritius	1.1	1.2	1.4	1.1	0.7	24.9	68.6	6.5	0.4	0.1	7	16
Mexico	83.2	103.8	124.7	1.6	1.1	31.6	63.2	5.2	0.5	0.1	5	19
Moldova	4.4	4.2	4.1	−0.2	−0.2	19.1	70.9	10.0	0.3	0.1	12	10
Mongolia	2.1	2.5	3.1	1.3	1.4	31.3	65.0	3.8	0.5	0.1	6	22
Morocco	23.9	29.8	38.3	1.6	1.6	31.5	63.8	4.8	0.5	0.1	6	23
Mozambique	13.4	19.4	25.5	2.6	1.7	44.1	52.6	3.3	0.8	0.1	20	39
Myanmar	40.8	50.0	57.1	1.5	0.8	30.1	65.0	4.9	0.5	0.1	10	20
Namibia	1.4	2.0	2.4	2.6	1.1	42.1	54.4	3.4	0.8	0.1	6	23
Nepal	19.1	26.6	35.7	2.4	1.8	39.5	56.9	3.6	0.7	0.1	8	29
Netherlands	15.0	16.3	17.0	0.6	0.3	18.3	67.7	14.0	0.3	0.2	8	12
New Zealand	3.4	4.1	4.4	1.2	0.5	21.7	66.1	12.2	0.3	0.2	7	14
Nicaragua	4.0	5.4	7.2	2.2	1.8	39.5	57.2	3.3	0.7	0.1	5	28
Niger	8.5	13.5	22.6	3.3	3.2	49.0	49.0	2.0	1.0	0.0[a]	21	54
Nigeria	90.6	128.7	175.8	2.5	1.9	44.5	52.5	3.0	0.8	0.1	19	41
Norway	4.2	4.6	5.0	0.6	0.5	19.7	65.3	15.0	0.3	0.2	9	12
Oman	1.8	2.5	3.5	2.3	2.0	34.9	62.7	2.5	0.6	0.0[a]	3	25
Pakistan	108.0	152.1	211.7	2.4	2.1	38.9	57.3	3.8	0.7	0.1	7	27
Panama	2.4	3.2	4.0	2.0	1.5	30.6	63.5	5.9	0.5	0.1	5	22
Papua New Guinea	4.1	5.8	7.6	2.4	1.7	40.7	56.9	2.4	0.7	0.0[a]	10	30
Paraguay	4.2	6.0	8.3	2.5	2.0	38.0	58.3	3.7	0.7	0.1	5	29
Peru	21.8	27.6	34.2	1.7	1.4	32.7	62.1	5.2	0.5	0.1	6	23
Philippines	61.1	81.6	103.3	2.1	1.5	35.7	60.5	3.8	0.6	0.1	5	25
Poland	38.1	38.2	37.7	0.0[a]	−0.1	16.8	70.3	12.8	0.2	0.2	10	9
Portugal	9.9	10.5	10.9	0.4	0.2	15.9	67.2	16.9	0.2	0.3	10	10
Puerto Rico	3.5	3.9	4.2	0.7	0.5	22.5	65.6	11.9	0.3	0.2	8	14

2.1 Population dynamics

	Total population			Average annual population growth rate		Population age composition			Dependency ratio		Crude death rate	Crude birth rate
	millions			%		%			dependents as proportion of working-age population		per 1,000 people	per 1,000 people
						Ages 0–14	Ages 15–64	Ages 65+	Young	Old		
	1990	2004	2020	1990–2004	2004–20	2004	2004	2004	2004	2004	2004	2004
Romania	23.2	21.7	20.4	–0.5	–0.4	15.9	69.5	14.6	0.2	0.2	12	10
Russian Federation	148.3	143.8	133.1	–0.2	–0.5	15.7	70.7	13.6	0.2	0.2	16	11
Rwanda	7.1	8.9	12.4	1.6	2.1	44.1	53.5	2.4	0.8	0.0[a]	18	41
Saudi Arabia	16.4	24.0	34.0	2.7	2.2	37.8	59.4	2.9	0.6	0.0[a]	4	27
Senegal	8.0	11.4	16.0	2.5	2.1	43.0	53.9	3.1	0.8	0.1	11	36
Serbia and Montenegro	10.5[b]	8.1	10.3	0.1[c]	1.5	18.6	67.4	14.0	0.3	0.2	14	11
Sierra Leone	4.1	5.3	7.7	1.9	2.3	42.8	53.9	3.3	0.8	0.1	23	46
Singapore	3.0	4.2	5.0	2.4	1.0	20.2	71.6	8.2	0.3	0.1	4	10
Slovak Republic	5.3	5.4	5.4	0.1	0.0[a]	17.2	71.1	11.7	0.2	0.2	10	10
Slovenia	2.0	2.0	1.9	0.0[a]	–0.3	14.2	70.4	15.4	0.2	0.2	9	9
Somalia	6.7	8.0	12.3	1.3	2.7	44.1	53.3	2.6	0.8	0.0[a]	17	45
South Africa	35.2	45.5	48.1	1.8	0.3	32.8	63.1	4.1	0.5	0.1	22	24
Spain	38.8	42.7	44.4	0.7	0.2	14.3	69.2	16.5	0.2	0.2	9	11
Sri Lanka	17.0	19.4	22.9	0.9	1.0	24.5	68.4	7.1	0.4	0.1	6	19
Sudan	26.1	35.5	47.5	2.2	1.8	39.5	56.9	3.6	0.7	0.1	11	32
Swaziland	0.8	1.1	1.0	2.7	–0.8	41.6	55.0	3.4	0.8	0.1	20	34
Sweden	8.6	9.0	9.5	0.4	0.3	17.7	65.1	17.1	0.3	0.3	10	11
Switzerland	6.7	7.4	7.4	0.7	0.0[a]	16.8	67.6	15.7	0.2	0.2	8	10
Syrian Arab Republic	12.8	18.6	26.0	2.6	2.1	37.4	59.5	3.1	0.6	0.1	3	28
Tajikistan	5.3	6.4	8.2	1.4	1.5	39.7	56.5	3.8	0.7	0.1	7	29
Tanzania	26.2	37.6	49.3	2.6	1.7	42.9	53.9	3.2	0.8	0.1	17	37
Thailand	54.6	63.7	71.0	1.1	0.7	24.1	69.0	6.9	0.3	0.1	7	16
Togo	4.0	6.0	8.7	3.0	2.4	43.7	53.2	3.1	0.8	0.1	12	38
Trinidad and Tobago	1.2	1.3	1.3	0.5	0.2	22.0	70.7	7.2	0.3	0.1	8	14
Tunisia	8.2	9.9	11.6	1.4	1.0	26.7	67.1	6.2	0.4	0.1	6	17
Turkey	56.2	71.7	86.8	1.7	1.2	29.5	65.1	5.4	0.5	0.1	6	19
Turkmenistan	3.7	4.8	5.8	1.9	1.2	32.7	62.7	4.7	0.5	0.1	8	22
Uganda	17.8	27.8	50.6	3.2	3.7	50.4	47.1	2.5	1.1	0.1	15	50
Ukraine	51.9	47.5	39.6	–0.6	–1.1	15.4	68.8	15.8	0.2	0.2	16	9
United Arab Emirates	1.8	4.3	6.1	6.4	2.2	22.4	76.5	1.1	0.3	0.0[a]	1	16
United Kingdom	57.6	59.9	62.5	0.3	0.3	18.2	65.9	15.9	0.3	0.2	10	12
United States	249.6	293.7	338.4	1.2	0.9	20.9	66.8	12.3	0.3	0.2	8	14
Uruguay	3.1	3.4	3.8	0.7	0.6	24.4	62.4	13.2	0.4	0.2	9	15
Uzbekistan	20.5	26.2	32.5	1.7	1.3	34.0	61.3	4.7	0.6	0.1	7	21
Venezuela, RB	19.8	26.1	33.5	2.0	1.5	31.7	63.4	4.9	0.5	0.1	5	22
Vietnam	66.2	82.2	99.9	1.5	1.2	30.3	64.2	5.5	0.5	0.1	6	18
West Bank and Gaza	2.0	3.5	5.7	4.1	3.0	45.7	51.1	3.1	0.9	0.1	4	35
Yemen, Rep.	12.1	20.3	32.7	3.7	3.0	46.7	51.0	2.3	0.9	0.0[a]	8	40
Zambia	8.4	11.5	15.1	2.3	1.7	46.0	51.0	3.0	0.9	0.1	22	41
Zimbabwe	10.6	12.9	14.1	1.4	0.6	40.5	55.9	3.6	0.7	0.1	23	30
World	**5,256.3 s**	**6,365.0 s**	**7,573.5 s**	**1.4 w**	**1.1 w**	**28.5 w**	**64.2 w**	**7.3 w**	**0.4 w**	**0.1 w**	**9 w**	**20 w**
Low income	1,763.4	2,343.0	3,084.4	2.0	1.7	36.8	58.9	4.3	0.6	0.1	11	29
Middle income	2,589.4	3,017.8	3,427.1	1.1	0.8	25.4	67.4	7.2	0.4	0.1	7	16
Lower middle income	2,082.8	2,441.6	2,796.9	1.1	0.8	25.5	67.6	6.8	0.4	0.1	7	16
Upper middle income	506.6	576.2	630.2	0.9	0.6	24.9	66.3	8.8	0.4	0.1	10	16
Low & middle income	4,352.8	5,360.8	6,511.5	1.5	1.2	30.4	63.7	5.9	0.5	0.1	9	22
East Asia & Pacific	1,596.1	1,869.5	2,107.6	1.1	0.7	24.5	68.7	6.8	0.4	0.1	7	15
Europe & Central Asia	466.1	472.5	476.9	0.1	0.1	20.2	68.2	11.6	0.3	0.2	12	13
Latin America & Carib.	437.6	545.9	660.3	1.6	1.2	30.4	63.6	5.9	0.5	0.1	6	21
Middle East & N. Africa	225.5	300.3	399.1	2.0	1.8	34.0	61.8	4.2	0.6	0.1	6	25
South Asia	1,113.1	1,446.8	1,834.9	1.9	1.5	33.8	61.4	4.8	0.6	0.1	8	25
Sub-Saharan Africa	514.4	725.8	1,032.7	2.5	2.2	43.7	53.2	3.1	0.8	0.1	18	40
High income	903.5	1,004.2	1,062.0	0.8	0.4	18.4	67.0	14.6	0.3	0.2	8	12
Europe EMU	293.3	309.3	315.7	0.4	0.1	15.6	66.9	17.5	0.2	0.3	9	10

a. Less than 0.05. b. Includes population of Kosovo until 1999. c. Data are for 1990–99.

About the data

Population estimates are usually based on national population censuses, but the frequency and quality of these vary by country. Most countries conduct a complete enumeration no more than once a decade. Estimates for the years before and after the censuses are interpolations or extrapolations based on demographic models. Errors and undercounting occur even in high-income countries; in developing countries such errors may be substantial because of limits in the transport, communications, and other resources required to conduct and analyze a full census.

The quality and reliability of official demographic data are also affected by the public trust in the government, the government's commitment to full and accurate enumeration, the confidentiality and protection against misuse accorded to census data, and the independence of census agencies from undue political influence. Moreover, the international comparability of population indicators is limited by differences in the concepts, definitions, data collection procedures, and estimation methods used by national statistical agencies and other organizations that collect population data.

Of the 152 economies listed in the table, 119 (about 78 percent) conducted a census between 1995 and 2005. The currentness of a census, along with the availability of complementary data from surveys or registration systems, is one of many objective ways to judge the quality of demographic data. In some European countries registration systems offer complete information on population in the absence of a census. See *Primary data documentation* for the most recent census or survey year and for the completeness of registration.

Current population estimates for developing countries that lack recent census-based data, and pre- and post-census estimates for countries with census data, are provided by the United Nations Population Division, national statistical offices, and other agencies. The standard estimation method requires fertility, mortality, and net migration data, which are often collected from sample surveys, some of which may be small or limited in coverage. The population estimates are the product of demographic modeling and so are susceptible to biases and errors because of shortcomings in the model as well as in the data. Population projections are made using the cohort component method.

The growth rate of the total population conceals the fact that different age groups may grow at very different rates. In many developing countries the population under age 15 was previously growing rapidly but is now starting to shrink. Previously high fertility rates and declining mortality rates are now reflected in the larger share of the working-age population.

Dependency ratios take into account variations in the different age groups: the proportions of children, elderly people, and working-age people in the population. Separate calculations of young-age and old-age dependency suggest the burden of dependency that the working-age population must bear in relation to children and the elderly. But dependency ratios show only the age composition of a population, not economic dependency. Some children and elderly people are part of the labor force, and many working-age people are not.

The vital rates shown in the table are based on data derived from birth and death registration systems, censuses, and sample surveys conducted by national statistical offices and other organizations, or on demographic analysis. The estimates for 2004 for many countries are national projections based on extrapolations of levels and trends measured in earlier years.

Vital registers are the preferred source of these data, but in many developing countries systems for registering births and deaths do not exist or are incomplete because of deficiencies in the coverage of events or of geographic areas. Many developing countries carry out special household surveys that estimate vital rates by asking respondents about births and deaths in the recent past. Estimates derived in this way are subject to sampling errors as well as errors due to inaccurate recall by the respondents.

The United Nations Statistics Division monitors the completeness of vital registration systems. The share of countries with at least 90 percent complete vital registration increased from 45 percent in 1988 to 54 percent in 2004. Still, some of the most populous developing countries—China, India, Indonesia, Brazil, Pakistan, Bangladesh, Nigeria—do not have complete vital registration systems. Fewer than 30 percent of births and deaths and fewer than 40 percent of infant deaths worldwide are thought to be registered and reported.

International migration is the only other factor besides birth and death rates that directly determines a country's population growth. From 1990 to 2000 the number of migrants in high-income countries increased by 23 million. About 175 million people currently live outside their home country, accounting for about 3 percent of the world's population. Estimating international migration is difficult. At any time many people are located outside their home country as tourists, workers, or refugees or for other reasons. Standards relating to the duration and purpose of international moves that qualify as migration vary, and accurate estimates require information on flows into and out of countries that is difficult to collect.

Definitions

• **Total population** of an economy includes all residents regardless of legal status or citizenship—except for refugees not permanently settled in the country of asylum, who are generally considered part of the population of their country of origin. The values shown are midyear estimates for 1990 and 2004 and projections for 2020. • **Average annual population growth rate** is the exponential change for the period indicated. See *Statistical methods* for more information. • **Population age composition** refers to the percentage of the total population that is in specific age groups. • **Dependency ratio** is the ratio of dependents—people younger than 15 or older than 64—to the working-age population—those ages 15–64. • **Crude death rate** and **crude birth rate** are the number of deaths and the number of live births occurring during the year, per 1,000 population, estimated at midyear. Subtracting the crude death rate from the crude birth rate provides the rate of natural increase, which is equal to the population growth rate in the absence of migration.

Data sources

The World Bank's population estimates are compiled and produced by its Human Development Network and Development Data Group in consultation with its operational staff and country offices. Important inputs to the World Bank's demographic work come from the United Nations Population Division's *World Population Prospects: The 2004 Revision*; census reports and other statistical publications from national statistical offices; household surveys conducted by national agencies, Macro International, and the U.S. Centers for Disease Control and Prevention; Eurostat, *Demographic Statistics* (various years); Centro Latinoamericano de Demografía, *Boletín Demográfico* (various years); and U.S. Bureau of the Census, International Database.

2.2 Labor force structure

	Labor force participation rate				Labor force				
	% ages 15–64				Total millions		Ages 15 and older average annual % growth	Female % of labor force	
	Male		Female						
	1990	2004	1990	2004	1990	2004	1990–2004	1990	2004
Afghanistan	88.7	..	38.2	..	5.0	..	..	28.4	..
Albania	86.3	76.3	63.3	55.1	1.6	1.4	–1.0	40.2	42.1
Algeria	81.0	83.3	23.7	37.0	7.2	12.9	4.2	22.6	30.2
Angola	90.9	92.2	76.0	75.7	4.5	6.8	2.9	46.4	45.8
Argentina	84.7	82.4	43.5	59.9	13.0	17.9	2.3	34.4	42.4
Armenia	89.7	66.4	76.7	55.6	1.9	1.3	–3.0	47.7	48.9
Australia	84.4	81.0	61.5	67.0	8.4	10.2	1.3	41.3	45.3
Austria	80.1	77.6	55.3	63.3	3.5	3.9	0.8	40.8	44.4
Azerbaijan	80.6	78.0	68.5	65.5	3.3	4.0	1.4	47.4	47.4
Bangladesh	89.8	88.1	64.5	55.4	46.9	62.4	2.0	40.2	37.0
Belarus	82.2	72.5	72.4	66.5	5.3	4.8	–0.7	48.6	49.2
Belgium	71.3	72.7	46.2	56.9	3.9	4.5	0.9	39.0	43.2
Benin	90.0	86.7	59.2	55.0	2.0	3.2	3.3	40.8	38.5
Bolivia	80.9	84.0	49.9	63.9	2.5	4.0	3.4	39.2	43.5
Bosnia and Herzegovina	82.4	78.3	66.1	69.4	2.3	2.0	–0.7	44.7	47.8
Botswana	76.0	68.6	58.9	47.2	0.5	0.6	1.3	45.2	41.9
Brazil	88.8	84.1	47.6	60.6	62.4	89.9	2.6	35.0	42.5
Bulgaria	77.8	63.0	72.3	53.3	4.4	3.1	–2.5	48.0	46.2
Burkina Faso	92.1	90.4	79.3	79.5	3.8	5.6	2.8	46.3	46.6
Burundi	90.7	93.0	91.8	92.8	2.8	3.7	1.9	52.6	52.2
Cambodia	86.7	81.3	81.0	78.0	4.4	6.6	2.9	52.6	51.5
Cameroon	83.5	81.6	58.2	54.1	4.4	6.2	2.4	41.5	39.8
Canada	84.9	82.5	68.3	72.4	14.7	17.4	1.2	44.0	46.2
Central African Republic	89.4	89.4	71.7	70.9	1.4	1.8	2.1	47.0	46.2
Chad	79.0	77.4	64.7	66.0	2.3	3.6	3.0	46.0	46.8
Chile	80.9	76.7	35.2	40.6	5.0	6.4	1.8	30.5	34.6
China	88.9	88.0	79.1	76.2	650.1	768.0	1.2	44.8	44.6
Hong Kong, China	85.5	81.4	53.0	61.2	2.9	3.6	1.7	36.3	45.8
Colombia	85.0	85.3	48.5	65.0	14.1	21.8	3.1	36.9	44.0
Congo, Dem. Rep.	91.2	91.1	62.6	63.1	15.0	22.3	2.8	41.6	41.2
Congo, Rep.	86.3	86.6	57.7	56.2	1.0	1.5	3.0	41.5	40.3
Costa Rica	87.6	84.9	35.3	47.2	1.2	1.9	3.5	27.6	34.5
Côte d'Ivoire	90.3	89.1	44.5	40.2	4.6	6.7	2.6	30.2	29.3
Croatia	76.9	71.4	55.0	57.4	2.2	2.0	–0.9	42.1	44.8
Cuba	79.5	82.4	43.5	50.5	4.5	5.3	1.2	34.8	37.3
Czech Republic	82.2	77.7	74.1	63.7	5.5	5.2	–0.4	47.4	44.9
Denmark	87.1	82.9	77.6	74.3	2.9	2.8	–0.2	46.1	46.6
Dominican Republic	85.6	84.1	37.8	47.5	2.6	3.8	2.5	29.6	35.3
Ecuador	85.9	85.2	33.6	62.7	3.7	6.2	3.7	27.8	42.0
Egypt, Arab Rep.	76.7	76.6	27.6	21.6	16.6	22.3	2.1	26.3	21.8
El Salvador	81.9	79.5	53.5	49.7	2.0	2.7	2.3	41.2	39.6
Eritrea	92.6	90.7	63.1	59.9	1.2	1.7	2.4	42.4	41.1
Estonia	83.0	73.7	76.0	64.3	0.9	0.7	–1.8	49.9	49.3
Ethiopia	92.3	90.9	74.5	73.5	22.6	30.9	2.2	44.9	44.9
Finland	79.0	76.8	72.2	72.7	2.6	2.6	0.2	47.2	47.8
France	75.0	73.8	57.0	62.4	24.8	26.9	0.6	43.3	45.9
Gabon	85.5	84.0	65.5	64.2	0.4	0.6	2.7	43.9	43.4
Gambia, The	86.2	86.7	63.3	60.4	0.4	0.6	3.5	43.4	41.7
Georgia	78.2	76.2	79.1	53.7	2.9	2.3	–1.7	52.3	43.9
Germany	81.4	79.2	56.8	66.5	38.3	40.8	0.5	40.4	44.9
Ghana	80.5	75.8	77.5	72.0	6.7	9.6	2.5	48.9	48.1
Greece	76.7	78.6	43.1	54.8	4.2	5.1	1.4	36.2	40.5
Guatemala	90.7	84.8	30.2	35.1	2.9	4.0	2.3	24.7	31.1
Guinea	90.8	88.9	82.8	82.7	3.0	4.3	2.6	46.2	46.5
Guinea-Bissau	91.4	93.0	60.5	62.9	0.4	0.6	2.9	40.3	40.9
Haiti	82.7	83.1	59.1	57.4	2.6	3.6	2.2	43.3	41.7

Labor force structure 2.2

	Labor force participation rate				Labor force				
	% ages 15–64				Total millions		Ages 15 and older average annual % growth	Female % of labor force	
	Male		Female						
	1990	2004	1990	2004	1990	2004	1990–2004	1990	2004
Honduras	89.0	90.5	34.6	54.6	1.6	3.0	4.4	27.7	36.9
Hungary	74.4	66.9	57.3	53.4	4.5	4.2	–0.5	44.5	45.0
India	86.6	84.4	40.3	36.1	335.1	427.2	1.7	29.9	28.3
Indonesia	82.9	87.0	52.1	52.8	75.3	105.1	2.4	38.4	37.8
Iran, Islamic Rep.	82.3	75.4	22.5	39.1	15.6	26.2	3.7	20.2	33.0
Iraq	77.8	..	16.4	..	4.7	..	..	16.8	..
Ireland	77.9	80.1	42.3	60.7	1.3	2.0	2.9	34.3	42.5
Israel	68.1	65.9	46.8	58.1	1.6	2.7	3.4	40.5	46.8
Italy	76.7	74.5	44.6	49.3	23.9	24.0	0.0	37.1	39.6
Jamaica	83.0	78.4	71.3	60.0	1.1	1.2	0.3	46.8	43.7
Japan	83.1	85.0	57.1	60.4	63.9	67.0	0.3	40.6	41.0
Jordan	71.3	79.5	18.6	28.3	0.8	1.8	6.3	18.8	24.1
Kazakhstan	81.6	80.1	68.0	73.1	7.7	8.0	0.2	46.3	49.4
Kenya	90.6	89.6	76.2	71.4	9.8	15.1	3.1	46.0	44.0
Korea, Dem. Rep.	84.0	80.7	56.4	50.0	9.7	10.6	0.6	39.3	38.6
Korea, Rep.	75.3	77.3	49.7	54.0	19.1	24.1	1.7	39.3	40.7
Kuwait	83.1	86.5	35.6	49.3	0.9	1.3	3.2	21.8	24.8
Kyrgyz Republic	78.0	77.6	65.0	60.0	1.8	2.2	1.4	46.2	44.3
Lao PDR	81.6	82.3	56.3	56.4	1.5	2.3	2.8	41.3	40.7
Latvia	83.4	71.9	75.0	62.8	1.5	1.1	–2.0	49.5	48.6
Lebanon	81.5	83.7	34.4	35.0	0.9	1.4	2.7	31.8	30.0
Lesotho	86.8	74.3	59.4	49.2	0.6	0.6	0.4	46.5	44.7
Liberia	85.2	84.0	55.9	55.7	0.8	1.2	2.9	39.4	39.9
Libya	81.4	82.3	19.9	32.3	1.3	2.2	4.2	17.3	26.3
Lithuania	81.7	72.8	70.4	65.9	1.9	1.6	–1.1	48.1	49.1
Macedonia, FYR	77.5	73.2	52.8	47.8	0.9	0.9	0.1	40.0	39.1
Madagascar	83.6	86.3	79.5	79.8	5.4	8.3	3.1	49.2	48.4
Malawi	91.7	90.0	86.2	86.0	4.5	5.8	1.9	50.3	49.8
Malaysia	82.7	83.8	45.3	47.6	7.1	10.7	2.9	34.8	35.6
Mali	90.7	85.9	75.1	74.7	3.8	5.3	2.5	46.0	47.3
Mauritania	87.6	85.0	57.8	56.5	0.8	1.2	2.7	40.7	40.4
Mauritius	86.6	84.4	45.2	46.4	0.5	0.6	1.4	33.9	35.3
Mexico	85.4	83.8	36.2	42.2	29.5	42.4	2.6	30.6	34.7
Moldova	81.5	75.8	70.4	65.4	2.1	2.1	0.0	48.6	47.8
Mongolia	83.7	83.2	59.3	56.3	0.8	1.2	2.4	41.0	40.2
Morocco	83.9	83.8	25.6	28.5	7.5	10.9	2.7	23.7	25.4
Mozambique	88.0	83.1	88.1	85.1	6.3	9.1	2.6	54.0	53.5
Myanmar	89.2	87.7	71.2	70.0	20.0	26.9	2.1	44.6	44.9
Namibia	67.1	65.0	50.6	48.8	0.4	0.6	2.6	44.1	43.6
Nepal	82.5	80.6	50.4	52.3	7.1	10.2	2.6	37.9	40.3
Netherlands	80.0	84.5	53.1	69.0	6.9	8.6	1.5	39.1	44.0
New Zealand	83.0	83.4	63.2	70.5	1.7	2.1	1.7	43.1	46.3
Nicaragua	87.0	87.2	36.8	36.7	1.3	2.0	3.1	30.1	29.7
Niger	94.7	95.5	72.4	72.9	3.6	5.7	3.4	42.6	41.9
Nigeria	86.9	85.9	49.0	46.8	32.7	46.7	2.5	36.2	34.8
Norway	82.5	83.7	69.9	77.2	2.2	2.5	0.9	44.7	47.2
Oman	83.8	82.8	15.7	22.7	0.6	0.9	3.6	11.1	15.6
Pakistan	88.1	85.7	28.8	33.0	35.2	54.5	3.1	23.3	26.5
Panama	82.7	83.4	41.6	53.8	0.9	1.4	3.1	32.5	38.3
Papua New Guinea	75.9	75.1	72.3	72.7	1.8	2.5	2.5	46.4	47.6
Paraguay	85.7	86.9	54.4	67.7	1.6	2.8	3.7	38.3	43.1
Peru	82.0	83.5	48.6	60.3	8.5	13.0	3.0	37.0	41.6
Philippines	83.7	84.6	48.7	55.5	23.4	35.9	3.1	36.6	39.4
Poland	79.2	69.2	65.1	57.8	18.6	17.3	–0.5	45.8	45.7
Portugal	82.6	79.6	59.2	67.1	4.8	5.5	1.0	42.7	46.2
Puerto Rico	67.4	67.8	35.0	44.0	1.2	1.4	1.6	35.8	41.2

2.2 Labor force structure

	Labor force participation rate				Labor force				
	% ages 15–64				Total millions		Ages 15 and older average annual % growth	Female % of labor force	
	Male		Female						
	1990	2004	1990	2004	1990	2004	1990–2004	1990	2004
Romania	77.2	68.8	61.1	55.6	11.0	10.4	–0.4	44.3	46.1
Russian Federation	81.6	75.2	71.7	66.9	77.2	73.1	–0.4	48.3	49.0
Rwanda	88.3	85.1	87.4	82.4	3.1	4.1	2.0	51.0	51.4
Saudi Arabia	81.3	80.5	15.6	18.2	5.1	7.7	2.9	11.4	14.8
Senegal	87.8	83.9	63.4	58.7	3.1	4.5	2.6	43.4	42.4
Serbia and Montenegro	77.0	75.9	54.9	53.3	4.9[a]	3.9	0.0[b]	41.7	41.7
Sierra Leone	90.2	94.4	55.6	58.3	1.7	2.3	2.1	38.5	38.4
Singapore	83.9	83.2	54.2	56.7	1.6	2.2	2.3	38.8	39.8
Slovak Republic	82.5	76.5	70.6	62.4	2.6	2.7	0.1	46.3	45.2
Slovenia	76.9	75.2	63.3	66.1	1.0	1.0	0.3	45.5	46.2
Somalia	95.8	95.1	63.1	61.0	2.8	3.4	1.3	39.9	39.3
South Africa	81.6	82.1	57.4	49.7	14.4	19.1	2.0	41.6	38.4
Spain	80.3	80.5	41.9	56.3	16.0	20.3	1.7	34.3	40.8
Sri Lanka	82.9	81.8	48.2	38.6	7.3	8.3	0.9	34.8	30.5
Sudan	78.9	72.6	27.8	24.2	7.8	10.3	2.0	26.0	24.8
Swaziland	79.6	74.9	39.6	33.2	0.2	0.3	2.7	38.0	33.1
Sweden	86.0	79.2	81.9	75.1	4.7	4.7	–0.1	47.7	47.4
Switzerland	90.2	88.0	62.8	74.7	3.7	4.2	0.9	40.4	46.3
Syrian Arab Republic	83.7	88.8	29.7	39.3	3.7	7.3	4.9	26.2	30.4
Tajikistan	77.6	66.1	56.2	49.7	1.9	2.1	0.8	42.2	43.6
Tanzania	92.1	90.8	90.2	88.4	12.8	18.9	2.8	50.2	49.5
Thailand	90.6	84.6	79.2	70.7	30.4	35.3	1.1	46.6	46.0
Togo	90.8	90.4	55.2	51.9	1.5	2.4	3.1	38.5	37.0
Trinidad and Tobago	79.7	82.2	45.9	51.2	0.5	0.6	2.0	36.1	38.9
Tunisia	79.2	78.3	22.1	30.4	2.4	3.7	3.0	21.5	27.1
Turkey	84.5	80.3	36.2	29.0	21.0	26.5	1.7	29.4	26.4
Turkmenistan	80.0	76.5	69.1	65.0	1.5	2.1	2.4	46.9	46.6
Uganda	92.4	87.8	82.0	81.2	7.8	11.5	2.8	47.5	48.2
Ukraine	79.7	72.3	70.7	63.1	26.3	22.4	–1.1	49.2	49.1
United Arab Emirates	92.4	92.1	25.9	38.2	0.9	2.6	7.5	9.8	13.2
United Kingdom	87.9	82.2	67.2	69.2	29.4	30.4	0.2	44.0	45.9
United States	85.1	81.7	67.5	70.1	129.3	153.7	1.2	44.4	46.2
Uruguay	85.9	86.1	54.3	65.7	1.4	1.7	1.6	39.9	43.9
Uzbekistan	78.5	75.6	64.4	60.2	8.2	11.1	2.2	45.4	44.5
Venezuela, RB	82.4	85.5	39.8	60.1	7.3	12.4	3.8	31.8	40.3
Vietnam	85.5	82.6	79.4	77.6	31.3	43.1	2.3	48.3	48.5
West Bank and Gaza	67.0	69.0	9.5	10.9	0.4	0.7	4.5	11.9	13.1
Yemen, Rep.	76.1	77.4	28.6	30.4	3.0	5.7	4.7	27.3	27.7
Zambia	90.4	91.5	67.8	68.3	3.5	4.9	2.4	43.2	42.4
Zimbabwe	81.0	85.1	69.9	64.8	4.3	5.7	2.1	47.2	44.2
World	**85.5 w**	**83.9 w**	**58.9 w**	**57.8 w**	**2,390.7 t**	**2,981.1 t**	**1.6 w**	**39.9 w**	**40.0 w**
Low income	87.0	85.0	50.7	47.8	709.0	956.4	2.1	35.7	35.0
Middle income	85.8	84.3	64.0	62.7	1,254.1	1,536.1	1.4	41.8	42.1
Lower middle income	86.6	85.5	66.3	65.2	1,033.5	1,280.1	1.5	42.0	42.4
Upper middle income	82.5	78.9	54.7	52.4	220.6	256.0	1.1	40.5	40.5
Low & middle income	86.3	84.6	59.0	56.7	1,963.1	2,492.5	1.7	39.6	39.3
East Asia & Pacific	87.8	87.2	74.3	71.6	856.8	1,049.4	1.4	44.1	43.8
Europe & Central Asia	80.8	74.6	65.1	58.1	223.8	218.5	–0.2	45.6	44.9
Latin America & Carib.	85.9	83.8	43.8	55.3	171.0	248.8	2.7	34.0	40.2
Middle East & N. Africa	79.9	79.1	24.5	30.5	64.9	104.6	3.4	22.9	27.2
South Asia	86.9	84.9	41.7	38.0	437.0	572.7	1.9	30.6	29.3
Sub-Saharan Africa	87.8	86.4	65.1	62.7	209.7	298.5	2.5	43.0	42.2
High income	82.1	80.6	58.6	63.5	427.6	488.5	1.0	41.3	43.6
Europe EMU	78.5	77.5	51.6	60.4	130.5	144.5	0.7	39.5	43.4

a. Includes population of Kosovo until 1999. b. Data are for 1990–99.

Labor force structure 2.2

About the data

The labor force is the supply of labor available for the production of goods and services in an economy. It includes people who are currently employed and people who are unemployed but seeking work as well as first-time job-seekers. Not everyone who works is included, however. Unpaid workers, family workers, and students are among those usually omitted, and in some countries members of the military are not counted. The size of the labor force tends to vary during the year as seasonal workers enter and leave it.

Data on the labor force are compiled by the International Labour Organization (ILO) from labor force surveys, censuses, establishment censuses and surveys, and various types of administrative records such as employment exchange registers and unemployment insurance schemes. For some countries a combination of these sources is used. While the resulting statistics may provide rough estimates of the labor force, they are not comparable across countries because of the noncomparability of the original data and the different ways the original sources may be combined.

For international comparisons the most comprehensive source is labor force surveys, which can be designed to cover all noninstitutionalized civilians, all branches and sectors of the economy, and all categories of workers, including people who hold multiple jobs. Despite the ILO's efforts to encourage the use of international standards, labor force data are not fully comparable because of differences among countries, and sometimes within countries, in both concepts and methodologies. Most important to data comparability is the nature of the data source. Labor force data obtained from population censuses are often based on a limited number of questions on the economic characteristics of individuals, with little scope to probe. The resulting data are often contrary to labor force survey data and often vary considerably from economy to economy, depending on the scope and coverage of the census. Establishment censuses and surveys on the other hand provide data only on the employed population, leaving out unemployed workers, workers in small establishments, and workers in the informal sector (ILO, *Key Indicators of the Labour Market 2001–2002*).

The reference period of the census or survey is another important source of differences: in some countries data refer to people's status on the day of the census or survey or during a specific period before the inquiry date, while in others the data are recorded without reference to any period. In developing countries, where the household is often the basic unit of production and all members contribute to output, but some at low intensity or irregular intervals, the estimated labor force may be significantly smaller than the numbers actually working.

The labor force estimates in the table were calculated by World Bank staff by applying labor force participation rates from the ILO database to population estimates to create a series consistent with these population estimates. This procedure sometimes results in estimates of labor force size that differ slightly from those in the ILO's *Yearbook of Labour Statistics*. The labor force estimates in this year's *World Development Indicators* are for the population ages 15 and older. In previous editions the labor force included children under age 15. For this reason, labor force estimates are not comparable across editions. The labor force participation rate of the population ages 15–64 provides an indication of the relative size of the supply of labor. But in many developing countries children under age 15 work full or part time. And in some high-income countries many workers postpone retirement past age 65. As a result, labor force participation rates calculated in this way may systematically over- or under-estimate actual rates.

In general, estimates of women in the labor force are lower than those of men and are not comparable internationally, reflecting the fact that for women demographic, social, legal, and cultural trends and norms determine whether their activities are regarded as economic. In many countries large numbers of women work on farms or in other family enterprises without pay, while others work in or near their homes, mixing work and family activities during the day. Countries differ in the criteria used to determine the extent to which such workers are to be counted as part of the labor force. In most economies the gap between male and female labor force participation rates has been narrowing since 1980. This stems from both falling rates for men and rising rates for women. The largest gap between men and women in labor force participation is observed in the Middle East and North Africa, where low participation of women in the work force also brings down the overall labor force participation rate.

Definitions

• **Labor force participation rate** is the proportion of the population ages 15–64 that is economically active: all people who supply labor for the production of goods and services during a specified period. • **Total labor force** comprises people ages 15 and older who meet the ILO definition of the economically active population. It includes both the employed and the unemployed. While national practices vary in the treatment of such groups as the armed forces and seasonal or part-time workers, the labor force generally includes the armed forces, the unemployed, and first-time job-seekers, but excludes homemakers and other unpaid caregivers and workers in the informal sector. • **Average annual growth rate of the labor force** is calculated using the exponential endpoint method (see *Statistical methods* for more information). • **Females as a percentage of the labor force** show the extent to which women are active in the labor force.

Data sources

The labor force participation rates are from the ILO database *Estimates and Projections of the Economically Active Population, 1980–2020*, fifth edition. The ILO publishes estimates of the economically active population in its *Yearbook of Labour Statistics*. Labor force numbers were calculated by World Bank staff, applying labor force participation rates from the ILO database to population estimates.

2.3 Employment by economic activity

	Agriculture				Industry				Services			
	Male % of male employment		Female % of female employment		Male % of male employment		Female % of female employment		Male % of male employment		Female % of female employment	
	1990–92[a]	2000–04[a]	1990–92[a]	2000–04[a]	1990–92[a]	2000–04[a]	1990–92[a]	2000–04[a]	1990–92[a]	2000–04[a]	1990–92[a]	2000–04[a]
Afghanistan	..	..	..	..	..	..	..	..	..	..	..	..
Albania	..	..	..	..	..	..	..	..	..	..	..	..
Algeria	..	..	..	..	..	..	..	..	..	..	..	..
Angola	..	..	..	..	..	..	..	..	..	..	..	..
Argentina	0[b, c]	2[c]	0[b, c]	1[b, c]	40[c]	28[c]	18[c]	9[c]	59[c]	70[c]	81[c]	90[c]
Armenia	..	..	..	..	..	..	..	..	..	..	..	..
Australia	6	5[c]	4	3[c]	32	30[c]	12	10[c]	62	65[c]	85	87[c]
Austria	6	5	8	6	47	43	20	13	46	51	72	81
Azerbaijan	..	41	..	39	..	15	..	8	..	44	..	54
Bangladesh	54	53	85	77	16	8	9	9	26	30	2	12
Belarus	..	..	..	..	..	..	..	..	..	..	..	..
Belgium	3	2	2	1	38	35	13	12	57	63	84	87
Benin	..	..	..	..	..	..	..	..	..	..	..	..
Bolivia	3[c]	6	1[c]	3	42[c]	39	17[c]	14	55[c]	55	82[c]	82
Bosnia and Herzegovina	..	..	..	..	..	..	..	..	..	..	..	..
Botswana	..	17	..	6	..	31	..	17	..	51	..	76
Brazil	31[c]	23[c]	25[c]	16[c]	27[c]	28[c]	10[c]	13[c]	43[c]	49[c]	65[c]	71[c]
Bulgaria	..	12	..	8	..	37	..	29	..	51	..	64
Burkina Faso	..	..	..	..	..	..	..	..	..	..	..	..
Burundi	..	..	..	..	..	..	..	..	..	..	..	..
Cambodia	..	72	..	75	..	7	..	10	..	20	..	15
Cameroon	53	..	68	..	14	..	4	..	26	..	23	..
Canada	6[c]	4[c]	3[c]	2[c]	31[c]	32[c]	11[c]	11[c]	63[c]	64[c]	86[c]	87[c]
Central African Republic	..	..	..	..	..	..	..	..	..	..	..	..
Chad	..	..	..	..	..	..	..	..	..	..	..	..
Chile	24	18	6	5	32	29	15	12	45	53	79	83
China	..	..	..	..	..	..	..	..	..	..	..	..
Hong Kong, China	1	0[b]	0[b]	0[b]	37	25	27	8	63	75	73	92
Colombia	2[c]	31[c]	1[c]	8[c]	35[c]	21[c]	25[c]	17[c]	63[c]	49[c]	74[c]	75[c]
Congo, Dem. Rep.	..	..	..	..	..	..	..	..	..	..	..	..
Congo, Rep.	..	..	..	..	..	..	..	..	..	..	..	..
Costa Rica	32	21	5	4	27	26	25	14	41	52	69	81
Côte d'Ivoire	..	..	..	..	..	..	..	..	..	..	..	..
Croatia	..	16	..	18	..	39	..	19	..	45	..	64
Cuba	..	..	..	..	..	..	..	..	..	..	..	..
Czech Republic	9	6	7	3	55	50	33	27	36	45	61	70
Denmark	7	5[c]	3	2[c]	37	34[c]	16	12[c]	56	61[c]	81	86[c]
Dominican Republic	26	23	3	2	23	24	21	15	52	53	76	83
Ecuador	10[c]	11[c]	2[c]	5[c]	29[c]	28[c]	17[c]	14[c]	62[c]	61[c]	81[c]	81[c]
Egypt, Arab Rep.	35	28	52	28	25	23	10	10	41	50	37	62
El Salvador	48	29	15	4	23	27	23	22	29	45	63	74
Eritrea	..	..	..	..	..	..	..	..	..	..	..	..
Estonia	23	9	13	4	42	42	30	23	36	50	57	73
Ethiopia	..	..	..	..	..	..	..	..	..	..	..	..
Finland	12	7	6	3	39	39	15	13	49	54	78	84
France	..	..	..	..	..	..	..	..	..	..	..	..
Gabon	..	..	..	..	..	..	..	..	..	..	..	..
Gambia, The	..	..	..	..	..	..	..	..	..	..	..	..
Georgia	..	53	..	57	..	12	..	4	..	35	..	39
Germany	4	3	4	2	51	44	24	17	45	53	72	81
Ghana	66	60	59	50	10	14	10	15	23	27	32	36
Greece	20[c]	15[c]	26[c]	18[c]	32[c]	30[c]	17[c]	11[c]	48[c]	56[c]	56[c]	71[c]
Guatemala	..	50	..	18	..	18	..	23	..	27	..	56
Guinea	..	..	..	..	..	..	..	..	..	..	..	..
Guinea-Bissau	..	..	..	..	..	..	..	..	..	..	..	..
Haiti	..	..	..	..	..	..	..	..	..	..	..	..

Employment by economic activity

	Agriculture				Industry				Services			
	Male % of male employment		Female % of female employment		Male % of male employment		Female % of female employment		Male % of male employment		Female % of female employment	
	1990–92[a]	2000–04[a]	1990–92[a]	2000–04[a]	1990–92[a]	2000–04[a]	1990–92[a]	2000–04[a]	1990–92[a]	2000–04[a]	1990–92[a]	2000–04[a]
Honduras	53[c]	52[c]	6[c]	9[c]	18[c]	19[c]	25[c]	26[c]	29[c]	29[c]	69[c]	66[c]
Hungary	15	8	8	3	42	42	29	24	44	50	64	74
India	..	..	..	..	..	..	..	..	..	..	..	..
Indonesia	55	43	56	45	10	13	12	14	35	45	32	42
Iran, Islamic Rep.	..	..	..	..	..	..	..	..	..	..	..	..
Iraq	..	..	..	..	..	..	..	..	..	..	..	..
Ireland	19	10	3	2	33	39	18	13	48	51	78	85
Israel	5	3	2	1	38	33	15	11	57	64	83	88
Italy	8	6	9	4	38	40	22	20	54	55	70	76
Jamaica	36	28	16	8	25	26	12	6	39	46	72	84
Japan	6	5	7	5	40	36	27	19	54	59	65	75
Jordan	..	..	..	..	..	..	..	..	..	..	..	..
Kazakhstan	..	36	..	34	..	23	..	10	..	40	..	56
Kenya	19[c]	..	20[c]	..	23[c]	..	9[c]	..	58[c]	..	71[c]	..
Korea, Dem. Rep.	..	..	..	..	..	..	..	..	..	..	..	..
Korea, Rep.	12[c]	8[c]	17[c]	10[c]	41[c]	34[c]	28[c]	18[c]	47[c]	58[c]	55[c]	72[c]
Kuwait	..	..	..	..	..	..	..	..	..	..	..	..
Kyrgyz Republic	..	43	..	43	..	19	..	10	..	38	..	47
Lao PDR	..	..	..	..	..	..	..	..	..	..	..	..
Latvia	25	17	14	10	37	35	26	18	38	47	59	71
Lebanon	..	..	..	..	..	..	..	..	..	..	..	..
Lesotho	..	..	..	..	..	..	..	..	..	..	..	..
Liberia	..	..	..	..	..	..	..	..	..	..	..	..
Libya	..	..	..	..	..	..	..	..	..	..	..	..
Lithuania	..	21	..	15	..	35	..	22	..	44	..	64
Macedonia, FYR	..	22	..	22	..	36	..	31	..	42	..	47
Madagascar	..	77	..	79	..	7	..	6	..	16	..	15
Malawi	..	..	..	..	..	..	..	..	..	..	..	..
Malaysia	23	16	20	11	31	35	32	27	46	49	48	62
Mali	..	..	..	..	..	..	..	..	..	..	..	..
Mauritania	..	..	..	..	..	..	..	..	..	..	..	..
Mauritius	17	11	11	6	32	36	64	40	48	53	24	54
Mexico	33	22	10	5	25	28	19	20	41	50	71	75
Moldova	..	44	..	42	..	20	..	12	..	35	..	46
Mongolia	..	44	..	40	..	17	..	14	..	39	..	46
Morocco	..	39	..	57	..	21	..	19	..	40	..	25
Mozambique	..	..	..	..	..	..	..	..	..	..	..	..
Myanmar	..	..	..	..	..	..	..	..	..	..	..	..
Namibia	45	33	52	29	21	17	8	7	34	49	40	63
Nepal	..	..	..	..	..	..	..	..	..	..	..	..
Netherlands	5	4	3	2	33	29	10	9	60	64	82	87
New Zealand	13[c]	10[c]	8[c]	6[c]	31[c]	32[c]	13[c]	11[c]	56[c]	58[c]	80[c]	83[c]
Nicaragua	..	43	..	10	..	19	..	17	..	32	..	52
Niger	..	..	..	..	..	..	..	..	..	..	..	..
Nigeria	..	..	..	..	..	..	..	..	..	..	..	..
Norway	8	6	3	2	35	35	10	9	57	60	86	89
Oman	..	7	..	5	..	11	..	14	..	82	..	80
Pakistan	45	38	69	65	20	22	15	16	35	40	16	20
Panama	35	25	3	4	20	22	11	9	45	53	85	88
Papua New Guinea	..	..	..	..	..	..	..	..	..	..	..	..
Paraguay	3[c]	39	0[b, c]	20	33[c]	19	19[c]	10	64[c]	42	80[c]	70
Peru	1[c]	1[c]	0[b, c]	0[c]	30[c]	28[c]	13[c]	11[c]	69[c]	71[c]	87[c]	89[c]
Philippines	53	45	32	25	17	18	14	12	29	37	55	63
Poland	..	19	..	18	..	38	..	17	..	43	..	65
Portugal	11[c]	12	13[c]	14	40[c]	43	24[c]	20	49[c]	45	63[c]	66
Puerto Rico	5	3	0[b]	0[b]	27	26	19	12	67	71	80	88

2.3 Employment by economic activity

	Agriculture				Industry				Services			
	Male % of male employment		Female % of female employment		Male % of male employment		Female % of female employment		Male % of male employment		Female % of female employment	
	1990–92[a]	2000–04[a]	1990–92[a]	2000–04[a]	1990–92[a]	2000–04[a]	1990–92[a]	2000–04[a]	1990–92[a]	2000–04[a]	1990–92[a]	2000–04[a]
Romania	29	34	38	37	44	34	30	25	28	32	33	38
Russian Federation	..	12	..	8	..	39	..	23	..	48	..	70
Rwanda	..	..	..	..	..	..	..	..	..	..	..	..
Saudi Arabia	..	5	..	1	..	24	..	1	..	71	..	98
Senegal	..	..	..	..	..	..	..	..	..	..	..	..
Serbia and Montenegro	..	..	..	..	..	..	..	..	..	..	..	..
Sierra Leone	..	..	..	..	..	..	..	..	..	..	..	..
Singapore	1	0[b]	0[b]	0[b]	36	29	32	18	63	70	68	82
Slovak Republic	..	8[c]	..	4[c]	..	49[c]	..	26[c]	..	43[c]	..	71[c]
Slovenia	..	8	..	8	..	46	..	26	..	45	..	65
Somalia	..	..	..	..	..	..	..	..	..	..	..	..
South Africa	..	13	..	7	..	33	..	14	..	54	..	79
Spain	11	7	8	4	41	42	16	14	48	52	76	82
Sri Lanka	..	32[c]	..	40[c]	..	40[c]	..	35[c]	..	29[c]	..	25[c]
Sudan	..	..	..	..	..	..	..	..	..	..	..	..
Swaziland	..	..	..	..	..	..	..	..	..	..	..	..
Sweden	5	3	2	1	40	35	12	10	55	62	86	89
Switzerland	5	5	4	3	39	33	15	12	57	62	81	85
Syrian Arab Republic	..	24	..	58	..	31	..	7	..	45	..	35
Tajikistan	..	..	..	..	..	..	..	..	..	..	..	..
Tanzania	78[c]	80[c]	90[c]	84[c]	7[c]	4[c]	1[c]	1[c]	15[c]	16[c]	8[c]	15[c]
Thailand	59	47	62	43	17	21	13	19	24	33	25	39
Togo	..	..	..	..	..	..	..	..	..	..	..	..
Trinidad and Tobago	15	10	6	2	34	37	14	14	51	53	80	84
Tunisia	..	..	..	..	..	..	..	..	..	..	..	..
Turkey	33	24	72	59	26	26	11	13	41	49	17	28
Turkmenistan	..	..	..	..	..	..	..	..	..	..	..	..
Uganda	91	60	91	77	4	11	6	5	5	29	3	18
Ukraine	..	21	..	17	..	38	..	21	..	41	..	62
United Arab Emirates	..	9	..	0[b]	..	36	..	14	..	55	..	86
United Kingdom	3	2	1	1	41	35	16	10	55	64	82	89
United States	4[c]	4[c]	1[c]	1[c]	33[c]	31[c]	14[c]	11[c]	62[c]	65[c]	85[c]	88[c]
Uruguay	7[c]	7[c]	1[c]	2[c]	36[c]	29[c]	21[c]	12[c]	57[c]	65[c]	78[c]	86[c]
Uzbekistan	..	..	..	..	..	..	..	..	..	..	..	..
Venezuela, RB	17	16	2	2	32	25	16	11	52	59	82	86
Vietnam	..	58	..	62	..	20	..	13	..	23	..	25
West Bank and Gaza	..	12	..	34	..	30	..	8	..	57	..	57
Yemen, Rep.	..	..	..	..	..	..	..	..	..	..	..	..
Zambia	..	..	..	..	..	..	..	..	..	..	..	..
Zimbabwe	..	..	..	..	..	..	..	..	..	..	..	..
World	.. w	.. w	.. w	.. w	.. w	.. w	.. w	.. w	.. w	.. w	.. w	.. w
Low income	..	..	..	..	..	..	..	..	..	..	..	..
Middle income	..	..	..	..	..	..	..	..	..	..	..	..
Lower middle income	..	..	..	..	..	..	..	..	..	..	..	..
Upper middle income	..	16	..	11	..	33	..	19	..	51	..	71
Low & middle income	..	..	..	..	..	..	..	..	..	..	..	..
East Asia & Pacific	..	..	..	..	..	..	..	..	..	..	..	..
Europe & Central Asia	..	20	..	19	..	35	..	20	..	45	..	61
Latin America & Carib.	20	21	14	9	30	27	14	14	50	52	72	76
Middle East & N. Africa	..	..	..	..	..	..	..	..	..	..	..	..
South Asia	..	..	..	..	..	..	..	..	..	..	..	..
Sub-Saharan Africa	..	..	..	..	..	..	..	..	..	..	..	..
High income	6	4	4	3	38	35	19	14	56	60	77	83
Europe EMU	7	5	7	4	43	42	21	17	49	53	72	80

Note: Data across sectors may not sum to 100 percent because of workers not classified by sectors.
a. Data are for the most recent year available. b. Less than 0.5. c. Limited coverage.

Employment by economic activity

About the data

The International Labour Organization (ILO) classifies economic activity using the International Standard Industrial Classification (ISIC) of All Economic Activities, revision 2 (1968) and revision 3 (1990). Because this classification is based on where work is performed (industry) rather than on what type of work is performed (occupation), all of an enterprise's employees are classified under the same industry, regardless of their trade or occupation. The categories should add up to 100 percent. Where they do not, the differences arise because of workers who cannot be classified by economic activity.

Data on employment are drawn from labor force surveys, household surveys, establishment censuses and surveys, administrative records of social insurance schemes, and official national estimates. The concept of employment generally refers to people above a certain age who worked, or who held a job, during a reference period. Employment data include both full-time and part-time workers.

There are many differences in how countries define and measure employment status, particularly for students, part-time workers, members of the armed forces, and household or contributing family workers. Where the armed forces are included, they are allocated to the service sector, causing that sector to be somewhat overstated relative to the service sector in economies where they are excluded. Where data are obtained from establishment surveys, they cover only employees; thus self-employed and contributing family workers are excluded. In such cases the employment share of the agricultural sector is severely underreported. Moreover, the age group and area covered could differ by country or change over time within a country. For detailed information on breaks in series, consult the original source.

Countries also take different approaches to the treatment of unemployed people. In most countries unemployed people with previous job experience are classified according to their last job. But in some countries the unemployed and people seeking their first job are not classifiable by economic activity. Because of these differences, the size and distribution of employment by economic activity may not be fully comparable across countries.

The ILO's *Yearbook of Labour Statistics* and its database Key Indicators of the Labour Market report data by major divisions of the ISIC revision 2 or revision 3. In this table the reported divisions or categories are aggregated into three broad groups: agriculture, industry, and services. Such broad classification may obscure fundamental shifts within countries' industrial patterns. Most economies report economic activity according to the ISIC revision 2, although a group of economies moved to ISIC revision 3. The use of one classification or another should not have a significant impact on the information for the three broad sectors presented in this table.

The distribution of economic wealth in the world remains strongly correlated with employment by economic activity. The wealthier economies are those with the largest share of total employment in services, whereas the poorer economies are largely agriculture based.

The distribution of economic activity by gender reveals some clear patterns. Industry accounts for a larger share of male employment than female employment worldwide, whereas a higher proportion of women work in the services sector. Employment in agriculture is also male-dominated, although not as much as industry. Segregating one sex in a narrow range of occupations significantly reduces economic efficiency by reducing labor market flexibility and thus the economy's ability to adapt to change. This segregation is particularly harmful for women, who have a much narrower range of labor market choices and lower levels of pay than men. But it is also detrimental to men when job losses are concentrated in industries dominated by men and job growth is centered in service occupations, where women often dominate, as has been the recent experience in many countries.

There are several explanations for the rising importance of service jobs for women. Many service jobs—such as nursing and social and clerical work—are considered "feminine" because of a perceived similarity to women's traditional roles. Women often do not receive the training needed to take advantage of changing employment opportunities. And the greater availability of part-time work in service industries may lure more women, although it is unclear whether this is a cause or an effect.

Definitions

• **Agriculture** corresponds to division 1 (ISIC revision 2) or tabulation categories A and B (ISIC revision 3) and includes hunting, forestry, and fishing. • **Industry** corresponds to divisions 2–5 (ISIC revision 2) or tabulation categories C–F (ISIC revision 3) and includes mining and quarrying (including oil production), manufacturing, construction, and public utilities (electricity, gas, and water). • **Services** correspond to divisions 6–9 (ISIC revision 2) or tabulation categories G–P (ISIC revision 3) and include wholesale and retail trade and restaurants and hotels; transport, storage, and communications; financing, insurance, real estate, and business services; and community, social, and personal services.

Data sources

Data on employment are from the ILO database Key Indicators of the Labour Market, fourth edition.

2.4 Child labor

	Survey year	Economically active children					Employment by economic activity[a]					
			% of children ages 7–14		% of economically active children ages 7–14		% of economically active children ages 7–14					
							Agriculture		Manufacturing		Services	
		Total	Male	Female	Work only	Work and study	Male	Female	Male	Female	Male	Female
Afghanistan		..	..	..	..	..	..	..	..	..	..	..
Albania	2000	36.6	41.1	31.8	43.1	56.9	..	..	..	..	..	..
Algeria		..	..	..	..	..	..	..	..	..	..	..
Angola	1995	5.2	4.9	5.6	77.6	22.4	5.7	7.9	6.2	8.4	82.4	79.9
Argentina	1997	20.7	25.4	16.0	8.6	91.4	..	..	..	..	..	..
Armenia		..	..	..	..	..	..	..	..	..	..	..
Australia		..	..	..	..	..	..	..	..	..	..	..
Austria		..	..	..	..	..	..	..	..	..	..	..
Azerbaijan	2000	9.7	12.0	7.3	4.2	95.8	..	..	..	..	..	..
Bangladesh	2003	17.5	20.9	13.9	63.3	36.7	61.4	64.0	11.6	15.5	25.2	18.3
Belarus		..	..	..	..	..	..	..	..	..	..	..
Belgium		..	..	..	..	..	..	..	..	..	..	..
Benin		..	..	..	..	..	..	..	..	..	..	..
Bolivia	2000	19.2	20.4	18.0	19.7	80.3	77.8	72.9	4.3	3.5	15.0	23.6
Bosnia and Herzegovina	2000	20.2	22.8	17.6	4.0	96.0	..	..	..	..	..	..
Botswana		..	..	..	..	..	..	..	..	..	..	..
Brazil	2003	7.1	9.5	4.6	5.8	94.2	64.3	49.8	6.5	9.1	26.8	40.9
Bulgaria		..	..	..	..	..	..	..	..	..	..	..
Burkina Faso[b]	1998	66.5	65.4	67.7	95.9	4.1	98.0	98.2	0.6	0.5	1.3	1.2
Burundi	2000	37.0	38.4	35.7	48.3	51.7	..	..	..	..	..	..
Cambodia	2001	52.3	52.4	52.1	16.5	83.5	78.5	73.6	4.7	5.4	15.7	20.4
Cameroon[b]	2001	15.9	14.5	17.4	52.5	47.5	90.4	86.3	1.9	2.3	5.1	8.8
Canada		..	..	..	..	..	..	..	..	..	..	..
Central African Republic	2000	67.0	66.5	67.6	54.9	45.1	..	..	..	..	..	..
Chad	2000	69.9	73.5	66.5	44.6	55.4	..	..	..	..	..	..
Chile	2003	8.8	10.5	6.9	4.0	96.0	31.5	11.9	7.6	5.8	58.5	80.6
China		..	..	..	..	..	..	..	..	..	..	..
Hong Kong, China		..	..	..	..	..	..	..	..	..	..	..
Colombia	2001	12.2	16.6	7.7	23.0	77.0	..	..	..	..	..	..
Congo, Dem. Rep.	2000	39.8	39.9	39.8	35.7	64.3	..	..	..	..	..	..
Congo, Rep.		..	..	..	..	..	..	..	..	..	..	..
Costa Rica	2002	6.7	9.7	3.5	20.8	79.2	56.5	55.2	8.7	2.7	28.0	42.1
Côte d'Ivoire	2000	40.7	40.9	40.5	46.4	53.6	..	..	..	..	..	..
Croatia		..	..	..	..	..	..	..	..	..	..	..
Cuba		..	..	..	..	..	..	..	..	..	..	..
Czech Republic		..	..	..	..	..	..	..	..	..	..	..
Denmark		..	..	..	..	..	..	..	..	..	..	..
Dominican Republic	2000	12.5	16.7	8.1	7.2	92.8	..	..	..	..	..	..
Ecuador	2001	17.9	22.1	13.6	25.0	75.0	65.1	69.2	10.7	8.6	21.2	22.1
Egypt, Arab Rep.	1998	6.4	4.0	8.9	60.9	39.1	..	..	..	..	..	..
El Salvador	2003	12.7	17.1	8.1	19.5	80.5	66.4	17.6	10.8	16.1	21.2	66.3
Eritrea		..	..	..	..	..	..	..	..	..	..	..
Estonia		..	..	..	..	..	..	..	..	..	..	..
Ethiopia	2001	57.1	67.9	45.9	63.5	36.5	96.5	88.7	0.5	2.8	2.5	6.2
Finland		..	..	..	..	..	..	..	..	..	..	..
France		..	..	..	..	..	..	..	..	..	..	..
Gabon		..	..	..	..	..	..	..	..	..	..	..
Gambia, The	2000	25.3	25.4	25.3	41.6	58.4	..	..	..	..	..	..
Georgia		..	..	..	..	..	..	..	..	..	..	..
Germany		..	..	..	..	..	..	..	..	..	..	..
Ghana	2000	28.5	28.5	28.4	36.4	63.6	81.0	59.1	4.5	7.6	13.8	32.0
Greece		..	..	..	..	..	..	..	..	..	..	..
Guatemala	2000	20.1	25.9	13.9	38.5	61.5	74.5	39.8	5.9	20.1	14.7	40.0
Guinea	1994	48.3	47.2	49.5	98.6	1.4	..	..	..	..	..	..
Guinea-Bissau	2000	67.5	67.4	67.5	63.7	36.3	..	..	..	..	..	..
Haiti		..	..	..	..	..	..	..	..	..	..	..

Child labor 2.4

	Survey year	Economically active children					Employment by economic activity[a]					
			% of children ages 7–14		% of economically active children ages 7–14		% of economically active children ages 7–14					
							Agriculture		Manufacturing		Services	
		Total	Male	Female	Work only	Work and study	Male	Female	Male	Female	Male	Female
Honduras	2002	11.4	16.5	6.1	41.9	58.1	73.6	19.8	5.9	24.4	18.6	55.7
Hungary		..	..	..	..	..	..	..	..	..	..	..
India	2000	5.2	5.3	5.1	89.8	10.2	70.5	76.6	10.0	15.4	15.9	6.5
Indonesia		..	..	..	..	..	..	..	..	..	..	..
Iran, Islamic Rep.		..	..	..	..	..	..	..	..	..	..	..
Iraq	2000	13.7	17.4	9.7	51.7	48.3	..	..	..	..	..	..
Ireland		..	..	..	..	..	..	..	..	..	..	..
Israel		..	..	..	..	..	..	..	..	..	..	..
Italy		..	..	..	..	..	..	..	..	..	..	..
Jamaica		..	..	..	..	..	..	..	..	..	..	..
Japan		..	..	..	..	..	..	..	..	..	..	..
Jordan		..	..	..	..	..	..	..	..	..	..	..
Kazakhstan	1996	29.7	30.3	29.1	4.4	95.6	..	..	..	..	..	..
Kenya	1999	6.7	6.9	6.4	44.8	55.2	87.3	74.4	2.5	0.3	8.8	25.3
Korea, Dem. Rep.		..	..	..	..	..	..	..	..	..	..	..
Korea, Rep.		..	..	..	..	..	..	..	..	..	..	..
Kuwait		..	..	..	..	..	..	..	..	..	..	..
Kyrgyz Republic	1998	8.6	9.7	7.6	7.0	93.0	93.0	96.3	0.0	0.0	7.0	2.7
Lao PDR		..	..	..	..	..	..	..	..	..	..	..
Latvia		..	..	..	..	..	..	..	..	..	..	..
Lebanon		..	..	..	..	..	..	..	..	..	..	..
Lesotho	2000	30.8	34.2	27.5	17.6	82.4	..	..	..	..	..	..
Liberia		..	..	..	..	..	..	..	..	..	..	..
Libya		..	..	..	..	..	..	..	..	..	..	..
Lithuania		..	..	..	..	..	..	..	..	..	..	..
Macedonia, FYR		..	..	..	..	..	..	..	..	..	..	..
Madagascar	2001	25.6	26.1	25.1	85.1	14.9	94.1	93.9	0.6	1.4	2.0	2.9
Malawi	2000	10.6	9.4	11.6	17.1	82.9	..	..	..	..	..	..
Malaysia		..	..	..	..	..	..	..	..	..	..	..
Mali	2001	25.3	32.3	18.6	68.7	31.3	..	..	..	..	..	..
Mauritania		..	..	..	..	..	..	..	..	..	..	..
Mauritius		..	..	..	..	..	..	..	..	..	..	..
Mexico[c]	1996	14.7	20.0	9.5	45.6	54.4	61.3	38.3	11.4	12.9	22.6	48.2
Moldova	2000	33.5	34.1	32.8	3.8	96.2	..	..	..	..	..	..
Mongolia	2000	22.0	23.5	20.6	28.2	71.8	..	..	..	..	..	..
Morocco	1998-99	13.2	13.5	12.8	93.2	6.8	60.8	60.3	8.1	8.5	13.5	6.4
Mozambique		..	..	..	..	..	..	..	..	..	..	..
Myanmar		..	..	..	..	..	..	..	..	..	..	..
Namibia	1999	15.4	16.2	14.7	9.5	90.5	91.5	91.7	0.4	0.4	8.1	8.0
Nepal	1999	47.2	42.2	52.4	35.6	64.4	89.0	86.1	1.2	1.5	9.7	12.3
Netherlands		..	..	..	..	..	..	..	..	..	..	..
New Zealand		..	..	..	..	..	..	..	..	..	..	..
Nicaragua	2001	12.1	17.5	6.5	33.3	66.7	73.2	32.0	3.0	10.2	23.3	57.8
Niger		..	..	..	..	..	..	..	..	..	..	..
Nigeria		..	..	..	..	..	..	..	..	..	..	..
Norway		..	..	..	..	..	..	..	..	..	..	..
Oman		..	..	..	..	..	..	..	..	..	..	..
Pakistan		..	..	..	..	..	..	..	..	..	..	..
Panama	2000	4.0	6.4	1.4	37.5	62.5	71.1	38.4	1.4	8.0	27.2	49.5
Papua New Guinea		..	..	..	..	..	..	..	..	..	..	..
Paraguay	1999	8.1	11.7	4.4	24.2	75.7	61.2	30.9	3.8	4.6	33.1	64.5
Peru	1994	17.7	20.4	15.2	7.3	92.7	78.9	76.3	3.6	3.4	17.5	20.3
Philippines	2001	13.3	16.3	10.0	14.8	85.2	72.6	53.6	3.6	5.3	22.1	41.0
Poland		..	..	..	..	..	..	..	..	..	..	..
Portugal	2001	3.6	4.6	2.6	3.6	96.4	52.7	40.7	11.4	10.7	25.6	47.7
Puerto Rico		..	..	..	..	..	..	..	..	..	..	..

2.4 Child labor

	Survey year	Economically active children					Employment by economic activity[a]					
			% of children ages 7–14		% of economically active children ages 7–14		% of economically active children ages 7–14					
							Agriculture		Manufacturing		Services	
		Total	Male	Female	Work only	Work and study	Male	Female	Male	Female	Male	Female
Romania		..	..	..	..	..	..	..	..	..	..	..
Russian Federation		..	..	..	..	..	..	..	..	..	..	..
Rwanda	2000	33.1	36.1	30.3	27.5	72.5	..	..	..	..	..	..
Saudi Arabia		..	..	..	..	..	..	..	..	..	..	..
Senegal	2000	35.4	43.2	27.7	56.2	43.8	..	..	..	..	..	..
Serbia and Montenegro		..	..	..	..	..	..	..	..	..	..	..
Sierra Leone	2000	74.0	24.7	72.7	53.8	46.2	..	..	..	..	..	..
Singapore		..	..	..	..	..	..	..	..	..	..	..
Slovak Republic		..	..	..	..	..	..	..	..	..	..	..
Slovenia		..	..	..	..	..	..	..	..	..	..	..
Somalia		..	..	..	..	..	..	..	..	..	..	..
South Africa	1999	27.7	29.0	26.4	5.1	94.9	..	..	..	..	..	..
Spain		..	..	..	..	..	..	..	..	..	..	..
Sri Lanka		..	..	..	..	..	..	..	..	..	..	..
Sudan	2000	19.1	21.5	16.8	55.9	44.1	..	..	..	..	..	..
Swaziland	2000	11.2	11.4	10.9	14.0	86.0	..	..	..	..	..	..
Sweden		..	..	..	..	..	..	..	..	..	..	..
Switzerland		..	..	..	..	..	..	..	..	..	..	..
Syrian Arab Republic		..	..	..	..	..	..	..	..	..	..	..
Tajikistan		..	..	..	..	..	..	..	..	..	..	..
Tanzania	2001	40.4	41.5	39.2	40.0	60.0	83.5	73.1	0.1	0.2	16.3	26.7
Thailand		..	..	..	..	..	..	..	..	..	..	..
Togo	2000	72.5	73.4	71.6	28.4	71.6	..	..	..	..	..	..
Trinidad and Tobago	2000	3.9	5.2	2.8	12.8	87.2	..	..	..	..	..	..
Tunisia		..	..	..	..	..	..	..	..	..	..	..
Turkey	1999	4.5	5.2	3.8	66.8	33.2	52.7	83.4	19.9	10.2	10.2	1.8
Turkmenistan		..	..	..	..	..	..	..	..	..	..	..
Uganda	2002–03	13.1	15.0	11.3	18.3	81.7	94.3	92.3	1.5	1.3	3.2	6.0
Ukraine		..	..	..	..	..	..	..	..	..	..	..
United Arab Emirates		..	..	..	..	..	..	..	..	..	..	..
United Kingdom		..	..	..	..	..	..	..	..	..	..	..
United States		..	..	..	..	..	..	..	..	..	..	..
Uruguay		..	..	..	..	..	..	..	..	..	..	..
Uzbekistan	2000	18.1	22.0	14.0	4.1	95.9	..	..	..	..	..	..
Venezuela, RB	2003	9.1	11.4	6.6	17.6	82.4	35.2	9.2	7.3	9.5	53.9	81.0
Vietnam		..	..	..	..	..	..	..	..	..	..	..
West Bank and Gaza		..	..	..	..	..	..	..	..	..	..	..
Yemen, Rep.	1999	13.1	12.4	14.0	64.3	35.7	87.2	96.6	1.2	0.8	10.8	1.8
Zambia	1999	14.4	15.0	13.9	72.8	27.2	92.7	88.1	0.3	0.8	6.6	11.0
Zimbabwe		..	..	..	..	..	..	..	..	..	..	..

a. Shares by major industrial category do not sum to 100 percent because of a residual category not included in the table. b. Data are for children ages 10–14. c. Data are for children ages 12–14.

About the data

The data in the table refer to children's economic activity, a broader concept than child labor. According to a gradually emerging consensus, child labor is a subset of children's economic activity or children's work that is injurious and therefore targeted for elimination.

In line with the international definition of employment, the threshold for classifying a child as economically active is spending one hour on economic activity during the reference week. Economic activity is as defined by the 1993 United Nations System of National Accounts (revision 3) and corresponds to the international definition of employment adopted by the Thirteenth International Conference of Labor Statisticians in 1982. Economic activity covers all market production and certain types of nonmarket production, including production of goods for own use. It excludes household chores performed by children in their own household. But some forms of economic activity are not captured by household surveys and so are not reflected in the estimates. These include unconditional forms of child labor, such as child commercial sexual exploitation and child slavery, which require different data collection methodologies.

The data used to develop the indicators are from household surveys conducted by the International Labor Organization (ILO), the United Nations Children's Fund (UNICEF), the World Bank, and national statistical offices. These surveys yield a variety of data in education, employment, health, expenditure, and consumption that relate to child work. But they do not provide information on unconditional forms of children's work.

Household survey data generally include information on work type—for example, whether a child is working for pay in cash or in kind or is involved in unpaid work, whether a child is working for someone who is not a member of the household, whether a child is involved in any type of family work (on the farm or in a business), and the like. The ages used in country surveys to define child labor range from 5 to 14 years old. The data in the table have been recalculated to present statistics for children ages 7–14.

Although efforts are made to harmonize the definition of employment and the questions on employment used in survey questionnaires, some differences remain among the survey instruments used to collect the information on working children. Differences exist not only among different household surveys in the same country, but also within the same type of survey carried out in different countries.

Because of the differences in the underlying survey instruments and in survey dates, estimates of the economically active child population are not fully comparable across countries. Caution should be exercised in drawing conclusions concerning relative levels of child economic activity across countries or regions based on the published estimates.

The table aggregates the distribution of working children by the industrial categories of the International Standard Industrial Classification (ISIC): agriculture, industry, and services. The residual category, which includes mining and quarrying; electricity, gas, and water; construction; extraterritorial organization; and other inadequately defined activities, is not presented in the table, and so the broad groups do not add up to 100 percent. The use of either ISIC revision 2 or revision 3 is strictly related to the codification applied by each country in describing the economic activity. The use of two different classifications does not affect the definition of the groups presented in the table.

2.4a

Of children who work, some combine work and schooling

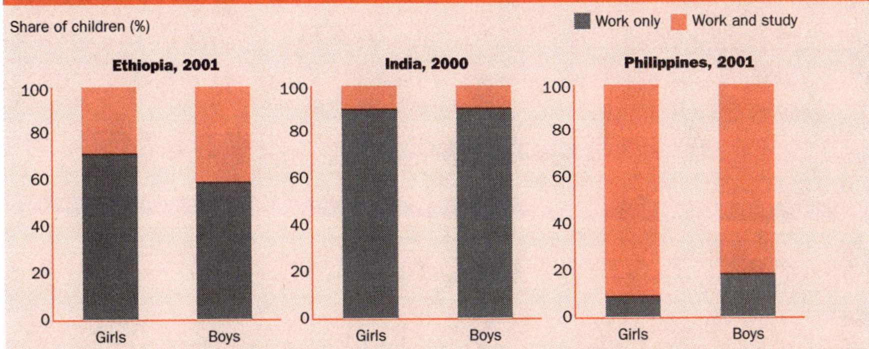

A little light work that does not interfere with education is not necessarily bad, but long working hours are likely to have serious health and developmental consequences for children. Studies suggest more children who work are working long hours.

Source: Understanding Children's Work project.

Definitions

• **Economically active children** refer to children involved in economic activity for at least one hour in the reference week of the survey. • **Work only** refers to children involved in economic activity and not attending school. • **Work and study** refer to children attending school in combination with economic activity. • **Employment by economic activity** refers to the distribution of economically active children by the major industrial categories (ISIC revision 2 or revision 3). • **Agriculture** corresponds to division 1 (ISIC revision 2) or categories A and B (ISIC revision 3) and includes agriculture and hunting, forestry and logging, and fishing. • **Manufacturing** corresponds to division 3 (ISIC revision 2) or category D (ISIC revision 3). • **Services** correspond to divisions 6–9 (ISIC revision 2) or categories G–P (ISIC revision 3) and include wholesale and retail trade, hotels and restaurants, transport, financial intermediation, real estate, public administration, education, health and social work, other community services, and private household activity.

Data sources

Estimates are produced by the Understanding Children's Work project based on household survey datasets made available by the ILO's International Programme on the Elimination of Child Labour under its Statistical Monitoring Programme on Child Labour, UNICEF under its Multiple Indicator Cluster Survey program, the World Bank under its Living Standards Measurement Study program, and national statistical offices. Information on how the data were collected and some indication of their reliability can be found at www.ilo.org/public/english/standards/ipec/simpoc/, www.childinfo.org, and www.worldbank.org/lsms. Detailed country statistics can be found at www.ucw-project.org.

2.5 Unemployment

	Unemployment						Long-term unemployment			Unemployment by educational attainment		
	Male % of male labor force		Female % of female labor force		Total % of total labor force		% of total unemployment			% of total unemployment		
							Male	Female	Total	Primary	Secondary	Tertiary
	1990–92[a]	2000–04[a]	1990–92[a]	2000–04[a]	1990–92[a]	2000–04[a]	2000–03[a]	2000–03[a]	2000–03[a]	2000–04[a]	2000–04[a]	2000–04[a]
Afghanistan	..	..	..	..	..	..	..	..	..	..	..	..
Albania	..	13.1	..	18.3	..	15.2	..	..	..	56.4	38.4	3.4
Algeria	24.2	26.6	20.3	31.4	23.0	27.3	..	..	..	..	..	..
Angola	..	..	..	..	..	..	..	..	..	..	..	..
Argentina	6.4[b]	16.3[b]	7.0[b]	14.7[b]	6.7[b]	15.6[b]	..	..	..	42.8[b]	38.5[b]	17.7[b]
Armenia	..	..	..	..	..	..	72.2[b]	70.8[b]	71.6[b]	5.2	81.5	13.3
Australia	11.3	5.3[b]	9.5	5.5[b]	10.5	5.4[b]	27.1[b]	17.0[b]	22.5[b]	48.3	32.7	19.0
Austria	3.5	4.5	3.8	5.4	3.6	4.9	25.0	23.9	24.5	37.3	55.7	7.0
Azerbaijan	..	..	..	..	..	..	..	..	..	4.6	31.4	64.1
Bangladesh	..	3.2	..	3.3	..	3.3	..	..	..	54.3	22.7	8.4
Belarus	..	..	..	..	..	..	..	..	..	10.2	40.6	49.1
Belgium	4.8	6.6	9.5	8.3	6.7	7.4	44.8	48.2	46.3	43.7	38.1	18.2
Benin	..	..	..	..	..	..	..	..	..	..	..	..
Bolivia	5.5[b]	4.3	5.6[b]	6.9	5.5[b]	5.5	..	..	..	60.2[b]	32.5[b]	4.4[b]
Bosnia and Herzegovina	..	..	..	..	..	..	..	..	..	..	..	..
Botswana	11.7	15.7	17.3	22.3	13.9	18.6	..	..	..	63.8	23.8	..
Brazil	5.4[b]	7.8[b]	7.9[b]	12.3[b]	6.4[b]	9.7[b]	..	..	..	..	..	..
Bulgaria	..	14.1	..	13.2	..	13.7	..	..	..	37.8	50.9	11.4
Burkina Faso	..	..	..	..	..	..	..	..	..	46.8	19.3	5.6
Burundi	..	..	..	..	..	..	..	..	..	..	..	..
Cambodia	..	1.4	..	2.0	..	1.8	..	..	..	..	..	..
Cameroon	..	8.2	..	6.7	..	7.5	..	..	..	..	..	..
Canada	12.1[b]	7.5[b]	10.2[b]	6.8[b]	11.2[b]	7.2[b]	11.4[b]	8.4[b]	10.1[b]	29.0[b]	30.8[b]	40.2[b]
Central African Republic	..	..	..	..	..	..	..	..	..	..	..	..
Chad	..	..	..	..	..	..	..	..	..	..	..	..
Chile	3.9	6.9	5.3	8.3	4.4	7.4	..	..	..	18.5	59.0	21.8
China	..	..	..	..	2.3[b]	4.0[b]	..	..	..	..	..	..
Hong Kong, China	2.0[b]	9.3[b]	1.9[b]	6.2[b]	2.0[b]	7.9[b]	..	..	..	48.6	39.4	10.1
Colombia	6.7	11.0	13.0	18.5	9.4	14.2	..	..	..	26.9	52.9	16.5
Congo, Dem. Rep.	..	..	..	..	..	..	..	..	..	..	..	..
Congo, Rep.	..	..	..	..	..	..	..	..	..	..	..	..
Costa Rica	3.4	5.8	5.4	8.2	4.0	6.7	8.9	13.3	10.9	62.2	24.1	9.9
Côte d'Ivoire	..	..	..	..	..	..	..	..	..	..	..	..
Croatia	..	13.1	..	15.7	..	14.3	..	..	56.4	21.5	68.4	9.8
Cuba	..	..	..	..	4.6	3.3	..	..	..	..	..	..
Czech Republic	..	7.0	..	9.9	..	8.3	47.4	51.9	49.9	24.6	71.8	3.5
Denmark	8.3	5.0	9.9	5.4	9.0	5.2	21.8	17.9	19.9	25.9	46.6	25.5
Dominican Republic	11.7	9.4	34.9	26.0	20.3	15.6	2.2	1.3	1.6	..	..	..
Ecuador	6.0[b]	9.0[b]	13.2[b]	15.0[b]	8.9[b]	11.4[b]	..	..	..	28.8	47.7	21.9
Egypt, Arab Rep.	6.4	6.3	17.0	23.9	9.0	11.0	..	..	..	..	..	..
El Salvador	8.4[b]	9.3	7.2[b]	3.5	7.9[b]	6.9	..	..	..	..	..	..
Eritrea	..	..	..	..	..	..	..	..	..	..	..	..
Estonia	3.9	10.2	3.5	9.9	3.7	10.0	..	..	..	20.9	62.1	16.8
Ethiopia	..	..	..	..	..	..	..	..	..	..	..	..
Finland	13.6	8.8	9.7	9.0	11.7	8.9	27.7	21.4	24.7	35.8	46.3	17.5
France	7.9[b]	9.0[b]	12.7[b]	11.1[b]	10.0[b]	9.9[b]	43.1[b]	42.8[b]	42.9[b]	40.6	39.9	17.7
Gabon	..	..	..	..	..	..	..	..	..	..	..	..
Gambia, The	..	..	..	..	..	..	..	..	..	..	..	..
Georgia	..	11.5	..	11.5	..	11.5	..	..	..	5.8	57.6	36.5
Germany	5.3	10.2	8.4	9.3	6.6	9.8	48.3	52.3	50.0	27.1	60.5	12.4
Ghana	..	7.5	..	8.7	..	8.2	..	..	..	..	..	..
Greece	4.9	6.4	12.9	15.9	7.8	10.2	49.2	61.0	56.5	34.2	50.0	15.1
Guatemala	2.6[b]	2.2	4.6[b]	3.7	3.2[b]	2.8	..	..	..	..	..	..
Guinea	..	..	..	..	..	..	..	..	..	..	..	..
Guinea-Bissau	..	..	..	..	..	..	..	..	..	..	..	..
Haiti	11.2	..	13.6	..	12.2	..	..	..	..	..	..	..

Unemployment 2.5

	Unemployment						Long-term unemployment			Unemployment by educational attainment		
	Male % of male labor force		Female % of female labor force		Total % of total labor force		% of total unemployment			% of total unemployment		
							Male	Female	Total	Primary	Secondary	Tertiary
	1990–92[a]	2000–04[a]	1990–92[a]	2000–04[a]	1990–92[a]	2000–04[a]	2000–03[a]	2000–03[a]	2000–03[a]	2000–04[a]	2000–04[a]	2000–04[a]
Honduras	3.3[b]	..	3.0[b]	..	3.2[b]	5.1[b]	..	..	..	..	..	..
Hungary	11.0	6.1	8.7	6.1	9.9	6.1	42.2	42.2	42.2	33.5	61.2	5.4
India	..	4.4[b]	..	4.1[b]	..	4.3[b]	..	..	..	27.0	41.1	31.9
Indonesia	3.5	8.1	4.5	12.9	3.9	9.9	..	..	..	26.3	52.8	6.7
Iran, Islamic Rep.	..	10.1	..	20.4	..	11.6	..	..	..	38.3	37.1	19.3
Iraq	..	30.2	..	16.0	..	28.1	..	..	..	..	..	..
Ireland	15.2	4.9	15.2	3.7	15.2	4.4	40.9	26.0	35.4	48.2	24.9	24.0
Israel	9.2	10.2	13.9	11.3	11.2	10.7	..	..	..	20.2	48.8	27.0
Italy	8.1	6.4	17.3	10.5	11.6	8.0	57.5	58.9	58.2	49.4	41.4	7.5
Jamaica	9.4	8.1	22.2	15.7	15.4	11.4	24.4	36.2	31.7	13.0	5.4	6.1
Japan	2.1[b]	4.9[b]	2.2[b]	4.4[b]	2.2[b]	4.7[b]	38.9[b]	24.6[b]	33.5[b]	70.8	0.0	29.2
Jordan	..	11.8	..	20.7	..	13.2	..	..	..	..	..	..
Kazakhstan	..	7.2	..	10.4	..	8.8	..	..	..	7.9	53.2	38.9
Kenya	..	..	..	..	..	..	..	..	..	..	..	..
Korea, Dem. Rep.	..	..	..	..	..	..	..	..	..	..	..	..
Korea, Rep.	2.8	3.7	2.1	3.1	2.5	3.5	0.7	0.3	0.6	17.0	53.4	29.6
Kuwait	..	..	..	..	..	..	..	..	..	27.5	39.9	6.1
Kyrgyz Republic	..	9.4	..	10.5	..	9.9	47.8	54.3	50.9	7.7	77.7	18.5
Lao PDR	..	..	..	..	..	..	..	..	..	..	..	..
Latvia	..	10.7	..	10.5	..	10.6	..	..	..	22.4	68.5	8.8
Lebanon	..	..	..	..	..	..	..	..	..	..	..	..
Lesotho	..	..	..	..	..	..	..	..	..	..	..	..
Liberia	..	..	..	..	..	..	..	..	..	..	..	..
Libya	..	..	..	..	..	..	..	..	..	..	..	..
Lithuania	..	12.7	..	12.2	..	12.4	..	..	57.8	15.0	68.5	16.5
Macedonia, FYR	..	37.0	..	36.3	..	36.7	..	..	..	..	..	..
Madagascar	..	3.5	..	5.6	..	4.5	..	..	..	42.7	18.8	6.1
Malawi	..	..	..	..	..	..	..	..	..	..	..	..
Malaysia	..	..	..	..	3.7	3.5	..	..	..	32.0	48.8	15.6
Mali	..	..	..	..	..	..	..	..	..	..	..	..
Mauritania	..	..	..	..	..	..	..	..	..	..	..	..
Mauritius	3.2	9.0	3.6	12.6	3.3	10.2	..	..	..	71.5[b]	28.2[b]	..
Mexico	2.7	2.9	4.0	3.4	3.1	3.0	1.1	0.8	1.0	13.7	30.1	46.4
Moldova	..	9.6	..	6.4	..	7.9	..	..	..	..	..	..
Mongolia	..	14.3	..	14.1	..	14.2	..	..	..	35.0	45.8	18.4
Morocco	13.0[b]	10.6	25.3[b]	11.4	16.0[b]	10.8	..	..	..	50.9[b]	20.6[b]	19.3[b]
Mozambique	..	..	..	..	..	..	..	..	..	..	..	..
Myanmar	..	..	..	..	..	..	..	..	..	..	..	..
Namibia	20.0	26.8	19.0	35.9	19.0	31.1	..	..	..	..	..	..
Nepal	..	..	..	..	..	..	..	..	..	..	..	..
Netherlands	4.3	4.1	7.3	4.4	5.5	4.3	30.1	28.1	29.2	46.3	35.1	17.4
New Zealand	11.0[b]	3.5[b]	9.6[b]	4.4[b]	10.4[b]	3.9[b]	15.5[b]	11.0[b]	13.3[b]	1.0	48.8	16.0
Nicaragua	11.3	7.6	19.4	8.0	14.4	7.8	..	..	..	50.8[b]	24.8[b]	19.7[b]
Niger	..	..	..	..	..	..	..	..	..	..	..	..
Nigeria	..	..	..	..	..	..	..	..	..	..	..	..
Norway	6.6	4.8	5.1	3.8	5.9	4.4	7.1	5.4	6.4	21.7	54.7	21.7
Oman	..	..	..	..	..	..	..	..	..	..	..	..
Pakistan	4.3	6.2	14.2	16.4	5.8	7.8	..	..	..	14.7	12.3	24.1
Panama	10.8	10.5	22.3	18.8	14.7	13.6	24.0	35.7	29.3	35.9	37.3	26.0
Papua New Guinea	9.0	4.3	5.9	1.3	7.7	2.8	..	..	..	..	..	..
Paraguay	6.3[b]	6.7	3.8[b]	8.9	5.2[b]	7.6	..	..	..	..	..	..
Peru	7.5[b]	9.0[b]	12.5[b]	11.9[b]	9.4[b]	10.3[b]	..	..	..	9.4[b]	61.4[b]	28.6[b]
Philippines	7.9	9.4	9.9	10.3	8.6	9.8	..	..	..	..	..	..
Poland	12.2	18.2	14.7	19.9	13.3	19.0	48.6	50.8	49.7	18.0	75.4	6.7
Portugal	3.5[b]	5.8	5.0[b]	7.6	4.1[b]	6.7	31.2	32.7	32.0	70.7	14.6	8.8
Puerto Rico	19.1[b]	12.8[b]	13.3[b]	10.9[b]	16.9[b]	12.0[b]	..	..	..	..	..	..

2.5 Unemployment

	Unemployment						Long-term unemployment			Unemployment by educational attainment		
	Male % of male labor force		Female % of female labor force		Total % of total labor force		Male	Female % of total unemployment	Total	Primary	Secondary % of total unemployment	Tertiary
	1990–92[a]	2000–04[a]	1990–92[a]	2000–04[a]	1990–92[a]	2000–04[a]	2000–03[a]	2000–03[a]	2000–03[a]	2000–04[a]	2000–04[a]	2000–04[a]
Romania	..	7.5	..	6.4	..	7.0	..	..	..	26.0	66.9	5.4
Russian Federation	5.2	9.9	5.2	8.8	5.2	8.6	..	..	..	..	..	..
Rwanda	0.6	..	0.2	..	0.3	..	..	..	..	60.7	24.1	5.9
Saudi Arabia	..	4.2	..	11.5	..	5.2	..	..	..	38.3	34.7	20.1
Senegal	..	..	..	..	..	..	..	..	..	..	..	..
Serbia and Montenegro	..	14.4[b]	..	16.4[b]	..	15.2[b]	..	..	..	..	..	..
Sierra Leone	..	..	..	..	..	..	..	..	..	..	..	..
Singapore	2.7	5.5	2.6	5.3	2.7	5.4	..	..	..	22.4	25.0	38.8
Slovak Republic	..	17.3	..	19.1	..	18.1	60.2	62.1	61.1	24.1	71.7	4.3
Slovenia	..	6.2	..	6.6	..	6.6	..	..	..	26.2	63.9	8.2
Somalia	..	..	..	..	..	..	..	..	..	..	..	..
South Africa	..	25.5[b]	..	31.7[b]	..	28.4[b]	..	..	..	50.2	41.0	5.1
Spain	13.9	8.2	25.8	15.0	18.1	11.0	34.3	43.9	39.8	56.0	20.4	22.7
Sri Lanka	10.1[b]	6.2[b]	19.9[b]	14.7[b]	13.3[b]	9.0[b]	..	..	..	47.2	0.0	52.8
Sudan	..	..	..	..	..	..	..	..	..	..	..	..
Swaziland	..	..	..	..	..	..	..	..	..	..	..	..
Sweden	6.8	6.9	4.6	6.2	5.7	6.5	19.6	15.3	17.8	23.2	58.1	17.5
Switzerland	2.3	3.9	3.5	4.8	2.8	4.3	21.6	32.6	27.0	28.7	54.5	16.9
Syrian Arab Republic	..	8.3	..	24.1	..	11.7	..	..	..	75.2	10.3	9.8
Tajikistan	..	..	..	..	..	..	..	..	..	..	..	..
Tanzania	2.7[b]	4.4	4.2[b]	5.8	3.5[b]	5.1	..	..	..	..	..	..
Thailand	1.3	1.6	1.5	1.4	1.4	1.5	..	..	..	40.0	47.2	0.2
Togo	..	..	..	..	..	..	..	..	..	..	..	..
Trinidad and Tobago	17.0	7.8	23.9	14.5	19.6	10.4	20.3	34.7	27.6	55.5	40.5	1.8
Tunisia	..	..	..	..	..	14.3	..	..	..	43.4	37.4	10.0
Turkey	8.8	10.5	7.8	9.7	8.5	10.3	22.1	30.9	24.4	53.5	29.2	12.7
Turkmenistan	..	..	..	..	..	..	..	..	..	..	..	..
Uganda	..	2.5	..	3.9	..	3.2	..	..	..	..	..	..
Ukraine	..	8.9	..	8.3	..	8.6	..	..	..	13.5	54.3	32.2
United Arab Emirates	..	2.2	..	2.6	..	2.3	..	..	..	..	..	..
United Kingdom	11.5[b]	5.0[b]	7.3[b]	4.2[b]	9.7[b]	4.6[b]	26.5	17.1	23.0	30.3	44.4	14.6
United States	7.9[b]	5.6[b]	7.0[b]	5.4[b]	7.5[b]	5.5[b]	12.5[b]	11.0[b]	11.8[b]	18.4	34.3	47.3
Uruguay	6.8[b]	13.5[b]	11.8[b]	20.8[b]	9.0[b]	16.8[b]	..	..	..	54.8[b]	31.3[b]	13.9[b]
Uzbekistan	..	..	..	..	..	..	..	..	..	..	..	..
Venezuela, RB	8.1	14.4	6.8	20.3[b]	7.7	16.8[b]	..	..	..	..	..	..
Vietnam	..	1.9	..	2.4	..	2.1	..	..	..	..	..	..
West Bank and Gaza	..	26.9	..	18.6	..	25.6	..	..	..	57.5	14.5	17.6
Yemen, Rep.	..	..	..	..	..	..	..	..	..	..	..	..
Zambia	16.3	..	22.4	..	18.9	..	..	..	..	..	..	..
Zimbabwe	..	10.4	..	6.1	..	8.2	..	..	..	..	..	..
World	.. w	.. w	.. w	.. w	.. w	6.5 w	.. w	.. w	.. w	.. w	.. w	.. w
Low income	..	..	..	..	..	..	..	..	..	..	..	..
Middle income	..	..	..	..	4.1	6.8	..	..	..	..	..	..
Lower middle income	..	..	..	..	3.6	5.9	..	..	..	..	..	..
Upper middle income	6.2	11.0	6.8	13.4	6.3	12.0	..	..	..	38.2	47.3	11.5
Low & middle income	..	..	..	..	..	5.6	..	..	..	..	..	..
East Asia & Pacific	..	..	..	..	2.5	4.4	..	..	..	..	..	..
Europe & Central Asia	..	11.1	..	10.7	..	10.6	..	..	..	..	..	..
Latin America & Carib.	5.5	8.0	8.5	11.8	6.7	9.5	..	..	..	..	..	..
Middle East & N. Africa	..	12.7	..	21.9	..	13.6	..	..	..	..	..	..
South Asia	..	4.4	..	5.0	..	4.5	..	..	..	30.0	33.8	27.4
Sub-Saharan Africa	..	..	..	..	..	..	..	..	..	..	..	..
High income	7.0	6.2	7.9	6.6	7.4	6.4	27.3	23.9	26.0	34.8	34.4	29.7
Europe EMU	7.5	8.2	12.6	10.6	9.5	9.2	44.2	46.4	45.5	40.4	42.3	16.4

a. Data are for the most recent year available. b. Limited coverage.

About the data

Unemployment and total employment in an economy are the broadest indicators of economic activity as reflected by the labor market. The International Labour Organization (ILO) defines the unemployed as members of the economically active population who are without work but available for and seeking work, including people who have lost their jobs and those who have voluntarily left work. Some unemployment is unavoidable in all economies. At any time some workers are temporarily unemployed—between jobs as employers look for the right workers and workers search for better jobs. Such unemployment, often called frictional unemployment, results from the normal operation of labor markets.

Changes in unemployment over time may reflect changes in the demand for and supply of labor, but they may also reflect changes in reporting practices. Ironically, low unemployment rates can often disguise substantial poverty in a country, while high unemployment rates can occur in countries with a high level of economic development and low incidence of poverty. In countries without unemployment or welfare benefits, people eke out a living in the informal sector. In countries with well-developed safety nets, workers can afford to wait for suitable or desirable jobs. But high and sustained unemployment indicates serious inefficiencies in the allocation of resources.

The ILO definition of unemployment notwithstanding, reference periods, the criteria for those considered to be seeking work, and the treatment of people temporarily laid off and those seeking work for the first time vary across countries. In many developing countries it is especially difficult to measure employment and unemployment in agriculture. The timing of a survey, for example, can maximize the effects of seasonal unemployment in agriculture. And informal sector employment is difficult to quantify where informal activities are not registered and tracked.

Data on unemployment are drawn from labor force sample surveys and general household sample surveys, censuses, and other administrative records such as social insurance statistics, employment office statistics, and official estimates, which are usually based on information drawn from one or more of the above sources. Labor force surveys generally yield the most comprehensive data because they include groups not covered in other unemployment statistics, particularly people seeking work for the first time. These surveys generally use a definition of unemployment that follows the international recommendations more closely than that used by other sources and therefore generate statistics that are more comparable internationally. But the age group and area covered could differ by country or change over time within a country. For detailed information on breaks in series, consult the original source.

In contrast, the quality and completeness of data from employment offices and social insurance programs vary widely. Where employment offices work closely with social insurance schemes and registration with such offices is a prerequisite for receipt of unemployment benefits, the two sets of unemployment estimates tend to be comparable. Where registration is voluntary and where employment offices function only in more populous areas, employment office statistics do not give a reliable indication of unemployment. Most commonly excluded from both these sources are discouraged workers who have given up their job search because they believe that no employment opportunities exist or do not register as unemployed after their benefits have been exhausted. Thus measured unemployment may be higher in countries that offer more or longer unemployment benefits.

Women tend to be excluded from the unemployment count for various reasons. Women suffer more from discrimination and from structural, social, and cultural barriers that impede them from actively seeking work. Also, women are often responsible for the care of children and the elderly or for other household affairs. They may not be available for work during the short reference period, as they need to make arrangements before starting work. Furthermore, women are considered to be employed when they are working part-time or in temporary jobs in the informal sector, despite the instability of these jobs or their active searching for more secure employment.

Long-term unemployment is measured by the length of time that an unemployed person has been without work and looking for a job. The underlying assumption is that shorter periods of joblessness are of less concern, especially when the unemployed are covered by unemployment benefits or similar forms of welfare support. The length of time that a person has been unemployed is difficult to measure, because the ability to recall that time diminishes as the period of joblessness extends. Women's long-term unemployment is likely to be lower in countries where women constitute a large share of the unpaid family workforce. Women in such countries have more access than men to nonmarket work and are more likely to drop out of the labor force and not be counted as unemployed.

Unemployment by level of educational attainment provides insights into the relationship between the educational attainment of workers and unemployment and may be used to draw inferences about changes in employment demand. Information on education attainment is the best available indicator of skill levels of the labor force.

Besides the limitations to comparability raised for measuring unemployment, the different ways of classifying the level of education across countries may also cause inconsistency. The level of education is supposed to be classified according to International Standard Classification of Education 1997 (ISCED97). For more information on ISCED97, see *About the data* for table 2.10.

Definitions

• **Unemployment** refers to the share of the labor force without work but available for and seeking employment. Definitions of labor force and unemployment differ by country (see *About the data*). • **Long-term unemployment** refers to the number of people with continuous periods of unemployment extending for a year or longer, expressed as a percentage of the total unemployed. • **Unemployment by educational attainment** shows the unemployed by level of educational attainment, as a percentage of the total unemployed. The levels of educational attainment accord with the International Standard Classification of Education 1997 of the United Nations Educational, Cultural, and Scientific Organization.

Data sources

Data on unemployment are from the ILO database Key Indicators of the Labour Market, fourth edition.

2.6 Wages and productivity

	Hours worked		Minimum wage		Agricultural wage		Labor cost per worker in manufacturing		Value added per worker in manufacturing	
	average per week		$ per year		$ per year		$ per year		$ per year	
	1980–84	1995–99[a]	1980–84	1995–99[a]	1980–84	1995–99[a]	1980–84	1995–99[a]	1980–84	1995–99[a]
Afghanistan	..	..	..	..	..	..	..	..	..	..
Albania	..	..	..	..	..	..	..	..	..	..
Algeria	..	..	..	*1,340*	..	..	6,242	*2,638*	11,306	..
Angola	..	..	..	..	..	..	..	..	..	..
Argentina	41	*40*	..	2,400	..	..	6,768	*7,338*	33,694	*37,480*
Armenia	..	..	..	..	..	..	..	..	..	..
Australia	37	*39*	..	*12,712*	11,212	*15,124*	14,749	26,087	27,801	*57,857*
Austria	33	*32*	..	b	..	..	11,949	*28,342*	20,956	*53,061*
Azerbaijan	..	..	..	..	..	..	..	..	..	..
Bangladesh	..	*52*	..	*492*	192	*360*	556	*671*	1,820	*1,711*
Belarus	..	..	..	..	1,641	410	2,233	754	..	..
Belgium	..	*38*	7,661	15,882	6,399	..	12,805	*24,132*	25,579	*58,678*
Benin	..	..	..	..	..	..	..	..	..	..
Bolivia	..	*46*	..	529	..	..	4,432	*2,343*	21,519	*26,282*
Bosnia and Herzegovina	..	..	..	..	..	..	..	..	..	..
Botswana	45	..	894	961	650	*1,223*	3,250	*2,884*	7,791	..
Brazil	..	..	1,690	1,308	..	..	10,080	*14,134*	43,232	*61,595*
Bulgaria	..	..	..	*573*	..	*1,372*	2,485	*1,179*	..	..
Burkina Faso	..	..	695	585	..	..	3,282	..	15,886	..
Burundi	..	..	..	..	..	..	..	..	..	..
Cambodia	..	..	..	..	..	..	..	..	..	..
Cameroon	..	..	..	..	..	..	..	..	..	..
Canada	38	*38*	4,974	7,897	20,429	*30,625*	17,710	*28,424*	36,903	*60,712*
Central African Republic	..	..	..	..	..	..	..	..	..	..
Chad	..	..	..	..	..	..	..	..	..	..
Chile	43	45	663	1,781	..	..	6,234	*5,822*	32,805	*32,977*
China	..	..	..	..	349	*325*	472	729	3,061	*2,885*
Hong Kong, China	48	*46*	..	..	..	..	4,127	*10,353*	7,886	32,611
Colombia	..	..	..	*1,128*	..	..	2,988	*2,507*	15,096	*17,061*
Congo, Dem. Rep.	..	..	..	..	..	..	..	..	..	..
Congo, Rep.	..	..	..	..	..	..	..	..	..	..
Costa Rica	..	*47*	1,042	*1,638*	982	*1,697*	2,433	*2,829*	7,185	*7,184*
Côte d'Ivoire	..	..	1,246	871	..	..	5,132	*9,995*	16,158	..
Croatia	..	..	..	..	..	..	..	..	..	..
Cuba	..	..	..	..	..	..	..	..	..	..
Czech Republic	43	43	..	942	2,277	3,090	2,306	3,815	5,782	*5,094*
Denmark	..	*37*	9,170	19,933	..	..	16,169	*29,235*	27,919	*49,273*
Dominican Republic	44	44	..	*1,439*	..	..	2,191	*1,806*	8,603	..
Ecuador	..	..	1,637	*492*	..	..	5,065	*3,738*	12,197	*9,747*
Egypt, Arab Rep.	58	..	343	*415*	..	..	2,210	*1,863*	3,691	*5,976*
El Salvador	..	..	..	*790*	..	..	3,654	..	14,423	..
Eritrea	..	..	..	..	..	..	..	..	..	..
Estonia	..	..	..	..	..	..	..	..	..	..
Ethiopia	..	..	..	..	..	..	..	*1,596*	..	*7,094*
Finland	..	*38*	..	b	..	..	11,522	*26,615*	25,945	*55,037*
France	40	*39*	6,053	*12,072*	..	..	18,488	..	26,751	*61,019*
Gabon	..	..	..	..	..	..	..	..	..	..
Gambia, The	..	..	..	..	..	..	..	..	..	..
Georgia	..	..	..	..	..	..	..	..	..	..
Germany	41	*40*	..	b	..	..	15,708	*33,226*	34,945	*79,616*
Ghana	..	..	..	..	1,470	..	2,306	..	12,130	..
Greece	..	*41*	..	6,057	..	..	6,461	*12,296*	14,561	*30,429*
Guatemala	..	..	..	*459*	..	..	2,605	*1,802*	11,144	*9,235*
Guinea	40	..	..	..	..	..	..	..	..	..
Guinea-Bissau	48	..	..	..	..	..	..	..	..	..
Haiti	..	..	..	..	..	..	..	..	..	..

Wages and productivity 2.6

	Hours worked		Minimum wage		Agricultural wage		Labor cost per worker in manufacturing		Value added per worker in manufacturing	
	average per week		$ per year		$ per year		$ per year		$ per year	
	1980–84	1995–99[a]	1980–84	1995–99[a]	1980–84	1995–99[a]	1980–84	1995–99[a]	1980–84	1995–99[a]
Honduras	..	*44*	..	..	1,623	..	2,949	*2,658*	7,458	*7,427*
Hungary	35	*33*	1,186	1,132	1,186	2,676	1,410	3,755	4,307	10,918
India	46	..	..	*408*	205	*245*	1,035	*1,192*	2,108	*3,118*
Indonesia	40	43	..	*241*	..	..	898	3,054	3,807	*5,139*
Iran, Islamic Rep.	..	..	..	..	..	..	9,737	*30,562*	17,679	*89,787*
Iraq	..	..	..	..	..	..	4,624	*13,288*	13,599	*34,316*
Ireland	41	*41*	5,556	12,087	..	..	10,190	*22,681*	26,510	*86,036*
Israel	36	*36*	..	*5,861*	4,582	*7,906*	13,541	*21,150*	23,459	*35,526*
Italy	..	*32*	..	[b]	..	..	9,955	*34,859*	24,580	*50,760*
Jamaica	..	*39*	782	*692*	..	..	5,218	*3,655*	12,056	*11,091*
Japan	47	47	3,920	12,265	..	..	12,306	*31,687*	34,456	*92,582*
Jordan	..	*50*	[b]	[b]	..	..	4,643	2,082	16,337	*11,906*
Kazakhstan	..	..	..	..	..	..	..	..	..	..
Kenya	41	*39*	..	551	508	*568*	1,043	810	2,345	1,489
Korea, Dem. Rep.	..	..	..	..	..	..	..	..	..	..
Korea, Rep.	52	*48*	..	3,903	..	..	3,153	*10,743*	11,617	*40,916*
Kuwait	..	..	..	*8,244*	..	..	10,281	..	30,341	..
Kyrgyz Republic	..	..	..	65	1,695	168	2,287	687	..	..
Lao PDR	..	..	..	..	..	..	..	..	..	..
Latvia	..	..	..	..	..	..	..	*366*	..	..
Lebanon	..	..	..	..	..	..	..	..	..	..
Lesotho	..	*45*	..	..	..	..	1,442	..	6,047	..
Liberia	..	..	..	..	..	..	..	..	..	..
Libya	..	..	..	..	..	..	8,648	..	21,119	..
Lithuania	..	..	..	..	..	..	..	..	..	..
Macedonia, FYR	..	..	..	..	..	..	..	..	..	..
Madagascar	..	*40*	..	..	..	..	1,575	..	3,542	..
Malawi	..	..	..	..	..	..	..	..	..	..
Malaysia	..	..	..	[b]	1,435	..	2,519	*3,429*	8,454	*12,661*
Mali	..	..	321	*459*	..	..	2,983	..	10,477	..
Mauritania	..	..	..	..	..	..	..	..	..	..
Mauritius	..	..	..	..	..	..	1,465	*1,973*	2,969	*4,217*
Mexico	43	*45*	1,343	768	1,031	*908*	3,772	7,607	17,448	*25,931*
Moldova	..	..	..	..	..	..	..	..	..	..
Mongolia	..	..	..	..	..	..	..	..	..	..
Morocco	..	..	..	*1,672*	..	..	2,583	*3,391*	6,328	*9,089*
Mozambique	..	..	..	..	..	..	..	..	..	..
Myanmar	..	..	..	..	..	..	..	..	..	..
Namibia	..	..	..	..	..	..	..	..	..	..
Nepal	..	..	..	..	..	..	371	..	1,523	..
Netherlands	40	*40*	9,074	15,170	..	..	18,891	*34,326*	27,491	*56,801*
New Zealand	39	*39*	3,309	9,091	..	..	10,605	*18,419*	16,835	*32,723*
Nicaragua	..	*44*	..	..	..	..	..	..	..	..
Niger	40	..	..	..	..	..	4,074	..	22,477	..
Nigeria	..	..	..	*300*	..	..	4,812	..	20,000	..
Norway	35	*35*	..	[b]	..	..	14,935	38,415	24,905	*51,510*
Oman	..	..	..	..	..	..	..	*3,099*	..	*61,422*
Pakistan	48	..	..	*600*	427	*416*	1,264	..	6,214	..
Panama	..	..	..	..	..	..	4,768	*6,351*	15,327	*17,320*
Papua New Guinea	44	..	..	..	..	..	4,825	..	13,563	..
Paraguay	36	*39*	..	..	1,606	*1,210*	2,509	*3,241*	..	*14,873*
Peru	48	..	..	..	..	*944*	2,988	..	15,962	..
Philippines	47	*43*	915	1,472	382	..	1,240	*2,450*	5,266	*10,781*
Poland	36	*33*	320	1,584	1,726	*1,301*	1,682	*1,714*	6,242	*7,637*
Portugal	39	*40*	1,606	4,086	..	..	3,115	*6,237*	7,161	*17,273*
Puerto Rico	..	..	..	..	..	..	..	..	..	..

2.6 Wages and productivity

	Hours worked		Minimum wage		Agricultural wage		Labor cost per worker in manufacturing		Value added per worker in manufacturing	
	average per week		$ per year		$ per year		$ per year		$ per year	
	1980–84	1995–99[a]	1980–84	1995–99[a]	1980–84	1995–99[a]	1980–84	1995–99[a]	1980–84	1995–99[a]
Romania	34	*34*	..	*531*	1,669	*1,864*	1,757	*1,190*	..	*3,482*
Russian Federation	..	..	863	297	2,417	659	2,524	1,528	..	..
Rwanda	..	..	..	..	..	..	1,871	..	9,835	..
Saudi Arabia	..	..	..	..	..	..	9,814	..	..	..
Senegal	..	..	993	848	..	..	2,828	*7,754*	6,415	..
Serbia and Montenegro	..	..	..	..	..	..	..	..	..	..
Sierra Leone	44	..	..	..	..	..	1,624	..	7,807	..
Singapore	46	47	..	..	..	*4,856*	5,576	21,317	16,442	*40,674*
Slovak Republic	43	*40*	..	..	2,277	*1,885*	2,306	*1,876*	5,782	*5,094*
Slovenia	..	..	..	..	..	..	..	*9,632*	..	*12,536*
Somalia	..	..	..	..	..	..	..	..	..	..
South Africa	42	*41*	..	b	888	..	6,261	*8,475*	12,705	*16,612*
Spain	38	*37*	3,058	5,778	..	..	8,276	*19,329*	18,936	*47,016*
Sri Lanka	50	*53*	..	..	198	*264*	447	*604*	2,057	*3,405*
Sudan	..	..	..	..	..	..	..	..	..	..
Swaziland	..	..	..	..	..	..	..	..	..	..
Sweden	36	*37*	..	..	9,576	*27,098*	13,038	*26,601*	32,308	*56,675*
Switzerland	44	*42*	..	b		..	..	..	..	*61,848*
Syrian Arab Republic	..	..	..	..	..	..	2,844	*4,338*	9,607	*9,918*
Tajikistan	..	..	..	..	..	..	..	..	..	..
Tanzania	..	..	..	..	..	..	1,123	..	3,339	..
Thailand	50	47	749	*1,159*	..	..	2,305	3,868	11,072	*19,946*
Togo	..	..	..	..	..	..	..	..	..	..
Trinidad and Tobago	..	*40*	..	*2,974*	..	..	..	..	14,008	..
Tunisia	..	..	1,381	*1,525*	668	*968*	3,344	*3,599*	7,111	..
Turkey	..	*48*	594	1,254	1,015	*2,896*	3,582	*7,958*	13,994	*32,961*
Turkmenistan	..	..	..	..	..	..	..	..	..	..
Uganda	43	..	..	..	..	..	253	..	..	..
Ukraine	..	..	..	..	..	..	..	..	..	..
United Arab Emirates	..	..	..	..	..	..	6,968	..	20,344	..
United Kingdom	42	*40*	..	b	..	..	11,406	*23,843*	24,716	*55,060*
United States	40	*41*	6,006	8,056	..	..	19,103	*28,907*	47,276	*81,353*
Uruguay	48	*42*	1,262	1,027	1,289	..	4,128	*3,738*	13,722	*16,028*
Uzbekistan	..	..	..	..	..	..	..	..	..	..
Venezuela, RB	41	..	1,869	*1,463*	..	..	11,188	*4,667*	37,063	*24,867*
Vietnam	..	47	..	134	..	442	..	711	..	..
West Bank and Gaza	..	..	..	..	..	..	..	..	..	..
Yemen, Rep.	..	..	..	..	..	..	4,492	1,291	17,935	5,782
Zambia	..	*45*	..	..	..	..	3,183	*4,292*	11,753	*16,615*
Zimbabwe	..	..	..	..	1,065	..	4,097	*3,422*	9,625	*11,944*

Note: Data are period averages.

a. Figures in italics refer to 1990–94. b. Country has sectoral minimum wage but no minimum wage policy.

About the data

Much of the data on labor markets are collected through national reporting systems that depend on plant-level surveys. Even when these data are compiled and reported by international agencies such as the International Labour Organization or the United Nations Industrial Development Organization, differences in definitions, coverage, and units of account limit their comparability across countries. The indicators in this table are the result of a research project at the World Bank that has compiled results from more than 300 national and international sources to provide a set of uniform and representative labor market indicators. Nevertheless, many differences in reporting practices persist, some of which are described below. The purpose of the table is to explore the relationship between labor markets and economic growth in the long run, not to follow labor market developments in the short run.

Analyses of labor force participation, employment, and underemployment often rely on the number of hours worked per week, which is the time spent at the workplace working, preparing for work, or waiting for work to be supplied or for a machine to be fixed. It also includes the time spent at the workplace when no work is being performed but for which payment is made under a guaranteed work contract and time spent on short periods of rest. Hours paid for but not spent at the workplace—such as paid annual and sick leave, paid holidays, paid meal breaks, and time spent commuting—are not included. When this information is not available, the number of hours paid for—the hours actually worked plus the hours paid for but not spent in the workplace—is reported. Data on hours worked are influenced by differences in methods of compilation and coverage and by national practices relating to number of days worked and overtime, making comparisons across countries difficult.

Wages refer to remuneration in cash and in kind paid to employees at regular intervals. They exclude employer contributions to social security and pension schemes as well as other benefits received by employees under these schemes. In some countries the national minimum wage represents a "floor," with higher minimum wages for particular occupations and skills sets through collective bargaining. In those countries the agreements reached by employers associations and trade unions are extended by the government to all firms in the sector or at least to large firms. Changes in the national minimum wage are generally associated with parallel changes in the minimum wages set through collective bargaining.

In many developing countries agricultural workers are hired on a casual or daily basis and lack any social security benefits. International comparisons of agricultural wages should be subject to more caution than those of wages in other activities. The nature of the work carried out by different categories of agricultural workers and the length of the workday and workweek vary considerably from one country to another. Seasonal fluctuations in agricultural wages are more important in some countries than in others. And the methods followed in different countries for estimating the monetary value of payments in kind are not uniform.

Labor cost per worker in manufacturing is sometimes used as a measure of international competitiveness. The indicator reported in the table is the ratio of total compensation to the number of workers in the manufacturing sector. Compensation includes direct wages, salaries, other remuneration paid directly by employers, and all contributions by employers to social security programs on behalf of their employees. But there are unavoidable differences in concepts and reference periods and in reporting practices. Remuneration for time not worked, bonuses and gratuities, and housing and family allowances should be considered part of the compensation costs, along with severance and termination pay. These indirect labor costs can vary substantially from country to country, depending on labor laws and collective bargaining agreements.

International competitiveness also depends on productivity, which is often measured by value added per worker in manufacturing. The indicator reported in the table is the ratio of total value added in manufacturing to the number of employees engaged in that sector. Total value added is estimated as the difference between the value of industrial output and the value of materials and supplies for production (including fuel and purchased electricity) and cost of industrial services received.

Observations on labor costs and value added per worker are from plant surveys covering relatively large establishments, usually employing 10 or more workers and mostly in the formal sector. In high-income countries the coverage of these surveys tends to be quite good. In developing countries there is often a substantial bias toward very large establishments in the formal sector. As a result, the data may not be strictly comparable across countries. The data are converted into U.S. dollars using the average exchange rate for each year.

Definitions

• **Hours worked** are average hours per week actually worked, hours paid for, or statutory hours of work in a normal workweek for all workers (male and female) in nonagricultural activities or, if unavailable, in manufacturing. • **Minimum wage** corresponds to the most general regime for nonagricultural activities. When rates vary across sectors, only that for manufacturing (or commerce, if the manufacturing wage is unavailable) is reported. • **Agricultural wage** is the daily wage in agriculture. To ensure comparability with the other wage series, full employment over the year is assumed, although many wage earners in agriculture are employed seasonally. • **Labor cost per worker in manufacturing** is the total payroll of manufacturing establishments divided by the number of people employed or engaged in those establishments. • **Value added per worker in manufacturing** is the value added of manufacturing establishments divided by the number of people employed or engaged in those establishments.

Data sources

Data on wages and productivity are drawn from Martin Rama and Raquel Artecona's "Database of Labor Market Indicators across Countries" (2002).

Poverty

	National poverty line								International poverty line				
		Population below the poverty line				Population below the poverty line							
	Survey year	Rural %	Urban %	National %	Survey year	Rural %	Urban %	National %	Survey year	Population below $1 a day %	Poverty gap at $1 a day %	Population below $2 a day %	Poverty gap at $2 a day %
Afghanistan		..	..	..		..	..	..		..	..	..	..
Albania	2002	29.6	19.8	25.4		..	..	..	2002[a]	<2	<0.5	11.8	2.0
Algeria	1988	16.6	7.3	12.2	1995	30.3	14.7	22.6	1995[a]	<2	<0.5	15.1	3.8
Angola		..	..	..		..	..	..		..	..	..	..
Argentina	1995	..	28.4		1998	..	29.9	..	2003[b]	7.0	2.0	23.0	8.4
Armenia	1998–99	50.8	58.3	55.1	2001	48.7	51.9	50.9	2003[a]	<2	<0.5	31.1	7.1
Australia		..	..	..		..	..	..		..	..	..	..
Austria		..	..	..		..	..	..		..	..	..	..
Azerbaijan	1995	..	..	68.1	2001	42.0	55.0	49.0	2002[a]	<2	<0.5	<2	<0.5
Bangladesh	1995–96	55.2	29.4	51.0	2000	53.0	36.6	49.8	2000[a]	36.0	8.1	82.8	36.3
Belarus	2000	..	..	41.9		..	..	..	2002[a]	<2	<0.5	<2	<0.5
Belgium		..	..	..		..	..	..		..	..	..	..
Benin	1995	25.2	28.5	26.5	1999	33.0	23.3	29.0	2003[a]	30.9	8.2	73.7	31.7
Bolivia	1997	77.3	53.8	63.2	1999	81.7	50.6	62.7	2002[b]	23.2	13.6	42.2	23.2
Bosnia and Herzegovina	2001–02	19.9	13.8	19.5		..	..	..		..	..	..	..
Botswana		..	..	..		..	..	..	1993[a]	23.5	7.7	50.1	22.8
Brazil	1996	54.0	15.4	23.9	1998	51.4	14.7	22.0	2003[b]	7.5	3.4	21.2	8.5
Bulgaria	1997	..	..	36.0	2001	..	..	12.8	2003[a]	<2	<0.5	6.1	1.5
Burkina Faso	1998	61.1	22.4	54.6	2003	52.4	19.2	46.4	2003[a]	27.2	7.3	71.8	30.4
Burundi	1990	36.0	43.0	36.4		..	..	..	1998[a]	54.6	22.7	87.6	48.9
Cambodia	1997	40.1	21.1	36.1	1999	40.1	13.9	35.9	1997[a]	34.1	9.7	77.7	34.5
Cameroon	1996	59.6	41.4	53.3	2001	49.9	22.1	40.2	2001[a]	17.1	4.1	50.6	19.3
Canada		..	..	..		..	..	..		..	..	..	..
Central African Republic		..	..	..		..	..	..	1993[a]	66.6	38.1	84.0	58.4
Chad	1995–96	67.0	63.0	64.0		..	..	..		..	..	..	..
Chile	1996	..	..	19.9	1998	..	..	17.0	2000[b]	<2	<0.5	9.6	2.5
China	1996	7.9	<2	6.0	1998	4.6	<2	4.6	2001[a]	16.6	3.9	46.7	18.4
Hong Kong, China		..	..	..		..	..	..		..	..	..	..
Colombia	1995	79.0	48.0	60.0	1999	79.0	55.0	64.0	2003[b]	7.0	3.1	17.8	7.7
Congo, Dem. Rep.		..	..	..		..	..	..		..	..	..	..
Congo, Rep.		..	..	..		..	..	..		..	..	..	..
Costa Rica	1992	25.5	19.2	22.0		..	..	..	2001[b]	2.2	0.8	7.5	2.8
Côte d'Ivoire		..	..	..		..	..	..	2002[a]	14.8	4.1	48.8	18.4
Croatia		..	..	..		..	..	..	2001[a]	<2	<0.5	<2	<0.5
Cuba		..	..	..		..	..	..		..	..	..	..
Czech Republic		..	..	..		..	..	..	1996[b]	<2	<0.5	<2	<0.5
Denmark		..	..	..		..	..	..		..	..	..	..
Dominican Republic	1992	49.0	19.3	33.9	1998	42.1	20.5	28.6	2003[b]	2.5	0.8	11.0	3.6
Ecuador	1995	56.0	19.0	34.0	1998	69.0	30.0	46.0	1998[b]	15.8	6.3	37.2	15.8
Egypt, Arab Rep.	1995–96	23.3	22.5	22.9	1999–2000	..	..	16.7	1999–2000[a]	3.1	<0.5	43.9	11.3
El Salvador	1992	55.7	43.1	48.3		..	..	..	2002[b]	19.0	9.3	40.6	17.7
Eritrea	1993–94	..	..	53.0		..	..	..		..	..	..	..
Estonia	1995	14.7	6.8	8.9		..	..	..	2003[a]	<2	<0.5	7.5	1.9
Ethiopia	1995–96	47.0	33.3	45.5	1999–2000	45.0	37.0	44.2	1999–2000[a]	23.0	4.8	77.8	29.6
Finland		..	..	..		..	..	..		..	..	..	..
France		..	..	..		..	..	..		..	..	..	..
Gabon		..	..	..		..	..	..		..	..	..	..
Gambia, The	1992	..	..	64.0	1998	61.0	48.0	57.6	1998[a]	59.3	28.8	82.9	51.1
Georgia	2002	55.4	48.5	52.1	2003	52.7	56.2	54.5	2003[a]	6.5	2.1	25.3	8.6
Germany		..	..	..		..	..	..		..	..	..	..
Ghana	1992	..	..	50.0	1998–99	49.9	18.6	39.5	1998–99[a]	44.8	17.3	78.5	40.8
Greece		..	..	..		..	..	..		..	..	..	..
Guatemala	1989	71.9	33.7	57.9	2000	74.5	27.1	56.2	2002[b]	13.5	5.5	31.9	13.8
Guinea	1994	..	..	40.0		..	..	..		..	..	..	..
Guinea-Bissau		..	..	..		..	..	..		..	..	..	..
Haiti	1987	..	..	65.0	1995	66.0	..	..	2001[b]	53.9	26.6	78.0	47.4

	National poverty line								International poverty line				
		Population below the poverty line				Population below the poverty line							
	Survey year	Rural %	Urban %	National %	Survey year	Rural %	Urban %	National %	Survey year	Population below $1 a day %	Poverty gap at $1 a day %	Population below $2 a day %	Poverty gap at $2 a day %
Honduras	1997	58.0	35.0	47.0	1999	58.0	37.0	48.0	1999[b]	20.7	7.5	44.0	20.2
Hungary	1993	..	..	14.5	1997	..	..	17.3	2002[a]	<2	<0.5	<2	<0.5
India	1993–94	37.3	32.4	36.0	1999–2000	30.2	24.7	28.6	1999–2000[a]	34.7	8.2	52.4	15.7
Indonesia	1996	..	..	15.7	1999	34.4	16.1	27.1	2002[a]	7.5	0.9	52.4	15.7
Iran, Islamic Rep.		..	..	..		..	..	..	1998[a]	<2	<0.5	7.3	1.5
Iraq		..	..	..		..	..	..		..	..	..	..
Ireland		..	..	..		..	..	..		..	..	..	..
Israel		..	..	..		..	..	..		..	..	..	..
Italy		..	..	..		..	..	..		..	..	..	..
Jamaica	1995	37.0	18.7	27.5	2000	25.1	12.8	18.7	2000[a]	<2	<0.5	13.3	2.7
Japan		..	..	..		..	..	..		..	..	..	..
Jordan	1991	..	..	15.0	1997	..	..	11.7	2002–03[a]	<2	<0.5	7.0	1.5
Kazakhstan	1996	39.0	30.0	34.6		..	..	..	2003[a]	<2	<.5	16.0	3.8
Kenya	1994	47.0	29.0	40.0	1997	53.0	49.0	52.0	1997[a]	22.8	5.9	58.3	23.9
Korea, Dem. Rep.		..	..	..		..	..	..		..	..	..	..
Korea, Rep.		..	..	..		..	..	..	1998[b]	<2	<0.5	<2	<0.5
Kuwait		..	..	..		..	..	..		..	..	..	..
Kyrgyz Republic	2000	56.4	43.9	52.0	2001	51.0	41.2	47.6	2003[a]	<2	<0.5	21.4	4.4
Lao PDR	1993	48.7	33.1	45.0	1997–98	41.0	26.9	38.6	2002[a]	27.0	6.1	74.1	30.2
Latvia		..	..	..		..	..	..	2003[a]	<2	<0.5	4.7	1.2
Lebanon		..	..	..		..	..	..		..	..	..	..
Lesotho		..	..	..		..	..	..	1995[a]	36.4	19.0	56.1	33.1
Liberia		..	..	..		..	..	..		..	..	..	..
Libya		..	..	..		..	..	..		..	..	..	..
Lithuania		..	..	..		..	..	..	2003[a]	<2	<0.5	7.8	1.8
Macedonia, FYR		..	..	..		..	..	..	2003[a]	<2	<0.5	<2	<0.5
Madagascar	1997	76.0	63.2	73.3	1999	76.7	52.1	71.3	2001[a]	61.0	27.9	85.1	51.8
Malawi	1990–91	..	..	54.0	1997–98	66.5	54.9	65.3	1997–98[a]	41.7	14.8	76.1	38.3
Malaysia	1989	..	..	15.5		..	..	..	1997[b]	<2	<0.5	9.3	2.0
Mali	1998	75.9	30.1	63.8		..	..	..	1994[a]	72.3	37.4	90.6	60.5
Mauritania	1996	65.5	30.1	50.0	2000	61.2	25.4	46.3	2000[a]	25.9	7.6	63.1	26.8
Mauritius		..	..	..		..	..	..		..	..	..	..
Mexico	1996	52.4	26.5	37.1	2002	34.8	11.4	20.3	2002[a]	4.5	1.2	20.4	6.5
Moldova	2001	64.1	58.0	62.4	2002	67.2	42.6	48.5	2001[a]	22.0	5.8	63.7	25.1
Mongolia	1995	33.1	38.5	36.3	1998	32.6	39.4	*35.6*	1998[a]	27.0	8.1	74.9	30.6
Morocco	1990–91	18.0	7.6	13.1	1998–99	27.2	12.0	19.0	1999[a]	<2	<0.5	14.3	3.1
Mozambique	1996–97	71.3	62.0	69.4		..	..	..	1996[a]	37.9	12.0	78.4	36.8
Myanmar		..	..	..		..	..	..		..	..	..	..
Namibia		..	..	..		..	..	..	1993[b]	34.9	14.0	55.8	30.4
Nepal	1995–96	43.3	21.6	41.8	2003–04	34.6	9.6	30.9	2003–04[a]	24.1	5.4	68.5	26.8
Netherlands		..	..	..		..	..	..		..	..	..	..
New Zealand		..	..	..		..	..	..		..	..	..	..
Nicaragua	1993	76.1	31.9	50.3	1998	68.5	30.5	47.9	2001[a]	45.1	16.7	79.9	41.2
Niger	1989–93	66.0	52.0	63.0		..	..	..	1995[a]	60.6	34.0	85.8	54.6
Nigeria	1985	49.5	31.7	43.0	1992–93	36.4	30.4	34.1	2003[a]	70.8	34.5	92.4	59.5
Norway		..	..	..		..	..	..		..	..	..	..
Oman		..	..	..		..	..	..		..	..	..	..
Pakistan	1993	33.4	17.2	28.6	1998–99	35.9	24.2	32.6	2002[a]	17.0	3.1	73.6	26.1
Panama	1997	64.9	15.3	37.3		..	..	..	2002[b]	6.5	2.3	17.1	6.9
Papua New Guinea	1996	41.3	16.1	37.5		..	..	..		..	..	..	..
Paraguay	1991	28.5	19.7	21.8		..	..	..	2002[b]	16.4	7.4	33.2	16.2
Peru	1994	67.0	46.1	53.5	1997	64.7	40.4	49.0	2002[b]	12.5	4.4	31.8	13.4
Philippines	1994	53.1	28.0	40.6	1997	50.7	21.5	36.8	2000[a]	15.5	3.0	47.5	17.8
Poland	1993	..	..	23.8		..	..	..	2002[a]	<2	<0.5	<2	<0.5
Portugal		..	..	..		..	..	..	1994[b]	<2	<0.5	<2	<0.5
Puerto Rico		..	..	..		..	..	..		..	..	..	..

2.7 Poverty

	National poverty line								International poverty line				
		Population below the poverty line				Population below the poverty line							
	Survey year	Rural %	Urban %	National %	Survey year	Rural %	Urban %	National %	Survey year	Population below $1 a day %	Poverty gap at $1 a day %	Population below $2 a day %	Poverty gap at $2 a day %
Romania	1994	27.9	20.4	21.5		..	..	..	2003[a]	<2	0.5	12.9	3.0
Russian Federation	1994	..	..	30.9		..	..	..	2002[a]	<2	<0.5	12.1	3.1
Rwanda	1993	..	..	51.2	1999–2000	65.7	14.3	60.3	1999–2000[a]	51.7	20.0	83.7	45.5
Saudi Arabia		..	..	..		..	..	..		..	..	..	..
Senegal	1992	40.4	23.7	33.4		..	..	..	1995[a]	22.3	5.7	63.0	25.2
Serbia and Montenegro		..	..	..		..	..	..		..	..	..	..
Sierra Leone	1989	..	..	82.8	2003–04	79.0	56.4	70.2	1989[a]	57.0	39.5	74.5	51.8
Singapore		..	..	..		..	..	..		..	..	..	..
Slovak Republic		..	..	..		..	..	..	1996[b]	<2	<0.5	2.9	0.8
Slovenia		..	..	..		..	..	..	1998[a]	<2	<0.5	<2	<0.5
Somalia		..	..	..		..	..	..		..	..	..	..
South Africa		..	..	..		..	..	..	2000[a]	10.7	1.7	34.1	12.6
Spain		..	..	..		..	..	..		..	..	..	..
Sri Lanka	1990–91	22.0	15.0	20.0	1995–96	27.0	15.0	25.0	2002[a]	5.6	0.8	41.6	11.9
Sudan		..	..	..		..	..	..		..	..	..	..
Swaziland		..	..	..		..	..	..		..	..	..	..
Sweden		..	..	..		..	..	..		..	..	..	..
Switzerland		..	..	..		..	..	..		..	..	..	..
Syrian Arab Republic		..	..	..		..	..	..		..	..	..	..
Tajikistan		..	..	..		..	..	..	2003[a]	7.4	1.3	42.8	13.0
Tanzania	1991	40.8	31.2	38.6	2000–01	38.7	29.5	35.7	2000–01[a]	57.8	20.7	89.9	49.3
Thailand	1990	..	..	18.0	1992	15.5	10.2	13.1	2002[a]	<2	<0.5	25.2	6.2
Togo	1987–89	..	..	32.3		..	..	..		..	..	..	..
Trinidad and Tobago	1992	20.0	24.0	21.0		..	..	..	1992[b]	12.4	3.5	39.0	14.6
Tunisia	1990	13.1	3.5	7.4	1995	13.9	3.6	7.6	2000[a]	<2	<0.5	6.6	1.3
Turkey	1994	..	..	28.3	2002	34.5	22.0	27.0	2003[a]	3.4	0.8	18.7	5.7
Turkmenistan		..	..	..		..	..	..		..	..	..	..
Uganda	1999–2000	37.4	9.6	33.8	2002–03	41.7	12.2	37.7		..	..	..	..
Ukraine	2000	34.9		31.5	2003	28.4	..	19.5	2003[b]	<2	<0.5	4.9	0.9
United Arab Emirates		..	..	..		..	..	..		..	..	..	..
United Kingdom		..	..	..		..	..	..		..	..	..	..
United States		..	..	..		..	..	..		..	..	..	..
Uruguay	1994	..	20.2	..	1998	..	24.7	..	2003[b]	<2	<0.5	5.7	1.6
Uzbekistan	2000	30.5	22.5	27.5		..	..	..		..	..	..	..
Venezuela, RB	1989	..	..	31.3		..	..	..	2000[b]	8.3	2.8	27.6	10.2
Vietnam	1998	45.5	9.2	37.4	2002	35.6	6.6	28.9		..	..	..	..
West Bank and Gaza		..	..	..		..	..	..		..	..	..	..
Yemen, Rep.	1998	45.0	30.8	41.8		..	..	..	1998[a]	15.7	4.5	45.2	15.0
Zambia	1996	82.8	46.0	69.2	1998	83.1	56.0	72.9	2002–03[a]	75.8	36.4	94.1	62.2
Zimbabwe	1990–91	35.8	3.4	25.8	1995–96	48.0	7.9	34.9	1995–96[a]	56.1	24.2	83.0	48.2

a. Expenditure base. b. Income base.

2.7a

Regional poverty estimates

Region	1981	1984	1987	1990	1993	1996	1999	2002[a]
People living on less than $1 a day (millions)								
East Asia & Pacific	796	562	426	472	415	287	282	214
China	634	425	308	375	334	212	223	180
Europe & Central Asia	3	2	2	2	17	20	30	10
Latin America & Caribbean	36	46	45	49	52	52	54	47
Middle East & North Africa	9	8	7	6	4	5	8	5
South Asia	475	460	473	462	476	461	429	437
Sub-Saharan Africa	164	198	219	227	242	271	294	303
Total	**1,482**	**1,277**	**1,171**	**1,218**	**1,208**	**1,097**	**1,096**	**1,015**
Excluding China	848	852	863	844	873	886	873	835
Share of people living on less than $1 a day (%)								
East Asia & Pacific	57.7	38.9	28.0	29.6	24.9	16.6	15.7	11.6
China	63.8	41.0	28.5	33.0	28.4	17.4	17.8	14.0
Europe & Central Asia	0.7	0.5	0.4	0.5	3.7	4.3	6.3	2.1
Latin America & Caribbean	9.7	11.8	10.9	11.3	11.3	10.7	10.5	8.9
Middle East & North Africa	5.1	3.8	3.2	2.3	1.6	2.0	2.6	1.6
South Asia	51.5	46.8	45.0	41.3	40.1	36.6	32.2	31.2
Sub-Saharan Africa	41.6	46.3	46.8	44.6	44.0	45.6	45.7	44.0
Total	**40.4**	**32.8**	**28.4**	**27.9**	**26.3**	**22.8**	**21.8**	**19.4**
Excluding China	31.7	29.8	28.4	26.1	25.6	24.6	23.1	21.1
People living on less than $2 a day (millions)								
East Asia & Pacific	1,170	1,109	1,028	1,116	1,079	922	900	748
China	876	814	731	825	803	650	627	533
Europe & Central Asia	20	18	15	23	81	98	113	76
Latin America & Caribbean	99	119	115	125	136	117	127	123
Middle East & North Africa	52	50	53	51	52	61	70	61
South Asia	821	859	911	958	1,005	1,029	1,039	1,091
Sub-Saharan Africa	288	326	355	382	410	447	489	516
Total	**2,450**	**2,480**	**2,478**	**2,654**	**2,764**	**2,674**	**2,739**	**2,614**
Excluding China	1,574	1,666	1,747	1,829	1,961	2,024	2,111	2,082
Share of people living on less than $2 a day (%)								
East Asia & Pacific	84.8	76.6	67.7	69.9	64.8	53.3	50.3	40.7
China	88.1	78.5	67.4	72.6	68.1	53.4	50.1	41.6
Europe & Central Asia	4.7	4.1	3.3	4.9	17.2	20.7	23.8	16.1
Latin America & Caribbean	26.9	30.4	27.8	28.4	29.5	24.1	25.1	23.4
Middle East & North Africa	28.9	25.2	24.2	21.4	20.2	22.3	24.3	19.8
South Asia	89.1	87.2	86.7	85.5	84.5	81.7	78.1	77.8
Sub-Saharan Africa	73.3	76.1	76.1	75.0	74.6	75.1	76.1	74.9
Total	**66.7**	**63.7**	**60.1**	**60.8**	**60.2**	**55.5**	**54.4**	**50.0**
Excluding China	58.8	58.4	57.5	56.6	57.4	56.3	55.8	52.7

Note: Estimates are computed based on population data from *World Development Indicators 2005*.
a. Preliminary estimates not strictly comparable with earlier estimates. See *About the data* for more information.

2.7 Poverty

About the data

The World Bank produced its first global poverty estimates for developing countries for *World Development Report 1990* using household survey data for 22 countries (Ravallion, Datt, and van de Walle 1991). Incorporating survey data collected during the last 15 years, the database has expanded considerably and now includes 440 surveys representing almost 100 developing countries. Some 1.1 million randomly sampled households were interviewed in these surveys, representing 93 percent of the population of developing countries. The surveys asked detailed questions on sources of income and how it was spent and on other household characteristics such as the number of people sharing that income. Most interviewas were conducted by staff of government statistics offices. Along with improvements in data coverage and quality, the underlying methodology has also improved, resulting in better and more comprehensive estimates.

Data availability

Since 1979 there has been considerable expansion in the number of countries that field such surveys, the frequency of the surveys, and the quality of their data. The number of data sets rose dramatically from a mere 13 between 1979 and 1981 to 100 between 1997 and 1999. The drop to 41 available surveys after 1999 reflects the lag between the time data are collected and the time they become available for analysis, not a reduction in data collection. Data coverage is improving in all regions, but Sub-Saharan Africa continues to lag, with only 28 of 48 countries having at least one data set available. A complete overview of data availability by year and country can be obtained at http://iresearch.worldbank.org/povcalnet/.

Data quality

The problems of estimating poverty and comparing poverty rates do not end with data availability. Several other issues, some related to data quality, also arise in measuring household living standards from survey data. One relates to the choice of income or consumption as a welfare indicator. Income is generally more difficult to measure accurately, and consumption comes closer to the notion of standard of living. And income can vary over time even if the standard of living does not. But consumption data are not always available. Another issue is that household surveys can differ widely, for example, in the number of consumer goods they identify. And even similar surveys may not be strictly comparable because of differences in timing or the quality and training of survey enumerators.

Comparisons of countries at different levels of development also pose a potential problem because of differences in the relative importance of consumption of nonmarket goods. The local market value of all consumption in kind (including own production, particularly important in underdeveloped rural economies) should be included in total consumption expenditure. Similarly, imputed profit from the production of nonmarket goods should be included in income. This is not always done, though such omissions were a far bigger problem in surveys before the 1980s. Most survey data now include valuations for consumption or income from own production. Nonetheless, valuation methods vary. For example, some surveys use the price in the nearest market, while others use the average farmgate selling price.

Whenever possible, the table uses consumption data for deciding who is poor and income surveys only when consumption data are unavailable. In recent editions there has been a change in how income surveys are used. In the past, average household income was adjusted to accord with consumption and income data from national accounts. But in testing this approach using data for some 20 countries for which income and consumption expenditure data were both available from the same surveys, income was found to yield a higher mean than consumption but also higher inequality. When poverty measures based on consumption and income were compared, these two effects roughly cancelled each other out: statistically, there was no significant difference. So recent editions use income data to estimate poverty directly, without adjusting average income measures.

International poverty lines

International comparisons of poverty estimates entail both conceptual and practical problems. Countries have different definitions of poverty, and consistent comparisons across countries can be difficult. Local poverty lines tend to have higher purchasing power in rich countries, where more generous standards are used, than in poor countries. Is it reasonable to treat two people with the same standard of living—in terms of their command over commodities—differently because one happens to live in a better-off country?

Poverty measures based on an international poverty line attempt to hold the real value of the poverty line constant across countries, as is done when making comparisons over time. The commonly used $1 a day standard, measured in 1985 international prices and adjusted to local currency using purchasing power parities (PPPs), was chosen for the World Bank's *World Development Report 1990: Poverty* because it is typical of the poverty lines in low-income countries. PPP exchange rates, such as those from the Penn World Tables or the World Bank, are used because they take into account the local prices of goods and services not traded internationally. But PPP rates were designed for comparing aggregates from national accounts, not for making international poverty comparisons. As a result, there is no certainty that an international poverty line measures the same degree of need or deprivation across countries.

Early editions of *World Development Indicators* used PPPs from the Penn World Tables. Recent editions use 1993 consumption PPP estimates produced by the World Bank. Recalculated in 1993 PPP terms, the original international poverty line of $1 a day in 1985 PPP terms is now about $1.08 a day. Any revisions in the PPP of a country to incorporate better price indexes can produce dramatically different poverty lines in local currency.

Issues also arise when comparing poverty measures within countries. For example, the cost of living is typically higher in urban than in rural areas. One reason is that food staples tend to be more expensive in urban areas. So the urban monetary poverty line should be higher than the rural poverty line. But it is not always clear that the difference between urban and rural poverty lines found in practice reflects only differences in the cost of living. In some countries the urban poverty line in common use has a higher real value—meaning that it allows the purchase of more commodities for consumption—than does the rural poverty line. Sometimes the difference has been so large as to imply that the incidence of poverty is greater in urban than in rural areas, even though the reverse is found when adjustments are made only for differences in the cost of living. As with international comparisons, when the real value of the poverty line varies it is not clear how meaningful such urban-rural comparisons are.

By combining all this information, a team in the World Bank's Development Research Group calculates the number of people living below various international poverty lines, as well as other poverty and inequality measures that are published in *World Development Indicators*. The database is updated annually as new survey data become available, and a major reassessment of progress against poverty is made about every three years.

Do it yourself: PovcalNet

Recently, this research team developed *PovcalNet*, an interactive Web-based computational tool that allows users to replicate the calculations by the World Bank's researchers in estimating the extent of absolute poverty in the world. *PovcalNet* is self-contained and powered by reliable built-in software that performs the relevant calculations from a primary database. The underlying software can also be downloaded from the site and used with distributional data of various formats. The *PovcalNet* primary database consists of distributional data calculated directly from household survey data. Detailed information for each of these is also available from the site.

Estimation from distributional data requires an interpolation method. The method chosen was Lorenz curves with flexible functional forms, which have proved reliable in past work. The Lorenz curve can be graphed as the cumulative percentages of total consumption or income against the cumulative number of people, starting with the poorest individual. The empirical Lorenz curves estimated by *PovcalNet* are weighted by household size, so they are based on percentiles of population, not households.

PovcalNet also allows users to calculate poverty measures under different assumptions. For example, instead of $1 a day, users can specify a different poverty line, say $1.50 or $3. Users can also specify different PPP rates and aggregate the estimates using alternative country groupings (for example, UN country groupings or groupings based on average incomes) or a selected set of individual countries. *PovcalNet* is available online at http://iresearch.worldbank.org/povcalnet/.

Note on the 2002 estimates

The 2002 estimates are adapted from *Global Economic Prospects 2006* (page 9, table 1.3). Note that a typesetting error occurred in the printed edition of *Global Economic Prospects 2006*; the 2002 poverty rate estimates reported in table 2.7a are the correct estimates.

Definitions

• **Survey year** is the year in which the underlying data were collected. • **Rural poverty rate** is the percentage of the rural population living below the national rural poverty line. • **Urban poverty rate** is the percentage of the urban population living below the national urban poverty line. • **National poverty rate** is the percentage of the population living below the national poverty line. National estimates are based on population-weighted subgroup estimates from household surveys. • **Population below $1 a day** and **population below $2 a day** are the percentages of the population living on less than $1.08 a day and $2.15 a day at 1993 international prices. As a result of revisions in PPP exchange rates, poverty rates for individual countries cannot be compared with poverty rates reported in earlier editions. • **Poverty gap** is the mean shortfall from the poverty line (counting the nonpoor as having zero shortfall), expressed as a percentage of the poverty line. This measure reflects the depth of poverty as well as its incidence.

Data sources

The poverty measures are prepared by the World Bank's Development Research Group. The national poverty lines are based on the World Bank's country poverty assessments. The international poverty lines are based on nationally representative primary household surveys conducted by national statistical offices or by private agencies under the supervision of government or international agencies and obtained from government statistical offices and World Bank Group country departments. The World Bank Group has prepared an annual review of its poverty work since 1993. For details on data sources and methods used in deriving the World Bank's latest estimates, see Chen and Ravallion (2004), "How Have the World's Poorest Fared Since the Early 1980s?"

2.8 Distribution of income or consumption

	Survey year	Gini index	Percentage share of income or consumption						
			Lowest 10%	Lowest 20%	Second 20%	Third 20%	Fourth 20%	Highest 20%	Highest 10%
Afghanistan		..	..	..	..	..	..	..	..
Albania	2002[a]	28.2	3.8	9.1	13.5	17.3	22.8	37.4	22.4
Algeria	1995[a]	35.3	2.8	7.0	11.6	16.1	22.7	42.6	26.8
Angola		..	..	..	..	..	..	..	..
Argentina[b]	2003[c]	52.8	1.1	3.2	7.0	12.1	20.7	56.8	39.6
Armenia	2003[a]	33.8	3.6	8.5	12.3	15.7	20.6	42.8	29.0
Australia	1994[c]	35.2	2.0	5.9	12.0	17.2	23.6	41.3	25.4
Austria	2000[c]	29.1	3.3	8.6	13.3	17.4	22.9	37.8	23.0
Azerbaijan	2002[a]	19.0	5.4	12.2	15.8	18.7	22.2	31.1	18.0
Bangladesh	2000[a]	31.8	3.9	9.0	12.5	15.9	21.2	41.3	26.7
Belarus	2002[a]	29.7	3.4	8.5	13.2	17.3	22.7	38.3	23.5
Belgium	2000[c]	33.0	3.4	8.5	13.0	16.3	20.8	41.4	28.1
Benin	2003[a]	36.5	3.1	7.4	11.3	15.4	21.5	44.5	29.0
Bolivia	2002[c]	60.1	0.3	1.5	5.9	10.9	18.7	63.0	47.2
Bosnia and Herzegovina	2001[a]	26.2	3.9	9.5	14.2	17.9	22.6	35.8	21.4
Botswana	1993[a]	63.0	0.7	2.2	4.9	8.2	14.4	70.3	56.6
Brazil	2003[c]	58.0	0.8	2.6	6.2	10.7	18.4	62.1	45.8
Bulgaria	2003[a]	29.2	3.4	8.7	13.7	17.2	22.1	38.3	23.9
Burkina Faso	2003[a]	39.5	2.8	6.9	10.9	14.5	20.5	47.2	32.2
Burundi	1998[a]	42.4	1.7	5.1	10.3	15.1	21.5	48.0	32.8
Cambodia	1997[a]	40.4	2.9	6.9	10.7	14.7	20.1	47.6	33.8
Cameroon	2001[a]	44.6	2.3	5.6	9.3	13.7	20.4	50.9	35.4
Canada	2000[c]	32.6	2.6	7.2	12.7	17.2	23.0	39.9	24.8
Central African Republic	1993[a]	61.3	0.7	2.0	4.9	9.6	18.5	65.0	47.7
Chad		..	..	..	..	..	..	..	..
Chile	2000[c]	57.1	1.2	3.3	6.6	10.5	17.4	62.2	47.0
China	2001[a]	44.7	1.8	4.7	9.0	14.2	22.1	50.0	33.1
Hong Kong, China	1996[c]	43.4	2.0	5.3	9.4	13.9	20.7	50.7	34.9
Colombia	2003[c]	58.6	0.7	2.5	6.2	10.6	18.0	62.7	46.9
Congo, Dem. Rep.		..	..	..	..	..	..	..	..
Congo, Rep.		..	..	..	..	..	..	..	..
Costa Rica	2001[c]	49.9	1.3	3.9	8.1	12.8	20.4	54.8	38.4
Côte d'Ivoire	2002[a]	44.6	2.0	5.2	9.1	13.7	21.3	50.7	34.0
Croatia	2001[a]	29.0	3.4	8.3	12.8	16.8	22.6	39.6	24.5
Cuba		..	..	..	..	..	..	..	..
Czech Republic	1996[c]	25.4	4.3	10.3	14.5	17.7	21.7	35.9	22.4
Denmark	1997[c]	24.7	2.6	8.3	14.7	18.2	22.9	35.8	21.3
Dominican Republic	2003[c]	51.7	1.4	3.9	7.8	12.1	19.4	56.8	41.3
Ecuador	1998[a]	43.7	0.9	3.3	7.5	11.7	19.4	58.0	41.6
Egypt, Arab Rep.	1999–2000[a]	34.4	3.7	8.6	12.1	15.4	20.4	43.6	29.5
El Salvador	2002[c]	52.4	0.7	2.7	7.5	12.8	21.2	55.9	38.8
Eritrea		..	..	..	..	..	..	..	..
Estonia	2003[a]	35.8	2.5	6.7	11.8	16.3	22.4	42.8	27.6
Ethiopia	1999–00[a]	30.0	3.9	9.1	13.2	16.8	21.5	39.4	25.5
Finland	2000[c]	26.9	4.0	9.6	14.1	17.5	22.1	36.7	22.6
France	1995[c]	32.7	2.8	7.2	12.6	17.2	22.8	40.2	25.1
Gabon		..	..	..	..	..	..	..	..
Gambia, The	1998[a]	50.2	1.8	4.8	8.7	12.8	20.3	53.4	37.0
Georgia	2003[a]	40.4	2.0	5.6	10.5	15.3	22.3	46.4	30.3
Germany	2000[c]	28.3	3.2	8.5	13.7	17.8	23.1	36.9	22.1
Ghana	1998–99[a]	40.8	2.1	5.6	10.1	14.9	22.9	46.6	30.0
Greece	2000[c]	34.3	2.5	6.7	11.9	16.8	23.0	41.5	26.0
Guatemala	2002[c]	55.1	0.9	2.9	7.0	11.6	19.0	59.5	43.4
Guinea	1994[a]	40.3	2.6	6.4	10.4	14.8	21.2	47.2	32.0
Guinea-Bissau	1993[a]	47.0	2.1	5.2	8.8	13.1	19.4	53.4	39.3
Haiti	2001[c]	59.2	0.7	2.4	6.2	10.4	17.7	63.4	47.7

Distribution of income or consumption 2.8

	Survey year	Gini index	Percentage share of income or consumption						
			Lowest 10%	Lowest 20%	Second 20%	Third 20%	Fourth 20%	Highest 20%	Highest 10%
Honduras	2003[c]	53.8	1.2	3.4	7.1	11.6	19.6	58.3	42.2
Hungary	2002[a]	26.9	4.0	9.5	13.9	17.6	22.4	36.5	22.2
India	1999–2000[a]	32.5	3.9	8.9	12.3	16.0	21.2	43.3	28.5
Indonesia	2002[a]	34.3	3.6	8.4	11.9	15.4	21.0	43.3	28.5
Iran, Islamic Rep.	1998[a]	43.0	2.0	5.1	9.4	14.1	21.5	49.9	33.7
Iraq		..	..	..	..	..	..	..	..
Ireland	2000[c]	34.3	2.9	7.4	12.3	16.3	21.9	42.0	27.2
Israel	2001[c]	39.2	2.1	5.7	10.5	15.9	23.0	44.9	28.8
Italy	2000[c]	36.0	2.3	6.5	12.0	16.8	22.8	42.0	26.8
Jamaica	2000[a]	37.9	2.7	6.7	10.7	15.0	21.7	46.0	30.3
Japan	1993[c]	24.9	4.8	10.6	14.2	17.6	22.0	35.7	21.7
Jordan	2002–03[a]	38.8	2.7	6.7	10.8	14.9	21.3	46.3	30.6
Kazakhstan	2003[a]	33.9	3.0	7.4	11.9	16.4	22.8	41.5	25.9
Kenya	1997[a]	42.5	2.5	6.0	9.8	14.3	20.8	49.1	33.9
Korea, Dem. Rep.		..	..	..	..	..	..	..	..
Korea, Rep.	1998[c]	31.6	2.9	7.9	13.6	18.0	23.1	37.5	22.5
Kuwait		..	..	..	..	..	..	..	..
Kyrgyz Republic	2003[a]	30.3	3.8	8.9	12.8	16.4	22.5	39.4	24.3
Lao PDR	2002[a]	34.6	3.4	8.1	11.9	15.6	21.1	43.3	28.5
Latvia	2003[a]	37.7	2.5	6.6	11.2	15.5	22.0	44.7	29.1
Lebanon		..	..	..	..	..	..	..	..
Lesotho	1995[a]	63.2	0.5	1.5	4.3	8.9	18.8	66.5	48.3
Liberia		..	..	..	..	..	..	..	..
Libya		..	..	..	..	..	..	..	..
Lithuania	2003[a]	36.0	2.7	6.8	11.6	16.0	22.3	43.2	27.7
Macedonia, FYR	2003[a]	39.0	2.4	6.1	10.8	15.5	22.2	45.5	29.6
Madagascar	2001[a]	47.5	1.9	4.9	8.5	12.7	20.4	53.5	36.6
Malawi	1997[a]	50.3	1.9	4.9	8.5	12.3	18.3	56.1	42.2
Malaysia	1997[c]	49.2	1.7	4.4	8.1	12.9	20.3	54.3	38.4
Mali	1994[a]	50.5	1.8	4.6	8.0	11.9	19.3	56.2	40.4
Mauritania	2000[a]	39.0	2.5	6.2	10.6	15.2	22.3	45.7	29.5
Mauritius		..	..	..	..	..	..	..	..
Mexico	2002[a]	49.5	1.6	4.3	8.3	12.6	19.7	55.1	39.4
Moldova	2003[a]	33.2	3.2	7.8	12.2	16.5	22.1	41.4	26.4
Mongolia	1998[a]	30.3	2.1	5.6	10.0	13.8	19.4	51.2	37.0
Morocco	1998–99[a]	39.5	2.6	6.5	10.6	14.8	21.3	46.6	30.9
Mozambique	1996–97[a]	39.6	2.5	6.5	10.8	15.1	21.1	46.5	31.7
Myanmar		..	..	..	..	..	..	..	..
Namibia	1993[c]	74.3	0.5	1.4	3.0	5.4	11.5	78.7	64.5
Nepal	2003–04[a]	47.2	2.6	6.0	9.0	12.4	18.0	54.6	40.6
Netherlands	1999[c]	30.9	2.5	7.6	13.2	17.2	23.3	38.7	22.9
New Zealand	1997[c]	36.2	2.2	6.4	11.4	15.8	22.6	43.8	27.8
Nicaragua	2001[a]	43.1	2.2	5.6	9.8	14.2	21.1	49.3	33.8
Niger	1995[a]	50.5	0.8	2.6	7.1	13.9	23.1	53.3	35.4
Nigeria	2003[a]	43.7	1.9	5.0	9.6	14.5	21.7	49.2	33.2
Norway	2000[c]	25.8	3.9	9.6	14.0	17.2	22.0	37.2	23.4
Oman		..	..	..	..	..	..	..	..
Pakistan	2002[a]	30.6	4.0	9.3	13.0	16.3	21.1	40.3	26.3
Panama	2002[c]	56.4	0.8	2.5	6.4	11.2	19.6	60.3	43.6
Papua New Guinea	1996[a]	50.9	1.7	4.5	7.9	11.9	19.2	56.5	40.5
Paraguay	2002[c]	57.8	0.6	2.2	6.3	11.3	18.8	61.3	45.4
Peru	2002[c]	54.6	1.1	3.2	7.1	11.8	19.3	58.7	43.2
Philippines	2000[a]	46.1	2.2	5.4	8.8	13.1	20.5	52.3	36.3
Poland	2002[a]	34.5	3.1	7.5	11.9	16.1	22.2	42.2	27.0
Portugal	1997[c]	38.5	2.0	5.8	11.0	15.5	21.9	45.9	29.8
Puerto Rico		..	..	..	..	..	..	..	..

2.8 Distribution of income or consumption

	Survey year	Gini index	Percentage share of income or consumption						
			Lowest 10%	Lowest 20%	Second 20%	Third 20%	Fourth 20%	Highest 20%	Highest 10%
Romania	2003[a]	31.0	3.3	8.1	12.9	17.1	22.7	39.2	24.4
Russian Federation	2002[a]	39.9	2.4	6.1	10.5	14.9	21.8	46.6	30.6
Rwanda	1983–85[a]	28.9	4.2	9.7	13.2	16.5	21.6	39.1	24.2
Saudi Arabia		..	..	..	..	..	..	..	..
Senegal	1995[a]	41.3	2.6	6.4	10.3	14.5	20.6	48.2	33.5
Serbia and Montenegro		..	..	..	..	..	..	..	..
Sierra Leone	1989[a]	62.9	0.5	1.1	2.0	9.8	23.7	63.4	43.6
Singapore	1998[c]	42.5	1.9	5.0	9.4	14.6	22.0	49.0	32.8
Slovak Republic	1996[c]	25.8	3.1	8.8	14.9	18.7	22.8	34.8	20.9
Slovenia	1998–99[c]	28.4	3.6	9.1	14.2	18.1	22.9	35.7	21.4
Somalia		..	..	..	..	..	..	..	..
South Africa	2000[a]	57.8	1.4	3.5	6.3	10.0	18.0	62.2	44.7
Spain	2000[c]	34.7	2.6	7.0	12.1	16.4	22.5	42.0	26.6
Sri Lanka	1999–2000[a]	33.2	3.4	8.3	12.5	16.0	21.0	42.2	27.8
Sudan		..	..	..	..	..	..	..	..
Swaziland	1994[c]	60.9	1.0	2.7	5.8	10.0	17.1	64.4	50.2
Sweden	2000[c]	25.0	3.6	9.1	14.0	17.6	22.7	36.6	22.2
Switzerland	2000[c]	33.7	2.9	7.6	12.2	16.3	22.6	41.3	25.9
Syrian Arab Republic		..	..	..	..	..	..	..	..
Tajikistan	2003[a]	32.6	3.3	7.9	12.3	16.5	22.4	40.8	25.6
Tanzania	2000–01[a]	34.6	2.9	7.3	12.0	16.1	22.3	42.4	26.9
Thailand	2002[a]	42.0	2.7	6.3	9.9	14.0	20.8	49.0	33.4
Togo		..	..	..	..	..	..	..	..
Trinidad and Tobago	1992[c]	40.3	2.1	5.5	10.3	15.5	22.7	45.9	29.9
Tunisia	2000[a]	39.8	2.3	6.0	10.3	14.8	21.7	47.3	31.5
Turkey	2003[a]	43.6	2.0	5.3	9.7	14.2	21.0	49.7	34.1
Turkmenistan	1998[a]	40.8	2.6	6.1	10.2	14.7	21.5	47.5	31.7
Uganda	1999[a]	43.0	2.3	5.9	10.0	14.0	20.3	49.7	34.9
Ukraine	2003[a]	28.1	3.9	9.2	13.6	17.3	22.4	37.5	23.0
United Arab Emirates		..	..	..	..	..	..	..	..
United Kingdom	1999[c]	36.0	2.1	6.1	11.4	16.0	22.5	44.0	28.5
United States	2000[c]	40.8	1.9	5.4	10.7	15.7	22.4	45.8	29.9
Uruguay[b]	2003[c]	44.9	1.9	5.0	9.1	14.0	21.5	50.5	34.0
Uzbekistan	2000[a]	26.8	3.6	9.2	14.1	17.9	22.6	36.3	22.0
Venezuela, RB	2000[c]	44.1	1.6	4.7	9.4	14.5	22.1	49.3	32.8
Vietnam	2002[a]	37.0	3.2	7.5	11.2	14.8	21.1	45.4	29.9
West Bank and Gaza		..	..	..	..	..	..	..	..
Yemen, Rep.	1998[a]	33.4	3.0	7.4	12.2	16.7	22.5	41.2	25.9
Zambia	2002–03[a]	42.1	2.4	6.1	10.2	14.2	20.7	48.8	33.7
Zimbabwe	1995[a]	50.1	1.8	4.6	8.1	12.2	19.3	55.7	40.3

a. Refers to expenditure shares by percentiles of population, ranked by per capita expenditure. b. Urban data. c. Refers to income shares by percentiles of population, ranked by per capita income.

Distribution of income or consumption 2.8

About the data

Inequality in the distribution of income is reflected in the percentage shares of income or consumption accruing to portions of the population ranked by income or consumption levels. The portions ranked lowest by personal income receive the smallest shares of total income. The Gini index provides a convenient summary measure of the degree of inequality.

Data on the distribution of income or consumption come from nationally representative household surveys. Where the original data from the household survey were available, they have been used to directly calculate the income or consumption shares by quintile. Otherwise, shares have been estimated from the best available grouped data.

For most countries the income distribution indicators are based on the same data used to derive the $1 and $2 a day poverty estimates in table 2.7. This table contains additional countries for which poverty estimates are not provided in table 2.7, either because no reasonable purchasing power parity estimates are available or because the international poverty lines are not relevant for high-income economies.

The distribution data have been adjusted for household size, providing a more consistent measure of per capita income or consumption. No adjustment has been made for spatial differences in cost of living within countries, because the data needed for such calculations are generally unavailable. For further details on the estimation method for low- and middle-income economies, see Ravallion and Chen (1996).

Because the underlying household surveys differ in method and type of data collected, the distribution data are not strictly comparable across countries. These problems are diminishing as survey methods improve and become more standardized, but achieving strict comparability is still impossible (see *About the data* for table 2.7).

Two sources of noncomparability should be noted in particular. First, the surveys can differ in many respects, including whether they use income or consumption expenditure as the living standard indicator. The distribution of income is typically more unequal than the distribution of consumption. In addition, the definitions of income used differ more often among surveys. Consumption is usually a much better welfare indicator, particularly in developing countries. Second, households differ in size (number of members) and in the extent of income sharing among members. And individuals differ in age and consumption needs. Differences among countries in these respects may bias comparisons of distribution.

World Bank staff have made an effort to ensure that the data are as comparable as possible. Wherever possible, consumption has been used rather than income. Income distribution and Gini indexes for high-income countries are calculated directly from the Luxembourg Income Study database, using an estimation method consistent with that applied for developing countries.

Definitions

• **Survey year** is the year in which the underlying data were collected. • **Gini index** measures the extent to which the distribution of income (or consumption expenditure) among individuals or households within an economy deviates from a perfectly equal distribution. A Lorenz curve plots the cumulative percentages of total income received against the cumulative number of recipients, starting with the poorest individual. The Gini index measures the area between the Lorenz curve and a hypothetical line of absolute equality, expressed as a percentage of the maximum area under the line. Thus a Gini index of 0 represents perfect equality, while an index of 100 implies perfect inequality. • **Percentage share of income or consumption** is the share of total income or consumption that accrues to subgroups of population indicated by deciles or quintiles. Percentage shares by quintile may not sum to 100 because of rounding.

Data sources

Data on distribution are compiled by the World Bank's Development Research Group using primary household survey data obtained from government statistical agencies and World Bank country departments. Data for high-income economies are from the Luxembourg Income Study database.

2.9 Assessing vulnerability and security

	Urban informal sector employment		Youth unemployment		Female-headed households	Pension contributors		Public expenditure on pensions			
	% of urban employment		Male	Female							
	Male	Female	% of male labor force ages 15–24	% of female labor force ages 15–24	% of total	Year	% of labor force	Year	% of GDP	Year	Average pension % of per capita income
	1995–2003[a]	1995–2003[a]	2000–04[a]	2000–04[a]	1990–2004[a]						
Afghanistan	..	..	..	..	..		..		..		..
Albania	..	..	42	27	..	2004	40.7	2004	4.6	1995	36.4
Algeria	..	..	..	..	..	2002	38.9	1997	2.1	1991	75.0
Angola	..	..	..	..	..		..		..		..
Argentina	..	..	34	34	..	2004	34.9	1994	6.2		..
Armenia	..	..	..	..	29	1995	66.6	2004	3.4	1996	18.7
Australia	..	..	12	11	..	2003	92.6	1997	5.9	1989	37.3
Austria	..	..	9	10	..	2004	86.8	1995	14.9	1993	69.3
Azerbaijan	..	..	..	..	..	1996	52.0	2003	3.0	1996	51.4
Bangladesh	..	..	11	10	10	1993	3.5	1992	0.0		..
Belarus	..	..	..	..	..	1992	97.0	2004	10.6	1995	31.2
Belgium	..	..	16	20	..	1995	86.2	1997	12.9		..
Benin	50	41	..	..	21	1996	4.8	2003	1.3	1993	189.7
Bolivia	..	..	7	10	20	2002	10.8	2000	4.5		..
Bosnia and Herzegovina	..	..	..	..	..	2004	37.7	2003	7.4		..
Botswana	..	..	34	46	..		..	1996	2.7		..
Brazil	27	27	15	22	20	2004	56.4	1997	9.8		..
Bulgaria	..	..	31	25	..	1994	64.0	2005	8.9	1995	39.3
Burkina Faso	..	..	..	..	9	1993	3.1	1992	0.3	1992	207.3
Burundi	..	..	..	..	..	1993	3.3	1991	0.2	1991	57.4
Cambodia	..	..	..	..	25		..		..		..
Cameroon	..	..	..	..	24	1993	13.7	2004	0.1		..
Canada	..	..	15	12	..	2003	68.3	1997	5.4	1994	54.3
Central African Republic	..	..	..	..	21		..	1990	0.3		..
Chad	..	..	..	..	22	1990	1.1	1997	0.1		..
Chile	..	..	17	23	..	2003	56.2	2001	2.9	1993	56.1
China	..	..	..	..	..	1994	17.6	1996	2.7		..
Hong Kong, China	..	..	19	11	..		..		..		..
Colombia	..	..	..	..	28	1999	20.7	1994	1.1	1989	72.2
Congo, Dem. Rep.	..	..	..	..	..		..		..		..
Congo, Rep.	..	..	..	..	..	1992	5.8	1992	0.9		..
Costa Rica	..	..	13	18	..	2004	62.5	1997	4.2	1993	76.1
Côte d'Ivoire	..	..	..	..	14	1997	9.3	1997	0.3		..
Croatia	..	..	35	40	..	2004	100.0	2005	12.3		..
Cuba	..	..	..	..	..		..	1992	12.6		..
Czech Republic	..	..	21	20	..	1995	85.0	2003	8.5	1996	37.0
Denmark	..	..	9	7	..	2003	91.4	1997	8.8	1994	46.7
Dominican Republic	..	..	16	34	28	2001	26.8	2000	0.8	2000	42.0
Ecuador	..	..	19	25	..	2004	30.9	2002	1.4	2002	55.3
Egypt, Arab Rep.	..	..	19	51	12	2004	65.0	1994	2.5	1994	45.0
El Salvador	..	..	14	8	..	2003	25.1	1997	1.3		..
Eritrea	..	..	..	..	47		..	2001	0.3		..
Estonia	..	..	17	26	..	1995	76.0	2003	6.1	1995	56.7
Ethiopia	39	65	..	..	24		..	2003	0.4	..	..
Finland	..	..	22	19	..	2003	91.2	1997	12.1	1994	57.4
France	..	..	22	24	..	2003	90.1	1997	13.4		..
Gabon	..	..	..	..	26	1995	15.0		..		..
Gambia, The	..	..	..	..	..		..		..		..
Georgia	21	7	20	32	..	2004	25.9	2004	3.0	1996	12.6
Germany	..	..	13	10	..	2003	87.9	1997	12.1	1995	62.8
Ghana	..	..	13	19	34	2003	7.4	2004	0.6		..
Greece	..	..	19	36	..	2002	81.9	1993	11.9	1990	85.6
Guatemala	..	..	..	..	20	2000	16.4	1995	0.7	1995	27.6
Guinea	..	..	..	..	13	1993	1.5		..		..
Guinea-Bissau	..	..	..	..	..		..		..		..
Haiti	..	..	..	..	43		..		..		..

Assessing vulnerability and security 2.9

	Urban informal sector employment		Youth unemployment		Female-headed households	Pension contributors		Public expenditure on pensions			
	% of urban employment		Male	Female							Average pension
	Male	Female	% of male labor force ages 15–24	% of female labor force ages 15–24	% of total	Year	% of labor force	Year	% of GDP	Year	% of per capita income
	1995–2003[a]	**1995–2003[a]**	**2000–04[a]**	**2000–04[a]**	**1990–2004[a]**						
Honduras	..	..	6	12	..	1999	20.6	1994	0.6		..
Hungary	..	..	16	14	..	1996	77.0	2001	11.0	1996	33.6
India	54	41	10	10	10	1992	10.6		..		..
Indonesia	..	..	..	..	12	1995	8.0		..		..
Iran, Islamic Rep.	..	..	..	..	..	2000	35.1	2001	1.5		..
Iraq	..	..	..	..	..	2004	18.4		..		..
Ireland	..	..	9	7	..	2002	100.0	1997	4.6	1993	77.9
Israel	..	..	22	22	..	1992	82.0	1996	5.9	1992	48.1
Italy	..	..	21	27	..	2003	86.0	1997	17.6		..
Jamaica	..	..	22	32	..	1999	44.4	1996	..	1989	25.9
Japan	..	..	11	8	..	2003	92.8	1997	6.9	1989	33.9
Jordan	..	..	..	..	12	2001	36.0	2003	1.9	1995	144.0
Kazakhstan	..	..	13	16	33	2004	35.4	2004	4.9	2001	23.0
Kenya	..	..	..	..	32	1995	18.0	2003	6.4		..
Korea, Dem. Rep.	..	..	..	..	..		..		..		..
Korea, Rep.	..	..	12	9	..	2003	88.7	1997	1.3		..
Kuwait	..	..	..	..	..		..	1990	3.5		..
Kyrgyz Republic	52	48	15	16	33	1997	44.0	1997	6.4	2001	45.0
Lao PDR	..	..	..	..	..		..		..		..
Latvia	..	..	17	20	..	1995	60.5	2002	8.2	1994	47.6
Lebanon	..	..	..	..	..	2003	26.1		..		..
Lesotho	..	..	..	..	..		..		..		..
Liberia	..	..	..	..	..		..		..		..
Libya	..	..	..	..	..	2003	72.8		..		..
Lithuania	50	27	23	28	..	2004	70.7	2003	6.2	1995	21.3
Macedonia, FYR	..	..	65	67	..	1995	49.0	1998	8.7	1996	91.6
Madagascar	..	..	..	..	22	1993	5.4	1990	0.2		..
Malawi	..	..	..	..	27		..		..		..
Malaysia	..	..	8	8	..	1993	48.7	2004	0.7		..
Mali	..	..	..	..	11	1990	2.5	1991	0.4		..
Mauritania	..	..	..	..	29	1995	5.0	1996	0.2		..
Mauritius	..	..	..	..	..	1995	60.0	2002	4.5		..
Mexico	18	22	6	8	..	2002	25.1	2001	7.8		..
Moldova	..	..	17	13	..		..	2003	8.0		..
Mongolia	..	..	20	21	..		..	2004	8.3		..
Morocco	..	..	17	16	17	2003	19.2	2002	2.5	1994	118.0
Mozambique	..	..	..	..	26	1995	2.0	2004	1.4		..
Myanmar	..	..	..	..	..		..		..		..
Namibia	..	..	40	49	42		..		..		..
Nepal	60	76	..	..	16		..		..		..
Netherlands	..	..	8	8	..	2002	100.0	1997	11.1	1989	48.5
New Zealand	..	..	9	10	..	2003	95.7	1997	6.5		..
Nicaragua	..	..	11	16	31	2001	14.9	1996	2.5		..
Niger	..	..	..	..	13	1992	1.3	1992	0.1		..
Nigeria	..	..	..	..	17	1993	1.3	2002	1.5	1991	40.5
Norway	..	..	13	11	..	2003	95.3	1997	8.2	1994	49.9
Oman	..	..	..	..	..		..		..		..
Pakistan	64	61	12	21	7	1993	3.5	2004	0.9		..
Panama	..	..	24	38	..	1998	51.6	1996	4.3		..
Papua New Guinea	..	..	..	..	..		..		..		..
Paraguay	..	..	12	17	17	2004	14.3	2001	0.7[b]		..
Peru	..	..	18	21	20	2003	20.8	2000	2.6		..
Philippines	16	19	24	31	15	1996	28.3	1993	1.0		..
Poland	..	..	39	43	..	1996	68.0	2003	13.9	1995	61.2
Portugal	..	..	14	18	..	2003	94.7	1997	10.0	1989	44.6
Puerto Rico	..	..	24	25	..		..		..		..

Assessing vulnerability and security

	Urban informal sector employment		Youth unemployment		Female-headed households	Pension contributors		Public expenditure on pensions			
	% of urban employment Male 1995–2003[a]	% of urban employment Female 1995–2003[a]	Male % of male labor force ages 15–24 2000–04[a]	Female % of female labor force ages 15–24 2000–04[a]	% of total 1990–2004[a]	Year	% of labor force	Year	% of GDP	Year	Average pension % of per capita income
Romania	..	..	18	19	..	1994	55.0	2002	7.1	1994	34.1
Russian Federation	10	9	..	..	..		..	2004	5.8	1995	18.3
Rwanda	..	..	..	..	36	1993	9.3		..		..
Saudi Arabia	..	..	..	..	..		..		..		..
Senegal	..	..	..	..	18	2003	4.1	1998	1.5	1997	85.0[b]
Serbia and Montenegro	..	..	..	..	..		..	2004	10.3		..
Sierra Leone	..	..	..	..	..	2004	3.5		..		..
Singapore	..	..	6	10	..	1995	73.0	1999	0.5		..
Slovak Republic	..	..	34	31	..	2000	70.9	2003	7.4	1994	44.5
Slovenia	..	..	13	15	..	1995	86.0	2003	10.1	1996	49.3
Somalia	..	..	..	..	..		..		..		..
South Africa	16	28	56	65	42		..		..		..
Spain	..	..	19	26	..	2003	91.2	1997	10.9	1995	54.1
Sri Lanka	..	..	22	36	..	1992	28.8	2005	1.8		..
Sudan	..	..	..	..	..	1995	12.1		..		..
Swaziland	..	..	..	..	..		..		..		..
Sweden	..	..	18	16	..	2003	87.1	1997	11.1	1994	78.0
Switzerland	..	..	8	7	..	2003	100.0	1997	13.4	1993	44.4
Syrian Arab Republic	..	..	21	39	..		..	1991	0.5		..
Tajikistan	..	..	..	..	..		..	1996	3.0		..
Tanzania	60	85	..	..	23	1996	2.0		..		..
Thailand	..	..	5	4	..	1999	18.0		..		..
Togo	..	..	..	..	24	1997	15.9	1997	0.6	1993	178.8
Trinidad and Tobago	..	..	17	26	..		..	1996	0.6	..	..
Tunisia	..	..	..	..	..	2003	48.2	2000	4.2	1991	89.5
Turkey	10	6	20	19	10	2002	33.2	2002	7.1	1993	56.0
Turkmenistan	..	..	..	..	27		..	1996	2.3		..
Uganda	..	..	..	..	28	1994	8.2	2003	0.3		..
Ukraine	5	5	16	17	..	2005	67.5	2005	15.4	1995	30.9
United Arab Emirates	..	..	..	..	..		..		..		..
United Kingdom	..	..	12	10	..	2003	96.2	1997	10.3		..
United States	..	..	13	11	..	2003	92.2	1997	7.5	1989	33.0
Uruguay	..	..	34	44	..	2004	37.1	1996	15.0	1996	64.1
Uzbekistan	..	..	..	..	22		..	2004	0.1	1995	45.8
Venezuela, RB	..	..	24	35	..	2004	29.3	2001	2.7		..
Vietnam	..	..	4	5	26	1998	8.4	1998	1.6		..
West Bank and Gaza	..	..	43	37	..	2000	18.6		..		..
Yemen, Rep.	..	..	..	..	9	1999	13.5	1994	0.1		..
Zambia	..	..	..	..	23	1994	10.2	1993	0.1		..
Zimbabwe	..	..	28	21	34	1995	12.0		..		..
World			.. w	.. w							
Low income			..	..							
Middle income			..	..							
Lower middle income			..	..							
Upper middle income			19	20							
Low & middle income			..	..							
East Asia & Pacific			..	..							
Europe & Central Asia			..	..							
Latin America & Carib.			12	17							
Middle East & N. Africa			..	..							
South Asia			10	13							
Sub-Saharan Africa			..	..							
High income			14	13							
Europe EMU			18	20							

a. Data are for the most recent year available. b. Refers to system covering private sector workers.

Assessing vulnerability and security 2.9

About the data

As traditionally defined and measured, poverty is a static concept, and vulnerability a dynamic one. Vulnerability reflects a household's resilience in the face of shocks and the likelihood that a shock will lead to a decline in well-being. Thus, it depends primarily on the household's asset endowment and insurance mechanisms. Because poor people have fewer assets and less diversified sources of income than the better-off, fluctuations in income affect them more.

Enhancing security for poor people means reducing their vulnerability to such risks as ill health, providing them the means to manage risk themselves, and strengthening market or public institutions for managing risk. The tools include microfinance programs, old age assistance and pensions, and public provision of education and basic health care (see tables 2.10 and 2.14).

Poor households face many risks, and vulnerability is thus multidimensional. The indicators in the table focus on individual risks—informal sector employment, youth unemployment, female-headed households, income insecurity in old age, and the extent to which publicly provided services may be capable of mitigating some of these risks. Poor people face labor market risks, often having to take up precarious, low-quality jobs in the informal sector and to increase their household's labor market participation by sending their children to work. Income security is a prime concern for the elderly.

For informal sector employment, the data are from labor force and special informal sector surveys, various household surveys, surveys of household industries or economic activities, surveys of small and micro enterprises, and official estimates. The international comparability of the data is affected by differences among countries in definitions and coverage and in the treatment of domestic workers and those who have a secondary job in the informal sector. The data in the table are based on national definitions of urban areas established by countries. For details on these definitions, see *Data sources*.

Youth unemployment is an important policy issue for many economies. Experiencing unemployment may permanently impair a young person's productive potential and future employment opportunities. The table presents unemployment among youth ages 15–24, but the lower age limit for young people in a country could be determined by the minimum age for leaving school, so age groups could differ across countries. Also, since this age group is likely to include school leavers, the level of youth unemployment varies considerably over the year as a result of different school opening and closing dates. The youth unemployment rate shares similar limitations on comparability as the general unemployment rate. For further information, see *About the data* for table 2.5.

The data on female-headed households are from recent Demographic and Health Surveys. The definition and concept of the female-headed household differ greatly across economies, making cross-country comparison difficult. In some cases it is assumed that a woman cannot be the head of any household in which an adult male is present, because of sex-biased stereotype. Users need to be cautious when interpreting the data.

The data on pension contributors come from national sources, the International Labour Organization (ILO), and International Monetary Fund country reports. Coverage by pension schemes may be broad or even universal where eligibility is determined by citizenship, residency, or income status. In contribution-related schemes, however, eligibility is usually restricted to individuals who have made contributions for a minimum number of years. Definitional issues—relating to the labor force, for example—may arise in comparing coverage by contribution-related schemes over time and across countries (for country-specific information, see Palacios and Pallares-Miralles 2000). The share of the labor force covered by a pension scheme may be overstated in countries that do not attempt to count informal sector workers as part of the labor force.

Public interventions and institutions can provide services directly to poor people, although whether these work well for the poor is debated. State action is often ineffective, in part because governments can influence only a few of the many sources of well-being and in part because of difficulties in delivering good and services. The effectiveness of public provision is further constrained by the fiscal resources at governments' disposal and the fact that state institutions may not be responsive to the needs of poor people.

The data on public pension spending are from national sources and cover all government expenditures, including the administrative costs of pension programs. They cover noncontributory pensions or social assistance targeted to the elderly and disabled and spending by social insurance schemes for which contributions had previously been made. The pattern of spending in a country is correlated with its demographic structure—spending increases as the population ages.

Definitions

• **Urban informal sector employment** is broadly characterized as employment in urban areas in units that produce goods or services on a small scale with the primary objective of generating employment and income for those concerned. These units typically operate at a low level of organization, with little or no division between labor and capital as factors of production. Labor relations are based on casual employment, kinship, or social relationships rather than contractual arrangements. • **Youth unemployment** refers to the share of the labor force ages 15–24 without work but available for and seeking employment. Definitions of labor force and unemployment may differ by country (see *About the data*). • **Female-headed households** refer to the percentage of households with a female head. • **Pension contributors** refer to the share of the labor force covered by a pension scheme. • **Public expenditure on pensions** includes all government expenditures on cash transfers to the elderly, the disabled, and survivors and the administrative costs of these programs. • **Average pension** is estimated by dividing total pension expenditure by the number of pensioners.

Data sources

Data on urban informal sector employment and youth unemployment are from the ILO database Key Indicators of the Labour Market, fourth edition. Data on female-headed household are from Demographic and Health Surveys by Macro International. Data on pension contributors and pension spending are from Robert Palacios and Montserrat Pallares-Miralles's "International Patterns of Pension Provision" (2000) and updates. Further updates, notes, and sources will be available under "Knowledge and information" on the World Bank's Web site on pensions (www.worldbank.org/pensions).

2.10 Education inputs

	Public expenditure per student						Public expenditure on education		Trained teachers in primary education	Primary pupil-teacher ratio
	% of GDP per capita									
	Primary[a]		Secondary		Tertiary		% of GDP	% of total government expenditure	% of total	pupils per teacher
	1991	2004[b]	1999	2004[b]	1999	2004[b]	2004[b]	2004[b]	2004[b]	2004[b]
Afghanistan	..	..	..	..	..	..	..	..	..	65
Albania	..	*7.7*	..	*11.9*	..	*36.3*	*2.8*	..	..	*21*
Algeria	..	*11.3*	..	*17.1*	..	..	..	..	98.3	27
Angola	..	..	..	..	..	..	..	..	..	..
Argentina	..	*10.9*	16.4	*14.9*	17.7	*13.1*	*4.0*	*13.8*	..	*17*
Armenia	..	*8.9*	*12.4*	*11.1*	*29.1*	*38.3*	*3.2*	..	66.7	22
Australia	..	*16.4*	14.9	*14.6*	26.3	*22.6*	*4.9*	..	..	..
Austria	18.6	*23.9*	30.7	*28.2*	53.0	*47.0*	*5.7*	..	..	*13*
Azerbaijan	..	*7.6*	17.2	*13.4*	19.3	*12.8*	3.3	*19.2*	99.8	14
Bangladesh	..	7.2	12.7	13.7	47.2	*33.8*	2.2	*15.5*	*51.2*	*54*
Belarus	..	13.7	..	22.9	..	27.6	5.8	13.0	98.5	15
Belgium	16.3	*19.0*	24.4	*25.2*	46.0	*38.6*	*6.3*	..	..	*12*
Benin	..	*12.2*	*26.1*	*22.1*	*202.9*	..	*3.3*	..	72.2	52
Bolivia	..	16.4	11.7	13.0	44.1	35.9	6.4	*18.1*	..	24
Bosnia and Herzegovina	..	..	..	..	..	..	..	..	..	..
Botswana	..	..	*5.6*	..	*92.6*	..	..	..	*89.7*	*26*
Brazil	..	..	10.5	..	63.2	..	..	..	..	*24*
Bulgaria	22.4	*16.2*	*18.8*	*19.0*	*18.0*	*18.7*	*3.6*	..	..	*17*
Burkina Faso	..	..	..	..	..	..	..	..	89.5	49
Burundi	13.4	19.9	..	75.8	1,190.1	442.1	5.2	*13.0*	..	51
Cambodia	..	6.5	*6.8*	..	*46.8*	..	2.0	..	96.5	55
Cameroon	..	..	18.6	..	71.3	75.7	3.8	17.2	68.5	53
Canada	..	..	..	..	49.3	..	..	..	..	*17*
Central African Republic	11.9	..	..	..	..	..	..	..	..	..
Chad	8.0	..	33.6	..	..	..	..	..	..	69
Chile	..	*15.3*	*14.9*	*16.3*	*19.4*	*15.3*	*4.1*	*19.1*	..	*34*
China	..	..	12.7	..	99.2	..	..	..	*96.8*	*21*
Hong Kong, China	..	16.0	*18.2*	22.0	*62.9*	67.9	4.7	23.3	91.8	19
Colombia	..	16.7	17.0	16.0	39.9	26.3	4.9	11.7	..	28
Congo, Dem. Rep.	..	..	..	..	..	..	..	..	..	..
Congo, Rep.	..	*7.9*	..	*18.3*	404.9	*245.9*	*3.2*	..	62.2	83
Costa Rica	7.8	17.1	23.2	19.7	55.0	36.3	4.9	18.5	97.4	22
Côte d'Ivoire	..	..	54.5	..	212.8	..	..	..	*100.0*	*42*
Croatia	..	*24.0*	..	*23.5*	41.3	*34.5*	*4.5*	*10.0*	*100.0*	*18*
Cuba	21.4	..	41.3	..	86.4	..	..	19.4	100.0	10
Czech Republic	..	*12.0*	22.1	*23.0*	34.4	*31.8*	*4.4*	..	..	*17*
Denmark	..	*24.9*	38.3	*36.1*	66.2	*74.6*	*8.5*	..	..	..
Dominican Republic	..	5.0	*2.5*	1.3	..	..	1.1	6.3	79.4	21
Ecuador	..	..	9.6	..	..	..	..	..	70.9	23
Egypt, Arab Rep.	..	..	..	..	..	..	..	..	..	*22*
El Salvador	..	*9.4*	*7.9*	*9.0*	*9.3*	*11.1*	2.8	*20.0*	..	..
Eritrea	..	9.8	*37.2*	17.4	*428.9*	855.5	3.8	..	83.1	47
Estonia	..	*19.8*	28.0	*25.5*	32.7	*24.9*	*5.7*	..	..	*14*
Ethiopia	32.0	..	..	..	..	..	6.1	20.4	..	65
Finland	21.9	*18.3*	26.4	*27.4*	41.3	*38.1*	*6.4*	..	..	*16*
France	12.0	*17.8*	29.0	*28.6*	30.2	*29.3*	*5.6*	..	..	*19*
Gabon	..	..	..	..	..	..	..	..	*100.0*	36
Gambia, The	13.7	7.1	..	8.7	..	229.7	1.9	*8.9*	..	..
Georgia	..	..	..	..	..	..	2.9	13.1	*97.4*	22
Germany	..	*16.7*	20.8	*22.6*	41.1	*43.0*	*4.8*	..	..	*14*
Ghana	..	..	..	..	..	..	..	..	60.7	32
Greece	7.6	*15.6*	17.4	..	29.5	*26.8*	*4.0*	..	..	*12*
Guatemala	..	4.7	*4.2*	3.7	..	..	..	..	..	31
Guinea	..	..	..	..	..	..	..	..	..	45
Guinea-Bissau	..	..	..	..	..	..	..	..	..	..
Haiti	9.1	..	..	..	..	..	..	..	..	..

	Public expenditure per student						Public expenditure on education		Trained teachers in primary education	Primary pupil-teacher ratio
	% of GDP per capita									
	Primary[a]		Secondary		Tertiary		% of GDP	% of total government expenditure	% of total	pupils per teacher
	1991	2004[b]	1999	2004[b]	1999	2004[b]	2004[b]	2004[b]	2004[b]	2004[b]
Honduras	..	..	..	..	..	..	..	..	87.2	34
Hungary	21.1	20.8	19.1	21.4	34.3	36.1	5.5	..	..	10
India	..	..	21.6	..	75.7	..	..	..	..	41
Indonesia	..	2.9	8.7	5.6	21.9	15.6	1.1	9.0	..	20
Iran, Islamic Rep.	..	10.5	10.9	11.5	38.4	26.5	4.8	17.7	100.0	20
Iraq	..	..	..	..	..	..	..	..	100.0	21
Ireland	11.6	12.4	16.9	18.1	28.8	26.6	4.3	..	..	19
Israel	11.9	23.0	22.7	23.5	32.1	26.6	7.5	13.7	..	15
Italy	15.3	25.4	26.8	28.1	25.6	27.4	4.7	..	..	11
Jamaica	9.9	15.5	25.6	24.8	85.9	44.6	5.3	9.5	..	30
Japan	..	22.2	20.5	21.7	14.9	17.1	3.6	..	..	20
Jordan	..	15.2	16.4	18.0	..	..	..	..	..	20
Kazakhstan	..	10.1	..	7.9	..	6.2	2.4	..	..	18
Kenya	13.4	25.2	18.4	25.1	255.5	409.2	7.0	29.2	98.8	40
Korea, Dem. Rep.	..	..	..	..	..	..	..	..	..	..
Korea, Rep.	11.8	16.3	15.6	23.7	8.3	5.0	4.2	15.5	..	30
Kuwait	34.8	25.9	..	28.3	..	178.1	8.2	17.4	100.0	13
Kyrgyz Republic	..	7.7	11.9	14.5	27.7	21.2	4.6	23.0	57.9	24
Lao PDR	..	6.7	4.3	8.9	66.9	82.4	2.3	11.0	79.4	31
Latvia	..	22.4	23.5	25.9	23.0	19.0	5.8	..	..	14
Lebanon	..	..	6.2	..	12.9	14.7	2.6	12.7	13.5	14
Lesotho	..	20.8	69.1	48.6	1,249.9	603.3	9.0	..	66.8	44
Liberia	..	..	..	..	..	..	..	..	..	..
Libya	..	..	..	..	23.8	..	..	..	..	..
Lithuania	..	..	..	..	34.4	32.9	5.9	..	..	16
Macedonia, FYR	..	23.6	..	7.7	..	23.7	3.5	..	..	20
Madagascar	..	..	39.9	..	180.9	184.2	3.3	18.2	..	52
Malawi	7.4	14.4	..	30.3	..	..	6.0	..	..	..
Malaysia	10.1	20.2	22.3	28.3	83.3	102.4	8.1	20.3	..	19
Mali	..	..	61.6	..	265.0	..	..	..	..	52
Mauritania	..	..	45.4	..	99.9	..	3.4	..	100.0	45
Mauritius	10.3	13.6	15.6	20.3	41.2	45.3	4.7	15.7	100.0	22
Mexico	4.9	14.4	14.5	16.2	48.8	49.8	5.3	..	..	27
Moldova	..	17.1	21.2	26.2	19.0	20.7	4.9	21.4	..	19
Mongolia	..	15.7	19.5	14.6	36.4	25.0	7.5	19.1	..	35
Morocco	15.8	19.3	51.4	46.9	109.6	87.2	6.3	27.8	..	28
Mozambique	..	..	..	..	..	..	..	..	..	65
Myanmar	..	..	7.1	..	29.0	..	..	..	65.0	33
Namibia	..	21.3	37.4	25.5	161.7	112.6	7.2	..	49.5	28
Nepal	..	12.7	13.5	10.7	144.9	72.7	3.4	14.9	30.5	40
Netherlands	12.6	18.0	21.8	22.9	44.2	39.8	5.1	..	..	..
New Zealand	17.2	18.7	24.3	22.2	41.6	35.6	6.7	15.1	..	18
Nicaragua	..	9.1	..	10.7	..	..	3.1	15.0	74.6	35
Niger	..	19.0	88.4	64.3	344.8	345.1	2.3	..	75.6	44
Nigeria	..	..	..	..	..	..	..	..	50.7	36
Norway	32.8	20.5	27.0	30.7	46.3	48.5	7.6	..	..	10
Oman	11.7	13.1	22.2	20.5	47.5	53.8	4.6	26.1	99.8	19
Pakistan	..	..	..	..	..	..	2.0	..	..	47
Panama	11.3	9.9	19.1	12.6	33.6	27.0	3.9	8.9	74.3	24
Papua New Guinea	..	..	..	..	..	..	..	..	..	35
Paraguay	..	12.3	17.3	13.7	55.2	28.2	4.4	11.4	..	27
Peru	..	6.4	9.2	8.7	21.3	14.0	3.0	17.1	..	25
Philippines	..	11.1	10.7	9.2	15.0	14.5	3.2	17.8	..	35
Poland	..	23.5	11.6	20.8	21.5	22.1	5.6	12.8	..	13
Portugal	17.2	24.0	29.1	31.6	29.7	26.0	5.8	..	..	11
Puerto Rico	..	..	..	..	..	..	..	..	..	..

2.10 Education inputs

	Public expenditure per student						Public expenditure on education		Trained teachers in primary education	Primary pupil-teacher ratio
	% of GDP per capita							% of total government expenditure		
	Primary[a]		Secondary		Tertiary		% of GDP		% of total	pupils per teacher
	1991	2004[b]	1999	2004[b]	1999	2004[b]	2004[b]	2004[b]	2004[b]	2004[b]
Romania	..	9.9	15.9	15.1	32.4	26.5	3.5	..	..	17
Russian Federation	..	..	..	..	..	..	3.8	10.7	99.0	17
Rwanda	..	..	28.4	..	..	..	..	..	81.7	62
Saudi Arabia	..	..	31.4	..	..	..	..	..	..	12
Senegal	19.4	..	..	..	..	..	4.0	..	50.9	43
Serbia and Montenegro	..	..	..	..	..	..	..	..	..	..
Sierra Leone	..	..	..	..	..	..	..	..	..	..
Singapore	..	..	..	..	..	..	..	..	..	..
Slovak Republic	..	11.3	18.5	18.8	33.0	31.1	4.3	..	..	18
Slovenia	16.8	..	..	..	28.7	26.3	6.0	..	..	13
Somalia	..	..	..	..	..	..	..	..	..	..
South Africa	..	13.7	21.5	20.3	65.2	47.1	5.4	18.1	78.7	34
Spain	11.7	19.2	25.3	24.7	20.4	23.1	4.5	..	..	14
Sri Lanka	..	..	..	..	..	..	..	..	..	23
Sudan	..	..	..	..	..	..	..	..	..	29
Swaziland	7.6	11.0	26.7	47.4	397.3	260.5	6.2	..	90.6	31
Sweden	46.5	24.4	26.4	26.7	53.3	50.6	7.7	..	..	11
Switzerland	36.5	24.3	27.7	29.2	54.5	59.9	5.8	..	..	..
Syrian Arab Republic	..	14.5	22.1	26.8	..	..	..	..	..	18
Tajikistan	..	6.7	..	9.2	..	8.8	2.8	16.9	84.1	22
Tanzania	..	..	..	..	..	..	..	..	100.0	58
Thailand	11.6	13.8	11.5	13.0	35.5	22.7	4.2	27.5	..	21
Togo	..	6.7	30.9	..	317.9	..	2.6	13.6	45.0	44
Trinidad and Tobago	..	16.0	12.2	..	147.6	..	4.3	..	81.0	18
Tunisia	..	15.5	26.7	23.6	78.7	62.8	6.4	..	..	22
Turkey	10.9	13.9	14.4	9.4	46.0	50.3	3.6	..	..	..
Turkmenistan	..	..	..	..	..	..	..	..	..	..
Uganda	..	11.6	..	34.9	..	194.1	5.2	18.3	80.4	50
Ukraine	..	10.4	11.2	15.7	36.4	27.1	4.6	18.3	99.7	19
United Arab Emirates	..	7.7	11.6	13.3	..	2.2	1.6	22.5	60.9	15
United Kingdom	14.9	16.4	15.7	15.5	26.2	28.9	5.3	11.5	..	17
United States	..	21.8	22.7	25.2	27.2	26.2	5.7	..	..	15
Uruguay	7.8	7.9	11.4	9.0	19.3	19.0	2.6	9.6	..	21
Uzbekistan	..	..	..	..	..	..	..	..	..	..
Venezuela, RB	..	..	..	..	..	..	..	..	..	20
Vietnam	..	..	..	..	..	..	4.4	17.1	87.0	23
West Bank and Gaza	..	..	..	..	..	..	..	..	..	27
Yemen, Rep.	..	..	..	..	..	..	..	..	..	..
Zambia	..	9.3	19.9	11.9	168.2	..	2.8	14.8	100.0	49
Zimbabwe	21.3	..	20.0	..	200.4	..	..	..	..	39
World	.. m	15.2 m	20.0 m	18.9 m	38.5 m	34.5 m	4.4 m	.. m	.. m	29 m
Low income	..	..	..	..	..	..	..	..	..	43
Middle income	..	13.1	16.3	16.3	37.8	32.5	4.4	..	..	22
Lower middle income	..	11.3	14.1	13.6	..	29.9	3.5	..	..	22
Upper middle income	..	14.4	17.8	19.6	33.9	32.7	4.5	..	..	22
Low & middle income	..	12.4	..	..	..	..	4.1	..	..	31
East Asia & Pacific	..	9.5	8.4	..	34.3	..	3.2	..	95.4	22
Europe & Central Asia	..	12.0	16.4	16.4	31.1	25.7	4.1	..	..	17
Latin America & Carib.	..	12.3	14.9	14.3	37.5	29.0	4.3	15.3	..	25
Middle East & N. Africa	..	14.5	..	20.5	..	..	..	..	..	24
South Asia	..	..	13.5	..	86.7	..	2.4	..	..	42
Sub-Saharan Africa	..	..	..	..	..	..	..	..	..	49
High income	16.3	19.1	24.3	24.7	32.1	28.9	5.6	..	..	16
Europe EMU	14.0	18.3	25.3	26.3	30.2	29.3	5.1	..	..	14

a. Break in series between 1997 and 1998 due to change from International Standard Classification of Education (ISCED) 1976 to ISCED97. b. Provisional data.

About the data

Data on education are compiled by the United Nations Educational, Scientific, and Cultural Organization (UNESCO) Institute for Statistics from official responses to surveys and from reports provided by education authorities in each country. Such data are used for monitoring, policymaking, and resource allocation. For a variety of reasons, however, education statistics generally fail to provide a complete and accurate picture of a country's education system. Statistics often lag by two to three years, though an effort is being made to shorten the delay. Moreover, coverage and data collection methods vary across countries and over time within countries, so comparisons should be interpreted with caution.

The data on education spending in the table refer solely to public spending—government spending on public education plus subsidies for private education. The data generally exclude foreign aid for education. They may also exclude spending by religious schools, which play a significant role in many developing countries. Data for some countries and for some years refer to spending by the ministry of education only (excluding education expenditures by other ministries and departments and local authorities).

Many developing countries have sought to supplement public funds for education. Some countries have adopted tuition fees to recover part of the cost of providing education services or to encourage development of private schools. Charging fees raises difficult questions relating to equity, efficiency, access, and taxation, however, and some governments have used scholarships, vouchers, and other methods of public finance to counter criticism. For most countries, the data reflect only public spending. Data for a few countries include private spending, although national practices vary with respect to whether parents or schools pay for books, uniforms, and other supplies. For greater detail, see the country- and indicator-specific notes in the source.

The share of public expenditure devoted to education allows an assessment of the priority a government assigns to education relative to other public investments. It also reflects a government's commitment to investing in human capital development. However, returns on investment to education, especially primary and lower secondary education, cannot be understood simply by comparing current education indicators with national income. It takes a long time before currently enrolled children can productively contribute to the national economy (Hanushek 2002).

The share of trained teachers in primary education measures the quality of the teaching staff. It does not take account of competencies acquired by teachers through their professional experience or self-instruction or of such factors as work experience, teaching methods and materials, or classroom conditions, which may affect the quality of teaching. Since the training teachers receive varies greatly (pre-service or in-service), care should be taken in comparing across countries.

The primary pupil-teacher ratio reflects the average numbers of pupils per teacher. It is different from the average class size because of the different practices countries employ, such as part-time teaching, school shifts, and multigrade classes. The comparability of pupil-teacher ratios across countries is affected by the definition of teachers and by differences in class size by grade and in the number of hours taught, as well as the different practices mentioned above. Moreover, the underlying enrollment levels are subject to a variety of reporting errors (for further discussion of enrollment data, see *About the data* for table 2.11). While the pupil-teacher ratio is often used to compare the quality of schooling across countries, it is often weakly related to the value added of schooling systems (Behrman and Rosenzweig 1994).

In 1998 UNESCO introduced the new International Standard Classification of Education (ISCED) 1997. Thus the time-series data for the years through 1997 are not consistent with those for 1998 and later. Any time-series analysis should therefore be undertaken with extreme caution.

And in 2006 the UNESCO Institute for Statistics changed its convention for citing the reference year of education data and indicators to the calendar year in which the academic or financial year ends. Data that used to be listed for 2003/04, for example, is now listed for 2004. This change was implemented to present the most recent data available and to align the data reporting with that of other international organizations (in particular the Organisation for Economic Co-operation and Development and Eurostat).

2.10a

Estimated impact of HIV/AIDS on education in three Sub-Saharan countries, 2005

	Kenya			Tanzania			Zambia		
	Low	Medium	High	Low	Medium	High	Low	Medium	High
Teacher deaths due to AIDS	700	1,620	3,020	605	1,290	2,010	580	1,030	1,500
Share of teacher attrition (%)	7.5	18	29.6	9.3	19.9	31	23.3	40.4	48.8
Teacher-years of absenteeism due to AIDS	690	1,590	2,930	610	1,290	2,200	605	1,090	1,580
Share of total teacher-years (%)	0.4	0.8	1.8	0.5	1.1	2.3	1.3	2.2	3.9

In the best-case scenario (low estimate) Kenya, Tanzania, and Zambia will lose 600–700 teacher-years through absenteeism caused by HIV/AIDS. In the worst-case scenario (high estimate) they will lose 1,200–3,000 teacher-years.

Note: The teacher infection rate is half the general population infection rate for the low estimate, the same as the general population infection rate for the medium estimate, and twice the general population infection rate for the high estimate. All estimates are modeled estimates.

Source: Desai and Jukes 2005 cited in UNESCO 2006 (p.88).

Definitions

• **Public expenditure per student** is public current spending on education divided by the number of students by level, as a percentage of gross domestic product (GDP) per capita. • **Public expenditure on education** is current and capital public expenditure on education, as a percentage of GDP and as a percentage of total government expenditure. • **Trained teachers in primary education** are the percentage of primary school teachers who have received the minimum organized teacher training (pre-service or in-service) required for teaching in their country. • **Primary pupil-teacher ratio** is the number of pupils enrolled in primary school divided by the number of primary school teachers (regardless of their teaching assignment).

Data sources

Data on education inputs are from the UNESCO Institute for Statistics, which compiles international data on education in cooperation with national commissions and national statistical services. Data for latest years are provisional, as of January 2006.

2.11 Participation in education

	Gross enrollment ratio				Net enrollment ratio				Children out of school	
	% of relevant age group				% of relevant age group				thousand primary-school-age children	
	Preprimary	Primary	Secondary	Tertiary	Primary[a]		Secondary[a]		Male	Female
	2004[b]	2004[b]	2004[b]	2004[b]	1991	2004[b]	1991	2004[b]	2004	2004
Afghanistan	1	90	13	1	..	..	..	..	..	..
Albania	49	104	78	16	95	96	..	74	5	6
Algeria	5	112	81	20	89	97	53	66	0	41
Angola	..	..	..	1	50	..	..	..	..	..
Argentina	62	118	99	61	..	..	..	81	3	11
Armenia	31	101	91	26	..	97	..	89	3	0
Australia	100	102	154	74	99	95	79	85	51	44
Austria	88	105	100	49	88	..	..	89	..	..
Azerbaijan	28	97	83	15	89	84	..	77	50	51
Bangladesh	12	106	51	7	..	..	..	48	..	..
Belarus	100	101	93	61	86	95	..	87	13	19
Belgium	116	105	160	61	96	100	87	97	4	4
Benin	4	99	26	..	41	83	..	..	..	..
Bolivia	48	113	89	41	..	95	..	74	25	18
Bosnia and Herzegovina	..	..	..	..	..	..	..	..	..	..
Botswana	..	104	74	6	83	82	35	60	29	22
Brazil	55	145	110	20	85	97	17	75	..	..
Bulgaria	77	105	99	41	86	94	63	88	6	7
Burkina Faso	1	53	12	1	29	40	..	10	590	681
Burundi	1	80	12	2	53	57	..	8	240	278
Cambodia	9	137	26	3	69	98	..	25	..	..
Cameroon	20	114	44	5	74	..	..	..	..	..
Canada	65	101	105	57	98	..	89	..	..	..
Central African Republic	3	64	12	..	52	..	..	..	..	..
Chad	..	71	15	..	35	57	..	11	243	413
Chile	50	99	88	43	89	86	55	78	119	124
China	36	115	70	15	97	..	..	..	..	..
Hong Kong, China	70	108	85	32	..	97	..	78	1	12
Colombia	38	111	75	27	69	83	34	55	379	334
Congo, Dem. Rep.	1	..	..	..	54	..	..	..	..	..
Congo, Rep.	6	89	32	4	79	..	..	..	..	..
Costa Rica	64	112	68	19	87	92	38	50	22	18
Côte d'Ivoire	3	72	25	..	45	56	..	20	519	705
Croatia	47	94	88	39	79	87	63	85	7	7
Cuba	116	100	93	54	93	96	70	87	9	20
Czech Republic	104	102	97	37	87	87	..	90	38	36
Denmark	90	103	127	67	98	100	87	95	0[c]	0
Dominican Republic	32	112	68	33	57	86	..	49	77	63
Ecuador	77	117	61	..	98	99	..	52	11	0
Egypt, Arab Rep.	14	100	87	29	84	94	..	79	78	218
El Salvador	50	113	60	18	..	91	..	48	35	32
Eritrea	7	66	28	1	16	48	..	19	135	156
Estonia	109	100	96	64	99	95	..	88	1	1
Ethiopia	2	77	28	2	22	46	..	25	..	..
Finland	57	102	127	87	98	100	93	94	1	1
France	113	105	110	55	100	100	..	95	7	3
Gabon	14	130	50	..	85	..	..	..	..	..
Gambia, The	18	..	..	1	48	..	..	33	..	..
Georgia	49	95	82	41	97	93	..	69	14	14
Germany	99	99	100	50	84	..	..	..	..	..
Ghana	46	81	42	3	54	58	..	36	624	597
Greece	67	100	96	72	95	98	83	84	2	2
Guatemala	28	113	49	10	..	93	..	34	32	80
Guinea	6	79	26	2	27	64	..	21	228	291
Guinea-Bissau	..	..	..	..	38	..	..	..	..	..
Haiti	..	..	..	..	22	..	..	..	..	..

Participation in education

	Gross enrollment ratio				Net enrollment ratio				Children out of school	
		% of relevant age group			% of relevant age group				thousand primary-school-age children	
	Preprimary	Primary	Secondary	Tertiary	Primary[a]		Secondary[a]		Male	Female
	2004[b]	2004[b]	2004[b]	2004[b]	1991	2004[b]	1991	2004[b]	2004	2004
Honduras	33	118	..	16	89	91	21	..	57	45
Hungary	79	99	103	52	91	89	75	92	9	8
India	34	107	52	11	..	87	..	..	..	..
Indonesia	22	116	62	16	97	96	39	55	0	215
Iran, Islamic Rep.	37	103	82	22	92	89	..	78	400	402
Iraq	6	98	45	15	94	88	..	38	..	..
Ireland	..	106	109	55	90	96	80	85	9	8
Israel	110	112	93	57	92	99	..	89	7	6
Italy	101	101	99	59	100	99	..	91	4	9
Jamaica	81	93	84	19	96	88	64	75	20	18
Japan	84	100	102	52	100	100	97	100	6	0
Jordan	30	100	88	35	94	93	..	82	18	11
Kazakhstan	31	109	98	48	89	98	..	92	4	6
Kenya	53	111	48	..	..	76	..	..	618	607
Korea, Dem. Rep.	..	..	..	..	..	..	..	..	..	..
Korea, Rep.	87	105	91	89	100	100	86	88	0[c]	9
Kuwait	71	96	90	22	49	86	..	78	9	6
Kyrgyz Republic	12	98	88	40	92	90	..	..	10	9
Lao PDR	8	116	46	6	63	84	..	37	50	68
Latvia	75	95	95	71	92	87	..	87	6	6
Lebanon	74	107	89	48	73	93	..	..	10	10
Lesotho	31	131	36	3	71	86	15	23	27	18
Liberia	..	..	..	..	..	..	..	..	..	..
Libya	8	112	104	56	96	..	..	..	..	..
Lithuania	62	100	103	69	..	92	..	94	5	4
Macedonia, FYR	31	98	84	27	94	92	..	81	2	1
Madagascar	10	134	..	3	64	89	..	..	136	136
Malawi	..	125	29	0[c]	48	95	..	25	71	19
Malaysia	99	93	70	29	..	93	..	70	113	107
Mali	3	64	22	2	21	46	5	..	557	615
Mauritania	2	94	20	3	35	74	..	14	58	60
Mauritius	95	103	80	17	91	95	..	75	4	2
Mexico	81	109	79	22	98	100	44	62	25	8
Moldova	50	85	74	32	89	78	..	69	23	22
Mongolia	33	102	93	39	90	84	..	82	13	11
Morocco	53	106	47	11	56	87	..	35	204	302
Mozambique	..	95	11	1	43	71	..	4	475	614
Myanmar	..	93	38	11	98	85	..	34	408	374
Namibia	29	101	58	6	..	74	..	37	59	47
Nepal	17	114	43	6	..	..	..	..	..	..
Netherlands	87	108	122	58	95	99	84	89	0[c]	8
New Zealand	90	102	119	72	98	100	85	92	1	1
Nicaragua	35	112	64	18	73	88	..	41	25	23
Niger	1	45	8	1	22	39	5	7	609	717
Nigeria	15	99	35	10	..	88	..	28	..	..
Norway	82	99	114	80	100	99	88	95	1	1
Oman	6	87	86	13	69	78	..	75	38	33
Pakistan	45	82	27	3	33	66	..	..	2,294	3,834
Panama	55	112	70	46	..	100	..	64	2	3
Papua New Guinea	59	75	26	..	..	..	..	..	..	..
Paraguay	30	110	65	26	94	89	26	51	46	42
Peru	58	118	90	..	..	100	..	69	3	0
Philippines	39	113	84	29	96	94	..	59	385	269
Poland	51	100	105	59	97	98	76	91	33	25
Portugal	75	118	109	56	98	..	..	82	2	4
Puerto Rico	..	..	..	..	..	..	..	..	..	..

2.11 Participation in education

	Gross enrollment ratio				Net enrollment ratio				Children out of school	
	% of relevant age group				% of relevant age group				thousand primary-school-age children	
	Preprimary	Primary	Secondary	Tertiary	Primary[a]		Secondary[a]		Male	Female
	2004[b]	2004[b]	2004[b]	2004[b]	1991	2004[b]	1991	2004[b]	2004	2004
Romania	76	100	85	36	81	90	..	81	33	34
Russian Federation	67	118	93	65	99	..	..	..	..	..
Rwanda	3	119	14	3	66	73	7	..	205	185
Saudi Arabia	5	67	68	28	59	53	31	52	824	806
Senegal	6	76	19	5	43	66	..	15	296	320
Serbia and Montenegro	..	..	..	..	69	..	62	..	..	..
Sierra Leone	..	..	..	2	43	..	..	..	..	..
Singapore	..	..	..	..	..	..	..	..	..	..
Slovak Republic	88	100	92	34	..	85	..	88	21	19
Slovenia	68	111	112	70	96	96	..	95	1	1
Somalia	..	..	..	..	9	..	..	..	..	..
South Africa	33	105	90	15	90	89	45	..	287	200
Spain	109	107	117	64	100	100	..	95	2	10
Sri Lanka	..	102	81	..	..	99	..	..	9	13
Sudan	23	60	33	..	40	..	..	..	..	..
Swaziland	..	101	42	4	75	77	30	29	24	23
Sweden	80	109	137	82	100	100	85	98	1	3
Switzerland	93	103	93	45	84	94	80	83	5	3
Syrian Arab Republic	10	123	63	..	91	98	43	58	0	32
Tajikistan	9	100	82	16	77	98	..	79	3	17
Tanzania	25	101	..	1	49	86	..	..	465	518
Thailand	92	99	77	41	76	87	..	..	365	433
Togo	2	101	39	..	64	79	15	..	..	..
Trinidad and Tobago	86	102	84	12	91	92	..	72	2	2
Tunisia	22	111	77	26	94	97	..	64	10	9
Turkey	7	95	85	28	89	89	42	..	332	548
Turkmenistan	..	..	..	..	..	..	..	..	..	..
Uganda	3	125	19	3	..	98	..	15	..	..
Ukraine	82	95	93	66	80	86	..	84	162	155
United Arab Emirates	64	84	66	22	99	71	60	62	41	42
United Kingdom	77	101	170	63	98	100	81	95	0[c]	1
United States	60	100	95	83	97	94	85	89	740	584
Uruguay	64	109	106	38	91	90	..	73	16	15
Uzbekistan	28	100	95	15	78	..	..	..	..	..
Venezuela, RB	55	105	72	39	87	92	18	61	109	89
Vietnam	47	98	73	10	90	93	..	..	..	..
West Bank and Gaza	30	93	94	38	..	86	..	89	22	19
Yemen, Rep.	1	87	48	9	51	75	..	..	..	..
Zambia	..	99	26	..	..	80	..	24	221	214
Zimbabwe	43	96	36	4	..	82	..	34	224	206
World	37 w	104 w	66 w	24 w	84 w	.. w	.. w	.. w	53,784 s	61,590 s
Low income	27	100	46	9	..	79	..	..	..	..
Middle income	38	111	75	24	92	..	..	..	..	..
Lower middle income	35	112	72	20	92	..	..	..	..	..
Upper middle income	53	106	87	40	94	..	..	..	..	..
Low & middle income	32	105	61	17	82	..	..	..	52,451[d]	60,508[d]
East Asia & Pacific	36	113	69	17	96	..	..	..	5,158[d]	4,870[d]
Europe & Central Asia	45	102	92	47	90	..	..	..	1,439[d]	1,669[d]
Latin America & Carib.	57	121	87	26	85	96	30	65	1,789[d]	1,497[d]
Middle East & N. Africa	23	104	67	23	84	89	..	..	2,585[d]	3,807[d]
South Asia	33	103	49	10	..	88	..	..	18,742[d]	23,552[d]
Sub-Saharan Africa	16	93	30	5	47	64	..	..	22,738[d]	25,112[d]
High income	76	100	105	67	95	95	85	90	1,333[d]	1,083[d]
Europe EMU	101	104	108	57	95	99	..	92	..	..

a. Break in series between 1997 and 1998 due to change from International Standard Classification of Education (ISCED) 1976 to ISCED97. b. Provisional data. c. Less than 0.5. d. Data are for 2001/02.

About the data

School enrollment data are reported to the United Nations Educational, Scientific, and Cultural Organization (UNESCO) Institute for Statistics by national education authorities and statistical offices. Enrollment ratios help to monitor two important issues for universal primary education: whether a country is on track to achieve the Millennium Development Goal of universal primary completion by 2015, which implies achieving a net primary enrollment ratio of 100 percent, and whether an education system has sufficient capacity to meet the needs of universal primary education, as indicated in part by its gross enrollment ratios.

Enrollment ratios, while a useful measure of participation in education, also have some limitations. They are based on data collected during annual school surveys, which are typically conducted at the beginning of the school year. They do not reflect actual rates of attendance or dropouts during the school year. And school administrators may report exaggerated enrollments, especially if there is a financial incentive to do so. Often the number of teachers paid by the government is related to the number of pupils enrolled.

Also as international indicators, the gross and net primary enrollment ratios have an inherent weakness: the length of primary education differs significantly across countries, although the International Standard Classification of Education tries to minimize the difference. A relatively short duration for primary education tends to increase the ratio, whereas a relatively long duration tends to decrease it (in part because there are more dropouts among older children).

Overage or underage enrollments frequently occur, particularly when parents prefer, for cultural or economic reasons, to have children start school at other than the official age. Children's age at enrollment may be inaccurately estimated or misstated, especially in communities where registration of births is not strictly enforced. Parents who want to enroll an underage child in primary school may do so by overstating the child's age. And in some education systems ages for children repeating a grade may be underreported.

Other problems affecting cross-country comparisons of enrollment data stem from errors in estimates of school-age populations. Age-gender structures from censuses or vital registration systems, the primary sources of data on school-age populations, are commonly subject to underenumeration (especially of young children) aimed at circumventing laws or regulations. Errors are also introduced when parents round up children's ages. While census data are often adjusted for age bias, adjustments are rarely made for inadequate vital registration systems. Compounding these problems, pre- and post-census estimates of school-age children are interpolations or projections based on models that may miss important demographic events (see the discussion of demographic data in *About the data* for table 2.1).

In using enrollment data, it is also important to consider repetition rates. These rates are quite high in some developing countries, leading to a substantial number of overage children enrolled in each grade and raising the gross enrollment ratio.

Thus gross enrollment ratios indicate the capacity of each level of the education system, but a high ratio does not necessarily mean a successful education system. The net enrollment ratio excludes overage students in an attempt to capture more accurately the system's coverage and internal efficiency. It does not solve the problem completely, however, because some children fall outside the official school age because of late or early entry rather than because of grade repetition. The difference between gross and net enrollment ratios shows the incidence of overage and underage enrollments.

Out of school children are children in the primary school age group who are not enrolled in primary or in secondary education. The data are calculated by the UNESCO Institute for Statistics using administrative data. Children out of school include dropouts and children who never enrolled as well as children of primary age enrolled in pre-primary education. The large number of children out of school creates pressure for the education system to enroll children and to provide classrooms, teachers, and educational materials, a task made difficult in many developing countries by limited education budgets.

In 2006 the UNESCO Instiitute for Statistics changed its convention for citing the reference year. For more information, see *About the data* for table 2.10.

Definitions

• **Gross enrollment ratio** is the ratio of total enrollment, regardless of age, to the population of the age group that officially corresponds to the level of education shown. • **Preprimary education** refers to the initial stage of organized instruction, designed primarily to introduce very young children to a school-type environment. • **Primary education** provides children with basic reading, writing, and mathematics skills along with an elementary understanding of such subjects as history, geography, natural science, social science, art, and music. • **Secondary education** completes the provision of basic education that began at the primary level and aims at laying the foundations for lifelong learning and human development by offering more subject- or skill-oriented instruction using more specialized teachers. • **Tertiary education**, whether or not leading to an advanced research qualification, normally requires, as a minimum condition of admission, the successful completion of education at the secondary level. • **Net enrollment ratio** is the ratio of children of official school age based on the International Standard Classification of Education 1997 who are enrolled in school to the population of the corresponding official school age. • **Children out of school** are the number of primary-school-age children not enrolled in primary or secondary school.

Data sources

Data on gross and net enrollment ratios and out of school children are from the UNESCO Institute for Statistics. Data on gross and net enrollment ratios for latest years are provisional, as of January 2006.

2.12 Education efficiency

	Gross intake rate in grade 1		Share of cohort reaching grade 5				Repeaters in primary school		Transition to secondary education	
	% of relevant age group		% of grade 1 students				% of enrollment		% of enrollment in last year of primary	
	Male	Female	Male[a]		Female[a]		Male	Female	Male	Female
	2004[b]	2004[b]	1991	2003[b]	1991	2003[b]	2004[b]	2004[b]	2004[b]	2004[b]
Afghanistan	..	..	..	..	..	..	..	..	..	..
Albania	103	102	..	..	..	..	3	2	98	100
Algeria	103	100	95	95	94	97	14	9	76	83
Angola	..	..	..	..	..	..	..	..	..	..
Argentina	112	112	..	91	..	93	7	5	..	..
Armenia	96	101	..	..	..	..	0[c]	0[c]	99	97
Australia	106	104	98	98	99	100	0	0	100	100
Austria	..	..	..	..	..	..	..	..	..	..
Azerbaijan	96	93	..	..	..	..	0[c]	0[c]	99	99
Bangladesh	134	128	..	51	..	54	7	7	92	99
Belarus	103	102	..	..	..	..	0[c]	0[c]	100	97
Belgium	101	101	90	..	92	..	..	..	..	..
Benin	112	94	54	70	56	69	23	23	51	51
Bolivia	119	120	..	87	..	86	2	1	92	91
Bosnia and Herzegovina	..	..	..	..	..	..	..	..	..	..
Botswana	110	107	81	87	87	92	6	4	97	97
Brazil	127	117	..	..	..	..	..	..	..	..
Bulgaria	106	106	91	..	90	..	3	2	96	95
Burkina Faso	76	66	71	74	68	78	13	13	42	37
Burundi	95	86	65	64	58	62	28	31	35	33
Cambodia	154	143	..	58	..	61	12	9	85	80
Cameroon	115	100	..	64	..	63	26	25	47	49
Canada	..	..	95	..	98	..	..	..	..	..
Central African Republic	75	52	24	..	22	..	..	..	..	..
Chad	98	70	56	51	41	39	24	25	60	46
Chile	98	96	94	100	91	98	2	1	95	98
China	100	99	58	100	78	98	0[c]	0[c]	92	92
Hong Kong, China	101	95	..	100	..	100	1	1	100	100
Colombia	126	120	..	75	..	80	5	4	100	100
Congo, Dem. Rep.	..	..	58	..	50	..	..	..	..	..
Congo, Rep.	66	63	56	65	65	67	25	24	78	78
Costa Rica	108	107	83	92	85	93	8	6	93	90
Côte d'Ivoire	75	68	75	..	70	..	17	18	..	..
Croatia	99	97	..	..	..	..	0[c]	0[c]	100	100
Cuba	105	103	..	98	..	97	1	0	98	99
Czech Republic	94	93	..	97	..	98	1	1	99	99
Denmark	98	98	94	100	94	99	..	..	100	99
Dominican Republic	118	104	..	52	..	70	9	6	92	84
Ecuador	136	134	..	75	..	77	2	2	76	71
Egypt, Arab Rep.	100	98	..	96	..	100	6	3	83	86
El Salvador	134	130	56	67	60	70	8	6	94	94
Eritrea	63	52	..	86	..	73	21	22	85	76
Estonia	97	98	..	98	..	99	3	1	93	98
Ethiopia	106	93	16	59	23	54	12	11	90	88
Finland	100	98	100	100	100	100	1	0[c]	100	100
France	..	..	69	..	95	..	..	..	..	..
Gabon	94	94	..	68	..	71	35	34	..	..
Gambia, The	95	101	..	..	..	..	..	..	..	..
Georgia	104	102	..	..	..	..	0[c]	0[c]	98	99
Germany	101	100	..	..	..	..	2	2	..	..
Ghana	87	89	81	62	79	65	6	6	95	100
Greece	..	..	100	..	100	..	..	..	..	..
Guatemala	129	125	..	79	..	76	14	13	97	95
Guinea	87	79	64	87	48	76	10	11	49	45
Guinea-Bissau	..	..	..	..	..	..	..	..	..	..
Haiti	..	..	..	..	..	..	..	..	..	..

Education efficiency

	Gross intake rate in grade 1		Share of cohort reaching grade 5				Repeaters in primary school		Transition to secondary education	
	% of relevant age group		% of grade 1 students				% of enrollment		% of enrollment in last year of primary	
	Male	Female	Male[a]		Female[a]		Male	Female	Male	Female
	2004[b]	2004[b]	1991	2003[b]	1991	2003[b]	2004[b]	2004[b]	2004[b]	2004[b]
Honduras	129	127	..	63	..	69	9	7	..	..
Hungary	99	98	77	..	98	..	3	2	99	99
India	135	129	..	60	..	64	4	4	85	89
Indonesia	120	120	34	88	78	90	4	4	80	83
Iran, Islamic Rep.	102	118	91	94	89	94	3	2	97	95
Iraq	110	103	..	..	..	..	9	7	..	..
Ireland	104	104	99	98	100	100	1	1	..	..
Israel	97	98	..	100	..	99	2	1	72	73
Italy	98	97	..	96	..	97	0[c]	0[c]	100	100
Jamaica	90	88	..	88	..	93	4	3	..	..
Japan	..	..	100	..	100	..	..	..	..	..
Jordan	99	100	..	97	..	98	0[c]	0[c]	97	98
Kazakhstan	106	105	..	..	..	..	0[c]	0[c]	100	100
Kenya	122	119	75	78	78	73	11	10	..	..
Korea, Dem. Rep.	..	..	..	..	..	..	..	..	..	..
Korea, Rep.	103	103	99	100	100	100	0	0	99	99
Kuwait	96	97	..	..	..	..	3	2	95	95
Kyrgyz Republic	99	97	..	..	..	..	0[c]	0[c]	98	100
Lao PDR	123	114	..	62	..	63	21	18	80	76
Latvia	92	90	..	..	..	..	2	1	99	99
Lebanon	100	99	..	95	..	100	12	9	83	89
Lesotho	144	131	58	58	73	69	21	16	64	62
Liberia	..	..	..	..	..	..	..	..	..	..
Libya	..	..	..	..	..	..	..	..	..	..
Lithuania	97	97	..	..	..	..	1	0[c]	99	99
Macedonia, FYR	98	96	..	..	..	..	0[c]	0[c]	98	97
Madagascar	168	164	22	56	21	58	31	29	56	55
Malawi	164	178	71	50	57	38	18	18	..	..
Malaysia	93	92	97	87	97	87	..	..	..	..
Mali	69	58	71	78	67	70	19	19	62	57
Mauritania	106	105	76	81	75	83	14	15	47	44
Mauritius	95	95	97	98	98	100	6	4	..	..
Mexico	108	107	35	92	71	94	6	4	94	92
Moldova	89	88	..	..	..	..	0[c]	0[c]	97	99
Mongolia	113	115	..	..	..	..	1	1	99	99
Morocco	100	96	75	82	76	80	16	11	78	81
Mozambique	138	129	36	53	32	45	21	21	..	..
Myanmar	124	125	..	64	..	66	1	1	74	66
Namibia	99	99	60	87	65	90	15	12	87	88
Nepal	115	105	51	63	51	67	22	22	80	76
Netherlands	98	97	..	100	..	100	..	..	..	..
New Zealand	..	..	..	..	..	..	..	..	..	..
Nicaragua	144	135	11	52	37	61	12	9	..	..
Niger	68	51	61	75	65	72	5	5	43	41
Nigeria	120	103	..	33	..	38	3	3	..	..
Norway	99	99	99	100	100	99	0	0	..	..
Oman	74	75	97	97	96	98	1	1	99	99
Pakistan	126	95	..	..	..	..	..	..	..	..
Panama	121	118	..	82	..	87	6	5	63	65
Papua New Guinea	101	90	70	72	68	66	0	0	77	77
Paraguay	109	106	73	68	75	71	9	6	..	..
Peru	113	114	..	85	..	83	10	10	..	..
Philippines	140	130	..	72	..	80	3	1	98	97
Poland	97	98	89	..	96	..	..	..	..	..
Portugal	..	..	..	..	..	..	..	..	..	..
Puerto Rico	..	..	..	..	..	..	..	..	..	..

2.12 Education efficiency

	Gross intake rate in grade 1		Share of cohort reaching grade 5				Repeaters in primary school		Transition to secondary education	
	% of relevant age group		% of grade 1 students				% of enrollment		% of enrollment in last year of primary	
	Male	Female	Male[a]		Female[a]		Male	Female	Male	Female
	2004[b]	2004[b]	1991	2003[b]	1991	2003[b]	2004[b]	2004[b]	2004[b]	2004[b]
Romania	107	106	..	..	..	..	3	2	98	98
Russian Federation	..	..	..	..	..	..	..	..	..	..
Rwanda	183	183	61	43	59	49	19	19	..	..
Saudi Arabia	66	66	82	94	84	93	5	3	100	93
Senegal	89	91	..	79	..	77	13	13	49	45
Serbia and Montenegro	..	..	..	..	..	..	..	..	..	..
Sierra Leone	..	..	..	..	..	..	..	..	..	..
Singapore	..	..	..	..	..	..	..	..	..	..
Slovak Republic	96	94	..	..	..	..	3	2	98	98
Slovenia	122	120	..	..	..	..	1	0[c]	100	99
Somalia	..	..	..	..	..	..	..	..	..	..
South Africa	118	112	..	82	..	87	6	4	94	96
Spain	..	..	..	..	..	..	..	..	..	..
Sri Lanka	..	..	92	..	93	..	..	..	96	98
Sudan	73	62	90	92	99	92	1	4	88	92
Swaziland	110	104	74	74	80	80	19	14	76	78
Sweden	97	97	100	..	100	..	..	..	..	..
Switzerland	89	92	..	..	..	..	2	2	100	100
Syrian Arab Republic	122	118	97	93	95	92	8	7	93	95
Tajikistan	98	94	..	..	..	..	0[c]	0[c]	98	97
Tanzania	118	114	81	86	82	90	5	5	34	33
Thailand	..	..	..	..	..	..	..	..	..	..
Togo	90	82	52	79	42	73	24	24	67	61
Trinidad and Tobago	97	96	..	66	..	76	6	4	96	99
Tunisia	98	100	94	96	77	97	11	7	86	90
Turkey	..	..	98	..	97	..	..	..	..	..
Turkmenistan	..	..	..	..	..	..	..	..	..	..
Uganda	164	163	..	63	..	64	14	14	..	..
Ukraine	105	105	..	..	..	..	0[c]	0[c]	..	..
United Arab Emirates	89	88	80	94	80	95	3	2	96	96
United Kingdom	..	..	..	..	..	..	..	..	..	..
United States	..	..	..	..	..	..	..	..	..	..
Uruguay	109	107	96	91	98	95	10	7	..	..
Uzbekistan	102	102	..	..	..	..	0	0	100	99
Venezuela, RB	103	100	82	89	90	94	9	6	97	100
Vietnam	101	95	..	90	..	88	3	2	99	100
West Bank and Gaza	85	84	..	..	..	..	0	0	100	100
Yemen, Rep.	122	97	..	78	..	67	5	4	..	..
Zambia	110	110	..	..	..	..	7	7	..	..
Zimbabwe	122	118	72	68	81	71	..	..	69	70
World	**116 w**	**110 w**	**.. w**	**.. w**	**.. w**	**.. w**	**4 w**	**4 w**	**.. w**	**.. w**
Low income	125	115	..	63	..	65	6	6	82	83
Middle income	107	106	61	93	81	93	3	2	91	91
Lower middle income	107	106	59	94	80	93	3	2	90	91
Upper middle income	..	..	..	..	..	..	..	..	..	..
Low & middle income	117	111	..	..	..	..	4	4	87	87
East Asia & Pacific	107	106	55	94	78	93	1	1	90	90
Europe & Central Asia	..	..	..	..	..	..	..	..	..	..
Latin America & Carib.	120	115	..	..	..	..	..	..	..	..
Middle East & N. Africa	106	105	..	92	..	92	8	5	87	89
South Asia	132	122	..	59	..	63	4	4	86	90
Sub-Saharan Africa	113	104	..	..	..	..	11	11	..	..
High income	..	..	..	..	..	..	..	..	..	..
Europe EMU	..	..	..	..	..	..	..	..	..	..

a. Break in series between 1997 and 1998 due to change from International Standard Classification of Education (ISCED) 1976 to ISCED97. b. Provisional data. c. Less than 0.5.

About the data

Indicators of students' progress through school are estimated by the United Nations Educational, Scientific, and Cultural Organization (UNESCO) Institute for Statistics and the World Bank. These indicators measure an education system's success in extending coverage to all students, maintaining the flow of students from one grade to the next, and imparting a particular level of education.

Gross intake rate indicates the general level of access to primary education. It also indicates the capacity of the education system to provide access to primary education. Low gross intake rates in grade 1 reflect the fact that many children do not enter primary school even though school attendance, at least through the primary level, is mandatory in all countries. Because the gross intake rate includes all new entrants regardless of age, it can be more than 100 percent. Once enrolled, students drop out for a variety of reasons, including low quality of schooling, discouragement over poor performance, and the direct and indirect costs of schooling. Students' progress to higher grades may also be limited by the availability of teachers, classrooms, and educational materials.

The share of cohort reaching grade 5 (cohort survival rate) is estimated as the proportion of an entering cohort of grade 1 students that eventually reaches grade 5. It measures the holding power and internal efficiency of an education system. Cohort survival rates approaching 100 percent indicate a high level of retention and a low level of dropout.

Cohort survival rates are typically estimated from data on enrollment and repetition by grade for two consecutive years, in a procedure called the reconstructed cohort method. This method makes three simplifying assumptions: dropouts never return to school; promotion, repetition, and dropout rates remain constant over the entire period in which the cohort is enrolled in school; and the same rates apply to all pupils enrolled in a given grade, regardless of whether they previously repeated a grade (Fredricksen 1993). Given these assumptions, cross-country comparisons should be made with caution, because other flows—caused by new entrants, reentrants, grade skipping, migration, or school transfers during the school year—are not considered.

The UNESCO Institute for Statistics measures the share of cohort reaching grade 5 because research suggests that five to six years of schooling is a critical threshold for the achievement of sustainable basic literacy and numeracy skills. But the indicator only indirectly reflects the quality of schooling, and a high rate does not guarantee these learning outcomes. Measuring actual learning outcomes requires setting curriculum standards and measuring students' learning progress against those standards through standardized assessments or tests.

The data on repeaters are often used to indicate the internal efficiency of the education system. Repeaters not only increase the cost of education for the family and for the school system, but also use limited school resources. Countries have different policies on repetition and promotion; in some cases the number of repeaters is controlled because of limited capacity. Care should be taken in interpreting this indicator.

The transition rate from primary school to secondary school conveys the degree of access or transition between the two levels of education. A low transition rate can signal problems such as an inadequate promotion and examination system or insufficient capacity in secondary schools. The quality of data on the transition rate is affected when new entrants and repeaters are not correctly distinguished in the first grade of secondary school. Students who interrupt their studies for one or more years after completing primary school could also affect the quality of the data.

In 2006 the UNESCO Instiitute for Statistics changed its convention for citing the reference year. For more information, see *About the data* for table 2.10.

Definitions

• **Gross intake rate in grade 1** is the number of new entrants in the first grade of primary education regardless of age, expressed as a percentage of the population of the official primary school entrance age. • **Share of cohort reaching grade 5** is the percentage of children enrolled in the first grade of primary school who eventually reach grade 5. The estimate is based on the reconstructed cohort method (see *About the data*). • **Repeaters in primary school** are the number of students enrolled in the same grade as in the previous year, as a percentage of all students enrolled in primary school. • **Transition to secondary education** refers to the number of new entrants to the first grade of secondary school in a given year, as a percentage of the number of students enrolled in the final grade of primary school in the previous year.

Data sources

Data on education efficiency are from the UNESCO Institute for Statistics. Data for latest years are provisional, as of January 2006.

2.13 Education completion and outcomes

	Primary completion rate						Youth literacy rate				Adult literacy rate	
	% of relevant age group						% ages 15–24				% ages 15 and older	
	Total[a]		Male[a]		Female[a]		Male		Female		Male	Female
	1991	2004	1991	2004	1991	2004	1990	2002	1990	2002	2002	2002
Afghanistan	25	..	37	..	13	..	..	..	..	..	..	..
Albania	..	99	..	99	..	99	97	99[b]	92	99[b]	99[b]	98[b]
Algeria	79	94	86	94	73	94	86	94[c]	68	86[c]	79[c]	60[c]
Angola	35	..	..	..	..	..	..	83[c]	..	63[c]	82[c]	54[c]
Argentina	..	102	..	100	..	105	98	99[b]	98	99[b]	97[b]	97[b]
Armenia	90	107	..	106	..	108	100	100[b]	99	100[b]	100[b]	99[b]
Australia	..	100	..	100	..	100	..	..	..	..	..	..
Austria	..	..	..	..	..	..	..	..	..	..	..	..
Azerbaijan	..	96	..	97	..	95	..	..	..	..	..	..
Bangladesh	49	73	..	70	..	75	51	58	33	41	50	31
Belarus	95	101	95	103	96	99	100	..	100	..	..	..
Belgium	79	..	76	..	82	..	..	..	..	..	..	..
Benin	21	49	28	59	13	38	57	58[b]	25	33[b]	46[b]	23[b]
Bolivia	71	100	78	102	64	98	96	99[b]	89	96[b]	93[b]	80[b]
Bosnia and Herzegovina	..	..	..	..	..	..	..	100[c]	..	100[c]	98[c]	91[c]
Botswana	79	92	71	89	87	94	79	85	87	93	76	82
Brazil	93	111	..	110	..	111	91	96[c]	93	98[c]	88[c]	89[c]
Bulgaria	90	97	89	98	92	96	100	98[b]	99	98[b]	99[b]	98[b]
Burkina Faso	21	29	26	34	16	25	..	..	..	..	..	..
Burundi	46	33	49	39	43	27	58	76[c]	45	69[c]	67[c]	52[c]
Cambodia	..	82	..	85	..	78	81	88[c]	66	79[c]	85[c]	64[c]
Cameroon	56	72	60	77	52	66	86	..	76	..	77[c]	60[c]
Canada	..	..	..	..	..	..	..	..	..	..	..	..
Central African Republic	27	..	35	..	18	..	66	70[c]	39	47[c]	65[c]	33[c]
Chad	18	29	30	41	7	18	58	55[c]	38	23[c]	41[c]	13[c]
Chile	..	97	..	98	..	97	98	99[b]	98	99[b]	96[b]	96[b]
China	103	99	..	99	..	100	97	99[b]	93	99[b]	95[b]	87[b]
Hong Kong, China	102	111	..	113	..	108	..	..	..	..	..	..
Colombia	71	94	60	92	82	96	94	97[c]	96	98[c]	94[c]	95[c]
Congo, Dem. Rep.	46	..	58	..	34	..	80	77[c]	58	61[c]	80[c]	52[c]
Congo, Rep.	54	66	59	70	49	63	95	98	90	97	89	77
Costa Rica	74	92	77	91	81	94	97	98	98	99	96	96
Côte d'Ivoire	43	43	55	52	32	34	65	70[c]	40	51[c]	60[c]	38[c]
Croatia	85	91	..	92	..	91	100	100[b]	100	100[b]	99[b]	97[b]
Cuba	96	93	..	93	..	92	99	100[b]	99	100[b]	100[b]	100[b]
Czech Republic	..	102	..	103	..	101	..	..	..	..	..	..
Denmark	98	103	98	103	98	104	..	..	..	..	..	..
Dominican Republic	61	91	..	88	..	93	87	93[b]	88	95[b]	87[b]	87[b]
Ecuador	91	101	91	100	92	101	96	96[b]	95	96[b]	92[b]	90[b]
Egypt, Arab Rep.	..	93	..	95	..	91	71	..	51	..	..	..
El Salvador	41	84	38	84	43	85	85	90	83	88	82	77
Eritrea	19	44	22	53	17	36	73	..	49	..	..	..
Estonia	93	103	93	105	94	101	100	100[b]	100	100[b]	100[b]	100[b]
Ethiopia	21	51	26	58	16	43	52	63	34	52	49	34
Finland	97	102	98	102	97	102	..	..	..	..	..	..
France	104	..	..	..	..	..	..	..	..	..	..	..
Gabon	58	66	55	65	61	68	..	..	..	..	..	..
Gambia, The	44	..	55	..	33	..	50	..	34	..	..	..
Georgia	..	86	..	84	..	87	..	..	..	..	..	..
Germany	100	97	99	97	100	97	..	..	..	..	..	..
Ghana	63	65	70	65	55	67	88	..	75	..	63[b]	46[b]
Greece	99	..	99	..	98	..	99	99[c]	100	100[c]	94[c]	88[c]
Guatemala	..	70	..	75	..	65	80	86[b]	66	78[b]	75[b]	63[b]
Guinea	17	48	24	58	9	39	62	..	26	..	..	..
Guinea-Bissau	..	27	..	35	..	19	..	..	..	..	..	..
Haiti	27	..	29	..	26	..	56	66	54	67	54	50

Education completion and outcomes

	Primary completion rate						Youth literacy rate				Adult literacy rate	
	% of relevant age group						% ages 15–24				% ages 15 and older	
	Total[a]		Male[a]		Female[a]		Male		Female		Male	Female
	1991	2004	1991	2004	1991	2004	1990	2002	1990	2002	2002	2002
Honduras	65	79	67	77	62	82	78	87[b]	81	91[b]	80[b]	80[b]
Hungary	82	96	88	97	90	96	100	99[b]	100	100[b]	99[b]	99[b]
India	..	84	..	88	..	79	73	84[b]	54	68[b]	73[b]	48[b]
Indonesia	91	101	..	101	..	101	97	99	93	98	92	83
Iran, Islamic Rep.	91	95	97	92	85	97	92	..	81	..	84[c]	70[c]
Iraq	59	74	64	85	53	63	56	..	25	..	..	..
Ireland	..	101	..	101	..	100	..	..	..	..	..	..
Israel	..	101	..	101	..	101	99	100[c]	98	99[c]	98[c]	96[c]
Italy	104	103	104	103	104	102	..	..	..	..	..	..
Jamaica	90	84	86	84	94	89	87	91	95	98	84	91
Japan	101	..	101	..	102	..	..	..	..	..	..	..
Jordan	101	97	101	97	101	96	98	99	95	99	95	85
Kazakhstan	..	110	..	110	..	109	100	..	100	..	..	..
Kenya	..	89	..	90	..	89	93	80	87	81	78	70
Korea, Dem. Rep.	..	..	..	..	..	..	..	..	..	..	..	..
Korea, Rep.	98	105	98	104	98	106	..	..	..	..	..	..
Kuwait	57	91	58	91	56	92	88	92	87	94	85	81
Kyrgyz Republic	..	93	..	93	..	93	..	..	..	..	..	..
Lao PDR	43	74	48	78	38	70	79	83[c]	61	75[c]	77[c]	61[c]
Latvia	..	98	..	99	..	97	..	100[b]	..	100[b]	100[b]	100[b]
Lebanon	..	94	..	92	..	96	95	..	89	..	..	..
Lesotho	58	71	41	60	75	82	77	..	97	..	74[c]	90[c]
Liberia	..	..	..	..	..	..	75	86	39	55	72	39
Libya	..	..	..	..	..	..	99	100	83	94	92	71
Lithuania	89	105	..	105	..	105	100	100[b]	100	100[b]	100[b]	100[b]
Macedonia, FYR	98	97	..	97	..	97	..	99[b]	..	98[b]	98[b]	94[b]
Madagascar	33	45	33	45	34	46	78	72[c]	67	68[c]	76[c]	65[c]
Malawi	31	58	35	60	28	57	76	..	51	..	..	..
Malaysia	90	95	90	95	90	95	95	97[b]	94	97[b]	92[b]	85[b]
Mali	11	44	13	58	9	30	..	..	..	..	..	..
Mauritania	33	43	40	45	26	41	56	68[b]	36	55[b]	60[b]	31[b]
Mauritius	102	100	103	98	102	102	91	94[b]	91	95[b]	88[b]	81[b]
Mexico	86	97	89	97	90	98	96	98[c]	94	97[c]	92[c]	89[c]
Moldova	..	83	..	82	..	83	100	98[b]	100	99[b]	97[b]	95[b]
Mongolia	..	95	..	95	..	96	..	97[b]	..	98[b]	98[b]	98[b]
Morocco	46	67	54	71	37	63	68	77	42	61	63	38
Mozambique	26	29	32	35	21	23	66	77	32	49	62	31
Myanmar	..	72	..	72	..	73	90	96[c]	86	93[c]	94[c]	86[c]
Namibia	78	81	70	76	86	85	86	87[b]	89	92[b]	81[b]	81[b]
Nepal	51	71	70	76	41	65	67	81[b]	27	60[b]	63[b]	35[b]
Netherlands	..	100	..	101	..	99	..	..	..	..	..	..
New Zealand	100	..	100	..	99	..	..	..	..	..	..	..
Nicaragua	41	73	43	70	59	77	68	84[c]	69	89[c]	77[c]	77[c]
Niger	17	25	21	30	12	20	25	26[b]	9	14[b]	20[b]	9[b]
Nigeria	..	76	..	83	..	69	81	91	66	87	74	59
Norway	100	103	100	102	100	103	..	..	..	..	..	..
Oman	74	91	78	93	70	90	95	100	75	97	82	65
Pakistan	..	..	..	..	..	..	63	75[c]	31	54[c]	62[c]	35[c]
Panama	86	97	86	96	86	97	96	97[b]	95	96[b]	93[b]	91[b]
Papua New Guinea	50	55	56	59	44	51	74	69[b]	62	64[b]	63[b]	51[b]
Paraguay	65	89	64	88	65	90	96	96[c]	95	96[c]	93[c]	90[c]
Peru	..	96	..	97	..	95	97	98[c]	92	96[c]	93[c]	82[c]
Philippines	86	98	84	94	84	102	97	94[b]	97	96[b]	93[b]	93[b]
Poland	96	100	..	..	..	..	..	..	..	..	..	..
Portugal	95	..	94	..	95	..	..	..	..	..	..	..
Puerto Rico	..	..	..	..	..	..	..	..	..	..	..	..

2.13 Education completion and outcomes

	Primary completion rate						Youth literacy rate				Adult literacy rate	
	% of relevant age group						% ages 15–24				% ages 15 and older	
	Total[a]		Male[a]		Female[a]		Male		Female		Male	Female
	1991	2004	1991	2004	1991	2004	1990	2002	1990	2002	2002	2002
Romania	96	90	96	90	96	89	99	98[b]	99	98[b]	98[b]	96[b]
Russian Federation	93	..	92	..	93	..	100	100[b]	100	100[b]	100[b]	99[b]
Rwanda	47	37	47	38	46	37	78	77[c]	67	76[c]	70[c]	59[c]
Saudi Arabia	56	62	60	62	51	61	91	98[c]	79	94[c]	87[c]	69[c]
Senegal	39	45	47	49	30	42	50	58[c]	30	41[c]	51[c]	29[c]
Serbia and Montenegro	71	96	..	97	..	96	..	99[b]	..	99[b]	99[b]	94[b]
Sierra Leone	..	..	..	..	..	..	..	47[c]	..	30[c]	40[c]	21[c]
Singapore	..	..	..	..	..	..	99	99[b]	99	100[b]	97[b]	89[b]
Slovak Republic	96	101	95	102	96	100	..	100[b]	..	100[b]	100[b]	100[b]
Slovenia	95	102	..	103	..	102	100	100	100	100	100	100
Somalia	..	..	..	..	..	..	..	..	..	..	..	..
South Africa	75	96	71	94	80	98	89	..	88	..	..	..
Spain	..	..	..	..	..	..	..	..	..	..	..	..
Sri Lanka	94	..	94	..	94	..	96	95[b]	94	96[b]	92[b]	89[b]
Sudan	40	49	45	53	36	44	76	82[c]	54	69[c]	69[c]	50[c]
Swaziland	62	61	59	58	65	64	85	87[c]	85	89[c]	80[c]	78[c]
Sweden	96	..	96	..	96	..	..	..	..	..	..	..
Switzerland	53	96	53	95	54	97	..	..	..	..	..	..
Syrian Arab Republic	89	107	94	109	84	104	92	97[c]	67	93[c]	91[c]	74[c]
Tajikistan	..	92	..	94	..	90	100	100[b]	100	100[b]	100[b]	99[b]
Tanzania	61	57	60	57	62	56	89	81[b]	77	76[b]	78[b]	62[b]
Thailand	..	..	..	..	..	..	..	98[b]	..	98[b]	95[b]	91[b]
Togo	35	66	48	78	22	55	79	83[c]	48	63[c]	68[c]	38[c]
Trinidad and Tobago	100	94	97	93	102	95	100	100	100	100	99	98
Tunisia	74	94	79	94	69	94	93	96[b]	75	92[b]	83[b]	65[b]
Turkey	90	..	93	..	86	..	97	98[c]	88	95[c]	96[c]	81[c]
Turkmenistan	..	..	..	..	..	..	..	..	..	..	..	..
Uganda	..	57	..	61	..	53	80	86	60	74	79	59
Ukraine	92	91	98	..	97	..	100	100[b]	100	100[b]	100[b]	99[b]
United Arab Emirates	95	75	95	77	94	74	82	88	89	95	76	81
United Kingdom	..	..	..	..	..	..	..	..	..	..	..	..
United States	..	..	..	..	..	..	..	..	..	..	..	..
Uruguay	95	94	92	92	97	97	98	99	99	99	97	98
Uzbekistan	..	98	..	98	..	98	100	100	100	100	100	99
Venezuela, RB	81	89	76	87	86	92	95	96[b]	97	98[b]	93[b]	93[b]
Vietnam	..	101	..	104	..	98	94	..	94	..	..	..
West Bank and Gaza	..	98	..	98	..	99	..	99[c]	..	99[c]	96[c]	87[c]
Yemen, Rep.	..	62	..	78	..	46	74	84	25	51	69	29
Zambia	..	66	..	71	..	61	86	..	76	..	..	..
Zimbabwe	91	80	94	82	89	79	97	99	91	96	94	86
World	.. w	.. w	.. w	.. w	.. w	.. w	.. w	.. w	.. w	.. w	.. w	.. w
Low income	66	74	75	78	59	70	73	81	55	67	73	50
Middle income	92	97	93	97	92	96	95	98	91	97	94	87
Lower middle income	93	98	94	98	92	96	95	98	90	97	93	86
Upper middle income	88	96	88	95	90	96	97	98	95	97	95	94
Low & middle income	81	86	86	88	78	84	86	90	77	83	86	74
East Asia & Pacific	97	99	98	99	96	97	97	98	93	97	95	87
Europe & Central Asia	92	94	92	95	93	94	99	99	97	98	99	99
Latin America & Carib.	86	97	85	96	89	97	93	96	93	97	91	90
Middle East & N. Africa	78	88	83	89	71	86	80	..	59	..	..	..
South Asia	73	82	87	85	65	78	70	82	50	65	72	46
Sub-Saharan Africa	51	62	55	66	47	56	76	..	61	..	..	..
High income	..	..	..	..	..	..	..	..	..	..	..	..
Europe EMU	..	..	..	..	..	..	..	..	..	..	..	..

a. Break in series between 1997 and 1998 due to change from International Standard Classification of Education (ISCED) 1976 to ISCED97. b. Based on census data. c. Based on survey data.

Education completion and outcomes 2.13

About the data

Many governments collect and publish statistics that indicate how their education systems are working and developing—statistics on enrollment and on such efficiency indicators as repetition rates, pupil-teacher ratios, and cohort progression through school.

The World Bank and the United Nations Educational, Scientific, and Cultural Organization (UNESCO) Institute for Statistics worked jointly to develop the primary completion rate indicator. Increasingly used as a core indicator of an education system's performance, it reflects both the coverage of the education system and the educational attainment of students. The indicator is vital as a key measure of educational outcome at the primary level and of progress on the Millennium Development Goals and the Education for All initiative. However, because curricula and standards for school completion vary across countries, a high rate of primary completion does not necessarily mean high levels of student learning.

The primary completion rate reflects the primary cycle as defined by the International Standard Classification of Education (ISCED), ranging from three or four years of primary education (in a very small number of countries) to five or six years (in most countries) and seven (in a small number of countries). For the countries that changed the primary cycle, the most recent ISCED primary cycle is applied consistently to the whole series.

The data in the table are for the proxy primary completion rate, calculated by subtracting the number of students who repeat the final primary grade from the number of students in that grade and dividing the result by the number of children of official graduation age in the population. Data limitations preclude adjusting this number for students who drop out during the final year of primary school. Thus proxy rates should be taken as an upper-bound estimate of the actual primary completion rate.

The numerator may include late entrants and overage children who have repeated one or more grades of primary school but are now graduating as well as children who entered school early. The denominator is the number of children of official graduation age, which could cause the primary completion rate to exceed 100 percent. There are other data limitations that contribute to completion rates exceeding 100 percent, such as the use of estimates for the population, the conduct of school and population surveys at different times of year, and other discrepancies in the numbers used in the calculation.

Basic student outcomes include achievements in reading and mathematics judged against established standards. In many countries national learning assessments are enabling ministries of education to monitor progress in these outcomes. Internationally, the UNESCO Institute for Statistics has established literacy as an outcome indicator based on an internationally agreed definition.

The literacy rate is defined as the percentage of people who can, with understanding, both read and write a short, simple statement about their everyday life. In practice, literacy is difficult to measure. To estimate literacy using such a definition requires census or survey measurements under controlled conditions. Many countries estimate the number of literate people from self-reported data. Some use educational attainment data as a proxy but apply different lengths of school attendance or levels of completion. Because definition and methodologies of data collection differ across countries, data need to be used with caution.

The reported literacy data are compiled by the UNESCO Institute for Statistics based on national censuses and household surveys during 1995–2004. When countries did not report data, the estimates generated in July 2002 by UNESCO Institute for Statistics are used. The data for 1990 are also from the model estimation. The estimation methodology can be reviewed at www.uis.unesco.org.

Literacy statistics for most countries cover the population ages 15 and older, by five-year age groups, but some include younger ages or are confined to age ranges that tend to inflate literacy rates. As an alternative, the UNESCO Institute for Statistics has proposed the narrower age range of 15–24, which better captures the ability of participants in the formal education system. The youth literacy rate reported in the table measures the accumulated outcomes of primary education over the previous 10 years or so by indicating the proportion of people who have passed through the primary education system and acquired basic literacy and numeracy skills.

Definitions

• **Primary completion rate** is the percentage of students completing the last year of primary school. It is calculated by taking the total number of students in the last grade of primary school, minus the number of repeaters in that grade, divided by the total number of children of official graduation age. • **Youth literacy rate** is the percentage of people ages 15–24 who can, with understanding, both read and write a short, simple statement about their everyday life. • **Adult literacy rate** is the literacy rate among people ages 15 and older.

Data sources

Data on the primary completion rate for 1991 and 2004 are primarily from the UNESCO Institiute for Statistics. The data for the latest years are provisional, as of January 2006. Data on literacy rates are from the UNESCO Institiute for Statistics.

2.14 Health expenditure, services, and use

	Health expenditure						Physicians		Health worker density index	Hospital beds	
	Total	Public		Out of pocket	External resources	Per capita			physicians, nurses, and midwives		
	% of GDP	% of GDP	% of total	% of private	% of total	$	per 1,000 people		per 1,000 people	per 1,000 people	
	2003	2003	2003	2003	2003	2003	1990	1997–2004[a]	2000–03[a]	1990	2000–03[a]
Afghanistan	6.5	2.6	39.5	76.5	45.6	11	0.1	0.2	0.4	0.2	0.4
Albania	6.5	2.7	41.7	99.8	3.4	118	1.4	1.3	5.4	4.0	3.1
Algeria	4.1	3.3	80.8	95.3	0.0	89	0.9	1.1	..	2.5	..
Angola	2.8	2.4	84.2	100.0	6.7	26	0.0[b]	0.1	..	1.3	..
Argentina	8.9	4.3	48.6	55.6	0.2	305	2.7	3.0	..	4.6	4.1
Armenia	6.0	1.2	20.2	80.6	17.2	55	3.9	3.6	8.8	9.1	4.4
Australia	9.5	6.4	67.5	67.8	0.0	2,519	*2.3*	2.5	10.8	*9.2*	7.4
Austria	7.5	5.1	67.6	59.2	0.0	2,358	2.2	3.4	9.3	10.2	8.3
Azerbaijan	3.6	0.9	23.8	96.8	1.9	32	3.9	3.5	12.0	10.1	8.3
Bangladesh	3.4	1.1	31.3	85.8	12.4	14	0.2	0.3	0.5	0.3	..
Belarus	6.4	4.9	75.9	80.5	0.1	116	3.6	4.6	17.5	13.2	11.3
Belgium	9.4	6.3	67.2	66.6	0.0	2,796	3.3	3.9	15.6	8.0	6.9
Benin	4.4	1.9	43.1	90.3	11.5	20	0.1	0.0[b]	..	0.8	..
Bolivia	6.7	4.3	64.0	79.3	7.3	61	0.4	1.2	1.1	1.3	1.0
Bosnia and Herzegovina	9.5	4.8	50.7	100.0	1.5	168	1.6	1.3	5.7	4.5	3.1
Botswana	5.6	3.3	58.2	28.8	2.9	232	*0.2*	0.4	..	1.6	..
Brazil	7.6	3.4	45.3	64.2	0.3	212	1.4	2.1	2.6	3.3	2.7
Bulgaria	7.5	4.1	54.5	98.4	1.0	191	3.2	3.6	8.3	9.8	6.3
Burkina Faso	5.6	2.6	46.8	98.1	7.4	19	*0.0*[b]	0.1	0.3	0.3	..
Burundi	3.1	0.7	23.3	100.0	14.1	3	0.1	0.0[b]	0.3	*0.7*	..
Cambodia	10.9	2.1	19.3	86.2	18.5	33	*0.1*	0.2	1.0	2.1	0.5
Cameroon	4.2	1.2	28.9	98.3	3.2	37	0.1	0.2	..	2.6	..
Canada	9.9	6.9	69.9	49.6	0.0	2,669	2.1	2.1	12.2	6.0	3.7
Central African Republic	4.0	1.5	38.6	95.3	2.9	12	0.0[b]	0.1	..	0.9	..
Chad	6.5	2.6	39.9	96.3	11.8	16	*0.0*[b]	0.0[b]	0.2	*0.7*	..
Chile	6.1	3.0	48.8	46.2	0.0	282	1.1	1.1	1.7	3.2	2.6
China	5.6	2.0	36.2	87.6	0.1	61	1.5	1.6	2.7	2.6	2.5
Hong Kong, China	..	..	..	..	..	..	..	..	..	..	..
Colombia	7.6	6.4	84.1	47.2	0.0	138	1.1	1.4	1.9	1.4	1.1
Congo, Dem. Rep.	4.0	0.7	18.3	100.0	15.1	4	0.1	0.1	..	1.4	..
Congo, Rep.	2.0	1.3	64.2	100.0	2.2	19	0.3	0.2	..	3.3	..
Costa Rica	7.3	5.8	78.8	88.7	2.7	305	1.3	1.3	2.4	2.5	1.4
Côte d'Ivoire	3.6	1.0	27.6	90.5	3.4	28	0.1	0.1	..	0.8	..
Croatia	7.8	6.5	83.6	100.0	0.6	494	2.1	2.4	7.7	7.4	5.6
Cuba	7.3	6.3	86.8	75.2	0.2	211	3.6	5.9	13.4	5.4	4.9
Czech Republic	7.5	6.8	90.0	83.9	0.0	667	2.8	3.5	13.4	11.3	8.8
Denmark	9.0	7.5	83.0	92.5	0.0	3,534	3.1	2.9	13.6	5.6	4.0
Dominican Republic	7.0	2.3	33.2	70.8	1.5	132	1.5	1.9	3.7	1.9	2.1
Ecuador	5.1	2.0	38.6	88.1	0.9	109	1.5	1.5	3.1	1.6	1.5
Egypt, Arab Rep.	*5.9*	*2.2*	*37.0*	*99.0*	*0.8*	*64*	0.8	0.5	4.9	2.1	2.2
El Salvador	8.1	3.7	46.1	93.5	1.0	183	0.8	1.2	2.0	1.5	..
Eritrea	4.4	2.0	45.5	100.0	19.6	8	..	0.1	..	..	..
Estonia	5.3	4.1	77.1	88.3	0.1	366	3.5	3.2	9.8	11.6	6.0
Ethiopia	5.9	3.4	58.4	78.7	26.0	5	*0.0*[b]	0.0[b]	0.2	0.2	..
Finland	7.4	5.7	76.5	81.2	0.0	2,307	2.4	2.6	25.6	12.5	7.2
France	10.1	7.7	76.3	42.2	0.0	2,981	2.6	3.4	10.2	9.7	7.7
Gabon	4.4	2.9	66.6	100.0	0.7	196	*0.5*	0.3	..	3.2	..
Gambia, The	8.1	3.2	40.0	67.0	21.8	21	..	0.1[b]	..	0.6	..
Georgia	4.0	1.0	23.9	98.2	5.3	35	4.9	4.1	7.9	9.8	4.2
Germany	11.1	8.7	78.2	47.9	0.0	3,204	3.1	3.4	13.2	10.4	8.9
Ghana	4.5	1.4	31.8	100.0	15.8	16	*0.0*[b]	0.2	0.9	1.5	..
Greece	9.9	5.1	51.3	95.4	..	1,556	3.4	4.4	7.5	5.1	4.7
Guatemala	5.4	2.1	39.7	91.9	3.8	112	0.8	0.9	..	1.1	0.5
Guinea	5.4	0.9	16.6	99.4	7.3	22	0.1	0.1	0.6	0.6	..
Guinea-Bissau	5.6	2.6	45.8	80.2	26.8	9	..	0.1	..	1.5	..
Haiti	7.5	2.9	38.1	69.5	12.4	26	0.1	0.2	..	0.8	0.8

Health expenditure, services, and use

	Health expenditure						Physicians		Health worker density index	Hospital beds	
	Total	Public		Out of pocket	External resources	Per capita			physicians, nurses, and midwives		
	% of GDP	% of GDP	% of total	% of private	% of total	$	per 1,000 people		per 1,000 people	per 1,000 people	
	2003	2003	2003	2003	2003	2003	1990	1997–2004[a]	2000–03[a]	1990	2000–03[a]
Honduras	7.1	4.0	56.5	85.8	9.3	72	0.7	0.6	..	1.0	1.0
Hungary	8.4	6.1	72.4	88.9	0.4	684	2.9	3.2	11.9	..	7.8
India	4.8	1.2	24.8	97.0	1.6	27	*0.5*	0.6	..	*0.8*	0.9
Indonesia	3.1	1.1	35.9	74.3	1.4	30	0.1	0.1	0.7	0.7	..
Iran, Islamic Rep.	6.5	3.1	47.3	94.8	0.1	131	*0.3*	0.4	..	1.4	1.6
Iraq	2.7	1.4	51.8	100.0	3.8	23	0.6	0.7	3.6	1.7	1.3
Ireland	7.3	5.8	78.9	61.9	0.0	2,860	1.6	2.8	19.0	6.1	4.3
Israel	8.9	6.1	68.2	89.1	3.4	1,514	3.2	3.8	10.3	6.2	6.1
Italy	8.4	6.3	75.1	83.3	0.0	2,139	4.7	4.2	10.5	7.2	4.4
Jamaica	5.3	2.7	50.6	64.7	1.2	164	0.6	0.8	2.5	2.2	1.4
Japan	7.9	6.4	81.0	90.1	0.0	2,662	1.7	2.0	10.4	..	14.3
Jordan	9.4	4.2	45.2	74.0	4.2	177	*1.3*	2.0	4.8	1.8	1.7
Kazakhstan	3.5	2.0	57.3	100.0	1.2	73	4.0	3.5	9.5	13.7	7.7
Kenya	4.3	1.7	38.7	82.6	15.3	20	0.0[b]	0.1	..	1.6	..
Korea, Dem. Rep.	5.8	5.3	91.2	100.0	19.1	1	..	3.3	..	..	..
Korea, Rep.	5.6	2.8	49.4	82.8	0.0	705	0.8	1.6	5.4	3.1	7.1
Kuwait	3.5	2.7	77.5	91.2	0.0	580	0.2	1.5	5.4	*3*	2.2
Kyrgyz Republic	5.0	*2.2*	43.6	..	..	..	3.4	2.5	10.1	12.0	5.3
Lao PDR	3.2	1.2	38.5	75.5	30.0	11	0.2	..	..	2.6	1.2
Latvia	6.4	3.3	51.3	94.3	0.4	301	4.1	3.0	8.2	14.1	7.8
Lebanon	10.2	3.0	29.3	79.4	0.1	573	*1.3*	3.3	4.4	1.7	3.0
Lesotho	5.2	4.1	79.7	18.2	8.2	31	0.0[b]	0.0[b]	..	..	..
Liberia	4.7	2.7	56.7	98.5	32.3	6	..	0.0[b]	..	..	..
Libya	4.1	2.6	62.9	100.0	0.0	171	1.1	1.3	..	4.2	3.9
Lithuania	6.6	5.0	76.0	96.6	1.3	351	4.0	4.0	12.4	12.5	8.7
Macedonia, FYR	7.1	6.0	84.5	100.0	1.7	161	2.2	2.2	8.1	5.9	4.8
Madagascar	2.7	1.7	63.4	91.7	22.0	8	0.1	0.3	0.4	0.9	0.4
Malawi	9.3	3.3	35.2	42.7	25.1	13	0.0[b]	0.0[b]	0.3	1.6	..
Malaysia	3.8	2.2	58.2	73.8	0.1	163	0.4	0.7	2.4	2.1	1.9
Mali	4.8	2.8	57.4	89.3	13.7	16	0.1	0.1	0.2	..	..
Mauritania	4.2	3.2	76.8	100.0	4.7	17	0.1	0.1	..	0.7	..
Mauritius	3.7	2.2	60.8	100.0	1.0	172	0.8	1.1	..	*2.9*	..
Mexico	6.2	2.9	46.4	94.2	0.4	372	1.1	1.5	3.9	1.0	1.0
Moldova	7.2	3.9	54.5	96.1	2.5	34	3.6	2.6	9.2	13.1	6.7
Mongolia	6.7	4.3	63.8	91.1	3.2	33	2.5	2.6	6.0	*11.5*	..
Morocco	5.1	1.7	33.1	76.1	1.0	72	*0.2*	0.5	1.5	1.3	0.8
Mozambique	4.7	2.9	61.7	38.8	40.8	12	0.0[b]	0.0[b]	0.3	0.9	..
Myanmar	2.8	0.5	19.4	99.7	2.2	394	0.1	0.4	0.8	0.6	0.6
Namibia	6.7	4.7	70.0	19.2	5.3	145	*0.2*	0.3	..	..	..
Nepal	5.3	1.5	27.8	92.2	9.9	12	0.1	0.2	0.3	0.2	..
Netherlands	9.8	6.1	62.4	20.8	0.0	3,088	2.5	3.1	16.7	5.8	4.7
New Zealand	8.1	6.3	78.3	72.1	0.0	1,618	1.9	2.2	10.9	8.5	6.1
Nicaragua	7.7	3.7	48.4	95.7	11.2	60	0.7	0.4	1.8	1.8	0.9
Niger	4.7	2.5	53.0	89.2	32.8	9	0.0[b]	0.0[b]	0.3	..	..
Nigeria	5.0	1.3	25.5	91.2	5.3	22	*0.2*	0.3	1.5	1.7	..
Norway	10.3	8.6	83.7	95.4	0.0	4,976	*2.6*	3.1	24.9	4.6	3.8
Oman	3.2	2.7	83.0	56.1	0.0	278	0.6	1.3	4.2	2.1	2.0
Pakistan	2.4	0.7	27.7	98.0	2.5	13	0.5	0.7	1.1	0.6	0.7
Panama	7.6	5.0	66.4	82.2	0.2	315	1.6	1.5	3.2	2.5	2.5
Papua New Guinea	3.4	3.0	88.9	87.2	28.3	23	0.1	0.1	0.6	4.0	..
Paraguay	7.3	2.3	31.5	74.6	1.8	75	0.6	1.1	1.4	0.9	1.2
Peru	4.4	2.1	48.3	79.0	3.2	98	1.1	1.2	..	1.4	1.4
Philippines	3.2	1.4	43.7	78.2	3.8	31	0.1	1.2	7.4	1.4	1.0
Poland	6.5	4.5	69.9	87.8	0.0	354	2.1	2.5	7.7	5.7	5.6
Portugal	9.6	6.7	69.7	95.7	0.0	1,348	2.8	3.3	7.0	4.1	3.6
Puerto Rico	..	..	..	..	..	..	..	..	..	..	..

2.14 Health expenditure, services, and use

	Health expenditure						Physicians		Health worker density index	Hospital beds	
	Total % of GDP	Public % of GDP	Public % of total	Out of pocket % of private	External resources % of total	Per capita $	per 1,000 people		physicians, nurses, and midwives per 1,000 people	per 1,000 people	
	2003	**2003**	**2003**	**2003**	**2003**	**2003**	**1990**	**1997–2004[a]**	**2000–03[a]**	**1990**	**2000–03[a]**
Romania	6.1	3.8	62.9	90.4	3.8	159	1.8	1.9	6.2	8.9	6.6
Russian Federation	5.6	3.3	59.0	71.1	0.2	167	4.1	4.3	12.5	13.1	10.5
Rwanda	3.7	1.6	43.5	41.7	54.5	7	*0.0[b]*	0.0[b]	0.2	1.7	..
Saudi Arabia	*3.3*	*2.5*	*75.4*	*31.0*	..	*348*	1.4	1.4	4.4	2.5	2.2
Senegal	5.1	2.1	41.8	95.3	15.4	29	0.1	0.1	..	0.7	..
Serbia and Montenegro	9.6	7.2	75.5	85.3	0.5	181	2.0	2.1	..	5.9	6.0
Sierra Leone	3.5	2.0	58.3	100.0	15.5	7	..	0.0[b]	..	..	..
Singapore	4.5	1.6	36.1	97.1	0.0	964	1.3	1.4	5.6	3.6	2.9
Slovak Republic	5.9	5.2	88.3	100.0	0.0	360	2.9	3.1	10.6	7.4	7.2
Slovenia	8.8	6.7	76.3	41.1	0.1	1,218	2.0	2.3	9.4	6.0	5.0
Somalia	*2.6*	*1.2*	*44.6*	*100.0*	*9.3*	*8*	..	0.0[b]	..	0.8	..
South Africa	8.4	3.2	38.6	17.1	0.5	295	*0.6*	0.8	4.6	..	..
Spain	7.7	5.5	71.3	82.0	0.0	1,541	2.3	3.2	6.8	4.6	3.8
Sri Lanka	3.5	1.6	45.0	88.9	2.3	31	*0.1*	0.5	1.2	2.7	..
Sudan	4.3	1.9	43.2	96.3	2.2	21	..	0.2	1.0	1.1	0.7
Swaziland	5.8	3.3	57.3	42.4	5.5	107	0.1	0.2	3.4	..	..
Sweden	9.4	8.0	85.2	92.1	0.0	3,149	2.9	3.3	13.5	12.4	3.6
Switzerland	11.5	6.7	58.5	76.0	0.0	5,035	3.0	3.6	12.1	*19.9*	6.0
Syrian Arab Republic	5.1	2.5	48.2	100.0	0.2	59	0.8	1.4	3.3	1.1	1.5
Tajikistan	4.4	0.9	20.8	100.0	14.9	11	2.6	2.0	7.2	10.7	6.1
Tanzania	4.3	2.4	55.4	81.1	21.9	12	..	0.0[b]	0.4	1.0	..
Thailand	3.3	2.0	61.6	74.8	0.3	76	0.2	0.4	..	1.6	..
Togo	5.6	1.4	24.8	88.0	2.3	16	*0.1*	0.0[b]	0.3	1.5	..
Trinidad and Tobago	3.9	1.5	37.8	88.6	1.4	316	0.7	0.8	..	4.0	3.4
Tunisia	5.6	2.8	50.0	..	..	126	0.5	1.3	..	1.9	1.7
Turkey	7.6	5.4	71.6	69.9	0.0	257	0.9	1.4	4.2	2.4	2.6
Turkmenistan	3.9	2.6	67.4	100.0	0.4	89	3.6	4.2	..	11.5	..
Uganda	7.3	2.2	30.4	52.8	28.5	18	*0.0[b]*	0.1	0.1	*0.9*	..
Ukraine	5.7	3.8	65.9	78.6	0.1	60	4.3	3.0	11.2	13.0	8.8
United Arab Emirates	3.3	2.5	74.7	70.4	0.0	661	0.8	2.0	6.2	2.6	2.2
United Kingdom	8.0	6.9	85.7	76.7	0.0	2,428	1.4	2.2	..	5.9	4.2
United States	15.2	6.8	44.6	24.3	0.0	5,711	2.4	2.3	13.2	4.9	3.3
Uruguay	9.8	2.7	27.2	25.0	0.4	323	3.7	3.7	4.5	4.5	1.9
Uzbekistan	5.5	2.4	43.0	95.5	3.0	21	3.4	2.7	13.7	12.5	5.5
Venezuela, RB	4.5	2.0	44.3	95.5	0.1	146	1.6	1.9	2.6	2.7	0.8
Vietnam	5.4	1.5	27.8	74.2	2.6	26	0.4	0.5	1.3	3.8	2.4
West Bank and Gaza	..	..	..	..	..	..	..	0.8	..	..	..
Yemen, Rep.	5.5	2.2	40.9	95.5	8.8	32	0.0[b]	0.3	0.7	0.8	0.6
Zambia	5.4	2.8	51.4	68.2	44.7	21	0.1	0.1	..	..	..
Zimbabwe	7.9	2.8	35.9	56.7	6.8	40	0.1	0.2	0.6	0.5	..
World	**10.2 w**	**5.9 w**	**60.4 w**	**43.4 w**	**0.1 w**	**588 w**	**1.6 w**	**1.5 w**	**.. w**	**3.7 w**	**.. w**
Low income	4.6	1.3	29.1	95.1	4.4	30	*0.5*	0.4	..	..	..
Middle income	6.0	3.0	49.5	77.5	0.5	116	1.6	1.7	..	3.5	..
Lower middle income	5.6	2.5	43.7	81.4	0.6	77	1.4	1.5	..	2.9	..
Upper middle income	6.5	3.7	57.6	72.0	0.3	280	2.4	2.4	7.6	6.6	5.6
Low & middle income	5.8	2.8	46.4	81.6	1.2	79	1.3	1.1	..	3.1	..
East Asia & Pacific	5.0	1.9	39.0	88.3	0.8	64	1.2	1.3	3.0	2.3	2.4
Europe & Central Asia	6.5	4.5	67.3	79.9	0.5	194	3.2	3.0	10.3	10.2	7.6
Latin America & Carib.	6.8	3.3	48.2	75.3	0.6	222	1.4	1.9	..	2.5	..
Middle East & N. Africa	5.6	2.7	50.9	89.2	0.8	92	..	1.2	..	1.8	..
South Asia	4.4	1.1	26.3	96.2	2.7	24	*0.5*	0.5	..	*0.7*	0.9
Sub-Saharan Africa	6.1	2.4	41.2	47.4	5.5	36	..	0.1	..	1.2	..
High income	11.2	6.7	63.9	37.0	0.0[b]	3,449	2.3	3.7	..	6.2	6.4
Europe EMU	9.6	7.1	74.1	57.6	0.0	2,552	3.1	3.9	12.2	8.1	6.6

a. Data are for the most recent year available. b. Less than 0.05.

Health expenditure, services, and use 2.14

About the data

National health accounts track financial flows in the health sector, including public and private expenditures, by source of funding. In contrast with high-income countries, few developing countries have health accounts that are methodologically consistent with national accounting approaches. The difficulties in creating national health accounts go beyond data collection. To establish a national health accounting system, a country needs to define the boundaries of the health care system and to define a taxonomy of health care delivery institutions. The accounting system should be comprehensive and standardized, providing not only accurate measures of financial flows but also information on the equity and efficiency of health financing to inform health policy.

The absence of consistent national health accounting systems in most developing countries makes cross-country comparisons of health spending difficult. Compiling estimates of public health expenditures is complicated in countries where state or provincial and local governments are involved in financing and delivering health care, because the data on public spending often are not aggregated. There are a number of potential data sources related to external resources for health, including government expenditure accounts, government records on external assistance, routine surveys of external financing assistance, and special surveys. Survey data are the major source of information about out of pocket expenditure on health. The data in the table are the product of an effort by the World Health Organization (WHO), the Organisation for Economic Co-operation and Development (OECD), and the World Bank to collect all available information on health expenditures from national and local government budgets, national accounts, household surveys, insurance publications, international donors, and existing tabulations.

Indicators on health services (physicians, health worker density, and hospital beds per 1,000 people) come from a variety of sources (see *Data sources*). Data are lacking for many countries, and for others comparability is limited by differences in definitions. In estimates of health personnel, for example, some countries incorrectly include retired physicians (because deletions to physician rosters are made only periodically) or those working outside the health sector. There is no universally accepted definition of hospital beds. Moreover, figures on physicians and hospital beds are indicators of availability, not of quality or use. They do not show how well trained the physicians are or how well equipped the hospitals or medical centers are. And physicians and hospital beds tend to be concentrated in urban areas, so these indicators give only a partial view of health services available to the entire population.

The WHO receives data on health professionals from ministries of health through its six regional offices, often in cooperation with national statistical offices. The data are scrutinized using such additional recources as national and international employment surveys, records from professional associations, and other publications. Significant inconsistenties are returned to national authorities for validation and resubmission.

The health worker density index indicates the overall level of health workers (physicians, nurses, and midwives) in the country. Dentists and pharmacists are not included. Comparability of the index across countries is affected by differences in the definition of health workers. Many countries continue to use national definitions and classifications for data collection, and some countries provide information only for public sector workers.

2.14a

In Uganda most births in rural areas take place at home

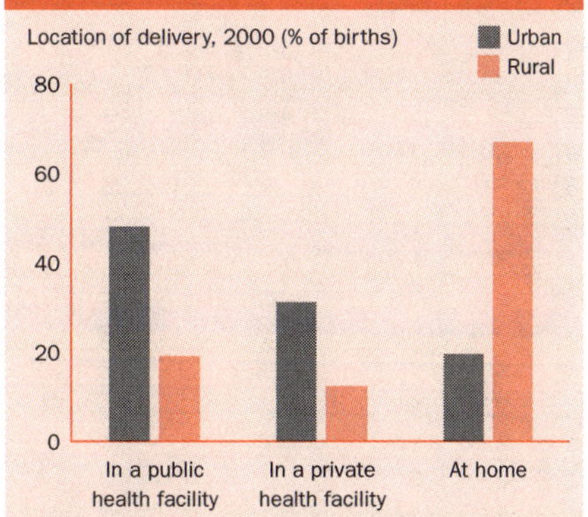

Rural areas lack accessibile medical facilities, as shown by the low share of births in public or private health facilities

Source: Demographic and Health Survey.

Definitions

• **Total health expenditure** is the sum of public and private health expenditure. It covers the provision of health services (preventive and curative), family planning activities, nutrition activities, and emergency aid designated for health but does not include provision of water and sanitation. • **Public health expenditure** consists of recurrent and capital spending from government (central and local) budgets, external borrowings and grants (including donations from international agencies and nongovernmental organizations), and social (or compulsory) health insurance funds. • **Out of pocket health expenditure** is any direct outlay by households, including gratuities and in-kind payments, to health practitioners and suppliers of pharmaceuticals, therapeutic appliances, and other goods and services whose primary intent is to contribute to the restoration or enhancement of the health status of individuals or population groups. It is a part of private health expenditure. • **External resources for health** are funds or services in kind that are provided by entities not part of the country in question. The resources may come from international organizations, other countries through bilateral arrangements, or foreign nongovernmental organizations. These resources are part of total health expenditure. • **Health expenditure per capita** is total health expenditure divided by number of people in the country. • **Physicians** are graduates of any faculty or school of medicine who are working in the country in any medical field (practice, teaching, or research). • **Health worker density index** reflects a combined density of physicians, nurses, and midwives per 1,000 people. • **Hospital beds** include inpatient beds available in public, private, general, and specialized hospitals and rehabilitation centers. In most cases beds for both acute and chronic care are included.

Data sources

Data on health expenditure come mostly from the WHO's *World Health Report 2006* and from the OECD for its member countries, supplemented by World Bank poverty assessments and country and sector studies. Data are also drawn from World Bank public expenditure reviews, the International Monetary Fund's Government Finance Statistics database, and other studies. Data on out of pocket expenditure in developing countries are drawn largely from household surveys conducted by governments or by statistical or international organizations. Data on physicians are from the WHO's *World Health Report 2006* and Global Atlas of the Health Workforce database, OECD, and TransMONEE, supplemented by country data. Data for the health worker density index are from the Joint Learning Initiative's *Human Resources for Health*. Data on hospital beds are from the WHO's *World Health Statistics 2005*, OECD's *Health Data 2005*, and TransMONEE, supplemented by country data.

2.15 Disease prevention coverage and quality

	Access to an improved water source % of population		Access to improved sanitation facilities % of population		Child immunization rate % of children ages 12–23 months[b]		Children with acute respiratory infection taken to health provider % of children under age 5 with ARI	Children with diarrhea who received oral rehydration and continued feeding % of children under age 5 with diarrhea	Children sleeping under treated bednets[a] % of children under age 5	Children with fever receiving antimalarial drugs % of children under age 5 with fever	Tuberculosis treatment success rate % of registered cases	DOTS detection rate % of estimated cases
	1990	2002	1990	2002	Measles 2004	DPT 2004	2000–04[c]	1998–2004[c]	2000–04[c]	2000–04[c]	2003	2004
Afghanistan	..	13	..	8	61	66	28	48	..	..	86	19
Albania	97	97	..	89	96	97	83	51	..	..	91	34
Algeria	95	87	88	92	81	86	52	..	..	..	90	105
Angola	32	50	30	30	64	59	58	32	2.3	63.0	68	94
Argentina	94	..	82	..	95	90	..	..	..	..	66	65
Armenia	..	92	..	84	92	91	25	48	..	..	77	44
Australia	100	100	100	100	93	92	..	..	..	..	82	33
Austria	100	100	100	100	74	83	..	..	..	..	68	42
Azerbaijan	66	77	..	55	98	96	36	40	1.4	1.0	70	47
Bangladesh	71	75	23	48	77	85	20	35	..	..	85	44
Belarus	100	100	..	..	99	99	..	..	..	..	73	42
Belgium	..	..	..	..	82	95	..	..	..	..	73	65
Benin	60	68	11	32	85	83	29	42	7.4	60.0	81	82
Bolivia	72	85	33	45	64	81	52	54	..	..	81	71
Bosnia and Herzegovina	98	98	..	93	88	84	80	23	..	..	94	96
Botswana	93	95	38	41	90	97	14	7	..	..	77	67
Brazil	83	89	70	75	99	96	..	..	..	..	83	47
Bulgaria	100	100	100	100	81	90	..	..	..	..	91	104
Burkina Faso	39	51	13	12	78	88	36	..	2.0	50.0	66	18
Burundi	69	79	44	36	75	74	40	16	1.3	31.0	79	29
Cambodia	..	34	..	16	80	85	35	59	..	..	93	61
Cameroon	50	63	21	48	64	73	40	33	1.3	66.1	*70*	91
Canada	100	100	100	100	95	91	..	..	..	..	35	58
Central African Republic	48	75	23	27	35	40	32	47	1.5	69.0	59	4
Chad	20	34	6	8	56	50	12	50	0.6	32.0	78	16
Chile	90	95	85	92	95	94	..	..	..	..	85	114
China	70	77	23	44	84	91	..	..	..	..	94	63
Hong Kong, China	..	..	..	..	..	..	..	..	..	..	78	55
Colombia	92	92	82	86	92	89	51	44	0.7	..	83	17
Congo, Dem. Rep.	43	46	18	29	64	64	36	17	0.7	45.0	83	70
Congo, Rep.	..	46	..	9	65	67	38	..	..	..	69	65
Costa Rica	..	97	..	92	88	90	..	..	..	..	94	153
Côte d'Ivoire	69	84	31	40	49	50	38	34	4.0	57.5	72	38
Croatia	..	..	..	..	96	96	..	..	..	..	..	..
Cuba	..	91	98	98	99	88	..	..	..	..	93	90
Czech Republic	..	..	..	..	97	98	..	..	..	..	79	61
Denmark	100	100	..	..	96	95	..	..	..	..	84	78
Dominican Republic	86	93	48	57	79	71	61	53	..	..	81	71
Ecuador	69	86	56	72	99	90	..	..	..	..	84	42
Egypt, Arab Rep.	94	98	54	68	97	97	70	29	..	..	80	61
El Salvador	67	82	51	63	93	90	62	..	..	..	88	57
Eritrea	40	57	8	9	84	83	44	54	4.2	4.0	85	14
Estonia	..	..	..	..	96	94	..	..	..	..	70	74
Ethiopia	25	22	4	6	71	80	16	38	..	3.0	70	36
Finland	100	100	100	100	97	98	..	..	..	..	..	..
France	..	..	..	..	86	97	..	..	..	..	..	..
Gabon	..	87	..	36	55	38	48	44	..	..	34	81
Gambia, The	..	82	..	53	90	92	75	38	14.7	55.0	75	66
Georgia	..	76	..	83	86	78	99	..	..	..	66	79
Germany	100	100	..	..	92	97	..	..	..	..	71	51
Ghana	54	79	43	58	83	80	44	40	4.0	63.0	66	37
Greece	..	..	..	..	88	88	..	..	..	..	..	..
Guatemala	77	95	50	61	75	84	64	22	..	..	91	55
Guinea	42	51	17	13	73	69	33	44	4.0	56.0	75	52
Guinea-Bissau	..	59	..	34	80	80	64	23	7.4	58.0	80	75
Haiti	53	71	15	34	54	43	26	41	..	12.0	78	49

Disease prevention coverage and quality

	Access to an improved water source		Access to improved sanitation facilities		Child immunization rate		Children with acute respiratory infection taken to health provider	Children with diarrhea who received oral rehydration and continued feeding	Children sleeping under treated bednets[a]	Children with fever receiving antimalarial drugs	Tuberculosis treatment success rate	DOTS detection rate
	% of population		% of population		% of children ages 12–23 months[b]		% of children under age 5 with ARI	% of children under age 5 with diarrhea	% of children under age 5	% of children under age 5 with fever	% of registered cases	% of estimated cases
					Measles	DPT						
	1990	2002	1990	2002	2004	2004	2000–04[c]	1998–2004[c]	2000–04[c]	2000–04[c]	2003	2004
Honduras	83	90	49	68	92	89	..	..	..	..	87	83
Hungary	99	99	..	95	99	99	..	..	..	..	48	47
India	68	86	12	30	56	64	..	22	..	..	86	57
Indonesia	71	78	46	52	72	70	61	61	0.1	1.0	87	53
Iran, Islamic Rep.	91	93	83	84	96	99	93	..	..	..	84	58
Iraq	83	81	81	80	90	81	76	..	..	..	85	20
Ireland	..	..	..	..	81	89	..	..	..	..	..	..
Israel	100	100	..	..	96	96	..	..	..	..	80	34
Italy	..	..	..	..	84	96	..	..	..	..	95	58
Jamaica	92	93	75	80	80	77	39	21	..	..	53	79
Japan	100	100	100	100	99	99	..	..	..	..	76	45
Jordan	98	91	..	93	99	95	72	44	..	..	87	79
Kazakhstan	86	86	72	72	99	82	..	22	..	..	75	79
Kenya	45	62	42	48	73	73	46	33	5.0	27.0	80	46
Korea, Dem. Rep.	100	100	..	59	95	72	93	..	..	..	88	103
Korea, Rep.	..	92	..	..	99	88	..	..	..	..	82	21
Kuwait	..	..	..	..	97	98	..	..	..	..	62	83
Kyrgyz Republic	..	76	..	60	99	99	..	..	..	..	84	62
Lao PDR	..	43	..	24	36	45	36	37	18.0	9.0	79	55
Latvia	..	..	..	..	99	98	..	..	..	..	74	83
Lebanon	100	100	..	98	96	92	74	..	..	..	92	82
Lesotho	..	76	37	37	70	78	..	29	..	..	70	86
Liberia	56	62	38	26	42	31	70	..	..	..	73	58
Libya	71	72	97	97	99	97	..	..	..	..	62	169
Lithuania	..	..	..	..	98	94	..	..	..	..	74	89
Macedonia, FYR	..	..	..	..	96	94	..	..	..	..	84	73
Madagascar	40	45	12	33	59	61	48	47	0.2	34.0	71	74
Malawi	41	67	36	46	80	89	27	51	2.9	27.0	73	40
Malaysia	..	95	96	..	95	99	..	..	..	..	72	69
Mali	34	48	36	45	75	76	43	45	8.4	38.0	65	19
Mauritania	41	56	28	42	64	70	39	28	..	33.4	58	43
Mauritius	100	100	99	99	98	98	..	..	..	..	87	33
Mexico	80	91	66	77	96	98	..	..	..	..	83	71
Moldova	..	92	..	68	96	98	78	52	..	..	65	59
Mongolia	62	62	..	59	96	99	78	66	..	..	87	80
Morocco	75	80	57	61	95	97	35	50	..	..	86	80
Mozambique	..	42	..	27	77	72	51	..	..	..	76	46
Myanmar	48	80	21	73	78	82	66	48	..	..	81	83
Namibia	58	80	24	30	70	81	53	39	3.4	14.0	63	88
Nepal	69	84	12	27	73	80	24	43	..	..	87	67
Netherlands	100	100	100	100	96	98	..	..	..	..	86	61
New Zealand	97	..	..	..	85	90	..	..	..	..	36	59
Nicaragua	69	81	47	66	84	79	57	49	..	2.0	84	87
Niger	40	46	7	12	74	62	27	43	5.8	48.0	70	46
Nigeria	49	60	39	38	35	25	31	28	1.0	34.0	59	21
Norway	100	100	..	..	88	91	..	..	..	..	97	46
Oman	77	79	83	89	98	99	..	..	..	..	90	123
Pakistan	83	90	38	54	67	65	..	..	..	..	75	27
Panama	..	91	..	72	99	99	..	..	..	..	74	133
Papua New Guinea	39	39	45	45	44	46	..	..	..	..	58	19
Paraguay	62	83	58	78	89	76	..	..	..	..	85	21
Peru	74	81	52	62	89	87	58	46	..	..	89	83
Philippines	87	85	54	73	80	79	55	76	..	..	88	73
Poland	..	..	..	..	97	99	..	..	..	..	78	56
Portugal	..	..	..	..	95	95	..	..	..	..	84	78
Puerto Rico	..	..	..	..	..	..	..	..	..	..	66	76

2.15 Disease prevention coverage and quality

	Access to an improved water source		Access to improved sanitation facilities		Child immunization rate		Children with acute respiratory infection taken to health provider	Children with diarrhea who received oral rehydration and continued feeding	Children sleeping under treated bednets[a]	Children with fever receiving antimalarial drugs	Tuberculosis treatment success rate	DOTS detection rate
	% of population		% of population		% of children ages 12–23 months[b]		% of children under age 5 with ARI	% of children under age 5 with diarrhea	% of children under age 5	% of children under age 5 with fever	% of registered cases	% of estimated cases
					Measles	DPT						
	1990	2002	1990	2002	2004	2004	2000–04[c]	1998–2004[c]	2000–04[c]	2000–04[c]	2003	2004
Romania	..	57	..	51	97	97	..	..	31.0	..	80	41
Russian Federation	94	96	87	87	98	97	..	..	..	..	61	13
Rwanda	58	73	37	41	84	89	20	16	5.0	13.0	67	29
Saudi Arabia	90	..	..	..	97	96	..	..	..	..	79	40
Senegal	66	72	35	52	57	87	27	33	1.7	36.0	70	52
Serbia and Montenegro	93	93	87	87	96	97	97	..	..	..	89	32
Sierra Leone	..	57	..	39	64	61	50	39	1.5	61.0	83	36
Singapore	..	..	..	..	94	94	..	..	..	..	77	67
Slovak Republic	100	100	100	100	98	99	..	..	..	..	87	34
Slovenia	..	..	..	..	94	92	..	..	..	..	85	66
Somalia	..	29	..	25	40	30	..	..	..	..	90	44
South Africa	83	87	63	67	81	93	..	37	..	..	67	83
Spain	..	..	..	..	97	96	..	..	..	..	..	..
Sri Lanka	68	78	70	91	96	97	..	..	..	..	81	70
Sudan	64	69	33	34	59	55	57	38	0.4	50.0	82	35
Swaziland	..	52	..	52	70	83	60	24	0.1	26.0	42	38
Sweden	100	100	100	100	94	99	..	..	..	..	83	69
Switzerland	100	100	100	100	82	95	..	..	..	..	..	..
Syrian Arab Republic	79	79	76	77	98	99	66	..	..	..	88	46
Tajikistan	..	58	..	53	89	82	51	29	1.9	69.0	86	12
Tanzania	38	73	47	46	94	95	..	38	10.0	58.0	81	47
Thailand	81	85	80	99	96	98	..	..	..	..	73	71
Togo	49	51	37	34	70	71	30	25	2.0	60.0	63	17
Trinidad and Tobago	92	91	100	100	95	94	74	31	..	..	..	..
Tunisia	77	82	75	80	95	97	43	..	..	..	91	95
Turkey	81	93	84	83	81	85	41	19	..	..	93	3
Turkmenistan	..	71	..	62	97	97	51	..	..	..	82	38
Uganda	44	56	43	41	91	87	67	29	0.2	..	68	43
Ukraine	..	98	99	99	99	99	..	..	..	..	..	..
United Arab Emirates	..	..	100	100	94	94	..	..	..	..	64	17
United Kingdom	..	..	..	..	..	..	..	..	..	..	..	..
United States	100	100	100	100	93	96	..	..	..	..	70	85
Uruguay	..	98	..	94	95	95	..	..	..	..	86	86
Uzbekistan	89	89	58	57	98	99	57	33	..	..	81	28
Venezuela, RB	..	83	..	68	80	86	72	51	..	..	82	77
Vietnam	72	80	32	41	97	96	71	39	15.8	7.0	92	89
West Bank and Gaza	..	94	..	76	..	..	65	..	..	..	80	1
Yemen, Rep.	69	69	21	30	76	78	47	..	..	..	82	40
Zambia	50	55	41	45	84	80	69	48	6.5	52.0	75	54
Zimbabwe	77	83	49	57	80	85	..	80	..	..	66	42
World	**75 w**	**82 w**	**43 w**	**54 w**	**76 w**	**79 w**		**.. w**				**55 w**
Low income	64	75	20	36	64	67		24				47
Middle income	77	83	48	61	87	89		..				68
Lower middle income	75	81	42	57	86	88		..				65
Upper middle income	88	93	80	81	91	93		37				74
Low & middle income	71	79	37	50	74	77		..				55
East Asia & Pacific	71	78	30	49	82	87		..				77
Europe & Central Asia	..	91	86	82	93	93		22				51
Latin America & Carib.	82	89	68	75	92	91		..				62
Middle East & N. Africa	87	88	69	75	92	93		..				50
South Asia	70	84	16	35	61	67		23				42
Sub-Saharan Africa	49	58	32	36	64	64		..				51
High income	..	99	..	..	93	96		..				57
Europe EMU	..	..	..	..	89	96		..				..

a. For malaria prevention only. b. Refers to children who were immunized before 12 months or, in some cases, at any time before the survey (12–23 months). c. Data are for the most recent year available.

Disease prevention coverage and quality

About the data

The indicators in the table are based on data provided to the World Health Organization (WHO) by member states as part of their efforts to monitor and evaluate progress in implementing national health strategies. Because reliable, observation-based statistical data for these indicators do not exist in some developing countries, some of the data are estimated.

People's health is influenced by the environment in which they live. Lack of clean water and basic sanitation is the main reason diseases transmitted by feces are so common in developing countries. The data on access to an improved water source measure the share of the population with ready access to water for domestic purposes. The data are based on surveys and estimates provided by governments to the Joint Monitoring Programme of the WHO and United Nations Children's Fund (UNICEF). The coverage rates for water and sanitation are based on information from service users on the facilities their households actually use rather than on information from service providers, who may include nonfunctioning systems. Access to drinking water from an improved source does not ensure that the water is safe or adequate, as these characteristics are not tested at the time of the surveys.

Governments in developing countries usually finance immunization against measles and diphtheria, pertussis (whooping cough), and tetanus (DPT) as part of the basic public health package. In many developing countries, lack of precise information on the size of the cohort of one-year-old children makes immunization coverage difficult to estimate from program statistics. The data shown here are based on an assessment of national immunization coverage rates by the WHO and UNICEF. The assessment considered both administrative data from service providers and household survey data on children's immunization histories. Based on the data available, consideration of potential biases, and contributions of local experts, the most likely true level of immunization coverage was determined for each year.

Acute respiratory infection continues to be a leading cause of death among young children, killing about 2 million children under age five in developing countries in 2000. An estimated 60 percent of these deaths can be prevented by the selective use of antibiotics by appropriate health care providers. Data are drawn mostly from household health surveys in which mothers report on number of episodes and treatment for acute respiratory infection.

Since 1990 diarrhea-related deaths among children have declined tremendously. Most diarrhea-related deaths are due to dehydration, and many of these deaths can be prevented with the use of oral rehydration salts at home. However, recommendations for the use of oral rehydration therapy have changed over time based on scientific progress, so it is difficult to accurately compare use rates among countries. Until the current recommended method for home management of diarrhea is adopted and applied in all countries, the data should be used with caution. Also, the prevalence of diarrhea may vary by season. Since country surveys are administered at different times, data comparability is further affected.

Malaria is endemic to the poorest countries in the world, mainly in tropical and subtropical regions of Africa, Asia, and the Americas. An estimated 300–500 million clinical malaria cases and more than 1 million malaria deaths occur each year—the vast majority in Sub-Saharan Africa and among children under age five. Insecticide-treated bednets, if properly used and maintained, are one of the most important malaria-preventive strategies to limit human-mosquito contact. Studies have emphasized that mortality rates could be reduced by about 25–30 percent if every child under age five in malaria-risk areas such as Africa slept under a treated bednet every night.

Prompt and effective treatment of malaria is a critical elemet of malaria control. It is vital that sufferers, especially children under age five, start treatment within 24 hours of the onset of symptoms, to prevent progression—often rapid—to severe malaria and death.

Data on the success rate of tuberculosis treatment are provided for countries that have implemented the recommended control strategy: directly observed treatment, short course (DOTS). Countries that have not adopted DOTS or have only recently done so are omitted because of lack of data or poor comparability or reliability of reported results. The treatment success rate for tuberculosis provides a useful indicator of the quality of health services. A low rate or no success suggests that infectious patients may not be receiving adequate treatment. An essential complement to the tuberculosis treatment success rate is the DOTS detection rate, which indicates whether there is adequate coverage by the recommended case detection and treatment strategy. A country with a high treatment success rate may still face big challenges if its DOTS detection rate remains low.

2.15a

Deaths from diarrhea can be sharply reduced with improvements in drinking water and sanitation

Percent change, 2005

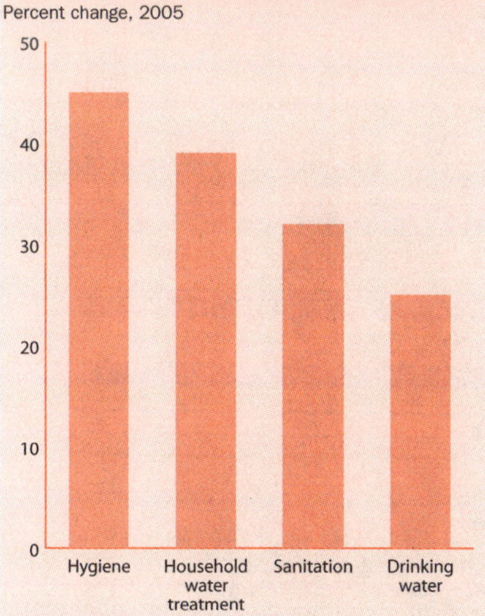

Source: WHO/UNICEF 2005.

Definitions

• **Access to an improved water source** refers to the percentage of the population with reasonable access to an adequate amount of water from an improved source, such as a household connection, public standpipe, borehole, protected well or spring, or rainwater collection. Unimproved sources include vendors, tanker trucks, and unprotected wells and springs. Reasonable access is defined as the availability of at least 20 liters a person a day from a source within 1 kilometer of the dwelling. • **Access to improved sanitation facilities** refers to the percentage of the population with at least adequate access to excreta disposal facilities that can effectively prevent human, animal, and insect contact with excreta. Improved facilities range from simple but protected pit latrines to flush toilets with a sewerage connection. To be effective, facilities must be correctly constructed and properly maintained. • **Child immunization rate** is the percentage of children ages 12–23 months who received vaccinations before 12 months or at any time before the survey for four diseases—measles and diphtheria, pertussis (whooping cough), and tetanus (DPT). A child is considered adequately immunized against measles after receiving one dose of vaccine and against DPT after receiving three doses. • **Children with acute respiratory infection taken to a health provider** refer to the percentage of children under age five with acute respiratory infection in the two weeks prior to the survey who were taken to an appropriate health provider, including hospital, health center, dispensary, village health worker, clinic, and private physician • **Children with diarrhea who received oral rehydration and continued feeding** refer to the percentage of children under age five with diarrhea in the two weeks prior to the survey who received either oral rehydration therapy or increased fluids, with continued feeding. • **Children sleeping under treated bednets** refer to the percentage of children under age five who slept under an insecticide-treated bednet to prevent malaria. • **Children with fever receiving antimalarial drugs** refer to the percentage of children under age five who were ill with fever in the last two weeks and received any appropriate (locally defined) antimalarial drugs. • **Tuberculosis treatment success rate** is the percentage of new, registered smear-positive (infectious) cases that were cured or in which a full course of treatment was completed. • **DOTS detection** rate is the percentage of estimated new infectious tuberculosis cases detected under the directly observed treatment, short course case detection and treatment strategy.

Data sources

Data on water and sanitation are from the WHO and UNICEF's *Meeting the MDG Drinking Water and Sanitation Target* (www.unicef.org/wes/mdgreport). Data on immunization are from WHO and UNICEF estimates of national immunization coverage. Data on children with acute respiratory infection, children with diarrhea, children sleeping under treated bednets, and children receiving antimalarial drugs are from UNICEF's *State of the World's Children 2006*, Childinfo, and Demographic and Health Surveys by Macro International. Data on tuberculosis are from the WHO's *Global Tuberculosis Control Report 2006*.

2.16 Reproductive health

	Total fertility rate		Adolescent fertility rate	Unmet need for contraception	Contraceptive prevalence rate	Tetanus vaccinations	Births attended by skilled health staff		Maternal mortality ratio	
	births per woman		births per 1,000 women ages 15–19	% of married women ages 15–49	% of women ages 15–49	% of pregnant women	% of total		per 100,000 live births	
									National estimates	Modeled estimates
	1990	2004	2004	1995–2004[a]	1996–2004[a]	2004	1990–92[a]	2000–04[a]	1990–2004[a]	2000
Afghanistan	8.0	..	..	..	10	35	..	14	1,600	1,900
Albania	2.9	2.2	16	..	75	..	..	98	23	55
Algeria	4.6	2.5	8	..	57	..	77	96	120	140
Angola	7.1	6.6	141	..	6	75	..	45	..	1,700
Argentina	3.0	2.3	59	..	..	..	96	99	44	82
Armenia	2.5	1.3	30	12	61	..	..	97	9	55
Australia	1.9	1.8	15	..	..	..	100	..	..	8
Austria	1.5	1.4	13	..	51	..	..	..	..	4
Azerbaijan	2.7	2.0	31	..	55	..	..	84	25	94
Bangladesh	4.3	3.0	123	11	59	45	..	13	380	380
Belarus	1.9	1.2	26	..	..	..	..	100	18	35
Belgium	1.6	1.6	8	..	..	..	..	..	..	10
Benin	6.7	5.7	130	27	19	69	..	66	500	850
Bolivia	4.9	3.7	82	23	58	..	..	67	230	420
Bosnia and Herzegovina	1.7	1.3	23	..	48	..	97	100	..	31
Botswana	4.4	3.1	76	..	48	..	..	94	330	100
Brazil	2.8	2.3	89	7	77	..	72	96	64	260
Bulgaria	1.8	1.3	44	..	42	..	..	99	15	32
Burkina Faso	7.3	6.5	159	29	14	65	..	38	480	1,000
Burundi	6.8	6.8	50	..	16	45	..	25	..	1,000
Cambodia	5.5	4.0	48	30	24	51	..	32	440	450
Cameroon	5.9	4.8	114	20	26	60	58	62	..	730
Canada	1.8	1.5	14	..	..	..	..	98	..	6
Central African Republic	5.6	4.8	126	16	28	42	..	44	1,100	1,100
Chad	6.7	6.4	192	10	3	42	..	14	830	1,100
Chile	2.6	2.0	61	..	..	..	..	100	17	31
China	2.1	1.8	5	..	87	..	..	96	51	56
Hong Kong, China	1.3	0.9	5	..	..	..	..	..	..	..
Colombia	3.1	2.4	77	6	77	*86*	82	*91*	78	130
Congo, Dem. Rep.	6.7	6.7	227	..	31	58	..	61	1,300	990
Congo, Rep.	6.3	6.3	145	..	..	65	..	..	..	510
Costa Rica	3.2	2.0	75	..	80	..	98	98	33	43
Côte d'Ivoire	6.5	4.8	123	28	15	75	..	68	600	690
Croatia	1.6	1.4	15	..	..	..	..	100	..	8
Cuba	1.7	1.5	50	..	73	..	..	100	34	33
Czech Republic	1.9	1.2	12	..	72	..	..	100	..	9
Denmark	1.7	1.8	7	..	..	..	..	..	10	5
Dominican Republic	3.3	2.8	91	11	70	..	93	98	180	150
Ecuador	3.6	2.7	84	..	66	..	..	..	80	130
Egypt, Arab Rep.	4.3	3.2	43	11	60	71	41	69	84	84
El Salvador	3.7	2.8	85	..	67	..	..	92	170	150
Eritrea	6.2	5.3	93	27	8	62	..	28	..	630
Estonia	2.0	1.4	23	..	..	..	..	100	46	63
Ethiopia	6.9	5.4	90	35	8	45	..	6	870	850
Finland	1.8	1.8	10	..	..	..	..	100	6	6
France	1.8	1.9	9	..	..	..	..	..	10	17
Gabon	5.3	3.8	106	28	33	45	..	86	520	420
Gambia, The	5.8	4.5	119	..	18	..	44	55	730	540
Georgia	2.1	1.4	33	..	41	..	..	..	52	32
Germany	1.5	1.4	10	..	..	..	..	..	8	8
Ghana	5.7	4.2	64	34	25	70	..	47	..	540
Greece	1.4	1.3	9	..	..	..	..	..	1	9
Guatemala	5.6	4.4	112	23	43	..	..	41	150	240
Guinea	6.5	5.8	191	24	7	77	31	56	530	740
Guinea-Bissau	7.1	7.1	194	..	8	56	..	35	910	1,100
Haiti	5.2	3.8	62	40	27	52	..	24	520	680

Reproductive health 2.16

	Total fertility rate		Adolescent fertility rate	Unmet need for contraception	Contraceptive prevalence rate	Tetanus vaccinations	Births attended by skilled health staff		Maternal mortality ratio	
	births per woman		births per 1,000 women ages 15–19	% of married women ages 15–49	% of women ages 15–49	% of pregnant women	% of total		per 100,000 live births National estimates	Modeled estimates
	1990	2004	2004	1995–2004[a]	1996–2004[a]	2004	1990–92[a]	2000–04[a]	1990–2004[a]	2000
Honduras	5.1	3.6	99	..	62	..	45	56	110	110
Hungary	1.8	1.3	21	..	..	..	..	100	..	16
India	3.8	2.9	73	16	47	80	..	43	540	540
Indonesia	3.1	2.3	54	9	57	54	32	72	310	230
Iran, Islamic Rep.	4.8	2.1	20	..	74	..	..	90	37	76
Iraq	5.9	4.6	40	..	44	70	..	72	290	250
Ireland	2.1	2.0	14	..	..	..	..	100	6	5
Israel	2.8	2.9	15	..	..	..	..	..	5	17
Italy	1.3	1.3	7	..	60	..	..	..	7	5
Jamaica	2.9	2.4	79	..	65	..	..	97	110	87
Japan	1.5	1.3	4	..	..	..	100	..	8	10
Jordan	5.4	3.4	26	11	56	..	87	100	41	41
Kazakhstan	2.7	1.8	29	9	66	..	..	..	50	210
Kenya	5.8	5.0	96	25	39	70	..	42	410	1,000
Korea, Dem. Rep.	2.4	2.0	2	..	..	..	..	97	110	67
Korea, Rep.	1.6	1.2	3	..	81	..	98	..	20	20
Kuwait	3.4	2.5	24	..	50	..	..	..	5	5
Kyrgyz Republic	3.7	2.5	33	12	60	..	..	99	..	110
Lao PDR	6.0	4.6	89	..	32	30	..	19	..	650
Latvia	2.0	1.2	17	..	..	..	..	..	25	42
Lebanon	3.1	2.3	26	..	63	..	..	..	..	150
Lesotho	4.8	3.5	37	..	30	..	..	60	..	550
Liberia	6.9	6.8	224	..	10	35	..	51	..	760
Libya	4.7	2.9	7	..	..	..	..	..	..	97
Lithuania	2.0	1.3	21	..	..	..	..	100	13	13
Macedonia, FYR	2.1	1.7	23	..	..	..	..	99	7	23
Madagascar	6.2	5.1	124	24	27	55	57	51	470	550
Malawi	7.0	5.9	158	30	31	70	55	61	1,100	1,800
Malaysia	3.8	2.8	18	..	..	..	..	97	30	41
Mali	7.4	6.8	201	26	8	50	..	41	580	1,200
Mauritania	6.1	5.7	99	32	8	33	40	57	750	1,000
Mauritius	2.3	2.0	32	..	76	..	..	98	22	24
Mexico	3.3	2.2	67	..	73	..	..	95	65	83
Moldova	2.4	1.4	31	..	62	..	..	..	44	36
Mongolia	4.0	2.4	53	..	69	..	..	99	99	110
Morocco	4.0	2.5	*42*	10	63	..	31	63	230	220
Mozambique	6.2	5.4	102	18	17	60	..	48	410	1,000
Myanmar	4.0	2.3	19	..	34	85	..	57	230	360
Namibia	5.9	3.8	53	22	44	67	68	76	270	300
Nepal	5.1	3.5	114	28	38	42	7	15	540	740
Netherlands	1.6	1.7	5	..	75	..	..	..	7	16
New Zealand	2.2	2.0	24	..	..	..	..	..	15	7
Nicaragua	4.8	3.2	120	15	69	..	..	67	83	230
Niger	8.2	7.7	260	17	14	43	15	16	590	1,600
Nigeria	6.7	5.6	142	17	13	51	31	35	..	800
Norway	1.9	1.8	10	..	..	..	..	..	6	16
Oman	6.5	3.6	46	..	32	..	..	95	23	87
Pakistan	5.8	4.3	69	..	28	45	19	23	530	500
Panama	3.0	2.6	86	..	..	..	..	93	70	160
Papua New Guinea	5.1	3.9	60	..	26	10	..	41	..	300
Paraguay	4.7	3.7	65	..	57	..	67	77	180	170
Peru	3.9	2.8	53	10	69	..	..	59	190	410
Philippines	4.3	3.1	36	17	49	70	..	60	170	200
Poland	2.0	1.2	15	..	..	..	..	100	4	13
Portugal	1.4	1.4	19	..	..	..	..	100	8	5
Puerto Rico	2.2	1.9	56	..	..	..	..	..	..	25

Reproductive health

	Total fertility rate		Adolescent fertility rate	Unmet need for contraception	Contraceptive prevalence rate	Tetanus vaccinations	Births attended by skilled health staff		Maternal mortality ratio	
	births per woman		births per 1,000 women ages 15–19	% of married women ages 15–49	% of women ages 15–49	% of pregnant women	% of total		per 100,000 live births	
									National estimates	Modeled estimates
	1990	2004	2004	1995–2004[a]	1996–2004[a]	2004	1990–92[a]	2000–04[a]	1990–2004[a]	2000
Romania	1.8	1.3	35	..	64	..	..	99	31	49
Russian Federation	1.9	1.3	29	..	..	..	..	99	..	67
Rwanda	7.4	5.5	47	36	13	76	26	31	1,100	1,400
Saudi Arabia	5.9	4.0	33	..	21	..	..	..	..	23
Senegal	6.4	4.8	82	35	11	85	..	58	560	690
Serbia and Montenegro	2.1	1.7	23	..	58	..	..	93	7	11
Sierra Leone	6.5	6.5	179	..	4	76	..	42	1,800	2,000
Singapore	1.9	1.2	5	..	..	..	..	..	6	30
Slovak Republic	2.1	1.3	21	..	..	..	..	99	16	3
Slovenia	1.5	1.2	6	..	..	..	100	100	17	17
Somalia	6.8	6.3	69	..	..	60	..	25	..	1,100
South Africa	3.3	2.7	67	15	56	61	..	..	150	230
Spain	1.3	1.3	9	..	..	..	..	..	6	4
Sri Lanka	2.5	1.9	19	..	70	..	..	96	92	92
Sudan	5.6	4.2	52	..	7	37	69	87	..	590
Swaziland	5.3	4.0	37	..	48	..	..	74	230	370
Sweden	2.1	1.8	7	..	..	..	..	..	5	2
Switzerland	1.6	1.4	5	..	..	..	..	..	5	7
Syrian Arab Republic	5.2	3.3	34	..	48	..	..	..	65	160
Tajikistan	5.1	3.6	30	..	34	..	..	71	45	100
Tanzania	6.1	4.8	110	22	25	90	44	46	580	1,500
Thailand	2.2	1.9	48	..	72	..	..	99	24	44
Togo	6.4	5.1	98	32	26	61	..	61	480	570
Trinidad and Tobago	2.4	1.6	36	..	38	..	..	96	45	160
Tunisia	3.5	2.0	7	..	66	..	..	90	69	120
Turkey	3.0	2.2	41	10	71	41	..	83	..	70
Turkmenistan	4.2	2.7	16	10	62	..	..	97	14	31
Uganda	7.2	7.1	208	35	23	53	..	39	510	880
Ukraine	1.8	1.2	29	..	89	..	..	100	13	35
United Arab Emirates	4.3	2.2	20	..	..	..	..	..	3	54
United Kingdom	1.8	1.7	26	..	..	..	..	..	7	13
United States	2.1	2.0	50	..	64	..	..	..	8	17
Uruguay	2.5	2.1	69	..	..	..	..	..	26	27
Uzbekistan	4.1	2.4	36	14	68	..	..	96	34	24
Venezuela, RB	3.4	2.7	91	..	77	..	..	94	68	96
Vietnam	3.6	1.8	20	5	79	85	..	90	170	130
West Bank and Gaza	*6.3*	4.9	..	..	42	..	..	97	..	..
Yemen, Rep.	7.5	5.9	93	39	23	21	16	27	370	570
Zambia	6.5	5.5	128	27	34	83	51	43	730	750
Zimbabwe	5.2	3.4	92	13	54	70	..	..	700	1,100
World	**3.1 w**	**2.6 w**	**58 w**		**60 w**		**.. w**	**60 w**		**410 w**
Low income	4.7	3.7	95		40		..	40		682
Middle income	2.6	2.1	32		76		..	87		142
Lower middle income	2.6	2.1	28		76		..	86		153
Upper middle income	2.7	2.0	47		69		..	95		92
Low & middle income	3.4	2.8	62		60		..	60		450
East Asia & Pacific	2.5	2.0	16		78		..	86		117
Europe & Central Asia	2.3	1.6	30		69		..	94		58
Latin America & Carib.	3.2	2.5	78		72		77	87		194
Middle East & N. Africa	4.8	3.0	33		59		42	72		183
South Asia	4.1	3.1	80		46		..	36		564
Sub-Saharan Africa	6.2	5.3	135		22		..	42		921
High income	1.8	1.7	25		64		41	..		14
Europe EMU	1.5	1.5	9		..		..	..		10

a. Data are for the most recent year available.

About the data

Reproductive health is a state of physical and mental well-being in relation to the reproductive system and its functions and processes. Means of achieving reproductive health include education and services during pregnancy and childbirth, provision of safe and effective contraception, and prevention and treatment of sexually transmitted diseases. Complications of pregnancy and childbirth are the leading cause of death and disability among women of reproductive age in developing countries. Reproductive health services will need to expand rapidly over the next two decades, when the number of women and men of reproductive age is projected to increase by about 500 million.

Total and adolescent fertility rates are based on data on registered live births from vital registration systems or, in the absence of such systems, from censuses or sample surveys. As long as the surveys are fairly recent, the estimated rates are generally considered reliable measures of fertility in the recent past. Where no empirical information on age-specific fertility rates is available, a model is used to estimate the share of births to adolescents. For countries without vital registration systems, fertility rates are generally based on extrapolations from trends observed in censuses or surveys from earlier years.

An increasing number of couples in the developing world want to limit or postpone childbearing but are not using effective contraceptive methods. These couples have an unmet need for contraception, shown in the table as the percentage of married women of reproductive age who do not want to become pregnant but are not using contraception (Bulatao 1998). Information on this indicator is collected through surveys and excludes women not exposed to the risk of unintended pregnancy because of menopause, infertility, or postpartum anovulation. Common reasons for not using contraception are lack of knowledge about contraceptive methods and concerns about possible health side-effects.

Contraceptive prevalence reflects all methods—ineffective traditional methods as well as highly effective modern methods. Contraceptive prevalence rates are obtained mainly from household surveys, including Demographic and Health Surveys, Multiple Indicator Cluster Surveys, and contraceptive prevalence surveys (see *Primary data documentation* for the most recent survey year). Unmarried women are often excluded from such surveys, which may bias the estimates.

Neonatal tetanus is an important cause of infant mortality in some developing countries. It can be prevented through immunization of the mother during pregnancy. Recommended doses for full protection are generally two tetanus shots during the first pregnancy and one booster shot during each subsequent pregnancy, with five doses considered adequate for lifetime protection. Information on tetanus shots during pregnancy is collected through surveys in which pregnant respondents are asked to show antenatal cards on which tetanus shots have been recorded. Because not all women have antenatal cards, respondents are also asked about their receipt of these injections. Poor recall may result in a downward bias in estimates of the share of births protected. But in settings where receiving injections is common, respondents may erroneously report having received tetanus shots.

The share of births attended by skilled health staff is an indicator of a health system's ability to provide adequate care for pregnant women. Good antenatal and postnatal care improve maternal health and reduce maternal and infant mortality. But data may not reflect such improvements because health information systems are often weak, maternal deaths are underreported, and rates of maternal mortality are difficult to measure.

Maternal mortality ratios are generally of unknown reliability, as are many other cause-specific mortality indicators. Household surveys such as the Demographic and Health Surveys attempt to measure maternal mortality by asking respondents about survivorship of sisters. The main disadvantage of this method is that the estimates of maternal mortality that it produces pertain to 12 years or so before the survey, making them unsuitable for monitoring recent changes or observing the impact of interventions. In addition, measurement of maternal mortality is subject to many types of errors. Even in high-income countries with vital registration systems, misclassification of maternal deaths has been found to lead to serious underestimation.

The maternal mortality ratios shown in the table as national estimates are based on national surveys, vital registration, or surveillance or are derived from community and hospital records. Those shown as modeled estimates are based on an exercise by the World Health Organization (WHO), United Nations Children's Fund (UNICEF), and United Nations Population Fund (UNFPA). For countries with national data reported maternal mortality was adjusted by a factor of under- or over-estimation and misclassification. For countries with no national data maternal mortality was estimated with a regression model using information on fertility, birth attendants, and GDP. Neither set of ratios can be assumed to provide an accurate estimate of maternal mortality for any of the countries in the table.

Definitions

• **Total fertility rate** is the number of children that would be born to a woman if she were to live to the end of her childbearing years and bear children in accordance with current age-specific fertility rates. • **Adolescent fertility rate** is the number of births per 1,000 women ages 15–19. • **Unmet need for contraception** is the percentage of fertile, married women of reproductive age who do not want to become pregnant and are not using contraception. • **Contraceptive prevalence rate** is the percentage of women who are practicing, or whose sexual partners are practicing, any form of contraception. It is usually measured for married women ages 15–49 only. • **Tetanus vaccinations** refer to the percentage of pregnant women who receive two tetanus toxoid injections during their first pregnancy and one booster shot during each subsequent pregnancy, with five doses considered adequate for a lifetime. • **Births attended by skilled health staff** are the percentage of deliveries attended by personnel trained to give the necessary supervision, care, and advice to women during pregnancy, labor, and the postpartum period; to conduct deliveries on their own; and to care for newborns. • **Maternal mortality ratio** is the number of women who die from pregnancy-related causes during pregnancy and childbirth, per 100,000 live births.

Data sources

Data on fertility rates are compiled and estimated by the World Bank's Development Data Group. Important inputs come from the following sources: the United Nations Population Division's *World Population Prospects: The 2004 Revision*; census reports and other statistical publications from national statistical offices; and household surveys such as Demographic and Health Surveys. Data on women with unmet need for contraception and contraceptive prevalence rates are from household surveys, including Demographic and Health Surveys by Macro International and Multiple Indicator Cluster Surveys by UNICEF. Data on tetanus vaccinations and births attended by skilled health staff and national estimates of maternal mortality ratios are from UNICEF's *State of the World's Children 2006* and Childinfo, and Demographic and Health Surveys by Macro International. Modeled estimates for maternal mortality ratios are from Carla AbouZahr and Tessa Wardlaw's "Maternal Mortality in 2000: Estimates Developed by WHO, UNICEF, and UNFPA" (2003).

2.17 Nutrition

	Prevalence of undernourishment		Prevalence of child malnutrition		Prevalence of overweight children	Low-birthweight babies	Exclusive breastfeeding	Consumption of iodized salt	Vitamin A supplementation
	% of population		% of children under age 5		% of children under age 5	% of births	% of children under 6 months	% of households	% of children 6–59 months
			Underweight	Stunting					
	1990–92	2001–03	1995–2004[a]	1995–2004[a]	1995–2004[a]	1998–2004[a]	1998–2004[a]	1998–2004[a]	2003
Afghanistan	..	..	39.3	47.6	4.0	..	..	28	86
Albania	5[b]	6	14.0	35.1	22.4	3	6	62	..
Algeria	5	5	10.4	19.1	10.1	7	13	69	..
Angola	58	38	30.5	45.2	0.5	12	11	35	68
Argentina	<3	<3	5.4	12.4	9.2	8	..	..	..
Armenia	52[b]	29	2.6	12.9	10.4	7	30	84	..
Australia	..	..	0.0	0.0	5.2	7	..	..	..
Austria	..	..	..	..	..	7	..	..	..
Azerbaijan	34[b]	10	6.8	13.3	2.6	11	7	26	..
Bangladesh	35	30	47.5	43.0	0.8	36	36	70	87
Belarus	<3[b]	3	..	..	..	5	..	55	..
Belgium	..	..	..	..	..	..	..	..	..
Benin	20	14	22.9	30.7	1.8	16	38	72	98
Bolivia	28	23	7.6	26.7	5.6	7	54	90	38
Bosnia and Herzegovina	9[b]	9	4.1	9.7	13.2	4	6	77	..
Botswana	23	30	12.5	23.1	6.9	10	34	66	*85*
Brazil	12	8	5.7	10.5	4.9	..	..	88	..
Bulgaria	8[b]	9	..	..	..	10	..	98	..
Burkina Faso	21	17	37.7	38.7	2.9	19	19	45	95
Burundi	48	67	45.1	56.8	0.7	16	62	96	95
Cambodia	43	33	45.2	44.6	2.0	11	12	14	47
Cameroon	33	25	18.1	31.7	5.2	11	21	61	86
Canada	..	..	..	..	..	6	..	..	..
Central African Republic	50	45	24.3	28.4	0.8	14	17	86	84
Chad	58	33	36.7	40.9	1.5	31	2	58	*85*
Chile	8	4	0.7	1.4	8.1	5	63	100	..
China	16	12	7.8	14.2	2.6	4	51	93	..
Hong Kong, China	..	..	..	..	..	5	..	..	..
Colombia	17	14	*7.0*	*12.0*	3.7	*6*	26	*43*	..
Congo, Dem. Rep.	31	72	31.0	38.1	3.9	12	24	72	80
Congo, Rep.	54	34	13.0	..	..	..	4[c]	..	89
Costa Rica	6	4	5.1	6.1	6.2	7	..	..	..
Côte d'Ivoire	18	14	17.2	25.1	2.5	17	5	31	*97*
Croatia	16[b]	7	0.6	0.8	5.9	6	..	90	..
Cuba	8	<3	3.9	4.6	..	6	41	88	..
Czech Republic	<3[b]	<3	..	..	..	7	..	..	..
Denmark	..	..	..	..	..	5	..	..	..
Dominican Republic	27	27	5.3	8.9	6.5	11	10	18	40
Ecuador	8	5	11.6	26.4	..	16	35	99	*50*
Egypt, Arab Rep.	4	3	8.6	15.6	6.7	12	30	56	..
El Salvador	12	11	10.3	18.9	3.6	7	24	..	..
Eritrea	..	73	39.6	37.6	0.7	..	52	68	52
Estonia	9[b]	3	..	..	..	4	..	..	..
Ethiopia	..	46	47.2	51.5	1.2	15	55	28	65
Finland	..	..	..	..	..	4	..	..	..
France	..	..	..	..	..	7	..	..	..
Gabon	10	5	11.9	20.7	3.7	14	6	36	30
Gambia, The	22	27	17.2	19.2	1.5	17	26	8	91
Georgia	44[b]	13	3.1	11.7	12.7	7	18[c]	68	..
Germany	..	..	..	..	..	7	..	..	..
Ghana	37	12	22.1	29.9	2.9	16	53	28	78
Greece	..	..	..	..	..	8	..	..	..
Guatemala	16	23	22.7	49.3	5.4	12	51	67	*33*
Guinea	39	24	32.7	26.1	2.7	16	23	68	98
Guinea-Bissau	24	37	25.0	30.5	3.3	22	37	2	*80*
Haiti	65	47	17.2	22.7	2.0	21	24	11	25

Nutrition 2.17

	Prevalence of undernourishment		Prevalence of child malnutrition		Prevalence of overweight children	Low-birthweight babies	Exclusive breastfeeding	Consumption of iodized salt	Vitamin A supplementation
	% of population		% of children under age 5		% of children under age 5	% of births	% of children under 6 months	% of households	% of children 6–59 months
	1990–92	2001–03	Underweight 1995–2004[a]	Stunting 1995–2004[a]	1995–2004[a]	1998–2004[a]	1998–2004[a]	1998–2004[a]	2003
Honduras	23	22	16.6	29.2	2.2	14	35	80	35
Hungary	<3[b]	<3	..	..	..	9	..	..	..
India	25	20	46.7	44.9	2.2	30	37[c]	50	45[d]
Indonesia	9	6	28.2	42.2	4.0	9	40	73	62
Iran, Islamic Rep.	4	4	10.9	15.4	4.3	..	44	94	..
Iraq	..	..	15.9	22.1	3.0	15	12	40	..
Ireland	..	..	..	..	..	6	..	..	..
Israel	..	..	..	..	..	8	..	..	..
Italy	..	..	..	..	..	6	..	..	..
Jamaica	14	10	3.6	4.4	3.8	10	..	100	..
Japan	..	..	..	..	..	8	..	..	..
Jordan	4	7	4.4	8.5	3.5	..	27	88	..
Kazakhstan	<3[b]	8	4.2	9.7	3.0	8	36	83	..
Kenya	39	31	19.9	30.3	3.7	10	13	91	33
Korea, Dem. Rep.	18	35	23.9	38.6	0.6	7	65	40	95
Korea, Rep.	<3	<3	..	..	..	4	..	..	..
Kuwait	24	5	1.7	3.2	5.7	7	..[c]	..	..
Kyrgyz Republic	21[b]	4	6.7	24.8	6.3	..	..	42	..
Lao PDR	29	21	40.4	42.4	1.2	14	23	75	64
Latvia	3[b]	3	..	..	..	5	..	..	..
Lebanon	<3	3	3.0	12.2	..	6	27[c]	87	..
Lesotho	17	12	18.0	46.1	12.1	14	15	69	75
Liberia	34	49	26.5	39.5	2.3	..	35	..	*40*
Libya	<3	<3	4.7	15.1	..	..	..	..	..
Lithuania	4[b]	<3	..	..	..	4	..	..	..
Macedonia, FYR	15[b]	7	5.9	6.9	4.9	6	99	80	95
Madagascar	35	38	41.9	47.7	2.0	17	67	75	91
Malawi	50	34	21.9	49.0	4.3	16	44	49	92
Malaysia	3	3	10.6	15.6	3.3	9	..[c]	..	..
Mali	29	28	33.2	38.2	1.5	23	25	74	61
Mauritania	15	10	31.8	34.5	..	..	20	2	*89*
Mauritius	6	6	14.9	9.7	4.0	14	21[c]	..	..
Mexico	5	5	7.5	17.7	5.3	8	..	91	..
Moldova	5[b]	11	3.2	..	..	5	..	33	..
Mongolia	34	28	12.7	24.6	4.8	7	51	75	87
Morocco	6	6	10.2	18.1	9.2	..	31	41	..
Mozambique	66	45	23.7	41.0	3.0	15	30	54	50
Myanmar	10	5	31.8	32.2	1.6	15	15[c]	60	87
Namibia	34	23	24.0	23.6	2.2	14	19	63	93
Nepal	20	17	48.3	50.5	0.2	21	68	63	96
Netherlands	..	..	..	..	..	..	..	..	..
New Zealand	..	..	..	..	..	6	..	83	..
Nicaragua	30	27	9.6	20.2	4.7	12	31	97	91
Niger	41	32	40.1	39.7	0.8	13	1	15	95
Nigeria	13	9	28.7	38.3	3.6	14	17	97	27
Norway	..	..	..	..	..	5	..	..	..
Oman	..	..	17.8	10.4	1.0	8	..	61	*97*
Pakistan	24	23	37.8	36.8	2.1	..	..	17	95
Panama	21	25	8.1	18.2	4.2	10	..	95	..
Papua New Guinea	15	13	..	..	..	..	..	..	1
Paraguay	18	15	4.6	..	..	..	22	88	..
Peru	42	12	7.1	25.4	7.6	..	67	..	*6*
Philippines	26	19	27.6	32.1	1.0	20	34	56	76
Poland	<3[b]	<3	..	..	..	6	..	..	..
Portugal	..	..	..	..	..	8	..	..	..
Puerto Rico	..	..	..	..	..	14	..	..	..

Nutrition

	Prevalence of undernourishment		Prevalence of child malnutrition		Prevalence of overweight children	Low-birthweight babies	Exclusive breastfeeding	Consumption of iodized salt	Vitamin A supplementation
	% of population		% of children under age 5		% of children under age 5	% of births	% of children under 6 months	% of households	% of children 6–59 months
			Underweight	Stunting					
	1990–92	2001–03	1995–2004[a]	1995–2004[a]	1995–2004[a]	1998–2004[a]	1998–2004[a]	1998–2004[a]	2003
Romania	<3[b]	<3	3.2	10.1	5.5	9	..	53	..
Russian Federation	4[b]	3	5.5	10.6	..	6	..	35	..
Rwanda	43	36	24.3	42.6	4.0	9	84	90	86
Saudi Arabia	4	4	14.3	..	..	..	..[c]	..	..
Senegal	23	23	22.7	25.4	2.2	18	24[c]	16	*83*
Serbia and Montenegro	5[b]	10	1.9	5.1	12.9	4	11[c]	73	..
Sierra Leone	46	50	27.2	33.8	..	23	4	23	84
Singapore	..	..	3.4	2.2	2.2	8	..	..	..
Slovak Republic	4[b]	6	..	..	..	7	..	..	..
Slovenia	3[b]	3	..	..	..	6	..	..	..
Somalia	..	..	25.8	23.3	..	..	9	..	*60*
South Africa	..	..	11.5	24.9	6.2	15	7	62	..
Spain	..	..	..	..	..	..	..	..	..
Sri Lanka	28	22	29.7	13.9	..	22	84	88	..
Sudan	31	27	40.7	43.3	3.4	31	16	1	34
Swaziland	14	19	10.3	30.2	..	9	24	59	80
Sweden	..	..	..	..	..	4	..	..	..
Switzerland	..	..	..	..	..	6	..	..	..
Syrian Arab Republic	5	4	6.9	18.8	..	6	81[c]	79	..
Tajikistan	22[b]	61	..	36.2	..	15	50	28	..
Tanzania	37	44	29.4	43.8	1.7	13	41	67	91
Thailand	30	21	17.6	13.4	2.8	9	..	63	..
Togo	33	25	25.1	21.7	1.5	18	18	67	84
Trinidad and Tobago	13	11	5.9	3.6	..	23	2	1	..
Tunisia	<3	<3	4.0	12.3	4.5	7	47	97	..
Turkey	<3	3	3.9	16.0	2.2	16	21	64	..
Turkmenistan	12[b]	8	12.0	22.3	..	6	13	100	..
Uganda	24	19	22.9	39.1	2.6	12	63	95	*46*
Ukraine	<3[b]	3	1.0	2.7	20.1	5	22	32	..
United Arab Emirates	4	<3	7.0	..	..	..	..	..	..
United Kingdom	..	..	..	..	..	8	..	..	..
United States	..	..	1.6	1.1	5.6	8	..	..	..
Uruguay	7	3	4.5	..	..	8	..	..	..
Uzbekistan	8[b]	26	7.9	21.1	14.4	7	19	19	93
Venezuela, RB	11	18	4.4	12.8	3.2	9	7[c]	90	..
Vietnam	31	17	28.4	36.5	2.7	9	15	83	99[d]
West Bank and Gaza	..	16	4.1	7.3	2.3	..	..	..	..
Yemen, Rep.	34	37	45.6	51.7	1.9	..	12	30	36
Zambia	48	47	23.0	46.8	3.0	12	40	77	73
Zimbabwe	45	45	13.0	26.5	7.0	11	33	93	46
World	**20 w**	**16 w**	**.. w**	**.. w**		**.. w**	**.. w**	**.. w**	**.. w**
Low income	27	24	43.4	43.1		22	33	..	61
Middle income	14	10	11.1	26.9		..	..	..	..
Lower middle income	15	11	11.2	15.1		..	43	70	..
Upper middle income	..	4	..	..		10	18	..	..
Low & middle income	20	16	..	..		..	36	62	..
East Asia & Pacific	17	12	11.5	17.1		11	..	..	..
Europe & Central Asia	6[b]	6	..	..		..	22	..	..
Latin America & Carib.	13	10	9.1	19.1		11	..	..	..
Middle East & N. Africa	6	7	14.7	20.0		..	31	67	..
South Asia	26	21	48.5	46.1		..	38	..	58
Sub-Saharan Africa	31	32	..	..		25	28	56	62
High income	..	..	..	..		..	12	..	..
Europe EMU	..	..	..	..		..	..	..	..

a. Data are for the most recent year available. b. Data are for 1993–95. c. Refers to exclusive breastfeeding for less than four months. d. Country's vitamin A supplementation programs do not target children all the way up to 59 months of age.

About the data

Data on undernourishment are produced by the Food and Agriculture Organization (FAO) of the United Nations based on the calories available from local food production, trade, and stocks; the number of calories needed by different age and gender groups; the proportion of the population represented by each age group; and a coefficient of distribution to take account of inequality in access to food (FAO 2000). From a policy and program standpoint, however, this measure has its limits. First, food insecurity exists even where food availability is not a problem because of inadequate access of poor households to food. Second, food insecurity is an individual or household phenomenon, and the average food available to each person, even corrected for possible effects of low income, is not a good predictor of food insecurity among the population. And third, nutrition security is determined not only by food security but also by the quality of care of mothers and children and the quality of the household's health environment (Smith and Haddad 2000).

Estimates of child malnutrition, based on weight for age (underweight) and height for age (stunting), are from national survey data. The proportion of children who are underweight is the most common indicator of malnutrition. Being underweight, even mildly, increases the risk of death and inhibits cognitive development in children. Moreover, it perpetuates the problem from one generation to the next, as malnourished women are more likely to have low-birthweight babies. Height for age reflects linear growth achieved pre- and post-natally, and a deficit indicates long-term, cumulative effects of inadequacies of health, diet, or care. It is often argued that stunting is a proxy for multifaceted deprivation and is a better indicator of long-term changes in malnutrition.

Estimates of children who are overweight are also from national survey data. Overweight in children has become a growing concern in developing countries. Researchers show an association between obesity in childhood and a high prevalence of diabetes, respiratory disease, high blood pressure, and psychosocial and orthopedic disorders (de Onis and Blossner 2000). The survey data were analyzed in a standardized way by the World Health Organization (WHO) to allow comparisons across countries.

Low birthweight, which is associated with maternal malnutrition, raises the risk of infant mortality and stunts growth in infancy and childhood. There is also emerging evidence that low-birthweight babies are more prone to noncommunicable diseases such as diabetes and cardiovascular heart diseases. Estimates of low-birthweight infants are drawn mostly from hospital records and household surveys. Many births in developing countries take place at home, and these births are seldom recorded. A hospital birth may indicate higher income and therefore better nutrition, or it could indicate a higher-risk birth, possibly skewing the data on birthweights downward. The data should therefore be treated with caution.

It is estimated that improved breastfeeding practice can save some 1.5 million children a year. Breast milk alone contains all the nutrients, antibodies, hormones, and antioxidants an infant needs to thrive. It protects babies from diarrhea and acute respiratory infections, stimulates their immune systems and response to vaccination, and according to some studies confers cognitive benefits as well. The data on breastfeeding are derived from national surveys.

Iodine deficiency is the single most important cause of preventable mental retardation, and it contributes significantly to the risk of stillbirth and miscarriage. Iodized salt is the best source of iodine, and a global campaign to iodize edible salt is significantly reducing the risks (UNICEF, *State of the World's Children 1999*).

Vitamin A is essential for the functioning of the immune system. A child deficient in vitamin A faces a 25 percent greater risk of dying from a range of childhood ailments such as measles, malaria, and diarrhea. Improving the vitamin A status of pregnant women helps reduce anemia, improves their resistance to infection, and may reduce their risk of dying during pregnancy and childbirth. Giving vitamin A to new mothers who are breastfeeding helps to protect their children during the first months of life. Food fortification with vitamin A is being introduced in many developing countries.

Definitions

• **Prevalence of undernourishment** is the percentage of the population that is undernourished. • **Prevalence of child malnutrition** is the percentage of children under age five whose weight for age (underweight) or height for age (stunting) is more than two standard deviations below the median for the international reference population ages 0–59 months. For children up to two years old height is measured by recumbent length. For older children height is measured by stature while standing. The reference population, adopted by the WHO in 1983, is based on children from the United States, who are assumed to be well nourished. • **Prevalence of overweight children** is the percentage of children under age five whose weight for height is more than two standard deviations above the median for the international reference population of the corresponding age, established by the U.S. National Center for Health Statistics and the WHO. • **Low-birthweight babies** are the percentage of newborns weighing less than 2,500 grams, with the measurement taken within the first hours of life, before significant postnatal weight loss has occurred. • **Exclusive breastfeeding** refers to the percentage of children less than six months old who are fed breast milk alone (no other liquids). • **Consumption of iodized salt** refers to the percentage of households that use edible salt fortified with iodine. • **Vitamin A supplementation** refers to the percentage of children ages 6–59 months old who received at least one high-dose vitamin A capsule in the previous six months.

Data sources

Data on undernourishment are from www.fao.org/faostat/foodsecurity/index_en.htm. Data on malnutrition and overweight are from WHO's *Global Database on Child Growth and Malnutrition*. Data on low-birthweight babies, breastfeeding, iodized salt consumption, and vitamin A supplementation are from the WHO's *World Health Report 2004* and the United Nations Children's Fund's *State of the World's Children 2006*.

2.18 Health risk factors and public health challenges

	Prevalence of smoking		Incidence of tuberculosis	Prevalence of diabetes	Mortality caused by road traffic injury	Prevalence of HIV			
	% of adults		per 100,000 people	% of population ages 20–79	per 100,000 people	Total % of population ages 15–49		Female % of population with HIV	
	Male 2000–05[a]	Female 2000–05[a]	2004	2003	1998–2003[a]	2001	2003	2001	2003
Afghanistan	..	..	333	8.2	..	..	..	..	..
Albania	60	18	22	3.8	11.1	..	..	..	..
Algeria	32	0[b]	54	4.1	..	<0.1	0.1	11.8	15.6
Angola	..	..	259	2.7	..	3.7	3.9	55.0	59.1
Argentina	32	25	43	5.4	..	0.7	0.7	19.2	20.0
Armenia	62	2	78	8.1	5.6	0.1	0.1	35.0	36.0
Australia	19	16	6	6.2	8.2	0.1	0.1	6.7	7.1
Austria	..	..	14	9.6	11.5	0.2	0.3	22.2	22.0
Azerbaijan	..	1	75	6.9	6.9	..	<0.1	..	..
Bangladesh	55	27	229	3.9	..	..	..	..	..
Belarus	53	7	60	6.9	14.3	..	..	..	..
Belgium	30	25	13	4.2	13.1	0.2	0.2	35.8	35.0
Benin	..	..	87	2.1	..	1.9	1.9	57.6	56.5
Bolivia	..	..	217	4.8	..	0.1	0.1	27.5	27.1
Bosnia and Herzegovina	49	30	53	9.6	..	..	<0.1	..	..
Botswana	..	..	670	3.6	..	38.0	37.3	57.6	57.6
Brazil	22	14	60	5.2	..	0.6	0.7	37.1	36.9
Bulgaria	44	23	36	10.0	10.2	..	0.1	..	..
Burkina Faso	..	..	191	2.7	..	4.2	1.8[c]	56.0	55.6
Burundi	..	..	343	1.3	..	6.2	6.0	54.5	59.1
Cambodia	..	..	510	2.0	..	2.7	2.6	30.0	30.0
Cameroon	..	..	179	0.8	..	7.0	5.5[d]	56.0	55.8
Canada	22	17	5	9.0	8.7	0.3	0.3	25.0	23.6
Central African Republic	..	..	322	2.3	..	13.5	13.5	56.5	54.2
Chad	..	..	279	2.7	..	4.9	4.8	57.1	55.6
Chile	48	37	16	5.6	10.7	0.3	0.3	32.0	33.5
China	67	4	101	2.7	19.0	0.1	0.1	20.0	22.9
Hong Kong, China	22	4	75	8.8	..	0.1	0.1	30.8	34.6
Colombia	..	..	50	4.3	24.2	0.5	0.7	33.3	34.4
Congo, Dem. Rep.	..	..	366	2.5	..	4.2	4.2	56.8	57.0
Congo, Rep.	..	..	377	2.6	..	5.3	4.9	56.3	56.3
Costa Rica	29	10	14	6.9	20.1	0.6	0.6	31.8	33.3
Côte d'Ivoire	..	..	393	2.3	..	6.7	7.0	56.3	56.6
Croatia	34	27	41	5.8	11.4	..	<0.1	..	..
Cuba	..	..	10	13.2	13.9	0.1	0.1	31.3	33.3
Czech Republic	31	20	11	9.5	14.2	<0.1	0.1	35.7	32.0
Denmark	31	25	8	6.9	8.0	0.2	0.2	17.4	18.0
Dominican Republic	16	11	91	10.0	41.1	1.8	1.0[e]	26.4	27.1
Ecuador	..	..	131	4.8	16.9	0.3	0.3	32.6	34.0
Egypt, Arab Rep.	40	18	27	9.8	7.5	<0.1	<0.1	10.9	13.3
El Salvador	42	15	54	6.2	41.7	0.6	0.7	32.1	34.3
Eritrea	..	..	271	1.9	..	2.8	2.7	56.4	56.4
Estonia	45	18	46	9.7	14.8	0.7	1.1	32.0	33.8
Ethiopia	6	0[b]	353	1.9	..	4.1	4.4	55.8	55.0
Finland	26	19	9	7.2	7.3	0.1	0.1	..	..
France	30	21	12	6.2	10.2	0.4	0.4	27.3	26.7
Gabon	..	..	280	2.9	..	6.9	8.1	56.8	57.8
Gambia, The	..	..	233	2.2	..	1.2	1.2	55.6	57.1
Georgia	53	6	82	9.0	6.2	<0.1	0.1	..	33.3
Germany	37	28	8	10.2	8.0	0.1	0.1	19.8	22.1
Ghana	7	1	206	3.3	..	3.1	2.2[c]	54.8	56.3
Greece	47	29	19	6.1	19.3	0.2	0.2	20.5	20.0
Guatemala	21	2	77	5.5	..	1.1	1.1	41.5	41.9
Guinea	..	..	240	2.0	..	2.8	3.2	59.0	55.4
Guinea-Bissau	..	..	199	2.0	..	..	..	..	..
Haiti	15	6	306	5.7	..	5.5	5.6	58.3	57.7

Health risk factors and public health challenges 2.18

	Prevalence of smoking		Incidence of tuberculosis	Prevalence of diabetes	Mortality caused by road traffic injury	Prevalence of HIV			
	% of adults		per 100,000 people	% of population ages 20–79	per 100,000 people	Total % of population ages 15–49		Female % of population with HIV	
	Male 2000–05[a]	Female 2000–05[a]	2004	2003	1998–2003[a]	2001	2003	2001	2003
Honduras	..	..	77	5.7	..	1.6	1.8	56.3	55.9
Hungary	41	28	26	9.7	13.1	..	0.1	..	..
India	47	17	168	5.9	..	0.8	0.9	39.5	38.0
Indonesia	58	3	245	1.9	..	0.1	0.1	12.1	13.6
Iran, Islamic Rep.	22	2	27	3.6	..	0.1	0.1	10.6	12.3
Iraq	..	..	132	7.7	8.4	..	<0.1	..	..
Ireland	28	26	11	3.4	10.1	0.1	0.1	31.8	30.8
Israel	32	18	9	7.1	5.9	..	0.1	..	..
Italy	31	17	7	6.6	10.5	0.5	0.5	32.3	32.1
Jamaica	..	..	7	7.2	..	0.8	1.2	51.4	47.6
Japan	47	15	30	6.9	7.0	<0.1	<0.1	22.5	24.2
Jordan	51	8	5	7.0	..	<0.1	<0.1	..	..
Kazakhstan	65	9	151	5.5	..	0.1	0.2	34.0	33.5
Kenya	21	1	619	2.5	..	8.0	6.7[c]	62.5	65.5
Korea, Dem. Rep.	..	..	178	5.2	..	..	..	..	..
Korea, Rep.	..	..	90	6.4	15.1	<0.1	<0.1	10.7	10.8
Kuwait	..	..	26	12.8	23.7	..	..	..	..
Kyrgyz Republic	51	5	122	4.3	12.9	<0.1	0.1	..	..
Lao PDR	59	13	156	1.1	..	<0.1	0.1	..	..
Latvia	51	19	68	9.9	22.7	0.5	0.6	32.2	33.3
Lebanon	42	31	11	6.4	..	0.1	0.1	..	..
Lesotho	..	..	696	3.1	..	29.6	28.9	56.7	56.7
Liberia	..	..	310	2.0	..	5.1	5.9	56.3	56.3
Libya	..	..	20	3.7	..	..	0.3	..	..
Lithuania	44	13	63	9.4	19.3	0.1	0.1	..	..
Macedonia, FYR	..	..	30	4.9	5.1	<0.1	<0.1	..	..
Madagascar	..	..	218	2.5	..	1.3	1.7	56.1	58.5
Malawi	21	5	413	1.7	..	14.3	14.2	57.1	56.8
Malaysia	43	2	103	9.4	..	0.4	0.4	15.4	16.7
Mali	..	..	281	2.0	..	1.8[f]	1.9	54.2	59.2
Mauritania	..	..	287	3.5	..	0.5	0.6	55.9	57.3
Mauritius	32	1	64	10.7	14.7	..	..	..	..
Mexico	13	5	32	7.4	11.8	0.3	0.3	32.7	33.1
Moldova	34	2	138	9.3	14.1	..	0.2	..	..
Mongolia	68	26	192	1.4	..	<0.1	<0.1	..	..
Morocco	29	0[b]	110	4.2	..	..	0.1	..	..
Mozambique	..	..	460	3.1	..	12.1	12.2	58.2	55.8
Myanmar	36	12	171	1.1	..	1.0	1.2	28.9	30.3
Namibia	23	10	717	3.1	..	21.3	21.3	52.6	55.0
Nepal	49	24	184	4.1	..	0.4	0.5	20.7	26.7
Netherlands	36	28	8	3.7	6.4	0.2	0.2	19.4	20.0
New Zealand	24	22	11	7.6	11.5	0.1	0.1	..	..
Nicaragua	..	5	63	6.1	20.1	0.2	0.2	32.7	33.9
Niger	..	..	157	3.1	..	1.1	1.2	56.9	56.3
Nigeria	..	1	290	2.2	..	5.5	5.4	58.1	57.6
Norway	27	25	5	6.7	6.1	0.1	0.1	..	..
Oman	..	..	11	11.4	..	0.1	0.1	..	..
Pakistan	..	..	181	8.5	..	0.1	0.1	6.9	12.2
Panama	..	..	45	7.3	16.4	0.7	0.9	37.3	41.3
Papua New Guinea	..	..	233	1.9	..	0.4	0.6	29.0	30.0
Paraguay	23	7	71	3.9	..	0.4	0.5	27.0	26.0
Peru	..	..	178	5.1	17.6	0.4	0.5	31.4	33.8
Philippines	41	8	293	2.4	..	<0.1	<0.1	20.9	22.5
Poland	40	25	29	9.0	14.8	..	0.1	..	..
Portugal	..	..	42	7.8	14.8	0.4	0.4	20.0	19.5
Puerto Rico	17	10	5	13.2	..	..	..	..	..

2.18 Health risk factors and public health challenges

	Prevalence of smoking		Incidence of tuberculosis	Prevalence of diabetes	Mortality caused by road traffic injury	Prevalence of HIV			
	% of adults		per 100,000 people	% of population ages 20–79	per 100,000 people	Total % of population ages 15–49		Female % of population with HIV	
	Male 2000–05[a]	Female 2000–05[a]	2004	2003	1998–2003[a]	2001	2003	2001	2003
Romania	32	10	146	9.3	16.8	..	<0.1	..	..
Russian Federation	60	16	115	9.2	19.4	0.7	1.1	32.1	33.7
Rwanda	..	..	371	1.1	..	5.1	5.1	54.5	56.5
Saudi Arabia	19	8	40	9.4	..	..	..	..	..
Senegal	..	..	245	2.3	..	0.8	0.8	55.3	56.1
Serbia and Montenegro	48	34	33	5.6	..	0.2	0.2	20.0	20.0
Sierra Leone	..	..	443	2.2	..	..	..	..	..
Singapore	24	4	40	12.3	5.2	0.2	0.2	23.5	24.4
Slovak Republic	..	..	19	8.7	11.3	..	<0.1	..	..
Slovenia	28	20	15	9.6	12.1	<0.1	<0.1	..	..
Somalia	..	..	411	2.3	..	..	..	..	..
South Africa	23	8	718	3.4	..	20.9	15.6[e]	56.3	56.9
Spain	39	25	25	9.9	12.8	0.6	0.7	20.0	20.8
Sri Lanka	23	2	60	2.1	..	<0.1	<0.1	..	17.1
Sudan	..	..	220	3.2	..	1.9	2.3	56.7	57.9
Swaziland	11	3	1,226	3.0	..	38.2	38.8	57.9	55.0
Sweden	17	18	4	7.3	5.9	0.1	0.1	27.3	25.7
Switzerland	27	23	7	9.5	7.5	0.4	0.4	30.0	30.0
Syrian Arab Republic	..	..	41	6.2	..	..	<0.1	..	..
Tajikistan	..	..	177	3.7	5.6	..	<0.1	..	..
Tanzania	..	..	347	2.3	..	9.0	7.0[d]	58.6	56.0
Thailand	49	3	142	2.1	..	1.7	1.5	32.3	35.7
Togo	..	..	355	2.1	..	4.3	4.1	56.4	56.3
Trinidad and Tobago	..	..	9	7.9	..	3.0	3.2	50.0	50.0
Tunisia	50	2	22	4.6	..	<0.1	<0.1	..	..
Turkey	49	18	28	7.0	..	..	..	..	..
Turkmenistan	..	..	65	4.0	10.3	..	<0.1	..	..
Uganda	25	3	402	1.5	..	5.1	4.1	59.6	60.0
Ukraine	53	11	101	9.7	10.8	1.2	1.4	32.0	33.3
United Arab Emirates	17	1	17	20.1	..	..	..	..	..
United Kingdom	27	25	12	3.9	6.1	0.2	0.2	28.2	29.8
United States	24	19	5	8.0	14.7	0.6	0.6	20.2	25.5
Uruguay	35	24	28	6.8	10.0	0.3	0.3	32.7	32.8
Uzbekistan	24	1	117	4.0	9.8	<0.1	0.1	33.3	33.6
Venezuela, RB	..	..	42	5.2	23.1	0.6	0.7	32.4	32.0
Vietnam	35	2	176	1.0	..	0.3	0.4	27.3	32.5
West Bank and Gaza	..	..	23	..	..	..	..	..	..
Yemen, Rep.	..	..	89	7.7	..	..	0.1	..	..
Zambia	16	1	680	3.0	..	16.7	15.6[g]	56.3	56.6
Zimbabwe	20	2	674	2.6	..	24.9	24.6	56.3	58.1
World	**.. w**	**.. w**	**139 w**	**5.1 w**	**.. w**	**1.1 w**	**1.1 w**	**29.4 w**	**30.8 w**
Low income	..	15	224	4.7	..	2.1	2.1	41.2	41.1
Middle income	..	..	114	4.4	..	0.7	0.7	23.7	25.7
Lower middle income	..	..	114	3.6	..	0.3	0.3	21.9	24.1
Upper middle income	..	..	112	7.6	..	2.7	2.6	33.3	34.2
Low & middle income	..	..	162	4.5	..	1.2	1.2	30.8	32.0
East Asia & Pacific	67	4	138	2.6	19.0	0.2	0.2	20.2	22.9
Europe & Central Asia	..	..	83	8.3	..	..	0.7	..	..
Latin America & Carib.	..	..	64	5.9	..	0.6	0.7	34.0	34.5
Middle East & N. Africa	..	..	54	6.2	..	..	0.1	..	..
South Asia	47	18	177	5.9	..	0.7	0.8	35.5	34.5
Sub-Saharan Africa	..	..	363	2.4	..	7.3	7.2	57.1	57.3
High income	..	..	17	7.6	10.9	0.3	0.4	22.0	24.2
Europe EMU	..	..	13	7.8	9.9	0.3	0.3	24.5	25.0

a. Data are for the most recent year available. b. Less than 0.5. c. Survey data, 2003. d. Survey data, 2004. e. Survey data, 2002. f. Survey data, 2001. g. Survey data, 2001/02.

About the data

The limited availability of data on health status is a major constraint in assessing the health situation in developing countries. Surveillance data are lacking for many major public health concerns. Estimates of prevalence and incidence are available for some diseases but are often unreliable and incomplete. National health authorities differ widely in their capacity and willingness to collect or report information. To compensate for the paucity of data and ensure reasonable reliability and international comparability, the World Health Organization (WHO) prepares estimates in accordance with epidemiological models and statistical standards.

Smoking is the most common form of tobacco use in many countries, and the prevalence of smoking is therefore a good measure of the extent of the tobacco epidemic (Corrao and others 2000). While the prevalence of smoking has been declining in some high-income countries, it has been increasing in many developing countries. Tobacco use causes heart and other vascular diseases and cancers of the lung and other organs. Given the long delay between starting to smoke and the onset of disease, the health impact of smoking in developing countries will increase rapidly in the next few decades. Because the data present a one-time estimate, with no information on the intensity or duration of smoking, and because the definition of adult varies across countries, the data should be interpreted with caution.

Tuberculosis is one of the main causes of death from a single infectious agent among adults in developing countries. In high-income countries tuberculosis has reemerged largely as a result of cases among immigrants. The estimates of tuberculosis incidence in the table are based on a new approach in which reported cases are adjusted using the ratio of case notifications to the estimated share of cases detected by panels of 80 epidemiologists convened by the WHO.

Diabetes, an important cause of ill health and a risk factor for other diseases in developed countries, is spreading rapidly in developing countries. While diabetes is most common among the elderly, prevalence rates are rising among younger and productive populations in developing countries. Economic development has led to the greater adoption of Western lifestyles and diet in developing countries, resulting in a substantial increase in diabetes. Without effective prevention and control programs, diabetes will likely continue to increase. Data are based on sample surveys.

Data for mortality caused by road traffic injury are collected by the WHO based on vital registries. There is considerable difference in completeness of the vital registry data. In some countries the vital registry system covers only part of the country. In some, not all deaths are registered. In addition, mortality from different causes is difficult to measure. For countries with incomplete vital registry systems, the WHO has used demographic techniques to estimate deaths.

Adult HIV prevalence rates reflect the rate of HIV infection in each country's population. Low national prevalence rates can be very misleading, however. They often disguise serious epidemics that are initially concentrated in certain localities or among specific population groups and threaten to spill over into the wider population. In many parts of the developing world most new infections occur in young adults, with young women especially vulnerable.

Estimates from recent Demographic and Health Surveys that have collected data on HIV/AIDS differ from those of the Joint United Nations Programme on HIV/AIDS (UNAIDS) and the WHO, which are based on surveillance systems that focus on pregnant women who attend sentinel antenatal clinics. There are reasons to be cautious about comparing the two sets of estimates. Demographic and Health Survey is a household survey that uses a representative sample from the whole population, whereas surveillance data from antenatal clinics is limited to pregnant women. Representative household surveys also frequently provide better coverage of rural populations. However, the fact that some respondents refuse to participate or are absent from the household adds considerable uncertainty to survey-based HIV estimates, because the possible association of absence or refusal with higher HIV prevalence is unknown. UNAIDS and WHO estimates are generally based on surveillance systems that focus on pregnant women who attend sentinel antenatal clinics. UNAIDS and the WHO use a methodology to estimate HIV prevalence for the adult population (ages 15–49) that assumes that prevalence among pregnant women is a good approximation of prevalence among men and women. However, this assumption might not apply to all countries or over time. There are also other potential biases associated with the use of antenatal clinic data, such as differences among women who attend antenatal clinics and those who do not.

Definitions

• **Prevalence of smoking** is the percentage of men and women who smoke cigarettes. The age range varies, but in most countries is 18 and older or 15 and older. • Incidence of tuberculosis is the estimated number of new tuberculosis cases (pulmonary, smear positive, extrapulmonary). • **Incidence of tuberculosis** is the estimated number of new pulmonary, smear positive, and extrapulmonary tuberculosis cases. • **Prevalence of diabetes** refers to the percentage of people ages 20–79 who have type 1 or type 2 diabetes. • **Mortality caused by road traffic injury** refers to the number of deaths per 100,000 people caused by road traffic injury. • **Prevalence of HIV** is the percentage of people who are infected with HIV.

Data sources

Data on smoking are from the American Cancer Society's *Tobacco Atlas*, 2nd edition. Data on tuberculosis are from the WHO's *Global Tuberculosis Control Report 2006*. Data on diabetes are from the International Diabetes Federation's e-Atlas. Data on mortality caused by road traffic injury are from the WHO and the World Bank's *World Report on Road Traffic Injury Prevention* and the Organisation for Economic Co-operation and Development. Data on HIV are from UNAIDS and the WHO's *2004 Report on the Global AIDS Epidemic*.

2.19 Mortality

	Life expectancy at birth		Infant mortality rate		Under-five mortality rate		Child mortality rate		Adult mortality rate		Survival to age 65	
	years		per 1,000 live births		per 1,000		per 1,000		per 1,000		% of cohort	
							Male	Female	Male	Female	Male	Female
	1990	2004	1990	2004	1990	2004	1997–2004[a]	1997–2004[a]	2002–04[a]	2002–04[a]	2003	2003
Afghanistan	45	..	168	..	260	..	..	..	..	..	..	..
Albania	72	74	37	17	45	19	..	..	99	56	77	85
Algeria	67	71	54	35	69	40	..	..	138	121	74	79
Angola	40	41	154	154	260	260	..	..	512	462	34	39
Argentina	72	75	26	16	29	18	..	..	180	92	75	87
Armenia	68	71	52	29	60	32	5	3	209	95	71	84
Australia	77	80	8	5	10	6	..	..	89	50	85	92
Austria	76	79	8	5	10	5	..	..	120	59	83	92
Azerbaijan	71	72	84	75	105	90	..	..	230	107	59	72
Bangladesh	55	63	100	56	149	77	24	29	252	220	59	62
Belarus	71	68	13	9	17	11	..	..	366	131	55	81
Belgium	76	79	8	4	10	5	..	..	125	67	82	91
Benin	53	55	111	90	185	152	72	79	325	292	43	50
Bolivia	59	65	89	54	125	69	25	29	262	199	61	69
Bosnia and Herzegovina	72	74	18	13	22	15	..	..	159	82	75	86
Botswana	64	35	45	84	58	116	..	..	823	793	13	18
Brazil	66	71	50	32	60	34	..	..	268	139	62	79
Bulgaria	72	72	15	12	19	15	..	..	216	91	69	84
Burkina Faso	48	48	113	97	210	192	110	113	427	400	28	32
Burundi	44	44	114	114	190	190	..	..	534	513	25	28
Cambodia	54	57	80	97	115	141	34	30	391	214	42	49
Cameroon	52	46	85	87	139	149	73	72	513	493	35	40
Canada	77	80	7	5	8	6	..	..	97	60	84	92
Central African Republic	48	39	102	115	168	193	..	..	658	649	24	29
Chad	46	44	117	117	203	200	106	99	500	471	39	44
Chile	74	78	17	8	21	8	..	..	136	68	79	89
China	69	71	38	26	49	31	..	..	145	91	73	79
Hong Kong, China	77	82	..	..	..	..	..	..	83	36	85	92
Colombia	68	73	30	18	36	21	4	3	191	108	71	84
Congo, Dem. Rep.	46	44	129	129	205	205	..	..	497	471	32	36
Congo, Rep.	54	52	83	81	110	108	..	..	469	444	36	45
Costa Rica	77	79	16	11	18	13	..	..	121	68	82	90
Côte d'Ivoire	52	46	103	117	157	194	83	58	475	457	31	34
Croatia	72	75	11	6	12	7	..	..	173	70	71	87
Cuba	75	77	11	6	13	7	..	..	132	86	81	88
Czech Republic	71	76	11	4	13	4	..	..	167	74	76	88
Denmark	75	77	8	4	9	5	..	..	121	74	80	88
Dominican Republic	66	68	50	27	65	32	9	9	280	151	63	76
Ecuador	69	75	43	23	57	26	..	..	188	109	70	81
Egypt, Arab Rep.	63	70	76	26	104	36	15	16	181	113	70	76
El Salvador	66	71	47	24	60	28	..	..	227	142	69	81
Eritrea	48	54	88	52	147	82	55	50	482	405	37	43
Estonia	69	72	12	6	16	8	..	..	310	101	60	85
Ethiopia	45	42	131	110	204	166	83	86	453	420	26	31
Finland	75	79	6	3	7	4	..	..	133	61	80	91
France	77	80	7	4	9	5	..	..	137	61	83	92
Gabon	60	54	60	60	92	91	31	33	418	397	46	51
Gambia, The	50	56	103	89	154	122	..	..	335	290	41	47
Georgia	70	71	43	41	47	45	..	..	219	84	72	87
Germany	75	78	7	4	9	5	..	..	119	61	82	91
Ghana	56	57	75	68	122	112	44	52	351	334	48	52
Greece	77	79	10	4	11	5	..	..	115	51	83	91
Guatemala	62	68	60	33	82	45	15	18	304	175	59	72
Guinea	47	54	145	101	240	155	101	98	316	285	32	33
Guinea-Bissau	42	45	153	126	253	203	..	..	464	411	34	39
Haiti	49	52	102	74	150	117	52	54	477	460	38	48

Mortality 2.19

	Life expectancy at birth		Infant mortality rate		Under-five mortality rate		Child mortality rate		Adult mortality rate		Survival to age 65	
	years		per 1,000 live births		per 1,000		per 1,000		per 1,000		% of cohort	
							Male	Female	Male	Female	Male	Female
	1990	2004	1990	2004	1990	2004	1997–2004[a]	1997–2004[a]	2002–04[a]	2002–04[a]	2003	2003
Honduras	65	68	44	31	59	41	..	..	259	214	59	73
Hungary	69	73	15	7	17	8	..	..	253	108	67	85
India	59	63	80	62	123	85	25	37	241	161	62	65
Indonesia	62	67	60	30	91	38	13	11	221	167	64	72
Iran, Islamic Rep.	65	71	54	32	72	38	..	..	166	114	72	76
Iraq	62	..	40	..	50	..	..	..	..	..	..	..
Ireland	75	78	8	5	9	6	..	..	100	59	80	89
Israel	76	79	10	5	12	6	..	..	91	49	84	90
Italy	77	80	8	4	9	5	..	..	96	49	82	91
Jamaica	71	71	17	17	20	20	..	..	241	194	81	87
Japan	79	82	5	3	6	4	..	..	95	45	86	94
Jordan	68	72	33	23	40	27	5	5	175	134	75	81
Kazakhstan	68	65	53	63	63	73	11	6	351	158	48	71
Kenya	58	48	64	79	97	120	42	39	522	587	28	32
Korea, Dem. Rep.	65	64	42	42	55	55	..	..	320	219	55	63
Korea, Rep.	71	77	8	5	9	6	..	..	152	59	73	87
Kuwait	75	77	14	10	16	12	..	..	91	60	82	88
Kyrgyz Republic	68	68	68	58	80	68	10	11	273	129	57	76
Lao PDR	50	55	120	65	163	83	..	..	330	280	45	51
Latvia	69	71	14	10	18	12	..	..	300	116	61	85
Lebanon	69	72	32	27	37	31	..	..	160	107	71	79
Lesotho	57	36	74	80	104	112	..	..	837	758	15	19
Liberia	43	42	157	157	235	235	..	..	528	477	33	37
Libya	68	74	35	18	41	20	..	..	146	100	73	83
Lithuania	71	72	10	8	13	8	..	..	303	106	67	87
Macedonia, FYR	72	74	33	13	38	14	..	..	145	84	75	85
Madagascar	51	56	103	76	168	123	45	45	335	286	49	55
Malawi	46	40	146	110	241	175	101	102	651	652	19	23
Malaysia	70	73	16	10	22	12	..	..	164	94	72	83
Mali	46	48	140	121	250	219	132	125	366	329	25	29
Mauritania	49	53	85	78	133	125	38	38	353	295	43	49
Mauritius	69	73	20	14	23	15	..	..	218	115	71	85
Mexico	71	75	37	23	46	28	..	..	164	91	75	86
Moldova	68	68	30	23	40	28	..	..	302	154	59	76
Mongolia	62	65	78	41	108	52	..	..	252	178	66	72
Morocco	64	70	69	38	89	43	9	11	170	117	68	76
Mozambique	43	42	158	104	235	152	61	64	591	558	25	30
Myanmar	56	61	91	76	130	106	..	..	305	208	47	58
Namibia	62	47	60	47	86	63	22	20	600	560	21	25
Nepal	55	62	100	59	145	76	28	40	261	237	58	57
Netherlands	77	79	7	5	9	6	..	..	94	66	84	90
New Zealand	75	79	8	5	11	7	..	..	99	65	83	90
Nicaragua	64	70	52	31	68	38	10	9	230	155	67	77
Niger	40	45	191	152	320	259	184	202	368	337	30	37
Nigeria	46	44	120	101	230	197	120	123	504	494	32	36
Norway	77	80	7	4	9	4	..	..	99	59	84	91
Oman	70	75	25	10	32	13	..	..	121	91	79	85
Pakistan	59	65	100	80	130	101	..	..	191	162	65	71
Panama	72	75	27	19	34	24	..	..	156	87	79	86
Papua New Guinea	52	56	74	68	101	93	..	..	406	367	49	53
Paraguay	68	71	33	21	41	24	..	..	165	111	70	80
Peru	66	70	60	24	80	29	19	17	193	127	69	79
Philippines	66	71	41	26	62	34	14	9	179	126	70	78
Poland	71	74	19	7	18	8	..	..	201	78	72	87
Portugal	74	77	11	4	14	5	..	..	130	60	78	89
Puerto Rico	75	77	..	..	..	..	..	..	198	73	77	91

2.19 Mortality

	Life expectancy at birth		Infant mortality rate		Under-five mortality rate		Child mortality rate		Adult mortality rate		Survival to age 65	
	years		per 1,000 live births		per 1,000		per 1,000		per 1,000		% of cohort	
							Male	Female	Male	Female	Male	Female
	1990	2004	1990	2004	1990	2004	1997–2004[a]	1997–2004[a]	2002–04[a]	2002–04[a]	2003	2003
Romania	70	71	27	17	31	20	..	..	234	101	65	81
Russian Federation	69	65	23	17	29	21	..	..	450	166	49	77
Rwanda	31	44	103	118	173	203	105	97	522	462	23	25
Saudi Arabia	68	72	35	21	44	27	..	..	157	110	76	83
Senegal	53	56	90	78	148	137	76	74	319	271	38	47
Serbia and Montenegro	72	73	24	13	28	15	..	..	172	94	73	83
Sierra Leone	39	41	175	165	302	283	..	..	442	387	25	29
Singapore	74	79	7	3	8	3	..	..	90	53	83	90
Slovak Republic	71	74	12	6	14	9	..	..	209	79	70	86
Slovenia	73	77	8	4	10	4	..	..	151	66	77	89
Somalia	42	47	133	133	225	225	..	..	409	357	38	45
South Africa	62	45	45	54	60	67	18	13	615	542	26	33
Spain	77	80	8	3	9	5	..	..	117	49	83	93
Sri Lanka	71	74	26	12	32	14	..	..	139	82	77	85
Sudan	53	57	74	63	120	91	..	..	335	288	53	58
Swaziland	57	42	78	108	110	156	..	..	862	837	25	29
Sweden	78	80	6	3	7	4	..	..	82	52	86	92
Switzerland	77	81	7	5	9	5	..	..	87	47	85	93
Syrian Arab Republic	68	74	35	15	44	16	..	..	138	97	69	79
Tajikistan	63	64	92	75	119	93	..	..	223	149	62	75
Tanzania	53	46	102	78	161	126	61	58	517	516	27	30
Thailand	68	71	31	18	37	21	..	..	258	129	67	78
Togo	57	55	88	78	152	140	73	65	388	316	38	43
Trinidad and Tobago	71	70	28	18	33	20	..	..	268	175	74	82
Tunisia	70	73	41	21	52	25	..	..	141	82	76	83
Turkey	66	70	67	28	82	32	10	13	193	121	69	79
Turkmenistan	63	63	80	80	97	103	19	17	311	161	57	73
Uganda	46	49	93	80	160	138	78	70	527	528	25	28
Ukraine	70	68	19	14	26	18	..	..	421	161	57	81
United Arab Emirates	73	79	12	7	14	8	..	..	83	55	80	86
United Kingdom	76	79	8	5	10	6	..	..	101	63	82	90
United States	75	77	9	7	11	8	..	..	144	84	81	90
Uruguay	73	75	20	15	25	17	..	..	169	87	74	88
Uzbekistan	69	67	65	57	79	69	..	..	252	149	63	77
Venezuela, RB	71	74	24	16	27	19	..	..	192	98	75	86
Vietnam	65	70	38	17	53	23	10	7	182	130	68	78
West Bank and Gaza	69	73	..	..	..	..	..	..	146	109	74	84
Yemen, Rep.	55	61	98	82	142	111	33	36	282	237	50	53
Zambia	46	38	101	102	180	182	89	74	690	728	16	21
Zimbabwe	59	37	53	79	80	129	35	31	780	796	18	20
World	**65 w**	**67 w**	**64 w**	**54 w**	**95 w**	**79 w**			**222 w**	**153 w**	**66 w**	**73 w**
Low income	56	59	94	79	147	122			300	246	54	58
Middle income	68	70	43	30	57	37			202	121	68	78
Lower middle income	67	70	45	32	61	40			182	114	70	78
Upper middle income	69	69	34	23	42	28			289	152	63	78
Low & middle income	63	65	69	59	103	86			241	171	62	70
East Asia & Pacific	67	70	43	29	59	37			169	111	70	77
Europe & Central Asia	69	69	40	28	49	34			316	134	60	80
Latin America & Carib.	68	72	43	27	54	31			219	124	69	82
Middle East & N. Africa	64	69	60	44	81	55			179	128	69	75
South Asia	59	63	86	66	129	92			237	169	61	65
Sub-Saharan Africa	49	46	111	100	185	168			489	467	32	36
High income	76	79	9	6	11	7			122	65	82	91
Europe EMU	76	79	8	4	9	5			117	57	82	91

a. Data are for the most recent year available.

About the data

Mortality rates for different age groups (infants, children, and adults) and overall indicators of mortality (life expectancy at birth or survival to a given age) are important indicators of health status in a country. Because data on the incidence and prevalence of diseases (morbidity data) are frequently unavailable, mortality rates are often used to identify vulnerable populations. And they are among the indicators most frequently used to compare levels of socioeconomic development across countries.

The main sources of mortality data are vital registration systems and direct or indirect estimates based on sample surveys or censuses. A "complete" vital registration system—one covering at least 90 percent of vital events in the population—is the best source of age-specific mortality data. But such systems are fairly uncommon in developing countries. Thus estimates must be obtained from sample surveys or derived by applying indirect estimation techniques to registration, census, or survey data. Survey data are subject to recall error, and surveys estimating infant deaths require large samples because households in which a birth or an infant death has occurred during a given year cannot ordinarily be preselected for sampling. Indirect estimates rely on estimated actuarial "life" tables that may be inappropriate for the population concerned. Because life expectancy at birth is constructed using infant mortality data and model life tables, similar reliability issues arise for this indicator.

Life expectancy at birth and age-specific mortality rates are generally estimates based on vital registration or the most recent census or survey available (see *Primary data documentation*). Extrapolations based on outdated surveys may not be reliable for monitoring changes in health status or for comparative analytical work.

To produce harmonized estimates of infant and under-five mortality rates that make use of all available information in a transparent way, the United Nations Children's Fund (UNICEF) and the World Bank developed and adopted a methodology that fits a regression line to the relationship between mortality rates and their reference dates using weighted least squares. (For further discussion of methodology for childhood mortality estimates, see Hill and others 1999.)

Infant and child mortality rates are higher for boys than for girls in countries in which parental gender preferences are insignificant. Child mortality captures the effect of gender discrimination better than does infant mortality, as malnutrition and medical interventions are more important in this age group. Where female child mortality is higher, as in some countries in South Asia, girls probably have unequal access to resources.

Adult mortality rates have increased in many countries in Sub-Saharan Africa and Europe and Central Asia. In Sub-Saharan Africa the increase stems from AIDS-related mortality and affects both men and women. In Europe and Central Asia the causes are more diverse and affect men more. They include a high prevalence of smoking, a high-fat diet, excessive alcohol use, and stressful conditions related to the economic transition.

The percentage of a cohort surviving to age 65 reflects both child and adult mortality rates. Like life expectancy, it is a synthetic measure based on current age-specific mortality rates and used in the construction of life tables. It shows that even in countries where mortality is high, a certain share of the current birth cohort will live well beyond the life expectancy at birth, while in low-mortality countries close to 90 percent will reach at least age 65.

Definitions

• **Life expectancy at birth** is the number of years a newborn infant would live if prevailing patterns of mortality at the time of its birth were to stay the same throughout its life. • **Infant mortality rate** is the number of infants dying before reaching one year of age, per 1,000 live births in a given year. • **Under-five mortality rate** is the probability that a newborn baby will die before reaching age five, if subject to current age-specific mortality rates. The probability is expressed as a rate per 1,000. • **Child mortality rate** is the probability of dying between the ages of one and five, if subject to current age-specific mortality rates. The probability is expressed as a rate per 1,000. • **Adult mortality rate** is the probability of dying between the ages of 15 and 60—that is, the probability of a 15-year-old dying before reaching age 60—if subject to current age-specific mortality rates between those ages. • **Survival to age 65** refers to the percentage of a cohort of newborn infants that would survive to age 65, if subject to current age-specific mortality rates.

Data sources

Data on infant and under-five mortality are the harmonized estimates of the World Health Organization, UNICEF, and the World Bank, based mainly on household surveys, censuses, and vital registration, supplemented by the World Bank's estimates based on household surveys and vital registration. Other estimates are compiled and produced by the World Bank's Human Development Network and Development Data Group in consultation with its operational staff and country offices. Important inputs to the World Bank's demographic work come from the United Nations Population Division's *World Population Prospects: The 2004 Revision*, census reports and other statistical publications from national statistical offices, and Demographic and Health Surveys by Macro International.

3 ENVIRONMENT

Development and economic growth have improved the quality of life for many people, but the gains have been uneven and economic growth has often had negative environmental consequences, with profound impact on poor people. Using the environment wisely is crucial for reducing poverty. Many poor people depend on the environment for their livelihoods. Because poor people control far fewer natural and produced resources, environmental degradation affects them disproportionately. The indicators in this section measure environmental resources and the goods and services produced from them—helping to establish the link between growth and environmental change and pointing the way toward sustainable development.

Environmental changes and their impact

Income derived from the environment is a major source of livelihood for many people, particularly for the rural population—a majority of the people who live on less than $1 a day. Despite rapid urbanization in most regions, almost half the world's population still lives in rural areas. In South Asia more than 70 percent of people live in rural areas, and in Sub-Saharan Africa more than 60 percent do. An estimated 75 percent of poor people live in rural areas. The sustainability and proper management of natural resources are crucial for maintaining rural livelihoods and safety nets in difficult times. Without proper management of natural resources and environmentally sustainable development, it would be difficult to reverse environmental losses—one of the main Millennium Development Goals.

At the same time, the environment is a source of vulnerability. Increasing use of fossil energy—mainly by industrial economies—and the resulting climate change add to poor people's vulnerability. The adverse impact of environmental change will be most striking in developing countries—and particularly among the poor—because of their high dependence on natural resources, their limited capacity to adapt to a changing climate, and their limited resources to remedy the impact of such changes or to implement mitigating policies.

Low-income families and regions are more vulnerable not only to human-induced environmental hazards but also to natural disasters and environmental risks such as the impact of global climate changes. Water scarcity is already a major problem for the world's poor, and changes in rainfall and temperature associated with climate change will likely make this scarcity worse. Crop yields are expected to decline in most tropical and subtropical regions as rainfall and temperature patterns change with a changing climate (IPCC 2001b, p. 84). The Food and Agriculture Organization estimates that land suitable for rainfed agriculture may shrink by 11 percent in developing countries by 2080 due to climate change (FAO 2005, p. 2). There is also some evidence that disease vectors such as malaria-bearing mosquitoes will spread more widely (IPCC 2001a, p. 455). Global warming may bring an increase in severe weather events like cyclones and torrential rains. The inadequate construction and exposed locations of poor people's dwellings often make poor people the most likely victims of such disasters. Hence mitigating the consequences of environmental changes that affect their livelihoods must be an integral part of poverty reduction efforts.

The following discussion highlights selected issues related to the indicators in the tables in this section, issues with profound impact on the livelihoods of the populace, particularly poor people:

- Agriculture and land use.
- Water quality and availability.
- Shrinking forests.
- Mix of energy use.

Natural resources—a major source of livelihoods

In many developing countries agriculture is still a major source of employment and income. While globally 44 percent of the active workforce is engaged in agriculture, the importance of this sector as a source of employment varies by region and income. About 60 percent of the active workforce is employed in agriculture, fisheries, and livestock in the Sub-Saharan Africa and Asia and Pacific regions, but only 19 percent in Latin America, where the urban population share is as high as in high-income Europe. In high-income countries only 7 percent of the workforce is engaged in these activities.

These variations are even more profound across countries: 2 percent in the United Kingdom and United States, 59 percent in India, 67 percent in China, and 93 percent in Nepal.

Population growth in developing countries will put further pressure on agriculture as rising demand for food requires more land and more forests to be turned to agricultural use. Greater numbers of poor people will be forced to live and work on marginal and fragile lands. In 2002 almost 1.4 billion people were living on fragile lands—more than three-fourths in Africa and Asia (figure 3a). This has an important impact on food production and food security in these regions—particularly in Sub-Saharan Africa, where food production barely keeps up with population growth.

3a

More than three-fourths of the 1.4 billion people living on fragile lands are in Asia and Africa

Rural population living on fragile lands as a share of world total

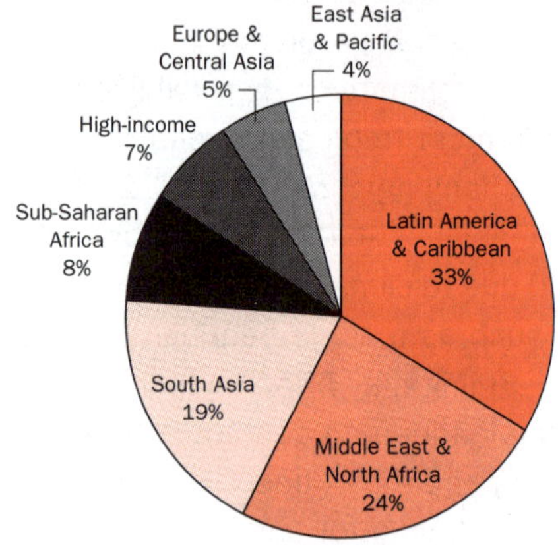

Source: World Bank 2003.

Climate change makes the situation even worse, and the region appears to be the most vulnerable to the consequences of global warming. In the past 30 years Africa has experienced at least one major drought each decade. Changes in rainfall—there are already indications of significant changes in the last decades—could also have serious consequences for parts of Africa that depend on hydroelectricity.

Climate variability and associated floods and droughts increase the risk of crop failure, reducing food security and increasing the incidence of malnutrition and disease. In Ethiopia, for example, the 1984 drought affected 8.7 million people: 1 million people died and millions more suffered from malnutrition and famine (UNEP 2002, p. 218). Nearly 1.5 million livestock also died (FAO 2000). The 1991–92 drought in southern Africa reduced the cereal harvest by more than half and exposed more than 17 million people to the risk of starvation. More than 100,000 people died in the Sahelian drought of the 1970s and 1980s (UNEP 2002, p. 219). Crop failure and livestock losses increase the dependence on imports and foreign aid, reducing economic performance and the ability to cope with future environmental disasters.

Water is life, but water is getting dirtier and scarcer

Water scarcity is a major reason for the low levels of food production in most parts of Africa. Average per capita renewable water resources in Africa are below the world average, and the distribution of surface water and ground water is uneven (figure 3b). By 2020 an estimated two-thirds of the world's

3b

Water withdrawal is skewed toward agriculture in every developing region

Annual water withdrawal per capita, 2002 (cubic meters)

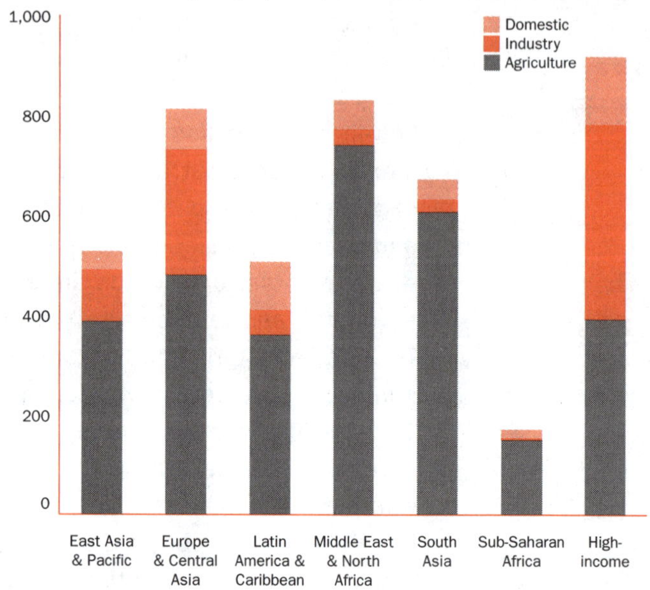

Source: Tables 2.1 and 3.5.

people will be living in water-stressed countries (CSD 1997 as cited in UNEP 2002, p. 150). By then, water use is expected to have increased 40 percent, and 17 percent more water will be required for food production to meet the needs of growing populations (World Water Council 2000; UNEP 2002, p. 151).

Population growth, expansion of irrigated agriculture, and industrial development are all behind the growing demand for water. Globally, agriculture accounts for 70 percent of freshwater withdrawal. Most is used for irrigation, which provides about 40 percent of world food production (CSD 1997 as cited in UNEP 2002). In Africa agriculture uses more than 85 percent of total water withdrawal, and population growth and demand for food are continuing to put more pressure on water availability. Without efficient and comprehensive water resources management that considers all aspects of water use, the projected water scarcity will have an even more profound impact.

Water quality can often be as severe a problem as water availability, but it receives less attention, particularly in developing regions. For many of the world's poorest populations, one of the greatest environmental threats to health remains the use of untreated water. While the share of people with access to an improved water source increased from 75 percent in 1990 to 82 percent in 2002, 1.1 billion people still lack access to safe drinking water (figure 3c) and 2.8 billion lack access to improved sanitation (table 3.10). Most of them are in Africa and Asia. Lack of access to safe water and sanitation results in hundreds of millions of cases of water-related diseases and more than 5 million deaths every year (UNEP 2002, p. 153).

3c

Many more people lack access to an improved water source in rural than in urban areas

Population without access to improved water, 2002 (millions)

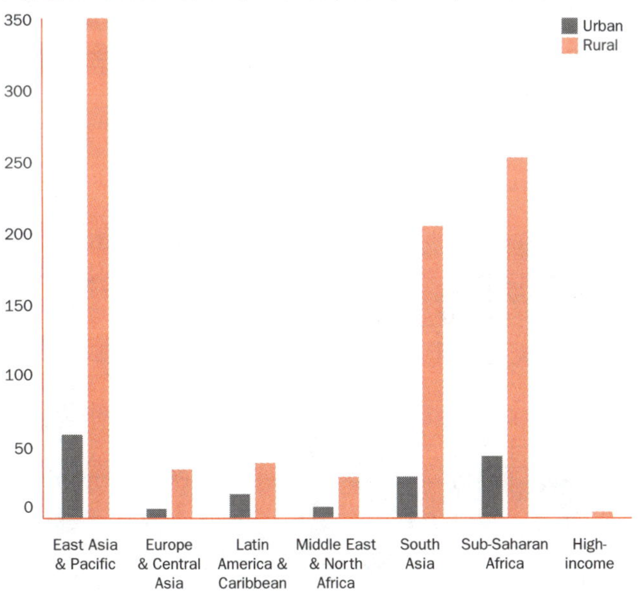

Source: WHO and World Bank database.

Forests are still shrinking—but the rate of net loss is slowing

In developing regions population growth, increasing demand for food, particularly meat and dairy products, and declining growth in agricultural productivity are maintaining the pressure for deforestation. Total forest area in 2005 was just under 4 billion hectares, covering 30 percent of total land area, for an average of 0.62 hectare per capita. But forest area is unevenly distributed. For example, 64 countries with a combined population of 2 billion have less than 0.1 hectare of forest per capita. The 10 most forest-rich countries account for two-thirds of total forest area, while 7 countries or territories have no forest at all, and an additional 57 have forest on less than 10 percent of their land area.

Deforestation, mainly for conversion to agricultural land, continues—about 13 million hectares a year. At the same time, forest planting, landscape restoration, and natural expansion of forests have reduced the net loss of forest area. The net change in forest area during 2000–05 is estimated at a loss of 7.3 million hectares a year (an area about the size of Panama or Sierra Leone), an improvement from 8.9 million hectares a year during 1990–2000. Africa and Latin America continued to have the largest net loss of forests, while forest area in Europe continued to expand, although at a slower rate. Asia, which had a net loss in the 1990s, reported a net gain of forests in 2000–05, due primarily to large-scale reforestation reported by China.

Forests contribute directly and indirectly to the livelihoods of many people. Recognizing that, countries in most regions understand the need for more efficient forest management (box 3d). This effort has been very slow in developing regions, however, particularly in Asia and Sub-Saharan Africa.

Energy—the mix affects the impact

Economic growth and energy use move together. Energy, especially electricity, is important in raising people's standard of living. High-income countries use more than five times as much energy per capita as developing countries do, and with only 15 percent of the world's population they use more than half of its energy. Despite high and increasing energy costs, and the Kyoto Protocol, which calls for reduction in carbon dioxide emissions, fossil fuels are still the main source of energy—and their use has been rising faster than that of any other source of energy (figure 3e).

How energy is generated largely determines the resulting environmental damages. Generating energy from fossil fuels produces emissions of carbon dioxide, the main greenhouse gas contributing to global warming and climate change. Human-induced carbon dioxide emissions result primarily from fossil fuel combustion and cement manufacturing, with high-income countries contributing half (figure 3f). Burning coal releases twice as much carbon dioxide as burning an equivalent amount of natural gas. Sub-Saharan Africa uses coal as its main source of electricity generation (more than two-thirds). So do East Asia and the Pacific and South Asia. Even though the low-income countries contribute less than 8 percent of global carbon dioxide emissions, they are affected by the consequences of climate change. Furthermore, there are local impacts from the type of energy use as well.

Most low-income countries depend on biomass energy for cooking and heating, a health hazard to billions of people. More than 3 million deaths a year are caused by air pollution, mostly due to particulate pollution. Many of these deaths are among children in developing countries, who die of acute respiratory infections due to indoor air pollution resulting from burning fuelwood, crop residues, or animal dung for cooking and heating. Sub-Saharan Africa has the highest death rate from respiratory disease followed by North Africa and Asia (figure 3g).

In South Africa children living in homes with wood stoves are almost five times more likely than others to develop respiratory infections severe enough to require hospitalization. In

3d

Sustainable management of forests is spreading

Regulatory pressure, social activism, and consumer preferences have encouraged producers and marketers to provide a range of sustainably produced forest products, including timber, coffee, and fruit. Some products are certified as having been produced in an environmentally and socially responsible manner. About 2 percent of forests worldwide are now certified as managed for sustainable yield and for providing wildlife habitat, watershed protection, biodiversity, and other ecological services. While the market share for certified products is small, it is growing rapidly, although developed country regions are far ahead of developing regions in product certification (see figure).

Developing regions lag far behind developed regions in certifying forest area

Certified forest area, 2000 (millions of hectares)

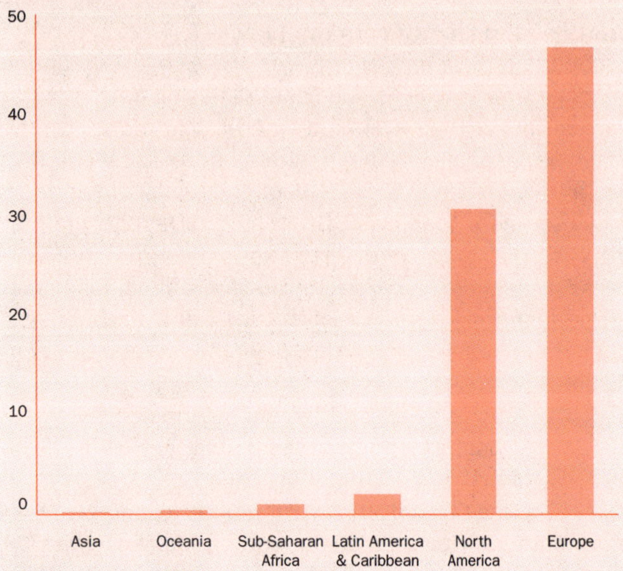

Source: FAO 2001.

3e

Use of fossil fuels continues to rise faster than that of other sources of energy

Energy use, 1990, 2003, and 2030 (billions of metric tons of oil equivalent)

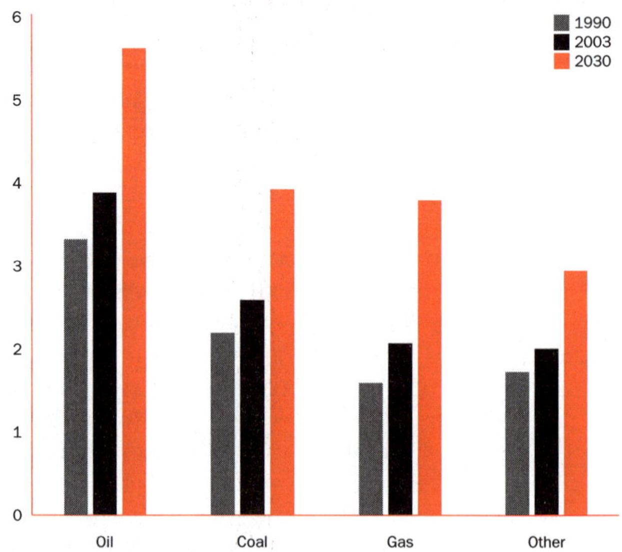

Source: International Energy Agency.

3f

High-income countries are the leading source of carbon dioxide emissions

Carbon dioxide emissions per capita, 1990 and 2002 (metric tons)

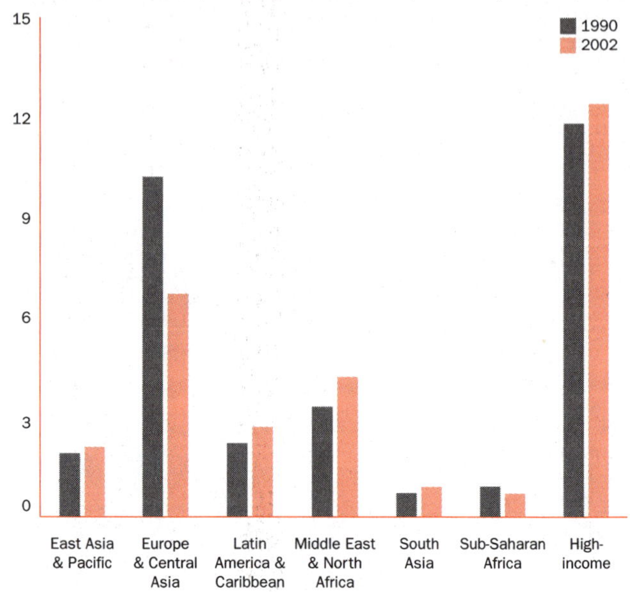

Source: Table 3.8.

Tanzania children under age 5 who die of acute respiratory infection are three times more likely to have been sleeping in a room with an open cookstove than are healthy children. In The Gambia children carried on their mothers' backs as they cook over smoky stoves contract pneumonia at a rate 2.5 times higher than unexposed children (WRI 2005). Efforts to reduce indoor air pollution focus on improved cookstoves (box 3h).

The use of cleaner energy sources is another path toward sustainable energy use. Use of renewable energy is growing, but it is still a very small share of the total (figure 3i). About 4.5 percent of global energy production comes from modern renewable energy sources, up from 3.2 percent in 1971. Hydropower is the largest renewable energy source, but large-scale hydropower can have major adverse environmental and social impacts. Modern biomass and geothermal energy are the other major renewable sources and have substantial growth potential. Wind and solar energy, while growing rapidly, provide only about 0.02 percent each of the global energy supply.

3g

Sub-Sarahan Africa has the highest death rate from respiratory disease

Deaths per 100,000 people, 2002

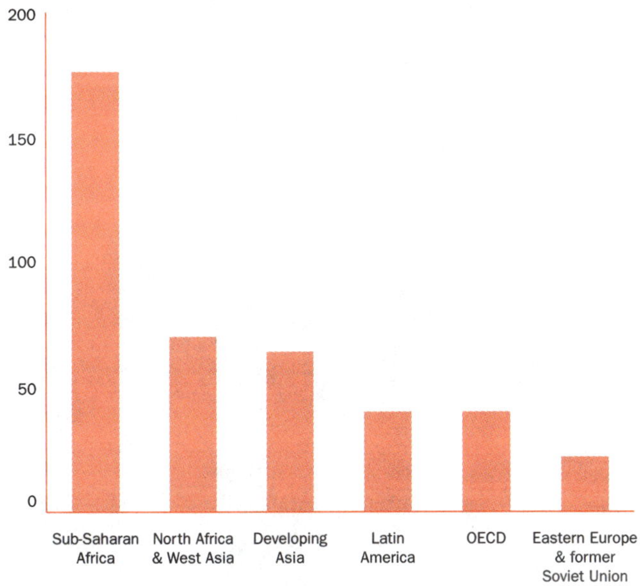

Source: World Health Organization.

3h

More efficient use of traditional biomass is improving the lives of women

For most poor households in rural Africa and Asia improved biomass cookstoves are the most feasible option for reducing death and disease from traditional biomass cooking. They also conserve biomass resources and reduce the time and energy needed for collecting fuel and cooking, thus freeing women's time for other productive activities. The Upesi stove developed in Kenya, for example, with a clay liner in a mud and stone hearth, uses 40 percent less fuel than the traditional three-stone stove and emits 60 percent less smoke. For higher income rural households, expanding the distribution networks for canisters of liquefied petroleum gas can improve the welfare of women and children.

Source: United Nations 2002.

3i

Use of renewable sources of energy is growing, but is still small

Sources of energy, 2003 (%)

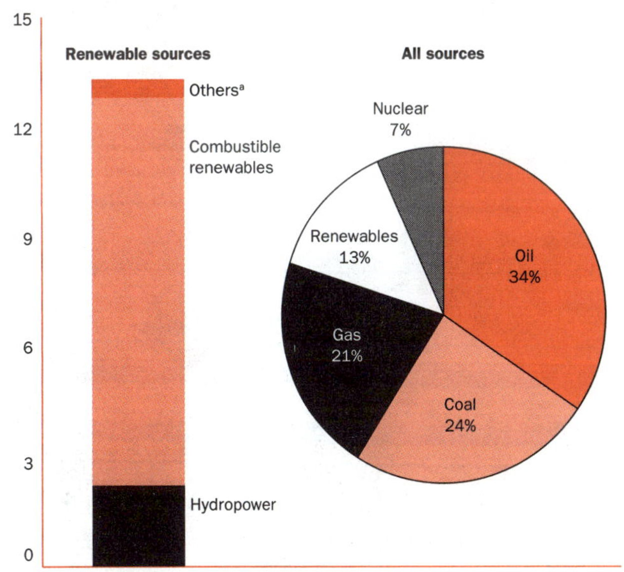

a. Includes wind, solar, and geothermal sources.

Source: International Energy Agency.

Rural population and land use

	Rural population			Land area	Land use							
	% of total		average annual % growth	thousand sq. km	% of land area						Arable land hectares per capita	
					Forest area		Permanent cropland		Arable land			
	1990	2004	1990–2004	2004	1990	2005	1990	2003	1990	2003	1989–91	2001–03
Afghanistan	82	..	..	652	2.0	1.3	0.2	0.2	12.1	12.1	0.54	0.31
Albania	64	56	–1.4	27	28.8	29.0	4.6	4.4	21.1	21.1	0.18	0.19
Algeria	49	41	0.5	2,382	0.8	1.0	0.2	0.3	3.0	3.2	0.28	0.24
Angola	74	64	1.7	1,247	48.9	47.4	0.4	0.2	2.3	2.7	0.28	0.21
Argentina	13	10	–1.0	2,737	12.9	12.1	0.4	0.4	9.7	10.2	0.81	0.74
Armenia	33	36	–0.6	28	12.3	10.0	2.7	2.1	17.7	17.7	..	0.16
Australia	15	8	–3.5	7,682	21.9	21.3	0.0	0.0	6.2	6.2	2.76	2.49
Austria	34	34	0.4	82	45.8	46.8	1.0	0.9	17.3	16.9	0.19	0.17
Azerbaijan	46	50	1.6	83	11.3	11.3	3.5	2.7	18.1	21.6	..	0.22
Bangladesh	80	75	1.6	130	6.8	6.7	2.3	3.4	70.2	61.3	0.09	0.06
Belarus	34	29	–1.5	207	35.6	38.1	0.9	0.6	29.3	26.8	..	0.57
Belgium	4	3	–1.6	33	20.6	20.3	0.5[a]	0.6	23.3[a]	26.6	..	..
Benin	66	55	2.0	111	30.0	21.3	1.0	2.4	14.6	24.0	0.31	0.33
Bolivia	44	36	0.7	1,084	57.9	54.2	0.1	0.2	1.9	2.8	0.31	0.35
Bosnia and Herzegovina	61	55	–1.4	51	..	42.7	*2.9*	1.9	*16.6*	19.6	..	0.26
Botswana	58	48	0.2	567	24.2	21.1	0.0	0.0	0.7	0.7	0.29	0.21
Brazil	25	16	–1.6	8,459	61.5	56.5	0.8	0.9	6.0	7.0	0.34	0.33
Bulgaria	34	30	–1.7	111	30.1	32.8	2.7	1.9	34.9	30.0	0.44	0.43
Burkina Faso	86	82	2.5	274	26.2	24.8	0.2	0.2	12.9	17.7	0.41	0.39
Burundi	94	90	1.5	26	11.3	5.9	14.0	14.2	36.2	38.6	0.16	0.14
Cambodia	87	81	1.9	177	73.3	59.2	0.6	0.6	20.9	21.0	0.38	0.28
Cameroon	60	48	0.7	465	52.7	45.7	2.6	2.6	12.8	12.8	0.51	0.39
Canada	23	19	–0.4	9,094	34.1	34.1	0.7	0.7	5.0	5.0	1.64	1.46
Central African Republic	63	57	1.3	623	37.3	36.5	0.1	0.2	3.1	3.1	0.64	0.50
Chad	79	75	2.8	1,259	10.4	9.5	0.0	0.0	2.6	2.9	0.54	0.41
Chile	17	13	–0.5	749	20.4	21.5	0.3	0.4	3.7	2.7	0.22	0.13
China[b]	73	60	–0.4	9,327	16.9	21.2	0.8	1.3	13.3	15.3	0.11	0.11
Hong Kong, China	0	0	..	..	..	..	..	..	..	..	..	..
Colombia	31	23	–0.4	1,039	59.2	58.5	1.6	1.5	3.2	2.2	0.09	0.05
Congo, Dem. Rep.	72	68	2.4	2,267	62.0	58.9	0.5	0.5	2.9	3.0	0.18	0.13
Congo, Rep.	52	46	2.4	342	66.6	65.8	0.1	0.2	1.4	1.5	0.20	0.13
Costa Rica	46	39	1.1	51	50.2	46.8	4.9	5.9	5.1	4.4	0.08	0.05
Côte d'Ivoire	60	55	1.8	318	32.1	32.7	11.0	11.3	7.6	10.4	0.19	0.19
Croatia	46	41	–1.4	56	..	38.2	*2.0*	2.2	*21.7*	26.1	..	0.33
Cuba	26	24	–0.2	110	18.7	24.7	7.4	6.6	27.6	27.9	0.29	0.28
Czech Republic	25	26	0.1	77	..	34.3	..	3.1	..	39.6	..	0.30
Denmark	15	15	0.1	42	10.5	11.8	0.2	0.2	60.4	53.4	0.50	0.42
Dominican Republic	45	40	0.8	48	28.4	28.4	9.3	10.3	21.7	22.7	0.15	0.13
Ecuador	45	38	0.5	277	49.9	39.2	4.8	4.9	5.8	5.9	0.16	0.13
Egypt, Arab Rep.	57	58	2.1	995	0.0	0.1	0.4	0.5	2.3	2.9	0.04	0.04
El Salvador	51	40	0.3	21	18.1	14.4	12.6	12.1	26.5	31.9	0.11	0.10
Eritrea	84	80	2.0	101	..	15.4	..	0.0	..	5.6	..	0.15
Estonia	29	30	–0.7	42	51.0	53.9	0.3	0.4	26.3	12.9	..	0.45
Ethiopia	87	84	2.0	1,000	..	13.0	..	0.7	..	11.1	..	0.16
Finland	39	39	0.4	305	72.9	73.9	0.0	0.0	7.5	7.3	0.46	0.42
France	26	24	–0.3	550	26.4	28.3	2.2	2.0	32.7	33.5	0.32	0.31
Gabon	32	16	–2.6	258	85.1	84.5	0.6	0.7	1.1	1.3	0.31	0.25
Gambia, The	75	74	3.1	10	44.2	47.1	0.5	0.5	18.2	31.5	0.20	0.23
Georgia	45	48	–0.8	69	39.7	39.7	4.8	3.8	11.4	11.5	..	0.17
Germany	15	12	–1.4	349	30.8	31.7	1.3	0.6	34.3	33.9	0.15	0.14
Ghana	64	54	1.3	228	32.7	24.3	6.6	9.7	11.9	18.4	0.17	0.20
Greece	41	39	0.2	129	25.6	29.1	8.3	8.8	22.5	20.9	0.28	0.25
Guatemala	59	53	1.6	108	43.8	36.3	4.5	5.6	12.0	13.3	0.15	0.12
Guinea	75	64	1.7	246	30.2	27.4	2.0	2.7	3.0	4.5	0.12	0.12
Guinea-Bissau	76	65	1.9	28	78.8	73.7	4.2	8.9	10.7	10.7	0.30	0.21
Haiti	71	62	0.5	28	4.2	3.8	11.6	11.6	28.3	28.3	0.11	0.10

Rural population and land use

	Rural population			Land area	Land use							
					% of land area						Arable land	
	% of total		average annual % growth	thousand sq. km	Forest area		Permanent cropland		Arable land		hectares per capita	
	1990	2004	1990–2004	2004	1990	2005	1990	2003	1990	2003	1989–91	2001–03
Honduras	60	54	1.9	112	66.0	41.5	3.2	3.2	13.1	9.6	0.30	0.16
Hungary	38	34	–0.9	92	19.5	21.5	2.5	2.1	54.7	50.1	0.49	0.45
India	74	71	1.4	2,973	21.5	22.8	2.2	3.1	54.8	54.0	0.19	0.15
Indonesia	69	53	–0.5	1,812	64.4	48.9	6.5	7.4	11.2	11.6	0.11	0.10
Iran, Islamic Rep.	44	33	–0.6	1,636	6.8	6.8	0.8	1.3	9.3	9.9	0.29	0.23
Iraq	30	..	..	437	1.8	1.9	0.7	0.6	12.1	13.2	0.29	0.22
Ireland	43	40	0.5	69	6.4	9.7	0.0	0.0	15.1	17.2	0.30	0.29
Israel	10	8	1.6	22	7.1	7.9	4.1	4.0	15.8	15.8	0.07	0.05
Italy	33	33	–0.1	294	28.5	33.9	10.1	9.3	30.6	27.1	0.16	0.14
Jamaica	49	48	0.6	11	31.9	31.3	9.2	10.2	11.0	16.1	0.05	0.07
Japan	37	34	–0.3	365	68.4	68.2	1.3	0.9	13.1	12.1	0.04	0.03
Jordan	28	21	1.8	88	0.9	0.9	1.0	1.2	3.3	3.3	0.09	0.05
Kazakhstan	43	44	–0.4	2,700	1.3	1.2	0.1	0.1	13.0	8.4	..	1.51
Kenya	75	60	0.9	569	6.5	6.2	0.9	1.0	7.4	8.2	0.18	0.14
Korea, Dem. Rep.	42	39	0.4	120	68.1	51.4	1.5	1.7	19.0	22.4	0.12	0.12
Korea, Rep.	26	19	–1.3	99	64.5	63.5	1.6	2.0	19.8	16.7	0.05	0.03
Kuwait	5	4	–1.3	18	0.2	0.3	0.1	0.2	0.2	0.8	0.00	0.01
Kyrgyz Republic	62	66	1.4	192	4.4	4.5	0.3	0.3	7.0	6.8	..	0.26
Lao PDR	85	79	1.9	231	75.0	69.9	0.3	0.4	3.5	4.1	0.19	0.17
Latvia	30	34	–0.1	62	44.7	47.4	0.4	0.5	27.2	29.4	..	0.78
Lebanon	17	12	–0.4	10	11.8	13.3	11.9	14.0	17.9	16.6	0.07	0.05
Lesotho	83	82	0.8	30	0.2	0.3	0.1	0.1	10.4	10.9	0.20	0.18
Liberia	58	53	2.3	96	42.1	32.8	2.2	2.3	4.2	4.0	0.19	0.12
Libya	20	13	–0.8	1,760	0.1	0.1	0.2	0.2	1.0	1.0	0.42	0.33
Lithuania	32	33	–0.3	63	31.0	33.5	0.9	0.9	47.8	46.7	..	0.84
Macedonia, FYR	42	40	0.1	25	..	35.6	*2.2*	1.8	*23.8*	22.3	..	0.28
Madagascar	76	73	2.6	582	23.5	22.1	1.0	1.0	4.7	5.1	0.23	0.17
Malawi	88	83	1.6	94	41.4	36.2	1.2	1.5	19.3	26.0	0.19	0.19
Malaysia	50	36	–0.1	329	68.1	63.6	16.0	17.6	5.2	5.5	0.10	0.08
Mali	76	67	1.9	1,220	11.5	10.3	0.0	0.0	1.7	3.8	0.23	0.38
Mauritania	56	37	–0.2	1,025	0.4	0.3	0.0	0.0	0.4	0.5	0.20	0.17
Mauritius	60	56	0.7	2	19.2	18.2	3.0	3.0	49.3	49.3	0.09	0.08
Mexico	28	24	0.7	1,909	36.2	33.7	1.0	1.3	12.6	13.0	0.29	0.25
Moldova	53	54	–0.2	33	9.7	10.0	14.2	9.1	52.8	56.1	..	0.43
Mongolia	43	43	1.3	1,567	7.3	6.5	0.0	0.0	0.9	0.8	0.65	0.49
Morocco	52	42	0.1	446	9.6	9.8	1.7	2.0	19.5	19.0	0.36	0.30
Mozambique	79	63	1.1	784	25.5	24.6	0.3	0.3	4.4	5.6	0.26	0.22
Myanmar	75	70	1.0	658	59.6	49.0	0.8	1.4	14.6	15.4	0.23	0.20
Namibia	73	67	1.9	823	10.6	9.3	0.0	0.0	0.8	1.0	0.47	0.42
Nepal	91	85	1.8	143	33.7	25.4	0.5	0.9	16.0	16.5	0.12	0.09
Netherlands	40	34	–0.6	34	10.2	10.8	0.9	0.9	25.9	26.9	0.06	0.06
New Zealand	15	14	0.6	268	28.8	31.0	5.1	7.0	9.4	5.6	0.73	0.38
Nicaragua	47	42	1.4	121	53.9	42.7	1.6	1.9	10.7	15.9	0.33	0.37
Niger	84	77	2.7	1,267	1.5	1.0	0.0	0.0	8.7	11.4	1.28	1.15
Nigeria	65	53	1.0	911	18.9	12.2	2.8	3.2	32.4	33.5	0.33	0.24
Norway	28	20	–1.7	306	29.8	30.7	..	..	2.8	2.9	0.21	0.19
Oman	38	22	–1.6	310	0.0	0.0	0.2	0.1	0.1	0.1	0.02	0.02
Pakistan	69	66	2.0	771	3.3	2.5	0.6	0.9	26.6	25.2	0.19	0.14
Panama	46	43	1.4	74	58.8	57.7	2.1	2.0	6.7	7.4	0.21	0.18
Papua New Guinea	87	87	2.4	453	69.6	65.0	1.3	1.4	0.4	0.5	0.05	0.04
Paraguay	51	42	1.1	397	53.3	46.5	0.2	0.2	5.3	7.7	0.50	0.53
Peru	31	26	0.4	1,280	54.8	53.7	0.3	0.5	2.7	2.9	0.16	0.14
Philippines	51	38	0.0	298	35.5	24.0	14.8	16.8	18.4	19.1	0.09	0.07
Poland	39	38	–0.2	306	29.2	30.0	1.1	1.0	47.3	41.1	0.38	0.35
Portugal	53	45	–0.8	92	33.9	41.3	8.5	7.9	25.6	17.4	0.24	0.16
Puerto Rico	28	3	–15.0	9	45.6	46.0	5.6	5.6	7.3	3.7	0.02	0.01

3.1 Rural population and land use

	Rural population			Land area	Land use							
							% of land area					
	% of total		average annual % growth	thousand sq. km	Forest area		Permanent cropland		Arable land		Arable land hectares per capita	
	1990	2004	1990–2004	2004	1990	2005	1990	2003	1990	2003	1989–91	2001–03
Romania	47	45	–0.7	230	27.8	27.7	2.6	2.0	41.2	40.9	0.41	0.43
Russian Federation	27	27	–0.2	16,381	49.4	49.4	0.1	0.1	8.1	7.5	..	0.85
Rwanda	95	80	0.4	25	12.9	19.5	12.4	10.9	35.7	48.6	0.12	0.13
Saudi Arabia	22	12	–1.6	2,150	1.3	1.3	0.0	0.1	1.6	1.7	0.21	0.16
Senegal	60	50	1.2	193	48.6	45.1	0.1	0.2	12.1	12.8	0.29	0.23
Serbia and Montenegro	49	48	–2.0	102	..	26.4	*3.5*	3.2	*36.5*	33.2	..	0.42
Sierra Leone	70	60	0.9	72	42.5	38.5	0.8	1.1	6.8	8.0	0.12	0.11
Singapore	0	0	..	1	3.0	3.0	1.5	1.5	1.5	1.5	0.00	0.00
Slovak Republic	44	42	–0.1	48	..	..	..	..	..	..	..	..
Slovenia	49	49	0.0	20	..	62.8	*1.8*	1.4	*9.9*	8.6	..	0.09
Somalia	71	65	0.6	627	13.2	11.4	0.0	0.0	1.6	1.7	0.15	0.14
South Africa	51	43	0.5	1,214	7.6	7.6	0.7	0.8	11.1	12.2	0.38	0.33
Spain	25	23	0.3	499	27.0	35.9	9.7	10.0	30.7	27.5	0.40	0.33
Sri Lanka	79	79	1.0	65	36.4	29.9	15.9	15.5	13.5	14.2	0.05	0.05
Sudan	73	60	0.8	2,376	32.2	28.4	0.1	0.2	5.5	7.2	0.50	0.48
Swaziland	77	76	2.6	17	27.4	31.5	0.7	0.8	10.5	10.4	0.24	0.16
Sweden	17	17	0.2	410	66.7	67.1	0.0	0.0	6.9	6.5	0.33	0.30
Switzerland	32	32	0.9	40	28.9	30.5	0.5	0.6	9.8	10.2	0.06	0.06
Syrian Arab Republic	51	50	2.5	184	2.0	2.5	4.0	4.5	26.6	25.0	0.38	0.26
Tajikistan	68	75	2.1	140	2.9	2.9	0.9	0.9	6.1	6.6	..	0.15
Tanzania	78	64	1.1	884	46.9	39.9	1.0	1.2	4.0	4.5	0.13	0.11
Thailand	71	68	0.8	511	31.3	28.4	6.1	7.0	34.2	27.7	0.32	0.24
Togo	72	64	2.2	54	12.6	7.1	1.7	2.2	38.6	46.2	0.53	0.44
Trinidad and Tobago	31	24	–1.3	5	45.8	44.1	9.0	9.2	14.4	14.6	0.06	0.06
Tunisia	42	36	0.3	155	4.1	6.8	12.5	13.8	18.7	18.0	0.36	0.28
Turkey	41	33	0.3	770	12.6	13.2	3.9	3.5	32.0	30.4	0.44	0.34
Turkmenistan	55	54	1.8	470	8.8	8.8	0.1	0.1	2.9	4.7	..	0.42
Uganda	89	88	3.1	197	25.0	18.4	9.4	10.9	25.4	26.4	0.28	0.20
Ukraine	33	33	–0.8	579	16.0	16.5	1.9	1.6	57.6	56.1	..	0.67
United Arab Emirates	17	15	5.2	84	2.9	3.7	0.2	2.3	0.4	0.8	0.02	0.02
United Kingdom	11	11	0.0	242	10.8	11.8	0.3	0.2	27.4	23.4	0.12	0.10
United States	25	20	–0.5	9,159	32.6	33.1	0.2	0.2	20.3	18.9	0.74	0.60
Uruguay	11	7	–2.3	175	5.2	8.6	0.3	0.2	7.2	7.8	0.41	0.40
Uzbekistan	60	63	2.2	425	7.2	7.8	0.9	0.8	10.5	11.1	..	0.18
Venezuela, RB	16	12	0.0	882	59.0	54.1	0.9	0.9	3.2	3.0	0.14	0.10
Vietnam	80	74	1.0	325	28.8	39.7	3.2	7.1	16.4	20.5	0.08	0.08
West Bank and Gaza	..	..	..	..	..	..	..	..	..	..	..	..
Yemen, Rep.	79	74	3.3	528	1.0	1.0	0.2	0.3	2.9	2.9	0.12	0.08
Zambia	61	64	2.6	743	66.1	57.1	0.0	0.0	7.1	7.1	0.63	0.47
Zimbabwe	71	65	0.8	387	57.5	45.3	0.3	0.3	7.5	8.3	0.27	0.25
World	**57 w**	**51 w**	**0.6 w**	**129,663 s**	**31.6 w**	**30.5 w**	**0.9 w**	**1.1 w**	**10.8 w**	**10.8 w**	**0.24 w**	**0.23 w**
Low income	74	69	1.6	29,192	27.8	24.8	1.0	1.2	12.9	13.5	0.21	0.17
Middle income	56	47	–0.2	67,543	34.5	33.6	1.0	1.2	9.6	9.7	0.18	0.22
Lower middle income	62	51	–0.2	38,470	32.1	30.7	1.3	1.6	10.0	10.5	0.15	0.17
Upper middle income	31	28	0.1	28,983	37.7	37.3	0.6	0.6	9.0	8.7	0.37	0.45
Low & middle income	63	57	0.7	96,645	32.5	30.9	1.0	1.2	10.5	10.8	0.20	0.20
East Asia & Pacific	71	59	–0.2	15,885	28.8	28.4	2.2	2.8	12.1	13.3	0.12	0.12
Europe & Central Asia	37	36	0.0	23,371	38.2	38.3	0.4	0.4	12.3	11.4	..	0.57
Latin America & Carib.	29	23	–0.1	20,057	49.0	45.6	0.9	1.0	6.6	7.1	0.30	0.27
Middle East & N. Africa	48	44	1.3	8,955	2.2	2.4	0.7	0.9	5.6	5.8	0.23	0.18
South Asia	75	72	1.6	4,781	16.5	16.8	1.8	2.4	42.6	41.7	0.18	0.14
Sub-Saharan Africa	72	64	1.6	23,596	30.0	26.5	0.8	0.9	6.3	7.5	0.31	0.25
High income	25	22	–0.4	33,018	28.9	29.3	0.7	0.7	11.4	10.8	0.43	0.37
Europe EMU	26	24	–0.3	2,435	33.2	37.0	4.7	4.5	27.1	25.8	0.23	0.21

a. Includes Luxembourg. b. Includes Taiwan, China.

Rural population and land use

About the data

Indicators of rural development are sparse, as few indicators are disaggregated between rural and urban areas (for some that are, see tables 2.7 and 3.10). This table shows indicators of rural population and land use. Rural population is approximated as the midyear nonurban population.

The data in the table show that land use patterns are changing. They also indicate major differences in resource endowments and uses among countries.

True comparability of the data is limited, however, by variations in definitions, statistical methods, and the quality of data collection. Countries use different definitions of rural population and land use, for example. The Food and Agriculture Organization (FAO), the primary compiler of these data, occasionally adjusts its definitions of land use categories and sometimes revises earlier data. Because the data reflect changes in reporting procedures as well as actual changes in land use, apparent trends should be interpreted with caution.

Satellite images show land use that differs from that given by ground-based measures in both area under cultivation and type of land use. Moreover, land use data in countries such as India are based on reporting systems that were designed for the collection of tax revenue. Because taxes on land are no longer a major source of government revenue, the quality and coverage of land use data (except for cropland) have declined. Data on forest area may be particularly unreliable because of differences in definitions and irregular surveys (see *About the data* for table 3.4).

3.1a

Ten countries with the largest forest area, 2005

Country	Million hectares
Russian Federation	809
Brazil	478
Canada	310
United States	303
China	197
Australia	164
Congo, Dem. Rep.	134
Indonesia	88
Peru	69
India	68

Source: Food and Agricultural Organization's Global Forest Resources Assessment.

3.1b

Five countries had more than half the world's forest in 2005

Forest area as share of world total

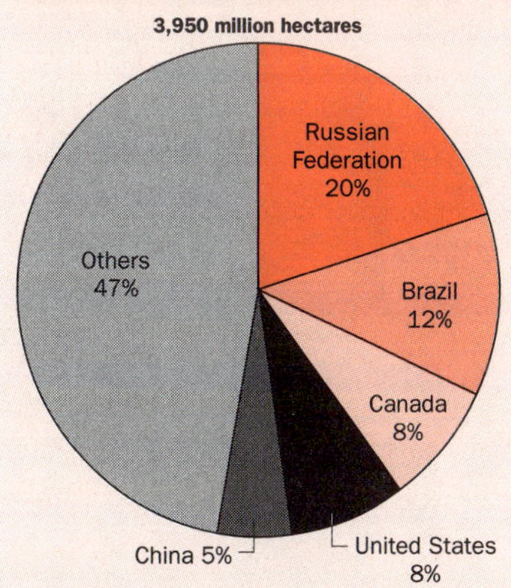

Source: Food and Agricultural Organization's Global Forest Resources Assessment.

Definitions

• **Rural population** is calculated as the difference between the total population and the urban population (see *Definitions* for tables 2.1 and 3.10). • **Land area** is a country's total area, excluding area under inland water bodies, national claims to the continental shelf, and exclusive economic zones. In most cases the definition of inland water bodies includes major rivers and lakes. (See table 1.1 for the total surface area of countries.) • **Land use** is broken into three categories. • **Forest area** is land under natural or planted stands of trees, whether productive or not. • **Permanent cropland** is land cultivated with crops that occupy the land for long periods and need not be replanted after each harvest, such as cocoa, coffee, and rubber. This category includes land under flowering shrubs, fruit trees, nut trees, and vines, but excludes land under trees grown for wood or timber. • **Arable land** includes land defined by the FAO as land under temporary crops (double-cropped areas are counted once), temporary meadows for mowing or for pasture, land under market or kitchen gardens, and land temporarily fallow. Land abandoned as a result of shifting cultivation is excluded.

Data sources

Data on urban population shares used to estimate rural population come from the United Nations Population Division's *World Urbanization Prospects: The 2005 Revision*. The total population figures are World Bank estimates. Data on land area and land use are from the FAO's electronic files. The FAO gathers these data from national agencies through annual questionnaires and by analyzing the results of national agricultural censuses. Data on forest area are from the FAO's Global Forest Resources Assessment.

3.2 Agricultural inputs

	Agricultural land		Irrigated land		Land under cereal production		Fertilizer consumption		Agricultural employment		Agricultural machinery	
	% of land area		% of cropland		thousand hectares		hundred grams per hectare of arable land		% of total employment		Tractors per 100 sq. km of arable land	
	1989–91	2001–03	1989–91	2001–03	1989–91	2003–05	1989–91	2000–02	1989–91	2001–03	1989–91	2001–03
Afghanistan	58.3	58.3	33.8	33.8	..	..	63	19	..	..	1	1
Albania	40.9	41.4	58.9	49.6	295	144	1,378	420	..	..	195	141
Algeria	16.2	16.8	5.8	6.9	2,807	2,784	157	130	..	21.1	125	129
Angola	46.1	46.1	2.3	2.3	883	1,372	46	2	..	..	35	33
Argentina	46.6	47.0	5.7	5.4	8,557	9,633	61	295	0.3	1.0	103	108
Armenia	..	49.5	..	51.1	168	194	..	157	20.5	..	..	288
Australia	60.5	58.2	4.0	5.1	12,823	18,360	272	465	5.4	4.4	67	64
Austria	42.7	41.2	0.3	0.3	940	783	2,001	1,533	7.7	5.7	2,378	2,368
Azerbaijan	..	56.8	..	72.5	627	794	..	63	31.4	40.1	..	169
Bangladesh	76.5	69.5	30.5	54.3	11,083	11,624	1,049	1,738	65.7	..	6	7
Belarus	..	43.1	..	2.3	2,578	2,066	..	1,325	21.6	..	..	111
Belgium	44.0[a]	46.3	2.3[a]	4.5	367[a]	314	4,969[a]	3,322[a]	2.7	1.7	1,530[a]	1,202[a]
Benin	20.4	30.4	0.6	0.4	658	948	54	154	..	..	1	1
Bolivia	32.8	34.2	5.4	4.1	620	748	37	37	1.7	..	25	20
Bosnia and Herzegovina	..	41.7	..	0.3	..	340	..	356	..	..	..	289
Botswana	45.9	45.8	0.3	0.3	203	137	22	122	..	12.3	135	159
Brazil	28.6	31.2	4.6	4.4	20,101	19,772	653	1,201	23.0	20.2	142	137
Bulgaria	55.7	48.7	30.1	16.5	2,152	1,760	1,698	500	18.9	18.0	135	95
Burkina Faso	35.0	39.2	0.5	0.5	2,743	3,249	59	30	..	..	2	4
Burundi	82.8	90.8	1.2	1.6	218	211	32	33	..	..	2	2
Cambodia	30.1	30.1	6.3	7.1	1,860	2,247	9	0	..	70.2	3	7
Cameroon	19.7	19.7	0.3	0.4	755	863	38	75	60.6	..	1	1
Canada	7.5	7.4	1.4	1.5	21,446	17,276	470	549	4.3	2.8	165	160
Central African Republic	8.0	8.3	0.0	0.1	110	187	5	3	..	..	0	0
Chad	38.4	38.6	0.5	0.8	1,170	1,887	20	49	..	..	1	0
Chile	21.3	20.4	51.8	82.4	778	687	1,082	2,386	19.3	13.6	129	272
China	57.0	59.5	36.0	35.4	93,047	79,896	2,222	2,578	55.8	44.7	67	65
Hong Kong, China	..	..	..	..	..	..	..	..	0.9	0.2	..	..
Colombia	43.4	44.2	13.1	22.6	1,655	1,195	1,770	2,605	1.3	21.6	98	89
Congo, Dem. Rep.	10.1	10.1	0.1	0.1	1,840	2,049	11	7	..	..	4	4
Congo, Rep.	30.8	30.9	0.2	0.4	15	11	24	67	..	..	14	14
Costa Rica	55.6	56.1	15.1	20.6	89	58	4,256	6,455	25.9	15.5	248	311
Côte d'Ivoire	59.4	62.4	1.1	1.1	1,401	1,638	152	256	..	..	15	12
Croatia	..	56.2	..	0.4	..	701	..	1,303	..	15.8	..	25
Cuba	61.5	60.6	23.2	22.5	233	326	1,771	476	24.9	25.5	256	249
Czech Republic	..	55.3	..	0.7	..	1,557	..	1,186	11.4	4.7	..	305
Denmark	65.5	62.9	16.9	19.6	1,564	1,493	2,436	1,393	5.6	3.2	639	540
Dominican Republic	74.0	76.4	15.1	17.2	135	150	859	848	20.3	15.4	22	17
Ecuador	28.3	29.2	27.9	29.0	828	844	465	1,531	7.1	8.5	65	91
Egypt, Arab Rep.	2.6	3.4	100.0	100.0	2,280	2,846	4,181	4,478	37.6	28.0	250	309
El Salvador	70.1	82.2	4.9	5.0	428	330	1,392	1,054	9.3	19.9	62	52
Eritrea	..	74.6	..	3.7	..	371	..	119	..	..	..	8
Estonia	..	19.0	..	0.6	454	267	..	432	20.5	6.7	..	889
Ethiopia	..	31.3	..	2.6	..	7,233	..	145	..	..	..	3
Finland	7.9	7.3	2.8	2.9	1,144	1,168	1,904	1,353	8.9	5.3	1,059	882
France	55.6	53.9	10.3	13.3	9,244	9,158	3,217	2,221	6.4	..	799	685
Gabon	20.0	20.0	1.0	1.4	14	20	33	9	..	..	50	46
Gambia, The	63.8	77.9	0.7	0.6	92	182	64	26	..	..	2	1
Georgia	..	43.2	..	44.1	249	332	..	412	..	53.8	..	254
Germany	50.8	48.7	4.0	4.0	6,864	6,983	3,070	2,245	4.1	2.5	1,314	801
Ghana	55.4	64.4	0.7	0.5	1,066	1,376	36	60	..	..	15	9
Greece	71.4	65.6	30.3	37.4	1,473	1,278	2,307	1,580	23.8	15.9	752	939
Guatemala	39.5	42.7	6.6	6.4	726	666	999	1,427	49.9	38.7	32	30
Guinea	48.7	50.4	7.2	5.6	603	778	18	32	..	..	5	5
Guinea-Bissau	53.2	57.9	4.1	4.6	106	134	22	80	..	..	1	1
Haiti	58.0	57.7	7.6	8.4	408	458	32	181	..	..	3	2

Agricultural inputs 3.2

	Agricultural land		Irrigated land		Land under cereal production		Fertilizer consumption		Agricultural employment		Agricultural machinery	
	% of land area		% of cropland		thousand hectares		hundred grams per hectare of arable land		% of total employment		Tractors per 100 sq. km of arable land	
	1989–91	2001–03	1989–91	2001–03	1989–91	2003–05	1989–91	2000–02	1989–91	2001–03	1989–91	2001–03
Honduras	29.9	26.2	3.8	5.6	475	391	191	1,193	44.1	35.1	31	49
Hungary	70.1	63.7	3.8	4.8	2,827	2,934	1,459	992	..	6.0	126	246
India	60.9	60.8	27.6	32.7	102,279	97,569	739	1,044	68.7	..	61	141
Indonesia	24.1	24.9	14.2	13.3	13,442	15,140	1,227	1,321	55.7	44.8	15	45
Iran, Islamic Rep.	37.3	37.5	41.1	44.1	9,503	9,013	760	921	26.0	..	136	168
Iraq	21.9	22.9	57.3	58.6	..	..	350	968	..	..	72	80
Ireland	76.2	63.6	..	..	306	292	6,609	5,308	14.6	6.8	1,624	1,360
Israel	26.6	26.2	47.0	45.4	111	84	2,877	2,598	4.1	1.9	795	718
Italy	56.4	52.2	21.9	24.9	4,481	4,124	2,135	1,819	8.9	5.1	1,593	2,031
Jamaica	44.0	47.4	11.3	8.8	2	1	2,079	1,258	..	19.9	252	177
Japan	15.6	14.2	54.3	54.7	2,469	2,001	3,865	3,066	7.2	4.7	4,306	4,588
Jordan	13.3	12.9	16.5	18.8	101	53	663	977	..	..	213	212
Kazakhstan	..	76.9	..	15.8	22,152	13,794	..	23	22.5	35.4	..	22
Kenya	45.7	46.5	1.2	1.8	1,776	2,101	258	320	19.0	..	24	28
Korea, Dem. Rep.	20.9	24.2	57.5	50.9	1,604	1,296	3,577	1,018	..	..	299	241
Korea, Rep.	22.1	19.5	46.8	47.2	1,427	1,093	4,888	4,317	17.4	9.4	215	1,239
Kuwait	7.9	8.6	60.0	77.0	1	2	417	711	..	..	222	69
Kyrgyz Republic	..	56.0	..	78.3	578	568	..	213	33.8	48.4	..	171
Lao PDR	7.2	8.1	15.7	17.6	643	819	18	95	..	..	11	12
Latvia	40.8	39.9	1.1	1.1	699	451	995	300	17.6	14.8	..	305
Lebanon	31.0	32.2	28.2	33.2	41	61	1,510	2,838	..	..	175	488
Lesotho	76.3	76.9	0.6	0.9	199	247	161	309	..	..	59	61
Liberia	27.1	27.0	0.4	0.5	179	120	25	0	..	..	8	9
Libya	8.8	8.8	20.2	21.9	418	341	445	349	..	..	179	219
Lithuania	..	55.6	..	0.2	1,134	880	..	579	..	17.7	..	349
Macedonia, FYR	..	48.8	..	9.0	..	195	..	502	..	23.0	..	954
Madagascar	47.0	47.4	30.1	30.6	1,308	1,423	32	31	..	78.0	11	12
Malawi	40.1	45.8	1.0	2.3	1,415	1,694	317	400	..	..	8	6
Malaysia	22.0	24.0	5.0	4.8	696	699	5,386	6,548	27.4	14.8	153	241
Mali	26.3	28.4	3.7	5.0	2,340	3,275	78	89	..	..	10	6
Mauritania	38.7	38.8	12.2	9.8	156	121	95	40	..	..	8	8
Mauritius	55.7	55.7	16.0	20.1	1	0	2,867	3,035	15.8	10.0	36	37
Mexico	54.2	56.2	21.6	23.2	10,014	10,946	716	727	24.2	17.0	124	131
Moldova	..	77.1	..	14.0	676	882	..	86	..	47.9	..	223
Mongolia	80.3	83.3	5.7	7.0	647	185	116	31	33.8	45.0	79	42
Morocco	67.8	68.0	13.5	15.5	5,545	5,578	369	440	..	44.2	45	58
Mozambique	60.8	61.8	2.8	2.7	1,561	2,112	10	53	..	..	17	14
Myanmar	15.8	16.8	10.2	17.9	5,154	6,827	84	146	67.5	..	13	10
Namibia	47.0	47.2	0.6	1.0	214	244	0	4	48.2	..	46	39
Nepal	29.0	29.5	41.6	47.1	3,013	3,333	320	333	82.8	..	22	24
Netherlands	59.0	57.2	61.0	59.9	192	222	6,506	4,286	4.6	3.0	2,074	1,641
New Zealand	65.3	64.3	7.3	8.5	161	121	1,525	5,704	10.6	8.7	301	507
Nicaragua	52.0	57.5	4.0	2.8	305	502	281	177	38.7	37.0	20	15
Niger	25.9	30.4	0.6	0.5	6,232	7,138	2	3	..	..	0	0
Nigeria	79.2	78.8	0.7	0.8	15,596	21,508	135	66	..	..	8	10
Norway	3.2	3.4	..	..	357	326	2,388	2,100	6.3	3.9	1,741	1,498
Oman	3.5	3.5	72.6	88.4	2	2	2,185	2,491	..	..	41	50
Pakistan	33.7	34.4	76.8	83.9	11,794	12,507	921	1,377	49.9	45.3	127	154
Panama	28.5	30.0	4.8	6.2	179	208	656	545	28.2	17.7	103	148
Papua New Guinea	2.0	2.3	..	..	2	3	671	556	..	..	60	53
Paraguay	58.6	62.5	3.0	2.2	447	782	92	319	1.7	32.2	72	55
Peru	16.3	16.6	30.5	27.9	802	1,118	320	759	1.1	0.8	37	36
Philippines	37.3	40.9	15.7	14.5	7,113	6,562	955	1,313	45.2	37.4	19	20
Poland	61.7	56.1	0.7	0.7	8,541	8,276	1,383	1,140	25.3	18.9	815	1,025
Portugal	43.3	41.5	20.2	27.5	832	465	1,152	1,234	18.1	12.6	563	1,029
Puerto Rico	49.0	25.5	34.5	48.2	1	0	..	..	3.7	2.0	..	..

3.2 Agricultural inputs

	Agricultural land % of land area		Irrigated land % of cropland		Land under cereal production thousand hectares		Fertilizer consumption hundred grams per hectare of arable land		Agricultural employment % of total employment		Agricultural machinery Tractors per 100 sq. km of arable land	
	1989–91	2001–03	1989–91	2001–03	1989–91	2003–05	1989–91	2000–02	1989–91	2001–03	1989–91	2001–03
Romania	64.4	64.4	31.1	31.1	5,927	5,655	1,077	355	28.9	38.1	147	178
Russian Federation	..	13.2	..	3.7	59,541	39,476	..	121	14.1	10.5	..	52
Rwanda	75.8	74.8	0.3	0.7	250	330	20	48	90.1	..	1	1
Saudi Arabia	56.7	80.9	45.6	42.7	1,009	646	1,461	1,067	..	5.4	19	28
Senegal	41.9	42.4	3.6	4.6	1,211	1,165	58	140	..	..	2	3
Serbia and Montenegro	..	54.8	..	0.8	..	2,047	..	732	..	..	..	1,023
Sierra Leone	38.3	39.1	5.2	5.0	462	253	24	5	..	..	6	2
Singapore	3.0	3.0	..	..	..	..	54,333	25,920	0.4	0.3	620	650
Slovak Republic	..	..	..	..	..	..	..	..	..	6.0	..	..
Slovenia	..	25.2	..	1.5	..	99	..	4,239	..	9.3	..	6,314
Somalia	70.2	70.3	19.2	18.7	..	..	18	5	..	..	21	16
South Africa	79.7	82.0	8.4	9.5	6,192	4,469	573	558	..	10.7	108	46
Spain	61.1	60.2	16.8	20.3	7,756	6,570	1,282	1,605	11.5	6.0	481	689
Sri Lanka	36.2	36.4	27.5	34.4	810	873	2,127	2,862	44.6	34.7	75	113
Sudan	51.9	56.4	13.7	11.0	5,376	9,365	48	40	..	..	7	7
Swaziland	74.3	80.9	22.9	26.0	80	64	697	371	..	..	233	222
Sweden	8.3	7.7	4.0	4.3	1,235	1,099	1,148	1,010	3.4	2.1	604	616
Switzerland	50.5	38.1	6.1	5.8	210	164	4,297	2,272	4.3	4.1	2,874	2,644
Syrian Arab Republic	73.5	74.8	12.9	24.1	3,969	3,194	581	718	..	30.3	129	225
Tajikistan	..	30.4	..	68.2	266	391	..	175	63.4	..	..	233
Tanzania	53.7	54.4	3.3	3.5	2,990	3,243	378	31	84.2	82.1	19	19
Thailand	41.9	38.4	20.6	26.6	10,991	11,152	537	1,039	63.2	45.7	33	144
Togo	58.4	66.7	0.3	0.3	625	767	57	74	..	..	0	0
Trinidad and Tobago	25.5	25.9	3.3	3.3	6	2	833	631	12.6	7.4	355	360
Tunisia	56.9	62.3	6.7	8.0	1,375	1,377	328	372	..	..	86	126
Turkey	51.8	51.0	14.5	19.5	13,679	13,809	736	768	47.4	35.5	278	410
Turkmenistan	..	69.7	..	89.1	331	948	..	543	42.4	..	..	256
Uganda	60.6	62.7	0.1	0.1	1,078	1,532	1	14	80.1	69.1	9	9
Ukraine	..	71.4	..	6.8	12,542	13,089	..	154	..	19.5	..	124
United Arab Emirates	3.3	6.8	128.1	29.2	1	0	4,247	5,149	..	..	55	55
United Kingdom	75.3	70.1	2.4	3.0	3,677	3,039	3,553	3,141	2.2	1.3	762	877
United States	46.6	44.7	11.1	12.7	63,775	57,028	1,006	1,101	2.9	2.5	248	273
Uruguay	84.7	85.5	9.6	14.3	508	567	586	849	..	4.3	262	241
Uzbekistan	..	64.2	..	87.4	1,225	1,753	..	1,614	40.6	..	..	373
Venezuela, RB	24.8	24.5	13.1	16.9	819	1,040	1,579	1,132	13.1	10.0	169	189
Vietnam	20.7	29.3	44.8	33.8	6,549	8,378	1,183	3,172	74.7	61.9	51	245
West Bank and Gaza	..	..	..	..	..	..	..	..	..	14.2	..	..
Yemen, Rep.	33.4	33.5	22.4	31.4	781	638	134	95	..	..	40	43
Zambia	47.4	47.5	0.6	2.9	929	861	128	84	..	..	11	11
Zimbabwe	52.1	53.1	3.5	5.2	1,606	1,610	562	443	..	..	60	75
World	**38.4 w**	**38.4 w**	**16.8 w**	**18.0 w**	**690,883 s**	**669,691 s**	**992 w**	**986 w**	**41.7 w**	**.. w**	**187 w**	**194 w**
Low income	43.4	44.6	21.8	23.8	205,135	230,127	529	663	65.9	..	47	83
Middle income	36.2	35.6	17.9	17.7	341,823	305,289	1,124	1,057	46.8	35.8	123	130
Lower middle income	40.6	43.1	22.7	23.1	226,040	208,050	1,324	1,431	50.5	40.3	90	105
Upper middle income	30.8	25.7	9.04	8.6	115,782	97,239	788	471	20.8	14.2	187	171
Low & middle income	38.4	38.3	19.3	20.0	546,957	535,416	887	910	50.6	..	93	112
East Asia & Pacific	48.4	50.6	..	..	141,839	133,283	1,767	2,148	56.0	45.1	56	73
Europe & Central Asia	38.5	28.6	11.6	11.1	137,259	113,303	1,098	345	23.8	20.2	231	184
Latin America & Carib.	34.6	36.1	11.1	11.4	48,262	50,630	602	895	17.9	17.2	121	123
Middle East & N. Africa	22.5	23.0	28.9	32.9	26,822	25,887	651	841	..	..	113	144
South Asia	54.8	54.7	33.0	39.0	129,072	125,982	745	1,066	66.6	..	62	130
Sub-Saharan Africa	42.9	44.0	3.6	3.6	63,703	86,332	142	123	..	..	20	13
High income	38.3	38.5	10.5	11.9	143,926	134,275	1,248	1,208	6.0	3.9	420	436
Europe EMU	50.6	48.4	14.4	16.9	33,599	31,385	2,524	2,040	8.7	4.8	997	980

a. Includes Luxembourg.

About the data

Agricultural activities provide developing countries with food and revenue, but they also can degrade natural resources. Poor farming practices can cause soil erosion and loss of soil fertility. Efforts to increase productivity through the use of chemical fertilizers, pesticides, and intensive irrigation have environmental costs and health impacts. Excessive use of chemical fertilizers can alter the chemistry of soil. Pesticide poisoning is common in developing countries. And salinization of irrigated land diminishes soil fertility. Thus inappropriate use of inputs for agricultural production has far-reaching effects.

This table provides indicators of major inputs to agricultural production: land, fertilizer, labor, and agricultural machinery. There is no single correct mix of inputs: appropriate levels and application rates vary by country and over time, depending on the type of crops, the climate and soils, and the production process used.

The data shown here and in table 3.3 are collected by the Food and Agriculture Organization (FAO) through annual questionnaires. The FAO tries to impose standard definitions and reporting methods, but exact consistency across countries and over time is not possible. Data on agricultural employment, in particular, should be used with caution. In many countries much agricultural employment is informal and unrecorded, including substantial work performed by women and children.

Fertilizer consumption measures the quantity of plant nutrients. Consumption is calculated as production plus imports minus exports. Because some chemical compounds used for fertilizers have other industrial applications, the consumption data may overstate the quantity available for crops.

To smooth annual fluctuations in agricultural activity, the indicators in the table have been averaged over three years.

3.2a

Irrigated lands have increased in all income groups and most regions, putting further pressure on water resources

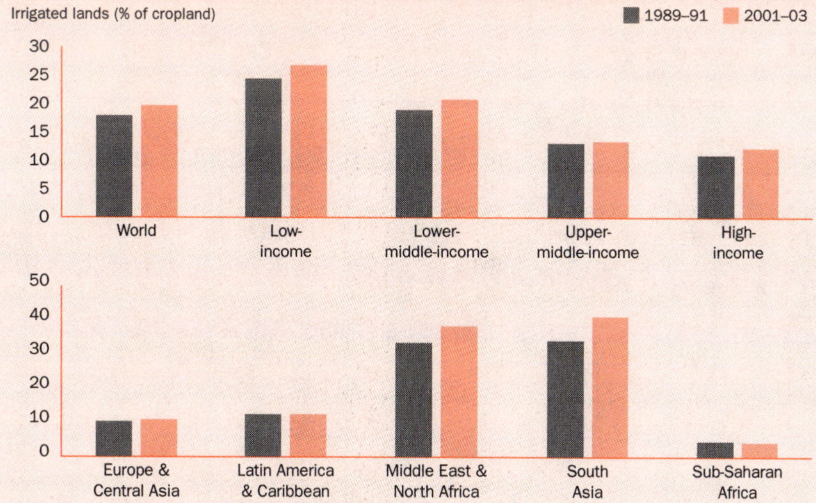

Note: Data are not available for East Asia and Pacific.
Source: Table 3.2.

Definitions

• **Agricultural land** refers to the share of land area that is arable, under permanent crops, and under permanent pastures. Arable land includes land defined by the FAO as land under temporary crops (double-cropped areas are counted once), temporary meadows for mowing or for pasture, land under market or kitchen gardens, and land temporarily fallow. Land abandoned as a result of shifting cultivation is excluded. Land under permanent crops is land cultivated with crops that occupy the land for long periods and need not be replanted after each harvest, such as cocoa, coffee, and rubber. This category includes land under flowering shrubs, fruit trees, nut trees, and vines, but excludes land under trees grown for wood or timber. Permanent pasture is land used for five or more years for forage, including natural and cultivated crops.• **Irrigated land** refers to areas purposely provided with water, including land irrigated by controlled flooding. • **Cropland** refers to arable land and permanent cropland (see table 3.1). • **Land under cereal production** refers to harvested areas, although some countries report only sown or cultivated area. • **Fertilizer consumption** is the quantity of plant nutrients used per unit of arable land. Fertilizer products cover nitrogenous, potash, and phosphate fertilizers (including ground rock phosphate). Traditional nutrients—animal and plant manures—are not included. The time reference for fertilizer consumption is the crop year (July through June). • **Agricultural employment** refers to employment in agriculture, forestry, hunting, and fishing (see table 2.3 for more detail). • **Agricultural machinery** refers to wheel and crawler tractors (excluding garden tractors) in use in agriculture at the end of the calendar year specified or during the first quarter of the following year.

Data sources

Data on agricultural inputs are from electronic files that the FAO makes available to the World Bank and that may contain more recent information than those published in the FAO's *Production Yearbook*.

3.3 Agricultural output and productivity

	Crop production index 1999–2001 = 100		Food production index 1999–2001 = 100		Livestock production index 1999–2001 = 100		Cereal yield kilograms per hectare		Agricultural productivity Agriculture value added per worker 2000 $	
	1992–94	2002–04	1992–94	2002–04	1992–94	2002–04	1993–95	2003–05	1992–94	2002–04
Afghanistan	..	..	..	..	..	..	..	..	..	..
Albania	85.1	100.6	81.1	105.9	78.7	108.9	2,662	3,491	916	1,469
Algeria	85.3	122.9	84.5	113.2	85.4	103.3	774	1,468	1,743	1,983
Angola	67.9	119.4	71.3	113.0	79.4	100.0	323	547	99	168
Argentina	68.8	106.4	76.0	101.4	92.5	92.0	2,821	3,771	7,335	9,311
Armenia	106.2	119.2	103.5	121.8	96.9	123.2	1,646	2,122	1,464	2,717
Australia	60.2	81.6	73.0	91.7	85.4	96.9	1,706	1,960	20,693	27,058
Austria	89.5	99.1	90.9	99.0	96.3	99.6	5,338	5,738	12,882	21,083
Azerbaijan	115.6	122.7	90.8	118.6	88.1	113.6	1,586	2,633	922	1,061
Bangladesh	74.8	104.7	74.0	104.6	80.2	103.2	2,572	3,533	251	309
Belarus	115.1	124.7	127.7	107.2	135.3	99.7	2,377	2,850	1,964	2,612
Belgium	87.8[a]	106.0	98.4[a]	101.3	98.7[a]	99.7	6,726[a]	8,710	..	..
Benin	66.0	125.4	67.9	126.3	92.5	109.2	988	1,147	391	599
Bolivia	68.2	116.4	72.6	111.6	77.5	107.9	1,513	1,857	678	749
Bosnia and Herzegovina	97.6	101.1	108.7	96.0	109.4	86.6	3,569	3,393	2,951	5,709
Botswana	95.8	111.5	111.9	104.8	115.4	103.4	325	514	532	409
Brazil	82.1	119.6	76.9	118.0	73.4	116.8	2,384	3,149	1,839	3,111
Bulgaria	116.1	110.9	113.7	101.7	117.7	96.2	2,794	3,157	2,153	6,639
Burkina Faso	76.6	126.6	79.1	116.2	75.6	108.1	858	959	157	166
Burundi	108.0	107.0	108.1	106.3	137.2	100.2	1,329	1,336	115	103
Cambodia	64.1	105.8	66.1	106.3	75.8	103.5	1,520	2,062	276	289
Cameroon	76.2	103.0	78.8	104.2	85.7	103.1	1,034	1,720	720	1,177
Canada	89.1	93.8	84.1	94.8	80.4	103.6	2,647	2,962	29,378	38,509
Central African Republic	76.7	97.7	74.6	106.9	73.7	113.5	902	1,046	292	415
Chad	68.8	110.9	73.9	110.2	84.1	105.4	611	711	189	199
Chile	85.7	110.5	81.5	108.6	76.0	107.0	4,403	5,621	4,235	3,222
China	75.0	110.6	68.5	113.2	61.2	116.1	4,581	5,057	273	373
Hong Kong, China	..	..	..	..	..	..	..	..	..	..
Colombia	97.5	107.4	85.7	106.8	82.2	107.1	2,552	3,567	3,207	2,751
Congo, Dem. Rep.	127.8	97.2	124.8	97.5	103.2	99.2	778	767	227	197
Congo, Rep.	83.2	105.1	82.2	107.0	79.6	114.5	770	806	295	337
Costa Rica	77.1	99.6	77.6	101.0	82.8	101.4	3,671	4,001	3,364	4,285
Côte d'Ivoire	73.4	96.2	75.2	100.0	78.1	110.9	946	1,266	608	757
Croatia	83.8	97.2	96.7	98.9	116.4	108.2	4,255	4,179	5,189	9,237
Cuba	82.0	112.6	83.2	108.1	98.9	92.7	1,697	3,076	..	..
Czech Republic	97.1	94.8	111.6	96.6	114.9	95.8	4,099	4,816	3,531	4,543
Denmark	94.4	97.7	96.8	100.6	93.9	102.8	5,833	6,080	22,271	37,443
Dominican Republic	114.7	110.0	104.8	106.1	86.1	103.7	3,739	4,177	2,482	4,169
Ecuador	90.7	95.9	80.4	106.5	70.9	115.3	1,983	2,485	1,027	1,478
Egypt, Arab Rep.	74.3	104.2	72.5	107.7	71.0	115.3	5,920	7,528	1,575	2,007
El Salvador	102.7	90.6	87.9	102.9	77.7	108.5	1,883	2,462	1,639	1,607
Eritrea	91.9	67.7	83.5	83.2	76.4	97.1	487	296	91	56
Estonia	115.3	89.9	161.6	100.4	166.6	101.7	1,815	2,274	2,693	3,199
Ethiopia	69.7	106.7	71.5	110.6	78.8	117.7	1,106	1,261	123	118
Finland	91.9	102.4	99.2	103.3	101.3	104.3	3,534	3,284	17,815	31,339
France	92.2	98.8	96.0	99.5	97.4	100.4	6,504	6,876	24,724	40,521
Gabon	86.7	101.9	88.6	101.6	88.5	100.5	1,848	1,641	1,535	1,747
Gambia, The	55.5	65.2	59.7	68.7	102.1	102.6	1,129	1,155	204	204
Georgia	119.4	91.9	98.6	100.9	74.5	110.3	1,978	2,152	2,127	1,442
Germany	83.8	95.1	91.8	97.5	96.8	101.0	5,882	6,497	13,908	23,616
Ghana	69.1	117.0	70.2	116.9	90.9	108.7	1,341	1,437	301	341
Greece	93.9	90.4	97.0	92.2	101.0	98.2	3,717	3,699	8,315	9,303
Guatemala	79.8	102.6	78.7	105.5	80.2	100.6	1,873	1,747	2,178	2,275
Guinea	80.5	107.5	80.0	110.7	68.5	111.8	1,178	1,476	175	229
Guinea-Bissau	73.1	104.9	75.9	105.1	86.1	106.6	1,410	1,149	211	224
Haiti	101.9	98.8	95.7	101.9	76.7	111.6	930	824	682	427

Agricultural output and productivity 3.3

	Crop production index		Food production index		Livestock production index		Cereal yield		Agricultural productivity	
	1999–2001 = 100		1999–2001 = 100		1999–2001 = 100		kilograms per hectare		Agriculture value added per worker 2000 $	
	1992–94	**2002–04**	**1992–94**	**2002–04**	**1992–94**	**2002–04**	**1993–95**	**2003–05**	**1992–94**	**2002–04**
Honduras	96.6	118.9	90.6	111.9	77.5	105.8	1,393	1,095	992	1,163
Hungary	89.1	99.7	93.6	100.9	101.9	101.9	3,706	4,718	2,825	3,986
India	84.5	100.0	80.8	102.5	74.5	110.5	2,104	2,391	362	391
Indonesia	88.0	112.7	90.3	113.1	99.4	127.3	3,875	4,278	498	564
Iran, Islamic Rep.	83.0	118.1	82.1	113.3	77.6	103.3	1,782	2,411	2,042	2,438
Iraq	..	..	..	..	..	..	..	..	..	2,271
Ireland	89.8	100.3	95.1	96.4	94.8	96.1	6,183	7,390	..	..
Israel	91.5	103.3	81.8	106.5	79.5	113.1	2,678	3,725	..	..
Italy	98.8	92.6	98.4	94.3	95.3	99.4	4,732	5,057	13,672	21,553
Jamaica	102.2	96.7	94.9	97.9	81.9	102.8	1,447	1,162	2,162	1,916
Japan	108.8	95.0	106.9	97.4	107.0	100.2	5,627	5,807	19,958	26,557
Jordan	106.8	136.6	97.1	124.1	92.8	94.1	1,363	1,354	1,810	1,192
Kazakhstan	121.7	108.4	140.6	106.4	178.3	111.6	803	994	1,585	1,420
Kenya	88.8	103.2	86.4	106.4	82.5	110.4	1,711	1,409	301	317
Korea, Dem. Rep.	124.4	108.4	118.5	109.1	113.7	114.2	4,455	3,408	..	..
Korea, Rep.	89.1	91.3	84.2	92.8	80.3	100.4	5,780	6,233	6,257	9,996
Kuwait	39.1	110.6	35.6	122.0	39.2	115.7	5,998	1,975	..	13,898
Kyrgyz Republic	60.0	102.9	71.0	101.0	101.4	98.4	1,968	2,984	625	942
Lao PDR	63.4	115.3	63.4	115.9	72.1	107.5	2,447	3,180	376	461
Latvia	127.4	119.4	186.1	111.0	219.0	101.1	1,778	2,225	1,566	2,415
Lebanon	116.9	94.1	107.4	100.4	68.1	120.4	2,264	2,377	15,726	25,189
Lesotho	74.1	100.8	94.6	100.4	125.8	100.0	855	906	447	495
Liberia	56.9	97.7	72.9	96.2	89.9	107.8	1,106	889	..	..
Libya	81.9	96.9	79.4	101.6	76.7	101.0	683	626	..	..
Lithuania	88.8	113.1	136.5	111.0	154.3	107.8	1,907	3,183	..	4,280
Macedonia, FYR	90.9	93.3	94.8	96.2	105.8	103.3	2,571	3,053	2,105	3,034
Madagascar	95.4	103.5	93.4	101.8	95.2	97.1	1,939	2,321	183	174
Malawi	57.7	84.3	49.3	87.1	85.2	101.8	1,233	1,150	73	131
Malaysia	78.1	114.0	78.6	113.7	98.8	115.1	3,051	3,293	3,918	4,690
Mali	75.6	107.4	81.8	105.8	85.2	112.9	797	872	205	229
Mauritania	84.4	97.2	81.8	107.6	80.9	109.3	763	1,075	283	282
Mauritius	107.3	101.6	100.4	104.9	82.4	116.8	3,942	3,436	4,034	4,996
Mexico	83.4	103.8	81.6	105.5	78.3	107.8	2,559	2,872	2,295	2,727
Moldova	147.6	112.2	151.4	112.6	170.3	103.2	3,001	2,572	902	732
Mongolia	173.0	107.3	83.3	96.4	81.4	95.9	780	808	697	661
Morocco	95.2	133.4	91.1	122.6	80.7	102.0	864	1,282	1,275	1,582
Mozambique	60.5	106.1	65.5	103.0	91.5	100.9	579	921	98	142
Myanmar	71.7	114.7	71.9	115.2	68.2	115.1	2,895	3,420	..	..
Namibia	68.6	111.4	104.8	109.8	112.0	109.3	299	441	845	1,097
Nepal	75.2	111.2	77.2	109.4	82.4	107.3	1,841	2,284	191	208
Netherlands	98.3	97.9	107.4	94.8	106.4	92.6	7,644	8,036	27,857	39,358
New Zealand	86.4	101.9	84.3	112.1	85.8	112.1	5,457	7,360	20,319	27,660
Nicaragua	73.7	115.3	69.7	119.4	65.3	119.9	1,731	1,778	1,221	1,916
Niger	73.4	119.5	77.9	116.3	85.9	104.7	311	394	165	172
Nigeria	79.4	103.4	79.6	103.7	82.8	106.6	1,165	1,057	610	863
Norway	113.4	103.4	101.3	98.6	98.1	97.3	3,768	4,121	23,252	32,779
Oman	69.2	87.3	67.0	89.9	75.3	94.0	2,185	2,332	1,000	1,128
Pakistan	80.3	102.5	77.3	106.0	75.6	109.1	1,946	2,438	603	688
Panama	110.2	104.2	96.7	101.8	80.2	101.1	1,863	1,958	2,450	3,570
Papua New Guinea	83.8	101.6	84.5	105.9	85.3	110.1	2,865	3,539	451	482
Paraguay	81.3	120.7	80.1	110.3	92.5	98.2	2,074	2,245	2,165	2,453
Peru	57.4	108.1	61.3	110.7	70.0	114.1	2,745	3,399	1,169	1,764
Philippines	87.3	109.6	81.5	112.2	67.4	120.7	2,263	2,946	907	1,001
Poland	101.3	91.6	99.2	103.6	99.4	105.0	2,781	3,191	1,026	1,408
Portugal	88.1	98.6	90.4	99.1	88.9	98.2	2,142	2,683	4,414	5,735
Puerto Rico	160.5	114.6	121.6	97.8	113.2	94.1	1,548	1,731	..	..

3.3 Agricultural output and productivity

	Crop production index		Food production index		Livestock production index		Cereal yield		Agricultural productivity	
	1999–2001 = 100		1999–2001 = 100		1999–2001 = 100		kilograms per hectare		Agriculture value added per worker 2000 $	
	1992–94	**2002–04**	**1992–94**	**2002–04**	**1992–94**	**2002–04**	**1993–95**	**2003–05**	**1992–94**	**2002–04**
Romania	94.6	112.2	101.1	110.7	112.7	107.6	2,760	3,255	2,312	3,519
Russian Federation	113.9	116.0	122.0	110.2	142.8	103.2	1,439	1,839	1,746	2,297
Rwanda	86.5	117.6	85.0	117.2	74.3	107.3	1,208	989	183	229
Saudi Arabia	126.0	114.8	100.6	116.0	70.4	104.9	4,264	4,430	8,905	14,284
Senegal	72.3	68.3	74.1	74.9	83.9	98.2	820	1,013	236	235
Serbia and Montenegro	99.8	110.0	106.1	106.0	101.7	94.9	3,385	4,056	..	1,446
Sierra Leone	123.0	113.5	114.7	112.3	88.6	105.2	1,181	1,223	..	..
Singapore	116.1	100.0	240.4	69.3	235.0	74.2	..	..	28,729	32,267
Slovak Republic	..	..	..	..	..	..	..	..	..	..
Slovenia	101.1	110.2	86.4	105.8	83.1	103.6	4,433	5,247	12,494	32,311
Somalia	..	..	..	..	..	..	..	..	..	..
South Africa	80.9	102.4	85.2	105.7	93.8	108.2	2,052	2,907	1,764	2,414
Spain	81.6	106.1	83.6	105.3	81.0	107.2	2,267	3,040	12,611	19,132
Sri Lanka	89.4	98.8	94.4	100.0	107.5	109.9	2,993	3,428	713	743
Sudan	80.8	110.8	77.6	107.6	75.4	106.3	479	481	364	688
Swaziland	94.5	100.1	106.1	105.3	140.4	111.9	1,607	1,114	1,040	1,161
Sweden	94.0	102.1	96.3	100.0	97.2	97.7	4,336	4,835	21,654	31,716
Switzerland	112.2	95.3	104.3	100.1	103.3	101.9	6,220	6,150	21,565	22,190
Syrian Arab Republic	83.9	117.1	81.0	122.2	69.6	115.6	1,558	1,786	2,356	2,977
Tajikistan	119.0	132.9	128.5	132.6	176.0	139.2	994	2,252	367	401
Tanzania	87.9	103.6	87.0	105.0	87.7	109.4	1,292	1,469	242	287
Thailand	85.6	106.1	88.6	106.0	98.9	105.5	2,383	2,725	481	599
Togo	81.4	110.3	81.6	104.2	83.6	106.7	816	1,040	360	409
Trinidad and Tobago	116.8	91.9	91.7	122.1	76.1	142.6	3,533	2,722	1,748	2,368
Tunisia	91.5	104.2	84.9	103.0	66.7	99.9	1,069	1,539	2,365	2,415
Turkey	88.1	104.0	90.2	103.2	94.6	101.6	2,068	2,399	1,772	1,793
Turkmenistan	115.6	116.5	68.4	125.2	71.4	121.7	2,215	3,011	1,179	..
Uganda	81.4	106.6	82.5	107.7	86.1	112.9	1,536	1,667	192	231
Ukraine	127.5	114.0	134.8	108.1	155.5	108.1	2,881	2,436	1,235	1,442
United Arab Emirates	31.8	56.0	34.1	62.2	65.5	116.9	1,485	3,119	11,659	34,739
United Kingdom	102.3	100.3	106.3	98.9	106.1	98.5	6,618	7,097	23,089	26,897
United States	92.2	101.5	88.7	102.7	87.1	102.6	4,836	6,444	22,868	36,863
Uruguay	78.7	112.7	82.2	104.3	88.3	98.3	2,880	4,279	6,213	7,102
Uzbekistan	105.1	109.0	92.6	107.9	103.1	104.7	1,730	3,461	1,263	1,567
Venezuela, RB	79.9	96.0	77.3	98.9	79.2	100.4	2,949	3,329	4,781	5,899
Vietnam	67.0	116.6	70.1	118.3	64.7	124.9	3,463	4,651	225	294
West Bank and Gaza	..	..	..	..	..	..	..	..	..	..
Yemen, Rep.	83.0	100.1	79.1	107.4	73.7	115.5	1,102	772	383	511
Zambia	88.8	102.4	92.5	104.1	87.3	99.2	1,684	1,584	160	206
Zimbabwe	72.0	69.3	75.2	85.7	86.4	100.1	1,154	676	238	242
World	**85.0 w**	**105.7 w**	**84.8 w**	**106.2 w**	**85.7 w**	**107.0 w**	**2,789 w**	**3,254 w**	**770 w**	**864 w**
Low income	82.4	103.5	80.6	105.2	77.8	109.6	1,820	2,083	336	378
Middle income	83.4	110.2	82.6	110.5	83.4	111.0	2,815	3,318	576	719
Lower middle income	81.4	111.7	78.0	112.5	74.2	114.1	3,217	3,644	456	588
Upper middle income	90.8	104.9	97.3	104.3	107.5	102.7	2,028	2,619	2,227	2,650
Low & middle income	83.1	108.1	82.0	109.0	82.0	110.6	2,420	2,787	477	568
East Asia & Pacific	77.0	110.8	72.1	112.4	63.8	116.6	4,031	4,466	..	..
Europe & Central Asia	105.9	107.1	114.7	106.1	128.8	104.1	1,902	2,331	1,602	1,914
Latin America & Carib.	80.7	111.5	79.1	110.4	78.7	108.9	2,493	3,159	2,234	2,812
Middle East & N. Africa	84.1	113.7	80.9	112.5	74.8	107.7	1,877	2,439	1,589	1,975
South Asia	83.8	101.0	80.3	103.5	75.0	109.8	2,128	2,505	364	401
Sub-Saharan Africa	80.3	103.9	81.7	105.1	85.9	107.1	1,034	1,087	294	341
High income	91.0	98.2	91.1	99.9	91.7	101.2	4,297	5,115	..	..
Europe EMU	90.6	97.8	93.3	98.8	96.2	99.7	4,855	5,427	14,186	21,695

a. Includes Luxembourg.

Agricultural output and productivity 3.3

About the data

The agricultural production indexes in the table are prepared by the Food and Agriculture Organization (FAO). The FAO obtains data from official and semiofficial reports of crop yields, area under production, and livestock numbers. If data are not available, the FAO makes estimates. The indexes are calculated using the Laspeyres formula: production quantities of each commodity are weighted by average international commodity prices in the base period and summed for each year. Because the FAO's indexes are based on the concept of agriculture as a single enterprise, estimates of the amounts retained for seed and feed are subtracted from the production data to avoid double counting. The resulting aggregate represents production available for any use except as seed and feed. The FAO's indexes may differ from other sources because of differences in coverage, weights, concepts, time periods, calculation methods, and use of international prices.

To ease cross-country comparisons, the FAO uses international commodity prices to value production. These prices, expressed in international dollars (equivalent in purchasing power to the U.S. dollar), are derived using a Geary-Khamis formula applied to agricultural outputs (see Inter-Secretariat Working Group on National Accounts 1993, sections 16.93–96). This method assigns a single price to each commodity so that, for example, one metric ton of wheat has the same price regardless of where it was produced. The use of international prices eliminates fluctuations in the value of output due to transitory movements of nominal exchange rates unrelated to the purchasing power of the domestic currency.

Data on cereal yield may be affected by a variety of reporting and timing differences. The FAO allocates production data to the calendar year in which the bulk of the harvest took place. But most of a crop harvested near the end of a year will be used in the following year. Cereal crops harvested for hay or harvested green for food, feed, or silage, and those used for grazing, are generally excluded. But millet and sorghum, which are grown as feed for livestock and poultry in Europe and North America, are used as food in Africa, Asia, and countries of the former Soviet Union. So some cereal crops are excluded from the data for some countries and included elsewhere, depending on their use.

Agricultural productivity is measured by value added per unit of input. (For further discussion of the calculation of value added in national accounts, see *About the data* for tables 4.1 and 4.2.) Agricultural value added includes that from forestry and fishing. Thus interpretations of land productivity should be made with caution. To smooth annual fluctuations in agricultural activity, the indicators in the table have been averaged over three years.

Definitions

• **Crop production index** shows agricultural production for each period relative to the base period 1999–2001. It includes all crops except fodder crops. The regional and income group aggregates for the FAO's production indexes are calculated from the underlying values in international dollars, normalized to the base period 1999–2001. The data in this table are three-year averages. • **Food production index** covers food crops that are considered edible and that contain nutrients. Coffee and tea are excluded because, although edible, they have no nutritive value. • **Livestock production index** includes meat and milk from all sources, dairy products such as cheese, and eggs, honey, raw silk, wool, and hides and skins. • **Cereal yield**, measured in kilograms per hectare of harvested land, includes wheat, rice, maize, barley, oats, rye, millet, sorghum, buckwheat, and mixed grains. Production data on cereals refer to crops harvested for dry grain only. Cereal crops harvested for hay or harvested green for food, feed, or silage, and those used for grazing, are excluded. • **Agricultural productivity** refers to the ratio of agricultural value added, measured in constant 2000 U.S. dollars, to the number of workers in agriculture.

3.3a

The 10 countries with the highest cereal yield in 2003–05—and the 10 with the lowest

Country	Kilograms per hectare	Country	Kilograms per hectare
Belgium	8,710	Eritrea	296
Netherlands	8,036	Niger	394
Egypt, Arab Rep.	7,528	Namibia	441
Ireland	7,390	Sudan	481
New Zealand	7,360	Botswana	514
United Kingdom	7,097	Angola	547
France	6,876	Libya	626
Germany	6,497	Zimbabwe	676
United States	6,444	Chad	711
Korea, Rep.	6,233	Congo, Dem. Rep.	767

Source: Table 3.3.

Data sources

The agricultural production indexes are prepared by the FAO and published annually in its *Production Yearbook*. The FAO makes these data and the data on cereal yield and agricultural employment available to the World Bank in electronic files that may contain more recent information than the published versions. For sources of data on agricultural value added, see *Data sources* for table 4.2.

Deforestation and biodiversity

	Average annual deforestation[a] thousand sq. km 1990–2005	Average annual deforestation[a] % 1990–2005	Mammals Total known species 2004	Mammals Threatened species 2004	Birds Total known species 2004	Birds Threatened species 2004	Higher plants[b] Total known species 2004	Higher plants[b] Threatened species 2004	GEF benefits index for biodiversity 2005	Nationally protected areas thousand sq. km 2004[c]	Nationally protected areas % of total land area 2004[c]	Marine protected areas thousand sq. km 2004[c]	Marine protected areas % of surface area 2004[c]
Afghanistan	295	2.3	144	12	434	17	4,000	1	24.1	2.0	0.3	..	..
Albania	–3	0.0	73	1	303	9	3,031	0	1.3	1.0	3.8	0.3	1.0
Algeria	–325	–1.8	100	12	372	11	3,164	2	19.9	119.1	5.0	0.9	0.0
Angola	1,248	0.2	296	11	930	20	5,185	26	63.4	82.3	6.6	29.1	2.3
Argentina	1,494	0.4	375	32	1,038	55	9,372	42	122.9	180.6	6.6	7.8	0.3
Armenia	42	1.2	78	9	302	12	3,553	1	1.7	2.1	7.6	..	..
Australia	2,817	0.2	376	63	851	60	15,638	56	635.5	1,029.4	13.4	680.8	8.8
Austria	–57	–0.2	101	5	412	8	3,100	3	2.3	27.3	33.1	..	..
Azerbaijan	0	0.0	82	11	364	11	4,300	0	5.7	5.3	6.4	1.2	1.4
Bangladesh	7	0.1	131	22	604	23	5,000	12	10.5	1.0	0.8	0.3	0.2
Belarus	–345	–0.5	71	6	226	4	2,100	0	0.1	13.1	6.3	..	..
Belgium[d]	7	0.1	92	9	427	10	1,550	0	0.1	..	..	0.0	0.0
Benin	647	2.0	159	6	485	2	2,500	14	1.6	12.6	11.4	..	..
Bolivia	2,703	0.4	361	26	1,414	30	17,367	70	91.9	145.3	13.4	..	..
Bosnia and Herzegovina	17	0.1	78	8	312	8	..	1	2.5	0.3	0.5	..	..
Botswana	1,183	0.9	169	6	570	9	2,151	0	9.9	104.9	18.5	..	..
Brazil	28,219	0.5	578	74	1,712	120	56,215	381	663.7	566.6	6.7	47.5	0.6
Bulgaria	–199	–0.6	106	12	379	11	3,572	0	6.1	5.0	4.5	0.0	0.0
Burkina Faso	240	0.3	129	6	452	2	1,100	2	1.9	31.5	11.5	..	..
Burundi	91	3.2	116	7	597	9	2,500	2	3.3	1.5	5.7	..	..
Cambodia	1,666	1.3	127	23	521	24	..	31	25.8	32.7	18.5	1.9	1.1
Cameroon	2,200	0.9	322	42	936	18	8,260	334	88.4	20.9	4.5	3.9	0.8
Canada	0	0.0	211	16	472	19	3,270	1	147.3	1,023.5	11.3	362.7	3.6
Central African Republic	299	0.1	187	11	663	3	3,602	15	11.0	54.2	8.7	..	..
Chad	793	0.6	104	12	531	5	1,600	2	14.1	114.6	9.1	..	..
Chile	–572	–0.4	159	22	445	32	5,284	40	107.3	141.5	18.9	114.5	15.1
China	–26,766	–1.7	502	80	1,221	82	32,200	443	430.4	727.5	7.8	16.0	0.2
Hong Kong, China	..	..	57	1	306	20	..	6	..	..	..	0.3	26.5
Colombia	474	0.1	467	39	1,821	86	51,220	222	380.0	106.0	10.2	8.1	0.7
Congo, Dem. Rep.	4,614	0.3	430	29	1,148	30	11,007	65	113.0	113.4	5.0	..	..
Congo, Rep.	170	0.1	166	14	597	4	6,000	35	22.8	22.2	6.5	..	..
Costa Rica	115	0.5	232	13	838	18	12,119	110	73.6	11.7	23.0	4.8	9.4
Côte d'Ivoire	–122	–0.1	229	23	702	11	3,660	105	25.7	19.1	6.0	0.3	0.1
Croatia	–13	–0.1	96	7	365	9	4,288	0	3.6	4.2	7.5	2.5	4.4
Cuba	–437	–2.1	65	11	358	18	6,522	163	89.8	75.9	69.1	31.7	28.6
Czech Republic	–12	–0.1	88	6	386	9	1,900	4	0.9	12.4	16.1	..	..
Denmark	–37	–0.8	81	4	427	10	1,450	3	1.1	14.4	34.0	5.1	11.8
Dominican Republic	0	0.0	36	5	224	16	5,657	30	45.0	25.1	51.9	8.6	17.6
Ecuador	1,976	1.4	341	34	1,515	69	19,362	1	199.4	50.7	18.3	141.0	49.7
Egypt, Arab Rep.	–15	–3.5	118	6	481	17	2,076	2	21.5	96.6	9.7	76.7	7.7
El Salvador	51	1.4	137	2	434	3	2,911	25	5.5	0.1	0.4	0.1	0.4
Eritrea	45	0.3	70	9	537	7	..	3	6.0	4.3	4.3	..	..
Estonia	–81	–0.4	67	4	267	3	1,630	0	0.3	5.0	11.8	..	..
Ethiopia	1,409	0.9	288	35	839	20	6,603	22	56.7	169.0	16.9	..	..
Finland	–204	–0.1	80	3	421	10	1,102	1	1.2	28.3	9.3	1.1	0.3
France	–677	–0.5	148	16	517	15	4,630	2	26.1	73.2	13.3	0.5	0.1
Gabon	101	0.1	166	11	632	5	6,651	107	22.8	1.8	0.7	1.0	0.4
Gambia, The	–19	–0.4	133	3	535	2	974	4	0.7	0.2	2.3	0.2	2.0
Georgia	0	0.0	98	11	268	8	4,350	0	4.6	1.6	2.3	0.0	0.1
Germany	–223	–0.2	126	9	487	14	2,682	12	4.4	113.8	32.6	9.1	2.6
Ghana	1,287	1.7	249	15	729	8	3,725	117	13.0	12.7	5.6	..	..
Greece	–302	–0.9	118	11	412	14	4,992	2	20.0	4.6	3.6	2.5	1.9
Guatemala	540	1.1	193	7	684	10	8,681	85	58.9	21.7	20.0	0.1	0.1
Guinea	456	0.6	215	18	640	10	3,000	22	17.0	1.7	0.7	..	..
Guinea-Bissau	96	0.4	101	5	459	1	1,000	4	4.6	..	..	..	..
Haiti	7	0.6	41	4	271	15	5,242	28	38.4	0.1	0.4	..	..

Deforestation and biodiversity 3.4

	Average annual deforestation[a]		Mammals		Birds		Higher plants[b]		GEF benefits index for biodiversity	Nationally protected areas		Marine protected areas	
	thousand sq. km 1990–2005	% 1990–2005	Total known species 2004	Threatened species 2004	Total known species 2004	Threatened species 2004	Total known species 2004	Threatened species 2004	2005	thousand sq. km 2004[c]	% of total land area 2004[c]	thousand sq. km 2004[c]	% of surface area 2004[c]
Honduras	1,825	2.5	201	10	699	6	5,680	111	52.7	7.2	6.4	1.9	1.7
Hungary	–117	–0.7	88	7	367	9	2,214	1	1.2	6.5	7.0	..	..
India	–2,508	–0.4	422	85	1,180	79	18,664	246	291.3	154.6	5.2	16.1	0.5
Indonesia	18,715	1.6	667	146	1,604	121	29,375	383	597.0	373.2	20.6	130.1	6.8
Iran, Islamic Rep.	0	0.0	158	21	498	18	8,000	1	52.2	78.5	4.8	6.2	0.4
Iraq	–12	–0.2	102	9	396	18	..	0	11.2	0.0	0.0	..	..
Ireland	–152	–3.5	63	4	408	8	950	1	5.0	1.2	1.7	0.0	0.0
Israel	–11	–0.7	115	13	534	18	2,317	0	5.7	3.3	15.0	0.1	0.6
Italy	–1,064	–1.3	132	12	478	15	5,599	3	28.9	23.2	7.9	1.5	0.5
Jamaica	4	0.1	35	5	298	12	3,308	208	32.8	..	..	8.2	74.5
Japan	55	0.0	171	37	592	53	5,565	12	274.6	24.8	6.8	10.6	2.8
Jordan	0	0.0	93	7	397	14	2,100	0	2.3	3.0	3.4	0.0	0.1
Kazakhstan	57	0.2	145	15	497	23	6,000	1	36.1	72.9	2.7	0.5	0.0
Kenya	124	0.3	407	33	1,103	28	6,506	103	65.9	45.5	8.0	3.1	0.5
Korea, Dem. Rep.	1,343	1.6	105	12	369	22	2,898	3	4.7	3.1	2.6	..	..
Korea, Rep.	71	0.1	89	12	423	34	2,898	0	12.2	6.8	6.9	3.5	3.5
Kuwait	–2	–6.7	23	1	358	12	234	0	0.9	0.3	1.5	0.3	1.5
Kyrgyz Republic	–22	–0.3	58	6	207	4	4,500	1	7.8	28.9	15.0	..	..
Lao PDR	781	0.5	215	30	704	21	8,286	19	35.7	6.9	3.0	..	..
Latvia	–111	–0.4	68	4	325	8	1,153	0	0.3	8.3	13.4	0.2	0.2
Lebanon	–10	–0.8	70	5	377	10	3,000	0	1.2	0.1	0.5	0.0	0.1
Lesotho	–2	–4.0	59	3	311	7	1,591	1	2.0	0.1	0.2	..	..
Liberia	603	1.5	183	20	576	11	2,200	46	19.5	1.6	1.7	0.6	0.5
Libya	0	0.0	87	5	326	7	1,825	1	11.5	1.8	0.1	0.5	0.0
Lithuania	–103	–0.5	71	5	227	4	1,796	0	0.2	6.7	10.7	0.5	0.8
Macedonia, FYR	0	0.0	89	9	291	9	3,500	0	1.5	1.8	7.1	..	..
Madagascar	569	0.4	165	49	262	34	9,505	276	208.7	25.0	4.3	0.2	0.0
Malawi	329	0.9	207	7	658	13	3,765	14	26.1	10.5	11.2	..	..
Malaysia	991	0.4	337	50	746	40	15,500	683	98.5	18.7	5.7	5.0	1.5
Mali	1,000	0.7	134	12	624	5	1,741	6	10.3	45.2	3.7	..	..
Mauritania	99	2.4	94	7	521	5	1,100	0	9.5	17.4	1.7	15.0	1.5
Mauritius	1	0.3	14	3	137	13	750	87	27.9	..	..	0.1	4.4
Mexico	3,185	0.5	544	72	1,026	57	26,071	261	503.1	194.7	10.2	82.1	4.2
Moldova	–7	–0.2	50	4	203	8	1,752	0	0.1	0.5	1.4	..	..
Mongolia	827	0.7	140	13	387	22	2,823	0	29.5	180.2	11.5	..	..
Morocco	–50	–0.1	129	12	430	13	3,675	2	26.5	3.1	0.7	0.5	0.1
Mozambique	500	0.3	228	12	685	23	5,692	46	54.4	65.9	8.4	22.5	2.8
Myanmar	4,665	1.2	288	39	1,047	41	7,000	38	70.5	2.0	0.3	0.2	0.0
Namibia	734	0.8	192	10	619	18	3,174	24	39.1	112.0	13.6	74.0	9.0
Nepal	787	1.6	203	29	..	31	6,973	7	14.9	12.7	8.9	..	..
Netherlands	–13	–0.4	95	9	444	11	1,221	0	0.6	4.8	14.2	0.8	1.9
New Zealand	–393	–0.5	73	8	351	74	2,382	21	147.8	79.3	29.6	22.7	8.4
Nicaragua	899	1.4	181	6	632	8	7,590	39	23.7	21.6	17.8	1.3	1.0
Niger	453	2.3	123	10	493	2	1,460	2	6.0	97.5	7.7	..	..
Nigeria	4,097	2.4	290	25	899	9	4,715	170	43.6	30.1	3.3	..	..
Norway	–171	–0.2	83	9	442	6	1,715	2	10.7	20.9	6.8	1.3	0.4
Oman	0	0.0	74	12	483	14	1,204	6	29.3	43.3	14.0	29.6	9.6
Pakistan	417	1.7	195	17	625	30	4,950	2	33.6	37.8	4.9	2.2	0.3
Panama	55	0.1	241	17	904	20	9,915	195	78.0	16.2	21.7	10.0	13.3
Papua New Guinea	1,391	0.4	260	58	720	33	11,544	142	183.7	10.4	2.3	3.5	0.8
Paraguay	1,788	0.9	168	11	696	27	7,851	10	22.2	13.9	3.5	..	..
Peru	943	0.1	441	46	1,781	94	17,144	274	241.0	78.1	6.1	3.4	0.3
Philippines	2,275	2.2	222	50	590	70	8,931	212	224.0	17.0	5.7	16.6	5.5
Poland	–207	–0.2	110	12	424	12	2,450	4	3.8	37.8	12.3	0.7	0.2
Portugal	–456	–1.5	105	15	501	15	5,050	15	25.1	6.0	6.6	2.0	2.2
Puerto Rico	–3	–0.1	38	2	310	12	2,493	52	25.1	..	..	1.7	19.1

3.4 Deforestation and biodiversity

	Average annual deforestation[a]		Mammals		Birds		Higher plants[b]		GEF benefits index for biodiversity	Nationally protected areas		Marine protected areas	
	thousand sq. km 1990–2005	% 1990–2005	Total known species 2004	Threatened species 2004	Total known species 2004	Threatened species 2004	Total known species 2004	Threatened species 2004	2005	thousand sq. km 2004[c]	% of total land area 2004[c]	thousand sq. km 2004[c]	% of surface area 2004[c]
Romania	1	0.0	101	15	365	13	3,400	1	..	10.8	4.7	6.1	2.6
Russian Federation	107	0.0	296	43	645	47	11,400	7	246.4	1,317.3	8.0	301.8	1.8
Rwanda	–108	–3.4	206	13	665	9	2,288	3	7.0	1.5	6.2	..	..
Saudi Arabia	0	0.0	94	9	433	17	2,028	3	22.8	823.3	38.3	5.2	0.2
Senegal	450	0.5	191	11	612	5	2,086	7	8.5	22.3	11.6	0.9	0.4
Serbia and Montenegro	–90	–0.4	96	10	381	10	4,082	1	..	..	..	0.1	0.1
Sierra Leone	193	0.6	197	12	626	10	2,090	47	10.1	1.5	2.1	..	..
Singapore	0	0.0	73	3	400	10	2,282	54	1.0	0.0	4.5	0.0	0.2
Slovak Republic	–5	0.0	87	7	332	11	3,124	2	0.8	..	..	..	..
Slovenia	–51	–0.4	87	7	350	7	3,200	0	1.1	1.2	6.0	0.0	0.0
Somalia	767	0.9	182	15	642	13	3,028	17	44.2	5.0	0.8	3.3	0.5
South Africa	0	0.0	320	29	829	36	23,420	75	156.1	67.2	5.5	3.4	0.3
Spain	–2,957	–2.2	132	20	515	20	5,050	14	44.0	42.5	8.5	1.8	0.4
Sri Lanka	278	1.2	123	21	381	16	3,314	280	43.9	8.7	13.5	2.3	3.5
Sudan	5,890	0.8	302	16	952	10	3,137	17	36.4	123.6	5.2	0.3	0.0
Swaziland	–46	–1.0	124	6	490	6	2,715	11	0.9	..	..	..	..
Sweden	–107	0.0	85	5	457	9	1,750	3	2.2	37.5	9.1	4.3	1.0
Switzerland	–44	–0.4	93	4	382	8	3,030	2	1.7	11.9	29.7	..	..
Syrian Arab Republic	–59	–1.6	82	3	350	11	3,000	0	6.2	..	..	..	..
Tajikistan	–1	0.0	76	7	351	9	5,000	2	4.9	5.9	4.2	..	..
Tanzania	4,123	1.0	375	34	1,056	37	10,008	239	100.4	263.3	29.8	2.3	0.2
Thailand	963	0.6	300	36	971	42	11,625	84	53.0	71.0	13.9	5.8	1.1
Togo	199	2.9	175	7	565	2	3,085	10	2.5	4.3	7.9	..	..
Trinidad and Tobago	6	0.3	116	1	435	2	2,259	1	16.0	0.3	6.0	0.1	1.3
Tunisia	–275	–4.3	78	10	360	9	2,196	0	3.5	0.5	0.3	0.2	0.1
Turkey	–330	–0.3	145	15	436	14	8,650	3	39.6	12.3	1.6	4.5	0.6
Turkmenistan	0	0.0	103	12	318	13	..	0	13.0	19.7	4.2	..	..
Uganda	865	1.8	360	29	1,015	15	4,900	38	22.1	48.5	24.6	..	..
Ukraine	–201	–0.2	120	14	325	13	5,100	1	2.8	22.6	3.9	3.1	0.5
United Arab Emirates	–45	–1.8	30	5	268	11	..	0	1.4	0.0	0.0	..	..
United Kingdom	–156	–0.6	103	10	557	10	1,623	13	14.2	50.3	20.8	22.5	9.2
United States	–2,961	–0.1	468	40	888	71	19,473	240	599.1	2,372.2	25.9	909.5	9.5
Uruguay	–401	–4.4	118	6	414	24	2,278	1	9.5	0.5	0.3	0.1	0.0
Uzbekistan	–167	–0.6	91	7	343	16	4,800	1	7.9	8.3	2.0	..	..
Venezuela, RB	2,875	0.6	353	26	1,392	25	21,073	67	178.2	562.8	63.8	21.3	2.3
Vietnam	–2,379	–2.5	279	41	837	41	10,500	145	77.4	12.0	3.7	0.7	0.2
West Bank and Gaza	..	..	..	..	..	..	..	..	..	..	..	..	..
Yemen, Rep.	0	0.0	74	6	385	14	1,650	159	22.3	..	..	..	..
Zambia	4,448	0.9	255	11	770	12	4,747	8	33.4	237.1	31.9	..	..
Zimbabwe	3,129	1.4	222	8	661	10	4,440	17	13.7	46.8	12.1	..	..
World	**83,484 s**	**0.1 w**	..	..	..	..	..	..	..	**13,740.8 s**	**10.7 w**	**4,348.9 s**	**3.0 w**
Low income	48,343	0.5	..	..	..	..	..	..	..	2,203.2	7.7	79.0	..
Middle income	42,278	0.1	..	..	..	..	..	..	..	5,703.8	8.5	1,228.0	1.9
Lower middle income	33,970	0.2	..	..	..	..	..	..	..	2,947.4	7.7	633.5	1.7
Upper middle income	8,308	0.1	..	..	..	..	..	..	..	2,756.4	..	594.5	2.1
Low & middle income	90,621	0.2	..	..	..	..	..	..	..	7,907.0	8.3	1,307.0	1.6
East Asia & Pacific	4,939	–0.2	..	..	..	..	..	..	..	1,454.8	..	192.1	1.3
Europe & Central Asia	–1,789	0.0	..	..	..	..	..	..	..	1,610.2	6.9	321.6	1.4
Latin America & Carib.	45,753	0.4	..	..	..	..	..	..	..	2,228.7	11.1	495.8	2.7
Middle East & N. Africa	–747	–0.5	..	..	..	..	..	..	..	345.9	4.2	114.7	1.5
South Asia	–831	–0.2	..	..	..	..	..	..	..	228.6	4.8	20.9	0.5
Sub-Saharan Africa	43,296	0.6	..	..	..	..	..	..	..	2,038.8	8.7	162.0	..
High income	–7,137	–0.1	..	..	..	..	..	..	..	5,833.9	..	3,041.9	6.1
Europe EMU	–6,101	–0.8	..	..	..	..	..	..	..	324.9	13.5	19.5	0.8

a. Negative numbers indicate an increase in forest area. b. Flowering plants only. c. Data may refer to earlier years. They are the most recent reported by the World Conservation Monitoring Centre in 2004. d. Includes Luxembourg.

About the data

Biological diversity is defined in terms of the variability in genes, species, and ecosystems. Faced with mounting threats to biodiversity, the international community has increasingly focused on conserving this diversity. Deforestation is a major cause of loss of biodiversity, and habitat conservation is vital for stemming this loss. Conservation efforts traditionally have focused on protecting areas of high biodiversity.

The estimates of forest area are from the Food and Agriculture Organization's (FAO) Global Forest Resources Assessment, which provides information on forest cover in 2005 and estimates of forest cover in 1990 and 2000. The current survey is the latest global forest assessment and uses a uniform global definition of forest. No breakdown of forest cover between natural forest and plantation is shown in the table because of space limitations. (This breakdown is provided by the FAO only for developing countries.) For this reason the deforestation data in the table may underestimate the rate at which natural forest is disappearing in some countries.

Measures of species richness are among the most straightforward ways to indicate the importance of an area for biodiversity. The number of threatened species is also an important measure of the immediate need for conservation efforts in a geographic area. Global analyses of the status of threatened species have been carried out for few groups of organisms. Only for mammals, birds, and amphibians has the status of virtually all known species been assessed. Threatened species are defined according to the World Conservation Union's (IUCN) classification categories: endangered (in danger of extinction and unlikely to survive if causal factors continue operating), vulnerable (likely to move into the endangered category in the near future if causal factors continue operating), rare (not endangered or vulnerable but at risk), indeterminate (known to be endangered, vulnerable, or rare but not enough information is available to say which), out of danger (formerly included in one of the above categories but now considered relatively secure because appropriate conservation measures are in effect), and insufficiently known (suspected but not definitely known to belong to one of the above categories).

While the number of birds and mammals is fairly well known, it is difficult to make an accurate count of plants. The number of plant species is highly debated. The IUCN's *2004 IUCN Red List of Threatened Plants* provides the most comprehensive list of threatened species on a global scale, the result of more than 20 years' work by botanists from around the world. Only 5 percent of plant species have been evaluated, and 70 percent of these are threatened with extinction. Plant species data should be interpreted with caution since they are not necessarily comparable across countries because of differences in taxonomic concepts and coverage. However, they do identify countries that are major sources of global biodiversity and that show national commitments to habitat protection.

Setting priorities for conserving biodiversity requires a broader set of information than species richness. With the support of the World Bank's Development Research Group and in close collaboration with scientific nongovernmental organizations, the Global Environment Facility (GEF) developed the GEF benefits index for biodiversity, a comprehensive indicator of national biodiversity status, to guide its biodiversity priorities. This indicator incorporates information on individual species range maps available from the IUCN for virtually all mammals (4,612), amphibians (5,327), and endangered birds (1,098); country-level data from the World Resources Institute (WRI) for reptiles and vascular plants; country-level data from FishBase for 27,669 fish species; and the ecological characteristics of 867 terrestial ecoregions of the world from World Wildlife Federation (WWF) International. For each country the biodiversity indicator incorporates the best available and comparable information in four relevant dimensions: represented species, threatened species, represented ecoregions, and threatened ecoregions. To combine these dimensions into one measure, the indicator uses dimensional weights that reflect the consensus of conservation scientists in the GEF, IUCN, WWF International, and other nongovernmental organizations. Each unit of the index represents 0.01 percent of the total global biodiversity value,

The table shows information on protected areas, numbers of certain species, and numbers of those species under threat. The World Conservation Monitoring Centre (WCMC) compiles these data from a variety of sources. Because of differences in definitions and reporting practices, cross-country comparability is limited. Compounding these problems, available data cover different periods.

Nationally protected areas are areas of at least 1,000 hectares that fall into one of five management categories defined by the WCMC:

- Scientific reserves and strict nature reserves with limited public access.
- National parks of national or international significance and not materially affected by human activity.
- Natural monuments and natural landscapes with unique aspects.
- Managed nature reserves and wildlife sanctuaries.
- Protected landscapes (which may include cultural landscapes) and areas managed mainly for the sustainable use of natural systems to ensure long-term protection and maintenance of biological diversity.

Designating land as a protected area does not necessarily mean that protection is in force. For small countries that may only have protected areas smaller than 1,000 hectares, this size limit in the definition will result in an underestimate of the extent and number of protected areas.

The dataset on protected areas is tentative and is being revised. Due to variations in consistency and methodology of collection, the quality of the data are highly variable across countries. Some countries update their information more frequently than others, some may have more accurate data on extent of coverage, and many underreport the number or extent of protected areas.

Definitions

• **Average annual deforestation** refers to the permanent conversion of natural forest area to other uses, including shifting cultivation, permanent agriculture, ranching, settlements, and infrastructure development. Deforested areas do not include areas logged but intended for regeneration or areas degraded by fuelwood gathering, acid precipitation, or forest fires. Negative numbers indicate an increase in forest area. • **Mammals** exclude whales and porpoises. • **Birds** are listed for countries included within their breeding or wintering ranges. • **Higher plants** refer to native vascular plant species. • **Threatened species** are the number of species classified by the IUCN as endangered, vulnerable, rare, indeterminate, out of danger, or insufficiently known. • **GEF benefits index for biodiversity** is a composite index of relative biodiversity potential for each country based on the species represented in each country, their threat status, and the diversity of habitat types in each country. • **Nationally protected areas** are totally or partially protected areas of at least 1,000 hectares that are designated as scientific reserves with limited public access, national parks, natural monuments, nature reserves or wildlife sanctuaries, and protected landscapes. Marine areas, unclassified areas, and litoral (intertidal) areas are not included. The data also do not include sites protected under local or provincial law. Total land area is used to calculate the percentage of total area protected (see table 3.1). • **Marine protected areas** are areas of intertidal or subtidal terrain—and overlying water and associated flora and fauna and historical and cultural features—which have been reserved by law or other effective means to protect part or all of the enclosed environment.

Data sources

Data on deforestation are from the FAO's Global Forest Resources Assessment 2005. Data on species are from the WCMC's electronic files and the IUCN's *2002 IUCN Red List of Threatened Animals* and *1997 IUCN Red List of Threatened Plants*. The GEF benefits index for biodiversity is from Kiran Dev Pandey, Piet Buys, Ken Chomitz, and David Wheeler's, "Biodiversity Conservation Indicators: New Tools for Priority Setting at the Global Environment Facility" (2006). Data on protected areas are from the United Nations Environment Programme and WCMC.

3.5 Freshwater

	Renewable internal freshwater resources[a]		Annual freshwater withdrawals[b]					Water productivity		
									GDP/water use 2000 $ per cu. m	
	Flows billion cu. m 2004	Per capita cu. m 2004	billion cu. m 1987–2002	% of internal resources 1987–2002	% for agriculture 1987–2002	% for industry 1987–2002	% for domestic 1987–2002	Total 1987–2004	Agriculture 1987–2004	Industry 1987–2004
Afghanistan	55	..	23.3	42.3	98	0	2	..	..	..
Albania	27	8,645	1.7	6.4	62	11	27	2.4	1.0	3.7
Algeria	11	348	6.1	54.0	65	13	22	9.4	1.3	38.4
Angola	148	9,555	0.4	0.2	60	17	23	30.8	3.3	130.7
Argentina	276	7,193	29.2	10.6	74	10	17	8.3	0.6	21.6
Armenia	9	2,998	3.0	32.5	66	4	30	0.8	0.3	6.1
Australia	492	24,464	23.9	4.9	75	10	15	17.4	*0.6*	*41.2*
Austria	55	6,729	2.1	3.8	1	64	35	93.6	183.0	40.8
Azerbaijan	8	977	17.3	212.6	68	28	5	0.4	0.1	0.6
Bangladesh	105	754	79.4	75.6	96	1	3	0.6	0.2	25.3
Belarus	37	3,786	2.8	7.5	30	47	23	5.0	1.9	3.7
Belgium	12	1,152	..	..	..	..	..	..	..	..
Benin	10	1,260	0.1	1.3	45	23	32	19.3	15.4	12.1
Bolivia	304	33,692	1.4	0.5	81	7	13	6.1	1.0	22.5
Bosnia and Herzegovina	36	9,080	..	..	..	..	..	..	..	..
Botswana	2	1,357	0.2	8.1	41	18	41	29.9	1.8	77.0
Brazil	5,418	29,460	59.3	1.1	62	18	20	10.5	1.0	12.6
Bulgaria	21	2,706	10.5	50.0	19	78	3	1.3	0.8	0.4
Burkina Faso	13	975	0.8	6.4	86	1	13	3.6	1.3	76.7
Burundi	10	1,382	0.3	2.9	77	6	17	2.5	1.5	9.5
Cambodia	121	8,738	4.1	3.4	98	1	2	1.0	0.3	52.1
Cameroon	273	17,022	1.0	0.4	74	8	18	9.8	5.8	24.8
Canada	2,850	89,134	46.0	1.6	12	69	20	16.4	*2.5*	*7.1*
Central African Republic	141	35,374	0.0	0.0	4	16	80	38.4	517.4	46.8
Chad	15	1,588	0.2	1.5	83	0	17	7.3	*2.9*	..
Chile	884	54,826	12.6	1.4	64	25	11	6.4	0.4	9.1
China	2,812	2,170	630.3	22.4	68	26	7	2.2	0.4	4.0
Hong Kong, China	..	..	..	..	..	..	..	..	..	..
Colombia	2,112	47,022	10.7	0.5	46	4	50	8.1	2.0	56.0
Congo, Dem. Rep.	900	16,114	0.4	0.0	31	17	53	12.1	*23.9*	*15.4*
Congo, Rep.	222	57,173	0.1	0.0	9	22	70	76.0	47.0	233.6
Costa Rica	112	26,428	2.7	2.4	53	17	30	6.2	0.9	9.9
Côte d'Ivoire	77	4,299	0.9	1.2	65	12	24	11.0	3.9	19.2
Croatia	38	8,487	..	..	..	..	..	..	..	..
Cuba	38	3,390	8.2	21.5	69	12	19	..	..	..
Czech Republic	13	1,287	2.6	19.6	2	57	41	22.5	32.1	13.6
Denmark	6	1,110	1.3	21.2	43	25	32	126.8	6.8	112.4
Dominican Republic	21	2,395	3.4	16.1	66	2	32	6.3	1.1	113.3
Ecuador	432	33,129	17.0	3.9	82	5	13	1.0	0.1	6.5
Egypt, Arab Rep.	2	25	68.3	3,794.4	86	6	8	1.6	0.3	8.2
El Salvador	18	2,625	1.3	7.2	59	16	25	10.7	1.6	21.1
Eritrea	3	662	0.3	10.7	97	0	3	2.3	0.3	..
Estonia	13	9,423	0.2	1.2	5	38	57	39.5	31.3	26.5
Ethiopia	122	1,744	5.6	4.6	94	0	6	1.3	0.6	29.2
Finland	107	20,466	2.5	2.3	3	84	14	50.0	60.5	17.6
France	179	2,956	40.0	22.4	10	75	16	34.3	8.8	9.4
Gabon	164	120,382	0.1	0.1	42	8	50	42.1	7.0	274.9
Gambia, The	3	2,030	0.0	1.0	65	12	23	14.1	5.2	15.7
Georgia	58	12,866	3.6	6.2	59	21	20	0.9	0.3	1.0
Germany	107	1,297	47.1	44.0	20	68	12	40.9	2.3	15.9
Ghana	30	1,399	1.0	3.2	66	10	24	5.5	3.0	14.8
Greece	58	5,246	7.8	13.4	80	3	16	15.6	1.1	97.2
Guatemala	109	8,882	2.0	1.8	80	13	7	10.0	2.8	14.5
Guinea	226	24,561	1.5	0.7	90	2	8	2.2	0.6	39.5
Guinea-Bissau	16	10,392	0.2	1.1	82	5	13	1.1	0.8	3.9
Haiti	13	1,548	1.0	7.6	94	1	5	*3.7*	*1.0*	*56.7*

Freshwater 3.5

	Renewable internal freshwater resources[a]		Annual freshwater withdrawals[b]					Water productivity		
									GDP/water use 2000 $ per cu. m	
	Flows billion cu. m 2004	Per capita cu. m 2004	billion cu. m 1987–2002	% of internal resources 1987–2002	% for agriculture 1987–2002	% for industry 1987–2002	% for domestic 1987–2002	Total 1987–2004	Agriculture 1987–2004	Industry 1987–2004
Honduras	96	13,610	0.9	0.9	80	12	8	7.3	*1.3*	*16.8*
Hungary	6	594	7.6	127.3	32	59	9	6.6	0.8	3.1
India	1,261	1,167	645.8	51.2	87	6	8	0.8	0.2	3.5
Indonesia	2,838	13,043	82.8	2.9	91	1	8	2.2	0.4	145.0
Iran, Islamic Rep.	129	1,918	72.9	56.7	91	2	7	1.6	0.2	26.2
Iraq	35	..	42.7	121.3	92	5	3	0.5	*0.0*	*10.0*
Ireland	49	12,045	1.1	2.3	0	77	23	94.5	..	..
Israel	1	110	2.1	273.3	62	7	31	55.5	..	..
Italy	183	3,170	44.4	24.3	45	37	18	24.7	1.3	17.2
Jamaica	9	3,556	0.4	4.4	49	17	34	20.1	2.5	34.2
Japan	430	3,366	88.4	20.6	63	18	20	53.6	*1.2*	*91.9*
Jordan	1	125	1.0	148.5	75	4	21	9.3	0.3	58.0
Kazakhstan	75	5,030	35.0	46.4	82	17	2	0.7	0.1	1.5
Kenya	21	619	1.6	7.6	64	6	30	8.4	3.8	20.0
Korea, Dem. Rep.	67	2,993	9.0	13.5	55	25	20	..	..	..
Korea, Rep.	65	1,349	18.6	28.7	48	16	36	30.6	2.4	66.7
Kuwait	0	0	0.4	..	52	2	46	84.0	*0.8*	*2,070.0*
Kyrgyz Republic	46	9,121	10.1	21.7	94	3	3	0.1	0.1	1.2
Lao PDR	190	32,878	3.0	1.6	90	6	4	0.6	0.4	2.8
Latvia	17	7,238	0.3	1.8	13	33	53	29.6	8.6	19.0
Lebanon	5	1,356	1.4	28.8	67	1	33	12.9	1.1	368.3
Lesotho	5	2,909	0.1	1.0	20	40	40	18.4	13.9	17.8
Liberia	200	61,717	0.1	0.1	55	18	27	5.4	..	..
Libya	1	105	4.3	711.3	83	3	14	8.7	..	..
Lithuania	16	4,529	0.3	1.7	7	15	78	47.9	41.4	91.3
Macedonia, FYR	5	2,659	..	..	..	..	..	..	..	..
Madagascar	337	18,606	15.0	4.4	96	2	3	0.2	0.1	1.9
Malawi	16	1,280	1.0	6.3	80	5	15	1.7	0.7	5.0
Malaysia	580	23,298	9.0	1.6	62	21	17	10.5	1.5	24.2
Mali	60	4,572	6.6	10.9	90	1	9	0.4	0.2	11.8
Mauritania	0	134	1.7	425.0	88	3	9	0.7	0.1	7.9
Mauritius	3	2,229	0.6	22.2	..	..	30	8.1	..	..
Mexico	409	3,940	78.2	19.1	77	6	17	7.5	0.4	33.2
Moldova	1	237	2.3	231.0	33	58	10	0.6	0.5	0.2
Mongolia	35	13,839	0.4	1.3	52	27	21	2.3	0.9	2.1
Morocco	29	972	12.6	43.4	87	3	10	2.9	0.6	31.9
Mozambique	100	5,164	0.6	0.6	87	2	11	7.3	2.0	120.3
Myanmar	881	17,611	33.2	3.8	98	1	1	..	..	..
Namibia	6	3,066	0.3	4.9	71	5	24	12.4	1.6	69.7
Nepal	198	7,454	10.2	5.1	97	1	3	0.6	0.2	19.0
Netherlands	11	676	7.9	72.2	34	60	6	47.6	3.3	18.5
New Zealand	327	80,522	2.1	0.6	42	10	48	26.7	*5.2*	*66.0*
Nicaragua	190	35,293	1.3	0.7	83	2	15	3.1	0.7	34.4
Niger	4	259	2.2	62.3	95	1	4	0.9	*0.4*	*33.7*
Nigeria	221	1,717	8.0	3.6	69	10	21	5.5	2.3	20.7
Norway	382	83,205	2.2	0.6	11	67	23	79.2	14.5	43.6
Oman	1	389	1.4	138.1	90	2	7	16.0	0.3	388.6
Pakistan	52	345	169.4	323.3	96	2	2	0.5	0.1	4.7
Panama	147	46,426	0.8	0.6	28	5	67	14.6	3.8	46.7
Papua New Guinea	801	138,775	0.1	0.0	..	..	..	..	..	..
Paraguay	94	15,622	0.5	0.5	71	8	20	15.8	4.9	46.5
Peru	1,616	58,631	20.1	1.2	82	10	8	2.8	0.3	7.7
Philippines	479	5,869	28.5	6.0	74	9	17	2.8	0.6	9.2
Poland	54	1,404	16.2	30.2	8	79	13	10.5	4.2	3.7
Portugal	38	3,618	11.3	29.6	78	12	10	9.7	0.4	20.2
Puerto Rico	7	1,823	..	..	..	..	..	..	..	..

3.5 Freshwater

	Renewable internal freshwater resources[a]		Annual freshwater withdrawals[b]					Water productivity		
	Flows billion cu. m 2004	Per capita cu. m 2004	billion cu. m 1987–2002	% of internal resources 1987–2002	% for agriculture 1987–2002	% for industry 1987–2002	% for domestic 1987–2002	Total 1987–2004	GDP/water use 2000 $ per cu. m Agriculture 1987–2004	Industry 1987–2004
Romania	42	1,951	23.2	54.8	57	34	9	1.8	0.4	1.7
Russian Federation	4,313	29,981	76.7	1.8	18	64	19	3.7	1.3	2.0
Rwanda	10	1,070	0.2	1.6	68	8	24	14.1	9.1	35.9
Saudi Arabia	2	100	17.3	721.7	89	1	10	11.0	0.6	482.0
Senegal	26	2,266	2.2	8.6	93	3	4	2.1	0.3	17.8
Serbia and Montenegro	44	5,401	..	..	..	..	..	..	..	..
Sierra Leone	160	29,982	0.4	0.2	92	3	5	1.9	..	..
Singapore	1	142	..	..	..	..	..	..	..	..
Slovak Republic	13	2,341	..	..	..	..	..	..	..	..
Slovenia	19	9,349	..	..	..	..	..	..	..	..
Somalia	6	753	3.3	54.8	100	0	0	..	..	..
South Africa	45	984	12.5	27.9	63	6	31	11.3	0.5	53.0
Spain	111	2,605	35.6	32.0	68	19	13	17.3	0.9	24.9
Sri Lanka	50	2,575	12.6	25.2	95	3	2	1.3	0.2	12.7
Sudan	30	845	37.3	124.4	97	1	3	0.4	*0.1*	*11.2*
Swaziland	3	2,357	1.0	39.5	97	1	2	1.4	0.1	37.6
Sweden	171	19,017	3.0	1.7	9	54	37	83.4	16.7	39.4
Switzerland	40	5,467	2.6	6.4	2	74	24	97.1	*67.5*	*36.5*
Syrian Arab Republic	7	377	20.0	285.0	95	2	3	1.0	0.3	13.9
Tajikistan	66	10,311	12.0	18.0	92	5	4	0.1	*0.0*	*0.8*
Tanzania	84	2,232	5.2	6.2	89	1	10	2.0	0.9	61.7
Thailand	210	3,297	87.1	41.5	95	3	3	1.5	0.1	26.2
Togo	12	1,920	0.2	1.5	45	2	53	8.2	6.5	63.8
Trinidad and Tobago	4	2,951	0.3	8.1	7	26	68	28.1	6.4	55.5
Tunisia	4	422	2.6	62.9	82	4	14	7.9	1.0	55.2
Turkey	227	3,165	37.5	16.5	74	11	15	5.3	1.0	10.4
Turkmenistan	1	285	24.7	1,812.5	98	1	2	..	..	..
Uganda	39	1,402	0.3	0.8	40	17	43	22.4	18.3	25.2
Ukraine	53	1,119	37.5	70.7	53	35	12	1.0	0.3	0.9
United Arab Emirates	0	35	2.3	1,533.3	68	9	23	34.5	1.5	197.8
United Kingdom	145	2,422	9.5	6.6	3	75	22	157.0	49.0	49.2
United States	2,800	9,535	479.3	17.1	41	46	13	20.9	*0.5*	*9.6*
Uruguay	59	17,154	3.2	5.3	96	1	3	5.6	0.4	115.2
Uzbekistan	16	623	58.3	357.0	93	2	5	0.3	0.1	2.5
Venezuela, RB	722	27,652	8.4	1.2	47	7	46	13.2	1.2	83.8
Vietnam	367	4,461	71.4	19.5	68	24	8	0.5	0.2	0.8
West Bank and Gaza	0	13	..	..	..	..	..	..	..	..
Yemen, Rep.	4	202	6.6	161.7	95	1	4	1.5	0.2	116.0
Zambia	80	6,987	1.7	2.2	76	8	17	2.0	0.5	6.7
Zimbabwe	12	948	4.2	34.3	79	7	14	1.6	0.3	4.3
World	**43,507 s**	**6,872 w**	**3,807.4 s**	**9.0 w**	**70 w**	**20 w**	**10 w**	**8.6 w**	**1.0 w**	**18.7 w**
Low income	8,095	3,456	1,245.4	15.5	88	5	6	0.8	0.3	7.0
Middle income	25,971	8,611	1,662.3	6.4	71	19	10	3.3	0.6	19.0
Lower middle income	17,807	7,295	1,355.8	7.7	75	17	8	2.5	0.4	17.9
Upper middle income	8,164	14,190	306.4	3.8	53	28	19	7.2	1.4	23.7
Low & middle income	34,066	6,358	2,907.7	8.6	78	13	8	2.3	0.5	14.0
East Asia & Pacific	9,454	5,062	958.9	10.2	74	20	7	2.1	0.5	19.2
Europe & Central Asia	5,255	11,123	383.2	7.5	59	31	10	2.7	1.0	2.9
Latin America & Carib.	13,429	24,619	265.3	2.0	71	10	19	7.6	0.7	26.3
Middle East & N. Africa	228	761	239.8	105.0	89	4	7	2.0	0.3	24.7
South Asia	1,816	1,255	941.1	51.8	90	4	6	0.7	0.2	5.9
Sub-Saharan Africa	3,884	5,353	119.3	3.1	87	3	10	3.1	1.0	*21.8*
High income	9,441	9,703	899.7	10.4	43	43	15	28.2	*2.7*	*33.6*
Europe EMU	910	2,942	199.7	22.3	38	48	15	30.3	5.7	20.3

a. River flows from other countries are not included because of data unreliability. b. Data are for the most recent year available for 1987–2004 (see *Primary data documentation*).

About the data

The data on freshwater resources are based on estimates of runoff into rivers and recharge of groundwater. These estimates are based on different sources and refer to different years, so cross-country comparisons should be made with caution. Because the data are collected intermittently, they may hide significant variations in total renewable water resources from one year to the next. The data also fail to distinguish between seasonal and geographic variations in water availability within countries. Data for small countries and countries in arid and semiarid zones are less reliable than those for larger countries and countries with greater rainfall.

Caution is also needed in comparing data on annual freshwater withdrawals, which are subject to variations in collection and estimation methods. In addition, inflows and outflows are estimated at different times and at different levels of quality and precision, requiring caution in interpreting the data, particularly for water-short countries, notably in the Middle East.

Water productivity is an indication only of the efficiency by which each country uses its water resources. Given the different economic structure of each country, these indicators should be used with proper caution, taking into account the countries' sectoral activities and natural resource endowments.

3.5a

Agriculture uses 70 percent of freshwater globally

Share of annual freshwater withdrawals, most recent year available

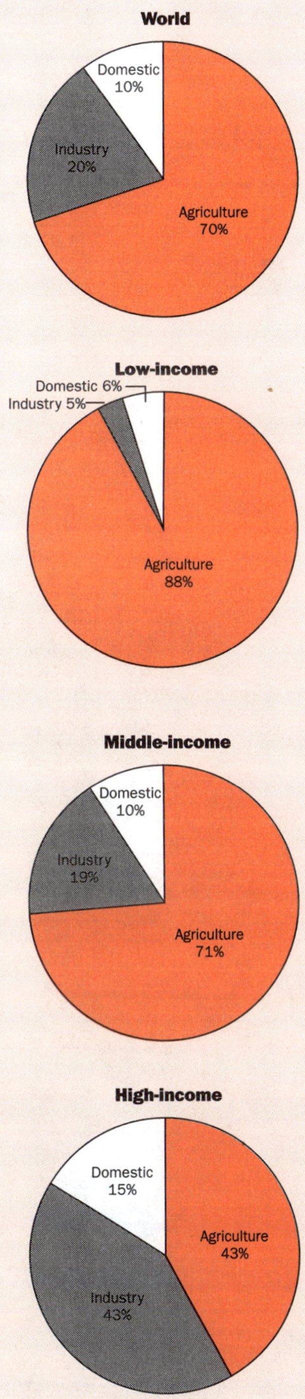

Note: Components may not sum to 100 percent because of rounding.

Source: Table 3.5.

Definitions

• **Renewable internal freshwater resources flows** refer to internal renewable resources (internal river flows and groundwater from rainfall) in the country. • **Renewable internal freshwater resources per capita** are calculated using the World Bank's population estimates (see table 2.1). • **Annual freshwater withdrawals** refer to total water withdrawals, not counting evaporation losses from storage basins. Withdrawals also include water from desalination plants in countries where they are a significant source. Withdrawals can exceed 100 percent of internal renewable resources because river flows from other countries are not included, because extraction from nonrenewable aquifers or desalination plants is considerable, or because there is significant water reuse. Withdrawals for agriculture and industry are total withdrawals for irrigation and livestock production and for direct industrial use (including withdrawals for cooling thermoelectric plants). Withdrawals for domestic uses include drinking water, municipal use or supply, and use for public services, commercial establishments, and homes. • **Water productivity** is calculated as GDP in constant prices divided by annual total water withdrawal. Sectoral water productivity is calculated as annual value added in agriculture or industry divided by water withdrawal in each sector.

Data sources

Data on freshwater resources and withdrawals are compiled by the World Resources Institute from various sources and published in *World Resources 2005* (produced in collaboration with the United Nations Environment Programme, United Nations Development Programme, and World Bank). These data are supplemented by the Food and Agriculture Organization's AQUASTAT data.

3.6 Water pollution

	Emissions of organic water pollutants				Industry shares of emissions of organic water pollutants							
					% of total							
	kilograms per day		kilograms per day per worker		Primary metals	Paper and pulp	Chemicals	Food and beverages	Stone, ceramics, and glass	Textiles	Wood	Other
	1990	2003[a]	1990	2003[a]	2003[a]	2003[a]	2003[a]	2003[a]	2003[a]	2003[a]	2003[a]	2003[a]
Afghanistan	5,864	236	0.16	0.21	..	37.7	17.5	31.1	0.4	13.2	..	..
Albania	34,785	..	0.14	..	..	..	..	..	..	..	..	..
Algeria	106,977	..	0.25	..	..	..	..	..	..	..	..	..
Angola	4,544	..	0.19	..	..	..	..	..	..	..	..	..
Argentina	186,686	149,455	0.20	0.23	4.9	7.2	4.2	71.1	0.0	6.6	1.5	4.3
Armenia	37,900	7,104	0.11	0.28	..	..	0.0	77.6	..	22.4	..	..
Australia	186,110	111,658	0.18	0.18	..	..	5.6	77.1	0.2	5.1	5.3	6.5
Austria	94,121	93,463	0.15	0.14	14.6	17.8	10.9	35.6	0.4	4.5	5.3	10.8
Azerbaijan	53,251	17,511	0.15	0.17	17.6	5.5	15.2	41.6	0.3	12.3	1.1	6.2
Bangladesh	171,087	..	0.17	..	..	..	..	..	..	..	..	..
Belarus	..	..	..	..	..	..	..	..	..	..	..	..
Belgium	117,978	102,460	0.16	0.17	13.7	18.0	12.0	40.4	0.2	6.0	2.0	7.5
Benin	..	..	..	..	..	..	..	..	..	..	..	..
Bolivia	8,404	12,759	0.24	0.25	0.9	20.5	6.6	61.4	0.3	7.1	2.4	0.5
Bosnia and Herzegovina	50,741	..	0.14	..	..	..	..	..	..	..	..	..
Botswana	4,509	5,204	0.19	0.18	2.0	7.2	5.1	55.7	0.3	25.8	1.5	2.2
Brazil	780,395	..	0.19	..	..	..	..	..	..	..	..	..
Bulgaria	149,381	97,137	0.11	0.17	8.5	9.9	7.0	45.1	0.2	21.7	2.1	5.3
Burkina Faso	..	2,598	..	0.22	3.5	1.1	5.4	73.8	0.1	4.1	10.1	1.7
Burundi	1,570	..	0.24	..	..	..	..	..	..	..	..	..
Cambodia	11,823	..	0.14	..	..	..	..	..	..	..	..	..
Cameroon	13,989	10,714	0.28	0.20	3.1	6.3	28.3	52.7	0.0	3.6	5.6	0.2
Canada	321,471	313,431	0.17	0.16	9.7	22.8	8.3	38.5	0.1	6.1	5.2	9.1
Central African Republic	998	..	0.18	..	..	..	..	..	..	..	..	..
Chad	..	..	..	..	..	..	..	..	..	..	..	..
Chile	66,783	72,850	0.22	0.24	6.9	11.3	8.9	62.7	0.1	5.0	2.6	2.3
China	7,038,131	6,088,663	0.14	0.14	20.4	10.9	14.8	28.1	0.5	15.5	0.9	8.8
Hong Kong, China	86,124	38,698	0.12	0.21	1.4	41.6	3.4	34.5	-	14.4	0.2	4.3
Colombia	93,253	93,879	0.19	0.21	3.1	16.2	9.7	53.2	0.2	14.2	1.0	2.2
Congo, Dem. Rep.	..	..	..	..	..	..	..	..	..	..	..	..
Congo, Rep.	2,456	..	0.32	..	..	..	..	..	..	..	..	..
Costa Rica	27,249	31,236	0.20	0.22	1.6	10.0	8.2	65.7	0.1	10.2	1.3	2.7
Côte d'Ivoire	7,874	..	0.22	..	..	..	..	..	..	..	..	..
Croatia	80,034	42,734	0.15	0.17	6.7	15.3	7.6	47.5	0.2	12.8	3.6	6.1
Cuba	172,973	..	0.25	..	..	..	..	..	..	..	..	..
Czech Republic	205,102	158,462	0.13	0.14	15.6	7.0	7.9	43.6	0.3	10.4	3.9	11.2
Denmark	91,871	83,591	0.18	0.17	4.4	29.1	7.9	44.2	0.2	2.2	3.5	8.3
Dominican Republic	47,900	..	0.36	..	..	..	..	..	..	..	..	..
Ecuador	25,567	41,171	0.23	0.28	2.2	10.1	5.6	73.7	0.1	5.6	1.4	1.0
Egypt, Arab Rep.	211,531	186,059	0.20	0.20	10.8	8.2	9.0	50.7	0.3	17.7	0.6	2.5
El Salvador	7,663	22,760	0.22	0.18	2.1	10.2	8.1	43.5	0.1	34.1	0.5	1.2
Eritrea	..	..	..	..	..	..	..	..	..	..	..	..
Estonia	..	..	..	..	..	..	..	..	..	..	..	..
Ethiopia	18,593	22,085	0.23	0.23	2.3	11.0	5.5	61.0	0.3	17.3	2.0	0.4
Finland	79,514	68,819	0.18	0.16	9.0	39.6	6.6	27.7	0.2	2.6	4.0	10.1
France	653,455	281,747	0.15	0.10	14.7	31.0	23.0	..	0.3	9.0	2.8	19.1
Gabon	2,018	..	0.25	..	..	..	..	..	..	..	..	..
Gambia, The	832	..	0.34	..	..	..	..	..	..	..	..	..
Georgia	..	..	..	..	..	..	..	..	..	..	..	..
Germany	835,019	1,020,145	0.12	0.14	9.0	20.9	11.3	38.7	0.2	2.8	2.5	14.5
Ghana	13,667	..	0.17	..	..	..	..	..	..	..	..	..
Greece	63,479	57,178	0.18	0.20	6.3	11.8	9.1	54.0	0.2	13.2	1.5	3.7
Guatemala	16,070	19,253	0.27	0.28	4.9	7.2	6.1	72.8	0.1	6.9	0.8	0.9
Guinea	..	..	..	..	..	..	..	..	..	..	..	..
Guinea-Bissau	..	..	..	..	..	..	..	..	..	..	..	..
Haiti	5,427	..	0.20	..	..	..	..	..	..	..	..	..

Water pollution 3.6

	Emissions of organic water pollutants				Industry shares of emissions of organic water pollutants							
					% of total							
	kilograms per day		kilograms per day per worker		Primary metals	Paper and pulp	Chemicals	Food and beverages	Stone, ceramics, and glass	Textiles	Wood	Other
	1990	2003[a]	1990	2003[a]	2003[a]	2003[a]	2003[a]	2003[a]	2003[a]	2003[a]	2003[a]	2003[a]
Honduras	17,824	..	0.23	..	..	..	..	..	..	..	..	..
Hungary	178,002	155,386	0.16	0.16	7.9	11.9	8.4	47.1	0.2	13.8	2.3	8.2
India	1,410,617	1,515,683	0.20	0.20	12.4	7.2	9.4	53.9	0.2	12.7	0.4	3.6
Indonesia	495,594	720,326	0.19	0.18	2.6	8.1	9.3	51.5		21.0	5.1	2.2
Iran, Islamic Rep.	102,689	141,982	0.16	0.16	17.2	7.1	10.8	43.8	0.6	12.5	0.8	7.0
Iraq	20,352	..	0.16	..	..	..	..	..	..	..	..	..
Ireland	34,610	49,144	0.18	0.15	1.3	14.2	11.4	56.4	0.2	3.1	1.6	11.7
Israel	46,359	51,740	0.16	0.16	3.4	21.5	10.6	45.6	0.1	6.6	1.5	10.5
Italy	358,084	504,492	0.13	0.12	9.4	16.8	10.8	29.9	0.3	15.9	3.7	13.1
Jamaica	18,736	..	0.29	..	..	..	..	..	..	..	..	..
Japan	1,556,648	1,279,287	0.14	0.15	7.0	21.9	9.0	43.2	0.2	5.0	1.6	12.0
Jordan	8,325	18,516	0.19	0.19	4.8	17.2	12.0	52.6	0.5	9.7	0.5	2.5
Kazakhstan	..	..	..	..	..	..	..	..	..	..	..	..
Kenya	42,588	54,246	0.23	0.25	..	11.8	5.7	69.0	0.1	9.9	1.8	1.5
Korea, Dem. Rep.	..	..	..	..	..	..	..	..	..	..	..	..
Korea, Rep.	369,193	309,517	0.12	0.12	11.4	18.2	12.9	26.0	0.2	14.4	1.4	15.4
Kuwait	9,052	11,897	0.16	0.17	2.1	16.6	11.1	50.2	0.4	11.6	2.8	5.0
Kyrgyz Republic	30,885	20,801	0.12	0.21	8.5	5.9	3.3	65.6	0.3	11.6	1.0	3.6
Lao PDR	..	..	..	..	..	..	..	..	..	..	..	..
Latvia	39,887	29,166	0.12	0.19	4.1	14.6	3.2	55.4	0.1	9.8	9.4	3.2
Lebanon	..	14,899	..	0.19	0.9	15.6	4.0	60.7	0.5	10.2	4.6	3.3
Lesotho	2,958	3,123	0.16	0.16	1.2	4.0	0.7	39.7	0.1	51.3	0.6	2.2
Liberia	615	..	0.30	..	..	..	..	..	..	..	..	..
Libya	..	..	..	..	..	..	..	..	..	..	..	..
Lithuania	53,818	37,477	0.13	0.18	1.0	10.3	5.1	54.8	0.2	18.3	6.1	4.0
Macedonia, FYR	32,419	..	0.18	..	..	..	..	..	..	..	..	..
Madagascar	11,043	..	0.27	..	..	..	..	..	..	..	..	..
Malawi	10,024	11,805	0.29	0.29	-	16.0	3.7	70.0	-	7.8	1.7	0.5
Malaysia	104,728	170,662	0.13	0.12	7.9	14.4	15.1	34.4	0.2	8.0	7.1	12.8
Mali	..	..	..	..	..	..	..	..	..	..	..	..
Mauritania	..	..	..	..	..	..	..	..	..	..	..	..
Mauritius	17,813	17,700	0.16	0.15	0.9	6.6	2.6	32.8	0.1	55.4	0.6	0.9
Mexico	174,266	296,093	0.18	0.20	7.8	12.5	10.4	55.6	0.2	7.5	0.9	4.9
Moldova	55,887	21,409	0.15	0.45	..	2.0	..	98.0	..	..	..	..
Mongolia	10,160	..	0.18	..	..	..	..	..	..	..	..	..
Morocco	41,710	69,060	0.14	0.16	2.2	8.6	6.4	42.1	0.3	36.3	1.2	2.7
Mozambique	20,414	10,230	0.27	0.31	1.1	7.1	2.7	81.2	0.1	5.8	1.4	0.3
Myanmar	7,663	6,159	0.17	0.18	56.5	4.6	13.2	14.9	0.4	2.9	1.7	5.6
Namibia	7,350	..	0.35	..	..	..	..	..	..	..	..	..
Nepal	20,894	26,908	0.13	0.16	3.5	9.7	5.9	55.1	1.4	21.7	1.7	0.8
Netherlands	136,686	124,182	0.18	0.18	7.3	26.7	11.3	43.0	0.2	2.3	1.2	7.8
New Zealand	50,243	46,099	0.22	0.22	3.2	21.7	5.2	57.3	0.1	4.6	3.6	4.1
Nicaragua	10,465	..	0.27	..	..	..	..	..	..	..	..	..
Niger	..	..	..	..	..	..	..	..	..	..	..	..
Nigeria	52,350	..	0.23	..	..	..	..	..	..	..	..	..
Norway	54,996	51,693	0.20	0.19	9.0	31.3	4.7	42.8	0.1	1.4	3.1	7.4
Oman	360	5,739	0.11	0.17	7.3	13.4	10.2	54.0	0.9	8.4	2.4	3.2
Pakistan	104,095	..	0.18	..	..	..	..	..	..	..	..	..
Panama	9,700	11,692	0.26	0.32	1.5	13.2	4.6	76.6	0.2	3.2	0.4	..
Papua New Guinea	5,729	..	0.25	..	..	..	..	..	..	..	..	..
Paraguay	3,250	..	0.28	..	..	..	..	..	..	..	..	..
Peru	56,144	..	0.20	..	..	..	..	..	..	..	..	..
Philippines	228,301	..	0.21	..	..	..	..	..	..	..	..	..
Poland	428,894	416,934	0.14	0.16	12.8	11.4	6.3	45.4	0.4	12.7	3.4	7.4
Portugal	147,873	133,570	0.15	0.14	3.9	15.8	4.9	36.2	0.4	26.5	5.5	6.7
Puerto Rico	19,026	15,367	0.15	0.14	1.9	14.9	21.9	34.4	0.2	15.5	1.4	9.7

3.6 Water pollution

	Emissions of organic water pollutants				Industry shares of emissions of organic water pollutants							
					% of total							
	kilograms per day		kilograms per day per worker		Primary metals	Paper and pulp	Chemicals	Food and beverages	Stone, ceramics, and glass	Textiles	Wood	Other
	1990	2003[a]	1990	2003[a]	2003[a]	2003[a]	2003[a]	2003[a]	2003[a]	2003[a]	2003[a]	2003[a]
Romania	413,864	38,395	0.12	0.07	..	17.6	..	5.1	..	28.7	12.5	36.0
Russian Federation	1,911,348	1,518,704	0.13	0.16	18.1	7.7	8.6	48.0	0.4	5.9	2.5	8.6
Rwanda	1,624	..	0.25	..	..	..	..	..	..	..	..	..
Saudi Arabia	18,476	..	0.15	..	..	..	..	..	..	..	..	..
Senegal	10,309	6,603	0.32	0.30	5.8	8.4	10.7	70.1	0.1	4.2	0.4	-
Serbia and Montenegro	137,795	98,696	0.15	0.16	9.9	11.8	8.2	47.4	0.3	12.7	2.2	7.3
Sierra Leone	4,170	..	0.32	..	..	..	..	..	..	..	..	..
Singapore	32,364	33,644	0.09	0.09	1.3	25.9	16.2	22.8	0.1	4.1	1.8	27.7
Slovak Republic	77,174	45,011	0.13	0.14	4.2	15.0	8.4	44.2	0.4	15.0	1.7	11.0
Slovenia	55,640	38,390	0.16	0.16	33.7	14.7	8.3	23.7	0.2	10.8	2.0	6.4
Somalia	6,177	..	0.38	..	..	..	..	..	..	..	..	..
South Africa	261,618	221,256	0.17	0.18	15.1	18.0	10.5	36.0	0.1	10.9	3.9	5.3
Spain	320,262	374,589	0.17	0.15	6.7	19.8	8.9	42.5	0.3	9.3	4.0	8.3
Sri Lanka	53,024	88,943	0.19	0.18	0.5	7.0	6.4	52.3	0.2	31.2	1.1	1.1
Sudan	..	..	..	..	..	..	..	..	..	..	..	..
Swaziland	6,586	..	0.33	..	..	..	..	..	..	..	..	..
Sweden	109,582	103,913	0.15	0.14	11.3	35.0	7.8	26.6	0.1	1.3	3.0	14.8
Switzerland	146,038	..	0.16	..	..	..	..	..	..	..	..	..
Syrian Arab Republic	21,702	15,115	0.22	0.20	4.1	1.5	3.9	69.8	0.9	19.4	0.2	-
Tajikistan	..	..	..	..	..	..	..	..	..	..	..	..
Tanzania	31,125	35,155	0.24	0.25	1.5	9.4	2.7	69.3	0.1	14.0	1.5	1.3
Thailand	291,552	..	0.17	..	..	..	..	..	..	..	..	..
Togo	..	..	..	..	..	..	..	..	..	..	..	..
Trinidad and Tobago	9,951	7,945	0.26	0.23	6.5	18.8	11.9	55.3	0.2	3.8	2.0	1.3
Tunisia	44,551	54,191	0.18	0.14	2.8	6.5	6.7	35.6	0.4	41.9	1.9	4.1
Turkey	177,264	188,199	0.18	0.16	11.5	7.3	7.7	42.6	0.3	24.4	1.4	4.6
Turkmenistan	..	..	..	..	..	..	..	..	..	..	..	..
Uganda	16,728	..	0.30	..	..	..	..	..	..	..	..	..
Ukraine	692,373	445,758	0.14	0.18	28.1	4.2	7.0	46.8	0.4	5.4	1.1	6.8
United Arab Emirates	5,638	..	0.14	..	..	..	..	..	..	..	..	..
United Kingdom	739,562	615,410	0.15	0.15	6.7	28.5	11.4	33.8	0.2	5.5	2.5	11.3
United States	2,565,226	1,897,480	0.15	0.13	9.8	10.9	13.8	40.3	0.2	6.3	4.1	14.5
Uruguay	38,661	16,362	0.23	0.28	1.2	7.2	6.7	75.9	0.1	8.2	0.6	..
Uzbekistan	..	..	..	..	..	..	..	..	..	..	..	..
Venezuela, RB	96,495	94,175	0.21	0.21	13.7	10.4	10.2	53.1	0.3	7.5	1.5	3.1
Vietnam	..	..	..	..	..	..	..	..	..	..	..	..
West Bank and Gaza	..	..	..	..	..	..	..	..	..	..	..	..
Yemen, Rep.	6,873	13,082	0.27	0.22	-	5.1	7.6	76.0	0.5	7.6	1.3	1.7
Zambia	15,880	..	0.23	..	..	..	..	..	..	..	..	..
Zimbabwe	37,149	..	0.20	..	..	..	..	..	..	..	..	..

Note: Industry shares may not sum to 100 percent because data may be for different years.
a. Data refer to any year from 1993 to 2003.

About the data

Emissions of organic pollutants from industrial activities are a major cause of degradation of water quality. Water quality and pollution levels are generally measured in terms of concentration or load—the rate of occurrence of a substance in an aqueous solution. Polluting substances include organic matter, metals, minerals, sediment, bacteria, and toxic chemicals. This table focuses on organic water pollution resulting from industrial activities. Because water pollution tends to be sensitive to local conditions, the national-level data in the table may not reflect the quality of water in specific locations.

The data in the table come from an international study of industrial emissions that may be the first to include data from developing countries (Hettige, Mani, and Wheeler 1998). These data were updated through 2003 by the World Bank's Development Research Group. Unlike estimates from earlier studies based on engineering or economic models, these estimates are based on actual measurements of plant-level water pollution. The focus is on organic water pollution caused by organic waste, measured in terms of biochemical oxygen demand (BOD), because the data for this indicator are the most plentiful and the most reliable for cross-country comparisons of emissions. BOD measures the strength of an organic waste by the amount of oxygen consumed in breaking it down. A sewage overload in natural waters exhausts the water's dissolved oxygen content. Wastewater treatment, by contrast, reduces BOD.

Data on water pollution are more readily available than other emissions data because most industrial pollution control programs start by regulating emissions of organic water pollutants. Such data are fairly reliable because sampling techniques for measuring water pollution are more widely understood and much less expensive than those for air pollution.

Hettige, Mani, and Wheeler (1998) used plant- and sector-level information on emissions and employment from 13 national environmental protection agencies and sector-level information on output and employment from the United Nations Industrial Development Organization (UNIDO). Their econometric analysis found that the ratio of BOD to employment in each industrial sector is about the same across countries. This finding allowed the authors to estimate BOD loads across countries and over time. The estimated BOD intensities per unit of employment were multiplied by sectoral employment numbers from UNIDO's industry database for 1980–98. The estimates of sectoral emissions were then totaled to get daily emissions of organic water pollutants in kilograms per day for each country and year. The data in the table were derived by updating these estimates through 2003.

Definitions

• **Emissions of organic water pollutants** are measured in terms of biochemical oxygen demand, which refers to the amount of oxygen that bacteria in water will consume in breaking down waste. This is a standard water treatment test for the presence of organic pollutants. Emissions per worker are total emissions divided by the number of industrial workers. • **Industry shares of emissions of organic water pollutants** refer to emissions from manufacturing activities as defined by two-digit divisions of the International Standard Industrial Classification (ISIC) revision 2: primary metals (ISIC division 37); paper and pulp (34); chemicals (35); food and beverages (31); stone, ceramics, and glass (36); textiles (32); wood (33); and other (38 and 39).

3.6a

Emission of organic water pollutants declined in most countries from 1990 to 2003

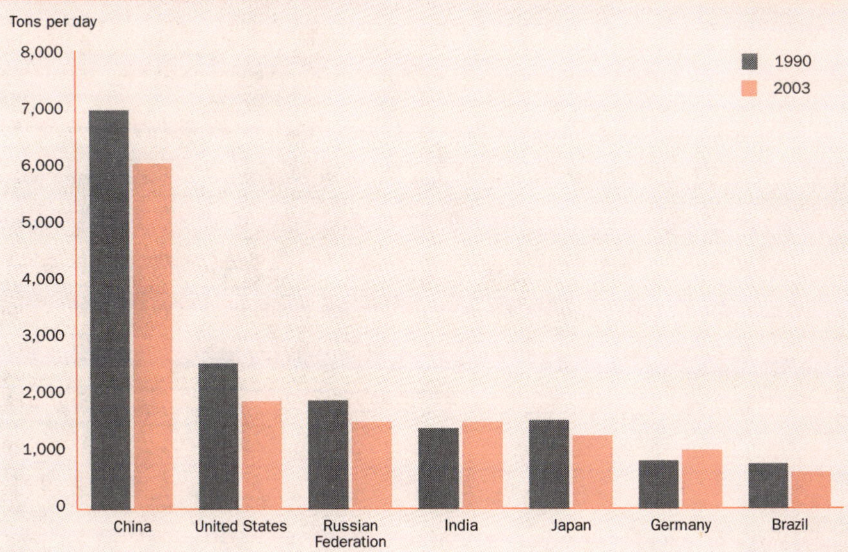

Source: Table 3.6.

Data sources

Data on water pollution come from a 1998 study by Hemamala Hettige, Muthukumara Mani, and David Wheeler, "Industrial Pollution in Economic Development: Kuznets Revisited" (available at www.worldbank.org/nipr). The data were updated through 2003 by the World Bank's Development Research Group using the same methodology as the initial study. Sectoral employment numbers are from UNIDO's industry database.

3.7 Energy production and use

	Total energy production		Energy use								Net energy imports[a]	
	thousand metric tons of oil equivalent		Total thousand metric tons of oil equivalent		Combustible renewables and waste % of total		average annual % growth	Per capita kilograms of oil equivalent		average annual % growth	% of energy use	
	1990	2003	1990	2003	1990	2003	1990–2003	1990	2003	1990–2003	1990	2003
Afghanistan	..	..	..	..	..	..	..	..	..	..	..	..
Albania	2,449	899	2,662	2,084	13.6	6.8	–1.9	809	674	–1.4	8	57
Algeria	104,439	163,271	23,858	32,998	0.1	0.2	2.5	943	1,036	0.7	–338	–395
Angola	28,652	50,730	6,280	9,115	68.8	66.4	2.9	596	606	0.1	–356	–457
Argentina	48,456	84,318	46,110	59,851	3.7	5.3	2.0	1,415	1,575	0.8	–5	–41
Armenia	*263*	692	*4,298*	2,004	*0.0*	0.1	..	*1,246*	660	..	*94*	65
Australia	157,712	253,534	87,536	112,645	4.5	4.4	1.9	5,130	5,668	0.8	–80	–125
Austria	8,104	10,025	25,026	33,183	9.9	11.1	2.2	3,246	4,086	1.8	68	70
Azerbaijan	*18,150*	19,826	*16,675*	12,290	*0.0*	0.0	..	*2,259*	1,493	..	*–9*	–61
Bangladesh	10,758	17,532	12,826	21,682	53.5	36.9	4.0	123	159	1.9	16	19
Belarus	*4,103*	3,497	*39,703*	25,797	*1.5*	4.2	..	*3,886*	2,613	..	*90*	86
Belgium	12,481	13,381	49,109	59,157	1.4	2.0	1.4	4,927	5,701	1.1	75	77
Benin	1,774	1,584	1,678	2,310	93.2	68.6	2.5	324	292	–0.8	–6	31
Bolivia	4,923	7,728	2,774	4,451	27.2	16.2	3.6	416	504	1.5	–77	–74
Bosnia and Herzegovina	*3,642*	3,109	*4,474*	4,453	*3.6*	4.2	..	*1,130*	1,137	..	*19*	30
Botswana	..	..	..	..	..	..	..	..	..	..	..	..
Brazil	97,554	171,139	133,469	193,245	30.8	25.9	2.9	893	1,065	1.4	27	11
Bulgaria	9,613	10,062	28,820	19,510	0.6	3.6	–3.0	3,306	2,494	–2.2	67	48
Burkina Faso	..	..	..	..	..	..	..	..	..	..	..	..
Burundi	..	..	..	..	..	..	..	..	..	..	..	..
Cambodia	..	..	..	..	..	..	..	..	..	..	..	..
Cameroon	12,090	12,135	5,032	6,754	75.9	78.8	2.3	432	429	–0.1	–140	–80
Canada	273,695	385,291	209,104	260,641	3.9	4.5	1.7	7,524	8,240	0.7	–31	–48
Central African Republic	..	..	..	..	..	..	..	..	..	..	..	..
Chad	..	..	..	..	..	..	..	..	..	..	..	..
Chile	7,638	8,336	14,064	26,268	19.0	15.4	4.8	1,067	1,647	3.3	46	68
China	902,689	1,380,786	879,923	1,409,377	22.8	15.5	3.6	775	1,094	2.7	–3	2
Hong Kong, China	43	48	10,662	16,515	0.5	0.3	3.4	1,869	2,428	2.0	100	100
Colombia	48,479	74,363	25,048	28,371	23.2	17.4	1.0	716	642	–0.9	–94	–162
Congo, Dem. Rep.	12,019	16,547	11,903	15,884	84.0	93.5	2.2	315	293	–0.6	–1	–4
Congo, Rep.	9,005	12,112	1,056	1,028	69.4	62.1	–0.2	425	273	–3.4	–753	–1,078
Costa Rica	1,032	1,626	2,025	3,675	36.6	8.2	4.6	658	880	2.2	49	56
Côte d'Ivoire	3,382	6,690	4,408	6,577	72.1	65.7	3.1	348	374	0.5	23	–2
Croatia	*4,346*	3,745	*6,714*	8,779	*3.8*	4.3	..	*1,502*	1,976	..	*35*	57
Cuba	6,271	6,661	16,535	11,216	33.7	22.3	–3.0	1,569	1,000	–3.5	62	41
Czech Republic	38,474	33,002	47,379	44,117	*1.2*	2.7	–0.6	4,572	4,324	–0.4	19	25
Denmark	9,996	28,498	17,847	20,755	6.4	10.7	1.2	3,472	3,853	0.8	44	–37
Dominican Republic	1,031	1,546	4,139	7,971	24.2	18.1	5.0	584	923	3.5	75	81
Ecuador	16,474	23,617	6,128	9,105	13.5	7.1	3.1	597	708	1.3	–169	–159
Egypt, Arab Rep.	54,869	60,998	31,895	52,356	3.3	2.6	3.8	573	735	1.9	–72	–17
El Salvador	1,722	2,390	2,535	4,487	48.2	32.1	4.4	496	675	2.4	32	47
Eritrea	..	..	..	..	..	..	..	..	..	..	..	..
Estonia	*4,118*	3,661	*6,271*	4,915	*2.9*	10.6	..	*4,091*	3,631	..	*34*	26
Ethiopia	14,158	18,903	15,151	20,509	92.9	91.2	2.3	296	299	0.1	7	8
Finland	12,081	15,976	29,171	37,554	15.6	19.5	1.9	5,851	7,204	1.6	59	57
France	111,445	136,003	227,282	271,287	4.9	4.4	1.4	4,006	4,519	0.9	51	50
Gabon	14,630	12,418	1,243	1,685	59.8	58.8	2.3	1,298	1,256	–0.3	–1,077	–637
Gambia, The	..	..	..	..	..	..	..	..	..	..	..	..
Georgia	*1,470*	1,376	*8,757*	2,727	*7.7*	23.7	..	*1,642*	597	..	*83*	50
Germany	186,159	134,520	356,221	347,118	1.4	2.8	–0.2	4,485	4,205	–0.5	48	61
Ghana	4,392	5,991	5,337	8,493	73.1	66.6	3.6	345	400	1.2	18	29
Greece	9,200	9,915	22,181	29,887	4.0	3.3	2.3	2,183	2,709	1.7	59	67
Guatemala	3,390	5,469	4,478	7,293	67.9	53.3	3.8	504	608	1.5	24	25
Guinea	..	..	..	..	..	..	..	..	..	..	..	..
Guinea-Bissau	..	..	..	..	..	..	..	..	..	..	..	..
Haiti	1,253	1,673	1,585	2,237	76.5	73.8	2.7	231	270	1.2	21	25

Energy production and use

	Total energy production		Energy use								Net energy imports[a]	
	thousand metric tons of oil equivalent		Total thousand metric tons of oil equivalent		Combustible renewables and waste % of total		average annual % growth	Per capita kilograms of oil equivalent		average annual % growth	% of energy use	
	1990	2003	1990	2003	1990	2003	1990–2003	1990	2003	1990–2003	1990	2003
Honduras	1,694	1,659	2,416	3,597	62.0	40.9	3.1	496	522	0.4	30	54
Hungary	14,325	10,411	28,553	26,341	1.3	3.1	–0.6	2,755	2,600	–0.4	50	60
India	334,056	453,147	365,377	553,390	48.1	38.2	3.2	430	520	1.5	9	18
Indonesia	162,556	249,955	96,085	161,553	38.8	26.8	4.0	539	753	2.6	–69	–55
Iran, Islamic Rep.	179,738	265,400	68,775	136,443	1.0	0.6	5.3	1,264	2,055	3.7	–161	–95
Iraq	104,933	68,448	19,060	25,750	0.1	0.1	2.3	1,029	..	..	–451	–166
Ireland	3,467	1,896	10,424	15,092	1.0	1.1	2.9	2,973	3,777	1.8	67	87
Israel	433	751	12,112	20,638	0.0	0.0	4.1	2,599	3,086	1.3	96	96
Italy	25,312	27,660	148,031	181,026	0.6	1.7	1.6	2,610	3,140	1.4	83	85
Jamaica	485	468	2,943	4,059	16.2	11.3	2.5	1,231	1,543	1.7	84	88
Japan	75,745	84,643	445,336	517,103	1.3	1.3	1.2	3,605	4,053	0.9	83	84
Jordan	162	285	3,498	5,450	0.1	0.1	3.4	1,103	1,027	–0.6	95	95
Kazakhstan	*89,007*	105,522	*79,661*	49,829	*0.1*	0.2	..	*4,846*	3,342	..	*–12*	–112
Kenya	10,272	13,492	12,479	16,170	78.4	77.5	2.0	533	494	–0.6	18	17
Korea, Dem. Rep.	28,725	18,760	32,874	19,944	2.9	5.1	–3.8	1,670	896	–4.8	13	6
Korea, Rep.	21,908	36,920	92,650	205,300	*0.3*	0.4	6.1	2,161	4,291	5.3	76	82
Kuwait	50,401	120,722	8,110	22,924	0.1	..	8.0	3,816	9,566	7.1	–521	–427
Kyrgyz Republic	*1,818*	1,366	*5,066*	2,661	*0.1*	0.2	..	*1,114*	528	..	*64*	49
Lao PDR	..	..	..	..	..	..	..	..	..	..	..	..
Latvia	*794*	1,977	*4,258*	4,375	13.2	28.9	..	*1,618*	1,881	..	81	55
Lebanon	143	251	2,309	5,956	4.5	2.1	7.3	842	1,700	5.4	94	96
Lesotho	..	..	..	..	..	..	..	..	..	..	..	..
Liberia	..	..	..	..	..	..	..	..	..	..	..	..
Libya	73,173	77,498	11,541	17,963	1.1	0.8	3.4	2,663	3,191	1.4	–534	–331
Lithuania	*4,298*	5,216	*11,017*	8,930	*2.6*	7.6	..	*2,978*	2,585	..	*61*	42
Macedonia, FYR	..	..	..	..	..	..	..	..	..	..	..	..
Madagascar	..	..	..	..	..	..	..	..	..	..	..	..
Malawi	..	..	..	..	..	..	..	..	..	..	..	..
Malaysia	48,753	83,843	22,637	56,655	9.4	4.6	7.1	1,269	2,318	4.6	–115	–48
Mali	..	..	..	..	..	..	..	..	..	..	..	..
Mauritania	..	..	..	..	..	..	..	..	..	..	..	..
Mauritius	..	..	..	..	..	..	..	..	..	..	..	..
Mexico	194,783	242,511	124,341	159,935	5.9	5.1	1.9	1,494	1,564	0.4	–57	–52
Moldova	*58*	61	*6,884*	3,267	*0.5*	1.8	..	*1,575*	772	..	*99*	98
Mongolia	..	..	..	..	..	..	..	..	..	..	..	..
Morocco	773	637	6,725	10,891	4.7	4.1	3.7	281	378	2.3	89	94
Mozambique	6,846	7,990	7,203	8,198	94.4	86.1	1.0	536	430	–1.7	5	3
Myanmar	10,651	18,345	10,683	13,673	84.4	73.5	1.9	262	276	0.4	0	–34
Namibia	*218*	308	*652*	1,262	*16.0*	14.5	..	*449*	635	..	*67*	76
Nepal	5,501	7,795	5,806	8,751	93.4	86.8	3.2	304	336	0.8	5	11
Netherlands	60,447	58,465	66,623	80,829	1.3	2.4	1.5	4,456	4,982	0.9	9	28
New Zealand	12,019	13,171	13,769	17,372	4.0	4.8	1.8	3,993	4,333	0.6	13	24
Nicaragua	1,495	1,805	2,118	3,099	53.3	49.9	2.9	535	588	0.7	29	42
Niger	..	..	..	..	..	..	..	..	..	..	..	..
Nigeria	150,453	214,580	70,905	97,789	79.8	79.4	2.5	783	777	–0.1	–112	–119
Norway	120,304	233,205	21,492	23,347	4.8	6.6	0.6	5,067	5,100	0.1	–460	–899
Oman	38,313	59,824	4,562	12,492	..	..	7.8	2,475	4,975	5.4	–740	–379
Pakistan	34,360	55,494	43,424	69,309	43.2	37.3	3.6	402	467	1.2	21	20
Panama	612	689	1,490	2,607	28.3	17.1	4.3	618	836	2.3	59	74
Papua New Guinea	..	..	..	..	..	..	..	..	..	..	..	..
Paraguay	4,578	6,623	3,083	3,989	72.3	54.4	2.0	731	679	–0.6	–48	–66
Peru	10,596	9,444	9,952	12,003	26.9	18.7	1.4	457	442	–0.3	–6	21
Philippines	13,701	22,503	26,159	42,124	29.2	24.5	3.7	428	525	1.6	48	47
Poland	99,228	79,969	99,847	93,666	2.2	5.6	–0.5	2,619	2,452	–0.5	1	15
Portugal	3,393	4,340	17,746	25,778	14.0	11.0	2.9	1,793	2,469	2.5	81	83
Puerto Rico	..	..	..	..	..	..	..	..	..	..	..	..

3.7 Energy production and use

	Total energy production		Energy use								Net energy imports[a]	
	thousand metric tons of oil equivalent		Total thousand metric tons of oil equivalent		Combustible renewables and waste % of total		average annual % growth	Per capita kilograms of oil equivalent		average annual % growth	% of energy use	
	1990	2003	1990	2003	1990	2003	1990–2003	1990	2003	1990–2003	1990	2003
Romania	40,834	28,927	62,403	39,009	1.0	7.5	–3.6	2,689	1,794	–3.1	35	26
Russian Federation	*1,118,707*	1,106,924	*774,823*	639,717	*1.6*	1.0	..	*5,211*	4,424	..	*–44*	–73
Rwanda	..	..	..	..	..	..	..	..	..	..	..	..
Saudi Arabia	376,342	533,664	64,976	130,783	0.0	0.0	5.4	3,967	5,607	2.7	–479	–308
Senegal	1,362	1,744	2,238	3,193	60.6	53.0	2.7	281	287	0.2	39	45
Serbia and Montenegro	*11,835*	11,474	*15,002*	16,235	*5.0*	4.9	..	*1,435*	1,991	..	*21*	29
Sierra Leone	..	..	..	..	..	..	..	..	..	..	..	..
Singapore	..	140	13,357	22,427	..	..	4.0	4,384	5,359	1.5	..	99
Slovak Republic	5,281	6,401	21,434	18,521	0.8	1.9	–1.1	4,057	3,443	–1.3	75	65
Slovenia	*2,765*	3,285	*5,008*	7,021	1.9	6.7	..	*2,508*	3,518	..	57	53
Somalia	..	..	..	..	..	..	..	..	..	..	..	..
South Africa	114,534	154,480	91,229	118,566	11.4	11.1	2.0	2,592	2,587	0.0	–26	–30
Spain	34,513	32,995	91,073	136,102	4.5	3.5	3.1	2,345	3,240	2.5	62	76
Sri Lanka	4,191	4,294	5,516	8,110	71.0	49.5	3.0	324	421	2.0	24	47
Sudan	8,775	26,974	10,642	16,615	81.7	80.6	3.4	408	477	1.2	18	–62
Swaziland	..	..	..	..	..	..	..	..	..	..	..	..
Sweden	29,754	31,664	47,566	51,532	11.6	17.1	0.6	5,557	5,754	0.3	37	39
Switzerland	9,830	11,999	25,105	27,075	4.1	6.2	0.6	3,740	3,689	–0.1	61	56
Syrian Arab Republic	22,319	33,989	11,677	17,882	0.0	0.0	3.3	909	986	0.6	–91	–90
Tajikistan	*1,553*	1,450	*9,087*	3,187	..	..	..	*1,647*	501	..	*83*	55
Tanzania	9,063	16,027	9,808	17,154	91.0	92.0	4.3	374	465	1.7	8	7
Thailand	26,496	48,255	43,860	88,762	33.4	16.5	5.4	803	1,406	4.3	40	46
Togo	1,203	1,873	1,447	2,598	82.6	71.3	4.5	365	445	1.5	17	28
Trinidad and Tobago	12,612	28,842	6,037	11,096	0.8	0.2	4.7	4,968	8,553	4.2	–109	–160
Tunisia	6,127	6,452	5,536	8,240	18.7	12.7	3.1	679	837	1.6	–11	22
Turkey	25,857	23,635	53,005	78,954	13.6	7.3	3.1	944	1,117	1.3	51	70
Turkmenistan	*48,822*	58,551	*11,314*	17,203	..	..	..	*2,912*	3,662	..	*–332*	–240
Uganda	..	..	..	..	..	..	..	..	..	..	..	..
Ukraine	*110,170*	75,537	*218,376*	132,555	*0.1*	0.2	..	*4,187*	2,772	..	*50*	43
United Arab Emirates	109,446	159,162	19,618	39,226	*0.2*	0.0	5.3	11,065	9,707	–1.0	–458	–306
United Kingdom	207,007	246,083	212,176	231,954	0.3	1.2	0.7	3,686	3,893	0.4	2	–6
United States	1,650,464	1,631,383	1,927,628	2,280,791	3.2	3.0	1.3	7,722	7,843	0.1	14	28
Uruguay	1,149	1,161	2,251	2,519	24.3	17.0	0.9	725	738	0.1	49	54
Uzbekistan	*40,461*	55,735	*44,994*	52,254	..	..	..	*2,092*	2,023	..	*10*	–7
Venezuela, RB	148,854	179,622	43,918	54,227	1.2	1.0	1.6	2,224	2,112	–0.4	–239	–231
Vietnam	24,711	54,528	24,324	44,260	77.7	53.0	4.6	367	544	3.0	–2	–23
West Bank and Gaza	..	..	..	..	..	..	..	..	..	..	..	..
Yemen, Rep.	9,384	21,895	2,543	5,697	3.0	1.4	6.2	210	289	2.5	–269	–284
Zambia	4,923	6,352	5,470	6,688	73.4	80.8	1.6	653	592	–0.8	10	5
Zimbabwe	8,550	8,532	9,384	9,668	50.4	60.5	0.2	888	752	–1.3	9	12
World	8,804,865 t	10,672,009 t	8,615,951 t	10,543,712 t	10.8 w	10.4 w	1.6 w	1,685 w	1,734 w	0.2 w	–2 w	–1 w
Low income	816,190	1,148,130	793,735	1,107,697	54.8	48.9	2.6	464	501	0.6	–3	–4
Middle income	4,378,339	5,234,462	3,499,414	4,114,859	11.6	10.8	1.3	1,349	1,373	0.1	–25	–27
Lower middle income	2,198,061	3,004,295	1,987,670	2,639,085	17.4	14.6	2.2	953	1,090	1.0	–11	–14
Upper middle income	2,181,284	2,230,191	1,511,828	1,474,925	3.8	3.9	–0.2	2,980	2,574	–1.1	–44	–51
Low & middle income	5,190,966	6,370,660	4,284,003	5,204,041	18.9	18.2	1.5	1,008	1,014	0.0	–21	–22
East Asia & Pacific	1,229,840	1,894,782	1,147,328	1,853,770	25.6	17.7	3.7	722	1,007	2.6	–7	–2
Europe & Central Asia	1,890,157	1,659,437	1,736,190	1,318,474	1.9	2.4	–2.1	3,726	2,794	–2.2	–9	–26
Latin America & Carib.	617,444	865,000	459,196	617,665	18.1	15.0	2.3	1,050	1,148	0.7	–34	–40
Middle East & N. Africa	601,905	768,565	194,412	336,326	1.8	1.3	4.2	861	1,144	2.2	–210	–129
South Asia	392,146	542,802	436,601	666,820	48.7	38.8	3.3	394	474	1.4	10	19
Sub-Saharan Africa	489,789	693,529	321,812	435,623	56.7	57.4	2.3	693	681	–0.1	–52	–59
High income	3,654,490	4,351,438	4,363,308	5,377,597	2.9	3.0	1.6	4,842	5,410	0.9	16	19
Europe EMU	466,633	445,236	1,046,458	1,221,275	3.1	3.9	1.2	3,568	3,964	0.8	55	64

a. A negative value indicates that a country is a net exporter.

About the data

In developing countries growth in energy use is closely related to growth in the modern sectors—industry, motorized transport, and urban areas—but energy use also reflects climatic, geographic, and economic factors (such as the relative price of energy). Energy use has been growing rapidly in low- and middle-income countries, but high-income countries still use more than five times as much energy on a per capita basis.

Energy data are compiled by the International Energy Agency (IEA). IEA data for countries that are not members of the Organisation for Economic Co-operation and Development (OECD) are based on national energy data adjusted to conform to annual questionnaires completed by OECD member governments.

Total energy use refers to the use of primary energy before transformation to other end-use fuels (such as electricity and refined petroleum products). It includes energy from combustible renewables and waste—solid biomass and animal products, gas and liquid from biomass, and industrial and municipal waste. Biomass is defined as any plant matter used directly as fuel or converted into fuel, heat, or electricity. (The data series published in *World Development Indicators 1998* and earlier editions did not include energy from combustible renewables and waste.) Data for combustible renewables and waste are often based on small surveys or other incomplete information. Thus the data give only a broad impression of developments and are not strictly comparable between countries. The IEA reports (see *Data sources*) include country notes that explain some of these differences. All forms of energy—primary energy and primary electricity—are converted into oil equivalents. To convert nuclear electricity into oil equivalents, a notional thermal efficiency of 33 percent is assumed; for hydroelectric power 100 percent efficiency is assumed.

The IEA makes these estimates in consultation with national statistical offices, oil companies, electricity utilities, and national energy experts. The IEA occasionally revises its time series to reflect political changes. Since 1990, for example, it has constructed energy statistics for countries of the former Soviet Union. In addition, energy statistics for other countries have undergone continuous changes in coverage or methodology as more detailed energy accounts have become available in recent years. Breaks in series are therefore unavoidable.

Definitions

• **Total energy production** refers to forms of primary energy—petroleum (crude oil, natural gas liquids, and oil from nonconventional sources), natural gas, solid fuels (coal, lignite, and other derived fuels), and combustible renewables and waste—and primary electricity, all converted into oil equivalents (see *About the data*). • **Energy use** refers to use of primary energy before transformation to other end-use fuels, which is equal to indigenous production plus imports and stock changes, minus exports and fuels supplied to ships and aircraft engaged in international transport (see *About the data*). • **Combustible renewables and waste** comprise solid biomass, liquid biomass, biogas, industrial waste, and municipal waste, measured as a percentage of total energy use. • **Net energy imports** are estimated as energy use less production, both measured in oil equivalents.

3.7a

In 2003 high-income economies, with 15 percent of world population, used 52 percent of world energy—and produced 41 percent

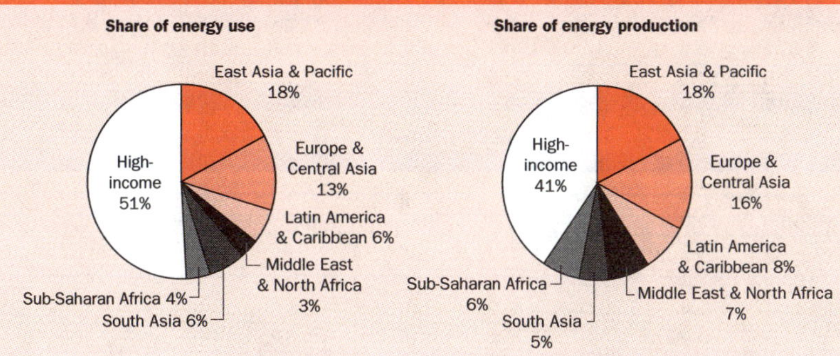

Source: Table 3.7.

Data sources

Data on energy production and use come from IEA electronic files. The IEA's data are published in its annual publications, *Energy Statistics and Balances of Non-OECD Countries*, *Energy Statistics of OECD Countries*, and *Energy Balances of OECD Countries*.

Energy efficiency and emissions

	GDP per unit of energy use		Carbon dioxide emissions						Methane emissions		Nitrous oxide emissions	
	2000 PPP $ per kilogram of oil equivalent		Total million metric tons		Per capita metric tons		kilograms per 2000 PPP $ of GDP		million metric tons of carbon dioxide equivalent	% change	thousand metric tons of carbon dioxide equivalent	% change
	1990	2003	1990	2002	1990	2002	1990	2002	2000	1990–2000	2000	1990–2000
Afghanistan	..	..	2.6	0.6	0.2	..	..	..	13.2	53.5	7,482	33.8
Albania	3.8	6.4	7.3	2.6	2.2	0.8	0.7	0.2	0.5	–37.5	52	–5.5
Algeria	5.7	5.6	77.0	92.0	3.0	2.9	0.6	0.5	28.5	40.4	9,196	14.2
Angola	3.7	3.1	4.7	7.7	0.4	0.5	0.2	0.3	15.8	16.2	6,135	20.0
Argentina	6.4	7.2	109.7	133.1	3.4	3.5	0.4	0.3	86.7	7.4	63,384	12.0
Armenia	*1.6*	5.2	*3.7*	2.9	*1.1*	1.0	*0.5*	0.3	2.8	–20.0	291	–41.1
Australia	4.0	4.8	272.2	355.8	16.0	18.1	0.8	0.7	113.2	0.5	26,974	33.7
Austria	7.1	7.2	57.7	63.6	7.5	7.9	0.3	0.3	9.7	–16.4	2,802	9.8
Azerbaijan	..	2.3	*47.1*	28.0	*6.4*	3.4	..	1.1	11.9	–23.7	782	–42.2
Bangladesh	9.8	10.4	15.4	34.5	0.2	0.3	0.1	0.2	47.6	8.9	44,800	37.0
Belarus	*1.2*	2.2	*94.6*	59.9	*9.3*	6.0	*2.0*	1.1	21.6	–10.7	8,318	–34.3
Belgium	4.7	4.9	100.6	91.5	10.1	8.9	0.4	0.3	11.7	–4.1	13,282	0.9
Benin	2.6	3.5	0.7	1.9	0.1	0.3	0.2	0.3	3.3	22.2	2,704	27.4
Bolivia	5.1	4.9	5.5	10.1	0.8	1.2	0.4	0.5	21.3	11.5	5,824	–0.9
Bosnia and Herzegovina	..	5.3	*4.7*	18.6	*1.2*	4.7	..	0.8	1.4	–30.0	556	–51.1
Botswana	..	..	2.2	4.1	1.5	2.3	0.3	0.3	7.0	12.9	4,842	9.8
Brazil	7.3	6.9	202.6	313.2	1.4	1.8	0.2	0.2	297.2	9.1	207,696	10.9
Bulgaria	2.1	2.8	75.3	41.9	8.6	5.3	1.2	0.8	10.0	–63.0	18,483	–22.4
Burkina Faso	..	..	1.0	1.1	0.1	0.1	0.1	0.1	8.8	20.6	11,733	23.1
Burundi	..	..	0.2	0.3	0.0	0.0	0.0	0.1	1.8	20.0	1,212	9.1
Cambodia	..	..	0.5	0.6	0.1	0.0	..	0.0	68.0	10.4	105	36.4
Cameroon	4.7	4.6	1.6	3.5	0.1	0.2	0.1	0.1	11.8	12.4	9,821	18.5
Canada	3.0	3.4	415.8	516.3	15.0	16.5	0.7	0.6	123.4	57.6	57,464	9.2
Central African Republic	..	..	0.2	0.3	0.1	0.1	0.1	0.1	6.6	15.8	5,055	18.1
Chad	..	..	0.1	0.1	0.0	0.0	0.0	0.0	9.6	15.7	8,699	21.6
Chile	5.5	5.9	35.3	57.2	2.7	3.6	0.5	0.4	14.5	15.1	7,474	35.6
China	2.1	4.5	2,398.9	3,507.4	2.1	2.7	1.3	0.6	802.9	18.1	644,725	23.8
Hong Kong, China	10.6	10.9	26.2	35.4	4.6	5.2	0.2	0.2	..	..	..	..
Colombia	8.4	10.1	56.8	57.3	1.6	1.3	0.3	0.2	55.5	11.7	41,220	48.0
Congo, Dem. Rep.	5.0	2.1	4.0	1.8	0.1	0.0	0.1	0.1	32.9	5.8	17,186	–0.3
Congo, Rep.	2.3	3.3	1.2	2.3	0.5	0.6	0.5	0.7	3.2	18.5	1,031	25.7
Costa Rica	9.7	9.9	2.9	5.8	1.0	1.4	0.2	0.2	3.6	–2.7	3,555	–9.9
Côte d'Ivoire	5.2	3.8	5.4	6.4	0.4	0.4	0.2	0.3	6.5	20.4	2,892	17.7
Croatia	*5.0*	5.6	*16.8*	21.1	*3.8*	4.8	*0.5*	0.5	3.8	–5.0	3,363	–12.1
Cuba	..	..	32.1	23.6	3.0	2.1	..	..	9.1	–8.1	9,288	–33.3
Czech Republic	*3.1*	3.9	*135.4*	114.4	*13.1*	11.2	*1.0*	0.7	10.8	–34.9	8,186	–48.1
Denmark	6.9	7.5	49.8	47.5	9.7	8.9	0.4	0.3	6.0	–3.2	9,331	–15.3
Dominican Republic	7.1	7.4	9.6	21.5	1.4	2.5	0.3	0.4	5.9	11.3	4,287	3.6
Ecuador	5.9	4.9	16.6	24.8	1.6	2.0	0.5	0.6	16.2	18.3	2,878	–2.7
Egypt, Arab Rep.	5.1	5.2	75.4	143.5	1.4	2.1	0.5	0.6	34.3	40.6	15,965	39.4
El Salvador	7.3	6.9	2.6	6.2	0.5	1.0	0.1	0.2	3.2	18.5	2,208	6.7
Eritrea	..	..	..	0.7	..	0.2	..	0.2	0.0	..	..	..
Estonia	*1.6*	3.4	*24.9*	15.9	*16.2*	11.7	*2.4*	1.0	2.4	–44.2	444	–57.8
Ethiopia	2.1	2.1	3.0	6.2	0.1	0.1	0.1	0.1	47.5	20.3	12,170	65.9
Finland	3.8	3.7	51.2	62.6	10.3	12.0	0.5	0.5	4.3	–33.9	7,302	–14.9
France	5.5	5.9	362.4	367.7	6.4	6.2	0.3	0.2	59.3	–11.0	72,265	–16.5
Gabon	4.8	4.9	6.0	3.5	6.3	2.6	1.0	0.4	3.8	22.6	1,847	–0.4
Gambia, The	..	..	0.2	0.3	0.2	0.2	0.1	0.1	0.7	16.7	506	3.1
Georgia	*1.2*	4.1	*15.1*	3.3	*2.8*	0.7	*1.4*	0.3	4.4	–18.5	1,129	–44.4
Germany	4.7	6.1	980.6	850.0	12.3	10.3	0.6	0.4	62.7	–44.2	60,468	–32.1
Ghana	4.6	5.0	3.8	7.5	0.2	0.4	0.2	0.2	7.1	34.0	7,431	63.8
Greece	6.7	7.3	72.2	94.0	7.1	8.5	0.5	0.5	10.9	23.9	11,198	2.4
Guatemala	6.7	6.5	5.1	10.3	0.6	0.9	0.2	0.2	6.2	5.1	5,165	8.1
Guinea	..	..	1.0	1.3	0.2	0.2	0.1	0.1	5.7	18.8	2,409	29.4
Guinea-Bissau	..	..	0.2	0.3	0.2	0.2	0.2	0.3	0.9	0.0	776	24.4
Haiti	10.4	6.4	1.0	1.8	0.1	0.2	0.1	0.1	3.4	17.2	2,632	6.7

Energy efficiency and emissions

	GDP per unit of energy use		Carbon dioxide emissions						Methane emissions		Nitrous oxide emissions	
	2000 PPP $ per kilogram of oil equivalent		Total million metric tons		Per capita metric tons		kilograms per 2000 PPP $ of GDP		million metric tons of carbon dioxide equivalent	% change	thousand metric tons of carbon dioxide equivalent	% change
	1990	**2003**	**1990**	**2002**	**1990**	**2002**	**1990**	**2002**	**2000**	**1990–2000**	**2000**	**1990–2000**
Honduras	5.0	4.9	2.6	5.9	0.5	0.9	0.2	0.4	4.9	–2.0	3,540	–0.4
Hungary	4.2	5.6	60.1	56.6	5.8	5.6	0.5	0.4	11.3	–24.7	12,896	136.1
India	4.0	5.3	677.9	1,218.9	0.8	1.2	0.5	0.5	445.3	16.3	398,980	26.4
Indonesia	4.2	4.3	165.7	306.0	0.9	1.4	0.4	0.5	169.2	13.7	38,747	10.1
Iran, Islamic Rep.	3.6	3.2	218.3	359.6	4.0	5.5	0.9	0.9	96.9	67.4	43,768	14.9
Iraq	..	..	48.5	79.3	2.6	..	..	..	14.4	6.7	6,461	1.4
Ireland	5.2	9.3	30.6	43.1	8.7	11.0	0.6	0.3	12.9	–0.8	9,787	5.9
Israel	7.0	7.1	33.1	69.5	7.1	10.6	0.4	0.5	11.4	32.6	1,672	20.1
Italy	8.4	8.2	389.6	432.3	6.9	7.5	0.3	0.3	37.0	–7.0	43,522	5.7
Jamaica	3.0	2.5	8.0	10.8	3.3	4.1	0.9	1.1	1.3	8.3	1,251	2.8
Japan	6.5	6.5	1,070.7	1,201.6	8.7	9.4	0.4	0.4	21.8	–17.1	36,982	–6.3
Jordan	3.5	4.0	10.2	16.7	3.2	3.2	0.8	0.8	7.9	9.7	232	91.7
Kazakhstan	*1.0*	1.9	*252.7*	147.7	*15.4*	9.9	*3.2*	1.8	27.3	–44.9	7,830	–65.0
Kenya	2.2	2.1	5.8	7.2	0.3	0.2	0.2	0.2	21.5	10.8	22,588	3.5
Korea, Dem. Rep.	..	..	244.6	143.0	12.4	6.5	..	..	33.5	3.4	6,535	–39.9
Korea, Rep.	4.5	4.2	241.2	445.5	5.6	9.4	0.6	0.5	25.0	–1.6	16,094	47.7
Kuwait	*1.2*	1.8	45.2	59.8	21.3	25.6	*1.5*	1.6	9.9	65.0	159	140.9
Kyrgyz Republic	*1.7*	3.2	*11.0*	5.0	*2.4*	1.0	*1.3*	0.6	2.2	–24.1	82	12.3
Lao PDR	..	..	0.2	1.3	0.1	0.2	0.1	0.1	6.2	8.8	52	26.8
Latvia	*3.5*	5.3	*12.7*	6.3	*4.8*	2.7	*0.9*	0.3	2.6	–39.5	1,245	–66.0
Lebanon	2.7	3.0	9.1	16.4	3.3	4.7	1.4	1.0	1.3	85.7	1,149	54.6
Lesotho	..	..	..	..	..	..	..	..	1.2	20.0	1,519	4.5
Liberia	..	..	0.5	0.5	0.2	0.1	..	..	1.2	–7.7	840	8.8
Libya	..	..	37.8	50.3	8.7	9.1	..	..	9.6	9.1	2,534	–11.4
Lithuania	*2.9*	4.3	*21.4*	12.6	*5.8*	3.6	*0.7*	0.4	5.9	–42.2	3,516	167.6
Macedonia, FYR	..	..	*10.6*	10.2	*5.5*	5.1	*0.9*	0.9	1.3	0.0	1,063	15.0
Madagascar	..	..	0.9	2.3	0.1	0.1	0.1	0.2	18.9	14.6	11,600	11.7
Malawi	..	..	0.6	0.8	0.1	0.1	0.1	0.1	3.6	16.1	2,277	13.2
Malaysia	4.4	3.9	55.3	151.4	3.1	6.3	0.6	0.7	30.4	42.7	13,304	14.7
Mali	..	..	0.4	0.6	0.1	0.0	0.1	0.1	12.0	9.1	13,764	24.2
Mauritania	..	..	2.6	3.1	1.3	1.1	0.9	0.7	4.4	12.8	6,427	13.1
Mauritius	..	..	1.5	3.1	1.4	2.6	0.2	0.3	0.3	50.0	856	17.4
Mexico	5.1	5.6	375.2	383.1	4.5	3.8	0.6	0.4	111.7	–0.5	10,027	10.6
Moldova	*1.4*	1.9	*20.9*	6.7	*4.8*	1.6	*2.2*	1.1	2.6	–40.9	1,576	–59.5
Mongolia	..	..	10.0	8.3	4.7	3.4	3.1	2.1	8.2	17.1	12,072	37.2
Morocco	11.9	10.2	23.5	43.6	1.0	1.5	0.3	0.4	10.0	9.9	15,673	5.6
Mozambique	1.3	2.5	1.0	1.5	0.1	0.1	0.1	0.1	11.1	18.1	3,234	9.8
Myanmar	..	..	4.3	7.6	0.1	0.2	..	..	61.1	23.9	12,470	32.2
Namibia	*12.3*	9.9	0.0	2.2	0.0	1.1	0.0	0.2	4.5	4.7	4,170	–1.5
Nepal	3.4	4.0	0.6	3.8	0.0	0.2	0.0	0.1	16.4	15.5	11,301	15.5
Netherlands	5.2	5.8	139.6	150.6	9.3	9.3	0.4	0.3	21.6	–22.9	17,242	3.0
New Zealand	4.1	4.8	23.6	33.9	6.9	8.6	0.4	0.4	36.2	–5.0	12,411	5.4
Nicaragua	5.3	5.5	2.7	3.9	0.7	0.8	0.2	0.2	5.3	12.8	4,048	7.8
Niger	..	..	1.1	1.2	0.1	0.1	0.2	0.1	6.5	25.0	4,999	28.2
Nigeria	1.1	1.3	45.3	52.0	0.5	0.4	0.6	0.5	72.5	41.9	41,556	18.7
Norway	5.1	6.8	46.9	63.1	11.1	13.9	0.4	0.4	7.1	6.0	5,123	0.1
Oman	4.3	2.8	11.2	30.1	6.1	12.1	0.6	0.9	3.7	85.0	1,033	19.3
Pakistan	3.9	4.2	68.0	108.5	0.6	0.8	0.4	0.4	94.7	25.1	84,591	34.0
Panama	7.4	7.6	3.1	6.2	1.3	2.0	0.3	0.4	3.3	10.0	2,694	7.0
Papua New Guinea	..	..	2.4	2.5	0.6	0.5	0.3	0.2	3.9	39.3	2,349	18.0
Paraguay	6.5	6.4	2.3	4.1	0.5	0.7	0.1	0.2	12.3	5.1	10,157	1.8
Peru	8.4	11.3	21.7	25.5	1.0	1.0	0.3	0.2	19.6	15.3	21,919	80.2
Philippines	9.1	7.8	43.9	73.7	0.7	0.9	0.2	0.2	34.2	6.9	20,795	33.4
Poland	3.0	4.6	347.6	295.9	9.1	7.7	1.2	0.7	47.2	–21.7	23,921	–22.3
Portugal	7.9	7.2	42.3	62.2	4.3	6.0	0.3	0.3	14.3	2.9	8,073	3.4
Puerto Rico	..	..	11.8	13.6	3.3	3.5	0.2	*0.1*	..	..	..	..

3.8 Energy efficiency and emissions

	GDP per unit of energy use		Carbon dioxide emissions						Methane emissions		Nitrous oxide emissions	
	2000 PPP $ per kilogram of oil equivalent		Total million metric tons		Per capita metric tons		kilograms per 2000 PPP $ of GDP		million metric tons of carbon dioxide equivalent	% change	thousand metric tons of carbon dioxide equivalent	% change
	1990	2003	1990	2002	1990	2002	1990	2002	2000	1990–2000	2000	1990–2000
Romania	2.5	4.0	155.1	86.6	6.7	4.0	1.0	0.6	36.1	–16.6	7,160	–66.1
Russian Federation	*1.6*	1.9	*1,984.0*	1,430.6	*13.3*	9.9	*1.6*	1.3	298.7	–46.0	51,508	–37.1
Rwanda	..	..	0.5	0.6	0.1	0.1	0.1	0.1	2.2	–15.4	1,170	–14.2
Saudi Arabia	2.9	2.2	179.9	340.0	11.0	15.0	0.9	1.3	54.4	56.8	8,666	15.2
Senegal	5.0	5.2	3.1	4.2	0.4	0.4	0.3	0.3	8.4	25.4	6,598	38.1
Serbia and Montenegro	..	..	..	..	..	..	..	..	9.5	–26.4	6,089	–34.7
Sierra Leone	..	..	0.3	0.6	0.1	0.1	0.1	0.3	2.6	8.3	941	30.2
Singapore	3.3	4.5	45.1	57.3	14.8	13.7	1.0	0.6	1.2	71.4	897	460.6
Slovak Republic	2.7	3.7	*43.1*	36.8	*8.1*	6.8	*0.9*	0.6	4.2	–31.2	3,172	–48.9
Slovenia	*4.9*	5.2	*12.3*	15.3	*6.2*	7.7	*0.5*	0.4	2.5	–7.4	1,978	22.6
Somalia	..	..	0.0	..	0.0	..	..	..	..	..	..	..
South Africa	3.8	3.9	285.5	344.8	8.1	7.6	0.8	0.8	37.4	6.6	25,752	1.4
Spain	7.4	7.0	211.8	304.1	5.5	7.4	0.3	0.3	39.6	22.6	30,094	15.2
Sri Lanka	7.3	8.8	3.8	10.3	0.2	0.5	0.1	0.2	13.3	29.1	2,884	19.8
Sudan	2.7	3.7	5.4	8.8	0.2	0.3	0.2	0.2	46.6	17.1	47,090	19.5
Swaziland	..	..	0.4	1.0	0.6	0.9	0.1	0.2	1.1	10.0	1,216	11.9
Sweden	4.0	4.6	49.5	51.8	5.8	5.8	0.3	0.2	7.1	–10.1	7,096	–3.6
Switzerland	8.2	8.1	42.7	40.8	6.4	5.6	0.2	0.2	5.0	–10.7	3,720	2.6
Syrian Arab Republic	2.9	3.4	35.8	49.0	2.8	2.8	1.1	0.8	9.7	67.2	9,359	19.7
Tajikistan	*0.9*	2.1	*20.6*	4.7	*3.7*	0.8	*2.6*	0.8	1.4	7.7	54	14.9
Tanzania	1.4	1.3	2.3	3.6	0.1	0.1	0.2	0.2	31.7	17.8	27,110	16.3
Thailand	5.7	5.0	95.7	231.6	1.8	3.7	0.4	0.6	75.9	4.3	13,083	6.9
Togo	4.3	3.2	0.8	1.7	0.2	0.3	0.1	0.2	2.1	16.7	2,294	15.1
Trinidad and Tobago	1.4	1.2	16.9	41.2	13.9	31.8	2.0	3.4	3.1	24.0	287	–15.8
Tunisia	6.7	8.1	13.3	22.0	1.6	2.3	0.4	0.4	4.8	29.7	5,176	14.4
Turkey	5.8	6.0	143.8	207.7	2.6	3.0	0.5	0.5	97.4	21.1	40,615	–11.7
Turkmenistan	*1.6*	*1.3*	*28.0*	42.1	*7.2*	9.1	*1.5*	*2.1*	27.1	17.3	573	–13.8
Uganda	..	..	0.8	1.7	0.1	0.1	0.1	0.1	12.4	25.3	12,891	26.9
Ukraine	*1.7*	1.9	*600.0*	306.3	*11.5*	6.4	*1.6*	1.3	153.5	–22.4	19,874	–42.8
United Arab Emirates	2.2	2.3	60.7	94.0	34.2	25.0	1.4	1.2	35.2	70.9	136	32.0
United Kingdom	5.9	7.1	569.3	542.7	9.9	9.2	0.5	0.3	51.1	–33.3	43,775	–35.4
United States	3.7	4.5	4,817.5	5,834.5	19.3	20.2	0.7	0.6	613.4	–4.8	429,959	8.2
Uruguay	9.9	10.5	3.9	4.1	1.3	1.2	0.2	0.2	18.3	19.6	673	29.7
Uzbekistan	*0.7*	0.8	*113.4*	122.1	*5.3*	4.8	*3.4*	3.0	46.2	15.2	13,478	19.1
Venezuela, RB	2.6	2.3	117.3	108.0	5.9	4.3	1.0	0.8	95.1	24.3	6,870	–5.4
Vietnam	3.3	4.4	21.4	66.2	0.3	0.8	0.3	0.4	68.1	15.0	12,873	52.2
West Bank and Gaza	..	..	..	..	..	..	..	..	..	..	..	..
Yemen, Rep.	3.0	2.8	9.6	13.0	0.8	0.7	1.2	0.8	8.7	89.1	5,591	9.5
Zambia	1.5	1.4	2.4	2.0	0.3	0.2	0.3	0.2	11.2	14.3	5,502	12.8
Zimbabwe	3.1	2.6	16.7	12.4	1.6	1.0	0.6	0.4	11.0	1.9	8,576	–5.0
World	3.9 w	4.7 w	21,254.1 t	24,355.2 t	4.0 w	3.9 w	0.6 w	0.5 t	5,835.0 t	–5.5 w	3,454,338 t	3.0 w
Low income	3.5	4.2	1,368.2	1,898.2	0.8	0.8	0.4	0.4	1,367.4	18.3	928,766	26.5
Middle income	3.0	4.2	9,255.9	9,795.3	3.5	3.3	0.9	0.6	3,007.8	8.3	1,528,288	9.7
Lower middle income	3.1	4.6	5,086.8	6,250.2	2.5	2.6	0.8	0.6	2,092.1	15.0	1,231,441	16.3
Upper middle income	2.8	3.5	4,176.7	3,547.9	8.1	6.2	1.0	0.7	916.0	–0.9	297,173	0.8
Low & middle income	3.1	4.2	10,622.4	11,693.5	2.4	2.2	0.8	0.6	4,375.1	9.7	2,456,507	12.1
East Asia & Pacific	2.6	4.6	3,047.9	4,506.5	1.9	2.5	1.0	0.6	1,365.1	17.3	779,925	21.9
Europe & Central Asia	2.1	2.7	4,827.8	3,118.8	10.2	6.7	1.3	1.0	844.1	–20.3	236,256	–19.4
Latin America & Carib.	6.0	6.2	1,038.5	1,264.8	2.4	2.4	0.4	0.3	800.5	7.7	419,712	13.8
Middle East & N. Africa	4.6	4.2	576.5	926.3	2.6	3.2	0.7	0.7	233.0	42.2	118,262	19.0
South Asia	4.2	5.3	768.6	1,378.1	0.7	1.0	0.4	0.4	631.7	17.2	550,313	27.9
Sub-Saharan Africa	2.8	2.8	418.3	511.2	0.8	0.7	0.5	0.4	501.5	15.3	353,802	11.8
High income	4.7	5.2	10,654.1	12,685.3	11.8	12.8	0.5	0.5	1,432.7	–9.0	960,933	0.9
Europe EMU	5.8	6.4	2,448.7	2,531.1	8.4	8.3	0.4	0.3	284.5	–17.6	276,251	–10.8

Energy efficiency and emissions

About the data

The ratio of GDP to energy use provides a measure of energy efficiency. To produce comparable and consistent estimates of real GDP across countries relative to physical inputs to GDP—that is, units of energy use—GDP is converted to 2000 constant international dollars using purchasing power parity (PPP) rates. Differences in this ratio over time and across countries reflect in part structural changes in the economy, changes in the energy efficiency of particular sectors, and differences in fuel mixes.

Because commercial energy is widely traded, it is necessary to distinguish between its production and its use. Net energy imports show the extent to which an economy's use exceeds its domestic production. High-income countries are net energy importers; middle-income countries have been their main suppliers.

Carbon dioxide emissions, largely a by-product of energy production and use (see table 3.7), account for the largest share of greenhouse gases, which are associated with global warming. Anthropogenic carbon dioxide emissions result primarily from fossil fuel combustion and cement manufacturing. In combustion, different fossil fuels release different amounts of carbon dioxide for the same level of energy use. Burning oil releases about 50 percent more carbon dioxide than burning natural gas, and burning coal releases about twice as much. Cement manufacturing releases about half a metric ton of carbon dioxide for each metric ton of cement produced.

Methane emissions, largely the result of agricultural activities and industrial production of methane, are expressed in carbon dioxide equivalents using the global warming potential, which allows the different gases to be compared on the basis of their effective contributions. A kilogram of methane is 23 times as effective at trapping heat in the earth's atmosphere as a kilogram of carbon dioxide within a time horizon of 100 years. The global warming potential of a kilogram of nitrous oxide is nearly 300 times that of a kilogram of carbon dioxide within the same time horizon.

The Carbon Dioxide Information Analysis Center (CDIAC), sponsored by the U.S. Department of Energy, calculates annual anthropogenic emissions of carbon dioxide. These calculations are based on data on fossil fuel consumption (from the World Energy Data Set maintained by the United Nations Statistics Division) and data on world cement manufacturing (from the Cement Manufacturing Data Set maintained by the U.S. Bureau of Mines). Emissions of carbon dioxide are often calculated and reported in terms of their content of elemental carbon. For this table these values were converted to the actual mass of carbon dioxide by multiplying the carbon mass by 3.664 (the ratio of the mass of carbon to that of carbon dioxide). Although the estimates of global carbon dioxide emissions are probably within 10 percent of actual emissions (as calculated from global average fuel chemistry and use), country estimates may have larger error bounds. Trends estimated from a consistent time series tend to be more accurate than individual values. Each year the CDIAC recalculates the entire time series from 1950 to the present, incorporating its most recent findings and the latest corrections to its database. Estimates do not include fuels supplied to ships and aircraft engaged in international transport because of the difficulty of apportioning these fuels among the countries benefiting from that transport.

Definitions

• **GDP per unit of energy use** is the PPP GDP per kilogram of oil equivalent of energy use. PPP GDP is gross domestic product converted to 2000 constant international dollars using purchasing power parity rates. An international dollar has the same purchasing power over GDP as a U.S. dollar has in the United States. • **Carbon dioxide emissions** are those stemming from the burning of fossil fuels and the manufacture of cement. They include carbon dioxide produced during consumption of solid, liquid, and gas fuels and gas flaring. • **Methane emissions** are those stemming from human activities such as agriculture and from industrial methane production. • **Nitrous oxide emissions** are those stemming from agriculture, biomass burning, industrial activities, and livestock management.

3.8a

The five largest producers of carbon dioxide . . .

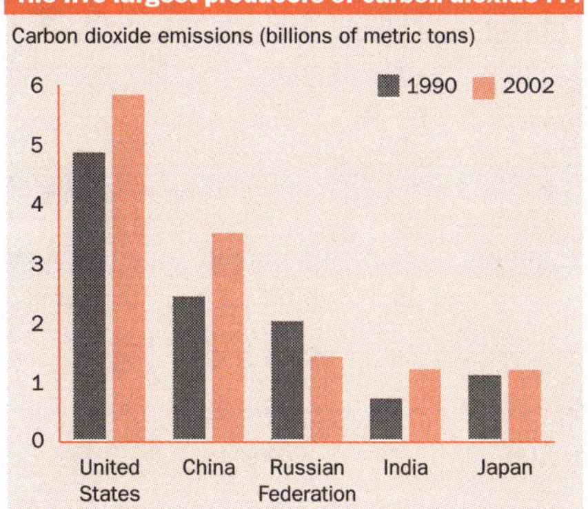

Source: Table 3.8.

3.8b

. . . differ significantly in per capita emissions

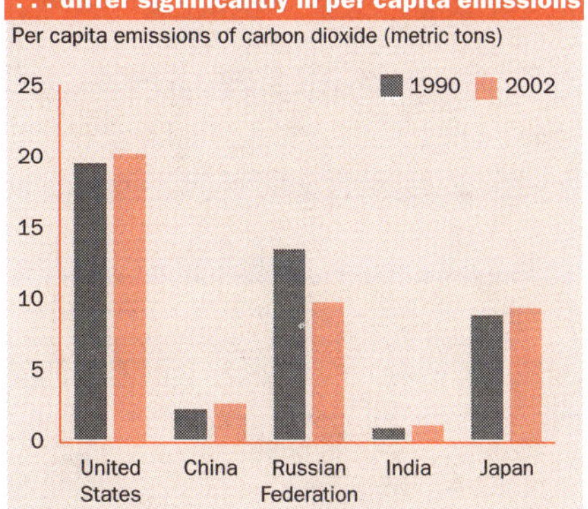

Source: Table 3.8.

Data sources

The underlying data on energy use are from electronic files of the International Energy Agency. Data on carbon dioxide emissions are from the CDIAC, Environmental Sciences Division, Oak Ridge National Laboratory, in the U.S. state of Tennessee. Data on methane and nitrous oxide emissions are compiled by the World Resources Institute.

Sources of electricity

	Electricity production		Sources of electricity[a]									
			% of total									
	billion kilowatt hours		Hydropower		Coal		Oil		Gas		Nuclear power	
	1990	**2003**	**1990**	**2003**	**1990**	**2003**	**1990**	**2003**	**1990**	**2003**	**1990**	**2003**
Afghanistan	..	..	..	..	..	..	..	..	..	..	..	..
Albania	3.2	5.2	89.1	98.8	..	..	10.9	1.2	..	..	..	..
Algeria	16.1	29.6	0.8	0.9	..	..	5.4	2.3	93.7	96.8	..	..
Angola	0.8	2.0	86.2	62.2	..	..	13.8	37.8	..	..	..	..
Argentina	51.0	92.1	35.6	36.8	1.3	1.0	9.7	1.1	39.0	51.7	14.3	8.2
Armenia	*10.0*	5.5	*33.8*	36.0	..	..	*43.3*	..	*22.9*	27.6	..	36.3
Australia	154.3	227.9	9.2	7.0	77.1	77.2	2.7	1.0	10.6	13.8	..	..
Austria	49.3	61.2	63.9	59.4	14.2	15.4	3.8	2.9	15.7	18.3	..	..
Azerbaijan	*21.8*	21.3	*8.9*	11.6	..	..	*91.1*	35.7	*0.5*	52.7	..	..
Bangladesh	7.7	19.7	11.4	5.7	..	..	4.3	6.7	84.3	87.5	..	..
Belarus	*41.6*	26.6	*0.0*	0.1	..	0.0	*52.1*	4.4	*47.9*	95.5	..	..
Belgium	70.3	83.6	0.4	0.3	28.2	13.9	1.9	1.2	7.7	25.9	60.8	56.7
Benin	0.0	0.1		2.6	..	..	100.0	97.4	..	..	..	..
Bolivia	2.1	4.3	55.3	60.3	..	..	5.3	19.1	37.6	18.5	..	..
Bosnia and Herzegovina	*6.5*	11.2	*52.2*	48.0	*47.8*	50.9	..	1.1	..	..	..	..
Botswana	..	..	..	..	..	..	..	..	..	..	..	..
Brazil	222.8	364.9	92.8	83.8	2.1	2.4	2.5	3.0	0.0	3.6	1.0	3.7
Bulgaria	42.1	42.3	4.5	7.0	50.3	46.1	2.9	1.9	7.6	4.2	34.8	40.9
Burkina Faso	..	..	..	..	..	..	..	..	..	..	..	..
Burundi	..	..	..	..	..	..	..	..	..	..	..	..
Cambodia	..	..	..	..	..	..	..	..	..	..	..	..
Cameroon	2.7	3.7	98.5	95.8	..	..	1.5	4.2	..	..	..	..
Canada	481.9	586.9	61.6	57.5	17.1	19.3	3.4	3.0	2.0	5.8	15.1	12.8
Central African Republic	..	..	..	..	..	..	..	..	..	..	..	..
Chad	..	..	..	..	..	..	..	..	..	..	..	..
Chile	18.4	48.8	55.1	46.3	34.4	13.5	7.6	1.3	1.3	35.4	..	..
China	621.2	1,907.4	20.4	14.9	71.2	79.4	7.9	3.0	0.5	0.3	*0.2*	2.3
Hong Kong, China	28.9	35.5	..	..	98.3	77.7	1.7	0.5	..	21.8	..	..
Colombia	36.2	47.1	76.0	76.8	9.8	8.1	1.0	0.3	12.4	13.6	..	..
Congo, Dem. Rep.	5.6	6.3	99.6	99.7	..	..	0.4	0.3	..	..	..	..
Congo, Rep.	0.5	0.3	99.4	99.7	..	..	0.6	0.3	..	..	..	..
Costa Rica	3.5	7.6	97.5	78.3	..	..	2.5	1.8	..	..	..	..
Côte d'Ivoire	2.0	5.1	66.7	36.0	..	..	33.3	0.1	..	63.9	..	..
Croatia	*8.9*	12.6	*48.8*	38.7	*5.0*	19.1	*35.8*	25.0	*15.4*	17.2	..	..
Cuba	15.0	15.9	0.6	0.6	..	..	91.5	94.3	0.2	0.0	..	..
Czech Republic	62.6	82.8	2.3	1.7	71.8	62.3	4.8	0.4	1.0	3.7	20.1	31.2
Denmark	26.0	46.3	0.1	0.0	90.3	54.7	3.7	5.1	2.7	21.2	..	..
Dominican Republic	3.7	13.5	9.4	8.9	1.2	21.1	88.6	69.5	..	0.1	..	..
Ecuador	6.3	11.5	78.5	62.2	..	..	21.5	29.7	..	8.1	..	..
Egypt, Arab Rep.	42.3	91.9	23.5	14.1	..	..	36.9	5.7	39.6	79.9	..	..
El Salvador	2.2	4.1	73.5	35.8	..	..	6.9	40.0	..	..	..	..
Eritrea	..	..	..	..	..	..	..	..	..	..	..	..
Estonia	*13.1*	10.2	*0.0*	0.1	*90.0*	92.2	*4.5*	0.4	*5.5*	6.9	..	..
Ethiopia	1.2	2.3	88.4	99.3	..	..	11.6	0.7	..	..	..	..
Finland	54.4	84.2	20.0	11.4	33.0	31.8	3.1	1.1	8.6	16.6	35.3	27.0
France	417.8	561.7	12.9	10.5	8.5	5.3	2.1	1.5	0.7	3.1	75.2	78.5
Gabon	1.0	1.5	72.1	59.8	..	..	11.2	22.8	16.4	16.9	..	..
Gambia, The	..	..	..	..	..	..	..	..	..	..	..	..
Georgia	*12.4*	7.1	*58.3*	91.7	..	..	*5.0*	0.4	*36.6*	7.9	..	..
Germany	547.7	594.3	3.2	3.2	58.8	52.9	1.9	0.8	7.4	9.8	27.8	27.8
Ghana	5.7	5.9	100.0	65.8	..	..	*0.3*	34.2	..	..	..	..
Greece	34.8	57.9	5.1	8.2	72.4	60.7	22.3	15.1	0.3	13.8	..	..
Guatemala	2.3	6.6	76.0	37.8	..	14.5	9.0	34.8	..	..	..	..
Guinea	..	..	..	..	..	..	..	..	..	..	..	..
Guinea-Bissau	..	..	..	..	..	..	..	..	..	..	..	..
Haiti	0.6	0.5	76.5	47.7	..	..	20.6	52.3	..	..	..	..

Sources of electricity

	Electricity production		Sources of electricity[a]									
	billion kilowatt hours		% of total									
			Hydropower		Coal		Oil		Gas		Nuclear power	
	1990	2003	1990	2003	1990	2003	1990	2003	1990	2003	1990	2003
Honduras	2.3	4.5	98.3	48.0	..	..	1.7	51.7	..	..	..	..
Hungary	28.4	34.1	0.6	0.5	30.5	27.1	4.8	4.8	15.7	34.8	48.3	32.3
India	289.4	633.3	24.8	11.9	65.3	68.3	4.3	4.6	3.4	11.5	2.1	2.8
Indonesia	33.3	112.9	20.2	8.0	31.5	41.1	42.7	24.9	2.3	20.3	..	..
Iran, Islamic Rep.	59.1	152.6	10.3	7.3	..	..	37.3	16.0	52.5	76.7	..	..
Iraq	24.0	28.3	10.8	1.5	..	..	89.2	98.5	..	..	..	..
Ireland	14.2	24.9	4.9	2.4	57.4	33.1	10.0	9.9	27.7	52.5	..	..
Israel	20.9	47.0	0.0	0.1	50.1	77.0	49.9	22.9	..	0.1	..	..
Italy	213.1	283.4	14.8	11.9	16.8	15.6	48.2	26.8	18.6	41.4	*0.1*	..
Jamaica	2.5	7.1	3.6	1.6	..	..	92.4	96.9	..	..	..	..
Japan	834.5	1,037.7	10.7	9.1	14.4	28.2	29.6	13.2	19.5	24.3	24.2	23.1
Jordan	3.6	8.5	0.3	0.5	..	..	87.8	90.7	11.9	8.8	..	..
Kazakhstan	*91.6*	63.8	*8.3*	13.5	*72.3*	69.9	*8.8*	6.0	*10.6*	10.6	..	..
Kenya	3.0	4.9	81.6	67.0	..	..	7.6	16.8	..	..	..	..
Korea, Dem. Rep.	27.7	21.0	56.3	55.7	40.1	39.4	3.6	4.9	..	..	..	..
Korea, Rep.	105.4	344.9	6.0	1.4	16.8	38.9	17.9	9.2	9.1	12.3	50.2	37.6
Kuwait	18.5	39.8	..	..	..	..	54.3	80.0	45.7	20.0	..	..
Kyrgyz Republic	*13.2*	14.0	*77.4*	92.7	*9.1*	3.6	..	..	*13.6*	3.6	..	..
Lao PDR	..	..	..	..	..	..	..	..	..	..	..	..
Latvia	*4.2*	4.0	*65.8*	57.0	*2.0*	0.6	*7.9*	2.1	*26.3*	38.5	..	..
Lebanon	1.5	10.5	33.3	12.9	..	..	66.7	87.1	..	..	..	..
Lesotho	..	..	..	..	..	..	..	..	..	..	..	..
Liberia	..	..	..	..	..	..	..	..	..	..	..	..
Libya	10.2	18.9	..	..	..	..	100.0	79.6	..	20.4	..	..
Lithuania	*20.7*	18.8	*2.5*	1.7	..	..	*12.4*	1.7	*6.7*	13.4	*78.2*	82.2
Macedonia, FYR	..	..	..	..	..	..	..	..	..	..	..	..
Madagascar	..	..	..	..	..	..	..	..	..	..	..	..
Malawi	..	..	..	..	..	..	..	..	..	..	..	..
Malaysia	23.0	78.4	17.3	7.3	12.3	14.4	50.0	4.3	20.4	74.0	..	..
Mali	..	..	..	..	..	..	..	..	..	..	..	..
Mauritania	..	..	..	..	..	..	..	..	..	..	..	..
Mauritius	..	..	..	..	..	..	..	..	..	..	..	..
Mexico	122.7	218.7	19.1	9.1	6.3	14.3	57.3	32.4	10.6	35.4	2.4	4.8
Moldova	*12.5*	3.4	*2.3*	1.9	*34.4*	5.4	*26.4*	0.5	*36.9*	92.2	..	..
Mongolia	..	..	..	..	..	..	..	..	..	..	..	..
Morocco	9.6	18.1	12.7	8.0	23.0	67.7	64.4	23.2	..	..	..	..
Mozambique	0.5	10.6	62.6	99.7	13.9	..	23.6	0.3	*0.2*	0.1	..	..
Myanmar	2.5	6.2	48.1	36.2	1.6	..	10.9	6.8	39.3	57.0	..	..
Namibia	*1.4*	1.5	*95.2*	96.9	*1.5*	0.4	*3.3*	2.7	..	..	..	..
Nepal	0.9	2.3	99.9	99.8	..	..	0.1	0.2	..	..	..	..
Netherlands	71.9	96.8	0.1	0.1	38.2	28.4	4.3	3.0	50.9	58.8	4.9	4.2
New Zealand	32.3	41.1	72.3	57.5	1.5	8.1	0.0	0.0	17.6	24.4	..	..
Nicaragua	1.4	2.7	28.8	11.0	..	..	39.8	75.2	..	..	..	..
Niger	..	..	..	..	..	..	..	..	..	..	..	..
Nigeria	13.5	20.2	32.6	38.8	0.1	..	13.7	22.7	53.7	38.5	..	..
Norway	121.6	106.7	99.6	98.9	0.2	0.1	0.0	0.0	*0.0*	0.3	..	..
Oman	4.5	10.7	..	..	..	..	18.4	18.0	81.6	82.0	..	..
Pakistan	37.7	80.8	44.9	33.3	0.1	0.2	20.6	15.7	33.6	48.5	0.8	2.2
Panama	2.7	5.6	83.2	50.6	..	..	14.7	49.0	..	..	..	..
Papua New Guinea	..	..	..	..	..	..	..	..	..	..	..	..
Paraguay	27.2	51.8	99.9	100.0	..	..	0.0	..	..	..	..	..
Peru	13.8	22.9	75.8	80.8	..	3.3	21.5	9.7	1.7	5.2	..	..
Philippines	25.2	52.9	24.0	14.9	7.7	27.5	46.7	14.2	..	24.9	..	..
Poland	134.4	150.0	1.1	1.1	97.5	95.1	1.2	1.6	0.1	1.6	..	..
Portugal	28.4	46.5	32.3	33.8	32.1	31.2	33.1	13.2	..	16.6	..	..
Puerto Rico	..	..	..	..	..	..	..	..	..	..	..	..

3.9 Sources of electricity

	Electricity production		Sources of electricity[a]									
			% of total									
	billion kilowatt hours		Hydropower		Coal		Oil		Gas		Nuclear power	
	1990	2003	1990	2003	1990	2003	1990	2003	1990	2003	1990	2003
Romania	64.3	55.1	17.7	24.0	28.8	42.9	18.4	6.6	35.1	17.6	..	8.9
Russian Federation	*1,116.7*	914.3	*17.0*	17.0	*15.3*	18.8	*9.9*	3.0	*45.7*	44.5	*11.9*	16.4
Rwanda	..	..	..	..	..	..	..	..	..	..	..	..
Saudi Arabia	69.2	153.0	..	..	..	..	56.5	53.6	43.5	46.4	..	..
Senegal	0.9	2.1	..	15.7	..	..	98.0	74.6	2.0	1.6	..	..
Serbia and Montenegro	*36.5*	35.4	*31.1*	27.9	*65.6*	69.9	*1.7*	0.8	*1.6*	1.5	..	..
Sierra Leone	..	..	..	..	..	..	..	..	..	..	..	..
Singapore	15.7	35.3	..	..	..	..	100.0	34.6	*0.0*	60.8	..	..
Slovak Republic	23.4	31.0	8.0	11.2	32.2	20.6	3.4	2.3	4.9	7.7	51.4	57.7
Slovenia	*12.1*	14.0	*28.2*	22.5	*36.2*	36.4	*2.5*	0.4	*0.2*	2.6	*32.9*	37.1
Somalia	..	..	..	..	..	..	..	..	..	..	..	..
South Africa	165.4	229.1	0.6	0.8	94.3	93.5	*0.0*	..	..	0.0	5.1	5.5
Spain	151.2	257.9	16.8	15.9	40.1	29.5	5.7	9.3	1.0	15.3	35.9	24.0
Sri Lanka	3.2	7.6	99.8	43.5	..	..	0.2	56.5	..	..	..	..
Sudan	1.5	3.4	63.2	34.7	..	..	36.8	65.3	..	..	..	..
Swaziland	..	..	..	..	..	..	..	..	..	..	..	..
Sweden	146.0	135.6	49.7	39.3	1.2	3.1	0.8	2.9	0.3	0.4	46.7	49.7
Switzerland	54.7	64.9	54.5	53.6	0.1	..	0.5	0.1	0.6	1.4	43.2	42.3
Syrian Arab Republic	11.6	29.5	23.5	9.5	..	..	56.0	41.7	20.5	48.9	..	..
Tajikistan	*18.6*	16.5	*94.7*	97.7	..	..	..	..	*5.3*	2.3	..	..
Tanzania	1.6	2.7	95.1	93.0	..	2.7	4.9	4.3	..	..	..	..
Thailand	44.2	117.0	11.3	6.2	25.0	15.8	23.5	2.7	40.2	73.0	..	..
Togo	0.2	0.3	60.1	82.8	..	..	39.9	17.2	..	..	..	..
Trinidad and Tobago	3.6	6.4	..	..	..	..	0.1	0.1	99.0	99.7	..	..
Tunisia	5.8	12.4	0.8	1.3	..	..	35.5	8.7	63.7	89.7	..	..
Turkey	57.5	140.6	40.2	25.1	35.1	22.9	6.9	6.5	17.7	45.2	..	..
Turkmenistan	*14.6*	10.8	*0.0*	0.0	..	..	..	..	*100.0*	100.0	..	..
Uganda	..	..	..	..	..	..	..	..	..	..	..	..
Ukraine	*279.6*	180.2	*3.2*	5.1	*18.1*	18.3	*9.1*	0.5	*40.4*	30.9	*29.2*	45.2
United Arab Emirates	17.1	49.5			..	..	4.0	0.6	96.0	99.4	..	..
United Kingdom	317.8	395.9	1.6	0.8	65.0	35.4	10.9	1.8	1.6	37.5	20.7	22.4
United States	3,202.8	4,054.4	8.5	6.9	53.1	51.4	4.1	3.4	11.9	16.5	19.1	19.4
Uruguay	7.4	8.6	94.2	99.4	..	..	5.1	0.2	..	0.0	..	..
Uzbekistan	*56.4*	49.4	*12.3*	12.8	*4.9*	2.9	*6.9*	11.4	*75.9*	72.9	..	..
Venezuela, RB	59.3	91.8	62.3	66.0	..	..	11.5	16.4	26.2	17.6	..	..
Vietnam	8.7	40.9	61.8	46.4	23.1	17.7	15.0	6.5	0.1	29.4	..	..
West Bank and Gaza	..	..	..	..	..	..	..	..	..	..	..	..
Yemen, Rep.	1.7	4.1	..	..	..	..	100.0	100.0	..	..	..	..
Zambia	8.0	9.6	99.2	99.5	0.5	0.2	0.3	0.4	..	..	..	..
Zimbabwe	9.4	8.8	46.7	60.9	53.3	38.9	..	0.2	..	..	..	..
World	**11,697.4**	**16,618.4**	**18.1**	**15.8**	**38.0**	**40.1**	**11.2**	**6.8**	**13.9**	**19.4**	**17.2**	**15.9**
Low income	535.1	981.1	34.4	23.8	40.9	46.3	7.3	7.2	14.5	20.0	1.2	2.0
Middle income	3,753.1	5,818.3	21.5	20.8	35.2	42.4	15.0	7.3	19.8	21.5	7.6	7.1
Lower middle income	1,817.8	3,591.1	27.4	23.3	37.4	49.4	16.8	7.2	14.0	14.4	5.1	4.5
Upper middle income	1,935.3	2,227.2	16.1	16.6	33.2	31.0	13.4	7.4	25.3	32.9	10.0	11.3
Low & middle income	4,288.2	6,799.4	23.1	21.2	35.9	42.9	14.0	7.3	19.1	21.3	6.8	6.4
East Asia & Pacific	785.8	2,336.8	21.7	14.8	61.3	69.4	12.7	4.4	3.5	8.6	*0.2*	1.9
Europe & Central Asia	2,143.0	1,946.4	12.9	15.7	31.9	29.8	12.6	3.6	29.2	34.0	12.3	16.8
Latin America & Carib.	607.0	1,037.0	63.7	56.4	3.8	5.4	19.0	14.2	9.5	18.1	2.1	3.0
Middle East & N. Africa	190.0	415.3	12.2	7.4	1.2	3.0	48.2	27.4	38.4	62.2	..	..
South Asia	338.8	743.7	27.6	14.7	55.8	58.2	6.1	6.4	8.6	17.4	1.9	2.6
Sub-Saharan Africa	223.5	320.3	18.5	20.1	72.1	68.0	2.2	4.0	3.3	3.5	3.8	4.0
High income	7,409.2	9,818.9	15.2	12.1	39.2	38.2	9.6	6.5	10.8	18.1	23.2	22.4
Europe EMU	1,653.6	2,155.1	11.0	10.2	34.4	27.7	9.5	6.4	8.7	17.0	35.5	34.4

a. Shares may not sum to 100 percent because some sources of generated electricity are not shown.

About the data

Use of energy is important in improving people's standard of living. But electricity generation also can damage the environment. Whether such damage occurs depends largely on how electricity is generated. For example, burning coal releases twice as much carbon dioxide—a major contributor to global warming—as does burning an equivalent amount of natural gas (see *About the data* for table 3.8). Nuclear energy does not generate carbon dioxide emissions, but it produces other dangerous waste products. The table provides information on electricity production by source. Shares may not sum to 100 percent because some sources of generated electricity (such as wind, solar, and geothermal) are not shown.

The International Energy Agency (IEA) compiles data on energy inputs used to generate electricity. IEA data for countries that are not members of the Organisation for Economic Co-operation and Development (OECD) are based on national energy data adjusted to conform to annual questionnaires completed by OECD member governments. In addition, estimates are sometimes made to complete major aggregates from which key data are missing, and adjustments are made to compensate for differences in definitions.

The IEA makes these estimates in consultation with national statistical offices, oil companies, electricity utilities, and national energy experts. The IEA occasionally revises its time series to reflect political changes. Since 1990, for example, it has constructed energy statistics for countries of the former Soviet Union. In addition, energy statistics for other countries have undergone continuous changes in coverage or methodology as more detailed energy accounts have become available in recent years. Breaks in series are therefore unavoidable.

Definitions

• **Electricity production** is measured at the terminals of all alternator sets in a station. In addition to hydropower, coal, oil, gas, and nuclear power generation, it covers generation by geothermal, solar, wind, and tide and wave energy as well as that from combustible renewables and waste. Production includes the output of electricity plants designed to produce electricity only, as well as that of combined heat and power plants. • **Sources of electricity** refer to the inputs used to generate electricity: hydropower, coal, oil, gas, and nuclear power. • **Hydropower** refers to electricity produced by hydroelectric power plants. • **Oil** refers to crude oil and petroleum products. • **Gas** refers to natural gas but not to natural gas liquids. • **Nuclear power** refers to electricity produced by nuclear power plants.

3.9a

Electricity sources have shifted since 1990 . . .

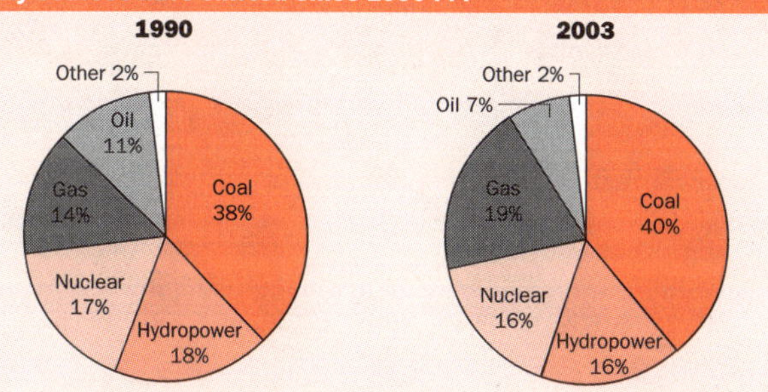

Source: Table 3.9.

3.9b

. . . with a more profound shift in low-income countries

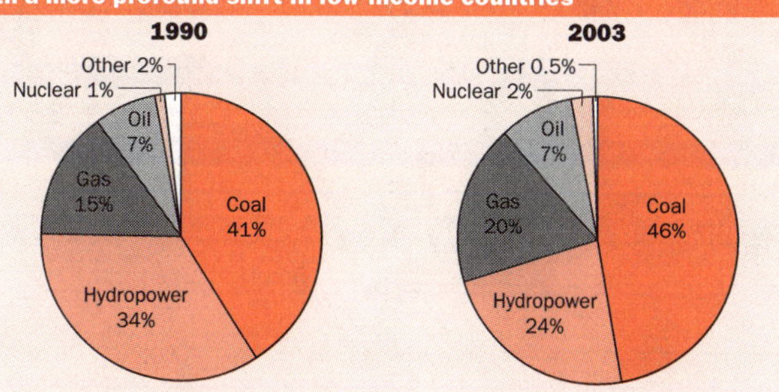

Source: Table 3.9.

Data sources

Data on electricity production are from the IEA's electronic files and its annual publications *Energy Statistics and Balances of Non-OECD Countries*, *Energy Statistics of OECD Countries*, and *Energy Balances of OECD Countries*.

3.10 Urbanization

	Urban population					Population in urban agglomerations of more than 1 million		Population in largest city		Access to improved sanitation facilities			
	millions		% of total population		average annual % growth	% of total population		% of urban population		% of urban population		% of rural population	
	1990	2004	1990	2004	1990–2004	1990	2005	1990	2005	1990	2002	1990	2002
Afghanistan	2.7	..	18	..	..	11	..	59	..	..	..	5	..
Albania	1.2	1.4	36	44	1.1	..	..	..	..	99	99	..	81
Algeria	13.0	19.2	51	59	2.8	8	10	15	17	99	99	76	82
Angola	2.8	5.6	26	36	5.1	15	18	58	48	62	56	19	16
Argentina	28.3	34.7	87	90	1.4	41	42	39	38	87	..	47	..
Armenia	2.4	1.9	67	64	–1.4	33	35	49	55	96	96	..	61
Australia	14.5	18.6	85	92	1.8	60	61	25	23	100	100	100	100
Austria	5.1	5.4	66	66	0.4	27	27	41	41	100	100	100	100
Azerbaijan	3.8	4.2	54	50	0.5	24	22	45	44	..	73	..	36
Bangladesh	20.6	34.3	20	25	3.7	9	13	32	35	71	75	11	39
Belarus	6.7	7.0	66	71	0.3	16	17	24	24	..	..	..	..
Belgium	9.6	10.1	96	97	0.4	..	..	10	10	..	..	..	..
Benin	1.8	3.7	34	45	5.2	..	..	..	..	31	58	1	12
Bolivia	3.7	5.8	56	64	3.1	25	31	29	26	49	58	13	23
Bosnia and Herzegovina	1.7	1.8	39	45	0.3	..	..	..	..	99	99	..	88
Botswana	0.6	0.9	42	52	3.0	..	..	..	..	61	57	21	25
Brazil	111.6	153.8	75	84	2.3	33	36	13	12	82	83	37	35
Bulgaria	5.8	5.4	66	70	–0.4	14	13	21	19	100	100	100	100
Burkina Faso	1.2	2.3	14	18	5.0	..	..	51	35	47	45	8	5
Burundi	0.4	0.7	6	10	5.3	..	..	..	..	42	47	44	35
Cambodia	1.2	2.6	13	19	5.5	6	8	..	..	..	53	..	8
Cameroon	4.7	8.4	40	52	4.1	16	23	21	23	43	63	7	33
Canada	21.3	25.8	77	81	1.4	34	37	18	19	100	100	99	99
Central African Republic	1.1	1.7	37	43	3.1	..	..	..	..	32	47	18	12
Chad	1.3	2.4	21	25	4.5	..	..	..	..	27	30	1	0
Chile	11.0	14.1	83	87	1.8	35	35	42	39	91	96	52	64
China	311.0	513.0	27	40	3.6	14	15	4	2	64	69	7	29
Hong Kong, China	5.7	6.9	100	100	1.4	100	100	100	100	..	..	..	..
Colombia	24.0	34.5	69	77	2.6	28	34	21	22	95	96	52	54
Congo, Dem. Rep.	10.6	18.0	28	32	3.8	9	10	32	30	56	43	3	23
Congo, Rep.	1.2	2.1	48	54	4.0	..	..	59	53	..	14	2	2
Costa Rica	1.6	2.6	54	61	3.3	..	..	45	43	..	89	97	97
Côte d'Ivoire	5.0	8.1	40	45	3.4	17	19	42	42	52	61	16	23
Croatia	2.6	2.6	54	59	0.2	..	..	..	..	..	..	..	..
Cuba	7.8	8.5	74	76	0.7	20	19	27	26	99	99	95	95
Czech Republic	7.8	7.6	75	74	–0.2	12	11	16	15	..	..	..	..
Denmark	4.4	4.6	85	85	0.4	26	20	31	24	..	..	..	..
Dominican Republic	3.9	5.2	55	60	2.1	21	22	39	36	60	67	33	43
Ecuador	5.7	8.1	55	62	2.6	26	29	28	29	73	80	36	59
Egypt, Arab Rep.	24.2	30.7	43	42	1.7	22	20	37	36	70	84	42	56
El Salvador	2.5	4.0	49	60	3.4	19	21	39	36	70	78	33	40
Eritrea	0.5	0.9	16	20	4.2	..	..	..	..	46	34	0	3
Estonia	1.1	0.9	71	70	–1.2	..	..	..	..	..	93	..	..
Ethiopia	6.5	11.1	13	16	3.8	3	4	28	25	14	19	2	4
Finland	3.1	3.2	61	61	0.3	17	21	28	35	100	100	100	100
France	42.0	46.2	74	76	0.7	23	23	22	21	..	..	..	..
Gabon	0.7	1.2	68	84	4.1	..	..	..	..	..	37	..	30
Gambia, The	0.2	0.4	25	26	3.6	..	..	..	..	..	72	..	46
Georgia	3.0	2.3	55	52	–1.8	22	23	41	45	96	96	..	69
Germany	67.8	72.9	85	88	0.5	40	42	9	9	..	..	..	..
Ghana	5.6	9.9	36	46	4.0	8	9	21	19	54	74	37	46
Greece	6.0	6.8	59	61	0.9	30	29	51	48	..	..	..	..
Guatemala	3.7	5.7	41	47	3.2	..	..	22	17	71	72	35	52
Guinea	1.6	3.3	25	36	5.2	14	16	56	43	27	25	13	6
Guinea-Bissau	0.2	0.5	24	35	5.7	..	..	..	..	..	57	..	23
Haiti	2.0	3.2	29	38	3.3	17	25	56	63	27	52	11	23

Urbanization

	Urban population					Population in urban agglomerations of more than 1 million		Population in largest city		Access to improved sanitation facilities			
	millions		% of total population		average annual % growth	% of total population		% of urban population		% of urban population		% of rural population	
	1990	2004	1990	2004	1990–2004	1990	2005	1990	2005	1990	2002	1990	2002
Honduras	2.0	3.2	40	46	3.6	..	..	36	32	77	89	31	52
Hungary	6.4	6.6	62	66	0.2	19	17	31	25	100	100	..	85
India	217.0	308.0	26	29	2.5	9	11	6	6	43	58	1	18
Indonesia	54.5	101.6	31	47	4.4	9	11	14	12	66	71	38	38
Iran, Islamic Rep.	30.6	45.1	56	67	2.8	22	22	21	16	86	86	78	78
Iraq	12.9	..	70	..	..	29	..	32	..	95	..	48	..
Ireland	2.0	2.4	57	60	1.5	..	..	46	41	..	..	..	..
Israel	4.2	6.2	90	92	2.8	48	58	43	48	100	100	..	..
Italy	37.8	38.8	67	67	0.2	23	20	12	10	..	..	..	..
Jamaica	1.2	1.4	51	52	0.8	..	..	..	..	85	90	64	68
Japan	77.9	83.8	63	66	0.5	42	44	42	42	100	100	100	100
Jordan	2.3	4.3	72	79	4.5	27	23	37	29	97	94	..	85
Kazakhstan	9.3	8.4	57	56	–0.8	7	7	12	13	87	87	52	52
Kenya	5.8	13.6	25	40	6.1	6	8	24	20	49	56	40	43
Korea, Dem. Rep.	11.5	13.8	58	61	1.3	16	20	22	24	..	58	..	60
Korea, Rep.	31.7	38.7	74	81	1.4	49	46	33	25	..	..	..	..
Kuwait	2.0	2.4	95	96	1.1	48	..	51	..	..	..	..	..
Kyrgyz Republic	1.7	1.7	38	34	0.2	..	..	38	48	..	75	..	51
Lao PDR	0.6	1.2	15	21	4.7	..	..	..	..	..	61	..	14
Latvia	1.9	1.5	70	66	–1.5	..	..	48	47	..	..	..	..
Lebanon	2.3	3.1	83	88	2.2	42	52	51	60	100	100	..	87
Lesotho	0.3	0.3	17	18	1.2	..	..	..	..	61	61	32	32
Liberia	0.9	1.5	42	47	3.8	..	..	..	..	59	49	24	7
Libya	3.5	5.0	80	87	2.6	35	36	43	41	97	97	96	96
Lithuania	2.5	2.3	68	67	–0.6	..	..	..	..	..	..	..	..
Macedonia, FYR	1.1	1.2	58	60	0.7	..	..	..	..	..	..	..	..
Madagascar	2.8	4.9	24	27	3.8	8	10	33	36	25	49	8	27
Malawi	1.1	2.1	12	17	4.6	..	..	..	..	52	66	34	42
Malaysia	8.9	16.0	50	64	4.2	6	5	13	8	94	..	98	98
Mali	2.1	4.3	24	33	5.1	8	10	35	30	50	59	32	38
Mauritania	0.9	1.9	44	63	5.3	..	..	..	..	31	64	26	9
Mauritius	0.4	0.5	41	44	1.6	..	..	..	..	100	100	99	99
Mexico	60.3	78.6	72	76	1.9	32	34	25	24	84	90	20	39
Moldova	2.0	1.9	47	46	–0.3	..	..	..	..	..	86	..	52
Mongolia	1.2	1.4	57	57	1.3	..	..	48	58	..	75	..	37
Morocco	11.6	17.3	48	58	2.9	21	25	23	21	87	83	28	31
Mozambique	2.8	7.1	21	37	6.6	6	7	27	18	..	51	14	14
Myanmar	10.1	15.0	25	30	2.8	7	8	29	26	39	96	15	63
Namibia	0.4	0.7	27	33	4.1	..	..	..	..	68	66	8	14
Nepal	1.7	4.1	9	15	6.2	..	..	..	..	62	68	7	20
Netherlands	9.0	10.8	60	66	1.3	14	14	12	11	100	100	100	100
New Zealand	2.9	3.5	85	86	1.3	25	28	30	33	..	..	88	..
Nicaragua	2.1	3.1	53	58	2.8	19	21	35	36	64	78	27	51
Niger	1.4	3.1	16	23	5.8	..	..	33	31	35	43	2	4
Nigeria	31.7	61.1	35	47	4.7	11	13	15	18	50	48	33	30
Norway	3.1	3.7	72	80	1.3	..	..	22	22	..	..	..	..
Oman	1.1	2.0	62	78	3.9	..	..	..	..	97	97	61	61
Pakistan	33.0	52.4	31	34	3.3	16	18	22	22	81	92	19	35
Panama	1.3	1.8	54	57	2.4	..	..	65	51	..	89	..	51
Papua New Guinea	0.5	0.8	13	13	2.5	..	..	..	..	67	67	41	41
Paraguay	2.1	3.5	49	58	3.8	22	28	45	49	71	94	46	58
Peru	15.0	20.5	69	74	2.2	27	29	39	39	68	72	15	33
Philippines	29.8	50.4	49	62	3.8	14	14	27	21	63	81	46	61
Poland	23.2	23.7	61	62	0.2	14	13	15	12	..	..	..	..
Portugal	4.6	5.8	47	55	1.6	30	31	40	34	..	..	..	..
Puerto Rico	2.6	3.8	72	97	2.8	44	60	60	62	..	..	..	..

Urbanization

	Urban population					Population in urban agglomerations of more than 1 million		Population in largest city		Access to improved sanitation facilities			
	millions		% of total population		average annual % growth	% of total population		% of urban population		% of urban population		% of rural population	
	1990	2004	1990	2004	1990–2004	1990	2005	1990	2005	1990	2002	1990	2002
Romania	12.4	11.9	53	55	–0.3	9	8	17	15	..	86	..	10
Russian Federation	108.8	105.4	73	73	–0.2	18	20	8	10	93	93	70	70
Rwanda	0.4	1.8	5	20	11.1	..	..	..	..	49	56	36	38
Saudi Arabia	12.8	21.1	78	88	3.6	30	44	18	25	100	100	..	..
Senegal	3.2	5.7	40	50	4.2	18	20	46	39	52	70	23	34
Serbia and Montenegro	5.4	4.3	51	52	–1.6	11	14	21	26	97	97	77	77
Sierra Leone	1.2	2.1	30	40	3.9	..	..	47	45	..	53	..	30
Singapore	3.0	4.2	100	100	2.4	99	100	99	100	100	100	..	..
Slovak Republic	3.0	3.1	56	58	0.3	..	..	..	..	100	100	100	100
Slovenia	1.0	1.0	51	51	0.0	..	..	..	..	..	..	..	..
Somalia	2.0	2.8	29	35	2.6	11	15	39	43	..	47	..	14
South Africa	17.2	26.1	49	57	3.0	23	30	11	13	85	86	42	44
Spain	29.3	32.7	75	77	0.8	23	22	16	15	..	..	..	..
Sri Lanka	3.6	4.1	21	21	0.9	..	..	..	..	89	98	64	89
Sudan	6.9	14.2	27	40	5.1	9	12	34	30	53	50	26	24
Swaziland	0.2	0.3	23	24	2.9	..	..	..	..	..	78	..	44
Sweden	7.1	7.5	83	83	0.4	17	19	21	23	100	100	100	100
Switzerland	4.6	5.0	68	68	0.6	..	..	18	20	100	100	100	100
Syrian Arab Republic	6.3	9.3	49	50	2.8	26	25	25	26	97	97	56	56
Tajikistan	1.7	1.6	32	25	–0.4	..	..	..	..	..	71	..	47
Tanzania	5.7	13.7	22	36	6.3	5	7	23	19	51	54	45	41
Thailand	16.1	20.5	29	32	1.7	11	10	37	32	95	97	74	100
Togo	1.1	2.1	29	36	4.6	..	..	..	..	71	71	24	15
Trinidad and Tobago	0.8	1.0	69	76	1.2	..	..	..	..	100	100	100	100
Tunisia	4.7	6.4	58	64	2.1	19	21	33	32	95	90	47	62
Turkey	33.2	47.9	59	67	2.6	22	25	20	20	96	94	67	62
Turkmenistan	1.7	2.2	45	46	2.0	..	..	..	..	..	77	..	50
Uganda	2.0	3.4	11	12	3.9	4	5	38	38	54	53	41	39
Ukraine	34.6	31.9	67	67	–0.6	14	15	7	8	100	100	97	97
United Arab Emirates	1.5	3.7	83	85	6.6	..	..	32	26	100	100	100	100
United Kingdom	51.1	53.4	89	89	0.3	24	22	15	14	..	..	..	..
United States	188.0	236.2	75	80	1.6	40	42	9	8	100	100	100	100
Uruguay	2.8	3.2	89	93	1.0	41	39	46	42	95	95	..	85
Uzbekistan	8.2	9.6	40	37	1.1	10	8	25	22	73	73	48	48
Venezuela, RB	16.6	23.0	84	88	2.3	31	34	17	14	..	71	..	48
Vietnam	13.4	21.6	20	26	3.4	13	13	30	23	46	84	16	26
West Bank and Gaza	..	..	..	..	..	..	..	..	..	..	..	..	..
Yemen, Rep.	2.6	5.3	21	26	5.1	6	8	26	29	59	76	11	14
Zambia	3.3	4.2	39	36	1.6	12	12	30	34	64	68	26	32
Zimbabwe	3.1	4.6	29	35	2.9	10	12	34	33	69	69	40	51
World	**2,259.9 s**	**3,091.5 s**	**43 w**	**49 w**	**2.2 w**	**.. w**	**.. w**	**17 w**	**16 w**	**76 w**	**79 w**	**22 w**	**35 w**
Low income	454.7	717.1	26	31	3.3	10	12	17	17	49	61	10	24
Middle income	1,146.2	1,604.3	44	53	2.4	..	..	16	14	79	81	25	41
Lower middle income	797.7	1,187.9	38	49	2.8	16	17	14	12	75	78	22	39
Upper middle income	348.5	416.4	69	72	1.3	..	..	20	20	91	91	58	61
Low & middle income	1,600.9	2,321.4	37	43	2.7	..	..	16	15	71	74	18	32
East Asia & Pacific	459.5	759.0	29	41	3.6	..	..	10	7	65	72	15	35
Europe & Central Asia	293.2	300.4	63	64	0.2	16	18	14	15	94	93	72	63
Latin America & Carib.	310.9	420.8	71	77	2.2	31	34	24	22	83	84	35	44
Middle East & N. Africa	115.5	167.2	52	56	2.6	21	21	28	25	86	89	51	56
South Asia	278.6	409.9	25	28	2.8	10	12	10	11	50	64	5	23
Sub-Saharan Africa	143.2	264.3	28	36	4.4	..	..	26	25	53	55	24	26
High income	659.0	770.1	75	78	1.1	..	..	20	19	..	..	..	..
Europe EMU	216.5	235.5	74	76	0.6	28	27	17	16	..	..	..	..

About the data

The population of a city or metropolitan area depends on the boundaries chosen. For example, in 1990 Beijing, China, contained 2.3 million people in 87 square kilometers of "inner city" and 5.4 million in 158 square kilometers of "core city." The population of "inner city and inner suburban districts" was 6.3 million, and that of "inner city, inner and outer suburban districts, and inner and outer counties" was 10.8 million. (For most countries the last definition is used.)

Estimates of the world's urban population would change significantly if China, India, and a few other populous nations were to change their definition of urban centers. According to China's State Statistical Bureau, by the end of 1996 urban residents accounted for about 43 percent of China's population, while in 1994 only 20 percent of the population was considered urban. In addition to the continuous migration of people from rural to urban areas, one of the main reasons for this shift was the rapid growth in the hundreds of towns reclassified as cities in recent years. Because the estimates in the table are based on national definitions of what constitutes a city or metropolitan area, cross-country comparisons should be made with caution. To estimate urban populations, UN ratios of urban to total population were applied to the World Bank's estimates of total population (see table 2.1).

The urban population with access to improved sanitation facilities is defined as people with access to at least adequate excreta disposal facilities that can effectively prevent human, animal, and insect contact with excreta. The rural population with access is included to allow comparison of rural and urban access. This definition and the definition of urban areas vary, however, so comparisons between countries can be misleading.

Definitions

• **Urban population** is the midyear population of areas defined as urban in each country and reported to the United Nations (see *About the data*). • **Population in urban agglomerations of more than 1 million** is the percentage of a country's population living in metropolitan areas that in 2000 had a population of more than 1 million. • **Population in largest city** is the percentage of a country's urban population living in that country's largest metropolitan area. • **Access to improved sanitation facilities** refers to the percentage of the urban or rural population with access to at least adequate excreta disposal facilities (private or shared but not public) that can effectively prevent human, animal, and insect contact with excreta. Improved facilities range from simple but protected pit latrines to flush toilets with a sewerage connection. To be effective, facilities must be correctly constructed and properly maintained.

3.10a

The urban population in developing countries has increased substantially since 1990

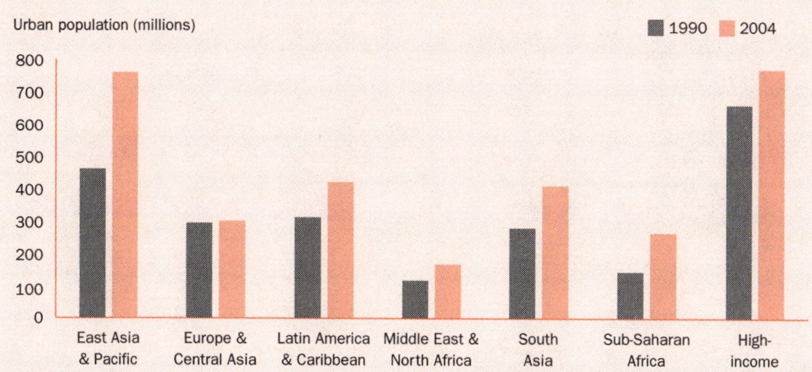

Source: Table 3.10.

Data sources

Data on urban population and the population in urban agglomerations and in the largest city are from the United Nations Population Division's *World Urbanization Prospects: The 2005 Revision*. The total population figures are World Bank estimates. Data on access to sanitation in urban and rural areas are from the World Health Organization.

3.11 Urban housing conditions

	Census year	Household size: number of people		Overcrowding: People living in overcrowded dwellings[a] % of total		Durable dwelling units: Buildings with durable structure % of total		Home ownership: Privately owned dwellings % of total		Multiunit dwellings: % of total		Vacancy rate: Unoccupied dwellings % of total	
		National	Urban	National	Urban	National	Urban	National	Urban	National	Urban	National	Urban
Afghanistan	..	..	..	..	..	..	..	..	..	..	..	..	..
Albania	2001	4.2	3.9	..	..	..	..	65[b]	30[b]	..	..	12	13
Algeria	1998	4.9	..	..	..	..	..	67	..	..	..	19	..
Angola	..	..	..	..	..	..	..	..	..	..	..	..	..
Argentina	2001	3.6	..	19	..	97	..	..	..	4	..	16[b]	..
Armenia	2001	4.1	4.0	4	6	93	93	95	90	1	1	..	..
Australia	2001	3.8	..	1	..	..	..	..	..	..	..	..	..
Austria	1991	2.6	..	2	..	..	..	..	..	50	..	13	..
Azerbaijan	1999	4.7	4.4	..	..	..	..	74	62	4	5	..	..
Bangladesh	2001	4.8	4.8	..	..	21[b]	42[b]	88[b]	61[b]	..	..	..	..
Belarus	1999	..	..	..	..	..	..	..	..	..	..	..	..
Belgium	2001	2.6	..	0[b]	..	..	..	67	..	32[b]	..	..	..
Benin	1992	5.9	..	..	..	26	..	59	..	..	..	..	..
Bolivia	2001	4.2	4.3	40	..	43	58	70	59	3[b]	5[b]	6	4
Bosnia and Herzegovina	..	..	..	..	..	..	..	..	..	..	..	..	..
Botswana	2001	4.2	3.9	27	47	88	90[b]	61	47	1	..	..	..
Brazil	2000	3.8	3.7	..	..	..	..	74	75	..	..	..	..
Bulgaria	2001	2.7	2.7	..	..	79	89	98	98	..	..	23	17
Burkina Faso	1996	6.2	5.8	30	53	..	..	..	..	..	..	..	..
Burundi	1990	4.7	..	..	..	..	..	..	..	..	..	..	..
Cambodia	1998	5.2	..	..	..	..	..	..	..	..	..	..	..
Cameroon	1987	5.2	5.1	67	77	77	..	73	48	27	42	..	..
Canada	2001	2.6	..	..	..	..	..	64	..	32	..	8	..
Central African Republic	2003	5.2	5.8	32	36[b]	78	92	85	74	..	..	..	..
Chad	1993	5.1	5.1	..	..	..	..	..	..	..	..	..	..
Chile	2002	3.4	3.5	..	..	91	92	66	65	13	15	11	10
China	2000	3.4	3.2	..	..	82	..	88	74	..	..	1	..
Hong Kong, China	..	..	..	..	..	..	..	..	..	..	..	..	..
Colombia	1993	4.8	..	27[b]	..	83[b]	..	68[b]	..	13	..	10[b]	..
Congo, Dem. Rep.	1984	5.4	..	55	..	..	..	..	..	..	..	..	..
Congo, Rep.	1984	10.5	..	..	..	..	..	76	..	..	..	..	..
Costa Rica	2000	4.0	..	22	..	88	..	72	..	2	3	9	6
Côte d'Ivoire	1998	5.4	..	..	..	..	..	..	..	..	..	..	..
Croatia	2001	3.0	..	..	..	..	..	..	..	..	..	12	..
Cuba	1981	4.2	4.2	..	..	..	..	..	..	15	21	0	0
Czech Republic	2001	2.4	..	..	..	..	..	52	..	49	..	12	..
Denmark	2001	2.2	..	..	..	..	..	..	..	..	..	..	..
Dominican Republic	2002	3.9	..	..	..	97	..	..	..	8	..	11	..
Ecuador	2001	3.5	3.7	30	..	81	88	68[b]	58[b]	9	14	12	7
Egypt, Arab Rep.	1996	4.7	..	..	..	..	..	..	..	75	..	..	..
El Salvador	1992	..	..	63	..	67	83	70	68	3	6	11	11
Eritrea	..	..	..	..	..	..	..	..	..	..	..	..	..
Estonia	2000	2.4	2.3	3	..	..	..	..	..	72	..	13	..
Ethiopia	1994	4.8	4.7	..	..	..	23	..	54	..	..	..	..
Finland	2000	2.2	..	..	..	..	..	64	..	44	..	..	..
France	1999	2.5	..	..	..	..	..	55	..	..	..	7	..
Gabon	2003	5.2	..	..	..	..	..	..	..	..	..	..	..
Gambia, The	1993	8.9	..	..	..	18	..	68	..	..	..	..	..
Georgia	2002	3.5	3.5	..	..	..	..	..	..	..	..	..	..
Germany	2001	2.3	..	..	..	..	..	43	..	..	..	7	..
Ghana	2000	5.1	5.1	..	..	45	..	57	..	53	..	5	..
Greece	2001	3.0	..	1	..	..	..	..	..	..	..	..	..
Guatemala	2002	4.4	4.7	..	..	67	80	81	74	2	4	13	11
Guinea	..	..	..	..	..	..	..	..	..	..	..	..	..
Guinea-Bissau	..	..	..	..	..	..	..	..	..	..	..	..	..
Haiti	1982	4.2	..	26	..	..	..	92	68	..	..	9	19

Urban housing conditions

	Census year	Household size		Overcrowding		Durable dwelling units		Home ownership		Multiunit dwellings		Vacancy rate	
		number of people		People living in overcrowded dwellings[a] % of total		Buildings with durable structure % of total		Privately owned dwellings % of total		% of total		Unoccupied dwellings % of total	
		National	Urban	National	Urban	National	Urban	National	Urban	National	Urban	National	Urban
Honduras	2001	4.4	..	..	..	69	85	..	..	..	..	14	..
Hungary	1990	2.7	..	..	..	..	..	..	..	..	..	4	..
India	2001	5.3	5.3	77	71	83	81	87	67	..	..	6	9
Indonesia	2000	4.0	..	..	..	..	..	..	..	..	..	..	..
Iran, Islamic Rep.	1996	4.8	4.6	33[b]	26[b]	72	76	73	67	..	..	..	..
Iraq	1997	7.7	7.2	..	..	88	96	70	66	4	5	13	15
Ireland	2002	3.0	..	..	..	..	..	..	..	8[b]	..	..	..
Israel	1995	3.5	..	..	..	..	..	..	..	..	..	..	..
Italy	2001	2.8	..	..	..	..	..	..	..	..	..	21	..
Jamaica	2001	3.5	..	..	..	98[b]	..	58[b]	..	2[b]	..	..	..
Japan	2000	2.7	..	..	..	..	..	61	..	37	..	..	..
Jordan	1994	6.2	6.0	1	..	97	97	69	64	57	67	..	..
Kazakhstan	..	..	..	..	..	..	..	..	..	..	..	..	..
Kenya	1999	4.6	3.4	..	..	35	72	72	25	..	..	39	17
Korea, Dem. Rep.	2000	3.8	..	23	..	..	..	50	..	15	..	..	..
Korea, Rep.	1993	4.4	..	..	..	..	..	..	..	..	..	..	..
Kuwait	1995	6.4	..	..	..	..	..	..	..	9[b]	..	11	..
Kyrgyz Republic	1999	4.4	3.6	..	..	..	..	..	..	..	..	..	..
Lao PDR	1995	6.1	6.1	..	..	49	77	96	86	..	..	..	..
Latvia	2000	3.0	2.6	4	..	88	..	58	..	74	..	0	..
Lebanon	..	..	..	..	..	..	..	..	..	..	..	..	..
Lesotho	2001	5.0	..	10[b]	..	..	..	84	..	0	..	..	..
Liberia	1974	4.8	..	31	..	20	..	1	..	..	..	..	..
Libya	..	6.4	..	..	..	..	..	..	..	..	..	7	..
Lithuania	2001	2.6	..	7	..	..	..	..	..	..	..	..	..
Macedonia, FYR	2002	3.6	3.6[b]	8[b]	..	95[b]	95[b]	48[b]	..	..	..	7[b]	3[b]
Madagascar	1993	4.9	4.8	64	57	..	..	81	59	..	..	..	..
Malawi	1998	4.4	4.4	30	..	48	84	86	47	..	..	..	..
Malaysia	2000	4.5	4.4	..	..	..	..	..	..	10[b]	16[b]	..	..
Mali	1998	5.6	..	..	..	..	..	..	..	..	..	..	..
Mauritania	1988	..	..	..	..	..	..	..	..	..	..	..	..
Mauritius	2000	3.9	3.8	6	7	91	94	87	81	..	..	7	6
Mexico	2000	4.4	..	27[b]	..	87	..	78	..	6	..	..	..
Moldova	2003	..	..	..	..	..	..	..	..	..	..	..	..
Mongolia	2000	4.4	4.5	..	..	..	..	..	..	48	56	..	..
Morocco	1982	5.9	5.3	..	..	..	..	..	..	..	..	..	..
Mozambique	1997	4.4	4.9	37	28	7	20	92	83	1	1	0	..
Myanmar	..	..	..	..	..	..	..	..	..	..	..	..	..
Namibia	2001	5.3	..	..	..	..	..	..	..	..	..	..	..
Nepal	2001	5.4	4.9	..	..	..	..	88	..	..	..	0	..
Netherlands	..	..	..	..	..	..	..	..	..	..	..	..	..
New Zealand	2001	2.8	..	1[b]	..	..	..	65	..	17	..	10	..
Nicaragua	1995	5.3	..	..	..	79	87	84	86	0	0	8	..
Niger	2001	6.4	6.0	..	..	..	..	77	40	..	..	..	..
Nigeria	1991	5.0	4.7	..	..	..	..	..	..	..	..	..	..
Norway	1980	2.7	..	1	..	..	..	67	..	38	..	..	..
Oman	2003	7.1	..	..	..	..	..	..	..	..	..	..	..
Pakistan	1998	6.8	6.8	..	..	58	86	81	..	..	..	..	..
Panama	2000	4.1	..	28[b]	..	88	98[b]	80	66[b]	10[b]	10[b]	14	..
Papua New Guinea	1990	4.5[b]	6.5	..	..	..	..	..	44	..	8	..	..
Paraguay	2002	4.6	4.5	38[b]	..[b]	95[b]	98[b]	79	75	1[b]	2[b]	6[b]	6[b]
Peru	1993	..	..	..	..	49	64	..	..	..	..	7	3
Philippines	1990	5.3	5.3	..	..	62	..	83	76	6	11	4	4
Poland	1988	3.2	..	..	..	..	..	..	..	..	..	1	..
Portugal	2001	2.8	..	..	..	..	..	76	..	86	..	..	..
Puerto Rico	1990	3.3	..	..	..	..	..	72	..	..	..	11	..

Urban housing conditions

	Census year	Household size		Overcrowding		Durable dwelling units		Home ownership		Multiunit dwellings		Vacancy rate	
		number of people		People living in overcrowded dwellings[a] % of total		Buildings with durable structure % of total		Privately owned dwellings % of total		% of total		Unoccupied dwellings % of total	
		National	Urban	National	Urban	National	Urban	National	Urban	National	Urban	National	Urban
Romania	1992	3.1	3.1	..	..	58	..	87	77	39	71	6	4
Russian Federation	2002	2.8	2.7	7	5	..	..	..	..	73	86	..	..
Rwanda	1991	4.7	..	..	..	79	78	92	73	19	25	..	..
Saudi Arabia	1992	6.1	..	..	..	92	..	42	..	..	..	..	..
Senegal	..	..	..	..	..	..	..	..	..	..	..	..	..
Serbia and Montenegro	2001	2.9	2.2	..	..	..	..	..	..	..	..	..	..
Sierra Leone	1985	6.8	..	..	..	34	..	68	..	..	..	..	..
Singapore	2000	4.4	..	..	..	..	..	..	..	..	..	..	..
Slovak Republic	..	..	..	..	..	..	..	..	..	..	..	..	..
Slovenia	1991	3.1	..	..	..	..	..	69	..	37	..	9	..
Somalia	1975	..	..	..	..	..	..	..	..	..	..	..	..
South Africa	2001	4.0	..	..	..	..	..	..	..	7	..	..	..
Spain	1991	3.3	..	0	..	..	..	78	..	..	..	..	..
Sri Lanka	2001	3.8	..	..	..	93[b]	92[b]	70[b]	58[b]	1	14[b]	13	1[b]
Sudan	1993	5.8	6.0	..	..	..	..	86[b]	58[b]	0[b]	1[b]	..	..
Swaziland	1997	5.4	3.7	..	..	..	..	..	..	..	..	..	..
Sweden	1990	2.0	..	..	..	..	..	..	..	54	..	1	..
Switzerland	1990	2.4	2.1	..	..	..	..	31	24	28	32	11	7
Syrian Arab Republic	1981	6.3	6.0	..	..	..	..	..	..	..	..	..	..
Tajikistan	2000	..	..	..	..	..	..	..	..	..	..	..	..
Tanzania	2002	4.9	4.5[b]	33[b]	7[b]	..	..	82[b]	43[b]	..	..	..	..
Thailand	2000	3.8	..	..	..	93	93	81	62	3	..	3	..
Togo	..	..	..	..	..	..	..	..	..	..	..	..	..
Trinidad and Tobago	2000	3.7	..	9[b]	..	98[b]	..	74[b]	..	17[b]	..	..	..
Tunisia	1994	8.0	..	..	..	99	..	71	89[b]	6	10[b]	15	12[b]
Turkey	1990	5.0	..	..	..	..	..	70	..	..	..	..	..
Turkmenistan	..	..	..	..	..	..	..	..	..	..	..	..	..
Uganda	1991	4.9	4.0[b]	..	..	21[b]	..	80[b]	24[b]	0[b]	2[b]	..	..
Ukraine	2003	..	..	..	..	..	..	..	..	..	..	..	..
United Arab Emirates	..	..	..	..	..	..	..	..	..	..	..	..	..
United Kingdom	2001	..	2.4	..	..	..	..	..	69	..	19	..	..
United States	2000	2.7	..	..	..	..	..	66	..	..	..	9	7
Uruguay	1996	3.3	3.4[b]	22[b]	..	..	..	57[b]	57[b]	..	..	13[b]	13[b]
Uzbekistan	..	..	..	..	..	..	..	..	..	..	..	..	..
Venezuela, RB	2001	4.4	..	..	..	..	..	78	..	14	..	16	..
Vietnam	1999	4.6	4.5	..	..	77	89	95	86	..	..	..	..
West Bank and Gaza	1997	7.1	..	..	..	..	..	78	..	45	..	..	..
Yemen, Rep.	1994	6.7	6.8	54[b]	6[b]	..	..	88[b]	68[b]	3[b]	11[b]	..	..
Zambia	2000	5.3	5.9	..	..	..	..	94	30	..	..	..	..
Zimbabwe	1992	4.8	4.2	..	..	..	..	94	30	6	..	..	..

a. More than two people per room. b. Data are from previous census.

About the data

Urbanization can yield important social benefits, improving access to public services and the job market. At the same time it also leads to significant demands for services. Inadequate living quarters and demand for housing and shelter are major concerns for policymakers. The unmet demand for affordable housing, along with urban poverty, has led to the emergence of slums in many poor countries. Improving the shelter situation requires a better understanding of the mechanisms governing housing markets and the processes governing housing availability. That requires good data and adequate policy-oriented analysis so that housing policy can be formulated in a global comparative perspective and drawn from the lessons learned in other countries. Housing policies and outcomes affect such broad socioeconomic conditions as the infant mortality rate, performance in school, household saving, productivity levels, capital formation, and government budget deficits. A good understanding of housing conditions thus requires an extensive set of indicators within a reasonable framework.

There is a strong demand for quantitative indicators that can measure housing conditions on a regular basis to monitor progress. However, data deficiencies and lack of rigorous quantitative analysis hamper informed decisionmaking on desirable policies to improve housing conditions. The data in the table are from housing and population censuses, collected using similar definitions. The table will incorporate household survey data in future editions. The table focuses attention on urban areas, where housing conditions are typically most severe. Not all the compiled indicators are presented in the table because of space limitations. Additional indicators for more countries will be available in the online version of *World Development Indicators* and on the companion CD-ROM.

3.11a

Selected housing indicators for smaller economies

	Census year	Household size number of people	Overcrowding People living in overcrowded dwellings[a] % of total	Durable dwelling units Buildings with durable structure % of total	Home ownership Privately owned dwellings % of total	Multiunit dwellings % of total	Vacancy rate Unoccupied dwellings % of total
Antigua and Barbuda	2001	3.0	..	99[b]	65[b]	3[b]	22
Bahamas, The	1990	3.8	12	99	55	13	14
Bahrain	2001	5.9	..	94[b]	51	28	6
Barbados	1990	3.5	3	100	76	9	9
Belize	2000	4.6	..	93	63	4	..
Cape Verde	1990	5.1	28	78	72	2	..
Cayman Islands	1999	3.1	..	100	53	38	19
Equatorial Guinea	1993	7.5	14	56[b]	75	14	..
Fiji	1996	5.4	..	60	65	7	..
Guam	2000	4.0	2[b]	93	48	29	19
Isle of Man	2001	2.4	0	..	68	16	..
Maldives	2000	6.6	..	93	..	1	15
Marshall Islands	1999	7.8	..	95	72	12	8
Netherlands Antilles	2001	2.9	24[b]	99	60	16	12
New Caledonia	1989	4.1	..	77	53	9	13
Northern Mariana Islands	1995	4.9	9[b]	99	33	27	17
Palau	2000	5.7	8	76	79	11	3
Seychelles	1997	4.2	15[b]	97	78	..	0
Solomon Islands	1999	6.3	51	23	85	1	..
St. Vincent & Grenadines	1991	3.9	..	98	71	7	..
Turks and Caicos	1990	3.3	4	96	66	11	..
Virgin Islands (U.K.)	1991	3.0	2	99	40	46	..
Western Samoa	1991	7.3	..	42	90	47	30

a. More than two people per room. b. Data are from previous census.
Source: National population and housing censuses.

Definitions

• **Household size** refers to the average number of people within a household. It is calculated by dividing total population by the number of households in the country and in urban areas. • **Overcrowding** refers to the number of households living in dwellings with two or more people per room as a percentage of the total number of households in the country and in urban areas. • **Durable dwelling units** refer to the number of housing units in structures made of durable building materials (concrete, stone, cement, brick, asbestos, zinc, and stucco) expected to maintain their stability for 20 years or longer under local conditions with normal maintenance and repair, taking into account location and environmental hazards such as floods, mudslides, and earthquakes as a percentage of total dwellings. • **Home ownership** refers to the number of privately owned dwellings as a percentage of total dwellings or the number of households that own housing units as a percentage of total households. This category includes privately owned and owner-occupied units, depending on the definition used in the census data. State- and community-owned units, rented, squatted, and rent-free units are not included. • **Multiunit dwellings** refer to the number of multiunit dwellings, such as apartments, flats, condominiums, barracks, boarding houses, orphanages, retirement houses, hostels, hotels, and collective dwellings, as a percentage of total occupied dwellings. • **Vacancy rate** refers to the percentage of completed dwelling units that are currently unoccupied. It includes all vacant units, whether on the market or not (such as second homes).

Data sources

Data on urban housing conditions are from national population and housing censuses.

3.12 Traffic and congestion

	Motor vehicles				Passenger cars		Two-wheelers		Road traffic		Particulate matter concentrations	
	per 1,000 people		per kilometer of road		per 1,000 people		per 1,000 people		million vehicle kilometers		Urban-population-weighted PM10 micrograms per cubic meter	
	1990	2003[a]	1990	2003[a]	1990	2003[a]	1990	2003[a]	1990	2003[a]	1990	2002
Afghanistan	3	..	3	..	2	..	..	..	..	..	34	27
Albania	11	70	3	12	2	47	3	1	..	..	93	58
Algeria	55	..	15	..	26	..	..	..	..	..	123	65
Angola	19	..	3	..	14	..	..	..	..	..	142	113
Argentina	181	181	27	37	134	140	1	..	43,119	27,458	105	78
Armenia	5	..	2	..	1	..	2	..	..	316	..	84
Australia	530	..	11	..	450	..	18	18	138,501	..	22	18
Austria	421	545	30	33	387	501	71	73	..	49,800	39	37
Azerbaijan	52	57	7	17	36	45	5	1	..	5,263	..	64
Bangladesh	1	1	0	1	0	0	1	1	..	..	229	157
Belarus	61	168	13	18	59	168	45	51	10,026	5,650	7	9
Belgium	423	527	30	37	385	470	14	31	150,750	156,633	31	28
Benin	3	..	2	..	2	..	34	..	..	..	75	51
Bolivia	41	10	6	1	25	3	9	0	1,139	..	119	92
Bosnia and Herzegovina	114	..	24	..	101	..	..	..	..	..	41	22
Botswana	18	92	3	6	10	38	1	1	..	..	40	25
Brazil	88	170	8	17	84	137	..	28	..	..	41	35
Bulgaria	163	335	39	26	146	295	55	28	..	285	109	69
Burkina Faso	4	..	3	..	2	..	9	..	..	..	140	97
Burundi	..	..	..	..	..	..	..	..	..	..	168	99
Cambodia	..	30	0	31	..	25	9	127	314	7,210	83	51
Cameroon	10	..	3	..	6	..	..	..	..	..	118	86
Canada	605	577	20	34	468	561	12	11	..	..	25	21
Central African Republic	1	..	0	..	1	..	0	..	1,494	..	29	24
Chad	2	..	0	..	1	..	0	..	..	..	103	73
Chile	81	136	13	26	52	89	2	2	..	..	85	56
China	5	15	4	11	1	10	3	46	..	659,390	113[b]	80[b]
Hong Kong, China	66	79	253	287	42	59	4	5	8,192	10,781	..	38
Colombia	39	51	13	19	21	43	8	12	50,945	41,587	37	24
Congo, Dem. Rep.	..	..	..	..	..	..	..	..	..	..	70	57
Congo, Rep.	18	..	3	..	12	..	..	..	..	..	126	74
Costa Rica	87	185	7	21	55	103	14	29	..	..	50	40
Côte d'Ivoire	24	..	6	..	15	..	..	..	..	..	94	38
Croatia	..	324	..	50	..	291	..	22	..	18,104	52	35
Cuba	37	..	16	..	18	..	19	..	..	..	43	25
Czech Republic	246	391	46	31	228	358	113	75	37,350	..	70	25
Denmark	368	424	27	32	320	360	9	15	36,304	46,520	29	22
Dominican Republic	75	..	48	..	21	..	..	..	..	..	44	36
Ecuador	35	53	8	16	31	47	2	2	10,306	19,604	37	28
Egypt, Arab Rep.	29	..	33	..	21	..	6	..	..	..	227	136
El Salvador	33	..	14	..	17	..	0	..	2,002	..	46	40
Eritrea	1	..	1	..	1	..	..	..	..	..	178	109
Estonia	211	386	22	9	154	321	66	6	5,455	6,843	18	17
Ethiopia	1	2	2	4	1	1	0	0	..	1,495	175	88
Finland	441	450	29	30	386	433	12	47	39,750	49,790	24	22
France	494	596	32	40	405	495	55	..	422,000	548,900	18	15
Gabon	32	..	4	..	19	..	..	..	..	..	21	13
Gambia, The	13	8	5	3	6	6	..	..	..	..	189	138
Georgia	107	63	27	16	89	50	5	0	4,620	..	204	46
Germany	405	578	53	206	386	545	18	45	446,000	639,100	28	22
Ghana	8	..	4	..	5	..	..	..	..	15,320	39	42
Greece	248	435	22	34	171	331	120	229	..	79,377	70	48
Guatemala	21	57	16	45	11	52	10	12	3,243	4,547	64	76
Guinea	4	..	1	..	2	..	..	..	..	..	87	63
Guinea-Bissau	7	..	2	..	4	..	..	..	..	..	114	84
Haiti	8	..	14	..	5	..	..	..	..	..	69	47

Traffic and congestion

	Motor vehicles				Passenger cars		Two-wheelers		Road traffic		Particulate matter concentrations	
	per 1,000 people		per kilometer of road		per 1,000 people		per 1,000 people		million vehicle kilometers		Urban-population-weighted PM10 micrograms per cubic meter	
	1990	2003[a]	1990	2003[a]	1990	2003[a]	1990	2003[a]	1990	2003[a]	1990	2002
Honduras	22	*61*	10	*28*	*5*	*52*	..	*14*	*3,288*	..	44	46
Hungary	212	313	21	*19*	188	274	16	10	22,898	*23,260*	35	22
India	4	*9*	2	*3*	2	*6*	15	*35*	..	..	109	84
Indonesia	16	..	10	..	7	..	34	*59*	..	..	137	114
Iran, Islamic Rep.	34	..	14	..	25	..	*36*	..	..	..	85	68
Iraq	14	..	6	..	1	..	..	..	..	..	150	167
Ireland	270	447	10	11	227	382	6	9	24,205	*33,915*	25	20
Israel	210	284	74	110	174	231	8	11	18,212	38,273	70	53
Italy	529	*610*	99	*73*	476	*545*	*45*	*125*	344,726	*65,983*	43	33
Jamaica	*52*	..	*7*	..	*43*	..	..	..	..	..	57	43
Japan	469	582	52	*63*	283	433	146	105	628,581	*790,829*	42	33
Jordan	60	99	26	71	*44*	67	*0*	0	*1,098*	*526,677*	124	69
Kazakhstan	76	96	8	6	50	77	..	5	18,248	*4,087*	12	27
Kenya	12	*11*	5	*5*	10	*8*	1	*1*	5,170	..	66	38
Korea, Dem. Rep.	..	..	..	..	..	..	..	..	..	..	203	88
Korea, Rep.	79	304	60	150	48	215	32	36	30,464	..	83	43
Kuwait	*474*	332	*165*	..	*368*	326	..	..	..	..	77	129
Kyrgyz Republic	44	*38*	10	*10*	44	*38*	*16*	*2*	5,220	*1,992*	..	36
Lao PDR	9	..	3	..	6	..	*18*	..	..	..	35	25
Latvia	135	329	6	11	106	280	76	10	3,932	..	30	17
Lebanon	321	..	183	..	300	..	13	..	..	..	41	43
Lesotho	11	..	4	..	3	..	..	..	*445*	..	176	94
Liberia	14	..	4	..	7	..	..	..	..	..	57	39
Libya	*165*	..	*10*	..	*96*	..	*0*	..	..	..	109	121
Lithuania	160	397	12	17	133	364	52	6	..	*2,709*	28	22
Macedonia, FYR	132	..	30	..	121	..	1	..	3,102	..	36	29
Madagascar	6	..	2	..	4	..	..	..	41,500	..	101	51
Malawi	4	..	4	..	2	..	..	..	..	..	169	88
Malaysia	124	254	26	*75*	101	222	167	249	..	..	36	28
Mali	3	..	2	..	2	..	..	..	..	..	144	102
Mauritania	10	..	3	..	7	..	..	..	..	..	55	42
Mauritius	59	119	35	72	44	88	54	103	..	*78*	85	47
Mexico	119	201	41	59	82	133	3	*4*	55,095	..	70	43
Moldova	53	78	17	26	48	60	45	3	*891*	*678*	..	41
Mongolia	21	*41*	1	*2*	6	*26*	22	*10*	340	*2,321*	22	16
Morocco	37	*45*	15	*23*	28	*45*	1	*1*	..	*14,242*	33	27
Mozambique	4	..	2	..	3	..	..	..	1,889	..	108	44
Myanmar	*2*	..	*3*	..	*1*	..	..	..	..	..	130	75
Namibia	71	*82*	1	*4*	39	*42*	1	*2*	1,896	..	74	50
Nepal	..	..	..	..	..	..	..	..	..	..	67	43
Netherlands	405	*427*	58	*58*	368	*383*	44	*25*	90,150	*109,955*	47	40
New Zealand	524	*730*	19	*31*	436	*613*	24	*21*	..	..	16	16
Nicaragua	19	39	5	11	10	16	3	8	108	*412*	49	32
Niger	6	..	4	..	5	..	..	..	178	..	112	86
Nigeria	*30*	..	*21*	..	*12*	..	*5*	..	..	..	172	95
Norway	458	527	22	26	380	424	48	64	*28,136*	35,047	26	18
Oman	130	..	9	..	83	..	3	..	..	..	163	124
Pakistan	6	*8*	4	*5*	4	*7*	8	*11*	*25,317*	*205,385*	226	165
Panama	75	*107*	18	*27*	60	*76*	2	..	..	..	58	58
Papua New Guinea	*27*	..	*6*	..	*7*	..	..	..	..	..	12	11
Paraguay	*27*	*88*	*4*	*15*	*16*	*52*	..	..	..	..	109	103
Peru	*128*	46	*43*	16	*62*	30	..	9	..	*23,360*	98	68
Philippines	10	*34*	4	*13*	7	*9*	6	*18*	*6,189*	*9,548*	55	34
Poland	168	354	18	*33*	138	294	36	22	59,608	*138,100*	59	39
Portugal	222	*463*	34	*278*	162	*429*	5	*56*	28,623	*47,943*	53	31
Puerto Rico	*295*	..	*79*	..	*242*	..	..	..	..	*741,445*	70	62

Traffic and congestion

	Motor vehicles				Passenger cars		Two-wheelers		Road traffic		Particulate matter concentrations	
	per 1,000 people		per kilometer of road		per 1,000 people		per 1,000 people		million vehicle kilometers		Urban-population-weighted PM10 micrograms per cubic meter	
	1990	2003[a]	1990	2003[a]	1990	2003[a]	1990	2003[a]	1990	2003[a]	1990	2002
Romania	72	*168*	11	*19*	56	*144*	13	*12*	23,907	*35,675*	36	20
Russian Federation	*87*	*174*	*14*	*48*	*65*	*140*	..	*43*	..	*56,455*	13	25
Rwanda	2	..	1	..	1	..	..	..	..	..	162	100
Saudi Arabia	165	..	19	..	98	..	0	..	*94,141*	..	105	91
Senegal	11	*14*	6	*9*	8	*11*	0	*0*	..	*4,013*	99	93
Serbia and Montenegro	137	..	31	..	133	..	*3*	..	..	..	26	17
Sierra Leone	10	*4*	4	*2*	7	*2*	2	*0*	*996*	..	101	69
Singapore	130	135	142	111	89	100	40	32	..	16,133	107	48
Slovak Republic	194	286	57	36	163	252	61	9	*8,127*	*10,992*	40	20
Slovenia	306	490	42	25	289	446	8	21	5,620	10,261	..	33
Somalia	2	..	1	..	1	..	..	..	..	..	81	35
South Africa	139	*144*	26	*24*	97	*92*	8	*4*	..	..	34	24
Spain	360	558	43	34	309	455	79	37	100,981	*224,370*	42	40
Sri Lanka	21	*34*	4	..	7	*13*	24	*49*	3,468	*15,630*	97	93
Sudan	9	..	22	..	8	..	..	..	..	..	291	219
Swaziland	66	83	18	*24*	35	40	3	3	..	..	117	71
Sweden	464	504	29	11	426	455	11	24	61,040	*58,992*	15	14
Switzerland	491	553	46	57	449	511	114	103	48,660	59,052	37	27
Syrian Arab Republic	26	36	10	7	10	12	..	6	..	..	151	89
Tajikistan	3	..	1	..	0	..	..	..	..	*1,092*	..	57
Tanzania	5	..	2	..	1	..	..	..	..	..	57	38
Thailand	46	..	36	..	14	..	86	..	45,769	..	87	77
Togo	24	..	11	..	16	..	8	..	..	..	50	45
Trinidad and Tobago	*117*	..	*19*	..	*98*	..	..	..	..	..	124	22
Tunisia	48	*88*	19	*43*	23	*60*	..	*1*	..	*19,231*	71	46
Turkey	50	90	8	101	34	66	10	15	27,041	52,344	76	56
Turkmenistan	..	..	..	..	..	..	..	..	..	..	..	73
Uganda	2	*5*	..	*4*	1	*2*	0	*3*	..	..	60	33
Ukraine	63	137	20	39	63	114	*59*	28	59,500	*13,755*	45	29
United Arab Emirates	121	..	52	..	97	..	..	..	..	..	233	109
United Kingdom	400	442	64	42	341	439	14	19	399,000	484,722	25	17
United States	758	*808*	30	*36*	573	*482*	17	*17*	2,527,441	*4,208,594*	30	24
Uruguay	138	..	45	..	122	..	74	..	..	..	235	154
Uzbekistan	..	..	..	..	..	..	..	..	..	..	95	81
Venezuela, RB	*93*	..	*25*	..	*73*	..	..	..	*563*	..	22	12
Vietnam	..	..	..	..	..	..	45	..	..	..	127	66
West Bank and Gaza	..	..	..	..	..	..	..	..	..	..	..	..
Yemen, Rep.	34	..	8	..	14	..	..	..	8,681	..	..	82
Zambia	14	..	3	..	8	..	..	..	..	..	133	71
Zimbabwe	*32*	*50*	*4*	*7*	*29*	*44*	*33*	*4*	..	..	60	43
World	118 w	*141* w	..	..	91 w	*100* w	..	..	..	..	77 w	60 w
Low income	5	*8*	..	..	3	*6*	..	..	..	..	129	89
Middle income	37	*69*	..	..	24	*51*	..	..	..	..	79	62
Lower middle income	22	*39*	..	..	10	*29*	..	..	..	..	92	70
Upper middle income	*121*	*187*	..	..	*91*	*143*	..	..	..	..	50	40
Low & middle income	25	*47*	..	..	16	*35*	..	..	..	..	93	70
East Asia & Pacific	9	20	..	..	4	14	..	..	..	..	112	80
Europe & Central Asia	*97*	*170*	..	..	*79*	*142*	..	..	..	..	39	35
Latin America & Carib.	100	*153*	..	..	*72*	*108*	..	..	..	..	60	43
Middle East & N. Africa	36	..	..	..	24	..	..	..	..	..	126	89
South Asia	4	*10*	..	..	2	*6*	..	..	..	..	131	99
Sub-Saharan Africa	21	..	..	..	15	..	..	..	..	..	114	73
High income	499	*623*	..	..	390	*433*	..	..	..	..	37	29
Europe EMU	429	570	..	..	379	502	..	..	..	..	33	27

a. Data are for 2003 or most recent year available. b. Includes data for Hong Kong, China; Macao, China; and Taiwan, China.

About the data

Traffic congestion in urban areas constrains economic productivity, damages people's health, and degrades the quality of their lives. The particulate air pollution emitted by motor vehicles—the dust and soot in exhaust—is proving to be far more damaging to human health than was once believed. (For information on particulate matter and other air pollutants, see table 3.13.)

In recent years ownership of passenger cars has increased, and the expansion of economic activity has led to the transport by road of more goods and services over greater distances (see table 5.8). These developments have increased demand for roads and vehicles, adding to urban congestion, air pollution, health hazards, traffic accidents, and injuries.

Congestion, the most visible cost of expanding vehicle ownership, is reflected in the indicators in the table. Other relevant indicators—such as average vehicle speed in major cities or the cost of traffic congestion, which takes a heavy toll on economic productivity—are not included because data are incomplete or difficult to compare.

The data in the table—except those on fuel prices—are compiled by the International Road Federation (IRF) through questionnaires sent to national organizations. The IRF uses a hierarchy of sources to gather as much information as possible. The primary sources are national road associations. Where such an association lacks data or does not respond, other agencies are contacted, including road directorates, ministries of transport or public works, and central statistical offices. As a result, the compiled data are of uneven quality. The coverage of each indicator may differ across countries because of differences in definitions. Comparability also is limited when time-series data are reported. Moreover, the data do not capture the quality or age of vehicles or the condition or width of roads. Thus comparisons over time and between countries should be made with caution.

Estimates of particulate matter concentrations weighted by urban population represent the average annual exposure level of the average urban resident to outdoor particulate matter under 10 microns (PM10). Data for countries and aggregates for regions and income groups are urban-population-weighted PM10 levels in residential areas of cities with more than 100,000 residents; they are available at www.worldbank.org/research. Data for selected cities are in table 3.13.

Significant uncertainties exist around these estimates, and caution should be used in interpreting them. But they do allow for cross-country comparisons of the relative risk of particulate matter pollution that urban residents face. Major sources of urban outdoor particulate matter pollution are emissions from traffic and industrial sources, but nonanthropogenic sources such as dust storms may also be a significant contributor for some cities. Estimates of economic damages from death and illness due to particulate matter pollution are shown in table 3.15.

3.12a

The 15 countries with the fewest passenger cars per 1,000 people in 2003—and the 15 with the most

Country	Number of cars	Country	Number of cars
Bangladesh	0.5	New Zealand	613
Ethiopia	1	Canada	561
Sierra Leone	2	Germany	545
Uganda	2	Italy	545
Bolivia	3	Switzerland	511
Gambia, The	6	Austria	501
India	6	France	495
Pakistan	7	United States	482
Kenya	8	Belgium	470
Afghanistan	9	Spain	455
Philippines	9	Sweden	455
China	10	Slovenia	446
Senegal	11	United Kingdom	439
Syrian Arab Republic	12	Finland	433
Sri Lanka	13	Japan	433

Source: Table 3.12.

Definitions

• **Motor vehicles** include cars, buses, and freight vehicles but not two-wheelers. Population figures refer to the midyear population in the year for which data are available. Roads refer to motorways, highways, main or national roads, and secondary or regional roads. A motorway is a road specially designed and built for motor traffic that separates the traffic flowing in opposite directions. • **Passenger cars** refer to road motor vehicles, other than two-wheelers, intended for the carriage of passengers and designed to seat no more than nine people (including the driver). • **Two-wheelers** refer to mopeds and motorcycles. • **Road traffic** is the number of vehicles multiplied by the average distances they travel. • **Particulate matter concentrations** refer to fine suspended particulates less than 10 microns in diameter that are capable of penetrating deep into the respiratory tract and causing significant health damage. The state of a country's technology and pollution controls is an important determinant of particulate matter concentrations.

Data sources

Data on vehicles and traffic are from the IRF's electronic files and its annual *World Road Statistics*. Data on particulate matter concentrations are from Kiran Dev Pandey, David Wheeler, Bart Ostro, Uwe Deichmann, Kirk Hamilton, and Katie Bolt's "Ambient Particulate Matter Concentrations in Residential and Pollution Hotspot Areas of World Cities: New Estimates Based on the Global Model of Ambient Particulates (GMAPS)" (2006).

3.13 Air pollution

	City	City population thousands 2005	Particulate matter micrograms per cubic meter 2002	Sulfur dioxide micrograms per cubic meter 1995–2001[a]	Nitrogen dioxide micrograms per cubic meter 1995–2001[a]
Argentina	Cordoba City	1,592	58	..	97
Australia	Melbourne	3,663	13	..	30
	Perth	1,484	13	5	19
	Sydney	4,388	22	28	81
Austria	Vienna	2,190	44	14	42
Belgium	Brussels	1,027	30	20	48
Brazil	Rio de Janeiro	11,469	42	129	..
	Sao Paulo	18,333	49	43	83
Bulgaria	Sofia	1,045	76	39	122
Canada	Montreal	3,511	20	10	42
	Toronto	5,060	24	17	43
	Vancouver	2,125	14	14	37
Chile	Santiago	5,623	62	29	81
China	Anshan	1,459	92	115	88
	Beijing	10,849	99	90	122
	Changchun	3,092	82	21	64
	Chengdu	3,478	95	77	74
	Chongquing	4,975	137	340	70
	Dalian	2,709	55	61	100
	Guangzhu	976	70	57	136
	Guiyang	2,467	78	424	53
	Harbin	2,898	85	23	30
	Jinan	2,654	104	132	45
	Kunming	1,748	78	19	33
	Lanzhou	1,788	101	102	104
	Liupanshui	2,118	65	102	..
	Nanchang	1,742	87	69	29
	Pinxiang	1,562	74	75	..
	Quingdao	2,431	68	190	64
	Shanghai	12,665	81	53	73
	Shenyang	4,916	112	99	73
	Taiyuan	2,516	98	211	55
	Tianjin	9,346	139	82	50
	Urumqi	1,467[b]	57	60	70
	Wuhan	6,003	88	40	43
	Zhengzhou	2,250	108	63	95
	Zibo	2,775	82	198	43
Colombia	Bogota	5,442[b]	32	..	..
Croatia	Zagreb	908[b]	37	31	..
Cuba	Havana	2,192	28	1	5
Czech Republic	Prague	1,164	25	14	33
Denmark	Copenhagen	1,091	23	7	54
Ecuador	Guayaquil	2,387	25	15	..
	Quito	1,514	33	22	..
Egypt, Arab Rep.	Cairo	11,146	159	69	..
Finland	Helsinki	1,103	23	4	35
France	Paris	9,854	12	14	57
Germany	Berlin	3,328	25	18	26
	Frankfurt	668[b]	22	11	45
	Munich	2,318	22	8	53
Ghana	Accra	1,970	40	..	..
Greece	Athens	3,238	51	34	64
Hungary	Budapest	1,670	23	39	51
Iceland	Reykjavik	164[b]	20	5	42
India	Ahmedabad	5,171	98	30	21
	Bangalore	6,532	53	..	..

About the data

In many towns and cities exposure to air pollution is the main environmental threat to human health. Long-term exposure to high levels of soot and small particles in the air contributes to a wide range of health effects, including respiratory diseases, lung cancer, and heart disease. Particulate pollution, on its own or in combination with sulfur dioxide, leads to an enormous burden of ill health.

Emissions of sulfur dioxide and nitrogen oxides lead to the deposition of acid rain and other acidic compounds over long distances. Acid deposition changes the chemical balance of soils and can lead to the leaching of trace minerals and nutrients critical to trees and plants.

Where coal is the primary fuel for power plants, steel mills, industrial boilers, and domestic heating, the result is usually high levels of urban air pollution—especially particulates and sometimes sulfur dioxide—and, if the sulfur content of the coal is high, widespread acid deposition. Where coal is not an important primary fuel or is used in plants with effective dust control, the worst emissions of air pollutants stem from the combustion of petroleum products.

The data on sulfur dioxide and nitrogen dioxide concentrations are based on reports from urban monitoring sites. Annual means (measured in micrograms per cubic meter) are average concentrations observed at these sites. Coverage is not comprehensive because not all cities have monitoring systems.

The data on concentrations of particulate matter are estimates, for selected cities, of average annual concentrations in residential areas away from air pollution "hotspots," such as industrial districts and transport corridors. The data have been extracted from a complete set of estimates developed by the World Bank's Development Research Group and Environment Department in a study of annual ambient concentrations of particulate matter in world cities with populations exceeding 100,000 (Pandey and others 2006).

Pollutant concentrations are sensitive to local conditions, and even in the same city different monitoring sites may register different concentrations. Thus these data should be considered only a general indication of air quality in each city, and cross-country comparisons should be made with caution. The current World Health Organization (WHO) air quality guidelines for annual mean concentrations are 50 micrograms per cubic meter for sulfur dioxide and 40 micrograms for nitrogen dioxide. The WHO has set no guidelines for particulate matter concentrations below which there are no appreciable health effects.

	City	City population	Particulate matter	Sulfur dioxide	Nitrogen dioxide
		thousands 2005	micrograms per cubic meter 2002	micrograms per cubic meter 1995–2001[a]	micrograms per cubic meter 1995–2001[a]
India	Calcutta	14,299	145	49	34
	Chennai	6,915	44	15	17
	Delhi	15,334	177	24	41
	Hyderabad	6,145	48	12	17
	Kanpur	3,040	128	15	14
	Lucknow	2,589	129	26	25
	Mumbai	18,336	74	33	39
	Nagpur	2,359	65	6	13
	Pune	4,485	55	..	..
Indonesia	Jakarta	13,194	115	..	..
Iran, Islamic Rep.	Tehran	7,352	68	209	..
Ireland	Dublin	1,033	21	20	..
Italy	Milan	4,007	36	31	248
	Rome	2,628	35	..	..
	Torino	969[b]	53	..	..
Japan	Osaka	2,626[b]	37	19	63
	Tokyo	35,327	42	18	68
	Yokohama	3,366	32	100	13
Kenya	Nairobi	2,818	42	..	..
Korea, Rep	Pusan	3,527	44	60	51
	Seoul	9,592	46	44	60
	Taegu	2,510	50	81	62
Malaysia	Kuala Lumpur	1,392	28	24	..
Mexico	Mexico City	19,013	55	74	130
Netherlands	Amsterdam	1,157	40	10	58
New Zealand	Auckland	1,152	15	3	20
Norway	Oslo	808	19	8	43
Philippines	Manila	10,432[b]	42	33	..
Poland	Lodz	943	39	21	43
	Warsaw	2,204	43	16	32
Portugal	Lisbon	1,977	28	8	52
Romania	Bucharest	1,764	22	10	71
Russian Federation	Moscow	10,672	25	109	..
	Omsk	1,132	27	20	34
Singapore	Singapore	4,372	48	20	30
Slovak Republic	Bratislava	456[b]	19	21	27
South Africa	Capetown	3,103	15	21	72
	Durban	2,643	29	31	..
	Johannesburg	3,288	30	19	31
Spain	Barcelona	4,424	43	11	43
	Madrid	5,145	37	24	66
Sweden	Stockholm	1,729	13	3	20
Switzerland	Zurich	984	26	11	39
Thailand	Bangkok	6,604	83	11	23
Turkey	Ankara	3,593	54	55	46
	Istanbul	9,760	64	120	..
Ukraine	Kiev	2,623	38	14	51
United Kingdom	Birmingham	2,215	26	9	45
	London	7,615	23	25	77
	Manchester	2,193	17	26	49
United States	Chicago	8,711	26	14	57
	Los Angeles	12,146	36	9	74
	New York	18,498	22	26	79
Venezuela, RB	Caracas	3,276	17	33	57

a. Data are for the most recent year available. b. Data are for 2000.

Definitions

• **City population** is the number of residents of the city or metropolitan area as defined by national authorities and reported to the United Nations. • **Particulate matter** refers to fine suspended particulates less than 10 microns in diameter that are capable of penetrating deep into the respiratory tract and causing significant health damage. The state of a country's technology and pollution controls is an important determinant of particulate matter concentrations. • **Sulfur dioxide** is an air pollutant produced when fossil fuels containing sulfur are burned. It contributes to acid rain and can damage human health, particularly that of the young and the elderly. • **Nitrogen dioxide** is a poisonous, pungent gas formed when nitric oxide combines with hydrocarbons and sunlight, producing a photochemical reaction. These conditions occur in both natural and anthropogenic activities. Nitrogen dioxide is emitted by bacteria, motor vehicles, industrial activities, nitrogenous fertilizers, combustion of fuels and biomass, and aerobic decomposition of organic matter in soils and oceans.

Data sources

Data on city population are from the United Nations Population Division. Data on particulate matter concentrations are from a recent World Bank study by Kiran D. Pandey, David Wheeler, Bart Ostro, Uwe Deichman, Kirk Hamilton, and Kathrine Bolt, "Ambient Particulate Matter Concentration in Residential and Pollution Hotspot Areas of World Cities: New Estimates Based on the Global Model of Ambient Particulates (GMAPS)" (2006). Data on sulfur dioxide and nitrogen dioxide concentrations are from the WHO's Healthy Cities Air Management Information System and the World Resources Institute, which relies on various national sources as well as, among others, the Organisation for Economic Co-operation and Development's *OECD Environmental Data Compendium 1999*, the U.S. Environmental Protection Agency's *National Air Quality and Emissions Trends Report 1995*, the Aerometric Information Retrieval System Executive International database, and the United Nations Centre for Human Settlements' Urban Indicators database.

3.14 Government commitment

	Environmental strategies or action plans	Biodiversity assessments, strategies, or action plans	Participation in treaties[a]								
			Climate change[b]	Ozone layer	CFC control	Law of the Sea[c]	Biological diversity[b]	Kyoto Protocol	CITES	CCD	Stockholm Convention
Afghanistan	..	..	2002	2004[f]	2004[f]	..	2002	..	1985[f]	1995[f]	..
Albania	1993	..	1995	1999[f]	1999[f]	2003[f]	1994[f]	2005[f]	2003[f]	2000[f]	2004
Algeria	2001	..	1994	1992[f]	1992[f]	1996	1995	2005[f]	1983[f]	1996	..
Angola	..	..	2000	2000[f]	2000[f]	1994	1998	..	..	1997	..
Argentina	1992	..	1994	1990	1990	1995	1994	2001	1981	1997	2005
Armenia	..	..	1994	1999[f]	1999[f]	2002[f]	1993[d]	2003[f]	..	1997	2003
Australia	1992	1994	1994	1987[f]	1989	1994	1993	..	1976	2000	2004
Austria	..	..	1994	1987	1989	1995	1994	2002	1982[f]	1997[f]	2002
Azerbaijan	1998	..	1995	1996[f]	1996[f]	..	2000[e]	2000[f]	1998[f]	1998[f]	2004[f]
Bangladesh	1991	1990	1994	1990[f]	1990[f]	2001	1994	2001[f]	1981	1996	..
Belarus	..	..	2000	1986[d]	1988[d]	..	1993	..	1995[f]	2001[f]	2004[f]
Belgium	..	..	1996	1988	1988	1998	1996	2002	1983	1997[f]	..
Benin	1993	..	1994	1993[f]	1993[f]	1997	1994	2002[f]	1984[f]	1996	2004
Bolivia	1994	1988	1995	1994[f]	1994[f]	1995	1994	1999	1979	1996	2003
Bosnia and Herzegovina	..	..	2000	1992[g]	1992[g]	1994[g]	2002[f]	..	2002	2002[f]	..
Botswana	1990	1991	1994	1991[f]	1991[f]	1994	1995	2003[f]	1977[f]	1996	2002[f]
Brazil	..	1988	1994	1990[f]	1990[f]	1994	1994	2002	1975	1997	2004
Bulgaria	..	1994	1995	1990[f]	1990[f]	1996	1996	2002	1991[f]	2001[f]	2004
Burkina Faso	1993	..	1994	1989	1989	2005	1993	2005[f]	1989[f]	1996	2004
Burundi	1994	1989	1997	1997[f]	1997[f]	..	1997	2001[f]	1988[f]	1997	2005
Cambodia	1999	..	1996	2001[f]	2001[f]	..	1995[f]	2002[f]	1997	1997	..
Cameroon	..	1989	1995	1989[f]	1989[f]	1994	1994	2002[f]	1981[f]	1997	..
Canada	1990	1994	1994	1986	1988	2003	1992	2002	1975	1995	2001
Central African Republic	..	..	1995	1993[f]	1993[f]	..	1995	..	1980[f]	1996	..
Chad	1990	..	1994	1989[f]	1994	..	1994	..	1989[f]	1996	2004
Chile	..	1993	1995	1990	1990	1997	1994	2002	1975	1997	2005
China	1994	1994	1994	1989[f]	1991[f]	1996	1993	2002[e]	1981[f]	1997	2004
Hong Kong, China	..	..	..	..	..	..	..	..	..	..	..
Colombia	1998	1988	1995	1990[f]	1993[f]	..	1994	2001[f]	1981	1999	..
Congo, Dem. Rep.	..	1990	1995	1994[f]	1994[f]	1995	1996	2005[f]	1976[f]	1997	2005[f]
Congo, Rep.	..	1990	1997	1994[f]	1994[f]	..	1994	..	1983[f]	1999	..
Costa Rica	1990	1992	1994	1991[f]	1991[f]	1994	1994	2002	1975	1998	..
Côte d'Ivoire	1994	1991	1995	1993[f]	1993[f]	1994	1994	..	1994[f]	1997	2004
Croatia	2001	2000	1996	1991[d]	1991[d]	1994[g]	1996	..	2000[f]	2000[d]	..
Cuba	..	..	1994	1992[f]	1992[f]	1994	1994	2002	1990[f]	1997	..
Czech Republic	1994	..	1994	1993[d]	1993[d]	1996	1993[e]	2001[e]	1993[g]	2000[f]	2002
Denmark	1994	..	1994	1988	1988	2004	1993	2002	1977	1995[f]	2003
Dominican Republic	..	1995	1999	1993[f]	1993[f]	..	1996	2002[f]	1986[f]	1997[f]	..
Ecuador	1993	1995	1994	1990[f]	1990[f]	..	1993	2000	1975	1995	2004
Egypt, Arab Rep.	1992	1988	1995	1988	1988	1994	1994	2005[f]	1978	1995	2003
El Salvador	1994	1988	1996	1992	1992	..	1994	1998	1987[f]	1997[f]	..
Eritrea	1995	..	1995	2005[f]	2005[f]	..	1996[f]	2005[f]	1994[f]	1996	2005[f]
Estonia	1998	..	1994	1996[f]	1996[f]	2005[f]	1994	2002	1992[f]	..	..
Ethiopia	1994	1991	1994	1994[f]	1994[f]	..	1994	2005[f]	1989[f]	1997	2003
Finland	1995	..	1994	1986	1988	1996	1994[d]	2002	1976[f]	1995[d]	2002[d]
France	1990	..	1994	1987[e]	1988[e]	1996	1994	2002[e]	1978	1997	2004[e]
Gabon	..	1990	1998	1994[f]	1994[f]	1998	1997	..	1989[f]	1996[f]	..
Gambia, The	1992	1989	1994	1990[f]	1990[f]	1994	1994	2001[f]	1977[f]	1996	..
Georgia	1998	..	1994	1996[f]	1996[f]	1996[f]	1994[f]	1999[f]	1996[f]	1999	..
Germany	..	..	1994	1988	1988	1994[f]	1993	2002	1976	1996	2002
Ghana	1992	1988	1995	1989[f]	1989	1994	1994	2003[f]	1975	1996	2003
Greece	..	..	1994	1988	1988	1995	1994	2002	1992[f]	1997	..
Guatemala	1994	1988	1996	1987[f]	1989[f]	1997	1995	1999	1979	1998[f]	..
Guinea	1994	1988	1994	1992[f]	1992[f]	1994	1993	2000[f]	1981[f]	1997	..
Guinea-Bissau	1993	1991	1996	2002[f]	2002[f]	1994	1995	..	1990[f]	1995	..
Haiti	1999	..	1996	2000[f]	2000[f]	1996	1996	2005[f]	..	1996	..

Government commitment

	Environmental strategies or action plans	Biodiversity assessments, strategies, or action plans	Participation in treaties[a]								
			Climate change[b]	Ozone layer	CFC control	Law of the Sea[c]	Biological diversity[b]	Kyoto Protocol	CITES	CCD	Stockholm Convention
Honduras	1993	..	1996	1993[f]	1993[f]	1994	1995	2000	1985[f]	1997	2005
Hungary	1995	..	1994	1988[f]	1989[f]	2002	1994	2002[f]	1985[f]	1999[f]	..
India	1993	1994	1994	1991[f]	1992[f]	1995	1994	2002[f]	1976	1996	..
Indonesia	1993	1993	1994	1992[f]	1992	1994	1994	2004	1978[f]	1998	..
Iran, Islamic Rep.	..	..	1996	1990[f]	1990[f]	..	1996	2005[f]	1976	1997	..
Iraq	..	..	..	..	..	1994	..	..	..	..	..
Ireland	..	..	1994	1988[f]	1988	1996	1996	2002	2002	1997	..
Israel	..	..	1996	1992[f]	1992	..	1995	2004	1979	1996	..
Italy	..	..	1994	1988	1988	1995	1994	2002	1979	1997	..
Jamaica	1994	..	1995	1993[f]	1993[f]	1994	1995	1999[f]	1997[f]	1997[f]	..
Japan	..	..	1994	1988[f]	1988	1996	1993[d]	2002[d]	1980	1998[d]	2002[f]
Jordan	1991	..	1994	1989[f]	1989[f]	1995[f]	1993	2003[f]	1978[f]	1996	2004
Kazakhstan	..	..	1995	1998[f]	1998[f]	..	1994	..	2000[f]	1997	..
Kenya	1994	1992	1994	1988[f]	1988	1994	1994	2005[f]	1978	1997	2004
Korea, Dem. Rep.	..	..	1995	1995[f]	1995[f]	..	1994[e]	2005[f]	..	2003[f]	2002[f]
Korea, Rep.	..	..	1994	1992	1992	1996	1994	2002	1993[f]	1999	..
Kuwait	..	..	1995	1992[f]	1992[f]	1994	2002	2005[f]	2002	1997	..
Kyrgyz Republic	1995	..	2000	2000[f]	2000[f]	..	1996[e]	2003[f]	..	1997[f]	..
Lao PDR	1995	..	1995	1998[f]	1998[f]	1998	1996[e]	2003[f]	2004[f]	1996[d]	..
Latvia	..	..	1995	1995[f]	1995[f]	2004[f]	1995	2002	1997[f]	2002[f]	2004
Lebanon	..	..	1995	1993[f]	1993[f]	1995	1994	..	..	1996	2003
Lesotho	1989	..	1995	1994[f]	1994[f]	..	1995	2000[f]	2003	1995	2002
Liberia	..	..	2003	1996[f]	1996[f]	..	2000	2002[f]	1981[f]	1998[f]	2002[f]
Libya	..	..	1999	1990[f]	1990[f]	..	2001	..	2003[f]	1996	2005[f]
Lithuania	..	..	1995	1995[f]	1995[f]	2003[f]	1996	2003	2001[f]	2003[f]	..
Macedonia, FYR	..	..	1998	1994[g]	1994[g]	1994[g]	1997[f]	2004[f]	2000[f]	2002[f]	2004
Madagascar	1988	1991	1999	1996[f]	1996[f]	2001	1996	2003[f]	1975	1997	..
Malawi	1994	..	1994	1991[f]	1991[f]	..	1994	2001[f]	1982[f]	1996	..
Malaysia	1991	1988	1994	1989[f]	1989[f]	1996	1994	2002	1977[f]	1997	..
Mali	..	1989	1995	1994[f]	1994[f]	1994	1995	2002	1994[f]	1995	2003
Mauritania	1988	..	1994	1994[f]	1994[f]	1996	1996	2005[f]	1998[f]	1996	2005
Mauritius	1990	..	1994	1992[f]	1992[f]	1994	1992	2001[f]	1975	1996	2004
Mexico	..	1988	1994	1987	1988	1994	1993	2000	1991[f]	1995	2003
Moldova	2002	..	1995	1996[f]	1996[f]	..	1995	2003[f]	2001[f]	1999[f]	2004
Mongolia	1995	..	1994	1996[f]	1996[f]	1996	1993	1999[f]	1996[f]	1996	2004
Morocco	..	1988	1996	1995	1995	..	1995	2002[f]	1975	1996	2004
Mozambique	1994	..	1995	1994[f]	1994[f]	1997	1995	2005[f]	1981[f]	1997	2005
Myanmar	..	1989	1995	1993[f]	1993[f]	1996	1995	2003[f]	1997[f]	1997[f]	2004[f]
Namibia	1992	..	1995	1993[f]	1993[f]	1994	1997	2003[f]	1990[f]	1997	2005[f]
Nepal	1993	..	1994	1994[f]	1994[f]	1998	1993	2005[f]	1975[f]	1996	..
Netherlands	1994	..	1994	1988[f]	1988[d]	1996	1994[d]	2002[f]	1984	1995[d]	2002[d]
New Zealand	1994	..	1994	1987	1988	1996	1993	2002	1989[f]	2000[f]	2004
Nicaragua	1994	..	1996	1993[f]	1993[f]	2000	1995	1999	1977[f]	1998	..
Niger	..	1991	1995	1992[f]	1992[f]	..	1995	2004	1975	1996	..
Nigeria	1990	1992	1994	1988[f]	1988[f]	1994	1994	2004[f]	1974	1997	2004
Norway	..	1994	1994	1986	1988	1996	1993	2002	1976	1996	2002
Oman	..	..	1995	1999[f]	1999[f]	1994	1995	2005[f]	..	1996[f]	2005
Pakistan	1994	1991	1994	1992[f]	1992[f]	1997	1994	2005[f]	1976[f]	1997	..
Panama	1990	..	1995	1989[f]	1989	1996	1995	1999	1978	1996	2003
Papua New Guinea	1992	1993	1994	1992[f]	1992[f]	1997	1993	2002	1975[f]	2000[f]	2003
Paraguay	..	..	1994	1992[f]	1992[f]	1994	1994	1999	1976	1997	2004
Peru	..	1988	1994	1989	1993[f]	..	1993	2002	1975	1995	2005
Philippines	1989	1989	1994	1991[f]	1991	1994	1993	2003	1981	2000	2004
Poland	1993	1991	1994	1990[f]	1990[f]	1998	1996	2002	1989	2001[f]	..
Portugal	1995	..	1994	1988[f]	1988	1997	1993	2002[e]	1980	1996	2004[d]
Puerto Rico	..	..	..	..	..	..	..	..	..	..	..

3.14 Government commitment

	Environmental strategies or action plans	Biodiversity assessments, strategies, or action plans	Participation in treaties[a]								
			Climate change[b]	Ozone layer	CFC control	Law of the Sea[c]	Biological diversity[b]	Kyoto Protocol	CITES	CCD	Stockholm Convention
Romania	1995	..	1994	1993[f]	1993[f]	1996	1994	2001	1994[f]	1998[f]	2004
Russian Federation	1999	1994	1995	1986[d]	1988[d]	1997	1995	2004	1992	2003[f]	..
Rwanda	1991	..	1998	2001[f]	2001[f]	..	1996	2004[f]	1980[f]	1998	2002[f]
Saudi Arabia	..	..	1995	1993[f]	1993[f]	1996	2001[e]	2005[f]	1996[f]	1997[f]	..
Senegal	1984	1991	1995	1993[f]	1993	1994	1994	2001[f]	1977[f]	1995	2003
Serbia and Montenegro	..	..	2001	2001[g]	2001[g]	2001[g]	2002	..	2002	..	2002
Sierra Leone	1994	..	1995	2001[f]	2001[f]	1994	1994[e]	..	1994[f]	1997	2003[f]
Singapore	1993	1995	1997	1989[f]	1989[f]	1994	1995	..	1986[f]	1999[f]	2005
Slovak Republic	..	..	1994	1993[g]	1993[g]	1996	1994[e]	2002	1993	2001[f]	2002
Slovenia	1994	..	1996	1992[g]	1992[g]	1995[g]	1996	2002	2000[f]	2001[f]	2004
Somalia	..	..	..	2001[f]	2001[f]	1994	..	..	1985[f]	2002[f]	..
South Africa	1993	..	1997	1990[f]	1990[f]	1997	1995	2002[f]	1975	1997	2002
Spain	..	..	1994	1988[f]	1988	1997	1995	2002	1986[f]	1996	2004
Sri Lanka	1994	1991	1994	1989[f]	1989[f]	1994	1994	2002[f]	1979[f]	1998[f]	..
Sudan	..	..	1994	1993[f]	1993[f]	1994	1995	2004[f]	1982	1995	..
Swaziland	..	..	1997	1992[f]	1992[f]	..	1994	..	1997[f]	1996	..
Sweden	..	..	1994	1986	1988	1996	1993	2002	1974	1995	2002
Switzerland	..	..	1994	1987	1988	..	1994	2003	1974	1996	2003
Syrian Arab Republic	1999	..	1996	1989[f]	1989[f]	..	1996	..	2003[f]	1997	2005
Tajikistan	..	..	1998	1996[f]	1998[f]	..	1997[e]	..	..	1997[f]	..
Tanzania	1994	1988	1996	1993[f]	1993[f]	1994	1996	2002[f]	1979	1997	2004
Thailand	..	..	1995	1989[f]	1989	..	2004	2002	1983	2001[f]	2005
Togo	1991	..	1995	1991[f]	1991	1994	1995[d]	2004[f]	1978	1995[d]	2004
Trinidad and Tobago	..	..	1994	1989[f]	1989[f]	1994	1996	1999	1984[f]	2000[f]	2002[f]
Tunisia	1994	1988	1994	1989[f]	1989[f]	1994	1993	2003[f]	1974	1995	2004
Turkey	1998	..	2004	1991[f]	1991[f]	..	1997	..	1996[f]	1998	..
Turkmenistan	..	..	1995	1993[f]	1993[f]	..	1996[e]	1999	..	1996	..
Uganda	1994	1988	1994	1988[f]	1988	1994	1993	2002[f]	1991[f]	1997	2004[f]
Ukraine	1999	..	1997	1986[d]	1988[d]	1999	1995	2004	1999[f]	2002[f]	..
United Arab Emirates	..	..	1996	1989[f]	1989[f]	..	2000	2005[f]	1990[f]	1998[f]	2002
United Kingdom	1995	1994	1994	1987	1988	1997[f]	1994	2002	1976	1996	2005
United States	1995	1995	1994	1986	1988	..	..	..	1974	2000	..
Uruguay	..	..	1994	1989[f]	1991[f]	1994	1993	2001	1975	1999[f]	2004
Uzbekistan	..	..	1994	1993[f]	1993[f]	..	1995[e]	1999	1997[f]	1995	..
Venezuela, RB	..	..	1995	1988[f]	1989	..	1994	..	1977	1998[f]	2005
Vietnam	..	1993	1995	1994[f]	1994[f]	1994	1994	2002	1994[f]	1998[f]	2002
West Bank and Gaza	..	..	..	..	..	..	..	..	..	..	..
Yemen, Rep.	1996	1992	1996	1996[f]	1996[f]	1994	1996	2004[f]	1997[f]	1997[f]	2004
Zambia	1994	..	1994	1990[f]	1990[f]	1994	1993	..	1980[f]	1996	..
Zimbabwe	1987	..	1994	1992[f]	1992[f]	1994	1994	..	1981[f]	1997	..

a. Ratification of the treaty. b. Years shown refer to the year the treaty entered into force in that country. c. Convention became effective November 16, 1994. d. Acceptance. e. Approval. f. Accession. g. Succession.

About the data

National environmental strategies and participation in international treaties on environmental issues provide some evidence of government commitment to sound environmental management. But the signing of these treaties does not always imply ratification, nor does it guarantee that governments will comply with treaty obligations.

In many countries efforts to halt environmental degradation have failed, primarily because governments have neglected to make this issue a priority, a reflection of competing claims on scarce resources. To address this problem, many countries are preparing national environmental strategies—some focusing narrowly on environmental issues, and others integrating environmental, economic, and social concerns. Among such initiatives are conservation strategies and environmental action plans. Some countries have also prepared country environmental profiles and biodiversity strategies and profiles.

National conservation strategies—promoted by the World Conservation Union (IUCN)—provide a comprehensive, cross-sectoral analysis of conservation and resource management issues to help integrate environmental concerns with the development process. Such strategies discuss current and future needs, institutional capabilities, prevailing technical conditions, and the status of natural resources in a country.

National environmental action plans, supported by the World Bank and other development agencies, describe a country's main environmental concerns, identify the principal causes of environmental problems, and formulate policies and actions to deal with them. These plans are a continuing process in which governments develop comprehensive environmental policies, recommend specific actions, and outline the investment strategies, legislation, and institutional arrangements required to implement them.

Biodiversity profiles—prepared by the World Conservation Monitoring Centre and the IUCN—provide basic background on species diversity, protected areas, major ecosystems and habitat types, and legislative and administrative support. In an effort to establish a scientific baseline for measuring progress in biodiversity conservation, the United Nations Environment Programme (UNEP) coordinates global biodiversity assessments.

To address global issues, many governments have also signed international treaties and agreements launched in the wake of the 1972 United Nations Conference on Human Environment in Stockholm and the 1992 United Nations Conference on Environment and Development (the Earth Summit) in Rio de Janeiro, which produced Agenda 21—an array of actions to address environmental challenges:

- The Framework Convention on Climate Change aims to stabilize atmospheric concentrations of greenhouse gases at levels that will prevent human activities from interfering dangerously with the global climate.
- The Vienna Convention for the Protection of the Ozone Layer aims to protect human health and the environment by promoting research on the effects of changes in the ozone layer and on alternative substances (such as substitutes for chlorofluorocarbons) and technologies, monitoring the ozone layer, and taking measures to control the activities that produce adverse effects.
- The Montreal Protocol for Chlorofluorocarbon Control requires that countries help protect the earth from excessive ultraviolet radiation by cutting chlorofluorocarbon consumption by 20 percent over their 1986 level by 1994 and by 50 percent over their 1986 level by 1999, with allowances for increases in consumption by developing countries.
- The United Nations Convention on the Law of the Sea, which became effective in November 1994, establishes a comprehensive legal regime for seas and oceans, establishes rules for environmental standards and enforcement provisions, and develops international rules and national legislation to prevent and control marine pollution.
- The Convention on Biological Diversity promotes conservation of biodiversity through scientific and technological cooperation among countries, access to financial and genetic resources, and transfer of ecologically sound technologies.

But 10 years after Rio the World Summit on Sustainable Development in Johannesburg recognized that many of the proposed actions have yet to materialize. To help developing countries comply with their obligations under these agreements, the Global Environment Facility (GEF) was created to focus on global improvement in biodiversity, climate change, international waters, and ozone layer depletion. The UNEP, United Nations Development Programme (UNDP), and the World Bank manage the GEF according to the policies of its governing body of country representatives. The World Bank is responsible for the GEF Trust Fund and is chair of the GEF.

Definitions

• **Environmental strategies and action plans** provide a comprehensive, cross-sectoral analysis of conservation and resource management issues to help integrate environmental concerns with the development process. They include national conservation strategies, national environmental action plans, national environmental management strategies, and national sustainable development strategies. The year shown for a country refers to the year in which a strategy or action plan was adopted. • **Biodiversity assessments, strategies, and action plans** include biodiversity profiles (see *About the data*). • **Participation in treaties** covers nine international treaties (see *About the data*). • **Climate change** refers to the Framework Convention on Climate Change (signed in New York in 1992). • **Ozone layer** refers to the Vienna Convention for the Protection of the Ozone Layer (signed in 1985). • **CFC control** refers to the Montreal Protocol for Chlorofluorocarbon Control (formally, the Protocol on Substances That Deplete the Ozone Layer, signed in 1987). • **Law of the Sea** refers to the United Nations Convention on the Law of the Sea (signed in Montego Bay, Jamaica, in 1982). • **Biological diversity** refers to the Convention on Biological Diversity (signed at the Earth Summit in Rio de Janeiro in 1992). • **Kyoto Protocol** refers to the protocol on climate change adopted at the third conference of the parties to the United Nations Framework Convention on Climate Change, held in Kyoto, Japan, in December 1997. • **CITES** refers to the Convention on International Trade in Endangered Species of Wild Fauna and Flora, an agreement between governments to ensure that the survival of wild animals and plants is not threatened by uncontrolled exploitation. • **CCD** refers to the United Nations Convention to Combat Desertification, an international convention dedicated to addressing the problems of land degradation in the world's drylands. Adopted in Paris on June 17, 1994, it entered into force on December 26, 1996. • **Stockholm Convention** is an international legally binding instrument designed to protect human health and the environment from persistent organic pollutants. It was adopted on May 22, 2001, and entered into force May 17, 2004.

Data sources

Data on environmental strategies and participation in international environmental treaties are from the Secretariat of the United Nations Framework Convention on Climate Change, the Ozone Secretariat of the UNEP, the World Resources Institute, the UNEP, the Center for International Earth Science Information Network, and the United Nations Treaty Series.

3.15 Toward a broader measure of savings

	Gross savings	Consumption of fixed capital	Net savings	Education expenditure	Energy depletion	Mineral depletion	Net forest depletion	Carbon dioxide damage	Particulate emission damage	Adjusted net savings
	% of GNI 2004	% of GNI 2004	% of GNI 2004	% of GNI 2004	% of GNI 2004	% of GNI 2004	% of GNI 2004	% of GNI 2004	% of GNI 2004	% of GNI 2004
Afghanistan	..	7.7	..	..	0.0	..	1.3	0.1	0.1	..
Albania	17.1	10.8	6.3	2.8	1.2	0.0	0.0	0.2	0.3	7.4
Algeria	47.6	11.6	36.0	4.5	35.2	0.0	0.1	0.8	0.7	3.6
Angola	18.4	11.5	6.9	3.1	45.0	0.0	0.0	0.3	1.1	–36.3
Argentina	22.2	12.4	9.8	4.3	8.2	0.3	0.0	0.6	2.3	2.7
Armenia	13.7	9.8	3.9	3.0	0.0	0.7	0.0	0.9	3.0	2.4
Australia	19.5	15.0	4.5	4.8	1.5	1.3	0.0	0.4	0.1	6.0
Austria	24.3	14.4	9.9	5.6	0.1	0.0	0.0	0.1	0.5	14.7
Azerbaijan	26.3	10.8	15.5	3.3	54.6	0.0	0.0	3.4	0.7	–40.0
Bangladesh	29.0	8.2	20.8	1.9	2.4	0.0	0.7	0.4	0.5	18.7
Belarus	23.6	11.0	12.6	5.4	2.1	0.0	0.0	2.1	..	13.8[a]
Belgium	23.2	15.6	7.5	3.0	0.0	0.0	0.0	0.2	0.3	10.1
Benin	12.5	9.0	3.5	2.4	0.1	0.0	0.0	0.3	0.5	5.1
Bolivia	18.2	10.3	7.9	6.3	15.4	1.0	0.0	0.7	1.0	–3.9
Bosnia and Herzegovina	3.9	10.6	–6.7	..	0.1	0.0	..	1.6	0.2	..
Botswana	40.0	12.5	27.5	5.6	0.0	2.0	0.0	0.4	..	30.8[a]
Brazil	24.0	11.8	12.1	4.1	3.7	1.1	0.0	0.4	0.4	10.7
Bulgaria	16.3	11.6	4.7	3.5	0.2	0.7	0.0	1.4	2.4	3.5
Burkina Faso	..	8.6	..	2.4	0.0	0.0	1.2	0.2	0.5	..
Burundi	15.5	6.8	8.7	3.7	0.0	0.0	14.6	0.3	0.3	–2.9
Cambodia	19.6	8.9	10.8	1.8	0.0	0.0	0.8	0.1	0.1	11.6
Cameroon	15.4	10.0	5.5	3.5	10.8	0.0	0.0	0.2	0.9	–3.0
Canada	20.7[b]	14.7	6.0	5.2	5.1	0.3	0.0	0.4	0.3	5.2
Central African Republic	14.1	8.3	5.8	1.6	0.0	0.0	0.0	0.1	0.1	7.2
Chad	10.0	13.7	–3.8	1.4	79.1	0.0	0.0	0.0	0.7	–82.2
Chile	22.7	12.5	10.2	3.9	0.2	10.8	0.0	0.5	1.2	1.5
China	42.3	10.4	31.9	2.0	3.0	0.2	0.0	1.4	1.5	27.8
Hong Kong, China	31.7	13.8	17.9	3.7	0.0	0.0	0.0	0.2	..	21.5[a]
Colombia	17.6	11.4	6.2	5.0	7.2	0.8	0.0	0.4	0.1	2.6
Congo, Dem. Rep.	7.6	7.3	0.3	0.9	2.8	0.9	0.0	0.3	0.6	–3.3
Congo, Rep.	36.0	13.3	22.7	3.8	54.1	0.0	0.0	0.2	..	–27.8[a]
Costa Rica	17.8	6.1	11.7	4.2	0.0	0.0	0.3	0.2	0.5	14.9
Côte d'Ivoire	15.5	10.2	5.4	4.6	2.9	0.0	0.6	0.3	0.3	5.7
Croatia	24.6	12.9	11.8	4.1	1.0	0.0	0.2	0.5	0.3	13.8
Cuba	..	..	..	8.1	..	..	..	..	0.2	..
Czech Republic	23.6	13.7	9.9	4.2	0.1	0.0	0.0	0.8	0.1	13.0
Denmark	22.7	15.4	7.3	8.1	1.3	0.0	0.0	0.1	0.1	13.9
Dominican Republic	29.3	11.8	17.5	2.2	0.0	2.2	0.0	0.9	0.3	16.3
Ecuador	28.4	11.6	16.8	1.4	19.0	0.1	0.0	0.6	0.2	–1.6
Egypt, Arab Rep.	21.1	10.0	11.1	4.4	10.6	0.1	0.3	1.2	1.7	1.6
El Salvador	9.4	11.3	–2.0	2.8	0.0	0.0	0.6	0.3	0.3	–0.2
Eritrea	–8.9	8.0	–16.9	1.6	0.0	0.0	1.2	0.5	0.6	–17.6
Estonia	19.9	13.5	6.4	5.1	0.6	0.0	1.0	1.2	0.1	8.6
Ethiopia	13.5	6.9	6.6	3.0	0.0	0.0	11.9	0.5	0.3	–3.2
Finland	23.7	16.2	7.5	5.9	0.0	0.0	0.0	0.2	0.1	13.1
France	19.0	12.6	6.4	5.2	0.1	0.0	0.0	0.1	0.0	11.2
Gabon	34.6	14.0	20.6	3.3	25.5	0.0	0.0	0.4	..	–2.0
Gambia, The	19.1	8.6	10.5	2.6	0.0	0.0	0.6	0.5	1.1	10.8
Georgia	18.0	9.9	8.1	4.3	0.6	0.0	0.0	0.7	1.1	10.0
Germany	20.7	14.9	5.7	4.5	0.1	0.0	0.0	0.2	0.1	9.7
Ghana	28.1	8.7	19.3	2.8	0.1	0.2	2.3	0.5	0.3	18.8
Greece	17.7	8.7	9.0	3.1	0.0	0.0	0.0	0.3	1.0	10.8
Guatemala	13.4	11.1	2.4	1.6	1.2	0.0	0.9	0.3	0.4	1.2
Guinea	8.0	8.8	–0.8	2.0	0.0	1.9	1.8	0.2	0.8	–3.5
Guinea-Bissau	8.8	7.9	0.9	..	0.0	0.0	0.0	0.6	1.0	..
Haiti	20.1	8.5	11.6	1.5	0.0	0.0	1.0	0.3	0.3	11.5

Toward a broader measure of savings

	Gross savings % of GNI 2004	Consumption of fixed capital % of GNI 2004	Net savings % of GNI 2004	Education expenditure % of GNI 2004	Energy depletion % of GNI 2004	Mineral depletion % of GNI 2004	Net forest depletion % of GNI 2004	Carbon dioxide damage % of GNI 2004	Particulate emission damage % of GNI 2004	Adjusted net savings % of GNI 2004
Honduras	..	10.3	..	3.5	0.0	0.2	0.0	0.6	0.3	..
Hungary	15.4	13.8	1.7	5.2	0.5	0.0	0.0	0.4	0.3	5.7
India	23.0	9.3	13.7	4.0	2.5	0.4	0.7	1.3	0.8	12.0
Indonesia	24.6	10.4	14.2	1.1	9.4	1.6	0.0	0.7	0.9	2.6
Iran, Islamic Rep.	39.7	11.0	28.7	4.4	36.0	0.2	0.0	1.7	0.9	–5.6
Iraq	..	..	..	..	..	..	..	..	2.7	..
Ireland	29.9[b]	11.0	18.9	4.8	0.0	0.0	0.0	0.2	0.1	23.3
Israel	10.0[b]	14.0	–4.0	7.3	0.0	0.0	0.0	0.4	1.2	1.6
Italy	19.5	13.9	5.6	4.5	0.1	0.0	0.0	0.2	0.3	9.5
Jamaica	26.6	12.1	14.5	5.0	0.0	1.3	0.0	0.9	0.3	17.0
Japan	26.3	14.4	12.0	3.1	0.0	0.0	0.0	0.2	0.6	14.4
Jordan	21.0	10.7	10.3	5.6	0.3	0.1	0.0	1.0	0.9	13.5
Kazakhstan	27.0	12.0	15.0	4.4	39.9	1.6	0.0	3.0	0.5	–25.5
Kenya	13.7	9.0	4.7	6.6	0.0	0.0	0.2	0.4	0.2	10.5
Korea, Dem. Rep.	..	..	..	..	..	..	..	..	2.0	..
Korea, Rep.	34.3	13.3	20.9	3.8	0.0	0.0	0.0	0.5	1.3	22.9
Kuwait	47.2[b]	12.6	34.7	5.0	46.8	0.0	0.0	0.7	2.7	–10.5
Kyrgyz Republic	9.8	9.1	0.7	4.4	1.0	0.0	0.0	1.6	0.2	2.2
Lao PDR	10.7	9.1	1.7	1.3	0.0	0.0	0.0	0.4	0.1	2.5
Latvia	..	..	..	..	..	..	..	..	..	..
Lebanon	2.4	12.9	–10.5	2.6	0.0	0.0	0.0	0.6	0.9	–9.3
Lesotho	..	..	..	..	..	..	..	..	..	..
Liberia	35.8	9.2	26.7	..	0.0	0.0	6.3	0.5	0.2	..
Libya	..	12.6	..	..	60.7	0.0	0.0	1.2	..	..
Lithuania	15.3	12.8	2.6	5.7	0.5	0.0	0.3	0.5	0.4	6.6
Macedonia, FYR	15.2	11.2	3.9	4.9	0.0	0.0	0.2	1.4	0.3	6.9
Madagascar	17.6	8.1	9.5	2.1	0.0	0.0	0.0	0.4	0.3	10.8
Malawi	–7.9	7.5	–15.4	5.0	0.0	0.0	2.1	0.3	0.3	–13.1
Malaysia	37.3	12.6	24.6	5.1	14.1	0.0	0.0	0.9	0.1	14.5
Mali	11.3	8.9	2.3	2.7	0.0	0.0	0.0	0.1	0.6	4.4
Mauritania	–6.3	8.5	–14.9	3.2	0.0	10.9	0.7	1.5	0.6	–25.3
Mauritius	23.8	12.0	11.8	3.3	0.0	0.0	0.0	0.4	..	14.8[a]
Mexico	21.1	12.6	8.6	5.3	7.4	0.1	0.0	0.4	0.6	5.3
Moldova	18.8	8.2	10.6	6.9	0.0	0.0	0.0	1.8	0.7	14.9
Mongolia	40.8	9.3	31.6	8.1	0.9	8.4	0.0	3.8	0.0	26.6
Morocco	28.0	10.7	17.3	6.1	0.0	0.3	0.0	0.6	0.3	22.3
Mozambique	6.6	8.8	–2.2	1.8	0.0	0.0	0.0	0.2	0.4	–1.0
Myanmar	..	..	..	0.8	..	..	..	..	0.6	..
Namibia	39.2	11.1	28.1	7.3	0.0	0.6	0.0	0.3	0.2	34.3
Nepal	26.9	8.1	18.8	2.6	0.0	0.0	2.8	0.4	0.1	18.2
Netherlands	23.6	16.0	7.6	4.9	1.0	0.0	0.0	0.2	0.7	10.6
New Zealand	22.6[b]	14.8	7.8	7.1	0.8	0.1	0.0	0.3	0.0	13.7
Nicaragua	10.8	10.1	0.7	2.9	0.0	0.0	1.0	0.6	0.1	1.8
Niger	8.0	7.9	0.1	2.3	0.0	0.0	3.0	0.3	0.5	–1.4
Nigeria	32.6	10.9	21.7	0.9	49.1	0.0	0.1	0.6	1.0	–28.2
Norway	32.5	13.7	18.9	7.0	10.9	0.0	0.0	0.1	0.1	14.8
Oman	29.4[b]	13.4	16.0	4.2	58.8	0.0	0.0	0.8	1.1	–40.6
Pakistan	23.6	8.2	15.4	2.3	5.3	0.0	0.5	0.8	1.4	9.7
Panama	13.8	12.8	1.1	4.4	0.0	0.0	0.0	0.4	0.5	4.6
Papua New Guinea	..	10.4	..	..	10.7	25.1	0.0	0.5	..	..
Paraguay	22.9	10.1	12.8	4.2	0.0	0.0	0.0	0.4	0.7	16.0
Peru	19.2	11.7	7.6	2.9	1.5	2.1	0.0	0.3	1.0	5.6
Philippines	34.1	9.2	24.8	2.8	0.3	0.4	0.2	0.6	0.3	25.9
Poland	18.9	12.6	6.3	5.3	0.5	0.3	0.1	0.9	0.7	9.1
Portugal	15.6	18.2	–2.6	5.7	0.0	0.0	0.0	0.2	0.5	2.3
Puerto Rico	..	..	..	..	..	..	..	..	..	..

3.15 Toward a broader measure of savings

	Gross savings % of GNI 2004	Consumption of fixed capital % of GNI 2004	Net savings % of GNI 2004	Education expenditure % of GNI 2004	Energy depletion % of GNI 2004	Mineral depletion % of GNI 2004	Net forest depletion % of GNI 2004	Carbon dioxide damage % of GNI 2004	Particulate emission damage % of GNI 2004	Adjusted net savings % of GNI 2004
Romania	18.2	11.7	6.5	3.2	3.3	0.0	0.0	0.9	0.2	5.3
Russian Federation	32.1	7.1	25.0	3.5	29.7	0.6	0.0	2.0	0.6	–4.4
Rwanda	17.7	7.9	9.8	3.5	0.0	0.0	3.7	0.2	0.2	9.1
Saudi Arabia	46.6[b]	13.0	33.6	7.2	50.1	0.0	0.0	0.9	1.0	–11.1
Senegal	17.2	9.6	7.5	3.4	0.0	0.0	0.2	0.4	1.4	8.9
Serbia and Montenegro	4.6	11.4	–6.8	..	0.9	0.0	..	0.3	0.1	..
Sierra Leone	11.4	7.9	3.4	1.0	0.0	0.0	4.3	0.4	0.6	–1.0
Singapore	46.6[b]	15.0	31.7	2.7	0.0	0.0	0.0	0.4	0.9	33.0
Slovak Republic	23.4	21.8	1.6	4.2	0.1	0.0	0.4	0.7	0.1	4.6
Slovenia	25.9	13.6	12.3	5.6	0.0	0.0	0.2	0.3	0.2	17.2
Somalia	..	..	..	..	..	..	..	..	0.2	..
South Africa	14.7	12.1	2.6	5.3	0.0	0.6	0.3	1.2	0.3	5.6
Spain	23.4	14.5	8.9	4.1	0.0	0.0	0.0	0.2	0.6	12.2
Sri Lanka	19.4	10.3	9.1	2.6	0.0	0.0	0.4	0.4	0.5	10.4
Sudan	15.8	9.9	5.9	0.9	15.1	0.0	0.0	0.3	0.8	–9.4
Swaziland	16.8	11.0	5.8	5.5	0.0	0.0	0.0	0.3	0.2	10.8
Sweden	23.6	12.1	11.6	8.0	0.0	0.1	0.0	0.1	0.0	19.4
Switzerland	..	13.9	..	5.0	0.0	0.0	0.0	0.1	0.3	..
Syrian Arab Republic	20.7	10.5	10.1	2.6	38.6	0.1	0.0	1.5	1.0	–28.4
Tajikistan	5.7	8.7	–3.0	2.8	0.4	0.0	0.0	2.0	0.2	–2.8
Tanzania	8.5	8.2	0.3	2.4	0.0	0.1	0.0	0.2	0.3	2.0
Thailand	31.8	11.3	20.5	4.9	2.4	0.0	0.2	1.0	0.6	21.2
Togo	8.6	8.6	0.0	2.6	0.0	0.1	3.0	0.6	0.3	–1.3
Trinidad and Tobago	28.5	12.3	16.2	4.0	46.2	0.0	0.0	2.3	0.0	–28.3
Tunisia	23.5	11.8	11.7	5.9	4.2	0.2	0.1	0.6	0.4	12.1
Turkey	20.0	11.8	8.2	3.5	0.2	0.0	0.0	0.5	1.4	9.4
Turkmenistan	33.6[b]	10.4	23.3	..	..	0.0	..	4.0	0.6	..
Uganda	9.9	8.2	1.7	1.9	0.0	0.0	6.4	0.2	0.0	–2.9
Ukraine	29.9	10.4	19.6	4.4	5.7	0.0	0.0	4.5	0.9	12.8
United Arab Emirates	39.2[b]	14.1	25.2	..	29.2	0.0	..	0.7	2.5	..
United Kingdom	14.5	10.3	4.1	5.3	1.1	0.0	0.0	0.2	0.1	8.1
United States	13.4	12.2	1.2	4.8	1.3	0.0	0.0	0.3	0.4	4.0
Uruguay	12.0	12.2	–0.2	2.6	0.0	0.0	0.3	0.3	2.7	–0.8
Uzbekistan	30.2	8.9	21.3	9.4	59.3	0.0	0.0	7.6	0.7	–37.0
Venezuela, RB	35.2	12.2	23.0	4.4	34.7	0.4	0.0	0.9	0.0	–8.6
Vietnam	32.7	9.2	23.6	2.8	9.5	0.0	0.6	1.1	0.5	14.6
West Bank and Gaza	..	..	..	..	..	..	..	..	..	..
Yemen, Rep.	12.9	10.0	2.9	..	44.2	0.0	0.0	0.7	0.5	..
Zambia	13.3	9.4	3.9	2.5	0.0	3.7	0.0	0.3	1.0	1.4
Zimbabwe	3.2	8.6	–5.5	6.9	0.6	1.3	0.0	1.6	0.4	–2.5
World	**20.8 w**	**12.7 w**	**8.1 w**	**4.4 w**	**2.8 w**	**0.1 w**	**0.0 w**	**0.4 w**	**0.5 w**	**8.7 w**
Low income	22.7	9.2	13.5	3.4	6.7	0.4	0.7	1.1	0.8	7.3
Middle income	28.3	11.1	17.2	3.6	8.4	0.5	0.0	1.0	0.9	9.8
Lower middle income	32.1	10.8	21.3	2.9	6.5	0.5	0.0	1.1	1.0	15.1
Upper middle income	23.1	11.5	11.6	4.5	11.2	0.6	0.0	0.9	0.7	2.6
Low & middle income	27.5	10.8	16.6	3.5	8.2	0.5	0.1	1.0	0.9	9.4
East Asia & Pacific	39.1	10.5	28.6	2.3	4.1	0.4	0.0	1.2	1.2	23.9
Europe & Central Asia	23.4	10.7	12.7	4.1	12.0	0.3	0.0	1.4	0.7	2.3
Latin America & Carib.	22.7	12.1	10.6	4.4	7.2	1.1	0.0	0.5	0.6	5.6
Middle East & N. Africa	30.0	11.2	18.8	4.5	27.3	0.1	0.1	1.2	0.9	–6.2
South Asia	23.6	9.1	14.4	3.6	2.7	0.3	0.7	1.2	0.8	12.4
Sub-Saharan Africa	17.1	10.9	6.2	3.9	9.8	0.4	0.6	0.7	0.5	–2.0
High income	19.4	13.2	6.2	4.6	1.4	0.0	0.0	0.3	0.4	8.7
Europe EMU	20.8	14.2	6.6	4.6	0.1	0.0	0.0	0.2	0.3	10.6

a. Adjusted net savings do not include particulate emission damage. b. World Bank staff estimate.

Toward a broader measure of savings 3.15

About the data

Adjusted net savings measure the change in value of a specified set of assets, excluding capital gains. If a country's net savings are positive and the accounting includes a sufficiently broad range of assets, economic theory suggests that the present value of social welfare is increasing. Conversely, persistently negative adjusted net savings indicate that an economy is on an unsustainable path.

The table provides a test to check the extent to which today's rents from a number of natural resources and changes in human capital are balanced by net savings, that is, this generation's bequest to future generations.

Adjusted net savings are derived from standard national accounting measures of gross savings by making four adjustments. First, estimates of capital consumption of produced assets are deducted to obtain net savings. Second, current public expenditures on education are added to net savings (in standard national accounting these expenditures are treated as consumption). Third, estimates of the depletion of a variety of natural resources are deducted to reflect the decline in asset values associated with their extraction and harvest. And fourth, deductions are made for damages from carbon dioxide and particulate emissions.

The exercise treats public education expenditures as an addition to savings effort. The adjustment made to savings goes in the right direction. However, because of the wide variability in the effectiveness of government education expenditures, these figures cannot be construed as the value of investments in human capital. The reader should bear in mind that current expenditure of $1 on education does not necessarily yield $1 of human capital. The calculation should also consider private education expenditure, but data are not available for a large number of countries.

While extensive, the accounting of natural resource depletion and pollution costs still has some gaps. Key estimates missing on the resource side include the value of fossil water extracted from aquifers, net depletion of fish stocks, and depletion and degradation of soils. Important pollutants affecting human health and economic assets are excluded because no internationally comparable data are widely available on damage from ground-level ozone or from sulfur oxides.

Estimates of resource depletion are based on the calculation of unit resource rents. An economic rent represents an excess return to a given factor of production—in this case the returns from resource extraction or harvest are higher than the normal rate of return on capital. Natural resources give rise to rents because they are not produced; in contrast, for produced goods and services competitive forces will expand supply until economic profits are driven to zero. For each type of resource and each country, unit resource rents are derived by taking the difference between world prices and the average unit extraction or harvest costs (including a "normal" return on capital). Unit rents are then multiplied by the physical quantity extracted or harvested in order to arrive at a depletion figure. This figure is one of a range of depletion estimates that are possible, depending on the assumptions made about future quantities, prices, and costs, and there is reason to believe that it is at the high end of the range. World prices are used in order to reflect the social opportunity cost of depleting minerals and energy. Researchers should keep this in mind when using the depletion estimates. In general, the data on energy and mineral depletion should not be considered a substitute for energy and mineral gross domestic product.

A positive net depletion figure for forest resources implies that the harvest rate exceeds the rate of natural growth; this is not the same as deforestation, which represents a change in land use (see *Definitions* for table 3.4). In principle, there should be an addition to savings in countries where growth exceeds harvest, but empirical estimates suggest that most of this net growth is in forested areas that cannot be exploited economically at present. Because the depletion estimates reflect only timber values, they ignore all the external and nontimber benefits associated with standing forests.

Pollution damage from emissions of carbon dioxide is calculated as the marginal social cost per unit multiplied by the increase in the stock of carbon dioxide. The unit damage figure represents the present value of global damage to economic assets and to human welfare over the time the unit of pollution remains in the atmosphere.

Pollution damage from particulate emissions is estimated by valuing the human health effects from exposure to particulate matter pollution in urban areas. The estimates are calculated as willingness to pay to avoid mortality and morbidity from cardiopulmonary disease and lung cancer in adults and acute respiratory infections in children that is attributable to particulate emissions.

For a detailed methodological note, see www.worldbank.org/data.

Definitions

• **Gross savings** are the difference between gross national income and public and private consumption, plus net current transfers. • **Consumption of fixed capital** represents the replacement value of capital used up in the process of production. • **Net savings** are gross savings minus the value of consumption of fixed capital. • **Education expenditure** refers to public current operating expenditures in education, including wages and salaries and excluding capital investments in buildings and equipment. • **Energy depletion** is the product of unit resource rents and the physical quantities of energy extracted. It covers coal, crude oil, and natural gas. • **Mineral depletion** is the product of unit resource rents and the physical quantities of minerals extracted. It refers to tin, gold, lead, zinc, iron, copper, nickel, silver, bauxite, and phosphate. • **Net forest depletion** is the product of unit resource rents and the excess of roundwood harvest over natural growth. • **Carbon dioxide damage** is estimated to be $20 per ton of carbon (the unit damage in 1995 U.S. dollars) times the number of tons of carbon emitted. • **Particulate emission damage** is the willingness to pay to avoid mortality and morbidity attributable to particulate emissions. • **Adjusted net savings** are net savings plus education expenditure and minus energy depletion, mineral depletion, net forest depletion, and carbon dioxide and particulate emissions damage.

Data sources

Gross savings are derived from the World Bank's national accounts data files, described in the *Economy* section. Consumption of fixed capital is from the United Nations Statistics Division's *National Accounts Statistics: Main Aggregates and Detailed Tables, 1997,* extrapolated to 2004. Data on education expenditure are from the United Nations Statistics Division's *Statistical Yearbook 1997* and from the United Nations Educational, Scientific, and Cultural Organization Institute for Statistics online database. Missing data are estimated. The wide range of data sources and estimation methods used to arrive at resource depletion estimates are described in a World Bank working paper, "Estimating National Wealth" (Kunte and others 1998). The unit damage figure for carbon dioxide emissions is from Fankhauser (1995). The estimates of damage from particulate emissions are from Pandey and others (2006). The conceptual underpinnings of the savings measure appear in Hamilton and Clemens (1999).

4 ECONOMY

The world economy continued to recover in 2004 from the slowdown of 2000–01. Gross domestic product (GDP) rose 4.1 percent, more than a full percentage point higher than in 2003 and the fastest rate of growth of global output in 15 years. High-income economies grew at an average annual rate of 3.4 percent, while developing countries averaged a remarkable 7.1 percent, the highest rate of growth since 1970.

The recovery has been widespread throughout the developing world. East Asia and Pacific grew fastest—9 percent over 2003. But all regions grew at nearly 6 percent or higher, except Sub-Saharan Africa, which grew at 4.8 percent. Fourteen countries registered growth rates of 10 percent or higher, and only four countries experienced negative growth (figure 4a). Many of the fastest growing economies are oil and gas producers and exporters, which benefited from the run-up in energy prices. Iraq's GDP increased more than 40 percent after four years of falling output, and Chad's grew by 30 percent.

Factors contributing to growth in 2004

The high growth throughout the developing world in 2004 was due in part to increased prices of primary commodities and supportive monetary conditions. Increases in the prices of oil, metals and minerals, and agricultural commodities boosted growth in a wide range of commodity producers. Oil prices rose 30 percent in 2004 even as production increased. While higher oil revenues were responsible for strong economic performance by oil producers, the impact on oil-importing countries was cushioned by increased volumes and prices of other primary commodities. For example, Brazil, an oil-importing country, achieved a growth rate of 4.9 percent in 2004. Argentina, Brazil, and South Africa saw their barter terms of trade improve by 10–20 percent over 2000 (table 6.2).

Meanwhile, global short-term interest rates declined sharply as major central banks reduced policy rates to support economic expansion. Inflation rates remained low, however, because of improved fiscal and monetary discipline. The median inflation rate was below 10 percent in all regions, well below the average of about 15 percent or higher in 1990 in three regions (table 4b). The number of countries with double-digit inflation was 38, the same as in 2003 despite the oil price hikes. The combination of reduced global interest rates and stable or falling inflation led to substantial declines in real interest rates (table 4c).

Long-term growth trends

Although growth was higher in most regions in 2000–04 than in the preceding decade, the continuing recovery in Sub-Saharan Africa remains one of the most remarkable stories of the past five years (figure 4d). By 2004 the region had experienced five years of continuous positive growth in per capita incomes, after two decades of decline (except for a slight increase in 1997). Increasing prices of primary commodities, particularly oil, but also important agricultural crops, get much of the credit. Oil and natural gas producers achieved very rapid growth, including Chad and Equatorial Guinea, where GDP rose more than 10 percent, and Nigeria, where GDP increased 6 percent. Countries left out of the commodity boom such

4a

Fast growing—and backsliding—economies in 2004

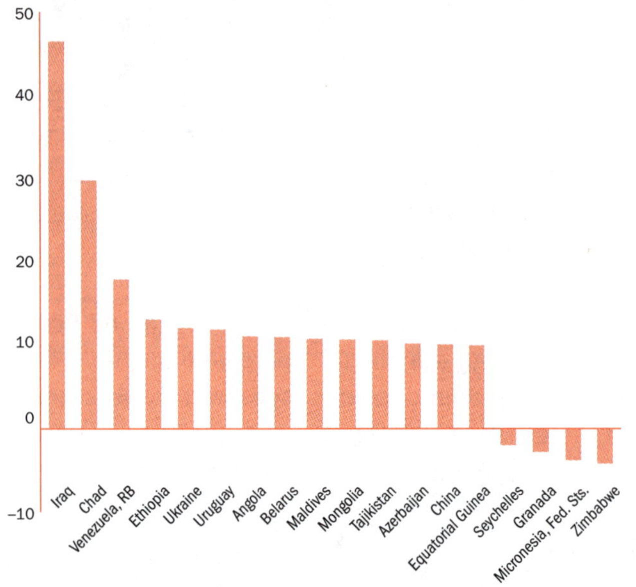

Source: World Bank data files.

4d

Accelerating regional growth

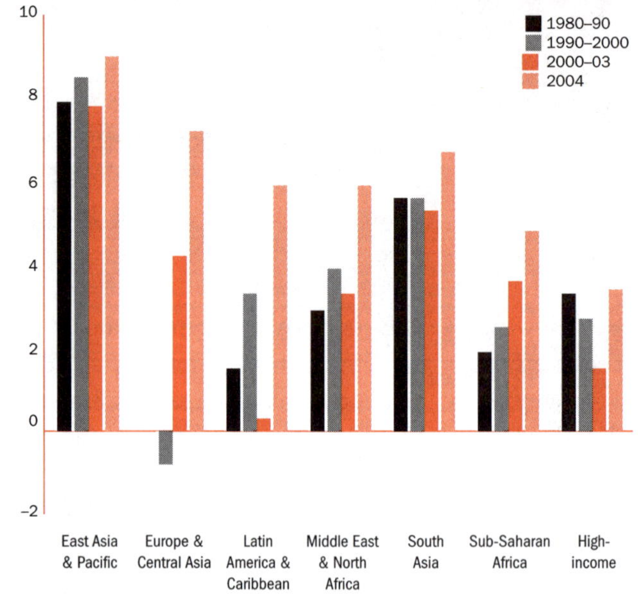

Source: World Bank data files.

as Central African Republic, Côte d'Ivoire, Eritrea, and Niger have done less well, with growth below 2 percent. Average rates of investment have also risen: from 17 percent of GDP in 2000 to 19 percent in 2004, reversing the falling trend of the 1980s and 1990s.

But even at this broad regional level Sub-Saharan Africa's macroeconomic indicators remain weak, with the lowest regional gross savings rates, at 16 percent of GDP, and the highest government consumption rate, at 17 percent. And despite a few years of economic growth, Sub-Saharan Africa still has the highest poverty rate in the world. A large proportion of the population in more than half the countries in Sub-Saharan Africa is still in need of food aid according to the World Food Programme.

Strong growth of 5 percent in Europe and Central Asia in 2000–04 was also assisted by higher oil prices. GDP in the Middle East and North Africa rose 3.8 percent over the period, about the same as in the 1980s and 1990s, again driven by increasing oil prices. But East Asia and Pacific, which has grown at about 8 percent a year during the past 20 years, continues to be the top performer. The region's exceptional performance was due largely to rapid growth in China. Similarly strong performance by India enabled South Asia to grow at nearly 6 percent over the same period. Despite rapid growth in 2004, Latin America and the Caribbean is the only region that failed to improve on growth rates of the 1990s because of low or negative growth in 2001 and 2002.

In achieving consistently high rates of growth over a long period, India and China have become more important in the world economy, as both consumers and producers. Growth has brought increasing demand for energy inputs, and growing imports of fuel have been blamed for rising fuel prices. But too much may be made of this. While China and India are now among the top 10 fuel importers and account for a large share of the increased demand for oil, they remain relatively small consumers compared with the major industrial countries. China and India accounted for only about 11 percent of the global increase in fuel imports between 2000 and 2004,

4b

Inflation, median annual growth of GDP deflator (%)

Region	1990	1995	2000	2003	2004
East Asia	5.8	7.9	2.5	3.9	5.7
Europe & Central Asia	14.8	46.4	8.5	4.7	6.1
Latin America & Caribbean	21.2	11.0	5.2	6.5	7.6
Middle East & North Africa	17.0	9.4	9.8	5.9	9.6
South Asia	8.5	9.1	4.6	4.5	5.0
Sub-Saharan Africa	9.7	10.7	6.1	6.5	6.0

Source: World Bank data files and table 4.14.

4c

Real interest rates (%)

Country	2000	2001	2002	2003	2004
Brazil	44.7	46.7	47.8	45.3	43.2
China	3.7	3.7	4.7	2.6	–1.2
India	8.2	8.4	7.4	8.0	5.4
Japan	3.6	3.3	3.2	3.2	4.0
Mexico	4.3	6.5	1.2	–1.5	1.1
Russian Federation	–9.6	1.2	0.2	–0.9	–5.6
United States	6.9	4.4	3.0	2.2	1.7

Note: Real interest rates are computed as the difference between the prime rate charged by banks and the rate of inflation measured by the growth of the GDP deflator.
Source: World Bank data files and table 4.13.

4e

Raising demand for energy supplies

Economy	Fuel imports ($ billions) 1995	2000	2004	Fuel imports as share of merchandise imports (%) 1995	2000	2004	Increase in fuel imports (%) 2000–04	Share of global increase in fuel imports (%) 2000–04
Brazil	7	9	12	12.1	15.1	18.8	40	1
China	5	21	48	3.9	9.2	8.5	131	7
India	8	19	34	23.8	36.7	34.6	78	4
Japan	54	77	99	16.1	20.4	21.7	28	6
United States	63	140	216	8.2	11.1	14.2	55	20
European Union	136	219	347	6.5	8.8	9.4	59	33
World	386	690	1,075	7.4	10.4	11.5	56	100

Source: World Bank data files.

whereas the United States alone accounted for 20 percent (table 4e). And in both China and India the share of fuel in merchandise imports has declined slightly since 2000.

Changes from the last edition

Interest and exchange rate indicators (table 5.7), which used to appear in section 5, *States and markets*, have moved to the *Economy* section, resulting in an additional table on monetary indicators (table 4.14), while the table showing growth in merchandise trade and terms of trade (table 4.4) has moved to section 6, *Global links* (table 6.2). *Economy* now shows the growth of exports and imports of goods and services from the national accounts data. Household final consumption expenditure in dollar terms has been dropped from table 4.8. However, these data are still available on the *World Development Indicators* CD-ROM and World Development Indicators Online database. In table 4.8 gross savings, which has been changed to conform to the System of National Accounts definition, now includes net income as well as transfers. In table 4.14 the food price index data, which were inconsistent with the consumer price index data from the International Monetary Fund's *International Financial Statistics*, were replaced by wholesale price index data from the *International Financial Statistics*. Total debt service ratios replace public and publicly guaranteed debt service ratios in table 4.17.

4f

China's data revision

Recently, the national accounts of China have been revised by the National Bureau of Statistics (NBS), incorporating new information from the 2005 National Economic Census. The earlier economic census was taken in 1993.

As the information from the 2005 census has been incorporated, the revised national accounts have for the first time been able to capture the growing private sector, including the services industry. The revised accounts show not only that the size of the economy is larger, but also that it is growing at a slightly higher rate then previously shown.

The NBS has not only revised the estimates for 2004, but has also revised time series back to 1993. So far, however, revised data are available only for production. The old data are retained here for the expenditure accounts, and the differences are shown as a statistical discrepancy. As a result of this large statistical discrepancy final household consumption is larger than it will be when the final set of data is released. While the constant price series for the years before 1993 were scaled upward using the previous growth rates to yield a consistent series for calculating long-term growth trends, the current price series contains a break in the series in 1993, as current price data beyond 1993 are unadjusted.

As a result of the revision, Chinese GDP for 2004 is about $1.93 trillion, some 17 percent higher than earlier published estimates. In real terms the economy grew at 10.1 percent, slightly higher than the previously published growth data. By the revised value-added estimates the service sector accounts for 41 percent of the economy, up from earlier estimates of 37 percent, and the industrial sector has declined from 49 percent to 46 percent, and agriculture from 14 percent to 13 percent. By the old data China's manufacturing sector was the fastest growing sector, contrary to trends in emerging economies like India, where the service sector has been growing faster. Now though still lower, the service sector is growing at almost the same rate as the manufacturing sector, nearly 10 percent in 2004.

China was ranked sixth in the global economy based on gross national income (GNI) in the last two editions of the *World Development Indicators*. The revised GNI estimates move China ahead of France to become the fifth largest economy in 2004 and, according to projections, will move it ahead of the United Kingdom next year to become the fourth largest. While still a lower-middle-income country, China has a more important role in the global economy than many of the largest industrial countries. For example, China is the fourth largest receiver of foreign direct investment, its reserves are second only to those of Japan, and its merchandise exports in dollar terms exceed all countries except Germany and the United States.

4.a

Recent economic performance

	Gross domestic product		Exports of goods and services		Imports of goods and services		GDP deflator		Current account balance		Total reserves[a]	
	average annual % growth		average annual % growth		average annual % growth		% growth		% of GDP		$ millions	months of import coverage
	2004	2005	2004	2005	2004	2005	2004	2005	2004	2005	2005	2005
Algeria	5.2	5.3	3.4	6.0	13.3	17.8	10.2	14.9	..	18.3	56,461	24.9
Argentina	9.0	7.5	8.2	15.1	39.8	18.6	9.2	8.2	2.2	–0.1	..	..
Armenia	7.0	13.9	14.8	22.0	8.5	17.2	0.6	3.1	–5.3	–3.6	755	4.2
Azerbaijan	10.2	24.3	10.7	76.1	23.3	18.2	6.4	12.0	–30.4	–5.2	1,178	3.3
Bangladesh	6.3	5.4	12.5	11.9	10.6	10.7	4.2	5.0	–0.5	–0.5	2,944	2.5
Bolivia	3.6	3.9	16.1	5.5	5.4	12.5	8.5	5.3	3.3	2.0	1,798	6.8
Bosnia and Herzegovina	6.2	5.3	8.9	11.5	2.8	5.2	2.9	2.5	–22.5	–23.9	2,668	4.0
Botswana	4.9	3.8	–0.3	19.5	2.7	12.0	4.8	9.3	..	8.9	5,865	19.3
Brazil	4.9	2.5	18.0	21.5	14.3	11.2	8.2	6.0	1.9	2.0	62,779	6.0
Bulgaria	5.6	5.6	13.1	4.7	14.1	11.4	4.2	3.6	–8.5	–14.9	8,701	4.6
Cameroon	4.3	3.9	1.7	3.1	4.1	4.8	0.4	–0.6	..	–2.4	124	0.3
Chile	6.1	5.2	22.0	5.1	–2.3	5.1	6.6	2.4	1.5	0.5	15,047	5.5
China	10.1	9.9	28.4	24.4	22.5	17.7	6.9	5.9	3.6	5.6	818,900	13.0
Colombia	4.1	4.0	10.2	15.5	16.7	16.7	7.1	5.1	–1.0	–1.1	14,956	6.7
Congo, Dem. Rep.	6.3	7.0	..	..	..	..	5.9	22.1	..	–4.2	360	1.2
Congo, Rep.	3.6	9.2	8.1	14.9	62.1	16.4	6.9	7.2	..	4.9	75	0.2
Costa Rica	4.2	3.5	7.1	6.8	7.8	13.1	11.6	10.8	–4.5	–4.7	2,080	2.2
Côte d'Ivoire	1.6	–0.3	15.7	–1.5	12.6	4.4	0.8	3.9	2.0	3.0	330	3.4
Croatia	3.8	3.7	5.4	6.1	3.5	3.5	3.3	3.4	–4.8	–3.8	9,082	5.1
Ecuador	7.0	3.3	15.1	4.2	9.8	5.3	4.1	2.8	–0.5	0.3	2,147	2.9
Egypt, Arab Rep.	4.2	4.9	27.6	25.6	22.0	30.7	11.5	5.4	5.0	3.3	19,302	8.0
El Salvador	1.5	2.5	6.6	3.3	3.4	3.3	4.3	4.0	–3.9	–3.6	2,139	3.1
Estonia	7.8	5.6	16.0	5.7	14.6	2.0	3.1	–1.5	–12.7	–6.5	1,780	2.4
Gabon	1.4	2.2	3.3	–5.8	3.8	1.8	7.0	8.9	..	7.0	..	..
Ghana	5.8	5.8	3.5	4.0	4.5	7.3	14.1	14.8	–2.7	–1.3	1,747	3.9
Guatemala	2.7	3.2	12.4	5.8	15.8	5.3	8.2	6.0	–4.3	–4.1	3,375	4.0
India	6.9	8.5	7.9	26.6	47.1	34.6	5.3	4.2	..	–3.7	142,489	7.2
Indonesia	5.1	5.9	8.5	14.5	25.0	15.2	7.1	7.5	1.2	1.0	47,088	5.1
Iran, Islamic Rep.	5.6	5.9	12.2	27.5	5.0	12.8	16.6	17.6	..	6.4	47,410	9.4
Jamaica	0.9	1.8	..	..	..	..	12.6	16.0	–5.7	–7.8	1,975	5.8
Jordan	7.7	7.5	13.0	8.7	27.4	8.1	5.2	4.0	–0.2	–10.4	5,396	5.8
Kazakhstan	9.4	9.4	10.5	11.5	14.5	13.9	9.9	16.1	1.3	5.3	7,070	3.4
Kenya	4.3	5.0	19.8	22.2	15.3	40.6	6.9	5.7	–2.4	–9.3	2,327	2.3
Latvia	8.3	6.0	9.3	7.5	15.6	4.5	7.2	0.3	–13.0	–8.5	..	..
Lebanon	6.3	1.0	23.4	–4.0	7.1	0.0	2.9	1.0	..	–18.1	10,556	12.3
Lesotho	2.3	0.0	0.7	5.5	1.5	3.7	1.7	2.1	–5.8	–5.5	447	3.8

	Gross domestic product		Exports of goods and services		Imports of goods and services		GDP deflator		Current account balance		Total reserves[a]	
	average annual % growth		average annual % growth		average annual % growth		% growth		% of GDP		$ millions	months of import coverage
	2004	2005	2004	2005	2004	2005	2004	2005	2004	2005	2005	2005
Lithuania	6.7	6.0	11.7	8.6	12.1	7.7	3.3	–0.7	–7.8	–4.4	3,041	2.6
Macedonia, FYR	2.9	3.6	11.7	11.0	10.6	–0.8	1.5	3.4	–7.8	–0.9	1,328	4.3
Malawi	6.7	2.6	–4.6	8.9	–5.3	12.7	11.6	15.3	..	–14.3	159	1.8
Malaysia	7.1	5.0	16.3	8.1	20.7	6.4	6.2	1.5	..	13.8	80,739	7.1
Mauritius	4.2	4.0	–1.7	1.7	2.0	0.0	6.0	5.4	–1.8	–0.4	1,485	4.7
Mexico	4.4	3.0	11.5	9.1	10.2	7.3	6.1	5.4	–1.1	–1.1	70,158	3.3
Moldova	7.3	7.0	8.3	15.3	0.4	27.0	8.0	7.0	–2.7	–5.5	597	2.7
Morocco	4.2	1.5	4.7	3.4	8.8	6.0	1.5	2.0	1.9	0.1	18,671	9.2
Nicaragua	5.2	4.0	15.8	9.9	9.4	12.1	10.2	12.0	–17.0	–18.0	782	2.7
Nigeria	6.0	4.0	3.1	–3.7	2.3	26.1	19.9	26.6	17.0	9.8	26,400	8.4
Pakistan	6.4	7.8	–1.5	16.9	–8.6	38.5	7.8	9.3	–0.8	–3.2	10,143	3.0
Panama	6.2	6.0	6.7	18.1	8.1	15.5	0.5	1.8	–8.2	–7.9	677	0.7
Paraguay	4.0	3.2	4.1	0.1	5.5	6.0	9.2	10.0	0.3	–0.3	981	3.9
Peru	4.8	6.7	14.7	14.2	10.4	9.9	5.7	3.5	0.0	1.3	14,097	14.0
Philippines	6.1	5.1	14.1	2.3	5.9	1.8	6.1	6.0	2.5	1.6	18,400	3.8
Poland	5.4	3.2	10.2	11.3	8.7	5.3	2.9	1.7	–4.3	–1.6	42,571	5.2
Romania	8.3	4.5	15.9	5.4	18.3	15.7	15.8	12.1	–7.6	–8.9	21,395	5.7
Russian Federation	7.1	6.4	12.3	2.5	23.5	19.2	18.1	19.7	10.3	11.3	182,200	17.5
Senegal	6.2	5.7	4.8	5.8	6.0	5.2	1.9	2.5	..	–7.6	1,092	3.5
Serbia and Montenegro	8.2	4.8	38.2	22.0	38.1	4.0	8.9	17.3	..	–9.0	5,900	6.2
Slovak Republic	5.5	6.0	11.5	9.0	12.7	8.7	4.6	1.6	..	–6.3	15,400	5.3
South Africa	3.7	5.0	2.9	11.3	12.9	9.5	5.9	4.3	–3.3	–4.2	658	3.5
Sri Lanka	5.4	5.3	7.8	7.5	9.3	8.7	9.4	9.7	–3.2	–5.6	2,571	2.9
Swaziland	2.1	1.8	1.1	–3.4	1.4	1.7	5.3	4.5	4.8	–1.6	230	1.1
Syrian Arab Republic	2.0	3.8	13.3	–9.2	27.0	6.7	10.5	9.6	0.9	1.2	4,790	5.8
Thailand	6.2	4.5	9.6	4.6	13.5	8.5	3.3	7.5	4.1	–2.1	52,066	5.3
Trinidad and Tobago	6.2	6.7	14.3	9.1	25.4	17.2	12.5	122.4	..	18.8	3,893	7.0
Tunisia	5.8	5.0	5.2	3.4	3.7	4.7	3.0	2.5	–2.0	–2.6	..	..
Turkey	8.9	6.0	12.5	5.0	24.7	10.6	9.9	7.7	–5.1	–6.2	52,433	5.4
Uganda	5.7	5.6	6.2	5.7	3.7	9.5	6.0	9.0	–2.9	–1.2	1,326	6.0
Ukraine	12.1	2.4	13.8	4.0	8.6	–9.0	15.1	15.0	10.5	2.7	19,395	5.5
Uruguay	11.9	6.0	22.9	16.2	29.7	21.0	7.4	5.0	–0.8	–0.8	2,837	6.8
Uzbekistan	7.7	7.0	21.8	11.5	19.3	7.3	15.1	15.9	..	9.5	2,889	7.9
Venezuela, RB	17.9	9.0	11.8	9.0	60.0	18.3	31.2	16.2	12.6	18.1	35,667	12.3
Zambia	4.7	5.1	12.6	16.3	10.3	18.1	20.2	18.9	..	–11.9	303	1.4

Note: Data for 2005 are the latest preliminary estimates and may differ from those in earlier World Bank publications.

a. International reserves including gold valued at London gold price.

Source: World Bank staff estimates.

4.1 Growth of output

	Gross domestic product		Agriculture		Industry		Manufacturing		Services	
	average annual % growth		average annual % growth		average annual % growth		average annual % growth		average annual % growth	
	1990–2000	2000–04	1990–2000	2000–04	1990–2000	2000–04	1990–2000	2000–04	1990–2000	2000–04
Afghanistan[a]	..	*16.8*	..	..	..	..	..	..	..	..
Albania	3.5	5.4	4.3	5.1	–0.5	4.8	..	..	7.0	7.7
Algeria	1.9	4.8	3.6	7.5	1.8	3.7	–2.1	–0.2	1.9	5.5
Angola[a]	1.6	8.1	–1.4	13.7	4.4	8.6	–0.3	11.3	–2.3	4.3
Argentina	4.3	–0.1	3.5	1.2	3.8	1.3	2.7	1.7	4.5	–1.2
Armenia	–1.9	11.3	0.4	5.0	–7.9	12.6	–4.3	8.4	–5.8	15.8
Australia	3.9	3.5	3.6	*–2.8*	2.9	*3.7*	2.2	*2.4*	4.3	*3.7*
Austria	2.4	1.2	1.6	0.6	2.7	1.8	2.7	*0.8*	2.3	0.9
Azerbaijan	–6.3	10.6	*–2.1*	6.7	*–0.8*	12.8	*–12.0*	9.5	*–2.3*	8.2
Bangladesh[a]	4.8	5.2	2.9	2.4	7.3	7.1	7.2	6.4	4.5	5.5
Belarus	–1.7	6.8	–4.0	6.1	–1.8	9.7	–0.7	10.2	–0.4	4.7
Belgium	2.1	1.4	2.8	1.3	1.7	0.3	*2.8*	*0.3*	1.9	1.8
Benin[a]	4.8	4.5	5.8	5.7	4.1	6.5	5.8	5.9	4.2	2.7
Bolivia[a]	4.0	2.6	2.9	3.3	4.1	2.3	3.8	2.8	4.3	2.2
Bosnia and Herzegovina	..	4.9	..	0.0	..	3.2	..	4.1	..	5.0
Botswana	4.9	5.5	–1.2	1.5	3.6	5.2	4.3	1.6	7.8	4.5
Brazil	2.9	2.0	3.3	5.4	2.6	2.1	1.5	3.1	3.0	–1.1
Bulgaria	–1.8	4.8	3.0	1.8	–5.0	5.3	..	8.2	–5.2	4.9
Burkina Faso	4.0	5.2	4.2	5.1	2.3	*2.7*	1.6	*2.2*	4.5	11.9
Burundi	–2.6	2.7	–1.6	1.9	–5.6	..	*–8.0*	..	–2.0	..
Cambodia[a]	*7.1*	6.3	*3.9*	2.8	*14.3*	14.2	*18.6*	14.6	*7.1*	3.9
Cameroon	1.7	4.5	5.5	6.0	–0.9	6.9	1.2	8.6	0.2	2.3
Canada	3.1	2.6	1.1	*–1.5*	3.2	*0.5*	4.5	*–0.6*	3.0	*3.5*
Central African Republic	2.0	–2.0	3.8	3.0	0.7	4.6	–0.2	*4.0*	–0.3	–16.0
Chad	1.9	14.1	4.4	..	2.2	..	..	..	1.0	6.2
Chile[a]	6.6	3.7	–2.7	–0.5	7.1	7.6	6.7	2.8	6.8	1.7
China[a, b]	10.6	9.4	4.1	3.4	13.7	10.6	..	..	10.2	9.8
Hong Kong, China	4.1	3.2	..	–1.0	..	–3.6	..	–6.9	..	4.3
Colombia[a]	2.8	2.9	–2.6	1.2	1.5	3.9	–2.5	2.7	4.5	2.7
Congo, Dem. Rep.	–4.9	3.6	1.2	..	–9.0	..	*–13.4*	..	–11.5	..
Congo, Rep.[a]	1.2	3.1	1.0	5.5	3.2	1.4	–3.0	12.7	–0.6	4.2
Costa Rica	5.3	3.9	4.1	1.6	6.2	2.7	6.7	2.1	4.6	5.1
Côte d'Ivoire[a]	3.3	–0.7	3.3	0.5	5.7	–3.5	4.9	–4.0	2.4	–0.2
Croatia	0.6	4.5	–3.0	0.2	–2.5	5.5	–3.3	3.5	2.2	5.2
Cuba[a]	*4.2*	..	*5.2*	..	*6.6*	..	*6.3*	..	*2.5*	..
Czech Republic	1.1	2.8	2.4	1.2	–0.2	4.1	*3.8*	6.0	1.7	2.0
Denmark	2.5	1.1	2.9	0.2	2.4	–0.8	2.1	*0.1*	2.5	1.7
Dominican Republic[a]	6.1	2.4	3.8	6.9	7.1	–1.1	4.9	0.0	6.0	2.5
Ecuador[a]	1.9	4.2	–1.7	2.9	2.7	5.5	1.5	2.2	2.4	3.6
Egypt, Arab Rep.	4.7	3.4	3.1	3.7	5.1	2.3	6.4	2.9	4.1	4.1
El Salvador[a]	4.8	1.9	1.2	0.2	5.2	2.5	5.2	2.5	4.0	1.9
Eritrea	*5.7*	3.3	*1.5*	–0.5	*15.0*	4.1	*10.6*	6.6	*5.7*	2.0
Estonia	0.2	7.0	–3.4	–2.0	–3.3	10.5	*5.9*	11.6	3.1	5.9
Ethiopia	4.2	3.6	1.9	0.9	3.7	4.4	3.7	2.5	6.5	4.3
Finland	2.6	2.3	1.8	–0.6	3.9	1.8	5.8	*0.9*	2.2	2.5
France	2.0	1.5	2.0	–0.6	1.0	1.0	..	..	2.4	1.6
Gabon[a]	2.8	1.6	–1.4	5.1	2.5	2.7	*0.6*	..	3.9	–0.1
Gambia, The	3.0	3.8	3.3	–0.2	1.0	7.3	0.9	4.2	3.7	5.9
Georgia	–7.2	7.2	–11.0	2.6	–8.1	10.5	–7.0	5.9	–0.3	8.2
Germany	1.8	0.6	–0.2	–0.1	–0.1	–0.1	*–0.1*	*–0.4*	2.9	1.3
Ghana[a]	4.3	4.9	3.4	5.0	2.6	4.1	–3.2	2.0	5.7	5.0
Greece	2.2	4.2	0.5	–0.3	1.0	4.0	*2.0*	*2.7*	2.6	4.9
Guatemala[a]	4.2	2.3	2.8	2.1	4.3	1.4	2.8	1.1	4.7	2.7
Guinea	4.4	2.9	4.6	4.5	4.7	3.2	4.1	2.0	3.6	1.8
Guinea-Bissau	1.2	–1.2	3.9	3.3	–3.1	14.1	–2.0	14.6	–0.6	4.9
Haiti[a]	–1.5	*–0.4*	–7.4	*–1.2*	3.2	*0.5*	–8.4	*–2.2*	–1.2	*–0.3*

Growth of output 4.1

	Gross domestic product		Agriculture		Industry		Manufacturing		Services	
	average annual % growth		average annual % growth		average annual % growth		average annual % growth		average annual % growth	
	1990–2000	2000–04	1990–2000	2000–04	1990–2000	2000–04	1990–2000	2000–04	1990–2000	2000–04
Honduras	3.2	3.3	2.2	*4.4*	3.6	*2.2*	4.0	*3.8*	3.8	*3.6*
Hungary	1.6	4.0	–2.4	5.5	3.5	3.3	*7.9*	4.5	1.2	3.9
India	6.0	6.2	3.0	2.0	6.3	6.2	7.0	6.5	8.0	8.2
Indonesia[a]	4.2	4.6	2.1	3.9	5.3	3.8	6.7	5.1	4.0	5.7
Iran, Islamic Rep.	3.5	6.0	3.5	5.2	–3.3	8.3	4.9	10.7	8.9	4.9
Iraq	..	–11.4	..	*–3.6*	..	*–17.0*	..	*–12.8*	..	*5.9*
Ireland	7.5	5.1	..	..	..	..	..	..	..	..
Israel	5.3	1.0	..	..	..	..	..	..	..	..
Italy	1.6	0.8	1.6	–0.8	1.1	0.2	1.5	–0.9	1.7	1.2
Jamaica[a]	0.9	1.5	–0.3	–1.4	–1.0	1.8	–2.3	0.2	2.3	1.6
Japan	1.3	0.9	–3.1	*–2.2*	–0.1	*–0.1*	0.8	*0.7*	2.2	*0.6*
Jordan	5.0	5.5	–3.0	11.6	5.2	9.3	5.6	11.4	5.0	4.3
Kazakhstan	–4.1	10.3	–8.0	4.9	–9.3	11.5	*2.7*	9.2	–1.5	10.2
Kenya	2.2	2.7	1.9	1.9	1.2	3.5	1.3	2.5	3.2	3.1
Korea, Dem. Rep.	..	..	..	..	..	..	..	..	..	..
Korea, Rep.[a]	5.8	4.7	1.6	–1.0	6.0	6.2	7.3	6.6	5.6	4.0
Kuwait[a]	*4.7*	4.7	*1.0*	*15.1*	*0.3*	*1.9*	*–0.1*	*2.5*	*2.7*	*4.5*
Kyrgyz Republic	–4.1	4.5	1.5	4.1	–10.3	2.4	–7.5	3.6	–4.9	6.6
Lao PDR	6.5	6.0	4.8	3.3	11.1	10.8	11.7	10.9	6.6	6.4
Latvia	–1.6	7.4	–5.7	2.7	–8.7	8.6	–7.8	8.1	2.6	7.4
Lebanon	5.8	4.4	*2.1*	2.7	*–3.8*	4.2	*–5.2*	4.4	..	3.5
Lesotho	3.9	3.1	2.0	–1.8	5.1	4.7	6.6	3.9	4.4	3.2
Liberia	4.1	–8.7	..	..	..	..	..	..	..	..
Libya	..	5.5	..	..	..	..	..	..	..	..
Lithuania	–2.7	7.5	*–0.8*	2.7	*3.3*	10.5	*5.7*	9.6	*5.5*	6.4
Macedonia, FYR	–0.8	0.7	0.2	–0.6	–2.9	0.4	–5.4	–1.3	1.0	1.3
Madagascar	2.0	0.9	1.8	1.3	2.4	–0.2	2.0	1.4	2.4	0.3
Malawi	3.7	2.9	8.6	1.8	2.0	0.1	0.5	–0.8	1.6	2.5
Malaysia[a]	7.0	4.4	0.3	3.4	8.6	4.2	9.5	4.4	7.3	4.7
Mali	4.1	6.3	2.6	5.1	6.4	5.9	–1.4	5.3	3.0	5.9
Mauritania	4.6	4.7	4.4	–0.3	3.5	4.3	–1.9	–6.3	5.5	6.7
Mauritius	5.2	4.4	–0.5	2.8	5.4	2.9	5.3	2.0	6.4	6.1
Mexico[a]	3.1	1.5	1.5	2.6	3.8	0.0	4.4	–0.6	2.9	2.1
Moldova	–9.6	7.0	*–11.2*	1.3	*–13.6*	9.5	*–7.1*	8.8	*0.7*	6.0
Mongolia[a]	3.5	5.2	3.7	–3.3	2.3	8.4	*–9.7*	14.3	0.5	6.9
Morocco[a]	2.3	4.7	–0.8	12.6	3.2	3.6	2.7	3.5	2.8	3.5
Mozambique	6.4	8.8	4.8	8.9	12.8	11.8	*18.6*	15.2	4.8	7.5
Myanmar[a]	7.0	..	5.7	..	10.5	..	7.9	..	7.2	..
Namibia	4.0	4.7	3.8	1.2	2.4	7.3	2.6	6.7	4.5	4.5
Nepal	4.9	2.5	2.4	3.3	7.2	0.7	8.9	–1.4	6.2	2.3
Netherlands	2.9	0.5	2.0	0.1	1.5	–0.6	2.3	*–1.4*	3.3	1.0
New Zealand	3.2	4.0	2.9	*2.5*	2.5	*3.6*	2.2	*3.1*	3.4	*4.2*
Nicaragua[a]	3.7	2.5	4.9	2.5	3.9	3.2	3.5	3.8	3.0	3.3
Niger[a]	2.4	4.1	3.0	*6.4*	2.0	*3.1*	2.6	*3.9*	1.9	*4.3*
Nigeria	2.5	5.4	3.4	5.3	1.0	5.1	1.1	*8.8*	3.1	6.1
Norway	4.0	1.6	2.6	0.4	3.8	–0.2	1.6	..	4.0	2.6
Oman[a]	4.5	3.0	5.0	2.2	3.9	–0.5	6.0	9.3	5.0	5.9
Pakistan	3.8	4.1	4.4	1.3	4.1	5.3	3.8	8.0	4.4	4.8
Panama	4.7	3.3	3.1	4.2	6.0	1.5	2.7	–2.1	4.5	3.6
Papua New Guinea	4.3	0.6	4.1	*2.2*	5.6	*–3.6*	5.5	*–1.1*	1.5	*1.4*
Paraguay	2.2	1.4	2.5	6.1	3.2	–1.9	0.7	–0.4	1.6	0.1
Peru[a]	4.6	3.7	5.5	2.6	5.0	5.0	3.8	2.6	4.2	2.8
Philippines[a]	3.4	3.9	1.7	2.4	3.5	2.4	3.0	3.9	4.0	5.8
Poland	4.6	2.8	*0.9*	4.7	*7.3*	2.3	*10.0*	5.2	*4.6*	2.9
Portugal	2.7	0.3	0.0	0.9	3.0	–1.2	2.4	*–0.1*	2.2	1.3
Puerto Rico[a]	4.2	..	..	..	..	..	..	..	..	..

4.1 Growth of output

	Gross domestic product		Agriculture		Industry		Manufacturing		Services	
	average annual % growth		average annual % growth		average annual % growth		average annual % growth		average annual % growth	
	1990–2000	2000–04	1990–2000	2000–04	1990–2000	2000–04	1990–2000	2000–04	1990–2000	2000–04
Romania	–0.6	5.9	–1.9	8.9	–1.2	5.9	..	..	0.9	5.6
Russian Federation	–4.7	6.1	–4.9	5.4	–7.1	6.2	..	..	–1.7	6.0
Rwanda	–0.3	5.2	2.6	4.7	–3.7	6.1	–6.0	5.8	–1.2	5.4
Saudi Arabia[a]	2.1	3.4	1.6	1.1	2.2	3.6	5.6	5.5	2.2	3.6
Senegal[a]	3.2	4.4	2.9	0.0	4.1	6.8	3.1	5.9	3.0	5.1
Serbia and Montenegro	*1.5*	4.7	..	–5.5	..	1.2	..	..	..	7.2
Sierra Leone[a]	–6.1	7.2	*–13.0*	..	*–4.5*	..	*6.1*	..	*–2.9*	..
Singapore[a]	7.7	2.9	–2.6	–1.1	8.8	1.2	7.9	3.2	7.5	3.7
Slovak Republic[a]	1.9	4.6	*2.7*	3.6	*2.4*	5.2	*6.6*	5.7	*5.7*	4.4
Slovenia	2.7	3.2	–0.5	–1.2	1.6	3.9	1.4	4.7	3.2	3.3
Somalia	..	..	..	..	..	..	..	..	..	..
South Africa	2.1	3.2	1.0	–0.4	1.1	2.0	1.6	1.7	2.7	4.1
Spain	2.6	3.0	1.2	–0.4	2.1	2.8	..	1.0	2.8	3.1
Sri Lanka	5.3	3.7	1.8	0.4	7.0	2.5	8.1	2.0	5.7	5.6
Sudan	5.4	6.0	9.2	..	5.8	..	4.4	..	2.7	..
Swaziland	3.3	2.3	1.2	–0.3	3.8	2.0	2.9	1.8	3.6	3.5
Sweden	2.2	2.0	–0.7	2.5	4.2	3.1	*8.5*	..	1.8	1.4
Switzerland	1.0	0.6	–2.0	..	0.4	..	1.2	..	1.2	..
Syrian Arab Republic[a]	5.0	3.5	5.8	3.3	8.7	–4.7	..	..	2.0	9.0
Tajikistan	–10.4	10.0	–6.8	*12.3*	–10.8	*10.9*	–10.0	*11.0*	–4.0	*5.6*
Tanzania[c]	2.9	6.8	3.2	4.9	3.1	8.9	2.7	7.6	2.7	5.9
Thailand[a]	4.2	5.4	1.0	3.2	5.7	6.9	6.9	7.2	3.8	4.3
Togo	3.5	2.6	4.0	2.7	1.8	8.2	1.8	7.6	3.9	–0.2
Trinidad and Tobago[a]	3.2	7.2	2.7	–6.8	3.5	12.0	4.9	6.0	2.9	5.1
Tunisia	4.7	4.3	2.3	3.7	4.6	3.0	5.5	3.0	5.3	5.1
Turkey	3.8	4.2	1.4	0.6	4.1	3.4	4.9	5.2	4.0	4.4
Turkmenistan	–4.8	..	–5.7	..	–3.4	..	..	..	–5.4	..
Uganda	7.1	5.8	3.7	3.9	12.2	7.0	14.1	5.0	8.2	7.2
Ukraine	–9.3	8.6	–5.6	3.0	–12.9	10.8	–11.2	14.0	–8.1	8.8
United Arab Emirates	4.8	7.9	13.2	1.7	3.0	5.5	11.9	6.5	7.2	8.2
United Kingdom	2.7	2.3	–0.2	1.2	1.5	–0.1	..	..	3.5	2.9
United States	3.5	2.5	3.7	*–0.7*	3.7	*0.0*	..	*0.6*	3.4	*2.5*
Uruguay	3.4	–1.2	2.8	6.0	1.1	–2.1	–0.1	–0.8	4.6	–2.2
Uzbekistan	–0.2	4.8	0.5	6.7	–3.4	3.6	*0.7*	2.0	0.4	4.3
Venezuela, RB[a]	1.6	–1.2	1.3	–0.4	1.2	–2.8	4.5	–2.1	–0.1	1.4
Vietnam[a]	7.9	7.2	4.3	3.6	11.9	10.1	11.2	11.2	7.5	6.6
West Bank and Gaza	*3.4*	*–13.3*	*–3.4*	*–10.7*	*–0.6*	*–22.0*	*4.1*	*–16.2*	*4.7*	*–9.7*
Yemen, Rep.[a]	6.0	3.6	5.6	5.3	7.5	2.8	3.7	2.5	5.4	3.1
Zambia[a]	0.5	4.4	4.2	1.3	–4.2	8.9	0.8	5.9	2.5	4.0
Zimbabwe	2.1	–5.9	4.3	–9.0	0.4	–10.1	0.4	–11.1	2.9	–7.5
World	**2.9 w**	**2.5 w**	**1.8 w**	**2.1 w**	**2.4 w**	***1.4* w**	**.. w**	***1.0* w**	**3.1 w**	***2.3* w**
Low income	4.7	5.5	3.1	2.7	4.9	6.0	5.8	6.5	5.9	6.7
Middle income	3.8	4.7	2.0	3.4	4.3	5.6	..	..	3.9	4.1
Lower middle income	5.2	6.0	2.6	3.8	6.4	7.3	..	..	5.1	5.4
Upper middle income	2.1	2.7	0.3	2.2	1.5	2.5	4.5	2.1	2.8	2.7
Low & middle income	3.9	4.8	2.3	3.2	4.3	5.6	..	..	4.2	4.4
East Asia & Pacific	8.5	8.1	3.4	3.4	11.0	9.1	..	..	8.0	8.4
Europe & Central Asia	–0.8	5.0	–1.7	3.3	–3.0	5.3	..	..	0.8	4.8
Latin America & Carib.	3.3	1.6	1.8	3.1	3.2	1.4	2.9	1.1	3.3	0.7
Middle East & N. Africa	3.9	3.8	2.9	5.1	2.1	1.9	3.7	5.2	4.7	4.5
South Asia	5.6	5.8	3.1	1.9	6.2	6.1	6.6	6.5	7.1	7.5
Sub-Saharan Africa	2.5	3.9	3.3	3.6	1.9	4.0	1.9	2.3	2.7	3.9
High income	2.7	2.0	1.0	*–1.3*	1.9	*0.3*	..	*0.7*	3.0	*2.0*
Europe EMU	2.1	1.3	1.3	–0.4	1.0	0.6	1.8	*–0.2*	2.5	1.6

a. Components are at producer prices. b. China has revised its national accounts data from 1993 onwards. Data before 1993 are linked to the revised data on the basis of earlier growth rates. c. Data cover mainland Tanzania only.

About the data

An economy's growth is measured by the change in the volume of its output or in the real incomes of its residents. The 1993 United Nations System of National Accounts (1993 SNA) offers three plausible indicators for calculating growth: the volume of gross domestic product (GDP), real gross domestic income, and real gross national income. The volume of GDP is the sum of value added, measured at constant prices, by households, government, and industries operating in the economy. This year's edition of *World Development Indicators* continues to measure growth of the economy by the change in GDP measured at constant prices.

Each industry's contribution to growth in the economy's output is measured by growth in the industry's value added. In principle, value added in constant prices can be estimated by measuring the quantity of goods and services produced in a period, valuing them at an agreed set of base year prices, and subtracting the cost of intermediate inputs, also in constant prices. This double-deflation method, recommended by the 1993 SNA and its predecessors, requires detailed information on the structure of prices of inputs and outputs.

In many industries, however, value added is extrapolated from the base year using single volume indexes of outputs or, more rarely, inputs. Particularly in the services industries, including most of government, value added in constant prices is often imputed from labor inputs, such as real wages or number of employees. In the absence of well-defined measures of output, measuring the growth of services remains difficult.

Moreover, technical progress can lead to improvements in production processes and in the quality of goods and services that, if not properly accounted for, can distort measures of value added and thus of growth. When inputs are used to estimate output, as is the case for nonmarket services, unmeasured technical progress leads to underestimates of the volume of output. Similarly, unmeasured improvements in the quality of goods and services produced lead to underestimates of the value of output and value added. The result can be underestimates of growth and productivity improvement and overestimates of inflation. These issues are highly complex, and only a few high-income countries have attempted to introduce any GDP adjustments for these factors.

Informal economic activities pose a particular measurement problem, especially in developing countries, where much economic activity may go unrecorded. Obtaining a complete picture of the economy requires estimating household outputs produced for home use, sales in informal markets, barter exchanges, and illicit or deliberately unreported activities. The consistency and completeness of such estimates depend on the skill and methods of the compiling statisticians and the resources available to them.

Rebasing national accounts

When countries rebase their national accounts, they update the weights assigned to various components to better reflect the current pattern of production or uses of output. The new base year should represent normal operation of the economy—that is, it should be a year without major shocks or distortions. Some developing countries have not rebased their national accounts for many years. Using an old base year can be misleading because implicit price and volume weights become progressively less relevant and useful.

To obtain comparable series of constant price data, the World Bank rescales GDP and value added by industrial origin to a common reference year. This year's *World Development Indicators* continues to use 2000 as the reference year. Because rescaling changes the implicit weights used in forming regional and income group aggregates, aggregate growth rates in this year's *World Development Indicators* are not comparable with those from earlier publications with different base years.

Rescaling may result in a discrepancy between the rescaled GDP and the sum of the rescaled components. Because allocating the discrepancy would cause distortions in the growth rates, the discrepancy is left unallocated. As a result, the weighted average of the growth rates of the components generally will not equal the GDP growth rate.

Growth rates of GDP and its components are calculated using constant price data in the local currency. Regional and income group growth rates are calculated after converting local currencies to constant price U.S. dollars using an exchange rate in the common reference year. The growth rates in the table are average annual compound growth rates. Methods of computing growth rates and the alternative conversion factor are described in *Statistical methods*.

Changes in the System of National Accounts

World Development Indicators adopted the terminology of the 1993 SNA in 2001. Although many countries continue to compile their national accounts according to the SNA version 3 (referred to as the 1968 SNA), more and more are adopting the 1993 SNA. Some low-income countries still use concepts from the even older 1953 SNA guidelines, including valuations such as factor cost, in describing major economic aggregates. Countries that use the 1993 SNA are identified in *Primary data documentation*.

Definitions

• **Gross domestic product** (GDP) at purchaser prices is the sum of gross value added by all resident producers in the economy plus any product taxes (less subsidies) not included in the valuation of output. It is calculated without deducting for depreciation of fabricated capital assets or for depletion and degradation of natural resources. Value added is the net output of an industry after adding up all outputs and subtracting intermediate inputs. The industrial origin of value added is determined by the International Standard Industrial Classification (ISIC) revision 3. • **Agriculture** corresponds to ISIC divisions 1–5 and includes forestry and fishing. • **Industry** covers mining, manufacturing (also reported separately), construction, electricity, water, and gas (ISIC divisions 10–45). • **Manufacturing** corresponds to industries belonging to ISIC divisions 15–37. • **Services** correspond to ISIC divisions 50–99. This sector is derived as a residual (from GDP less agriculture and industry) and may not properly reflect the sum of services output, including banking and financial services. For some countries it includes product taxes (minus subsidies) and may also include statistical discrepancies.

Data sources

National accounts data for most developing countries are collected from national statistical organizations and central banks by visiting and resident World Bank missions. Data for high-income economies come from data files of the Organisation for Economic Co-operation and Development (for information on the OECD's national accounts series, see its *Annual National Accounts for OECD Member Countries: Data from 1970 Onwards*). The World Bank rescales constant price data to a common reference year. The complete national accounts time series is available on the *World Development Indicators 2006* CD-ROM. The United Nations Statistics Division publishes detailed national accounts for UN member countries in *National Accounts Statistics: Main Aggregates and Detailed Tables* and publishes updates in the *Monthly Bulletin of Statistics*.

4.2 Structure of output

	Gross domestic product		Agriculture		Industry		Manufacturing		Services	
	$ millions		% of GDP		% of GDP		% of GDP		% of GDP	
	1990	2004	1990	2004	1990	2004	1990	2004	1990	2004
Afghanistan[a]	..	5,761	..	..	..	..	..	..	..	..
Albania	2,102	7,590	36	25	48	19	..	*11*	16	56
Algeria	62,045	84,649	11	10	48	57	11	7	41	34
Angola[a]	10,260	19,493	18	9	41	58	5	4	41	33
Argentina	141,352	153,014	8	10	36	36	27	24	56	54
Armenia	2,257	3,079	17	23	52	37	33	23	31	40
Australia	310,518	637,327	4	*3*	29	*26*	14	*12*	67	*71*
Austria	164,984	292,328	4	2	32	31	21	*20*	64	67
Azerbaijan	8,858	8,523	29	12	33	55	19	9	38	32
Bangladesh[a]	30,129	56,585	30	21	22	27	13	16	48	52
Belarus	17,370	22,889	24	11	47	40	39	32	29	50
Belgium	197,176	352,312	2	1	33	25	..	*18*	65	73
Benin[a]	1,845	4,075	36	37	13	15	8	9	51	48
Bolivia[a]	4,868	8,773	17	16	35	31	19	14	49	54
Bosnia and Herzegovina	..	8,533	..	12	..	28	..	13	..	61
Botswana	3,792	8,974	5	3	61	51	5	5	34	47
Brazil	461,952	603,973	8	10	39	40	*25*	11	53	50
Bulgaria	20,731	24,131	17	11	49	31	..	19	34	58
Burkina Faso	3,120	4,824	28	31	20	20	15	14	52	49
Burundi	1,132	657	56	51	19	20	13	..	25	29
Cambodia[a]	1,115	4,884	..	33	..	29	..	22	..	38
Cameroon	11,152	14,391	25	44	30	16	15	8	46	40
Canada	574,192	977,968	3	..	32	..	17	..	65	..
Central African Republic	1,488	1,307	48	56	20	22	11	..	33	23
Chad	1,739	4,221	29	*64*	18	*8*	14	*6*	53	*29*
Chile[a]	30,323	94,105	9	4	42	45	20	19	50	52
China[a, b]	354,644	1,931,710	27	13	42	46	33	..	31	41
Hong Kong, China	75,433	163,005	0	*0*	25	*11*	18	*4*	74	*89*
Colombia[a]	40,274	97,718	17	12	38	31	21	14	45	58
Congo, Dem. Rep.	9,350	6,628	31	*58*	29	*19*	11	*4*	40	*22*
Congo, Rep.[a]	2,799	4,343	13	6	41	57	8	6	47	37
Costa Rica	5,713	18,496	18	9	29	29	22	21	53	63
Côte d'Ivoire[a]	10,796	15,475	33	22	23	21	21	17	44	58
Croatia	24,778	34,311	10	8	34	30	28	19	56	62
Cuba[a]	..	..	..	..	..	..	..	..	..	..
Czech Republic	34,880	107,015	6	3	49	38	..	26	45	59
Denmark	133,360	241,437	5	2	27	25	18	*16*	69	73
Dominican Republic[a]	7,074	18,673	13	11	31	26	18	13	55	63
Ecuador[a]	10,356	30,282	13	7	38	31	19	10	49	62
Egypt, Arab Rep.	43,130	78,796	19	15	29	37	18	18	52	48
El Salvador[a]	4,801	15,824	17	10	27	31	22	24	55	60
Eritrea	*477*	925	*31*	15	*12*	24	*8*	11	*57*	61
Estonia	5,010	11,239	17	4	50	29	42	18	34	67
Ethiopia	8,609	8,003	49	47	13	10	8	..	38	44
Finland	136,962	185,923	7	3	34	31	23	*23*	59	66
France	1,239,256	2,046,646	4	3	27	22	..	14	70	76
Gabon[a]	5,952	7,229	7	8	43	61	6	5	50	31
Gambia, The	317	415	29	32	13	14	7	5	58	54
Georgia	7,738	5,202	32	18	34	25	24	19	35	57
Germany	1,707,383	2,740,551	2	1	38	29	*28*	*23*	61	70
Ghana[a]	5,886	8,869	45	38	17	25	10	9	38	37
Greece	84,073	205,215	11	7	28	23	..	*12*	61	70
Guatemala[a]	7,650	27,451	26	23	20	19	15	13	54	58
Guinea	2,818	3,870	24	25	33	37	5	4	43	38
Guinea-Bissau	244	280	61	63	19	12	8	9	21	25
Haiti[a]	2,864	3,530	..	27	..	17	..	9	..	55

Structure of output 4.2

	Gross domestic product		Agriculture		Industry		Manufacturing		Services	
	$ millions		% of GDP		% of GDP		% of GDP		% of GDP	
	1990	2004	1990	2004	1990	2004	1990	2004	1990	2004
Honduras	3,049	7,371	22	*14*	26	*31*	16	*20*	51	*56*
Hungary	33,056	100,685	15	*3*	39	*31*	*23*	*23*	46	*66*
India	316,937	691,163	31	21	28	27	17	16	41	52
Indonesia[a]	114,426	257,641	19	15	39	44	21	28	42	41
Iran, Islamic Rep.	120,404	163,445	24	11	29	42	12	12	48	48
Iraq	*48,422*	*12,602*	..	*9*	..	*70*	..	*2*	..	*21*
Ireland	47,299	181,623	9	*3*	35	*41*	28	*31*	56	*56*
Israel	52,490	116,879	..	..	..	..	..	..	..	..
Italy	1,102,380	1,677,834	4	3	34	28	25	20	63	70
Jamaica[a]	4,592	8,865	8	6	46	33	21	14	59	62
Japan	3,039,693	4,622,771	3	*1*	39	*31*	27	*21*	58	*68*
Jordan	4,020	11,515	8	3	28	29	15	19	64	68
Kazakhstan	26,933	40,743	*27*	8	*45*	40	*9*	16	*29*	52
Kenya	8,591	16,088	30	27	19	17	12	11	51	56
Korea, Dem. Rep.	..	..	..	..	..	..	..	..	..	..
Korea, Rep.[a]	263,776	679,674	9	4	42	41	27	29	50	56
Kuwait[a]	18,428	55,718	1	*1*	52	*59*	12	*3*	47	*41*
Kyrgyz Republic	2,674	2,205	34	37	36	21	28	14	30	42
Lao PDR	866	2,452	61	47	15	28	10	20	24	26
Latvia	7,447	13,571	22	4	46	23	35	13	32	73
Lebanon	2,838	21,768	..	7	..	21	..	13	..	72
Lesotho	615	1,312	24	18	33	41	14	19	44	42
Liberia	384	492	54	*43*	17	*6*	..	*6*	29	*51*
Libya	28,905	29,119	..	..	..	..	..	..	..	..
Lithuania	10,506	22,263	27	6	31	34	21	21	42	60
Macedonia, FYR	4,478	5,355	9	13	45	28	36	16	47	59
Madagascar	3,081	4,364	29	29	13	16	11	14	59	55
Malawi	1,881	1,879	45	39	29	17	20	11	26	44
Malaysia[a]	44,024	118,318	15	10	42	50	24	31	43	40
Mali	2,421	4,863	46	36	16	26	9	3	39	39
Mauritania	1,020	1,534	30	18	29	34	10	10	42	48
Mauritius	2,383	6,034	13	6	33	30	25	21	54	64
Mexico[a]	262,710	676,497	8	4	28	26	21	18	64	70
Moldova	3,593	2,595	36	21	37	24	..	17	27	55
Mongolia[a]	..	1,612	17	21	30	30	..	5	52	49
Morocco[a]	25,784	50,031	18	16	32	30	18	17	50	54
Mozambique	2,463	6,086	37	22	18	31	10	13	45	47
Myanmar[a]	..	..	57	..	11	..	8	..	32	..
Namibia	2,350	5,712	12	10	38	32	14	14	50	58
Nepal	3,628	6,707	52	40	16	23	6	9	32	37
Netherlands	294,761	578,979	5	2	31	26	19	*15*	65	72
New Zealand	43,618	98,944	7	..	28	..	19	..	65	..
Nicaragua[a]	1,009	4,555	37	19	25	31	20	20	56	50
Niger[a]	2,481	3,081	35	*40*	16	*17*	7	*7*	49	*43*
Nigeria	28,472	72,053	33	17	41	57	6	*4*	26	27
Norway	116,108	250,052	4	2	36	39	13	*11*	61	59
Oman[a]	11,685	24,284	3	2	54	56	3	8	43	42
Pakistan	40,010	96,115	26	22	25	25	17	18	49	53
Panama	5,313	13,733	10	8	15	18	10	8	75	74
Papua New Guinea	3,221	3,909	29	*29*	30	*42*	9	*9*	41	*29*
Paraguay	5,265	7,343	28	27	25	24	17	14	47	49
Peru[a]	26,294	68,637	9	10	27	30	18	16	64	60
Philippines[a]	44,312	84,567	22	14	35	32	25	24	44	54
Poland	58,976	242,293	8	3	50	33	..	20	42	64
Portugal	71,462	167,716	9	4	32	27	22	*17*	60	70
Puerto Rico[a]	30,604	..	1	..	42	..	40	..	57	..

4.2 Structure of output

	Gross domestic product		Agriculture		Industry		Manufacturing		Services	
	$ millions		% of GDP		% of GDP		% of GDP		% of GDP	
	1990	2004	1990	2004	1990	2004	1990	2004	1990	2004
Romania	38,299	73,167	24	14	50	37	*34*	31	26	49
Russian Federation	516,814	581,447	17	5	48	35	..	..	35	60
Rwanda	2,584	1,845	33	41	25	22	18	10	43	38
Saudi Arabia[a]	116,778	250,557	6	4	49	59	9	10	46	37
Senegal[a]	5,699	7,775	20	17	19	20	13	12	61	63
Serbia and Montenegro	..	23,997	..	19	..	36	..	22	..	45
Sierra Leone[a]	650	1,075	47	..	19	..	5	..	34	..
Singapore[a]	36,901	106,818	..	0	..	35	..	29	..	65
Slovak Republic[a]	15,485	41,094	7	4	59	30	..	19	34	67
Slovenia	17,413	32,182	6	*3*	42	*37*	34	*27*	52	*61*
Somalia	917	..	66	..	..	..	5	..	..	..
South Africa	112,014	212,777	5	3	40	32	24	20	55	65
Spain	526,471	1,039,927	7	4	34	29	..	16	59	67
Sri Lanka	8,032	20,055	26	18	26	27	15	15	48	55
Sudan	13,167	21,098	..	39	..	25	..	6	..	36
Swaziland	882	2,396	13	13	42	47	35	39	45	40
Sweden	240,153	346,412	3	2	32	29	..	*21*	64	69
Switzerland	235,808	357,542	3	*1*	33	*29*	22	*20*	64	*70*
Syrian Arab Republic[a]	12,309	24,022	28	23	24	27	20	..	48	50
Tajikistan	2,629	2,073	33	24	38	31	25	22	29	45
Tanzania[c]	4,259	10,851	46	45	18	17	9	7	36	39
Thailand[a]	85,345	161,688	13	10	37	44	27	35	50	46
Togo	1,628	2,061	34	41	23	23	10	9	44	36
Trinidad and Tobago[a]	5,068	12,544	3	1	45	47	13	7	52	52
Tunisia	12,291	28,185	16	13	30	28	17	18	55	60
Turkey	150,642	302,786	18	13	30	22	20	14	52	65
Turkmenistan	3,232	6,167	32	*21*	30	*45*	..	*21*	38	*34*
Uganda	4,304	6,822	57	32	11	21	6	9	32	47
Ukraine	81,456	64,828	26	12	45	37	*39*	23	30	51
United Arab Emirates	33,653	104,204	2	3	64	55	8	13	35	42
United Kingdom	989,524	2,124,385	2	1	35	26	23	..	63	73
United States	5,757,200	11,711,834	2	*1*	28	*22*	19	*15*	70	*77*
Uruguay	9,287	13,215	9	11	33	29	27	21	58	60
Uzbekistan	13,361	11,960	33	31	33	25	*22*	10	34	44
Venezuela, RB[a]	47,027	110,104	6	*5*	61	*52*	15	*18*	34	*44*
Vietnam[a]	6,472	45,210	39	22	23	40	12	20	39	38
West Bank and Gaza	..	*3,454*	..	*6*	..	*12*	..	*10*	..	*82*
Yemen, Rep.[a]	4,828	12,834	24	14	27	38	9	5	49	49
Zambia[a]	3,288	5,402	21	21	51	27	36	12	28	52
Zimbabwe	8,784	4,696	17	18	33	23	23	14	50	60
World	**21,735,592 t**	**41,290,409 t**	**6 w**	***4* w**	**33 w**	***28* w**	**22 w**	***18* w**	**61 w**	***68* w**
Low income	609,821	1,239,169	32	23	26	28	15	15	42	49
Middle income	3,238,587	7,156,777	16	10	39	37	25	18	46	53
Lower middle income	1,656,377	4,165,291	19	12	39	41	27	..	42	46
Upper middle income	1,582,075	2,991,524	10	6	39	32	22	20	51	62
Low & middle income	3,849,026	8,395,211	18	12	37	36	23	18	45	52
East Asia & Pacific	665,783	2,650,867	25	13	40	45	30	..	35	42
Europe & Central Asia	1,107,862	1,769,739	16	8	43	32	..	19	41	60
Latin America & Carib.	1,101,298	2,021,995	9	9	36	34	*22*	16	55	58
Middle East & N. Africa	..	547,496	19	12	33	39	14	14	49	49
South Asia	401,923	880,212	31	21	27	27	17	16	43	52
Sub-Saharan Africa	298,442	523,310	20	16	34	32	17	15	47	52
High income	17,887,372	32,900,093	3	*2*	33	*26*	22	*18*	65	*72*
Europe EMU	5,583,289	9,500,919	4	2	33	27	..	*19*	63	71

a. Components are at producer prices. b. China has revised its national accounts data from 1993 onwards. Data before 1993 are not comparable with the later data. c. Data cover mainland Tanzania only.

About the data

An economy's gross domestic product (GDP) represents the sum of value added by all producers in that economy. Value added is the value of the gross output of producers less the value of intermediate goods and services consumed in production, before taking account of the consumption of fixed capital in the production process. The United Nations System of National Accounts calls for estimates of value added to be valued at either basic prices (excluding net taxes on products) or producer prices (including net taxes on products paid by producers but excluding sales or value added taxes). Both valuations exclude transport charges that are invoiced separately by producers. Total GDP shown in the table and elsewhere in this book is measured at purchaser prices. Value added by industry is normally measured at basic prices. When value added is measured at producer prices, this is noted in *Primary data documentation*.

While GDP estimates based on the production approach are generally more reliable than estimates compiled from the income or expenditure side, different countries use different definitions, methods, and reporting standards. World Bank staff review the quality of national accounts data and sometimes make adjustments to improve consistency with international guidelines. Nevertheless, significant discrepancies remain between international standards and actual practice. Many statistical offices, especially those in developing countries, face severe limitations in the resources, time, training, and budgets required to produce reliable and comprehensive series of national accounts statistics.

Data problems in measuring output

Among the difficulties faced by compilers of national accounts is the extent of unreported economic activity in the informal or secondary economy. In developing countries a large share of agricultural output is either not exchanged (because it is consumed within the household) or not exchanged for money.

Agricultural production often must be estimated indirectly, using a combination of methods involving estimates of inputs, yields, and area under cultivation. This approach sometimes leads to crude approximations that can differ from the true values over time and across crops for reasons other than climatic conditions or farming techniques. Similarly, agricultural inputs that cannot easily be allocated to specific outputs are frequently "netted out" using equally crude and ad hoc approximations. For further discussion of the measurement of agricultural production, see *About the data* for table 3.3.

Ideally, industrial output should be measured through regular censuses and surveys of firms. But in most developing countries such surveys are infrequent, so earlier survey results must be extrapolated using an appropriate indicator. The choice of sampling unit, which may be the enterprise (where responses may be based on financial records) or the establishment (where production units may be recorded separately), also affects the quality of the data. Moreover, much industrial production is organized in unincorporated or owner-operated ventures that are not captured by surveys aimed at the formal sector. Even in large industries, where regular surveys are more likely, evasion of excise and other taxes and nondisclosure of income lower the estimates of value added. Such problems become more acute as countries move from state control of industry to private enterprise, because new firms enter business and growing numbers of established firms fail to report. In accordance with the System of National Accounts, output should include all such unreported activity as well as the value of illegal activities and other unrecorded, informal, or small-scale operations. Data on these activities need to be collected using techniques other than conventional surveys of firms.

In industries dominated by large organizations and enterprises, such as public utilities, data on output, employment, and wages are usually readily available and reasonably reliable. But in the services industry the many self-employed workers and one-person businesses are sometimes difficult to locate, and they have little incentive to respond to surveys, let alone to report their full earnings. Compounding these problems are the many forms of economic activity that go unrecorded, including the work that women and children do for little or no pay. For further discussion of the problems of using national accounts data, see Srinivasan (1994) and Heston (1994).

Dollar conversion

To produce national accounts aggregates that are measured in the same standard monetary units, the value of output must be converted to a single common currency. The World Bank conventionally uses the U.S. dollar and applies the average official exchange rate reported by the International Monetary Fund for the year shown. An alternative conversion factor is applied if the official exchange rate is judged to diverge by an exceptionally large margin from the rate effectively applied to transactions in foreign currencies and traded products.

Definitions

• **Gross domestic product** (GDP) at purchaser prices is the sum of gross value added by all resident producers in the economy plus any product taxes (less subsidies) not included in the valuation of output. It is calculated without deducting for depreciation of fabricated assets or for depletion and degradation of natural resources. Value added is the net output of an industry after adding up all outputs and subtracting intermediate inputs. The industrial origin of value added is determined by the International Standard Industrial Classification (ISIC) revision 3. • **Agriculture** corresponds to ISIC divisions 1–5 and includes forestry and fishing. • **Industry** covers mining, manufacturing (also reported separately), construction, electricity, water, and gas (ISIC divisions 10–45). • **Manufacturing** corresponds to industries belonging to ISIC divisions 15–37. • **Services** correspond to ISIC divisions 50–99. This sector is derived as a residual (from GDP less agriculture and industry) and may not properly reflect the sum of services output, including banking and financial services. For some countries it includes product taxes (minus subsidies) and may also include statistical discrepancies.

Data sources

National accounts data for most developing countries are collected from national statistical organizations and central banks by visiting and resident World Bank missions. Data for high-income economies come from data files of the Organisation for Economic Co-operation and Development (for information on the OECD's national accounts series, see its *Annual National Accounts for OECD Member Countries: Data from 1970 Onwards*). The complete national accounts time series is available on the *World Development Indicators 2006* CD-ROM. The United Nations Statistics Division publishes detailed national accounts for UN member countries in *National Accounts Statistics: Main Aggregates and Detailed Tables* and publishes updates in the *Monthly Bulletin of Statistics*.

4.3 Structure of manufacturing

	Manufacturing value added		Food, beverages, and tobacco		Textiles and clothing		Machinery and transport equipment		Chemicals		Other manufacturing[a]	
	$ millions		% of total		% of total		% of total		% of total		% of total	
	1990	2002	1990	2002	1990	2002	1990	2002	1990	2002	1990	2002
Afghanistan	..	..	..	..	..	..	..	..	..	..	..	..
Albania	..	393	24	..	33	..	..	..	..	..	44	..
Algeria	6,452	4,109	13	..	17	..	..	..	..	..	70	..
Angola	513	404	..	..	..	..	..	..	..	..	..	..
Argentina	37,868	20,763	20	..	10	..	13	..	12	..	46	..
Armenia	681	483	..	..	..	..	..	..	..	..	..	..
Australia	38,871	44,802	18	15	6	12	20	25	7	7	49	42
Austria	31,439	37,308	15	20	7	17	28	18	8	9	43	37
Azerbaijan	1,561	463	..	..	..	..	..	..	..	..	..	..
Bangladesh	3,839	7,278	24	..	38	..	7	..	17	..	15	..
Belarus	6,630	3,790	..	..	..	..	..	..	..	..	..	..
Belgium	..	41,434	17	18	7	15	..	24	13	7	62	37
Benin	145	244	..	..	..	..	..	..	..	..	..	..
Bolivia	826	1,039	28	..	5	..	1	..	3	..	63	..
Bosnia and Herzegovina	..	559	12	..	15	..	18	..	7	..	49	..
Botswana	181	233	*51*	19	*12*	4	..	..	..	..	*36*	77
Brazil	*89,966*	53,032	14	..	12	..	27	..	..	..	48	..
Bulgaria	..	2,391	*22*	..	*9*	..	*19*	..	*5*	..	*45*	..
Burkina Faso	460	394	*1*	1	*8*	17	*1*	3	..	..	*90*	80
Burundi	134	..	83	..	9	..	..	..	2	..	7	..
Cambodia	58	755	..	..	..	..	..	..	..	..	..	..
Cameroon	1,581	845	61	..	–13	..	1	..	5	..	46	..
Canada	91,671	*118,620*	15	17	6	9	26	21	10	7	44	46
Central African Republic	154	*81*	58	..	6	..	2	..	6	..	28	..
Chad	239	263	..	..	..	..	..	..	..	..	..	..
Chile	5,613	12,348	25	25	8	18	5	12	10	8	52	37
China[b]	116,573	..	15	*15*	15	*12*	24	*32*	13	*12*	34	*28*
Hong Kong, China	12,639	7,033	8	11	36	20	21	25	2	3	33	41
Colombia	8,034	10,783	31	21	15	4	9	4	14	..	31	71
Congo, Dem. Rep.	1,029	220	..	..	..	..	..	..	..	..	..	..
Congo, Rep.	234	158	*58*	..	*4*	..	*3*	..	..	..	*35*	..
Costa Rica	1,107	3,277	47	45	8	5	7	6	9	11	30	33
Côte d'Ivoire	2,257	1,949	*38*	26	*7*	13	*8*	9	..	..	*47*	52
Croatia	6,475	3,771	22	..	15	..	20	..	8	..	36	..
Cuba	..	..	*67*	..	*5*	..	*1*	..	..	..	*27*	..
Czech Republic	..	17,407	..	..	..	..	..	..	..	..	..	..
Denmark	20,757	23,862	22	21	4	7	24	25	12	8	39	38
Dominican Republic	1,270	3,393	..	..	..	..	..	..	..	..	..	..
Ecuador	1,988	2,663	22	11	10	3	5	1	8	1	56	85
Egypt, Arab Rep.	7,296	16,250	19	..	16	..	9	..	14	..	43	..
El Salvador	1,043	3,318	*36*	44	*14*	27	*4*	3	*24*	9	*23*	17
Eritrea	*35*	66	*53*	*55*	*18*	*11*	*2*	*2*	*18*	*6*	*9*	*26*
Estonia	1,985	1,085	..	..	..	..	..	..	..	..	..	..
Ethiopia	624	..	..	..	*13*	..	*2*	..	*2*	..	*83*	..
Finland	27,531	27,212	13	*17*	4	*12*	24	*19*	8	*7*	52	*45*
France	..	192,279	13	13	6	12	31	22	9	7	41	45
Gabon	332	234	*45*	*28*	*2*	*4*	*1*	*3*	*7*	*2*	*45*	*63*
Gambia, The	18	19	..	..	..	..	..	..	..	..	..	..
Georgia	1,773	599	..	..	..	..	..	..	..	..	..	..
Germany	*456,405*	410,644	..	*8*	..	*2*	..	*41*	..	*10*	..	*38*
Ghana	575	556	..	38	..	11	..	4	..	8	..	39
Greece	..	13,845	22	24	20	21	12	13	10	8	36	35
Guatemala	1,151	2,985	*38*	41	*11*	10	*4*	4	*18*	14	*29*	31
Guinea	126	128	..	..	..	..	..	..	..	..	..	..
Guinea-Bissau	19	20	..	..	..	..	..	..	..	..	..	..
Haiti	..	268	*51*	..	*9*	..	..	..	..	..	*40*	..

Structure of manufacturing 4.3

	Manufacturing value added		Food, beverages, and tobacco		Textiles and clothing		Machinery and transport equipment		Chemicals		Other manufacturing[a]	
	$ millions		% of total		% of total		% of total		% of total		% of total	
	1990	2002	1990	2002	1990	2002	1990	2002	1990	2002	1990	2002
Honduras	443	1,172	45	33	10	3	3	0	6	..	36	64
Hungary	*6,613*	12,449	14	12	9	13	26	10	12	7	39	58
India	48,808	72,681	12	2	15	27	26	17	14	5	34	49
Indonesia	23,643	59,471	28	23	15	17	12	22	9	10	37	28
Iran, Islamic Rep.	14,503	13,938	12	36	20	30	20	9	8	2	40	23
Iraq	..	319	*20*	51	*16*	53	*4*	25	*11*	7	*49*	-35
Ireland	11,982	34,732	27	35	4	20	29	11	17	5	24	29
Israel	..	..	14	20	9	15	32	17	9	6	37	42
Italy	247,917	216,177	8	*9*	13	*13*	35	*27*	7	*8*	37	*44*
Jamaica	853	1,071	41	29	5	3	..	2	..	4	54	63
Japan	810,232	811,829	9	10	5	0	40	9	10	11	37	70
Jordan	520	1,393	28	27	7	9	4	5	15	17	47	42
Kazakhstan	*1,941*	3,566	..	..	..	..	..	..	..	..	..	..
Kenya	864	1,299	39	37	10	19	10	7	9	10	33	28
Korea, Dem. Rep.	..	..	..	..	..	..	..	..	..	..	..	..
Korea, Rep.	64,605	129,449	11	*27*	12	*20*	32	*6*	9	*10*	36	*37*
Kuwait	2,142	1,031	4	*10*	3	*5*	2	*5*	3	*3*	88	*76*
Kyrgyz Republic	706	210	..	..	..	..	..	..	..	..	..	..
Lao PDR	85	344	..	..	..	..	..	..	..	..	..	..
Latvia	2,474	1,128	..	*27*	..	*11*	..	*10*	..	*4*	..	*49*
Lebanon	..	2,114	..	..	..	..	..	..	..	..	..	..
Lesotho	71	128	..	..	..	..	..	..	..	..	..	..
Liberia	..	27	..	..	..	..	..	..	..	..	..	..
Libya	..	..	..	49	..	3	..	2	..	10	..	36
Lithuania	2,164	2,398	..	..	..	..	..	..	..	..	..	..
Macedonia, FYR	1,411	589	20	..	26	..	14	..	9	..	31	..
Madagascar	314	518	*39*	11	*36*	35	*3*	6	*8*	1	*14*	48
Malawi	313	197	38	62	10	12	1	1	18	8	33	17
Malaysia	10,665	29,095	13	*9*	7	*4*	31	*41*	11	*8*	39	*38*
Mali	200	98	..	..	..	..	..	..	..	..	..	..
Mauritania	94	112	..	..	..	..	..	..	..	..	..	..
Mauritius	491	922	30	..	46	..	2	..	4	..	17	..
Mexico	49,992	110,667	22	*25*	5	*4*	24	*27*	18	*15*	32	*28*
Moldova	..	247	..	59	..	10	..	6	..	..	..	25
Mongolia	..	70	33	..	37	..	1	..	1	..	27	..
Morocco	4,753	6,067	22	*33*	17	*18*	8	*8*	12	*13*	41	*28*
Mozambique	230	493	12	49	2	15	7	5	..	3	79	29
Myanmar	..	..	..	..	..	..	..	..	..	..	..	..
Namibia	292	314	..	..	..	..	..	..	..	..	..	..
Nepal	209	432	37	45	31	19	1	2	5	10	26	23
Netherlands	52,330	56,954	21	19	3	14	25	33	17	12	35	23
New Zealand	7,574	*8,037*	28	3	8	12	13	10	7	5	44	71
Nicaragua	170	721	56	53	10	8	0	0	6	10	28	29
Niger	163	143	37	..	29	..	..	..	..	..	34	..
Nigeria	1,562	2,075	*15*	..	*46*	..	*13*	..	*4*	..	*22*	..
Norway	13,450	18,563	18	1	2	10	25	21	9	3	46	65
Oman	343	1,564	..	9	..	2	..	3	..	5	..	82
Pakistan	6,184	10,440	24	23	28	2	9	5	15	11	25	59
Panama	502	974	51	52	8	7	2	3	8	4	31	35
Papua New Guinea	289	241	12	21	..	0	..	3	..	4	88	73
Paraguay	883	775	*56*	45	*16*	18	..	1	..	5	*29*	32
Peru	3,926	8,149	23	..	11	..	8	..	9	..	49	..
Philippines	11,003	17,735	39	*38*	11	*10*	13	*8*	12	*12*	26	*33*
Poland	..	29,220	21	20	9	19	26	23	7	6	37	32
Portugal	13,630	18,319	15	19	21	23	13	10	6	9	45	40
Puerto Rico	12,126	*27,099*	16	*8*	5	*2*	18	*18*	44	*61*	17	*12*

4.3 Structure of manufacturing

	Manufacturing value added		Food, beverages, and tobacco		Textiles and clothing		Machinery and transport equipment		Chemicals		Other manufacturing[a]	
	$ millions		% of total		% of total		% of total		% of total		% of total	
	1990	2002	1990	2002	1990	2002	1990	2002	1990	2002	1990	2002
Romania	*9,152*	*16,141*	19	..	18	..	14	..	4	..	45	..
Russian Federation	..	..	..	*19*	..	*2*	..	*24*	..	*5*	..	*50*
Rwanda	473	194	..	..	..	2	*10*	..	..	2	*90*	97
Saudi Arabia	10,049	19,460	*7*	..	*1*	..	*4*	..	*39*	..	*50*	*100*
Senegal	747	626	60	..	3	..	5	..	9	..	23	..
Serbia and Montenegro	..	2,596	..	36	..	6	..	14	..	11	..	33
Sierra Leone	28	*21*	..	..	..	..	..	..	..	..	..	..
Singapore	..	22,942	4	2	3	1	53	52	10	22	29	23
Slovak Republic	..	4,811	..	..	..	..	..	..	..	..	..	..
Slovenia	5,200	5,170	12	10	15	9	16	17	9	13	48	50
Somalia	41	..	*86*	50	*3*	3	..	..	..	..	*12*	47
South Africa	24,043	19,885	15	*16*	8	*13*	18	*15*	9	*9*	50	*48*
Spain	..	108,351	18	17	8	22	25	18	10	11	39	33
Sri Lanka	1,077	2,320	51	*39*	24	*31*	4	*6*	4	*4*	17	*21*
Sudan	..	930	16	..	4	..	0	..	21	..	59	..
Swaziland	250	283	69	..	8	..	1	..	*0*	..	22	..
Sweden	..	43,749	10	11	2	8	33	30	9	2	47	49
Switzerland	49,484	53,226	10	..	4	..	34	..	..	..	53	..
Syrian Arab Republic	2,508	..	35	35	29	43	..	2	..	1	36	19
Tajikistan	653	415	..	..	..	..	..	..	..	..	..	..
Tanzania[c]	361	660	51	42	3	27	7	3	11	3	29	26
Thailand	23,217	42,739	24	23	30	14	19	4	2	25	26	34
Togo	162	134	60	10	7	13	..	..	..	..	33	77
Trinidad and Tobago	681	692	31	..	3	..	3	..	19	..	44	..
Tunisia	2,075	3,910	19	*35*	20	*11*	5	*5*	4	*20*	52	*30*
Turkey	26,882	21,912	16	31	15	23	16	8	10	6	43	32
Turkmenistan	..	647	..	..	..	..	..	..	..	..	..	..
Uganda	230	535	*61*	19	*14*	1	*3*	2	*6*	*1*	*16*	79
Ukraine	*31,517*	7,582	..	..	..	..	..	..	..	..	..	..
United Arab Emirates	2,643	10,268	..	*5*	..	*2*	..	*6*	..	*4*	..	*84*
United Kingdom	206,719	*220,429*	13	*12*	5	*11*	32	*32*	11	*10*	38	*36*
United States	1,040,600	1,463,300	12	12	5	8	31	30	12	10	40	39
Uruguay	2,597	2,145	31	..	18	..	9	..	10	..	32	..
Uzbekistan	..	782	..	..	..	..	..	..	..	..	..	..
Venezuela, RB	6,921	15,270	17	*28*	5	*5*	5	*4*	9	..	64	*64*
Vietnam	793	7,218	..	*30*	..	*21*	..	*15*	..	*6*	..	*28*
West Bank and Gaza	..	341	..	..	..	..	..	..	..	..	..	..
Yemen, Rep.	449	507	..	*50*	..	*5*	..	*0*	..	..	..	*44*
Zambia	1,048	385	44	..	12	..	7	..	9	..	29	..
Zimbabwe	1,799	3,692	28	28	19	18	10	3	6	5	38	48
World	4,528,705 t	5,446,980 t										
Low income	83,631	123,365										
Middle income	..	..										
Lower middle income	..	..										
Upper middle income	265,244	386,586										
Low & middle income	..	..										
East Asia & Pacific	..	..										
Europe & Central Asia	..	..										
Latin America & Carib.	204,350	258,603										
Middle East & N. Africa	..	56,686										
South Asia	60,476	93,715										
Sub-Saharan Africa	43,316	40,599										
High income	3,627,337	4,286,603										
Europe EMU	838,928	1,159,441										

a. Includes unallocated data. b. China has revised its national accounts data from 1993 onwards. Data before 1993 are not comparable with the later data. c. Data cover mainland Tanzania only.

Structure of manufacturing 4.3

About the data

The data on the distribution of manufacturing value added by industry are provided by the United Nations Industrial Development Organization (UNIDO). UNIDO obtains data on manufacturing value added from a variety of national and international sources, including the United Nations Statistics Division, the World Bank, the Organisation for Economic Co-operation and Development, and the International Monetary Fund. To improve comparability over time and across countries, UNIDO supplements these data with information from industrial censuses, statistics supplied by national and international organizations, unpublished data that it collects in the field, and estimates by the UNIDO Secretariat. Nevertheless, coverage may be less than complete, particularly for the informal sector. To the extent that direct information on inputs and outputs is not available, estimates may be used, which may result in errors in industry totals. Moreover, countries use different reference periods (calendar or fiscal year) and valuation methods (basic or producer prices) to estimate value added. (See also *About the data* for table 4.2.)

The data on manufacturing value added in U.S. dollars are from the World Bank's national accounts files. These figures may differ from those used by UNIDO to calculate the shares of value added by industry, in part because of differences in exchange rates. Thus estimates of value added in a particular industry calculated by applying the shares to total manufacturing value added will not match those from UNIDO sources. The classification of manufacturing industries in the table accords with the United Nations International Standard Industrial Classification (ISIC) revision 2. First published in 1948, the ISIC has its roots in the work of the League of Nations Committee of Statistical Experts. The committee's efforts, interrupted by the Second World War, were taken up by the United Nations Statistical Commission, which at its first session appointed a committee on industrial classification. The latest revision, ISIC revision 3, was completed in 1989, and many countries have now switched to it. But revision 2 is still widely used for compiling cross-country data. Concordances matching ISIC categories to national systems of classification and to related systems such as the Standard International Trade Classification are readily available.

In establishing a classification system, compilers must define both the types of activities to be described and the organizational units whose activities are to be reported. There are many possibilities, and the choices made affect how the resulting statistics can be interpreted and how useful they are in analyzing economic behavior. The ISIC emphasizes commonalities in the production process and is explicitly not intended to measure outputs (for which there is a newly developed Central Product Classification). Nevertheless, the ISIC views an activity as defined by "a process resulting in a homogeneous set of products" (United Nations 1990 [ISIC, series M, no. 4, rev. 3], p. 9).

Firms typically use a multitude of processes to produce a final product. For example, an automobile manufacturer engages in forging, welding, and painting as well as advertising, accounting, and many other service activities. In some cases the processes may be carried out by different technical units within the larger enterprise, but collecting data at such a detailed level is not practical, nor would it be useful to record production data at the very highest level of a large, multiplant, multiproduct firm. The ISIC has therefore adopted as the definition of an establishment "an enterprise or part of an enterprise which independently engages in one, or predominantly one, kind of economic activity at or from one location . . . for which data are available . . ." (United Nations 1990, p. 25). By design, this definition matches the reporting unit required for the production accounts of the UN System of National Accounts.

4.3a

Manufacturing growth trends for selected Sub-Saharan countries

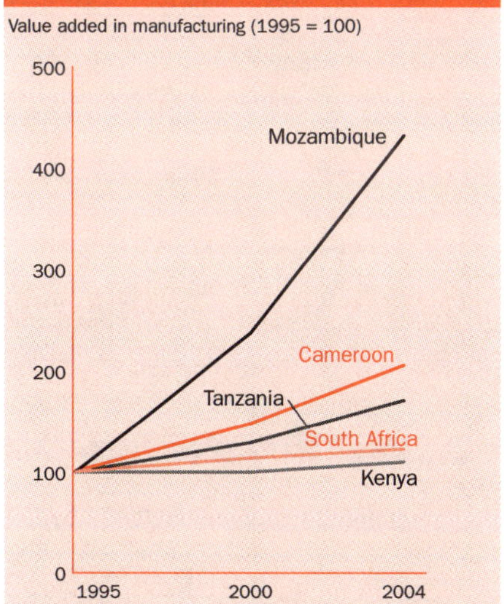

Mozambique had impressive growth in the manufacturing sector with over 15 percent growth between 1995 and 2004. By contrast, South Africa—with the largest manufacturing sector in the region—had modest growth of slightly more than 1.5 percent over the same period.

Source: World Bank data files.

Definitions

• **Manufacturing value added** is the sum of gross output less the value of intermediate inputs used in production for industries classified in ISIC major division 3. • **Food, beverages, and tobacco** correspond to ISIC division 31. • **Textiles and clothing** correspond to ISIC division 32. • **Machinery and transport equipment** correspond to ISIC groups 382–84. • **Chemicals** correspond to ISIC groups 351 and 352. • **Other manufacturing** covers wood and related products (ISIC division 33), paper and related products (ISIC division 34), petroleum and related products (ISIC groups 353–56), basic metals and mineral products (ISIC divisions 36 and 37), fabricated metal products and professional goods (ISIC groups 381 and 385), and other industries (ISIC group 390). When data for textiles and clothing, machinery and transport equipment, or chemicals are shown in the table as not available, they are included in "other manufacturing."

Data sources

Data on value added in manufacturing in U.S. dollars are from the World Bank's national accounts files. Data used to calculate shares of value added by industry are provided to the World Bank in electronic files by UNIDO. The most recent published source is UNIDO's *International Yearbook of Industrial Statistics 2005*. The ISIC system is described in the United Nations' *International Standard Industrial Classification of All Economic Activities, Third Revision* (1990). The discussion of the ISIC draws on Jacob Ryten's paper "Fifty Years of ISIC: Historical Origins and Future Perspectives" (1998).

4.4 Structure of merchandise exports

	Merchandise exports		Food		Agricultural raw materials		Fuels		Ores and metals		Manufactures	
	$ millions		% of total		% of total		% of total		% of total		% of total	
	1990	2004	1990	2004	1990	2004	1990	2004	1990	2004	1990	2004
Afghanistan	235	420	..	..	..	..	..	..	..	..	..	..
Albania	230	596	..	6	..	4	..	3	..	6	..	82
Algeria	12,930	32,298	0	0	0	0	96	97	0	0	3	2
Angola	3,910	13,850	0	..	0	..	93	..	6	..	0	..
Argentina	12,353	34,453	56	48	4	2	8	16	2	4	29	29
Armenia	..	705	..	12	..	2	..	3	..	21	..	62
Australia	39,752	86,423	22	19	10	4	20	19	20	16	26	25
Austria	41,265	117,417	3	6	4	3	1	3	3	3	88	84
Azerbaijan	..	3,615	..	4	..	1	..	82	..	1	..	10
Bangladesh	1,671	8,150	14	8	7	2	1	0	*0*	0	77	90
Belarus	..	13,752	..	8	..	3	..	27	..	1	..	60
Belgium	117,703[a]	306,509	9[a]	9	2[a]	1	3[a]	6	4[a]	3	77[a]	81
Benin	288	672	*15*	*41*	*56*	*49*	*15*	*0*	*0*	*0*	*13*	*9*
Bolivia	926	2,129	19	27	8	2	25	38	44	19	5	14
Bosnia and Herzegovina	*276*	1,789	..	..	..	..	..	..	..	..	..	..
Botswana	1,784	3,467	..	..	..	..	..	..	..	..	..	..
Brazil	31,414	96,475	28	28	3	4	2	5	14	9	52	54
Bulgaria	5,030	9,918	..	10	..	2	..	8	..	12	..	62
Burkina Faso	152	445	..	16	..	72	..	3	..	1	..	8
Burundi	75	47	..	92	..	1	..	0	..	2	..	5
Cambodia	86	2,798	..	1	..	2	..	0	..	0	..	97
Cameroon	2,002	2,700	20	19	14	24	50	47	7	5	9	5
Canada	127,629	316,547	9	7	9	5	10	17	9	5	59	60
Central African Republic	120	120	*31*	*2*	*24*	*25*	*0*	*0*	*1*	*36*	*44*	*37*
Chad	188	2,200	..	..	..	..	..	..	..	..	..	..
Chile	8,372	32,025	24	21	9	8	1	3	55	54	11	13
China†	62,091	593,329	13	4	3	1	8	2	2	2	72	91
Hong Kong, China[b]	82,390	265,670	4	1	1	1	1	0	1	1	92	96
Colombia	6,766	16,224	33	17	4	5	37	38	0	1	25	38
Congo, Dem. Rep.	2,326	1,413	..	..	..	..	..	..	..	..	..	..
Congo, Rep.	981	3,900	..	..	..	..	..	..	..	..	..	..
Costa Rica	1,448	6,297	58	33	5	3	1	0	1	1	27	63
Côte d'Ivoire	3,072	6,475	..	*56*	..	*9*	..	*13*	..	*0*	..	*20*
Croatia	*4,597*	8,022	*13*	9	*6*	4	*9*	11	*5*	3	*68*	72
Cuba	5,100	2,192	..	..	..	..	..	..	..	..	..	..
Czech Republic	*12,170*	68,657	..	3	..	2	..	3	..	2	..	90
Denmark	36,870	76,821	27	19	3	3	3	8	1	1	60	66
Dominican Republic	2,170	5,750	*21*	..	*0*	..	*0*	..	*0*	..	*78*	..
Ecuador	2,714	7,634	44	31	1	5	52	54	0	0	2	9
Egypt, Arab Rep.	3,477	7,682	10	10	10	7	29	43	9	4	42	31
El Salvador	582	3,295	57	32	1	1	2	4	3	3	38	60
Eritrea	*16*	35	..	..	..	..	..	..	..	..	..	..
Estonia	..	5,945	..	7	..	8	..	4	..	3	..	77
Ethiopia	298	639	..	*62*	..	*26*	..	*0*	..	*1*	..	*11*
Finland	26,571	61,334	2	2	10	6	1	4	4	3	83	83
France	216,588	448,714	16	11	2	1	2	3	3	2	77	83
Gabon	2,204	3,490	..	1	..	10	..	76	..	6	..	7
Gambia, The	31	22	..	*63*	..	*7*	..	*1*	..	*2*	..	*27*
Georgia	..	649	..	32	..	2	..	4	..	25	..	37
Germany	421,100	912,261	5	4	1	1	1	2	3	2	89	84
Ghana	897	2,580	*51*	*72*	*15*	*10*	*9*	*0*	*17*	*4*	*8*	*14*
Greece	8,105	15,198	30	20	3	3	7	7	7	8	54	59
Guatemala	1,163	2,938	67	45	6	4	2	8	0	0	24	42
Guinea	671	700	..	*2*	..	*1*	..	*0*	..	*72*	..	*25*
Guinea-Bissau	19	81	..	..	..	..	..	..	..	..	..	..
Haiti	160	391	14	..	1	..	0	..	0	..	85	..
†Data for Taiwan, China	67,245	182,424	4	1	2	1	1	3	1	2	93	93

Structure of merchandise exports 4.4

	Merchandise exports		Food		Agricultural raw materials		Fuels		Ores and metals		Manufactures	
	$ millions		% of total		% of total		% of total		% of total		% of total	
	1990	2004	1990	2004	1990	2004	1990	2004	1990	2004	1990	2004
Honduras	831	1,537	82	*63*	4	*4*	1	*0*	4	*6*	9	*27*
Hungary	10,000	54,857	23	7	3	1	3	2	6	2	63	88
India	17,969	75,595	16	10	4	1	3	9	5	7	70	73
Indonesia	25,675	72,330	11	14	5	6	44	18	4	7	35	56
Iran, Islamic Rep.	19,305	44,446	..	*4*	..	*0*	..	*85*	..	*1*	..	*9*
Iraq	12,380	17,810	..	..	..	..	..	..	..	..	..	..
Ireland	23,743	104,281	22	8	2	0	1	0	1	1	70	86
Israel	12,080	38,520	8	3	3	1	1	0	2	1	87	94
Italy	170,304	349,153	6	7	1	1	2	2	1	1	88	88
Jamaica	1,158	1,390	19	*23*	0	*0*	1	*3*	9	*10*	70	*65*
Japan	287,581	565,807	1	0	1	0	0	0	1	2	96	93
Jordan	1,064	3,887	10	14	1	0	0	1	33	12	56	72
Kazakhstan	..	20,093	..	4	..	1	..	65	..	14	..	16
Kenya	1,031	2,693	49	40	6	12	13	23	3	4	30	21
Korea, Dem. Rep.	1,857	1,380	..	..	..	..	..	..	..	..	..	..
Korea, Rep.	65,016	253,845	3	1	1	1	1	4	1	2	94	92
Kuwait	7,042	28,729	1	..	0	..	93	..	0	..	6	..
Kyrgyz Republic	..	719	..	18	..	12	..	19	..	7	..	43
Lao PDR	79	361	..	..	..	..	..	..	..	..	..	..
Latvia	..	3,951	..	9	..	19	..	5	..	3	..	61
Lebanon	494	1,747	..	*19*	..	*2*	..	*0*	..	*10*	..	*68*
Lesotho	62	726	..	..	..	..	..	..	..	..	..	..
Liberia	868	235	..	..	..	..	..	..	..	..	..	..
Libya	13,225	20,844	*1*	..	*0*	..	*95*	..	..	..	*4*	..
Lithuania	..	9,269	*24*	11	*6*	4	*8*	25	*1*	2	*59*	58
Macedonia, FYR	*1,199*	1,661	..	15	..	1	..	5	..	2	..	77
Madagascar	319	990	73	61	4	6	1	4	8	5	14	22
Malawi	417	441	91	78	2	5	0	0	0	0	7	16
Malaysia	29,452	126,503	12	8	14	2	18	12	2	1	54	76
Mali	359	1,123	36	..	62	..	..	..	0	..	2	..
Mauritania	469	410	..	..	..	..	..	..	..	..	..	..
Mauritius	1,194	2,004	32	27	1	0	1	0	0	0	66	71
Mexico	40,711	189,083	12	5	2	1	38	12	6	2	43	80
Moldova	..	986	..	53	..	7	..	2	..	2	..	36
Mongolia	661	880	..	*3*	..	*13*	..	*3*	..	*43*	..	*38*
Morocco	4,265	9,739	26	19	3	2	4	2	15	8	52	69
Mozambique	126	1,504	..	*19*	..	*6*	..	*16*	..	*55*	..	*3*
Myanmar	325	2,850	*51*	..	*36*	..	*0*	..	*2*	..	*11*	..
Namibia	1,085	1,833	..	*48*	..	*1*	..	*1*	..	*7*	..	*41*
Nepal	204	756	13	*21*	3	*1*	..	*0*	0	*4*	83	*74*
Netherlands	131,775	358,187	20	15	4	3	10	9	3	3	59	70
New Zealand	9,394	20,373	45	49	18	11	4	1	5	4	26	31
Nicaragua	330	756	77	85	14	2	0	1	1	1	8	11
Niger	282	370	..	*30*	..	*4*	..	*2*	..	*55*	..	*8*
Nigeria	13,596	23,657	*1*	*0*	*1*	*0*	*97*	*98*	*0*	*0*	*1*	*2*
Norway	34,047	81,752	7	6	2	1	48	64	10	7	32	19
Oman	5,508	13,342	1	4	0	0	92	83	1	1	5	12
Pakistan	5,615	13,379	9	10	10	2	1	3	0	0	79	85
Panama	340	944	75	84	1	1	0	1	1	4	21	10
Papua New Guinea	1,177	2,532	22	*21*	9	*3*	0	*22*	58	*49*	10	*6*
Paraguay	959	1,626	52	75	38	12	*0*	0	0	1	10	13
Peru	3,230	12,547	21	24	3	2	10	6	47	47	18	20
Philippines	8,117	39,689	19	6	2	1	2	1	8	2	38	55
Poland	14,320	74,854	*11*	8	*2*	1	*10*	5	*8*	4	*54*	81
Portugal	16,417	35,767	7	8	6	2	3	3	3	2	80	85
Puerto Rico	..	..	..	..	..	..	..	..	..	..	..	..

4.4 Structure of merchandise exports

	Merchandise exports		Food		Agricultural raw materials		Fuels		Ores and metals		Manufactures	
	$ millions		% of total		% of total		% of total		% of total		% of total	
	1990	2004	1990	2004	1990	2004	1990	2004	1990	2004	1990	2004
Romania	4,960	23,485	1	3	3	3	18	7	4	5	73	82
Russian Federation	..	183,452	..	1	..	3	..	50	..	8	..	21
Rwanda	110	99	..	*52*	..	*7*	..	*7*	..	*23*	..	*10*
Saudi Arabia	44,417	126,230	1	*1*	0	*0*	90	*86*	1	*0*	8	*12*
Senegal	761	1,529	53	35	3	3	12	19	9	4	23	39
Serbia and Montenegro	*2,929*	3,979	*19*	*23*	*3*	*4*	*6*	*3*	*10*	*12*	*62*	*57*
Sierra Leone	138	139	..	*92*	..	*1*	..	..	..	*0*	..	*7*
Singapore[b]	52,730	179,547	5	2	3	0	18	9	2	1	72	84
Slovak Republic	*6,355*	27,548	..	4	..	1	..	7	..	3	..	86
Slovenia	*6,681*	15,831	*7*	3	*2*	1	*3*	2	*3*	4	*86*	90
Somalia	..	..	..	..	..	..	..	..	..	..	..	..
South Africa	23,549	46,029	*8*[c]	9	*4*[c]	2	*7*[c]	9	*10*[c]	22	*29*[c]	58
Spain	55,642	178,607	15	14	2	1	4	4	2	2	75	77
Sri Lanka	1,912	5,757	34	21	6	2	1	0	2	3	54	74
Sudan	374	3,778	*60*	*10*	*38*	*6*	..	*81*	*0*	*0*	*2*	*2*
Swaziland	556	1,900	..	*15*	..	*8*	..	*1*	..	*0*	..	*76*
Sweden	57,540	122,537	2	3	7	4	3	4	3	3	83	81
Switzerland	63,784	118,527	3	3	1	0	0	0	3	3	94	93
Syrian Arab Republic	4,212	4,930	14	15	4	4	45	68	1	1	36	11
Tajikistan	..	915	..	..	..	..	..	..	..	..	..	..
Tanzania	331	1,338	..	53	..	13	..	2	..	12	..	20
Thailand	23,068	97,414	29	*14*	5	*5*	1	*2*	1	*1*	63	*75*
Togo	268	771	23	24	21	16	0	0	45	13	9	47
Trinidad and Tobago	1,960	6,349	5	*4*	0	*0*	67	*60*	1	*0*	27	*35*
Tunisia	3,526	9,685	11	11	1	1	17	10	2	1	69	78
Turkey	12,959	63,121	22	9	3	1	2	2	4	2	68	85
Turkmenistan	..	3,870	..	..	..	..	..	..	..	..	..	..
Uganda	152	635	..	64	..	15	..	5	..	0	..	15
Ukraine	..	32,672	..	*13*	..	*2*	..	*9*	..	*8*	..	*67*
United Arab Emirates	23,544	82,750	*2*	..	*0*	..	*7*	..	*78*	..	*12*	..
United Kingdom	185,172	346,863	7	6	1	1	8	9	3	3	79	76
United States	393,592	818,775	11	7	4	2	3	2	3	2	75	82
Uruguay	1,693	2,950	40	55	21	8	0	4	0	1	39	32
Uzbekistan	..	4,280	..	..	..	..	..	..	..	..	..	..
Venezuela, RB	17,497	34,210	2	1	0	0	80	85	7	3	10	12
Vietnam	2,404	25,625	..	*23*	..	*2*	..	*21*	..	*1*	..	*53*
West Bank and Gaza	..	..	..	..	..	..	..	..	..	..	..	..
Yemen, Rep.	692	4,150	*8*	4	*1*	0	*74*	92	*1*	0	*15*	3
Zambia	1,309	1,576	..	16	..	10	..	2	..	62	..	10
Zimbabwe	1,726	1,520	44	31	7	16	1	2	16	23	31	28
World	**3,475,089 t**	**9,145,027 t**	**10 w**	**7 w**	**3 w**	**2 w**	**9 w**	**8 w**	**3 w**	**3 w**	**73 w**	**77 w**
Low income	71,042	212,988	*15*	*15*	*4*	*3*	*27*	*28*	..	*3*	*49*	*50*
Middle income	549,007	2,259,406	17	9	4	2	22	17	5	5	50	64
Lower middle income	274,053	1,229,532	17	10	4	2	16	13	5	4	55	68
Upper middle income	276,680	1,029,873	*17*	8	*6*	2	*27*	21	*8*	5	*42*	60
Low & middle income	621,233	2,472,407	17	9	4	2	20	17	6	5	51	64
East Asia & Pacific	155,928	966,841	15	6	6	2	13	6	3	2	60	80
Europe & Central Asia[d]	..	623,360	..	5	..	2	..	24	..	5	..	57
Latin America & Carib.	143,296	463,326	21	16	3	2	30	19	10	7	36	56
Middle East & N. Africa	81,103	170,601	..	*6*	..	*1*	..	*70*	..	*2*	..	*20*
South Asia	27,754	104,394	16	11	5	1	2	6	4	5	71	76
Sub-Saharan Africa	68,368	143,866	..	*16*	..	*5*	..	*38*	..	*10*	..	*31*
High income	2,849,973	6,672,648	8	6	3	2	6	5	3	3	77	81
Europe EMU	1,234,747	2,903,656	11	8	2	1	3	4	3	2	80	82

Note: Components may not sum to 100 percent because of unclassified trade.

a. Includes Luxembourg. b. Includes re-exports. c. Refers to the South African Customs Union (Botswana, Lesotho, Namibia, South Africa, and Swaziland).

Structure of merchandise exports 4.4

About the data

Data on merchandise trade are from customs reports of goods movement into or out of an economy or from reports of the financial transactions related to merchandise trade recorded in the balance of payments. Because of differences in timing and definitions, estimates of trade flows from customs reports are likely to differ from those based on the balance of payments. Moreover, several international agencies process trade data, each correcting unreported or misreported data, and this leads to other differences in the available data.

The most detailed source of data on international trade in goods is the Commodity Trade (Comtrade) database maintained by the United Nations Statistics Division. In addition, the International Monetary Fund (IMF) collects customs-based data on exports and imports of goods. The value of exports is recorded as the cost of the goods delivered to the frontier of the exporting country for shipment—the free on board (f.o.b.) value. Many countries report trade data in U.S. dollars. When countries report in local currency, the United Nations Statistics Division applies the average offcial exchange rate for the period shown.

Countries may report trade according to the general or special system of trade (see *Primary data documentation*). Under the general system exports comprise outward-moving goods that are (a) goods wholly or partly produced in the country; (b) foreign goods, neither transformed nor declared for domestic consumption in the country, that move outward from customs storage; and (c) goods previously included as imports for domestic consumption but subsequently exported without transformation. Under the special system exports comprise categories a and c. In some compilations categories b and c are classified as re-exports. Because of differences in reporting practices, data on exports may not be fully comparable across economies.

The data on total exports of goods (merchandise) in this table come from the World Trade Organization (WTO). The WTO uses two main sources, national statistical offices and the IMF's *International Financial Statistics*. It supplements these with the Comtrade database and publications or databases of regional organizations, specialized agencies, economic groups, and private sources (such as Eurostat, the Food and Agriculture Organization, and country reports of the Economist Intelligence Unit). In recent years country Web sites and direct contacts through email have helped to improve the collection of up-to-date statistics for many countries, reducing the proportion of estimated figures. The WTO database now covers most of the major traders in Africa, Asia, and Latin America, which together with the high-income countries account for nearly 95 percent of total world trade. There has also been a remarkable improvement in the availability of reliable figures for countries in Europe and Central Asia.

The shares of exports by major commodity group are from Comtrade. The values of total exports reported here have not been fully reconciled with the estimates of exports of goods and services from the national accounts or those from the balance of payments.

The classification of commodity groups is based on the Standard International Trade Classification (SITC) revision 1. Most countries now report using later revisions of the SITC or the Harmonized System. Concordance tables are used to convert data reported in one system of nomenclature to another. The conversion process may introduce some errors of classification, but conversions from later to earlier systems are generally reliable.

Definitions

• **Merchandise exports** are the f.o.b. value of goods provided to the rest of the world, valued in U.S. dollars. • **Food** corresponds to the commodities in SITC sections 0 (food and live animals), 1 (beverages and tobacco), and 4 (animal and vegetable oils and fats) and SITC division 22 (oil seeds, oil nuts, and oil kernels). • **Agricultural raw materials** correspond to SITC section 2 (crude materials except fuels) excluding divisions 22, 27 (crude fertilizers and minerals excluding coal, petroleum, and precious stones), and 28 (metalliferous ores and scrap). • **Fuels** correspond to SITC section 3 (mineral fuels). • **Ores and metals** correspond to the commodities in SITC divisions 27, 28, and 68 (nonferrous metals). • **Manufactures** correspond to the commodities in SITC sections 5 (chemicals), 6 (basic manufactures), 7 (machinery and transport equipment), and 8 (miscellaneous manufactured goods), excluding division 68.

4.4a

Developing economies' share of world merchandise exports continues to increase

Share of world merchandise exports

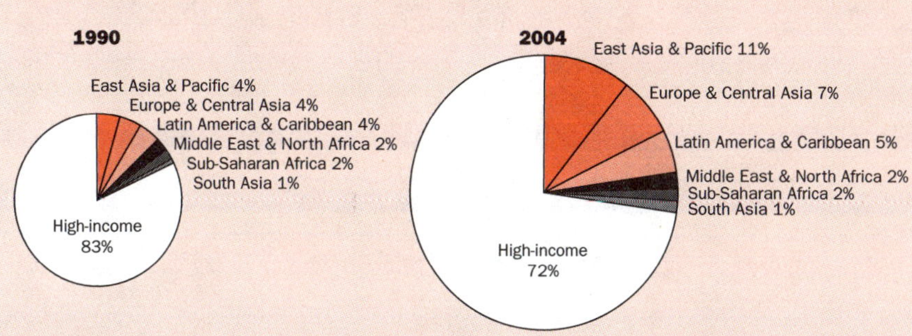

Developing economies' share of world merchandise exports increased by 11 percentage points from 1990 to 2004. East Asia and Pacific was the biggest gainer, capturing an additional 7 percentage points.

Source: World Trade Organization data files.

Data sources

The WTO publishes data on world trade in its *Annual Report*. The IMF publishes estimates of total exports of goods in its *International Financial Statistics* and *Direction of Trade Statistics*, as does the United Nations Statistics Division in its *Monthly Bulletin of Statistics*. And the United Nations Conference on Trade and Development publishes data on the structure of exports and imports in its *Handbook of International Trade and Development Statistics*. Tariff line records of exports and imports are compiled in the United Nations Statistics Division's Comtrade database.

4.5 Structure of merchandise imports

	Merchandise imports		Food		Agricultural raw materials		Fuels		Ores and metals		Manufactures	
	$ millions		% of total		% of total		% of total		% of total		% of total	
	1990	2004	1990	2004	1990	2004	1990	2004	1990	2004	1990	2004
Afghanistan	936	2,300	..	..	..	..	..	..	..	..	..	..
Albania	380	2,268	..	19	..	1	..	8	..	2	..	70
Algeria	9,780	18,199	24	22	5	2	1	1	2	1	68	74
Angola	1,578	6,500	..	..	..	..	..	..	..	..	..	..
Argentina	4,076	22,320	4	2	4	1	8	3	6	2	78	91
Armenia	..	1,318	..	22	..	1	..	17	..	1	..	59
Australia	41,985	109,376	5	5	2	1	6	9	1	1	84	82
Austria	49,146	117,765	5	6	3	2	6	10	4	4	81	78
Azerbaijan	..	3,516	..	12	..	1	..	11	..	2	..	74
Bangladesh	3,618	12,026	19	19	5	9	16	8	3	2	56	62
Belarus	..	16,346	..	10	..	2	..	28	..	4	..	55
Belgium	119,702[a]	285,450	10[a]	8	2[a]	1	8[a]	9	6[a]	4	68[a]	77
Benin	265	865	*38*	*24*	*4*	*5*	*1*	*17*	*1*	*1*	*56*	*53*
Bolivia	687	1,842	12	12	2	2	1	7	1	1	85	79
Bosnia and Herzegovina	*360*	5,907	..	..	..	..	..	..	..	..	..	..
Botswana	1,946	3,340	..	..	..	..	..	..	..	..	..	..
Brazil	22,524	65,921	9	5	3	2	27	19	5	4	56	70
Bulgaria	5,100	14,424	*8*	5	*3*	1	*36*	4	*4*	6	*49*	69
Burkina Faso	536	1,155	..	12	..	1	..	24	..	1	..	62
Burundi	231	176	..	9	..	1	..	16	..	1	..	72
Cambodia	164	3,170	..	8	..	2	..	10	..	0	..	79
Cameroon	1,400	2,100	19	18	0	2	2	18	1	1	78	61
Canada	123,244	279,779	6	6	2	1	6	7	3	3	81	81
Central African Republic	154	150	*19*	*23*	*1*	*5*	*7*	*11*	*2*	*4*	*71*	*56*
Chad	285	770	..	..	..	..	..	..	..	..	..	..
Chile	7,742	24,871	4	7	2	1	16	21	1	2	75	68
China†	53,345	561,230	9	4	6	4	2	8	3	7	80	77
Hong Kong, China	84,725	272,893	8	3	2	1	2	2	2	2	85	92
Colombia	5,590	16,746	7	11	4	2	6	2	3	2	77	82
Congo, Dem. Rep.	1,739	1,873	..	..	..	..	..	..	..	..	..	..
Congo, Rep.	621	1,720	..	..	..	..	..	..	..	..	..	..
Costa Rica	1,990	8,268	8	9	2	1	10	9	2	2	66	79
Côte d'Ivoire	2,097	3,783	..	*22*	..	*1*	..	*17*	..	*1*	..	*48*
Croatia	*4,500*	16,583	*12*	8	*4*	1	*10*	12	*4*	2	*70*	76
Cuba	4,600	5,286	*12*	..	*3*	..	*32*	..	*1*	..	*46*	..
Czech Republic	*12,880*	69,510	..	5	..	2	..	7	..	4	..	83
Denmark	33,333	68,191	12	12	3	2	7	5	2	2	73	77
Dominican Republic	3,006	7,845	..	..	..	..	..	..	..	..	..	..
Ecuador	1,861	7,861	9	9	3	1	2	7	2	1	84	81
Egypt, Arab Rep.	12,412	12,831	32	22	7	5	3	8	2	4	56	50
El Salvador	1,263	6,269	14	18	3	2	15	14	4	1	63	65
Eritrea	*351*	650	..	..	..	..	..	..	..	..	..	..
Estonia	..	8,728	..	9	..	4	..	7	..	2	..	79
Ethiopia	1,081	3,080	..	*21*	..	*1*	..	*12*	..	*2*	..	*64*
Finland	27,001	50,824	5	6	2	3	12	12	4	7	76	70
France	234,436	465,454	10	8	3	2	10	11	4	3	74	77
Gabon	918	1,280	..	24	..	1	..	3	..	1	..	70
Gambia, The	188	200	..	*38*	..	*2*	..	*11*	..	*1*	..	*49*
Georgia	..	1,847	..	21	..	0	..	17	..	1	..	59
Germany	355,686	716,926	10	7	3	1	8	9	4	3	72	69
Ghana	1,205	4,320	*11*	21	*1*	1	*17*	2	*0*	2	*70*	74
Greece	19,777	52,577	15	11	3	1	8	13	3	3	70	72
Guatemala	1,649	7,808	10	12	2	1	17	14	2	1	69	71
Guinea	723	690	..	*23*	..	*1*	..	*22*	..	*1*	..	*53*
Guinea-Bissau	86	86	..	..	..	..	..	..	..	..	..	..
Haiti	332	1,306	..	..	..	..	..	..	..	..	..	..
†Data for Taiwan, China	54,782	168,444	7	4	5	2	11	13	6	6	69	76

Structure of merchandise imports

	Merchandise imports		Food		Agricultural raw materials		Fuels		Ores and metals		Manufactures	
	$ millions		% of total		% of total		% of total		% of total		% of total	
	1990	2004	1990	2004	1990	2004	1990	2004	1990	2004	1990	2004
Honduras	935	3,916	10	*16*	1	*1*	16	*16*	1	*1*	71	*66*
Hungary	10,340	59,332	8	4	4	1	14	7	4	3	70	84
India	23,580	97,339	3	4	4	3	27	35	8	5	51	53
Indonesia	21,837	54,895	5	10	5	5	9	20	4	4	77	61
Iran, Islamic Rep.	20,322	34,705	..	*11*	..	*2*	..	*6*	..	*2*	..	*79*
Iraq	7,660	21,302	..	..	..	..	..	..	..	..	..	..
Ireland	20,669	60,651	11	8	2	1	6	5	2	1	76	78
Israel	16,793	42,864	8	6	2	1	9	11	3	2	77	80
Italy	181,968	351,034	12	9	6	3	11	10	5	4	64	70
Jamaica	1,928	3,772	15	*15*	1	*1*	20	*18*	1	*1*	61	*63*
Japan	235,368	454,543	15	12	7	2	24	22	9	6	44	57
Jordan	2,600	8,189	26	17	1	1	18	19	1	2	52	58
Kazakhstan	..	12,781	..	7	..	1	..	13	..	2	..	77
Kenya	2,223	4,553	9	10	3	2	20	24	2	2	66	61
Korea, Dem. Rep.	2,930	2,540	..	..	..	..	..	..	..	..	..	..
Korea, Rep.	69,844	224,463	6	5	8	2	16	22	7	7	63	63
Kuwait	3,972	12,005	17	..	1	..	1	..	2	..	79	..
Kyrgyz Republic	..	941	..	13	..	2	..	27	..	3	..	54
Lao PDR	185	506	..	..	..	..	..	..	..	..	..	..
Latvia	..	7,005	..	11	..	3	..	12	..	2	..	70
Lebanon	2,529	9,397	..	*18*	..	*2*	..	*16*	..	*2*	..	*62*
Lesotho	672	1,400	..	..	..	..	..	..	..	..	..	..
Liberia	570	900	..	..	..	..	..	..	..	..	..	..
Libya	5,336	5,650	*24*	17	*2*	1	*0*	1	*1*	1	*73*	81
Lithuania	..	12,283	*12*	8	*5*	2	*44*	19	*2*	2	*35*	68
Macedonia, FYR	*1,206*	2,875	..	14	..	1	..	13	..	2	..	58
Madagascar	651	1,230	11	14	1	0	17	23	1	0	69	62
Malawi	575	792	9	13	1	1	11	3	1	1	78	82
Malaysia	29,258	105,287	7	6	1	1	5	6	4	4	82	81
Mali	602	1,320	26	..	1	..	19	..	1	..	53	..
Mauritania	388	400	..	..	..	..	..	..	..	..	..	..
Mauritius	1,618	2,778	12	18	3	2	8	13	1	1	76	66
Mexico	43,548	206,423	15	6	4	1	4	4	3	3	64	85
Moldova	..	1,774	..	12	..	6	..	21	..	1	..	61
Mongolia	924	990	..	*14*	..	*1*	..	*20*	..	*1*	..	*65*
Morocco	6,922	17,625	10	11	6	3	17	17	6	3	61	67
Mozambique	878	1,970	..	*11*	..	*1*	..	*12*	..	*0*	..	*43*
Myanmar	270	2,220	*13*	..	*1*	..	*5*	..	*0*	..	*81*	..
Namibia	1,163	2,435	..	*15*	..	*1*	..	*10*	..	*4*	..	*69*
Nepal	672	1,870	15	*17*	7	*5*	9	*16*	2	*4*	67	*59*
Netherlands	126,098	319,330	13	10	2	2	10	12	3	3	71	73
New Zealand	9,501	23,201	7	8	1	1	8	6	3	2	81	82
Nicaragua	638	2,212	19	17	1	0	19	19	1	0	59	64
Niger	388	560	..	*34*	..	*4*	..	*17*	..	*1*	..	*44*
Nigeria	5,627	11,096	*6*	*15*	*1*	*1*	*0*	*16*	*2*	*2*	*67*	*66*
Norway	27,231	48,082	6	7	2	2	4	4	6	6	82	80
Oman	2,681	8,865	19	14	1	0	4	2	1	4	69	76
Pakistan	7,411	17,949	17	11	4	6	21	22	4	3	54	58
Panama	1,539	3,530	12	*14*	1	*1*	16	*12*	1	*1*	70	*72*
Papua New Guinea	1,193	1,680	18	*16*	0	*1*	7	*13*	1	*0*	73	*69*
Paraguay	1,352	2,652	8	9	0	1	14	16	1	1	77	74
Peru	2,634	10,101	24	13	2	2	12	19	1	1	61	66
Philippines	13,042	42,345	10	6	2	1	15	11	3	2	53	79
Poland	11,570	89,174	*12*	6	*4*	2	*13*	9	*5*	3	*58*	80
Portugal	25,263	54,914	12	12	4	2	11	11	2	2	71	72
Puerto Rico	..	..	..	..	..	..	..	..	..	..	..	..

Structure of merchandise imports

	Merchandise imports		Food		Agricultural raw materials		Fuels		Ores and metals		Manufactures	
	$ millions		% of total		% of total		% of total		% of total		% of total	
	1990	2004	1990	2004	1990	2004	1990	2004	1990	2004	1990	2004
Romania	7,600	32,664	12	6	4	1	38	12	6	3	39	78
Russian Federation	..	96,307	..	17	..	1	..	3	..	3	..	69
Rwanda	288	285	..	12	..	4	..	16	..	2	..	67
Saudi Arabia	24,069	44,576	15	16	1	1	0	0	3	3	81	79
Senegal	1,219	2,710	29	28	2	2	16	18	2	2	51	49
Serbia and Montenegro	4,634	11,752	9	11	3	2	23	17	3	3	62	67
Sierra Leone	149	286	..	23	..	8	..	40	..	1	..	29
Singapore	60,774	163,854	6	3	2	0	16	15	2	1	73	80
Slovak Republic	6,670	29,471	..	5	..	1	..	13	..	3	..	78
Slovenia	6,142	17,197	9	6	4	3	11	8	4	5	67	78
Somalia	..	..	..	..	..	..	..	..	..	..	..	..
South Africa	18,399	57,100	8[b]	5	2[b]	1	1[b]	14	1[b]	2	75[b]	69
Spain	87,715	249,308	11	10	3	1	12	11	4	3	71	74
Sri Lanka	2,688	7,973	19	12	2	1	13	15	1	3	65	69
Sudan	618	4,075	13	16	1	1	20	3	0	1	66	78
Swaziland	663	2,000	..	18	..	2	..	13	..	1	..	64
Sweden	54,264	99,324	6	8	2	2	9	10	3	3	79	75
Switzerland	69,681	111,603	6	6	2	1	5	5	3	4	84	84
Syrian Arab Republic	2,400	6,287	31	17	2	4	3	7	1	3	62	64
Tajikistan	..	1,375	..	..	..	..	..	..	..	..	..	..
Tanzania	1,027	2,490	..	15	..	2	..	16	..	1	..	66
Thailand	33,045	95,353	5	5	5	3	9	12	4	3	75	76
Togo	581	1,050	22	18	1	1	8	23	1	2	67	56
Trinidad and Tobago	1,109	4,894	19	9	1	1	11	27	6	3	62	59
Tunisia	5,513	12,738	11	9	4	3	9	10	4	3	72	76
Turkey	22,302	97,540	8	3	4	3	21	15	5	6	61	72
Turkmenistan	..	3,320	..	..	..	..	..	..	..	..	..	..
Uganda	288	1,491	..	17	..	2	..	10	..	2	..	70
Ukraine	..	28,996	..	6	..	1	..	39	..	3	..	48
United Arab Emirates	11,199	47,640	17	..	0	..	6	..	4	..	72	..
United Kingdom	222,977	463,467	10	9	3	1	6	6	4	2	75	77
United States	516,987	1,525,516	6	4	2	1	13	14	3	2	73	75
Uruguay	1,343	3,114	7	9	4	4	18	24	2	2	69	62
Uzbekistan	..	3,392	..	..	..	..	..	..	..	..	..	..
Venezuela, RB	7,335	14,995	11	15	4	2	3	1	4	2	77	80
Vietnam	2,752	31,091	..	6	..	3	..	11	..	3	..	77
West Bank and Gaza	..	..	..	..	..	..	..	..	..	..	..	..
Yemen, Rep.	1,571	4,190	27	28	1	1	40	13	1	1	31	56
Zambia	1,220	2,143	..	7	..	1	..	11	..	3	..	79
Zimbabwe	1,847	2,550	4	19	3	2	16	14	2	10	73	54
World	**3,550,315 t**	**9,376,651 t**	**9 w**	**7 w**	**3 w**	**2 w**	**11 w**	**11 w**	**4 w**	**3 w**	**71 w**	**74 w**
Low income	81,953	252,827	..	11	..	3	..	22	..	3	..	61
Middle income	509,902	2,161,147	10	7	4	2	9	9	3	4	70	77
Lower middle income	277,830	1,187,304	10	7	5	3	9	12	3	5	71	73
Upper middle income	228,653	973,843	11	7	3	2	8	7	4	3	70	79
Low & middle income	593,527	2,413,971	10	7	4	2	10	11	4	4	69	75
East Asia & Pacific	160,502	903,670	8	5	5	3	5	9	3	6	77	77
Europe & Central Asia[c]	164,871	631,428	..	7	..	2	..	10	..	4	..	75
Latin America & Carib.	120,374	436,972	12	7	3	2	10	8	3	3	66	80
Middle East & N. Africa	79,941	160,252	..	17	..	3	..	8	..	2	..	68
South Asia	39,124	140,502	8	8	4	4	24	28	6	4	54	56
Sub-Saharan Africa	57,641	141,150	..	12	..	1	..	14	..	2	..	67
High income	2,943,378	6,962,657	9	7	3	2	11	12	4	3	71	74
Europe EMU	1,255,515	2,744,049	11	8	3	2	9	10	4	3	71	73

Note: Components may not sum to 100 percent because of unclassified trade.
a. Includes Luxembourg. b. Refers to the South African Customs Union (Botswana, Lesotho, Namibia, South Africa, and Swaziland).

Structure of merchandise imports 4.5

About the data

Data on imports of goods are derived from the same sources as data on exports. In principle, world exports and imports should be identical. Similarly, exports from an economy should equal the sum of imports by the rest of the world from that economy. But differences in timing and definitions result in discrepancies in reported values at all levels. For further discussion of indicators of merchandise trade, see *About the data* for tables 4.4 and 6.2.

The value of imports is generally recorded as the cost of the goods when purchased by the importer plus the cost of transport and insurance to the frontier of the importing country—the cost, insurance, and freight (c.i.f.) value, corresponding to the landed cost at the point of entry of foreign goods into the country. A few countries, including Australia, Canada, and the United States, collect import data on a free on board (f.o.b.) basis and adjust them for freight and insurance costs. Many countries collect and report trade data in U.S. dollars. When countries report in local currency, the United Nations Statistics Division applies the average official exchange rate for the period shown.

Countries may report trade according to the general or special system of trade (see *Primary data documentation*). Under the general system imports include goods imported for domestic consumption and imports into bonded warehouses and free trade zones. Under the special system imports comprise goods imported for domestic consumption (including transformation and repair) and withdrawals for domestic consumption from bonded warehouses and free trade zones. Goods transported through a country en route to another are excluded.

The data on total imports of goods (merchandise) in this table come from the World Trade Organization (WTO). For further discussion of the WTO's sources and methodology, see *About the data* for table 4.4. The shares of imports by major commodity group are from the United Nations Statistics Division's Commodity Trade (Comtrade) database. The values of total imports reported here have not been fully reconciled with the estimates of imports of goods and services from the national accounts (shown in table 4.8) or those from the balance of payments (table 4.15).

The classification of commodity groups is based on the Standard International Trade Classification (SITC) revision 1. Most countries now report using later revisions of the SITC or the Harmonized System. Concordance tables are used to convert data reported in one system of nomenclature to another. The conversion process may introduce some errors of classification, but conversions from later to earlier systems are generally reliable. Shares may not sum to 100 percent because of unclassified trade.

Definitions

• **Merchandise imports** are the c.i.f. value of goods purchased from the rest of the world valued in U.S. dollars. • **Food** corresponds to the commodities in SITC sections 0 (food and live animals), 1 (beverages and tobacco), and 4 (animal and vegetable oils and fats) and SITC division 22 (oil seeds, oil nuts, and oil kernels). • **Agricultural raw materials** correspond to SITC section 2 (crude materials except fuels) excluding divisions 22, 27 (crude fertilizers and minerals excluding coal, petroleum, and precious stones), and 28 (metalliferous ores and scrap). • **Fuels** correspond to SITC section 3 (mineral fuels). • **Ores and metals** correspond to the commodities in SITC divisions 27, 28, and 68 (nonferrous metals). • **Manufactures** correspond to the commodities in SITC sections 5 (chemicals), 6 (basic manufactures), 7 (machinery and transport equipment), and 8 (miscellaneous manufactured goods), excluding division 68.

4.5a

Top 10 exporters in Sub-Saharan Africa in 2004

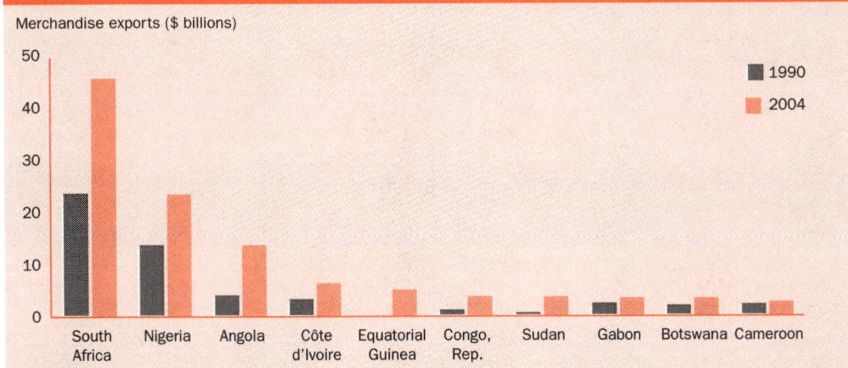

Sub-Saharan economies accounted for about 6 percent of developing economy exports and 1.6 percent of world exports.

Note: No data are available for Equatorial Guinea for 1990.

Source: World Trade Organization data files.

Data sources

The WTO publishes data on world trade in its *Annual Report*. The International Monetary Fund publishes estimates of total imports of goods in its *International Financial Statistics* and *Direction of Trade Statistics*, as does the United Nations Statistics Division in its *Monthly Bulletin of Statistics*. And the United Nations Conference on Trade and Development publishes data on the structure of exports and imports in its *Handbook of International Trade and Development Statistics*. Tariff line records of exports and imports are compiled in the United Nations Statistics Division's Comtrade database.

4.6 Structure of service exports

	Commercial service exports		Transport		Travel		Insurance and financial services		Computer, information, communications, and other commercial services	
	$ millions		% of commercial services		% of commercial services		% of commercial services		% of commercial services	
	1990	2004	1990	2004	1990	2004	1990	2004	1990	2004
Afghanistan	*1*	..	..	..	..	..	..	..	..	..
Albania	32	*695*	20.0	*9.9*	11.1	*75.2*	2.2	*3.4*	66.7	*11.5*
Algeria	479	..	41.7	..	13.4	..	5.9	..	39.0	..
Angola	65	323	48.8	5.5	20.6	20.4	4.6	..	26.1	74.1
Argentina	2,264	5,065	51.1	22.2	39.9	50.6	0.0	0.0	9.0	27.1
Armenia	*17*	238	..	30.9	..	35.9	..	5.0	..	28.3
Australia	9,833	24,774	35.5	23.6	43.2	51.3	4.2	5.0	17.2	20.1
Austria	22,755	48,297	6.4	19.4	59.0	31.7	2.9	6.1	31.7	42.9
Azerbaijan	..	453	..	45.4	..	14.4	..	1.7	..	38.6
Bangladesh	296	420	13.0	18.4	6.4	15.9	0.1	4.5	80.6	61.1
Belarus	*185*	1,729	*54.1*	58.9	*13.3*	16.6	*1.0*	0.2	*31.6*	24.3
Belgium	26,646[a]	50,459	27.5[a]	25.5	14.0[a]	18.2	18.2[a]	7.6	40.3[a]	48.7
Benin	109	*163*	33.4	*8.8*	50.2	*65.4*	6.9	*0.5*	9.5	*25.3*
Bolivia	133	384	35.8	30.0	43.6	46.0	10.0	12.4	10.6	11.6
Bosnia and Herzegovina	..	825	..	3.7	..	59.2	..	1.7	..	35.4
Botswana	183	*647*	20.4	*10.7*	64.1	*70.6*	8.2	*5.5*	7.3	*13.2*
Brazil	3,706	11,615	36.4	21.2	37.3	27.7	3.1	4.5	23.2	46.5
Bulgaria	837	4,083	27.5	29.1	38.2	52.4	3.1	1.6	31.2	16.9
Burkina Faso	34	*32*	37.1	*14.6*	34.1	*61.6*	..	*0.4*	28.9	*23.4*
Burundi	7	*2*	38.7	*31.6*	51.4	*32.2*	1.6	*0.6*	8.3	*35.6*
Cambodia	*50*	759	..	13.7	..	79.5	..	..	..	6.9
Cameroon	369	..	42.6	..	14.4	..	9.4	..	33.6	..
Canada	18,350	46,370	23.0	18.3	34.7	27.6	..	9.7	42.3	44.4
Central African Republic	17	..	50.9	..	16.0	..	18.8	..	14.3	..
Chad	23	..	18.4	..	34.1	..	0.2	..	47.3	..
Chile	1,786	5,872	40.0	56.2	29.8	18.6	4.9	3.1	25.3	22.1
China	5,748	62,056	47.1	19.5	30.2	41.5	4.0	0.8	18.7	38.3
Hong Kong, China	..	54,175	..	*29.8*	..	*15.4*	..	*8.9*	..	*46.0*
Colombia	1,548	2,179	31.3	31.2	26.2	47.3	17.1	1.4	25.5	20.0
Congo, Dem. Rep.	..	..	..	..	..	..	..	..	..	..
Congo, Rep.	65	*79*	53.9	*3.6*	12.9	*25.1*	..	*0.7*	33.2	*70.6*
Costa Rica	583	2,206	16.3	11.1	48.9	66.1	..	0.4	34.8	22.3
Côte d'Ivoire	425	631	62.4	22.2	12.1	12.0	8.3	..	17.2	65.8
Croatia	*2,216*	9,619	*29.2*	10.2	*59.1*	72.5	*1.4*	0.6	*10.3*	16.7
Cuba	..	..	..	..	..	..	..	..	..	..
Czech Republic	*4,679*	9,656	*26.5*	29.2	*33.3*	43.3	*9.6*	4.4	*30.6*	23.1
Denmark	12,731	36,304	32.5	47.1	26.2	15.6	2.3	..	39.0	37.4
Dominican Republic	1,086	3,463	5.6	2.9	66.9	91.8	0.2	0.1	27.3	5.2
Ecuador	508	847	47.6	40.2	37.0	43.4	9.3	0.3	6.1	16.1
Egypt, Arab Rep.	4,812	14,046	50.1	28.6	22.9	43.6	1.0	0.8	26.1	27.0
El Salvador	301	921	26.2	37.2	25.3	36.6	7.5	4.6	41.1	21.6
Eritrea	*73*	..	*85.7*	..	*1.0*	..	..	..	*13.3*	..
Estonia	*200*	2,786	*74.7*	43.2	*13.7*	31.5	*0.1*	1.4	*11.5*	24.0
Ethiopia	261	799	80.7	46.3	2.1	21.7	0.7	0.5	16.6	31.6
Finland	4,562	9,792	38.4	24.5	25.8	21.1	0.1	1.8	35.6	52.6
France	74,948	109,518	21.7	23.4	27.1	37.2	14.8	2.7	36.4	36.8
Gabon	214	*167*	33.4	*50.7*	1.4	*8.7*	5.8	*30.8*	59.4	*9.8*
Gambia, The	53	..	8.8	..	87.9	..	0.1	..	3.3	..
Georgia	..	492	..	50.8	..	35.9	..	5.6	..	7.8
Germany	50,561	133,856	29.2	24.8	28.3	20.6	1.0	6.8	41.5	47.8
Ghana	79	684	49.2	20.0	5.6	68.2	2.7	1.1	42.6	10.7
Greece	6,514	32,986	4.9	50.1	39.7	38.6	0.1	1.1	55.2	10.3
Guatemala	313	1,063	7.4	8.2	37.6	73.0	2.0	6.4	53.1	12.4
Guinea	91	31	14.2	21.8	32.6	*0.1*	0.1	0.4	53.2	77.8
Guinea-Bissau	4	*5*	5.4	*15.5*	..	*37.0*	..	*15.0*	94.6	*32.5*
Haiti	43	*116*	19.8	..	78.9	*80.2*	1.3	..	..	*19.8*

Structure of service exports

	Commercial service exports		Transport		Travel		Insurance and financial services		Computer, information, communications, and other commercial services	
	$ millions		% of commercial services		% of commercial services		% of commercial services		% of commercial services	
	1990	2004	1990	2004	1990	2004	1990	2004	1990	2004
Honduras	121	593	35.1	12.1	24.0	66.8	12.9	3.1	28.0	18.0
Hungary	2,677	10,255	1.6	13.0	36.8	39.3	0.2	2.8	61.4	44.9
India	4,610	39,638[b]	20.8	*13.3*	33.8	*16.8*	2.7	*3.5*	42.7	*66.4*
Indonesia	2,488	17,331	2.8	13.2	86.5	27.7	0.0	1.8	10.7	57.4
Iran, Islamic Rep.	343	..	10.5	..	8.2	..	6.4	..	74.9	..
Iraq	..	..	..	..	..	..	..	..	..	..
Ireland	3,286	52,158	31.1	4.5	44.4	8.2	0.0	29.1	24.5	58.2
Israel	4,546	14,830	30.8	21.5	30.7	16.1	-0.3	0.1	38.8	62.3
Italy	48,579	82,484	21.0	16.9	33.9	42.9	5.5	3.2	39.6	37.0
Jamaica	975	2,262	18.0	22.0	77.0	63.6	1.4	1.6	3.6	12.8
Japan	41,384	94,933	*40.4*	33.9	*7.9*	11.9	*-0.4*	5.8	*52.1*	48.5
Jordan	1,430	2,036	26.0	20.9	35.8	65.3	..	..	38.3	13.8
Kazakhstan	..	1,807	..	46.3	..	39.1	..	1.2	..	13.4
Kenya	774	1,150	32.1	48.9	60.2	43.0	0.7	1.2	7.1	6.8
Korea, Dem. Rep.	..	..	..	..	..	..	..	..	..	..
Korea, Rep.	9,155	40,047	34.7	56.0	34.5	14.3	0.1	2.9	30.7	26.8
Kuwait	1,054	2,067	87.5	84.7	12.5	8.7	..	3.8	..	2.8
Kyrgyz Republic	*9*	193	*25.1*	26.4	*3.8*	39.3	..	1.1	*71.1*	33.3
Lao PDR	11	*127*	74.8	*18.0*	24.3	*82.0*	0.9	..	..	..
Latvia	*290*	1,752	*94.9*	56.6	*2.5*	15.2	..	7.2	*2.6*	21.0
Lebanon	..	..	..	..	..	..	..	..	..	..
Lesotho	34	56	14.1	1.1	51.2	60.4	..	4.7	34.7	33.8
Liberia	*32*	..	*84.6*	..	*15.4*	..	..	..	..	..
Libya	83	351	83.8	18.0	7.7	62.1	..	17.1	8.5	2.9
Lithuania	*198*	2,431	*83.6*	55.7	*10.9*	31.9	..	0.5	*5.5*	11.9
Macedonia, FYR	..	384	..	29.3	..	18.7	..	2.0	..	50.0
Madagascar	129	*202*	32.1	*28.5*	31.3	*37.5*	0.3	*1.7*	36.4	*32.3*
Malawi	37	*49*	46.1	*32.7*	42.6	*67.3*	0.1	..	11.2	*0.0*
Malaysia	3,769	*13,459*	31.8	*20.6*	44.7	*43.8*	0.1	*2.5*	23.5	*33.1*
Mali	71	*208*	31.0	*20.5*	54.3	*61.6*	4.9	*1.5*	9.8	*16.4*
Mauritania	14	..	35.3	..	64.7	..	..	..	..	..
Mauritius	478	1,449	33.0	25.7	51.1	59.1	0.1	1.7	15.8	13.5
Mexico	7,222	13,931	12.4	9.8	76.5	77.2	4.6	6.2	6.5	6.8
Moldova	..	325	..	43.9	..	29.2	..	1.2	..	25.7
Mongolia	48	329	41.8	32.7	10.4	56.2	4.6	1.2	43.2	9.9
Morocco	1,871	6,304	9.6	16.3	68.4	62.2	0.8	1.5	21.2	20.0
Mozambique	103	246	61.3	32.5	..	38.7	..	0.8	38.7	28.1
Myanmar	94	232	10.3	36.8	20.9	36.2	0.5	..	68.3	27.0
Namibia	106	463	..	7.1	81.0	87.5	5.9	..	13.1	5.5
Nepal	166	356	3.6	9.1	65.6	64.7	..	0.1	30.8	26.1
Netherlands	28,478	71,784	45.4	27.0	14.6	14.4	0.8	1.7	39.2	56.9
New Zealand	2,415	7,753	43.4	19.1	42.7	65.4	-0.3	0.7	14.2	14.8
Nicaragua	34	254	19.2	14.4	35.5	73.9	0.0	1.0	45.4	10.7
Niger	22	*57*	5.2	*8.9*	59.5	*48.5*	13.5	*1.3*	21.8	*41.3*
Nigeria	965	3,336	3.9	20.2	2.5	0.6	0.3	0.2	93.3	79.0
Norway	12,452	25,893	68.7	57.5	12.6	11.3	0.4	4.0	18.3	27.2
Oman	68	830	15.3	34.7	84.7	62.4	..	0.4	..	2.5
Pakistan	1,218	1,697	59.3	54.2	12.0	10.5	1.4	3.5	27.3	31.9
Panama	907	2,690	64.9	57.0	18.9	24.2	3.8	9.7	12.4	9.1
Papua New Guinea	198	*285*	11.2	*7.5*	12.0	*1.8*	0.5	*1.8*	76.3	*88.9*
Paraguay	404	556	18.3	15.6	21.1	12.1	..	5.9	60.5	66.4
Peru	714	1,795	43.4	21.2	30.4	60.1	11.2	4.6	15.0	14.2
Philippines	2,897	4,101	8.5	27.3	16.1	49.1	0.5	1.4	74.9	22.2
Poland	3,200	13,437	57.3	31.3	11.2	43.4	4.0	1.7	27.6	23.6
Portugal	5,054	14,596	15.6	19.6	70.4	53.5	0.7	2.4	13.3	24.5
Puerto Rico	..	..	..	..	..	..	..	..	..	..

4.6 Structure of service exports

	Commercial service exports		Transport		Travel		Insurance and financial services		Computer, information, communications, and other commercial services	
	$ millions		% of commercial services		% of commercial services		% of commercial services		% of commercial services	
	1990	2004	1990	2004	1990	2004	1990	2004	1990	2004
Romania	610	3,590	50.5	43.4	17.4	14.0	5.6	2.8	26.6	39.8
Russian Federation	..	20,164	..	38.6	..	25.9	..	2.5	..	32.9
Rwanda	31	72	56.1	29.8	32.8	60.4	1.0	..	10.0	9.9
Saudi Arabia	3,027	5,852	..	..	..	..	..	..	..	..
Senegal	356	*488*	19.2	*15.7*	42.8	*42.7*	0.5	*2.0*	37.6	*39.7*
Serbia and Montenegro	..	..	..	..	..	..	..	..	..	..
Sierra Leone	45	61	9.7	2.3	76.2	94.8	..	0.8	14.1	2.1
Singapore	12,719	41,077	17.5	35.6	36.6	12.4	0.7	9.5	45.3	42.5
Slovak Republic	*1,939*	*3,270*	*23.7*	*43.2*	*19.8*	*26.4*	..	*2.3*	*56.5*	*28.1*
Slovenia	*1,219*	3,449	*22.6*	29.1	*55.0*	47.1	*1.2*	0.8	*21.2*	22.9
Somalia	..	..	..	..	..	..	..	..	..	..
South Africa	3,291	8,066	21.6	17.1	55.8	70.3	10.8	4.5	11.9	8.1
Spain	27,649	84,105	17.2	16.6	67.2	53.6	4.3	3.1	11.3	26.7
Sri Lanka	425	1,506	39.7	41.4	30.2	34.1	4.2	3.3	25.9	21.2
Sudan	134	35	14.1	27.4	15.7	60.7	0.5	2.5	69.7	9.5
Swaziland	102	485	24.5	5.5	29.2	19.6	..	60.3	46.3	14.7
Sweden	13,453	38,320	35.8	20.8	21.7	16.1	9.1	5.2	33.5	57.9
Switzerland	18,325	41,544	16.3	10.1	40.4	25.0	23.7	33.1	19.6	31.8
Syrian Arab Republic	740	2,222	29.8	9.5	43.3	81.0	..	1.2	27.0	8.3
Tajikistan	..	81	..	64.8	..	1.5	..	5.4	..	28.4
Tanzania	131	845	19.9	9.1	36.4	70.4	0.5	6.9	43.1	13.7
Thailand	6,292	18,932	21.1	23.0	68.7	53.1	0.2	0.7	10.0	23.3
Togo	114	*72*	26.9	*29.8*	50.8	*20.5*	13.7	*1.2*	8.6	*48.6*
Trinidad and Tobago	322	*672*	50.7	*36.7*	29.4	*37.0*	..	*16.1*	19.9	*10.2*
Tunisia	1,575	3,520	23.0	26.0	64.8	56.0	1.5	2.4	10.7	15.6
Turkey	7,882	23,806	11.7	13.7	40.9	66.7	..	2.4	47.4	17.2
Turkmenistan	..	..	..	..	..	..	..	..	..	..
Uganda	..	436	..	11.1	..	61.1	..	10.8	..	17.0
Ukraine	..	6,041	..	66.9	..	18.9	..	0.7	..	13.5
United Arab Emirates	..	..	..	..	..	..	..	..	..	..
United Kingdom	53,830	179,649	25.2	16.7	29.0	15.7	16.4	22.5	29.4	45.1
United States	132,880	321,837	28.1	17.3	37.9	29.2	3.5	8.7	30.5	44.8
Uruguay	460	959	36.9	34.9	51.8	51.5	1.0	6.8	10.3	6.9
Uzbekistan	..	..	..	..	..	..	..	..	..	..
Venezuela, RB	1,121	1,008	40.9	35.1	44.3	47.3	0.2	0.2	14.7	17.4
Vietnam	..	*2,948*	..	..	..	..	..	..	..	..
West Bank and Gaza	..	..	..	..	..	..	..	..	..	..
Yemen, Rep.	82	292	27.2	15.8	48.8	47.6	..	..	24.0	36.7
Zambia	94	..	68.9	..	13.6	..	4.1	..	13.4	..
Zimbabwe	253	..	44.3	..	25.3	..	1.2	..	29.2	..
World	**815,710 t**	**2,190,577 t**	**28.5 w**	**24.3 w**	**34.6 w**	**28.5 w**	**4.7 w**	**6.7 w**	**38.5 w**	**41.7 w**
Low income	13,854	67,030	24.7	*19.5*	23.1	*19.7*	2.0	*3.0*	50.4	*58.1*
Middle income	96,848	358,642	29.6	23.3	45.0	46.8	3.1	2.7	22.3	27.3
Lower middle income	46,348	197,288	32.3	22.8	39.3	40.8	3.3	1.6	25.2	34.9
Upper middle income	51,220	161,008	26.4	23.8	52.1	53.6	2.7	3.9	18.8	18.7
Low & middle income	110,619	423,636	29.2	23.5	43.0	45.6	3.0	2.6	24.9	28.4
East Asia & Pacific	22,615	129,117	32.3	19.9	43.5	42.2	2.0	1.0	22.2	37.0
Europe & Central Asia	..	121,538	..	34.1	..	35.5	..	2.4	..	28.1
Latin America & Carib.	26,062	61,844	25.8	19.4	56.2	58.4	4.1	4.3	13.9	17.9
Middle East & N. Africa	..	..	31.1	..	29.3	..	3.4	..	36.4	..
South Asia	6,847	44,325	26.8	*22.1*	28.2	*17.4*	2.3	*3.7*	42.7	*56.8*
Sub-Saharan Africa	9,561	24,238	25.7	18.1	31.6	40.2	5.4	2.9	37.9	39.2
High income	701,271	1,767,896	28.3	24.5	32.1	24.0	5.2	7.8	42.2	45.2
Europe EMU	311,131	723,009	27.1	22.5	30.3	27.7	5.9	5.6	36.7	45.1

a. Includes Luxembourg. b. World Trade Organization estimate.

Structure of service exports 4.6

About the data

Balance of payments statistics, the main source of information on international trade in services, have many weaknesses. Some large economies—such as the former Soviet Union—did not report data on trade in services until recently. Disaggregation of important components may be limited, and it varies significantly across countries. There are inconsistencies in the methods used to report items. And the recording of major flows as net items is common (for example, insurance transactions are often recorded as premiums less claims). These factors contribute to a downward bias in the value of the service trade reported in the balance of payments.

Efforts are being made to improve the coverage, quality, and consistency of these data. Eurostat and the Organisation for Economic Co-operation and Development, for example, are working together to improve the collection of statistics on trade in services in member countries. In addition, the International Monetary Fund (IMF) has implemented the new classification of trade in services introduced in the fifth edition of its *Balance of Payments Manual* (1993).

Still, difficulties in capturing all the dimensions of international trade in services mean that the record is likely to remain incomplete. Cross-border intrafirm service transactions, which are usually not captured in the balance of payments, have increased in recent years. One example of such transactions is transnational corporations' use of mainframe computers around the clock for data processing, exploiting time zone differences between their home country and the host countries of their affiliates. Another important dimension of service trade not captured by conventional balance of payments statistics is establishment trade—sales in the host country by foreign affiliates. By contrast, cross-border intrafirm transactions in merchandise may be reported as exports or imports in the balance of payments.

The data on exports of services in this table and on imports of services in table 4.7, unlike those in editions before 2000, include only commercial services and exclude the category "government services not included elsewhere." The data are compiled by the IMF based on returns from national sources. Data on total trade in goods and services from the IMF's Balance of Payments database are shown in table 4.15.

4.6a

Top 10 developing country exporters of commercial services in 2004

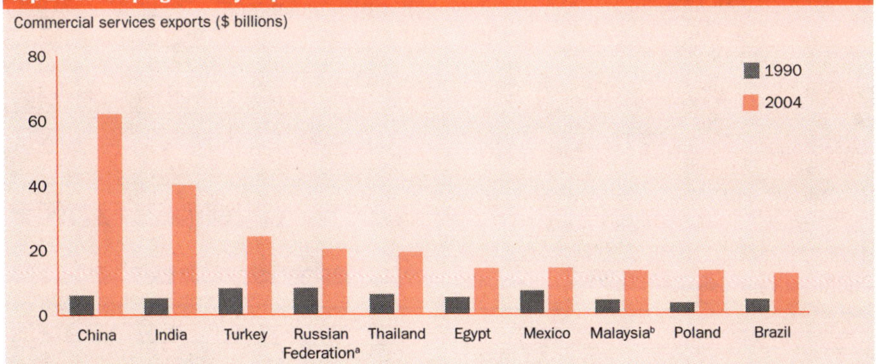

The top 10 developing country exporters accounted for about 55 percent of developing country commercial service exports and 11 percent of world commercial service exports.

a. Data are for 1994 and 2004.
b. Data are for 1990 and 2003.

Source: International Monetary Fund data files and staff estimates.

Definitions

• **Commercial service exports** are total service exports minus exports of government services not included elsewhere. International transactions in services are defined by the IMF's *Balance of Payments Manual* (1993) as the economic output of intangible commodities that may be produced, transferred, and consumed at the same time. Definitions may vary among reporting economies. • **Transport** covers all transport services (sea, air, land, internal waterway, space, and pipeline) performed by residents of one economy for those of another and involving the carriage of passengers, movement of goods (freight), rental of carriers with crew, and related support and auxiliary services. Excluded are freight insurance, which is included in insurance services; goods procured in ports by nonresident carriers and repairs of transport equipment, which are included in goods; repairs of harbors, railway facilities, and airfield facilities, which are included in construction services; and rental of carriers without crew, which is included in other services. • **Travel** covers goods and services acquired from an economy by travelers in that economy for their own use during visits of less than one year for business or personal purposes. Travel services include the goods and services consumed by travelers, such as meals, lodging, and transport (within the economy visited), including car rental. • **Insurance and financial services** cover freight insurance on goods exported and other direct insurance such as life insurance, financial intermediation services such as commissions, foreign exchange transactions, and brokerage services; and auxiliary services such as financial market operational and regulatory services. • **Computer, information, communications, and other commercial services** include such activities as international telecommunications and postal and courier services; computer data; news-related service transactions between residents and nonresidents; construction services; royalties and license fees; miscellaneous business, professional, and technical services; and personal, cultural, and recreational services.

Data sources

Data on exports of commercial services are from the IMF. The IMF publishes balance of payments data in its *International Financial Statistics* and *Balance of Payments Statistics Yearbook*.

4.7 Structure of service imports

	Commercial service imports		Transport		Travel		Insurance and financial services		Computer, information, communications, and other commercial services	
	$ millions		% of commercial services		% of commercial services		% of commercial services		% of commercial services	
	1990	2004	1990	2004	1990	2004	1990	2004	1990	2004
Afghanistan	*97*	..	*85.9*	..	..	..	*9.5*	..	*4.6*	..
Albania	29	*734*	26.3	*21.3*	..	*66.6*	2.9	*3.6*	70.8	*8.5*
Algeria	1,155	..	58.1	..	12.9	..	9.8	..	19.2	..
Angola	1,288	4,803	38.3	18.3	3.0	0.8	2.6	4.9	56.1	76.1
Argentina	2,876	6,596	32.6	24.8	40.7	44.9	..	3.8	26.7	26.5
Armenia	*40*	305	*89.2*	58.7	*0.9*	21.2	*9.9*	6.7	*0.0*	13.4
Australia	13,388	25,613	33.9	36.3	31.5	36.7	4.8	4.2	29.8	22.8
Austria	14,104	46,195	8.4	13.7	54.9	24.4	4.6	6.1	32.1	55.8
Azerbaijan	..	2,702	..	10.7	..	4.7	..	1.4	..	83.3
Bangladesh	554	1,835	71.1	77.3	14.1	8.8	6.6	7.8	8.3	6.1
Belarus	*125*	1,009	*34.0*	24.8	*44.6*	51.9	*12.3*	1.7	*9.2*	21.5
Belgium	25,924[a]	48,234	23.3[a]	22.9	21.1[a]	28.9	14.8[a]	7.9	40.8[a]	40.3
Benin	113	*244*	46.9	*70.0*	12.8	*8.7*	5.7	*13.4*	34.6	*7.9*
Bolivia	291	578	61.7	34.8	20.6	25.6	10.0	20.5	7.6	19.2
Bosnia and Herzegovina	..	438	..	45.2	..	28.4	..	14.0	..	12.4
Botswana	371	*652*	57.5	*38.1*	15.0	*35.2*	5.5	*4.2*	22.0	*22.5*
Brazil	6,733	16,111	44.4	27.6	22.4	17.8	2.7	7.1	30.5	47.4
Bulgaria	600	3,225	40.5	47.1	31.5	29.6	4.5	3.7	23.5	19.7
Burkina Faso	196	*135*	64.7	*65.1*	16.6	*16.1*	5.1	*14.7*	13.6	*4.2*
Burundi	59	*38*	62.6	*52.6*	29.0	*38.3*	6.3	*4.1*	2.2	*5.0*
Cambodia	*64*	462	*24.5*	62.8	..	10.3	..	5.0	*75.5*	22.0
Cameroon	1,018	..	45.3	..	27.5	..	7.2	..	20.1	..
Canada	27,479	56,571	21.1	21.6	39.8	28.3	..	12.2	39.2	38.0
Central African Republic	166	..	49.7	..	30.6	..	8.9	..	10.7	..
Chad	223	..	45.1	..	31.2	..	4.4	..	19.2	..
Chile	1,982	6,401	47.4	50.3	21.5	13.9	3.3	10.9	27.9	24.8
China	4,113	71,602	78.9	34.3	11.4	26.7	2.3	8.8	7.4	30.2
Hong Kong, China	..	30,016	..	*25.9*	..	*44.0*	..	*5.8*	..	*24.3*
Colombia	1,683	3,987	34.9	40.5	27.0	32.4	13.7	8.6	24.4	18.6
Congo, Dem. Rep.	..	..	..	..	..	..	..	..	..	..
Congo, Rep.	748	*537*	18.4	*12.6*	15.2	*9.8*	1.6	*8.1*	64.9	*69.6*
Costa Rica	540	1,293	41.2	39.8	28.8	31.4	6.0	6.3	24.0	22.6
Côte d'Ivoire	1,518	1,880	32.1	48.5	11.1	19.1	4.7	..	52.0	32.4
Croatia	*1,088*	3,583	*30.5*	19.0	*34.4*	23.4	*3.7*	3.6	*31.4*	54.1
Cuba	..	..	..	..	..	..	..	..	..	..
Czech Republic	*3,701*	9,130	*19.8*	16.5	*14.2*	25.0	*14.0*	12.5	*52.0*	46.0
Denmark	10,106	33,401	38.3	43.4	36.5	21.8	1.6	..	23.6	34.8
Dominican Republic	435	1,159	40.0	55.9	33.1	26.7	4.1	9.6	22.9	7.8
Ecuador	755	1,735	41.6	47.9	23.2	22.5	8.1	3.8	27.2	25.7
Egypt, Arab Rep.	3,327	7,470	44.0	40.0	3.9	16.8	4.6	8.2	47.5	35.0
El Salvador	296	1,056	45.9	45.8	20.6	22.7	12.1	12.9	21.5	18.6
Eritrea	*1*	..	..	..	..	..	..	..	..	..
Estonia	*123*	1,707	*76.3*	42.4	*15.4*	23.4	*0.3*	1.4	*8.0*	32.7
Ethiopia	348	938	76.5	62.4	3.3	6.4	3.4	5.1	16.9	26.1
Finland	7,432	12,129	26.1	27.9	37.2	23.3	1.8	1.6	34.8	47.3
France	59,560	96,452	29.4	27.2	20.7	29.6	19.2	4.9	30.7	38.3
Gabon	984	*821*	23.2	*32.3*	13.9	*23.6*	5.3	*5.7*	57.6	*38.4*
Gambia, The	35	..	65.1	..	23.1	..	9.0	..	2.8	..
Georgia	..	437	..	46.8	..	33.7	..	9.9	..	9.6
Germany	83,338	191,706	20.6	21.1	46.9	36.8	1.0	4.7	31.6	37.4
Ghana	226	881	55.1	45.6	5.9	21.2	11.2	5.3	27.8	27.9
Greece	2,756	13,560	34.0	52.5	39.5	21.2	5.4	5.0	21.0	21.3
Guatemala	363	1,247	41.0	50.7	27.4	31.3	3.4	12.2	28.2	5.8
Guinea	243	195	57.5	47.3	12.2	12.8	5.5	12.7	24.9	27.2
Guinea-Bissau	17	*36*	54.5	*59.4*	19.8	*37.1*	5.6	*1.0*	20.0	*2.6*
Haiti	71	*244*	47.9	*97.5*	52.1	..	..	..	..	*2.5*

Structure of service imports

	Commercial service imports		Transport		Travel		Insurance and financial services		Computer, information, communications, and other commercial services	
	$ millions		% of commercial services		% of commercial services		% of commercial services		% of commercial services	
	1990	2004	1990	2004	1990	2004	1990	2004	1990	2004
Honduras	213	736	45.4	49.0	17.6	28.5	15.0	..	22.0	22.5
Hungary	2,264	10,239	8.8	15.3	25.9	27.8	1.0	5.8	64.4	51.1
India	5,943	40,950[b]	57.5	*36.7*	6.6	*13.8*	5.8	*6.5*	30.1	*43.1*
Indonesia	5,898	28,265	47.4	19.5	14.2	12.4	4.0	3.4	34.5	64.7
Iran, Islamic Rep.	3,703	..	47.3	..	9.2	..	10.8	..	32.8	..
Iraq	..	..	..	..	..	..	..	..	..	..
Ireland	5,145	64,461	24.3	3.5	22.6	8.0	1.9	16.1	51.2	72.4
Israel	4,825	12,342	39.6	35.2	29.7	22.7	4.4	3.5	26.3	38.7
Italy	46,602	80,412	23.7	24.4	22.1	25.4	10.4	4.7	43.9	45.5
Jamaica	667	1,677	47.9	38.6	17.0	17.1	6.7	9.3	28.4	35.0
Japan	84,281	134,013	*30.8*	31.9	*27.9*	28.5	*2.1*	4.6	*39.3*	35.0
Jordan	1,118	1,972	52.0	56.1	30.1	26.6	5.2	8.3	12.7	9.1
Kazakhstan	..	4,933	..	17.7	..	15.4	..	2.6	..	64.4
Kenya	598	675	66.2	49.1	6.4	15.9	8.9	10.5	18.5	24.4
Korea, Dem. Rep.	..	..	..	..	..	..	..	..	..	..
Korea, Rep.	10,050	49,641	39.8	36.1	27.5	24.2	0.3	1.2	32.4	38.6
Kuwait	2,805	6,135	31.9	36.1	65.5	60.2	1.2	1.6	1.4	2.2
Kyrgyz Republic	*51*	226	*74.1*	39.2	*0.8*	22.2	*7.6*	14.3	*17.6*	24.3
Lao PDR	25	*5*	73.0	*99.0*	..	*1.0*	6.4	..	20.6	*0.0*
Latvia	*120*	1,164	*82.3*	35.5	*10.9*	32.4	*4.8*	5.8	*2.1*	26.3
Lebanon	..	..	..	..	..	..	..	..	..	..
Lesotho	48	86	67.9	64.6	24.7	35.3	5.6	..	1.7	0.1
Liberia	*74*	..	*60.8*	..	*33.7*	..	*5.6*	..	..	..
Libya	926	1,603	41.9	40.2	45.8	37.6	4.1	5.5	8.3	16.7
Lithuania	*177*	1,578	*90.7*	42.1	*6.9*	40.3	..	1.7	*2.4*	16.0
Macedonia, FYR	..	440	..	42.5	..	12.4	..	3.9	..	41.3
Madagascar	172	*405*	43.5	*58.4*	23.4	*15.8*	3.5	*3.6*	29.5	*22.2*
Malawi	268	*222*	81.8	*50.1*	5.9	*35.2*	8.7	*0.0*	3.7	*14.7*
Malaysia	5,394	*17,323*	46.9	*36.1*	26.9	*16.4*	..	*3.5*	26.2	*44.0*
Mali	352	*478*	57.4	*65.3*	15.8	*10.0*	1.9	*5.7*	24.9	*19.0*
Mauritania	126	..	76.9	..	18.3	..	3.1	..	1.7	..
Mauritius	407	1,005	51.6	46.7	23.0	25.4	5.5	6.1	19.9	21.9
Mexico	10,063	19,250	25.0	11.1	54.9	36.2	6.2	42.0	14.0	10.8
Moldova	..	352	..	33.0	..	38.2	..	1.3	..	27.6
Mongolia	155	496	56.2	40.2	0.8	38.8	6.3	8.2	36.8	12.8
Morocco	940	2,805	58.3	49.0	19.9	20.5	6.0	2.9	15.9	27.6
Mozambique	206	511	57.7	37.3	..	26.2	4.3	1.6	38.1	34.9
Myanmar	73	444	35.4	51.2	22.6	6.5	2.5	..	39.5	42.4
Namibia	341	376	46.9	36.1	17.9	23.3	6.8	5.5	28.5	35.1
Nepal	159	364	40.8	36.1	28.5	42.3	3.2	4.5	27.5	17.1
Netherlands	28,995	68,564	37.7	20.0	25.4	23.8	1.0	2.4	35.9	53.8
New Zealand	3,251	6,806	40.6	36.3	29.5	34.6	2.5	3.8	27.5	25.3
Nicaragua	73	375	70.7	56.5	20.1	22.8	7.9	3.6	1.4	17.2
Niger	209	*175*	68.3	*76.7*	10.4	*12.6*	4.3	*2.1*	17.1	*8.5*
Nigeria	1,901	4,969	33.6	29.5	30.3	23.4	3.1	..	32.9	47.2
Norway	12,247	23,988	44.6	36.2	30.0	35.0	1.7	3.8	23.7	25.1
Oman	719	2,740	36.6	37.1	6.5	22.5	4.1	9.4	52.8	31.1
Pakistan	1,863	5,089	67.0	40.4	23.1	24.9	1.4	3.3	8.6	31.5
Panama	666	1,402	66.6	55.2	14.8	17.0	10.2	13.1	8.4	14.6
Papua New Guinea	393	*662*	35.6	*26.1*	12.8	*5.8*	4.0	*7.3*	47.6	*60.8*
Paraguay	361	323	61.6	52.8	19.8	22.1	11.4	16.8	7.3	8.3
Peru	1,070	2,628	43.5	41.7	27.6	23.6	10.9	8.8	18.0	25.9
Philippines	1,721	5,081	56.9	48.1	6.5	25.9	3.4	5.5	33.2	20.5
Poland	2,847	12,272	52.4	24.0	14.9	31.3	1.0	5.1	31.8	39.6
Portugal	3,772	9,464	48.5	30.5	23.0	29.2	5.1	4.3	23.5	36.0
Puerto Rico	..	..	..	..	..	..	..	..	..	..

4.7 Structure of service imports

	Commercial service imports		Transport		Travel		Insurance and financial services		Computer, information, communications, and other commercial services	
	$ millions		% of commercial services		% of commercial services		% of commercial services		% of commercial services	
	1990	2004	1990	2004	1990	2004	1990	2004	1990	2004
Romania	787	3,829	65.5	39.2	13.1	14.1	7.3	5.9	14.1	40.9
Russian Federation	..	32,766	..	11.9	..	48.0	..	5.7	..	34.5
Rwanda	94	136	69.0	64.5	23.7	23.2	..	..	7.3	12.3
Saudi Arabia	12,677	11,057	18.1	30.1	..	..	2.2	3.3	79.7	66.6
Senegal	368	*567*	60.1	*56.8*	12.4	*9.8*	8.8	*11.1*	18.7	*22.3*
Serbia and Montenegro	..	..	..	..	..	..	..	..	..	..
Sierra Leone	67	84	29.5	34.4	32.7	35.3	4.8	6.1	33.0	24.2
Singapore	8,575	40,470	41.0	38.2	21.0	19.2	9.1	7.0	29.0	35.6
Slovak Republic	*1,666*	*3,012*	*17.3*	*29.8*	*13.1*	*19.0*	..	*8.7*	*69.6*	*42.4*
Slovenia	*1,034*	2,581	*42.5*	23.4	*27.3*	33.8	*2.5*	2.2	*27.8*	40.7
Somalia	*122*	..	*38.2*	..	..	..	*4.2*	..	*57.6*	..
South Africa	3,594	9,079	40.2	50.6	31.5	29.5	11.6	7.6	16.7	12.3
Spain	15,197	57,016	30.9	27.3	28.0	21.3	6.3	5.5	34.9	45.9
Sri Lanka	620	1,872	64.2	60.6	11.9	15.8	6.8	5.9	17.1	17.7
Sudan	202	1,023	31.9	82.2	25.4	17.2	4.9	0.2	37.8	0.5
Swaziland	171	517	6.1	14.0	20.6	10.0	..	49.0	73.4	27.0
Sweden	16,959	32,908	23.2	15.2	37.1	30.8	7.9	2.8	31.7	51.2
Switzerland	11,093	23,653	33.7	22.0	53.0	37.1	1.4	4.9	12.0	36.0
Syrian Arab Republic	702	1,813	54.5	55.2	35.5	35.9	4.4	3.5	5.7	5.4
Tajikistan	..	205	..	77.4	..	1.7	..	8.1	..	12.8
Tanzania	288	963	58.0	24.9	7.9	43.8	6.2	8.8	27.9	22.5
Thailand	6,160	22,948	58.1	47.3	23.3	19.7	5.5	5.6	13.3	27.4
Togo	217	*204*	56.9	*72.8*	18.4	*3.5*	9.1	*11.8*	15.6	*11.9*
Trinidad and Tobago	460	*335*	51.7	*48.2*	26.6	*32.0*	9.9	*0.0*	11.9	*19.8*
Tunisia	682	1,869	51.4	52.9	26.2	18.2	7.4	7.7	15.0	21.2
Turkey	2,794	10,299	32.2	42.1	18.6	24.5	..	11.8	49.2	21.6
Turkmenistan	..	..	..	..	..	..	..	..	..	..
Uganda	195	679	58.3	38.6	..	17.9	6.5	9.7	35.2	33.8
Ukraine	..	4,695	..	34.7	..	21.2	..	11.5	..	32.6
United Arab Emirates	..	..	..	..	..	..	..	..	..	..
United Kingdom	44,713	140,060	33.2	24.3	41.0	40.3	2.4	5.5	23.4	29.9
United States	97,950	263,598	36.3	29.5	38.9	26.4	4.5	13.2	20.4	30.9
Uruguay	363	649	48.2	45.2	30.7	29.8	1.5	6.4	19.6	18.5
Uzbekistan	..	..	..	..	..	..	..	..	..	..
Venezuela, RB	2,390	4,271	33.5	42.1	42.8	25.2	4.3	6.9	19.4	25.9
Vietnam	..	*3,698*	..	..	..	..	..	..	..	..
West Bank and Gaza	..	..	..	..	..	..	..	..	..	..
Yemen, Rep.	639	1,004	27.6	49.4	9.9	12.5	5.4	8.7	57.1	29.4
Zambia	370	..	76.8	..	14.6	..	5.3	..	3.3	..
Zimbabwe	460	..	51.8	..	14.4	..	3.4	..	30.4	..
World	**833,781 t**	**2,117,904 t**	**34.7 w**	**27.9 w**	**32.5 w**	**28.4 w**	**5.0 w**	**8.5 w**	**32.4 w**	**35.8 w**
Low income	23,328	84,535	55.6	*44.3*	13.4	*18.0*	5.2	*6.0*	26.2	*32.3*
Middle income	104,787	387,261	48.7	30.8	25.3	27.7	4.1	13.2	22.1	28.4
Lower middle income	50,060	221,076	61.7	37.4	15.8	23.2	4.3	7.4	18.2	32.0
Upper middle income	56,000	166,327	34.4	23.7	35.6	32.6	3.8	19.4	26.4	24.4
Low & middle income	128,523	468,869	49.3	31.7	24.1	27.3	4.2	12.8	22.5	28.3
East Asia & Pacific	25,043	160,657	65.5	36.8	15.8	23.9	2.6	7.4	16.2	32.0
Europe & Central Asia	*37,010*	113,048	*30.9*	26.6	*19.2*	30.0	*6.2*	7.5	*44.2*	35.9
Latin America & Carib.	33,523	74,822	34.0	24.5	40.8	30.4	5.9	24.7	19.6	20.5
Middle East & N. Africa	18,678	..	49.2	..	16.3	..	6.9	..	27.7	..
South Asia	9,262	50,739	60.5	*44.9*	10.7	*16.3*	5.3	*6.3*	23.5	*32.5*
Sub-Saharan Africa	18,321	38,142	45.1	44.7	22.6	24.3	7.6	6.5	25.5	24.7
High income	700,780	1,652,657	30.8	27.0	34.8	28.7	5.2	7.4	34.8	37.6
Europe EMU	300,933	708,916	26.3	23.3	31.1	28.5	7.7	5.2	35.0	43.9

a. Includes Luxembourg. b. World Trade Organization estimate.

Structure of service imports

About the data

Trade in services differs from trade in goods because services are produced and consumed at the same time. Thus services to a traveler may be consumed in the producing country (for example, use of a hotel room) but are classified as imports of the traveler's country. In other cases services may be supplied from a remote location; for example, insurance services may be supplied from one location and consumed in another. For further discussion of the problems of measuring trade in services, see *About the data* for table 4.6.

The data on exports of services in table 4.6 and on imports of services in this table, unlike those in editions before 2000, include only commercial services and exclude the category "government services not included elsewhere." The data are compiled by the International Monetary Fund (IMF) based on returns from national sources.

Definitions

• **Commercial service imports** are total service imports minus imports of government services not included elsewhere. International transactions in services are defined by the IMF's *Balance of Payments Manual* (1993) as the economic output of intangible commodities that may be produced, transferred, and consumed at the same time. Definitions may vary among reporting economies. • **Transport** covers all transport services (sea, air, land, internal waterway, space, and pipeline) performed by residents of one economy for those of another and involving the carriage of passengers, movement of goods (freight), rental of carriers with crew, and related support and auxiliary services. Excluded are freight insurance, which is included in insurance services; goods procured in ports by nonresident carriers and repairs of transport equipment, which are included in goods; repairs of harbors, railway facilities, and airfield facilities, which are included in construction services; and rental of carriers without crew, which is included in other services. • **Travel** covers goods and services acquired from an economy by travelers in that economy for their own use during visits of less than one year for business or personal purposes. Travel services include the goods and services consumed by travelers, such as meals, lodging, and transport (within the economy visited), including car rental. • **Insurance and financial services** cover freight insurance on goods imported and other direct insurance such as life insurance, financial intermediation services such as commissions, foreign exchange transactions, and brokerage services; and auxiliary services such as financial market operational and regulatory services. • **Computer, information, communications, and other commercial services** include such activities as international telecommunications, and postal and courier services; computer data; news-related service transactions between residents and nonresidents; construction services; royalties and license fees; miscellaneous business, professional, and technical services; and personal, cultural, and recreational services.

4.7a

The mix of commerical service imports is changing

Commercial service imports by developing economies (% of total)

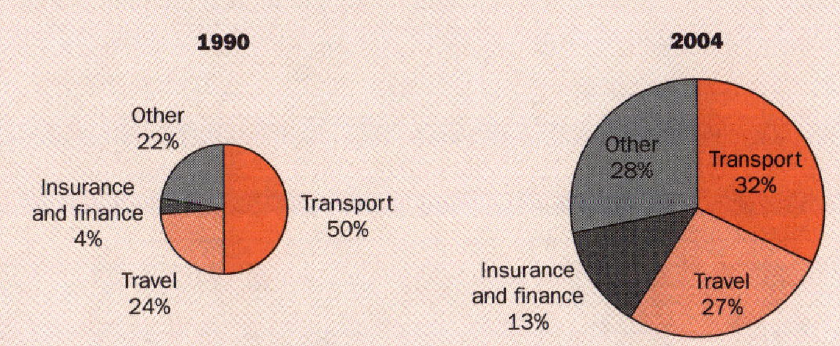

Between 1990 and 2004 travel, insurance and finance, and other services displaced transport as the most important service imports for developing economies.

Source: International Monetary Fund data files.

Data sources

Data on imports of commercial services are from the IMF. The IMF publishes balance of payments data in its *International Financial Statistics* and *Balance of Payments Statistics Yearbook*.

4.8 Structure of demand

	Household final consumption expenditure		General government final consumption expenditure		Gross capital formation		Exports of goods and services		Imports of goods and services		Gross savings	
	% of GDP		% of GDP		% of GDP		% of GDP		% of GDP		% of GDP	
	1990	2004	1990	2004	1990	2004	1990	2004	1990	2004	1990	2004
Afghanistan	..	..	..	..	..	..	..	..	..	..	..	..
Albania	61	89	19	9	29	24	15	21	23	43	21	17
Algeria	57	39	16	15	29	33	23	40	25	26	26	46
Angola	36	73	35	..[a]	12	12	39	71	21	55	9	16
Argentina	77	63	3	11	14	19	10	25	5	18	*13*	21
Armenia	46	82	18	11	47	20	35	39	46	53	..	14
Australia	59	*60*	19	*18*	22	*25*	17	*18*	17	*21*	18	*19*
Austria	57	56	19	18	24	22	38	51	37	46	24	24
Azerbaijan	51	58	18	12	27	55	44	50	39	74	..	24
Bangladesh	86	76	4	6	17	24	6	16	14	21	14	31
Belarus	47	57	24	20	27	28	46	69	44	74	29	24
Belgium	55	54	20	23	22	20	71	84	69	81	24	24
Benin	87	77	11	14	14	20	14	15	26	26	10	13
Bolivia	77	68	12	15	13	12	23	31	24	26	10	17
Bosnia and Herzegovina	..	84	..	25	..	21	..	26	..	55	..	4
Botswana	33	28	24	34	37	31	55	40	50	32	43	39
Brazil	59	55	19	19	20	21	8	18	7	13	19	23
Bulgaria	60	68	18	19	26	24	33	58	37	69	16	16
Burkina Faso	82	82	13	13	18	19	11	9	24	23	13	*6*
Burundi	95	98	11	8	15	11	8	9	28	25	..	15
Cambodia	91	80	7	5	8	26	6	65	13	76	6	19
Cameroon	67	72	13	12	18	17	20	26	17	26	16	15
Canada	56	*56*	23	*20*	21	*20*	26	*38*	26	*34*	18	*23*
Central African Republic	86	75	15	12	12	18	15	12	28	16	0	14
Chad	98	55	10	5	7	25	14	52	28	36	–3	6
Chile	62	58	10	12	25	23	35	36	31	30	23	22
China[b]	50	49[c]	12	10	35	39	19	34	16	31	39	42
Hong Kong, China	58	59	7	10	28	22	132	193	124	184	34	32
Colombia	66	62	9	20	19	19	21	21	15	22	22	17
Congo, Dem. Rep.	79	91	12	5	9	13	30	*19*	29	*22*	1	7
Congo, Rep.	62	33	14	16	16	24	54	85	46	57	7	27
Costa Rica	61	66	18	15	27	22	35	47	41	49	17	17
Côte d'Ivoire	72	71	17	8	7	11	32	48	27	38	–4	15
Croatia	*75*	58	*24*	20	*10*	30	*78*	48	*86*	56	–16	24
Cuba	..	..	..	..	..	..	..	..	..	..	..	..
Czech Republic	49	50	23	23	25	28	45	72	43	72	*28*	22
Denmark	49	48	26	27	20	20	36	44	31	38	22	23
Dominican Republic	80	73	4	5	25	21	34	50	44	49	22	27
Ecuador	68	65	11	9	21	28	33	27	32	29	11	27
Egypt, Arab Rep.	73	71	11	12	29	17	20	29	33	29	21	21
El Salvador	89	91	10	11	14	16	19	27	31	44	4	9
Eritrea	*104*	97	*22*	54	*8*	22	*11*	13	*45*	86	*10*	–9
Estonia	*51*	58	*16*	19	27	31	*60*	78	*54*	86	*40*	19
Ethiopia	74	83	19	17	12	21	8	19	12	40	10	13
Finland	51	53	22	22	29	19	23	37	24	32	24	24
France	57	56	22	24	22	20	21	26	23	26	20	19
Gabon	50	*52*	13	*7*	22	25	46	61	31	40	24	30
Gambia, The	76	75	14	11	22	24	60	42	72	52	5	18
Georgia	65	72	10	15	31	29	40	31	46	48	..	18
Germany	57	59	20	19	24	17	25	38	25	33	23	21
Ghana	85	76	9	16	14	28	17	35	26	54	7	28
Greece	72	66	15	17	23	26	18	21	28	30	22	18
Guatemala	84	92	7	4	14	18	21	18	25	32	10	13
Guinea	73	86	9	6	18	11	31	21	31	23	11	8
Guinea-Bissau	87	88	10	14	30	12	10	35	37	49	15	9
Haiti	81	*95*	8	*4*	13	*27*	18	*12*	20	*39*	*6*	21

4.8 Structure of demand

	Household final consumption expenditure		General government final consumption expenditure		Gross capital formation		Exports of goods and services		Imports of goods and services		Gross savings	
	% of GDP		% of GDP		% of GDP		% of GDP		% of GDP		% of GDP	
	1990	2004	1990	2004	1990	2004	1990	2004	1990	2004	1990	2004
Honduras	67	*74*	14	*14*	23	*29*	36	*37*	40	*54*	14	*21*
Hungary	61	69	11	10	25	24	31	64	29	68	26	15
India	66	68	12	11	24	24	7	19	9	23	22	23
Indonesia	59	65	9	8	31	23	25	31	24	27	28	24
Iran, Islamic Rep.	62	49	11	12	29	37	22	32	24	30	27	40
Iraq	..	..	..	..	..	..	..	..	..	..	..	..
Ireland	58	45	16	15	21	25	57	80	52	65	23	*23*
Israel	56	59	30	29	25	17	35	44	45	49	22	..
Italy	58	60	20	19	22	20	20	27	20	26	20	19
Jamaica	65	72	13	14	26	31	48	41	52	58	19	25
Japan	53	*57*	13	*18*	33	*24*	10	*12*	10	*10*	34	*27*
Jordan	74	93	25	16	32	24	62	48	93	80	22	21
Kazakhstan	*52*	55	*18*	12	*32*	24	*74*	55	*75*	46	..	25
Kenya	63	70	19	17	24	18	26	26	31	32	19	14
Korea, Dem. Rep.	..	..	..	..	..	..	..	..	..	..	..	..
Korea, Rep.	52	52	12	14	38	30	28	44	29	40	37	34
Kuwait	57	38	39	21	18	14	45	60	58	33	..	..
Kyrgyz Republic	71	79	25	17	24	14	29	43	50	53	4	9
Lao PDR	..	..	..	..	..	..	12	29	25	42	..	..
Latvia	53	63	9	20	40	33	48	44	49	60	*56*	18
Lebanon	140	82	25	17	18	21	18	21	100	41	22	2
Lesotho	138	94	14	22	53	42	17	48	122	105	60	28
Liberia	..	91	..	10	..	12	..	35	..	48	..	29
Libya	48	*58*	24	*17*	19	*14*	40	*47*	31	*36*	..	..
Lithuania	57	67	19	16	33	24	52	54	61	61	..	15
Macedonia, FYR	72	79	19	20	19	22	26	40	36	61	10	15
Madagascar	86	80	8	9	17	28	17	32	28	48	9	17
Malawi	72	95	15	17	23	11	24	27	33	49	14	–8
Malaysia	52	43	14	13	32	23	75	121	72	100	30	35
Mali	80	78	14	10	23	20	17	28	34	36	15	11
Mauritania	69	104	26	15	20	22	46	29	61	70	18	–7
Mauritius	64	62	13	14	31	24	64	56	71	56	26	24
Mexico	70	69	8	12	23	21	19	30	20	32	20	21
Moldova	*76*	90	..[a]	15	25	25	48	51	51	82	*58*	21
Mongolia	57	57	34	19	38	37	24	75	53	87	7	41
Morocco	65	60	16	21	25	25	27	33	33	39	25	28
Mozambique	92	78	14	10	22	20	8	30	36	38	2	6
Myanmar	*89*	..	..[a]	..	13	..	3	..	5	..	12	..
Namibia	51	49	31	25	34	26	52	46	67	45	35	40
Nepal	84	76	9	11	18	26	11	18	22	31	10	27
Netherlands	50	49	24	25	23	21	55	65	51	60	25	23
New Zealand	61	*60*	19	*18*	20	*23*	27	*29*	27	*29*	16	*18*
Nicaragua	59	89	44	10	19	28	25	26	46	54	–4	10
Niger	84	82	15	12	8	16	15	16	22	26	–2	8
Nigeria	56	38	15	22	15	22	43	55	29	37	19	27
Norway	49	45	21	22	23	19	40	44	34	30	25	33
Oman	46	45	22	23	12	18	47	57	28	43	..	..
Pakistan	74	73	15	8	19	17	16	16	23	15	22	23
Panama	57	68	18	13	17	21	87	63	79	65	24	13
Papua New Guinea	59	..	25	..	24	..	41	*71*	49	*60*	9	..
Paraguay	77	73	6	7	23	22	33	36	40	37	20	23
Peru	74	69	8	10	17	19	16	21	14	18	16	18
Philippines	72	72	10	10	24	17	28	52	33	51	20	37
Poland	48	64	19	18	26	20	29	39	22	41	*16*	19
Portugal	63	63	16	21	28	24	33	31	40	38	28	15
Puerto Rico	65	..	15	..	17	..	*72*	..	*70*	..	..	..

4.8 Structure of demand

	Household final consumption expenditure		General government final consumption expenditure		Gross capital formation		Exports of goods and services		Imports of goods and services		Gross savings	
	% of GDP		% of GDP		% of GDP		% of GDP		% of GDP		% of GDP	
	1990	2004	1990	2004	1990	2004	1990	2004	1990	2004	1990	2004
Romania	66	70	13	15	30	25	17	37	26	47	22	18
Russian Federation	49	50	21	17	30	21	18	35	18	22	*36*	31
Rwanda	84	84	10	13	15	21	6	10	14	27	11	17
Saudi Arabia	47	30	29	23	15	19	41	53	32	25	18	*29*
Senegal	76	77	15	13	14	23	25	28	30	41	6	17
Serbia and Montenegro	..	93	..	18	..	17	..	24	..	52	..	5
Sierra Leone	84	87	8	14	10	16	22	23	24	39	3	11
Singapore	47	41	10	11	36	18	..	..	..	..	45	..
Slovak Republic	54	56	22	20	33	26	27	77	36	80	..	23
Slovenia	53	54	17	20	17	27	91	60	79	61	*24*	26
Somalia	112	..	..[a]	..	16	..	10	..	38	..	*17*	..
South Africa	57	63	20	20	18	18	24	27	19	27	20	14
Spain	60	58	16	18	27	28	16	26	20	29	24	23
Sri Lanka	77	76	10	8	23	25	29	36	38	46	17	19
Sudan	..	71	..	12	..	20	..	18	..	21	..	15
Swaziland	73	65	18	25	19	18	75	84	87	92	27	17
Sweden	49	48	27	28	24	16	30	46	29	38	22	24
Switzerland	57	*61*	11	*12*	31	*20*	36	*44*	34	*37*	34	*29*
Syrian Arab Republic	69	64	14	14	17	21	28	35	28	34	15	20
Tajikistan	74	101	9	9	25	9	28	46	35	65	*24*	6
Tanzania[d]	81	78	18	13	26	19	13	19	38	29	8	9
Thailand	57	57	9	11	41	27	34	71	42	66	33	31
Togo	71	86	14	10	27	18	34	34	45	47	20	9
Trinidad and Tobago	59	58	12	9	13	20	45	60	29	48	21	27
Tunisia	58	63	16	16	33	25	44	45	51	48	27	22
Turkey	69	67	11	13	24	26	13	29	18	35	24	20
Turkmenistan	49	52	23	14	40	26	..	66	..	57	..	*34*
Uganda	92	77	8	15	13	23	7	14	19	28	1	10
Ukraine	57	55	17	18	28	19	28	61	29	54	36	30
United Arab Emirates	38	48	16	13	21	22	66	82	41	65	..	..
United Kingdom	63	65	20	21	20	17	24	25	27	28	15	15
United States	67	*71*	17	*16*	18	*18*	10	*10*	11	*14*	15	*13*
Uruguay	70	74	12	11	12	13	24	30	18	28	14	12
Uzbekistan	61	56	25	17	32	20	29	40	48	33	*3*	30
Venezuela, RB	62	50	8	13	10	22	40	36	20	20	27	34
Vietnam	84	65	12	6	13	36	36	66	45	74	–2	32
West Bank and Gaza	..	*84*	..	*53*	..	*3*	..	*10*	..	*49*	..	*–13*
Yemen, Rep.	74	78	18	13	15	17	14	25	20	34	28	12
Zambia	64	69	19	13	17	26	36	20	37	27	7	13
Zimbabwe	63	74	19	21	17	13	23	36	23	44	16	3
World	**60 w**	***62 w***	**17 w**	***17 w***	**23 w**	***21 w***	**19 w**	***24 w***	**19 w**	***24 w***	**22 w**	***20 w***
Low income	70	69	13	11	21	23	13	24	17	27	18	22
Middle income	60	58	13	14	26	26	22	35	21	33	26	28
Lower middle income	58	56	14	13	29	29	19	33	19	31	28	32
Upper middle income	63	61	13	14	23	22	25	38	23	35	*21*	22
Low & middle income	61	60	13	13	25	25	21	33	20	32	25	27
East Asia & Pacific	53	52	12	10	34	34	24	43	23	40	35	39
Europe & Central Asia	56	60	17	16	27	23	24	42	24	42	*25*	23
Latin America & Carib.	67	62	12	14	19	21	17	26	15	23	20	22
Middle East & N. Africa	66	59	15	14	26	26	26	34	34	34	24	30
South Asia	69	69	11	11	23	23	9	19	12	22	21	24
Sub-Saharan Africa	64	65	18	18	18	19	27	32	26	33	16	16
High income	60	*63*	18	*18*	23	*20*	19	*23*	19	*23*	22	*19*
Europe EMU	57	57	20	20	24	20	27	37	28	34	22	21

a. Data on general government final consumption expenditure are not available separately; they are included in household final consumption expenditure. b. China has revised its national accounts data from 1993 onwards, but revised expenditure data are not available. The data shown here are based on earlier series. c. Includes the difference between the old and the new GDP series. d. Data cover mainland Tanzania only.

Structure of demand 4.8

About the data

Gross domestic product (GDP) from the expenditure side is made up of household final consumption expenditure, general government final consumption expenditure, gross capital formation (private and public investment in fixed assets, changes in inventories, and net acquisitions of valuables), and net exports (exports minus imports) of goods and services. Such expenditures are recorded in purchaser prices and include net taxes on products.

Because policymakers have tended to focus on fostering the growth of output, and because data on production are easier to collect than data on spending, many countries generate their primary estimate of GDP using the production approach. Moreover, many countries do not estimate all the separate components of national expenditures but instead derive some of the main aggregates indirectly using GDP (based on the production approach) as the control total.

Household final consumption expenditure (private consumption in the 1968 System of National Accounts, or SNA) is often estimated as a residual, by subtracting from GDP all other known expenditures. The resulting aggregate may incorporate fairly large discrepancies. When household consumption is calculated separately, many of the estimates are based on household surveys, which tend to be one-year studies with limited coverage. Thus the estimates quickly become outdated and must be supplemented by estimates using price- and quantity-based statistical procedures. Complicating the issue, in many developing countries the distinction between cash outlays for personal business and those for household use may be blurred. *World Development Indicators* includes in household consumption the expenditures of nonprofit institutions serving households.

General government final consumption expenditure (general government consumption in the 1968 SNA) includes expenditures on goods and services for individual consumption as well as those on services for collective consumption. Defense expenditures, including those on capital outlays (with certain exceptions), are treated as current spending.

Gross capital formation (gross domestic investment in the 1968 SNA) consists of outlays on additions to the economy's fixed assets plus net changes in the level of inventories. It is generally obtained from reports by industry of acquisition and distinguishes only the broad categories of capital formation. The 1993 SNA recognizes a third category of capital formation: net acquisitions of valuables. Included in gross capital formation under the 1993 SNA guidelines are capital outlays on defense establishments that may be used by the general public, such as schools, airfields, and hospitals, and intangibles such as computer software and mineral exploration outlays. Data on capital formation may be estimated from direct surveys of enterprises and administrative records or based on the commodity flow method using data from production, trade, and construction activities.

The quality of data on fixed capital formation by government depends on the quality of government accounting systems (which tend to be weak in developing countries). Measures of fixed capital formation by households and corporations—particularly capital outlays by small, unincorporated enterprises—are usually unreliable.

Estimates of changes in inventories are rarely complete but usually include the most important activities or commodities. In some countries these estimates are derived as a composite residual along with household final consumption expenditure. According to national accounts conventions, adjustments should be made for appreciation of the value of inventory holdings due to price changes, but this is not always done. In highly inflationary economies this element can be substantial.

Data on exports and imports are compiled from customs reports and balance of payments data. Although the data from the payments side provide reasonably reliable records of cross-border transactions, they may not adhere strictly to the appropriate definitions of valuation and timing used in the balance of payments or correspond to the change-of-ownership criterion. This issue has assumed greater significance with the increasing globalization of international business. Neither customs nor balance of payments data usually capture the illegal transactions that occur in many countries. Goods carried by travelers across borders in legal but unreported shuttle trade may further distort trade statistics.

Gross savings represent the difference between disposable income and consumption and replace gross domestic savings, a concept used by the World Bank and included in previous editions of *World Development Indicators*. The change was made to conform to the SNA concepts and definitions. For further discussion of the problems in compiling national accounts, see Srinivasan (1994), Heston (1994), and Ruggles (1994). For an analysis of the reliability of foreign trade and national income statistics, see Morgenstern (1963).

Definitions

• **Household final consumption expenditure** is the market value of all goods and services, including durable products (such as cars, washing machines, and home computers), purchased by households. It excludes purchases of dwellings but includes imputed rent for owner-occupied dwellings. It also includes payments and fees to governments to obtain permits and licenses. *World Development Indicators* includes in household consumption expenditure the expenditures of nonprofit institutions serving households, even when reported separately by the country. In practice, household consumption expenditure may include any statistical discrepancy in the use of resources relative to the supply of resources. • **General government final consumption expenditure** includes all government current expenditures for purchases of goods and services (including compensation of employees). It also includes most expenditures on national defense and security but excludes government military expenditures that potentially have wider public use and are part of government capital formation. • **Gross capital formation** consists of outlays on additions to the fixed assets of the economy, net changes in the level of inventories, and net acquisitions of valuables. Fixed assets include land improvements (fences, ditches, drains, and so on); plant, machinery, and equipment purchases; and the construction of roads, railways, and the like, including schools, offices, hospitals, private residential dwellings, and commercial and industrial buildings. Inventories are stocks of goods held by firms to meet temporary or unexpected fluctuations in production or sales, and "work in progress." • **Exports** and **imports of goods and services** are the value of all goods and other market services provided to, or received from, the rest of the world. They include the value of merchandise, freight, insurance, transport, travel, royalties, license fees, and other services, such as communication, construction, financial, information, business, personal, and government services. They exclude compensation of employees and investment income (factor services in the 1968 SNA) as well as transfer payments. • **Gross savings** are calculated as gross national income less total consumption, plus net transfers.

Data sources

National accounts indicators for most developing countries are collected from national statistical organizations and central banks by visiting and resident World Bank missions. Data for high-income economies come from Organisation for Economic Co-operation and Development data files (see the OECD's *Annual National Accounts for OECD Member Countries: Data from 1970 Onwards*). The United Nations Statistics Division publishes detailed national accounts for UN member countries in *National Accounts Statistics: Main Aggregates and Detailed Tables* and updates in the *Monthly Bulletin of Statistics*.

4.9 Growth of consumption investment, and trade

	Household final consumption expenditure average annual % growth		Household final consumption expenditure Per capita average annual % growth		General government final consumption expenditure average annual % growth		Gross capital formation average annual % growth		Goods and services average annual % growth Exports		Goods and services average annual % growth Imports	
	1990–2000	2000–04	1990–2000	2000–04	1990–2000	2000–04	1990–2000	2000–04	1990–2000	2000–04	1990–2000	2000–04
Afghanistan	..	..	..	..	..	..	..	..	..	..	..	..
Albania	4.3	2.5	5.2	2.1	2.4	0.7	25.8	3.3	17.9	16.9	15.8	16.8
Algeria	−0.1	6.4	−1.9	4.8	3.6	3.1	−0.9	11.9	3.3	4.1	−1.1	9.0
Angola	..	..	..	..	..	..	..	..	..	..	..	..
Argentina	2.7	−1.7	1.5	−2.6	2.2	−1.0	7.4	−1.4	8.7	4.9	15.6	−7.3
Armenia	−0.5	9.0	1.0	9.5	−1.7	6.6	26.2	13.3	−18.4	26.7	−12.5	15.7
Australia	3.6	4.2	2.8	2.9	2.8	2.9	6.3	11.0	7.2	−0.2	8.1	9.4
Austria	1.9	0.7	1.5	0.2	2.5	0.4	2.1	0.4	5.5	4.7	5.0	3.6
Azerbaijan	1.5	12.1	0.4	11.2	−1.7	6.1	42.9	48.5	6.8	11.1	15.5	33.0
Bangladesh	2.6	4.8	0.4	2.8	4.7	12.6	9.2	7.8	13.1	6.7	9.7	2.8
Belarus	−0.5	11.5	−0.3	12.0	−1.9	0.4	−7.5	12.5	−4.8	10.1	−8.7	12.8
Belgium	1.9	1.3	1.6	0.9	1.5	2.6	2.3	0.3	4.7	2.4	4.5	2.4
Benin	2.6	13.5	−0.7	10.0	4.4	9.5	12.2	6.4	1.8	4.4	2.1	3.7
Bolivia	3.6	2.0	1.4	0.0	3.6	2.5	8.5	−4.8	4.5	9.8	6.0	3.9
Bosnia and Herzegovina	..	..	..	..	..	..	..	4.7	..	5.3	..	2.3
Botswana	2.7	3.7	0.6	3.5	7.1	8.7	2.5	16.4	4.7	−5.8	3.8	−0.4
Brazil[a]	4.8	−0.2	3.3	−1.6	−0.4	4.3	3.4	−0.2	6.1	12.4	11.1	−1.6
Bulgaria	−3.7	5.0	−3.0	5.9	−8.5	3.7	−4.9	12.5	3.9	9.1	2.7	11.7
Burkina Faso	4.2	3.6	1.3	0.3	−0.5	2.6	7.0	7.7	0.0	7.5	1.4	13.2
Burundi	−2.3	..	−3.5	..	−2.1	..	0.4	..	7.9	10.6	1.1	..
Cambodia[a]	6.0	2.8	3.4	0.7	7.2	4.4	10.9	23.4	21.7	13.9	14.8	12.7
Cameroon	3.1	6.1	0.7	4.1	0.7	6.5	0.4	7.8	3.2	1.5	5.1	5.0
Canada	2.6	3.1	1.6	2.1	0.3	3.4	4.5	3.6	8.7	−1.1	7.2	0.2
Central African Republic[a]	..	..	..	..	..	..	..	..	..	..	..	..
Chad[a]	0.6	16.9	−2.4	12.8	−2.8	5.8	4.4	12.8	1.2	39.2	−1.1	27.4
Chile	6.4	1.2	4.7	0.1	9.6	2.1	4.7	6.4	9.4	4.7	10.4	−1.8
China[b]	9.0	7.0	7.8	6.3	8.8	7.2	11.2	15.0	13.0	24.2	14.3	22.2
Hong Kong, China	3.9	1.1	2.1	0.3	3.3	2.6	5.8	0.1	8.1	9.2	8.4	8.0
Colombia	2.2	3.0	0.3	1.3	10.5	1.1	2.0	12.6	5.3	1.6	9.0	7.8
Congo, Dem. Rep.[a]	−4.5	..	−7.1	..	−17.4	..	−0.7	..	−0.5	..	−2.4	..
Congo, Rep.[a]	−1.7	15.4	−4.8	11.9	−2.0	12.7	0.4	21.3	5.1	3.8	2.9	24.9
Costa Rica[a]	5.0	2.8	2.5	0.8	1.9	1.9	4.7	9.1	11.0	4.0	9.0	4.2
Côte d'Ivoire	4.0	−2.2	1.1	−3.8	0.8	3.7	8.6	−4.6	1.5	3.5	6.9	6.3
Croatia	2.6	5.1	3.5	4.8	1.4	−2.0	5.4	15.5	5.9	6.1	4.6	8.6
Cuba	..	..	..	..	..	..	..	..	7.1	..	7.9	..
Czech Republic	2.9	3.2	2.9	3.3	−0.6	2.8	4.7	4.2	8.8	9.9	12.1	10.0
Denmark	2.2	1.3	1.8	1.0	2.3	1.6	5.6	2.2	4.4	2.6	6.0	3.9
Dominican Republic[a]	3.4	−95.7	1.8	−95.7	15.9	−14.9	10.5	−10.2	13.2	5.7	11.4	1.2
Ecuador[a]	2.1	4.3	0.3	2.8	−1.5	1.9	−0.7	14.5	5.3	3.8	2.8	10.6
Egypt, Arab Rep.	4.5	2.8	2.5	0.8	2.1	3.3	5.9	−0.2	3.4	6.7	2.7	3.8
El Salvador	5.3	2.1	3.1	0.2	2.8	2.0	7.1	1.0	13.4	4.2	11.6	3.5
Eritrea	−5.0	1.8	−6.7	−2.5	22.6	5.0	19.1	−13.5	−2.5	−7.4	7.5	−3.7
Estonia	0.6	7.7	2.2	8.1	4.9	5.3	0.2	12.1	11.2	5.0	12.0	7.6
Ethiopia	5.5	4.3	3.2	2.1	9.7	−1.3	6.4	12.1	7.1	16.7	5.8	13.2
Finland	1.7	2.8	1.4	2.5	0.8	2.4	1.3	0.5	9.9	2.5	6.2	2.4
France	1.6	2.0	1.3	1.4	1.8	2.4	..	..	7.5	1.0	5.7	2.5
Gabon[a]	1.2	5.1	−1.7	3.3	5.4	1.6	3.8	1.0	1.5	2.9	0.7	3.0
Gambia, The	3.5	1.8	0.0	−1.1	−2.2	4.2	1.9	2.3	−0.2	3.2	−0.8	4.5
Georgia	6.1	6.4	7.6	7.6	12.0	0.3	−12.5	17.1	12.2	3.8	11.2	4.6
Germany	1.9	0.3	1.6	0.2	1.8	0.4	1.1	−2.8	6.0	4.9	5.8	2.5
Ghana	0.2	9.2	−2.3	6.9	4.8	4.2	1.3	7.6	10.1	1.0	10.4	3.3
Greece	2.2	3.4	1.4	3.1	2.1	2.4	4.1	7.8	7.6	−0.4	7.4	1.1
Guatemala[a]	4.2	4.2	1.9	1.7	5.1	−2.0	6.2	2.3	6.2	0.8	9.2	6.6
Guinea	3.6	5.0	0.5	2.7	5.0	6.7	2.8	−7.7	4.6	1.0	1.3	1.5
Guinea-Bissau	2.6	7.1	−0.4	4.0	1.9	−3.9	−6.5	−8.6	15.4	3.8	−0.5	−6.3
Haiti	..	..	..	..	..	..	8.6	1.5	−10.3	7.7	−5.2	10.6

Growth of consumption, investment, and trade 4.9

	Household final consumption expenditure				General government final consumption expenditure		Gross capital formation		Goods and services			
	average annual % growth		Per capita average annual % growth		average annual % growth		average annual % growth		average annual % growth Exports		Imports	
	1990–2000	2000–04	1990–2000	2000–04	1990–2000	2000–04	1990–2000	2000–04	1990–2000	2000–04	1990–2000	2000–04
Honduras[a]	3.0	*3.4*	0.1	*1.0*	2.0	*4.1*	7.0	*2.0*	1.6	*1.6*	3.8	*2.4*
Hungary	–0.2	6.8	0.1	6.7	0.9	3.7	10.0	–1.4	9.8	8.0	11.4	8.7
India	4.9	6.2	3.0	4.6	6.6	2.6	7.0	7.7	12.3	12.0	14.4	15.8
Indonesia	6.6	4.0	5.0	2.6	0.1	8.7	–0.7	5.2	5.9	3.8	5.7	4.9
Iran, Islamic Rep.	2.9	5.5	1.3	4.1	5.2	3.4	3.1	11.8	–1.3	4.4	–11.6	11.7
Iraq	..	..	..	..	..	..	..	..	..	..	..	..
Ireland	5.3	3.3	4.5	1.6	4.1	6.1	10.4	2.9	15.5	4.0	14.3	2.2
Israel	*4.5*	2.1	*1.9*	0.2	*3.0*	1.0	*1.5*	–6.9	*10.6*	2.2	*7.4*	0.2
Italy	1.6	0.9	1.4	1.0	0.1	2.2	–0.3	16.9	6.1	–0.6	4.7	0.8
Jamaica	..	..	..	..	..	..	..	..	..	..	..	..
Japan	1.5	*0.6*	1.2	*0.4*	3.1	*2.3*	–0.2	*–2.6*	4.2	*3.6*	4.1	*1.5*
Jordan	5.9	6.0	1.9	3.2	1.7	3.7	1.1	8.8	2.4	9.1	2.0	8.8
Kazakhstan[a]	–8.1	9.4	–7.0	9.2	–7.1	7.5	–18.3	14.2	–2.6	9.8	–11.2	2.8
Kenya	3.6	1.9	0.8	–0.3	6.9	1.8	6.1	1.5	1.1	9.5	9.4	4.8
Korea, Dem. Rep.	..	..	..	..	..	..	..	..	..	..	..	..
Korea, Rep.	4.9	2.8	3.9	2.2	4.7	4.5	3.4	3.4	16.0	11.8	10.0	9.3
Kuwait	*5.0*	*6.1*	*1.2*	*3.1*	*–2.9*	*7.1*	*–4.4*	*5.5*	*–1.6*	*0.2*	*0.8*	*8.3*
Kyrgyz Republic	–6.5	10.9	–7.4	9.9	–8.8	0.8	–3.9	–10.6	*–1.6*	6.2	*–8.2*	8.9
Lao PDR	..	..	..	..	..	..	..	..	..	..	..	..
Latvia	–3.9	8.0	–2.7	8.7	1.8	2.2	–3.9	18.3	*4.2*	6.4	*7.6*	11.2
Lebanon	4.6	3.4	2.3	2.3	1.2	–1.6	8.2	8.4	7.2	16.2	3.1	5.7
Lesotho	0.1	1.4	–1.1	1.2	6.2	6.7	1.5	–7.3	11.1	12.4	0.9	4.8
Liberia	..	..	..	..	..	..	..	..	..	..	..	..
Libya	..	..	..	..	..	..	..	..	..	..	..	..
Lithuania[a]	*5.2*	6.6	*6.0*	7.1	*1.9*	4.3	*11.1*	14.3	*4.9*	14.1	*7.5*	13.8
Macedonia, FYR	2.2	3.4	1.7	3.1	–0.4	1.3	3.1	3.6	4.2	–2.3	7.4	0.1
Madagascar	2.3	2.0	–0.7	–0.9	0.0	3.8	3.4	11.2	3.9	–5.8	4.3	8.4
Malawi	5.4	5.2	3.5	2.8	–4.4	7.8	–8.4	–4.8	4.0	0.3	–1.1	5.6
Malaysia	5.3	5.9	2.6	3.8	4.8	11.2	5.3	1.4	12.0	4.5	10.3	5.2
Mali	3.0	1.9	0.2	–1.1	3.2	25.2	0.4	4.7	10.0	8.2	3.5	5.0
Mauritania	3.6	..	0.9	..	0.2	..	9.3	..	–1.5	..	–0.6	..
Mauritius	5.1	3.9	3.9	2.9	4.8	4.6	4.7	3.6	5.4	6.6	5.2	3.6
Mexico	2.4	2.7	0.7	1.3	1.8	–0.5	4.7	–2.1	14.6	2.7	12.3	2.3
Moldova[a]	*9.9*	9.3	*10.2*	9.7	*–12.4*	10.4	*–15.5*	7.6	*0.7*	16.3	*5.6*	16.0
Mongolia[a]	..	..	..	..	..	..	..	..	*30.9*	*8.4*	*29.3*	*7.8*
Morocco	1.6	3.8	0.1	2.1	3.8	4.4	2.9	6.6	5.4	4.4	4.4	3.8
Mozambique[a]	4.8	6.5	1.8	4.3	3.1	9.3	15.5	4.8	11.0	23.3	6.3	10.8
Myanmar	*3.9*	..	..	..	..	..	15.3	..	10.0	..	5.8	..
Namibia	4.8	–0.1	1.7	–1.5	3.3	1.3	6.9	12.3	3.8	8.7	5.4	2.3
Nepal	..	..	..	..	..	..	..	..	..	..	..	..
Netherlands	2.8	0.4	2.2	–0.1	2.0	2.5	3.2	–1.6	6.8	2.2	6.6	2.4
New Zealand	3.2	*4.4*	2.0	*3.0*	2.5	*3.4*	5.8	*8.9*	5.1	*4.0*	6.3	*7.5*
Nicaragua[a]	6.1	4.1	3.8	2.0	–1.5	–0.5	11.3	–3.7	9.3	5.7	12.2	3.2
Niger	*1.8*	..	..	..	*0.8*	..	*4.0*	..	*3.1*	..	*–2.1*	..
Nigeria	*0.2*	*5.7*	..	..	*–1.8*	*2.2*	*5.4*	*12.4*	4.4	4.7	4.5	9.5
Norway	3.5	3.0	2.9	2.4	2.8	3.1	6.0	–1.2	5.6	1.5	5.8	2.8
Oman	5.4	1.3	2.4	0.4	2.4	6.1	4.0	17.0	6.2	7.0	5.9	12.8
Pakistan	4.9	2.3	2.3	–0.2	0.7	5.7	1.8	1.9	1.7	13.1	2.5	2.8
Panama[a]	6.4	3.7	4.2	1.9	1.7	6.4	10.4	1.1	–0.4	0.3	1.2	0.4
Papua New Guinea	*5.6*	..	..	..	*2.7*	..	*0.5*	..	*4.3*	..	*2.8*	..
Paraguay	3.7	1.5	1.0	–0.9	6.4	–4.1	0.2	–2.5	–1.0	5.7	3.2	4.9
Peru[a]	4.0	3.3	2.2	1.8	5.2	1.7	7.5	2.2	8.5	8.3	9.0	4.5
Philippines	3.7	4.7	1.5	2.8	3.8	–1.5	4.1	–0.6	7.8	4.3	7.8	6.2
Poland[a]	5.1	3.0	5.0	3.3	3.5	1.1	10.6	–1.6	11.3	8.3	16.7	4.1
Portugal	2.8	1.0	2.5	0.3	2.8	1.7	5.4	–3.9	5.6	3.3	7.3	1.5
Puerto Rico	..	..	..	..	..	..	..	..	*1.6*	..	*4.5*	..

4.9 Growth of consumption, investment, and trade

	Household final consumption expenditure				General government final consumption expenditure		Gross capital formation		Goods and services			
	average annual % growth		Per capita average annual % growth		average annual % growth		average annual % growth		average annual % growth			
									Exports		Imports	
	1990–2000	2000–04	1990–2000	2000–04	1990–2000	2000–04	1990–2000	2000–04	1990–2000	2000–04	1990–2000	2000–04
Romania[a]	1.4	7.5	1.7	8.4	0.8	2.8	–5.1	10.4	8.1	12.5	6.0	14.8
Russian Federation	–0.9	8.7	–0.8	9.1	–2.2	1.7	–19.1	8.9	0.8	10.1	–6.1	18.1
Rwanda[a]	1.2	3.4	–0.1	0.9	–1.7	13.1	1.4	0.4	–3.8	5.8	5.0	–0.6
Saudi Arabia	..	*1.9*	..	*–0.9*	..	*0.6*	..	*6.2*	..	*2.2*	..	*2.2*
Senegal	2.4	5.1	–0.2	2.6	2.1	4.9	7.9	9.0	6.3	4.6	3.5	8.1
Serbia and Montenegro	..	9.5	..	9.4	..	6.1	..	15.3	..	14.5	..	23.1
Sierra Leone	*1.2*	13.5	*0.3*	8.8	*10.4*	..	*–5.6*	..	*–11.2*	..	*–0.2*	..
Singapore	5.7	4.0	2.6	2.7	9.1	1.2	7.7	–10.9	..	..	..	..
Slovak Republic	*4.7*	3.1	*4.5*	3.1	*2.9*	3.5	*7.9*	3.6	*9.0*	11.7	11.7	10.4
Slovenia	3.8	2.1	3.8	2.0	2.1	2.4	11.3	6.2	2.2	6.7	4.8	6.5
Somalia	..	..	..	..	..	..	..	..	..	..	..	..
South Africa	2.9	3.9	0.7	3.0	0.3	5.3	5.0	7.1	5.6	0.8	7.1	6.6
Spain	2.2	3.1	1.8	1.7	2.8	4.6	2.8	4.5	10.6	2.9	9.0	5.4
Sri Lanka[a]	*5.7*	..	..	..	*7.5*	..	6.9	4.6	7.5	3.9	8.6	6.1
Sudan	*6.2*	..	*3.7*	..	*0.2*	..	*11.3*	19.5	*14.2*	7.4	*8.8*	*4.5*
Swaziland[a]	3.8	2.1	0.6	0.3	5.5	–2.2	2.7	4.2	3.8	2.0	4.5	0.8
Sweden	1.3	1.3	1.0	1.0	0.6	1.2	1.8	–1.0	8.6	4.0	6.2	1.7
Switzerland	1.1	*0.9*	0.5	*0.1*	0.8	*3.0*	1.4	*–1.9*	4.0	*0.0*	4.2	*0.2*
Syrian Arab Republic	2.9	4.6	0.1	2.0	1.9	7.0	3.2	12.0	12.0	–0.5	4.4	7.8
Tajikistan	*–4.2*	..	*–5.5*	..	*–19.2*	..	–17.5	*26.9*	*–1.4*	12.8	*–3.9*	*1.7*
Tanzania[c]	2.1	1.8	–0.8	–0.2	3.4	19.3	–1.6	9.6	7.1	4.2	0.3	6.1
Thailand	3.7	5.6	2.5	4.6	5.1	2.3	–4.0	9.1	9.5	6.6	4.6	8.0
Togo	5.0	0.6	1.8	–2.1	0.0	0.2	–0.1	5.8	1.2	6.1	1.1	3.2
Trinidad and Tobago	0.7	9.5	0.1	9.1	0.3	5.4	12.5	2.7	6.9	4.3	9.9	7.1
Tunisia	4.3	4.9	2.6	3.9	4.0	4.5	3.5	3.8	5.2	1.4	3.8	2.1
Turkey	3.5	2.6	1.7	1.0	4.9	–0.8	5.0	9.1	11.7	12.1	11.0	10.9
Turkmenistan	..	..	..	..	..	..	*2.2*	..	*–6.1*	10.9	*0.6*	10.4
Uganda	6.2	5.4	3.0	1.9	7.1	6.8	8.9	6.2	14.7	9.9	10.1	5.4
Ukraine	–6.9	11.1	–6.4	12.0	–4.1	5.2	–18.5	7.1	–3.6	9.1	–6.6	8.0
United Arab Emirates	*7.1*	12.9	*0.7*	5.1	*6.9*	0.8	*5.5*	5.5	*5.5*	12.2	*6.4*	13.6
United Kingdom	2.9	2.9	2.6	2.9	1.1	3.5	4.6	2.3	6.6	1.5	6.8	3.8
United States	3.6	*3.0*	2.4	*1.9*	0.7	*3.7*	7.4	*–1.3*	7.3	*–2.0*	9.8	*1.8*
Uruguay[a]	5.0	–3.2	4.2	–3.9	2.3	–4.1	6.3	–4.2	6.0	0.1	9.9	–5.5
Uzbekistan	..	..	..	..	..	..	–2.6	4.3	*2.4*	3.3	*–1.2*	3.2
Venezuela, RB	0.6	0.6	–1.5	–1.2	3.7	5.0	11.0	–9.1	1.0	–2.8	8.2	–3.2
Vietnam	*5.4*	7.0	*3.8*	5.8	*3.2*	6.6	19.8	11.6	24.1	15.3	28.2	19.4
West Bank and Gaza	*2.9*	*–10.4*	*–1.3*	*–14.1*	*16.1*	*–1.7*	*–1.7*	*–53.9*	*1.0*	*–19.5*	*2.4*	*–13.5*
Yemen, Rep.	3.4	8.2	–0.7	4.9	1.3	5.3	10.9	6.7	16.5	–4.8	8.0	4.5
Zambia	–3.6	1.5	–5.9	–0.3	–8.1	6.9	5.4	6.1	2.8	13.1	1.5	6.4
Zimbabwe	0.0	–3.3	–1.7	–3.9	–2.2	–7.9	–2.5	–8.3	10.5	–5.7	9.4	–4.2
World	**2.9 w**	***2.4 w***	**1.5 w**	***1.1 w***	**1.7 w**	***2.9 w***	**3.2 w**	***1.2 w***	**7.0 w**	***5.0 w***	**6.9 w**	***3.3 w***
Low income	4.2	5.4	2.0	3.4	4.2	3.6	6.1	7.3	8.2	9.6	8.9	11.9
Middle income	3.8	3.6	2.6	2.7	2.6	3.5	2.5	7.4	7.2	10.1	6.3	9.3
Lower middle income	4.9	4.2	3.6	3.2	3.3	4.9	4.6	10.4	6.9	14.0	5.2	12.4
Upper middle income	2.6	2.9	1.6	2.1	1.7	1.6	–0.4	2.0	7.6	5.9	7.4	6.0
Low & middle income	3.8	3.9	2.2	2.5	2.7	3.5	2.8	7.4	7.3	10.1	6.5	9.6
East Asia & Pacific	7.4	6.3	6.1	5.4	7.1	6.8	7.9	13.0	11.0	15.3	10.4	15.0
Europe & Central Asia	1.0	5.6	0.9	5.5	0.1	1.7	–7.3	6.6	3.5	9.8	1.9	10.9
Latin America & Carib.	3.4	0.9	1.8	–0.6	1.6	2.0	5.0	–0.6	8.5	4.4	10.6	1.1
Middle East & N. Africa	3.2	4.1	1.1	2.2	3.5	3.5	3.0	8.3	3.4	4.5	–1.6	6.7
South Asia	4.7	5.5	2.6	3.7	5.8	3.2	6.5	7.1	10.0	11.2	11.2	12.6
Sub-Saharan Africa	2.7	3.9	0.2	1.6	0.5	5.2	4.0	7.0	4.8	3.3	5.5	6.8
High income	2.8	*2.2*	2.0	*1.5*	1.6	*2.8*	3.4	*–0.1*	6.9	*1.8*	7.0	*2.3*
Europe EMU	1.9	1.3	1.6	0.8	1.6	2.0	1.4	3.7	6.9	2.7	6.1	2.5

a. Household final consumption expenditure includes statistical discrepancy. b. China has revised its national accounts data from 1993 onwards, but revised expenditure data are not available. The data shown here are based on earlier series. c. Data cover mainland Tanzania only.

Growth of consumption, investment, and trade 4.9

About the data

Measures of growth in consumption and capital formation are subject to two kinds of inaccuracy. The first stems from the difficulty of measuring expenditures at current price levels, as described in *About the data* for table 4.8. The second arises in deflating current price data to measure volume growth, where results depend on the relevance and reliability of the price indexes and weights used. Measuring price changes is more difficult for investment goods than for consumption goods because of the one-time nature of many investments and because the rate of technological progress in capital goods makes capturing change in quality difficult. (An example is computers—prices have fallen as quality has improved.) Several countries estimate capital formation from the supply side, identifying capital goods entering an economy directly from detailed production and international trade statistics. This means that the price indexes used in deflating production and international trade, reflecting delivered or offered prices, will determine the deflator for capital formation expenditures on the demand side.

Growth rates of household final consumption expenditure, household final consumption expenditure per capita, general government final consumption expenditure, gross capital formation, and exports and imports of goods and services are estimated using constant price data. (Consumption, capital formation, and exports and imports of goods and servces as shares of GDP are shown in table 4.8.)

To obtain government consumption in constant prices, countries may deflate current values by applying a wage (price) index or extrapolate from the change in government employment. Neither technique captures improvements in productivity or changes in the quality of government services. Deflators for household consumption are usually calculated on the basis of the consumer price index. Many countries estimate household consumption as a residual that includes statistical discrepancies associated with the estimation of other expenditure items, including changes in inventories; thus these estimates lack detailed breakdowns of household consumption expenditures.

4.9a

Gross capital formation and government consumption are both on the rise in Sub-Saharan Africa

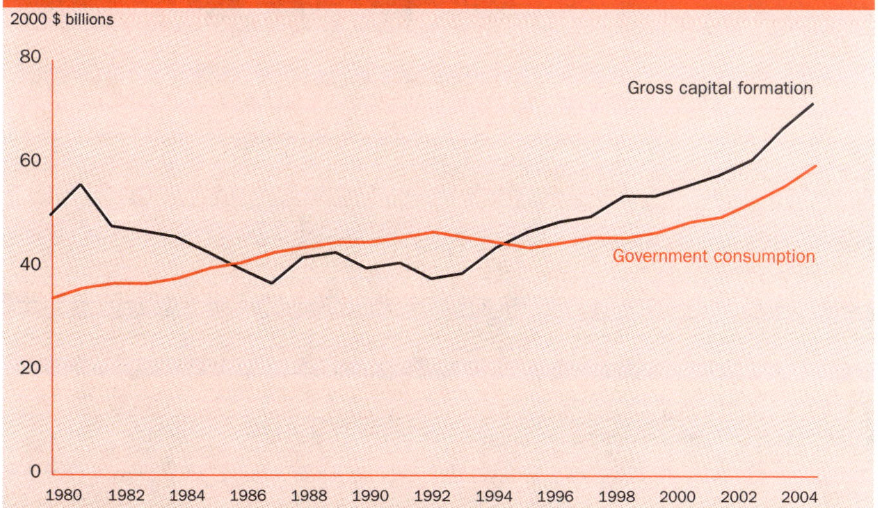

Gross capital formation has been increasing in Sub-Saharan Africa since the mid-1990s, after a decline in the previous decade.

Source: World Bank data files.

Definitions

• **Household final consumption expenditure** is the market value of all goods and services, including durable products (such as cars, washing machines, and home computers), purchased by households. It excludes purchases of dwellings but includes imputed rent for owner-occupied dwellings. It also includes payments and fees to governments to obtain permits and licenses. *World Development Indicators* includes in household consumption expenditure the expenditures of nonprofit institutions serving households, even when reported separately by the country. In practice, household consumption expenditure may include any statistical discrepancy in the use of resources relative to the supply of resources. • **General government final consumption expenditure** includes all government current expenditures for purchases of goods and services (including compensation of employees). It also includes most expenditures on national defense and security but excludes government military expenditures that potentially have wider public use and are part of government capital formation. • **Gross capital formation** consists of outlays on additions to the fixed assets of the economy, net changes in the level of inventories, and net acquisitions of valuables. Fixed assets include land improvements (fences, ditches, drains, and so on); plant, machinery, and equipment purchases; and the construction of roads, railways, and the like, including schools, offices, hospitals, private residential dwellings, and commercial and industrial buildings. Inventories are stocks of goods held by firms to meet temporary or unexpected fluctuations in production or sales, and "work in progress." • **Exports and imports of goods and services** represent the value of all goods and other market services provided to, or received from, the rest of the world. They include the value of merchandise, freight, insurance, transport, travel, royalties, license fees, and other services, such as communication, construction, financial, information, business, personal, and government services. They exclude compensation of employees and investment income (factor services in the 1968 SNA) as well as transfer payments.

Data sources

National accounts indicators for most developing countries are collected from national statistical organizations and central banks by visiting and resident World Bank missions. Data for high-income economies come from data files of the Organisation for Economic Co-operation and Development (see the OECD's *Annual National Accounts for OECD Member Countries: Data from 1970 Onwards*). The United Nations Statistics Division publishes detailed national accounts for UN member countries in *National Accounts Statistics: Main Aggregates and Detailed Tables* and updates in the *Monthly Bulletin of Statistics*.

4.10 Central government finances

	Revenue[a]		Expense		Cash surplus or deficit		Net incurrence of liabilities				Debt and interest payments	
	% of GDP		% of GDP		% of GDP		% of GDP Domestic		% of GDP Foreign		Total debt % of GDP	Interest payments % of revenue
	1995	2004	1995	2004	1995	2004	1995	2004	1995	2004	2004	2004
Afghanistan	..	4.6	..	13.2	..	–0.7	..	0.3	..	3.4	10.6	0.2
Albania[b]	21.2	..	25.6	..	–8.9	..	7.4	..	2.1	..	..	..
Algeria[b]	30.2	36.0	24.2	24.6	–1.3	1.2	–7.4	1.8	8.6	–1.7	48.1	8.6
Angola	..	..	..	..	..	..	..	..	..	..	..	..
Argentina	..	18.1	..	18.3	..	–0.5	..	1.4	..	1.5	..	26.5
Armenia[b]	..	19.9	..	18.6	..	–0.9	..	0.3	..	2.0	35.5	2.7
Australia	..	26.4	..	25.5	..	0.8	1.7	..	0.7	..	22.4	4.0
Austria	37.4	38.2	40.6	40.1	–2.9	–1.9	..	2.2	28.0	..	65.3	7.9
Azerbaijan[b]	18.0	..	19.8	..	–3.1	..	..	..	..	..	..	..
Bangladesh[b]	..	10.0	..	8.8	..	–0.7	..	2.3	..	0.9	36.2	16.4
Belarus[b]	30.0	30.6	28.7	28.5	–2.7	–0.2	2.2	0.7	0.4	0.5	12.3	1.5
Belgium	43.5	43.7	45.0	43.9	–1.2	–0.3	..	–4.6	..	1.8	139.8	11.4
Benin	..	..	..	..	..	..	..	..	..	..	..	..
Bolivia	..	20.2	..	27.2	..	–5.4	..	3.6	..	3.6	93.8	10.4
Bosnia and Herzegovina	..	41.2	..	38.6	..	1.8	..	0.1	..	1.0	..	1.5
Botswana[b]	40.5	..	30.3	..	4.9	..	0.2	..	–0.4	..	..	..
Brazil[b]	26.9	..	32.9	..	–2.7	..	..	..	..	..	..	..
Bulgaria[b]	35.5	38.2	39.4	35.3	–5.1	1.6	7.4	0.9	–0.8	–3.0	..	4.6
Burkina Faso	..	..	..	..	..	..	..	..	..	..	..	..
Burundi[b]	19.3	..	23.6	..	–4.7	..	3.0	..	4.0	..	..	..
Cambodia	..	10.7	..	9.1	..	–2.2	..	–0.7	..	2.6	..	1.9
Cameroon	11.3	..	13.1	..	–2.9	..	–0.4	..	3.5	..	..	..
Canada[b]	20.6	19.9	24.6	18.3	–4.4	1.4	5.0	–1.0	0.0	0.3	48.7	7.9
Central African Republic	..	..	..	..	..	..	..	..	..	..	..	..
Chad	..	..	..	..	..	..	..	..	..	..	..	..
Chile	..	22.3	..	18.4	..	2.2	..	–1.0	..	0.2	15.7	4.4
China	5.4	8.8	..	10.4	..	–2.4	1.6	..	..	..	..	7.6
Hong Kong, China	..	..	..	..	..	..	..	..	..	..	..	..
Colombia	..	17.1	..	22.9	..	–8.0	..	7.5	..	–1.7	57.7	27.4
Congo, Dem. Rep.[b]	5.3	7.9	8.2	7.8	0.0	–0.1	0.0	..	0.2	..	..	..
Congo, Rep.[b]	..	30.9	..	19.9	..	6.4	..	..	..	..	0.2	18.1
Costa Rica[b]	20.3	22.4	21.3	22.7	–2.1	–1.3	..	..	–0.8	1.4	38.3	18.3
Côte d'Ivoire	20.1	17.1	..	17.5	..	0.1	–1.2	2.4	3.8	6.8	104.3	15.5
Croatia[b]	43.1	41.9	42.5	42.0	–1.3	–4.0	–2.7	2.0	0.8	2.0	..	5.0
Cuba	..	..	..	..	..	..	..	..	..	..	..	..
Czech Republic	..	32.4	..	36.1	..	–3.3	..	0.6	..	3.0	21.4	3.1
Denmark	39.4	36.5	38.5	35.2	1.5	1.8	..	–2.5	..	..	42.8	8.4
Dominican Republic[b]	16.0	16.3	10.2	13.2	0.8	1.4	0.0	1.0	–1.0	2.3	..	9.4
Ecuador	14.1	..	12.0	..	..	..	..	..	..	..	..	..
Egypt, Arab Rep.[b]	34.8	..	28.1	..	3.4	..	..	..	..	..	..	..
El Salvador	..	15.5	..	17.0	..	–3.3	..	2.0	..	0.6	49.0	14.4
Eritrea	..	..	..	..	..	..	..	..	..	..	..	..
Estonia[b]	32.8	28.0	32.0	26.7	0.6	0.9	–0.2	0.0	0.9	–0.1	2.5	0.6
Ethiopia[b]	..	18.5	..	26.7	..	–9.8	..	1.2	..	9.2	..	7.6
Finland	40.2	39.1	38.9	36.9	1.9	2.5	0.3	–0.6	–1.3	3.8	45.9	4.3
France	43.3	43.3	46.5	47.1	–2.9	–3.5	..	2.0	..	1.6	70.7	5.9
Gabon	..	..	..	..	..	..	..	..	..	..	..	..
Gambia, The	..	..	..	..	..	..	..	..	..	..	..	..
Georgia[b]	12.2	15.8	15.4	14.4	–4.3	0.5	2.2	0.1	2.4	0.3	43.2	8.2
Germany	29.9	28.6	38.6	31.3	–8.3	–2.4	–0.6	..	3.2	..	..	6.1
Ghana	17.0	23.8	..	20.9	..	–2.9	..	..	..	3.3	..	14.4
Greece	45.4	..	45.6	..	–2.6	..	..	..	..	..	..	..
Guatemala[b]	8.4	10.6	7.6	11.1	–0.5	–0.9	..	0.8	0.4	1.7	19.0	10.9
Guinea	13.4	..	10.5	..	–3.2	..	–0.1	..	4.2	..	..	..
Guinea-Bissau	..	..	..	..	..	..	..	..	..	..	..	..
Haiti	..	..	..	..	..	..	..	..	..	..	..	..

Central government finances

	Revenue[a]		Expense		Cash surplus or deficit		Net incurrence of liabilities				Debt and interest payments	
	% of GDP		% of GDP		% of GDP		% of GDP Domestic		Foreign		Total debt % of GDP	Interest payments % of revenue
	1995	2004	1995	2004	1995	2004	1995	2004	1995	2004	2004	2004
Honduras	..	..	..	..	..	..	..	..	..	..	..	..
Hungary	..	*37.1*	..	*41.6*	..	*-6.2*	..	*0.3*	..	*5.4*	*58.2*	*10.9*
India[b]	12.3	12.6	14.5	15.9	-2.2	-3.6	5.2	3.6	0.0	0.3	65.8	31.9
Indonesia[b]	17.7	18.3	9.7	16.8	3.0	-1.1	*-0.6*	0.0	-0.4	-0.4	28.7	14.8
Iran, Islamic Rep.[b]	23.0	28.9	15.1	20.2	1.1	3.6	..	1.2	0.1	-1.8	..	0.8
Iraq	..	..	..	..	..	..	..	..	..	..	..	..
Ireland[b]	25.4	..	28.6	..	-2.0	..	..	..	..	..	..	..
Israel	..	41.6	..	48.8	..	-4.8	4.9	..	0.1	..	*98.1*	13.3
Italy	*38.9*	*37.7*	*41.7*	*40.0*	*-2.9*	*-2.3*	..	..	..	..	..	*13.8*
Jamaica[b]	..	*32.0*	33.3	*41.1*	..	*-9.7*	..	..	..	..	*145.0*	*59.2*
Japan	*20.6*	..	..	..	..	..	*1.5*	..	..	..	..	..
Jordan[b]	28.2	25.6	26.1	31.9	0.9	-1.4	-2.5	3.0	6.1	-3.0	88.2	5.8
Kazakhstan[b]	*14.0*	16.0	*18.7*	14.9	*-1.8*	0.2	*0.8*	1.2	*2.8*	-0.9	*13.2*	3.6
Kenya[b]	26.0	*18.2*	25.5	*20.6*	-1.1	*-2.4*	*4.3*	*4.5*	0.0	*-4.1*	..	*18.0*
Korea, Dem. Rep.	..	..	..	..	..	..	..	..	..	..	..	..
Korea, Rep.[b]	17.8	*22.8*	14.3	*18.6*	2.4	*2.9*	-0.3	*-2.3*	-0.1	*-0.1*	..	*5.1*
Kuwait[b]	36.8	*54.4*	46.4	*43.3*	-13.6	*6.5*	..	..	..	..	..	*0.3*
Kyrgyz Republic[b]	16.7	*16.1*	25.6	*15.8*	-10.8	*-0.8*	..	..	..	..	*99.3*	*8.4*
Lao PDR	..	..	..	..	..	..	..	..	..	..	..	..
Latvia[b]	25.8	25.9	28.3	28.1	-2.7	-1.0	2.4	0.4	1.5	1.7	*13.8*	2.4
Lebanon	..	*20.6*	..	*30.8*	..	*-13.4*	..	*5.2*	..	*6.9*	..	*80.0*
Lesotho[b]	49.8	49.7	34.4	38.0	5.1	5.3	*0.0*	..	6.2	..	..	3.8
Liberia	..	..	..	..	..	..	..	..	..	..	..	..
Libya	..	..	..	..	..	..	..	..	..	..	..	..
Lithuania	..	28.1	..	28.8	..	-1.6	..	-0.3	..	0.6	23.6	3.4
Macedonia, FYR	..	..	..	..	..	..	..	..	..	..	..	..
Madagascar	..	60.4	..	63.0	..	-22.5	..	-3.6	..	31.8	*483.8*	14.5
Malawi	..	..	..	..	..	..	..	..	..	..	..	..
Malaysia[b]	24.4	*23.7*	17.2	*20.1*	2.4	*-4.3*	..	..	-0.8	..	..	*10.5*
Mali	..	..	..	..	..	..	..	..	..	..	..	..
Mauritania	..	..	..	..	..	..	..	..	..	..	..	..
Mauritius[b]	21.6	21.8	19.9	21.8	-1.3	-3.2	3.1	-1.6	-0.6	-0.3	42.7	13.9
Mexico[b]	15.3	..	15.0	..	-0.6	..	..	..	5.5	..	..	..
Moldova[b]	28.4	28.8	*38.4*	27.1	*-6.3*	0.4	*3.0*	2.4	*2.7*	-1.9	52.0	8.2
Mongolia	..	*37.9*	..	*30.8*	..	*-0.5*	..	*11.3*	..	*-6.8*	*119.8*	*3.1*
Morocco[b]	27.6	..	28.6	..	-4.5	..	5.6	..	-0.7	..	..	..
Mozambique	..	..	..	..	..	..	..	..	..	..	..	..
Myanmar	6.4	*4.7*	..	..	..	..	..	..	..	..	..	..
Namibia[b]	31.7	*28.1*	*35.7*	*31.1*	*-5.0*	*-6.8*	..	*-20.0*	..	*-0.1*	..	*9.1*
Nepal	10.5	12.2	..	..	..	..	*0.6*	0.1	*2.5*	1.4	66.7	11.7
Netherlands	..	41.1	..	42.6	..	-1.7	..	0.9	3.3	..	54.3	5.5
New Zealand	..	35.8	..	31.5	..	3.7	..	-0.4	..	-0.3	45.4	4.7
Nicaragua[b]	15.0	21.3	16.3	19.7	0.6	-1.0	..	..	*3.4*	..	..	8.3
Niger	..	..	..	..	..	..	..	..	..	..	..	..
Nigeria	..	..	..	..	..	..	..	..	..	..	..	..
Norway	..	49.3	..	37.2	..	11.8	..	*2.3*	..	*6.9*	*37.7*	2.1
Oman[b]	27.8	*27.0*	32.4	*26.9*	-8.9	*-2.8*	-0.1	*3.0*	0.0	*-2.1*	*19.9*	*4.5*
Pakistan[b]	17.2	13.8	19.1	14.7	-5.3	-2.0	..	..	..	..	..	39.9
Panama[b]	26.1	*25.6*	22.0	*23.2*	1.5	*0.9*	..	..	..	..	..	*19.3*
Papua New Guinea[b]	23.9	*23.8*	25.8	*23.4*	-0.5	*-2.4*	1.5	*5.2*	-0.7	*-2.3*	*73.9*	*19.9*
Paraguay[b]	15.3	16.9	13.0	12.9	0.1	1.4	*0.0*	-1.2	*-0.8*	-0.2	..	6.2
Peru[b]	17.1	16.7	17.1	16.9	-1.3	-1.2	*0.2*	1.1	3.9	3.6	..	11.9
Philippines[b]	17.7	14.8	*15.9*	..	*-0.8*	..	-0.5	4.0	-0.7	1.8	70.1	39.7
Poland[b]	..	*35.0*	..	*39.3*	..	*-3.4*	..	*3.7*	..	*0.4*	*43.2*	*7.7*
Portugal	*37.1*	*37.8*	*39.7*	*41.9*	*-3.1*	*-2.3*	*-3.7*	*1.2*	*4.3*	*3.2*	..	*7.5*
Puerto Rico	..	..	..	..	..	..	..	..	..	..	..	..

Central government finances

	Revenue[a]		Expense		Cash surplus or deficit		Net incurrence of liabilities				Debt and interest payments	
							% of GDP					Interest payments
	% of GDP		% of GDP		% of GDP		Domestic		Foreign		Total debt % of GDP	% of revenue
	1995	2004	1995	2004	1995	2004	1995	2004	1995	2004	2004	2004
Romania[b]	..	25.8	..	25.9	..	–2.0	..	0.4	..	1.7	..	8.4
Russian Federation	..	27.3	..	21.9	..	5.4	..	–0.1	..	–1.3	41.4	4.0
Rwanda	10.6	..	15.0	..	–5.6	..	2.9	..	..	..	..	..
Saudi Arabia	..	..	..	..	..	..	..	..	..	..	..	..
Senegal[b]	16.6	18.0	..	15.6	..	–2.2	..	1.4	..	1.6	73.6	4.6
Serbia and Montenegro[b]	..	35.8	..	39.9	..	–3.0	..	..	..	..	..	2.6
Sierra Leone	9.4	..	..	..	..	..	0.3	..	..	..	..	..
Singapore[b]	26.8	20.2	12.5	15.5	19.9	4.2	10.3	9.3	0.0	..	109.6	0.8
Slovak Republic	..	35.2	..	36.8	..	–3.3	..	2.9	..	–0.2	46.5	7.0
Slovenia[b]	37.2	40.7	35.7	41.2	–0.2	–1.3	–0.4	2.3	0.3	–0.8	..	3.6
Somalia	..	..	..	..	..	..	..	..	..	..	..	..
South Africa[b]	..	27.8	..	29.4	..	–1.9	..	2.9	..	0.4	36.9	12.7
Spain	29.2	26.0	33.0	29.7	–2.6	0.6	3.4	0.1	..	..	..	6.6
Sri Lanka[b]	20.4	16.4	26.0	22.9	–7.6	–7.6	5.2	7.0	3.2	0.1	105.5	43.6
Sudan[b]	7.0	..	6.6	..	–0.4	..	0.3	..	..	..	..	..
Swaziland[b]	..	25.5	..	23.2	..	–2.3	..	..	..	..	..	4.7
Sweden	40.7	38.0	39.3	37.5	2.2	0.3	..	1.6	..	0.5	62.4	5.3
Switzerland[b]	22.7	19.4	25.8	19.1	–0.6	0.6	–0.5	–0.6	..	..	28.5	4.5
Syrian Arab Republic[b]	22.9	..	..	..	..	..	..	..	..	..	..	..
Tajikistan[b]	9.3	13.5	11.4	13.8	–3.3	–6.6	0.1	–0.2	2.3	0.2	79.8	5.1
Tanzania	..	..	..	..	..	..	..	..	..	..	..	..
Thailand	..	19.6	..	17.1	..	0.6	..	4.0	..	–0.3	26.1	6.7
Togo	..	..	..	..	..	..	..	..	..	..	..	..
Trinidad and Tobago[b]	27.2	..	25.3	..	–0.1	..	2.8	..	2.6	..	..	..
Tunisia[b]	30.1	29.7	28.4	28.4	–2.5	–2.4	0.9	0.9	2.9	0.6	59.6	9.4
Turkey[b]	17.9	..	21.0	..	–4.1	..	5.5	..	..	..	..	..
Turkmenistan	..	..	..	..	..	..	..	..	..	..	..	..
Uganda[b]	10.6	12.1	..	22.8	..	–3.8	..	0.5	..	4.2	..	6.5
Ukraine[b]	..	30.7	..	33.0	..	–3.2	..	2.9	..	0.2	..	2.8
United Arab Emirates[b]	10.1	..	9.3	..	0.5	..	..	..	..	..	..	..
United Kingdom	37.3	36.6	37.2	39.9	0.3	–3.2	–0.3	3.6	0.0	0.0	..	5.4
United States	..	17.2	..	20.9	..	–3.8	..	0.1	..	3.0	38.1	11.0
Uruguay[b]	27.6	26.5	27.1	27.5	–1.2	–2.5	7.9	–0.5	1.1	1.8	88.5	18.5
Uzbekistan	..	..	..	..	..	..	..	..	..	..	..	..
Venezuela, RB[b]	16.9	24.0	18.5	25.2	–2.3	–4.1	1.1	6.3	0.1	0.2	..	19.5
Vietnam	..	..	..	..	..	..	..	..	..	..	..	..
West Bank and Gaza	..	..	..	..	..	..	..	..	..	..	..	..
Yemen, Rep.[b]	17.3	..	19.1	..	–3.9	..	..	..	..	..	..	..
Zambia[b]	20.0	..	21.4	..	–3.1	..	28.0	..	16.2	..	..	..
Zimbabwe[b]	26.7	..	32.1	..	–5.4	..	–1.4	..	1.6	..	..	..
World	.. w	24.6 w	.. w	27.3 w	.. w	–2.7 w	.. m	.. m	.. m	.. m	.. m	7.9 m
Low income	13.5	13.0	15.5	15.5	–2.6	–3.2	..	..	..	..	..	..
Middle income	17.3	..	..	..	..	..	..	1.1	..	0.8	..	9.1
Lower middle income	16.7	..	..	..	..	..	..	0.9	..	1.1	..	8.5
Upper middle income	..	..	..	..	..	..	..	2.9	..	0.6	..	10.5
Low & middle income	16.7	..	..	..	..	..	..	..	..	..	..	..
East Asia & Pacific	8.4	11.5	..	12.0	..	–2.1	..	..	..	..	..	7.6
Europe & Central Asia	..	31.0	..	31.1	..	–1.2	..	0.9	..	0.4	..	3.5
Latin America & Carib.	20.9	..	23.0	..	–0.4	..	..	1.0	..	2.3	..	11.9
Middle East & N. Africa	28.3	..	23.5	..	0.0	..	..	..	..	..	..	..
South Asia	13.2	12.4	15.4	15.1	–2.7	–3.1	3.8	1.3	1.1	1.1	65.8	16.4
Sub-Saharan Africa	..	..	..	..	..	..	..	..	..	..	..	..
High income	..	26.0	..	28.9	..	–2.8	..	1.2	..	..	..	6.0
Europe EMU	36.3	35.7	38.8	38.6	–2.3	–2.3	..	1.1	..	..	..	6.4

a. Excluding grants. b. Data were reported on a cash basis and have been adjusted to the accrual framework.

Central government finances 4.10

About the data

Tables 4.10–4.12 present an overview of the size and role of central governments relative to national economies. The data in these tables are based on the concepts and recommendations of the second edition of the International Monetary Fund's (IMF) *Government Finance Statistics Manual 2001*. Before 2005, *World Development Indicators* reported data derived on the basis of the 1986 manual. The 2001 manual, which is harmonized with the 1993 System of National Accounts, recommends an accrual accounting method instead of the cash-based method of the 1986 manual. The new manual focuses on all economic events affecting assets, liabilities, revenues, and expenses, instead of only those represented by cash transactions. The new manual takes all stocks into account, so that the stock data at the end of an accounting period is equal to the stock data at the beginning of the period plus the flows during the period. The 1986 manual considered only the debt stock data. Further, the new manual does not distinguish between current and capital revenue or expenditures, unlike the 1986 manual. The new manual also introduces the concepts of nonfinancial and financial assets. Most countries still follow the previous manual, however. The IMF has reclassified historical *Government Finance Statistics Yearbook* data to conform to the format of the 2001 manual. Because of differences in reporting, the reclassified data understate both revenue and expense.

Government Finance Statistics Manual 2001 describes the economic functions of a government as the provision of goods and services to the community on a nonmarket basis for collective or individual consumption, and the redistribution of income and wealth through transfer payments. The activities of government are financed mainly by taxation and other transfers of income, though other forms of financing such as borrowing for temporary periods can also be used. The definition of government excludes public corporations and quasi corporations (such as the central bank).

Units of government meeting this definition exist at many levels, from local administrative units to the highest level of national government, but inadequate statistical coverage precludes the presentation of subnational data. Although data for general government are available for a few countries under the 2001 manual, only data for the central government are shown to minimize disparities. However, cross-country comparisons are potentially misleading due to different accounting concepts of central government.

Central government can refer to one of two accounting concepts: consolidated or budgetary. For most countries central government finance data have been consolidated into one account, but for others only budgetary central government accounts are available. Countries reporting budgetary data are noted in *Primary data documentation*. Because budgetary accounts do not necessarily include all central government units (such as extrabudgetary accounts and social security funds), the picture they provide of central government activities is usually incomplete.

Data on government revenues and expenditures are collected by the IMF through questionnaires distributed to member governments and by the Organisation for Economic Co-operation and Development. Despite the IMF's efforts to systematize and standardize the collection of public finance data, statistics on public finance are often incomplete, untimely, and not comparable across countries.

Government finance statistics are reported in local currency. The indicators here are shown as percentages of GDP. Many countries report government finance data by fiscal year; see *Primary data documentation* for information on fiscal year end by country.

4.10a

Selected developing countries with large cash deficits

Central government cash deficit as a share of GDP (%)

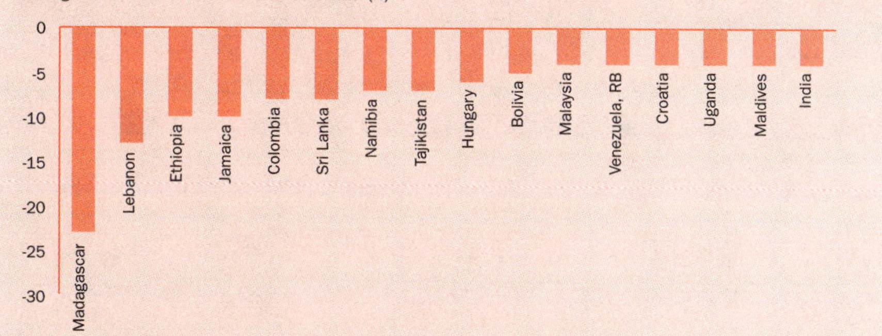

Sixteen developing economies had a cash deficit of about 4 percent of GDP.

Note: Data for 2004 refer to the most recent year for which dara are available in 2002–04.

Source: International Monetary Fund, Government Finance Statistics data files.

Definitions

• **Revenue** is cash receipts from taxes, social contributions, and other revenues such as fines, fees, rent, and income from property or sales. Grants are also considered as revenue but are excluded here. • **Expense** is cash payments for operating activities of the government in providing goods and services. It includes compensation of employees (such as wages and salaries), interest and subsidies, grants, social benefits, and other expenses such as rent and dividends. • **Cash surplus or deficit** is revenue (including grants) minus expense, minus net acquisition of nonfinancial assets. In the earlier version nonfinancial assets were included under revenue and expenditure in gross terms. This cash surplus or deficit is closest to the earlier overall budget balance (still missing is lending minus repayments, which are brought in below as a financing item under net acquisition of financial assets). • **Net incurrence of government liabilities** includes **domestic financing** (obtained from residents) and **foreign financing** (obtained from nonresidents), or the means by which a government provides financial resources to cover a budget deficit or allocates financial resources arising from a budget surplus. The net incurrence of liabilities should be offset by the net acquisition of financial assets (a third financing item). The difference between the cash surplus or deficit and the three financing items is the net change in the stock of cash. • **Total debt** is the entire stock of direct government fixed-term contractual obligations to others outstanding on a particular date. It includes domestic and foreign liabilities such as currency and money deposits, securities other than shares, and loans. It is the gross amount of government liabilities reduced by the amount of equity and financial derivatives held by the government. Because debt is a stock rather than a flow, it is measured as of a given date, usually the last day of the fiscal year. • **Interest payments** include interest payments on government debt—including long-term bonds, long-term loans, and other debt instruments —to domestic and foreign residents.

Data sources

Data on central government finances are from the IMF's *Government Finance Statistics Yearbook, 2005* and IMF data files. Each country's accounts are reported using the system of common definitions and classifications in the IMF's *Government Finance Statistics Manual 2001*. See these sources for complete and authoritative explanations of concepts, definitions, and data sources.

4.11 Central government expenses

	Goods and services % of expense		Compensation of employees % of expense		Interest payments % of expense		Subsidies and other transfers % of expense		Other expense % of expense	
	1995	2004	1995	2004	1995	2004	1995	2004	1995	2004
Afghanistan	..	51	..	42	..	0	..	5	..	2
Albania[a]	18	..	14	..	9	..	59	..	0	..
Algeria[a]	6	6	39	32	13	12	34	50	8	..
Angola	..	..	..	..	..	..	..	..	..	..
Argentina	..	5	..	12	..	26	..	50	..	7
Armenia[a]	..	42	..	17	..	3	..	32	..	6
Australia	..	10	..	10	..	4	..	70	..	5
Austria	7	5	13	13	8	8	65	70	7	5
Azerbaijan[a]	49	..	10	..	0	..	41	..	0	..
Bangladesh[a]	..	17	..	25	..	20	..	29	..	9
Belarus[a]	39	19	5	13	1	2	55	64	0	3
Belgium	2	3	7	7	15	11	71	75	4	4
Benin	..	..	..	..	..	..	..	..	..	..
Bolivia	..	17	..	24	..	9	..	44	..	5
Bosnia and Herzegovina	..	24	..	28	..	2	..	42	..	5
Botswana[a]	32	..	30	..	2	..	36	..	2	..
Brazil[a]	12	..	9	..	14	..	66	..	..	..
Bulgaria[a]	18	22	7	11	37	5	38	59	2	3
Burkina Faso	..	..	..	..	..	..	..	..	..	..
Burundi[a]	20	..	30	..	6	..	14	..	10	..
Cambodia	..	32	..	36	..	3	..	18	..	12
Cameroon	13	..	47	..	24	..	13	..	..	..
Canada[a]	8	8	10	11	18	9	64	66	..	6
Central African Republic	..	..	..	..	..	..	..	..	..	..
Chad	..	..	..	..	..	..	..	..	..	..
Chile	..	9	..	22	..	5	..	55	..	8
China	..	..	..	..	..	7	..	62	..	0
Hong Kong, China	..	..	..	..	..	..	..	..	..	..
Colombia	..	8	..	14	..	20	..	25	..	32
Congo, Dem. Rep.[a]	37	36	58	21	1	..	2	43	..	..
Congo, Rep.[a]	..	29	..	37	..	29	..	5	..	0
Costa Rica[a]	12	12	38	43	20	18	26	26	4	2
Côte d'Ivoire	..	30	..	39	..	16	..	16	..	1
Croatia[a]	35	7	27	27	3	5	32	55	3	6
Cuba	..	..	..	..	..	..	..	..	..	..
Czech Republic	..	6	..	8	..	3	..	74	..	9
Denmark	8	10	13	13	13	9	62	64	4	4
Dominican Republic[a]	16	16	41	45	9	12	19	15	6	12
Ecuador	6	..	49	..	26	..	..	..	..	..
Egypt, Arab Rep.[a]	18	..	22	..	26	..	6	..	..	..
El Salvador	..	13	..	42	..	13	..	5	..	27
Eritrea	..	..	..	..	..	..	..	..	..	..
Estonia[a]	33	32	14	10	1	1	46	58	0	0
Ethiopia[a]	..	24	..	14	..	7	..	42	..	14
Finland	10	10	10	10	9	5	65	68	7	7
France	7	7	23	22	6	5	58	58	5	7
Gabon	..	..	..	..	..	..	..	..	..	..
Gambia, The	..	..	..	..	..	..	..	..	..	..
Georgia[a]	52	22	11	16	10	10	26	50	..	1
Germany	4	4	5	5	6	6	66	81	20	4
Ghana	..	..	..	45	..	21	..	5	..	..
Greece	10	..	24	..	20	..	40	..	6	..
Guatemala[a]	15	12	50	28	12	11	18	21	6	29
Guinea	31	..	47	..	13	..	10	..	0	..
Guinea-Bissau	..	..	..	..	..	..	..	..	..	..
Haiti	..	..	..	..	..	..	..	..	..	..

Central government expenses

	Goods and services		Compensation of employees		Interest payments		Subsidies and other transfers		Other expense	
	% of expense		% of expense		% of expense		% of expense		% of expense	
	1995	2004	1995	2004	1995	2004	1995	2004	1995	2004
Honduras	..	..	..	..	..	..	..	..	..	..
Hungary	..	*8*	..	*14*	..	*10*	..	*60*	..	*8*
India[a]	14	15	10	10	27	26	33	..	0	..
Indonesia[a]	21	8	20	13	16	16	41	63	2	0
Iran, Islamic Rep.[a]	21	12	56	45	0	1	..	34	..	7
Iraq	..	..	..	..	..	..	..	..	..	..
Ireland[a]	5	..	13	..	15	..	63	..	4	..
Israel	..	26	..	24	..	12	..	29	..	8
Italy	*4*	*4*	*15*	*16*	*19*	*13*	*57*	*61*	*5*	*5*
Jamaica[a]	22	*13*	24	*32*	32	*46*	1	*2*	21	*8*
Japan	..	..	..	..	..	..	..	..	..	..
Jordan[a]	7	6	67	58	11	6	12	18	4	12
Kazakhstan[a]	..	25	..	9	*3*	4	*58*	54	..	8
Kenya[a]	17	*32*	32	*47*	30	*17*	..	*1*	1	*3*
Korea, Dem. Rep.	..	..	..	..	..	..	..	..	..	..
Korea, Rep.[a]	16	*12*	15	*11*	3	*6*	63	*56*	3	*15*
Kuwait[a]	33	*27*	31	*34*	5	*0*	24	*27*	7	*13*
Kyrgyz Republic[a]	32	*34*	36	*41*	5	*9*	27	*17*	..	..
Lao PDR	..	..	..	..	..	..	..	..	..	..
Latvia[a]	20	12	20	16	3	2	56	44	0	25
Lebanon	..	*3*	..	*30*	..	*54*	..	*12*	..	*2*
Lesotho[a]	32	31	45	38	5	5	*8*	26	*3*	..
Liberia	..	..	..	..	..	..	..	..	..	..
Libya	..	..	..	..	..	..	..	..	..	..
Lithuania	..	12	..	18	..	3	..	58	..	8
Macedonia, FYR	..	..	..	..	..	..	..	..	..	..
Madagascar	..	14	..	39	..	23	..	11	..	13
Malawi	..	..	..	..	..	..	..	..	..	..
Malaysia[a]	23	*26*	34	*30*	17	*12*	27	*31*	1	*1*
Mali	..	..	..	..	..	..	..	..	..	..
Mauritania	..	..	..	..	..	..	..	..	..	..
Mauritius[a]	12	12	45	39	12	14	28	32	2	3
Mexico[a]	9	..	19	..	19	..	..	..	..	..
Moldova[a]	*10*	18	*8*	15	*11*	9	*71*	49	*1*	9
Mongolia	..	*36*	..	*30*	..	*4*	..	*31*	..	*0*
Morocco[a]	17	..	39	..	21	..	19	..	4	..
Mozambique	..	..	..	..	..	..	..	..	..	..
Myanmar	..	..	..	..	..	..	..	..	..	..
Namibia[a]	*28*	*28*	*53*	*49*	*1*	*8*	..	*14*	*4*	*2*
Nepal	..	..	..	..	..	..	..	..	..	..
Netherlands	..	7	..	8	..	5	..	76	..	3
New Zealand	..	26	..	25	..	5	..	36	..	6
Nicaragua[a]	16	15	23	30	15	10	34	42	13	2
Niger	..	..	..	..	..	..	..	..	..	..
Nigeria	..	..	..	..	..	..	..	..	..	..
Norway	..	12	..	16	..	3	..	64	..	5
Oman[a]	55	*54*	30	*32*	7	*5*	8	*10*	0	..
Pakistan[a]	..	31	..	5	28	39	2	25	..	..
Panama[a]	16	*16*	45	*37*	8	*21*	30	*25*	1	..
Papua New Guinea[a]	19	*35*	36	*28*	20	*21*	26	*16*	*1*	..
Paraguay[a]	12	8	51	52	5	8	31	28	0	3
Peru[a]	21	21	18	21	19	12	33	44	8	2
Philippines[a]	*15*	..	*34*	..	*33*	..	*15*	..	..	..
Poland[a]	..	*13*	..	*12*	..	*7*	..	*60*	..	*7*
Portugal	*7*	*7*	*30*	*32*	*10*	*7*	*41*	*45*	*11*	*9*
Puerto Rico	..	..	..	..	..	..	..	..	..	..

4.11 Central government expenses

	Goods and services		Compensation of employees		Interest payments		Subsidies and other transfers		Other expense	
	% of expense		% of expense		% of expense		% of expense		% of expense	
	1995	2004	1995	2004	1995	2004	1995	2004	1995	2004
Romania[a]	..	*22*	..	*16*	..	*8*	..	*43*	..	*12*
Russian Federation	..	23	..	18	..	5	..	46	..	8
Rwanda	*52*	..	*36*	..	*12*	..	*5*	..	..	..
Saudi Arabia	..	..	..	..	..	..	..	..	..	..
Senegal[a]	..	*25*	..	*34*	..	*6*	..	*34*	..	..
Serbia and Montenegro[a]	..	*10*	..	*14*	..	*2*	..	*68*	..	*6*
Sierra Leone	..	..	..	..	..	..	..	..	..	..
Singapore[a]	38	35	39	31	8	1	15	33	..	..
Slovak Republic	..	*12*	..	*13*	..	*7*	..	*63*	..	*5*
Slovenia[a]	19	16	21	19	3	4	55	59	3	2
Somalia	..	..	..	..	..	..	..	..	..	..
South Africa[a]	..	12	..	14	..	12	..	56	..	6
Spain	*5*	*6*	*18*	*17*	*11*	*7*	*59*	*66*	*7*	*4*
Sri Lanka[a]	23	*14*	20	*25*	22	*32*	24	*22*	10	*7*
Sudan[a]	*44*	..	*38*	..	*8*	..	*10*	..	..	..
Swaziland[a]	..	*4*	..	*44*	..	*5*	..	*22*	..	*25*
Sweden	*11*	*12*	*9*	*11*	*13*	*5*	*62*	*65*	*5*	*7*
Switzerland[a]	24	*9*	6	*7*	4	*5*	66	*74*	0	*5*
Syrian Arab Republic[a]	..	..	..	..	..	..	..	..	..	..
Tajikistan[a]	*47*	29	*8*	9	*12*	5	*33*	27	..	30
Tanzania	..	..	..	..	..	..	..	..	..	..
Thailand	..	21	..	32	..	8	..	33	..	7
Togo	..	..	..	..	..	..	..	..	..	..
Trinidad and Tobago[a]	20	..	36	..	20	..	24	..	*1*	..
Tunisia[a]	7	7	37	40	13	10	36	..	7	..
Turkey[a]	8	..	32	..	13	..	*31*	..	*4*	..
Turkmenistan	..	..	..	..	..	..	..	..	..	..
Uganda[a]	..	*36*	..	*11*	..	*6*	..	*47*	..	..
Ukraine[a]	..	11	..	16	..	3	..	62	..	8
United Arab Emirates[a]	*50*	..	*37*	..	..	..	..	..	..	..
United Kingdom	*22*	19	*7*	13	*9*	5	*53*	53	*9*	10
United States	..	16	..	13	..	9	..	60	..	2
Uruguay[a]	13	14	17	22	6	18	64	46	0	..
Uzbekistan	..	..	..	..	..	..	..	..	..	..
Venezuela, RB[a]	6	*8*	22	*19*	27	*19*	*61*	*53*	2	*2*
Vietnam	..	..	..	..	..	..	..	..	..	..
West Bank and Gaza	..	..	..	..	..	..	..	..	..	..
Yemen, Rep.[a]	8	..	67	..	16	..	8	..	*0*	..
Zambia[a]	*32*	..	*35*	..	*16*	..	*19*	..	*0*	..
Zimbabwe[a]	16	..	34	..	31	..	19	..	..	..
World	.. m	.. m	.. m	.. m	.. m	.. m	.. m	.. m	.. m	.. m
Low income	..	..	..	..	..	..	..	..	..	..
Middle income	..	..	..	..	..	..	..	..	..	..
Lower middle income	..	..	..	..	..	..	..	..	..	..
Upper middle income	..	*13*	..	*20*	..	*13*	..	*50*	..	..
Low & middle income	..	..	..	..	..	..	..	..	..	..
East Asia & Pacific	..	..	..	..	..	..	..	..	..	..
Europe & Central Asia	..	20	..	16	..	4	..	52	..	8
Latin America & Carib.	*14*	*13*	*36*	*29*	*15*	*14*	..	*26*	..	..
Middle East & N. Africa	13	..	39	..	13	..	12	..	..	..
South Asia	32	38	23	26	22	12	15	8	..	..
Sub-Saharan Africa	..	..	..	..	..	..	..	..	..	..
High income	..	*10*	..	*16*	..	..	..	*61*	..	..
Europe EMU	*7*	*6*	*15*	*13*	*9*	*6*	*59*	*68*	*6*	*5*

Note: Components may not sum to 100 percent because of missing data.
a. Data were reported on a cash basis and have been adjusted to the accrual framework.

Central government expenses

About the data

The term *expense* replaced *expenditure* in this table in the 2005 edition of *World Development Indicators* in accordance with use in the International Monetary Fund's (IMF) *Government Finance Statistics Manual 2001*. Government expenses include all nonrepayable payments, whether current or capital, requited or unrequited. Total central government expense as presented in the IMF's *Government Finance Statistics Yearbook* is comparable to the concept used in the 1993 System of National Accounts.

Expenses can be measured either by function (health, defense, education) or by economic type (interest payments, wages and salaries, purchases of goods and services). Functional data are often incomplete, and coverage varies by country because functional responsibilities stretch across levels of government for which no data are available. Defense expenses, usually the central government's responsibility, are shown in table 5.7. For more information on education expenses, see table 2.10; for more on health expenses, see table 2.14.

The classification of expenses by economic type in this table shows whether the government produces goods and services and distributes them, purchases the goods and services from a third party and distributes them, or transfers cash to households to make the purchases directly. When the government produces and provides goods and services, the cost is reflected in compensation of employees, use of goods and services, and consumption of fixed capital. Purchases from a third party and cash transfers to households are shown as subsidies and other transfers, and other expenses. The economic classification can be problematic. For example, the distinction between current and capital expense may be arbitrary, and subsidies to public corporations or banks may be disguised as capital financing. Subsidies may also be hidden in special contractual pricing for goods and services. For further discussion of government finance statistics, see *About the data* for tables 4.10 and 4.12.

4.11a

Interest payments are a large part of government expenditure for some developing economies

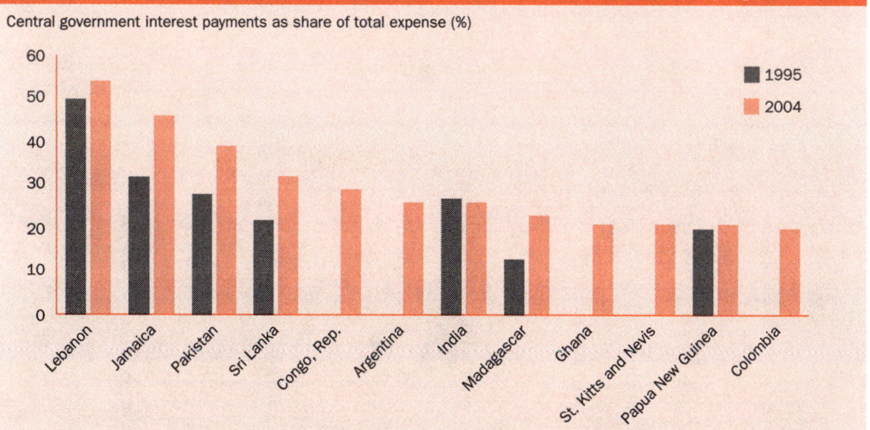

Interest payments accounted for over 20 percent of total expense in 2004 for 12 countries.

Note: Data for 2004 refer to the most recent year for which data are available in 2002–04. For Lebanon and Madagascar data for 1995 refer to 2000. And no data for 1995 are available for Republic of Congo, Argentina, Ghana, St. Kitts and Nevis, and Colombia.

Source: International Monetary Fund, Government Finance Statistics data files.

Definitions

• **Goods and services** include all government payments in exchange for goods and services used for the production of market and nonmarket goods and services. Own-account capital formation is excluded. • **Compensation of employees** consists of all payments in cash, as well as in kind (such as food and housing), to employees in return for services rendered, and government contributions to social insurance schemes such as social security and pensions that provide benefits to employees. • **Interest payments** are payments made to nonresidents, to residents, and to other general government units for the use of borrowed money. (Repayment of principal is shown as a financing item, and commission charges are shown as purchases of services.) • **Subsidies and other transfers** include all unrequited, nonrepayable transfers on current account to private and public enterprises; grants to foreign governments, international organizations, and other government units; and social security, social assistance benefits, and employer social benefits in cash and in kind. • **Other expense** is spending on dividends, rent, and other miscellaneous expenses, including provision for consumption of fixed capital.

Data sources

Data on central government expenses are from the IMF's *Government Finance Statistics Yearbook, 2005* and IMF data files. Each country's accounts are reported using the system of common definitions and classifications in the IMF's *Government Finance Statistics Manual 2001*. See these sources for complete and authoritative explanations of concepts, definitions, and data sources.

4.12 Central government revenues

	Taxes on income, profits, and capital gains % of revenue		Taxes on goods and services % of revenue		Taxes on international trade % of revenue		Other taxes % of revenue		Social contributions % of revenue		Grants and other revenue % of revenue	
	1995	2004	1995	2004	1995	2004	1995	2004	1995	2004	1995	2004
Afghanistan	..	3	..	3	..	18	..	1	..	1	..	75
Albania[a]	8	..	39	..	14	..	1	..	15	..	22	..
Algeria[a]	65	*66*	10	*9*	18	*13*	1	*1*	..	..	5	*11*
Angola	..	..	..	..	..	..	..	..	..	..	..	..
Argentina	..	19	..	29	..	16	..	14	..	17	..	5
Armenia[a]	..	15	..	31	..	3	..	25	..	14	..	12
Australia	..	62	..	25	..	2	..	2	..	..	..	9
Austria	*24*	*25*	*24*	*25*	*0*	*0*	*4*	*4*	*42*	*40*	*6*	*6*
Azerbaijan[a]	31	..	34	..	33	..	2	..	..	..	0	..
Bangladesh[a]	..	12	..	29	..	33	..	4	..	..	..	22
Belarus[a]	16	8	33	36	6	7	11	10	31	35	3	4
Belgium	*37*	*35*	*23*	*23*	..	..	*2*	*1*	*35*	*34*	*3*	*7*
Benin	..	..	..	..	..	..	..	..	..	..	..	..
Bolivia	..	7	..	38	..	3	..	13	..	8	..	31
Bosnia and Herzegovina	..	2	..	36	..	10	..	6	..	34	..	12
Botswana[a]	21	..	4	..	15	..	0	..	..	..	59	..
Brazil[a]	*14*	..	*24*	..	*2*	..	*4*	..	*31*	..	*26*	..
Bulgaria[a]	17	15	28	40	8	2	3	0	21	27	23	16
Burkina Faso	..	..	..	..	..	..	..	..	..	..	..	..
Burundi[a]	14	..	30	..	20	..	1	..	5	..	30	..
Cambodia	..	6	..	38	..	24	..	0	..	..	..	33
Cameroon	*24*	..	*23*	..	*22*	..	*4*	..	*4*	..	*21*	..
Canada[a]	50	52	17	18	2	1	..	..	22	23	10	6
Central African Republic	..	..	..	..	..	..	..	..	..	..	..	..
Chad	..	..	..	..	..	..	..	..	..	..	..	..
Chile	..	18	..	45	..	2	..	6	..	6	..	22
China	9	*21*	61	*79*	7	*-8*	0	*1*	..	..	22	*7*
Hong Kong, China	..	..	..	..	..	..	..	..	..	..	..	..
Colombia	..	35	..	35	..	5	..	5	..	0	..	20
Congo, Dem. Rep.[a]	21	*25*	12	*24*	21	*27*	5	*1*	*1*	..	41	*23*
Congo, Rep.[a]	..	*4*	..	*16*	..	*7*	..	*1*	..	*4*	..	*69*
Costa Rica[a]	11	15	32	38	15	5	1	2	28	32	12	8
Côte d'Ivoire	15	*8*	14	*18*	58	*46*	3	*13*	5	*8*	5	*7*
Croatia[a]	11	7	42	47	9	2	1	1	33	34	4	9
Cuba	..	..	..	..	..	..	..	..	..	..	..	..
Czech Republic	..	20	..	27	..	0	..	1	..	45	..	6
Denmark	*34*	38	*40*	44	..	..	*7*	2	*5*	4	*14*	12
Dominican Republic[a]	16	*24*	34	*41*	36	*21*	1	*2*	4	*3*	9	*9*
Ecuador	*50*	..	*26*	..	*11*	..	*1*	..	..	..	*12*	..
Egypt, Arab Rep.[a]	17	..	13	..	10	..	10	..	10	..	41	..
El Salvador	..	21	..	41	..	7	..	1	..	14	..	16
Eritrea	..	..	..	..	..	..	..	..	..	..	..	..
Estonia[a]	19	*13*	39	*41*	0	*0*	0	..	31	*35*	10	*11*
Ethiopia[a]	..	*15*	..	*12*	..	*27*	..	*0*	..	*5*	..	*41*
Finland	*21*	21	*34*	35	*0*	0	*2*	2	*32*	30	*12*	11
France	*23*	23	*26*	24	*0*	0	*3*	4	*40*	41	*7*	7
Gabon	..	..	..	..	..	..	..	..	..	..	..	..
Gambia, The	..	..	..	..	..	..	..	..	..	..	..	..
Georgia[a]	*7*	2	*48*	47	*10*	8	..	0	*13*	23	*22*	21
Germany	16	16	20	22	..	..	0	..	58	59	6	3
Ghana	*15*	22	*31*	22	*24*	29	..	2	..	..	*9*	26
Greece	*20*	..	*30*	..	*0*	..	*3*	..	*30*	..	*16*	..
Guatemala[a]	19	25	46	58	23	10	3	1	2	2	6	4
Guinea	*11*	..	*20*	..	*36*	..	*0*	..	..	..	*32*	..
Guinea-Bissau	..	..	..	..	..	..	..	..	..	..	..	..
Haiti	..	..	..	..	..	..	..	..	..	..	..	..

Central government revenues 4.12

	Taxes on income, profits, and capital gains		Taxes on goods and services		Taxes on international trade		Other taxes		Social contributions		Grants and other revenue	
	% of revenue		% of revenue		% of revenue		% of revenue		% of revenue		% of revenue	
	1995	2004	1995	2004	1995	2004	1995	2004	1995	2004	1995	2004
Honduras	..	..	..	..	..	..	..	..	..	..	..	..
Hungary	..	*19*	..	*36*	..	*2*	..	*2*	..	*33*	..	*8*
India[a]	23	35	28	31	24	14	0	0	0	0	25	19
Indonesia[a]	46	28	33	32	4	3	1	4	6	3	9	30
Iran, Islamic Rep.[a]	12	9	5	2	9	8	1	1	6	13	66	66
Iraq	..	..	..	..	..	..	..	..	..	..	..	..
Ireland[a]	38	..	35	..	..	..	3	..	14	..	10	..
Israel	..	29	..	29	..	1	..	6	..	17	..	18
Italy	*33*	*31*	*23*	*24*	..	*0*	*6*	*6*	*33*	*34*	*5*	*5*
Jamaica[a]	..	*30*	..	*34*	..	*9*	..	*7*	..	*7*	..	*0*
Japan	*35*	..	*14*	..	*1*	..	*5*	..	*26*	..	*18*	..
Jordan[a]	10	8	23	32	22	11	9	10	..	1	36	38
Kazakhstan[a]	*11*	40	*28*	40	*3*	5	*5*	0	*48*	..	*6*	15
Kenya[a]	34	*34*	36	*50*	15	*3*	1	*0*	*0*	*0*	14	*12*
Korea, Dem. Rep.	..	..	..	..	..	..	..	..	..	..	..	..
Korea, Rep.[a]	31	*25*	32	*31*	7	*4*	10	*7*	8	*15*	12	*18*
Kuwait[a]	1	*0*	0	..	2	*2*	0	*0*	..	..	97	*97*
Kyrgyz Republic[a]	26	*16*	56	*55*	5	*2*	1	..	..	..	11	*26*
Lao PDR	..	..	..	..	..	..	..	..	..	..	..	..
Latvia[a]	7	12	41	36	3	1	0	0	35	31	13	20
Lebanon	..	*10*	..	*46*	..	*8*	..	*12*	..	*1*	..	*24*
Lesotho[a]	15	20	12	17	49	45	1	0	..	..	24	17
Liberia	..	..	..	..	..	..	..	..	..	..	..	..
Libya	..	..	..	..	..	..	..	..	..	..	..	..
Lithuania	..	22	..	36	..	0	..	0	..	32	..	9
Macedonia, FYR	..	..	..	..	..	..	..	..	..	..	..	..
Madagascar	..	6	..	16	..	27	..	4	..	..	..	46
Malawi	..	..	..	..	..	..	..	..	..	..	..	..
Malaysia[a]	37	*47*	26	*21*	12	*6*	5	*0*	1	..	19	*26*
Mali	..	..	..	..	..	..	..	..	..	..	..	..
Mauritania	..	..	..	..	..	..	..	..	..	..	..	..
Mauritius[a]	12	13	25	43	34	20	6	5	6	4	16	16
Mexico[a]	27	..	54	..	4	..	2	..	14	..	16	..
Moldova[a]	*6*	3	*38*	48	*5*	5	*1*	0	*38*	27	2	17
Mongolia	..	*16*	..	*35*	..	*6*	..	*0*	..	*16*	..	*27*
Morocco[a]	20	..	40	..	15	..	3	..	9	..	13	..
Mozambique	..	..	..	..	..	..	..	..	..	..	..	..
Myanmar	20	*16*	26	*22*	12	*2*	..	..	..	..	42	*60*
Namibia[a]	27	*38*	32	*20*	28	*32*	2	*2*	..	*1*	11	*8*
Nepal	10	11	33	30	26	22	4	5	..	..	27	33
Netherlands	..	23	..	29	..	1	..	3	..	37	..	8
New Zealand	..	53	..	29	..	3	..	0	..	0	..	15
Nicaragua[a]	8	18	46	41	6	4	0	0	10	16	29	21
Niger	..	..	..	..	..	..	..	..	..	..	..	..
Nigeria	..	..	..	..	..	..	..	..	..	..	..	..
Norway	..	31	..	26	..	0	..	1	..	20	..	22
Oman[a]	21	*21*	1	*1*	3	*3*	2	*2*	..	..	74	*73*
Pakistan[a]	18	20	27	33	24	11	7	9	..	..	24	27
Panama[a]	20	*15*	*17*	*9*	*11*	*9*	3	*4*	16	*20*	34	*44*
Papua New Guinea[a]	40	*50*	8	*13*	27	*26*	2	*3*	0	*0*	23	*8*
Paraguay[a]	15	12	36	39	18	12	4	3	6	6	22	30
Peru[a]	15	24	49	53	10	7	8	4	11	9	10	12
Philippines[a]	33	40	26	25	29	18	4	3	..	..	8	15
Poland[a]	..	*14*	..	*34*	..	*1*	..	*0*	..	*40*	..	*11*
Portugal	*23*	*23*	*32*	*32*	*0*	*0*	*2*	*2*	*29*	*31*	*14*	*12*
Puerto Rico	..	..	..	..	..	..	..	..	..	..	..	..

Central government revenues

	Taxes on income, profits, and capital gains		Taxes on goods and services		Taxes on international trade		Other taxes		Social contributions		Grants and other revenue	
	% of revenue		% of revenue		% of revenue		% of revenue		% of revenue		% of revenue	
	1995	2004	1995	2004	1995	2004	1995	2004	1995	2004	1995	2004
Romania[a]	..	*9*	..	*33*	..	*3*	..	*1*	..	*42*	..	*13*
Russian Federation	..	4	..	26	..	19	..	0	..	27	..	24
Rwanda	*11*	..	*25*	..	*23*	..	*3*	..	*2*	..	*36*	..
Saudi Arabia	..	..	..	..	..	..	..	..	..	..	..	..
Senegal[a]	*17*	*20*	*19*	*30*	*36*	*33*	*2*	*4*	..	..	*26*	*13*
Serbia and Montenegro[a]	..	*13*	..	*39*	..	*7*	..	*4*	..	*29*	..	*9*
Sierra Leone	15	..	34	..	39	..	0	..	..	..	12	..
Singapore[a]	26	28	20	24	1	0	15	11	..	..	38	38
Slovak Republic	..	*17*	..	*29*	..	*1*	..	*0*	..	*40*	..	*13*
Slovenia[a]	13	15	33	33	9	1	0	4	42	38	3	10
Somalia	..	..	..	..	..	..	..	..	..	..	..	..
South Africa[a]	..	51	..	35	..	3	..	4	..	2	..	5
Spain	*26*	*23*	*23*	*15*	*0*	*0*	*0*	*0*	*40*	*41*	*10*	*22*
Sri Lanka[a]	12	*14*	49	*56*	17	*12*	4	*1*	1	*1*	18	*16*
Sudan[a]	*17*	..	*41*	..	*27*	..	*1*	..	..	..	*14*	..
Swaziland[a]	..	*29*	..	*15*	..	*50*	..	*0*	..	..	..	*6*
Sweden	*15*	*5*	*26*	*34*	*0*	..	*12*	*12*	*35*	*38*	*13*	*10*
Switzerland[a]	11	*16*	21	*30*	1	*1*	2	*3*	49	*39*	17	*11*
Syrian Arab Republic[a]	23	..	37	..	13	..	8	..	0	..	19	..
Tajikistan[a]	*6*	3	*63*	54	*12*	11	*0*	1	*13*	12	*5*	18
Tanzania	..	..	..	..	..	..	..	..	..	..	..	..
Thailand	..	32	..	40	..	8	..	1	..	5	..	14
Togo	..	..	..	..	..	..	..	..	..	..	..	..
Trinidad and Tobago[a]	50	..	26	..	6	..	1	..	2	..	15	..
Tunisia[a]	16	23	20	35	28	7	4	4	15	18	17	12
Turkey[a]	31	..	39	..	4	..	3	..	..	..	23	..
Turkmenistan	..	..	..	..	..	..	..	..	..	..	..	..
Uganda[a]	*10*	*12*	*45*	*24*	*7*	*16*	*2*	*0*	..	..	*37*	*48*
Ukraine[a]	..	15	..	21	..	5	..	0	..	38	..	20
United Arab Emirates[a]	..	..	*15*	..	..	..	..	..	*1*	..	*84*	..
United Kingdom	*39*	36	*31*	32	..	..	*6*	6	*19*	22	*5*	4
United States	..	51	..	4	..	1	..	1	..	40	..	3
Uruguay[a]	10	10	32	49	4	5	10	6	31	19	8	12
Uzbekistan	..	..	..	..	..	..	..	..	..	..	..	..
Venezuela, RB[a]	38	*13*	33	*23*	9	*4*	0	*8*	4	*2*	19	*50*
Vietnam	..	..	..	..	..	..	..	..	..	..	..	..
West Bank and Gaza	..	..	..	..	..	..	..	..	..	..	..	..
Yemen, Rep.[a]	17	..	10	..	18	..	3	..	..	..	51	..
Zambia[a]	27	..	22	..	36	..	0	..	0	..	15	..
Zimbabwe[a]	36	..	22	..	17	..	3	..	2	..	19	..
World	.. m	.. m	.. m	.. m	.. m	.. m	.. m	.. m	.. m	.. m	.. m	.. m
Low income	..	..	..	..	..	..	..	..	..	..	..	..
Middle income	..	..	..	..	..	..	..	..	..	..	..	..
Lower middle income	..	..	..	..	..	..	..	..	..	..	..	..
Upper middle income	..	*15*	..	*34*	..	*4*	..	*2*	..	..	..	*12*
Low & middle income	..	..	..	..	..	..	..	..	..	..	..	..
East Asia & Pacific	..	..	..	..	..	..	..	..	..	..	..	..
Europe & Central Asia	..	10	..	36	..	5	..	0	..	*33*	..	15
Latin America & Carib.	*16*	..	*29*	..	*12*	*7*	*3*	..	..	*10*	*14*	..
Middle East & N. Africa	17	..	13	..	15	..	3	..	..	..	36	..
South Asia	11	12	28	29	24	18	2	1	..	..	26	33
Sub-Saharan Africa	..	..	..	..	..	..	..	..	..	..	..	..
High income	..	..	..	*28*	..	..	..	..	..	..	..	*11*
Europe EMU	*23*	*24*	*24*	*24*	*0*	*0*	*3*	*3*	*35*	*37*	*7*	*7*

Note: Components may not sum to 100 percent because of missing data or adjustment to tax revenue.
a. Data were reported on a cash basis and have been adjusted to the accrual framework.

About the data

The International Monetary Fund (IMF) classifies government revenues as taxes, grants, and property income. Taxes are classified by the base on which the tax is levied, grants by the source, and property income by type (for example, interest, dividends, or rent). The most important source of revenue is taxes. Grants are unrequited, nonrepayable, noncompulsory receipts from other government units and foreign governments or from international organizations. Transactions are generally recorded on an accrual basis.

The IMF's *Government Finance Statistics Manual 2001* describes taxes as compulsory, unrequited payments made to governments by individuals, businesses, or institutions. Taxes are classified in six major groups by the base on which the tax is levied: income, profits, and capital gains; payroll and workforce; property; goods and services; international trade and transactions; and other taxes. However, the distinctions are not always clear. Taxes levied on the income and profits of individuals and corporations are classified as direct taxes, and taxes and duties levied on goods and services are classified as indirect taxes. This distinction may be a useful simplification, but it has no particular analytical significance except with respect to the capacity to fix tax rates. Direct taxes tend to be progressive, whereas indirect taxes are proportional.

Social security taxes do not reflect compulsory payments made by employers to provident funds or other agencies with a like purpose. Similarly, expenditures from such funds are not reflected in government expenses (see table 4.11). For further discussion of taxes and tax policies, see *About the data* for table 5.6. For further discussion of government revenues and expenditures, see *About the data* for tables 4.10 and 4.11.

4.12a

Rich countries rely more on direct taxes

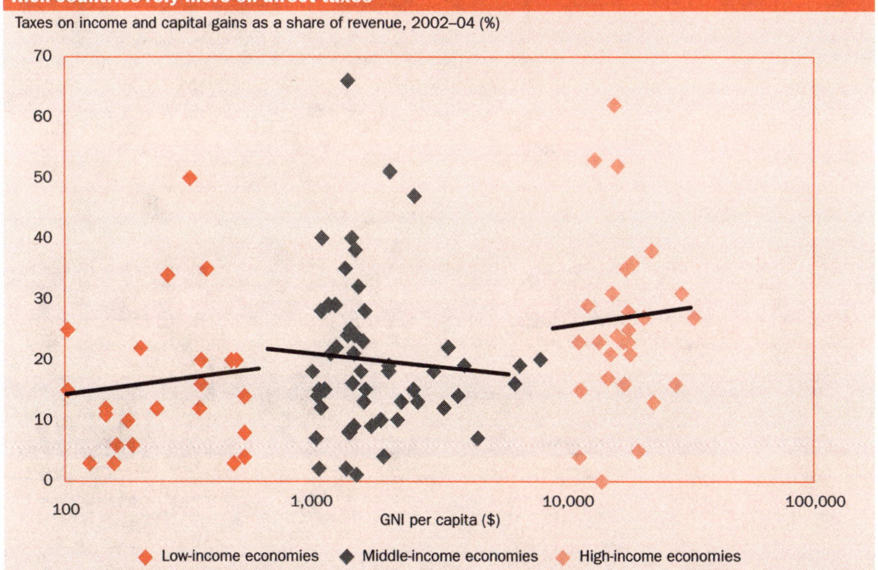

High-income economies prefer to tax income and property. Low-income economies tend to rely on indirect taxes on international trade and goods and services. But in all groups there are exceptions.

Source: International Monetary Fund, Government Finance Statistics data files and World Bank data files.

Definitions

• **Taxes on income, profits, and capital gains** are levied on the actual or presumptive net income of individuals, on the profits of corporations and enterprises, and on capital gains, whether realized or not, on land, securities, and other assets. Intragovernmental payments are eliminated in consolidation. • **Taxes on goods and services** include general sales and turnover or value added taxes, selective excises on goods, selective taxes on services, taxes on the use of goods or property, taxes on extraction and production of minerals, and profits of fiscal monopolies. • **Taxes on international trade** include import duties, export duties, profits of export or import monopolies, exchange profits, and exchange taxes. • **Other taxes** include employer payroll or labor taxes, taxes on property, and taxes not allocable to other categories, such as penalties for late payment or nonpayment of taxes. • **Social contributions** include social security contributions by employees, employers, and self-employed individuals, and other contributions whose source cannot be determined. They also include actual or imputed contributions to social insurance schemes operated by governments. • **Grants and other revenue** include grants from other foreign governments, international organizations, and other government units; interest; dividends; rent; requited, nonrepayable receipts for public purposes (such as fines, administrative fees, and entrepreneurial income from government ownership of property); and voluntary, unrequited, nonrepayable receipts other than grants.

Data sources

Data on central government revenues are from the IMF's *Government Finance Statistics Yearbook, 2005* and IMF data files. Each country's accounts are reported using the system of common definitions and classifications in the IMF's *Government Finance Statistics Manual 2001*. The IMF receives additional information from the Organisation for Economic Co-operation and Development on the tax revenues of some of its members. See the IMF sources for complete and authoritative explanations of concepts, definitions, and data sources.

4.13 Monetary indicators

	Money and quasi money		Claims on private sector		Claims on governments and other public entities		Interest rate					
							%					
	annual % growth		Annual growth % of M2		Annual growth % of M2		Deposit		Lending		Real	
	1990	2004	1990	2004	1990	2004	1990	2004	1990	2004	1990	2004
Afghanistan	..	..	..	..	..	..	..	..	..	..	..	..
Albania	..	13.1	..	4.2	..	2.0	*18.5*	6.6	*20.6*	11.8	*–65.5*	5.7
Algeria	11.4	11.3	12.2	2.6	*3.2*	–11.5	8.0	2.5	..	8.0	..	–2.0
Angola	..	37.0	..	19.9	..	–15.0	..	15.4	..	82.3	..	28.3
Argentina	1,113.3	21.4	1,444.7	5.4	1,573.2	5.8	1,517.9	2.6	..	6.8	..	–2.2
Armenia	*1,076.8*	22.3	*92.0*	16.9	534.3	–1.1	..	4.9	..	18.6	..	17.9
Australia	12.8	11.7	13.8	14.8	–2.2	0.5	13.5	3.6	17.9	8.9	13.9	5.2
Austria[a]	..	..	..	..	..	..	3.4	..	..	..	..	..
Azerbaijan	*825.8*	46.1	*134.1*	28.2	*574.2*	–1.2	..	9.2	..	15.7	..	8.8
Bangladesh	10.4	16.3	9.2	11.5	–0.1	3.8	12.0	7.1	16.0	14.8	9.1	10.1
Belarus	..	45.6	..	42.6	..	3.5	*65.1*	12.7	*71.6*	16.9	*–85.1*	–4.0
Belgium[a]	..	..	..	..	..	..	6.1	*1.6*	13.0	6.7	9.9	4.3
Benin	28.6	–9.3	–1.3	3.3	12.4	–0.4	7.0	3.5	16.0	..	14.2	..
Bolivia	52.8	2.2	40.8	–3.3	17.5	0.8	23.8	7.4	41.8	14.5	22.0	5.5
Bosnia and Herzegovina	..	22.4	..	13.7	..	0.3	..	3.7	..	10.3	..	7.2
Botswana	–14.0	16.0	12.6	10.8	–51.9	9.2	6.1	9.9	7.9	15.8	1.5	10.4
Brazil	1,306.0	19.4	1,841.5	13.4	3,178.2	–1.0	9,394.3	15.4	..	54.9	..	43.2
Bulgaria	*51.7*	24.0	*37.5*	27.5	*43.1*	–6.6	*39.5*	3.0	*52.5*	8.8	*–53.3*	4.4
Burkina Faso	–0.5	–8.3	3.6	6.4	–1.5	–4.6	7.0	3.5	16.0	..	14.4	..
Burundi	9.6	17.8	15.4	1.5	–6.9	34.2	*4.0*	..	12.3	18.3	6.0	11.2
Cambodia	..	30.4	..	14.5	..	*–2.4*	..	1.8	..	17.6	..	11.7
Cameroon	–1.7	6.4	0.9	1.1	–3.0	–1.5	7.5	5.0	18.5	18.0	16.6	17.5
Canada	7.8	10.2	9.2	13.1	0.5	0.8	9.9	0.8	14.1	4.0	10.5	0.9
Central African Republic	–3.7	14.2	–1.6	9.0	2.3	4.7	7.5	5.0	18.5	18.0	15.9	20.2
Chad	–2.4	3.5	1.3	3.3	–17.3	–0.8	7.5	5.0	18.5	18.0	9.7	4.1
Chile	24.2	8.3	21.7	23.7	16.3	–0.4	40.4	1.9	48.9	5.1	22.8	–1.4
China	28.9	14.8	26.5	8.6	1.5	1.6	8.6	2.3	9.4	5.6	3.5	–1.2
Hong Kong, China	*8.5*	7.3	*7.9*	2.2	–1.0	0.7	6.7	0.0	10.0	5.0	0.5	8.0
Colombia	33.0	18.2	*8.7*	7.7	*–7.5*	5.1	36.4	7.8	45.2	15.1	15.2	7.5
Congo, Dem. Rep.	195.4	72.6	18.0	16.1	429.7	–15.9	..	..	..	*66.8*	..	*31.5*
Congo, Rep.	18.5	17.4	5.1	–0.7	–12.6	3.9	7.5	5.0	18.5	18.0	19.7	10.4
Costa Rica	27.5	33.8	7.3	15.5	8.2	9.8	21.2	9.5	32.6	23.4	11.8	10.6
Côte d'Ivoire	–2.6	9.6	–3.9	4.9	–3.0	–3.9	7.0	3.5	16.0	..	21.5	..
Croatia	..	8.2	..	11.1	..	0.3	*658.5*	1.9	*1,157.8*	11.7	*81.0*	8.1
Cuba	..	..	..	..	..	..	..	..	..	..	..	..
Czech Republic	..	4.4	..	5.3	..	–5.0	*7.0*	1.3	*14.1*	6.0	*–3.6*	2.9
Denmark	6.5	11.0	3.0	26.5	*–3.1*	–5.4	7.9	*2.4*	14.1	*7.1*	10.1	*5.4*
Dominican Republic	42.5	9.0	19.1	–1.2	1.1	21.2	*20.0*	21.1	*35.3*	32.6	*–14.5*	–12.3
Ecuador	50.3	24.2	9.3	23.4	–26.5	–11.7	43.5	4.1	37.5	9.6	29.9	5.3
Egypt, Arab Rep.	28.7	14.4	6.3	2.1	25.3	8.7	12.0	7.7	19.0	13.4	0.5	1.7
El Salvador	–17.5	1.6	–24.2	4.5	10.2	0.7	18.0	..	21.2	..	15.7	..
Eritrea	..	11.6	..	3.7	..	11.3	..	..	..	..	..	..
Estonia	*76.5*	15.8	*27.6*	36.2	*–7.4*	–2.0	..	2.2	*30.5*	5.7	*–86.6*	2.5
Ethiopia	19.9	19.3	0.3	4.5	21.8	10.9	*3.6*	3.4	6.0	7.0	2.5	–2.3
Finland[a]	..	..	..	..	..	..	7.5	1.0	11.6	3.7	4.9	2.9
France[a]	..	..	..	..	..	..	4.5	2.3	10.6	6.6	8.2	4.9
Gabon	3.3	11.4	0.7	–8.5	–20.6	–14.5	7.5	5.0	18.5	18.0	2.7	10.3
Gambia, The	8.4	18.3	7.8	–3.9	–35.4	–13.2	11.3	22.0	26.5	36.5	13.0	18.6
Georgia	..	42.4	..	20.3	..	–4.5	..	7.2	..	31.2	..	19.7
Germany[a]	..	..	..	..	..	..	7.1	*2.7*	11.6	*9.7*	8.1	*8.1*
Ghana	13.3	27.4	4.9	13.0	9.9	23.2	*21.3*	13.6	*25.6*	..	*–5.9*	..
Greece[a]	..	..	..	..	..	..	19.5	2.3	27.6	*6.8*	5.7	*3.2*
Guatemala	25.8	9.4	15.0	8.8	0.5	*–5.2*	18.2	4.2	23.3	13.8	–12.3	5.2
Guinea	–17.4	36.5	*13.1*	1.8	*2.9*	19.2	21.0	8.9	21.2	..	–2.2	..
Guinea-Bissau	574.6	42.8	90.5	–1.3	460.7	–17.7	32.7	3.5	45.8	..	11.9	..
Haiti	2.5	5.2	–0.6	1.2	0.4	0.2	..	10.8	..	34.1	..	*2.9*

Monetary indicators

	Money and quasi money		Claims on private sector		Claims on governments and other public entities		Interest rate					
	annual % growth		Annual growth % of M2		Annual growth % of M2		% Deposit		Lending		Real	
	1990	2004	1990	2004	1990	2004	1990	2004	1990	2004	1990	2004
Honduras	21.4	20.7	13.0	11.0	–10.9	–3.2	8.8	11.1	17.1	19.9	–3.4	11.3
Hungary	29.2	8.9	23.0	16.7	69.4	–2.9	24.7	9.1	28.8	12.8	2.5	7.9
India	15.1	16.7	5.9	15.3	10.5	0.8	..	..	16.5	10.9	5.4	5.4
Indonesia	44.6	8.2	66.9	11.7	–6.7	0.7	17.5	6.4	20.8	14.1	12.2	6.6
Iran, Islamic Rep.	18.0	23.0	14.7	27.6	5.8	–4.3	..	11.7	..	16.7	..	0.1
Iraq	..	..	..	..	..	..	..	..	..	..	..	..
Ireland[a]	..	..	..	..	..	..	6.3	0.0	11.3	2.6	12.1	–0.9
Israel	19.4	3.6	18.5	3.9	4.9	–3.9	14.4	3.6	26.4	7.4	9.1	7.6
Italy[a]	..	..	..	..	..	..	6.8	*0.9*	14.1	*5.0*	5.4	*2.0*
Jamaica	21.5	14.0	12.5	7.3	–16.0	–18.7	23.9	8.0	30.5	18.1	4.3	4.9
Japan	8.2	1.6	9.7	–1.9	1.5	0.5	3.6	0.1	7.0	1.8	4.4	4.0
Jordan	8.3	10.5	4.7	9.4	1.0	2.9	8.2	2.5	10.3	8.3	–1.0	2.9
Kazakhstan	..	69.3	..	58.9	..	–17.1	..	..	..	..	..	..
Kenya	20.1	13.7	8.0	14.5	21.5	–1.2	13.7	2.4	18.8	12.5	7.3	5.2
Korea, Dem. Rep.	..	..	..	..	..	..	..	..	..	..	..	..
Korea, Rep.	17.2	–0.6	36.1	1.6	–1.2	*1.4*	10.0	3.9	10.0	5.9	–0.5	3.2
Kuwait	*4.8*	12.1	*0.4*	13.9	–1.6	–9.7	*7.4*	2.7	*8.4*	5.6	*10.3*	–14.2
Kyrgyz Republic	..	32.1	..	18.1	..	–30.6	..	6.7	..	29.3	..	23.4
Lao PDR	7.8	21.6	3.6	4.9	7.0	–0.2	30.0	7.9	*26.0*	29.3	*11.4*	17.2
Latvia	..	26.7	..	47.3	..	–2.9	*34.8*	3.3	*86.4*	7.4	*21.3*	0.3
Lebanon	55.1	10.1	27.6	1.7	18.5	5.8	16.9	7.4	39.9	10.8	21.2	7.7
Lesotho	8.4	3.3	6.8	1.9	–14.9	–23.3	13.0	4.2	20.4	12.4	10.8	10.5
Liberia	*21.1*	45.7	*19.0*	15.8	*31.8*	204.7	*6.8*	3.8	*13.8*	18.1	*10.2*	15.7
Libya	19.0	17.9	2.0	–0.1	15.0	–115.9	5.5	2.1	7.0	6.1	*0.4*	–11.5
Lithuania	..	24.1	..	26.0	..	1.7	*88.3*	1.2	*91.8*	5.7	*–52.8*	2.4
Macedonia, FYR	..	16.1	..	14.3	..	–0.3	..	6.5	..	12.4	..	10.8
Madagascar	4.5	25.2	23.8	13.9	–14.8	–13.2	20.5	15.2	25.8	25.5	12.9	9.8
Malawi	11.1	29.7	15.5	11.5	–12.9	10.2	12.1	13.7	21.0	36.8	9.3	22.7
Malaysia	10.6	19.3	20.8	22.5	–1.2	–4.5	5.7	3.0	8.8	6.0	4.8	–0.2
Mali	–4.9	–2.6	0.1	4.1	–13.4	1.7	7.0	3.5	16.0	..	10.6	..
Mauritania	11.5	*10.5*	20.2	*18.7*	1.5	*–15.8*	5.0	*8.0*	10.0	*21.0*	7.2	*10.8*
Mauritius	21.2	13.2	10.8	7.6	0.8	8.9	12.6	8.1	18.0	21.0	6.6	14.2
Mexico	83.8	10.7	48.4	3.8	7.3	3.3	30.4	2.7	*17.7*	7.2	*7.5*	1.1
Moldova	*358.0*	39.8	*53.3*	13.6	*447.0*	9.8	..	15.1	..	20.9	..	12.0
Mongolia	*31.6*	20.5	*40.2*	24.2	*29.8*	–8.5	300.0	14.2	*300.0*	25.4	*10.4*	6.1
Morocco	21.5	7.8	*12.4*	4.4	–4.9	–1.6	8.5	3.6	9.0	11.5	2.1	9.9
Mozambique	37.2	5.8	22.0	1.6	–6.8	–13.7	..	9.9	..	22.1	..	8.4
Myanmar	37.7	32.4	12.8	5.6	23.9	29.3	5.9	9.5	8.0	15.0	–8.9	*–6.2*
Namibia	*30.3*	*20.7*	*15.4*	*30.3*	*–4.7*	*9.5*	*12.8*	6.4	*23.4*	11.4	*17.9*	8.2
Nepal	18.5	12.6	5.7	..	7.3	2.4	11.9	2.7	14.4	8.5	3.2	3.8
Netherlands[a]	..	..	..	..	..	..	3.3	2.3	11.8	2.8	9.3	1.5
New Zealand	12.5	5.6	4.2	14.6	–1.6	0.5	11.7	5.8	16.0	10.4	13.3	6.4
Nicaragua	7,677.8	17.2	4,932.9	15.2	..	–6.0	9.5	4.7	22.0	13.5	–97.6	3.0
Niger	–4.1	19.7	–5.1	9.5	1.4	10.7	7.0	3.5	16.0	..	17.9	..
Nigeria	32.7	14.0	7.8	15.7	26.3	–38.1	19.8	13.7	25.3	19.2	16.9	–0.6
Norway	5.6	*3.4*	5.0	*10.4*	–0.1	*–5.4*	9.7	1.5	14.2	4.0	9.9	–0.8
Oman	10.0	4.0	9.6	7.0	–10.9	–4.2	8.3	2.3	9.7	7.6	–12.1	–1.4
Pakistan	11.6	20.5	5.0	18.6	7.6	4.1	..	..	..	..	..	..
Panama	36.6	8.4	0.8	6.6	–25.7	4.8	8.4	2.2	12.0	8.8	11.4	8.3
Papua New Guinea	4.3	12.4	–1.1	–2.0	8.6	3.9	8.7	1.7	15.5	13.3	10.9	12.5
Paraguay	54.4	14.2	32.0	6.6	–9.2	–1.4	22.9	5.1	31.0	33.5	–3.9	22.3
Peru	6,384.9	3.1	2,123.7	–0.2	2,127.1	–4.8	2,439.6	3.0	4,774.5	14.5	–29.7	8.3
Philippines	22.4	9.9	15.6	5.0	3.4	5.9	19.5	6.2	24.1	10.1	9.9	3.7
Poland	160.1	6.9	158.7	2.5	–20.6	–1.2	41.7	3.8	504.2	7.6	*–0.4*	4.5
Portugal[a]	..	..	..	..	..	..	14.0	..	21.8	..	7.6	..
Puerto Rico	..	..	..	..	..	..	..	..	..	..	..	..

Monetary indicators

	Money and quasi money		Claims on private sector		Claims on governments and other public entities		Interest rate					
	annual % growth		Annual growth % of M2		Annual growth % of M2		% Deposit		% Lending		Real	
	1990	2004	1990	2004	1990	2004	1990	2004	1990	2004	1990	2004
Romania	26.4	39.9	..	12.8	*51.2*	–10.5	..	..	..	..	..	..
Russian Federation	..	33.7	..	33.7	..	–16.9	..	3.8	..	11.4	..	–5.6
Rwanda	5.6	*15.4*	–10.0	*8.4*	26.8	*13.3*	6.9	*8.1*	13.2	..	–0.3	..
Saudi Arabia	4.6	17.3	–4.5	20.6	*4.2*	–10.3	8.0	1.7	..	..	..	..
Senegal	–4.8	12.2	–8.4	5.5	–5.3	–3.1	7.0	3.5	16.0	..	14.6	..
Serbia and Montenegro	..	..	..	..	..	..	..	..	..	..	..	..
Sierra Leone	74.0	20.1	4.9	9.2	228.7	–10.5	40.5	10.1	52.5	22.1	–10.6	5.3
Singapore	20.0	6.2	13.7	4.0	–4.9	–2.1	4.7	0.4	7.4	5.3	2.8	1.7
Slovak Republic	..	6.8	..	3.2	..	3.2	*8.0*	4.1	*14.4*	9.1	*–11.0*	4.3
Slovenia	*123.0*	7.6	*96.1*	15.4	–10.4	2.7	*682.5*	3.8	*824.6*	8.7	*374.3*	5.5
Somalia	..	..	..	..	..	..	..	..	..	..	..	..
South Africa	11.4	13.7	13.7	13.7	1.8	–0.2	18.9	6.6	21.0	11.3	4.7	5.1
Spain[a]	..	..	..	..	..	..	10.7	*2.5*	16.0	*4.3*	8.1	*–0.1*
Sri Lanka	19.9	19.6	16.2	15.8	4.4	6.3	19.4	5.1	13.0	9.5	–5.9	0.1
Sudan	48.8	30.8	12.6	19.3	29.4	–9.5	..	..	..	..	..	..
Swaziland	0.6	10.4	20.5	23.0	–13.1	4.8	8.7	4.6	14.5	11.3	–0.4	5.7
Sweden	0.8	2.4	13.6	13.4	–12.2	16.0	9.9	1.0	16.7	4.0	7.3	3.2
Switzerland	0.8	2.9	11.7	4.7	1.0	0.0	8.3	0.4	7.4	3.2	2.9	2.7
Syrian Arab Republic	26.1	*7.8*	3.4	*3.0*	11.4	*2.5*	4.0	*4.0*	9.0	*9.0*	–8.7	*10.6*
Tajikistan	..	9.8	..	102.8	..	–13.8	..	9.7	..	20.3	..	2.9
Tanzania	41.9	19.2	22.6	10.2	80.6	*–2.5*	*17.0*	4.2	*31.0*	13.9	*8.6*	9.5
Thailand	26.7	5.1	30.0	4.4	–4.0	0.6	12.3	1.0	14.4	5.5	8.2	2.1
Togo	9.5	18.1	1.8	2.8	6.9	–3.7	7.0	3.5	16.0	..	12.6	..
Trinidad and Tobago	6.2	14.1	2.7	14.5	–1.9	–19.8	6.0	2.8	12.9	9.3	–2.3	–2.8
Tunisia	7.6	11.3	5.9	10.9	1.8	2.3	*7.4*	..	*4.8*	..	*–3.7*	..
Turkey	53.2	22.1	42.9	18.5	0.1	6.0	47.5	24.3	..	..	..	..
Turkmenistan	..	*23.8*	..	*3.4*	..	*–10.3*	..	..	..	..	..	..
Uganda	60.2	11.1	*23.3*	3.5	*0.8*	–4.6	31.3	7.7	38.7	20.6	–4.0	13.8
Ukraine	*1,809.2*	32.8	*78.3*	22.4	*1,554.7*	–2.0	*148.6*	7.8	*184.3*	17.4	*–91.7*	2.0
United Arab Emirates	–8.2	23.8	1.3	19.7	–4.8	–0.3	..	*3.6*	..	*8.1*	..	*18.4*
United Kingdom	10.5	10.3	13.1	14.1	1.9	0.7	12.5	..	14.8	4.4	6.7	2.2
United States	4.9	3.0	–0.4	8.9	1.4	–0.5	..	..	10.0	4.3	5.9	1.7
Uruguay	118.5	–1.7	56.2	–11.9	25.5	1.5	147.5	6.2	163.8	23.7	27.5	15.1
Uzbekistan	..	..	..	..	..	..	..	..	..	..	..	..
Venezuela, RB	64.9	46.9	17.6	37.6	45.3	–8.2	27.8	12.6	35.5	18.5	–4.4	–9.7
Vietnam	*12.3*	31.1	*19.6*	32.6	23.7	–6.5	*22.0*	*6.6*	*32.2*	*9.5*	*12.6*	*2.6*
West Bank and Gaza	..	..	..	..	..	..	..	..	..	..	..	..
Yemen, Rep.	*11.3*	14.6	*1.4*	5.9	*10.2*	–2.4	..	13.0	..	18.5	..	3.6
Zambia	47.9	32.1	22.8	16.4	195.2	13.0	25.7	11.5	35.1	30.7	–34.5	8.7
Zimbabwe	15.1	229.3	13.5	103.2	5.0	180.7	8.8	103.2	11.7	278.9	–2.6	–15.8

a. As members of the European Monetary Union, these countries share a single currency, the euro.

About the data

Money and the financial accounts that record the supply of money lie at the heart of a country's financial system. There are several commonly used definitions of the money supply. The narrowest, M1, encompasses currency held by the public and demand deposits with banks. M2 includes M1 plus time and savings deposits with banks that require a notice for withdrawal. M3 includes M2 as well as various money market instruments, such as certificates of deposit issued by banks, bank deposits denominated in foreign currency, and deposits with financial institutions other than banks. However defined, money is a liability of the banking system, distinguished from other bank liabilities by the special role it plays as a medium of exchange, a unit of account, and a store of value.

The banking system's assets include its net foreign assets and net domestic credit. Net domestic credit includes credit extended to the private sector and general government and credit extended to the nonfinancial public sector in the form of investments in short- and long-term government securities and loans to state enterprises; liabilities to the public and private sectors in the form of deposits with the banking system are netted out. Net domestic credit also includes credit to banking and nonbank financial institutions.

Domestic credit is the main vehicle through which changes in the money supply are regulated, with central bank lending to the government often playing the most important role. The central bank can regulate lending to the private sector in several ways—for example, by adjusting the cost of the refinancing facilities it provides to banks, by changing market interest rates through open market operations, or by controlling the availability of credit through changes in the reserve requirements imposed on banks and ceilings on the credit provided by banks to the private sector.

Monetary accounts are derived from the balance sheets of financial institutions—the central bank, commercial banks, and nonbank financial intermediaries. Although these balance sheets are usually reliable, they are subject to errors of classification, valuation, and timing and to differences in accounting practices. For example, whether interest income is recorded on an accrual or a cash basis can make a substantial difference, as can the treatment of nonperforming assets. Valuation errors typically arise with respect to foreign exchange transactions, particularly in countries with flexible exchange rates or in those that have undergone a currency devaluation during the reporting period. The valuation of financial derivatives and the net liabilities of the banking system can also be difficult. The quality of commercial bank reporting also may be adversely affected by delays in reports from bank branches, especially in countries where branch accounts are not computerized. Thus the data in the balance sheets of commercial banks may be based on preliminary estimates subject to constant revision. This problem is likely to be even more serious for nonbank financial intermediaries.

Many interest rates coexist in an economy, reflecting competitive conditions, the terms governing loans and deposits, and differences in the position and status of creditors and debtors. In some economies interest rates are set by regulation or administrative fiat. In economies with imperfect markets, or where reported nominal rates are not indicative of effective rates, it may be difficult to obtain data on interest rates that reflect actual market transactions. Deposit and lending rates are collected by the International Monetary Fund (IMF) as representative interest rates offered by banks to resident customers. The terms and conditions attached to these rates differ by country, however, limiting their comparability. Real interest rates are calculated by adjusting nominal rates by an estimate of the inflation rate in the economy. A negative real interest rate indicates a loss in the purchasing power of the principal. The real interest rates in the table are calculated as $(i - P) / (1 + P)$, where i is the nominal lending interest rate and P is the inflation rate (as measured by the GDP deflator).

Definitions

• **Money and quasi money** comprise the sum of currency outside banks, demand deposits other than those of the central government, and the time, savings, and foreign currency deposits of resident sectors other than the central government. This definition of the money supply, often called M2, corresponds to lines 34 and 35 in the IMF's *International Financial Statistics* (IFS). The change in money supply is measured as the difference in end-of-year totals relative to M2 in the preceding year. • **Claims on private sector** (IFS line 32d) include gross credit from the financial system to individuals, enterprises, nonfinancial public entities not included under net domestic credit, and financial institutions not included elsewhere. • **Claims on governments and other public entities** (IFS line 32an + 32b + 32bx + 32c) usually comprise direct credit for specific purposes, such as financing the government budget deficit; loans to state enterprises; advances against future credit authorizations; and purchases of treasury bills and bonds, net of deposits by the public sector. Public sector deposits with the banking system also include sinking funds for the service of debt and temporary deposits of government revenues. • **Deposit interest rate** is the rate paid by commercial or similar banks for demand, time, or savings deposits. • **Lending interest rate** is the rate charged by banks on loans to prime customers. • **Real interest rate** is the lending interest rate adjusted for inflation as measured by the GDP deflator.

Data sources

Monetary and financial data are published by the IMF in its monthly *International Financial Statistics* and annual *International Financial Statistics Yearbook*. The IMF collects data on the financial systems of its member countries. The World Bank receives data from the IMF in electronic files that may contain more recent revisions than the published sources. The discussion of monetary indicators draws from an IMF publication by Marcello Caiola, *A Manual for Country Economists* (1995). Also see the IMF's *Monetary and Financial Statistics Manual* (2000) for guidelines for the presentation of monetary and financial statistics. World Bank data on the GDP deflator are used to derive real interest rates.

4.14 Exchange rates and prices

	Official exchange rate		Purchasing power parity (PPP) conversion factor		Ratio of PPP conversion factor to official exchange rate	Real effective exchange rate	GDP implicit deflator		Consumer price index		Wholesale price index	
	local currency units to $		local currency units to international $			Index 2000 = 100	average annual % growth		average annual % growth		average annual % growth	
	2004	2005	1990	2004	2004	2004	1990–2000	2000–04	1990–2000	2000–04	1990–2000	2000–04
Afghanistan	47.85	541.20	..	..	..	..	..	*8.5*	..	..	..	..
Albania	102.78	94.58[a]	2.0	49.5	0.5	..	23.9	4.2	*17.3*	3.5	..	..
Algeria	72.06	73.28	5.0	29.0	0.4	85.9	14.1	6.0	11.6	2.8	*0.5*	0.4
Angola	83.54	85.64[a]	0.0	52.1	0.6	..	459.4	94.1	446.2	97.7	..	..
Argentina	2.92	2.90	0.3	0.9	0.3	..	5.2	13.3	7.1	12.0	*7.0*	26.9
Armenia	533.45	457.69	0.0	147.1	0.3	80.7	102.5	3.0	*31.4*	2.4	*3.1*	1.0
Australia	1.36	1.31	1.4	1.4	1.0	121.9	2.0	3.1	2.4	3.1	1.3	1.6
Austria[b]	0.81	0.80	0.9	0.9	1.1	105.6	1.5	1.6	2.0	1.9	0.7	1.6
Azerbaijan	4,913.48	4,727.10	..	1,211.5	0.2	..	100.6	4.5	*76.8*	3.1	..	..
Bangladesh	59.51	64.33	9.5	12.7	0.2	..	3.7	4.2	4.9	3.7	..	..
Belarus	2,160.26	2,153.82	0.0	728.2	0.3	..	224.9	41.6	*163.7*	36.3	*168.6*	41.7
Belgium[b]	0.81	0.80	0.9	0.9	1.1	106.5	1.8	1.9	1.9	1.9	1.6	0.9
Benin	528.29	527.47	159.8	277.2	0.5	..	6.7	3.2	*6.0*	2.2	..	..
Bolivia	7.94	8.07	1.3	2.9	0.4	80.1	7.0	4.8	6.6	2.5	..	..
Bosnia and Herzegovina	1.58	1.57	..	0.5	0.3	..	*3.3*	3.6	..	..	..	..
Botswana	4.69	5.11	1.2	2.5	0.5	..	8.4	6.2	9.4	7.9	..	..
Brazil	2.93	2.43	0.0	1.2	0.4	..	102.7	10.6	98.3	9.6	105.4	18.3
Bulgaria	1.58	1.57	0.0	0.6	0.4	121.6	67.5	4.0	75.1	5.1	60.7	3.8
Burkina Faso	528.29	527.47	135.5	169.1	0.3	..	4.5	3.0	4.3	2.2	..	..
Burundi	1,100.91	1,106.17[a]	49.4	145.9	0.1	63.2	11.7	6.6	13.9	5.7	..	..
Cambodia	4,016.25	4,092.50	..	576.9	0.1	..	*2.9*	2.1	*4.0*	2.0	..	..
Cameroon	528.29	527.47	171.0	221.6	0.4	112.7	4.1	2.3	5.5	..	..	..
Canada	1.30	1.21	1.3	1.3	1.0	111.1	1.7	2.1	1.9	2.4	2.2	0.5
Central African Republic	528.29	527.47	135.9	158.3	0.3	111.7	3.7	2.2	4.1	2.3	*6.0*	5.3
Chad	528.29	527.47	107.3	113.3	0.2	..	6.5	5.3	5.6	2.3	..	..
Chile	609.37	560.09	148.7	312.9	0.5	83.0	7.0	5.0	6.7	2.5	6.7	6.1
China	8.28	8.19	1.3[c]	1.9[c]	0.2[c]	95.0	5.5	2.7	5.5	1.0	..	..
Hong Kong, China	7.79	7.78	6.4	6.0	0.8	..	1.1	–3.9	3.0	–2.1	0.0	–0.8
Colombia	2,628.61	2,320.75	117.9	793.5	0.3	88.4	16.9	7.1	16.1	6.8	13.9	7.2
Congo, Dem. Rep.	401.04	441.74[a]	0.0	66.6	0.2	32.0	523.0	55.8	496.4	53.0	..	..
Congo, Rep.	528.29	527.47	385.8	606.3	1.1	..	7.5	–2.8	*6.7*	1.6	..	..
Costa Rica	437.91	477.79	32.8	202.3	0.5	91.0	14.4	9.2	13.7	10.3	12.6	10.5
Côte d'Ivoire	528.29	527.47	167.1	320.7	0.6	117.6	6.7	2.9	5.6	3.1	..	..
Croatia	6.04	5.95	0.0	3.8	0.6	104.7	46.4	3.3	*19.7*	2.3	44.3	1.4
Cuba	..	..	..	..	..	..	..	..	..	..	..	..
Czech Republic	25.70	23.96	*7.4*	13.9	0.5	115.8	9.1	3.2	*5.6*	2.1	5.8	1.4
Denmark	5.99	6.00	8.3	8.4	1.4	109.5	2.0	1.9	2.2	2.1	1.3	0.9
Dominican Republic	42.12	30.41	2.5	12.1	0.3	79.3	10.2	20.6	9.8	20.7	..	..
Ecuador	1.00	1.00	0.4	0.6	0.6	146.4	4.0	11.9	36.0	13.6	*38.5*	5.9
Egypt, Arab Rep.	6.20	5.78	0.8	1.6	0.3	..	6.7	4.9	6.8	4.8	5.6	9.7
El Salvador	8.75	8.75	2.4	4.0	0.5	..	4.9	2.7	6.2	2.8	..	1.8
Eritrea	13.79	13.79[a]	*1.0*	2.7	0.2	..	*10.8*	15.8	..	..	..	..
Estonia	12.60	12.58	0.1	7.3	0.6	..	31.5	3.7	*13.3*	3.2	*4.9*	1.6
Ethiopia	8.64	8.64[a]	0.7	1.2	0.1	..	5.1	1.9	4.0	4.4	..	..
Finland[b]	0.81	0.80	1.0	1.0	1.2	106.1	2.0	1.1	1.6	1.3	1.0	–0.1
France[b]	0.81	0.80	1.0	0.9	1.1	107.8	1.3	1.8	1.6	2.0	..	0.9
Gabon	528.29	527.47	339.4	413.9	0.8	108.2	4.9	1.2	3.3	1.2	..	..
Gambia, The	30.03	29.81[a]	1.8	4.3	0.1	51.1	6.9	18.9	4.8	10.9	..	..
Georgia	1.92	1.81	0.0	0.7	0.4	..	156.4	5.8	*13.9*	5.2	..	..
Germany[b]	0.81	0.80	1.0	0.9	1.2	108.1	1.3	1.0	*1.7*	1.5	*0.8*	1.3
Ghana	9,004.63	9,072.54	95.6	1,592.3	0.2	100.4	26.0	25.0	26.3	21.3	..	..
Greece[b]	0.81	0.80	0.3	0.7	0.8	111.3	7.1	3.6	6.8	3.4	*3.4*	2.8
Guatemala	7.95	7.63	1.4	4.1	0.5	..	9.1	7.2	8.8	7.1	..	..
Guinea	2,225.03	2,550.00[a]	223.9	493.6	0.2	..	5.8	8.7	..	..	..	..
Guinea-Bissau	528.29	527.47	11.0	133.9	0.3	..	20.5	0.0	22.1	0.7	..	..
Haiti	38.35	40.45	1.1	9.7	0.3	..	19.0	*15.1*	19.7	21.6	..	..

Exchange rates and prices

	Official exchange rate		Purchasing power parity (PPP) conversion factor		Ratio of PPP conversion factor to official exchange rate	Real effective exchange rate	GDP implicit deflator		Consumer price index		Wholesale price index	
	local currency units to $		local currency units to international $			Index 2000 = 100	average annual % growth		average annual % growth		average annual % growth	
	2004	2005	1990	2004	2004	2004	1990–2000	2000–04	1990–2000	2000–04	1990–2000	2000–04
Honduras	18.21	18.83	1.3	6.7	0.4	..	15.4	7.3	15.7	8.2	..	..
Hungary	202.75	199.58	20.9	120.6	0.6	131.4	15.4	7.4	15.9	6.2	12.7	1.9
India	45.32	44.10	4.8	9.2	0.2	..	6.6	3.9	7.5	3.9	6.3	4.7
Indonesia	8,938.85	9,704.74	639.3	2,953.7	0.3	..	16.1	7.9	13.5	9.1	15.2	5.9
Iran, Islamic Rep.	8,613.99	8,963.96	179.5	2,775.3	0.3	122.1	24.3	18.9	22.0	14.4	22.1	9.3
Iraq	*0.31*	..	..	..	..	..	..	*0.3*	..	..	..	..
Ireland[b]	0.81	0.80	0.8	0.9	1.1	118.5	3.8	3.6	2.8	3.9	1.4	–0.9
Israel	4.48	4.49	1.5	3.2	0.7	77.2	7.5	1.7	7.1	2.0	6.4	3.5
Italy[b]	0.81	0.80	0.7	0.8	1.0	111.0	3.3	2.9	3.2	2.5	2.5	1.3
Jamaica	61.20	62.28	4.9	46.8	0.8	..	18.1	10.6	17.3	9.3	..	..
Japan	108.19	110.22	186.2	132.5	1.2	81.6	–0.5	–1.5	0.3	–0.5	–1.0	–1.1
Jordan	0.71	0.71	0.3	0.3	0.5	..	2.5	2.0	2.8	2.1	..	..
Kazakhstan	136.04	132.88	0.0	49.4	0.4	..	104.4	9.2	*33.6*	6.7	*12.6*	6.1
Kenya	79.17	75.55	9.0	35.8	0.5	..	12.2	4.0	12.0	6.9	..	..
Korea, Dem. Rep.	..	..	..	..	..	..	..	..	..	..	..	..
Korea, Rep.	1,145.32	1,024.12	543.9	793.8	0.7	..	4.5	2.9	4.4	3.4	2.9	1.7
Kuwait	0.30	0.29	*0.4*	*0.3*	*1.0*	..	*3.0*	4.8	1.8	1.1	1.2	2.0
Kyrgyz Republic	42.65	41.01	0.0	9.6	0.2	..	63.7	4.2	*14.7*	3.7	*25.0*	6.9
Lao PDR	10,585.54	10,655.17	174.2	2,296.5	0.2	..	27.9	11.1	29.0	11.5	..	..
Latvia	0.54	0.56	0.0	0.3	0.5	..	27.9	3.9	*17.0*	3.2	*6.9*	3.3
Lebanon	1,507.50	1,507.50	305.4	1,354.5	0.9	..	11.1	2.7	..	..	..	..
Lesotho	6.46	6.36	1.0	1.9	0.3	88.7	9.0	6.3	*8.7*	*11.1*	..	..
Liberia	54.91	57.10	..	..	..	..	49.7	12.9	..	..	..	..
Libya	1.31	1.31	..	..	..	..	..	16.3	1.9	–5.9	..	..
Lithuania	2.78	2.77	0.0	1.4	0.5	..	40.1	0.4	*16.7*	0.2	*12.9*	–0.5
Macedonia, FYR	49.41	49.28	0.0	19.6	0.4	98.5	42.9	2.4	*6.3*	2.0	*5.5*	0.5
Madagascar	1,868.86	2,003.03	102.7	553.1	0.3	..	15.3	9.6	15.1	8.3	..	..
Malawi	108.90	108.94[a]	1.4	27.9	0.3	74.6	29.9	15.0	29.7	14.0	..	..
Malaysia	3.80	3.79	1.5	1.8	0.5	91.9	3.4	2.8	3.0	1.4	2.9	3.8
Mali	528.29	527.47	140.7	209.0	0.4	..	5.7	4.7	4.0	1.5	..	..
Mauritania	265.23[a]	..	36.0	55.2	*0.2*	..	6.9	7.0	5.6	5.7	..	..
Mauritius	27.50	29.50	6.5	11.3	0.4	..	5.8	5.3	6.3	5.1	..	..
Mexico	11.29	10.90	1.4	7.5	0.7	..	15.8	7.0	15.7	5.1	15.0	6.6
Moldova	12.33	12.60	0.0	4.4	0.4	97.6	70.0	11.4	*17.0*	9.5	..	..
Mongolia	1,185.28	1,211.77[a]	2.3	352.7	0.3	..	34.6	10.8	*26.3*	4.7	..	..
Morocco	8.87	8.87	3.2	3.5	0.4	92.9	2.1	0.8	2.9	1.5	2.2	*–0.6*
Mozambique	22,581.34	23,060.98	316.9	5,312.1	0.2	..	23.7	13.5	23.4	13.4	..	..
Myanmar	5.75	5.76	..	..	..	..	24.6	..	25.7	31.8	..	..
Namibia	6.46	6.36	1.0	2.7	0.4	..	9.8	6.5	..	..	..	..
Nepal	73.67	71.37	6.8	13.2	0.2	..	6.6	3.8	7.0	3.7	..	..
Netherlands[b]	0.81	0.80	0.9	0.9	1.1	111.9	2.4	3.1	2.6	2.7	1.6	2.0
New Zealand	1.51	1.42	1.6	1.6	1.1	128.5	1.9	2.4	1.9	2.3	1.8	1.3
Nicaragua	15.94	16.73	0.0	3.7	0.2	82.6	26.5	6.5	20.4	5.9	..	..
Niger	528.29	527.47	121.2	160.7	0.3	..	4.9	1.9	4.6	1.1	..	..
Nigeria	132.89	132.36[a]	3.7	61.6	0.5	107.2	23.2	15.3	24.5	14.9	..	..
Norway	6.74	6.44	8.2	9.6	1.4	106.0	3.2	1.4	2.2	1.8	1.3	0.6
Oman	0.39	0.38	0.3	*0.2*	*0.6*	..	1.2	1.8	0.1	–0.5	..	..
Pakistan	58.26	59.51	6.2	16.5	0.3	91.3	10.2	5.1	7.7	4.0	8.4	5.4
Panama	1.00	1.00	0.6	0.6	0.6	..	2.6	0.9	1.1	0.9	0.8	–0.2
Papua New Guinea	3.22	3.14[a]	0.5	0.9	0.3	99.2	7.5	7.4	10.3	10.1	..	..
Paraguay	5,974.58	6,177.96	400.1	1,513.4	0.3	73.6	11.3	12.4	11.5	9.7	*12.2*	15.9
Peru	3.41	3.30	0.1	1.5	0.4	..	16.3	2.3	16.6	1.9	14.6	1.5
Philippines	56.04	55.09	5.6	12.8	0.2	79.6	7.5	4.5	6.7	4.5	*7.9*	8.1
Poland	3.66	3.24	0.2	1.8	0.5	99.8	16.6	2.0	17.5	2.6	13.6	2.9
Portugal[b]	0.81	0.80	0.4	0.7	0.8	109.9	4.6	3.5	3.9	3.4	..	1.5
Puerto Rico	..	..	0.7	..	..	..	3.1	..	..	..	..	..

4.14 Exchange rates and prices

	Official exchange rate		Purchasing power parity (PPP) conversion factor		Ratio of PPP conversion factor to official exchange rate	Real effective exchange rate	GDP implicit deflator		Consumer price index		Wholesale price index	
	local currency units to $		local currency units to international $			Index 2000 = 100	average annual % growth		average annual % growth		average annual % growth	
	2004	2005	1990	2004	2004	2004	1990–2000	2000–04	1990–2000	2000–04	1990–2000	2000–04
Romania	32,636.57	29,136.53	6.6	13,095.7	0.4	109.9	71.8	23.3	72.3	20.4	69.5	24.0
Russian Federation	28.81	28.28	0.0	11.9	0.4	136.5	94.7	15.8	*59.4*	15.3	*37.9*	–13.3
Rwanda	574.62	555.94	31.9	95.0	0.2	..	10.3	5.0	*11.7*	5.7	..	..
Saudi Arabia	3.75	3.75	2.8	2.9	0.8	82.3	2.2	4.0	0.5	0.1	0.9	0.8
Senegal	528.29	527.47	185.1	222.0	0.4	..	4.0	1.9	3.9	1.4	..	..
Serbia and Montenegro	..	..	..	..	..	..	*51.3*	29.3	..	..	..	..
Sierra Leone	2,701.30	2,889.59	29.5	653.4	0.2	74.4	25.8	13.1	20.9	4.4	..	..
Singapore	1.69	1.66	1.8	1.5	0.9	92.8	0.6	0.5	1.3	0.6	0.0	0.8
Slovak Republic	32.26	31.02	5.9	16.9	0.5	97.4	8.9	4.3	*8.1*	6.5	7.8	5.1
Slovenia	192.38	192.71	*16.0*	149.2	0.8	..	19.2	6.4	*9.7*	6.3	*7.5*	4.9
Somalia	..	..	..	..	..	..	..	..	..	..	..	..
South Africa	6.46	6.36	1.0	2.7	0.4	107.8	9.0	7.1	7.7	5.9	7.3	6.4
Spain[b]	0.81	0.80	0.6	0.8	0.9	111.6	3.8	4.2	3.4	3.2	2.2	1.7
Sri Lanka	101.19	100.50	10.2	25.0	0.2	..	8.9	8.5	9.5	9.1	7.6	8.9
Sudan	257.91	243.61	0.7	78.4	0.3	..	43.8	8.3	46.1	8.0	..	..
Swaziland	6.46	6.36	0.8	2.8	0.4	..	11.9	10.5	9.2	*8.7*	..	..
Sweden	7.35	7.47	9.1	9.6	1.3	100.7	1.9	1.8	1.7	1.8	2.2	1.0
Switzerland	1.24	1.25	2.0	1.8	1.5	105.4	0.9	1.0	1.3	0.7	–0.3	0.2
Syrian Arab Republic	11.23	11.23	10.2	16.5	1.5	..	6.6	3.2	4.9	..	3.2	..
Tajikistan	2.97	3.12	0.0	0.8	0.3	..	136.2	23.9	..	..	..	..
Tanzania	1,089.34	1,128.93	75.7	488.8	0.4	..	16.5	5.9	14.9	2.4	..	..
Thailand	40.22	40.22	10.8	12.9	0.3	..	3.2	1.8	3.9	1.6	3.6	3.5
Togo	528.29	527.47	93.8	127.5	0.2	112.8	5.0	0.7	6.1	1.5	..	..
Trinidad and Tobago	6.30	6.28	3.1	5.0	0.8	101.5	5.2	3.6	5.1	4.2	2.3	1.3
Tunisia	1.25	1.30	0.4	0.5	0.4	90.3	3.8	2.4	3.8	2.7	3.1	2.6
Turkey	1.43[d]	1.34[d]	1,560.9	778,515.9	0.5	..	65.0	31.9	68.4	32.6	..	..
Turkmenistan	..	..	0.0	1,931.0	..	..	329.1	..	..	..	..	..
Uganda	1,810.31	1,780.67	109.1	327.9	0.2	82.7	8.3	3.8	7.4	3.3	..	..
Ukraine	5.32	5.12	0.0	1.1	0.2	81.7	133.5	8.9	*73.3*	5.9	*75.5*	8.9
United Arab Emirates	3.67	3.67	3.4	..	..	..	2.7	2.7	..	..	..	..
United Kingdom	0.55	0.55	0.5	0.6	1.2	100.8	2.7	2.8	2.7	2.3	1.7	0.9
United States	1.00	1.00	1.0	1.0	1.0	92.6	1.9	2.1	2.6	2.3	1.4	2.3
Uruguay	28.70	24.48	0.6	11.8	0.4	59.6	22.4	13.4	23.9	12.6	22.1	24.8
Uzbekistan	..	..	*0.0*	251.3	..	..	144.3	33.1	..	..	..	..
Venezuela, RB	1,891.33	2,089.75	24.4	1,323.1	0.7	66.2	38.3	27.8	39.3	22.7	37.6	35.2
Vietnam	*15,509.58*	15,776.00[a]	641.1	3,209.5	*0.2*	..	10.9	5.1	*3.0*	3.5	..	..
West Bank and Gaza	..	..	..	..	..	..	*8.9*	*10.9*	..	..	..	..
Yemen, Rep.	184.78	185.58[a]	20.3	135.1	0.7	..	18.1	8.0	20.8	*11.7*	..	..
Zambia	4,778.88	4,463.50	18.6	2,653.0	0.6	109.5	39.4	20.9	42.4	21.0	..	..
Zimbabwe	5,068.66	22,363.64	0.9	..	..	..	53.7	207.2	36.1	..	*25.9*	..

Note: Inconsistencies in the growth rates of the GDP deflator and the consumer and wholesale price indexes are due mainly to uneven coverage of the time period.

a. Latest quarterly or monthly data available. b. As members of the European Monetary Union, these countries share a single currency, the euro. c. Based on a 1986 bilateral comparison of China and the United States (Rouen and Kai 1995), employing a different methodology than that used for other countries. This interim methodology will be revised in the next rfew years. d. New liras per dollar.

Exchange rates and prices 4.14

About the data

In a market-based economy the choices that households, producers, and governments make about the allocation of resources are influenced by relative prices, including the real exchange rate, real wages, real interest rates, and a host of other prices in the economy. Relative prices also reflect, to a large extent, the choices of these agents. Thus relative prices convey vital information about the interaction of economic agents in an economy and with the rest of the world.

The exchange rate is the price of one currency in terms of another. Official exchange rates and exchange rate arrangements are established by governments. (Other exchange rates fully recognized by governments include market rates, which are determined largely by legal market forces, and for countries maintaining multiple exchange arrangements, principal rates, secondary rates, and tertiary rates.) Also see *Statistical methods* for information on alternative conversion factors used in the *World Bank Atlas* method of calculating gross national income (GNI) per capita in U.S. dollars.

The official or market exchange rate is often used to compare prices in different currencies. Since exchange rates reflect at best the relative prices of tradable goods, the volume of goods and services that a U.S. dollar buys in the United States may not correspond to what a U.S. dollar converted to another country's currency at the official exchange rate would buy in that country. Since identical volumes of goods and services in different countries correspond to different values (and vice versa) when offcial exchange rates are used, an alternative method of comparing prices across countries has been developed. In this method national currency estimates of GNI are converted to a common unit of account by using conversion factors that reflect equivalent purchasing power. Purchasing power parity (PPP) conversion factors are based on price and expenditure surveys conducted by the International Comparison Program and represent the conversion factors applied to equalize price levels across countries. See *About the data* for table 1.1 for further discussion of the PPP conversion factor.

The ratio of the PPP conversion factor to the official exchange rate (also referred to as the national price level) makes it possible to compare the cost of the bundle of goods that make up gross domestic product (GDP) across countries. These national price levels vary systematically, rising with GNI per capita.

Real effective exchange rates represent a nominal effective exchange rate index adjusted for relative movements in national price or cost indicators of the home country, selected countries, and the euro area. A nominal effective exchange rate index represents the ratio (expressed on the base 2000 = 100) of an index of a currency's period-average exchange rate to a weighted geometric average of exchange rates for currencies of selected countries and the euro area. For most high-income countries, weights are derived from trade in manufactured goods among industrial countries. The data are compiled from the nominal effective exchange rate index and a cost indicator of relative normalized unit labor costs in manufacturing. For selected other countries the nominal effective exchange rate index is based on each country's trade in both manufactured goods and primary products with its partner or competitor countries. For these countries the real effective exchange rate index is derived from the nominal index adjusted for relative changes in consumer prices. An increase in the real effective exchange rate represents an appreciation of the local currency. Because of conceptual and data limitations, changes in real effective exchange rates should be interpreted with caution.

Controlling inflation is one of the primary goals of monetary policy and is intimately linked to the growth in money supply. Inflation is measured by the rate of increase in a price index, but actual price change can be negative. Which index is used depends on which set of prices in the economy is being examined. The GDP deflator reflects changes in prices for total gross domestic product. The most general measure of the overall price level, it takes into account changes in government consumption, capital formation (including inventory appreciation), international trade, and the main component, household final consumption expenditure. The GDP deflator is usually derived implicitly as the ratio of current to constant price GDP, resulting in a Paasche index. It is defective as a general measure of inflation for use in policy because of the long lags in deriving estimates and because it is often only an annual measure.

Consumer price indexes are produced more frequently and so are more current. They are also constructed explicitly, based on surveys of the cost of a defined basket of consumer goods and services. Nevertheless, consumer price indexes should be interpreted with caution. The definition of a household, the basket of goods chosen, and the geographic (urban or rural) and income group coverage of consumer price surveys can all vary widely across countries. In addition, the weights are derived from household expenditure surveys, which, for budgetary reasons, tend to be conducted infrequently in developing countries, leading to poor comparability over time. Although useful for measuring consumer price inflation within a country, consumer price indexes are of less value in making comparisons across countries. Food price indexes, like consumer price indexes, should be interpreted with caution because of the high variability across countries in the items covered.

Wholesale price indexes are based on the prices of commodities that have some significance in the output or consumption of the country at the first commercial transaction. The prices are farm gate prices for agricultural commodities and ex-factory prices for industrial goods. Preference should be given to indexes that provide the broadest coverage of the economy.

The least-squares method is used to calculate the growth rates of the GDP implicit deflator, consumer price index, and wholesale price index.

Definitions

• **Official exchange rate** is the exchange rate determined by national authorities or the rate determined in the legally sanctioned exchange market. It is calculated as an annual average based on monthly averages (local currency units relative to the U.S. dollar). • **Purchasing power parity (PPP) conversion factor** is the number of units of a country's currency required to buy the same amount of goods and services in the domestic market as a U.S. dollar would buy in the United States. • **Ratio of PPP conversion factor to official exchange rate** is the result obtained by dividing the PPP conversion factor by the official exchange rate. • **Real effective exchange rate** is the nominal effective exchange rate (a measure of the value of a currency against a weighted average of several foreign currencies) divided by a price deflator or index of costs. • **GDP implicit deflator** measures the average annual rate of price change in the economy as a whole for the periods shown. • **Consumer price index** reflects changes in the cost to the average consumer of acquiring a basket of goods and services that may be fixed or may change at specified intervals, such as yearly. The Laspeyres formula is generally used. • **Wholesale price index** refers to a mix of agricultural and industrial goods at various stages of production and distribution, including import duties. The Laspeyres formula is generally used.

Data sources

Data on official and real effective exchange rates and consumer and wholesale price indexes are from the International Monetary Fund's *International Financial Statistics*. PPP conversion factors and GDP deflators are from the World Bank's data files.

4.15 Balance of payments current account

	Goods and services ($ millions)				Net income ($ millions)		Net current transfers ($ millions)		Current account balance ($ millions)		Total reserves[a] ($ millions)	
	Exports		Imports									
	1990	2004	1990	2004	1990	2004	1990	2004	1990	2004	1990	2004
Afghanistan	*261*	..	*727*	..	*12*	..	*311*	..	*–143*	..	638	..
Albania	354	*1,167*	485	*2,586*	–2	*170*	15	*842*	–118	*–407*	..	1,388
Algeria	13,462	..	10,106	..	–2,268	..	333	..	1,420	..	2,703	45,692
Angola	3,992	13,798	3,385	10,635	–765	–2,484	–77	7	–236	686	..	1,374
Argentina	14,800	39,702	6,846	28,152	–4,400	–8,884	998	688	4,552	3,353	6,222	19,660
Armenia	..	985	..	1,514	..	37	..	330	..	–162	*1*	576
Australia	49,843	112,514	53,056	131,417	–13,176	–20,487	439	–269	–15,950	–39,658	19,319	36,926
Austria	63,694	161,062	61,580	155,304	–942	–2,237	–6	–2,756	1,166	765	17,228	12,188
Azerbaijan	..	4,235	..	6,312	..	–701	..	*188*	..	–2,589	..	1,090
Bangladesh	2,064	9,234	3,960	13,089	–116	–371	1,613	3,948	–398	–279	660	3,222
Belarus	..	15,666	..	17,019	..	26	..	285	..	–1,043	..	837
Belgium	138,605[b]	297,953	135,098[b]	284,718	2,316[b]	5,631	–2,197[b]	–6,952	3,627[b]	11,914	23,789	13,991
Benin	364	713	454	1073	–25	–38	97	66	–18	–331	69	640
Bolivia	977	2,546	1,086	2,319	–249	–385	159	*444*	–199	285	511	1,271
Bosnia and Herzegovina	..	2,914	..	7,111	..	446	..	1,833	..	–1,918	..	2,408
Botswana	2,005	*3,689*	1,987	*2,780*	–106	*–716*	69	*290*	–19	*483*	3,331	5,661
Brazil	35,170	109,059	28,184	80,069	–11,608	–20,520	799	3,268	–3,823	11,738	9,200	52,935
Bulgaria	6,950	13,975	8,027	16,465	–758	–658	125	1,094	–1,710	–2,053	*670*	9,337
Burkina Faso	349	..	758	..	0	..	332	..	–77	..	305	669
Burundi	89	*43*	318	*175*	–15	*–17*	174	124	–69	*–25*	112	66
Cambodia	*314*	3,243	*507*	3,663	*–21*	–239	*120*	442	*–93*	–217	..	1,118
Cameroon	2,508	..	2,475	..	–558	..	–26	..	–551	..	37	842
Canada	149,538	377,646	149,118	336,733	–19,388	–19,167	–796	254	–19,764	22,000	23,530	34,476
Central African Republic	220	..	410	..	–22	..	123	..	–89	..	123	153
Chad	271	..	488	..	–21	..	192	..	–46	..	132	227
Chile	10,221	37,981	9,166	29,542	–1,737	–8,101	198	1,051	–485	1,390	6,784	15,997
China†	57,374	655,827	46,706	606,543	1,055	–3,523	274	22,898	11,997	68,659	34,476	622,949
Hong Kong, China	..	314,438	..	299,591	..	3,491	..	–1,981	..	16,357	24,656	123,569
Colombia	8,679	19,496	6,858	19,929	–2,305	–4,183	1,026	3,650	542	–967	4,869	13,537
Congo, Dem. Rep.	..	..	..	..	..	..	..	..	..	..	261	..
Congo, Rep.	1,488	*1,546*	1,282	*995*	–460	*–546*	3	*–8*	–251	*–3*	10	124
Costa Rica	1,963	8,610	2,346	9,140	–233	–517	192	*216*	–424	–831	525	1,919
Côte d'Ivoire	3,503	7,650	3,445	6,181	–1,091	–705	–181	–462	–1,214	303	21	1,694
Croatia	..	17,828	..	20,180	..	–772	..	1,483	..	–1,641	*167*	8,758
Cuba	..	..	..	..	..	..	..	..	..	..	..	..
Czech Republic	..	76,569	..	76,966	..	–5,433	..	*235*	..	–5,595	..	28,451
Denmark	48,902	111,355	41,415	98,925	–5,708	–2,330	–408	–4,159	1,372	5,941	11,226	40,021
Dominican Republic	1,832	9,283	2,233	9,049	–249	–1,332	371	*2,498*	–280	1,399	69	806
Ecuador	3,262	8,734	2,519	9,306	–1,210	–1,479	107	1,894	–360	–157	1,009	1,440
Egypt, Arab Rep.	9,895	26,516	14,091	26,915	–1,022	–246	7,545	*4,567*	2,327	3,922	3,620	15,339
El Salvador	973	4,301	1,624	7,029	–132	–459	631	2,576	–152	–612	595	1,938
Eritrea	..	..	..	..	..	..	..	..	..	..	..	35
Estonia	*664*	8,794	*711*	9,674	*–13*	–718	*97*	165	*36*	–1,432	*198*	1,792
Ethiopia	597	1,684	1,271	3,778	–69	–29	449	1,372	–294	–751	55	1,497
Finland	31,180	71,099	33,456	60,636	–3,735	238	–952	–1,003	–6,962	9,698	10,415	13,010
France	285,389	531,488	283,238	526,635	–3,896	8,540	–8,199	–21,775	–9,944	–8,382	68,291	77,353
Gabon	2,730	*3,351*	1,812	*1,882*	–617	*–713*	–134	–181	168	*575*	279	449
Gambia, The	168	..	192	..	–11	..	59	..	23	..	55	84
Georgia	..	1,631	..	2,491	..	97	..	414	..	–349	..	383
Germany	473,670	1,051,303	427,621	912,587	20,593	283	–21,954	–35,229	44,688	103,770	104,547	97,170
Ghana	983	3,487	1,506	5,356	–111	–198	411	1,831	–223	–236	309	1,750
Greece	13,018	48,824	19,564	61,380	–1,709	–5,097	4,718	*4,504*	–3,537	–13,148	4,721	2,708
Guatemala	1,568	4,608	1,812	8,483	–196	–319	227	*3,006*	–213	–1,188	362	3,522
Guinea	829	811	953	964	–149	–27	70	18	–203	–162	*145*	*263*
Guinea-Bissau	26	*71*	88	*102*	–22	*–9*	39	*39*	–45	*0*	18	73
Haiti	318	*469*	515	*1,375*	–18	*–14*	193	*907*	–22	*–13*	10	115
†Data for Taiwan, China	74,172	198,943	67,015	187,757	4,362	11,245	–596	–3,826	10,923	18,606	77,653	247,699

Balance of payments current account

	Goods and services				Net income		Net current transfers		Current account balance		Total reserves[a]	
	$ millions				$ millions		$ millions		$ millions		$ millions	
	Exports		Imports									
	1990	2004	1990	2004	1990	2004	1990	2004	1990	2004	1990	2004
Honduras	1,032	3,066	1,127	4,430	–237	–279	280	*1,230*	–51	–413	47	1,980
Hungary	12,035	66,351	11,017	69,425	–1,427	–6,086	787	317	379	–8,842	1,185	15,951
India	22,911	*82,735*	29,527	*93,918*	–3,257	*–4,451*	2,837	*22,488*	–7,036	*6,853*	5,637	131,631
Indonesia	29,295	89,789	27,511	79,116	–5,190	–8,704	418	1,139	–2,988	3,108	8,657	36,311
Iran, Islamic Rep.	19,741	..	22,292	..	378	..	2,500	..	327	..	..	..
Iraq	..	..	..	..	..	..	..	..	..	..	..	..
Ireland	26,786	152,172	24,576	124,724	–4,955	–29,269	2,384	397	–361	–1,423	5,362	2,908
Israel	17,312	51,445	20,228	52,040	–1,981	–4,162	5,060	6,230	163	1,474	6,598	27,094
Italy	219,971	435,871	218,573	423,241	–14,712	–18,204	–3,164	*–9,563*	–16,479	–15,137	88,595	62,386
Jamaica	2,217	3,899	2,390	5,272	–430	–583	291	1,446	–312	–509	168	1,846
Japan	323,692	636,610	297,306	542,380	22,492	85,703	–4,800	–7,875	44,078	172,059	87,828	844,667
Jordan	2,511	5,983	3,569	9,407	–214	190	1,045	3,216	–227	–18	1,139	5,447
Kazakhstan	..	22,602	..	18,800	..	–2,784	..	–488	..	530	..	9,277
Kenya	2,228	4,202	2,705	5,115	–418	–114	368	649	–527	–378	236	1,520
Korea, Dem. Rep.	..	..	..	..	..	..	..	..	..	..	..	..
Korea, Rep.	73,297	299,174	76,373	269,782	–88	725	1,150	–2,504	–2,014	27,613	14,916	199,195
Kuwait	8,268	33,543	7,169	18,510	7,738	6,400	–4,951	–2,548	3,886	18,884	2,929	9,354
Kyrgyz Republic	..	942	..	1,135	..	–90	..	209	..	–75	..	565
Lao PDR	102	..	212	..	–1	..	56	..	–55	..	8	275
Latvia	*1,090*	6,001	*997*	8,180	*2*	–272	*96*	685	*191*	–1,766	..	2,021
Lebanon	..	..	..	..	..	..	..	..	..	..	4,210	15,774
Lesotho	100	771	754	1,398	433	303	286	*248*	65	–76	72	503
Liberia	..	..	..	..	..	..	..	..	..	..	1	19
Libya	11,468	17,862	8,960	10,532	174	–1,301	–481	–2,324	2,201	3,705	7,225	27,714
Lithuania	..	11,751	..	13,321	..	–612	..	458	..	–1,725	*107*	3,594
Macedonia, FYR	..	2,080	..	3,247	..	–39	..	791	..	–415	..	991
Madagascar	471	*1,126*	809	*1,654*	–161	*–79*	234	*299*	–265	*–309*	92	504
Malawi	443	*472*	549	*795*	–80	*–38*	99	161	–86	*–201*	142	139
Malaysia	32,665	*118,577*	31,765	*96,820*	–1,872	*–5,928*	102	*–2,447*	–870	*13,381*	10,659	66,897
Mali	420	*1,152*	830	*1,471*	–37	*–160*	225	*207*	–221	*–271*	198	861
Mauritania	471	..	520	..	–46	..	86	..	–10	..	59	*420*
Mauritius	1,722	3,460	1,916	3,603	–23	–14	97	49	–119	–107	761	1,633
Mexico	48,805	202,003	51,915	216,589	–8,316	–9,812	3,975	17,044	–7,451	–7,354	10,217	64,202
Moldova	..	1,331	..	2,122	..	357	..	*365*	..	–69	*2*	470
Mongolia	493	1,211	1,096	1,405	–44	–11	7	269	–640	63	*23*	250
Morocco	6,239	16,632	7,783	19,860	–988	–671	2,336	4,868	–196	970	2,338	16,647
Mozambique	229	1,759	996	2,381	–97	–300	448	*314*	–415	–607	232	1,159
Myanmar	319	3,181	603	2,458	–192	–745	39	134	–436	112	410	773
Namibia	1,220	2,310	1,584	2,495	37	151	354	669	28	634	*50*	345
Nepal	422	1,224	834	2,186	14	–15	109	1,173	–289	197	354	1,529
Netherlands	159,304	388,899	147,652	341,622	–620	15,088	–2,943	*–7,952*	8,089	54,414	34,401	21,050
New Zealand	11,683	28,305	11,699	28,791	–1,576	–5,793	138	79	–1,453	–6,199	4,129	5,294
Nicaragua	392	1,653	682	2,851	–217	–192	202	*619*	–305	–772	166	668
Niger	533	*415*	728	*681*	–54	*–26*	14	73	–236	*–219*	226	258
Nigeria	14,550	26,993	6,909	16,064	–2,738	–916	85	2,252	4,988	12,264	4,129	17,257
Norway	47,078	109,104	38,910	73,557	–2,700	1,544	–1,476	–2,645	3,992	34,445	15,788	44,308
Oman	5,577	14,175	3,342	10,613	–254	–1,293	–874	*–1,826*	1,106	443	1,784	3,598
Pakistan	6,835	16,079	10,205	22,057	–1,084	–2,362	2,794	7,532	–1,661	–808	1,046	10,718
Panama	4,438	8,859	4,193	9,172	–255	–1,042	219	228	209	–1,127	344	631
Papua New Guinea	1,381	..	1,509	..	–103	..	156	..	–76	..	427	660
Paraguay	2,514	3,397	2,169	3,540	2	–31	43	194	390	20	675	1,168
Peru	4,120	14,530	4,087	12,581	–1,733	–3,421	281	1,461	–1,419	–11	1,891	12,665
Philippines	11,430	42,829	13,967	50,492	–872	147	714	*9,596*	–2,695	2,080	2,036	16,234
Poland	19,037	95,333	15,095	99,935	–3,386	–11,399	2,511	5,644	3,067	–10,357	4,674	36,773
Portugal	21,554	51,899	27,146	65,411	–96	–3,095	5,507	3,449	–181	–13,158	20,579	11,684
Puerto Rico	..	..	..	..	..	..	..	..	..	..	..	..

4.15 Balance of payments current account

	Goods and services ($ millions)				Net income ($ millions)		Net current transfers ($ millions)		Current account balance ($ millions)		Total reserves[a] ($ millions)	
	Exports		Imports									
	1990	2004	1990	2004	1990	2004	1990	2004	1990	2004	1990	2004
Romania	6,380	27,099	9,901	34,029	161	–1,766	106	*3,107*	–3,254	–5,589	1,374	16,095
Russian Federation	..	203,741	..	130,144	..	–13,000	..	–677	..	59,920	..	126,258
Rwanda	143	201	354	493	–16	–27	143	314	–85	–6	44	315
Saudi Arabia	47,381	131,849	43,880	66,746	7,968	478	–15,616	–13,655	–4,147	51,926	13,437	29,304
Senegal	1,453	*1,826*	1,840	*2,657*	–129	*–136*	153	530	–363	*–437*	22	1,386
Serbia and Montenegro	..	..	..	..	..	..	..	..	..	..	..	..
Sierra Leone	210	215	215	342	–71	–67	7	119	–69	–74	5	125
Singapore	67,489	238,522	64,953	206,796	1,006	–2,686	–421	*–1,144*	3,122	27,897	27,748	112,232
Slovak Republic	..	*25,241*	..	*25,649*	..	*–119*	..	*245*	..	*–282*	..	14,912
Slovenia	*7,900*	19,519	*6,930*	19,927	*–38*	–300	*46*	38	*978*	–670	*112*	8,900
Somalia	*68*	..	*468*	..	*–84*	..	*328*	..	*–157*	..	*23*	..
South Africa	27,160	56,734	21,017	57,888	–4,271	–4,343	–321	–1,485	1,552	–6,982	2,583	14,886
Spain	83,595	269,030	100,870	307,365	–3,533	–16,985	2,799	–60	–18,009	–55,380	57,238	19,759
Sri Lanka	2,293	7,284	2,965	9,108	–167	–204	541	1,380	–298	–648	447	2,205
Sudan	499	3,822	877	4,651	–136	–1,113	141	1,123	–372	–818	11	1,626
Swaziland	658	2,438	768	2,448	59	32	102	92	51	114	216	324
Sweden	70,560	163,934	70,490	134,855	–4,473	3,224	–1,936	–4,818	–6,339	27,485	20,324	24,740
Switzerland	97,033	181,568	96,389	146,291	7,878	30,974	–2,398	–6,005	6,124	60,246	61,284	74,568
Syrian Arab Republic	5,030	8,175	2,955	7,915	–401	–729	88	*679*	1,762	210	*535*	..
Tajikistan	..	1,220	..	1,445	..	–58	..	226	..	–57	..	172
Tanzania	538	2,179	1,474	3,196	–185	–39	562	618	–559	–437	193	2,296
Thailand	29,229	114,019	35,870	107,512	–853	–2,022	213	2,148	–7,281	6,632	14,258	49,847
Togo	663	*693*	847	*959*	–32	*–23*	132	*128*	–84	*–162*	358	360
Trinidad and Tobago	2,289	*5,890*	1,427	*4,283*	–397	*–681*	–6	*59*	459	*985*	513	3,195
Tunisia	5,203	13,308	6,039	14,099	–455	–1,298	828	1,534	–463	–555	867	4,031
Turkey	21,042	91,048	25,524	102,199	–2,508	–5,519	4,365	1,127	–2,625	–15,543	7,626	37,304
Turkmenistan	..	..	..	..	..	..	..	..	..	..	..	..
Uganda	178	1,153	686	2,154	–48	–172	293	974	–263	–200	44	1,308
Ukraine	..	39,719	..	34,846	..	–645	..	*2,576*	..	6,804	*469*	9,526
United Arab Emirates	..	..	..	..	..	..	..	..	..	..	4,891	18,530
United Kingdom	239,226	533,167	264,090	604,562	–5,154	48,582	–8,794	–19,697	–38,811	–42,511	43,146	49,740
United States	535,260	1,151,448	616,120	1,769,031	28,560	30,440	–26,660	–80,931	–78,960	–668,074	173,094	190,465
Uruguay	2,158	4,008	1,659	3,673	–321	–527	8	89	186	–103	1,446	2,512
Uzbekistan	..	..	..	..	..	..	..	..	..	..	..	..
Venezuela, RB	18,806	39,846	9,451	22,042	–774	–3,885	–302	–89	8,279	13,830	12,733	23,408
Vietnam	..	*19,654*	..	*21,458*	..	*–721*	..	*1,921*	..	*–604*	..	7,041
West Bank and Gaza	..	..	..	..	..	..	..	..	..	..	..	..
Yemen, Rep.	1,490	5,045	2,170	4,918	–372	–1,346	1,790	1,444	739	225	441	5,687
Zambia	1,360	..	1,897	..	–437	..	380	..	–594	..	201	337
Zimbabwe	2,012	..	2,001	..	–263	..	112	..	–140	..	295	*132*
World	4,323,913 t	11,238,500 t	4,305,881 t	11,096,960 t								
Low income	84,525	*224,181*	104,291	*247,585*								
Middle income	629,219	2,682,381	584,802	2,466,936								
Lower middle income	302,952	1,477,304	303,741	1,362,939								
Upper middle income	330,225	1,212,867	280,527	1,108,946								
Low & middle income	714,917	2,954,236	689,885	2,775,051								
East Asia & Pacific	167,280	1,105,736	166,172	1,026,871								
Europe & Central Asia[c]	..	764,285	..	729,833								
Latin America & Carib.	170,341	541,417	147,342	502,855								
Middle East & N. Africa	..	..	105,814	..								
South Asia	34,864	*114,362*	48,099	*131,775*								
Sub-Saharan Africa	78,044	166,824	72,993	166,946								
High income	3,593,864	8,314,172	3,592,267	8,352,618								
Europe EMU	1,523,198	3,491,397	1,484,793	3,286,395								

a. International reserves including gold valued at London gold price. b. Includes Luxembourg.

Balance of payments current account

About the data

The balance of payments records an economy's transactions with the rest of the world. Balance of payments accounts are divided into two groups: the current account, which records transactions in goods, services, income, and current transfers, and the capital and financial account, which records capital transfers, acquisition or disposal of nonproduced, nonfinancial assets, and transactions in financial assets and liabilities. The table presents data from the current account with the addition of gross international reserves.

The balance of payments is a double-entry accounting system that shows all flows of goods and services into and out of an economy; all transfers that are the counterpart of real resources or financial claims provided to or by the rest of the world without a quid pro quo, such as donations and grants; and all changes in residents' claims on and liabilities to nonresidents that arise from economic transactions. All transactions are recorded twice—once as a credit and once as a debit. In principle the net balance should be zero, but in practice the accounts often do not balance. In these cases a balancing item, net errors and omissions, is included.

Discrepancies may arise in the balance of payments because there is no single source for balance of payments data and therefore no way to ensure that the data are fully consistent. Sources include customs data, monetary accounts of the banking system, external debt records, information provided by enterprises, surveys to estimate service transactions, and foreign exchange records. Differences in collection methods—such as in timing, definitions of residence and ownership, and the exchange rate used to value transactions—contribute to net errors and omissions. In addition, smuggling and other illegal or quasi-legal transactions may be unrecorded or misrecorded. For further discussion of issues relating to the recording of data on trade in goods and services, see *About the data* for tables 4.4–4.7.

The concepts and definitions underlying the data in the table are based on the fifth edition of the International Monetary Fund's (IMF) *Balance of Payments Manual* (1993). The fifth edition redefined as capital transfers some transactions previously included in the current account, such as debt forgiveness, migrants' capital transfers, and foreign aid to acquire capital goods. Thus the current account balance now reflects more accurately net current transfer receipts in addition to transactions in goods, services (previously nonfactor services), and income (previously factor income). Many countries maintain their data collection systems according to the fourth edition. Where necessary, the IMF converts data reported in such systems to conform to the fifth edition (see *Primary data documentation*). Values are in U.S. dollars converted at market exchange rates.

The data in this table come from the IMF's Balance of Payments and International Financial Statistics databases, supplemented by estimates by World Bank staff for countries for which the IMF does not collect balance of payments statistics. In addition, World Bank staff make estimates of missing data for the current year for major countries to obtain meaningful aggregates.

Definitions

• **Exports and imports of goods and services** comprise all transactions between residents of an economy and the rest of the world involving a change in ownership of general merchandise, goods sent for processing and repairs, nonmonetary gold, and services. • **Net income** refers to receipts and payments of employee compensation for nonresident workers, and investment income (receipts and payments on direct investment, portfolio investment, and other investments and receipts on reserve assets). Income derived from the use of intangible assets is recorded under business services. • **Net current transfers** are recorded in the balance of payments whenever an economy provides or receives goods, services, income, or financial items without a quid pro quo. All transfers not considered to be capital are current. • **Current account balance** is the sum of net exports of goods and services, net income, and net current transfers. • **Total reserves** comprise holdings of monetary gold, special drawing rights, reserves of IMF members held by the IMF, and holdings of foreign exchange under the control of monetary authorities. The gold component of these reserves is valued at year-end (31 December) London prices ($385.00 an ounce in 1990, and $438.00 an ounce in 2004).

4.15a

Top 15 countries with the largest current account surplus, and top 15 countries with the largest current account deficit in 2003

Country	$ billions	% of GDP	Country	$ billions	% of GDP
Japan	136.2	3.2	United States	–519.7	–4.7
Germany	51.3	2.1	Spain	–31.7	–3.6
China	45.9	2.8	Austria	–30.7	–5.8
Switzerland	44.7	13.9	United Kingdom	–27.5	–1.5
Russian Federation	35.4	8.2	Italy	–19.4	–1.3
Netherlands	29.7	5.8	Greece	–12.6	–7.2
Taiwan, China	29.3	10.2	Portugal	–8.7	–5.9
Norway	28.3	12.8	Mexico	–8.6	–1.3
Saudi Arabia	28.1	13.1	Turkey	–8.0	–3.3
Singapore	27.0	29.2	Hungary	–7.2	–8.7
Sweden	22.8	7.6	Czech Republic	–5.8	–6.4
Hong Kong, China	16.5	10.6	Poland	–4.6	–2.2
Malaysia	13.4	12.9	New Zeland	–3.4	–4.2
Canada	13.4	1.6	Romania	–3.3	–5.8
Korea, Rep.	11.9	2.0	South Africa	–2.6	–1.6

Source: International Monetary Fund, Balance of Payments data files.

Data sources

Data on the balance of payments are published in the IMF's *Balance of Payments Statistics Yearbook* and *International Financial Statistics*. The World Bank exchanges data with the IMF through electronic files that in most cases are more timely and cover a longer period than the published sources. More information about the design and compilation of the balance of payments can be found in the IMF's *Balance of Payments Manual*, fifth edition (1993), *Balance of Payments Textbook* (1996a), and *Balance of Payments Compilation Guide* (1995). The IMF's International Financial Statistics and Balance of Payments databases are available on CD-ROM.

4.16 External debt

	Total external debt		Long-term debt		Public and publicly guaranteed debt				Private nonguaranteed external debt		Use of IMF credit	
					$ millions							
					Total		IBRD loans and IDA credits					
	$ millions		$ millions						$ millions		$ millions	
	1990	2004	1990	2004	1990	2004	1990	2004	1990	2004	1990	2004
Afghanistan	..	..	..	..	..	..	..	..	..	..	..	..
Albania	..	1,549	..	1,451	..	1,404	..	677	..	46	..	97
Algeria	28,149	21,987	26,688	20,913	26,688	20,249	1,208	909	0	664	670	643
Angola	8,592	9,521	7,604	8,631	7,604	8,631	0	318	0	0	0	0
Argentina	62,233	169,247	48,676	127,661	46,876	103,850	2,609	7,447	1,800	23,811	3,083	14,091
Armenia	..	1,224	..	984	..	961	..	780	..	24	..	218
Australia	..	..	..	..	..	..	..	..	..	..	..	..
Austria	..	..	..	..	..	..	..	..	..	..	..	..
Azerbaijan	..	1,986	..	1,640	..	1,409	..	493	..	230	..	208
Bangladesh	12,439	20,344	11,658	19,171	11,658	19,171	4,159	8,895	0	0	626	231
Belarus	..	3,717	..	772	..	744	..	73	..	29	..	9
Belgium	..	..	..	..	..	..	..	..	..	..	..	..
Benin	1,292	1,916	1,218	1,827	1,218	1,827	326	791	0	0	18	65
Bolivia	4,275	6,096	3,864	5,663	3,687	4,645	587	1,750	177	1,019	257	307
Bosnia and Herzegovina	..	3,202	..	2,734	..	2,644	..	1,454	..	90	..	109
Botswana	553	524	547	488	547	488	169	11	0	0	0	0
Brazil	119,964	222,026	94,427	171,729	87,756	97,865	8,427	8,668	6,671	73,864	1,821	25,029
Bulgaria	..	15,661	..	11,241	..	7,434	..	1,498	..	3,807	..	1,183
Burkina Faso	834	1,967	750	1,823	750	1,823	282	1,027	0	0	0	115
Burundi	907	1,385	851	1,325	851	1,325	398	793	0	0	43	41
Cambodia	1,845	3,377	1,683	3,016	1,683	3,016	0	467	0	0	27	97
Cameroon	6,657	9,496	5,577	8,557	5,347	7,924	871	1,200	230	632	121	333
Canada	..	..	..	..	..	..	..	..	..	..	..	..
Central African Republic	698	1,078	624	926	624	926	265	455	0	0	37	44
Chad	529	1,701	469	1,582	469	1,582	186	910	0	0	31	96
Chile	19,226	44,058	14,687	36,351	10,425	9,426	1,874	445	4,263	26,925	1,156	0
China	55,301	248,934	45,515	131,342	45,515	90,815	5,881	21,705	0	40,527	469	0
Hong Kong, China	..	..	..	..	..	..	..	..	..	..	..	..
Colombia	17,222	37,732	15,784	32,391	14,671	23,372	3,874	3,494	1,113	9,019	0	0
Congo, Dem. Rep.	10,259	11,841	8,994	10,532	8,994	10,532	1,161	1,993	0	0	521	818
Congo, Rep.	4,947	5,829	4,200	5,051	4,200	5,051	239	269	0	0	11	29
Costa Rica	3,756	5,700	3,367	4,013	3,063	3,859	412	72	304	154	11	0
Côte d'Ivoire	17,251	11,739	13,223	10,837	10,665	9,828	1,920	2,383	2,558	1,010	431	311
Croatia	..	31,548	..	29,338	..	11,668	..	856	..	17,670	..	0
Cuba	..	..	..	..	..	..	..	..	..	..	..	..
Czech Republic	..	45,561	..	28,470	..	12,020	..	52	..	16,450	..	0
Denmark	..	..	..	..	..	..	..	..	..	..	..	..
Dominican Republic	4,372	6,965	3,518	5,815	3,419	5,815	258	390	99	0	72	204
Ecuador	12,107	16,868	10,029	15,062	9,865	10,629	848	851	164	4,433	265	290
Egypt, Arab Rep.	33,017	30,291	28,439	27,353	27,439	27,353	2,401	1,968	1,000	0	125	0
El Salvador	2,149	7,250	1,938	5,470	1,913	5,384	164	361	26	86	0	0
Eritrea	..	681	..	666	..	666	..	352	..	0	..	0
Estonia	..	10,008	..	7,009	..	562	..	49	..	6,447	..	0
Ethiopia	8,630	6,574	8,479	6,351	8,479	6,351	851	3,488	0	0	6	183
Finland	..	..	..	..	..	..	..	..	..	..	..	..
France	..	..	..	..	..	..	..	..	..	..	..	..
Gabon	3,983	4,150	3,150	3,800	3,150	3,800	69	38	0	0	140	100
Gambia, The	369	674	308	622	308	622	102	247	0	0	45	25
Georgia	..	2,082	..	1,710	..	1,611	..	678	..	99	..	266
Germany	..	..	..	..	..	..	..	..	..	..	..	..
Ghana	3,734	7,035	2,670	5,861	2,637	5,861	1,423	4,312	33	0	745	469
Greece	..	..	..	..	..	..	..	..	..	..	..	..
Guatemala	2,849	5,532	2,368	3,916	2,241	3,796	293	478	127	120	67	0
Guinea	2,476	3,538	2,253	3,188	2,253	3,188	420	1,287	0	0	52	122
Guinea-Bissau	692	765	630	738	630	738	146	301	0	0	5	16
Haiti	910	1,225	772	1,186	772	1,186	324	504	0	0	38	11

External debt

	Total external debt		Long-term debt		Public and publicly guaranteed debt				Private nonguaranteed external debt		Use of IMF credit	
	$ millions		$ millions		$ millions Total		IBRD loans and IDA credits		$ millions		$ millions	
	1990	2004	1990	2004	1990	2004	1990	2004	1990	2004	1990	2004
Honduras	3,718	6,332	3,487	5,692	3,420	5,124	635	1,380	66	568	32	195
Hungary	21,202	63,159	17,931	50,829	17,931	20,725	1,512	220	0	30,103	330	0
India	83,628	122,723	72,462	115,199	70,974	88,699	20,996	28,507	1,488	26,499	2,623	0
Indonesia	69,872	140,649	58,242	106,463	47,982	72,917	10,385	9,939	10,261	33,546	494	9,686
Iran, Islamic Rep.	9,020	13,622	1,797	10,103	1,797	9,985	86	316	0	118	0	0
Iraq	..	..	..	..	..	..	..	..	..	..	..	..
Ireland	..	..	..	..	..	..	..	..	..	..	..	..
Israel	..	..	..	..	..	..	..	..	..	..	..	..
Italy	..	..	..	..	..	..	..	..	..	..	..	..
Jamaica	4,752	6,399	4,049	5,269	4,015	5,171	672	439	34	98	357	1
Japan	..	..	..	..	..	..	..	..	..	..	..	..
Jordan	8,333	8,175	7,202	7,234	7,202	7,234	593	1,018	0	0	94	338
Kazakhstan	..	32,310	..	28,738	..	3,209	..	1,275	..	25,528	..	0
Kenya	7,055	6,826	5,639	5,988	4,759	5,978	2,056	2,883	880	10	482	103
Korea, Dem. Rep.	..	..	..	..	..	..	..	..	..	..	..	..
Korea, Rep.	..	..	..	..	..	..	..	..	..	..	..	..
Kuwait	..	..	..	..	..	..	..	..	..	..	..	..
Kyrgyz Republic	..	2,100	..	1,885	..	1,740	..	579	..	145	..	207
Lao PDR	1,768	2,056	1,758	2,013	1,758	2,013	131	616	0	0	8	38
Latvia	..	12,661	..	5,008	..	1,587	..	187	..	3,421	..	0
Lebanon	1,779	22,177	358	18,206	358	17,460	34	387	0	746	0	0
Lesotho	396	764	378	726	378	726	112	284	0	0	15	38
Liberia	1,849	2,706	1,116	1,168	1,116	1,168	248	263	0	0	322	347
Libya	..	..	..	..	..	..	..	..	..	..	..	..
Lithuania	..	9,475	..	5,683	..	2,507	..	197	..	3,176	..	26
Macedonia, FYR	..	2,044	..	1,901	..	1,537	..	605	..	364	..	63
Madagascar	3,689	3,462	3,320	3,232	3,320	3,232	797	2,269	0	0	144	226
Malawi	1,558	3,418	1,385	3,297	1,382	3,297	854	2,076	3	0	115	93
Malaysia	15,328	52,145	13,422	40,713	11,592	25,560	1,102	638	1,830	15,153	0	0
Mali	2,468	3,316	2,337	3,132	2,337	3,132	498	1,441	0	0	69	145
Mauritania	2,113	2,297	1,806	2,046	1,806	2,046	264	694	0	0	70	90
Mauritius	984	2,294	910	941	762	859	195	88	148	82	22	0
Mexico	104,442	138,689	81,809	129,600	75,974	77,193	11,030	9,564	5,835	52,407	6,551	0
Moldova	..	1,868	..	1,168	..	754	..	386	..	415	..	126
Mongolia	..	1,517	..	1,306	..	1,306	..	287	..	0	..	44
Morocco	25,004	17,672	23,847	17,461	23,647	14,863	3,138	2,545	200	2,598	750	0
Mozambique	4,650	4,651	4,231	4,108	4,211	3,157	268	1,475	19	951	74	197
Myanmar	4,695	7,239	4,466	5,647	4,466	5,647	716	774	0	0	0	0
Namibia	..	..	..	..	..	..	..	..	..	..	..	..
Nepal	1,640	3,354	1,572	3,332	1,572	3,332	668	1,491	0	0	44	22
Netherlands	..	..	..	..	..	..	..	..	..	..	..	..
New Zealand	..	..	..	..	..	..	..	..	..	..	..	..
Nicaragua	10,745	5,145	8,313	4,403	8,313	4,125	299	1,167	0	278	0	248
Niger	1,726	1,950	1,487	1,811	1,226	1,772	461	1,106	261	39	85	135
Nigeria	33,439	35,890	31,935	31,304	31,545	31,304	3,321	1,994	391	0	0	0
Norway	..	..	..	..	..	..	..	..	..	..	..	..
Oman	2,736	3,872	2,400	2,565	2,400	1,209	52	0	0	1,356	0	0
Pakistan	20,663	35,687	16,643	32,566	16,506	31,029	3,922	9,278	138	1,537	836	1,876
Panama	6,493	9,469	3,842	9,047	3,842	7,305	462	246	0	1,742	272	36
Papua New Guinea	2,594	2,149	2,461	1,976	1,523	1,445	349	344	938	531	61	64
Paraguay	2,105	3,433	1,732	2,765	1,713	2,453	320	268	19	312	0	0
Peru	20,044	31,296	13,959	28,679	13,629	23,500	1,188	2,834	330	5,179	755	104
Philippines	30,580	60,550	25,241	54,748	24,040	35,564	4,044	3,531	1,201	19,184	912	756
Poland	49,364	99,190	39,261	82,343	39,261	36,595	55	1,912	0	45,748	509	0
Portugal	..	..	..	..	..	..	..	..	..	..	..	..
Puerto Rico	..	..	..	..	..	..	..	..	..	..	..	..

External debt

	Total external debt		Long-term debt		Public and publicly guaranteed debt				Private nonguaranteed external debt		Use of IMF credit	
					$ millions							
	$ millions		$ millions		Total		IBRD loans and IDA credits		$ millions		$ millions	
	1990	2004	1990	2004	1990	2004	1990	2004	1990	2004	1990	2004
Romania	1,140	30,034	230	24,756	223	13,667	0	2,522	7	11,089	0	443
Russian Federation	..	197,335	..	158,624	..	99,646	..	5,743	..	58,978	..	3,562
Rwanda	712	1,656	664	1,545	664	1,545	340	1,020	0	0	0	92
Saudi Arabia	..	..	..	..	..	..	..	..	..	..	..	..
Senegal	3,739	3,938	3,003	3,698	2,943	3,553	835	2,040	60	145	314	204
Serbia and Montenegro	..	15,882	..	13,052	..	9,508	..	3,302	..	3,545	..	964
Sierra Leone	1,196	1,723	940	1,520	940	1,520	92	591	0	0	108	196
Singapore	..	..	..	..	..	..	..	..	..	..	..	..
Slovak Republic	..	22,068	..	11,603	..	5,163	..	401	..	6,440	..	0
Slovenia	..	..	..	..	..	..	..	..	..	..	..	..
Somalia	2,370	2,849	1,926	1,949	1,926	1,949	419	444	0	0	159	174
South Africa	..	28,500	..	20,591	..	9,793	0	23	..	10,798	0	0
Spain	..	..	..	..	..	..	..	..	..	..	..	..
Sri Lanka	5,863	10,887	5,049	10,061	4,947	9,765	946	2,168	102	296	410	294
Sudan	14,762	19,332	9,651	12,220	9,155	11,724	1,048	1,300	496	496	956	593
Swaziland	298	470	294	456	294	456	44	27	0	0	0	0
Sweden	..	..	..	..	..	..	..	..	..	..	..	..
Switzerland	..	..	..	..	..	..	..	..	..	..	..	..
Syrian Arab Republic	17,259	21,521	15,108	15,742	15,108	15,742	523	24	0	0	0	0
Tajikistan	..	896	..	773	..	744	..	296	..	29	..	122
Tanzania	6,454	7,799	5,794	6,237	5,782	6,225	1,493	3,916	12	12	140	423
Thailand	28,095	51,307	19,771	39,819	12,460	15,323	2,530	559	7,311	24,496	1	0
Togo	1,281	1,812	1,081	1,597	1,081	1,597	398	716	0	0	87	27
Trinidad and Tobago	2,512	2,926	2,055	1,531	1,782	1,421	41	70	273	110	329	0
Tunisia	7,688	18,700	6,878	16,243	6,660	14,574	1,406	1,854	218	1,669	176	0
Turkey	49,424	161,595	39,924	108,188	38,870	68,212	6,429	6,230	1,054	39,976	0	21,507
Turkmenistan	..	..	..	..	..	..	..	..	..	..	..	..
Uganda	2,583	4,822	2,160	4,498	2,160	4,498	969	3,303	0	0	282	192
Ukraine	..	21,652	..	18,279	..	10,729	..	2,168	..	7,551	..	1,605
United Arab Emirates	..	..	..	..	..	..	..	..	..	..	..	..
United Kingdom	..	..	..	..	..	..	..	..	..	..	..	..
United States	..	..	..	..	..	..	..	..	..	..	..	..
Uruguay	4,415	12,376	3,114	7,712	3,045	7,251	359	785	69	462	101	2,684
Uzbekistan	..	5,007	..	4,810	..	4,302	..	317	..	508	..	19
Venezuela, RB	33,171	35,570	28,159	31,218	24,509	25,852	974	294	3,650	5,366	3,012	0
Vietnam	23,270	17,825	21,378	15,412	21,378	15,412	59	3,039	0	0	112	277
West Bank and Gaza	..	..	..	..	..	..	..	..	..	..	..	..
Yemen, Rep.	6,352	5,488	5,160	4,799	5,160	4,799	602	1,701	0	0	0	376
Zambia	6,905	7,279	4,543	6,257	4,541	5,871	813	2,637	2	386	949	890
Zimbabwe	3,279	4,797	2,681	3,604	2,496	3,558	449	983	185	46	7	293
World	.. s	.. s	.. s	.. s	.. s	.. s	.. s	.. s	.. s	.. s	.. s	.. s
Low income	332,618	426,945	285,169	379,869	277,476	346,191	56,639	110,191	7,692	33,678	10,818	10,888
Middle income	1,004,055	2,328,780	813,715	1,785,050	761,412	1,147,246	80,680	120,261	52,304	637,804	23,834	85,156
Lower middle income	553,760	1,140,272	456,404	859,746	423,325	589,496	53,183	84,079	33,079	270,250	8,305	43,131
Upper middle income	450,295	1,188,508	357,311	925,304	338,086	557,750	27,497	36,182	19,225	367,554	15,529	42,024
Low & middle income	1,336,673	2,755,725	1,098,884	2,164,919	1,038,888	1,493,438	137,319	230,452	59,996	671,482	34,652	96,044
East Asia & Pacific	234,078	588,888	194,619	403,085	172,984	269,630	25,307	42,041	21,635	133,455	2,085	10,964
Europe & Central Asia	217,224	794,943	176,378	603,687	171,457	321,739	10,429	32,978	4,921	281,947	1,305	30,735
Latin America & Carib.	444,629	778,970	352,716	639,331	327,698	433,342	35,877	41,926	25,018	205,989	18,298	43,307
Middle East & N. Africa	139,541	163,935	118,031	141,014	116,613	133,862	10,074	10,849	1,418	7,152	1,815	1,378
South Asia	124,396	193,933	107,527	181,227	105,800	152,895	30,717	50,465	1,727	28,332	4,537	2,423
Sub-Saharan Africa	176,805	235,056	149,612	196,576	144,336	181,970	24,916	52,193	5,276	14,606	6,612	7,238
High income												
Europe EMU												

About the data

Data on the external debt of developing countries are gathered by the World Bank through its Debtor Reporting System. World Bank staff calculate the indebtedness of these countries using loan-by-loan reports submitted by them on long-term public and publicly guaranteed borrowing, along with information on short-term debt collected by the countries or collected from creditors through the reporting systems of the Bank for International Settlements and the Organisation for Economic Co-operation and Development. These data are supplemented by information on loans and credits from major multilateral banks, loan statements from official lending agencies in major creditor countries, and estimates by World Bank and International Monetary Fund (IMF) staff. In addition, the table includes data on private nonguaranteed debt for 80 countries either reported to the World Bank or estimated by its staff.

The coverage, quality, and timeliness of debt data vary across countries. Coverage varies for both debt instruments and borrowers. With the widening spectrum of debt instruments and investors and the expansion of private nonguaranteed borrowing, comprehensive coverage of long-term external debt becomes more complex. Reporting countries differ in their capacity to monitor debt, especially private nonguaranteed debt. Even data on public and publicly guaranteed debt are affected by coverage and accuracy in reporting—again because of monitoring capacity and sometimes because of an unwillingness to provide information. A key part often underreported is military debt.

Because debt data are normally reported in the currency of repayment, they have to be converted into U.S. dollars to produce summary tables. Stock figures (amount of debt outstanding) are converted using end-of-period exchange rates, as published in the IMF's *International Financial Statistics* (line ae). Flow figures are converted at annual average exchange rates (line rf). Projected debt service is converted using end-of-period exchange rates. Debt repayable in multiple currencies, goods, or services and debt with a provision for maintenance of the value of the currency of repayment are shown at book value.

Because flow data are converted at annual average exchange rates and stock data at end-of-period exchange rates, year-to-year changes in debt outstanding and disbursed are sometimes not equal to net flows (disbursements less principal repayments); similarly, changes in debt outstanding, including undisbursed debt, differ from commitments less repayments. Discrepancies are particularly significant when exchange rates have moved sharply during the year. Cancellations and reschedulings of other liabilities into long-term public debt also contribute to the differences.

Variations in reporting rescheduled debt also affect cross-country comparability. For example, rescheduling under the auspices of the Paris Club of official creditors may be subject to lags between the completion of the general rescheduling agreement and the completion of the specific bilateral agreements that define the terms of the rescheduled debt. Other areas of inconsistency include country treatment of arrears and of nonresident national deposits denominated in foreign currency.

Definitions

• **Total external debt** is debt owed to nonresidents repayable in foreign currency, goods, or services. It is the sum of public, publicly guaranteed, and private nonguaranteed long-term debt, use of IMF credit, and short-term debt. Short-term debt includes all debt having an original maturity of one year or less and interest in arrears on long-term debt. • **Long-term debt** is debt that has an original or extended maturity of more than one year. It has three components: public, publicly guaranteed, and private nonguaranteed debt. • **Public and publicly guaranteed debt** comprises the long-term external obligations of public debtors, including the national government and political subdivisions (or an agency of either) and autonomous public bodies, and the external obligations of private debtors that are guaranteed for repayment by a public entity. • **IBRD loans and IDA credits** are extended by the World Bank. The International Bank for Reconstruction and Development (IBRD) lends at market rates. The International Development Association (IDA) provides credits at concessional rates. • **Private nonguaranteed external debt** consists of the long-term external obligations of private debtors that are not guaranteed for repayment by a public entity. • **Use of IMF credit** denotes repurchase obligations to the IMF for all uses of IMF resources (excluding those resulting from drawings on the reserve tranche). These obligations, shown for the end of the year specified, comprise purchases outstanding under the credit tranches (including enlarged access resources) and all special facilities (the buffer stock, compensatory financing, extended fund, and oil facilities), trust fund loans, and operations under the structural adjustment and enhanced structural adjustment facilities.

4.16a

GDP is outpacing external debt in Sub-Saharan countries

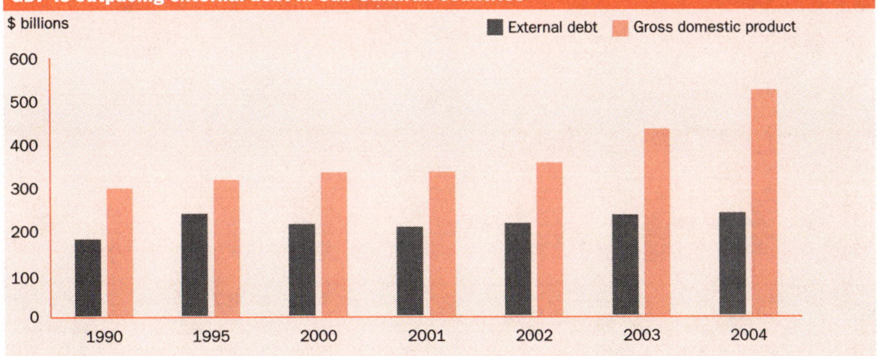

Source: World Bank data files.

Data sources

The main sources of external debt information are reports to the World Bank through its Debtor Reporting System from member countries that have received IBRD loans or IDA credits. Additional information is from the files of the World Bank and the IMF. Summary tables of the external debt of developing countries are published annually in the World Bank's *Global Development Finance* and on its *Global Development Finance* CD-ROM.

4.17 Debt ratios

	Present value of debt		Total debt service				Multilateral debt service		Short-term debt			
	% of GNI	% of exports of goods, sevices, and income	% of GNI		% of exports of goods, sevices, and income		% of public and publicly guaranteed debt		% of total debt		% of exports of goods, sevices, and income	
	2004	2004	1990	2004	1990	2004	1990	2004	1990	2004	1990	2004
Afghanistan	..	..	..	..	..	..	..	..	..	..	..	..
Albania	17	51	..	1.0	..	..	..	49.2	..	0.1	..	..
Algeria	32	80	14.7	7.1	63.4	..	5.0	28.1	2.8	2.0	5.7	..
Angola	68	82	4.0	11.9	8.1	14.8	2.2	0.6	11.5	9.4	24.7	6.4
Argentina	159	510	4.6	8.6	37.0	28.5	16.2	95.7	16.8	16.3	62.9	63.3
Armenia	50	130	..	3.4	..	8.1	..	41.7	..	1.8	..	1.7
Australia	..	..	..	..	..	..	..	..	..	..	..	..
Austria	..	..	..	..	..	..	..	..	..	..	..	..
Azerbaijan	23	45	..	3.0	..	5.3	..	31.5	..	7.0	..	3.1
Bangladesh	26	124	2.4	1.1	25.8	5.2	22.8	65.0	1.3	4.6	5.4	7.3
Belarus	20	30	..	1.4	..	2.1	..	16.9	..	79.0	..	18.6
Belgium	..	..	..	..	..	..	..	..	..	..	..	..
Benin	24[a]	113[a]	2.1	1.6	8.2	..	95.7	57.4	4.3	1.3	11.9	..
Bolivia	38[a]	136[a]	8.3	6.1	38.6	18.6	67.6	94.6	3.6	2.1	15.5	4.6
Bosnia and Herzegovina	34	63	..	2.0	..	3.7	..	66.5	..	11.2	..	7.5
Botswana	6	12	2.9	0.6	4.4	..	61.3	69.6	1.1	6.8	0.2	..
Brazil	47	258	1.8	9.2	22.2	46.8	43.5	21.4	19.8	11.4	64.4	22.0
Bulgaria	83	143	..	10.4	..	17.1	..	17.7	..	20.7	..	22.6
Burkina Faso	23[a]	203[a]	1.1	1.2	6.8	..	73.0	62.5	10.1	1.5	16.6	..
Burundi	15	203	3.8	13.7	43.4	..	51.1	90.3	1.5	1.4	13.7	..
Cambodia	68	99	2.7	0.6	..	0.8	0.0	71.2	7.3	7.8	..	7.7
Cameroon	20[a]	72[a]	4.9	4.6	20.5	..	43.5	22.7	14.4	6.4	37.9	..
Canada	..	..	..	..	..	..	..	..	..	..	..	..
Central African Republic	75	599	2.0	1.4	13.2	..	50.0	13.3	5.4	10.0	17.1	..
Chad	33[a]	79[a]	0.7	1.7	4.4	..	72.3	76.3	5.6	1.4	10.9	..
Chile	57	141	9.7	10.4	25.9	24.2	35.7	27.8	17.6	17.5	31.6	19.5
China	15	46	2.0	1.2	11.7	3.5	7.6	28.7	16.9	47.2	15.4	17.3
Hong Kong, China	..	..	..	..	..	..	..	..	..	..	..	..
Colombia	49	204	10.2	8.2	40.9	33.0	32.2	38.7	8.4	14.2	15.1	22.9
Congo, Dem. Rep.	36	131	4.1	1.9	..	..	49.6	50.9	7.3	4.1	..	..
Congo, Rep.	331	356	22.9	10.7	35.4	..	12.7	47.5	14.9	12.9	49.0	..
Costa Rica	36	70	9.2	3.8	23.9	7.3	36.1	38.2	10.1	29.6	18.0	17.9
Côte d'Ivoire	90	170	13.7	3.7	35.4	6.9	77.5	32.1	20.9	5.0	101.0	7.5
Croatia	110	194	..	15.8	..	27.2	..	9.1	..	7.0	..	11.3
Cuba	..	..	..	..	..	..	..	..	..	..	..	..
Czech Republic	51	71	..	8.2	..	10.5	..	7.1	..	37.5	..	21.6
Denmark	..	..	..	..	..	..	..	..	..	..	..	..
Dominican Republic	39	61	3.4	4.4	10.4	6.4	50.3	25.8	17.9	13.6	35.0	8.0
Ecuador	70	205	11.9	13.0	32.5	36.0	34.8	31.8	15.0	9.0	54.4	14.6
Egypt, Arab Rep.	32	108	7.3	3.0	20.4	7.6	18.7	23.0	13.5	9.7	29.6	9.7
El Salvador	54	123	4.4	4.0	15.3	8.8	60.2	53.4	9.8	24.6	15.5	25.5
Eritrea	53	154	..	2.1	..	..	..	50.3	..	2.1	..	..
Estonia	111	132	..	13.8	..	15.7	..	15.7	..	30.0	..	32.5
Ethiopia	30[a]	144[a]	2.8	1.2	39.0	5.3	14.6	77.7	1.7	0.6	24.0	2.1
Finland	..	..	..	..	..	..	..	..	..	..	..	..
France	..	..	..	..	..	..	..	..	..	..	..	..
Gabon	75	117	3.3	3.6	6.4	..	32.6	47.4	17.4	6.0	25.2	..
Gambia, The	108[a]	231[a]	12.9	8.6	22.2	..	25.4	65.6	4.3	4.0	9.3	..
Georgia	37	100	..	4.1	..	11.2	..	21.0	..	5.1	..	5.5
Germany	..	..	..	..	..	..	..	..	..	..	..	..
Ghana	32[a]	76[a]	6.3	2.7	38.1	6.6	31.2	35.7	8.6	10.0	33.5	19.5
Greece	..	..	..	..	..	..	..	..	..	..	..	..
Guatemala	23	88	3.1	2.0	13.6	7.4	33.4	54.6	14.5	29.2	24.4	22.0
Guinea	45[a]	186[a]	6.3	4.5	20.0	19.9	22.1	66.4	7.0	6.5	20.5	26.5
Guinea-Bissau	326[a]	779[a]	3.6	16.7	31.0	..	70.2	12.4	8.2	1.5	208.5	..
Haiti	29	76	1.3	3.7	11.0	..	69.2	92.9	11.1	2.3	31.0	..

Debt ratios

	Present value of debt		Total debt service				Multilateral debt service		Short-term debt			
	% of GNI	% of exports of goods, sevices, and income	% of GNI		% of exports of goods, sevices, and income		% of public and publicly guaranteed debt		% of total debt		% of exports of goods, sevices, and income	
	2004	2004	1990	2004	1990	2004	1990	2004	1990	2004	1990	2004
Honduras	38	68	13.7	4.7	35.3	7.8	90.7	70.9	5.4	7.0	18.1	10.5
Hungary	76	108	13.4	18.1	34.3	25.2	8.0	4.6	13.9	19.5	23.9	18.1
India	18	95	2.6	2.8	31.9	..	22.5	9.0	10.2	6.1	33.3	..
Indonesia	61	175	9.1	8.2	33.3	22.1	22.5	26.7	15.9	17.4	37.3	26.4
Iran, Islamic Rep.	9	31	0.5	1.2	3.2	..	30.5	5.1	80.1	25.8	35.8	..
Iraq	..	..	..	..	..	..	..	..	..	..	..	..
Ireland	..	..	..	..	..	..	..	..	..	..	..	..
Israel	..	..	..	..	..	..	..	..	..	..	..	..
Italy	..	..	..	..	..	..	..	..	..	..	..	..
Jamaica	89	141	15.9	9.9	26.9	14.8	38.6	23.0	7.3	17.6	14.1	20.0
Japan	..	..	..	..	..	..	..	..	..	..	..	..
Jordan	72	101	16.5	6.0	20.4	8.2	26.8	49.3	12.4	7.4	33.7	7.1
Kazakhstan	101	182	..	23.1	..	38.0	..	32.9	..	11.1	..	15.5
Kenya	34	136	9.6	2.3	35.4	8.6	44.7	41.8	13.2	10.8	41.8	17.3
Korea, Dem. Rep.	..	..	..	..	..	..	..	..	..	..	..	..
Korea, Rep.	..	..	..	..	..	..	..	..	..	..	..	..
Kuwait	..	..	..	..	..	..	..	..	..	..	..	..
Kyrgyz Republic	82	173	..	7.6	..	14.2	..	90.9	..	0.4	..	0.7
Lao PDR	76	276	1.1	2.3	8.7	..	53.6	74.3	0.1	0.2	2.1	..
Latvia	110	239	..	10.0	..	21.2	..	92.5	..	60.5	..	117.7
Lebanon	121	488	2.9	21.0	..	..	27.8	2.7	79.9	17.9	..	..
Lesotho	44	64	2.3	3.2	4.2	4.5	44.7	44.5	0.7	0.0	0.5	0.0
Liberia	760	2,133	..	0.2	..	..	100.0	..	22.2	44.0	..	..
Libya	..	..	..	..	..	..	..	..	..	..	..	..
Lithuania	53	96	..	8.2	..	14.3	..	22.7	..	39.8	..	30.7
Macedonia, FYR	39	94	..	4.6	..	10.5	..	40.9	..	4.0	..	3.5
Madagascar	38[a]	170[a]	7.5	1.9	45.5	..	23.7	67.4	6.1	0.1	46.0	..
Malawi	60[a]	186[a]	7.2	3.3	29.3	..	38.2	79.1	3.8	0.8	12.9	..
Malaysia	53	42	10.3	8.2	12.6	..	9.9	3.6	12.4	21.9	5.5	..
Mali	33[a]	98[a]	2.8	2.2	12.3	..	54.3	63.8	2.5	1.2	11.3	..
Mauritania	57[a]	186[a]	13.5	3.5	29.9	..	73.8	61.3	11.2	7.0	48.7	..
Mauritius	43	69	6.6	4.3	8.8	7.4	51.6	22.4	5.3	59.0	2.9	38.5
Mexico	24	77	4.5	7.7	20.7	22.9	26.0	14.6	15.4	6.6	29.5	4.1
Moldova[a]	75	108	..	8.5	..	12.1	..	40.7	..	30.7	..	28.1
Mongolia	86	108	..	2.6	..	2.9	..	40.5	..	11.0	..	11.7
Morocco	39	91	7.2	6.1	21.6	14.0	39.8	40.4	1.6	1.2	4.9	1.0
Mozambique	17[a]	54[a]	3.4	1.4	26.2	4.5	30.6	54.6	7.4	7.4	115.2	18.8
Myanmar	..	176	..	..	18.4	3.8	43.6	2.4	4.9	22.0	69.8	48.2
Namibia	..	..	..	..	..	..	..	..	..	..	..	..
Nepal	37	119	1.9	1.7	15.7	5.5	36.8	72.6	1.5	0.0	5.4	0.0
Netherlands	..	..	..	..	..	..	..	..	..	..	..	..
New Zealand	..	..	..	..	..	..	..	..	..	..	..	..
Nicaragua	35	78	1.6	2.9	3.9	5.8	21.1	55.5	22.6	9.6	602.0	22.7
Niger	25[a]	156[a]	4.1	1.7	17.4	..	71.3	83.8	8.9	0.2	27.1	..
Nigeria	71	140	13.0	4.0	22.6	8.2	15.5	20.2	4.5	12.8	10.2	15.6
Norway	..	..	..	..	..	..	..	..	..	..	..	..
Oman	18	29	6.5	4.3	12.3	6.9	5.1	38.8	12.3	33.8	5.6	9.1
Pakistan	35	156	4.6	4.6	21.3	21.2	40.3	65.2	15.4	3.5	35.6	6.2
Panama	94	129	6.8	11.0	6.2	14.3	90.6	16.7	36.6	4.1	42.5	3.9
Papua New Guinea	66	80	17.9	13.6	37.2	..	23.0	40.3	2.8	5.1	4.8	..
Paraguay	52	104	6.0	6.8	12.4	13.5	35.9	55.1	17.7	19.5	14.2	18.0
Peru	57	265	1.9	4.2	10.8	17.1	28.8	34.8	26.6	8.0	121.1	15.7
Philippines	73	124	8.2	12.8	27.0	20.9	28.7	12.4	14.5	8.3	33.3	9.1
Poland	45	121	1.7	14.5	4.9	34.6	9.2	24.6	19.4	17.0	48.9	16.9
Portugal	..	..	..	..	..	..	..	..	..	..	..	..
Puerto Rico	..	..	..	..	..	..	..	..	..	..	..	..

4.17 Debt ratios

	Present value of debt		Total debt service				Multilateral debt service		Short-term debt			
	% of GNI	% of exports of goods, sevices, and income	% of GNI		% of exports of goods, sevices, and income		% of public and publicly guaranteed debt		% of total debt		% of exports of goods, sevices, and income	
	2004	2004	1990	2004	1990	2004	1990	2004	1990	2004	1990	2004
Romania	51	136	0.1	6.6	0.3	17.2	..	28.5	79.8	16.1	13.9	17.6
Russian Federation	46	120	..	3.7	..	9.8	..	8.5	..	17.8	..	16.3
Rwanda	15[a]	150[a]	0.8	1.3	14.2	11.2	60.7	55.0	6.6	1.1	31.8	8.5
Saudi Arabia	..	..	..	..	..	..	..	..	..	..	..	..
Senegal	22[a]	61[a]	5.9	4.4	20.0	..	39.8	36.2	11.3	0.9	25.9	..
Serbia and Montenegro	77	209	..	4.1	..	..	..	81.0	..	11.8	..	..
Sierra Leone	37[a]	188[a]	3.7	2.5	10.1	10.9	26.1	31.4	12.4	0.4	70.6	3.0
Singapore	..	..	..	..	..	..	..	..	..	..	..	..
Slovak Republic	67	86	..	12.4	..	..	..	26.8	..	47.4	..	..
Slovenia	..	..	..	..	..	..	..	..	..	..	..	..
Somalia	..	..	1.3	..	..	..	100.0	..	12.0	25.5	..	..
South Africa	17	54	..	1.8	..	6.4	..	1.5	..	27.8	..	13.2
Spain	..	..	..	..	..	..	..	..	..	..	..	..
Sri Lanka	50	111	4.9	4.0	13.8	8.5	13.8	22.2	6.9	4.9	14.5	5.9
Sudan	151	625	0.4	1.6	8.7	6.0	100.0	18.3	28.2	33.7	724.8	124.3
Swaziland	27	25	4.9	1.8	5.7	1.7	72.9	50.1	1.5	3.0	0.6	0.5
Sweden	..	..	..	..	..	..	..	..	..	..	..	..
Switzerland	..	..	..	..	..	..	..	..	..	..	..	..
Syrian Arab Republic	101	249	10.0	1.4	21.8	3.5	3.5	33.5	12.5	26.9	39.4	62.5
Tajikistan	41	55	..	5.1	..	6.8	..	11.0	..	0.0	..	0.0
Tanzania	22[a, b]	115[a, b]	4.4	1.1	32.9	5.3	52.7	80.1	8.1	14.6	95.5	50.4
Thailand	35	50	6.3	7.8	16.9	10.6	22.1	42.0	29.6	22.4	26.6	9.8
Togo	83	191	5.4	1.0	11.9	..	40.8	45.7	8.8	10.4	15.6	..
Trinidad and Tobago	31	53	9.6	3.4	19.3	..	4.7	31.6	5.1	47.7	5.5	..
Tunisia	79	147	12.1	7.6	24.5	13.7	26.0	41.8	8.3	13.1	10.8	16.5
Turkey	69	221	4.9	11.3	29.4	35.9	23.3	7.8	19.2	19.7	37.7	33.8
Turkmenistan	..	..	..	..	..	..	..	..	..	..	..	..
Uganda	33[a]	162[a]	3.4	1.5	81.4	6.9	37.4	87.0	5.4	2.8	78.7	8.9
Ukraine	42	71	..	6.7	..	10.7	..	22.7	..	8.2	..	4.4
United Arab Emirates	..	..	..	..	..	..	..	..	..	..	..	..
United Kingdom	..	..	..	..	..	..	..	..	..	..	..	..
United States	..	..	..	..	..	..	..	..	..	..	..	..
Uruguay	108	351	11.0	12.2	40.8	34.9	16.2	37.3	27.2	16.0	49.7	44.8
Uzbekistan	45	123	..	7.1	..	..	..	13.3	..	3.6	..	..
Venezuela, RB	45	125	10.8	6.2	23.3	16.0	1.6	16.9	6.0	12.2	9.3	10.5
Vietnam	39	65	2.9	1.8	..	..	3.4	10.4	7.7	12.0	..	..
West Bank and Gaza	..	..	..	..	..	..	..	..	..	..	..	..
Yemen, Rep.	37	66	3.5	1.9	5.6	3.5	51.0	58.4	18.8	5.7	39.4	4.9
Zambia	36	112	6.7	8.3	14.7	..	41.0	48.2	20.5	1.8	103.8	..
Zimbabwe	33	264	5.5	2.0	23.2	..	24.0	32.9	18.0	18.8	29.0	..
World			.. w	.. w	.. w	.. w	.. w	.. w	.. w	.. w	.. w	..
Low income			3.9	3.0	22.4	10.1	27.7	24.8	11.0	8.5	39.9	17.7
Middle income			4.7	6.0	19.4	15.0	18.1	20.9	16.6	19.7	29.0	17.3
Lower middle income			4.1	4.5	24.3	13.1	22.3	26.9	16.1	20.8	30.1	16.5
Upper middle income			..	8.1	15.6	17.0	13.5	14.9	17.2	18.6	27.5	18.3
Low & middle income			4.5	5.6	19.8	14.5	19.4	21.4	15.2	18.0	30.5	17.3
East Asia & Pacific			4.8	3.0	17.5	6.8	17.7	23.0	16.0	29.7	20.5	16.8
Europe & Central Asia			..	8.9	..	19.6	10.0	14.3	18.2	20.2	36.0	19.8
Latin America & Carib.			4.2	8.1	23.8	26.4	27.6	24.4	16.6	12.4	39.7	16.2
Middle East & N. Africa			6.3	4.4	21.4	10.6	13.1	24.3	14.1	13.1	22.5	12.9
South Asia			2.9	2.9	27.6	12.4	25.3	21.2	9.9	5.3	30.1	6.1
Sub-Saharan Africa			..	2.9	13.5	7.9	30.0	23.0	11.6	13.3	..	18.0
High income												
Europe EMU												

a. Data are from debt sustainability analyses undertaken as part of the Heavily Indebted Poor Countries Initiative. Present value estimates for these countries are for public and publicly guaranteed debt only. b. Data refer to mainland Tanzania only.

About the data

The indicators in the table measure the relative burden on developing countries of servicing external debt. The present value of external debt provides a measure of future debt service obligations that can be compared with the current value of such indicators as gross national income (GNI) and exports of goods and services. The table shows the present value of total debt service both as a percentage of GNI in 2004 and as a percentage of exports in 2004. The ratios compare total debt service obligations with the size of the economy and its ability to obtain foreign exchange through exports. The ratios shown here may differ from those published elsewhere because estimates of exports and GNI have been revised to incorporate data available as of February 1, 2006. Exports refer to exports of goods, services, and income. Workers' remittances are not included here, though they are included with income receipts in other World Bank publications such as *Global Development Finance*.

The present value of external debt is calculated by discounting the debt service (interest plus amortization) due on long-term external debt over the life of existing loans. Short-term debt is included at its face value. The data on debt are in U.S. dollars converted at official exchange rates (see *About the data* for table 4.16). The discount rate applied to long-term debt is determined by the currency of repayment of the loan and is based on reference rates for commercial interest established by the Organisation for Economic Co-operation and Development. Loans from the International Bank for Reconstruction and Development (IBRD) and credits from the International Development Association (IDA) are discounted using a special drawing rights reference rate, as are obligations to the International Monetary Fund (IMF). When the discount rate is greater than the interest rate of the loan, the present value is less than the nominal sum of future debt service obligations.

The ratios in the table are used to assess the sustainability of a country's debt service obligations, but there are no absolute rules to determine what values are too high. Empirical analysis of the experience of developing countries and their debt service performance has shown that debt service difficulties become increasingly likely when the ratio of the present value of debt to exports reaches 200 percent. Still, what constitutes a sustainable debt burden varies from one country to another. Countries with fast-growing economies and exports are likely to be able to sustain higher debt levels.

The most indebted low-income countries may be eligible for debt relief under special programs, such as the Heavily Indebted Poor Countries Debt Initiative. Indebted countries may also apply to the Paris and London Clubs for renegotiation of obligations to public and private creditors. The World Bank no longer classifies countries by their level of indebtedness for the purposes of developing debt management startegies.

Definitions

• **Present value of debt** is the sum of short-term external debt plus the discounted sum of total debt service payments due on public, publicly guaranteed, and private nonguaranteed long-term external debt over the life of existing loans. • **Exports of goods, services, and income** refer to international transactions involving a change in ownership of general merchandise, goods sent for processing and repairs, nonmonetary gold, services, receipts of employee compensation for nonresident workers, and investment income. • **Total debt service** is the sum of principal repayments and interest actually paid on total long-term debt (public and publicly guaranteed and private nonguaranteed), use of IMF credit, and interest on short-term debt. • **Multilateral debt service** is the repayment of principal and interest to the World Bank, regional development banks, and other multilateral and intergovernmental agencies. • **Short-term debt** includes all debt having an original maturity of one year or less and interest in arrears on long-term debt.

4.17a

The debt burden of Sub-Saharan countries has been falling since 1995

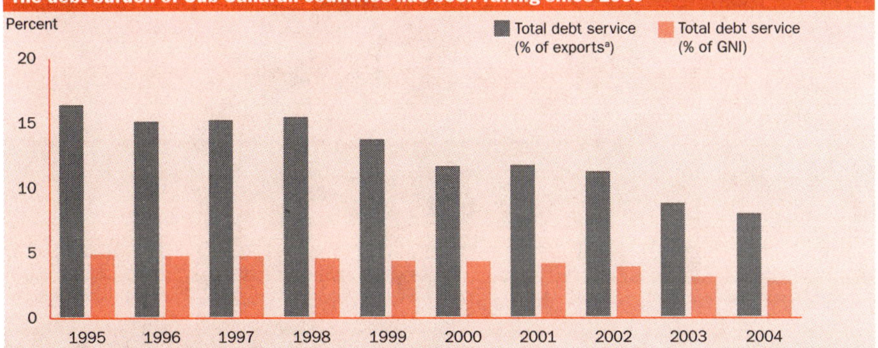

a. Includes goods, services, income, and workers' remittances.

Source: World Bank data files.

Data sources

The main sources of external debt information are reports to the World Bank through its Debtor Reporting System from member countries that have received IBRD loans or IDA credits. Additional information is from the files of the World Bank and the IMF. Data on GNI and exports of goods and services are from the World Bank's national accounts files and the IMF's Balance of Payments database. Summary tables of the external debt of developing countries are published annually in the World Bank's *Global Development Finance* and on its *Global Development Finance* CD-ROM.

5 STATES & MARKETS

Effective governments improve people's standard of living by ensuring access to essential services, such as health, education, water and sanitation, electricity, and transport, and the opportunity to live and work in peace and security. Countries confront different development challenges and face unique constraints. The main elements to get right are economic management, regulation, and taxation; efficient financial and labor markets; public safety and security; and the building and maintenance of infrastructure. Together, they provide an environment of incentives and opportunities in which firms and individuals can invest and work productively. This section brings together indicators that measure the actions of governments and the responses of markets through three cross-cutting development themes: managing the public sector, developing the private sector, and providing infrastructure.

Without good governance, other reforms have limited impact

In successful, high-growth economies such as Botswana, China, India, the Republic of Korea, Mauritius, and Singapore, the state has played an important role in attracting investment; improving productivity, technology, and competitiveness; and promoting property rights, contract enforcement, and economic and political stability. Institutions differ in each of these countries, as do the choices of legal regimes, balance between regulation and competition, size of the public sector, and flexibility of fiscal and monetary policies. Solutions that work in one place may not work in another. And while an accountable and capable state with strong institutions has come to be recognized as fundamental to economic and social development, it is still difficult to quantify what is meant by good governance or to measure the quality of institutions. More research is needed to understand the role of institutions and how to improve them in countries with weak institutions.

Many African leaders recognize that building strong institutions and improving public sector management are needed to encourage investment and economic growth and that poverty reduction is impossible without that. Improving public revenue and expenditure management is on the agenda of several African countries and is also a priority of the New Partnership for Africa's Development.

Many countries are using public expenditure tracking surveys to identify shortcomings in the delivery of public services, including Cameron, Ghana, Madagascar, Mozambique, Rwanda, Senegal, Tanzania, Uganda, and Zambia. Expenditure transactions can be complex, with leakages and diversions common in a range of processes, including procurement. Such surveys map and track specific expenditure flows from allocation through intended use. In Uganda a survey conducted in 1996–99 increased intended resources arriving at a school from an average of 13 percent to 78 percent (World Bank 2005c). Although such surveys are not a substitute for broad strengthening of public sector financial management, they can help in understanding weaknesses in public financial management capacity and accountability mechanisms at various levels.

Improving the investment climate for increased private sector investment, growth, and poverty reduction

Better policies, institutions, physical infrastructure, and human resources are needed to attract domestic and foreign investors and to improve the efficiency of firms. But the goal is an investment climate that benefits society, not just firms.

What can governments do to attract the investment needed for its citizens? They can create stability. Combat corruption by public officials, firms, and other interest groups. Foster trust and legitimacy through participatory policymaking and transparency. And develop policies that address current economic and business conditions. Investment climate surveys draw data directly from firms and cover both objective and subjective indicators. Investment climate indicators cover eight factors that influence investment decisions, from policy uncertainty and corruption to reliability of electricity and the availability of skilled labor and labor regulations (table 5.2).

In investment climate surveys senior managers ranked policy uncertainty as the main business constraint. These surveys tell us that, compared with other developing country regions, Sub-Saharan Africa is a high-cost, high-risk place to do business, resulting in less investment, less employment, lower incomes, less growth and competitiveness, and higher poverty. Overall, doing business in Africa costs about 20–40 percent more than in other developing country regions. Costs are higher because of burdensome regulations, difficulty securing property rights, ineffective courts, weak infrastructure, and uncompetitive services. Because 80 percent of investment is from domestic sources, institutions and policies in Africa need to focus on the domestic investment climate, especially for agriculture and in rural areas. In 14 African countries with investment climate surveys, the high cost of financing for firms is the number one complaint.

New studies of business regulations and their enforcement have been conducted in 155 countries jointly by the International Finance Corporation and World Bank through the Doing Business survey program. The Doing Business findings are based on responses to objective questions using standardized surveys of experts, usually lawyers and accountants. These surveys complement the investment climate surveys by comparing the ease of doing business in 10 areas ranging from starting a business and dealing with licenses to hiring and firing, protecting investors, trading across borders, enforcing contracts, and closing a business. Data on most of these dimensions of doing business are presented in tables 5.3 and 5.6 .

Doing Business surveys have been conducted in 33 African countries. One conclusion of the *Doing Business 2006* report: more reform is needed in Africa (figure 5a). Entrepreneurs face greater regulatory obstacles in Africa than in any other region. Of the 16 countries surveyed in West Africa just 2 carried out business regulation reforms. In the region as a whole for every three countries that improved regulation, one made it more burdensome.

5a

Africa had the lowest business environment reform intensity in 2004

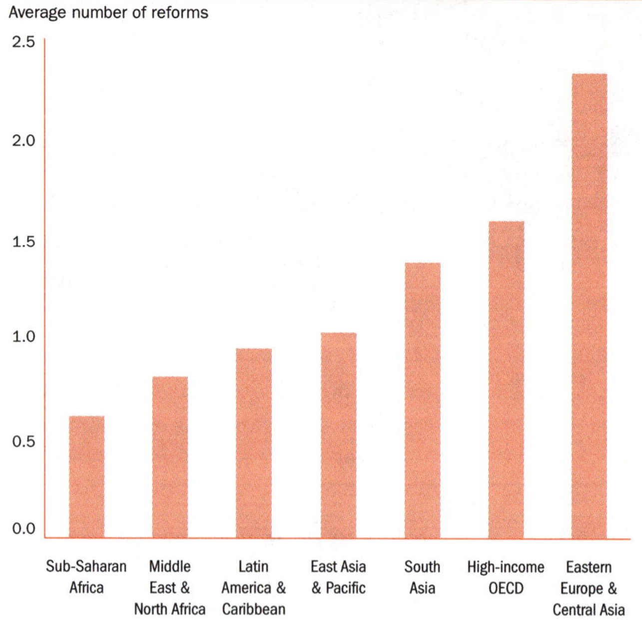

Source: Doing Business database.

But in some African countries, like Rwanda, reforms are paying off. In 2001 Rwanda introduced new company and labor laws. Land titling reforms followed in 2002. In 2004 Rwanda was among the top reformers: it streamlined customs procedures, improved credit registries, and simplified judicial procedures. Since initiating reform, Rwanda has had economic growth averaging 3.6 percent a year—among the highest for non-oil-producing states in Africa. Uganda has also benefited from an improved investment climate, posting GDP growth of about 7 percent a year during 1993–2002 and reducing poverty measured by a national poverty line from 55 percent in 1993 to 37.7 percent in 2000. Other African countries that have made progress in business reform include Mauritius, Namibia, Nigeria, and South Africa.

Infrastructure for development

Infrastructure services affect people in many ways—what they consume and produce; how they heat and light their homes; how they travel to work, to school, or to visit friends and family; and how they communicate, share information, and learn at home, school, and work. And the profitability and competitiveness of businesses depend on the cost and availability of infrastructure services such as the power and fuel used to operate machines or the transportation services needed to deliver raw materials to factories and finished products to market.

Physical isolation is a strong contributor to poverty. Populations without reliable access to social and economic services are poorer than those with reliable access. Problems of access are particularly severe in rural areas far from roads used regularly for motorized transport services. An estimated 900 million rural dwellers in developing countries, most of them poor, are without reliable access.

In many developing countries increasing agricultural productivity is central to rural development and poverty reduction strategies. Improved rural transport makes it easier for farmers to obtain inputs and advice at reasonable cost and to sell their products at good prices. Farmers with difficult access to local markets earn less for their products than farmers with easier access, and increases in output are associated with agricultural areas with improved roads.

An indicator has been developed to measure rural transport access based on the proportion of the rural populations that lives within 2 kilometers of an all-season road (a road that can be used all year by the prevailing means of rural transport, often a pick-up or other truck without four-wheel drive). Predictable interruptions of short duration during inclement weather (for example, heavy rainfall) are accepted, particularly on low-volume roads. The rural access index, calculated from representative household surveys, is shown for selected International Development Association (IDA)–eligible countries, in table 5b.

Values of the rural access index were also calculated on the basis of rural population, road length, and arable land area for more that 30 other countries (mainly non-IDA recipients) for which there are no suitable household survey results. The values for 64 countries (representing 85 percent of the world's rural population) show that 57 percent of rural inhabitants in IDA countries enjoy adequate access compared with 87 percent in non-IDA countries. Among developing country regions, Sub-Saharan Africa had the lowest level of rural access (30 percent), followed by Middle East and North Africa (34 percent),

5b

Rural access index for selected low-income countries (% of rural population)

Country	Index	Country	Index
Albania	31	Kenya	44
Azerbaijan	67	Lao PDR[a]	59
Bangladesh	37	Madagascar	25
Benin	32	Malawi	38
Burkina Faso	25	Mongolia	36
Burundi	19	Nicaragua	28
Cambodia[a]	87	Niger	37
Cameroon	20	Nigeria	47
Chad	5	Pakistan	77
Congo, Dem. Rep	26	Papua New Guinea	68
Ethiopia	17	Tajikistan	74
Gambia, The[b]	77	Tanzania	38
Ghana	34	Uzbekistan	57
Guinea[c]	22	Vietnam	73
India	60	Yemen, Rep.	21
Indonesia	94		

Note: Based on surveys between 1997 and 2003.
a. Nonstandard measurement process resulting in a higher index value.
b. Survey conducted during 1994–96.
c. Survey conducted in 2004.
Source: World Bank Transport Technical Paper based on household surveys.

Latin America and the Caribbean (54 percent), South Asia (58 percent), Europe and Central Asia (75 percent), and East Asia (94 percent).

Improvements in roads and transport services generally have significant positive effects on school attendance. In Morocco in the early 1990s a paved road in the community more than doubled girls' school attendance rates from 21 percent to 48 percent and raised boys' attendance rates from 58 percent to 76 percent, according to survey findings. In health, transport services play several important roles: ensuring adequate and reliable availability of food, providing medical supplies, transporting health personnel to facilities, and the most difficult role, bringing people to medical stations, whether for urgent care or regular treatment.

Information and communication technology has the potential for reducing poverty and fostering growth in developing countries. Mobile phones provide market information for farmers and businesspeople, the Internet delivers information to schools and hospitals, and computers improve public and private services and increase productivity and participation. Firms that use information and communication technology grow faster, invest more, and are more productive and profitable than those that do not. A survey of firms in developing countries found that sales growth is 3.4 percentage points higher and value added per employee is $3,400 higher in firms that use email to do business with clients and suppliers. And by making information accessible to more people, information and communication technology enhances social inclusion and promotes more effective, accountable governments.

Africa lags behind other regions in most infrastructure indicators. The high cost and poor quality of infrastructure services—transport, energy, water and sanitation, and information and communication technology—have limited growth potential. For Africa to reach the Millennium Development Goal of halving poverty by 2015, average growth rates need to reach 7 percent a year. That will require annual investment of $20 billion in infrastructure, about twice as much as Africa has historically invested. About 40 percent of that needs to go into roads and 20 percent each into energy and water (World Bank 2005c).

Financing these infrastructure needs in Africa will require a concerted effort from all funding sources, public and private. Led by the African Union and the New Partnership for Africa's Development, and including the African Development Bank and the World Bank, the Africa Infrastructure Consortium is working to mobilize and allocate infrastructure resources to support country and regional projects. The goal is to improve infrastructure, whether services are delivered by public or private providers or jointly. Reformers need to consider multiple factors—the strength of institutions, regulatory rules, fiscal health, investor interest, the competitiveness of markets, and other specific characteristics that influence the performance of public and private operators.

5.1 Private sector in the economy

	Investment in infrastructure projects with private participation[a]								Domestic credit to private sector		Micro, small, and medium-size enterprises[b]	
	$ millions											
	Telecommunications		Energy		Transport		Water and sanitation		% of GDP		number of firms	Employment % of total
	1995–99	**2000–04**	**1995–99**	**2000–04**	**1995–99**	**2000–04**	**1995–99**	**2000–04**	**1990**	**2004**	**2000–04**	**2000–04**
Afghanistan	..	204.0	..	..	..	..	..	..	..	..	..	..
Albania	..	443.2	0.0	8.0	..	..	..	0.0	..	9.9	35,694	56.7
Algeria	..	2,052.5	..	..	..	..	..	..	44.4	11.0	580,000	..
Angola	..	278.7	..	45.0	..	55.0	..	..	..	5.4	..	..
Argentina	10,498.6	5,130.2	13,093.6	3,389.5	8,848.1	200.2	3,473.6	688.9	15.6	10.5	..	..
Armenia	442.0	94.1	0.0	47.0	..	50.0	..	0.0	..	7.8	34,000	31.3
Australia	..	..	..	..	..	..	..	..	61.6	102.4	1,269,000	52.3
Austria	..	..	..	..	..	..	..	..	89.7	*105.6*	252,399	65.3
Azerbaijan	122.0	232.6	..	375.2	..	..	..	0.0	..	9.1	21,178	5.0
Bangladesh	438.1	651.3	554.9	501.5	0.0	0.0	..	..	16.7	30.1	177,000	80.0
Belarus	20.0	534.3	500.0	..	..	..	..	..	..	14.0	237,467	9.7
Belgium	..	..	..	..	..	..	..	..	37.0	*73.1*	437,000	69.3
Benin	..	106.9	..	..	..	..	..	..	20.3	14.5	..	..
Bolivia	528.0	471.5	2,777.3	679.8	168.7	16.6	682.0	..	24.0	42.2	..	..
Bosnia and Herzegovina	0.0	0.0	..	..	..	..	..	..	..	43.8	75,000	62.6
Botswana	97.0	85.0	..	..	..	..	..	..	9.4	19.0	16,466	..
Brazil	45,052.4	36,039.1	34,196.8	24,638.9	17,460.5	3,082.6	2,137.0	1,587.6	38.9	35.1	4,667,609	56.5
Bulgaria	202.5	1,418.6	..	1,246.0	..	..	..	152.0	..	37.1	224,211	64.7
Burkina Faso	..	41.9	5.6	..	..	..	..	..	16.8	14.9	..	..
Burundi	..	53.6	..	..	..	..	..	..	8.6	22.6	..	..
Cambodia	102.4	79.3	143.0	38.1	120.0	125.3	..	..	..	9.3	..	..
Cameroon	12.7	365.4	..	91.9	95.0	0.0	..	..	26.7	9.9	..	..
Canada	..	..	..	..	..	..	..	..	75.9	86.0	2,374,247	65.0
Central African Republic	1.1	..	..	..	..	..	..	..	7.2	7.2	..	..
Chad	2.0	11.0	..	0.0	..	..	..	..	7.3	3.3	..	..
Chile	3,489.0	3,134.6	6,808.6	1,224.2	3,104.1	4,499.0	3,111.2	1,563.0	47.2	63.1	700,000	95.0
China	5,970.0	8,495.0	16,916.2	5,359.1	10,802.8	5,201.1	719.8	2,332.8	87.7	120.1	25,110,000	78.0
Hong Kong, China	..	..	..	..	..	..	..	..	163.7	150.2	284,000	60.0
Colombia	1,384.3	715.5	6,964.8	107.6	995.5	1,160.5	233.0	237.3	30.8	22.8	967,315	49.0
Congo, Dem. Rep.	68.0	431.4	..	..	0.0	..	..	..	1.8	1.5	..	..
Congo, Rep.	12.2	61.8	325.0	..	..	..	..	..	15.7	3.2	..	..
Costa Rica	..	..	301.2	80.0	..	161.0	..	..	15.8	32.3	40,921	54.3
Côte d'Ivoire	752.3	114.9	260.6	..	178.0	140.0	..	..	36.5	14.4	..	..
Croatia	978.0	926.5	368.5	7.1	672.2	405.0	..	298.7	..	57.5	96,146	40.0
Cuba	..	60.0	165.0	..	..	0.0	..	600.0	..	..	..	..
Czech Republic	6,178.5	4,751.6	944.1	3,865.3	283.7	106.7	44.9	318.3	..	33.4	2,350,584	62.2
Denmark	..	..	..	..	..	..	..	..	52.2	160.3	205,000	78.4
Dominican Republic	163.0	306.8	979.0	1,264.1	..	898.9	..	..	27.5	27.9	..	..
Ecuador	696.4	197.0	30.0	302.0	686.8	20.0	..	550.0	13.6	22.5	..	..
Egypt, Arab Rep.	1,914.5	2,049.9	700.0	678.0	123.9	735.3	..	..	30.6	54.5	2,500,000	..
El Salvador	610.5	668.1	900.2	85.0	..	..	..	..	19.1	40.5	465,969	..
Eritrea	..	40.0	..	..	..	..	..	..	..	*32.8*	..	..
Estonia	628.2	244.7	26.5	..	1.0	298.4	..	81.0	..	42.4	32,801	55.0
Ethiopia	..	..	..	300.0	..	..	..	..	19.5	24.3	..	..
Finland	..	..	..	..	..	..	..	..	86.6	*68.7*	221,000	59.2
France	..	..	..	..	..	..	..	..	94.3	*90.8*	2,971,178	62.7
Gabon	8.4	26.6	624.8	..	46.7	85.6	..	..	13.0	8.6	..	..
Gambia, The	..	6.6	..	..	..	..	..	..	11.0	11.7	..	..
Georgia	61.0	142.8	159.0	13.0	..	..	..	..	..	9.7	25,593	50.6
Germany	..	..	..	..	..	..	..	..	88.7	*112.3*	3,008,000	70.4
Ghana	491.1	101.3	383.8	184.0	..	10.0	..	..	4.9	13.1	25,679	66.0
Greece	..	..	..	..	..	..	..	..	36.3	*78.6*	771,000	74.0
Guatemala	1,366.3	440.2	1,223.2	110.0	33.8	..	..	..	14.2	19.8	..	..
Guinea	120.3	18.0	36.4	..	..	..	0.0	..	..	3.6	..	..
Guinea-Bissau	..	21.3	..	..	..	..	..	..	22.0	1.5	..	..
Haiti	1.5	18.0	4.7	..	..	..	..	..	12.6	15.6	..	..

Private sector in the economy 5.1

	Investment in infrastructure projects with private participation[a] $ millions								Domestic credit to private sector		Micro, small, and medium-size enterprises[b]	
	Telecommunications		Energy		Transport		Water and sanitation		% of GDP		number of firms	Employment % of total
	1995–99	2000–04	1995–99	2000–04	1995–99	2000–04	1995–99	2000–04	1990	2004	2000–04	2000–04
Honduras	51.3	94.3	112.1	358.8	10.5	120.0	..	220.0	31.1	42.0	257,422	..
Hungary	6,430.2	4,632.7	3,812.1	260.6	135.0	..	178.5	0.0	46.6	46.5	855,058	55.8
India	7,456.8	14,321.9	7,165.6	7,559.8	1,272.8	1,854.3	..	223.2	25.2	37.1	..	..
Indonesia	9,103.9	4,989.6	9,942.1	315.6	2,223.1	590.3	882.8	36.7	46.9	23.6	41,362,315	..
Iran, Islamic Rep.	28.0	345.0	..	650.0	..	..	..	..	32.5	38.3	..	..
Iraq	..	420.0	..	..	..	..	..	..	..	..	..	..
Ireland	..	..	..	..	..	..	..	..	47.6	*136.9*	97,000	72.1
Israel	..	..	..	..	..	..	..	..	57.6	92.2	391,106	44.0
Italy	..	..	..	..	..	..	..	..	56.5	*87.8*	4,486,000	73.0
Jamaica	235.5	700.3	43.0	201.0	0.0	565.0	..	..	36.1	18.1	..	..
Japan	..	..	..	..	..	..	..	..	175.7	99.5	5,712,191	88.0
Jordan	39.9	1,351.0	..	..	182.0	0.0	0.0	169.0	72.3	72.1	139,844	54.5
Kazakhstan	1,633.5	669.2	1,825.0	300.0	..	..	..	40.0	..	28.3	..	..
Kenya	193.0	787.0	189.0	..	53.4	..	..	..	32.7	26.8	22,014	74.2
Korea, Dem. Rep.	..	..	..	..	..	..	..	..	..	..	..	..
Korea, Rep.	..	..	..	..	..	..	..	..	62.8	98.2	2,948,171	86.7
Kuwait	..	..	..	..	..	..	..	..	0.0	71.6	..	..
Kyrgyz Republic	100.0	9.1	..	..	..	..	..	..	..	7.1	22,670	62.2
Lao PDR	157.1	77.7	535.5	..	..	0.0	..	..	1.0	6.5	..	..
Latvia	600.9	609.4	106.0	71.1	75.0	..	..	..	..	44.8	32,571	36.6
Lebanon	485.7	138.1	..	..	..	153.0	..	0.0	79.4	75.9	..	..
Lesotho	15.7	85.4	..	0.0	..	..	..	..	15.8	6.5	..	..
Liberia	..	50.0	..	..	..	..	..	..	*0.0*	6.1	..	..
Libya	..	..	..	..	..	..	..	..	31.0	16.9	..	..
Lithuania	832.7	933.0	10.0	399.3	..	..	..	..	..	25.9	55,825	70.6
Macedonia, FYR	..	706.6	..	..	..	..	..	..	..	23.2	27,938	..
Madagascar	10.1	12.6	..	..	..	20.3	..	..	16.9	10.0	..	..
Malawi	23.1	11.3	..	..	6.0	..	..	..	10.9	8.4	747,396	38.0
Malaysia	4,187.6	2,253.0	1,610.2	5,048.1	8,200.1	3,347.3	1,084.4	48.1	69.4	130.1	204,669	..
Mali	..	82.6	..	747.0	..	..	..	..	12.8	20.1	..	..
Mauritania	..	119.7	..	..	..	..	..	..	43.5	*25.9*	..	..
Mauritius	..	406.0	109.3	..	42.6	..	..	..	35.6	59.5	75,267	..
Mexico	10,757.5	14,743.6	2,095.8	6,494.3	4,988.5	1,047.3	276.5	520.7	17.5	16.7	2,891,300	71.9
Moldova	84.6	..	60.0	25.3	..	..	..	..	..	21.3	20,518	8.2
Mongolia	21.9	21.6	..	..	..	..	..	..	..	32.0	..	..
Morocco	1,240.0	5,233.0	5,819.9	1,049.0	..	..	1,000.0	..	34.1	56.7	450,000	..
Mozambique	29.0	109.0	..	1,200.0	441.0	797.1	0.6	..	17.6	2.1	..	..
Myanmar	4.0	..	394.0	..	50.0	..	..	..	4.7	*12.1*	..	..
Namibia	53.2	35.2	4.0	1.0	..	450.0	..	0.0	22.6	50.4	..	..
Nepal	..	20.0	98.2	39.0	..	..	..	..	12.8	..	..	..
Netherlands	..	..	..	..	..	..	..	..	79.9	*166.3*	570,000	58.5
New Zealand	..	..	..	..	..	..	..	..	76.0	121.1	323,998	29.2
Nicaragua	24.5	240.3	232.4	115.0	..	104.0	..	..	*112.6*	26.8	..	..
Niger	..	99.9	..	..	..	..	..	4.9	12.3	6.2	..	..
Nigeria	69.0	4,639.7	..	709.0	..	22.8	..	..	9.4	15.6	..	..
Norway	..	..	..	..	..	..	..	..	81.7	9.9	288,368	56.9
Oman	..	..	183.0	1,364.3	77.5	473.8	..	..	20.6	*34.9*	..	..
Pakistan	75.5	1,877.7	4,298.3	..	421.3	47.0	..	..	24.2	29.3	..	..
Panama	1,429.2	10.7	669.2	395.7	994.6	51.4	25.0	..	46.7	91.2	..	..
Papua New Guinea	..	..	65.0	..	..	..	175.0	..	28.6	11.0	..	..
Paraguay	199.3	77.6	..	..	58.0	..	..	..	15.8	15.4	..	..
Peru	4,774.5	1,948.4	3,004.9	2,092.6	86.3	239.5	..	56.0	11.8	18.6	509,424	..
Philippines	5,154.6	3,719.0	6,998.0	2,793.7	1,364.0	1,060.5	5,847.7	0.0	22.3	34.8	806,866	70.4
Poland	4,751.1	15,673.7	628.1	2,277.5	169.4	657.5	6.1	21.8	21.1	27.7	1,654,822	68.0
Portugal	..	..	..	..	..	..	..	..	49.1	*150.3*	693,000	81.6
Puerto Rico	..	..	..	..	..	..	..	..	..	..	2,069	43.6

5.1 Private sector in the economy

	Investment in infrastructure projects with private participation[a] $ millions								Domestic credit to private sector % of GDP		Micro, small, and medium-size enterprises[b]	
	Telecommunications		Energy		Transport		Water and sanitation				number of firms	Employment % of total
	1995–99	2000–04	1995–99	2000–04	1995–99	2000–04	1995–99	2000–04	1990	2004	2000–04	2000–04
Romania	2,072.8	2,355.9	100.0	..	23.4	..	..	1,134.0	..	10.0	347,064	..
Russian Federation	4,665.6	13,404.3	2,281.3	14.0	406.0	109.4	108.0	480.5	..	24.5	8,441,000	49.0
Rwanda	8.0	39.3	..	0.0	..	..	..	..	6.9	*10.7*	..	..
Saudi Arabia	..	8,537.0	..	..	55.0	190.0	..	52.0	54.7	55.9	..	..
Senegal	273.9	342.6	124.0	..	..	..	6.3	0.0	26.5	21.2	..	..
Serbia and Montenegro	1,590.0	830.6	..	..	..	..	..	0.0	..	..	68,220	70.4
Sierra Leone	7.0	48.5	..	..	..	..	..	..	3.2	4.7	..	..
Singapore	..	..	..	..	..	..	..	..	96.8	106.9	134,098	51.2
Slovak Republic	488.5	2,359.8	..	3,323.6	..	..	0.0	..	..	31.2	70,553	66.0
Slovenia	..	..	..	..	..	..	..	..	..	46.3	93,392	64.1
Somalia	0.0	3.0	..	..	..	..	..	..	..	..	..	..
South Africa	5,978.3	9,144.0	3.0	1,244.3	1,386.4	504.7	209.3	3.2	81.0	141.3	..	..
Spain	..	..	..	..	..	..	..	..	77.7	*125.4*	3,058,631	..
Sri Lanka	601.9	524.3	176.3	132.0	240.0	..	..	..	19.6	31.5	131,387	27.6
Sudan	6.0	991.1	..	..	..	..	..	..	4.8	7.7	..	..
Swaziland	21.2	24.7	..	..	..	..	..	..	20.7	*19.5*	..	..
Sweden	..	..	..	..	..	..	..	..	127.4	105.9	868,497	39.3
Switzerland	..	..	..	..	..	..	..	..	162.6	161.2	343,000	75.3
Syrian Arab Republic	..	191.0	..	..	..	..	..	..	7.5	*10.2*	..	..
Tajikistan	1.2	8.5	..	16.0	..	..	..	..	..	17.4	92,964	25.0
Tanzania	100.2	391.1	150.0	340.0	16.5	6.5	..	4.8	13.9	9.0	2,700,000	..
Thailand	4,190.5	2,788.0	6,550.4	3,950.4	1,791.4	939.0	239.4	261.1	83.4	97.4	842,360	18.0
Togo	5.0	0.0	0.0	67.7	0.0	..	..	..	22.6	16.0	..	..
Trinidad and Tobago	146.7	..	207.0	..	..	..	0.0	120.0	40.0	27.8	..	..
Tunisia	..	610.0	265.0	..	..	..	..	..	55.1	65.2	..	..
Turkey	3,269.7	5,372.8	2,992.2	4,835.0	610.0	359.8	942.0	..	16.7	20.5	210,134	64.3
Turkmenistan	..	..	..	..	..	..	..	..	..	*1.9*	..	..
Uganda	119.3	242.6	..	18.1	..	..	..	0.0	0.0	6.8	160,453	..
Ukraine	1,094.6	1,473.5	..	160.0	..	..	..	..	..	25.0	283,398	20.2
United Arab Emirates	..	..	..	..	..	..	..	..	38.0	*53.5*	..	..
United Kingdom	..	..	..	..	..	..	..	..	115.8	156.3	4,352,275	39.5
United States	..	..	..	..	..	..	..	..	144.0	249.2	5,680,914	50.1
Uruguay	63.7	105.8	86.0	330.0	20.0	280.2	..	351.0	32.4	30.4	..	..
Uzbekistan	503.8	189.7	..	..	..	..	..	..	..	..	237,500	57.0
Venezuela, RB	4,877.9	2,639.5	103.0	30.0	268.0	34.0	29.0	15.0	26.2	11.2	11,314	..
Vietnam	248.0	380.0	435.5	2,192.0	85.0	30.0	38.8	174.0	..	58.9	59,831	85.7
West Bank and Gaza	265.0	256.7	..	150.0	..	..	9.5	..	..	..	..	..
Yemen, Rep.	..	358.0	..	..	190.0	..	..	..	6.1	7.7	..	..
Zambia	32.8	81.4	277.0	12.4	..	..	..	..	8.9	8.0	..	..
Zimbabwe	46.0	59.0	600.0	..	85.0	..	..	..	23.0	22.3	..	..
World	.. s	.. s	.. s	.. s	.. s	.. s	.. s	.. s	108.1 w	138.1 w	25,102,874 s	.. w
Low income	11,627.2	28,029.4	16,349.4	14,156.8	3,014.0	3,157.8	220.7	406.9	22.1	31.2	224,693	..
Middle income	162,329.7	171,333.8	137,624.9	81,914.1	66,579.6	28,069.2	21,239.7	11,956.8	43.1	59.7	7,160,980	..
Lower middle income	91,141.3	84,325.1	100,450.1	47,260.2	36,250.7	15,234.3	11,751.2	7,376.5	51.3	75.9	100,593	71.0
Upper middle income	71,188.4	87,008.7	37,174.8	34,653.9	30,328.9	12,834.9	9,488.5	4,580.3	32.4	37.7	7,060,387	..
Low & middle income	173,956.9	199,363.2	153,974.3	96,070.9	69,593.6	31,227.0	21,460.4	12,363.7	39.2	55.6	7,385,673	..
East Asia & Pacific	29,304.5	23,042.7	43,589.9	19,697.0	24,636.4	11,293.5	8,987.9	2,852.7	73.7	105.2	43,073,436	75.2
Europe & Central Asia	36,751.4	58,017.2	13,812.8	17,244.0	2,375.7	1,986.8	1,279.5	2,526.3	..	26.6	3,528,759	..
Latin America & Carib.	86,705.0	68,076.9	74,159.1	41,898.5	37,723.4	12,517.8	9,967.3	6,579.6	28.6	25.7	3,632,221	..
Middle East & N. Africa	3,973.1	13,005.2	6,967.9	3,891.3	573.4	1,412.1	1,009.5	169.0	34.5	39.8	139,844	..
South Asia	8,604.5	17,612.5	12,293.3	8,232.3	1,934.1	1,901.3	..	223.2	24.2	35.7	177,000	..
Sub-Saharan Africa	8,618.4	19,608.7	3,151.3	5,107.8	2,350.6	2,115.5	216.2	12.9	42.4	67.0	47,693	..
High income	..	8,537.0	..	..	55.0	190.0	..	52.0	119.8	159.1	17,717,201	60.4
Europe EMU	..	..	..	..	..	..	..	..	78.6	106.0	6,306,542	68.6

a. Data refer to total for the period shown. b. Data are for the most recent year available.

Private sector in the economy 5.1

About the data

Private sector development and investment—that is, tapping private sector initiative and investment for socially useful purposes—are critical for poverty reduction. In parallel with public sector efforts, private investment, especially in competitive markets, has tremendous potential to contribute to growth. Private markets are the engine of productivity growth, creating productive jobs and higher incomes. And with government playing a complementary role of regulation, funding, and service provision, private initiative and investment can help provide the basic services and conditions that empower poor people—by improving health, education, and infrastructure.

Private participation in infrastructure has made important contributions to easing fiscal constraints, improving the efficiency of infrastructure services, and extending their delivery to poor people. The privatization trend in infrastructure that began in the 1970s and 1980s took off in the 1990s, peaking in 1997. Developing countries have been at the head of this wave, pioneering better approaches to providing infrastructure services and reaping the benefits of greater competition and customer focus. Between 1990 and 2004 more than 2,900 projects in more than 130 developing countries introduced private participation in at least one infrastructure sector, with $866 billion in investments.

In 2004, 132 new infrastructure projects with private participation valued at $23 billion were implemented. In addition, $41 billion in investment projects reached financial closure between 1990 and 2003. Telecommunications attracted $45 billion in investment in 2004, mostly in standalone mobile operations. Except for water and sanitation, with $1.9 billion in investment in 2004 (up from about $1.4 billion in 2003), investment in other infrastructure sectors declined in 2004.

The data on investment in infrastructure projects with private participation refer to all investment (public and private) in projects in which a private company assumes operating risk during the operating period or assumes development and operating risk during the contract period. Foreign state-owned companies are considered private entities for the purposes of this measure. The data are from the World Bank's Private Participation in Infrastructure (PPI) Project Database, which tracks more than 3,200 projects, newly owned or managed by private companies, that reached financial closure in low- and middle-income economies in 1990–2004. Aggregates for geographic regions and income groups are calculated by the World Bank's Development Data Group. For more information, see http://ppi.worldbank.org/.

Credit is an important link in the money transmission process; it finances production, consumption, and capital formation, which in turn affect the level of economic activity. The data on domestic credit to the private sector are taken from the banking survey of the International Monetary Fund's (IMF) *International Financial Statistics* or, when data are unavailable, from its monetary survey. The monetary survey includes monetary authorities (the central bank), deposit money banks, and other banking institutions, such as finance companies, development banks, and savings and loan institutions. In some cases credit to the private sector may include credit to state-owned or partially state-owned enterprises.

Formal and informal micro, small, and medium-size enterprises employ more than half of the working population in many market economies and account for about 90 percent of all firms. And they contribute significantly to innovation. If small businesses are allowed to compete on an equal playing field, the good ones can become larger, workers can earn higher wages, and productivity will increase. A good investment climate—one that provides opportunities and incentives for firms, reduces legal and regulatory costs, lowers the costs of financial institutions in providing financial services, and facilitates the transfer of technology and knowledge and the upgrading of capabilities in small and medium-size firms—is important for economic progress, better jobs, and a more inclusive society.

Data on the activities of micro, small, and medium-size enterprises are collected by governments, international organizations, foundations, and small business organizations. These data have been collated by the International Finance Corporation (IFC) and are available in the Micro, Small, and Medium Enterprises: A Collection of Published Data database. This IFC initiative is a work in progress, improved and updated as new data become available. Because the concepts and definitions of micro, small, and medium-size enterprises vary by source, using these data for precise country rankings may be inappropriate. See www.ifc.org/ifcext/sme.nsf/Content/Resources for additional information on sources and precise firm size.

Definitions

• **Investment in infrastructure projects with private participation** refers to infrastructure projects in telecommunications, energy (electricity and natural gas transmission and distribution), transport, and water and sanitation that have reached financial closure and directly or indirectly serve the public. Incinerators, movable assets, stand-alone solid waste projects, and small projects such as windmills are excluded. Included are operation and management contracts, operation and management contracts with major capital expenditure, greenfield projects (in which a private entity or a public-private joint venture builds and operates a new facility), and divestitures. • **Domestic credit to private sector** refers to financial resources provided to the private sector—such as through loans, purchases of nonequity securities, and trade credits and other accounts receivable—that establish a claim for repayment. For some countries these claims include credit to public enterprises. • **Micro, small, and medium-size enterprises** are business that may be defined by the number of employees. There is no international standard definition of firm size; however, many institutions that collect information use the following size categories: micro enterprises have 0–9 employees, small enterprises have 10–49 employees, and medium-size enterprises have 50–249 employees.

Data sources

Data on investment in infrastructure projects with private participation are from the World Bank's PPI Project Database (http://ppi.worldbank.org). Data on domestic credit are from the IMF's *International Financial Statistics.* Data on micro, small, and medium-size enterprises are from the International Finance Corporation's micro, small, and medium-size enterprises database (www.ifc.org/ifcext/sme.nsf/Content/Resources).

5.2 Investment climate

	Survey year	Policy uncertainty	Corruption	Courts		Crime	Regulation and tax administration			Finance	Electricity	Labor	
		Major constraint %	Major constraint %	Major constraint %	Lack confidence courts uphold property rights %	Major constraint %	Tax rates as major constraint %	Time dealing with officials % of management time	Average time to clear customs days	Major constraint %	Major constraint %	Major constraint % Skills	Major constraint % Regulation
Afghanistan		..	..	..	..	..	..	..	..	..	..	..	..
Albania	2005	19.1	31.8	23.9	43.6	8.6	40.9	12.2	2.1	19.5	34.7	10.4	2.5
Algeria	2003	..	35.2	..	27.3	..	44.8	..	21.6	51.3	11.5	25.5	12.9
Angola		..	..	..	..	..	..	..	..	..	..	..	..
Argentina		..	..	..	..	..	..	..	..	..	..	..	..
Armenia	2005	12.2	20.1	12.4	47.5	2.3	38.4	10.4	4.4	20.8	3.2	2.3	2.9
Australia		..	..	..	..	..	..	..	..	..	..	..	..
Austria		..	..	..	..	..	..	..	..	..	..	..	..
Azerbaijan	2005	2.9	21.3	4.4	30.8	2.4	22.9	16.6	1.6	7.0	4.9	1.8	1.5
Bangladesh	2000	45.4	57.9	..	83.0	39.4	35.8	4.6	11.5	45.7	73.2	19.8	10.8
Belarus	2005	23.4	6.6	3.0	33.4	2.9	20.4	8.3	4.4	22.5	0.9	6.6	3.4
Belgium		..	..	..	..	..	..	..	..	..	..	..	..
Benin		..	..	..	..	..	..	..	..	..	..	..	..
Bolivia	2004	..	..	..	..	..	..	..	9.3	..	..	..	..
Bosnia and Herzegovina	2005	35.1	24.7	21.5	41.6	19.9	15.6	9.5	2.6	25.8	8.2	3.6	3.2
Botswana		..	..	..	..	..	..	..	..	..	..	..	..
Brazil	2003	75.9	67.2	32.8	39.6	52.2	84.5	9.4	13.8	71.7	20.3	39.6	56.9
Bulgaria	2005	27.6	19.0	17.2	56.7	11.5	20.4	7.4	2.9	22.0	6.4	10.4	7.8
Burkina Faso		..	..	..	..	..	..	..	..	..	..	..	..
Burundi		..	..	..	..	..	..	..	..	..	..	..	..
Cambodia	2003	40.1	55.9	31.4	61.0	41.7	18.6	14.6	..	9.9	12.7	6.6	5.9
Cameroon		..	..	..	..	..	..	..	..	..	..	..	..
Canada		..	..	..	..	..	..	..	..	..	..	..	..
Central African Republic		..	..	..	..	..	..	..	..	..	..	..	..
Chad		..	..	..	..	..	..	..	..	..	..	..	..
Chile		..	..	..	..	..	..	..	..	..	..	..	..
China	2002	32.9	27.3	..	17.5	20.0	36.8	12.6	7.9	22.3	29.7	30.7	20.7
Hong Kong, China		..	..	..	..	..	..	..	..	..	..	..	..
Colombia		..	..	..	..	..	..	..	..	..	..	..	..
Congo, Dem. Rep.		..	..	..	..	..	..	..	..	..	..	..	..
Congo, Rep.		..	..	..	..	..	..	..	..	..	..	..	..
Costa Rica		..	..	..	..	..	..	..	..	..	..	..	..
Côte d'Ivoire		..	..	..	..	..	..	..	..	..	..	..	..
Croatia	2005	17.9	18.5	29.3	26.0	3.9	12.0	7.5	3.7	12.7	2.1	7.2	3.0
Cuba		..	..	..	..	..	..	..	..	..	..	..	..
Czech Republic	2005	22.0	20.5	25.2	53.1	15.8	59.1	7.1	5.1	17.4	15.5	12.5	15.6
Denmark		..	..	..	..	..	..	..	..	..	..	..	..
Dominican Republic		..	..	..	..	..	..	..	..	..	..	..	..
Ecuador	2003	60.7	49.2	34.1	70.8	27.8	38.1	17.7	16.4	42.2	28.3	22.3	14.1
Egypt, Arab Rep.	2004	65.8	51.3	27.4	..	..	81.8	..	9.9	39.0	26.5	29.8	28.1
El Salvador	2004	28.4	35.1	16.4	46.6	49.0	22.6	9.3	6.2	29.6	21.5	20.0	3.9
Eritrea	2002	31.5	2.7	..	..	1.3	31.1	5.9	9.1	53.7	38.2	41.0	5.2
Estonia	2005	5.3	4.3	2.0	29.6	1.9	3.0	5.7	1.9	6.1	3.3	7.1	18.8
Ethiopia	2002	39.3	39.0	..	..	9.5	73.6	5.7	13.5	40.2	42.5	17.9	4.6
Finland		..	..	..	..	..	..	..	..	..	..	..	..
France		..	..	..	..	..	..	..	..	..	..	..	..
Gabon		..	..	..	..	..	..	..	..	..	..	..	..
Gambia, The		..	..	..	..	..	..	..	..	..	..	..	..
Georgia	2005	45.2	20.1	13.5	29.0	24.5	35.7	12.2	2.8	25.4	33.5	14.1	7.6
Germany	2005	5.8	3.9	2.3	10.3	1.9	29.6	3.5	5.7	16.7	1.0	6.9	9.6
Ghana		..	..	..	..	..	..	..	..	..	..	..	..
Greece	2005	9.3	10.0	4.7	18.2	5.2	27.5	8.4	5.9	16.3	4.6	8.6	7.7
Guatemala	2003	66.4	80.9	31.2	71.3	80.4	56.5	17.4	9.3	38.7	26.6	31.4	16.7
Guinea		..	..	..	..	..	..	..	..	..	..	..	..
Guinea-Bissau		..	..	..	..	..	..	..	..	..	..	..	..
Haiti		..	..	..	..	..	..	..	..	..	..	..	..

	Survey year	Policy uncertainty	Corruption	Courts		Crime	Regulation and tax administration			Finance	Electricity	Labor	
		Major constraint %	Major constraint %	Major constraint %	Lack confidence courts uphold property rights %	Major constraint %	Tax rates as major constraint %	Time dealing with officials % of management time	Average time to clear customs days	Major constraint %	Major constraint %	Major constraint % Skills	Major constraint % Regulation
Honduras	2003	47.0	62.8	21.8	56.1	60.9	35.6	14.2	5.1	55.4	36.4	26.4	14.2
Hungary	2005	26.3	9.4	7.4	49.8	5.6	50.6	8.3	7.7	27.9	2.1	12.9	10.3
India	2003	20.9	37.4	..	29.4	15.6	27.9	15.3	6.7	19.2	28.9	12.5	16.7
Indonesia	2004	48.2	41.5	24.7	40.8	22.0	29.5	14.6	5.8	23.0	22.3	18.9	25.9
Iran, Islamic Rep.		..	..	..	..	..	..	..	..	..	..	..	..
Iraq		..	..	..	..	..	..	..	..	..	..	..	..
Ireland	2005	5.6	3.0	2.8	28.3	4.8	17.4	5.8	3.3	9.0	6.4	15.6	9.6
Israel		..	..	..	..	..	..	..	..	..	..	..	..
Italy		..	..	..	..	..	..	..	..	..	..	..	..
Jamaica		..	..	..	..	..	..	..	..	..	..	..	..
Japan		..	..	..	..	..	..	..	..	..	..	..	..
Jordan		..	..	..	..	..	..	..	..	..	..	..	..
Kazakhstan	2005	9.2	12.7	8.2	42.7	5.3	15.6	10.7	6.0	14.9	2.7	8.6	2.5
Kenya	2003	51.5	73.8	..	51.3	69.8	68.2	13.8	8.9	58.3	48.1	27.6	22.5
Korea, Dem. Rep.	2005	40.9	8.5	3.6	37.2	3.5	15.1	1.3	8.0	12.5	8.3	6.8	4.1
Korea, Rep.		..	..	..	..	..	..	..	..	..	..	..	..
Kuwait		..	..	..	..	..	..	..	..	..	..	..	..
Kyrgyz Republic	2005	33.2	32.8	17.1	50.8	19.4	31.3	16.1	5.4	23.1	4.0	18.9	2.5
Lao PDR		..	..	..	..	..	..	..	..	..	..	..	..
Latvia	2005	22.3	9.6	5.8	51.3	3.1	29.4	8.0	3.3	6.5	4.5	17.8	3.5
Lebanon		..	..	..	..	..	..	..	..	..	..	..	..
Lesotho		..	..	..	..	..	..	..	..	..	..	..	..
Liberia		..	..	..	..	..	..	..	..	..	..	..	..
Libya		..	..	..	..	..	..	..	..	..	..	..	..
Lithuania	2005	23.2	14.0	15.3	49.7	9.5	40.9	8.3	2.0	10.3	3.9	15.3	8.9
Macedonia, FYR	2005	27.9	34.7	31.0	55.4	12.8	20.7	15.6	3.1	31.6	12.0	6.1	9.2
Madagascar	2005	41.5	46.6	34.8	44.6	37.7	44.9	25.4	7.0	62.9	41.3	30.5	14.8
Malawi		..	..	..	..	..	..	..	..	..	..	..	..
Malaysia	2005	22.4	14.5	..	19.1	11.4	21.7	10.2	3.7	17.8	14.8	25.0	14.5
Mali	2004	21.9	48.7	16.9	33.1	22.1	36.6	10.8	10.0	57.0	24.2	20.8	3.9
Mauritania		..	..	..	..	..	..	..	..	..	..	..	..
Mauritius		..	..	..	..	..	..	..	..	..	..	..	..
Mexico		..	..	..	..	..	..	..	..	..	..	..	..
Moldova	2005	31.6	17.6	22.1	64.2	10.1	37.8	10.9	2.8	31.9	2.9	12.0	8.2
Mongolia		..	..	..	..	..	..	..	..	..	..	..	..
Morocco	2004	..	16.9	29.1	23.5	7.6	62.6	10.5	3.0	78.5	8.9	21.1	16.2
Mozambique		..	..	..	..	..	..	..	..	..	..	..	..
Myanmar		..	..	..	..	..	..	..	..	..	..	..	..
Namibia		..	..	..	..	..	..	..	..	..	..	..	..
Nepal	2000	..	..	..	..	..	..	..	..	..	41.7	..	..
Netherlands		..	..	..	..	..	..	..	..	..	..	..	..
New Zealand		..	..	..	..	..	..	..	..	..	..	..	..
Nicaragua	2003	58.2	65.7	33.3	60.4	39.2	34.7	17.3	5.8	57.6	34.7	17.0	6.9
Niger		..	..	..	..	..	..	..	..	..	..	..	..
Nigeria	2001	..	..	..	..	36.3	..	..	17.8	..	97.4	..	..
Norway		..	..	..	..	..	..	..	..	..	..	..	..
Oman	2004	20.7	11.9	14.9	12.9	8.6	20.7	..	8.0	29.4	10.1	34.6	34.8
Pakistan	2002	40.1	40.4	..	62.6	21.5	45.6	10.6	17.1	40.1	39.2	12.8	15.0
Panama		..	..	..	..	..	..	..	..	..	..	..	..
Papua New Guinea		..	..	..	..	..	..	..	..	..	..	..	..
Paraguay		..	..	..	..	..	..	..	..	..	..	..	..
Peru	2002	71.1	59.6	..	34.7	51.6	..	..	7.9	55.8	11.1	12.5	..
Philippines	2003	29.5	35.2	..	33.8	26.5	30.4	11.0	9.1	18.2	33.4	11.9	24.7
Poland	2005	42.7	18.2	21.0	47.4	15.0	57.7	7.2	3.8	39.6	4.1	15.3	17.9
Portugal	2005	22.2	15.4	17.8	47.7	15.7	20.5	5.8	6.0	18.3	7.8	12.4	18.1
Puerto Rico		..	..	..	..	..	..	..	..	..	..	..	..

Investment climate

	Survey year	Policy uncertainty Major constraint %	Corruption Major constraint %	Courts Major constraint %	Courts Lack confidence courts uphold property rights %	Crime Major constraint %	Regulation and tax administration Tax rates as major constraint %	Regulation and tax administration Time dealing with officials % of management time	Regulation and tax administration Average time to clear customs days	Finance Major constraint %	Electricity Major constraint %	Labor Major constraint % Skills	Labor Major constraint % Regulation
Romania	2005	33.9	30.1	19.7	44.3	15.3	34.1	3.6	3.0	22.6	8.1	14.2	16.4
Russian Federation	2005	26.2	16.5	9.5	63.9	9.3	21.8	14.8	9.5	15.7	5.1	13.1	3.1
Rwanda		..	..	..	..	..	..	..	..	..	..	..	..
Saudi Arabia		..	..	..	..	..	..	..	..	..	..	..	..
Senegal	2004	31.3	39.9	13.3	40.5	15.4	50.8	13.8	7.0	60.3	30.7	18.5	16.3
Serbia and Montenegro	2005	61.2	25.5	30.0	43.1	13.5	29.5	12.4	5.7	43.9	4.7	10.7	13.4
Sierra Leone		..	..	..	..	..	..	..	..	..	..	..	..
Singapore		..	..	..	..	..	..	..	..	..	..	..	..
Slovak Republic	2005	13.0	10.6	13.1	44.4	5.1	8.3	9.3	3.9	7.9	2.7	8.2	4.6
Slovenia	2005	11.5	3.7	8.1	34.4	0.9	12.7	6.4	3.2	9.5	2.7	5.4	4.5
Somalia		..	..	..	..	..	..	..	..	..	..	..	..
South Africa	2004	17.9	16.1	8.8	20.8	29.0	18.6	10.7	6.5	14.5	9.0	35.5	32.9
Spain	2005	10.3	7.8	7.9	16.6	9.8	18.8	5.1	5.5	13.3	8.3	13.8	11.8
Sri Lanka	2003	34.0	16.9	..	31.2	14.0	19.1	4.7	4.1	20.4	41.3	21.3	25.6
Sudan		..	..	..	..	..	..	..	..	..	..	..	..
Swaziland		..	..	..	..	..	..	..	..	..	..	..	..
Sweden		..	..	..	..	..	..	..	..	..	..	..	..
Switzerland		..	..	..	..	..	..	..	..	..	..	..	..
Syrian Arab Republic	2004	27.0	57.6	..	..	..	62.5	14.5	15.8	24.8	57.5	36.3	33.8
Tajikistan	2005	5.6	15.7	4.9	35.9	4.1	22.2	8.1	5.9	7.2	10.1	4.6	1.5
Tanzania	2003	31.5	51.1	20.0	55.1	25.5	73.4	16.2	17.5	53.0	58.9	25.0	12.1
Thailand	2004	29.1	18.3	..	25.8	10.3	24.4	2.9	4.6	15.2	25.6	30.0	11.4
Togo		..	..	..	..	..	..	..	..	..	..	..	..
Trinidad and Tobago		..	..	..	..	..	..	..	..	..	..	..	..
Tunisia		..	..	..	..	..	..	..	..	..	..	..	..
Turkey	2005	31.5	17.0	12.4	28.5	14.7	37.8	11.7	6.4	17.5	9.2	9.8	12.2
Turkmenistan		..	..	..	..	..	..	..	..	..	..	..	..
Uganda	2003	27.6	38.2	..	30.1	26.8	48.3	5.0	..	52.8	44.5	30.8	10.8
Ukraine	2005	31.3	22.6	15.2	48.2	12.3	45.7	13.7	6.8	29.9	4.9	19.8	6.5
United Arab Emirates		..	..	..	..	..	..	..	..	..	..	..	..
United Kingdom		..	..	..	..	..	..	..	..	..	..	..	..
United States		..	..	..	..	..	..	..	..	..	..	..	..
Uruguay		..	..	..	..	..	..	..	..	..	..	..	..
Uzbekistan	2005	11.5	8.9	6.6	41.7	8.9	18.3	7.7	8.7	12.5	7.2	4.6	3.0
Venezuela, RB		..	..	..	..	..	..	..	..	..	..	..	..
Vietnam	2005	14.7	12.8	5.5	23.1	4.0	13.8	6.9	4.5	30.3	15.7	22.3	10.9
West Bank and Gaza		..	..	..	..	..	..	..	..	..	..	..	..
Yemen, Rep.	2005	31.1	62.8	32.0	58.4	28.7	71.9	21.3	13.3	31.8	47.6	23.6	12.8
Zambia	2003	57.0	46.4	38.6	36.0	48.8	57.5	14.1	4.8	67.7	39.6	35.7	16.9
Zimbabwe		..	..	..	..	..	..	..	..	..	..	..	..

Note: Data are based on enterprise surveys conducted by the World Bank and its partners during 2001–05. While averages are reported, there are significant variations across firms. Surveys of Eastern Europe and Central Asia were conducted under the joint World Bank–European Bank for Reconstruction and Development Business Environment and Enterprise Performance Surveys Initiative.

About the data

The table includes recently available data from World Bank–sponsored firm-level Investment Climate Surveys covering more than 50,000 firms in 63 developing countries for 2001–05. The data provide fresh insights into how investment climates vary around the world. In addition to these surveys, data from the Doing Business project, which benchmarks regulatory regimes in 155 countries, are presented in table 5.3.

A good investment climate requires government policies that provide an environment for firms and entrepreneurs to invest productively, create jobs, and contribute to growth and poverty reduction. The goal is to create a better investment climate that benefits society as a whole, not just firms.

Improving government policies and behaviors is key to shaping the investment climate because they are influential in driving growth and poverty reduction. Governments face four primary challenges in improving the investment climate and getting the balance right between society's interests and firms' incentives to invest. One is restraining corruption by public officials, firms, and other interest groups. Two is establishing credibility by maintaining economic and political stability and restraining arbitrary behavior by the key agencies of the state. Three is fostering public trust and legitimacy through open and participatory policymaking, transparency, and equity. Four is ensuring that government policies realistically reflect current conditions and continue to adapt to changing economic and business conditions.

Firms evaluating alternative investment options, governments interested in improving their investment climates, and economists seeking to understand the role of different factors in explaining economic performance have all grappled with defining and measuring the investment climate. The World Bank, working with client governments and others, recently pioneered new measures of the investment climate. The Investment Climate Surveys measure specific constraints facing firms and relate them to measures of firm performance, growth, and investment.

The indicators included in the table cover eight dimensions of the investment climate: policy uncertainty, corruption, courts, crime, regulation and tax administration, finance, infrastructure, and labor.

Firms in developing countries rate policy uncertainty as their dominant concern among investment climate constraints. It measures the credibility of governments and their policies and the ability to deliver what is promised. Corruption—the exploitation of public office for private gain—can harm the investment climate in several ways. It can distort policymaking, undermine government credibility, tax entrepreneurial activities, and divert resources from public coffers. Better courts reduce the risks firms face, so that firms are willing to invest more. And the importance of courts grows as the number of large and complex long-term transactions increases. Robbery, fraud, and other crimes against property and against the person undermine the investment climate. Crime retards entrepreneurial activity. In Latin America, more than 50 percent of surveyed firms judged crime to be a serious obstacle to doing business.

Most countries have room to improve regulation and taxation without compromising broader social interests. The investment climate is harmed when governments impose unnecessary costs, by increasing uncertainty and risk and by erecting unjustified barriers to competition. Improvements in the tax system may include broadening the tax base, simplifying tax structures, increasing the autonomy of tax agencies, and improving compliance through computerization. When financial markets work well, they connect firms to lenders and investors, which allows firms to seize business opportunities and grow their businesses. But too often government distortions introduced by state ownership or directed credit undermine financial sector development, productivity, and economic growth. Firms that have access to modern infrastructure—telecommunications, reliable electricity supplies, and efficient transportation—are more productive, and improvements in infrastructure services also benefit households. Ill-considered labor regulations can discourage firms from creating more jobs, and while some employees may benefit, the unemployed, the low skilled, and those working in the informal economy will not.

The Investment Climate Surveys follow a stratified random sampling methodology, drawing from registered establishments with at least 10 employees. Samples are stratified on sectors and size of firms. Sectors are selected based on their contribution to GDP and for comparability with sectors in other countries. Because the distribution of establishments in most countries is overwhelmingly populated by small and medium-size enterprises, surveys generally oversample large establishments. Sample sizes for recent surveys range from 250 to 1,800 businesses and average 550 establishments.

For more information on the investment climate, see http://econ.worldbank.org/wdr/wdr2005 and http://iresearch.worldbank.org/ics.

Definitions

• **Policy uncertainty** measures the share of senior managers who ranked economic and regulatory policy uncertainty as a major or very severe constraint. • **Corruption** measures the share of senior managers who ranked corruption as a major or very severe constraint. • **Courts** measure the share of senior managers who ranked courts and dispute resolution systems as a major or very severe constraint. • **Lack confidence courts uphold property rights** measures the share of managers who do not agree with the statement: "I am confident that the judicial system will enforce my contractual and property rights in business disputes." • **Crime** measures the share of senior managers who ranked crime, theft, and disorder as a major or very severe constraint. • **Tax rates as major constraint** measure the share of senior managers who ranked tax rates as a major or very severe constraint. • **Time dealing with officials** is the percentage of management time in a given week spent on requirements imposed by government regulations (taxes, customs, labor regulations, licensing and registration). • **Average time to clear customs** is the number of days to clear an imported good through customs. • **Finance** measures shares of senior managers who ranked access to finance or cost of finance as a major or very severe constraint. • **Electricity** measures the share of senior managers who ranked electricity as a major or severe constraint. • **Labor skills** measure the share of senior managers who ranked skills of available workers as a major or severe constraint. • **Labor regulations** measure the share of senior managers who ranked labor regulations as a major or severe constraint.

Data sources

Data on the investment climate are from the World Bank's Investment Climate Surveys (http://iresearch.worldbank.org/ics).

5.3 Business environment

	Starting a business			Registering property		Dealing with licenses		Hiring and firing workers	Enforcing contracts		Protecting investors	Closing a business
	Number of procedures January 2005	Time required days January 2005	Cost % of per capita income January 2005	Number of procedures January 2005	Time required days January 2005	Number of procedures to build a warehouse January 2005	Time required days January 2005	Rigidity of employment index 0 (less rigid) to 100 (more rigid) January 2005	Number of procedures January 2005	Time required days January 2005	Disclosure index 0 (less disclosure) to 10 (more disclosure) January 2005	Time to resolve insolvency years January 2005
Afghanistan	1	7	52.8	11	252	..	..	39	..	400	0	..
Albania	11	41	31.1	7	47	22	344	48	39	390	0	4.0
Algeria	14	26	25.3	16	52	25	244	51	49	407	8	3.5
Angola	14	146	642.8	7	334	15	326	64	47	1,011	5	6.2
Argentina	15	32	13.4	5	44	23	288	48	33	520	7	2.8
Armenia	10	25	6.1	4	6	20	176	49	24	185	..	1.9
Australia	2	2	1.9	5	5	16	121	17	11	157	8	1.0
Austria	9	29	5.7	3	32	14	195	44	20	374	2	1.1
Azerbaijan	14	115	12.5	7	61	28	212	38	25	267	0	2.7
Bangladesh	8	35	81.4	11	363	13	185	24	29	365	6	4.0
Belarus	16	79	22.9	7	231	18	354	27	28	225	1	5.8
Belgium	4	34	11.1	7	132	15	184	20	27	112	8	0.9
Benin	8	32	190.8	3	50	22	335	53	49	570	5	3.1
Bolivia	15	50	154.8	7	92	13	187	40	47	591	1	1.8
Bosnia and Herzegovina	12	54	40.9	7	331	17	476	42	36	330	3	3.3
Botswana	11	108	10.9	6	69	42	160	30	26	154	8	2.2
Brazil	17	152	10.1	15	47	19	460	56	24	546	5	10.0
Bulgaria	11	32	9.6	9	19	24	212	44	34	440	8	3.3
Burkina Faso	12	45	149.9	8	107	46	241	84	41	446	6	4.0
Burundi	11	43	200.7	5	94	18	302	69	47	433	..	4.0
Cambodia	10	86	276.1	7	56	28	247	59	31	401	5	..
Cameroon	12	37	172.8	5	93	15	444	56	58	585	8	3.2
Canada	2	3	0.9	6	10	15	87	14	17	346	8	0.8
Central African Republic	10	14	211.6	3	69	21	237	76	45	660	..	4.8
Chad	19	75	360.8	6	44	16	199	72	52	526	3	10.0
Chile	9	27	10.3	6	31	12	191	24	28	305	8	5.6
China	13	48	13.6	3	32	30	363	30	25	241	10	2.4
Hong Kong, China	5	11	3.4	5	83	22	230	0	16	211	10	1.1
Colombia	12	43	25.3	7	23	12	150	57	37	363	7	3.0
Congo, Dem. Rep.	13	155	503.3	8	106	16	306	90	51	909	3	5.2
Congo, Rep.	8	67	288.8	6	103	15	174	80	47	560	4	3.0
Costa Rica	11	77	23.8	6	21	19	120	39	34	550	2	3.5
Côte d'Ivoire	11	45	134.0	7	369	22	569	45	25	525	6	2.2
Croatia	12	49	13.4	5	956	28	278	57	22	415	2	3.1
Cuba	..	..	..	..	..	..	..	..	..	..	..	..
Czech Republic	10	40	9.5	4	123	31	245	24	21	290	2	9.2
Denmark	3	5	0.0	6	42	7	70	20	15	83	7	3.3
Dominican Republic	10	75	30.9	7	107	12	150	44	29	580	3	3.5
Ecuador	14	69	38.1	10	21	19	149	58	41	388	1	4.3
Egypt, Arab Rep.	10	34	104.9	7	193	30	263	53	55	410	5	4.2
El Salvador	12	40	118.0	5	52	22	144	41	41	275	6	4.0
Eritrea	13	91	128.6	6	91	19	187	27	27	385	4	1.7
Estonia	6	35	6.2	4	65	12	116	51	25	150	8	3.0
Ethiopia	7	32	65.1	15	56	12	133	41	30	420	1	2.4
Finland	3	14	1.2	3	14	17	56	48	27	228	6	0.9
France	7	8	1.2	9	183	10	185	66	21	75	10	1.9
Gabon	..	..	..	..	..	..	..	..	..	..	..	..
Gambia, The	..	..	..	..	..	..	..	..	..	..	..	..
Georgia	8	21	13.7	6	9	29	282	43	18	375	4	3.3
Germany	9	24	4.7	4	41	11	165	55	26	175	5	1.2
Ghana	12	81	78.6	7	382	16	127	34	23	200	7	1.9
Greece	15	38	24.6	12	23	17	176	66	14	151	1	2.0
Guatemala	15	39	58.4	5	69	22	294	40	37	1,459	1	4.0
Guinea	13	49	178.8	6	104	29	278	48	44	306	5	3.8
Guinea-Bissau	..	..	..	..	..	..	..	..	..	..	..	..
Haiti	12	203	153.1	5	683	12	186	24	35	368	4	5.7

Business environment 5.3

	Starting a business			Registering property		Dealing with licenses		Hiring and firing workers	Enforcing contracts		Protecting investors	Closing a business
	Number of procedures	Time required days	Cost % of per capita income	Number of procedures	Time required days	Number of procedures to build a warehouse	Time required days	Rigidity of employment index 0 (less rigid) to 100 (more rigid)	Number of procedures	Time required days	Disclosure index 0 (less disclosure) to 10 (more disclosure)	Time to resolve insolvency years
	January 2005	**January 2005**	**January 2005**	**January 2005**	**January 2005**	**January 2005**	**January 2005**	**January 2005**	**January 2005**	**January 2005**	**January 2005**	**January 2005**
Honduras	13	62	64.1	7	36	14	199	34	36	545	1	3.8
Hungary	6	38	22.4	4	78	25	213	37	21	365	1	2.0
India	11	71	61.7	6	67	20	270	62	40	425	7	10.0
Indonesia	12	151	101.7	7	42	19	224	57	34	570	8	5.5
Iran, Islamic Rep.	8	47	6.3	9	36	21	668	49	23	545	3	4.5
Iraq	11	77	37.4	5	8	14	210	69	65	320	4	..
Ireland	4	24	5.3	5	38	10	181	33	16	217	9	0.4
Israel	5	34	5.3	7	144	21	219	33	27	585	8	4.0
Italy	9	13	15.7	8	27	17	284	57	18	1,390	7	1.2
Jamaica	6	9	8.3	5	54	13	242	10	18	202	3	1.1
Japan	11	31	10.7	6	14	11	87	19	16	60	6	0.6
Jordan	11	36	45.9	8	22	17	122	34	43	342	5	4.3
Kazakhstan	7	24	8.6	8	52	32	258	23	47	380	7	3.3
Kenya	13	54	48.2	8	73	11	170	28	25	360	4	4.5
Korea, Dem. Rep.	12	22	15.2	7	11	14	60	45	29	75	7	1.5
Korea, Rep.	12	..	15.2	..	..	..	..	..	..	..	..	..
Kuwait	13	35	2.2	8	75	26	149	20	52	390	5	4.2
Kyrgyz Republic	8	21	10.4	7	10	16	152	38	46	492	8	3.5
Lao PDR	9	198	15.1	9	135	24	208	50	53	443	4	5.0
Latvia	7	18	4.2	9	54	21	160	59	20	186	5	1.1
Lebanon	6	46	110.6	8	25	16	275	24	39	721	8	4.0
Lesotho	9	92	56.1	6	101	12	254	42	49	285	2	2.6
Liberia	..	..	..	..	..	..	..	..	..	..	..	..
Libya	..	..	..	..	..	..	..	..	..	..	..	..
Lithuania	8	26	3.3	3	3	14	151	44	17	154	5	1.2
Macedonia, FYR	13	48	11.3	6	74	18	214	54	27	509	5	3.7
Madagascar	11	38	54.3	8	134	19	356	59	29	280	5	..
Malawi	10	35	139.6	6	118	23	205	21	16	277	4	2.6
Malaysia	9	30	20.9	4	143	25	226	10	31	300	10	2.2
Mali	13	42	190.7	5	44	17	260	66	28	340	6	3.6
Mauritania	11	82	143.6	4	49	19	152	73	28	410	..	8.0
Mauritius	6	46	8.8	5	210	21	132	37	17	367	6	2.0
Mexico	9	58	15.6	5	74	12	222	51	37	421	6	1.8
Moldova	10	30	17.1	6	48	20	122	68	37	340	7	2.8
Mongolia	8	20	6.2	5	11	18	96	34	26	314	..	4.0
Morocco	5	11	12.0	3	82	21	217	60	17	240	6	1.8
Mozambique	14	153	95.0	8	42	14	212	61	38	580	..	5.0
Myanmar	..	..	..	..	..	..	..	..	..	..	..	..
Namibia	10	95	18.8	9	28	11	169	27	31	270	8	1.0
Nepal	7	21	69.9	2	2	12	147	44	28	350	4	5.0
Netherlands	7	11	13.0	2	2	18	184	49	22	48	4	1.7
New Zealand	2	12	0.2	2	2	7	65	7	19	50	10	2.0
Nicaragua	8	42	139.1	7	65	12	192	47	20	155	4	2.2
Niger	13	35	465.4	5	49	27	165	90	33	330	6	5.0
Nigeria	9	43	73.8	21	274	16	465	38	23	730	6	1.5
Norway	4	13	2.7	1	1	13	97	38	14	87	7	0.9
Oman	9	34	4.8	4	16	16	271	35	41	455	8	7.0
Pakistan	11	24	18.6	5	49	12	218	46	46	395	6	2.8
Panama	7	19	24.8	7	44	22	128	63	45	355	3	2.0
Papua New Guinea	8	56	30.2	4	72	20	218	21	22	440	5	2.8
Paraguay	17	74	147.8	7	48	15	273	59	46	285	6	3.9
Peru	10	102	38.0	5	33	19	201	48	35	381	7	3.1
Philippines	11	48	20.3	8	33	23	197	45	25	360	1	5.7
Poland	10	31	22.2	6	197	25	322	37	41	980	7	1.4
Portugal	11	54	13.4	5	83	20	327	58	24	320	7	2.0
Puerto Rico	7	7	1.0	8	15	20	137	35	43	270	..	3.8

5.3 Business environment

	Starting a business			Registering property		Dealing with licenses		Hiring and firing workers	Enforcing contracts		Protecting investors	Closing a business
	Number of procedures January 2005	Time required days January 2005	Cost % of per capita income January 2005	Number of procedures January 2005	Time required days January 2005	Number of procedures to build a warehouse January 2005	Time required days January 2005	Rigidity of employment index 0 (less rigid) to 100 (more rigid) January 2005	Number of procedures January 2005	Time required days January 2005	Disclosure index 0 (less disclosure) to 10 (more disclosure) January 2005	Time to resolve insolvency years January 2005
Romania	5	11	5.3	8	170	15	291	59	43	335	8	4.6
Russian Federation	8	33	5.0	6	52	22	528	30	29	330	7	3.8
Rwanda	9	21	280.2	5	371	17	252	59	27	310	..	..
Saudi Arabia	13	64	68.5	4	4	18	131	13	44	360	8	2.8
Senegal	9	57	108.7	6	114	18	185	64	33	485	7	3.0
Serbia and Montenegro	10	15	6.0	6	111	21	212	28	33	635	7	2.7
Sierra Leone	9	26	835.4	8	58	48	236	80	58	305	3	2.6
Singapore	6	6	1.1	3	9	11	129	0	23	69	10	0.8
Slovak Republic	9	25	5.1	3	17	13	272	39	27	565	2	4.8
Slovenia	9	60	10.1	6	391	14	207	64	25	913	3	3.6
Somalia	..	..	..	..	..	..	..	..	..	..	..	..
South Africa	9	38	8.6	6	23	18	176	52	26	277	8	2.0
Spain	10	47	16.5	3	25	12	277	66	23	169	4	1.0
Sri Lanka	8	50	10.4	8	63	18	167	40	17	440	4	2.2
Sudan	10	38	68.1	..	..	..	..	43	67	915	..	..
Swaziland	..	..	..	..	..	..	..	..	..	..	..	..
Sweden	3	16	0.7	1	2	8	116	43	23	208	2	2.0
Switzerland	6	20	8.7	4	16	15	152	17	22	170	1	3.0
Syrian Arab Republic	12	47	34.5	4	34	20	134	40	47	672	5	4.1
Tajikistan	..	..	..	..	..	..	..	..	..	..	..	..
Tanzania	13	35	161.3	12	61	26	313	69	21	242	3	3.0
Thailand	8	33	6.1	2	2	9	147	18	26	390	10	2.7
Togo	13	53	218.3	6	212	14	273	79	37	535	4	3.0
Trinidad and Tobago	..	..	..	..	..	..	..	..	..	..	..	..
Tunisia	9	14	10.0	5	57	21	154	54	14	27	0	1.3
Turkey	8	9	27.7	8	9	32	232	55	22	330	8	5.9
Turkmenistan	..	..	..	..	..	..	..	..	..	..	..	..
Uganda	17	36	117.8	8	48	19	155	13	15	209	7	2.2
Ukraine	15	34	10.6	10	93	18	265	61	28	269	1	2.9
United Arab Emirates	12	54	44.3	3	9	21	125	33	53	614	4	5.1
United Kingdom	6	18	0.7	2	21	19	115	14	14	288	10	1.0
United States	5	5	0.5	4	12	19	70	3	17	250	7	2.0
Uruguay	11	45	43.9	8	66	17	146	31	39	620	3	2.1
Uzbekistan	9	35	15.5	12	97	..	..	34	35	368	4	4.0
Venezuela, RB	13	116	15.7	7	33	13	276	38	41	445	3	4.0
Vietnam	11	50	50.6	5	67	14	143	51	37	343	4	5.0
West Bank and Gaza	11	106	275.4	7	58	18	144	38	26	465	..	..
Yemen, Rep.	12	63	240.2	6	21	13	131	37	37	360	6	3.0
Zambia	6	35	18.1	6	70	16	165	10	16	274	10	3.1
Zimbabwe	10	96	1,442.5	4	30	21	481	24	33	350	8	2.2
World	**10 u**	**48 u**	**77.3 u**	**6 u**	**86 u**	**18 u**	**209 u**	**41 u**	**32 u**	**394 u**	**5 u**	**3.2 u**
Low income	10	60	167.6	7	114	19	231	50	36	421	5	3.7
Middle income	10	49	42.3	6	82	19	216	38	32	424	5	3.5
Lower middle income	10	52	54.2	6	74	18	216	39	32	433	4	3.6
Upper middle income	9	42	18.4	6	99	20	216	38	30	405	5	3.5
Low & middle income	10	53	94.8	6	95	19	222	43	34	423	5	3.6
East Asia & Pacific	9	56	47.2	5	64	17	147	28	31	426	5	3.7
Europe & Central Asia	10	36	13.6	6	117	22	254	44	30	372	5	3.5
Latin America & Carib.	12	66	58.8	7	79	16	210	41	35	470	4	3.5
Middle East & N. Africa	10	45	75.6	7	50	19	236	45	38	414	5	3.8
South Asia	8	35	39.7	7	124	16	195	39	30	386	5	5.1
Sub-Saharan Africa	11	64	215.3	7	118	20	251	53	36	439	5	3.3
High income	7	24	9.4	5	47	16	157	34	24	282	6	1.9
Europe EMU	8	27	10.2	6	55	15	201	51	22	296	6	1.3

About the data

The table presents key indicators on the environment for doing business. The indicators identify regulations that enhance or constrain business investment, productivity, and growth. The data are from the World Bank's Doing Business database.

A vibrant private sector is central to promoting growth and expanding opportunities for poor people. But encouraging firms to invest, improve productivity, and create jobs requires a legal and regulatory environment that fosters access to credit, protects property rights, and supports efficient judicial, taxation, and customs systems. The indicators in the table point to the administrative and regulatory reforms and institutions needed to create a favorable environment for doing business.

When entrepreneurs start a business, the first obstacles they face are the administrative and legal procedures required to register the new firm. Countries differ widely in how they regulate the entry of new businesses. In some countries the process is straightforward and affordable. But in others the procedures are so burdensome that entrepreneurs may opt to run their business informally. The data on starting a business cover the number of start-up procedures and the time required and cost to complete them.

Property registries were first developed to help raise tax revenue, but they have benefited entrepreneurs as well. Securing rights to land and buildings, a major source of wealth in most countries, strengthens incentives to invest and facilitates trade. More complex procedures to register property are associated with less perceived security of property rights, more informality, and more corruption. The data cover the number procedures required and time required to secure rights to property.

Lack of access to credit is one of the biggest barriers entrepreneurs face in starting and operating a business. Indicators covering financial access and financial information are presented in table 5.5.

There are many types of business licenses required, and striking the right balance between the ease of doing business and consumer safety requires continuous reform. Since construction is a large sector in most economies, the procedures required for a business in the construction industry to build a standardized warehouse are recorded. These include obtaining all necessary licenses and permits, completing all required notifications and inspections, and submitting the relevant documents to the authorities. The data cover the number of procedures and time needed by the construction firm to complete all procedures.

Every economy has a complex system of laws and institutions to protect the interests of workers and guarantee a minimum standard of living for its population. The rigidity of employment index focuses on the regulation of employment, specifically the hiring and firing of workers and the rigidity of working hours. This index is the average of three subindexes: a difficulty of hiring index, a rigidity of hours index, and a difficulty of firing index. All subindexes have several components and take values between 0 and 100, with higher values indicating more rigid regulation.

Contract enforcement is critical to enable businesses to engage with new borrowers or customers. Without good contract enforcement trade and credit will be restricted to a small community of people who have developed relationships through repeated dealings or the security of assets. The institution that enforces contracts between debtors and creditors, and suppliers and customers, is the court. The efficiency of contract enforcement is reflected in two indicators: number of judicial procedures to resolve a dispute and time to enforce a commercial contract.

What companies disclose to the public has a large impact on investor protection. Both investors and entrepreneurs benefit greatly from such legal protection. The disclosure index is based on measures that cover ownership disclosure, measures that reduce expropriation, and disclosures to help investors.

Unviable businesses prevent assets and human capital from being allocated to more productive uses in new companies or in viable companies that are financially distressed. The time to close a business (resolve an insolvency) captures the average time to complete a procedure, as estimated by insolvency lawyers. Information is collected on the sequence of bankruptcy procedures and on whether any procedures can be carried out simultaneously. Delays due to legal derailment tactics that parties to the insolvency may use, in particular extension of response periods or appeals, are taken into account.

To ensure cross-country comparability, several standard characteristics of a company are defined in all surveys, such as size, ownership, location, legal status, and type of activities. The data were collected through a study of laws and regulations in each country, surveys of regulators or private sector professionals on each topic, and cooperative arrangements with private consulting firms and business and law associations. These standard characteristics include limited liability company; operates in the country's most populous city; 100 percent domestically owned and has five owners, none of whom is a legal entity; start-up capital of 10 times income per capita at the end of 2004, paid in cash; performs general industrial or commercial activities, such as production or sale of products or services to the public; does not perform foreign trade activities or handle products subject to a special tax regime; does not use heavily polluting production processes; leases the commercial plant and offices and is not a proprietor of real estate; does not qualify for investment incentives or any special benefits; up to 50 employees within one month of commencement of operations, all of them nationals; turnover at least 100 times income per capita; and company deed 10 pages long.

Definitions

• **Number of procedures for starting a business** is the number of procedures required to start a business, including interactions required to obtain necessary permits and licenses and to complete all inscriptions, verifications, and notifications to start operations. Data are for businesses with specific characteristics of ownership, size, and type of production. • **Time required for starting a business** is the number of calendar days needed to complete the required procedures for legally operating a business. If a procedure can be speeded up at additional cost, the fastest procedure, independent of cost, is chosen. • **Cost for starting a business** is normalized by presenting it as a percentage of gross national income (GNI) per capita. • **Number of procedures to register property** is the number of procedures required for a business to secure rights to property. • **Time required for registering property** is the number of calendar days needed for a business to secure rights to property. • **Number of procedures to build a warehouse** is the number of interactions of a company's employees or managers with external parties, including government agency staff, public inspectors, notaries, land registry and cadastre staff, and technical experts apart from architects and engineers. • **Time required to build a warehouse** is the number of calendar days needed to complete the required procedures for building a warehouse. If a procedure can be speeded up at additional cost, the fastest procedure, independent of cost, is chosen. • **Rigidity of employment index** measures the regulation of employment, specifically the hiring and firing of workers and the rigidity of working hours. This index is the average of three subindexes: a difficulty of hiring index, a rigidity of hours index, and a difficulty of firing index. The index ranges from 0 to 100, with higher values indicating more rigid regulations. • **Number of procedures for enforcing contracts** is the number of independent actions, mandated by law or court regulation, that demand interaction between the parties to a contract or between them and the judge or court officer. • **Time required for enforcing contracts** is the number of calendar days from the filing of the lawsuit in court to the final determination and, in appropriate cases, payment. • **Disclosure index** measures the degree to which investors are protected through disclosure of ownership and financial information. The index ranges from 0 to 7, with higher values indicating more disclosure. • **Time to resolve insolvency** is the number of years from the time of filing for insolvency in court until resolution of distressed assets.

Data sources

Data on the business environment are from the World Bank's Doing Business project (http://rru.worldbank.org/DoingBusiness/).

5.4 Stock markets

	Market capitalization				Market liquidity		Turnover ratio		Listed domestic companies		S&P/EMDB indexes	
	$ millions		% of GDP		Value traded % of GDP		Value of shares traded % of market capitalization		number		% change	
	2000	2005	2000	2004	2000	2004	2000	2005	2000	2005	2004	2005
Afghanistan	..	..	..	..	..	..	..	..	..	..	..	..
Albania	..	..	..	..	..	..	..	..	..	..	..	..
Algeria	..	..	..	..	..	..	..	..	..	..	..	..
Angola	..	..	..	..	..	..	..	..	..	..	..	..
Argentina	166,068	61,478	58.4	30.3	2.1	5.0	4.8	29.7	127	101	24.6[a]	45.4[a]
Armenia	..	*18*	..	*0.6*	..	0.1	*4.6*	*3.9*	..	*194*	..	..
Australia	372,794	*776,403*	96.2	121.8	58.4	80.7	56.5	*75.5*	1,330	*1,515*	..	..
Austria	29,935	*85,815*	15.4	29.4	4.8	8.2	29.8	*34.0*	97	*99*	..	..
Azerbaijan	*4*	..	*0.1*	..	..	..	..	..	*2*	..	..	..
Bangladesh	1,186	3,035	2.6	5.9	1.7	1.6	74.4	32.3	221	262	104.3[b]	–27.7[b]
Belarus	..	..	..	..	..	..	..	..	..	..	..	..
Belgium	182,481	*768,377*	79.9	218.1	16.6	20.0	20.7	*14.9*	174	*170*	..	..
Benin	..	..	..	..	..	..	..	..	..	..	..	..
Bolivia	*1,742*	*1,988*	*20.7*	*22.7*	*0.0*	0.1	*1.0*	*0.2*	*26*	*34*	..	..
Bosnia and Herzegovina	..	..	..	..	..	..	..	..	..	..	..	..
Botswana	978	2,437	18.6	28.4	0.9	0.6	4.8	2.0	16	18	21.1[b]	–3.2[b]
Brazil	226,152	474,647	37.6	54.7	16.8	15.5	43.5	37.2	459	381	33.7[a]	47.6[a]
Bulgaria	617	5,086	4.9	11.6	0.5	2.1	9.2	35.2	503	331	82.7[b]	16.4[b]
Burkina Faso	..	..	..	..	..	..	..	..	..	..	..	..
Burundi	..	..	..	..	..	..	..	..	..	..	..	..
Cambodia	..	..	..	..	..	..	..	..	..	..	..	..
Cameroon	..	..	..	..	..	..	..	..	..	..	..	..
Canada	841,385	*1,177,518*	117.8	120.4	88.8	66.9	77.3	*63.1*	1,418	*3,597*	..	..
Central African Republic	..	..	..	..	..	..	..	..	..	..	..	..
Chad	..	..	..	..	..	..	..	..	..	..	..	..
Chile	60,401	136,446	79.7	124.4	8.0	12.3	9.4	15.5	258	245	18.3[a]	14.7[a]
China	580,991	780,763	48.5	33.1	60.2	38.7	158.3	82.6	1,086	1,387	–2.1[a]	13.3[a]
Hong Kong, China	623,398	*861,463*	377.0	528.5	228.5	269.3	61.3	*55.7*	779	*1,086*	..	..
Colombia	9,560	46,016	11.4	25.8	0.5	1.5	3.8	17.8	126	114	115.4[b]	108.1[b]
Congo, Dem. Rep.	..	..	..	..	..	..	..	..	..	..	..	..
Congo, Rep.	..	..	..	..	..	..	..	..	..	..	..	..
Costa Rica	*2,924*	*1,920*	*18.3*	*10.4*	..	0.7	*12.0*	..	*21*	23	..	..
Côte d'Ivoire	1,185	2,327	11.4	13.5	0.3	0.3	2.6	1.5	41	39	41.1[b]	16.9[b]
Croatia	2,742	12,918	14.9	31.9	1.0	1.4	7.4	6.6	64	145	–7.7[b]	7.4[b]
Cuba	..	..	..	..	..	..	..	..	..	..	..	..
Czech Republic	11,002	38,345	19.7	28.8	11.8	16.5	60.3	120.7	131	36	76.3[a]	43.5[a]
Denmark	107,666	*151,342*	68.0	62.7	57.9	40.4	86.0	*71.4*	225	*178*	..	..
Dominican Republic	*141*	..	*0.8*	..	..	..	..	..	*6*	..	..	..
Ecuador	704	3,214	4.4	8.5	0.1	0.3	5.5	5.0	30	32	46.7[b]	26.0[b]
Egypt, Arab Rep.	28,741	79,672	28.1	48.9	10.9	7.1	34.7	42.4	1,076	744	126.4[a]	158.0[a]
El Salvador	2,041	*2,643*	15.5	*16.7*	0.2	3.1	*2.7*	*0.3*	40	*32*	..	..
Eritrea	..	..	..	..	..	..	..	..	..	..	..	..
Estonia	1,846	3,495	33.7	55.2	6.0	7.4	18.9	51.5	23	15	70.5[b]	22.8[b]
Ethiopia	..	..	..	..	..	..	..	..	..	..	..	..
Finland	293,635	*183,765*	244.9	98.8	172.3	118.4	64.3	*124.3*	154	*134*	..	..
France	1,446,634	*1,857,235*	108.9	90.7	81.6	64.1	74.1	*81.7*	808	*701*	..	..
Gabon	..	..	..	..	..	..	..	..	..	..	..	..
Gambia, The	..	..	..	..	..	..	..	..	..	..	..	..
Georgia	24	*186*	0.8	*3.6*	..	0.5	..	*0.5*	269	*277*	..	..
Germany	1,270,243	*1,194,517*	66.8	43.6	56.3	51.3	79.1	*123.7*	1,022	*660*	..	..
Ghana	502	1,661	10.1	29.8	0.2	0.7	1.5	3.2	22	30	32.7[b]	–33.9[b]
Greece	110,839	*125,242*	98.9	61.0	84.8	21.2	63.7	*37.5*	329	*340*	..	..
Guatemala	240	..	1.2	..	0.0	..	*2.9*	..	44	*5*	..	..
Guinea	..	..	..	..	..	..	..	..	..	..	..	..
Guinea-Bissau	..	..	..	..	..	..	..	..	..	..	..	..
Haiti	..	..	..	..	..	..	..	..	..	..	..	..

Stock markets

	Market capitalization				Market liquidity		Turnover ratio		Listed domestic companies		S&P/EMDB indexes	
	$ millions		% of GDP		Value traded % of GDP		Value of shares traded % of market capitalization		number		% change	
	2000	2005	2000	2004	2000	2004	2000	2005	2000	2005	2004	2005
Honduras	*458*	..	*8.7*	..	..	..	..	..	46	..	..	..
Hungary	12,021	32,576	25.8	28.5	26.0	12.9	90.7	79.2	60	44	93.7[a]	16.1[a]
India	148,064	553,074	32.4	56.1	111.5	54.8	133.6	93.6	5,937	4,763	20.1[a]	33.6[a]
Indonesia	26,834	81,428	16.3	28.4	8.7	10.7	32.9	54.8	290	335	39.3[a]	9.1[a]
Iran, Islamic Rep.	7,350	*46,995*	7.3	*28.8*	4.9	8.1	*12.4*	*21.7*	304	*411*	..	..
Iraq	..	..	..	..	..	..	..	..	..	..	..	..
Ireland	81,882	*114,085*	86.2	62.8	15.2	24.4	19.2	*44.5*	76	*53*	..	..
Israel	64,081	120,114	55.5	81.7	20.3	39.6	36.3	55.4	654	572	13.4[a]	24.1[a]
Italy	768,364	*789,563*	71.5	47.1	72.4	47.9	104.0	*114.5*	291	*269*	..	..
Jamaica	3,582	13,028	44.6	162.6	0.9	5.4	2.5	3.1	46	39	107.4[b]	–14.1[b]
Japan	3,157,222	*3,678,262*	66.5	79.6	56.8	74.2	69.9	*103.5*	2,561	*3,220*	12.5[c]	21.7[c]
Jordan	4,943	37,639	58.4	159.6	4.9	46.3	7.7	85.0	163	201	55.0[b]	117.8[b]
Kazakhstan	1,342	*3,941*	7.3	*9.7*	0.5	2.4	*1.2*	*22.0*	23	*54*	..	..
Kenya	1,283	6,384	10.1	24.2	0.4	2.0	3.6	9.7	57	47	–15.0[b]	60.0[b]
Korea, Dem. Rep.	..	..	..	..	..	..	..	..	..	..	..	..
Korea, Rep.	171,587	718,180	33.5	63.1	208.7	94.0	233.2	210.8	1,308	1,620	25.7[a]	58.8[a]
Kuwait	20,772	..	56.3	..	11.4	..	21.3	..	77	..	..	..
Kyrgyz Republic	4	*34*	0.3	1.5	1.7	3.0	..	*205.3*	80	*6*	..	..
Lao PDR	..	..	..	..	..	..	..	..	..	..	..	..
Latvia	563	2,527	7.3	12.2	3.0	0.8	48.6	4.6	64	45	49.8[b]	32.8[b]
Lebanon	1,583	4,929	9.5	10.7	0.7	0.9	6.7	25.5	12	11	53.5[b]	111.8[b]
Lesotho	..	..	..	..	..	..	..	..	..	..	..	..
Liberia	..	..	..	..	..	..	..	..	..	..	..	..
Libya	..	..	..	..	..	..	..	..	..	..	..	..
Lithuania	1,588	8,183	13.9	29.0	1.8	2.1	14.8	10.2	54	43	56.2[b]	6.2[b]
Macedonia, FYR	7	*413*	0.2	*7.7*	0.1	*0.5*	*348.3*	*8.1*	*1*	*68*	..	..
Madagascar	..	..	..	..	..	..	..	..	..	..	..	..
Malawi	126	..	7.2	..	0.5	..	..	..	7	*8*	..	..
Malaysia	116,935	180,346	129.5	160.6	64.8	50.6	44.6	26.9	795	1,020	12.7[a]	–2.9[a]
Mali	..	..	..	..	..	..	..	..	..	..	..	..
Mauritania	..	..	..	..	..	..	..	..	..	..	..	..
Mauritius	1,331	2,617	30.1	39.4	1.7	1.6	5.0	6.1	40	42	17.8[b]	10.5[b]
Mexico	125,204	239,128	21.5	25.4	7.8	6.3	32.3	25.7	179	151	47.9[a]	43.9[a]
Moldova	*392*	*574*	*30.4*	*22.1*	1.9	2.1	*97.9*	*7.7*	*36*	*23*	..	..
Mongolia	*37*	*25*	*3.9*	*1.5*	..	0.0	*7.3*	*2.2*	*410*	*395*	..	..
Morocco	10,899	27,220	32.7	50.1	3.3	3.4	9.2	16.4	53	56	18.3[a]	8.4[a]
Mozambique	..	..	..	..	..	..	..	..	..	..	..	..
Myanmar	..	..	..	..	..	..	..	..	..	..	..	..
Namibia	311	415	9.1	7.7	0.6	0.3	4.5	1.6	13	13	36.7[b]	–1.1[b]
Nepal	790	576	14.4	8.6	0.6	0.4	*6.9*	..	110	*114*	..	..
Netherlands	640,456	*622,284*	172.8	*107.5*	182.7	104.4	101.4	*104.1*	234	*177*	..	..
New Zealand	18,866	*43,731*	36.2	44.2	20.7	15.6	45.9	*40.1*	142	*158*	..	..
Nicaragua	..	..	..	..	..	..	..	..	..	..	..	..
Niger	..	..	..	..	..	..	..	..	..	..	..	..
Nigeria	4,237	19,356	10.1	20.1	0.6	2.3	7.3	11.5	195	214	23.9[b]	20.7[b]
Norway	65,034	*141,430*	39.0	56.6	36.0	54.2	93.4	*114.7*	191	*148*	..	..
Oman	3,463	15,269	17.4	26.0	2.8	7.4	14.2	29.8	131	96	25.2[b]	38.0[b]
Pakistan	6,581	45,937	9.0	30.2	45.0	76.9	475.5	375.7	762	661	20.7[b]	58.5[b]
Panama	2,794	*3,401*	24.0	*24.8*	1.3	0.4	*1.5*	*1.5*	29	*22*	..	..
Papua New Guinea	..	2,942	..	75.3	..	0.1	..	..	..	9	..	..
Paraguay	*423*	212	*5.5*	2.9	..	0.0	*3.5*	..	*55*	52	..	..
Peru	10,562	35,995	19.9	29.3	2.9	1.6	12.6	7.1	230	196	–0.7[a]	29.8[a]
Philippines	25,957	40,153	34.2	34.2	10.8	4.3	15.8	20.4	228	235	25.0[a]	21.3[a]
Poland	31,279	93,873	18.8	29.3	8.8	6.8	49.9	37.3	225	248	59.3[a]	20.8[a]
Portugal	60,681	*73,404*	57.0	43.8	51.1	20.6	85.5	*52.5*	109	*56*	..	..
Puerto Rico	..	..	..	..	..	..	..	..	..	..	..	..

5.4 Stock markets

	Market capitalization				Market liquidity		Turnover ratio		Listed domestic companies		S&P/EMDB indexes	
	$ millions		% of GDP		Value traded % of GDP		Value of shares traded % of market capitalization		number		% change	
	2000	2005	2000	2004	2000	2004	2000	2005	2000	2005	2004	2005
Romania	1,069	20,588	2.9	16.1	0.6	1.3	23.1	28.8	5,555	3,747	99.3[b]	58.7[b]
Russian Federation	38,922	548,579	15.0	46.1	7.8	22.5	36.9	39.0	249	296	12.8[a]	64.9[a]
Rwanda	..	..	..	..	..	..	..	..	..	..	..	..
Saudi Arabia	67,171	646,104	35.6	122.2	9.2	188.8	27.1	231.7	75	77	83.6[b]	111.0[b]
Senegal	..	..	..	..	..	..	..	..	..	..	..	..
Serbia and Montenegro	..	*3,281*	..	*13.7*	0.3	1.8	*0.0*	*122.3*	6	*404*	..	..
Sierra Leone	..	..	..	..	..	..	..	..	..	..	..	..
Singapore	152,827	*171,555*	167.1	160.6	100.0	76.1	52.1	*51.2*	418	*489*	..	..
Slovak Republic	1,217	4,393	6.0	10.7	4.4	1.6	129.8	1.6	493	209	41.0[b]	16.6[b]
Slovenia	2,547	7,899	13.4	30.1	..	3.6	20.7	9.1	38	116	128.5[b]	–6.9[b]
Somalia	..	..	..	..	..	..	..	..	..	..	..	..
South Africa	204,952	565,408	154.2	214.1	58.3	76.5	33.9	41.6	616	388	50.1[a]	24.8[a]
Spain	504,219	*940,673*	86.8	90.5	169.8	114.9	210.7	*143.3*	1,019	*3,272*	..	..
Sri Lanka	1,074	5,720	6.6	18.2	0.9	2.9	11.0	23.7	239	239	–59.2[b]	29.3[b]
Sudan	..	..	..	..	..	..	..	..	..	..	..	..
Swaziland	*73*	*225*	*5.3*	*9.4*	0.0	0.0	*0.2*	*0.0*	6	*6*	..	..
Sweden	328,339	*376,781*	137.1	108.8	162.8	119.1	111.2	*123.7*	292	*256*	..	..
Switzerland	792,316	*825,849*	322.0	231.0	247.6	203.4	82.0	*93.7*	252	*282*	..	..
Syrian Arab Republic	..	..	..	..	..	..	..	..	..	..	..	..
Tajikistan	..	..	..	..	..	..	..	..	..	..	..	..
Tanzania	233	670	2.6	6.2	0.4	0.2	*3.4*	..	4	6	..	..
Thailand	29,489	123,539	24.0	71.4	19.0	67.5	53.2	75.2	381	468	–6.4[a]	3.8[a]
Togo	..	..	..	..	..	..	..	..	..	..	..	..
Trinidad and Tobago	4,330	16,972	53.1	135.9	1.7	4.2	3.1	4.0	27	37	36.8[b]	–1.3[b]
Tunisia	2,828	2,876	14.5	9.4	3.2	0.8	23.3	16.8	44	46	4.2[b]	11.1[b]
Turkey	69,659	161,537	35.0	32.5	89.9	48.7	206.2	153.9	315	302	32.9[a]	49.5[a]
Turkmenistan	..	..	..	..	..	..	..	..	..	..	..	..
Uganda	..	96	..	1.4	..	0.0	..	..	..	5	..	..
Ukraine	1,881	24,976	6.0	18.2	0.9	0.3	19.6	3.6	139	221	170.3[b]	52.8[b]
United Arab Emirates	5,727	30,363	8.1	34.3	0.2	4.3	..	..	54	30	..	..
United Kingdom	2,576,992	*2,815,928*	179.2	132.6	127.6	174.5	66.6	*140.5*	1,904	*2,486*	15.3[d]	4.4[d]
United States	15,104,037	*16,323,726*	154.7	139.4	326.3	165.3	200.8	*126.5*	7,524	*5,231*	9.0[e]	3.0[e]
Uruguay	*161*	*330*	*0.8*	*2.5*	*0.0*	0.0	*0.9*	*0.4*	*16*	*10*	..	..
Uzbekistan	32	*4*	0.2	*0.0*	0.1	0.0	..	*108.7*	5	*145*	..	..
Venezuela, RB	8,128	5,017	6.9	5.6	0.6	0.4	8.9	4.6	85	50	–50.4[b]	–22.0[b]
Vietnam	..	..	..	..	..	..	..	..	..	..	..	..
West Bank and Gaza	765	*1,097*	16.5	*18.8*	4.1	*1.7*	*20.9*	*1.7*	24	*27*	..	..
Yemen, Rep.	..	..	..	..	..	..	..	..	..	..	..	..
Zambia	236	430	7.3	8.0	0.2	0.1	*4.7*	..	9	11	..	..
Zimbabwe	2,432	2,402	32.9	41.3	3.8	2.9	10.8	6.4	69	79	–26.7[b]	36.6[b]
World	32,187,883 s	*38,904,431* s	103.1 w	96.3 w	153.6 w	97.0 w	122.3 w	53.7 w	47,884 s	*48,874* s	..	..
Low income	167,320	*450,544*	24.2	44.5	78.9	45.0	152.7	107.6	7,965	*6,756*	..	..
Middle income	1,851,805	*2,982,006*	37.5	43.7	26.9	23.9	71.5	41.6	15,497	*14,117*	..	..
Lower middle income	980,024	*1,426,779*	35.5	36.7	32.3	26.2	91.3	37.1	11,450	*10,584*	..	..
Upper middle income	871,781	*1,555,228*	40.0	52.8	20.1	20.9	47.4	44.3	4,047	*3,533*	..	..
Low & middle income	2,019,125	*3,432,550*	35.9	43.8	33.3	26.7	81.4	53.7	23,462	*20,873*	..	..
East Asia & Pacific	780,487	*1,050,879*	47.2	41.0	50.0	37.0	125.2	50.0	3,190	*3,794*	..	..
Europe & Central Asia	176,208	*561,440*	19.3	32.8	25.6	19.4	82.1	59.0	8,295	*7,023*	..	..
Latin America & Carib.	626,283	*767,136*	32.6	39.6	8.6	8.3	26.9	26.1	1,806	*1,525*	..	..
Middle East & N. Africa	60,573	*141,343*	19.8	*37.1*	6.3	7.4	*18.7*	*16.5*	1,807	*1,627*	..	..
South Asia	157,695	*424,403*	26.4	48.7	90.9	52.2	168.0	120.6	7,269	*6,000*	..	..
Sub-Saharan Africa	217,880	*487,349*	91.2	129.6	32.8	43.9	22.5	27.6	1,095	*904*	..	..
High income	30,168,757	*35,471,881*	117.8	108.9	179.9	113.9	130.9	*114.0*	24,422	*28,001*	..	..
Europe EMU	5,423,385	*6,805,103*	88.5	71.6	81.8	60.6	90.8	*102.0*	4,367	*5,973*	..	..

Note: Because aggregates for market capitalization are unavailable for 2005, those shown refer to 2004.

a. Data refer to the S&P/IFC Investable index. b. Data refer to the S&P/IFC Global index c. Data refer to the Nikkei 225 index. d. Data refer to the FT 100 index. e. Data refer to the S&P 500 index.

About the data

The development of an economy's financial markets is closely related to its overall development. Well functioning financial systems provide good and easily accessible information. That lowers transaction costs, which in turn improves resource allocation and boosts economic growth. Both banking systems and stock markets enhance growth, the main factor in poverty reduction. At low levels of economic development commercial banks tend to dominate the financial system, while at higher levels domestic stock markets tend to become more active and efficient relative to domestic banks.

Open economies with sound macroeconomic policies, good legal systems, and shareholder protection attract capital and therefore have larger financial markets. Recent research on stock market development shows that new communications technology and increased financial integration have resulted in more cross-border capital flows, a stronger presence of financial firms around the world, and the migration of stock exchange activities to international exchanges. Many firms in emerging markets now cross-list on international exchanges, which provides them with lower cost capital and more liquidity-traded shares. However, this also means that exchanges in emerging markets may not have enough financial activity to sustain them, putting pressure on them to rethink their operations.

The stock market indicators in the table include measures of size (market capitalization, number of listed domestic companies) and liquidity (value traded as a percentage of gross domestic product, value of shares traded as a percentage of market capitalization). The comparability of such indicators between countries may be limited by conceptual and statistical weaknesses, such as inaccurate reporting and differences in accounting standards. The percentage change in stock market prices in U.S. dollars, from the Standard & Poor's Emerging Markets Data Base (S&P/EMDB) indexes is an important measure of overall performance. Regulatory and institutional factors that can affect investor confidence, such as entry and exit restrictions, the existence of a securities and exchange commission, and the quality of laws to protect investors, may influence the functioning of stock markets but are not included in the table.

Stock market size can be measured in a number of ways, and each may produce a different ranking of countries. Market capitalization shows the overall size of the stock market in U.S. dollars and as a percentage of GDP. The number of listed domestic companies is another measure of market size. Market size is positively correlated with the ability to mobilize capital and diversify risk.

Market liquidity, the ability to easily buy and sell securities, is measured by dividing the total value traded by GDP. The turnover ratio—the value of shares traded as a percentage of market capitalization—is also a measure of liquidity as well as of transaction costs. (High turnover indicates low transaction costs.) The turnover ratio complements the ratio of value traded to GDP, because the turnover ratio is related to the size of the market and the value traded ratio to the size of the economy. A small, liquid market will have a high turnover ratio but a low value traded ratio. Liquidity is an important attribute of stock markets because, in theory, liquid markets improve the allocation of capital and enhance prospects for long-term economic growth. A more comprehensive measure of liquidity would include trading costs and the time and uncertainty in finding a counterpart in settling trades.

Standard & Poor's maintains a series of indexes for investors interested in investing in stock markets in developing countries. At the core of the S&P/EMDB indexes, the Global (S&P/IFCG) index is intended to represent the most active stocks in the markets it covers and to be the broadest possible indicator of market movements. The Investable (S&P/IFCI) index, which applies the same calculation methodology as the S&P/IFCG index, is designed to measure the returns that foreign portfolio investors might receive from investing in emerging market stocks that are legally and practically open to foreign portfolio investment.

The S&P/EMDB, the source for all the data in the table, provides regular updates on 53 emerging stock markets encompassing more than 2,613 stocks. The S&P/IFCG index includes 32 markets and 2,125 stocks, and the S&P/IFCI index covers 22 markets and 1,377 stocks. In addition 251 companies from 21 "frontier" markets are covered. These indexes are widely used benchmarks for international portfolio management. See Standard & Poor's (2001b) for further information on the indexes.

Because markets included in Standard & Poor's emerging markets category vary widely in level of development, it is best to look at the entire category to identify the most significant market trends. And it is useful to remember that stock market trends may be distorted by currency conversions, especially when a currency has registered a significant devaluation.

About the data is based on Demirgüç-Kunt and Levine (1996a), Beck and Levine (2001), and Claessens, Klingebiel, and Schmukler (2002).

Definitions

• **Market capitalization** (also known as market value) is the share price times the number of shares outstanding. • **Market liquidity** is the total value traded divided by GDP. Value traded is the total value of shares traded during the period. This indicator complements the market capitalization ratio by showing whether market size is matched by trading. • **Turnover ratio** is the total value of shares traded during the period divided by the average market capitalization for the period. Average market capitalization is calculated as the average of the end-of-period values for the current period and the previous period. • **Listed domestic companies** are the domestically incorporated companies listed on the country's stock exchanges at the end of the year. This indicator does not include investment companies, mutual funds, or other collective investment vehicles. • **S&P/EMDB indexes** measure the U.S. dollar price change in the stock markets covered by the S&P/IFCI and S&P/IFCG country indexes.

Data sources

Data on stock markets are from Standard & Poor's *Global Stock Markets Factbook 2005*, which draws on the Emerging Markets Data Base, supplemented by other data from Standard & Poor's. The firm collects data through an annual survey of the world's stock exchanges, supplemented by information provided by its network of correspondents and by Reuters. Data on GDP are from the World Bank's national accounts data files.

Financial access, stability, and efficiency

	Bank branches	Bank deposit accounts	Financial information infrastructure index	Banking system ownership		Bank capital to asset ratio	Bank nonperforming loans to total gross loans	Deposit insurance coverage	Domestic credit provided by banking sector	Interest rate spread	Risk premium on lending
				% of total banking assets							
	per 100,000 people	per 1,000 people	0 (less developed) to 10 (more developed)	Held by foreign-owned banks	Held by government-owned banks	%	%	% of GDP per capita	% of GDP	Lending rate minus deposit rate percentage points	Prime lending rate minus treasury bill rate percentage points
	2001–04[a]	2001–04[a]	2005	2001	2001	2004	2004	2003	2004	2004	2004
Afghanistan	..	..	..	..	..	..	..	..	..	..	..
Albania	2.1	161	..	46.0	54.0	..	..	3.0	45.7	5.2	5.0
Algeria	..	..	..	3.9	95.7	..	..	3.7	24.8	5.5	7.9
Angola	..	..	..	..	..	11.3	13.3	..	4.5	66.9	..
Argentina	10.0	369	7.5	31.8	31.9	..	18.6	3.1	45.5	4.2	..
Armenia	7.6	111	4.5	59.0	0.0	17.8	7.2	..	7.2	13.7	13.4
Australia	29.9	..	..	17.0	0.0	5.9	0.3	..	109.0	5.2	..
Austria	53.9	3,120	..	..	0.0	6.0	*2.2*	0.7	121.9	..	..
Azerbaijan	4.1	..	..	4.6	58.3	11.9	9.5	..	11.2	6.5	11.1
Bangladesh	4.5	229	..	..	..	2.7	17.6	4.6	41.1	7.6	..
Belarus	4.8	..	..	26.0	74.0	20.0	4.6	0.6	21.2	4.2	..
Belgium	53.2	3,080	..	..	0.0	3.2	2.2	0.8	104.9	5.2	4.7
Benin	..	..	3.0	91.0	0.0	..	..	..	9.9	..	..
Bolivia	1.5	41	5.5	36.3	0.0	11.5	14.0	..	52.5	7.1	7.1
Bosnia and Herzegovina	3.9	429	..	73.0	10.0	13.2	3.5	1.7	43.5	6.6	..
Botswana	3.8	..	..	100.0	0.0	9.7	2.8	..	–3.0	5.9	..
Brazil	14.6	631	4.0	29.9	32.0	16.0	3.9	2.3	98.8	39.5	37.8
Bulgaria	13.9	1,351	7.0	74.6	17.6	11.0	7.1	3.4	36.2	5.8	6.1
Burkina Faso	..	..	..	56.0	0.0	..	..	..	13.5	..	..
Burundi	..	..	..	..	..	..	..	..	38.4	..	..
Cambodia	..	..	1.0	..	..	..	..	..	8.2	15.8	..
Cameroon	..	..	3.0	..	..	..	..	..	15.2	13.0	..
Canada	45.6	..	..	4.8	0.0	4.4	0.7	1.6	97.0	3.2	1.8
Central African Republic	..	..	..	..	..	..	..	..	16.7	13.0	..
Chad	..	..	..	..	..	..	..	..	7.9	13.0	..
Chile	9.4	1,045	6.5	46.8	13.3	7.0	1.2	0.7	70.2	3.2	..
China	1.3	..	5.5	..	..	3.9	15.6	..	142.6	3.3	..
Hong Kong, China	..	..	..	..	0.0	12.3	2.2	..	149.3	5.0	4.9
Colombia	8.7	612	7.0	21.5	18.3	12.1	3.3	4.0	41.2	7.3	..
Congo, Dem. Rep.	..	..	..	..	..	..	..	..	1.2	..	..
Congo, Rep.	..	..	1.0	..	..	..	..	..	12.0	13.0	..
Costa Rica	9.6	..	6.5	23.3	62.2	11.9	2.0	..	42.3	13.9	..
Côte d'Ivoire	..	..	..	84.2	10.6	..	..	..	18.6	..	..
Croatia	23.4	..	..	89.3	5.0	8.5	4.5	2.3	68.2	9.9	..
Cuba	..	..	..	..	..	..	..	..	..	..	..
Czech Republic	11.2	1,923	3.5	90.0	3.8	5.6	4.1	3.4	45.8	4.7	3.5
Denmark	37.6	2,706	..	0.0	0.0	..	..	1.2	167.0	4.7	..
Dominican Republic	6.0	720	..	..	..	7.4	7.3	*0.2*	37.3	11.5	..
Ecuador	9.3	420	..	7.0	14.0	9.9	6.4	..	20.1	5.6	..
Egypt, Arab Rep.	3.6	..	3.5	13.3	64.7	5.1	24.2	..	106.3	5.7	3.5
El Salvador	4.6	457	5.5	12.3	4.2	8.0	12.0	3.0	49.2	..	..
Eritrea	..	..	..	..	..	..	..	..	141.9	..	..
Estonia	15.2	..	..	98.9	0.0	9.8	0.3	1.2	62.9	3.5	..
Ethiopia	0.4	..	..	..	..	..	..	..	61.1	3.6	6.4
Finland	19.1	..	..	6.2	0.0	8.2	0.4	0.9	70.7	2.7	..
France	43.2	1,801	..	..	0.0	6.5	*4.8*	2.7	106.4	4.4	*4.3*
Gabon	..	..	1.0	..	..	..	15.8	..	12.7	13.0	..
Gambia, The	..	..	..	95.8	..	..	..	..	19.9	14.5	..
Georgia	3.1	..	5.5	..	..	..	..	..	18.4	24.0	12.1
Germany	49.4	..	..	4.3	42.2	4.4	*5.3*	0.8	138.0	7.0	*6.7*
Ghana	1.6	..	..	53.5	12.1	12.4	16.1	..	30.5	..	..
Greece	30.8	2,418	..	10.8	22.8	7.9	7.1	1.4	106.0	4.3	*4.4*
Guatemala	10.1	404	7.0	9.0	3.0	..	..	1.3	16.1	9.6	..
Guinea	..	..	..	90.0	0.0	..	..	..	15.5	..	..
Guinea-Bissau	..	..	..	100.0	0.0	..	..	..	8.1	..	..
Haiti	..	..	..	..	..	..	..	..	31.7	23.3	21.8

Financial access, stability, and efficiency

	Bank branches	Bank deposit accounts	Financial information infrastructure index	Banking system ownership		Bank capital to asset ratio	Bank non-performing loans to total gross loans	Deposit insurance coverage	Domestic credit provided by banking sector	Interest rate spread	Risk premium on lending
				% of total banking assets						Lending rate minus deposit rate	Prime lending rate minus treasury bill rate
	per 100,000 people	per 1,000 people	0 (less developed) to 10 (more developed)	Held by foreign-owned banks	Held by government-owned banks	%	%	% of GDP per capita	% of GDP	percentage points	percentage points
	2001–04[a]	2001–04[a]	2005	2001	2001	2004	2004	2003	2004	2004	2004
Honduras	0.7	287	5.5	18.5	0.0	8.4	6.4	9.5	45.1	8.8	..
Hungary	28.3	..	5.5	88.8	9.0	8.9	2.7	1.6	59.0	3.7	1.5
India	6.3	..	5.5	7.3	75.3	5.9	6.6	3.9	60.1	..	..
Indonesia	8.4	..	6.5	..	..	9.3	13.4	..	48.8	7.7	..
Iran, Islamic Rep.	8.4	2,249	5.0	..	..	..	..	..	46.2	5.0	..
Iraq	..	..	..	..	..	..	..	..	..	..	..
Ireland	23.4	..	..	..	..	4.9	0.8	0.6	137.0	2.6	..
Israel	14.7	..	..	1.2	46.1	7.1	10.5	..	83.3	3.8	2.7
Italy	52.1	976	..	5.7	10.0	6.9	6.5	4.6	106.5	4.1	*2.8*
Jamaica	..	..	..	..	..	..	3.0	1.7	28.4	10.2	2.7
Japan	10.0	..	..	6.7	0.0	4.2	2.9	2.5	154.9	1.7	..
Jordan	10.0	465	..	64.3	0.0	*6.4*	*19.9*	7.6	91.5	5.8	..
Kazakhstan	2.5	..	5.5	17.9	0.5	8.0	29.9	1.3	18.6	..	..
Kenya	1.4	70	3.5	39.3	1.1	11.4	22.9	3.1	39.7	10.1	9.4
Korea, Dem. Rep.	..	..	..	..	..	..	..	..	..	..	..
Korea, Rep.	13.4	..	7.5	29.5	40.0	4.8	1.9	3.3	100.8	2.0	..
Kuwait	8.3	..	..	0.0	0.0	11.0	5.4	..	85.3	3.0	..
Kyrgyz Republic	3.1	..	..	24.7	16.0	..	..	..	8.4	22.6	24.3
Lao PDR	..	..	2.5	..	..	..	..	..	9.5	21.4	8.9
Latvia	..	..	4.5	65.2	3.2	8.2	1.1	*1.3*	54.7	4.2	*2.1*
Lebanon	18.0	383	6.0	15.9	2.0	5.7	10.1	0.8	179.0	3.4	5.6
Lesotho	..	..	..	100.0	0.0	..	..	..	–1.3	8.1	3.8
Liberia	..	..	..	..	..	..	..	..	219.7	14.3	..
Libya	..	..	..	..	..	..	..	..	–0.5	4.0	0.6
Lithuania	3.4	1,166	6.0	78.2	12.2	9.5	2.3	2.8	30.0	4.5	*3.2*
Macedonia, FYR	..	..	..	51.1	1.3	..	..	9.9	22.1	5.9	..
Madagascar	0.7	14	4.0	67.8	0.0	6.2	11.4	..	15.0	10.3	12.6
Malawi	..	..	..	..	..	..	..	..	22.8	23.1	8.3
Malaysia	9.8	1,250	6.5	19.0	0.0	8.1	11.8	..	138.7	3.0	3.7
Mali	..	..	..	67.0	21.8	..	..	..	17.7	..	..
Mauritania	..	..	..	..	..	..	..	..	–5.9	13.0	..
Mauritius	11.9	1,586	..	24.5	0.0	..	..	..	84.6	12.9	..
Mexico	7.6	310	8.0	82.7	0.0	11.5	2.5	489.1	38.4	4.5	0.4
Moldova	..	..	..	36.7	13.6	20.2	6.5	..	32.0	5.8	9.0
Mongolia	..	..	..	..	..	..	..	..	34.8	11.2	..
Morocco	6.6	..	3.0	20.8	35.0	7.6	19.4	..	82.6	7.9	..
Mozambique	..	..	5.0	..	..	6.5	6.4	..	5.4	12.2	9.7
Myanmar	..	..	..	..	..	..	..	..	..	5.5	..
Namibia	4.5	423	..	70.0	0.0	..	..	..	53.6	5.0	3.6
Nepal	1.7	..	3.5	..	..	..	..	..	..	5.8	6.1
Netherlands	34.2	..	..	2.2	3.9	3.9	1.8	0.7	178.8	0.4	..
New Zealand	28.0	..	..	99.1	0.0	..	..	..	121.5	4.6	4.5
Nicaragua	2.8	96	4.0	..	..	..	9.3	27.5	85.2	8.8	..
Niger	..	..	3.5	73.4	0.0	..	..	..	11.4	..	..
Nigeria	1.6	..	1.0	..	4.7	9.9	21.6	1.0	13.2	5.5	4.8
Norway	22.9	1,611	..	19.2	0.0	6.1	1.0	5.8	11.1	2.6	..
Oman	..	..	..	11.9	0.0	..	..	*6.5*	34.9	5.3	..
Pakistan	4.7	192	5.0	20.1	53.8	6.2	9.0	..	41.8	..	..
Panama	12.9	..	8.5	59.3	11.8	13.2	2.6	..	90.8	6.6	..
Papua New Guinea	1.6	120	..	..	..	..	..	..	21.9	11.5	4.4
Paraguay	..	..	..	83.5	9.2	10.5	10.8	9.7	18.3	28.4	..
Peru	4.2	316	7.5	42.5	0.0	9.8	9.5	8.8	17.4	11.5	..
Philippines	7.8	302	6.0	15.0	11.2	12.8	24.7	1.9	59.8	3.9	2.8
Poland	8.2	..	7.5	68.7	23.5	8.2	15.5	5.0	34.6	3.8	..
Portugal	51.6	..	..	17.7	22.8	6.1	2.2	1.9	153.9	..	..
Puerto Rico	..	..	..	30.4	0.7	..	..	..	..	..	..

5.5 Financial access, stability, and efficiency

	Bank branches	Bank deposit accounts	Financial information infrastructure index	Banking system ownership		Bank capital to asset ratio	Bank non-performing loans to total gross loans	Deposit insurance coverage	Domestic credit provided by banking sector	Interest rate spread	Risk premium on lending
				% of total banking assets						Lending rate minus deposit rate	Prime lending rate minus treasury bill rate
	per 100,000 people	per 1,000 people	0 (less developed) to 10 (more developed)	Held by foreign-owned banks	Held by government-owned banks	%	%	% of GDP per capita	% of GDP	percentage points	percentage points
	2001–04[a]	2001–04[a]	2005	2001	2001	2004	2004	2003	2004	2004	2004
Romania	13.8	1,208	8.0	47.3	41.8	8.5	8.1	1.4	15.3	..	..
Russian Federation	2.2	1,892	2.0	8.8	35.5	14.0	3.8	1.1	25.9	7.6	*7.6*
Rwanda	..	..	2.0	0.0	6.6	..	..	..	13.5	..	..
Saudi Arabia	5.4	214	..	20.7	21.4	8.0	3.1	..	64.2	..	..
Senegal	..	..	3.5	78.7	0.0	8.4	14.2	..	21.8	..	..
Serbia and Montenegro	..	..	..	13.2	3.8	..	22.8	0.0	..	..	..
Sierra Leone	..	..	..	..	..	11.6	14.8	..	30.3	11.9	−4.1
Singapore	9.1	1,671	..	..	0.0	9.7	2.9	..	80.2	4.9	4.3
Slovak Republic	10.3	..	3.5	85.5	4.4	7.2	5.4	4.2	44.0	4.9	..
Slovenia	2.2	..	..	20.6	12.2	7.5	5.7	1.8	55.7	4.8	4.5
Somalia	..	..	..	..	..	..	..	..	..	..	..
South Africa	6.0	..	6.0	7.7	0.0	7.0	1.8	..	86.7	4.7	3.8
Spain	95.9	2,076	..	8.5	0.0	8.5	0.8	1.1	140.6	1.8	*1.0*
Sri Lanka	6.9	..	4.0	..	..	..	..	1.1	44.6	4.4	1.8
Sudan	..	..	..	4.0	12.0	..	..	..	11.5	..	..
Swaziland	..	..	..	85.8	14.2	..	..	..	15.6	6.7	3.4
Sweden	21.8	..	..	..	0.0	6.3	0.9	0.9	113.1	3.0	*1.7*
Switzerland	38.0	1,986	..	10.7	14.1	5.0	1.6	0.5	176.1	2.8	2.8
Syrian Arab Republic	..	..	..	..	..	..	..	..	30.3	5.0	..
Tajikistan	..	..	..	50.0	4.6	..	..	..	16.5	10.6	..
Tanzania	0.6	..	2.0	..	..	..	..	0.9	9.2	9.7	5.6
Thailand	7.2	1,423	5.5	6.8	30.6	8.7	11.9	..	105.3	4.5	..
Togo	..	..	..	17.5	51.0	..	..	..	16.7	..	..
Trinidad and Tobago	9.2	1,073	..	2.4	14.5	..	..	1.0	18.8	6.5	4.5
Tunisia	..	..	3.5	15.7	42.7	..	23.7	..	70.9	..	..
Turkey	8.5	1,114	5.0	3.5	31.8	14.3	6.0	*12.6*	54.9	..	..
Turkmenistan	..	..	..	0.0	96.0	..	..	..	..	..	..
Uganda	0.5	47	..	..	..	10.1	2.2	6.5	11.0	12.9	11.6
Ukraine	..	..	3.5	10.5	12.0	13.1	30.0	0.3	30.8	9.6	..
United Arab Emirates	..	..	..	27.0	35.0	12.1	12.5	..	50.6	..	..
United Kingdom	18.3	..	..	46.0	0.0	*6.8*	2.2	1.9	159.1	..	0.0
United States	30.9	..	..	19.0	0.0	10.3	0.8	2.7	215.5	..	3.0
Uruguay	6.4	..	5.5	43.3	42.5	..	3.6	..	53.3	17.5	8.9
Uzbekistan	..	..	..	..	..	..	..	..	..	..	..
Venezuela, RB	4.4	487	4.5	43.2	6.9	12.5	2.8	1.9	11.0	5.9	..
Vietnam	..	..	5.5	..	..	..	..	4.0	58.4	*2.9*	*3.7*
West Bank and Gaza	3.3	254	..	..	..	..	..	..	..	..	..
Yemen, Rep.	..	..	3.5	..	..	..	..	..	5.2	5.5	4.7
Zambia	1.5	..	1.5	..	..	..	7.6	..	35.2	19.2	18.1
Zimbabwe	3.3	174	..	28.0	6.1	10.7	*4.7*	..	49.8	175.7	153.2
World	**9.8 w**	**.. w**	**.. m**	**25.4 m**	**5.5 m**	**8.5 m**	**6.4 m**	**.. m**	**143.7 w**	**6.5 m**	**.. m**
Low income	4.9	..	..	..	..	..	..	..	47.7	11.9	..
Middle income	5.0	..	..	30.9	10.6	9.7	7.1	2.3	78.5	6.5	..
Lower middle income	4.4	..	..	21.2	13.0	10.2	10.8	2.3	101.3	6.7	..
Upper middle income	7.1	1,096	..	45.0	5.9	8.9	3.2	2.1	47.4	5.8	5.3
Low & middle income	4.9	..	..	40.9	9.1	..	7.6	..	74.1	7.4	..
East Asia & Pacific	2.9	..	..	..	..	..	..	..	125.9	6.3	..
Europe & Central Asia	6.6	..	5.3	50.0	12.0	9.8	5.7	1.7	36.8	5.8	..
Latin America & Carib.	9.9	500	..	31.8	11.8	11.0	5.2	3.0	56.6	7.6	5.0
Middle East & N. Africa	..	..	..	15.7	35.0	..	..	..	59.4	5.5	..
South Asia	5.9	..	4.5	..	..	5.9	9.0	3.9	56.4	6.5	..
Sub-Saharan Africa	..	..	..	68.9	0.0	..	..	..	47.1	12.5	..
High income	33.0	..	..	10.8	0.0	6.4	2.2	1.4	161.3	4.1	..
Europe EMU	53.1	..	..	6.2	2.0	6.1	2.0	0.9	124.8	4.0	3.6

a. Data are for the most recent year available in the period shown.

Financial access, stability, and efficiency

About the data

This year the table includes new indicators from the World Bank and the International Monetary Fund (IMF) covering financial access, stability, and efficiency.

Financial sector development has positive impacts on economic growth and poverty. The size of the sector determines the amount of resources mobilized for investment. Access to finance can expand opportunities for all—not just the rich and well connected—with higher levels of access and use of banking services associated with lower financing obstacles for people and businesses. A stable financial system that promotes efficient savings and investment is also crucial for a thriving democracy and market economy. The banking system is the largest sector in the financial system in most countries, so most of the indicators in the table cover the banking system.

There are several aspects of access to financial services: availability, cost, and quality of services. Two measures of access and use are presented in the table: number of bank branches and bank deposit accounts. The number of bank branches measures the physical outreach of the banking sector to a country's population. As a measure of access to bank outlets, this indicator has limitations: it assumes a uniform distribution of bank outlets across a country's population. But in many countries bank branches are concentrated in urban areas, with accessibility limited for people who live in rural areas. The number of bank deposit accounts is an indicator of actual use of banking services. An individual can have more than one account, so it is still an imperfect measure. Further analysis and detailed explanation of the data can be found in Beck, Demirgüç-Kunt, and Martinez Peria (2005).

The development and growth of credit markets depend on access to timely, reliable, and accurate data on borrowers' credit experiences. For secured transactions, such as mortgages or vehicle loans, having rapid access to information in property registries is also vital, and for small business loans, corporate registry data are needed.

The financial information infrastructure index is based on both the quality and availability of data in credit reports, public registries, corporate registries, and court records. Basic consumer protections are also included in the index. The index ranges from 0 (less developed financial information infrastructure) to 10 (more developed financial information infrastructure). Data are from the World Bank's Financial Sector Operations and Policy Department.

The type of bank ownership—foreign, government, or domestic private—has important implications for the efficiency and stability of financial intermediation. Studies show that banking systems with more foreign-owned (more than half of assets owned by foreigners) and domestic private banks tend to be more efficient and resilient to crises than banking systems with mostly government-owned (more than half of assets owned by the government) banks. These data were collected through a survey of bank regulators conducted by Barth, Caprio, and Levine (2006).

The frequency and magnitude of financial crises over the past two decades have made it clear how important it is to monitor the strength of financial systems. Robust financial systems help increase economic activity and welfare, but unstable financial systems can disrupt financial activity and impose huge and widespread costs on the economy. The ratio of a bank's capital to its total assets measures the extent to which a bank can deal with unexpected losses. Aggregating the ratios across banks provides a measure of the solvency and resiliency of a country's banking system.

The share of bank nonperforming loans to total gross loans is a measure of bank health and efficiency. It helps to identify problems with asset quality in the loan portfolio. A high ratio may signal deterioration in the quality of the credit portfolio. International guidelines recommend that loans be classified as nonperforming when payments of principal and interest are past due by 90 days or more or when future payments are not expected to be received in full. See the IMF's *Global Financial Stability Report* for more detailed background information.

Deposit insurance is a tool used by governments to promote financial stability and to protect small depositors from losses due to bank failures. Almost all countries have financial safety nets that include explicit or implicit deposit insurance, bank regulation and supervision, central bank lender of last resort facilities, and bank insolvency resolution procedures. But deposit insurance can lead banks to take too much risk. Countries with excessive explicit deposit insurance are more likely to experience a financial crisis and to have poorer financial intermediation. Deposit insurance coverage as a percentage of GDP is presented in the table.

Domestic credit provided by the banking sector as a share of GDP is a measure of banking sector depth and financial sector development in terms of size. In a few countries governments may hold international reserves as deposits in the banking system rather than in the central bank. Since the claims on the central government are a net item (claims on the central government minus central government deposits), this net figure may be negative, resulting in a negative figure of domestic credit provided by the banking sector.

The interest rate spread—the margin between the cost of mobilizing liabilities and the earnings on assets—is a measure of the efficiency by which the financial sector intermediates funds. A narrow interest rate spread means low transaction costs, which lowers the overall cost of funds for investment, crucial to economic growth. The risk premium on lending is the spread between the lending rate to the private sector and the "risk-free" government rate. A small spread indicates that the market considers its best corporate customers to be low risk. Interest rate spreads are expressed as annual averages. In some countries this spread may be negative, indicating that the market considers its best corporate clients to be lower risk than the government.

Definitions

• **Bank branches** are deposit money bank branches. • **Bank deposit accounts** are deposit accounts, including checking, savings, and time deposit accounts for businesses, individuals, and others. • **Financial information infrastructure index** is based on 10 measures, 6 covering the scope, quality, and availability of credit reporting data (in private and public registries) and the existence of a basic legal framework for credit reporting, and 4 covering the availability of public registry data for collateral (fixed and moveable) and corporate registries and court records. • **Banking system ownership** refers to the shares of assets of foreign-owned banks and government-owned banks as percentages of total banking system assets in a country. • **Bank capital to asset ratio** is the ratio of bank capital and reserves to total assets. Capital and reserves include funds contributed by owners, retained earnings, general and special reserves, provisions, and valuation adjustments. Capital includes tier 1 capital (paid-up shares and common stock), which is a common feature in all countries' banking systems, and total regulatory capital, which includes several specified types of subordinated debt instruments that need not be repaid if the funds are required to maintain minimum capital levels (these comprise tier 2 and tier 3 capital). Total assets include all nonfinancial and financial assets. • **Bank nonperforming loans to total gross loans** are the value of nonperforming loans divided by the total value of the loan portfolio (including nonperforming loans before the deduction of specific loan-loss provisions). The loan amount recorded as nonperforming should be the gross value of the loan as recorded on the balance sheet, not just the amount that is overdue. • **Deposit insurance coverage** is the value of deposits per depositor protected by a formal deposit insurance scheme as a percentage of GDP per capita. • **Domestic credit provided by the banking sector** includes all credit to various sectors on a gross basis, except credit to the central government, which is net. The banking sector includes monetary authorities, deposit money banks, and other banking institutions for which data are available (including institutions that do not accept transferable deposits but do incur such liabilities as time and savings deposits). • **Interest rate spread** is the interest rate charged by banks on loans to prime customers minus the interest rate paid by commercial or similar banks for demand, time, or savings deposits. • **Risk premium on lending** is the interest rate charged by banks on loans to prime private sector customers minus the "risk free" treasury bill interest rate at which short-term government securities are issued or traded in the market.

Data sources

Data on bank branches, deposit accounts, financial information infrastructure, bank ownership, and deposit insurance coverage are collected from surveys of banking and regulatory institutions by the World Bank's Research Department and Financial Sector and Operations Policy Department. Data on bank capital and nonperforming loans are from the IMF's *Global Financial Stability Report*. Data on credit and interest rates are from the IMF's *International Financial Statistics*.

5.6 Tax policies

	Tax revenue collected by central government		Tax payments by businesses			Highest marginal tax rate[a]		
						Individual		
	% of GDP		Number of payments	Time to prepare and pay taxes hours	Total tax payable % of gross profit	%	On income over $	Corporate %
	2000	2004	January 2005	January 2005	January 2005	2004	2004	2004
Afghanistan	..	3.5	2	80	21.4	..	..	..
Albania[b]	*13.6*	..	53	240	71.6	..	..	..
Algeria[b]	37.9	*32.0*	63	504	58.5	..	..	..
Angola	..	..	30	656	32.5	..	..	..
Argentina	*9.8*	14.2	35	580	97.9	35	41,667	35
Armenia[b]	..	15.3	50	1,120	53.8	..	..	..
Australia	22.8	24.1	12	107	37.0	47	46,538	30
Austria	19.3	*20.5*	20	272	50.8	50	64,052	34
Azerbaijan[b]	*12.7*	..	35	756	41.4	35	7,307	24
Bangladesh[b]	*7.6*	8.1	17	640	50.4	..	..	..
Belarus[b]	16.6	18.6	113	1,188	121.8	..	..	..
Belgium	27.8	*25.8*	10	160	44.6	50	30,210	33
Benin	..	..	75	270	53.1	..	..	..
Bolivia	*13.2*	15.0	41	1,080	64.0	13	..	25
Bosnia and Herzegovina	..	22.4	73	100	19.7	..	..	..
Botswana[b]	..	..	24	140	52.9	25	20,950	15
Brazil[b]	*12.2*	..	23	2,600	147.9	28	8,843	15
Bulgaria[b]	18.3	22.3	27	616	38.6	29	4,550	20
Burkina Faso	..	..	40	270	48.3	..	..	..
Burundi[b]	*15.4*	..	41	140	173.5	..	..	..
Cambodia	*8.6*	8.6	27	97	31.1	20	36,356	20
Cameroon[b]	..	..	51	1,300	47.6	*60*	*10,726*	*39*
Canada[b]	15.3	14.2	10	119	32.5	29	809,718	21
Central African Republic	..	..	66	504	60.9	..	..	..
Chad	..	..	65	122	51.3	..	..	..
Chile	*16.6*	15.9	8	432	46.7	40	6,127	17
China[b]	6.8	*8.5*	34	584	46.9	45	12,082	*30*
Hong Kong, China	..	..	1	80	14.3	17	13,462	18
Colombia	*13.3*	13.8	54	432	75.1	35	29,426	37
Congo, Dem. Rep.[b]	3.5	*6.3*	34	312	134.7	50	6,056	40
Congo, Rep.[b]	*9.2*	*8.5*	94	576	66.9	..	..	..
Costa Rica[b]	12.1	13.4	41	402	54.3	30	16,860	30
Côte d'Ivoire[b]	14.6	*14.9*	71	270	46.9	10	3,837	35
Croatia[b]	26.2	24.1	39	232	47.1	45	35,171	..
Cuba	..	..	..	..	..	..	..	..
Czech Republic	15.7	16.1	14	930	40.1	32	12,910	28
Denmark	31.3	31.1	18	135	63.4	59	51,162	30
Dominican Republic	15.7[b]	15.1[c]	85	124	57.2	25	23,734	25
Ecuador[b]	..	..	33	600	33.9	25	57,600	25
Egypt, Arab Rep.[b]	..	..	39	504	32.1	*32*	*10,823*	*40*
El Salvador	*10.7*	11.0	65	224	32.2	..	..	..
Eritrea	..	..	18	216	66.3	..	..	..
Estonia[b]	16.0	..	11	104	39.5	26	1,354	35
Ethiopia[b]	*13.2*	*13.2*	20	52	43.6	..	..	..
Finland	25.0	23.0	19	..	52.1	34	68,517	29
France	23.6	22.4	29	72	42.8	48	60,673	33
Gabon	..	..	..	..	..	*50*	..	*35*
Gambia, The[b]	..	..	..	..	..	..	..	..
Georgia[b]	7.7	9.8	49	448	49.7	..	..	..
Germany	11.9	10.9	32	105	50.3	45	65,224	25
Ghana[b]	*17.2*	22.4	35	304	45.3	30	5,647	33
Greece	26.0	..	32	204	47.9	40	29,464	35
Guatemala[b]	10.1	10.1	50	260	53.4	31	35,853	31
Guinea[b]	..	..	55	416	51.2	..	..	..
Guinea-Bissau	..	..	..	..	..	..	..	..
Haiti	..	..	53	..	31.7	..	..	..

	Tax revenue collected by central government		Tax payments by businesses			Highest marginal tax rate[a]		
	% of GDP		Number of payments	Time to prepare and pay taxes hours	Total tax payable % of gross profit	Individual %	Individual On income over $	Corporate %
	2000	2004	January 2005	January 2005	January 2005	2004	2004	2004
Honduras	..	..	48	424	43.2	25	27,778	25
Hungary	22.7	*22.1*	24	304	56.8	38	7,214	16
India[b]	9.0	10.2	59	264	43.2	30	3,283	36
Indonesia[b]	*11.3*	12.3	52	560	38.8	35	22,371	30
Iran, Islamic Rep.[b]	6.4	6.0	28	292	14.6	35	125,345	25
Iraq	..	..	13	48	5.6	..	..	..
Ireland[b]	..	..	8	76	45.3	42	35,443	13
Israel	31.0	28.8	33	210	57.5	49	90,040	36
Italy	23.6	*22.9*	20	360	59.8	45	88,608	33
Jamaica[b]	24.7	*24.8*	72	414	49.4	25	1,993	33
Japan[b]	..	..	26	315	34.6	37	167,395	30
Jordan[b]	19.0	20.8	10	101	39.8	..	..	..
Kazakhstan[b]	10.2	14.7	34	156	41.6	20	47,552	30
Kenya[b]	18.8	*17.2*	17	372	68.2	30	5,841	30
Korea, Dem. Rep.	..	..	..	..	..	..	..	..
Korea, Rep.[b]	16.1	..	26	290	29.6	36	66,644	27
Kuwait[b]	*1.3*	*1.5*	14	..	8.2	*0*	..	*0*
Kyrgyz Republic[b]	11.7	..	95	204	59.4	..	..	..
Lao PDR	..	..	31	180	24.7	*40*	*7,894*	..
Latvia[b]	14.4	13.8	39	320	38.7	*25*	..	15
Lebanon	12.4	*15.5*	33	208	30.4	..	..	..
Lesotho[b]	32.4	43.5	19	564	37.7	..	..	..
Liberia	..	..	..	..	..	..	..	..
Libya	..	..	..	..	..	..	..	..
Lithuania	14.6	17.2	13	162	41.6	..	..	15
Macedonia, FYR	..	..	54	96	40.1	..	..	..
Madagascar	56.6	54.4	29	400	58.9	..	..	..
Malawi	..	..	33	782	56.5	..	..	..
Malaysia[b]	14.3	*17.6*	28	..	11.6	28	65,789	28
Mali	..	..	60	270	44.0	..	..	..
Mauritania	..	..	61	696	75.8	..	..	..
Mauritius[b]	18.4	17.8	7	158	38.2	25	951	25
Mexico	11.7	..	49	536	31.3	33	9,555	33
Moldova[b]	14.7	16.4	44	250	44.7	..	..	..
Mongolia	..	*22.6*	43	..	45.3	..	..	..
Morocco	*23.5*[b]	*21.9*[d]	28	690	54.8	*44*	*5,243*	*35*
Mozambique	..	..	35	230	50.9	32	42,314	32
Myanmar[b]	3.0	..	..	..	..	..	..	..
Namibia[b]	30.0	*25.9*	23	50	43.9	35	29,851	35
Nepal[b]	8.7	9.8	23	408	31.8	..	..	..
Netherlands	23.1	22.8	22	700	53.3	52	63,777	35
New Zealand	*29.8*	30.3	8	70	44.2	39	39,242	33
Nicaragua[b]	13.8	15.5	64	240	54.3	*25*	*31,545*	*25*
Niger	..	..	44	270	49.4	..	..	..
Nigeria	..	..	36	1,120	27.1	*25*	*1,553*	*30*
Norway	27.7	29.0	3	87	60.1	..	..	28
Oman[b]	7.2	..	13	52	5.2	0	..	12
Pakistan[b]	10.2	10.5	32	560	57.4	35	11,746	41
Panama[b]	10.2	..	45	424	32.9	30	200,000	30
Papua New Guinea[b]	19.4	*22.3*	43	198	36.7	*47*	*24,842*	*25*
Paraguay[b]	9.9	11.2	33	328	37.9	0	..	30
Peru[b]	12.3	13.3	53	424	50.7	30	49,899	30
Philippines[b]	13.7	12.6	62	94	46.4	32	8,995	32
Poland[b]	*16.4*	*17.3*	43	175	55.6	40	19,211	19
Portugal	22.7	*22.6*	7	328	45.4	40	67,139	25
Puerto Rico	..	..	41	140	17.8	33	50,000	20

5.6 Tax policies

	Tax revenue collected by central government		Tax payments by businesses			Highest marginal tax rate[a]		
	% of GDP		Number of payments	Time to prepare and pay taxes hours	Total tax payable % of gross profit	Individual %	Individual On income over $	Corporate %
	2000	2004	January 2005	January 2005	January 2005	2004	2004	2004
Romania[b]	*11.7*	*11.7*	62	188	51.1	40	4,617	25
Russian Federation	*13.7*	13.5	27	256	40.8	13	..	24
Rwanda[b]	..	..	42	168	53.9	..	..	..
Saudi Arabia	..	..	13	70	1.4	0	..	0
Senegal[b]	17.3	..	59	696	45.0	0	*22,469*	*35*
Serbia and Montenegro[b]	*23.0*	*23.0*	41	168	46.3	..	..	..
Sierra Leone[b]	*6.8*	..	20	399	163.9	..	..	..
Singapore[b]	15.6	12.5	16	30	19.5	22	188,191	20
Slovak Republic	..	*16.7*	31	344	39.5	38	14,087	25
Slovenia[b]	21.4	21.5	29	272	47.3	50	..	25
Somalia	..	..	..	..	..	..	..	..
South Africa[b]	24.0	26.0	32	350	43.8	40	38,060	30
Spain	15.9	*11.8*	7	56	48.4	29	56,962	35
Sri Lanka[b]	14.5	*14.0*	42	..	49.4	30	8,083	30
Sudan[b]	*6.3*	..	..	..	..	..	..	..
Swaziland	26.7	*24.9*	..	..	..	33	5,496	30
Sweden	19.9	*19.7*	5	122	52.6	25	59,756	28
Switzerland[b]	11.3	*10.0*	25	63	22.0	..	..	9
Syrian Arab Republic[b]	*17.4*	..	22	336	20.8	..	..	..
Tajikistan[b]	7.7	9.8	..	..	..	..	..	..
Tanzania	..	..	48	248	51.3	30	6,090	30
Thailand	..	15.9	44	52	29.2	37	101,420	30
Togo	..	..	51	270	50.9	..	..	..
Trinidad and Tobago[b]	..	..	..	..	..	30	7,937	30
Tunisia[b]	21.3	20.7	31	112	52.7	..	..	..
Turkey[b]	*20.2*	..	18	254	51.1	40	100,298	30
Turkmenistan	..	..	..	..	..	..	..	..
Uganda[b]	10.9	*11.9*	31	237	42.9	30	2,523	30
Ukraine[b]	14.1	13.3	84	2,185	51.0	13	*3,826*	25
United Arab Emirates[b]	*1.7*	..	15	12	8.9	*0*	..	*0*
United Kingdom	29.1	27.4	22	..	52.9	40	51,358	30
United States	*12.7*	9.8	9	325	21.5	35	319,100	35
Uruguay	16.7	18.5	54	300	80.2	*0*	..	35
Uzbekistan	..	..	118	152	75.6	30	666	18
Venezuela, RB[b]	13.3	*11.5*	68	864	48.9	34	60,324	34
Vietnam[b]	..	..	44	1,050	31.5	..	..	28
West Bank and Gaza	..	..	49	..	42.0	..	..	..
Yemen, Rep.[b]	*9.4*	..	32	248	128.8	..	..	..
Zambia[b]	*18.4*	..	36	132	38.6	30	368	35
Zimbabwe[b]	..	..	59	216	48.6	45	26,249	30
World	*15.7* w	*14.5* w	35 u	354 u	46.5 u			
Low income	10.0	10.5	44	385	54.4			
Middle income	*12.3*	*12.4*	38	406	44.5			
Lower middle income	*9.6*	*10.1*	42	444	44.5			
Upper middle income	..	..	30	333	44.4			
Low & middle income	*11.9*	*12.0*	40	398	48.5			
East Asia & Pacific	7.7	*10.0*	31	270	33.1			
Europe & Central Asia	*15.6*	*15.8*	48	438	50.3			
Latin America & Carib.	*11.8*	..	49	549	54.5			
Middle East & N. Africa	..	..	30	281	40.4			
South Asia	9.3	10.1	26	332	35.3			
Sub-Saharan Africa	..	..	41	394	58.1			
High income	*16.5*	14.6	18	181	38.8			
Europe EMU	19.2	*17.9*	19	233	49.2			

a. These data are from PricewaterhouseCoopers' *Individual Taxes: Worldwide Summaries 2004–2005* and *Corporate Taxes: Worldwide Summaries 2004–2005*, copyright 2004 by PricewaterhouseCoopers and used by permission of John Wiley and Sons, Inc. b. Data on central government tax revenue were reported on a cash basis and have been adjusted to the accrual framework of the *Government Finance Statistics Manual 2001*. c. World Bank staff estimate. d. International Monetary Fund staff estimate.

About the data

The table includes new information on taxes that businesses must pay and measures of the administrative burden in paying taxes. Data are from the World Bank's *Doing Business 2006*.

Taxes are the main source of revenue for many governments. The sources of tax revenue and their relative contributions are determined by government policy choices about where and how to impose taxes and by changes in the structure of the economy. Tax policy may reflect concerns about distributional effects, economic efficiency (including corrections for externalities), and the practical problems of administering a tax system. There is no ideal level of taxation. But taxes influence incentives and thus the behavior of economic actors and the economy's competitiveness.

Taxes are compulsory transfers to governments from individuals, businesses, or institutions. Certain compulsory transfers, such as fines, penalties, and most social security contributions are excluded from tax revenue.

The level of taxation is typically measured by tax revenue as a share of gross domestic product (GDP). Comparing levels of taxation across countries provides a quick overview of the fiscal obligations and incentives facing the private sector. The table shows only central government data, which may significantly understate the total tax burden, particularly in countries where provincial and municipal governments are large or have considerable tax authority.

Low ratios of tax revenue to GDP may reflect weak administration and large-scale tax avoidance or evasion. Low ratios may also reflect a sizable parallel economy with unrecorded and undisclosed incomes. Tax revenue ratios tend to rise with income, with higher income countries relying on taxes to finance a much broader range of social services and social security than lower income countries are able to.

The new indicators covering taxes paid by businesses go beyond the usual measures of tax rates, which capture only part of the taxpayer burden. In some countries tax systems are so complex that businesses must make more than 100 payments and spend up to 2,600 hours a year to prepare and pay taxes.

Taxes are measured at all levels of government and include corporate income tax, personal income tax withheld by businesses, value added or sales taxes, property transfer taxes, financial transactions taxes, dividend taxes, waste collection taxes, and vehicle and road taxes. To make the data comparable across countries, several assumptions are made about the business. The main assumptions are that they are limited liability companies, they operate in the country's most populous city, they are domestically owned, they perform general industrial or commercial activities, and they have a certain level of start-up capital, employees, and turnover. For details about the assumptions, see *Doing Business 2006*.

A potentially important influence on both domestic and international investors is a tax system's progressivity, as reflected in the highest marginal tax rate levied at the national level on individual and corporate income. Figures for individual marginal tax rates generally refer to employment income. In some countries the highest marginal tax rate is also the basic or flat rate, and other surtaxes, deductions, and the like may apply. And in many countries several different corporate tax rates may be levied, depending on the type of business (mining, banking, insurance, agriculture, manufacturing), ownership (domestic or foreign), volume of sales, or whether surtaxes or exemptions are included. The corporate tax rates in the table are mainly general rates applied to domestic companies. For more detailed information, see the country's laws, regulations, and tax treaties.

5.6a

Excessive paperwork adds to the time that businesses spend complying with taxes

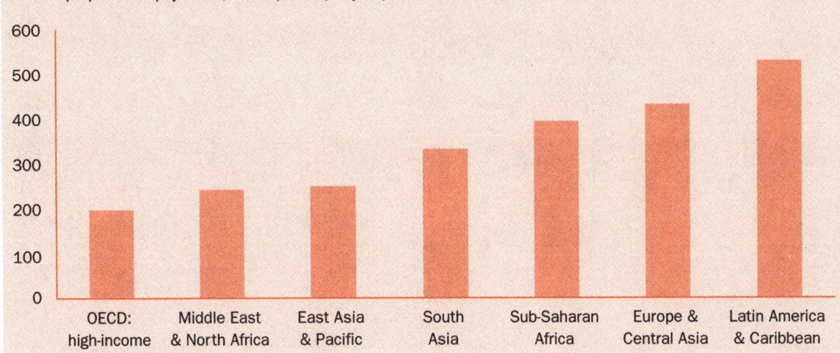

Source: Table 5.6.

Definitions

• **Tax revenue collected by central government** refers to compulsory transfers to the central government for public purposes. Certain compulsory transfers such as fines, penalties, and most social security contributions are excluded. Refunds and corrections of erroneously collected tax revenue are treated as negative revenue. The analytic framework of the International Monetary Fund's (IMF) *Government Finance Statistics Manual 2001* (GFSM 2001) is based on accrual accounting and balance sheets. For countries still reporting government finance data on a cash basis, the IMF adjusts reported data to the GFSM 2001 accrual framework. These countries are footnoted in the table. • **Tax payments by businesses** are the total number of taxes paid by businesses, including electronic filing. The tax is counted as paid once a year even if payments are more frequent. • **Time to prepare and pay taxes** is the time, in hours per year, it takes to prepare, file, and pay (or withhold) three major types of taxes: the corporate income tax, the value added or sales tax, and labor taxes, including payroll taxes and social security contributions. • **Total tax payable** is the total amount of taxes payable by the business (except for labor taxes) after accounting for deductions and exemptions as a percentage of gross profit. For further details on the method used for assessing the total tax payable, see *Doing Business 2006*. • **Highest marginal tax rate** is the highest rate shown on the national level schedule of tax rates applied to the annual taxable income of individuals and corporations. Also presented are the income levels for individuals above which the highest marginal tax rates levied at the national level apply.

Data sources

Data on central government tax revenues are from print and electronic editions of the IMF's *Government Finance Statistics Yearbook*. Data on taxes paid by businesses are from *Doing Business 2006*. Data on individual and corporate tax rates are from PricewaterhouseCoopers's *Individual Taxes: Worldwide Summaries 2004–2005* and *Corporate Taxes: Worldwide Summaries 2004–2005*.

5.7 Defense expenditures and arms transfers

	Military expenditures				Armed forces personnel				Arms transfers ($ millions, 1990 prices)			
	% of GDP		% of central government expenditure		thousands		% of labor force		Exports		Imports	
	1995	2004	1995	2004	1995	2004	1995	2004	1995	2004	1995	2004
Afghanistan	..	..	..	..	383	27	5.5	0.3	0	..	*0*	*0*
Albania	2.1	1.2	8.2	..	87	22	6.0	1.6	..	..	21	6
Algeria	3.0	3.3	12.2	*15.2*	163	318	1.8	2.5	..	..	342	282
Angola	18.1	9.1	..	..	122	118	2.3	1.7	*0*	*0*	1	5
Argentina	1.6	1.0	..	5.6	99	102	0.7	0.6	3	0	67	129
Armenia	4.1	2.9	..	15.5	61	49	4.2	3.8	..	..	49	68
Australia	2.0	1.8	..	7.2	57	52	0.6	0.5	20	52	147	334
Austria	0.9	0.7	..	*1.9*	56	39	1.4	1.0	*0*	1	23	46
Azerbaijan	2.3	1.8	11.7	..	127	81	3.8	2.0	..	..	*0*	*0*
Bangladesh	1.4	1.2	..	13.2	171	251	0.3	0.4	..	..	121	26
Belarus	1.6	1.2	5.5	4.1	106	182	2.1	3.8	8	50	*0*	0
Belgium	1.6	1.4	..	*2.9*	47	36	1.1	0.8	297	*0*	16	12
Benin	..	..	..	..	7	6	0.3	0.2	..	..	*0*	*0*
Bolivia	1.9	1.6	..	5.9	64	68	2.2	1.7	..	..	*0*	1
Bosnia and Herzegovina	..	2.4	..	6.2	92	24	5.2	1.2	*0*	*0*	*0*	0
Botswana	3.5	3.6	11.5	..	9	10	1.4	1.6	..	..	7	10
Brazil	2.1	1.4	*4.8*	..	681	687	0.9	0.8	40	100	226	38
Bulgaria	2.6	2.4	6.6	6.9	136	85	3.5	2.7	2	*0*	*0*	12
Burkina Faso	1.5	1.4	..	..	10	10	0.2	0.2	..	..	0	..
Burundi	4.2	5.8	17.8	..	15	81	0.5	2.2	..	..	*0*	*0*
Cambodia	5.4	2.2	..	24.1	309	192	6.2	2.9	*0*	0	*0*	0
Cameroon	1.4	1.5	11.7	..	24	23	0.5	0.4	..	..	*0*	*0*
Canada	1.6	1.2	6.3	6.5	76	71	0.5	0.4	378	543	146	340
Central African Republic	1.2	*1.1*	..	..	5	2	0.3	0.1	..	..	0	..
Chad	1.4	1.1	..	..	35	34	1.3	1.0	0	..	1	0
Chile	3.3	3.9	..	21.0	130	116	2.3	1.8	*0*	*0*	461	43
China	1.7[a]	1.9[a]	..[a]	*19.3*[a]	4,130	3,755	0.6	0.5	897	125	419	2,238
Hong Kong, China	..	..	..	..	..	..	..	..	..	..	..	..
Colombia	2.6	4.3	..	18.9	233	336	1.4	1.5	..	..	37	17
Congo, Dem. Rep.	*1.5*	..	*13.5*	..	65	64	0.4	0.3	..	..	*0*	*0*
Congo, Rep.	..	*1.4*	..	*6.9*	17	12	1.4	0.8	..	..	*0*	0
Costa Rica	..	..	..	..	16	0	1.2	*0.0*	..	..	0	*0*
Côte d'Ivoire	*0.8*	*1.6*	..	*8.9*	15	18	0.3	0.3	..	..	2	14
Croatia	9.4	1.7	22.2	4.1	150	30	7.2	1.5	*0*	0	22	8
Cuba	..	..	..	..	124	75	2.5	1.4	..	..	0	*0*
Czech Republic	1.7	*1.8*	..	*5.1*	92	27	1.8	0.5	156	*0*	*0*	18
Denmark	1.7	1.5	..	4.2	33	21	1.2	0.7	*0*	6	127	194
Dominican Republic	..	..	..	..	40	39	1.3	1.0	..	..	*0*	21
Ecuador	2.4	1.9	*20.1*	..	57	46	1.3	0.8	..	..	10	22
Egypt, Arab Rep.	3.5	2.8	12.5	..	610	798	3.5	3.6	16	0	1,696	398
El Salvador	1.0	0.7	..	3.9	39	15	1.8	0.6	0	..	3	*0*
Eritrea	20.8	*19.4*	..	..	55	201	4.4	11.7	*0*	0	3	382
Estonia	1.0	1.8	3.0	..	6	6	0.8	0.9	*0*	0	18	5
Ethiopia	2.2	4.3	..	*21.8*	120	182	0.5	0.6	0	..	*0*	162
Finland	1.5	1.2	..	3.3	35	31	1.4	1.2	20	17	159	57
France	3.0	2.5	..	5.4	502	358	2.0	1.3	681	2,122	43	89
Gabon	..	..	..	..	10	6	2.0	1.0	..	..	*0*	0
Gambia, The	0.8	0.4	..	..	1	1	0.2	0.1	..	..	0	*0*
Georgia	*2.2*	1.4	*8.2*	9.4	14	22	0.5	1.0	*0*	20	*0*	*0*
Germany	1.6	1.4	8.3	4.4	365	284	0.9	0.7	1,435	1,091	218	190
Ghana	0.8	0.8	..	3.8	13	7	0.2	0.1	..	..	*0*	27
Greece	4.3	*4.1*	..	..	202	167	4.5	3.3	*0*	*0*	865	1,434
Guatemala	1.0	0.4	13.1	3.6	57	48	1.8	1.2	..	..	3	0
Guinea	*1.4*	*2.9*	..	..	19	11	0.5	0.3	..	..	*0*	*0*
Guinea-Bissau	0.9	..	..	..	9	9	1.9	1.5	..	..	0	..
Haiti	..	..	..	..	7	0	0.2	*0.0*	..	..	..	..

Defense expenditures and arms transfers

	Military expenditures				Armed forces personnel				Arms transfers			
									$ millions 1990 prices			
	% of GDP		% of central government expenditure		thousands		% of labor force		Exports		Imports	
	1995	2004	1995	2004	1995	2004	1995	2004	1995	2004	1995	2004
Honduras	..	0.7	..	..	24	20	1.2	0.7	..	..	0	..
Hungary	1.6	1.7	..	*4.4*	73	46	1.8	1.1	6	0	21	15
India	2.2	2.3	15.1	14.8	2,150	2,617	0.6	0.6	2	22	945	2,375
Indonesia	1.6	1.4	16.2	8.3	461	582	0.5	0.6	30	50	334	85
Iran, Islamic Rep.	2.3	3.4	15.2	17.0	763	460	4.4	1.8	1	1	306	283
Iraq	..	..	..	..	407	179	7.0	2.2	0	..	*0*	82
Ireland	1.0	0.6	2.8	..	13	10	0.9	0.5	0	..	*0*	25
Israel	9.0	9.3	..	19.1	178	176	8.5	6.6	110	283	244	724
Italy	1.8	1.9	..	*4.7*	585	445	2.5	1.9	305	261	270	317
Jamaica	..	..	..	..	4	2	0.3	0.2	..	..	*0*	0
Japan	0.9	1.0	..	..	252	251	0.4	0.4	16	0	757	195
Jordan	12.4	7.6	47.5	24.0	129	110	10.2	6.1	*0*	72	19	132
Kazakhstan	1.1	1.0	*5.7*	7.0	75	99	1.0	1.2	24	5	99	27
Kenya	1.6	1.6	6.5	*7.9*	29	29	0.2	0.2	..	..	*0*	0
Korea, Dem. Rep.	..	..	..	..	1,243	1,295	12.4	12.2	52	*0*	72	5
Korea, Rep.	2.8	2.5	19.4	..	641	696	3.0	2.9	25	50	1,638	737
Kuwait	13.6	*7.5*	29.3	*20.9*	22	21	2.5	1.6	*0*	0	630	*0*
Kyrgyz Republic	1.6	2.9	6.1	..	7	17	0.4	0.8	61	*0*	*0*	5
Lao PDR	*2.9*	..	..	..	137	129	7.7	5.6	..	..	*0*	0
Latvia	0.9	1.7	3.1	6.0	11	5	0.9	0.5	*0*	0	12	14
Lebanon	6.7	3.8	..	*12.8*	63	85	5.5	6.2	*0*	*0*	34	0
Lesotho	3.7	2.6	10.7	6.8	2	2	0.3	0.3	..	..	*0*	1
Liberia	*31.2*	*7.5*	..	..	21	0	2.7	*0.0*	..	..	*0*	0
Libya	*4.1*	1.9	..	..	81	76	5.2	3.4	*0*	*0*	*0*	74
Lithuania	0.4	1.7	..	5.8	9	28	0.5	1.7	*0*	*0*	4	31
Macedonia, FYR	*3.0*	2.5	..	..	18	17	2.2	2.0	0	29	*0*	0
Madagascar	4.3	..	..	..	29	21	0.5	0.3	..	..	*0*	0
Malawi	0.8	..	..	..	10	6	0.2	0.1	*0*	0	*0*	0
Malaysia	2.8	2.3	16.0	*13.8*	140	130	1.7	1.2	*0*	0	900	277
Mali	2.2	1.9	..	..	15	11	0.4	0.2	..	..	*0*	*0*
Mauritania	2.6	1.2	..	..	21	20	2.3	1.7	..	..	1	0
Mauritius	0.4	0.2	1.8	0.9	2	0	0.4	*0.0*	..	..	*0*	0
Mexico	0.6	0.4	3.8	..	189	203	0.5	0.5	..	..	43	265
Moldova	0.9	0.4	*2.4*	1.3	15	9	0.8	0.4	*0*	0	6	0
Mongolia	1.7	*2.1*	..	..	31	15	3.3	1.3	..	..	0	*0*
Morocco	4.6	4.5	16.1	..	238	250	2.7	2.3	..	..	30	*0*
Mozambique	1.5	1.2	..	..	12	11	0.2	0.1	..	..	*0*	*0*
Myanmar	3.7	..	..	..	371	482	1.7	1.8	..	..	216	65
Namibia	2.0	2.4	..	*8.5*	8	15	1.5	2.3	..	..	2	53
Nepal	0.9	1.7	..	..	63	131	0.8	1.3	..	..	1	32
Netherlands	1.9	1.6	..	3.8	78	53	1.0	0.6	350	211	33	183
New Zealand	1.4	1.0	..	3.2	10	8	0.6	0.4	*0*	1	4	42
Nicaragua	1.1	0.7	6.8	3.5	12	14	0.8	0.7	5	0	0	*0*
Niger	1.0	*0.9*	..	..	11	10	0.3	0.2	..	..	*0*	0
Nigeria	0.7	0.8	..	..	89	160	0.2	0.3	0	..	2	10
Norway	2.4	1.9	..	5.0	31	25	1.4	1.0	22	51	83	1
Oman	14.6	*10.4*	45.2	..	48	45	6.2	4.8	*0*	0	157	123
Pakistan	6.0	4.1	31.4	28.1	846	921	2.2	1.7	*0*	10	..	..
Panama	1.2	..	5.6	..	12	0	1.1	*0.0*	..	..	*0*	0
Papua New Guinea	1.0	*0.6*	3.9	*2.1*	4	3	0.2	0.1	..	..	*0*	0
Paraguay	*1.1*	0.7	*10.0*	5.4	28	24	1.4	0.9	..	..	*0*	4
Peru	1.9	1.2	10.9	7.1	178	157	1.8	1.2	*0*	5	32	14
Philippines	1.4	0.9	*8.5*	..	149	146	0.5	0.4	..	..	32	59
Poland	2.0	1.9	..	*5.0*	302	162	1.7	0.9	187	86	125	256
Portugal	2.5	2.1	..	*5.1*	104	91	2.1	1.7	0	..	18	59
Puerto Rico	..	..	..	..	..	..	..	..	..	..	..	..

5.7 Defense expenditures and arms transfers

	Military expenditures				Armed forces personnel				Arms transfers			
	% of GDP		% of central government expenditure		thousands		% of labor force		$ millions 1990 prices Exports		Imports	
	1995	**2004**	**1995**	**2004**	**1995**	**2004**	**1995**	**2004**	**1995**	**2004**	**1995**	**2004**
Romania	2.8	2.2	..	*8.9*	297	176	2.4	1.7	6	*0*	*0*	276
Russian Federation	4.4	*3.9*	..	*17.9*	1,800	1,452	2.5	2.0	3,181	6,197	40	0
Rwanda	4.4	2.1	..	..	47	53	2.0	1.3	..	..	*0*	0
Saudi Arabia	9.3	7.7	..	..	178	214	3.0	2.8	*0*	0	974	838
Senegal	1.8	1.4	..	..	17	18	0.5	0.4	..	..	2	0
Serbia and Montenegro	*5.3*	3.4	..	*11.0*	165	110	3.5	*2.8*	*0*	0	18	0
Sierra Leone	2.9	1.6	..	..	7	13	0.4	0.6	..	..	15	0
Singapore	4.4	4.7	35.1	30.5	66	165	3.7	7.6	*0*	70	225	456
Slovak Republic	3.2	1.7	..	*5.2*	51	20	2.1	0.8	114	*0*	220	*0*
Slovenia	1.7	1.6	4.7	3.9	13	10	1.3	1.0	..	..	18	14
Somalia	..	..	..	..	225	0	8.3	0.0	..	..	*0*	0
South Africa	2.2	1.5	..	5.0	277	55	1.7	0.3	16	35	38	8
Spain	1.4	1.0	..	*3.7*	282	220	1.7	1.1	65	75	348	261
Sri Lanka	5.3	2.8	20.3	*13.6*	236	239	3.3	2.9	..	..	49	6
Sudan	1.9	*2.2*	..	..	134	121	1.6	1.2	..	..	3	270
Swaziland	2.4	..	..	..	3	..	1.1	..	..	..	*0*	0
Sweden	2.3	1.7	..	*4.7*	100	28	2.2	0.6	185	260	70	13
Switzerland	1.3	1.0	5.2	*5.4*	31	4	0.8	0.1	77	154	93	125
Syrian Arab Republic	7.1	*7.0*	..	..	531	415	11.2	5.7	*0*	0	43	*0*
Tajikistan	1.0	2.2	..	15.8	18	12	0.9	0.6	..	..	*0*	0
Tanzania	1.5	3.0	..	..	36	28	0.2	0.1	..	..	*0*	*0*
Thailand	2.3	1.2	..	6.7	421	419	1.3	1.2	*0*	5	562	105
Togo	2.4	1.5	..	..	8	9	0.4	0.4	..	..	3	0
Trinidad and Tobago	..	..	..	..	7	2	1.3	0.3	..	..	*0*	0
Tunisia	1.9	1.5	6.7	5.4	59	47	2.1	1.3	..	..	59	*0*
Turkey	3.9	3.9	18.6	..	690	616	3.0	2.3	*0*	18	1,288	418
Turkmenistan	2.3	..	..	..	11	26	0.7	1.2	..	..	0	20
Uganda	2.2	2.5	..	*11.1*	52	55	0.6	0.5	..	..	39	19
Ukraine	2.8	2.6	..	7.9	519	271	2.0	1.2	218	452	0	29
United Arab Emirates	5.2	*2.8*	49.2	..	71	50	5.5	1.9	27	3	432	1,246
United Kingdom	3.0	2.6	..	6.5	233	205	0.8	0.7	1,109	985	635	171
United States	3.8	4.0	..	19.0	1,636	1,473	1.2	1.0	9,690	5,453	389	533
Uruguay	1.7	1.4	6.3	5.0	27	25	1.8	1.4	*0*	0	7	*0*
Uzbekistan	1.1	*0.5*	..	..	42	75	0.5	0.7	*0*	170	*0*	*0*
Venezuela, RB	1.6	1.2	8.7	*5.4*	80	82	0.9	0.7	*0*	1	*0*	12
Vietnam	*2.6*	..	..	..	622	5,564	1.8	12.9	..	..	270	247
West Bank and Gaza	..	..	..	..	..	0	..	..	..	..	1	0
Yemen, Rep.	6.4	6.6	33.4	..	70	136	1.8	2.4	..	..	120	309
Zambia	2.2	..	..	..	23	16	0.6	0.3	0	*0*	*0*	*0*
Zimbabwe	3.6	3.4	11.2	..	68	50	1.4	0.9	..	..	*0*	*0*
World	**2.4 w**	**2.5 w**	**.. w**	**10.9 w**	**30,182 s**	**32,645 s**	**1.2 w**	**1.1 w**	**19,837 s**	**19,152 s**	**19,528 s**	**18,814 s**
Low income	2.4	2.3	17.0	15.6	7,768	13,185	1.0	1.4	120	202	1,822	3,949
Middle income	2.2	1.9	..	13.6	16,059	13,882	1.2	0.9	4,905	7,251	7,868	5,989
Lower middle income	2.1	2.0	..	16.4	11,683	10,550	1.0	0.8	1,242	914	4,404	4,283
Upper middle income	2.3	1.8	..	..	4,376	3,332	1.9	1.3	3,663	6,337	3,464	1,706
Low & middle income	2.2	2.0	..	13.7	23,826	27,067	1.1	1.1	5,025	7,453	9,690	9,938
East Asia & Pacific	1.8	1.8	..	17.3	8,021	12,716	0.9	1.2	979	180	2,813	3,081
Europe & Central Asia	2.8	2.3	..	11.0	4,971	3,669	2.3	1.7	3,963	7,027	1,943	1,208
Latin America & Carib.	1.8	1.3	5.3	..	2,112	2,066	1.1	0.8	48	106	889	566
Middle East & N. Africa	4.1	3.7	17.6	..	3,172	2,930	4.2	2.8	17	73	2,810	1,683
South Asia	2.7	2.5	17.8	15.9	3,852	4,186	0.8	0.7	2	32	1,116	2,439
Sub-Saharan Africa	2.3	1.9	..	..	1,698	1,500	0.7	0.5	16	35	119	961
High income	2.5	2.6	..	10.5	6,356	5,578	1.3	1.1	14,812	11,699	9,838	8,876
Europe EMU	2.0	1.7	..	4.4	2,270	1,736	1.7	1.2	3,153	3,778	1,993	2,673

Note: For some countries data are partial or uncertain or based on rough estimates; see SIPRI (2005).

a. Estimate differs from official statistics of the government of China, which has published the following estimates: military expenditure as 1.1 percent of GDP in 1995 and 1.6 percent in 2003 and 9.3 percent of central government expenditure in 1995 and 7.7 percent in 2003 (see National Bureau of Statistics of China, www.stats.gov.cn).

Defense expenditures and arms transfers 5.7

About the data

Although national defense is an important function of government and security from external threats contributes to economic development, high levels of defense spending burden the economy and may impede growth. Data on military expenditures as a share of gross domestic product (GDP) are a rough indicator of the portion of national resources used for military activities and of the burden on the national economy. Comparisons of defense spending between countries should take into account the many factors that influence perceptions of vulnerability and risk, including historical and cultural traditions, the length of borders that need defending, the quality of relations with neighbors, and the role of the armed forces in the body politic. As an "input" measure, military spending is not directly related to the "output" of military activities, capabilities, or military security.

Data on defense spending reported by governments are not compiled using standard definitions. They are often incomplete and unreliable. Even in countries where the parliament vigilantly reviews budgets and spending, defense spending and arms transfers rarely receive close scrutiny and full, public disclosure (see Ball 1984 and Happe and Wakeman-Linn 1994). The data on military expenditures as a share of GDP and a share of central government expenditure are estimated by the Stockholm International Peace Research Institute (SIPRI). Central government expenditures are from the International Monetary Fund (IMF). Therefore the data shown in the table may differ from comparable data published by national governments.

SIPRI's primary source of military expenditure data is offcial data provided by national governments. These data are derived from national budget documents, defense white papers, and other public documents from offcial government agencies, including governments' responses to questionnaires sent by SIPRI, the United Nations, or the Organization for Security and Co-operation in Europe. Secondary sources include international statistics, such as those of the North Atlantic Treaty Organization (NATO) and the IMF's *Government Finance Statistics Yearbook*. Other secondary sources include country reports of the Economist Intelligence Unit, country reports by IMF staff, and specialist journals and newspapers.

Lack of sufficiently detailed data makes it diffcult to apply a common definition of military expenditure globally, so SIPRI has adopted a definition (derived from the NATO definition) as a guideline (see *Definitions*). This definition cannot be applied for all countries, however, since that would require much more detailed information than is available about what is included in military budgets and off-budget military expenditure items. In the many cases where SIPRI cannot make independent estimates, it uses the national data provided. Because of the differences in definitions and the difficulty in verifying the accuracy and completeness of data, the data on military spending are not strictly comparable across countries.

The data on armed forces are from the International Institute for Strategic Studies' *The Military Balance 2005–2006*. These data refer to military personnel on active duty, including paramilitary forces. Reserve forces, which are units that are not fully staffed or operational in peace time, are not included. These data also exclude civilians in the defense establishment and so are not consistent with the data on military spending on personnel. Moreover, because data exclude personnel not on active duty, they underestimate the share of the labor force working for the defense establishment. Because governments rarely report the size of their armed forces, such data typically come from intelligence sources.

The data on arms transfers are from SIPRI's Arms Transfers Project, which reports on international flows of conventional weapons. Data are collected from open sources, and since publicly available information is inadequate for tracking all weapons and other military equipment, SIPRI covers only what it terms *major conventional weapons*.

SIPRI's data on arms transfers cover sales of weapons, manufacturing licenses, aid, and gifts; therefore the term *arms transfers* rather than *arms trade* is used. The transferred weapons must be transferred voluntarily by the supplier, must have a military purpose, and must be destined for the armed forces, paramilitary forces, or intelligence agencies of another country. SIPRI data also cover weapons supplied to or from rebel forces in an armed conflict as well as arms deliveries for which neither the supplier nor the recipient can be identified with an acceptable degree of certainty; these data are available in SIPRI's database.

SIPRI's estimates of arms transfers, presented in 1990 constant price U.S. dollars, are designed as a trend-measuring device in which similar weapons have similar values, reflecting both the value and quality of weapons transferred. The trends presented in the tables are based on actual deliveries only. SIPRI cautions that these estimated values do not reflect financial value (payments for weapons transferred) for three reasons: reliable data on the value of the transfer are not available; even when the value of a transfer is known, it usually includes more than the actual conventional weapons such as spares, support systems, and training; and even when the value of the transfer is known, details of the financial arrangements such as credit and loan conditions and discounts are usually not known.

Given these measurement issues, SIPRI's method of estimating the transfer of military resources includes an evaluation of the technical parameters of the weapons. Weapons for which a price is not known are compared with the same weapons for which actual acquisition prices are available ("core weapons") or for the closest match. These weapons are assigned a value in an index that reflects their military resource value in relation to the core weapons. These matches are based on such characteristics as size, performance, and type of electronics, and adjustments are made for second-hand weapons. More information on SIPRI's arms transfers project is available at www.sipri.org/contents/armstrad/.

Definitions

• **Military expenditures** data from SIPRI are derived from the NATO definition, which includes all current and capital expenditures on the armed forces, including peacekeeping forces; defense ministries and other government agencies engaged in defense projects; paramilitary forces, if these are judged to be trained and equipped for military operations; and military space activities. Such expenditures include military and civil personnel, including retirement pensions of military personnel and social services for personnel; operation and maintenance; procurement; military research and development; and military aid (in the military expenditures of the donor country). Excluded are civil defense and current expenditures for previous military activities, such as for veterans' benefits, demobilization, conversion, and destruction of weapons. This definition cannot be applied for all countries, however, since that would require much more detailed information than is available about what is included in military budgets and off-budget military expenditure items. (For example, military budgets might or might not cover civil defense, reserves and auxiliary forces, police and paramilitary forces, dual-purpose forces such as military and civilian police, military grants in kind, pensions for military personnel, and social security contributions paid by one part of government to another.) • **Armed forces personnel** are active duty military personnel, including paramilitary forces if the training, organization, equipment, and control suggest they may be used to support or replace regular military forces. • **Arms transfers** cover the supply of military weapons through sales, aid, gifts, and those made through manufacturing licenses. Data cover major conventional weapons such as aircraft, armored vehicles, artillery, radar systems, missiles, and ships designed for military use. Excluded are transfers of other military equipment such as small arms and light weapons, trucks, small artillery, ammunition, support equipment, technology transfers, and other services. See *About the data* for more detail.

Data sources

Data on military expenditures and arms transfers are from SIPRI's *Yearbook 2005: Armaments, Disarmament and International Security*. Data on armed forces personnel are from the International Institute for Strategic Studies' *The Military Balance 2005–2006*.

5.8 Transport services

	Roads				Railways			Ports	Air		
	Total road network km 1999–2003[a]	Paved roads % 1999–2003[a]	Passengers carried million passenger-km 1999–2003[a]	Goods hauled million ton-km 1999–2003[a]	Rail lines total route-km 2000–04[a]	Passengers carried million passenger-km 2000–04[a]	Goods hauled million ton-km 2000–04[a]	Port container traffic thousand TEU 2004	Registered carrier departures worldwide thousands 2004	Passengers carried thousands 2004	Air freight million ton-km 2004
Afghanistan	34,789	23.7	..	..	..	..	..	..	*3*	*150*	*8*
Albania	18,000	39.0	197	..	447	89	32	..	5	189	0
Algeria	104,000	68.9	..	..	3,572	950	1,945	*311.1*	49	3,236	21
Angola	51,429	10.4	166,045	4,709	2,761	..	..	..	5	223	64
Argentina	215,471	29.4	..	..	35,754	..	..	1,251.9	100	6,851	115
Armenia	7,633	..	1,867	280	711	48	452	..	6	510	7
Australia	811,601	..	..	..	9,474	1,347	41,314	5,129.8	325	41,597	1,898
Austria	133,718	100.0	82,330	26,411	5,801	8,375	19,047	..	137	7,619	502
Azerbaijan	27,016	47.0	9,862	53,738	2,122	584	6,980	..	11	1,007	34
Bangladesh	239,226	9.5	..	..	2,745	..	..	*625.2*	7	1,647	180
Belarus	93,055	100.0	10,739	12,710	5,498	13,893	40,331	..	6	274	1
Belgium	149,757	78.2	118,340	32,450	3,536	8,676	8,725	7,292.9	154	3,265	713
Benin	6,787	20.0	..	..	438	66	86	..	*1*	*46*	*7*
Bolivia	60,762	7.1	..	..	3,698	..	..	..	29	1,853	24
Bosnia and Herzegovina	21,846	52.3	..	332	1,032	53	293	..	*5*	*73*	0
Botswana	25,233	35.1	..	..	888	171	842	..	8	214	0
Brazil	1,724,929	5.5	..	..	30,403	..	..	5,058.6	486	35,264	1,499
Bulgaria	102,016	92.0	8,596	..	4,259	2,628	5,212	..	8	476	3
Burkina Faso	12,506	16.0	..	..	622	..	..	..	1	62	0
Burundi	14,480	7.1	..	..	..	..	..	..	..	..	..
Cambodia	12,323	16.2	201	308	650	45	92	..	4	163	4
Cameroon	80,932	6.7	..	..	974	308	1,115	..	10	358	23
Canada	1,408,900	..	..	184,774	49,422	3,122	323,600	3,926.1	989	40,701	1,657
Central African Republic	23,810	..	..	..	..	..	..	..	*1*	*46*	*7*
Chad	33,400	0.8	..	..	..	..	..	..	*1*	*46*	*7*
Chile	79,604	20.2	..	..	2,035	820	1,935	1,473.5	86	5,464	1,094
China	1,809,829	79.5	769,560	709,950	61,015	551,196	1,828,548	74,540.1[b]	1,216	119,789	8,188
Hong Kong, China	1,831	100.0	..	..	..	..	..	..	111	17,893	6,932
Colombia	112,988	14.4	..	..	3,154	..	..	1,073.1	156	8,965	1,079
Congo, Dem. Rep.	157,000	..	..	..	4,499	140	491	..	*5*	*95*	*7*
Congo, Rep.	12,800	9.7	..	..	1,026	76	307	..	*5*	*52*	0
Costa Rica	35,889	22.5	..	..	848	..	..	734.1	34	884	10
Côte d'Ivoire	50,400	9.7	..	..	639	148	129	670.0	*1*	*46*	*7*
Croatia	28,588	84.6	3,716	8,241	2,726	1,213	2,733	..	20	1,336	2
Cuba	60,856	49.0	..	..	4,382	..	..	..	11	773	33
Czech Republic	127,672	100.0	90,055	475	9,511	6,553	16,214	..	66	4,219	41
Denmark	71,847	100.0	61,258	17,766	2,141	5,390	1,888	997.5	100	6,429	175
Dominican Republic	12,600	49.4	..	..	1,743	..	..	537.3	..	..	..
Ecuador	43,197	16.9	10,276	5,170	966	..	..	564.1	12	478	1
Egypt, Arab Rep.	64,000	78.1	..	..	5,150	40,837	4,188	1,422.2	42	4,584	248
El Salvador	10,029	19.8	..	..	283	..	..	..	26	2,535	25
Eritrea	4,010	21.8	..	..	306	..	..	..	..	..	..
Estonia	56,849	23.4	2,299	6,364	959	192	9,567	..	8	510	1
Ethiopia	33,856	12.9	219,113	2,456	..	..	..	..	30	1,403	117
Finland	78,216	61.0	67,300	27,800	5,741	3,352	10,105	1,308.1	112	7,201	325
France	891,290	100.0	744,900	266,500	29,246	74,014	45,121	3,947.0	685	48,583	5,584
Gabon	32,333	3.7	..	..	650	92	1,949	..	8	433	62
Gambia, The	3,742	19.3	16	..	..	..	..	..	..	..	..
Georgia	20,247	39.4	4,987	22,500	1,565	401	5,065	..	4	203	3
Germany	231,581	100.0	1,062,700	227,197	34,729	70,286	77,640	12,457.7	942	82,156	8,064
Ghana	47,787	17.9	..	..	977	85	242	..	1	96	7
Greece	116,470	91.8	5,889	18,360	2,449	1,668	588	1,877.7	138	9,277	58
Guatemala	14,095	34.5	..	..	886	..	..	817.3	..	..	..
Guinea	44,348	9.8	..	..	837	..	..	..	..	..	..
Guinea-Bissau	4,400	10.3	..	..	..	..	..	..	..	..	..
Haiti	4,160	24.3	..	..	..	..	..	..	..	..	..

5.8 Transport services

	Roads				Railways			Ports	Air		
	Total road network km	Paved roads %	Passengers carried million passenger-km	Goods hauled million ton-km	Rail lines total route-km	Passengers carried million passenger-km	Goods hauled million ton-km	Port container traffic thousand TEU	Registered carrier departures worldwide thousands	Passengers carried thousands	Air freight million ton-km
	1999–2003[a]	1999–2003[a]	1999–2003[a]	1999–2003[a]	2000–04[a]	2000–04[a]	2000–04[a]	2004	2004	2004	2004
Honduras	13,600	20.4	..	..	699	..	..	555.5	..	..	..
Hungary	159,568	43.9	13,300	12,505	8,000	7,380	8,713	..	47	2,546	24
India	3,851,440	62.6	..	..	63,221	541,208	381,241	4,266.9	302	23,797	689
Indonesia	368,360	58.0	..	..	..	..	..	5,566.6	319	26,785	434
Iran, Islamic Rep.	178,152	66.3	..	..	6,405	10,012	18,182	1,220.7	104	12,234	98
Iraq	45,550	84.3	..	..	2,339	570	1,682	..	..	..	..
Ireland	95,736	100.0	39,440	6,500	1,919	1,582	399	924.9	262	34,783	124
Israel	17,237	100.0	..	..	493	1,423	1,173	1,607.9	34	4,954	1,355
Italy	479,688	100.0	759,200	184,756	16,235	46,768	21,581	*8,473.2*	384	35,932	1,393
Jamaica	18,700	70.1	..	..	272	..	..	1,360.6	23	2,008	38
Japan	1,177,278	77.7	955,412	312,028	20,060	242,300	22,200	15,937.5	646	103,116	8,938
Jordan	7,364	100.0	..	..	291	..	522	..	18	1,660	254
Kazakhstan	258,029	95.9	55,676	382	13,770	11,816	163,420	..	12	843	13
Kenya	63,942	12.1	..	22	1,917	226	1,399	..	26	2,005	193
Korea, Dem. Rep.	31,200	6.4	..	..	5,214	..	..	..	2	95	2
Korea, Rep.	97,252	76.8	9,404	565	3,129	28,641	10,641	14,299.4	233	33,390	7,969
Kuwait	4,450	80.6	..	..	..	..	..	..	19	2,317	224
Kyrgyz Republic	18,500	91.1	5,274	797	424	50	561	..	6	246	5
Lao PDR	32,620	14.1	1,290	121	..	..	..	..	9	276	2
Latvia	69,919	100.0	2,550	2,324	2,270	810	16,877	..	16	594	1
Lebanon	7,300	84.9	..	..	401	..	..	*299.4*	12	1,087	85
Lesotho	5,940	18.3	..	..	..	..	..	..	..	..	..
Liberia	10,600	6.2	..	..	490	..	..	..	..	..	..
Libya	83,200	57.2	..	..	2,757	..	..	..	8	850	0
Lithuania	78,893	27.4	20,982	11,462	1,782	443	11,637	..	11	448	1
Macedonia, FYR	8,684	63.8	..	..	699	94	426	..	2	211	0
Madagascar	49,827	11.6	..	..	883	10	12	..	18	514	13
Malawi	28,400	18.5	..	..	710	25	88	..	6	114	1
Malaysia	71,814	77.9	..	..	1,667	1,931	1,224	11,264.4	171	19,268	2,599
Mali	15,100	12.1	..	..	733	196	189	..	*1*	*46*	*7*
Mauritania	7,660	11.3	..	..	717	..	..	..	2	128	0
Mauritius	2,015	100.0	..	..	..	..	..	*381.5*	15	1,089	220
Mexico	349,038	33.5	399,000	195,200	26,656	..	..	1,905.9	333	21,240	403
Moldova	12,730	86.2	1,640	1,577	1,120	355	2,715	..	5	201	1
Mongolia	49,250	3.5	761	1,889	1,810	1,073	6,452	..	7	318	6
Morocco	57,694	56.4	..	18	1,907	2,614	5,535	560.7	42	3,004	62
Mozambique	30,400	18.7	..	..	2,072	137	808	..	9	299	5
Myanmar	27,966	78.0	2,028	9,493	..	..	..	..	25	1,408	3
Namibia	42,237	12.8	47	591	..	..	..	..	7	281	56
Nepal	15,905	53.9	..	..	59	..	..	..	6	449	7
Netherlands	116,500	90.0	193,900	481	2,811	14,097	4,026	8,482.4	250	25,304	4,773
New Zealand	92,662	63.8	..	..	3,898	..	3,853	1,614.9	197	11,305	749
Nicaragua	18,658	11.4	..	..	6	..	..	..	*1*	*61*	*1*
Niger	10,100	7.9	..	..	..	..	..	..	*1*	*46*	*7*
Nigeria	194,394	30.9	..	..	3,505	973	39	512.6	10	682	10
Norway	91,916	77.5	56,573	13,614	4,077	2,477	2,668	..	260	13,230	177
Oman	32,800	30.0	..	..	..	..	..	2,515.5	32	3,267	235
Pakistan	254,410	60.0	209,959	..	7,791	23,911	5,004	1,101.5	50	5,097	402
Panama	11,643	34.6	..	..	355	..	..	2,428.8	27	1,501	34
Papua New Guinea	19,600	3.5	..	..	..	..	..	..	19	759	23
Paraguay	29,500	50.8	..	..	441	..	..	..	9	373	0
Peru	78,672	13.1	..	72	2,123	..	..	695.6	43	2,666	200
Philippines	200,037	9.9	..	..	..	..	..	3,673.3	57	7,406	301
Poland	423,997	69.7	29,996	85,989	19,576	18,626	47,847	428.4	78	3,493	77
Portugal	72,600	86.0	98,328	20,470	2,849	3,415	2,675	865.7	127	9,052	237
Puerto Rico	24,023	94.0	..	10	96	..	..	1,671.3	..	..	..

5.8 Transport services

	Roads				Railways			Ports	Air		
	Total road network km	Paved roads %	Passengers carried million passenger-km	Goods hauled million ton-km	Rail lines total route-km	Passengers carried million passenger-km	Goods hauled million ton-km	Port container traffic thousand TEU	Registered carrier departures worldwide thousands	Passengers carried thousands	Air freight million ton-km
	1999–2003[a]	1999–2003[a]	1999–2003[a]	1999–2003[a]	2000–04[a]	2000–04[a]	2000–04[a]	2004	2004	2004	2004
Romania	198,817	50.4	5,283	25,350	10,844	8,633	14,262	..	30	1,338	5
Russian Federation	537,289	67.4	164	5,702	85,542	157,100	1,664,300	1,368.0	399	25,949	1,416
Rwanda	12,000	8.3	..	..	..	..	..	..	..	..	..
Saudi Arabia	152,044	29.9	..	..	1,390	364	1,173	3,185.7	113	14,943	957
Senegal	13,576	29.3	..	..	906	138	371	..	6	421	0
Serbia and Montenegro	45,290	62.0	..	..	3,809	..	..	..	25	1,414	6
Sierra Leone	11,300	8.0	..	..	..	..	..	..	0	16	8
Singapore	3,165	100.0	..	..	..	..	..	21,311.0	75	17,718	7,193
Slovak Republic	42,993	87.3	32,981	16,859	3,660	2,227	9,675	..	16	825	0
Slovenia	38,400	100.0	1,065	6,305	1,229	764	3,462	..	17	765	3
Somalia	22,100	11.8	..	..	..	..	..	..	..	..	..
South Africa	362,099	20.3	..	434	20,047	10,001	106,549	2,675.3	134	9,876	930
Spain	666,292	99.0	397,117	132,868	14,395	20,237	14,117	7,809.6	550	45,529	1,043
Sri Lanka	97,286	81.0	21,067	..	..	..	..	2,220.6	16	2,416	300
Sudan	11,900	36.3	..	..	5,478	32	889	..	8	476	41
Swaziland	3,594	..	..	..	301	..	..	..	*2*	*90*	*0*
Sweden	424,981	31.1	105,834	37,048	9,895	5,544	13,122	933.8	192	11,539	257
Switzerland	71,220	..	94,622	26,100	3,378	12,869	9,313	..	144	9,279	1,090
Syrian Arab Republic	91,795	20.1	589	..	2,798	635	1,924	..	16	1,141	20
Tajikistan	27,767	..	..	..	617	41	1,087	..	8	498	6
Tanzania	78,891	8.6	..	..	2,600[c]	471[c]	1,351[c]	..	6	248	2
Thailand	57,403	98.5	..	..	4,044	10,092	3,422	4,855.8	129	20,625	1,869
Togo	7,520	31.6	..	..	568	..	..	..	*1*	*46*	*7*
Trinidad and Tobago	8,320	51.1	..	..	..	..	..	*440.4*	17	1,132	42
Tunisia	18,997	65.4	..	16,611	1,909	1,242	2,173	..	21	1,940	20
Turkey	354,421	41.6	163,327	152,163	8,697	5,237	9,332	2,942.4	110	12,516	369
Turkmenistan	24,000	81.2	..	..	2,523	1,118	6,437	..	29	1,779	17
Uganda	70,746	23.0	..	..	259	..	218	..	0	46	27
Ukraine	169,739	97.0	40,131	24,387	22,011	51,726	233,961	..	34	1,924	23
United Arab Emirates	1,088	100.0	..	..	..	..	..	8,661.6	87	14,314	3,734
United Kingdom	619,398	100.0	666,000	159,000	16,514	42,626	20,700	7,480.9	970	86,055	5,698
United States	6,378,154	58.8	..	1,599,754	141,961	..	2,200,123[d]	35,612.7	9,566[e]	678,111[e]	37,450[e]
Uruguay	8,983	90.0	..	..	2,993	..	..	*301.6*	8	564	0
Uzbekistan	81,600	87.3	..	..	4,126	2,163	18,428	..	23	1,588	83
Venezuela, RB	96,155	33.6	..	..	433	..	32	920.9	129	4,592	2
Vietnam	215,628	..	18,116	4,772	2,600	4,376	2,682	2,138.8	51	5,050	217
West Bank and Gaza	..	..	..	..	..	..	..	..	..	..	..
Yemen, Rep.	67,000	11.5	..	..	..	..	..	*377.4*	16	995	60
Zambia	91,440	22.0	..	..	1,273[c]	186[c]	554[c]	..	5	49	0
Zimbabwe	97,267	19.0	..	..	..	..	..	..	4	238	17
World		36.3 m	.. m	.. m	.. s	.. m	.. m	326,382.9 s	23,754 s	1,886,515 s	140,242 s
Low income		13.3	..	..	..	..	..	8,435.5	696	49,908	2,157
Middle income		50.8	..	..	..	1,230	..	134,631.2	5,021	404,182	22,844
Lower middle income		50.1	..	..	..	..	..	104,722.1	3,087	272,310	15,055
Upper middle income		51.1	..	..	..	2,079	9,621	29,909.1	1,934	131,872	7,788
Low & middle income		29.5	..	..	..	..	..	143,321.1	5,718	454,090	25,001
East Asia & Pacific		32.3	1,659	..	..	..	2,662	102,039.0	2,079	203,261	13,730
Europe & Central Asia		74.0	9,603	11,400	216,994	2,227	9,675	..	985	65,135	2,139
Latin America & Carib.		26.8	..	..	..	..	..	19,377.2	1,561	98,165	4,629
Middle East & N. Africa		66.4	..	..	..	1,265	..	..	358	33,999	1,103
South Asia		53.9	..	..	..	..	..	7,589.0	389	33,527	1,579
Sub-Saharan Africa		12.5	..	..	..	..	..	..	347	20,003	1,821
High income		91.8	..	..	..	8,375	10,105	183,061.8	18,037	1,432,425	115,241
Europe EMU		99.5	108,334	26,460	120,432	8,676	10,105	44,966.0	3,783	309,557	27,487

a. Data are for the latest year available in the period shown. b. Includes Hong Kong, China. c. Excludes Tazara railway. d. Refers to Class 1 railways only. e. Data cover only those carriers designated by the U.S. Department of Transportation as major and national air carriers.

About the data

Transport infrastructure—highways, railways, ports and waterways, and airports and air traffic control systems—and the services that flow from it are crucial to the activities of households, producers, and governments. Because performance indicators vary significantly by transport mode and focus (whether physical infrastructure or the services flowing from that infrastructure), highly specialized and carefully specified indicators are required. The table provides selected indicators of the size, extent, and productivity of roads, railways, and air transport systems and of the volume of traffic in these modes as well as in ports.

Data for transport sectors are not always internationally comparable. Unlike for demographic statistics, national income accounts, and international trade data, the collection of infrastructure data has not been "internationalized." But data on roads are collected by the International Road Federation (IRF), and data on air transport by the International Civil Aviation Organization (ICAO).

National road associations are the primary source of IRF data. In countries where such an association is lacking or does not respond, other agencies are contacted, such as road directorates, ministries of transport or public works, or central statistical offices. As a result, due to differing definitions and data collections methods and quality, the compiled data are of uneven quality. Moreover, the quality of transport service (reliability, transit time, and condition of goods delivered) is rarely measured, though it may be as important as quantity in assessing an economy's transport system. Several new initiatives are under way to improve data availability and consistency. The IRF is collaborating with national and international development agencies to improve the quality and coverage of road statistics. To improve measures of progress and performance, the World Bank is also working on better measures of access, affordability, efficiency, quality, and fiscal and institutional aspects of infrastructure.

Unlike the road sector, where numerous qualified motor vehicle operators can operate anywhere on the road network, railways are a restricted transport system with vehicles confined to a fixed guideway. Considering their cost and service characteristics, railways generally are best suited to carry—and can effectively compete for—bulk commodities and containerized freight for distances of 500–5,000 kilometers, and passengers for distances of 50–1,000 kilometers. Below these limits road transport tends to be more competitive, while above these limits either air transport for passengers and freight or sea transport for freight tend to be more competitive. The railways indicators in the table focus on scale and output measures: total route-kilometers, passenger-kilometers, and goods (freight) hauled in ton-kilometers.

Measures of port container traffic, much of it commodities of medium to high value added, give some indication of economic growth in a country. But when traffic is merely transshipment, much of the economic benefit goes to the terminal operator and ancillary services for ships and containers rather than to the country more broadly. In transshipment centers empty containers may account for as much as 40 percent of traffic.

The air transport data represent the total (international and domestic) scheduled traffic carried by the air carriers registered in a country. Countries submit air transport data to ICAO on the basis of standard instructions and definitions issued by ICAO. In many cases, however, the data include estimates by ICAO for nonreporting carriers. Where possible, these estimates are based on previous submissions supplemented by information published by the air carriers, such as flight schedules.

The data cover the air traffic carried on scheduled services, but changes in air transport regulations in Europe have made it more difficult to classify traffic as scheduled or nonscheduled. Thus recent increases shown for some European countries may be due to changes in the classification of air traffic rather than actual growth. For countries with few air carriers or only one, the addition or discontinuation of a home-based air carrier may cause significant changes in air traffic.

Definitions

• **Total road network** covers motorways, highways, main or national roads, secondary or regional roads, and all other roads in a country. • **Paved roads** are roads surfaced with crushed stone (macadam) and hydrocarbon binder or bituminized agents, with concrete, or with cobblestones. • **Passengers carried by road** are the number of passengers transported by road times kilometers traveled. • **Goods hauled by road** are the volume of goods transported by road vehicles, measured in millions of metric tons times kilometers traveled. • **Rail lines** are the length of railway route available for train service, irrespective of the number of parallel tracks. • **Passengers carried by railway** are the number of passengers transported by rail times kilometers traveled. • **Goods hauled by railway** are the volume of goods transported by railway, measured in metric tons times kilometers traveled. • **Port container traffic** measures the flow of containers from land to sea transport modes and vice versa in twenty-foot-equivalent units (TEUs), a standard-size container. Data cover coastal shipping as well as international journeys. Transshipment traffic is counted as two lifts at the intermediate port (once to off-load and again as an outbound lift) and includes empty units. • **Registered carrier departures worldwide** are domestic takeoffs and takeoffs abroad of air carriers registered in the country. • **Air passengers carried** include both domestic and international passengers of air carriers registered in the country. • **Air freight** is the volume of freight, express, and diplomatic bags carried on each flight stage (operation of an aircraft from takeoff to its next landing), measured in metric tons times kilometers traveled.

Data sources

Data on roads are from the IRF's *World Road Statistics*, supplemented by World Bank staff estimates. Data on railways are from a database maintained by the World Bank's Transport and Urban Development Department, Transport Division. Data on port container traffic are from Containerisation International's *Containerisation International Yearbook*. And the data on air transport are from the ICAO's *Civil Aviation Statistics of the World* and ICAO staff estimates.

5.9 Power and communications

	Electric power		Telephones									
			Access				Quality	Affordability and efficiency				
	Consumption per capita kWh 2003	Transmission and distribution losses % of output 2003	per 1,000 people Fixed mainlines[a] 2004	per 1,000 people Mobile subscribers[a] 2004	Population covered by mobile telephony[a] % 2004	International voice traffic minutes per person[a] 2004	Faults per 100 mainlines[a] 2004	$ per month Price basket for residential fixed line[a] 2004	$ per month Price basket for mobile[b] 2004	Cost of call to U.S. $ per 3 minutes[a] 2004	Total telecommunications revenue[a] % of GDP 2004	Total telephone subscribers per employee[a] 2004
Afghanistan	..	..	2	21	..	..	..	..	..	..	..	..
Albania	1,311	40	82	356	90	442	57.2	5.6	24.3	1.34	5.6	319
Algeria	796	14	71	145	84	..	6.0	5.1	10.2	2.08	2.5	..
Angola	113	14	6	61	..	7	..	11.9	11.2	3.23	2.0	96
Argentina	2,185	15	227	352	95	40	..	6.6	8.3	..	2.4	625
Armenia	1,312	23	192	67	81	67	52.9	3.1	12.2	2.42	3.2	146
Australia	10,713	7	541	818	97	214	8.0	29.4	17.8	0.68	3.5	374
Austria	8,104	5	460	978	98	293	5.4	30.6	26.4	0.71	2.5	..
Azerbaijan	2,355	16	118	215	96	24	45.2	1.6	10.5	4.18	1.7	225
Bangladesh	128	12	6	31	50	5	..	7.2	3.7	1.21	1.3	..
Belarus	3,039	13	311	113	87	57	24.8	2.0	7.5	2.25	3.0	159
Belgium	8,412	4	456	876	99	316	5.6	34.6	24.9	0.75	2.6	759
Benin	61	..	9	30	23	8	6.2	12.2	15.5	4.80	2.6	..
Bolivia	422	13	69	200	60	24	..	7.9	6.3	1.89	3.8	..
Bosnia and Herzegovina	2,096	17	239	268	90	89	..	5.1	9.1	3.62	4.4	238
Botswana	..	..	77	319	85	62	..	11.3	11.1	2.88	3.0	341
Brazil	1,883	17	230	357	68	12	1.6	7.4	18.9	0.71	4.0	..
Bulgaria	3,965	14	357	609	98	36	2.6	8.5	17.3	0.57	5.9	199
Burkina Faso	..	..	6	31	60	6	51.8	11.9	15.4	1.14	2.0	138
Burundi	..	..	3	9	82	2	..	4.5	11.6	2.45	2.1	98
Cambodia	..	..	3	37	87	2	..	9.3	4.0	2.94	2.8	..
Cameroon	178	24	6	96	70	..	..	6.7	16.6	..	3.3	..
Canada	17,290	6	634	469	93	439	..	16.1	6.7	..	2.7	301
Central African Republic	..	..	3	15	..	2	56.0	32.8	12.7	1.99	1.0	54
Chad	..	..	1	13	8	2	60.8	12.8	27.7	9.11	4.0	..
Chile	2,880	6	206	593	99	57	25.0	16.4	17.0	2.18	3.8	567
China	1,379	6	241	258	73	6	..	3.6	3.7	2.90	3.2	656
Hong Kong, China	5,653	13	549	1,184	100	895	1.3	15.1	3.4	2.62	3.9	539
Colombia	834	19	195	232	74	44	33.0	5.8	9.1	..	4.9	..
Congo, Dem. Rep.	87	3	0	18	55	..	..	..	10.4	..	4.6	..
Congo, Rep.	122	..	4	99	65	..	..	..	17.5	5.39	..	..
Costa Rica	1,666	7	316	217	..	82	4.0	5.9	4.2	1.93	2.5	316
Côte d'Ivoire	174	14	14	86	55	15	81.0	28.2	23.9	2.25	3.7	..
Croatia	3,156	20	425	575	98	170	12.0	14.7	14.4	..	5.4	389
Cuba	1,200	15	68	7	50	28	9.5	12.4	20.0	7.35	2.6	..
Czech Republic	6,070	6	338	1,054	99	163	6.8	16.7	15.1	1.06	3.7	512
Denmark	6,602	5	643	956	99	244	9.0	25.7	19.9	0.89	2.6	437
Dominican Republic	1,060	32	107	289	88	232	..	16.9	7.0	0.22	7.5	..
Ecuador	677	34	124	348	88	51	35.3	9.0	10.6	1.75	2.1	..
Egypt, Arab Rep.	1,127	12	130	105	91	23	0.1	3.8	4.1	1.45	3.4	274
El Salvador	584	13	131	271	86	322	35.2	12.9	13.5	2.40	36.0	..
Eritrea	..	..	9	5	0	9	51.1	4.9	..	3.55	2.8	56
Estonia	5,224	12	329	931	99	128	16.3	14.2	11.4	0.90	6.3	..
Ethiopia	28	10	6	2	..	1	100.0	2.9	3.4	7.05	1.8	65
Finland	16,427	4	453	954	99	178	..	24.7	13.6	1.80	3.1	329
France	..	6	561	738	99	210	..	25.7	29.7	0.84	2.2	..
Gabon	922	18	28	359	24	54	50.2	27.8	16.8	5.68	2.6	..
Gambia, The	..	..	27	118	60	..	..	3.9	..	1.81	10.3	124
Georgia	1,507	16	151	186	79	57	17.2	4.6	6.5	0.68	4.0	191
Germany	6,896	5	661	864	99	191	..	17.5	30.6	0.43	2.9	526
Ghana	248	12	14	78	28	15	67.4	3.6	11.1	0.39	5.2	137
Greece	5,041	9	466	999	99	164	13.6	14.3	19.3	1.09	4.0	..
Guatemala	396	21	92	258	78	114	..	10.5	4.3	1.21	2.8	..
Guinea	..	..	3	12	..	7	1.6	9.4	..	4.61	1.1	150
Guinea-Bissau	..	..	7	1	..	9	70.5	..	..	..	..	..
Haiti	31	52	17	48	..	..	..	..	..	..	..	..

Power and communications

	Electric power		Telephones									
			Access				Quality	Affordability and efficiency				
	Consumption per capita kWh	Transmission and distribution losses % of output	per 1,000 people Fixed mainlines[a]	per 1,000 people Mobile subscribers[a]	Population covered by mobile telephony[a] %	International voice traffic minutes per person[a]	Faults per 100 mainlines[a]	$ per month Price basket for residential fixed line[a]	$ per month Price basket for mobile[b]	Cost of call to U.S. $ per 3 minutes[a]	Total telecommunications revenue[a] % of GDP	Total telephone subscribers per employee[a]
	2003	2003	2004	2004	2004	2004	2004	2004	2004	2004	2004	2004
Honduras	556	23	53	100	49	82	3.6	5.9	6.9	2.52	5.8	183
Hungary	3,637	12	354	863	99	49	8.7	20.3	13.3	1.01	5.6	508
India	435	27	41	44	41	3	126.0	3.2	3.2	1.19	1.9	..
Indonesia	440	16	46	138	85	5	20.0	6.2	4.6	2.79	2.3	665
Iran, Islamic Rep.	1,916	17	219	64	..	8	..	2.8	2.9	0.55	1.1	304
Iraq	977	6	37	20	..	..	..	..	..	..	..	..
Ireland	6,098	8	496	929	99	983	6.0	39.7	19.1	0.71	2.7	401
Israel	6,599	3	441	1,057	97	306	..	14.9	9.3	0.59	4.5	825
Italy	5,620	7	451	1,090	100	236	..	23.8	14.0	0.79	2.6	..
Jamaica	2,481	9	189	832	95	233	39.7	10.3	8.1	0.87	5.5	345
Japan	7,818	5	460	716	99	36	..	26.0	29.1	1.66	3.0	..
Jordan	1,453	9	113	293	99	104	12.6	10.0	9.4	1.44	8.2	303
Kazakhstan	3,510	16	167	184	94	26	..	3.8	4.7	..	3.0	108
Kenya	125	19	9	76	..	5	149.1	12.5	14.0	3.00	4.8	80
Korea, Dem. Rep.	795	16	44	0	..	..	..	..	..	..	..	..
Korea, Rep.	7,018	3	542	761	99	116	1.0	7.3	2.1	0.76	4.2	..
Kuwait	14,808	11	202	813	99	..	4.0	10.3	7.4	1.50	2.4	234
Kyrgyz Republic	1,647	29	79	59	..	14	..	1.4	10.8	8.92	3.8	71
Lao PDR	..	..	13	35	7	3	..	2.3	2.2	1.11	1.5	85
Latvia	2,456	23	273	664	97	66	20.3	15.6	14.9	1.63	6.4	415
Lebanon	2,558	15	178	251	..	..	..	20.4	20.1	2.19	4.9	304
Lesotho	..	..	21	88	80	..	75.0	18.6	14.3	3.28	2.5	..
Liberia	..	..	2	15	16	..	..	..	..	..	3.5	..
Libya	2,415	28	133	23	..	..	..	..	..	..	..	..
Lithuania	3,055	7	239	996	100	34	16.3	14.6	6.9	2.31	3.5	..
Macedonia, FYR	..	..	259	383	99	127	..	5.3	..	..	6.7	..
Madagascar	..	..	3	18	30	1	59.6	7.5	4.0	0.59	12.5	93
Malawi	..	..	7	18	70	5	..	4.5	20.0	3.56	2.0	49
Malaysia	3,061	5	179	587	96	85	40.0	8.7	5.6	0.71	4.4	728
Mali	..	..	6	30	15	6	177.6	8.5	13.5	12.28	3.0	71
Mauritania	..	..	13	175	..	20	..	12.3	..	..	7.5	..
Mauritius	..	..	287	413	99	92	41.5	7.4	4.8	1.67	3.8	373
Mexico	1,801	15	174	370	86	82	1.7	15.5	11.4	3.04	2.7	505
Moldova	1,166	57	205	187	92	61	5.2	1.8	27.6	2.21	7.5	169
Mongolia	..	..	53	124	64	4	20.6	2.5	9.6	4.92	3.5	82
Morocco	577	16	44	313	95	55	25.0	18.4	16.0	1.41	4.9	..
Mozambique	339	10	4	36	..	32	66.0	16.5	10.9	1.17	2.8	158
Myanmar	101	20	8	2	..	1	155.0	2.9	..	0.36	0.2	49
Namibia	1,277	18	64	142	88	57	40.4	15.8	14.7	4.28	4.4	181
Nepal	68	19	15	7	..	6	78.0	3.1	2.8	2.04	1.7	88
Netherlands	6,748	4	483	910	100	311	..	31.7	24.5	0.32	3.3	593
New Zealand	8,896	13	443	745	97	347	30.7	18.1	19.8	1.30	3.3	..
Nicaragua	361	29	40	137	48	44	4.6	14.3	16.0	3.20	2.5	196
Niger	..	..	2	11	13	..	104.6	9.1	19.3	8.77	0.9	..
Nigeria	107	33	8	71	58	2	20.6	13.7	11.2	1.49	4.4	192
Norway	23,169	9	487	910	99	236	..	29.9	6.4	0.31	1.8	412
Oman	3,505	18	95	318	..	108	..	12.9	5.1	1.87	2.6	319
Pakistan	408	25	30	33	45	11	..	6.1	2.9	1.03	2.1	97
Panama	1,401	18	118	270	87	55	13.9	10.9	18.1	3.64	4.7	188
Papua New Guinea	..	..	11	3	..	8	..	6.6	8.4	4.32	2.3	..
Paraguay	801	4	48	294	60	20	3.4	14.0	7.3	0.90	4.0	..
Peru	759	10	74	148	75	68	..	19.4	21.9	1.80	3.0	..
Philippines	574	13	42	404	80	29	..	12.2	4.0	1.20	3.7	..
Poland	3,329	10	322	605	98	61	17.2	17.3	7.7	0.99	3.5	603
Portugal	4,383	8	404	981	99	194	10.1	25.8	31.7	1.04	5.4	922
Puerto Rico	..	..	285	689	..	..	..	..	..	..	3.8	..

Power and communications

	Electric power		Telephones									
			Access				Quality	Affordability and efficiency				
	Consumption per capita kWh	Transmission and distribution losses % of output	per 1,000 people Fixed mainlines[a]	per 1,000 people Mobile subscribers[a]	Population covered by mobile telephony[a] %	International voice traffic minutes per person[a]	Faults per 100 mainlines[a]	$ per month Price basket for residential fixed line[a]	$ per month Price basket for mobile[b]	Cost of call to U.S. $ per 3 minutes[a]	Total telecommunications revenue[a] % of GDP	Total telephone subscribers per employee[a]
	2003	2003	2004	2004	2004	2004	2004	2004	2004	2004	2004	2004
Romania	2,221	9	202	471	97	*49*	*8.9*	*9.6*	8.8	0.82	*3.8*	*252*
Russian Federation	5,480	12	*256*	517	*78*	*15*	..	*7.8*	6.3	2.03	*3.2*	*193*
Rwanda	..	..	3	16	65	..	..	*7.9*	24.8	2.43	4.2	..
Saudi Arabia	6,259	5	154	383	*92*	*120*	*1.7*	*11.7*	9.6	*2.40*	3.2	..
Senegal	167	13	*21*	90	85	*21*	*17.3*	*14.5*	13.5	1.02	*7.1*	..
Serbia and Montenegro	3975	16	330	581	95	112	..	*2.3*	6.4	*2.08*	3.1	374
Sierra Leone	..	..	*5*	22	35	..	..	*3.0*	13.6	..	2.8	..
Singapore	7,977	6	440	910	100	*728*	*99.2*	6.7	5.7	0.69	*3.4*	403
Slovak Republic	5,010	6	232	794	99	*66*	*10.0*	*11.4*	10.3	1.06	4.0	508
Slovenia	6,817	4	*407*	871	99	..	*23.4*	*12.6*	11.7	0.65	*2.8*	*556*
Somalia	..	..	25	63	..	..	..	..	..	..	..	..
South Africa	4399	10	103	413	96	39	*48.2*	21.6	13.5	0.79	5.8	..
Spain	5,701	9	416	905	99	*117*	*14.2*	*20.3*	21.5	0.60	*4.4*	868
Sri Lanka	325	18	51	114	40	*20*	*6.8*	7.3	3.7	2.11	*2.2*	*166*
Sudan	81	16	29	30	*60*	11	..	*4.4*	3.2	*39.18*	2.4	*225*
Swaziland	..	..	*45*	109	90	*51*	*70.0*	8.3	16.6	2.97	*3.7*	*209*
Sweden	15,403	8	*767*	1,034	99	..	..	27.1	15.8	0.41	*1.9*	*780*
Switzerland	8,191	6	710	849	99	*665*	..	29.6	33.0	0.29	3.6	*516*
Syrian Arab Republic	1,243	24	143	126	99	*37*	*50.0*	*3.0*	48.2	*4.81*	*2.1*	..
Tajikistan	2,206	15	*39*	*7*	..	*10*	*144.0*	*1.0*	12.3	*6.96*	*2.1*	*57*
Tanzania	54	27	*4*	44	*25*	*1*	*24.0*	*11.6*	11.1	3.17	*2.4*	*262*
Thailand	1,752	7	107	430	*92*	12	2.5	8.3	6.8	0.67	*3.6*	..
Togo	94	30	*10*	*38*	80	*13*	*6.2*	*10.4*	13.4	3.98	*3.4*	*248*
Trinidad and Tobago	4,721	5	247	498	..	*334*	..	*7.0*	7.8	0.95	*3.7*	..
Tunisia	1,118	11	121	359	95	*61*	*30.0*	4.7	6.8	*2.28*	4.0	*224*
Turkey	1,656	17	267	484	*68*	*32*	*30.4*	*10.3*	6.4	*2.09*	*3.0*	*664*
Turkmenistan	1,750	14	*80*	*2*	..	*6*	*86.4*	*1.5*	..	..	*0.8*	*59*
Uganda	..	..	3	42	*70*	2	..	*16.6*	7.9	*3.51*	4.6	..
Ukraine	2,998	18	256	289	*75*	36	..	*2.5*	10.3	*1.65*	6.1	142
United Arab Emirates	10,992	10	275	853	99	..	*0.3*	5.0	3.5	1.73	*2.7*	500
United Kingdom	6,209	8	563	1,021	99	*262*	*11.0*	29.5	19.1	0.77	*3.9*	*358*
United States	13,078	7	606	617	95	201	*12.5*	25.0	10.8	..	2.5	344
Uruguay	1,781	21	291	174	99	60	..	9.0	7.4	0.52	2.9	..
Uzbekistan	1,741	9	*66*	21	*75*	6	*87.4*	*1.4*	4.6	*13.95*	2.1	87
Venezuela, RB	2,664	26	128	322	90	23	*2.0*	*16.2*	14.5	*0.84*	3.0	..
Vietnam	429	14	122	60	67	8	..	*4.3*	6.9	1.95	3.5	73
West Bank and Gaza	..	..	102	278	*95*	34	*94.0*	*9.4*	..	*1.03*	0.6	..
Yemen, Rep.	158	24	39	53	68	12	..	*3.0*	5.9	2.39	1.5	176
Zambia	576	3	*8*	26	*51*	7	*124.9*	*5.4*	13.1	*6.45*	1.9	..
Zimbabwe	819	16	25	31	..	19	*63.0*	*2.0*	17.8	*4.36*	1.6	138
World	**2,456 w**	**9 w**	**195 w**	**281 w**	**69 w**	**30 w**	**23.6 m**	**9.7 m**	**11.1 m**	**1.20 m**	**3.0 w**	**232 m**
Low income	358	24	34	42	43	5	..	6.6	11.6	5.58	3.4	*93*
Middle income	1,720	11	192	293	77	22	22.8	7.7	9.1	1.45	3.0	278
Lower middle income	1,329	10	189	249	76	16	25.0	5.5	8.9	1.62	2.4	191
Upper middle income	3,378	13	221	483	84	46	19.8	13.9	11.1	1.06	3.0	402
Low & middle income	1,159	13	125	187	64	12	35.3	7.3	10.5	1.65	3.0	166
East Asia & Pacific	1,184	7	191	244	73	8	..	4.5	5.1	1.20	2.6	..
Europe & Central Asia	3,531	13	242	463	82	35	*19.9*	3.5	10.3	1.61	3.0	150
Latin America & Carib.	1,615	16	180	318	76	44	4.7	9.0	9.1	1.96	3.9	..
Middle East & N. Africa	1,212	16	91	128	..	..	..	4.9	8.1	1.66	1.2	..
South Asia	394	26	35	41	43	4	*88.1*	3.2	3.2	1.21	1.9	*97*
Sub-Saharan Africa	513	12	16	78	..	8	61.6	8.5	13.5	2.43	3.6	*138*
High income	9,503	6	535	771	98	149	*7.0*	25.8	17.8	0.76	3.7	472
Europe EMU	6,506	6	525	904	99	199	*8.0*	31.2	24.5	0.75	3.0	487

a. Data are from the International Telecommunication Union's World Telecommunication Development Report database, and World Bank estimates. b. World Bank estimates.

Power and communications 5.9

About the data

The quality of an economy's infrastructure, including power and communications, is an important element in investment decisions for both domestic and foreign investors. Government effort alone is not enough to meet the need for investments in modern infrastructure; public-private partnerships, especially those involving local providers and financiers, are critical for lowering costs and delivering value for money. In telecommunications, competition in the marketplace, along with sound regulation, is lowering costs and improving the quality of and access to services around the globe.

An economy's production and consumption of electricity is a basic indicator of its size and level of development. Although a few countries export electric power, most production is for domestic consumption. Expanding the supply of electricity to meet the growing demand of increasingly urbanized and industrialized economies without incurring unacceptable social, economic, and environmental costs is one of the great challenges facing developing countries.

Data on electric power production and consumption are collected from national energy agencies by the International Energy Agency (IEA) and adjusted by the IEA to meet international definitions (for data on electricity production, see table 3.9). Electricity consumption is equivalent to production less power plants' own use and transmission, distribution, and transformation losses less exports plus imports. It includes consumption by auxiliary stations, losses in transformers that are considered integral parts of those stations, and electricity produced by pumping installations. Where data are available, it covers electricity generated by primary sources of energy—coal, oil, gas, nuclear, hydro, geo-thermal, wind, tide and wave, and combustible renewables. Neither production nor consumption data capture the reliability of supplies, including breakdowns, load factors, and frequency of outages.

Over the past decade new financing and technology, along with privatization and liberalization, have spurred dramatic growth in telecommunications in many countries. With the rapid development of mobile telephony and the global expansion of the Internet, information and communication technologies are increasingly recognized as essential tools of development, contributing to global integration and enhancing public sector effectiveness, efficiency, and transparency. The table presents telecommunications indicators covering access, quality, and affordability and efficiency.

Operators are the main source of telecommunications data, so information on subscribers is widely available for most countries. This gives a general idea of access, but a more precise measure is the penetration rate—the share of households with access to telecommunications. Also important are data on actual use of the telecommunications equipment. Ideally, statistics on telecommunications (and other information and communications technologies) should be compiled for all three measures: subscription and possession, access, and use. The quality of data varies among reporting countries as a result of differences in regulations covering the provision of data.

Globally there have been huge improvements in access to telecommunications, driven mainly by mobile telephony. By 2002 access to mobiles outpaced access to fixed-line telephones in developing countries, and rural areas are catching up with urban areas (although gaps are still large). By 2002 there were over a billion mobile subscribers and an estimated 4.7 billion people, or about 77 percent of the world's population, were covered by a mobile cellular signal.

Telephone mainline faults are a measure of telecommunications quality. The definition varies among countries: some operators define faults as including malfunctioning customer equipment while others include only technical faults.

Although access is the key to delivering telecommunications services to people, if that service is not affordable to most people, then goals of universal usage will not be met. Three indicators of telecommunications affordability are presented in the table (price basket for fixed-line telephone service, price basket for mobile service, and the cost of a local call). Telecommunications efficiency is measured by total telecommunications revenue as percent of GDP and by total telephone subscribers per employee.

Definitions

• **Electric power consumption** measures the production of power plants and combined heat and power plants less transmission, distribution, and transformation losses and own use by heat and power plants plus imports less exports. • **Electric power transmission and distribution losses** are losses in transmission between sources of supply and points of distribution and in distribution to consumers, including pilferage. • **Fixed telephone mainlines** are telephone lines connecting a subscriber to the telephone exchange equipment. • **Mobile telephone subscribers** are subscribers to a public mobile telephone service using cellular technology. • **Population covered by mobile telephony** is the percentage of people within range of a mobile cellular signal regardless of whether they are subscribers. • **International voice traffic** is the sum of international incoming and outgoing telephone traffic (in minutes) divided by total population. • **Telephone mainline faults** are the number of reported faults for the year divided by the number of telephone mainlines and multiplied by 100. • **Price basket for residential fixed line** is calculated as one-fifth of the installation charge, the monthly subscription charge, and the cost of local calls (15 peak and 15 off-peak calls of three minutes each). • **Price basket for mobile** is calculated as the pre-paid price for 25 calls per month spread over the same mobile network, other mobile networks, and mobile to fixed calls and during peak, off-peak, and weekend times. It also includes 30 text messages per month. • **Cost of call to U.S.** is the cost of a three-minute, peak rate, fixed-line call from the country to the United States. • **Total telecommunications revenue** is the revenue from the provision of telecommunications services such as fixed-line, mobile, and data divided by GDP. • **Total telephone subscribers per employee** are telephone subscribers (fixed-line plus mobile) divided by total telecommunications employees.

Data sources

Data on electricity consumption and losses are from the IEA's *Energy Statistics and Balances of Non-OECD Countries 2002–2003*, the IEA's *Energy Statistics of OECD Countries 2002–2003*, and the United Nations Statistics Division's *Energy Statistics Yearbook*. Data on telecommunications are from the International Telecommunication Union's World Telecommunication Development Report database and World Bank estimates.

5.10 The information age

	Daily newspapers	Households with television[a]	Personal computers and the Internet							Information and communications technology expenditures	
			Access			Quality		Application	Affordability		
	per 1,000 people	%	Personal computers[a] per 1,000 people	Internet users[a] per 1,000 people	Schools connected to the Internet %	Broadband subscribers per 1,000 people[a]	International Internet bandwidth bits per capita[a]	Secure Internet servers per million people	Price basket for Internet $ per month[b]	% of GDP	Per capita $
	2000	2004	2004	2004	2004	2004	2004	November 2005	2003	2004	2004
Afghanistan	..	..	..	1	..	0.0	1	0	..	..	..
Albania	..	90	12	24	..	0.0	4	0	28.6	..	..
Algeria	27	98	9	26	53	1.1	5	0	17.8	..	..
Angola	11	9	3	11	..	0.0	0	0	78.8	..	..
Argentina	40	97	96	133	..	13.5	319	11	13.3	5.6	224
Armenia	..	91	66	50	..	0.0	12	1	44.8	..	..
Australia	161	96	682	646	97	77.0	1,097	500	18.1	5.4	1,714
Austria	309	97	418	477	94	101.3	6,682	232	32.9	5.1	1,816
Azerbaijan	10	99	18	49	..	0.0	0	0	108.3	..	..
Bangladesh	..	29	12	2	..	0.0	0	0	20.0	2.9	12
Belarus	..	91	..	163	..	0.0	36	1	12.8	..	..
Belgium	153	97	348	403	93	155.4	11,279	118	28.6	5.3	1,783
Benin	5	20	4	12	..	0.0	6	0	46.4	..	..
Bolivia	99	..	36	39	..	0.0	44	2	22.3	5.6	55
Bosnia and Herzegovina	..	87	45	58	..	0.1	77	3	7.3	..	..
Botswana	25	15	45	34	..	0.0	23	1	27.0	..	..
Brazil	46	90	105	120	50	12.4	149	14	28.0	6.3	208
Bulgaria	173	97	59	283	60	5.6	80	9	12.4	3.8	117
Burkina Faso	1	7	2	4	..	0.0	4	0	45.4	..	..
Burundi	2	14	5	3	..	0.0	1	0	80.9	..	..
Cambodia	..	..	3	3	..	0.0	1	0	57.4	..	..
Cameroon	6	18	10	10	..	0.0	3	0	51.7	5.1	45
Canada	168	99	700	626	98	164.3	6,803	570	12.7	5.4	1,641
Central African Republic	2	2	3	2	..	0.0	0	..	175.0	..	..
Chad	0	2	2	6	..	0.0	0	..	68.9	..	..
Chile	..	95	133	267	62	29.7	788	21	21.8	5.8	340
China	59	91	41	73	..	16.5	57	0	10.1	4.4	66
Hong Kong, China	218	99	608	506	100	215.7	4,793	159	3.8	8.7	2,065
Colombia	26	92	67	80	50	2.8	124	4	18.6	8.3	180
Congo, Dem. Rep.	3	2	..	1	..	0.0	0	0	74.0	..	..
Congo, Rep.	6	6	4	9	..	0.0	0	1	121.2	..	..
Costa Rica	70	91	238	235	15	0.1	..	62	25.8	7.8	337
Côte d'Ivoire	16	35	15	17	..	0.0	2	0	67.2	..	..
Croatia	134	93	190	293	..	5.0	317	40	17.1	..	..
Cuba	54	..	27	13	..	0.0	8	0	57.8	..	..
Czech Republic	..	..	240	470	90	16.5	2,450	42	20.8	6.0	632
Denmark	283	98	656	696	100	168.6	34,870	411	17.6	5.6	2,487
Dominican Republic	28	88	0	91	..	3.8	..	6	33.0	..	..
Ecuador	98	89	56	48	..	0.0	38	4	31.8	3.6	83
Egypt, Arab Rep.	31	95	32	54	66	0.4	19	1	5.5	1.4	15
El Salvador	29	..	44	87	..	2.8	62	5	48.1	..	..
Eritrea	..	14	4	12	..	0.0	2	..	26.8	..	..
Estonia	192	93	921	497	75	102.8	3,410	102	13.6	..	..
Ethiopia	0	2	3	2	1	0.0	0	0	27.4	..	..
Finland	445	91	481	629	99	149.2	4,326	308	22.5	6.6	2,344
France	142	95	487	414	97	108.1	3,312	79	14.1	5.6	1,899
Gabon	29	54	29	29	..	0.0	33	6	121.9	..	..
Gambia, The	2	12	16	33	..	0.0	1	..	27.1	..	..
Georgia	5	76	42	39	..	0.3	..	4	26.2	..	..
Germany	291	94	561	500	99	83.7	6,860	274	14.1	5.5	1,822
Ghana	14	21	5	17	1	0.0	1	0	43.8	..	..
Greece	..	98	89	177	59	4.7	589	31	37.6	4.2	774
Guatemala	..	..	19	61	..	0.0	57	6	31.2	..	..
Guinea	..	9	5	5	..	0.0	0	..	63.3	..	..
Guinea-Bissau	5	26	..	17	..	0.0	..	..	105.1	..	..
Haiti	..	26	..	59	..	0.0	..	1	130.0	..	..

The information age

	Daily newspapers	Households with television[a]	Personal computers and the Internet								Information and communications technology expenditures	
			Access			Quality			Application	Affordability		
	per 1,000 people	%	per 1,000 people Personal computers[a]	per 1,000 people Internet users[a]	Schools connected to the Internet %	Broadband subscribers per 1,000 people[a]	International Internet bandwidth bits per capita[a]	Secure Internet servers per million people	Price basket for Internet $ per month[b]	% of GDP	Per capita $
	2000	2004	2004	2004	2004	2004	2004	November 2005	2003	2004	2004
Honduras	..	58	16	32	..	*0.0*	*3*	4	40.6	4.7	49
Hungary	162	92	146	267	*85*	36.2	989	30	10.2	5.9	588
India	*60*	37	12	32	..	0.6	11	1	8.7	3.8	24
Indonesia	*23*	66	14	67	..	0.3	10	0	22.3	3.1	37
Iran, Islamic Rep.	..	*77*	110	8	..	*0.2*	*15*	0	5.9	2.2	54
Iraq	..	..	*8*	1	..	*0.0*	..	..	..	..	..
Ireland	148	95	494	265	*99*	33.9	6,044	355	28.3	3.7	1,653
Israel	..	*93*	741	471	*95*	135.3	2,501	163	29.8	7.8	1,349
Italy	109	..	315	501	*88*	81.7	*2,078*	45	16.5	4.0	1,171
Jamaica	..	*70*	63	403	*10*	*9.6*	..	14	43.5	11.8	395
Japan	566	*99*	542	587	*99*	145.8	1,038	257	21.1	7.6	2,732
Jordan	*74*	*97*	55	110	*18*	*0.9*	57	4	26.3	8.4	178
Kazakhstan	..	95	..	27	..	*0.0*	*3*	1	34.5	..	..
Kenya	*8*	*19*	13	45	..	*0.0*	1	0	45.7	2.9	14
Korea, Dem. Rep.	..	..	..	..	..	*0.0*	..	..	..	..	..
Korea, Rep.	..	93	545	657	100	247.9	1,485	20	9.7	6.5	924
Kuwait	..	*95*	183	244	..	*5.4*	117	*21*	24.7	1.5	338
Kyrgyz Republic	..	..	17	52	..	*0.0*	*4*	1	15.0	..	..
Lao PDR	..	..	4	4	..	*0.0*	1	0	31.9	..	..
Latvia	138	*85*	217	350	*97*	16.9	972	38	58.1	..	..
Lebanon	63	*93*	113	169	*20*	*10.1*	56	10	36.9	..	..
Lesotho	*9*	*17*	..	24	..	*0.0*	*1*	..	43.4	..	..
Liberia	*14*	..	..	..	..	*0.0*	*0*	..	..	..	..
Libya	*14*	..	*24*	36	..	*0.0*	*1*	0	18.9	..	..
Lithuania	31	*97*	155	282	*56*	37.6	194	22	34.1	..	..
Macedonia, FYR	54	..	69	78	..	1.5	*25*	0	18.9	..	..
Madagascar	*5*	*8*	5	5	..	*0.0*	2	0	67.3	..	..
Malawi	*2*	*2*	2	4	*1*	*0.0*	0	0	62.0	..	..
Malaysia	95	98	197	397	..	10.1	128	15	8.4	6.7	316
Mali	*1*	*15*	3	4	..	*0.0*	1	0	58.0	..	..
Mauritania	..	*21*	14	5	..	*0.0*	*3*	0	38.6	..	..
Mauritius	116	94	279	146	*19*	2.0	146	18	15.0	..	..
Mexico	94	92	108	135	*60*	*3.1*	108	8	22.6	3.0	196
Moldova	*153*	*75*	27	96	*50*	0.7	43	4	19.0	..	..
Mongolia	18	*29*	124	80	*19*	*0.2*	*9*	3	17.8	..	..
Morocco	29	76	21	117	..	2.1	26	1	25.3	5.5	93
Mozambique	*3*	*6*	6	7	*0*	*0.0*	*1*	0	50.8	..	..
Myanmar	*9*	*3*	6	1	..	*0.0*	1	0	42.5	..	..
Namibia	*17*	*39*	109	37	*4*	0.0	4	7	33.4	..	..
Nepal	..	..	4	7	..	0.0	*1*	0	13.5	..	..
Netherlands	279	*99*	682	614	*92*	189.4	20,549	327	24.1	6.2	2,214
New Zealand	202	98	474	788	*99*	*18.0*	1,127	493	12.9	9.3	2,257
Nicaragua	..	..	37	23	..	*0.4*	186	2	51.0	..	..
Niger	*0*	*5*	1	2	..	*0.0*	0	0	96.8	..	..
Nigeria	*25*	*26*	7	14	..	*0.0*	*1*	0	85.5	..	..
Norway	569	*100*	573	390	*99*	*87.1*	9,370	309	26.3	5.0	2,716
Oman	..	*79*	47	97	..	*0.0*	*15*	4	23.6	..	..
Pakistan	39	*39*	5	13	..	0.0	5	0	15.6	7.1	45
Panama	..	*77*	41	94	..	5.8	292	56	36.0	9.3	400
Papua New Guinea	..	..	64	29	..	*0.0*	*1*	1	20.0	..	..
Paraguay	..	..	59	25	..	*0.1*	26	1	36.3	..	..
Peru	*23*	..	98	117	..	7.6	205	5	32.8	6.7	166
Philippines	..	*76*	45	54	..	*0.3*	39	3	17.0	6.4	67
Poland	102	*92*	193	236	*90*	32.7	560	22	15.7	4.3	270
Portugal	102	99	133	281	*92*	81.7	833	57	20.6	4.3	679
Puerto Rico	..	*97*	..	221	..	*5.9*	..	31	..	..	..

5.10 The information age

	Daily newspapers	Households with television[a]	Personal computers and the Internet							Information and communications technology expenditures	
			Access			Quality		Application	Affordability		
	per 1,000 people	%	per 1,000 people Personal computers[a]	per 1,000 people Internet users[a]	Schools connected to the Internet %	Broadband subscribers per 1,000 people[a]	International Internet bandwidth bits per capita[a]	Secure Internet servers per million people	Price basket for Internet $ per month[b]	% of GDP	Per capita $
	2000	**2004**	**2004**	**2004**	**2004**	**2004**	**2004**	**November 2005**	**2003**	**2004**	**2004**
Romania	..	..	113	208	57	0.7	186	5	26.4	2.6	88
Russian Federation	..	98	132	111	65	0.9	100	2	10.0	3.3	135
Rwanda	0	2	..	4	..	0.0	1	..	66.8	..	..
Saudi Arabia	..	99	354	66	..	0.3	31	3	34.7	2.2	235
Senegal	..	29	21	42	..	0.2	27	0	40.6	7.5	51
Serbia and Montenegro	..	92	48	147	70	0.0	87	2	13.2	..	..
Sierra Leone	..	7	..	2	..	0.0	0	..	12.0	..	..
Singapore	273	98	763	571	100	120.8	5,826	270	11.0	9.9	2,498
Slovak Republic	131	100	296	423	65	11.6	2,295	18	20.7	5.0	386
Slovenia	168	98	353	476	99	59.1	1,085	79	25.4	..	..
Somalia	..	8	6	25	..	0.0	0	..	..	..	..
South Africa	25	54	82	78	27	1.3	19	21	33.3	7.3	343
Spain	98	99	257	336	94	80.9	2,822	82	20.7	3.5	843
Sri Lanka	29	32	27	14	..	0.1	17	2	15.1	5.9	61
Sudan	..	49	17	32	..	0.1	6	..	160.6	..	..
Swaziland	..	18	32	32	..	0.0	1	2	20.6	..	..
Sweden	410	94	763	756	99	152.6	17,531	331	22.4	6.7	2,570
Switzerland	372	99	826	474	..	173.5	9,671	473	22.4	7.0	3,370
Syrian Arab Republic	..	80	32	43	..	0.0	1	..	55.2	..	..
Tajikistan	..	..	..	1	..	0.0	0	..	54.3	..	..
Tanzania	..	14	7	9	..	0.0	0	0	117.0	..	..
Thailand	197	92	58	109	37	0.2	47	5	7.0	3.6	91
Togo	2	51	29	37	..	0.0	2	0	30.4	..	..
Trinidad and Tobago	..	88	105	123	15	0.1	138	21	13.4	..	..
Tunisia	19	90	48	84	25	0.7	44	1	17.3	5.3	149
Turkey	..	..	52	142	40	0.8	124	17	19.8	6.9	293
Turkmenistan	7	94	..	8	..	0.0	0	..	20.2	..	..
Uganda	3	6	4	7	1	0.0	2	0	96.8	..	..
Ukraine	175	97	28	79	..	0.0	17	1	16.7	6.1	83
United Arab Emirates	..	86	116	321	..	13.0	351	49	13.1	..	..
United Kingdom	326	99	599	628	99	102.5	13,055	466	23.9	6.9	2,450
United States	196	97	749	630	99	129.0	3,305	783	14.9	9.0	3,595
Uruguay	..	..	125	198	50	3.2	291	26	26.5	6.7	259
Uzbekistan	..	..	..	34	..	0.1	1	0	20.2	..	..
Venezuela, RB	..	90	82	89	..	8.0	51	5	19.5	4.5	189
Vietnam	6	83	13	71	..	0.6	23	0	19.9	..	..
West Bank and Gaza	..	94	48	46	..	0.0	23	1	25.4	..	..
Yemen, Rep.	..	43	15	9	..	0.0	..	0	30.8	..	..
Zambia	22	26	10	20	..	0.0	1	0	32.6	..	..
Zimbabwe	..	26	77	63	..	0.4	151	0	23.3	16.0	58
World	**90 w**	**84 m**	**130 w**	**139 w**	**.. m**	**32.0 w**	**816 w**	**65 w**	**25.8 m**	**6.6 w**	**508 w**
Low income	44	16	11	24	..	0.1	10	0	45.5	4.2	..
Middle income	55	89	61	90	..	12.9	91	4	22.3	4.7	111
Lower middle income	61	89	46	74	..	12.5	60	2	25.4	4.7	79
Upper middle income	..	92	122	159	62	3.7	218	13	20.8	4.7	241
Low & middle income	49	54	41	62	..	7.7	59	3	27.4	4.6	82
East Asia & Pacific	60	80	38	74	..	13.4	48	1	19.9	4.4	67
Europe & Central Asia	..	92	110	138	..	2.4	210	9	19.8	4.7	202
Latin America & Carib.	61	88	92	115	..	5.2	159	11	31.5	5.1	200
Middle East & N. Africa	..	88	49	42	..	0.2	9	1	24.4	..	..
South Asia	59	32	12	26	..	0.6	10	1	15.1	4.2	26
Sub-Saharan Africa	12	15	15	19	..	0.1	6	2	51.2	..	..
High income	262	98	574	545	98	125.9	4,545	384	20.9	7.1	2,329
Europe EMU	188	97	421	443	94	93.7	5,788	149	22.5	5.0	1,530

a. Data are from the International Telecommunication Union's (ITU) World Telecommunication Development Report database, and World Bank estimates. b. Data are from the ITU's World Telecommunication Development Report database. Please cite the ITU for third-party use of these data.

About the data

The digital and information revolution has changed the way the world learns, communicates, does business, and treats illnesses. New information and communications technologies offer vast opportunities for progress in all walks of life in all countries—opportunities for economic growth, improved health, better service delivery, learning through distance education, and social and cultural advances. The table presents indicators of the penetration of the information economy (newspapers, televisions, personal computers, and Internet use), quality (broadband subscribers, international Internet bandwidth, and secure Internet servers), and some of the economics of the information age (Internet access charges and spending on information and communications technology).

The data on the number of daily newspapers in circulation are from surveys by the United Nations Educational, Scientific, and Cultural Organization (UNESCO) Institute for Statistics. In some countries definitions, classifications, and methods of enumeration do not entirely conform to UNESCO standards. For example, newspaper circulation data should refer to the number of copies distributed, but in some cases the figures reported are the number of copies printed.

The data for other electronic communications and information technology are from the International Telecommunication Union (ITU), the Internet Software Consortium, Netcraft, the World Information Technology and Services Alliance (WITSA), Global Insights, and World Bank staff estimates. Estimates of households with television are derived from household surveys; data presented in the table are from the ITU and World Bank staff estimates.

The estimates of personal computers are derived from an annual ITU questionnaire, supplemented by other sources. In many countries mainframe computers are used extensively. Since thousands of users can be connected to a single mainframe computer, the number of personal computers understates the total use of computers.

The data on Internet users and related Internet indicators are based on nationally reported data. Some countries derive these data from Internet surveys, but since survey questions and definitions differ across countries, the estimates may not be strictly comparable. For example, questions on the age of Internet users and frequency of use vary by country. Countries that do not have surveys generally derive their estimates from reported Internet service provider (ISP) subscriber counts, calculated by multiplying the number of subscribers by a selected multiplier. This method may undercount the actual number of people using the Internet, particularly in developing countries, where many commercial subscribers rent out computers connected to the Internet or prepaid cards are used to access the Internet.

The number of secure Internet servers, from the Netcraft Secure Server Survey, gives an indication of how many companies are conducting encrypted transactions over the Internet.

The data on information and communications technology expenditures cover the world's 70 largest buyers of such technology among countries and regions.

Ensuring universal access to information and communication technology is a goal of many countries, but not all countries regularly track accessibility. There is no common set of information and communications technology indicators and definitions, and data are often drawn from administrative records rather than from specific surveys. Access needs to be accurately measured in three major areas: individual, household, and community access.

Definitions

• **Daily newspapers** refer to those published at least four times a week and calculated as average circulation (or copies printed) per 1,000 people. • **Households with television** are the share of households with a television set. Some countries report only the number of households with a color television set, and therefore the true number may be higher than reported. • **Personal computers** are self-contained computers designed for use by a single individual. • **Internet users** are people with access to the worldwide network. • **Schools connected to the Internet** are the share of primary and secondary schools in the country that have access to the Internet. • **Broadband subscribers** are the total number of broadband subscibers with a digital subscriber line, cable modem, or other high-speed technologies. Reporting countries may have different definitions of broadband, so data are not strictly comparable across countries. • **International Internet bandwidth** is the contracted capacity of international connections between countries for transmitting Internet traffic. • **Secure Internet servers** are servers using encryption technology in Internet transactions. • **Information and communications technology expenditures** include computer hardware (computers, storage devices, printers, and other peripherals); computer software (operating systems, programming tools, utilities, applications, and internal software development); computer services (information technology consulting, computer and network systems integration, Web hosting, data processing services, and other services); and communications services (voice and data communications services) and wired and wireless communications equipment.

5.10a

Europe and Central Asia had the highest Internet use among developing country regions in 2004

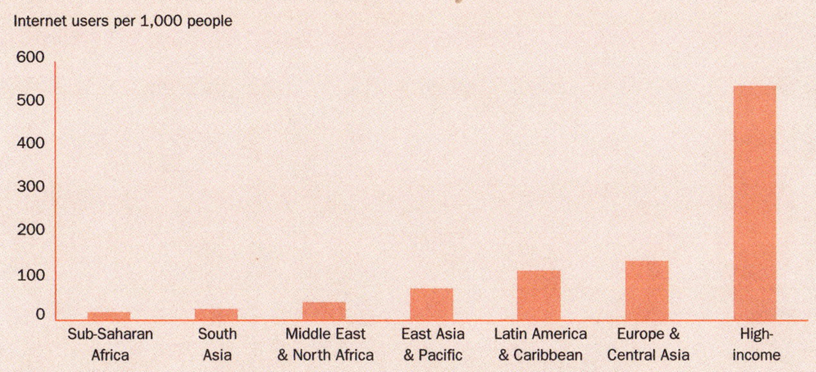

Source: Table 5.10 based on International Telecommunication Union and World Bank data.

Data sources

Data on newspapers are compiled by the UNESCO Institute for Statistics. Data on televisions, personal computers, Internet users, price basket for Internet, broadband subscribers, and international Internet bandwidth are from the ITU and are reported in the ITU's World Telecommunication Development Report database and World Bank estimates. Data on schools connected to the Internet are World Bank staff estimates. Data on secure Internet servers are from Netcraft (www.netcraft.com/). Data on information and communications technology expenditures are from *Digital Planet 2004: The Global Information Economy* by WITSA, and Global Insight, Inc.

5.11 Science and technology

	Researchers in R&D	Technicians in R&D	Scientific and technical journal articles	Expenditures for R&D	High-technology exports		Royalty and license fees		Patent applications filed[a]		Trademark applications filed[b]	
	per million people	per million people		% of GDP	$ millions	% of manufactured exports	Receipts $ millions	Payments $ millions	Residents	Non-residents	Residents	Non-residents
	1996–2004[c]	1996–2004[c]	2001	1996–2003[c]	2004	2004	2004	2004	2002	2002	2002	2002
Afghanistan	..	..	*0*	..	..	..	..	..	..	..	..	..
Albania	..	..	*17*	..	5	1	*5*	*8*	0	89,821	0	1,758
Algeria	..	..	225	..	7	1	..	..	42	88,839	1,313	3,088
Angola	..	..	*3*	..	..	..	227	2	..	..	..	..
Argentina	720	316	2,930	0.41	749	8	58	483	*0*	*6,634*	30,839	12,007
Armenia	1,537	103	152	0.25	4	1	..	..	204	89,361	388	2,084
Australia	3,670	..	14,788	1.63	3,128	14	472	1,437	10,823	96,434	26,831	17,113
Austria	2,968	1,254	4,526	2.22	10,597	12	170	1,241	3,313	250,719	7,272	9,996
Azerbaijan	1,236	195	68	0.30	8	2	..	*0*	0	89,337	144	2,051
Bangladesh	..	..	177	..	3	0	0	5	..	..	..	..
Belarus	1,871	207	528	0.62	215	3	2	10	908	89,686	1,730	4,548
Belgium	3,478	1,473	5,984	2.33	19,583	8	..	..	2,122	161,472	21,010[d]	10,695[d]
Benin	..	..	*20*	..	*1*	*2*	*0*	*2*	..	..	..	..
Bolivia	120	6	*33*	0.28	28	9	2	10	..	..	..	..
Bosnia and Herzegovina	..	..	*9*	..	..	..	..	..	0	89,872	0	3,283
Botswana	..	..	*41*	..	..	..	*3*	*12*	0	10	..	..
Brazil	344	332	7,205	0.98	5,929	12	114	1,197	6,521	95,225	81,036	13,218
Bulgaria	1,263	477	784	0.50	247	4	7	30	306	158,051	4,043	5,576
Burkina Faso	17	16	*23*	0.17	3	10	..	..	..	..	..	..
Burundi	..	..	*3*	..	0	6	*0*	*0*	..	..	20	132
Cambodia	..	..	*5*	..	4	0	..	6	..	..	333	1,305
Cameroon	..	..	75	..	2	1	..	..	..	..	..	..
Canada	3,597	..	22,626	1.94	25,625	14	3,019	5,528	5,934	102,418	17,068	19,664
Central African Republic	47	27	*4*	..	*0*	*0*	..	..	..	..	..	..
Chad	..	..	*2*	..	..	..	..	..	..	..	..	..
Chile	444	303	1,203	0.61	195	5	48	283	*241*	*2,879*	..	..
China	663	..	20,978	1.31	161,603	30	236	4,497	40,346	140,910	321,034	57,597
Hong Kong, China	1,564	225	*1,817*	0.60	80,109	32	*341*	*864*	112	9,018	5,903	14,543
Colombia	109	77	324	0.17	347	6	7	82	52	87,859	*7,265*	*7,096*
Congo, Dem. Rep.	..	..	*6*	..	..	..	..	..	..	..	..	..
Congo, Rep.	30	32	*13*	..	..	..	..	..	..	..	..	..
Costa Rica	368	..	92	0.39	1,374	37	1	51	0	89,225	..	..
Côte d'Ivoire	..	..	*40*	..	*93*	*8*	0	0	..	..	..	..
Croatia	1,296	455	710	1.14	759	13	41	146	444	89,877	843	5,600
Cuba	537	2,447	299	0.65	..	..	..	..	13	89,468	0	1,551
Czech Republic	1,594	879	2,622	1.27	7,662	13	57	172	608	158,592	8,114	9,756
Denmark	5,016	2,713	4,988	2.53	9,686	20	..	..	3,875	250,103	3,914	6,744
Dominican Republic	..	..	*6*	..	..	..	0	30	..	..	..	..
Ecuador	50	73	*20*	0.07	49	7	0	43	13	85,290	4,219	4,634
Egypt, Arab Rep.	..	..	1,548	0.19	15	1	100	108	627	798	0	2,496
El Salvador	47	..	*0*	0.08	37	4	0	18	..	..	..	..
Eritrea	..	..	*2*	..	..	..	..	..	..	..	..	..
Estonia	2,523	427	339	0.83	587	14	4	18	33	157,901	1,017	5,213
Ethiopia	..	..	93	..	*0*	*0*	0	0	*3*	*4*	..	..
Finland	7,992	3,472	5,098	3.49	10,625	21	850	805	2,941	248,668	2,830	6,095
France	3,213	..	31,317	2.19	64,871	19	5,070	3,142	21,959	160,056	58,035	12,774
Gabon	..	..	*20*	..	28	15	..	..	..	..	..	..
Gambia, The	..	..	*17*	..	*0*	*3*	..	..	0	177,146	..	..
Georgia	2,600	270	110	0.29	89	38	8	6	202	89,881	202	2,438
Germany	3,261	1,089	43,623	2.50	131,838	17	5,103	5,759	80,661	230,066	53,817	12,827
Ghana	..	..	90	..	*8*	*4*	0	0	0	177,371	..	..
Greece	1,413	895	3,329	0.65	1,031	11	32	466	614	162,387	5,290	6,075
Guatemala	..	..	*14*	..	88	7	0	0	*5*	0	*3,048*	*5,040*
Guinea	251	91	*2*	..	*0*	*0*	0	0	..	..	..	..
Guinea-Bissau	..	..	*6*	..	..	..	..	*0*	..	..	..	..
Haiti	..	..	*1*	..	..	..	*0*	*0*	..	..	..	..

	Researchers in R&D	Technicians in R&D	Scientific and technical journal articles	Expenditures for R&D	High-technology exports		Royalty and license fees		Patent applications filed[a]		Trademark applications filed[b]	
	per million people	per million people		% of GDP	$ millions	% of manufactured exports	Receipts $ millions	Payments $ millions	Residents	Non-residents	Residents	Non-residents
	1996–2004[c]	1996–2004[c]	2001	1996–2003[c]	2004	2004	2004	2004	2002	2002	2002	2002
Honduras	78	253	11	0.05	6	2	0	22	7	161	..	..
Hungary	1,472	457	2,479	0.95	14,158	29	551	949	962	91,497	4,316	9,546
India	119	102	11,076	0.85	2,840	5	25	421	220	91,704	..	..
Indonesia	..	..	207	..	5,809	16	221	990	0	90,922	..	..
Iran, Islamic Rep.	467	376	995	..	51	2	..	..	691	0	9,858	1,224
Iraq	..	..	21	..	..	..	..	..	..	..	..	..
Ireland	2,674	621	1,665	1.11	30,239	34	221	18,444	1,255	162,170	1,167	4,577
Israel	1,613	532	6,487	4.93	6,861	19	493	464	2,323	94,961	2,842	4,827
Italy	1,213	1,347	22,313	1.16	23,504	8	770	1,751	4,086	159,865	0	9,385
Jamaica	..	..	44	0.07	3	0	10	9	15	54	663	1,433
Japan	5,287	528	57,420	3.15	124,045	24	15,701	13,644	371,495	115,411	100,645	16,827
Jordan	1,927	709	240	..	147	5	..	..	..	..	..	..
Kazakhstan	629	92	116	0.22	72	2	0	26	2	89,421	1,809	2,902
Kenya	..	..	230	..	18	3	17	50	0	177,559	0	1,166
Korea, Dem. Rep.	..	..	1	..	..	..	..	..	0	88,052	0	1,913
Korea, Rep.	3,187	..	11,037	2.64	75,742	33	1,790	4,450	76,860	126,836	90,014	17,862
Kuwait	69	172	257	0.20	..	..	0	0	..	..	..	..
Kyrgyz Republic	406	51	10	0.20	2	2	5	4	123	89,357	67	1,850
Lao PDR	..	..	2	..	..	..	..	..	..	..	25	656
Latvia	1,434	318	157	0.38	130	5	8	14	8	140,637	1,262	5,699
Lebanon	..	..	202	..	17	2	..	..	0	104	..	..
Lesotho	42	26	1	0.01	..	..	17	0	0	177,309	0	774
Liberia	..	..	1	..	..	..	..	..	0	89,507	0	760
Libya	361	493	19	..	..	..	0	0	..	..	..	..
Lithuania	2,136	427	272	0.69	250	5	1	18	91	140,674	1,540	5,602
Macedonia, FYR	..	..	74	0.26	16	1	3	9	42	140,588	411	3,541
Madagascar	15	45	..	0.12	1	1	1	13	4	89,526	162	293
Malawi	..	..	36	..	2	2	0	0	0	177,315	138	440
Malaysia	299	58	494	0.69	52,868	55	20	782	..	..	..	..
Mali	..	..	11	..	..	..	0	1	..	..	..	..
Mauritania	..	..	2	..	..	..	..	..	..	..	..	..
Mauritius	201	126	16	0.35	61	4	0	4	..	..	..	..
Mexico	268	96	3,209	0.42	31,832	21	92	805	627	94,116	40,141	18,509
Moldova	172	201	77	0.81	13	4	2	3	240	89,396	1,391	2,690
Mongolia	681	69	8	0.28	0	0	..	..	121	89,864	255	3,260
Morocco	782	..	469	0.62	696	10	16	37	0	89,300	0	2,849
Mozambique	..	..	14	..	2	9	1	3	0	176,319	0	931
Myanmar	..	..	10	..	..	..	0	0	..	..	..	..
Namibia	..	..	13	..	15	3	0	3	..	..	..	..
Nepal	59	137	39	0.66	1	0	..	..	..	..	..	..
Netherlands	2,482	1,725	12,602	1.80	55,211	29	4,205	3,339	7,496	158,485	..	..
New Zealand	3,405	..	2,903	1.17	858	14	98	485	2,137	91,240	8,818	11,276
Nicaragua	44	39	8	0.05	5	6	0	0	..	..	..	..
Niger	..	..	21	..	1	3	..	0	..	..	..	..
Nigeria	..	..	332	..	9	2	..	64	..	..	..	..
Norway	4,587	1,754	3,252	1.75	2,759	18	242	485	504	90,712	0	6,981
Oman	..	..	96	..	22	1	..	..	0	75,825	..	..
Pakistan	86	13	282	0.22	150	1	10	95	58	0	5,342	1,560
Panama	97	387	37	0.34	2	2	0	49	7	153	..	..
Papua New Guinea	..	..	36	..	47	39	..	..	..	..	..	..
Paraguay	79	113	4	0.10	14	7	194	7	..	..	..	..
Peru	226	..	93	0.10	43	2	2	68	..	..	6,940	6,983
Philippines	..	..	158	..	13,913	64	12	270	0	81,697	..	..
Poland	1,581	282	5,686	0.56	1,932	3	27	880	2,324	92,176	12,355	11,607
Portugal	1,949	307	2,142	0.93	2,639	9	40	337	185	251,752	6,929	7,829
Puerto Rico	..	..	..	..	..	..	..	..	..	..	..	..

Science and technology

	Researchers in R&D	Technicians in R&D	Scientific and technical journal articles	Expenditures for R&D	High-technology exports		Royalty and license fees		Patent applications filed[a]		Trademark applications filed[b]	
	per million people	per million people		% of GDP	$ millions	% of manufactured exports	Receipts $ millions	Payments $ millions	Residents	Non-residents	Residents	Non-residents
	1996–2002[c]	1996–2002[c]	2001	1996–2002[c]	2003	2003	2002	2002	2002	2002	2002	2002
Romania	976	249	997	0.40	653	3	8	108	1,486	141,294	6,026	6,485
Russian Federation	3,319	557	15,846	1.28	3,432	9	227	1,094	24,049	96,315	29,279	14,215
Rwanda	..	..	*4*	..	*1*	*25*	0	0	..	..	..	..
Saudi Arabia	..	..	580	..	*122*	*2*	0	0	61	552	..	..
Senegal	..	..	62	..	33	6	*0*	*1*	..	..	..	..
Serbia and Montenegro	1,031	440	547	..	..	..	..	..	507	90,893	0	4,758
Sierra Leone	..	..	*3*	..	*1*	*31*	1	0	0	177,366	0	787
Singapore	4,745	381	2,603	2.15	87,742	59	224	5,647	511	93,748	3,344	20,282
Slovak Republic	1,984	460	955	0.59	1,217	5	*50*	*91*	276	157,652	2,350	7,742
Slovenia	2,543	1,600	876	1.53	794	6	12	123	332	136,912	1,086	6,612
Somalia	..	..	*0*	..	..	..	..	..	..	..	..	..
South Africa	307	73	2,327	0.76	1,300	6	48	381	184	90,471	..	..
Spain	2,195	861	15,570	1.11	9,932	7	486	3,032	4,330	251,260	66,471	12,460
Sri Lanka	181	44	76	0.18	60	1	..	..	0	89,759	..	..
Sudan	263	131	*43*	0.34	*0*	*0*	..	..	2	177,336	0	795
Swaziland	..	..	*6*	..	*4*	*1*	0	96	0	88,379	0	828
Sweden	5,416	..	10,314	3.98	17,022	17	3,459	1,420	9,443	246,886	0	5,976
Switzerland	3,601	2,319	8,107	2.57	24,121	22	..	..	7,977	246,451	0	10,592
Syrian Arab Republic	29	24	*55*	..	6	1	..	10	0	30	*0*	*0*
Tajikistan	..	..	*20*	..	..	..	1	0	40	89,352	0	1,522
Tanzania	..	..	87	..	3	2	*0*	1	0	176,850	*0*	*16*
Thailand	286	115	727	0.24	*18,203*	*30*	14	1,584	*1,117*	*4,548*	..	..
Togo	..	..	*11*	..	0	0	*0*	*1*	..	..	..	..
Trinidad and Tobago	399	889	*37*	0.12	*22*	*1*	..	..	2	89,901	340	1,317
Tunisia	1,013	34	344	0.63	370	5	18	8	0	72,604	..	..
Turkey	341	37	4,098	0.66	1,064	2	0	362	550	250,492	28,209	7,611
Turkmenistan	..	..	*0*	..	..	..	..	..	0	89,333	0	1,648
Uganda	24	14	91	0.81	12	13	6	6	0	177,305	*0*	*14*
Ukraine	1,774	463	2,256	1.16	*572*	*5*	40	268	37	90,563	0	5,285
United Arab Emirates	..	..	159	..	..	..	..	..	0	89,666	..	..
United Kingdom	2,706	..	47,660	1.89	64,295	24	12,019	8,368	33,671	251,239	51,399	17,135
United States	4,484	..	200,870	2.60	216,016	32	52,643	23,901	198,339	183,398	181,693	30,944
Uruguay	366	50	155	0.26	22	2	0	10	*44*	*572*	5,863	9,514
Uzbekistan	..	..	204	..	..	..	..	..	717	89,902	756	2,166
Venezuela, RB	236	..	535	0.28	118	3	0	219	*56*	*2,292*	..	..
Vietnam	..	..	158	..	*594*	*6*	..	..	2	90,135	0	1,929
West Bank and Gaza	..	..	..	..	..	..	..	..	..	..	..	..
Yemen, Rep.	..	..	*10*	..	17	13	..	9	..	..	..	..
Zambia	51	16	*26*	0.01	1	1	..	..	0	157,720	0	554
Zimbabwe	..	..	113	..	5	1	..	..	0	177,483	*1*	*17*
World	.. w	.. w	648,500 s	2.36 w	*1,269,586* s	20 w	109,808 s	120,273 s	936,630 s	12,882,065 s	1,316,564 s	604,897 s
Low income	..	..	13,147	0.73	..	*4*	59	248	1,469	3,003,874	8,489	26,165
Middle income	851	..	83,927	0.87	*266,410*	20	2,447	15,526	81,493	4,789,712	589,487	258,839
Lower middle income	609	..	39,520	1.02	..	23	1,282	9,566	51,330	2,439,396	423,019	134,156
Upper middle income	1,411	308	44,407	0.68	119,785	17	1,165	5,961	30,163	2,350,316	166,468	124,683
Low & middle income	..	..	97,074	0.85	*201,022*	18	2,506	15,774	82,962	7,793,586	597,976	285,004
East Asia & Pacific	663	..	22,722	1.31	..	34	484	7,347	40,469	581,580	321,648	66,765
Europe & Central Asia	1,907	379	39,077	0.98	32,514	9	992	4,118	34,159	3,071,921	106,252	137,176
Latin America & Carib.	..	..	16,045	0.57	40,852	13	563	3,425	7,255	1,166,254	163,101	62,928
Middle East & N. Africa	..	..	4,119	..	*1,152*	3	134	172	669	327,396	1,313	8,433
South Asia	119	102	11,611	0.75	..	4	17	100	220	181,463	5,342	2,242
Sub-Saharan Africa	..	..	3,500	..	..	*4*	317	612	190	2,464,972	320	7,460
High income	3,558	..	551,426	2.54	1,170,986	20	107,302	104,498	853,668	5,088,479	718,588	319,893
Europe EMU	2,607	1,230	148,169	2.20	361,128	16	17,110	38,459	129,155	2,448,271	222,821	92,713

Note: The original information on patent and trademark applications was provided by the World Intellectual Property Organization (WIPO). The International Bureau of WIPO assumes no responsibility with respect to the transformation of these data.

a. Excludes applications filed under the auspices of the African Regional Industrial Property Organization (3 by residents, 88,378 by nonresidents), European Patent Office (67,677 by residents, 97,737 by nonresidents), and the Eurasian Patent Organization (549 by residents, 88,857 by nonresidents). b. Excludes applications filed under the auspices of the Office for Harmonization in the Internal Market (29,345 by residents, 15,669 by nonresidents). c. Data are for the most recent year available. d. Includes Luxembourg and the Netherlands.

About the data

During the last century technological innovation in public health, nutrition, and agriculture has led to improvements in human welfare—child mortality rates have been reduced, and life expectancy has increased in all regions of the world. Knowledge is a key factor in economic development, and societies that are able to produce, select, adapt, and commercialize knowledge have better chances of achieving sustained growth and improved quality of life. Science, advancing rapidly in virtually all fields—particularly in biotechnology—is playing a growing economic role: countries able to access, generate, and apply scientific knowledge will have a competitive edge over those that cannot. And there is greater appreciation of the need for high-quality scientific input into public policy, such as regional and global environmental concerns.

Science and technology cover a range of issues too complex and too broad to be quantified by any single set of indicators, but those in the table shed light on countries' "technological base"—the availability of skilled human resources, the number of scientific and technical articles published, the competitive edge countries enjoy in high-technology exports, sales and purchases of technology through royalties and licenses, and the number of patent and trademark applications filed.

The United Nations Educational, Scientific, and Cultural Organization (UNESCO) Institute for Statistics collects data on researchers, technicians, and research and development (R&D) expenditure from countries and territories around the world through questionnaires and special surveys, supplemented by information from other international sources. Data for researchers and technicians are normally calculated in full-time equivalents.

R&D expenditures are all expenditures for R&D performed within a country, including both capital expenditures and current costs (annual wages, salaries, and associated costs of researchers, technicians, and supporting staff and noncapital purchases of materials, supplies, and R&D equipment such as utilities, books, journals, reference materials, subscriptions to libraries and scientific societies, and materials for laboratories).

The information does not reflect the quality of training and education, which varies widely. Similarly, R&D expenditures are no guarantee of progress; governments need to pay close attention to the practices that make R&D expenditures effective.

Scientific and technical journal article counts are from a set of journals classified and covered by the Institute for Scientific Information's Science Citation Index (SCI) and the Social Sciences Citation Index (SSCI). Article counts are based on fractional assignments; for example, an article with two authors from different countries is counted as half an article for each country (see *Definitions* for the fields covered). The SCI and SSCI databases cover the core set of scientific journals but may exclude some of regional or local importance. They may also reflect some bias toward English-language journals.

The method for determining a country's high-technology exports was developed by the Organisation for Economic Co-operation and Development in collaboration with Eurostat. The product approach method is based on calculation of R&D intensity (R&D expenditure divided by total sales) for groups of products from six countries (Germany, Italy, Japan, the Netherlands, Sweden, and the United States). Because industrial sectors characterized by a few high-technology products may also produce many low-technology products, the product approach is more appropriate for analyzing international trade than is a sectoral approach. To construct a list of high-technology manufactured products (services are excluded), R&D intensity was calculated for products classified at the three-digit level of the Standard International Trade Classification revision 3. The final list was determined at the four-and five-digit levels. At these levels final selection was based on patent data and expert opinion, since no R&D data were available. This method takes only R&D intensity into account. Other characteristics of high technology are also important, such as know-how, scientific and technical personnel, and technology embodied in patents; considering these characteristics would result in a different list. (See Hatzichronoglou 1997 for further details.) Moreover, the R&D for high-technology exports may not have occurred in the reporting country.

Most countries have adopted systems that protect patentable inventions. Most patent legislation requires that an idea, to be protected by law (patentable), be new in the sense that it has not already been published or publicly used; nonobvious (involve an inventive step) in the sense that it would not have occurred to any specialist in the industrial field had such a specialist been asked to find a solution to the problem; and capable of industrial application in the sense that it can be industrially manufactured or used. Information on patent applications filed is shown separately for residents and nonresidents.

A trademark provides protection to its owner by ensuring exclusive right to use it to identify goods or services or to authorize another to use it in return for payment. The period of protection varies, but a trademark can be renewed indefinitely by paying additional fees. The trademark system helps consumers identify and purchase a product or service whose nature and quality, indicated by its unique trademark, meet their needs.

Definitions

• **Researchers in R&D** are professionals engaged in the conception or creation of new knowledge, products, processes, methods, or systems and in the management of the projects concerned. Postgraduate PhD students (ISCED97 level 6) engaged in R&D are included. • **Technicians in R&D** and equivalent staff are people whose main tasks require technical knowledge and experience in engineering, physical and life sciences (technicians), or social sciences and humanities (equivalent staff). They participate in R&D by performing scientific and technical tasks involving the application of concepts and operational methods, normally under the supervision of researchers. • **Scientific and technical journal articles** refer to published scientific and engineering articles in physics, biology, chemistry, mathematics, clinical medicine, biomedical research, engineering and technology, and earth and space sciences. • **Expenditures for R&D** are current and capital expenditures on creative work undertaken systematically to increase knowledge, including knowledge of humanity, culture, and society, and the use of knowledge for new applications. R&D covers basic research, applied research, and experimental development. • **High-technology exports** are products with high R&D intensity, as in aerospace, computers, pharmaceuticals, and scientific instruments. • **Royalty and license fees** are payments and receipts between residents and nonresidents for the authorized use of intangible, nonproduced, nonfinancial assets and proprietary rights (patents, copyrights, trademarks, franchises, industrial processes) and for the use, through licensing agreements, of produced originals of prototypes (films, manuscripts). • **Patent applications filed** are applications filed with a national patent office for exclusive rights to an invention—a product or process that provides a new way of doing something or a new technical solution to a problem. A patent protects the invention for the patent owner for a set period, generally 20 years. • **Trademark applications filed** are applications to register a trademark with a national or regional trademark office. Trademarks are distinctive signs identifying goods or services as produced or provided by a specific person or enterprise. Trademarks protect owners of the mark by ensuring exclusive right to use it to identify goods or services or to authorize its use in return for payment.

Data sources

Data on researchers, technicians, and expenditures in R&D are from the UNESCO Institute for Statistics. Data on journal articles are from the National Science Foundation's *Science and Engineering Indicators 2004*. Data on high-technology exports are from the United Nations Statistics Division's Commodity Trade (Comtrade) database. Data on royalty and license fees are from the International Monetary Fund's *Balance of Payments Statistics Yearbook*. Data on patents and trademarks are from the World Intellectual Property Organization's Industrial Property Statistics database.

6 GLOBAL LINKS

In an era of uncertain alliances and global fears, it is striking that the world economy continues to become more integrated. Celebrated by some, deplored by others, globalization has been loudly debated over the past decade. But globalization is not a single process. It proceeds as people and institutions seek profits and competitive advantage through expanding trade in goods and services and cross-border flows of financial resources and people. It has been propelled by cheaper and faster transportation, more innovative information technology, fewer or lower trade barriers, and better economic management.

As the world becomes more integrated, decisions made in Washington, London, or Tokyo along with decisions made in New Delhi and Lagos and deals brokered in the virtual world of electronic communications can all have an impact on the lives and prospects of the world's people. But not all people have shared in the benefits of an expanding global economy. Compared with other developing country regions, Sub-Saharan Africa lags in this integration process and has not yet been able to take full advantage of opportunities brought by globalization.

Expanding trade

In an integrated world, trade spurs growth and growth spurs trade (figure 6a). The five fastest growing economies in the world from 1990 to 2004 measured by GDP per capita—Albania, Vietnam, Ireland, China, and Bosnia and Herzegovina—all experienced double-digit annual growth in trade. Rapid expansion of China's trade has not only been a driving force of China's continuous high growth, but has also helped its trading partners in East Asia and Pacific to integrate faster into the global manufacturing sector.

The global economy has become more open. In 1990 the total value of trade was less than 40 percent of global GDP; by 2004 the world economy had grown 50 percent and two-way trade exceeded 55 percent of global GDP. Trade in goods makes up 81 percent of trade and has been increasing 7 percent a year on average between 1990 and 2004. Although the nominal value of global trade in services nearly tripled over the same period and its share of GDP rose from less than 8 percent to more than 10 percent, its share of global trade has remained largely unchanged (table 6.1). In a world economy where services account for 70 percent of output, there appear to be unrealized opportunities for further trade.

During the last decade developing countries have become more important players in world trade. By 2004 low- and middle-income economies accounted for 28.5 percent of world trade, up from 22.3 percent in 1999. Between 1990 and 2004 their trade grew 11.5 percent a year compared with 7.2 percent for high-income economies. The middle-income economies were by far the fastest growing traders. Still, high-income economies, which account for more than 70 percent of world trade and almost 80 percent of global output (measured at market exchange rates), remain the most important markets (table 6.3).

6a

Trade spurs growth and growth spurs trade

Annual growth of real GDP per capita and real trade by size of economy, 1990–2004

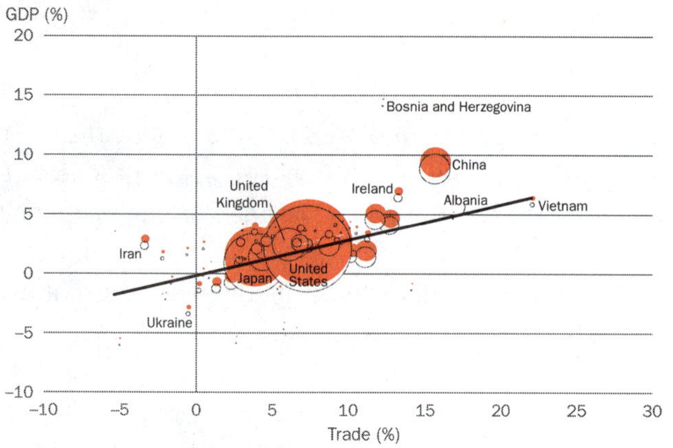

Source: World Bank staff estimates.

Many obstacles to trade remain, especially for low-income economies. Trade-supporting infrastructure is essential and is improving due to more efficient communication and transportation technology. But landlocked economies and those lacking suitable seaports remain at a disadvantage. Poor roads and high inland transportation costs have kept many people from trading with the outside world.

Other obstacles include an unfriendly business environment and inadequate policies and institutions. For example, in Sub-Saharan Africa it takes twice as long to comply with the procedures required to export or import goods as it does in East Asia and Pacific and four times as long as in high-income countries (World Bank 2006a; see also table 5.3). Lack of access to capital and a small entrepreneurial class willing or able to take risks also impede the growth of trade.

But the greatest barriers are those erected by high-income economies. Even in an era of falling tariffs (table 6.7), developing countries have a hard time reaching high-value markets. Tariff escalation is one of the rich countries' protectionist strategies. EU tariffs are almost zero for cocoa beans but rise to about 10 percent for semiprocessed cocoa and to about 30 percent for chocolate. So tariff escalation penalizes producers when they add value.

Subsidies paid by Organisation for Economic Co-operation and Development (OECD) governments to their agricultural produces (see table 1.4) are another source of formidable disadvantage for developing economies. Cotton subsidies, particularly in the United States, lower world prices and cost West African economies an estimated $250 million a year.

The economies of Sub-Saharan Africa are far from reaching their potential for trade. Their share in global trade is low—about 1.5 percent in 2004—and has changed little since 1999. However, the region's export structure is improving slowly. In 1984 primary products accounted for 88 percent of merchandise exports from Sub-Saharan Africa to high-income countries. By 2004 that share had fallen to 73 percent.

The decline of primary products in overall exports is more pronounced if petroleum exports and South Africa are excluded, dropping from 67 percent to 46 percent over the same period. Some Sub-Saharan countries have made significant progress in specific product sectors: cut flowers from Kenya; music from Mali; clothing and textiles from Mauritius, Lesotho, and Madagascar; and outsourced services from Ghana are making headway into world markets.

Within Sub-Saharan Africa intraregional trade is also limited. A recent study found that only 15 percent of merchandise exports go to other countries in the region, and only 10 percent of merchandise imports originate in the region (Newfarmer 2006). Because of gaps in the statistical reporting, it is hard to know whether intraregional trade is accurately estimated. The United Nations Statistics Division's Comtrade database shows no entries for three-quarters of all possible two-way trade flows between Sub-Saharan economies in 2004.

Although regional agreements have proliferated, significant barriers to trade remain because of imperfect implementation of agreements, high border and behind-the-border costs, absence of common standards, restrictive rules of origin even within customs unions, and inconsistent (and inconsistently applied) tax policies. All of these issues will have to be dealt with before Africa can achieve effective regional integration.

Expanding flows of financial resource

Global capital markets are expanding rapidly. One measure of financial market integration is the size of gross private capital flows recorded in the balance of payments (table 6.1). Between 1990 and 2004 flows to and from high-income economies tripled as a share of their GDP. Expansion has been slower for most developing countries. Gross capital flows as a share of GDP have more than doubled but remain less than half those in high-income countries.

For developing countries foreign direct investment (FDI) is the largest source of external funding, but portfolio equity and bond investments continue to expand following the turnaround in 2002 (figure 6b). Although low- and middle-income economies still receive only one-third of global FDI, the absolute level has increased nearly tenfold between 1990 and 2004, growing much faster than in high-income economies. But their net inflow as a share of GDP has still not fully recovered to the peak achieved before the East Asian financial crisis.

There are large differences in FDI inflows among developing economies. Middle-income economies received more than 90 percent of net FDI inflows in 2004, and if measured as a share of GDP, these inflows are twice those to low-income

6b

Foreign direct investment is the largest source of external finance for developing countries

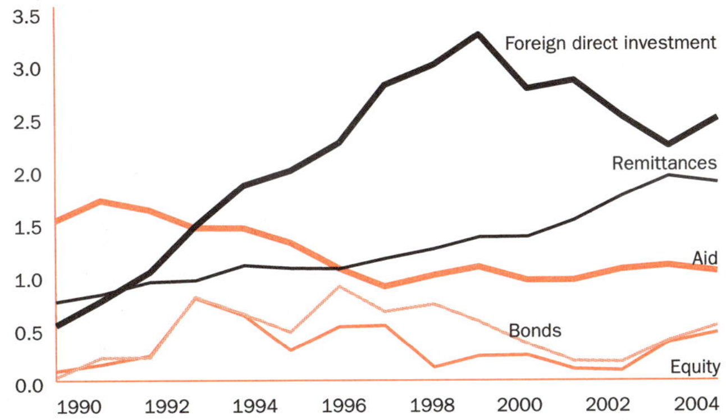

Source: World Bank staff estimates

6c

Aid is the largest source of external finance for Sub-Saharan Africa

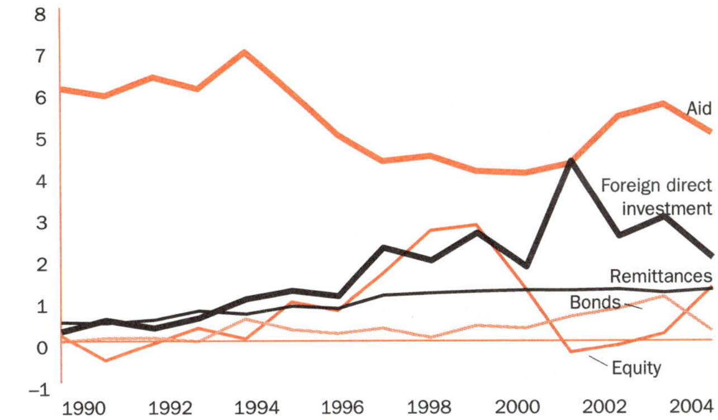

Source: World Bank staff estimates.

countries. The increase in FDI inflows has been greatest in Europe and Central Asia, followed by Latin America and the Caribbean and East Asia and Pacific. Although Sub-Saharan Africa has larger inflows than South Asia and the Middle East and North Africa, FDI in Sub-Saharan Africa is dominated by extractive industries, including oil and minerals. Four countries—Angola, Chad, Nigeria, and Sudan—together received nearly half of Sub-Saharan Africa's FDI inflows in 2004 (table 6.8).

Countries that have difficulty tapping financial markets must rely largely on aid flows to fund development programs. In 2004 developing countries received official development assistance and official aid totaling $85.5 billion, up from $76.7 billion in 2003 and $56.6 billion in 2000. Aid to Afghanistan (up from $141 million in 2000 to $2.19 billion in 2004) and Iraq (up from $116 million in 2000 to $4.66 billion in 2004) accounted for a large part of the overall increase in aid (table 6.11).

Even so, a substantial increase in aid flows and private capital flows will be required to help developing countries achieve the Millennium Development Goals. For example, aid is the largest source of external finance for the countries of Sub-Saharan Africa, but as a share of GDP aid declined from more than 6 percent at the beginning of the 1990s to 4 percent at the end of the decade (figure 6c). It has since increased to 5 percent.

If measured as a share of donors' gross national income, aid also declined sharply in the 1990s and rebounded somewhat after 2000. Only five rich countries have fulfilled the UN official development assistance target of 0.7 of GNI: Denmark, Luxembourg, the Netherlands, Norway, and Sweden. If donor countries follow through on their promises at the United Nations International Conference on Financing for Development, in Monterey, Mexico, in 2002 and at the more recent Group of Eight summit at Gleneagles, Scotland, aid is expected to rise to about $97 billion in 2006 and to reach $128 billion in 2010 (box 6d).

Movement of people

The movement of people across national borders is another mark of integration. International tourist arrivals worldwide for 2005 exceeded 800 million—an all-time high—and these tourists also spent considerable amounts of money on their trips. Receipts from international tourists were 6.5 percent of exports in 2004 for middle-income countries and as high as 17 percent for the Middle East and North Africa (table 6.15).

Meanwhile, an estimated 190 million people (3 percent of the world's population) are living in countries in which they were not born. International migration has enormous economic, social, and cultural implications in both origin and destination countries.

Demographic trends in both developed and developing countries point to significant potential gains from migration. In many developed countries the population is aging fast, while in many developing countries the population is young and growing rapidly. This imbalance is likely to create strong demand in developed country labor markets for developing country workers, especially to provide services that can be supplied only locally. The share of immigrants in the total population of high-income countries increased to 11 percent in 2005, up from 7 percent two decades ago, while the shares for low- and middle-income countries have remained about the same (figure 6e).

The large wage gap between developed and developing countries, especially for unskilled and semiskilled labor, indicates that migration from developing countries to developed countries can generate significant welfare gains. The flow of formal remittances from migrants back to their country of origin has been increasing rapidly and has become

6d

New promises of aid and debt relief

At the Group of Eight (G-8) summit at Gleneagles, Scotland, In 2005 commitments were made to relieve poor countries of their debts, increase aid and make it more effective, remove trade barriers, improve governance, and build stronger development partnerships.

Specific commitments included agreements to relieve 100 percent of the multilateral debts owed to the International Development Association, the African Development Bank, and the International Monetary Fund by all countries that have reached the completion point under the Heavily Indebted Poor Countries Debt Initiative. Also notable were EU commitments to spend at least 0.56 percent of gross national income on aid by 2010 and G-8 commitments to double aid to Africa.

The Organisation for Economic Co-operation and Development estimates that if all 2005 commitments to increase aid are met, official development assistance from Development Assistance Committee countries alone will rise by $50 billion in real terms between 2004 and 2010, to nearly $130 billion.

Aid commitments after the G-8 meeting at Gleneagles, Scotland

	2004		2010 projection			
					Real change in ODA compared with 2004	
Country	Net ODA ($ millions)	ODA/GNI (%)	Net ODA ($ millions)	ODA/GNI (%)	Amount ($ millions)	Percent
Denmark	2,037	0.85	2,185	0.80	148	7
France	8,473	0.41	14,110	0.61	5,638	67
Germany	7,534	0.28	15,509	0.51	7,975	106
Italy	2,462	0.15	9,262	0.51	6,801	276
Luxembourg	236	0.83	328	1.00	93	39
Netherlands	4,204	0.73	5,070	0.80	867	21
Spain	2,437	0.24	6,925	0.59	4,488	184
Sweden	2,722	0.78	4,025	1.00	1,303	48
United Kingdom	7,883	0.36	14,600	0.59	6,717	85
Other EU members[a]	4,899	0.36	9,206	0.60	4,306	88
EU members, total	**42,886**	**0.35**	**81,221**	**0.59**	**38,335**	**89**
Canada	2,599	0.27	3,648	0.33	1,049	40
Japan	8,906	0.19	11,906	0.22	3,000	34
Norway	2,199	0.87	2,876	1.00	677	31
United States	19,705	0.17	24,000	0.18	4,295	22
Other DAC members[b]	3,218	0.30	4,477	0.37	1,260	39
DAC members, total	**79,512**	**0.26**	**128,128**	**0.36**	**48,616**	**61**

a. Austria, Belgium, Finland, Greece, Ireland, and Portugal.
b. Australia, New Zealand, and Switzerland.
Source: *OECD Journal on Development* 2006.

the largest source of foreign capital for many developing countries.

Remittance flows have more than tripled since 1990, reaching $227.6 billion in 2004, with $161 billion going to developing countries (table 6.14). Already twice the size of foreign aid, remittances are expected to continue growing. Empirical studies have found that remittances typically boost income levels, especially for the poor, and may encourage investment in physical and human capital and help to buffer the impact of negative shocks.

Among these international migrants are millions of highly educated people who have moved to developed countries from developing countries that already suffer from low levels of human capital and skilled workers. The flight of human capital, or "brain drain," may increase the concentration of poverty and reduce the beneficial impact of globalization. A recent study estimates that highly skilled immigrants represented 34.6 percent of the OECD immigration stock in 2000, while only 11.3 percent of the world labor force had a tertiary education (Özden and Schiff 2006). The most affected areas are Sub-Saharan Africa and small island economies in the Caribbean. Although Sub-Saharan Africa's emigration rate is not particularly high, 13 percent of those who do migrate have a tertiary education. In Jamaica four of five trained doctors were employed outside the country.

6e

Immigrant populations are expanding in high-income economies

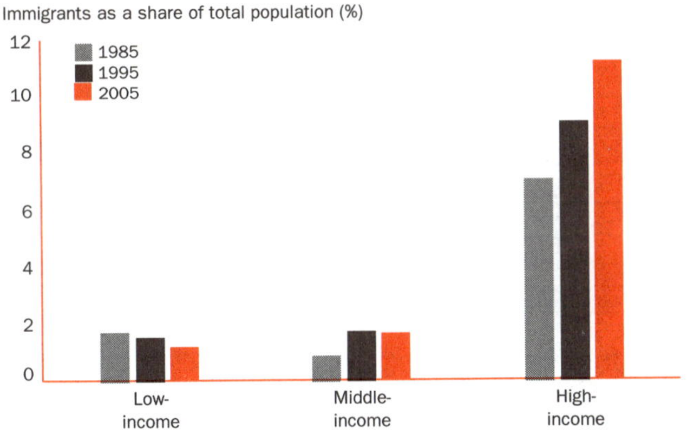

Source: World Bank staff estimates based on United Nations Population Fund data.

6f

Immigrants in OECD countries are better educated

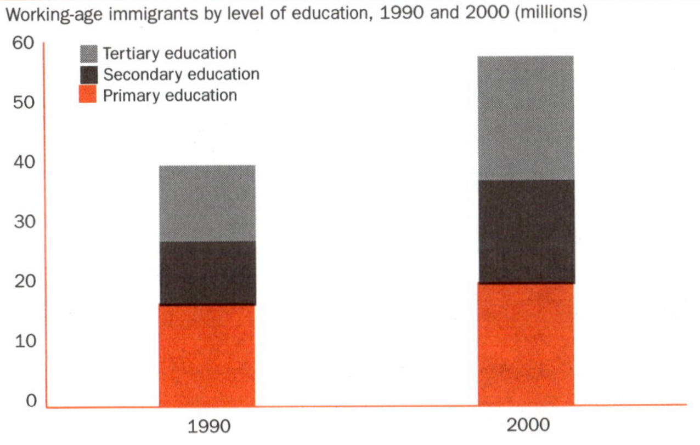

Source: Özden and Schiff 2005.

6.1 Integration with the global economy

	Merchandise trade		Trade in services		Growth in real trade less growth in real GDP	Gross private capital flows		Foreign direct investment			
	% of GDP		% of GDP		percentage points	% of GDP		% of GDP, Net inflows		% of GDP, Net outflows	
	1990	2004	1990	2004	1990–2004	1990	2004	1990	2004	1990	2004
Afghanistan	..	47.2	..	..	..	..	..	..	..	..	..
Albania	29.0	37.7	2.9	*26.6*	*12.8*	18.0	*6.2*	0.0	5.6	0.0	*0.0*
Algeria	36.6	59.7	2.9	..	0.1	2.6	..	0.1	1.0	0.0	..
Angola	53.5	104.4	18.7	26.3	..	10.1	25.7	–3.3	7.4	0.0	0.2
Argentina	11.6	37.1	3.9	7.8	4.1	8.2	15.6	1.3	2.7	0.0	0.2
Armenia	..	65.7	..	18.3	–7.6	..	13.9	0.2	7.1	..	0.1
Australia	26.3	30.7	7.7	8.1	*3.0*	9.3	32.0	2.6	6.7	0.3	2.8
Austria	54.8	80.5	22.7	32.6	3.3	9.6	41.9	0.4	1.4	1.0	2.5
Azerbaijan	..	83.7	..	37.8	*14.4*	..	100.4	*0.0*	41.7	..	14.1
Bangladesh	17.6	35.7	3.6	5.3	4.3	0.9	1.9	0.0	0.8	0.0	0.0
Belarus	..	131.5	..	12.2	–1.9	..	7.5	*0.0*	0.7	..	0.0
Belgium	120.4	168.0	26.4[a]	40.9[a]	2.2	81.5[a]	222.2[a]	3.9[a]	30.9[a]	3.0[a]	26.4[a]
Benin	30.0	37.7	13.9	*12.0*	–2.3	10.7	*5.7*	3.4	1.5	0.0	*0.1*
Bolivia	33.1	45.3	9.4	11.3	1.5	3.1	5.0	0.6	1.3	0.0	0.0
Bosnia and Herzegovina	..	90.2	..	15.0	*–3.8*	..	21.8	..	7.2	..	0.0
Botswana	98.4	75.9	15.4	*17.0*	–2.3	9.0	*20.6*	2.5	0.5	0.2	*2.7*
Brazil	11.7	26.9	2.4	4.9	4.6	1.9	8.8	0.2	3.0	0.1	1.6
Bulgaria	48.9	100.9	6.9	30.6	5.8	39.2	29.6	0.0	8.3	0.0	–0.9
Burkina Faso	22.0	33.2	9.1	..	–1.5	1.0	..	0.0	0.7	0.0	..
Burundi	27.0	34.0	12.9	*8.5*	*6.8*	3.7	*6.2*	0.1	0.5	0.0	*0.0*
Cambodia	22.4	122.2	*5.7*	25.3	*9.8*	*3.2*	8.1	*0.0*	2.7	..	0.2
Cameroon	30.5	33.4	12.8	..	2.0	15.5	..	–1.0	0.0	0.1	..
Canada	43.7	61.0	8.3	10.7	*3.3*	8.1	14.0	1.3	0.6	0.9	4.8
Central African Republic	18.4	20.7	16.0	..	..	2.2	..	0.1	–1.0	0.3	..
Chad	27.2	70.4	15.5	..	4.5	5.6	..	0.5	11.3	0.0	..
Chile	53.1	60.5	12.9	13.3	1.6	15.0	21.5	2.2	8.1	0.0	1.0
China	32.5	59.8	2.9	7.0	5.7	2.5	10.0	1.0	2.8	0.2	0.1
Hong Kong, China	221.5	330.4	..	51.6	3.6	..	145.5	..	20.9	..	24.4
Colombia	30.7	33.7	8.3	6.4	2.7	3.1	10.9	1.2	3.1	0.0	0.1
Congo, Dem. Rep.	43.5	49.6	..	..	*5.9*	..	..	–0.2	0.0	..	..
Congo, Rep.	57.2	129.4	31.0	*17.7*	3.4	6.6	*11.7*	0.8	0.0	0.0	*0.0*
Costa Rica	60.2	78.7	20.3	19.2	3.1	7.0	12.3	2.9	3.4	0.0	0.3
Côte d'Ivoire	47.9	66.3	20.5	17.8	0.7	3.5	5.2	0.4	1.1	0.0	0.0
Croatia	*88.8*	71.7	..	38.6	*4.0*	..	20.8	*0.0*	3.6	..	1.0
Cuba	..	..	..	..	..	..	..	..	..	..	..
Czech Republic	*83.6*	129.1	..	17.7	8.7	..	19.6	0.2	4.2	..	0.5
Denmark	52.6	60.1	17.3	28.9	3.4	15.1	38.0	0.8	–3.6	1.1	–4.1
Dominican Republic	73.2	72.8	21.7	25.4	3.4	5.0	13.5	1.9	3.5	0.0	0.0
Ecuador	44.2	51.2	13.0	9.0	1.9	11.0	13.1	1.2	3.8	0.0	0.0
Egypt, Arab Rep.	36.8	26.0	22.6	28.2	–1.7	6.8	13.3	1.7	1.6	0.0	0.2
El Salvador	38.4	60.4	13.4	13.0	6.2	2.0	12.5	0.0	2.9	0.0	0.0
Eritrea	*77.0*	74.1	..	..	*–1.9*	*53.0*	..	*0.0*	3.2	..	..
Estonia	..	130.6	*9.1*	40.6	*7.5*	*3.9*	51.9	*0.0*	9.3	*0.0*	2.4
Ethiopia	16.0	46.5	7.7	24.6	3.6	1.6	4.0	0.1	6.8	0.0	..
Finland	39.1	60.3	9.0	11.9	4.4	17.4	42.1	0.6	1.7	2.0	–0.8
France	36.4	44.7	11.1	10.2	4.2	20.2	26.1	1.1	1.2	2.8	2.3
Gabon	52.5	66.0	21.0	*16.7*	–1.4	18.0	*18.7*	1.2	4.5	0.5	*0.3*
Gambia, The	69.1	53.5	34.5	..	–3.3	0.9	..	4.5	14.5	0.0	..
Georgia	..	48.0	..	19.6	*10.2*	..	12.4	*0.0*	9.6	..	0.2
Germany	45.5	59.4	8.7	12.2	4.3	9.6	27.4	0.2	–1.3	1.4	–0.3
Ghana	35.7	77.8	6.6	19.9	3.1	2.9	6.8	0.3	1.6	0.0	0.0
Greece	33.2	33.0	11.4	23.0	3.7	3.9	32.3	1.2	0.7	0.0	0.3
Guatemala	36.8	39.1	9.7	9.0	2.9	2.9	11.6	0.6	0.6	0.0	0.0
Guinea	49.5	35.9	18.6	9.3	–1.2	3.9	1.6	0.6	2.6	..	0.0
Guinea-Bissau	43.0	59.6	11.0	*17.7*	4.0	23.0	*14.4*	0.8	1.8	0.0	*0.2*
Haiti	17.2	48.1	4.3	*13.4*	*–1.2*	1.1	*3.9*	0.3	0.2	–0.3	*0.0*

Integration with the global economy

	Merchandise trade		Trade in services		Growth in real trade less growth in real GDP	Gross private capital flows		Foreign direct investment			
	% of GDP		% of GDP		percentage points	% of GDP		% of GDP Net inflows		% of GDP Net outflows	
	1990	2004	1990	2004	1990–2004	1990	2004	1990	2004	1990	2004
Honduras	57.9	74.0	11.7	19.1	*–0.4*	7.2	8.0	1.4	4.0	0.0	0.0
Hungary	61.5	113.4	16.0	20.5	8.5	4.6	24.7	1.9	4.6	0.0	1.1
India	13.1	25.0	3.4	*8.2*	6.8	0.8	*5.9*	0.1	0.8	0.0	*0.2*
Indonesia	41.5	49.4	7.5	17.9	0.5	4.1	4.6	1.0	0.4	0.0	*0.0*
Iran, Islamic Rep.	32.9	48.4	3.7	..	–7.3	2.6	..	–0.3	0.3	0.0	..
Iraq	*55.4*	*155.9*	..	..	..	..	..	..	..	..	..
Ireland	93.9	90.8	18.2	64.4	5.7	22.2	314.1	1.3	6.1	0.8	8.7
Israel	55.0	69.6	18.1	23.5	*1.1*	6.5	18.7	0.3	1.4	0.4	2.7
Italy	32.0	41.7	8.8	9.9	2.7	10.6	10.4	0.6	1.0	0.7	1.1
Jamaica	67.2	58.2	37.5	45.4	..	8.4	45.5	3.0	6.8	0.0	0.7
Japan	17.2	22.1	4.1	5.0	*2.7*	5.4	14.4	0.1	0.2	1.7	0.7
Jordan	91.1	104.9	67.5	36.9	–1.6	6.3	18.1	0.9	5.4	–0.8	*0.0*
Kazakhstan	..	80.7	..	17.1	–2.6	..	41.8	*0.0*	10.1	..	–3.1
Kenya	37.9	45.0	21.4	14.1	2.7	3.5	7.2	0.7	0.3	0.0	0.0
Korea, Dem. Rep.	..	..	..	..	..	..	..	..	..	..	..
Korea, Rep.	51.1	70.4	7.5	13.5	6.3	5.3	8.5	0.3	1.2	0.4	0.7
Kuwait	59.8	73.1	25.2	19.6	*–3.2*	19.3	35.8	0.0	0.0	1.3	3.4
Kyrgyz Republic	..	75.3	..	19.9	*–1.5*	..	17.2	*0.0*	3.5	..	2.0
Lao PDR	30.5	35.4	5.8	..	..	3.7	..	0.7	0.7	0.0	..
Latvia	..	80.7	*9.2*	21.8	*5.1*	*2.3*	43.1	*0.0*	5.1	*0.0*	0.8
Lebanon	106.5	51.2	..	..	–0.7	..	..	0.2	1.3	..	..
Lesotho	119.3	162.0	19.8	12.2	–0.5	9.6	14.2	2.8	9.4	0.0	0.0
Liberia	374.1	230.6	..	..	..	..	..	58.6	4.1	..	..
Libya	64.2	91.0	5.2	7.6	..	7.3	24.5	..	..	0.4	–0.7
Lithuania	..	96.8	..	18.3	*8.2*	..	19.4	*0.0*	3.5	..	1.2
Macedonia, FYR	*103.8*	84.7	..	16.2	4.6	..	11.6	*0.0*	2.9	..	0.0
Madagascar	31.5	50.9	12.8	*14.9*	2.1	1.8	*1.1*	0.7	1.0	0.0	*0.0*
Malawi	52.7	65.6	16.2	*14.0*	–2.1	3.2	*3.1*	1.2	0.9	0.0	..
Malaysia	133.4	195.9	21.2	*29.9*	2.9	10.3	*22.6*	5.3	3.9	0.0	*1.3*
Mali	39.7	50.2	19.0	*16.3*	2.0	2.0	*8.4*	0.2	3.7	0.0	*0.0*
Mauritania	84.1	52.8	16.0	..	*–5.7*	48.8	..	0.7	19.6	0.0	..
Mauritius	118.0	79.2	38.0	41.1	0.1	8.0	6.5	1.7	0.2	0.0	0.5
Mexico	32.1	58.5	7.0	5.0	8.1	9.2	6.9	1.0	2.6	0.0	0.5
Moldova	..	106.4	..	27.4	*11.4*	..	16.9	*0.0*	3.1	..	0.1
Mongolia	..	116.0	..	52.2	*15.5*	..	26.1	..	5.8	..	0.0
Morocco	43.4	54.7	13.4	20.3	1.9	5.5	7.6	0.6	1.5	0.0	0.0
Mozambique	40.8	57.1	12.5	12.9	2.4	0.4	7.9	0.4	4.0	0.0	0.0
Myanmar	..	..	..	..	..	..	..	..	..	..	..
Namibia	95.6	74.7	20.7	15.2	0.2	16.5	23.5	..	..	0.1	–0.4
Nepal	24.1	39.2	10.2	12.4	..	3.5	6.8	0.2	0.0	0.0	..
Netherlands	87.5	117.0	20.0	24.7	3.4	29.8	66.6	3.6	0.1	4.7	3.0
New Zealand	43.3	44.0	13.3	14.9	*2.1*	17.8	15.4	4.0	2.3	3.7	–0.8
Nicaragua	95.9	65.2	17.0	15.1	5.5	9.0	6.1	0.1	5.5	0.0	0.0
Niger	27.0	30.2	10.9	*9.4*	..	2.8	*2.3*	1.7	0.0	0.0	*0.0*
Nigeria	67.5	48.2	10.3	11.5	1.5	5.9	11.0	2.1	2.6	0.0	..
Norway	52.8	51.9	21.6	20.1	1.3	11.9	31.8	0.9	0.2	1.3	0.8
Oman	70.1	91.4	6.7	14.7	2.5	3.5	8.6	1.2	–0.1	0.0	0.0
Pakistan	32.6	32.6	8.8	8.4	–0.8	4.2	3.5	0.6	1.2	0.0	0.1
Panama	35.4	32.6	33.5	30.4	–3.7	106.6	39.0	2.6	7.4	0.0	0.0
Papua New Guinea	73.6	107.8	18.9	..	..	5.7	..	4.8	0.7	0.0	..
Paraguay	43.9	58.3	16.2	12.6	–3.3	5.4	3.4	1.5	1.3	0.0	0.1
Peru	22.3	33.0	7.5	6.8	3.2	3.2	6.8	0.2	2.6	0.0	0.0
Philippines	47.8	97.0	11.3	11.2	2.6	4.4	13.7	1.2	0.6	0.0	0.5
Poland	43.9	67.7	10.3	10.7	7.5	11.0	18.1	0.2	5.2	0.0	0.3
Portugal	58.3	54.1	12.7	14.6	3.2	11.4	37.6	3.7	0.5	0.2	3.6
Puerto Rico	..	..	..	..	*–0.5*	..	..	..	..	..	..

6.1

Integration with the global economy

	Merchandise trade		Trade in services		Growth in real trade less growth in real GDP	Gross private capital flows		Foreign direct investment			
	% of GDP		% of GDP		percentage points	% of GDP		% of GDP			
								Net inflows		Net outflows	
	1990	2004	1990	2004	1990–2004	1990	2004	1990	2004	1990	2004
Romania	32.8	76.7	3.6	10.2	8.5	2.9	14.2	0.0	7.4	0.0	0.1
Russian Federation	..	48.1	..	9.3	3.3	..	16.0	*0.0*	2.1	..	1.8
Rwanda	15.4	20.8	6.6	18.3	−0.6	2.8	1.0	0.3	0.4	0.0	0.0
Saudi Arabia	58.6	68.2	21.8	12.6	..	8.8	20.0	..	..	0.0	0.0
Senegal	34.7	54.5	20.9	*15.5*	2.1	4.8	*4.9*	1.0	0.9	−0.2	*0.0*
Serbia and Montenegro	..	65.6	..	..	..	..	..	..	4.0	..	..
Sierra Leone	44.2	39.5	20.9	14.0	..	11.0	6.8	4.9	2.4	0.0	*0.0*
Singapore	307.6	321.5	58.1	76.6	..	54.2	116.9	15.1	15.0	5.5	9.9
Slovak Republic	*110.8*	138.8	..	*19.4*	*6.8*	..	*15.5*	*0.0*	2.7	..	*0.1*
Slovenia	*102.4*	102.6	*18.0*	18.8	1.9	*3.4*	22.4	*0.9*	2.6	*0.0*	1.7
Somalia	..	..	*11.2*	..	..	*21.3*	..	0.6	..	*0.0*	..
South Africa	37.4	48.5	6.4	8.3	2.6	2.2	8.6	−0.1	0.3	0.0	0.7
Spain	27.2	41.1	8.4	13.7	5.7	11.0	30.8	2.7	1.6	0.7	4.8
Sri Lanka	57.3	68.5	13.4	17.1	2.5	13.1	5.2	0.5	1.2	0.0	0.0
Sudan	7.5	37.2	3.0	5.3	*4.8*	0.3	10.4	−0.2	7.2	0.0	0.0
Swaziland	138.2	162.8	32.4	43.1	1.1	10.7	7.0	3.4	2.9	0.9	0.1
Sweden	46.6	64.0	12.8	20.7	4.2	33.9	44.8	0.8	−0.2	6.1	4.4
Switzerland	56.6	64.4	12.8	18.8	*2.9*	28.1	54.8	2.4	−0.2	2.3	7.3
Syrian Arab Republic	53.7	46.7	14.3	19.1	2.8	18.0	1.6	0.6	1.1	0.0	0.0
Tajikistan	..	110.5	..	16.2	*4.5*	..	16.1	*0.0*	13.1	..	0.0
Tanzania	31.9	35.3	9.8	17.6	−1.0	0.2	3.5	0.0	2.3	0.0	*0.0*
Thailand	65.7	119.2	14.9	26.1	2.9	13.5	7.9	2.9	0.9	0.2	0.1
Togo	52.1	88.4	24.1	*17.0*	−1.3	9.6	*14.8*	1.1	2.9	0.0	*−0.4*
Trinidad and Tobago	60.6	89.6	15.9	*10.1*	3.7	11.4	*25.2*	2.2	8.0	0.0	*−2.1*
Tunisia	73.5	79.6	20.6	19.9	−0.1	9.5	6.6	0.6	2.1	0.0	0.0
Turkey	23.4	53.1	7.4	11.7	7.0	4.3	12.8	0.5	0.9	0.0	0.3
Turkmenistan	..	116.6	..	..	*8.5*	..	..	..	..	..	..
Uganda	10.2	31.2	4.5	16.8	2.8	1.1	4.8	−0.1	3.3	0.0	0.0
Ukraine	..	95.1	..	17.6	3.6	..	34.2	*0.0*	2.6	..	0.0
United Arab Emirates	103.2	125.1	..	..	*1.9*	..	..	..	..	..	..
United Kingdom	41.2	38.1	10.6	15.4	3.4	35.3	91.7	3.4	3.4	2.0	3.8
United States	15.8	20.0	4.6	5.4	*4.0*	5.6	20.0	0.8	0.9	0.6	2.2
Uruguay	32.7	45.9	9.2	12.6	2.1	12.7	22.0	0.4	2.4	0.0	0.1
Uzbekistan	..	64.1	..	..	*−1.2*	..	..	*0.0*	1.2	..	..
Venezuela, RB	52.8	44.7	7.9	5.3	0.6	51.6	16.2	1.0	1.4	0.8	−0.3
Vietnam	79.7	125.4	..	*19.0*	14.6	..	*5.8*	2.8	3.6	..	*0.0*
West Bank and Gaza	..	..	..	..	*−3.1*	..	..	..	..	..	..
Yemen, Rep.	46.9	65.0	16.3	11.1	1.7	16.2	1.6	−2.7	1.1	..	*0.0*
Zambia	76.9	68.8	15.0	..	1.4	64.7	..	6.2	6.2	0.0	..
Zimbabwe	40.7	86.7	8.6	..	5.7	1.7	..	−0.1	1.3	0.0	..
World	**32.4 w**	**44.9 w**	**7.8 w**	**10.5 w**		**10.3 w**	**28.4 w**	**1.0 w**	**1.6 w**	**1.2 w**	**2.1 w**
Low income	24.1	37.8	6.5	*9.4*		2.7	*6.9*	0.4	1.4	0.0	*0.2*
Middle income	34.4	61.5	7.1	10.2		6.6	12.2	0.8	2.8	0.1	0.5
Lower middle income	31.5	57.5	6.2	10.3		4.3	10.7	0.7	2.7	0.1	0.3
Upper middle income	*38.3*	67.0	*8.1*	10.2		*8.0*	14.2	*1.0*	2.8	*0.3*	0.7
Low & middle income	32.5	58.1	7.0	10.3		5.9	11.9	0.7	2.6	0.1	0.5
East Asia & Pacific	47.0	71.1	7.3	9.6		5.0	9.4	1.6	2.5	0.2	0.1
Europe & Central Asia	*49.7*	70.9	*7.1*	13.4		*5.3*	18.8	*0.3*	3.5	*0.0*	0.9
Latin America & Carib.	23.3	44.6	5.8	6.9		8.0	10.4	0.8	3.0	0.1	0.7
Middle East & N. Africa	42.9	55.1	9.1	..		4.9	..	0.3	1.1	0.0	..
South Asia	16.5	27.9	4.2	*8.2*		1.4	*5.4*	0.1	0.8	0.0	*0.2*
Sub-Saharan Africa	42.4	54.7	11.0	12.1		5.1	9.5	0.4	2.2	0.0	*0.3*
High income	32.3	41.5	8.0	10.5		11.0	32.0	1.0	1.3	1.4	2.4
Europe EMU	44.4	59.4	11.1	14.8		13.4	41.3	1.1	1.3	1.7	2.6

a. Includes Luxembourg.

Integration with the global economy

About the data

The growing integration of societies and economies has helped reduce poverty in many countries. One indication of increasing global economic integration is the growing importance of trade in the world economy. Another is the increasing size and importance of private capital flows to developing countries that have liberalized their financial markets.

The table presents standardized measures of the size of trade and capital flows relative to gross domestic product (GDP). The numerators on trade and private capital flows are based on gross flows that capture the two-way flow of goods, services, and capital. In conventional balance of payments accounting exports are recorded as a credit and imports as a debit. And in the financial account inward investment is a credit and outward investment a debit. Thus net flows, the sum of credits and debits, represent a balance in which many transactions are canceled out. Gross flows are a better measure of integration because they show the total value of financial transactions during a given period.

Merchandise trade and trade in services (exports and imports) are shown relative to total GDP. Merchandise trade is an important part of global trade. Trade in services (such as transport, travel, finance, insurance, royalties, construction, communications, and cultural services) is an increasingly important element of global integration. The difference between the growth of real trade in goods and services and the growth of GDP helps to identify economies that have integrated with the global economy by liberalizing trade, lowering barriers to foreign investment, and harnessing their abundant labor to gain a competitive advantage in labor-intensive manufactures and services.

This year the table includes net inflows and outflows of foreign direct investment based on balance of payments data reported by the International Monetary Fund (IMF), supplemented by staff estimates using data reported by the United Nations Conference on Trade and Development and official national sources.

The internationally accepted definition of foreign direct investment is provided in the fifth edition of the IMF's *Balance of Payments Manual* (1993). For a more detailed explanation of foreign direct investment, see *About the data* for table 6.8.

Foreign direct investment may be understated in many developing countries. Some countries fail to report reinvested earnings, and the definition of long-term loans differs among countries. Underreporting of FDI outflows is more pervasive, particularly when investors are attempting to avoid controls on capital and foreign exchange or high taxes on investment income. Some countries do not identify FDI outflows in their balance of payments statistics. However, the quality and coverage of the data are improving as a result of continuous efforts by international and national statistics agencies.

Trade and capital flows are converted to U.S. dollars at the IMF's average official exchange rate for the year shown. An alternative conversion factor is applied if the official exchange rate diverges by an exceptionally large margin from the rate effectively applied to transactions in foreign currencies and traded products.

6.1a

Trade in services is becoming increasingly important

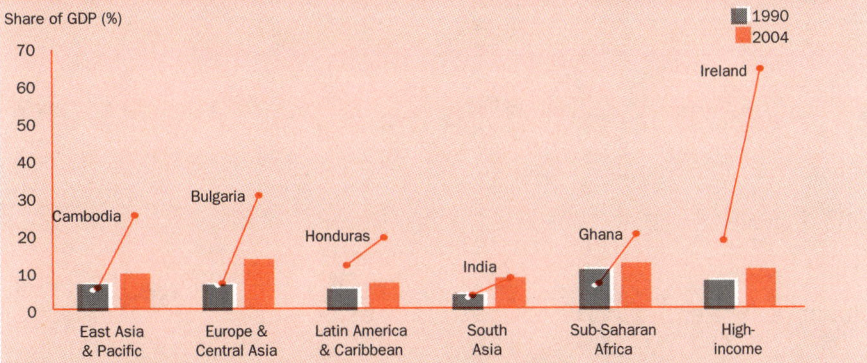

Although services trade makes up only 20 percent of global trade, it is rising fast in some regions. Some countries have benefited considerably from the fast-growing services trade.

Source: International Monetary Fund Balance of Payments database.

Definitions

• **Merchandise trade** is the sum of merchandise exports and imports divided by the value of GDP, all in current U.S. dollars. • **Trade in services** is the sum of services exports and imports divided by the value of GDP, all in current U.S. dollars. • **Growth in real trade less growth in real GDP** is the difference between annual growth in trade of goods and services and annual growth in GDP. Growth rates are calculated using constant price series taken from national accounts and are expressed as a percentage. • **Gross private capital flows** are the sum of the absolute values of direct, portfolio, and other investment inflows and outflows recorded in the balance of payments financial account, excluding changes in the assets and liabilities of monetary authorities and general government. The indicator is calculated as a ratio to GDP in U.S. dollars. • **Foreign direct investment net inflows** are the net inflows of investment to acquire a lasting management interest in an enterprise operating in an economy other than that of the investor. It is the sum of equity capital, reinvestment of earnings, and other short- and long-term capital, as shown in the balance of payments. This series shows net inflows in the reporting economy and is divided by the value of GDP. • **Foreign direct investment net outflows** are the net outflows of investment from the reporting economy to the rest of the world.

Data sources

Data on merchandise trade are from the World Trade Organization. Data on GDP are from the World Bank's national accounts files, converted from national currencies to U.S. dollars using the official exchange rate, supplemented by an alternative conversion factor if the official exchange rate is judged to diverge by an exceptionally large margin from the rate effectively applied to transactions in foreign currencies and traded products. Data on trade in services are from the IMF's Balance of Payments database. Data on real trade and GDP growth are from the World Bank's national accounts files. Gross private capital flows and foreign direct investment are reported in the World Bank Debtor Reporting System and are calculated using mainly the IMF's Balance of Payments database.

6.2 Growth of merchandise trade

	Export volume		Import volume		Export value		Import value		Net barter terms of trade index	
	average annual % growth		average annual % growth		average annual % growth		average annual % growth		2000 = 100	
	1980–90	1990–2004	1980–90	1990–2004	1980–90	1990–2004	1980–90	1990–2004	1990	2004
Afghanistan	..	..	..	..	..	..	..	..	..	..
Albania[a]	..	..	..	..	..	*14.6*	..	*16.6*	..	..
Algeria	4.7	2.7	–8.0	1.7	–3.1	5.8	–2.7	1.2	74	126
Angola	*9.0*	5.8	*–1.9*	8.2	6.4	9.6	0.7	9.3	94	121
Argentina	2.1	6.9	–9.6	6.4	2.1	7.8	–6.5	5.3	64	110
Armenia[a]	..	..	..	..	..	1.3	..	3.6	..	..
Australia[a]	6.3	5.5	6.0	7.6	6.6	4.8	6.4	6.0	116	116
Austria[a]	6.6	..	5.7	..	10.2	6.3	8.7	4.6	..	..
Azerbaijan[a]	..	..	..	..	..	*8.6*	..	*8.2*	..	..
Bangladesh	7.1	10.5	1.8	4.1	7.8	12.4	3.6	8.2	117	88
Belarus[a]	..	..	..	..	..	*13.2*	..	*13.2*	..	..
Belgium[a]	..	*5.8*	..	*5.4*	..	*6.2*	..	*6.4*	*106*	99
Benin	11.8	3.0	–9.9	5.9	18.8	3.6	–4.9	6.3	107	93
Bolivia	3.1	4.9	–1.3	5.2	–1.9	5.6	–0.3	5.8	102	108
Bosnia and Herzegovina	..	..	..	..	..	..	..	..	..	..
Botswana	14.8	3.8	11.5	2.3	18.8	3.4	11.1	1.3	98	92
Brazil	6.3	6.7	0.7	10.6	5.1	6.6	–1.9	7.6	66	110
Bulgaria[a]	..	..	..	..	*–12.3*	4.8	*–14.0*	8.2	..	..
Burkina Faso	–0.3	12.1	3.8	5.0	7.9	10.5	4.3	5.2	119	97
Burundi	3.5	8.0	1.0	6.3	2.5	–6.3	2.2	–3.9	128	84
Cambodia	..	..	..	..	..	..	..	..	..	..
Cameroon	7.0	3.3	4.8	7.2	1.4	2.7	0.1	4.6	81	112
Canada[a]	6.4	6.9	7.4	7.2	6.8	6.7	7.9	6.1	97	107
Central African Republic	0.0	14.7	4.2	1.6	3.5	1.7	7.9	–1.3	238	99
Chad	8.6	7.7	11.0	13.0	9.4	7.8	12.6	13.6	112	101
Chile	9.2	9.4	–3.0	6.8	8.1	8.2	2.8	7.1	114	115
China[†]	13.6	15.6	11.9	15.1	12.8	15.5	13.5	15.4	102	92
Hong Kong, China	15.4	7.4	13.7	7.5	16.8	6.5	15.0	6.7	100	99
Colombia	7.9	4.4	–2.1	6.2	7.7	5.9	0.0	6.6	81	93
Congo, Dem. Rep.	9.7	4.4	12.2	11.0	2.7	–3.3	3.1	1.5	86	94
Congo, Rep.	7.4	4.5	3.3	6.7	2.1	8.6	5.3	6.1	63	121
Costa Rica	3.8	10.1	5.2	11.8	4.6	11.3	4.4	11.0	75	102
Côte d'Ivoire	2.6	4.6	–2.1	0.7	1.7	6.0	–1.5	3.0	143	121
Croatia[a]	..	..	..	..	..	3.5	..	9.1	..	..
Cuba	..	..	..	..	..	..	..	..	..	..
Czech Republic[a]	..	..	..	..	..	*12.5*	..	*11.7*	..	..
Denmark[a]	4.1	5.1	3.1	5.1	9.0	4.1	6.8	4.2	102	102
Dominican Republic	–0.9	3.5	2.9	8.3	–2.1	4.2	5.4	8.6	96	95
Ecuador	7.1	4.7	–1.8	7.6	–0.4	6.2	–1.3	8.8	114	108
Egypt, Arab Rep.	13.4	3.4	8.1	–0.5	7.3	4.2	12.6	2.0	101	107
El Salvador	–4.6	3.2	4.6	6.6	–4.6	6.9	2.4	9.4	84	91
Eritrea	..	*–2.8*	..	*8.1*	..	*–4.2*	..	*7.2*	*99*	93
Estonia[a]	..	..	..	..	..	*16.0*	..	*16.7*	..	..
Ethiopia	*–1.0*	9.7	*4.0*	9.6	–1.1	7.6	4.3	10.2	121	91
Finland[a]	2.3	*9.3*	4.4	*4.3*	7.4	6.5	6.9	5.3	111	90
France[a]	3.6	3.6	3.7	3.6	7.5	4.2	6.5	4.1	103	111
Gabon	2.5	5.8	–3.5	1.3	–3.9	2.5	1.1	1.1	157	125
Gambia, The	2.2	–9.3	–6.0	–0.8	6.6	–9.1	2.5	–1.3	100	115
Georgia	..	..	..	..	..	*12.5*	..	*9.6*	..	..
Germany[a, b]	4.5	*5.9*	4.9	*4.3*	9.2	5.0	7.1	4.0	110	107
Ghana	–17.2	4.7	–19.3	6.5	–2.7	6.6	0.6	6.6	100	123
Greece[a]	5.0	*9.1*	6.4	*9.2*	5.8	2.8	6.6	5.6	99	103
Guatemala	–1.1	6.8	0.1	9.8	–2.2	6.7	0.6	10.7	115	93
Guinea	..	3.2	..	2.5	4.0	0.2	9.7	–0.5	122	106
Guinea-Bissau	–2.0	14.0	–0.3	–4.1	4.2	11.7	5.2	–3.1	146	94
Haiti	–0.4	11.6	–4.6	10.8	–1.2	11.2	–2.9	12.4	132	87
[†]Data for Taiwan, China	*26.1*	2.8	*30.3*	3.3	14.9	5.8	12.4	6.4	97	92

Growth of merchandise trade

	Export volume average annual % growth		Import volume average annual % growth		Export value average annual % growth		Import value average annual % growth		Net barter terms of trade index 2000 = 100	
	1980–90	**1990–2004**	**1980–90**	**1990–2004**	**1980–90**	**1990–2004**	**1980–90**	**1990–2004**	**1990**	**2004**
Honduras	4.1	2.7	1.6	10.5	1.6	4.9	0.6	11.6	78	90
Hungary[a]	3.4	11.6	1.3	11.9	1.6	13.8	0.1	13.8	111	99
India	4.2	11.5	4.7	10.8	7.3	9.7	4.2	10.3	86	76
Indonesia	7.6	5.9	*0.3*	3.3	–1.3	6.5	2.6	3.2	95	104
Iran, Islamic Rep.	..	..	..	..	7.2	4.8	0.2	0.8	..	..
Iraq	..	..	..	..	*2.0*	*23.6*	–2.8	*1.5*	..	..
Ireland[a]	9.3	12.8	4.8	9.0	12.8	12.0	7.0	8.9	106	97
Israel[a]	6.9	8.6	5.8	6.6	8.3	9.3	5.9	6.4	89	95
Italy[a]	4.3	3.2	5.3	3.6	8.7	4.5	6.9	4.4	94	103
Jamaica	–1.0	1.4	..	..	1.1	0.8	2.8	5.8	..	..
Japan[a]	5.0	2.6	6.6	4.8	8.9	3.3	5.1	4.2	105	92
Jordan	7.7	7.3	1.2	4.3	6.2	8.4	–1.9	6.4	94	87
Kazakhstan[a]	..	..	..	..	..	*14.9*	..	*9.9*	..	..
Kenya	1.7	5.0	2.5	6.1	–1.1	5.5	1.7	5.5	70	91
Korea, Dem. Rep.	..	..	..	..	..	..	..	..	..	..
Korea, Rep.	12.4	14.9	11.8	8.9	15.0	8.8	11.9	6.9	133	85
Kuwait	..	..	..	..	–7.7	13.2	–4.1	5.6	..	..
Kyrgyz Republic[a]	..	..	..	..	..	*4.8*	..	*4.8*	..	..
Lao PDR[a]	..	..	..	..	11.0	9.2	6.6	6.0	..	..
Latvia[a]	..	*7.5*	..	..	..	*11.7*	..	*16.5*	..	..
Lebanon	..	..	..	..	–5.2	8.2	–5.5	8.5	..	..
Lesotho	7.2	16.0	3.9	2.8	3.7	14.7	3.5	1.6	100	91
Liberia	..	..	..	..	..	..	..	..	..	..
Libya	*2.8*	*–3.3*	*–1.8*	*–1.3*	–7.4	*–1.7*	–4.4	*–1.9*	..	..
Lithuania[a]	..	..	..	..	..	*13.8*	..	*15.0*	..	..
Macedonia, FYR[a]	..	..	..	..	..	*2.4*	..	*5.5*	..	..
Madagascar	–2.5	4.6	–6.2	4.3	–1.2	7.9	–4.3	5.8	81	82
Malawi	2.4	3.0	–0.1	–0.3	2.0	0.8	3.3	1.0	148	82
Malaysia	4.8	11.4	8.5	8.5	8.6	9.3	7.7	7.2	103	99
Mali	4.4	*10.9*	3.0	*6.2*	6.0	8.6	2.7	5.7	135	*113*
Mauritania	3.9	1.2	–3.1	3.9	8.0	–3.0	–2.1	0.3	97	95
Mauritius	11.5	2.3	11.7	2.3	14.4	3.4	12.9	3.2	93	89
Mexico	15.3	12.4	0.9	11.1	5.9	12.9	6.4	11.6	102	98
Moldova[a]	..	..	..	..	..	*2.7*	..	*6.0*	..	..
Mongolia	..	..	..	..	5.0	3.3	5.5	4.9	..	..
Morocco	5.7	6.6	3.2	7.6	6.2	6.5	3.6	6.0	85	98
Mozambique	–9.5	21.5	–2.7	2.3	–9.6	16.3	0.1	3.1	175	94
Myanmar	*–8.4*	18.5	*–18.1*	8.6	–7.6	16.7	–4.7	14.8	252	102
Namibia	..	1.5	..	4.7	..	0.3	..	1.7	93	97
Nepal[a]	..	..	..	..	8.1	8.7	6.9	6.8	..	..
Netherlands[a]	4.4	6.0	4.3	5.5	4.6	5.6	4.4	5.2	101	96
New Zealand[a]	3.5	4.3	4.4	5.9	6.2	4.2	5.4	5.5	105	110
Nicaragua	–4.8	8.6	–3.5	7.2	–5.8	7.7	–3.1	9.3	155	91
Niger	–5.2	1.4	–5.2	–0.9	–5.4	0.8	–3.5	1.4	165	131
Nigeria	–4.4	1.9	–20.8	5.2	–8.4	5.7	–15.0	5.8	89	122
Norway[a]	4.2	5.3	3.5	6.5	5.3	6.2	6.2	3.7	67	100
Oman	*11.2*	*2.4*	..	..	3.3	7.4	0.7	6.5	..	136
Pakistan	8.0	4.7	2.7	2.2	8.1	4.9	3.0	3.7	109	85
Panama	–0.5	5.1	–6.7	4.2	–0.5	7.0	–3.6	5.3	69	94
Papua New Guinea	–0.6	–6.8	..	..	4.9	1.8	0.7	–0.7	..	113
Paraguay	12.8	1.9	10.4	*1.6*	11.6	3.6	4.2	2.7	103	*112*
Peru	2.7	10.0	–2.0	5.4	–1.5	8.9	1.3	5.9	114	109
Philippines	19.5	13.8	21.0	9.9	3.9	13.6	2.9	8.8	87	84
Poland[a]	4.8	10.9	1.5	14.7	1.4	11.8	–3.2	15.0	92	107
Portugal[a]	*11.9*	*0.1*	*15.1*	*–0.2*	15.1	4.8	10.3	4.3	103	*102*
Puerto Rico	..	..	..	..	..	..	..	..	..	..

Growth of merchandise trade

	Export volume		Import volume		Export value		Import value		Net barter terms of trade index	
	average annual % growth		average annual % growth		average annual % growth		average annual % growth		2000 = 100	
	1980–90	1990–2004	1980–90	1990–2004	1980–90	1990–2004	1980–90	1990–2004	1990	2004
Romania[a]	..	..	..	..	–4.0	11.0	–3.8	10.3	..	..
Russian Federation[a]	..	..	..	..	..	*9.8*	..	*5.0*	..	..
Rwanda	2.6	–2.6	1.8	–0.2	–0.9	–0.5	2.7	–0.9	40	89
Saudi Arabia	–8.3	1.1	..	..	–12.7	5.6	–6.1	2.3	..	135
Senegal	1.2	10.5	0.4	6.1	3.5	4.7	1.4	5.8	172	96
Serbia and Montenegro	..	..	..	..	..	..	..	..	..	..
Sierra Leone	..	..	..	..	..	..	..	..	..	78
Singapore	12.2	9.7	8.6	5.9	9.9	7.5	8.0	5.5	116	89
Slovak Republic[a]	..	..	..	..	..	*13.0*	..	*12.8*	..	..
Slovenia[a]	..	..	..	..	..	7.9	..	8.3	..	..
Somalia	..	..	..	..	..	..	..	..	..	..
South Africa	1.6	4.7	–0.9	7.1	0.7	3.5	–1.3	5.6	104	120
Spain	2.5	9.7	8.8	8.9	10.8	8.1	10.6	7.2	100	102
Sri Lanka	4.6	5.9	2.1	*6.4*	5.4	7.7	2.7	6.6	82	104
Sudan	..	..	..	..	..	..	..	..	..	121
Swaziland	7.6	4.0	2.4	2.0	4.7	4.6	–0.5	3.1	100	94
Sweden[a]	4.4	7.6	5.0	5.4	8.0	5.0	6.7	4.2	108	92
Switzerland[a]	*3.7*	..	*4.3*	..	9.5	3.6	8.8	2.8	..	..
Syrian Arab Republic	19.6	3.4	..	..	2.4	4.5	–8.4	3.1	..	113
Tajikistan	..	..	..	..	..	..	..	..	..	..
Tanzania	..	8.6	..	2.0	–5.1	8.7	–0.5	2.7	107	100
Thailand	13.8	8.9	11.1	2.8	14.0	8.8	12.7	5.2	119	92
Togo	–1.2	12.6	0.7	0.3	1.1	7.1	2.0	6.3	133	30
Trinidad and Tobago	0.1	..	–2.4	..	–9.4	9.2	–12.3	11.1	..	..
Tunisia	3.0	6.6	1.6	5.6	3.5	6.5	2.7	5.5	109	99
Turkey	19.4	11.6	15.6	9.6	14.0	10.2	9.3	9.4	109	102
Turkmenistan	..	..	..	..	..	..	..	..	..	..
Uganda	*–13.5*	14.4	*–6.8*	13.2	–4.0	9.8	4.5	12.7	146	88
Ukraine[a]	..	..	..	..	..	*9.5*	..	*7.9*	..	..
United Arab Emirates	..	..	..	..	–0.8	*8.1*	0.7	*10.7*	..	..
United Kingdom[a]	..	..	..	..	5.9	4.3	8.5	5.1	101	105
United States[a]	3.6	4.8	7.2	8.0	5.7	5.1	8.2	8.3	101	101
Uruguay	4.4	3.4	–0.5	3.4	4.5	2.9	–1.2	3.5	116	108
Uzbekistan	..	..	..	..	..	..	..	..	..	..
Venezuela, RB	3.4	2.4	–4.1	1.6	–4.4	5.7	–3.2	2.5	90	108
Vietnam	..	..	..	..	..	*15.8*	..	*13.7*	..	..
West Bank and Gaza	..	..	..	..	..	..	..	..	..	..
Yemen, Rep.	..	..	*–7.2*	6.3	–3.2	17.0	–5.0	2.9	..	117
Zambia	–0.5	6.5	2.0	6.6	0.9	–0.1	0.0	4.5	207	119
Zimbabwe	3.6	7.7	3.4	7.2	2.5	2.6	–0.5	1.9	98	104

a. Data are from the International Monetary Fund's International Financial Statistics database. b. Data prior to 1990 refer to the Federal Republic of Germany before unification.

About the data

Data on international trade in goods are available from each country's balance of payments and customs records. While the balance of payments focuses on the financial transactions that accompany trade, customs data record the direction of trade and the physical quantities and value of goods entering or leaving the customs area. Customs data may differ from data recorded in the balance of payments because of differences in valuation and the time of recording. The 1993 System of National Accounts and the fifth edition of the International Monetary Fund's (IMF) *Balance of Payments Manual* (1993) attempted to reconcile the definitions and reporting standards for international trade statistics, but differences in sources, timing, and national practices limit comparability. Real growth rates derived from trade volume indexes and terms of trade based on unit price indexes may therefore differ from those derived from national accounts aggregates.

Trade in goods, or merchandise trade, includes all goods that add to or subtract from an economy's material resources. Thus the total supply of goods in an economy is made up of gross output plus imports less exports (currency in circulation, titles of ownership, and securities are excluded, but nonmonetary gold is included). Trade data are collected on the basis of a country's customs area, which in most cases is the same as its geographic area. Goods provided as part of foreign aid are included, but goods destined for extraterritorial agencies (such as embassies) are not.

Collecting and tabulating trade statistics are difficult. Some developing countries lack the capacity to report timely data. This is a problem especially for countries that are landlocked and those whose territorial boundaries are porous. As a result, it is necessary to estimate their trade from the data reported by their partners. (For further discussion of the use of partner country reports, see *About the data* for table 6.3.) Countries that belong to common customs unions may need to collect data through direct inquiry of companies. In some cases economic or political concerns may lead national authorities to suppress or misrepresent data on certain trade flows, such as oil, military equipment, or the exports of a dominant producer. In other cases reported trade data may be distorted by deliberate under- or over-invoicing to effect capital transfers or avoid taxes. And in some regions smuggling and black market trading result in unreported trade flows.

By international agreement customs data are reported to the United Nations Statistics Division, which maintains the Commodity Trade (Comtrade) database. The United Nations Conference on Trade and Development (UNCTAD) compiles a variety of international trade statistics, including price and volume indexes, based on the Comtrade data. The IMF and the World Trade Organization also compile data on trade prices and volumes. The growth rates and terms of trade for low- and middle-income economies shown in the table were calculated from index numbers compiled by UNCTAD. Volume measures for high-income economies were derived by deflating the value of trade using deflators from the IMF's *International Financial Statistics*. In some cases price and volume indexes from different sources may vary significantly as a result of differences in estimation procedures. All indexes are rescaled to a 2000 base year. Terms of trade were computed from the same indicators.

The terms of trade measures the relative prices of a country's exports and imports. There are a number of ways to calculate terms of trade. The most common is the net barter (or commodity) terms of trade index, constructed as the ratio of the export price index to the import price index. When a country's net barter terms of trade index increases, its exports become more valuable or its imports cheaper.

Definitions

• **Export** and **import volumes** are average annual growth rates calculated for low- and middle-income economies from UNCTAD's quantum index series and for high-income economies from export and import data deflated by the IMF's trade price deflators. • **Export** and **import values** are average annual growth rates calculated from UNCTAD's value indexes or from current values of merchandise exports and imports. • **Net barter terms of trade index** is calculated as the ratio of the export price index to the corresponding import price index measured relative to the base year 2000.

6.2a

Exports are growing in developing countries

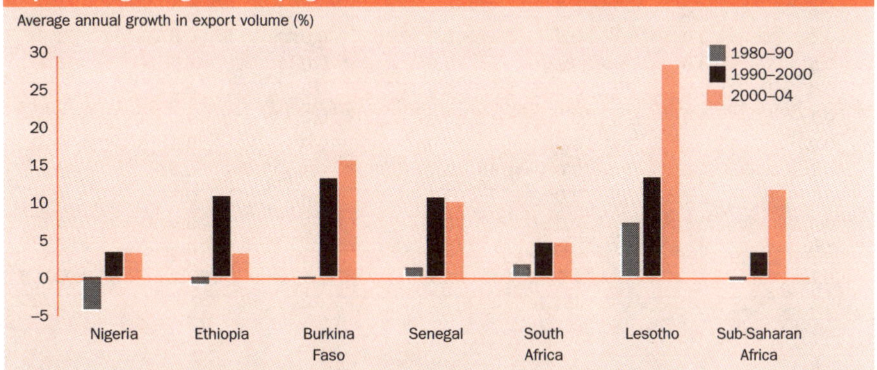

Sub-Saharan countries have reversed the decline of exports in goods since 1990 and experienced encouraging growth over the last five years.

Source: United Nations Conference on Trade and Development.

Data sources

The main source of trade data for developing countries is UNCTAD's annual *Handbook of Statistics*. The IMF's *International Financial Statistics* includes data on the export and import values and deflators for high-income and selected developing economies.

6.3 Direction and growth of merchandise trade

Direction of trade

High-income importers

% of world trade, 2004

Source of exports	European Union	Japan	United States	Other high-income	All high-income
High-income economies	30.7	2.7	9.9	12.5	55.8
European Union	24.3	0.6	3.3	3.8	32.1
Japan	1.0	..	1.5	2.0	4.5
United States	1.9	0.6	..	3.7	6.3
Other high-income economies	3.4	1.5	5.2	2.9	13.0
Low- and middle-income economies	7.7	1.9	6.2	5.3	21.0
East Asia & Pacific	1.8	1.5	2.2	3.9	9.3
China	1.1	0.8	1.4	2.2	5.6
Europe & Central Asia	3.6	0.1	0.3	0.4	4.3
Russian Federation	0.8	0.0	0.1	0.2	1.1
Latin America & Caribbean	0.7	0.1	2.9	0.3	4.0
Brazil	0.2	0.0	0.2	0.1	0.6
Middle East & N. Africa	0.9	0.1	0.2	0.2	1.5
Algeria	0.2	0.0	0.1	0.0	0.3
South Asia	0.3	0.0	0.2	0.3	0.8
India	0.2	0.0	0.1	0.2	0.6
Sub-Saharan Africa	0.4	0.1	0.4	0.1	1.0
South Africa	0.2	0.0	0.1	0.1	0.3
World	38.4	4.6	16.1	17.8	76.8

Low- and middle-income importers

% of world trade, 2004

Source of exports	East Asia & Pacific	Europe & Central Asia	Latin America & Caribbean	Middle East & N. Africa	South Asia	Sub-Saharan Africa	All low- & middle-income	World
High-income economies	6.8	4.2	1.6	1.3	0.9	0.9	15.7	71.5
European Union	1.1	3.6	0.5	0.8	0.3	0.5	6.9	39.0
Japan	1.5	0.1	0.2	0.1	0.1	0.1	1.9	6.4
United States	0.7	0.1	0.7	0.1	0.1	0.1	1.8	8.1
Other high-income economies	3.5	0.3	0.3	0.3	0.4	0.2	5.1	18.1
Low- and middle-income economies	2.2	2.4	1.1	0.6	0.5	0.5	7.5	28.5
East Asia & Pacific	1.3	0.4	0.2	0.2	0.3	0.2	2.5	11.8
China	0.4	0.3	0.1	0.1	0.1	0.1	1.1	6.7
Europe & Central Asia	0.2	1.8	0.0	0.2	0.1	0.0	2.4	6.7
Russian Federation	0.1	0.6	0.0	0.1	0.0	0.0	0.8	1.9
Latin America & Caribbean	0.2	0.1	0.8	0.1	0.0	0.0	1.2	5.2
Brazil	0.1	0.0	0.2	0.0	0.0	0.0	0.4	1.0
Middle East & N. Africa	0.2	0.1	0.0	0.1	0.0	0.0	0.5	2.0
Algeria	0.0	0.0	0.0	0.0	0.0	0.0	0.1	0.4
South Asia	0.1	0.0	0.0	0.0	0.1	0.1	0.3	1.2
India	0.1	0.0	0.0	0.0	0.1	0.0	0.3	0.9
Sub-Saharan Africa	0.2	0.0	0.1	0.0	0.0	0.2	0.5	1.5
South Africa	0.0	0.0	0.0	0.0	0.0	0.1	0.1	0.5
World	9.0	6.7	2.7	1.9	1.4	1.5	23.2	100.0

Direction and growth of merchandise trade

Nominal growth of trade

High-income importers

annual % growth, 1994–2004

Source of exports	European Union	Japan	United States	Other high-income	All high-income
High-income economies	7.8	3.8	6.3	5.6	6.8
European Union	8.5	4.9	9.4	6.4	8.3
Japan	3.3	..	0.8	3.9	2.6
United States	4.5	0.2	..	4.5	4.0
Other high-income economies	6.9	5.5	6.7	7.8	6.8
Low- and middle-income economies	11.9	8.2	11.9	10.1	11.0
East Asia & Pacific	13.2	9.5	13.1	10.1	11.2
China	20.5	13.1	19.3	14.8	16.5
Europe & Central Asia	15.4	5.9	11.9	12.1	14.6
Russian Federation	11.6	4.4	8.3	9.4	10.6
Latin America & Caribbean	5.8	2.6	11.6	9.7	9.9
Brazil	5.9	0.7	8.5	9.1	6.9
Middle East & N. Africa	10.3	7.1	14.6	9.9	10.5
Algeria	11.0	3.0	17.7	26.4	13.3
South Asia	8.4	–1.5	9.5	11.5	9.0
India	9.2	–0.1	10.7	13.7	10.5
Sub-Saharan Africa	4.5	4.9	9.3	4.8	6.0
South Africa	3.5	2.7	2.0	3.7	3.2
World	8.5	5.4	8.1	6.7	7.8

Low- and middle-income importers

annual % growth, 1994–2004

Source of exports	East Asia & Pacific	Europe & Central Asia	Latin America & Caribbean	Middle East & N. Africa	South Asia	Sub-Saharan Africa	All low- & middle-income	World
High-income economies	9.2	13.5	3.0	7.6	9.0	7.0	9.0	7.2
European Union	9.0	14.4	3.3	7.7	9.7	7.0	10.4	8.6
Japan	7.8	14.2	0.4	2.9	3.0	0.6	6.6	3.7
United States	8.4	4.4	3.8	1.7	9.5	6.8	5.7	4.3
Other high-income economies	10.0	11.1	2.4	11.7	9.6	9.8	9.6	7.5
Low- and middle-income economies	16.9	12.1	9.0	14.3	13.5	12.1	13.0	11.5
East Asia & Pacific	16.6	19.4	15.2	15.8	16.5	19.7	17.0	12.2
China	19.9	23.0	19.2	21.8	20.3	23.9	21.1	17.1
Europe & Central Asia	11.7	11.0	9.2	14.5	15.0	15.3	11.4	13.3
Russian Federation	12.5	8.2	5.7	19.9	20.2	16.9	9.6	10.2
Latin America & Caribbean	18.4	16.6	7.3	13.3	8.8	11.2	9.5	9.8
Brazil	14.3	17.8	6.9	14.4	1.5	11.4	9.5	7.9
Middle East & N. Africa	25.6	14.0	14.2	14.1	4.5	20.3	16.2	11.7
Algeria	48.9	21.7	23.6	9.5	–14.6	10.5	20.1	14.0
South Asia	18.6	9.0	16.9	15.2	15.7	17.4	15.8	10.6
India	20.6	7.7	20.3	19.7	15.6	18.2	17.1	12.2
Sub-Saharan Africa	18.8	10.2	16.8	5.6	3.7	6.2	10.3	7.2
South Africa	2.0	2.8	2.9	1.8	3.2	1.6	1.9	2.8
World	10.6	13.0	5.1	9.4	10.4	8.6	10.1	8.3

6.3 Direction and growth of merchandise trade

About the data

The table provides estimates of the flow of trade in goods between groups of economies. The data are from the International Monetary Fund's (IMF) Direction of Trade database. All developed and 23 developing countries report trade on a timely basis, covering about 80 percent of trade for recent years. Trade by less timely reporters and by countries that do not report is estimated using reports of trading partner countries. Because the largest exporting and importing countries are reliable reporters, a large portion of the missing trade flows can be estimated from partner reports. Partner country data may introduce discrepancies due to smuggling, confidentiality, different exchange rates, overreporting of transit trade, inclusion or exclusion of freight rates, and different points of valuation and times of recording.

In addition, estimates of trade within the European Union (EU) have been significantly affected by changes in reporting methods following the creation of a customs union. The current system for collecting data on trade between EU members—Intrastat, introduced in 1993—has less exhaustive coverage than the previous customs-based system and has resulted in some problems of asymmetry (estimated imports are about 5 percent less than exports). Despite these issues, only a small portion of world trade is estimated to be omitted from the IMF's *Direction of Trade Statistics Yearbook* and Direction of Trade database.

Most countries report their trade data in national currencies, which are converted into U.S. dollars using the IMF's published period average exchange rates (series rf or rh, monthly averages of the market or official rates) for the reporting country or, if those are not available, monthly average rates in New York. Because imports are reported at cost, insurance, and freight (c.i.f.) valuations, and exports at free on board (f.o.b.) valuations, the IMF adjusts country reports of import values by dividing them by 1.10 to estimate equivalent export values. This approximation is more or less accurate, depending on the set of partners and the items traded. Other factors affecting the accuracy of trade data include lags in reporting, recording differences across countries, and whether the country reports trade according to the general or special system of trade. (For further discussion of the measurement of exports and imports, see *About the data* for tables 4.4 and 4.5.)

The regional trade flows shown in the table were calculated from current price values. The growth rates are presented in nominal terms; that is, they include the effects of changes in both volumes and prices.

Definitions

• **Merchandise trade** includes all trade in goods; trade in services is excluded. • **High-income economies** are those classified as such by the World Bank (see inside front cover). • **European Union** is defined as all high-income EU members: Austria, Belgium, Cyprus, Denmark, Finland, France, Germany, Greece, Ireland, Italy, Luxembourg, Malta, the Netherlands, Portugal, Slovenia, Spain, Sweden, and the United Kingdom. • **Other high-income economies** include all high-income economies (OECD and non-OECD) except the European Union, Japan, and the United States. • **Low- and middle-income regional groupings** are based on World Bank classifications and may differ from those used by other organizations.

6.3a

Triangular trade in manufactures between China, selected other large East Asian economies, and the United States and Japan

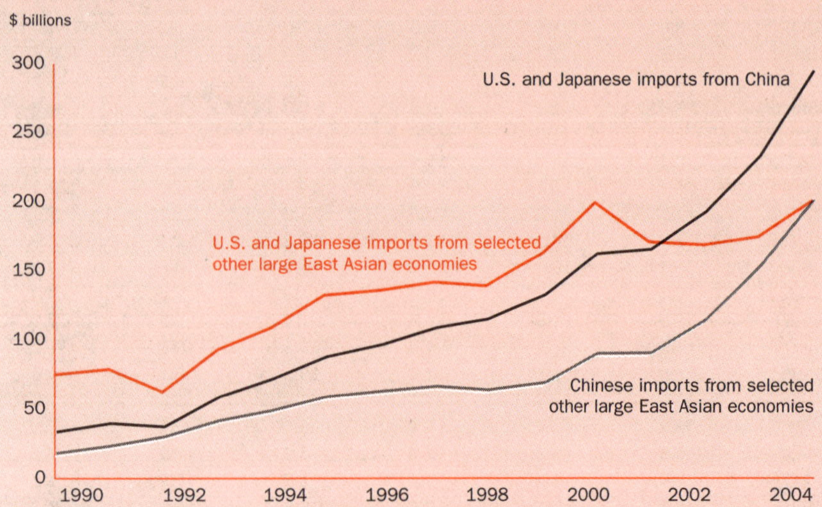

The strong rise in manufactured exports to China and Hong Kong, China, from selected large East Asian trading partners since the early 1990s has been accompanied by an almost equally strong rise in exports from China and Hong Kong, China, to the United States and Japan.

Note: Selected other large East Asian economies are Indonesia; Republic of Korea; Malaysia; Philippines; Taiwan, China; and Thailand.

Source: United Nations Statistic Division, Comtrade database.

Data sources

Intercountry trade flows are published in the IMF's *Direction of Trade Statistics Yearbook* and Direction of Trade Statistics Quarterly; the data in the table were calculated using the IMF's Direction of Trade database.

High-income trade with low- and middle-income economies

6.4

Exports to low-income economies

	High-income countries		European Union		Japan		United States	
	1994	2004	1994	2004	1994	2004	1994	2004
Total ($ billions)	**56.6**	**118.9**	**27.0**	**52.3**	**8.1**	**11.1**	**6.2**	**15.8**
% of total exports								
Food	9.0	6.8	9.4	7.4	0.7	0.5	22.8	13.3
Cereals	3.3	2.1	2.8	1.7	0.2	0.2	17.0	8.2
Agricultural raw materials	2.3	2.0	1.5	1.6	1.6	1.5	4.4	4.8
Ores and nonferrous metals	2.1	2.7	1.6	2.4	0.6	1.1	2.5	1.7
Fuels	4.7	5.8	2.5	3.5	0.9	0.8	0.8	1.8
Crude petroleum	0.0	0.5	0.0	0.0	0.0	0.0	0.0	0.0
Petroleum products	3.9	4.1	2.4	3.4	0.8	0.4	0.8	1.0
Manufactured goods	78.8	79.1	81.2	82.9	95.3	92.3	65.8	74.5
Chemical products	12.0	11.7	12.6	12.7	5.9	6.5	12.8	12.2
Iron and steel	3.6	3.1	4.3	3.0	5.9	9.9	1.0	1.3
Machinery and transport equipment	45.0	41.5	41.0	40.6	71.6	61.6	41.9	46.2
Furniture	0.2	0.3	0.3	0.4	0.1	0.2	0.1	0.2
Textiles	6.2	5.5	2.8	2.6	4.0	4.6	4.7	5.6
Footwear	0.2	0.1	0.2	0.1	0.0	0.0	0.1	0.1
Other	11.6	16.9	19.9	23.5	7.7	9.4	5.3	9.0
Miscellaneous goods	3.0	3.5	3.8	2.2	0.8	3.9	3.7	3.9

Imports from low-income economies

	High-income countries		European Union		Japan		United States	
	1994	2004	1994	2004	1994	2004	1994	2004
Total ($ billions)	**63.1**	**151.8**	**32.2**	**61.9**	**7.3**	**11.2**	**15.5**	**53.6**
% of total imports								
Food	19.7	12.4	22.7	16.9	26.9	19.0	9.4	6.8
Cereals	0.7	0.4	0.3	0.4	0.5	0.1	0.2	0.2
Agricultural raw materials	7.0	2.6	8.6	4.6	10.5	2.0	1.5	0.8
Ores and nonferrous metals	5.7	3.6	5.0	5.1	15.6	8.7	2.2	0.5
Fuels	22.9	25.2	17.1	11.9	13.7	31.0	36.3	37.7
Crude petroleum	21.4	21.4	16.6	9.0	10.3	27.5	33.5	34.6
Petroleum products	1.4	2.6	0.3	0.9	2.8	1.5	2.7	2.5
Manufactured goods	44.2	55.7	46.0	61.0	32.7	38.8	50.1	53.5
Chemical products	2.1	3.3	2.1	3.5	1.0	2.9	1.8	2.4
Iron and steel	1.0	1.9	0.4	2.1	2.0	1.6	1.2	1.9
Machinery and transport equipment	2.6	5.1	2.7	5.9	0.3	9.9	1.7	3.2
Furniture	0.2	1.4	0.2	1.5	0.4	1.7	0.1	1.4
Textiles	26.1	26.6	27.0	29.9	16.9	10.9	27.8	30.6
Footwear	1.1	3.5	1.6	6.4	0.2	2.3	0.6	1.2
Other	11.1	14.0	11.9	11.6	11.9	9.6	16.8	12.8
Miscellaneous goods	0.5	0.5	0.7	0.4	0.6	0.5	0.5	0.7

Simple applied tariff rates on imports from low-income economies (%)

	High-income countries		European Union		Japan		United States	
	1994	2004	1994	2004	1994	2004	1994	2004
Food	2.8	2.5	2.9	3.6	6.7	5.6	1.2	3.2
Cereals	5.3	2.3	13.0	1.5	13.0	11.3	1.0	1.0
Agricultural raw materials	0.3	0.6	0.2	0.2	0.3	0.4	0.2	0.3
Ores and nonferrous metals	0.4	0.5	0.2	0.5	0.2	0.1	0.2	0.2
Fuels	0.9	0.6	0.2	0.1	1.0	0.3	2.6	0.6
Crude petroleum	0.0	0.2	0.0	0.0	0.0	0.0	0.0	0.0
Petroleum products	1.5	0.9	0.3	0.1	1.6	0.6	2.6	1.1
Manufactured goods	3.9	3.1	1.2	0.9	2.5	2.7	5.4	4.6
Chemical products	1.3	1.3	0.5	0.5	0.9	0.4	2.0	1.7
Iron and steel	2.4	1.1	0.8	1.1	0.3	0.2	4.7	0.3
Machinery and transport equipment	0.8	0.8	0.2	0.2	0.0	0.0	0.6	0.3
Furniture	2.3	2.3	0.0	0.0	0.0	0.0	0.8	1.0
Textiles	8.9	6.9	4.1	3.0	4.9	5.8	11.6	10.3
Footwear	9.0	7.0	1.0	3.4	13.0	11.1	14.5	9.2
Other	5.0	4.0	1.8	1.3	2.9	3.6	6.6	5.8
Miscellaneous goods	0.6	0.2	0.5	0.5	0.0	0.0	1.7	0.1
Average	3.9	2.9	1.4	1.1	2.9	2.8	4.6	4.2

6.4 High-income trade with low- and middle-income economies

Exports to middle-income economies	High-income countries		European Union		Japan		United States	
	1994	2004	1994	2004	1994	2004	1994	2004
Total ($ billions)	**565.7**	**1,309.6**	**207.5**	**544.8**	**85.2**	**161.9**	**134.7**	**252.8**
% of total exports								
Food	7.2	4.8	9.0	5.0	0.4	0.3	9.7	8.7
Cereals	1.7	1.0	1.4	0.7	0.1	0.0	3.4	2.8
Agricultural raw materials	2.1	1.9	1.3	1.4	0.9	0.9	3.2	3.5
Ores and nonferrous metals	1.7	2.5	1.5	1.9	1.1	2.3	1.6	2.4
Fuels	2.5	2.4	1.7	1.5	0.8	0.7	2.1	2.9
Crude petroleum	0.2	0.1	0.2	0.0	0.0	0.0	0.0	0.0
Petroleum products	2.0	1.9	1.3	1.3	0.7	0.6	1.5	2.4
Manufactured goods	83.4	85.6	82.5	87.9	95.9	92.2	79.3	79.3
Chemical products	10.2	12.3	11.7	13.3	6.0	8.8	10.4	12.2
Iron and steel	3.0	3.0	2.9	3.2	6.5	6.3	1.0	1.0
Machinery and transport equipment	48.3	50.7	46.2	49.4	68.2	62.1	49.1	48.4
Furniture	0.6	0.5	0.9	0.8	0.1	0.2	0.7	0.5
Textiles	7.4	5.6	6.2	5.4	3.4	2.8	5.7	5.6
Footwear	0.3	0.2	0.5	0.3	0.0	0.0	0.1	0.0
Other	13.6	13.4	14.3	15.5	11.7	12.0	12.2	11.6
Miscellaneous goods	3.1	2.7	4.0	2.3	0.9	3.6	4.0	3.2
Imports from middle-income economies								
Total ($ billions)	**622.1**	**1,833.7**	**213.2**	**674.0**	**80.5**	**186.4**	**187.9**	**606.6**
% of total imports								
Food	12.7	6.7	16.1	8.3	19.5	9.8	8.7	4.9
Cereals	0.6	0.3	0.2	0.3	2.2	0.3	0.2	0.1
Agricultural raw materials	3.4	1.6	4.4	2.1	6.5	2.4	1.6	1.1
Ores and nonferrous metals	5.4	4.0	7.1	4.7	9.9	7.9	3.4	2.1
Fuels	14.5	15.6	19.2	18.6	20.6	15.8	12.4	15.8
Crude petroleum	9.5	10.1	12.1	12.2	11.8	7.2	9.1	12.0
Petroleum products	2.5	2.7	3.5	3.3	1.3	1.5	2.9	2.7
Manufactured goods	62.1	70.7	50.2	65.0	42.6	62.9	71.7	73.9
Chemical products	3.4	3.2	4.6	3.4	2.6	3.2	2.6	2.6
Iron and steel	2.4	2.6	2.4	3.0	1.8	1.4	2.3	2.3
Machinery and transport equipment	20.3	33.4	11.9	29.4	8.7	27.8	29.5	35.9
Furniture	1.4	2.4	1.5	2.3	1.6	1.7	1.6	3.4
Textiles	15.3	10.3	15.8	10.5	15.0	12.0	13.1	9.2
Footwear	3.2	1.7	1.8	1.3	1.4	1.2	4.6	2.4
Other	16.0	17.0	12.1	15.2	11.5	15.7	18.1	18.0
Miscellaneous goods	1.9	1.4	3.1	1.3	1.0	1.2	2.2	2.2
Simple applied tariff rates on imports from middle-income economies (%)								
Food	5.6	3.7	9.4	3.6	9.4	7.9	1.6	2.7
Cereals	6.5	3.1	18.2	1.5	15.6	13.7	1.3	0.9
Agricultural raw materials	0.7	0.6	0.9	0.2	0.3	0.4	0.5	0.3
Ores and nonferrous metals	1.1	0.5	1.4	0.5	0.3	0.1	0.8	0.5
Fuels	1.0	0.7	1.0	0.1	0.6	0.6	1.1	1.4
Crude petroleum	0.0	0.2	0.0	0.0	0.0	0.0	0.0	0.0
Petroleum products	1.6	1.0	1.5	0.1	1.4	1.0	1.7	2.2
Manufactured goods	5.0	2.7	3.6	0.9	1.8	2.2	4.6	2.8
Chemical products	2.8	1.1	3.1	0.5	0.8	0.4	2.3	1.0
Iron and steel	3.2	1.0	3.2	1.1	0.8	0.3	4.1	0.2
Machinery and transport equipment	2.2	1.1	1.6	0.2	0.0	0.0	1.2	0.3
Furniture	3.7	2.8	1.5	0.0	0.0	0.0	0.8	0.3
Textiles	11.4	7.1	8.5	2.9	5.0	6.8	11.5	8.7
Footwear	12.1	7.6	4.6	3.4	16.1	18.7	14.0	8.9
Other	6.3	3.7	4.5	1.3	2.5	3.3	5.9	4.0
Miscellaneous goods	1.5	0.5	1.9	0.5	0.0	0.0	1.3	0.3
Average	4.8	2.7	3.9	1.1	2.6	2.7	4.0	2.7

Note: Data for 1993 were used in the computation when data for 1994 were not available, and data for 2003 when data for 2004 were not available.

High-income trade with low- and middle-income economies

About the data

Developing countries are becoming increasingly important in the global trading system. Since the early 1990s trade between high-income countries and low- and middle-income economies has grown faster than trade among high-income economies. The increased trade benefits consumers and producers. But as the World Trade Organization's (WTO) Ministerial Conferences in Doha, Qatar, in October 2001, Cancun, Mexico, in September 2003, and Hong Kong, China, in December 2005 showed, achieving a more pro-development outcome from trade remains a challenge. Meeting it will require strengthening international consultation. Negotiations after the Doha meetings were launched on services, agriculture, manufactures, WTO rules, the environment, dispute settlement, intellectual property rights protection, and disciplines on regional integration. At the most recent negotiations in Hong Kong, China, trade ministers agreed to eliminate subsidies of agricultural exports by 2013; to abolish cotton export subsidies in 2006 and grant unlimited export access to selected cotton-growing countries in Sub-Saharan Africa; to cut more domestic farm supports in the European Union, Japan, and the United States; and to offer more aid to developing countries to help them compete in global trade.

Trade flows between high-income countries and low- and middle-income economies reflect the changing mix of exports to and imports from developing economies. While food and primary commodities have continued to fall as a share of high-income countries' imports, the share of manufactures in goods imports from both low- and middle-income countries has grown. Moreover, trade between developing countries has grown substantially over the past decade. This growth has resulted from many factors, including developing countries' increasing share of world output and the liberalization of their trade.

Yet trade barriers remain high. The table includes information about tariff rates by selected product groups. Applied tariff rates are the tariffs in effect for partners in preferential trade agreements such as the North American Free Trade Agreement. When these are unavailable, most favored nation rates are used. The difference between most favored nation and applied rates can be substantial. Simple averages of applied rates are shown because they are generally a better indicator of tariff protection.

The data are from the United Nations Conference on Trade and Development (UNCTAD). Partner country reports by high-income countries were used for both exports and imports. Exports are recorded free on board (f.o.b.); imports include insurance and freight charges (c.i.f.). Because of differences in sources of data, timing, and treatment of missing data, the numbers in the table may not be fully comparable with those used to calculate the direction of trade statistics in table 6.3 or the aggregate flows in tables 4.4, 4.5, and 6.2. Data are classified using the Harmonized System of trade at the six- or eight-digit level. Tariff line data were matched to Standard International Trade Classification (SITC) revision 1 codes to define commodity groups. For further discussion of merchandise trade statistics, see *About the data* for tables 4.4, 4.5, 6.2, and 6.3, and for information about tariff barriers, see table 6.7.

6.4a

Growing trade between developing countries

Trade among developing countries as a share of total developing country trade, 1975–2004 (%)

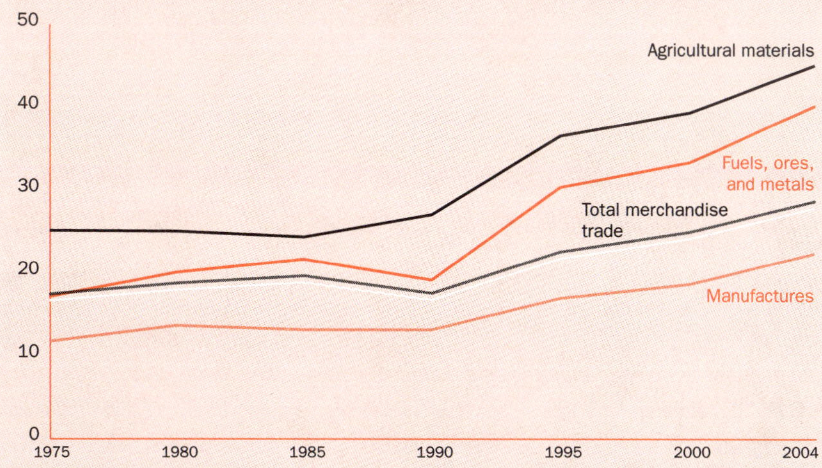

As developing countries' share in global trade has steadily increased over the past three decades, the share of trade among developing countries has greatly increased, especially since 1990.

Source: United Nations Statistics Division, Comtrade database.

Definitions

The product groups in the table are defined in accordance with the SITC revision 1: **food** (0, 1, 22, and 4) and **cereals** (04); **agricultural raw materials** (2 excluding 22, 27, and 28); **ores and nonferrous metals** (27, 28, and 68); **fuels** (3), **crude petroleum** (331), and **petroleum products** (332); **manufactured goods** (5–8 excluding 68), **chemical products** (5), **iron and steel** (67), **machinery and transport equipment** (7), **furniture** (82), **textiles** (65 and 84), **footwear** (85), and **other** manufactured goods (6 and 8 excluding 65, 67, 68, 82, 84, and 85); and **miscellaneous goods** (9). • **Exports** are all merchandise exports by high-income OECD countries to low-income and middle-income economies as recorded in the United Nations Statistics Division's Comtrade database. • **Imports** are all merchandise imports by high-income countries from low-income and middle-income economies as recorded in the United Nations Statistics Division's Comtrade database. • **High-, middle-, and low-income economies** are those classified as such by the World Bank (see inside front cover). • **European Union** is defined as all high-income EU members: Austria, Belgium, Cyprus, Denmark, Finland, France, Germany, Greece, Ireland, Italy, Luxembourg, Malta, the Netherlands, Portugal, Slovenia, Spain, Sweden, and the United Kingdom.

Data sources

Trade values are from United Nations Statistics Division's Comtrade database. Tariff data are from UNCTAD's Trade Analysis and Information System database and are calculated by World Bank staff using the World Integrated Trade Solution system.

6.5 Primary commodity prices

	1970	1980	1990	1995	2000	2001	2002	2003	2004	2005
World Bank commodity price index (1990 = 100)										
Nonenergy commodities	156	159	100	104	89	84	89	91	100	111
Agriculture	163	175	100	112	90	84	93	95	98	103
Beverages	203	230	100	129	91	76	91	87	88	107
Food	166	177	100	100	87	91	97	96	103	100
Raw materials	130	133	100	116	93	81	89	98	99	104
Fertilizers	108	164	100	88	109	105	108	106	118	123
Metals and minerals	144	120	100	87	85	80	78	82	105	130
Petroleum	19	204	100	64	127	113	117	126	154	213
Steel products[a]	111	100	100	91	79	71	73	79	114	126
MUV G-5 index	28	79	100	117	97	94	93	100	107	110
Commodity prices (1990 prices)										
Agricultural raw materials										
Cotton (cents/kg)	225	260	182	182	134	112	109	140	128	111
Logs, Cameroon ($/cu. m)[a]	153	319	344	290	283	282	..	..	..	..
Logs, Malaysian ($/cu. m)	154	248	177	218	195	169	175	187	184	185
Rubber (cents/kg)	145	181	86	135	69	61	82	108	122	137
Sawnwood, Malaysian ($/cu. m)	625	503	533	632	612	510	565	550	543	601
Tobacco ($/mt)	3,836	2,887	3,392	2,258	3,063	3,185	2,947	2,643	2,561	2,524
Beverages (cents/kg)										
Cocoa	240	330	127	122	93	113	191	175	145	140
Coffee, robustas	330	411	118	237	94	64	71	81	74	102
Coffee, Arabica	409	440	197	285	198	146	146	141	166	231
Tea, avg., 3 auctions	298	211	206	127	193	169	162	151	157	150
Energy										
Coal, Australian ($/mt)	..	50	40	34	27	34	29	28	51	45
Coal, U.S. ($/mt)	..	55	42	33	34	48	43	..	..	..
Natural gas, Europe ($/mmbtu)	..	4	3	2	4	4	3	4	4	6
Natural gas, U.S. ($/mmbtu)	1	2	2	1	4	4	4	5	6	8
Petroleum ($/bbl)	4	47	23	15	29	26	27	29	35	49

About the data

Primary commodities—raw or partially processed materials that will be transformed into finished goods—are often the most significant exports of developing countries, and revenues obtained from them have an important effect on living standards. Price data for primary commodities are collected from a variety of sources, including trade journals, international study groups, government market surveys, newspaper and wire service reports, and commodity exchange spot and near-term forward prices.

The table is based on frequently updated price reports. When possible, the prices received by exporters are used; if export prices are unavailable, the prices paid by importers are used. Annual price series are generally simple averages based on higher frequency data. The constant price series in the table is deflated using the manufactures unit value (MUV) index for the Group of Five (G-5) countries (see below).

The commodity price indexes are calculated as Laspeyres index numbers, in which the fixed weights are the 1987–89 export values for low- and middle-income economies, rebased to 1990. Each index represents a fixed basket of primary commodity exports. The nonenergy commodity price index contains 37 price series for 31 nonenergy commodities. Separate indexes are compiled for petroleum and steel products, which are not included in the nonenergy commodity price index.

The MUV index is a composite index of prices for manufactured exports from the five major (G-5) industrial countries (France, Germany, Japan, the United Kingdom, and the United States) to low- and middle-income economies, valued in U.S. dollars. The index covers products in groups 5–8 of the Standard International Trade Classification revision 1. To construct the MUV G-5 index, unit value indexes for each country are combined using weights determined by each country's export share.

Primary commodity prices

	1970	1980	1990	1995	2000	2001	2002	2003	2004	2005
Commodity prices (continued)										
(1990 prices)										
Fertilizers ($/mt)										
Phosphate rock	39	59	41	30	45	44	43	38	38	38
TSP	152	229	132	128	142	135	143	149	174	184
Food										
Fats and oils ($/mt)										
Coconut oil	1,417	855	337	572	463	337	452	467	617	562
Groundnut oil	1,350	1,090	964	846	734	721	738	1,242	1,085	968
Palm oil	927	740	290	536	319	303	419	443	440	385
Soybeans	417	376	247	221	218	208	228	264	286	250
Soybean meal	367	332	200	168	195	192	188	211	225	195
Soybean oil	1,021	758	447	534	348	375	488	553	576	497
Grains ($/mt)										
Sorghum	185	164	104	102	91	101	109	106	103	88
Maize	208	159	109	105	91	95	107	105	104	90
Rice	450	521	271	274	208	183	206	197	222	261
Wheat	196	219	136	151	117	134	159	146	147	139
Other food										
Bananas ($/mt)	590	481	541	380	436	618	568	374	490	550
Beef (cents/kg)	465	350	256	163	199	226	226	198	235	239
Oranges ($/mt)	599	496	531	454	374	631	606	680	803	800
Sugar, EU domestic (cents/kg)	40	62	58	59	57	56	59	60	63	61
Sugar, U.S. domestic (cents/kg)	59	84	51	43	44	50	50	47	42	43
Sugar, world (cents/kg)	29	80	28	25	19	20	16	16	15	20
Metals and minerals										
Aluminum ($/mt)	1,982	1,847	1,639	1,542	1,594	1,531	1,449	1,430	1,603	1,732
Copper ($/mt)	5,038	2,768	2,662	2,508	1,866	1,673	1,674	1,777	2,678	3,357
Iron ore (cents/dmtu)	35	36	33	24	30	32	31	32	35	59
Lead (cents/kg)	108	115	81	54	47	50	49	51	83	89
Nickel ($/mt)	10,148	8,270	8,864	7,028	8,888	6,303	7,271	9,617	12,915	13,453
Tin (cents/kg)	1,310	2,128	609	531	559	475	436	489	795	673
Zinc (cents/kg)	105	97	151	88	116	94	84	83	98	126

a. Series not included in the nonenergy index.

Definitions

• **Nonenergy commodity price index** covers the 31 nonenergy primary commodities that make up the agriculture, fertilizer, and metals and minerals indexes. • **Agriculture** includes beverages, food, and agricultural raw materials. • **Beverages** include cocoa, coffee, and tea. • **Food** includes rice, wheat, maize, sorghum, soybeans, soybean oil, soybean meal, palm oil, coconut oil, groundnut oil, bananas, beef, oranges, and sugar. • **Agricultural raw materials** include cotton, timber (logs and sawnwood), natural rubber, and tobacco. • **Fertilizers** include phosphate rock and triple superphosphate (TSP). • **Metals and minerals** include aluminum, copper, iron ore, lead, nickel, tin, and zinc. • **Petroleum price index** refers to the average spot price of Brent, Dubai, and West Texas Intermediate crude oils, equally weighted. • **Steel products price index** is the composite price index for eight steel products based on quotations free on board (f.o.b.) Japan excluding shipments to China and the United States, weighted by product shares of apparent combined consumption (volume of deliveries) for Germany, Japan, and the United States. • **MUV G-5 index** is the manufactures unit value index for G-5 country exports to low- and middle-income economies. • **Commodity prices**—for definitions and sources, see "Commodity Price Data" (also known as the "Pink Sheet") at the Global Prospects Web site (www.worldbank.org/prospects).

Data sources

Data on commodity prices and the MUV G-5 index are compiled by the World Bank's Development Prospects Group. Monthly updates of commodity prices are available on the Web at www.worldbank.org/prospects.

6.6 Regional trade blocs

Merchandise exports within bloc

	Year of creation	$ millions 1990	1995	1998	1999	2000	2001	2002	2003	2004
High-income and low- and middle-income economies										
APEC[a]	1989	901,560	1,688,708	1,734,386	1,896,213	2,261,791	2,070,973	2,168,705	2,420,758	2,903,670
CEFTA	1992	4,235	12,118	14,234	13,226	15,123	17,054	19,180	25,309	37,340
CIS	1991	..	29,943	27,037	20,842	27,043	22,264	28,029	36,466	40,340
EMFTA	1995	1,057,338	1,366,726	1,341,891	1,522,340	1,548,718	1,526,481	1,620,324	1,952,123	2,315,677
European Union	1957	981,260	1,259,699	1,223,801	1,396,574	1,409,464	1,398,298	1,480,493	1,782,423	2,089,442
FTAA	1994	300,700	525,346	682,067	734,848	857,300	812,144	787,492	830,495	969,106
NAFTA	1994	226,273	394,472	521,649	581,161	676,141	639,419	626,020	651,060	737,591
Africa										
CEMAC	1994	139	120	153	127	97	118	136	148	176
CEPGL	1976	7	8	8	9	10	11	13	15	19
COMESA	1994	963	1,386	1,501	1,348	1,536	1,496	1,786	2,189	2,848
Cross Border Initiative	1992	613	1,002	1,156	964	1,058	849	1,169	1,370	1,700
EAC	1996	230	530	555	438	485	453	479	573	753
ECCAS	1983	163	163	198	179	191	203	199	198	238
ECOWAS	1975	1,557	1,936	2,350	2,364	2,835	2,371	3,229	3,147	3,973
Indian Ocean Commission	1984	73	127	95	91	106	134	105	179	155
MRU	1973	0	1	2	4	5	4	5	5	6
SADC	1992	1,630	3,373	3,865	4,224	4,282	3,771	4,316	5,377	6,384
UDEAC	1964	139	120	152	126	96	117	134	146	174
UEMOA	1994	621	560	752	805	741	775	857	1,078	1,283
Latin America and the Caribbean										
ACS	1994	5,398	11,049	12,505	11,199	16,326	15,543	15,464	16,090	21,839
Andean Group	1969	1,312	4,812	5,408	3,929	5,310	5,623	5,070	5,203	7,094
CACM	1961	667	1,594	2,010	2,175	2,657	2,535	2,574	2,734	3,554
CARICOM	1973	448	867	1,020	1,136	1,050	1,420	1,184	1,410	1,797
Central American Group of Four	1993	399	1,026	1,230	1,369	1,838	1,712	1,737	1,843	2,297
Group of Three	1995	1,046	3,460	3,921	2,912	3,721	4,178	3,839	3,367	5,664
LAIA (ALADI)	1980	12,331	35,299	42,959	34,785	42,911	40,795	36,060	40,250	55,639
MERCOSUR	1991	4,127	14,199	20,352	15,313	17,829	15,156	10,228	12,732	17,470
OECS	1981	29	39	36	37	38	37	40	48	60
Middle East and Asia										
Arab Common Market	1964	911	1,368	978	951	1,312	1,728	1,998	1,797	6,297
ASEAN	1967	27,365	79,544	69,809	77,889	98,060	86,331	91,765	101,140	122,369
Bangkok Agreement	1975	4,476	12,066	12,851	14,463	16,844	16,733	17,957	21,809	24,925
EAEC	1990	281,067	634,606	549,010	612,415	772,423	698,552	779,390	940,963	1,177,295
ECO	1985	1,243	4,746	4,031	3,903	4,518	4,498	5,016	7,539	9,371
GAFTA	1997	13,313	13,129	13,548	13,752	16,238	17,528	19,195	21,511	36,027
GCC	1981	6,906	6,832	7,358	7,306	7,958	8,103	8,899	9,580	12,532
SAARC	1985	863	2,024	2,466	2,180	2,593	2,827	3,402	4,873	5,706
UMA	1989	958	1,109	881	919	1,094	1,137	1,202	1,338	1,372

Note: Regional bloc memberships are as follows: **Asia Pacific Economic Cooperation (APEC)**, Australia, Brunei Darussalam, Canada, Chile, China, Hong Kong (China), Indonesia, Japan, the Republic of Korea, Malaysia, Mexico, New Zealand, Papua New Guinea, Peru, the Philippines, the Russian Federation, Singapore, Taiwan (China), Thailand, the United States, and Vietnam; **Central European Free Trade Area (CEFTA)**, Bulgaria, the Czech Republic, Hungary, Poland, Romania, the Slovak Republic, and Slovenia; **Commonwealth of Independent States (CIS)**, Armenia, Azerbaijan, Belarus, Georgia, Kazakhstan, the Kyrgyz Republic, Moldova, the Russian Federation, Tajikistan, Ukraine, and Uzbekistan; **Euro-Mediterranean Free Trade Area (EMFTA)**, European Union, Algeria, Cyprus, Egypt, Israel, Jordan, Lebanon, Malta, Morocco, Syrian Arab Republic, Tunisia, Turkey, and West Bank and Gaza; **European Union (EU; formerly European Economic Community and European Community)**, Austria, Belgium, Denmark, Finland, France, Germany, Greece, Ireland, Italy, Luxembourg, the Netherlands, Portugal, Spain, Sweden, and the United Kingdom; **Free Trade Areas of the Americas (FTAA)**, Antigua and Barbuda, Argentina, Bahamas, Barbados, Belize, Bolivia, Brazil, Canada, Chile, Colombia, Costa Rica, Dominica, Dominican Republic, Ecuador, El Salvador, Grenada, Guatemala, Guyana, Haiti, Honduras, Jamaica, Mexico, Nicaragua, Panama, Paraguay, Peru, Republica Bolivariana de Venezuela, St. Kitts and Nevis, St. Lucia, St. Vincent and the Grenadines, Suriname, Trinidad and Tobago, the United States, and Uruguay; **North American Free Trade Area (NAFTA)**, Canada, Mexico, and the United States; **Economic and Monetary Community of Central Africa (CEMAC)**, Cameroon, the Central African Republic, Chad, the Republic of Congo, Equatorial Guinea, Gabon, and São Tomé and Principe; **Economic Community of the Countries of the Great Lakes (CEPGL)**, Burundi, the Democratic Republic of Congo, and Rwanda; **Common Market for Eastern and Southern Africa (COMESA)**, Angola, Burundi, Comoros, the Democratic Republic of Congo, Djibouti, the Arab Republic of Egypt, Eritrea, Ethiopia, Kenya, Madagascar, Malawi, Mauritius, Namibia, Rwanda, Seychelles, Sudan, Swaziland, Uganda, Tanzania, Zambia, and Zimbabwe; **Cross Border Initiative**, Burundi, Comoros, Kenya, Madagascar, Malawi, Mauritius, Namibia, Rwanda, Seychelles, Swaziland, Tanzania, Uganda, Zambia, and Zimbabwe; **East African Community (EAC)**, Kenya, Tanzania, and Uganda; **Economic Community of Central African States (ECCAS)**, Angola, Burundi, Cameroon, the Central African Republic, Chad, the Democratic Republic of Congo, the Republic of Congo, Equatorial Guinea, Gabon, Rwanda, and São Tomé and Principe; **Economic Community of West African States (ECOWAS)**, Benin, Burkina Faso, Cape Verde, Côte d'Ivoire, the Gambia, Ghana, Guinea, Guinea-Bissau, Liberia, Mali, Mauritania, Niger, Nigeria, Senegal, Sierra Leone, and Togo; **Indian Ocean Commission**, Comoros, Madagascar, Mauritius, Réunion, and Seychelles; **Mano River Union (MRU)**, Guinea, Liberia, and Sierra Leone; **Southern African Development Community (SADC; formerly Southern African Development Coordination Conference)**, Angola, Botswana, the Democratic Republic of Congo,

a. No preferential trade agreement.

Merchandise exports within bloc

	Year of creation	% of total bloc exports								
		1990	1995	1998	1999	2000	2001	2002	2003	2004
High-income and low- and middle-income economies										
APEC[a]	1989	68.3	71.8	69.7	71.8	73.1	72.6	73.4	72.6	72.0
CEFTA	1992	9.9	14.6	13.0	12.1	12.2	12.4	12.2	12.5	13.9
CIS	1991	..	27.6	26.6	20.7	19.2	18.2	18.8	19.6	16.7
EMFTA	1995	68.5	65.3	60.0	65.8	64.6	63.3	63.3	63.9	63.6
European Union	1957	65.9	62.4	56.8	62.9	61.6	60.8	60.6	61.2	60.7
FTAA	1994	46.6	52.5	58.1	59.7	60.7	60.6	60.8	60.1	60.1
NAFTA	1994	41.4	46.2	51.7	54.6	55.7	55.5	56.6	56.1	55.9
Africa										
CEMAC	1994	2.3	2.1	2.3	1.7	1.1	1.4	1.5	1.4	1.3
CEPGL	1976	0.5	0.5	0.6	0.8	0.8	0.8	0.9	1.3	1.2
COMESA	1994	6.6	7.7	8.7	7.4	5.7	6.4	6.4	6.6	6.7
Cross Border Initiative	1992	10.3	11.9	13.9	12.1	10.6	9.0	12.3	11.4	13.2
EAC	1996	13.4	17.4	19.0	14.4	16.1	13.7	13.3	14.0	14.6
ECCAS	1983	1.4	1.5	1.8	1.3	1.1	1.3	1.1	1.0	0.9
ECOWAS	1975	7.9	9.0	10.7	10.4	7.9	8.5	10.9	8.6	8.5
Indian Ocean Commission	1984	4.1	6.0	4.7	4.8	4.4	5.6	4.3	6.1	4.3
MRU	1973	0.0	0.1	0.1	0.4	0.4	0.3	0.2	0.3	0.3
SADC	1992	4.8	8.7	10.4	11.9	9.3	8.6	9.5	9.8	9.5
UDEAC	1964	2.3	2.1	2.3	1.7	1.0	1.4	1.4	1.4	1.2
UEMOA	1994	13.0	10.3	11.0	13.1	13.1	12.7	12.2	13.3	13.9
Latin America and the Caribbean										
ACS	1994	8.4	8.5	7.2	5.6	6.7	6.8	6.7	6.6	7.6
Andean Group	1969	4.1	12.0	12.8	8.8	8.8	10.6	9.5	8.6	8.7
CACM	1961	15.3	21.8	15.8	13.6	17.3	17.9	17.5	16.8	20.0
CARICOM	1973	8.1	12.1	17.3	16.9	14.7	16.5	13.8	12.4	12.5
Central American Group of Four	1993	13.7	22.2	17.1	14.6	19.2	18.7	18.4	18.2	20.0
Group of Three	1995	2.0	3.2	2.6	1.7	1.7	2.1	1.9	1.6	2.3
LAIA (ALADI)	1980	10.8	17.1	16.7	12.7	12.8	12.8	11.2	11.4	12.6
MERCOSUR	1991	8.9	20.3	25.0	20.6	20.0	17.1	11.5	11.9	12.6
OECS	1981	8.1	12.6	12.0	13.1	10.0	6.0	4.0	7.6	11.6
Middle East and Asia										
Arab Common Market	1964	2.7	6.7	4.8	3.3	2.9	4.4	5.1	4.1	7.9
ASEAN	1967	19.0	24.6	21.2	21.7	23.0	22.4	22.7	22.2	22.2
Bangkok Agreement	1975	3.7	5.0	5.0	5.1	5.1	5.5	5.5	5.7	5.2
EAEC	1990	39.7	47.9	42.0	43.8	46.6	46.6	48.2	49.4	49.8
ECO	1985	3.2	7.9	6.8	5.8	5.6	5.5	5.9	6.7	6.3
GAFTA	1997	10.3	9.9	11.0	8.9	7.2	8.4	9.3	8.5	10.2
GCC	1981	8.0	6.8	8.0	6.7	4.8	5.2	5.9	5.1	5.0
SAARC	1985	3.2	4.4	4.8	4.0	4.1	4.3	4.8	5.7	5.6
UMA	1989	2.9	3.8	3.3	2.5	2.3	2.6	2.8	2.4	1.9

Lesotho, Malawi, Mauritius, Mozambique, Namibia, Seychelles, South Africa, Swaziland, Tanzania, Zambia, and Zimbabwe; **Central African Customs and Economic Union (UDEAC; formerly Union Douanière et Economique de l'Afrique Centrale)**, Cameroon, the Central African Republic, Chad, the Republic of Congo, Equatorial Guinea, and Gabon; **West African Economic and Monetary Union (UEMOA)**, Benin, Burkina Faso, Côte d'Ivoire, Guinea-Bissau, Mali, Niger, Senegal, and Togo; **Association of Caribbean States (ACS)**, Antigua and Barbuda, the Bahamas, Barbados, Belize, Colombia, Costa Rica, Cuba, Dominica, the Dominican Republic, El Salvador, Grenada, Guatemala, Guyana, Haiti, Honduras, Jamaica, Mexico, Nicaragua, Panama, St. Kitts and Nevis, St. Lucia, St. Vincent and the Grenadines, Suriname, Trinidad and Tobago, and República Bolivariana de Venezuela; **Andean Group**, Bolivia, Colombia, Ecuador, Peru, and República Bolivariana de Venezuela; **Central American Common Market (CACM)**, Costa Rica, El Salvador, Guatemala, Honduras, and Nicaragua; **Caribbean Community and Common Market (CARICOM)**, Antigua and Barbuda, the Bahamas (part of the Caribbean Community but not of the Common Market), Barbados, Belize, Dominica, Grenada, Guyana, Jamaica, Montserrat, St. Kitts and Nevis, St. Lucia, St. Vincent and the Grenadines, Suriname, and Trinidad and Tobago; **Central American Group of Four**, El Salvador, Guatemala, Honduras, and Nicaragua; **Group of Three**, Colombia, Mexico, and República Bolivariana de Venezuela; **Latin American Integration Association (LAIA; formerly Latin American Free Trade Area)**, Argentina, Bolivia, Brazil, Chile, Colombia, Ecuador, Mexico, Paraguay, Peru, Uruguay, and República Bolivariana de Venezuela; **Southern Cone Common Market (MERCOSUR)**, Argentina, Brazil, Paraguay, and Uruguay; **Organization of Eastern Caribbean States (OECS)**, Antigua and Barbuda, Dominica, Grenada, Montserrat, St. Kitts and Nevis, St. Lucia, and St. Vincent and the Grenadines; **Arab Common Market**, the Arab Republic of Egypt, Iraq, Jordan, Libya, Mauritania, the Syrian Arab Republic, and the Republic of Yemen; **Association of South-East Asian Nations (ASEAN)**, Brunei, Cambodia, Indonesia, the Lao People's Democratic Republic, Malaysia, Myanmar, the Philippines, Singapore, Thailand, and Vietnam; **Bangkok Agreement**, Bangladesh, India, the Republic of Korea, the Lao People's Democratic Republic, the Philippines, Sri Lanka, and Thailand; **East Asia Economic Caucus (EAEC, formerly East Asia Economic Group)**, Brunei, China, Hong Kong (China), Indonesia, Japan, the Republic of Korea, Malaysia, the Philippines, Singapore, Taiwan (China), and Thailand; **Economic Cooperation Organization (ECO)**, Afghanistan, Azerbaijan, the Islamic Republic of Iran, Kazakhstan, the Kyrgyz Republic, Pakistan, Tajikistan, Turkey, Turkmenistan, and Uzbekistan; **Gulf Cooperation Council (GCC)**, Bahrain, Kuwait, Oman, Qatar, Saudi Arabia, and the United Arab Emirates; **South Asian Association for Regional Cooperation (SAARC)**, Bangladesh, Bhutan, India, Maldives, Nepal, Pakistan, and Sri Lanka; and **Arab Maghreb Union (UMA)**, Algeria, Libya, Mauritania, Morocco, and Tunisia.

6.6 Regional trade blocs

Total merchandise exports by bloc

	Year of creation	% of world exports								
		1990	1995	1998	1999	2000	2001	2002	2003	2004
High-income and low- and middle-income economies										
APEC[a]	1989	39.0	46.3	46.1	46.6	48.4	46.5	46.0	44.5	44.3
CEFTA	1992	1.3	1.6	2.0	1.9	1.9	2.2	2.4	2.7	2.9
CIS	1991	..	2.1	1.9	1.8	2.2	2.0	2.3	2.5	2.7
EMFTA	1995	45.6	41.2	41.4	40.8	37.5	39.2	39.9	40.7	40.0
European Union	1957	44.0	39.7	39.9	39.2	35.8	37.5	38.0	38.8	37.9
FTAA	1994	19.1	19.7	21.8	21.7	22.1	21.8	20.2	18.4	17.7
NAFTA	1994	16.2	16.8	18.7	18.8	19.0	18.7	17.2	15.5	14.5
Africa										
CEMAC	1994	0.2	0.1	0.1	0.1	0.1	0.1	0.1	0.1	0.2
CEPGL	1976	0.1	0.0	0.0	0.0	0.0	0.0	0.0	0.0	0.0
COMESA	1994	0.4	0.4	0.3	0.3	0.4	0.4	0.4	0.4	0.5
Cross Border Initiative	1992	0.2	0.2	0.2	0.1	0.2	0.2	0.1	0.2	0.1
EAC	1996	0.1	0.1	0.1	0.1	0.1	0.1	0.1	0.1	0.1
ECCAS	1983	0.3	0.2	0.2	0.2	0.3	0.3	0.3	0.3	0.3
ECOWAS	1975	0.6	0.4	0.4	0.4	0.6	0.5	0.5	0.5	0.5
Indian Ocean Commission	1984	0.1	0.0	0.0	0.0	0.0	0.0	0.0	0.0	0.0
MRU	1973	0.1	0.0	0.0	0.0	0.0	0.0	0.0	0.0	0.0
SADC	1992	1.0	0.8	0.7	0.6	0.7	0.7	0.7	0.7	0.7
UDEAC	1964	0.2	0.1	0.1	0.1	0.1	0.1	0.1	0.1	0.2
UEMOA	1994	0.1	0.1	0.1	0.1	0.1	0.1	0.1	0.1	0.1
Latin America and the Caribbean										
ACS	1994	1.9	2.6	3.2	3.5	3.8	3.7	3.6	3.3	3.2
Andean Group	1969	0.9	0.8	0.8	0.8	1.0	0.9	0.8	0.8	0.9
CACM	1961	0.1	0.1	0.2	0.3	0.2	0.2	0.2	0.2	0.2
CARICOM	1973	0.2	0.1	0.1	0.1	0.1	0.1	0.1	0.2	0.2
Central American Group of Four	1993	0.1	0.1	0.1	0.2	0.1	0.1	0.1	0.1	0.1
Group of Three	1995	1.5	2.1	2.8	3.0	3.3	3.2	3.1	2.8	2.7
LAIA (ALADI)	1980	3.4	4.1	4.8	4.8	5.3	5.2	5.0	4.7	4.8
MERCOSUR	1991	1.4	1.4	1.5	1.3	1.4	1.4	1.4	1.4	1.5
OECS	1981	0.0	0.0	0.0	0.0	0.0	0.0	0.0	0.0	0.0
Middle East and Asia										
Arab Common Market	1964	1.0	0.4	0.4	0.5	0.7	0.6	0.6	0.6	0.9
ASEAN	1967	4.3	6.4	6.1	6.3	6.7	6.3	6.3	6.1	6.1
Bangkok Agreement	1975	3.6	4.8	4.8	5.0	5.2	4.9	5.1	5.1	5.3
EAEC	1990	20.9	26.1	24.2	24.7	26.0	24.4	25.2	25.4	26.0
ECO	1985	1.1	1.2	1.1	1.2	1.3	1.3	1.3	1.5	1.6
GAFTA	1997	3.8	2.6	2.3	2.7	3.5	3.4	3.2	3.4	3.9
GCC	1981	2.5	2.0	1.7	1.9	2.6	2.5	2.3	2.5	2.7
SAARC	1985	0.8	0.9	0.9	1.0	1.0	1.1	1.1	1.1	1.1
UMA	1989	1.0	0.6	0.5	0.6	0.7	0.7	0.7	0.7	0.8

a. No preferential trade agreement.

About the data

Trade blocs are groups of countries that have established special preferential arrangements governing trade between members. Although in some cases the preferences—such as lower tariff duties or exemptions from quantitative restrictions—may be no greater than those available to other trading partners, such arrangements are intended to encourage exports by bloc members to one another—sometimes called intratrade.

Most countries are members of a regional trade bloc, and more than a third of the world's trade takes place within such arrangements. While trade blocs vary widely in structure, they all have the same main objective: to reduce trade barriers between member countries. But effective integration requires more than reducing tariffs and quotas. Economic gains from competition and scale may not be achieved unless other barriers that divide markets and impede the free flow of goods, services, and investments are lifted. For example, many regional trade blocs retain contingent protections or restrictions on intrabloc trade. These include antidumping, countervailing duties, and "emergency protection" to address balance of payments problems or to protect an industry from surges in imports. Other barriers include differing product standards, discrimination in public procurement, and cumbersome and costly border formalities.

Membership in a regional trade bloc may reduce the frictional costs of trade, increase the credibility of reform initiatives, and strengthen security among partners. But making it work effectively is challenging for any government. All sectors of an economy may be affected, and some sectors may expand while others contract, so it is important to weigh the potential costs and benefits that membership may bring.

The table shows the value of merchandise intratrade for important regional trade blocs (service exports are excluded) as well as the size of intratrade relative to each bloc's total exports of goods and the share of the bloc's total exports in world exports. Although the Asia Pacific Economic Cooperation (APEC) has no preferential arrangements, it is included in the table because of the volume of trade between its members.

The data on country exports are drawn from the International Monetary Fund's (IMF) Direction of Trade database and should be broadly consistent with those from other sources, such as the United Nations Statistics Division's Commodity Trade (Comtrade) database. However, trade flows between many developing countries, particularly in Sub-Saharan Africa, are not well recorded. Thus the value of intratrade for certain groups may be understated. Data on trade between developing and high-income countries are generally complete.

Membership in the trade blocs shown is based on the most recent information available, from the World Bank Policy Research Report *Trade Blocs* (2000a), from the World Bank's *Global Economic Prospects 2005*, and from consultation with the World Bank's international trade unit. This year, the date of each trade bloc's creation has also been included. Although bloc exports have been calculated back to 1990 on the basis of current membership, several of the blocs came into existence in later years and their membership may have changed over time. For this reason, and because systems of preferences also change over time, intratrade in earlier years may not have been affected by the same preferences as in recent years. In addition, some countries belong to more than one trade bloc, so shares of world exports exceed 100 percent. Exports of blocs include all commodity trade, which may include items not specified in trade bloc agreements. Differences from previously published estimates may be due to changes in bloc membership or to revisions in the underlying data.

Definitions

• **Merchandise exports within bloc** are the sum of merchandise exports by members of a trade bloc to other members of the bloc. They are shown both in U.S. dollars and as a percentage of total merchandise exports by the bloc. • **Total merchandise exports by bloc** as a share of world exports are the ratio of the bloc's total merchandise exports (within the bloc and to the rest of the world) to total merchandise exports by all economies in the world.

6.6a

Regional trade agreements are proliferating

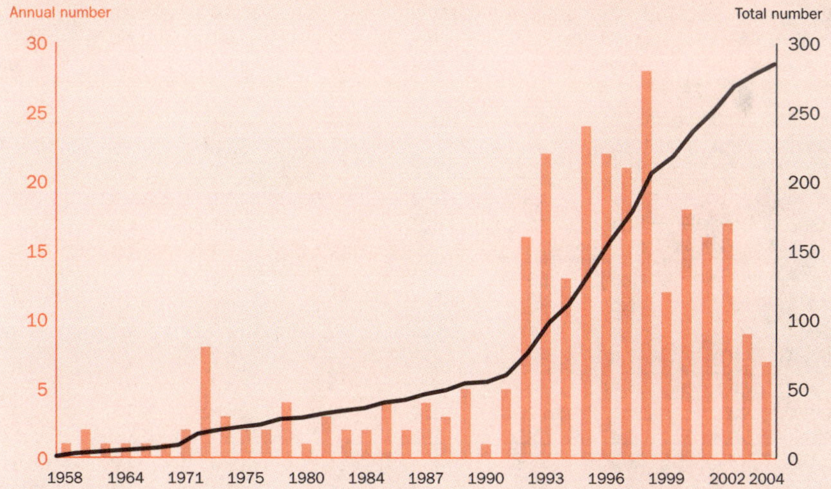

There are more than 250 regional trade agreements in force—six times as many as two decades ago. About a third of global trade takes place between countries that have some form of reciprocal regional trade agreement.

Source: World Bank 2005. *Global Economic Prospects 2005.*

Data sources

Data on merchandise trade flows are published in the IMF's *Direction of Trade Statistics Yearbook* and *Direction of Trade Statistics Quarterly*; the data in the table were calculated using the IMF's Direction of Trade database. The United Nations Conference on Trade and Development (UNCTAD) publishes data on intratrade in its *Handbook of International Trade and Development Statistics*. The information on trade bloc membership is from the World Bank Policy Research Report *Trade Blocs* (2000a), the World Bank's *Global Economic Prospects 2005*, and the World Bank's international trade unit.

6.7 Tariff barriers

	Most recent year	All products %						Primary products %		Manufactured products %	
		Binding coverage	Simple mean bound rate	Simple mean tariff	Weighted mean tariff	Share of lines with international peaks	Share of lines with specific rates	Simple mean tariff	Weighted mean tariff	Simple mean tariff	Weighted mean tariff
Albania	2002	100.0	7.0	8.3	8.4	0.0	0.0	9.2	7.7	8.2	8.7
Algeria	2003	..	..	17.9	12.0	39.4	0.0	18.1	10.5	17.8	12.5
Angola	2002	..	..	8.1	8.5	15.2	1.6	11.6	14.7	7.5	5.9
Argentina	2004[a]	100.0	31.9	11.4	9.3	35.5	0.0	8.4	2.4	11.7	9.9
Armenia	2001	100.0	8.5	3.2	2.2	0.0	0.0	6.5	3.3	2.6	1.3
Australia	2005[a]	97.1	10.0	4.2	3.1	5.6	0.2	1.5	0.7	4.6	3.6
Azerbaijan	2002	..	..	9.7	6.2	0.1	6.6	11.7	4.8	9.4	7.0
Bangladesh	2004	14.9	162.4	16.4	15.4	43.8	0.0	16.2	12.7	16.4	17.1
Belarus	2002	0.0	..	11.2	8.9	16.1	2.2	11.1	7.1	11.3	10.4
Belize	2003	..	..	12.9	11.4	38.9	0.4	20.1	13.3	11.7	10.8
Benin	2004	39.1	28.6	14.0	12.7	54.1	0.0	15.5	12.9	13.7	12.5
Bolivia	2004[a]	100.0	40.0	7.5	5.4	0.0	0.0	7.6	5.0	7.5	5.6
Bosnia and Herzegovina	2001[a]	..	..	5.1	4.9	0.0	0.0	3.7	5.3	5.3	4.7
Botswana	2001[a]	89.0	17.3	5.0	1.0	16.0	1.4	2.1	0.3	5.4	1.1
Brazil	2004[a]	100.0	31.4	13.1	7.6	37.0	0.0	9.0	1.8	13.5	9.9
Brunei	2004[a]	95.3	24.3	3.0	4.3	22.3	1.3	0.1	0.1	3.5	4.9
Bulgaria	2004[a]	100.0	24.7	10.2	9.6	24.5	2.5	15.4	10.7	9.6	9.3
Burkina Faso	2004	39.3	41.9	13.2	11.4	49.5	0.0	13.7	11.3	13.1	11.5
Burundi	2002[a]	20.9	67.6	20.0	14.7	32.6	0.6	22.4	10.6	19.6	16.9
Cambodia	2003[a]	..	..	15.6	16.4	24.8	0.0	16.8	15.6	15.4	16.6
Cameroon	2002	31.0	79.9	18.1	15.0	49.5	..	21.1	16.5	17.7	14.4
Canada	2005[a]	99.7	5.1	3.7	0.9	6.0	3.6	1.8	0.3	4.0	1.0
Chile	2004[a]	100.0	25.1	4.9	3.8	0.0	0.0	4.4	2.4	4.9	4.4
China	2004	100.0	10.0	9.6	6.0	14.9	0.0	9.6	6.2	9.5	5.8
Colombia	2004[a]	100.0	42.8	11.3	9.3	18.4	0.0	11.1	10.2	11.3	9.0
Congo, Dem. Rep.	2003	..	..	13.0	12.8	42.5	0.5	14.8	12.1	12.7	13.2
Costa Rica	2004[a]	100.0	42.9	5.7	3.8	0.9	0.0	8.3	5.8	5.4	3.4
Côte d'Ivoire	2004	33.2	11.2	12.7	10.7	44.9	0.0	14.7	11.5	12.3	10.1
Croatia	2004	100.0	5.9	4.1	3.2	5.7	3.9	6.5	3.6	3.7	3.1
Cuba	2004	31.0	21.3	10.7	9.9	11.6	..	11.1	8.8	10.6	10.4
Czech Republic	2003	100.0	5.0	5.1	4.4	4.8	0.0	5.7	4.1	4.9	4.3
Djibouti	2002	100.0	40.9	30.9	26.8	92.3	2.3	21.9	19.7	32.6	32.3
Dominican Republic	2004	100.0	34.9	10.3	8.1	32.5	0.2	13.5	7.1	9.8	8.7
Ecuador	2004[a]	99.9	21.8	11.5	9.0	20.5	0.0	10.7	6.6	11.5	9.5
Egypt, Arab Rep.	2002	99.0	37.2	18.9	13.9	46.2	6.8	18.1	7.9	19.0	16.9
El Salvador	2004[a]	100.0	36.6	5.4	4.3	8.0	0.0	6.4	3.8	5.3	4.5
Estonia	2003	100.0	8.7	1.0	0.9	5.4	0.0	8.2	4.0	0.0	0.0
Ethiopia	2002	..	..	19.4	13.5	52.0	0.2	22.0	6.7	19.1	15.7
European Union	2005[a]	100.0	4.2	1.8	1.7	1.8	10.3	2.6	0.9	1.7	2.1
Fiji	2004	51.4	40.1	..	..	..	..	..	..	..	..
Gabon	2002	100.0	21.4	18.6	14.7	52.3	..	23.2	19.7	17.9	13.5
Gambia, The	2002	13.6	100.6	..	..	..	..	..	..	..	..
Georgia	2004	100.0	7.2	7.3	9.1	5.3	1.4	12.0	13.2	6.5	6.3
Ghana	2004	14.3	92.1	13.1	11.0	45.0	0.2	17.6	17.1	12.3	8.8
Guatemala	2004[a]	34.9	36.5	5.1	4.9	1.4	0.0	7.3	5.1	4.8	4.8
Guinea	2004	39.0	20.1	..	..	..	..	..	..	..	..
Guinea-Bissau	2004	..	..	13.9	13.6	56.0	0.0	16.6	14.5	13.4	12.9
Guyana	2003	100.0	56.7	12.0	11.5	36.2	0.4	20.2	14.1	10.8	9.6
Honduras	2004[a]	100.0	32.5	5.2	5.4	1.1	0.0	7.2	8.0	4.9	4.0
Hungary	2002	96.2	9.8	8.9	7.9	10.9	0.0	17.9	6.7	7.7	8.0
Iceland	2003[a]	95.0	13.5	5.1	3.0	5.7	1.3	6.2	3.8	4.9	2.7
India	2004[a]	73.8	49.6	28.1	28.0	92.1	0.0	29.0	36.9	27.8	25.3
Indonesia	2004[a]	96.6	37.5	6.4	5.5	8.7	0.3	7.7	3.2	6.2	6.2
Iran, Islamic Rep.	2004	..	..	17.5	14.8	41.6	0.5	14.3	13.6	17.6	15.0
Israel	2005[a]	76.2	20.5	4.5	2.4	1.1	3.7	5.3	3.0	4.4	2.2
Jamaica	2003	100.0	49.8	9.4	9.8	36.5	0.3	16.0	11.0	8.4	9.3
Japan	2004[a]	99.6	3.0	2.9	2.4	8.1	2.8	5.3	3.9	2.4	1.6
Jordan	2003	100.0	16.3	14.4	11.4	40.8	0.2	20.0	11.9	13.6	11.0
Kenya	2004	14.0	95.1	16.2	10.3	39.1	0.1	19.5	10.1	15.8	10.2

	Most recent year	All products % Binding coverage	Simple mean bound rate	Simple mean tariff	Weighted mean tariff	Share of lines with international peaks	Share of lines with specific rates	Primary products % Simple mean tariff	Weighted mean tariff	Manufactured products % Simple mean tariff	Weighted mean tariff
Korea, Rep.	2002	94.4	15.8	9.3	10.0	5.2	0.4	19.5	19.0	7.7	5.0
Kuwait	2002	..	..	3.5	3.9	0.1	1.4	1.5	3.7	4.0	4.0
Kyrgyz Republic	2003	99.9	7.4	4.1	4.3	0.1	2.3	6.6	6.1	3.6	2.9
Lao PDR	2004[a]	..	..	8.5	12.1	8.4	0.1	13.6	13.8	7.8	11.4
Latvia	2001	100.0	12.8	3.2	2.6	2.9	0.0	8.0	5.5	2.5	1.5
Lebanon	2002[a]	..	..	7.2	6.3	12.5	0.4	13.6	6.1	6.3	6.4
Lesotho	2001[a]	..	..	10.8	17.8	42.1	2.9	16.0	9.2	10.5	17.8
Libya	2002	..	..	20.2	25.2	46.6	2.1	19.2	15.1	20.1	28.5
Lithuania	2003[a]	100.0	9.2	1.2	0.6	3.0	0.0	3.3	1.2	0.9	0.4
Macedonia, FYR	2004	..	..	10.2	7.6	26.0	3.4	12.2	8.4	9.9	7.2
Madagascar	2001	29.7	27.4	5.2	3.6	4.4	0.0	5.5	1.7	5.1	4.6
Malawi	2001[a]	30.2	75.0	12.9	10.2	40.4	0.0	12.6	9.0	12.9	10.7
Malaysia	2003[a]	83.7	14.5	7.4	4.1	21.2	0.9	4.6	2.1	7.8	4.5
Maldives	2003	97.1	37.1	21.3	20.7	71.4	0.0	17.8	18.5	22.2	21.9
Mali	2004	40.7	28.8	12.8	10.7	45.9	0.0	15.4	11.5	12.4	10.4
Mauritania	2001	39.4	19.6	12.8	9.3	51.5	0.0	12.6	7.9	12.8	10.0
Mauritius	2002	18.0	94.0	23.5	13.0	40.0	0.1	19.6	9.9	23.8	14.4
Mexico	2004[a]	100.0	35.0	14.6	3.7	38.5	0.0	13.0	2.6	14.7	3.8
Moldova	2001	..	..	4.6	2.8	0.1	0.9	8.3	2.6	4.0	2.9
Mongolia	2004	100.0	17.5	..	..	..	..	..	..	..	..
Morocco	2003	100.0	41.3	28.3	24.9	75.1	0.0	33.5	25.4	27.8	24.6
Mozambique	2003[a]	..	..	12.7	9.9	36.8	0.0	16.0	9.9	12.1	9.9
Myanmar	2004	16.5	83.2	4.4	4.1	3.3	0.0	7.2	4.6	4.1	3.9
Namibia	2001[a]	88.9	17.3	4.5	0.5	13.8	2.4	3.5	0.4	4.6	0.6
Nepal	2004	..	..	14.8	14.3	21.5	0.6	13.9	9.3	14.7	16.3
New Zealand	2004[a]	100.0	10.3	3.7	3.0	7.0	5.6	1.7	0.6	4.0	3.5
Nicaragua	2004[a]	100.0	41.7	4.9	3.8	0.9	0.0	7.0	3.9	4.7	3.6
Niger	2004	96.8	44.3	12.8	13.8	48.3	0.0	15.6	15.9	12.4	13.0
Nigeria	2002	19.3	118.0	24.8	18.5	51.8	1.0	36.8	26.7	23.2	15.7
Norway	2003[a]	100.0	3.0	0.5	0.4	0.5	5.5	1.5	1.4	0.3	0.2
Oman	2002	100.0	13.8	8.0	13.6	0.6	2.6	9.5	31.6	7.6	6.5
Pakistan	2004	44.8	52.2	16.1	13.2	50.3	0.1	14.7	9.4	16.2	15.7
Panama	2001	..	..	7.9	6.9	1.2	0.2	11.3	5.9	7.5	7.4
Papua New Guinea	2005	100.0	31.8	5.7	2.2	24.5	0.5	14.2	3.2	4.7	1.7
Paraguay	2004[a]	100.0	33.6	8.5	6.3	23.7	0.0	6.2	1.9	8.7	7.9
Peru	2004[a]	100.0	30.1	9.6	8.7	10.4	0.0	10.7	9.7	9.4	8.2
Philippines	2003	67.0	25.7	4.4	2.6	1.6	0.0	5.7	5.0	4.2	2.0
Poland	2003[a]	96.2	11.9	4.3	2.2	8.8	5.0	18.1	6.7	2.4	1.2
Qatar	2002	100.0	16.0	4.1	4.3	0.2	0.0	4.5	5.7	4.0	4.0
Romania	2004[a]	100.0	40.4	13.3	12.0	37.7	0.0	17.1	10.3	12.8	12.4
Russian Federation	2002	0.0	..	10.3	8.7	8.3	19.1	9.7	8.2	10.4	8.9
Rwanda	2003[a]	100.0	89.1	8.3	6.6	10.7	0.0	11.8	6.4	7.9	6.6
Saudi Arabia	2004	..	..	6.6	7.3	10.9	0.3	6.0	10.5	6.7	6.6
Senegal	2004	100.0	30.0	13.4	9.2	50.4	0.0	14.7	8.1	13.2	10.5
Serbia and Montenegro	2002	..	..	10.0	7.9	21.7	0.0	13.3	7.6	9.5	7.9
Seychelles	2001	..	..	27.2	23.4	57.6	0.3	38.8	46.6	25.4	18.5
Sierra Leone	2004	100.0	47.4	..	..	..	..	..	..	..	..
Singapore	2003	69.3	6.9	0.0	0.0	0.0	0.0	0.0	0.0	0.0	0.0
Slovak Republic	2002	100.0	5.0	22.1	21.2	51.0	0.0	19.5	12.8	22.4	23.6
Slovenia	2003[a]	100.0	23.7	3.9	1.6	10.4	1.4	6.1	3.3	3.5	1.1
South Africa	2001[a]	88.9	17.3	8.5	5.6	30.9	2.0	6.7	3.9	8.6	5.8
Sri Lanka	2004[a]	36.5	29.7	9.8	6.7	23.2	0.8	14.4	8.0	9.2	6.0
Sudan	2002	..	..	21.1	19.6	43.8	0.0	28.2	24.0	20.5	18.9
Suriname	2000	..	..	15.3	12.5	7.2	68.3	23.9	12.7	12.3	12.1
Swaziland	2001[a]	88.9	17.3	1.8	0.6	7.0	0.8	0.9	0.1	2.0	0.9
Sweden	1989	..	..	5.4	4.3	3.6	2.3	1.4	1.0	6.0	5.0
Switzerland[b]	2001[a]	99.8	1.7	3.2	1.5	..	37.7	15.0	9.5	1.1	0.2
Syrian Arab Republic	2002	..	..	14.6	15.5	23.2	0.1	14.2	11.7	14.5	16.6
Tanzania	2003[a]	13.4	120.0	14.1	8.2	37.4	0.0	15.2	7.4	14.0	8.6

Tariff barriers

	Most recent year	All products %						Primary products %		Manufactured products %	
		Binding coverage	Simple mean bound rate	Simple mean tariff	Weighted mean tariff	Share of lines with international peaks	Share of lines with specific rates	Simple mean tariff	Weighted mean tariff	Simple mean tariff	Weighted mean tariff
Thailand	2003[a]	74.8	25.8	13.3	8.3	46.4	0.7	15.4	4.4	12.9	9.3
Togo	2004	13.2	80.0	14.4	10.8	55.7	0.0	15.5	10.1	14.1	11.3
Trinidad and Tobago	2003	100.0	55.8	9.7	5.5	36.2	0.0	15.5	4.8	8.8	5.9
Tunisia	2004	57.8	57.7	25.3	22.3	65.6	0.0	36.8	18.4	24.2	23.5
Turkey	2003[a]	50.0	28.7	2.6	2.0	4.6	1.2	11.7	3.5	1.7	1.5
Turkmenistan	2002	..	..	5.1	2.9	13.7	3.3	15.6	13.2	3.6	1.1
Uganda	2004[a]	14.9	73.5	6.7	5.4	0.0	0.0	9.5	6.4	6.4	5.0
Ukraine	2002	..	..	7.6	3.9	11.2	10.5	6.8	1.5	7.6	6.4
United States	2005[a]	100.0	3.6	3.0	1.7	3.8	6.6	2.5	1.0	3.1	1.8
Uruguay	2004[a]	100.0	31.7	10.8	4.2	33.5	0.0	6.9	1.4	11.1	5.8
Uzbekistan	2001	..	..	10.4	5.9	26.7	0.0	10.4	4.6	10.5	6.2
Venezuela, RB	2004[a]	99.9	36.8	12.2	11.9	20.6	0.0	12.2	11.8	12.1	11.8
Vietnam	2004[a]	..	..	13.6	14.5	33.6	0.2	17.8	17.7	12.8	13.3
Yemen, Rep.	2000	..	..	12.7	11.8	10.9	0.0	13.5	10.8	12.6	12.4
Zambia	2005[a]	15.9	105.6	13.2	9.6	29.5	0.0	13.4	11.4	13.1	9.0
Zimbabwe	2003	20.8	91.3	15.9	18.7	36.3	5.7	19.2	27.2	15.4	15.7

a. Rates are either partially or fully recorded applied rates. All other simple and weighted tariff rates are most favored nation rates. b. Data for Switzerland include all specific rates converted to their ad valorem equivalents.

About the data

Poor people in developing countries work primarily in agriculture and labor-intensive manufactures, sectors that confront the greatest trade barriers. Removing barriers to merchandise trade could increase growth by about 0.8 percent a year in these countries—even more if trade in services (retailing, business, financial, and telecommunications services) were also liberalized.

In general, tariffs in high-income countries on imports from developing countries, though low, are twice the size of those collected from other high-income countries. But protection is also an issue for developing countries, which maintain high tariffs on agricultural commodities, labor-intensive manufactures, and other products and services. In some developing regions new trade policies could make the difference between achieving important Millennium Development Goals—reducing poverty, lowering maternal and child mortality rates, improving educational attainment—and falling far short.

Countries use a combination of tariff and nontariff measures to regulate imports. The most common form of tariff is an ad valorem duty, based on the value of the import, but tariffs may also be levied on a specific, or per unit, basis or may combine ad valorem and specific rates. Tariffs may be used to raise fiscal revenues or to protect domestic industries from foreign competition—or both. Nontariff barriers, which limit the quantity of imports of a particular good, include quotas, prohibitions, licensing schemes, export restraint arrangements, and health and quarantine measures.

Nontariff barriers are generally considered less desirable than tariffs because changes in an exporting country's efficiency and costs no longer result in changes in market share in the importing country. Further, the quotas or licenses that regulate trade become very valuable, and resources are often wasted in attempts to acquire these assets. A high percentage of products subject to nontariff barriers suggests a protectionist trade regime, but the frequency of nontariff barriers does not measure how much they restrict trade. Moreover, a wide range of domestic policies and regulations (such as health regulations) may act as nontariff barriers. Based on the difficulty of combining nontariff barriers into an aggregate indicator, they are not included in this table.

The tariff rates used in calculating the indicators in the table are most favored nation rates unless they are specified as applied rates. Effectively applied rates are those in effect for partners in preferential trade agreements such as the North American Free Trade Agreement. The difference between most favored nation and applied rates can be substantial. As more countries report their free trade agreements, suspensions of tariffs, or other special preferences, *World Development Indicators* will include their effectively applied rates. All estimates are calculated using the most up-to-date information, which is not necessarily updated every year. As a result, data for the same year may differ from data in last year's publication.

Three measures of average tariffs are shown: simple bound rates and the simple and the weighted mean tariffs. The most favored nation or applied rates are calculated using all traded items, while bound rates are based on all products in a country's tariff schedule. Weighted mean tariffs are weighted by the value of the country's trade with each trading partner. Simple averages are often a better indicator of tariff protection than weighted averages, which are biased downward because higher tariffs discourage trade and reduce the weights applied to these tariffs. Bound rates have resulted from trade negotiations that are incorporated into a country's schedule of concessions and are thus enforceable. If a contracting party raises a tariff to a higher level than its bound rate, beneficiaries of the earlier binding have a right to receive compensation, usually as reduced tariffs on other products they export to the country. If the beneficiaries are not compensated, they may retaliate by raising their own tariffs against an equivalent value of the original country's exports.

Some countries set fairly uniform tariff rates across all imports. Others are more selective, setting high tariffs to protect favored domestic industries. The share of tariff lines with international peaks (those for which ad valorem tariff rates exceed 15 percent) provides an indication of how selectively tariffs are applied. The effective rate of protection—the degree to which the value added in an industry is protected—may exceed the nominal rate if the tariff system systematically differentiates among imports of raw materials, intermediate products, and finished goods.

The share of tariff lines with specific duties shows the extent to which countries utilize tariffs based on physical quantities or other, non ad valorem measures. Some countries—for example, Switzerland—apply only specific duties. Specific duties are not included in the table, except for Switzerland. Work is under way to complete the estimations for ad valorem equivalents of specific duties for all countries.

The indicators were calculated from data supplied by the United Nations Conference on Trade and Development (UNCTAD) and the World Trade Organization (WTO). Data are classified using the Harmonized System of trade at the six- or eight-digit level. Tariff line data were matched to Standard International Trade Classification (SITC) revision 2 codes to define commodity groups and import weights. Import weights were calculated using the United Nations Statistics Division's Commodity Trade (Comtrade) database. Data are shown only for the last year for which complete data are available. To conserve space, data for the European Union are shown instead of data for individual members.

Definitions

• **Binding coverage** is the percentage of product lines with an agreed bound rate. • **Simple mean bound rate** is the unweighted average of all the lines in the tariff schedule in which bound rates have been set. • **Simple mean tariff** is the unweighted average of effectively applied rates or most favored nation rates for all products subject to tariffs calculated for all traded goods. • **Weighted mean tariff** is the average of effectively applied rates or most favored nation rates weighted by the product import shares corresponding to each partner country. • **Share of lines with international peaks** is the share of lines in the tariff schedule with tariff rates that exceed 15 percent. • **Share of lines with specific rates** is the share of lines in the tariff schedule that are set on a per unit basis or that combine ad valorem and per unit rates. • **Primary products** are commodities classified in SITC revision 2 sections 0–4 plus division 68 (nonferrous metals). • **Manufactured products** are commodities classified in SITC revision 2 sections 5–8 excluding division 68.

Data sources

All indicators in the table were calculated by World Bank staff using the World Integrated Trade Solution system. Data on tariffs were provided by UNCTAD and the WTO. Data on global imports are from the United Nations Statistics Division's Comtrade database.

6.8 Global private financial flows

	Foreign direct investment		Portfolio investment flows				Bank and trade-related lending	
	$ millions		$ millions				$ millions	
			Bonds		Equity			
	1990	2004	1990	2004	1990	2004	1990	2004
Afghanistan	..	..	..	..	..	..	..	..
Albania	0	426	..	0	0	0	..	30
Algeria	40	882	–16	0	0	0	–409	–479
Angola	–335	1,444	0	0	0	0	570	1,288
Argentina	1,836	4,084	–857	–671	0	–86	–1,195	–823
Armenia	4	219	..	0	0	1	..	0
Australia	8,111	42,469	..	..	..	..	..	..
Austria	653	4,022	..	..	..	..	..	..
Azerbaijan	..	3,556	..	0	0	0	..	117
Bangladesh	3	449	0	0	0	4	55	–16
Belarus	..	169	..	0	0	1	..	–62
Belgium	8,047[a]	118,758[a]	..	..	..	..	..	..
Benin	62	60	0	0	0	1	0	0
Bolivia	27	116	0	0	0	0	–24	3
Bosnia and Herzegovina	..	613	..	0	0	0	..	39
Botswana	96	47	0	0	0	10	–19	–1
Brazil	989	18,166	129	–4,436	103	2,081	–555	–178
Bulgaria	4	2,005	..	–548	0	0	..	1,618
Burkina Faso	0	35	0	0	0	0	–1	0
Burundi	1	3	0	0	0	0	–6	–5
Cambodia	..	131	0	0	0	0	0	0
Cameroon	–113	0	0	0	0	0	–12	24
Canada	7,581	6,284	..	..	..	..	..	..
Central African Republic	1	–13	0	0	0	0	–1	–4
Chad	9	478	0	0	0	0	–1	0
Chile	661	7,603	–7	1,451	367	8	1,194	–1,093
China	3,487	54,936	–48	3,690	0	10,923	4,668	4,280
Hong Kong, China	..	34,034	..	..	..	..	..	..
Colombia	500	3,052	–4	553	0	130	–151	–1,844
Congo, Dem. Rep.	–14	0	0	0	0	0	–12	–4
Congo, Rep.	23	0	0	0	0	0	–100	0
Costa Rica	163	620	–42	49	0	0	–99	–21
Côte d'Ivoire	48	175	–1	0	0	–1	10	–134
Croatia	..	1,243	..	910	0	177	..	2,808
Cuba	..	..	..	..	..	..	..	..
Czech Republic	72	4,454	..	2,696	0	738	..	–658
Denmark	1,132	–8,804	..	..	..	..	..	..
Dominican Republic	133	645	0	–20	0	0	–3	440
Ecuador	126	1,160	0	0	0	1	58	598
Egypt, Arab Rep.	734	1,253	–1	–100	0	26	–65	–128
El Salvador	2	466	0	294	0	0	6	–35
Eritrea	..	30	..	0	0	0	..	0
Estonia	..	1,049	..	857	0	176	..	1,570
Ethiopia	12	545	0	0	0	0	–57	71
Finland	812	3,075	..	..	..	..	..	..
France	13,183	24,521	..	..	..	..	..	..
Gabon	73	323	0	0	0	0	29	–23
Gambia, The	14	60	0	0	0	0	–8	0
Georgia	..	499	..	0	0	0	..	63
Germany	3,005	–34,903	..	..	..	..	..	..
Ghana	15	139	0	0	0	0	–23	31
Greece	1,005	1,355	..	..	..	..	..	..
Guatemala	48	155	–11	380	0	0	1	–16
Guinea	18	100	0	0	0	0	–19	0
Guinea-Bissau	2	5	0	0	0	0	0	0
Haiti	8	7	0	0	0	0	0	0

Global private financial flows

	Foreign direct investment		Portfolio investment flows				Bank and trade-related lending	
	$ millions		$ millions				$ millions	
			Bonds		Equity			
	1990	2004	1990	2004	1990	2004	1990	2004
Honduras	44	293	0	0	0	0	32	161
Hungary	623	4,608	921	2,875	0	1,491	–1,379	7,978
India	237	5,335	147	3,722	0	8,835	1,459	–40
Indonesia	1,093	1,023	26	1,520	0	2,129	1,804	–2,467
Iran, Islamic Rep.	–362	500	0	0	0	0	–30	652
Iraq	..	..	..	..	..	..	..	..
Ireland	627	11,040	..	..	..	..	..	..
Israel	151	1,664	..	..	..	..	..	..
Italy	6,411	16,772	..	..	..	..	..	..
Jamaica	138	602	0	641	0	0	–46	56
Japan	1,777	7,805	..	..	..	..	..	..
Jordan	38	620	0	–11	0	–120	214	–5
Kazakhstan	..	4,104	..	3,075	0	–14	..	5,102
Kenya	57	46	0	0	0	3	65	–111
Korea, Dem. Rep.	..	..	..	..	..	..	..	..
Korea, Rep.	788	8,189	..	..	..	..	..	..
Kuwait	0	–20	..	..	..	..	..	..
Kyrgyz Republic	..	77	..	0	0	0	..	–54
Lao PDR	6	17	0	0	0	0	0	0
Latvia	..	699	..	503	0	23	..	1,129
Lebanon	6	288	0	2,632	0	0	6	–48
Lesotho	17	123	0	0	0	0	0	–9
Liberia	225	20	0	0	0	0	0	0
Libya	..	..	..	..	..	..	..	..
Lithuania	..	773	..	696	0	8	..	598
Macedonia, FYR	..	157	..	0	0	15	..	27
Madagascar	22	45	0	0	0	0	–15	–2
Malawi	23	16	0	0	1	0	2	–2
Malaysia	2,332	4,624	–1,239	2,063	0	4,400	–617	–2,039
Mali	6	180	0	0	0	1	–1	1
Mauritania	7	300	0	0	0	0	–1	0
Mauritius	41	14	0	0	0	19	45	–40
Mexico	2,549	17,377	661	–1,904	1,995	–2,522	4,396	294
Moldova	..	81	..	–2	0	–2	..	–28
Mongolia	0	93	..	0	0	0	..	0
Morocco	165	769	0	–40	0	572	318	–532
Mozambique	9	245	0	0	0	0	26	–23
Myanmar	163	214	0	0	0	0	–8	–32
Namibia	..	..	..	..	..	..	..	..
Nepal	6	0	0	0	0	0	–14	0
Netherlands	10,676	377	..	..	..	..	..	..
New Zealand	1,735	2,271	..	..	..	..	..	..
Nicaragua	1	250	0	0	0	0	20	26
Niger	41	0	0	0	0	0	10	–7
Nigeria	588	1,875	0	0	0	0	–121	–145
Norway	1,003	502	..	..	..	..	..	..
Oman	142	–17	0	550	0	147	–400	–578
Pakistan	245	1,118	0	283	0	50	–63	–132
Panama	136	1,012	–2	769	–1	0	–4	11
Papua New Guinea	155	25	0	0	0	0	49	–214
Paraguay	77	92	0	0	0	0	–9	–129
Peru	41	1,816	0	1,242	0	–47	18	34
Philippines	530	469	395	1,823	0	418	–286	–252
Poland	89	12,613	0	3,370	0	1,913	–18	–100
Portugal	2,610	825	..	..	..	..	..	..
Puerto Rico	..	..	..	..	..	..	..	..

6.8 Global private financial flows

	Foreign direct investment $ millions		Portfolio investment flows $ millions				Bank and trade-related lending $ millions	
			Bonds		Equity			
	1990	2004	1990	2004	1990	2004	1990	2004
Romania	0	5,440	0	–187	0	111	4	4,152
Russian Federation	..	12,479	..	7,904	0	528	..	2,805
Rwanda	8	8	0	0	0	0	–2	0
Saudi Arabia	..	..	..	..	..	..	..	..
Senegal	57	70	0	0	1	4	–15	92
Serbia and Montenegro	..	966	..	0	0	0	..	1,191
Sierra Leone	32	26	0	0	0	0	4	0
Singapore	5,575	16,032	..	..	..	..	..	..
Slovak Republic	..	1,122	..	622	0	60	..	404
Slovenia	..	827	..	..	..	..	..	..
Somalia	6	9	0	0	0	0	0	0
South Africa	–76	585	..	1,249	389	6,661	..	–668
Spain	13,984	16,594	..	..	..	..	..	..
Sri Lanka	43	233	0	100	0	–100	10	–57
Sudan	–31	1,511	0	0	0	0	0	54
Swaziland	30	68	0	0	–2	0	–2	16
Sweden	1,982	–588	..	..	..	..	..	..
Switzerland	5,545	–797	..	..	..	..	..	..
Syrian Arab Republic	71	275	0	0	0	0	–9	–4
Tajikistan	..	272	..	0	0	0	..	–24
Tanzania	0	249	0	0	0	0	5	–4
Thailand	2,444	1,412	–87	597	440	–295	1,574	117
Togo	18	60	0	0	4	3	0	0
Trinidad and Tobago	109	1,001	–52	–150	0	0	–126	0
Tunisia	76	593	–60	282	5	24	–137	141
Turkey	684	2,733	597	2,109	89	1,427	466	5,826
Turkmenistan	..	..	..	..	..	..	..	..
Uganda	–6	222	0	0	0	1	16	7
Ukraine	..	1,715	..	856	0	–2,204	..	4,637
United Arab Emirates	..	..	..	..	..	..	..	..
United Kingdom	33,504	72,561	..	..	..	..	..	..
United States	48,490	106,831	..	..	..	..	..	..
Uruguay	42	311	–16	–186	0	0	–176	–123
Uzbekistan	..	140	..	0	0	0	..	–160
Venezuela, RB	451	1,518	345	872	0	–170	–922	–82
Vietnam	180	1,610	0	–13	0	0	0	23
West Bank and Gaza	..	..	..	..	..	..	..	..
Yemen, Rep.	–131	144	0	0	0	0	161	0
Zambia	203	334	0	–1	0	0	–9	–22
Zimbabwe	–12	60	–30	0	0	0	127	7
World	**201,413 s**	**624,797 s**	**.. s**	**.. s**	**.. s**	**.. s**	**.. s**	**.. s**
Low income	2,233	17,031	116	3,990	7	8,899	1,532	–844
Middle income	20,523	194,354	966	39,007	3,383	28,660	13,935	35,627
Lower middle income	10,307	111,023	388	9,711	545	13,653	6,535	18,478
Upper middle income	10,216	83,331	577	29,297	2,838	15,007	7,400	17,149
Low & middle income	22,756	211,385	1,081	42,997	3,390	37,559	15,467	34,784
East Asia & Pacific	10,505	64,563	–952	9,679	440	17,575	7,180	–594
Europe & Central Asia	1,476	62,211	1,893	25,738	89	4,450	4,281	38,901
Latin America & Carib.	8,244	60,843	101	–1,087	2,464	–606	2,430	–2,767
Middle East & N. Africa	780	5,340	–76	3,313	5	649	–350	–982
South Asia	541	7,151	147	4,105	1	8,789	1,446	–224
Sub-Saharan Africa	1,209	11,276	–31	1,249	393	6,701	479	450
High income	178,657	413,412	..	..	..	..	..	..
Europe EMU	61,012	122,354	..	..	..	..	..	..

a. Includes Luxembourg.

About the data

The data on foreign direct investment are based on balance of payments data reported by the International Monetary Fund (IMF), supplemented by staff estimates using data reported by the United Nations Conference on Trade and Development and official national sources.

The internationally accepted definition of foreign direct investment is provided in the fifth edition of the IMF's *Balance of Payments Manual* (1993). Under this definition foreign direct investment has three components: equity investment, reinvested earnings, and short- and long-term intercompany loans between parent firms and foreign affiliates. But many countries fail to report reinvested earnings, and the definition of long-term loans differs among countries. Foreign direct investment, as distinguished from other kinds of international investment, is made to establish a lasting interest in or effective management control over an enterprise in another country. As a guideline, the IMF suggests that investments should account for at least 10 percent of voting stock to be counted as foreign direct investment. In practice, many countries set a higher threshold.

The Organisation for Economic Co-operation and Development has also published a definition, in consultation with the IMF, Eurostat, and the United Nations. Because of the multiplicity of sources and differences in definitions and reporting methods, there may be more than one estimate of foreign direct investment for a country and data may not be comparable across countries.

Foreign direct investment data do not give a complete picture of international investment in an economy. Balance of payments data on foreign direct investment do not include capital raised locally, which has become an important source of financing for investment projects in some developing countries. In addition, foreign direct investment data capture only cross-border investment flows involving equity participation and thus omit nonequity crossborder transactions such as intrafirm flows of goods and services. For a detailed discussion of the data issues, see the World Bank's *World Debt Tables 1993–94* (volume 1, chapter 3).

Portfolio flow data are compiled from several market and official sources, including Euromoney databases and publications; Micropal; Lipper Analytical Services; published reports of private investment houses, central banks, national securities and exchange commissions, and national stock exchanges; and the World Bank's Debtor Reporting System.

Gross statistics on international bond and equity issues are produced by aggregating individual transactions reported by market sources. Transactions of public and publicly guaranteed bonds are reported through the Debtor Reporting System by World Bank member economies that have received either loans from the International Bank for Reconstruction and Development or credits from the International Development Association. Information on private nonguaranteed bonds is collected from market sources, because official national sources reporting to the Debtor Reporting System are not asked to report the breakdown between private nonguaranteed bonds and private nonguaranteed loans. Information on transactions by nonresidents in local equity markets is gathered from national authorities, investment positions of mutual funds, and market sources.

The volume of portfolio investment reported by the World Bank generally differs from that reported by other sources because of differences in the sources, in the classification of economies, and in the method used to adjust and disaggregate reported information. Differences in reporting arise particularly for foreign investments in local equity markets because clarity, adequate disaggregation, and comprehensive and periodic reporting are lacking in many developing economies. By contrast, capital flows through international debt and equity instruments are well recorded, and for these the differences in reporting lie primarily in the classification of economies, the exchange rates used, whether particular installments of the transactions are included, and the treatment of certain offshore issuances.

Net private capital flows—calculated as the sum of foreign direct investment, portfolio investment flows, and bank and trade-related lending—are no longer included in the table because they are likely to be overestimated. The source of overestimation is the possible double counting of intercompany lending, which is a debt liability but may also be included in foreign direct investment flows. There is currently no practical way to know when double counting has occured and therefore to adjust for it.

6.8a

Which developing countries received the most net inflows of foreign direct investment in 2004?

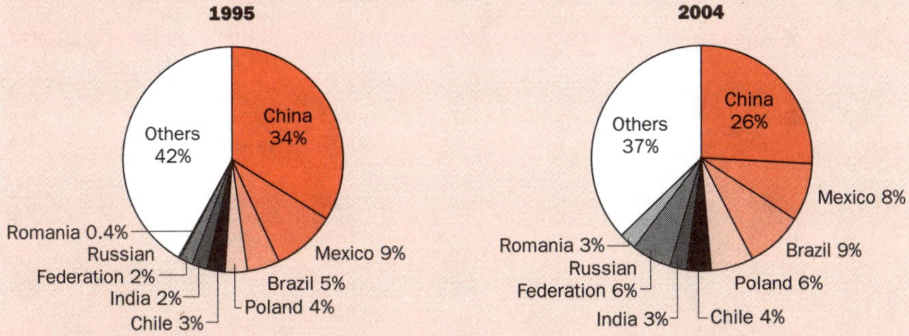

Economic integration in the past decade has boosted foreign direct investment (FDI) inflows to developing countries—particularly those with improved investment climates. FDI is also increasingly concentrated. The top eight FDI-receiving developing countries account for 63 percent of net FDI inflow in 2004, up from 58 percent in 1995.

Source: World Bank Debtor Reporting System.

Definitions

• **Foreign direct investment** is net inflows of investment to acquire a lasting management interest in an enterprise operating in an economy other than that of the investor. It is the sum of equity capital, reinvestment of earnings, other long-term capital, and short-term capital, as shown in the balance of payments. • **Portfolio investment flows** are net and include portfolio debt flows (public and publicly guaranteed and private nonguaranteed bond issues purchased by foreign investors) and non-debt-creating portfolio equity flows (the sum of country funds, depository receipts, and direct purchases of shares by foreign investors). • **Bank and trade-related lending** covers commercial bank lending (public and publicly guaranteed and private nonguaranteed) and other private credits.

Data sources

Data are compiled from a variety of public and private sources, including the World Bank's Debtor Reporting System, the IMF's International Financial Statistics and Balance of Payments databases, and other sources mentioned in *About the data*. These data are also published in the World Bank's *Global Development Finance 2006*.

6.9 Net financial flows from Development Assistance Committee members

Net flows to part I countries

$ millions	Official development assistance: Total 2004	Official development assistance: Bilateral grants 2004	Official development assistance: Bilateral loans 2004	Official development assistance: Contributions to multilateral institutions 2004	Other official flows 2004	Private flows: Total 2004	Private flows: Foreign direct investment 2004	Private flows: Bilateral portfolio investment 2004	Private flows: Multilateral portfolio investment 2004	Private flows: Private export credits 2004	Net grants by NGOs 2004	Total net flows 2004
Australia	1,460	1,191	..	270	35	482	506	–24	..	..	489	2,466
Austria	678	380	–28	325	–229	815	924	..	..	–109	89	1,352
Belgium	1,463	953	–50	561	–93	–735	–169	..	..	–566	181	816
Canada	2,599	2,022	–31	608	–794	3,542	3,613	–71	..	0	639	5,986
Denmark	2,037	1,192	11	835	21	518	518	..	..	..	58	2,634
Finland	655	353	9	293	..	..	..	..	..	..	..	..
France	8,473	6,067	–500	2,906	–216	4,342	1,534	2,831	..	–23	..	12,599
Germany	7,534	4,513	–690	3,712	–1,051	4,199	3,613	–278	–85	949	1,148	11,830
Greece	465	304	..	161	4	–14	–14	..	..	..	17	472
Ireland	607	410	..	198	..	3,010	..	3,010	..	..	234	3,851
Italy	2,462	855	–151	1,757	507	221	808	–2,269	..	1,682	49	3,239
Japan	8,906	7,131	–1,213	2,988	–2,372	4,392	9,171	–3,426	–3,020	1,667	425	11,351
Luxembourg	236	171	..	64	..	..	..	..	..	..	6	242
Netherlands	4,204	3,217	–547	1,534	151	9,339	1,986	3,086	559	3,708	412	14,106
New Zealand	212	159	..	53	5	25	25	..	..	..	29	271
Norway	2,199	1,496	41	662	0	586	635	..	..	–49	..	2,785
Portugal	1,031	179	694	158	–692	335	187	..	..	148	3	676
Spain	2,437	1,227	173	1,037	25	10,300	10,503	..	..	–203	..	12,762
Sweden	2,722	2,066	10	646	–64	266	594	..	..	–328	31	2,954
Switzerland	1,545	1,173	14	359	..	–2,810	–2,082	..	–966	238	316	–949
United Kingdom	7,883	5,239	100	2,544	–155	18,805	13,335	5,826	..	–356	390	26,922
United States	19,705	17,027	–777	3,455	–679	6,465	20,355	–12,343	–1,255	–293	6,792	32,283
Total	**79,512**	**57,322**	**–2,937**	**25,126**	**–5,599**	**64,082**	**66,041**	**–3,658**	**–4,766**	**6,465**	**11,307**	**148,646**

Net flows to part II countries

$ millions	Official aid: Total 2004	Official aid: Bilateral grants 2004	Official aid: Bilateral loans 2004	Official aid: Contributions to multilateral institutions 2004	Other official flows 2004	Private flows: Total 2004	Private flows: Foreign direct investment 2004	Private flows: Bilateral portfolio investment 2004	Private flows: Private export credits 2004	Net grants by NGOs 2004	Total net flows 2004
Australia	10	5	..	6	23	–1,478	–1,324	–154	..	..	–1,445
Austria	260	158	0	101	–2	3,702	3,778	0	–76	12	3,973
Belgium	190	8	..	182	–44	6,636	6,657	0	–21	..	6,782
Canada	93	93	0	..	–71	3,403	3,301	150	–48	..	3,425
Denmark	140	64	–21	97	5	767	767	..	..	5	918
Finland	92	45	..	47	..	..	..	..	..	..	92
France	2,358	1,532	32	795	–97	..	6,038	4,078	1,938	22	8,299
Germany	1,435	549	–74	959	–1,076	..	7,600	2,825	4,564	211	7,958
Greece	130	51	..	80	11	2	93	93	..	..	237
Ireland	3	3	..	..	..	..	..	..	..	..	3
Italy	664	14	..	650	–59	..	170	494	–1,758	1,434	775
Japan	121	129	–68	60	–90	..	5,671	5,344	1,081	–754	5,702
Luxembourg	15	3	..	13	..	..	..	..	..	..	15
Netherlands	222	64	–12	169	..	..	17,745	8,513	7,398	1,834	17,967
New Zealand	1	1	..	0	..	..	..	..	..	..	1
Norway	45	45	..	..	0	..	–1	..	..	–1	44
Portugal	62	1	..	61	–5	..	–82	–89	..	7	–24
Spain	15	15	..	..	..	..	2,169	2,169	..	..	2,184
Sweden	123	123	..	..	–13	..	862	724	..	138	972
Switzerland	100	85	4	12	1	13	8,262	8,312	0	–50	8,375
United Kingdom	834	70	0	764	..	4	20,667	4,284	16,648	–266	21,505
United States	1,605	1,702	–167	70	–278	3,577	9,124	18,713	–9,663	74	14,027
Total	**8,519**	**4,759**	**–305**	**4,065**	**–1,694**	**3,613**	**91,347**	**68,639**	**20,204**	**2,504**	**101,785**

Note: Data may not sum to totals because of gaps in reporting. A substantial part of the increase in private flows to part II countries is due to the transfer of countries from part I to part II of the Development Assistance Committee list of aid recipients.

Net financial flows from Development Assistance Committee members 6.9

About the data

The high-income members of the Development Assistance Committee (DAC) of the Organisation for Economic Co-operation and Development (OECD) are the main source of official external finance for developing countries. The table shows the flow of official and private financial resources from DAC members to official and private recipients in developing and transition economies.

DAC exists to help its members coordinate their development assistance and to encourage the expansion and improve the effectiveness of the aggregate resources flowing to recipient economies. In this capacity DAC monitors the flow of all financial resources, but its main concern is official development assistance (ODA). DAC has three criteria for ODA: It is undertaken by the official sector. It promotes the economic development and welfare of developing countries as a main objective. And it is provided on concessional terms, with a grant element of at least 25 percent on loans (calculated at a rate of discount of 10 percent).

This definition excludes nonconcessional flows from official creditors, which are classified as "other official flows," and military aid, which is not recorded in DAC statistics. The definition includes food aid, capital projects, emergency relief, technical cooperation, and postconflict peacekeeping efforts. Also included are contributions to multilateral institutions, such as the United Nations and its specialized agencies, and concessional funding to the multilateral development banks. In 1999, to avoid double counting extrabudgetary expenditures reported by DAC countries and flows reported by the United Nations, all UN agencies revised their data to include only regular budgetary expenditures since 1990 (except for the World Food Programme and the United Nations High Commissioner for Refugees, which revised their data from 1996 onward).

DAC maintains a list of countries and territories that are aid recipients. Part I of the list comprises developing countries and territories considered by DAC members to be eligible for ODA. Part II comprises economies in transition: more advanced countries of Central and Eastern Europe, the countries of the former Soviet Union, and certain advanced developing countries and territories. Flows to these recipients that meet the criteria for ODA are termed official aid.

The table was compiled from replies by DAC member countries to questionnaires issued by the DAC Secretariat. Net flows of ODA, official aid, and other official resources are defined as gross disbursements of grants and loans minus repayments of principal on earlier loans. Because the table is based on donor country reports, it does not provide a complete picture of the resources received by developing and transition economies, for two reasons. First, flows from DAC members are only part of the aggregate resource flows to these economies. Second, the data that record contributions to multilateral institutions measure the flow of resources made available to those institutions by DAC members, not the flow of resources from those institutions to developing and transition economies.

6.9a

Who were the largest donors in 2004?

Official development assistance as a share of total

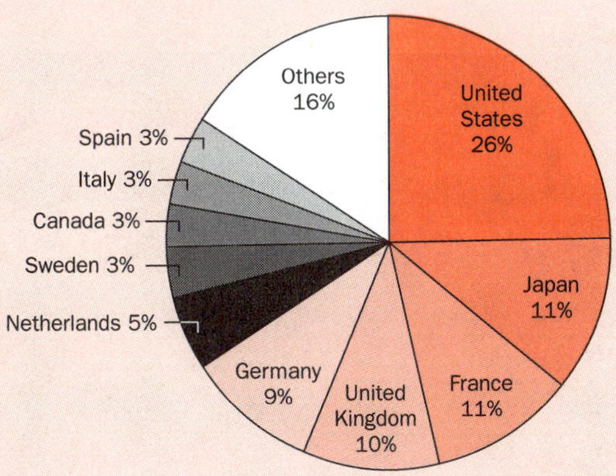

The United States is the largest donor, contributing a quarter of total official development assistance in 2004. The next four largest donors—Japan, France, the United Kingdom, and Germany—contributed 41 percent combined.

Source: Organisation for Economic Co-operation and Development, Development Assistance Committee.

Definitions

• **Official development assistance** comprises grants and loans (net of repayments of principal) that meet the DAC definition of ODA and are made to countries and territories in part I of the DAC list of aid recipients. • **Official aid** comprises grants and loans (net of repayments) that meet the criteria for ODA and are made to countries and territories in part II of the DAC list of aid recipients. • **Bilateral grants** are transfers of money or in kind for which no repayment is required. • **Bilateral loans** are loans extended by governments or official agencies that have a grant element of at least 25 percent (calculated at a rate of discount of 10 percent). • **Contributions to multilateral institutions** are concessional funding received by multilateral institutions from DAC members in the form of grants or capital subscriptions. • **Other official flows** are transactions by the official sector whose main objective is other than development or whose grant element is less than 25 percent. • **Private flows** consist of flows at market terms financed from private sector resources in donor countries. They include changes in holdings of private long-term assets by residents of the reporting country. • **Foreign direct investment** is investment by residents of DAC member countries to acquire a lasting management interest (at least 10 percent of voting stock) in an enterprise operating in the recipient country. The data reflect changes in the net worth of subsidiaries in recipient countries whose parent company is in the DAC source country. • **Bilateral portfolio investment** covers bank lending and the purchase of bonds, shares, and real estate by residents of DAC member countries in recipient countries. • **Multilateral portfolio investment** records the transactions of private banks and nonbanks in DAC member countries in the securities issued by multilateral institutions. • **Private export credits** are loans extended to recipient countries by the private sector in DAC member countries to promote trade; they may be supported by an official guarantee. • **Net grants by NGOs** are private grants by nongovernmental organizations, net of subsidies from the official sector. • **Total net flows** comprise ODA or official aid flows, other official flows, private flows, and net grants by nongovernmental organizations.

Data sources

Data on financial flows are compiled by DAC and published in its annual statistical report, *Geographical Distribution of Financial Flows to Aid Recipients*, and its annual *Development Cooperation Report*. Data are available electronically on the OECD's *International Development Statistics* CD-ROM and to registered users at www.oecd.org/dataoecd/50/17/5037721.htm.

6.10 Aid flows from Development Assistance Committee members

Net flows to part I countries

	Net official development assistance									Untied aid[a]	
	$ millions		% of GNI		average annual % change in volume[b]	Per capita of donor country[b] $		% of general government disbursement		% of bilateral ODA commitments	
	1999	2004	1999	2004	1998–99 to 2003–04	1999	2004	1999	2004	1999	2004
Australia	982	1,460	0.26	0.25	1.7	59	62	0.70	0.67	86.7	77.1
Austria	492	678	0.24	0.23	1.0	69	74	0.43	0.46	39.8	52.2
Belgium	760	1,463	0.30	0.41	11.4	84	125	0.60	0.84	39.0	92.7
Canada	1,706	2,599	0.28	0.27	1.7	65	73	0.61	0.66	29.6	56.7
Denmark	1,733	2,037	1.01	0.85	–2.0	378	336	1.78	1.50	70.8	88.8
Finland	416	655	0.33	0.35	5.0	91	113	0.63	0.70	84.7	..
France	5,639	8,473	0.38	0.41	3.3	109	122	0.73	0.77	70.6	94.2
Germany	5,515	7,534	0.26	0.28	2.5	74	82	0.54	0.59	84.7	92.2
Greece	194	465	0.15	0.23	12.2	21	37	0.32	0.44	3.3	23.0
Ireland	245	607	0.31	0.39	13.5	82	133	0.75	0.98	..	100.0
Italy	1,806	2,462	0.15	0.15	–0.6	37	38	0.31	0.30	22.6	..
Japan	12,163	8,906	0.27	0.19	–4.7	88	67	0.72	0.51	96.4	94.4
Luxembourg	119	236	0.66	0.83	8.8	320	466	1.43	1.61	96.1	..
Netherlands	3,134	4,204	0.79	0.73	0.7	244	233	1.68	1.49	94.1	86.8
New Zealand	134	212	0.27	0.23	1.7	42	44	0.63	0.64	..	81.2
Norway	1,370	2,199	0.88	0.87	2.5	399	430	1.80	1.89	99.1	100.0
Portugal	276	1,031	0.26	0.63	13.8	33	89	0.53	1.27	73.7	99.2
Spain	1,363	2,437	0.23	0.24	4.0	43	50	0.56	0.60	..	67.7
Sweden	1,630	2,722	0.70	0.78	7.0	202	272	1.08	1.38	91.5	87.5
Switzerland	984	1,545	0.35	0.41	4.7	160	192	1.07	1.20	96.8	96.8
United Kingdom	3,426	7,883	0.24	0.36	10.2	65	115	0.59	0.84	91.8	100.0
United States	9,145	19,705	0.10	0.17	12.7	36	66	0.29	0.47	..	..
Total or average	**53,233**	**79,512**	**0.22**	**0.26**	**4.3**	**69**	**84**	**0.56**	**0.63**	**85.8**	**90.6**

Net flows to part II countries

	Net official aid						
	$ millions		% of GNI		average annual % change in volume[b]	Per capita of donor country[b] $	
	1999	2004	1999	2004	1998–99 to 2003–04	1999	2004
Australia	3	10	0.00	0.00	33.3	0	0
Austria	184	260	0.09	0.09	2.8	26	28
Belgium	82	190	0.03	0.05	14.6	9	16
Canada	165	93	0.03	0.01	–13.2	6	3
Denmark	128	140	0.07	0.06	3.0	28	23
Finland	74	92	0.06	0.05	–1.0	16	16
France	745	2,358	0.05	0.11	19.0	14	34
Germany	729	1,434	0.03	0.05	10.6	10	16
Greece	11	131	0.01	0.06	45.2	1	10
Ireland	..	3	..	0.00	..	0	1
Italy	92	664	0.01	0.04	22.9	2	10
Japan	67	121	0.00	0.00	–187.9	0	1
Luxembourg	3	15	0.01	0.05	27.1	7	30
Netherlands	22	222	0.01	0.04	22.6	2	12
New Zealand	0	1	0.00	0.00	36.1	0	0
Norway	28	45	0.02	0.02	–3.0	8	9
Portugal	28	62	0.03	0.04	11.9	3	5
Spain	13	15	0.00	0.00	–3.6	0	0
Sweden	99	123	0.04	0.04	1.5	12	12
Switzerland	70	100	0.03	0.03	0.2	11	12
United Kingdom	407	834	0.03	0.04	8.8	8	12
United States	3,521	1,605	0.04	0.01	–14.9	14	5
Total or average	**6,468**	**8,519**	**0.03**	**0.03**	**1.6**	**8**	**9**

a. Excludes administrative costs and technical cooperation. b. At 2003 exchange rates and prices.

Aid flows from Development Assistance Committee members 6.10

About the data

Effective aid supports institutional development and policy reforms, which are at the heart of successful development. To be effective, especially in reducing global poverty, aid requires partnerships among recipient countries, aid agencies, and donor countries. It also requires improvements in economic policies and institutions. Where traditional methods of nurturing such reforms have failed, aid agencies need to find alternative approaches and new opportunities.

As part of its work, the Development Assistance Committee (DAC) of the Organisation for Economic Co-operation and Development (OECD) assesses the aid performance of member countries relative to the size of their economies. As measured here, aid comprises bilateral disbursements of concessional financing to recipient countries plus the provision by donor governments of concessional financing to multilateral institutions. Volume amounts, at constant prices and exchange rates, are used to measure the change in real resources provided over time. Aid flows to part I recipients—official development assistance (ODA)—are tabulated separately from those to part II recipients—official aid (see *About the data* for table 6.9 for more information on the distinction between the two types of aid flows).

Measures of aid flows from the perspective of donors differ from aid receipts from the perspective of recipients for two main reasons. First, aid flows include expenditure items about which recipients may have no precise information, such as development-oriented research, stipends and tuition costs for aid-financed students in donor countries, or payment of experts hired by donor countries. Second, donors record their concessional funding (usually grants) to multilateral agencies when they make payments, while the agencies make funds available to recipients with a time lag and in many cases in the form of soft loans where donors' grants have been used to reduce the interest burden over the life of the loan.

Aid as a share of gross national income (GNI), aid per capita, and ODA as a share of the general government disbursements of the donor are calculated by the OECD. The denominators used in calculating these ratios may differ from corresponding values elsewhere in this book because of differences in timing or definitions.

DAC members have progressively introduced the new United Nations System of National Accounts (adopted in 1993), which replaced gross national product (GNP) with GNI. Because GNI includes items not included in GNP, ratios of ODA to GNI are slightly smaller than the previously reported ratios of ODA to GNP.

The proportion of untied aid is reported here because tying arrangements may prevent recipients from obtaining the best value for their money and so reduce the value of the aid received. Tying arrangements require recipients to purchase goods and services from the donor country or from a specified group of countries. They may be justified on the grounds that they prevent a recipient from misappropriating or mismanaging aid receipts, but they may also be motivated by a desire to benefit suppliers in the donor country. The same volume of aid may have different purchasing power depending on the relative costs of suppliers in countries to which the aid is tied and the degree to which each recipient's aid basket is untied.

Definitions

• **Net official development assistance** (ODA) and **net official aid** record the actual international transfer by the donor of financial resources or of goods or services valued at the cost to the donor, less any repayments of loan principal during the same period. Data are shown at current prices and dollar exchange rates. • **Aid as a percentage of GNI** shows the donor's contributions of ODA or official aid as a share of its gross national income. • **Average annual percentage change in volume** and **aid per capita of donor country** are calculated using 2002 exchange rates and prices. • **Aid as a percentage of general government disbursements** shows the donor's contributions of ODA as a share of public spending. • **Untied aid** is the share of ODA that is not subject to restrictions by donors on procurement sources.

6.10a

Official development assistance from non-DAC donors, 2000–04 ($ millions)

Donor	2000	2001	2002	2003	2004
OECD members (non-DAC)					
Czech Republic	16	26	45	91	108
Hungary	..	..	..	21	55
Iceland	9	10	13	18	21
Korea, Rep.	212	265	279	366	423
Poland	29	36	14	27	118
Slovak Republic	6	8	7	15	28
Turkey	82	64	73	67	339
Arab countries					
Kuwait	165	73	20	133	209
Saudi Arabia	295	490	2,478	2,391	1,734
United Arab Emirates	150	127	156	188	181
Other donors					
Israel[a]	164	76	114	92	66
Other donors[b]	1	2	3	4	22
Total	**1,128**	**1,178**	**3,201**	**3,416**	**3,726**

Note: China also provides aid, but does not disclose the amount.
a. Includes $66.8 million in 2000, $50.1 million in 2001, $87.8 million in 2002, $68.8 million in 2003, and $47.9 million in 2004 for first-year sustenance expenses for people arriving from developing countries (many of which are experiencing civil war or severe unrest) or people who have left their country for humanitarian or political reasons.
b. Includes Estonia, Latvia, and Lithuania.

Source: Organisation for Economic Co-operation and Development.

Data sources

Data on financial flows are compiled by DAC and published in its annual statistical report, *Geographical Distribution of Financial Flows to Aid Recipients*, and its annual *Development Cooperation Report*. Data are available electronically on the OECD's *International Development Statistics* CD-ROM and to registered users at www.oecd.org/dataoecd/50/17/5037721.htm.

6.11 Aid dependency

	Net official development assistance or official aid		Aid per capita		Aid dependency ratios							
	$ millions		$		Aid as % of GNI		Aid as % of gross capital formation		Aid as % of imports of goods and services		Aid as % of central government expenditure	
	1999	2004	1999	2004	1999	2004	1999	2004	1999	2004	1999	2004
Afghanistan	143	2,190	6	..	..	38.0	..	..	..	..	..	288.8
Albania	488	362	159	116	13.8	4.7	70.7	20.2	43.9	..	..	..
Algeria	138	313	5	10	0.3	0.4	1.0	1.1	..	..	1.2	..
Angola	388	1,144	29	74	8.2	6.6	23.2	49.1	5.5	8.7	..	..
Argentina	100	91	3	2	0.0	0.1	0.2	0.3	0.2	0.2	..	0.3
Armenia	209	254	68	84	11.0	8.1	61.8	40.5	21.9	14.2	..	41.9
Australia												
Austria												
Azerbaijan	169	176	21	21	3.7	2.2	14.0	3.8	8.6	2.5	19.5	..
Bangladesh	1,215	1,404	10	10	2.6	2.4	11.9	10.3	13.2	10.4	..	28.7
Belarus	39	46	4	5	0.3	0.2	1.4	0.7	0.6	0.3	1.2	0.7
Belgium												
Benin	211	378	30	46	8.9	9.3	50.5	45.6	23.7	..	..	..
Bolivia	569	767	70	85	7.0	9.1	36.6	70.7	24.3	27.4	..	32.1
Bosnia and Herzegovina	1,040	671	277	172	21.0	7.7	79.3	37.8	23.2	9.3	..	20.4
Botswana	61	39	35	22	1.3	0.5	4.3	1.4	2.0	..	..	..
Brazil	187	285	1	2	0.0	0.0	0.2	0.2	0.2	0.3	..	..
Bulgaria	271	622	33	80	2.1	2.6	11.7	11.0	3.9	3.6	6.7	7.3
Burkina Faso	398	610	36	48	14.2	12.7	59.6	66.2	..	..	..	..
Burundi	74	351	12	48	10.6	54.6	114.1	501.4	55.5	..	44.5	..
Cambodia	277	478	22	35	8.1	10.3	45.2	38.0	11.0	12.1	..	107.3
Cameroon	435	762	30	47	5.0	5.4	25.3	31.8	..	..	..	..
Canada												
Central African Republic	118	105	32	26	11.4	7.9	78.0	45.6	..	..	..	..
Chad	188	319	24	34	12.4	11.8	121.6	30.6	..	..	..	..
Chile	70	49	5	3	0.1	0.1	0.5	0.2	0.3	0.1	..	0.3
China	2,394	1,661	2	1	0.2	0.1	0.6	0.2	1.1	0.3	..	..
Hong Kong, China	4	7	1	1	0.0	0.0	0.0	0.0	0.0	0.0	..	..
Colombia	302	509	7	11	0.4	0.5	2.7	2.8	1.9	2.1	..	2.3
Congo, Dem. Rep.	132	1,815	3	32	3.1	28.6	91.0	213.9	..	..	10.2	..
Congo, Rep.	142	116	43	30	8.6	3.5	21.7	11.0	7.2	..	..	..
Costa Rica	-8	13	-2	3	-0.1	0.1	-0.3	0.3	-0.1	0.1	-0.3	0.3
Côte d'Ivoire	448	154	27	9	3.8	1.0	27.2	9.2	8.7	2.2	..	..
Croatia	48	121	11	27	0.2	0.4	1.1	1.2	0.5	0.6	0.5	0.8
Cuba	59	90	5	8	..	..	..	..	..	..	..	..
Czech Republic	325	280	32	27	0.6	0.3	2.0	0.9	0.9	0.3	..	0.7
Denmark												
Dominican Republic	195	87	24	10	1.2	0.5	4.6	2.3	1.9	0.8	8.3	..
Ecuador	149	160	12	12	1.0	0.6	6.1	1.9	2.7	1.5	..	..
Egypt, Arab Rep.	1,582	1,458	24	20	1.7	1.9	8.1	11.1	7.0	5.3	..	..
El Salvador	184	211	30	31	1.5	1.4	9.0	8.6	3.6	2.8	..	68.7
Eritrea	149	260	43	61	20.3	28.5	60.0	129.0	24.1	..	..	..
Estonia	84	136	61	101	1.5	1.3	6.0	3.9	1.9	1.3	4.9	..
Ethiopia	643	1,823	10	26	10.0	23.0	58.4	107.7	33.8	47.5	..	..
Finland												
France												
Gabon	48	38	38	28	1.2	0.6	3.9	2.1	2.0	..	..	..
Gambia, The	34	63	26	43	8.2	16.0	43.6	63.3	..	..	..	..
Georgia	245	315	51	70	8.3	6.0	39.6	20.7	21.2	11.9	60.6	42.2
Germany	..	..	..	..	..	..	..	..	..	..	..	..
Ghana	609	1,358	31	63	8.1	15.4	37.9	54.9	15.0	24.3	..	73.2
Greece												
Guatemala	293	218	27	18	1.6	0.8	9.2	4.5	5.5	2.4	15.2	7.2
Guinea	238	279	29	30	7.0	7.3	31.1	68.6	22.6	27.9	..	..
Guinea-Bissau	52	76	39	50	24.9	28.3	139.0	219.4	..	..	..	..
Haiti	263	243	34	29	6.4	6.7	23.2	..	20.8	..	..	..

	Net official development assistance or official aid		Aid per capita		Aid dependency ratios							
	$ millions		$		Aid as % of GNI		Aid as % of gross capital formation		Aid as % of imports of goods and services		Aid as % of central government expenditure	
	1999	2004	1999	2004	1999	2004	1999	2004	1999	2004	1999	2004
Honduras	818	642	131	91	15.6	9.1	41.8	..	25.2	13.5	..	..
Hungary	249	303	25	30	0.6	0.3	1.8	1.3	0.7	0.4	..	..
India	1,491	691	1	1	0.3	0.1	1.4	0.4	2.2	..	2.2	0.6
Indonesia	2,125	84	10	0	1.6	0.0	13.3	0.1	3.9	0.1	9.3	0.2
Iran, Islamic Rep.	162	189	3	3	0.2	0.1	0.5	0.3	1.0	..	0.4	0.6
Iraq	76	4,658	3	..	..	..	..	..	..	..	..	..
Ireland												
Israel	906	479	148	70	0.9	0.4	3.8	2.4	1.9	0.8	..	0.8
Italy												
Jamaica	-22	75	-8	29	-0.3	0.9	-1.2	2.7	-0.5	1.2	-0.8	..
Japan												
Jordan	432	581	91	107	5.4	5.0	22.7	21.1	7.9	6.0	19.8	15.9
Kazakhstan	175	265	12	18	1.1	0.7	5.8	2.7	2.4	1.2	7.3	4.4
Kenya	310	635	10	19	2.4	4.0	15.5	21.6	8.9	12.0	13.4	..
Korea, Dem. Rep.	201	196	9	9	..	..	..	..	..	..	..	..
Korea, Rep.	-55	-68	-1	-1	0.0	0.0	0.0	0.0	0.0	0.0	-0.1	..
Kuwait	7	3	3	1	0.0	0.0	0.2	0.0	0.1	0.0	0.1	..
Kyrgyz Republic	283	258	58	51	24.1	12.2	125.8	84.9	35.8	20.9	127.8	..
Lao PDR	295	270	57	47	21.0	11.4	..	..	46.9	..	..	..
Latvia	100	165	42	71	1.4	1.2	5.9	3.7	2.6	1.8	4.3	4.3
Lebanon	194	265	58	75	1.1	1.3	5.1	5.7	..	..	..	..
Lesotho	31	102	18	57	2.7	6.3	7.0	18.8	3.4	6.9	..	20.5
Liberia	94	210	32	65	28.1	53.4	..	346.8	..	..	..	..
Libya	7	18	1	3	..	0.1	0.2	..	0.1	0.1	..	..
Lithuania	134	252	38	73	1.3	1.2	5.5	4.8	2.3	1.8	..	3.9
Macedonia, FYR	277	248	138	122	7.6	4.7	38.3	21.5	14.0	7.4	..	..
Madagascar	359	1,236	23	68	9.8	28.8	64.7	103.2	28.4	..	..	44.9
Malawi	447	476	40	38	25.8	25.9	171.7	229.4	55.1	..	..	..
Malaysia	144	290	6	12	0.2	0.3	0.8	1.1	0.2	..	1.0	..
Mali	355	567	31	43	14.0	12.2	65.1	59.2	32.9	..	..	..
Mauritania	219	180	85	60	20.1	11.1	120.2	54.5	..	..	..	..
Mauritius	42	38	36	31	1.0	0.6	3.8	2.6	1.4	1.0	4.4	2.9
Mexico	37	121	0	1	0.0	0.0	0.0	0.1	0.0	0.1	0.1	..
Moldova	107	118	25	28	9.0	4.0	40.0	18.0	12.1	5.2	31.5	16.8
Mongolia	222	262	93	104	24.9	16.4	66.4	44.3	33.5	18.3	..	..
Morocco	679	706	24	23	2.0	1.4	8.3	5.6	5.2	3.4	6.8	..
Mozambique	805	1,228	46	63	21.3	21.4	55.1	100.6	47.1	44.6	..	..
Myanmar	81	121	2	2	..	..	..	..	3.2	3.7	..	..
Namibia	179	179	97	89	5.3	3.1	22.7	12.3	9.2	6.6	15.8	..
Nepal	351	427	15	16	7.0	6.4	34.0	24.2	20.2	18.9	..	..
Netherlands												
New Zealand												
Nicaragua	673	1,232	138	229	19.0	28.3	46.9	95.3	28.3	40.4	93.8	137.0
Niger	187	536	16	40	9.4	17.5	90.7	109.3	36.8	..	..	..
Nigeria	152	573	1	4	0.5	1.0	1.9	3.6	1.0	3.3	..	..
Norway												
Oman	40	55	17	22	0.3	0.2	1.7	1.3	0.6	0.5	0.9	..
Pakistan	733	1,421	5	9	1.2	1.5	7.5	8.5	5.4	5.8	6.5	10.2
Panama	15	38	5	12	0.1	0.3	0.5	1.3	0.1	0.3	0.6	..
Papua New Guinea	216	266	42	46	6.6	7.6	38.6	..	10.3	..	21.4	..
Paraguay	78	0	15	0	1.0	0.0	4.4	0.0	2.3	0.0	6.1	0.0
Peru	451	487	18	18	0.9	0.7	4.1	3.8	4.2	3.0	5.1	4.2
Philippines	690	463	9	6	0.9	0.5	4.8	3.1	1.7	0.9	..	..
Poland	1,186	1,525	31	40	0.7	0.6	2.9	3.1	2.2	1.3	..	..
Portugal												
Puerto Rico												

6.11 Aid dependency

	Net official development assistance or official aid $ millions		Aid per capita $		Aid dependency ratios: Aid as % of GNI		Aid as % of gross capital formation		Aid as % of imports of goods and services		Aid as % of central government expenditure	
	1999	2004	1999	2004	1999	2004	1999	2004	1999	2004	1999	2004
Romania	387	916	17	42	1.1	1.3	6.8	5.0	3.2	2.5	..	..
Russian Federation	1,946	1,313	13	9	1.0	0.2	6.7	1.1	3.0	0.9	..	1.0
Rwanda	373	468	50	53	19.4	25.8	112.2	121.8	81.4	88.8	..	..
Saudi Arabia	29	32	1	1	0.0	0.0	0.1	0.1	0.1	0.0	..	..
Senegal	535	1,052	53	92	11.5	13.9	60.9	57.9	26.7	..	91.0	..
Serbia and Montenegro	676	1,170	64	144	6.6	4.9	56.9	29.0	..	..	..	..
Sierra Leone	74	360	17	67	11.5	34.3	204.7	211.3	36.5	87.1	..	..
Singapore	-1	9	0	2	0.0	0.0	0.0	0.0	0.0	0.0	0.0	0.1
Slovak Republic	319	235	59	44	1.6	0.6	5.7	2.2	2.3	..	..	..
Slovenia	31	62	16	31	0.1	0.2	0.5	0.7	0.3	0.3	0.4	0.5
Somalia	115	191	17	24	..	..	..	..	..	..	..	..
South Africa	541	617	13	14	0.4	0.3	2.5	1.6	1.5	0.9	..	1.0
Spain												
Sri Lanka	263	519	14	27	1.7	2.7	6.2	10.4	3.7	5.5	7.9	..
Sudan	243	882	8	25	2.6	4.5	13.9	20.9	14.7	15.3	30.0	..
Swaziland	29	117	28	104	2.0	4.9	11.2	26.6	2.2	4.5	8.1	..
Sweden												
Switzerland												
Syrian Arab Republic	228	110	14	6	1.5	0.5	6.8	2.2	3.7	1.2	..	..
Tajikistan	123	241	20	37	11.9	12.1	65.0	124.7	..	16.0	112.7	84.4
Tanzania	990	1,746	29	46	11.6	16.2	73.8	83.8	42.0	52.7	..	..
Thailand	1,014	-2	17	0	0.9	0.0	4.0	0.0	1.6	0.0	..	0.0
Togo	71	61	14	10	4.7	3.0	33.9	16.5	10.2	..	..	..
Trinidad and Tobago	26	-1	20	-1	0.4	0.0	1.8	0.0	0.8	..	..	..
Tunisia	253	328	27	33	1.3	1.2	4.6	4.7	2.5	2.1	4.4	4.1
Turkey	11	257	0	4	0.0	0.1	0.0	0.3	0.0	0.2	..	..
Turkmenistan	24	37	5	8	1.0	0.6	2.5	2.4	..	..	..	..
Uganda	590	1,159	25	42	9.9	17.3	50.3	75.5	37.6	49.1	70.6	..
Ukraine	569	360	11	8	1.9	0.6	10.3	2.9	3.5	1.0	7.2	1.7
United Arab Emirates	4	6	1	1	0.0	0.0	0.0	0.0	..	..	0.1	..
United Kingdom												
United States												
Uruguay	22	22	7	6	0.1	0.2	0.7	1.3	0.5	0.5	0.4	0.6
Uzbekistan	155	246	6	9	0.9	2.1	5.2	10.2	..	..	..	..
Venezuela, RB	44	49	2	2	0.0	0.0	0.2	0.2	0.2	0.2	0.2	..
Vietnam	1,429	1,830	18	22	5.0	4.1	18.0	11.4	10.1	..	..	..
West Bank and Gaza	516	1,136	182	324	10.2	..	35.1	..	..	..	..	..
Yemen, Rep.	458	252	26	12	6.6	2.1	25.6	11.5	12.8	4.0	27.7	..
Zambia	624	1,081	59	94	21.0	21.2	113.4	77.1	46.1	..	114.2	..
Zimbabwe	245	186	20	14	4.3	4.0	28.5	31.0	..	..	..	..
World	60,715 s	87,307 s	10 w	14 w	0.2 w	0.2 w	0.9 w	.. w	0.7 w	0.7 w	.. w	.. w
Low income	19,714	33,954	9	14	2.4	2.8	10.9	11.9	10.3	..	..	..
Middle income	27,137	31,603	9	10	0.6	0.4	2.4	1.6	1.9	1.2	..	..
Lower middle income	19,713	23,430	8	10	0.7	0.6	2.8	1.8	2.8	1.6	..	..
Upper middle income	6,158	6,766	11	12	0.3	0.2	1.4	1.0	0.8	0.5	..	..
Low & middle income	58,885	85,456	12	16	1.1	1.0	4.5	3.8	3.6	2.8	..	..
East Asia & Pacific	9,890	6,916	6	4	0.6	0.3	2.1	0.7	2.1	0.6	..	..
Europe & Central Asia	11,478	11,869	24	25	1.3	0.7	6.1	2.9	3.2	1.5	..	..
Latin America & Carib.	5,937	6,869	12	13	0.3	0.4	1.6	1.6	1.3	1.2	..	..
Middle East & N. Africa	5,149	10,517	19	35	1.1	1.7	4.7	6.4	4.0	..	..	..
South Asia	4,293	6,758	3	5	0.7	0.8	3.2	3.3	4.2	..	..	..
Sub-Saharan Africa	13,263	26,004	21	36	4.2	5.3	22.2	26.1	11.5	13.9	..	..
High income												
Europe EMU												

Note: Regional aggregates include data for economies not specified elsewhere. World and income group totals include aid not allocated by country or region.

About the data

Ratios of aid to gross national income (GNI), gross capital formation, imports, and government spending provide a measure of the recipient country's dependency on aid. But care must be taken in drawing policy conclusions. For foreign policy reasons, some countries have traditionally received large amounts of aid. Thus aid dependency ratios may reveal as much about a donor's interest as they do about a recipient's needs. Ratios in Sub-Saharan Africa are generally much higher than those in other regions, and they increased in the 1980s. These high ratios are due only in part to aid flows. Many African countries saw severe erosion in their terms of trade in the 1980s, which, along with weak policies, contributed to falling incomes, imports, and investment. Thus the increase in aid dependency ratios reflects events affecting both the numerator and the denominator.

As defined here, aid includes official development assistance (ODA) and official aid (see *About the data* for table 6.9). The data cover loans and grants from Development Assistance Committee (DAC) member countries, multilateral organizations, and non-DAC donors. They do not reflect aid given by recipient countries to other developing countries. As a result, some countries that are net donors (such as Saudi Arabia) are shown in the table as aid recipients (see table 6.10a).

The table does not distinguish among different types of aid (program, project, or food aid; emergency assistance; postconflict peacekeeping assistance; or technical cooperation), each of which may have very different effects on the economy. Expenditures on technical cooperation do not always directly benefit the economy to the extent that they defray costs incurred outside the country on the salaries and benefits of technical experts and the overhead costs of firms supplying technical services.

In 1999, to avoid double counting extrabudgetary expenditures reported by DAC countries and flows reported by the United Nations, all UN agencies revised their data since 1990 to include only regular budgetary expenditures (except for the World Food Programme and the United Nations High Commissioner for Refugees, which revised their data from 1996 onward). These revisions have affected net ODA and official aid and, as a result, aid per capita and aid dependency ratios.

Because the table relies on information from donors, it is not necessarily consistent with information recorded by recipients in the balance of payments, which often excludes all or some technical assistance—particularly payments to expatriates made directly by the donor. Similarly, grant commodity aid may not always be recorded in trade data or in the balance of payments. Moreover, DAC statistics exclude purely military aid.

The nominal values used here may overstate the real value of aid to the recipient. Changes in international prices and in exchange rates can reduce the purchasing power of aid. The practice of tying aid, still prevalent though declining in importance, also tends to reduce its purchasing power (see *About the data* for table 6.10).

The values for population, GNI, gross capital formation, imports of goods and services, and central government expenditure used in computing the ratios are taken from World Bank and International Monetary Fund (IMF) databases. The aggregates also refer to World Bank definitions. Therefore the ratios shown may differ somewhat from those computed and published by the Organisation for Economic Co-operation and Development (OECD). Aid not allocated by country or region—including administrative costs, research on development issues, and aid to nongovernmental organizations—is included in the world total. Thus regional and income group totals do not sum to the world total.

6.11a

More aid flows to developing countries

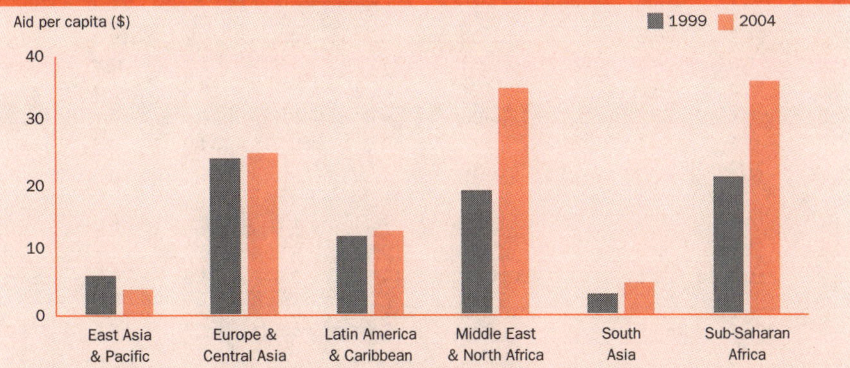

Between 1999 and 2004 the flow of aid to Sub-Saharan Africa and Middle East and North Africa increased while the flow of aid to other regions changed little.

Source: Organisation for Economic Co-operation and Development, Development Assistance Committee.

Definitions

• **Net official development assistance** consists of disbursements of loans made on concessional terms (net of repayments of principal) and grants by official agencies of the members of DAC, by multilateral institutions, and by non-DAC countries to promote economic development and welfare in countries and territories in part I of the DAC list of aid recipients. It includes loans with a grant element of at least 25 percent (calculated at a rate of discount of 10 percent). • **Net official aid** refers to aid flows (net of repayments) from official donors to countries and territories in part II of the DAC list of aid recipients: more advanced countries of Central and Eastern Europe, the countries of the former Soviet Union, and certain advanced developing countries and territories. Official aid is provided under terms and conditions similar to those for ODA. • **Aid per capita** includes both ODA and official aid. • **Aid dependency ratios** are calculated using values in U.S. dollars converted at official exchange rates. For definitions of GNI, gross capital formation, imports of goods and services, and central government expenditure, see *Definitions* for tables 1.1, 4.8, and 4.11.

Data sources

Data on financial flows are compiled by DAC and published in its annual statistical report, *Geographical Distribution of Financial Flows to Aid Recipients*, and in its annual *Development Cooperation Report*. Data are available in electronic format on the OECD's *International Development Statistics* CD-ROM and to registered users at www.oecd.org/dataoecd/50/17/5037721.htm. Data on population, GNI, gross capital formation, imports of goods and services, and central government expenditure are from World Bank and IMF databases.

6.12 Distribution of net aid by Development Assistance Committee members

	Total $ millions	Ten major DAC donors $ millions										Other DAC donors $ millions
		United States	France	Japan	United Kingdom	Germany	Netherlands	Sweden	Canada	Norway	Spain	
	2004	2004	2004	2004	2004	2004	2004	2004	2004	2004	2004	2004
Afghanistan	1,697.5	778.3	15.0	172.5	224.0	75.1	90.3	55.7	56.2	67.7	16.6	146.5
Albania	228.4	40.3	6.6	9.8	4.0	23.6	11.0	5.7	1.1	8.0	1.6	117.1
Algeria	234.6	3.8	172.9	–1.0	0.0	–2.6	0.1	2.0	1.1	1.6	12.7	44.6
Angola	1,015.0	121.3	21.9	25.5	15.1	13.0	19.6	17.3	4.8	24.8	9.3	743.2
Argentina	78.5	1.8	13.6	9.3	..	10.9	1.0	0.3	2.3	0.0	33.4	6.4
Armenia	133.9	73.1	4.0	4.7	6.6	18.7	9.2	2.3	0.6	3.3	1.4	10.4
Australia												
Austria												
Azerbaijan	91.9	47.6	2.4	9.6	0.2	17.0	3.5	0.5	0.9	5.7	0.1	5.1
Bangladesh	632.9	62.9	0.9	38.2	252.7	25.2	65.2	26.6	48.9	23.9	0.1	88.7
Belarus	31.4	2.0	4.4	0.2	0.2	12.6	1.5	6.0	0.2	..	0.0	4.8
Belgium												
Benin	210.3	27.9	62.9	11.2	..	24.5	10.4	0.1	6.4	0.2	0.3	67.1
Bolivia	557.4	137.6	17.8	50.8	50.8	75.3	48.1	29.0	11.9	3.4	54.5	78.8
Bosnia and Herzegovina	301.0	61.9	3.4	22.2	11.0	29.9	24.8	34.1	5.9	17.0	24.7	66.6
Botswana	32.6	21.1	1.9	–1.4	0.5	3.8	1.2	0.4	1.2	1.6	0.0	2.8
Brazil	147.3	–57.5	31.1	41.7	11.1	51.9	16.3	2.5	9.1	3.1	9.9	28.7
Bulgaria	246.0	38.9	24.7	28.7	3.0	106.5	3.5	0.8	1.7	1.2	0.5	37.1
Burkina Faso	331.3	17.6	83.6	8.5	6.5	38.5	55.0	12.2	16.2	0.2	2.3	91.3
Burundi	184.3	43.8	34.8	0.4	9.5	10.4	23.3	6.6	4.3	11.9	0.8	39.1
Cambodia	297.8	48.1	25.6	86.4	17.6	22.5	8.7	22.6	8.5	3.3	0.1	54.9
Cameroon	572.0	17.2	129.1	16.9	30.0	205.7	11.6	14.3	43.2	1.7	–5.6	108.5
Canada												
Central African Republic	54.8	12.0	36.6	0.1	..	2.4	0.6	0.7	0.4	0.5	0.1	2.0
Chad	162.2	47.4	46.3	0.7	8.1	31.0	4.4	1.5	1.7	..	3.1	18.7
Chile	25.9	–1.7	15.1	–34.6	1.1	27.4	1.4	0.8	3.5	3.9	3.4	6.2
China	1,585.4	21.5	102.8	964.7	72.2	260.5	25.6	18.2	34.9	14.8	12.7	58.2
Hong Kong, China	6.3	0.2	2.1	2.2	..	..	0.0	..	..	..	0.0	2.3
Colombia	470.0	375.6	5.6	–8.4	2.0	8.8	26.0	14.1	9.2	8.5	9.6	19.7
Congo, Dem. Rep.	1,164.4	189.6	134.7	48.5	301.0	59.3	58.8	23.3	20.3	18.0	6.1	305.5
Congo, Rep.	47.5	0.4	36.1	0.3	4.9	0.5	1.3	3.6	0.4	1.7	–0.3	–0.8
Costa Rica	11.2	–15.1	5.8	–5.2	–15.9	8.9	12.2	1.2	2.9	4.6	9.9	2.5
Côte d'Ivoire	196.0	31.8	62.2	1.9	5.9	14.5	1.9	1.6	4.7	3.0	3.9	65.2
Croatia	87.3	45.9	3.8	0.7	2.3	2.4	2.3	6.9	0.8	14.9	0.6	7.3
Cuba	69.3	10.6	4.3	3.4	3.3	2.9	1.4	2.7	8.2	4.5	16.6	12.1
Czech Republic	42.8	0.7	11.4	1.7	..	18.2	2.2	0.1	0.5	0.1	0.5	8.2
Denmark												
Dominican Republic	84.4	–4.1	6.6	15.3	0.2	10.5	1.9	0.1	2.8	0.6	45.1	5.9
Ecuador	159.8	74.5	1.5	–2.7	–14.8	15.6	12.9	1.3	7.8	2.4	31.5	30.6
Egypt, Arab Rep.	1,177.1	704.5	109.2	64.9	76.8	107.3	9.8	1.7	10.6	0.7	19.8	72.6
El Salvador	201.9	114.8	3.6	2.3	0.2	12.7	6.5	7.7	4.8	1.1	27.5	21.4
Eritrea	178.3	95.0	0.8	1.6	5.0	4.4	12.5	3.2	5.2	18.6	0.2	32.3
Estonia	27.4	2.9	2.3	0.8	..	4.5	0.6	4.6	0.4	0.4	0.1	11.5
Ethiopia	1,026.2	402.3	26.3	33.3	147.1	126.1	57.5	50.8	59.5	34.0	0.8	89.1
Finland												
France												
Gabon	23.5	2.9	13.7	2.7	..	1.0	0.8	..	1.7	0.1	0.0	1.2
Gambia, The	11.7	3.2	0.2	2.7	0.5	1.9	0.5	0.6	0.9	0.3	..	1.6
Georgia	210.3	92.3	3.9	10.6	3.1	58.4	7.5	4.1	2.5	4.8	0.1	23.5
Germany												
Ghana	896.9	80.4	74.5	115.4	263.5	65.6	152.6	0.5	48.5	1.7	19.1	75.6
Greece												
Guatemala	203.4	53.5	2.4	25.4	–0.3	23.3	20.9	16.0	7.6	13.0	22.4	19.7
Guinea	178.4	47.7	72.3	16.5	3.2	20.2	3.2	1.4	8.0	1.6	..	4.8
Guinea-Bissau	28.6	0.1	5.4	0.0	..	0.8	3.3	2.4	0.7	0.1	1.5	14.9
Haiti	208.7	91.2	25.0	5.9	3.5	7.5	7.1	2.2	37.4	7.0	4.5	18.0

Distribution of net aid by Development Assistance Committee members

	Total $ millions 2004	Ten major DAC donors ($ millions) United States 2004	France 2004	Japan 2004	United Kingdom 2004	Germany 2004	Netherlands 2004	Sweden 2004	Canada 2004	Norway 2004	Spain 2004	Other DAC donors $ millions 2004
Honduras	328.5	112.1	21.3	31.3	1.2	26.1	16.1	27.7	9.4	1.8	54.0	28.0
Hungary	61.0	1.5	12.8	4.7	..	22.9	1.8	1.1	0.8	0.1	4.4	11.4
India	20.9	50.5	–13.0	–82.1	370.2	–10.7	–315.8	11.6	33.6	13.3	9.5	–45.6
Indonesia	-145.6	68.9	–28.2	–318.5	8.5	–8.6	–0.5	9.1	9.3	7.4	10.9	96.9
Iran, Islamic Rep.	140.2	4.8	15.7	19.8	4.8	41.2	11.1	2.6	0.4	11.5	3.7	25.2
Iraq	4,392.1	3,022.0	4.2	662.1	275.1	10.2	140.8	21.3	72.0	18.5	59.4	107.0
Ireland												
Israel	477.9	501.1	9.1	0.7	..	–36.6	1.0	..	0.1	..	0.9	2.1
Italy												
Jamaica	7.8	11.6	–1.5	–15.8	7.5	–10.4	7.7	0.2	9.2	0.3	0.4	–0.9
Japan												
Jordan	432.9	374.0	6.3	–5.3	4.7	21.0	0.6	0.8	7.0	1.3	3.3	19.9
Kazakhstan	203.3	56.4	2.8	130.8	1.8	–0.6	3.3	1.2	0.5	1.5	4.5	1.7
Kenya	469.5	140.9	32.2	70.9	45.8	41.7	24.4	29.9	18.1	7.9	2.4	55.9
Korea, Dem. Rep.	137.1	55.7	–0.5	..	37.4	7.5	0.5	5.4	2.4	5.6	0.1	23.6
Korea, Rep.	-68.7	–44.4	18.2	–58.9	..	11.5	0.1	..	3.2	..	..	2.2
Kuwait	2.2	..	1.7	0.3	..	0.1	0.0	..	..	..	0.0	0.7
Kyrgyz Republic	108.8	39.9	0.9	26.7	6.3	13.7	3.1	2.5	0.3	3.1	0.1	12.8
Lao PDR	177.6	3.5	19.7	71.7	2.2	15.9	2.4	22.2	2.5	2.5	..	35.6
Latvia	29.1	2.8	2.0	0.7	..	6.0	0.6	5.7	0.2	0.3	0.0	11.4
Lebanon	128.2	28.8	58.6	8.1	0.3	12.0	0.2	0.7	2.7	6.4	3.3	7.6
Lesotho	35.1	4.0	–0.8	1.2	7.2	5.3	0.1	0.0	0.5	1.3	..	16.8
Liberia	161.9	102.5	0.8	..	16.5	–3.1	8.6	12.5	1.0	11.6	..	11.9
Libya	9.6	0.0	3.0	0.3	..	2.8	0.1	..	..	..	..	3.9
Lithuania	32.1	1.6	3.7	3.2	..	9.8	1.2	7.0	0.3	0.6	0.1	5.3
Macedonia, FYR	161.4	53.1	4.3	4.2	3.0	18.2	28.5	9.3	0.7	12.6	2.3	25.7
Madagascar	684.8	40.7	484.5	28.0	27.5	7.6	0.9	0.2	17.6	8.5	8.0	62.0
Malawi	308.4	56.8	1.3	19.0	119.5	24.6	15.8	15.9	16.0	27.2	–0.4	13.3
Malaysia	286.8	1.1	–2.4	256.5	0.5	7.3	0.2	..	0.3	0.9	0.9	22.1
Mali	327.5	45.5	81.5	13.7	0.4	26.4	64.1	14.9	44.1	8.0	1.3	28.2
Mauritania	82.6	11.0	29.2	11.1	0.5	11.3	0.8	0.4	2.1	0.7	11.5	4.5
Mauritius	14.7	0.3	12.3	1.5	0.2	–1.3	0.0	0.0	0.3	0.0	..	2.0
Mexico	78.9	42.8	18.7	13.0	0.2	23.3	0.2	0.2	5.1	0.4	–28.3	3.9
Moldova	76.9	32.8	4.2	3.3	4.9	6.3	5.6	7.2	0.6	1.3	0.0	11.3
Mongolia	154.7	25.9	5.3	65.6	7.4	26.5	9.5	2.4	1.3	1.2	2.8	7.4
Morocco	393.5	–10.3	218.1	66.3	0.1	34.5	6.5	0.7	4.6	0.8	51.0	21.7
Mozambique	728.1	110.0	14.6	19.4	65.9	38.7	54.7	67.9	27.3	61.1	32.5	236.6
Myanmar	81.4	5.7	2.0	26.8	12.0	4.7	2.8	3.7	0.6	7.1	..	16.5
Namibia	129.7	34.3	4.3	1.2	2.7	33.2	4.2	9.8	0.7	2.7	11.1	26.0
Nepal	318.5	35.4	–2.2	56.4	65.8	52.6	14.1	1.1	7.7	23.0	0.1	65.2
Netherlands												
New Zealand												
Nicaragua	858.0	69.7	65.3	29.9	13.4	278.0	40.8	41.1	9.0	12.6	207.7	91.2
Niger	305.7	19.3	195.8	14.1	8.4	16.7	5.5	0.1	7.6	1.9	1.0	35.8
Nigeria	314.2	120.2	7.4	8.7	126.1	13.7	3.8	1.2	15.2	5.5	0.6	12.6
Norway												
Oman	2.0	–5.0	1.0	5.3	..	0.2	..	..	..	..	..	1.0
Pakistan	382.7	76.9	5.1	134.1	90.8	20.4	7.9	2.1	15.5	8.1	0.1	22.2
Panama	25.3	9.3	0.5	6.2	0.0	1.3	0.3	..	0.7	..	6.6	0.8
Papua New Guinea	249.9	0.1	0.2	–6.1	..	1.9	0.8	0.1	0.6	0.4	0.1	252.3
Paraguay	5.4	14.8	–0.4	–3.3	–0.5	–19.1	1.9	1.7	2.1	0.6	6.4	1.8
Peru	460.2	177.9	12.8	89.8	5.3	40.7	18.1	4.6	14.2	1.3	56.2	40.0
Philippines	433.4	79.5	–6.9	211.4	0.4	39.1	16.9	6.3	12.4	1.9	14.1	59.0
Poland	413.0	–0.8	196.5	–4.0	..	72.9	1.0	1.3	49.6	0.4	2.1	94.6
Portugal												
Puerto Rico												

6.12 Distribution of net aid by Development Assistance Committee members

	Total $ millions	Ten major DAC donors ($ millions) United States	France	Japan	United Kingdom	Germany	Netherlands	Sweden	Canada	Norway	Spain	Other DAC donors $ millions
	2004	2004	2004	2004	2004	2004	2004	2004	2004	2004	2004	2004
Romania	209.3	38.0	42.1	34.2	8.5	51.4	2.3	1.0	1.9	0.8	1.5	28.0
Russian Federation	1,075.2	716.4	31.9	4.8	37.9	98.3	12.8	69.7	13.2	29.6	3.3	57.9
Rwanda	217.2	50.3	7.3	0.9	58.2	16.6	25.5	8.5	6.1	6.2	0.4	37.8
Saudi Arabia	8.5	0.1	6.8	–0.2	..	1.7	0.1	..	0.0	..	..	0.6
Senegal	755.4	49.8	509.8	50.4	9.1	33.1	16.9	8.9	24.6	1.0	18.3	34.0
Serbia and Montenegro	585.3	181.2	9.0	11.4	9.6	115.7	22.8	39.4	10.4	37.0	18.5	130.7
Sierra Leone	163.1	30.1	3.5	0.2	60.9	11.7	9.5	3.2	3.2	5.2	1.6	34.6
Singapore	9.1	..	3.6	2.7	0.1	1.9	..	..	0.0	..	0.1	1.3
Slovak Republic	58.9	1.1	6.7	22.8	0.0	11.9	2.5	0.1	1.2	0.1	0.3	12.7
Slovenia	4.3	0.9	1.5	0.1	0.1	–2.1	0.3	0.1	0.1	..	0.2	3.7
Somalia	139.3	31.9	0.4	..	11.8	2.5	18.9	13.7	1.8	33.7	..	25.1
South Africa	460.4	94.7	2.5	18.8	87.1	56.5	55.7	25.6	12.0	15.9	0.5	91.7
Spain												
Sri Lanka	337.8	–3.4	4.7	179.5	16.8	28.6	13.9	23.0	5.5	30.3	0.6	38.9
Sudan	744.8	377.6	11.6	1.6	116.6	48.3	0.3	26.5	26.3	57.2	7.9	71.5
Swaziland	104.5	1.2	0.1	4.9	1.4	–3.1	97.6	0.2	0.6	0.4	..	1.8
Sweden												
Switzerland												
Syrian Arab Republic	14.9	0.0	23.7	–26.5	0.1	–0.2	4.8	0.1	1.6	1.3	0.7	9.8
Tajikistan	92.5	47.5	0.3	6.6	1.5	5.4	1.2	3.1	6.9	1.5	..	19.0
Tanzania	1,029.5	89.5	120.0	52.5	215.6	56.4	117.6	83.6	32.7	59.6	5.8	196.7
Thailand	-24.9	10.1	–0.5	–55.6	–19.7	–1.5	4.0	6.4	4.0	2.2	0.7	25.6
Togo	52.3	3.6	26.5	0.8	0.3	9.7	1.2	0.2	6.0	0.3	0.7	3.8
Trinidad and Tobago	7.2	1.8	1.7	1.9	0.4	0.4	0.1	..	1.0	..	0.1	0.6
Tunisia	230.8	–15.7	141.4	59.7	..	12.3	–2.4	0.6	0.5	0.1	9.7	25.2
Turkey	-45.4	–29.7	10.7	–25.9	–3.7	–74.6	2.3	1.8	–2.4	1.6	49.5	25.6
Turkmenistan	11.3	6.5	0.8	2.2	0.1	1.2	0.0	..	0.1	0.1	..	0.8
Uganda	682.6	207.7	6.2	11.8	107.6	41.8	70.9	42.7	10.2	41.7	3.3	139.3
Ukraine	233.4	102.8	11.3	2.1	11.1	50.8	5.8	9.6	19.3	0.2	0.2	20.6
United Arab Emirates	5.2	0.3	3.6	0.2	..	1.0	..	..	..	..	0.0	0.5
United Kingdom												
United States												
Uruguay	9.4	–1.6	3.3	2.0	..	0.3	0.0	0.2	1.4	..	2.7	1.6
Uzbekistan	206.1	61.2	3.1	99.8	1.5	20.3	0.7	0.4	0.8	1.0	1.3	16.8
Venezuela, RB	28.3	9.0	6.6	4.6	0.4	2.1	0.1	0.0	0.9	0.3	2.8	2.1
Vietnam	1,181.5	30.5	106.8	615.3	67.7	74.8	52.3	26.8	25.3	12.1	6.3	164.2
West Bank and Gaza	605.1	273.9	25.2	9.0	29.5	31.2	20.9	39.4	22.4	53.8	23.8	76.6
Yemen, Rep.	152.6	43.3	3.7	18.2	12.7	35.8	29.8	0.3	0.6	0.4	2.6	5.8
Zambia	745.3	81.8	103.8	14.3	282.6	36.2	53.6	26.2	25.0	37.4	0.9	84.2
Zimbabwe	165.4	30.4	3.1	3.6	49.7	15.7	12.4	12.9	11.9	8.1	0.2	18.0
World	**58,838.7 s**	**17,785.0 s**	**7,130.4 s**	**5,977.9 s**	**5,408.9 s**	**4,298.3 s**	**2,722.8 s**	**2,198.7 s**	**2,084.1 s**	**1,581.5 s**	**1,415.0 s**	**8,236.1 s**
Low income	20,730.2	4,206.9	2,730.1	1,973.9	3,307.0	1,748.2	943.1	736.0	780.2	682.2	380.9	3,273.6
Middle income	21,485.4	8,147.2	2,055.1	2,768.1	785.4	1,764.1	839.2	532.3	467.9	430.8	776.2	2,977.5
Lower middle income	16,988.3	6,666.7	1,151.0	2,431.0	637.1	1,375.7	698.4	381.2	343.8	307.0	641.9	2,385.8
Upper middle income	3,359.0	948.1	659.5	333.8	147.3	329.3	101.0	127.6	106.5	82.2	114.6	434.1
Low & middle income	57,254.0	17,285.8	5,988.5	6,030.1	5,408.7	4,311.0	2,732.8	2,198.6	2,080.7	1,581.1	1,413.6	8,210.6
East Asia & Pacific	5,271.0	541.5	395.0	1,980.3	202.3	456.6	141.6	138.4	110.0	68.0	49.9	1,203.2
Europe & Central Asia	5,230.6	1,758.6	483.9	417.4	123.8	730.4	188.4	238.7	119.3	167.0	117.6	902.2
Latin America & Carib.	5,141.7	1,810.3	343.3	309.3	149.8	662.8	289.0	188.5	211.5	90.5	631.5	476.2
Middle East & N. Africa	8,073.3	4,437.9	862.3	888.7	407.6	313.9	225.3	78.0	126.2	98.2	208.6	434.9
South Asia	3,452.1	1,000.5	10.6	514.4	1,020.7	192.2	–112.1	121.0	168.5	167.5	26.9	346.4
Sub-Saharan Africa	17,125.5	3,497.9	3,011.6	641.3	2,329.4	1,246.5	1,210.8	671.2	614.5	623.5	180.6	3,124.9
High income												
Europe EMU												

Note: Regional aggregates include data for economies not specified elsewhere. World and income group totals include aid not allocated by country or region.

Distribution of net aid by Development Assistance Committee members

6.12

About the data

The table shows net bilateral aid to low- and middle-income economies from members of the Development Assistance Committee (DAC) of the Organisation for Economic Co-operation and Development (OECD). The DAC compilation of the data includes aid to some countries and territories not shown in the table and aid to unspecified economies that is recorded only at the regional or global level. Aid to countries and territories not shown in the table has been assigned to regional totals based on the World Bank's regional classification system. Aid to unspecified economies has been included in regional totals and, when possible, in income group totals. Aid not allocated by country or region—including administrative costs, research on development issues, and aid to nongovernmental organizations—is included in the world total. Thus regional and income group totals do not sum to the world total.

In 1999 all UN agencies revised their data since 1990 to include only regular budgetary expenditures (except for the World Food Programme and the United Nations High Commissioner for Refugees, which revised their data from 1996 onward). They did so to avoid double counting extrabudgetary expenditures reported by DAC countries and flows reported by the United Nations.

The table is based on donor country reports of bilateral programs, which may differ from reports by recipient countries. Recipients may lack access to information on such aid expenditures as development-oriented research, stipends and tuition costs for aid-financed students in donor countries, and payment of experts hired by donor countries. Moreover, a full accounting would include donor country contributions to multilateral institutions, the flow of resources from multilateral institutions to recipient countries, and flows from countries that are not members of DAC.

The expenditures that countries report as official development assistance (ODA) have changed. For example, some DAC members have reported as ODA the aid provided to refugees during the first 12 months of their stay within the donor's borders.

Some of the aid recipients shown in the table are also aid donors. See table 6.10a for a summary of ODA from non-DAC countries.

6.12a

The flow of bilateral aid from DAC members reflects global events and priorities

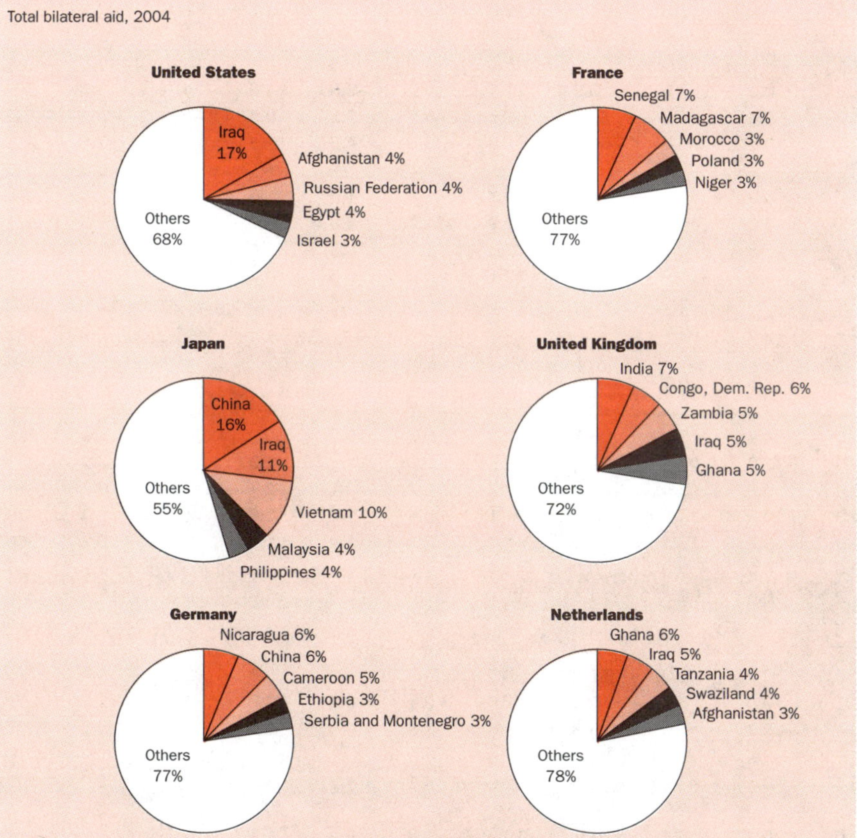

This figure shows the distribution of aid from the top six donors to their top five recipients in 2004.

Source: Organisation for Economic Co-operation and Development, Development Assistance Committee.

Definitions

• **Net aid** comprises net bilateral official development assistance to part I recipients and net bilateral official aid to part II recipients (see *About the data* for table 6.9). • **Other DAC donors** are Australia, Austria, Belgium, Denmark, Finland, Greece, Ireland, Luxembourg, New Zealand, Norway, Portugal, and Switzerland.

Data sources

Data on financial flows are compiled by DAC and published in its annual statistical report, *Geographical Distribution of Financial Flows to Aid Recipients*, and its annual *Development Cooperation Report*. Data are available electronically on the OECD's *International Development Statistics* CD-ROM and to registered users at www.oecd.org/dataoecd/50/17/5037721.htm.

6.13 Net financial flows from multilateral institutions

	International financial institutions							United Nations					Total
	$ millions							$ millions					$ millions
	World Bank		IMF		Regional development banks								
	IDA	IBRD	Concessional	Non-concessional	Concessional	Non-concessional	Others	UNDP	UNFPA	UNICEF	WFP	Others	
	2004	2004	2004	2004	2004	2004	2004	2004	2004	2004	2004	2004	2004
Afghanistan	..	..	..	..	..	..	..	5.8	3.3	11.1	0.2	53.7	74.1
Albania	64.3	0.0	2.4	0.0	0.0	11.2	22.3	2.0	0.3	0.7	0.4	1.5	105.2
Algeria	0.0	–149.2	0.0	–371.6	0.0	–679.6	–53.0	1.1	..	1.2	2.8	2.3	–1,246.0
Angola	12.9	0.0	0.0	0.0	0.6	–1.6	4.3	3.7	2.1	5.2	14.4	8.7	50.2
Argentina	0.0	–61.0	0.0	–2,035.0	0.0	–145.5	0.0	0.0	0.4	0.4	..	6.3	–2,234.4
Armenia	77.8	–0.6	1.9	–8.3	0.0	–7.8	–4.0	1.0	0.6	0.7	0.3	2.5	64.0
Australia													
Austria													
Azerbaijan	49.2	0.0	–21.7	–38.0	0.0	–8.5	7.7	2.4	0.6	1.1	1.4	2.4	–3.4
Bangladesh	474.3	–7.3	147.4	0.0	–20.8	71.8	13.1	19.6	6.8	11.0	9.9	7.7	733.3
Belarus	0.0	–13.5	0.0	–17.3	0.0	–13.2	0.0	0.6	0.3	0.6	..	1.7	–41.0
Belgium													
Benin	36.5	0.0	–5.6	0.0	33.7	–0.4	–12.5	2.3	2.3	2.1	2.3	2.9	63.7
Bolivia	116.6	0.2	–21.8	55.6	80.1	–69.3	103.2	1.4	2.6	2.1	2.2	2.3	275.1
Bosnia and Herzegovina	208.5	–24.4	0.0	–29.8	0.0	4.8	37.9	0.8	0.2	0.8	..	11.9	210.7
Botswana	–0.5	–1.7	0.0	0.0	1.0	–9.3	–10.2	0.5	1.2	0.6	..	4.2	–14.3
Brazil	0.0	–116.3	0.0	–4,356.8	0.0	–1,468.2	–4.5	1.1	0.9	1.7	..	132.4	–5,809.7
Bulgaria	0.0	123.7	0.0	–55.1	0.0	–10.9	80.6	0.6	0.3	..	..	1.9	141.0
Burkina Faso	128.6	0.0	2.2	0.0	37.6	–0.2	14.6	7.0	2.7	5.3	4.5	3.4	205.7
Burundi	29.3	0.0	39.1	–28.5	–13.3	–7.0	–0.6	8.9	1.6	3.4	3.8	9.6	46.3
Cambodia	46.3	0.0	–10.4	0.0	53.5	0.0	9.5	6.3	2.8	4.1	3.1	2.3	117.5
Cameroon	96.9	–29.7	–22.9	0.0	48.5	–26.1	2.6	3.6	..	2.7	1.4	5.2	82.1
Canada													
Central African Republic	0.0	0.0	–2.4	8.3	0.0	0.0	–1.6	4.2	1.8	2.7	3.8	5.3	21.9
Chad	69.9	5.9	–12.9	0.0	7.5	0.0	12.7	5.7	2.3	4.8	4.7	6.5	107.1
Chile	–0.7	18.8	0.0	0.0	–1.8	–49.8	–1.5	0.5	0.2	0.5	..	1.8	–32.0
China	–116.7	306.3	0.0	0.0	0.0	200.3	–201.5	9.0	4.8	12.3	6.3	7.3	228.2
Hong Kong, China	..	..	..	..	..	..	..	..	..	..	..	0.0	0.0
Colombia	–0.7	200.0	0.0	0.0	–17.3	–71.0	115.3	1.4	1.9	1.0	0.0	3.8	234.3
Congo, Dem. Rep.	166.6	0.0	79.1	0.0	44.4	0.0	–10.9	11.7	4.8	18.7	3.4	15.3	333.1
Congo, Rep.	23.6	–3.2	7.5	–7.8	–0.7	–74.7	–2.3	1.1	0.9	1.0	1.9	8.0	–44.7
Costa Rica	–0.2	–8.7	0.0	0.0	–11.8	1.7	39.1	0.5	0.5	0.6	..	2.0	23.8
Côte d'Ivoire	33.1	–38.4	–126.7	0.0	1.1	–0.4	–12.2	4.9	1.4	3.5	–0.4	12.0	–122.1
Croatia	0.0	36.0	0.0	0.0	0.0	43.6	19.0	0.4	..	0.2	..	5.3	104.5
Cuba	..	..	..	..	..	..	..	0.8	0.9	0.8	3.0	1.7	7.1
Czech Republic	0.0	–18.9	0.0	0.0	0.0	–13.4	87.1	..	..	..	..	2.4	57.2
Denmark													
Dominican Republic	–0.7	29.3	0.0	64.9	–20.3	208.7	2.6	0.6	0.8	0.9	0.2	4.9	291.8
Ecuador	–1.1	–52.9	0.0	–112.0	–27.0	–90.5	46.6	0.9	1.1	1.3	0.1	3.2	–230.3
Egypt, Arab Rep.	36.2	–51.8	0.0	0.0	15.4	0.3	–18.3	1.2	2.4	2.7	3.9	6.5	–1.4
El Salvador	–0.8	–24.3	0.0	0.0	–23.5	–20.6	–34.1	0.5	1.0	0.6	1.1	1.3	–98.8
Eritrea	35.1	0.0	0.0	0.0	19.1	0.0	–1.4	2.4	1.9	1.6	2.5	5.3	66.4
Estonia	0.0	–4.1	0.0	0.0	0.0	0.0	–3.4	..	0.0	..	..	0.3	–7.1
Ethiopia	189.2	0.0	21.9	0.0	68.3	–4.4	11.1	11.0	5.3	18.6	9.8	15.9	346.7
Finland													
France													
Gabon	0.0	–11.7	0.0	37.0	–0.2	52.6	5.0	0.5	0.2	0.6	..	5.4	89.5
Gambia, The	19.4	0.0	–11.2	0.0	6.7	0.0	7.6	2.1	0.7	0.9	0.9	2.5	29.7
Georgia	64.4	0.0	–20.4	–13.7	0.0	–6.3	–5.6	1.8	0.5	0.7	0.0	4.2	25.7
Germany													
Ghana	218.3	–1.6	15.5	0.0	47.9	6.6	32.9	4.1	4.2	3.9	0.8	6.7	339.2
Greece													
Guatemala	0.0	50.0	0.0	0.0	–18.4	61.1	10.3	0.8	4.4	1.1	0.4	1.2	111.0
Guinea	31.2	0.0	–19.1	0.0	1.3	–40.6	–24.2	1.1	2.0	2.8	2.5	13.5	–29.5
Guinea-Bissau	24.9	0.0	–3.1	–2.2	4.1	0.0	–0.7	2.6	1.0	1.3	2.2	2.0	32.1
Haiti	–40.5	0.0	–4.4	–2.7	–11.5	0.0	–1.4	3.8	2.2	4.2	6.9	1.7	–41.8

Net financial flows from multilateral institutions 6.13

	International financial institutions $ millions							United Nations $ millions					Total
	World Bank		IMF		Regional development banks								
	IDA	IBRD	Concessional	Non-concessional	Concessional	Non-concessional	Others	UNDP	UNFPA	UNICEF	WFP	Others	$ millions
	2004	2004	2004	2004	2004	2004	2004	2004	2004	2004	2004	2004	2004
Honduras	113.4	–15.1	21.0	0.0	114.5	–21.6	12.7	1.0	3.2	1.4	2.1	2.2	234.8
Hungary	0.0	–39.5	0.0	0.0	0.0	–3.1	478.7	..	..	..	..	2.7	438.7
India	422.3	616.2	0.0	0.0	0.0	423.4	–24.0	20.3	11.9	28.9	8.5	11.1	1,518.6
Indonesia	94.8	–825.6	0.0	–1,004.9	34.8	5.1	–36.3	7.8	5.3	5.5	0.6	6.9	–1,705.9
Iran, Islamic Rep.	0.0	–34.3	0.0	0.0	0.0	0.0	2.0	1.2	2.2	1.8	0.1	19.7	–7.3
Iraq	..	..	..	..	..	..	..	3.9	3.8	1.3	3.0	1.5	13.5
Ireland													
Israel	..	..	..	..	..	..	..	..	..	..	..	0.2	0.2
Italy													
Jamaica	0.0	–40.7	0.0	–8.0	–5.3	1.9	33.7	0.5	..	0.9	..	1.3	–15.6
Japan	..	..	..	..	..	..	..	..	..	..	..	..	..
Jordan	–2.6	–56.7	0.0	–98.0	0.0	0.0	–38.0	0.7	0.6	0.6	1.7	92.4	–99.3
Kazakhstan	0.0	–27.4	0.0	0.0	0.0	0.7	–17.9	0.7	0.6	1.0	..	2.0	–40.3
Kenya	26.7	–4.8	–14.1	0.0	16.6	–1.9	–7.5	5.0	2.7	5.3	7.4	18.4	53.8
Korea, Dem. Rep.	..	..	..	..	..	..	..	0.9	1.0	1.1	7.5	2.6	13.0
Korea, Rep.	..	..	..	..	..	..	..	0.1	..	..	..	0.9	1.0
Kuwait	..	..	..	..	..	..	..	..	..	..	..	0.4	0.4
Kyrgyz Republic	22.7	0.0	–3.9	0.0	54.4	–8.0	1.5	2.1	0.7	1.1	..	1.4	72.0
Lao PDR	29.2	0.0	–7.8	0.0	35.0	0.0	–2.7	3.3	1.2	1.8	2.0	2.5	64.4
Latvia	0.0	–8.0	0.0	–5.7	0.0	–2.5	–238.1	0.4	0.1	..	..	0.5	–253.3
Lebanon	0.0	14.2	0.0	0.0	0.0	0.0	–1.8	0.7	0.8	0.6	..	62.1	76.6
Lesotho	10.1	–2.4	9.8	0.0	9.0	–1.7	–0.3	1.3	0.4	1.5	6.3	1.8	35.7
Liberia	0.0	0.0	0.0	0.0	0.0	0.0	0.0	5.3	0.9	3.2	6.6	2.1	18.1
Libya	..	..	..	..	..	..	..	..	..	..	..	6.6	6.6
Lithuania	0.0	–92.8	0.0	–19.8	0.0	–0.6	–0.9	0.3	0.1	..	..	0.4	–113.4
Macedonia, FYR	13.6	32.2	–8.1	–0.4	0.0	4.1	27.7	1.0	..	0.7	..	3.0	73.8
Madagascar	216.7	0.0	45.5	0.0	46.8	–2.4	19.5	3.8	2.0	5.0	2.4	2.0	341.2
Malawi	50.9	–0.5	–9.5	0.0	23.4	–0.4	–6.2	5.6	4.0	4.9	4.9	3.7	80.8
Malaysia	0.0	–69.8	0.0	0.0	0.0	–43.1	49.5	0.2	0.4	0.5	..	1.1	–61.2
Mali	69.0	0.0	–16.1	0.0	38.2	0.0	14.2	8.3	2.3	6.0	3.0	3.3	128.1
Mauritania	36.8	0.0	–9.4	0.0	10.3	11.1	25.4	2.2	2.0	1.3	1.7	3.1	84.6
Mauritius	–0.6	–9.0	0.0	0.0	–0.1	–9.4	–2.6	0.1	0.1	..	..	1.0	–20.6
Mexico	0.0	–1,153.3	0.0	0.0	0.0	174.6	0.0	0.8	2.1	0.8	..	9.0	–966.0
Moldova	17.2	–10.4	0.0	–21.6	0.0	–8.0	–13.1	1.5	0.2	0.7	..	1.6	–32.0
Mongolia	47.2	0.0	–7.2	0.0	36.1	0.0	4.6	1.5	1.1	1.0	..	2.3	86.5
Morocco	–1.4	–338.2	0.0	0.0	3.9	120.0	59.9	0.8	2.6	1.8	0.2	3.6	–146.8
Mozambique	185.7	0.0	–6.7	0.0	86.0	–0.8	21.9	8.5	9.0	8.5	5.2	6.8	324.0
Myanmar	0.0	0.0	0.0	0.0	0.0	0.0	–1.7	7.5	4.0	7.0	1.3	5.1	23.2
Namibia	..	..	..	..	..	..	..	0.8	1.1	1.1	2.5	6.5	12.0
Nepal	45.3	0.0	9.8	0.0	–9.1	0.0	–2.0	7.4	5.8	5.4	9.6	5.9	78.1
Netherlands													
New Zealand													
Nicaragua	126.0	0.0	32.7	0.0	139.7	–1.5	9.7	2.9	3.4	0.8	4.5	1.9	320.0
Niger	63.2	0.0	5.8	0.0	27.6	12.5	2.2	5.9	3.1	6.9	5.6	2.6	135.3
Nigeria	137.2	–216.4	0.0	0.0	–1.2	–60.9	0.0	3.5	6.4	24.5	..	10.9	–96.0
Norway													
Oman	0.0	0.0	0.0	0.0	0.0	0.0	–135.2	..	..	..	..	1.1	–134.1
Pakistan	676.1	–303.1	146.9	–460.5	70.8	–950.5	92.0	7.1	5.0	12.6	8.6	28.6	–666.4
Panama	0.0	–25.4	0.0	–9.9	–8.9	–27.9	–6.0	0.6	0.6	0.6	..	15.1	–61.3
Papua New Guinea	–3.6	–13.0	0.0	–59.9	2.7	–3.6	–3.6	2.2	0.8	1.3	..	2.3	–74.2
Paraguay	–1.5	–16.7	0.0	0.0	–15.1	8.4	–3.1	0.4	1.1	0.8	..	0.6	–25.2
Peru	0.0	45.4	0.0	–39.6	–10.1	245.4	237.4	0.8	9.4	1.2	1.2	6.6	497.7
Philippines	–6.9	–226.4	0.0	–472.5	–15.7	–133.9	21.9	2.2	4.5	2.3	..	5.0	–819.5
Poland	0.0	–676.5	0.0	0.0	0.0	0.0	0.0	0.5	0.1	..	..	1.2	–674.7
Portugal													
Puerto Rico													

6.13 Net financial flows from multilateral institutions

	International financial institutions							United Nations					Total
	$ millions							$ millions					
	World Bank		IMF		Regional development banks								
	IDA	IBRD	Concessional	Non-concessional	Concessional	Non-concessional	Others	UNDP	UNFPA	UNICEF	WFP	Others	$ millions
	2004	2004	2004	2004	2004	2004	2004	2004	2004	2004	2004	2004	2004
Romania	0.0	142.0	0.0	–170.9	44.3	62.0	161.7	0.7	0.5	0.8	..	2.0	243.1
Russian Federation	0.0	–608.3	0.0	–1,656.0	0.0	143.8	0.0	0.8	0.7	1.3	1.6	9.3	–2,106.9
Rwanda	82.2	0.0	1.1	0.0	15.9	0.0	–1.9	5.1	2.1	3.6	7.0	6.9	121.9
Saudi Arabia	..	..	..	..	..	..	..	..	..	..	..	14.6	14.6
Senegal	158.0	0.0	–29.4	0.0	51.0	–1.7	79.8	4.4	2.2	2.5	2.5	4.2	273.4
Serbia and Montenegro	161.9	0.0	0.0	0.0	0.0	0.0	0.0	0.6	..	0.7	0.0	22.9	186.0
Sierra Leone	30.6	0.0	40.2	0.0	31.0	0.0	12.8	5.9	1.8	2.5	4.8	13.2	142.9
Singapore	..	..	..	..	..	..	..	..	..	..	..	0.1	0.1
Slovak Republic	0.0	74.4	0.0	0.0	0.0	–1.6	–152.4	0.5	..	..	..	1.7	–77.4
Slovenia	..	..	..	..	..	..	..	..	..	..	..	0.9	0.9
Somalia	0.0	0.0	0.0	0.0	0.0	0.0	0.0	5.0	0.4	4.8	1.7	3.9	15.7
South Africa	0.0	7.0	0.0	0.0	0.0	30.5	0.0	3.1	0.4	1.1	..	5.7	47.8
Spain													
Sri Lanka	29.9	–2.0	–8.3	–103.4	75.2	17.2	33.5	2.5	1.0	1.0	3.4	4.2	54.1
Sudan	–1.8	0.0	0.0	–31.3	0.0	–3.1	45.2	10.7	4.0	7.0	10.8	15.7	57.2
Swaziland	–0.3	8.8	0.0	0.0	–0.8	9.7	7.9	0.4	0.6	1.2	0.7	..	28.1
Sweden													
Switzerland													
Syrian Arab Republic	–1.5	–4.5	0.0	0.0	0.0	0.0	–47.2	1.4	2.4	1.0	1.7	35.1	–11.7
Tajikistan	54.6	0.0	17.1	0.0	19.1	0.0	13.2	3.6	0.6	1.3	1.7	1.9	113.1
Tanzania	329.9	–2.9	–16.2	0.0	58.6	0.0	6.3	7.2	5.9	10.0	3.5	3.1	405.5
Thailand	–3.4	–1,615.0	0.0	0.0	–3.0	–76.7	–15.0	1.4	0.9	0.9	..	6.4	–1,703.5
Togo	0.0	0.0	–16.1	0.0	0.0	9.9	7.1	2.1	1.3	1.6	..	1.9	7.8
Trinidad and Tobago	0.0	–15.2	0.0	0.0	–0.1	–16.1	–6.1	0.5	..	..	..	1.9	–35.2
Tunisia	–2.1	–88.7	0.0	0.0	0.0	72.2	223.0	0.5	0.8	0.8	..	2.2	208.7
Turkey	–5.9	919.5	0.0	–3,504.1	0.0	0.0	285.1	0.1	1.1	1.4	..	6.9	–2,296.0
Turkmenistan	..	..	..	..	..	..	..	0.7	0.5	1.1	..	1.3	3.5
Uganda	120.6	0.0	–26.2	0.0	52.9	0.0	–0.6	5.4	5.3	7.8	12.5	12.3	190.0
Ukraine	0.0	–132.9	0.0	–299.1	0.0	11.7	–62.6	2.2	0.5	1.1	..	3.6	–475.5
United Arab Emirates	..	..	..	..	..	..	..	..	..	..	..	0.3	0.3
United Kingdom													
United States													
Uruguay	0.0	63.6	0.0	151.9	–2.4	–57.2	–0.5	0.2	0.3	0.5	..	0.9	157.4
Uzbekistan	4.5	4.5	0.0	–24.6	2.6	85.6	5.0	2.3	0.7	1.9	..	1.9	84.3
Venezuela, RB	0.0	–191.4	0.0	0.0	0.0	–189.7	100.1	0.5	1.0	0.7	..	6.0	–272.9
Vietnam	435.7	0.0	–71.6	–1.5	145.6	–2.0	4.4	6.4	7.7	4.4	..	4.8	533.8
West Bank and Gaza	..	..	..	..	..	..	..	4.0	1.9	1.6	2.7	273.9	284.1
Yemen, Rep.	66.2	0.0	–31.4	–9.9	0.0	0.0	11.7	5.5	4.1	3.6	7.5	5.7	63.0
Zambia	140.7	–3.3	–4.5	0.0	9.2	–15.2	28.3	4.3	1.5	4.0	7.7	13.7	186.4
Zimbabwe	0.0	–1.7	–15.1	–5.8	–1.1	0.0	5.6	3.0	1.4	2.5	–2.4	4.9	–8.8
World	.. s	.. s	.. s	.. s	.. s	.. s	.. s	388.9 s	314.3 s	655.1 s	269.6 s	1,534.2 s	3,162.1 s
Low income	5,195.7	–11.8	117.5	–648.2	1,309.1	–594.7	389.3	289.2	159.4	293.4	209.3	400.3	7,108.4
Middle income	938.1	–4,782.7	–45.4	–14,114.9	234.3	–1,686.7	1,427.3	86.1	86.8	83.2	59.9	907.2	–16,806.9
Lower middle income	938.7	–2,921.1	–50.4	–7,073.3	260.0	–1,565.4	857.3	72.5	70.4	71.1	58.3	719.4	–8,562.4
Upper middle income	–0.6	–1,861.6	5.0	–7,041.6	–25.7	–121.3	569.9	12.7	11.7	11.6	1.6	165.0	–8,273.4
Low & middle income	6,133.9	–4,794.5	72.1	–14,763.1	1,543.4	–2,281.4	1,816.5	380.5	314.3	655.1	269.6	1,513.6	–9,139.9
East Asia & Pacific	525.6	–2,445.8	–97.0	–1,538.8	287.9	–47.3	–172.7	52.0	39.2	46.1	21.0	58.1	–3,271.8
Europe & Central Asia	732.8	–323.6	–32.6	–5,858.5	120.5	353.2	832.4	28.2	9.3	19.2	5.4	98.2	–4,015.6
Latin America & Carib.	323.6	–1,314.4	35.4	–6,291.7	202.0	–1,532.8	746.7	22.2	43.4	26.7	21.8	236.3	–7,480.7
Middle East & N. Africa	103.5	–709.2	–31.4	–479.6	21.8	–487.0	19.8	21.5	24.8	18.2	25.0	552.8	–919.7
South Asia	1,661.6	303.8	295.7	–564.0	122.7	–438.1	114.0	65.0	35.2	71.9	42.8	114.2	1,824.8
Sub-Saharan Africa	2,786.7	–305.4	–98.0	–30.5	788.4	–129.5	276.6	186.4	106.2	200.2	153.6	351.7	4,286.3
High income													
Europe EMU													

Note: The aggregates for the United Nations and total net financial flows include amounts for economies not specified elsewhere.

About the data

The table shows concessional and nonconcessional financial flows from the major multilateral institutions—the World Bank, the International Monetary Fund (IMF), regional development banks, UN agencies, and regional groups such as the Commission of the European Communities. Much of the data comes from the World Bank's Debtor Reporting System.

The multilateral development banks fund their nonconcessional lending operations primarily by selling low-interest, highly rated bonds (the World Bank, for example, has a AAA rating) backed by prudent lending and financial policies and the strong financial support of their members. These funds are then on-lent at slightly higher interest rates and with relatively long maturities (15–20 years) to developing countries. Lending terms vary with market conditions and the policies of the banks.

Concessional flows from bilateral donors are defined by the Development Assistance Committee (DAC) of the Organisation for Economic Co-operation and Development (OECD) as financial flows containing a grant element of at least 25 percent. The grant element of loans is evaluated assuming a nominal market interest rate of 10 percent. The grant element is nil for a loan carrying a 10 percent interest rate, and it is 100 percent for a grant, which requires no repayment. Concessional flows from multilateral development agencies are credits provided through their concessional lending facilities. The cost of these loans is reduced through subsidies provided by donors or drawn from other resources available to the agencies. Grants provided by multilateral agencies are not included in the net flows.

All concessional lending by the World Bank is carried out by the International Development Association (IDA). Eligibility for IDA resources is based on gross national income (GNI) per capita; countries must also meet performance standards assessed by World Bank staff. Since July 1, 2005, the GNI per capita cutoff has been set at $825, measured in 2003 using the *World Bank Atlas* method (see *Users guide*). In exceptional circumstances IDA extends eligibility temporarily to countries that are above the cutoff and are undertaking major adjustment efforts but are not creditworthy for lending by the International Bank for Reconstruction and Development (IBRD). An exception has also been made for small island economies. Lending by the International Finance Corporation is not included in this table.

The IMF makes concessional funds available through its Poverty Reduction and Growth Facility, which replaced the Enhanced Structural Adjustment Facility in 1999, and through the IMF Trust Fund. Eligibility is based principally on a country's per capita income and eligibility under IDA, the World Bank's concessional window.

Regional development banks also maintain concessional windows for funds. Loans from the major regional development banks—the African Development Bank, Asian Development Bank, and Inter-American Development Bank—are recorded in the table according to each institution's classification.

In 1999 all UN agencies revised their data since 1990 to include only regular budgetary expenditures (except for the World Food Programme and the United Nations High Commissioner for Refugees, which revised their data from 1996 onward). They did so to avoid double counting extrabudgetary expenditures reported by DAC countries and flows reported by the United Nations.

6.13a

Maintaining financial flows from the World Bank to developing countries

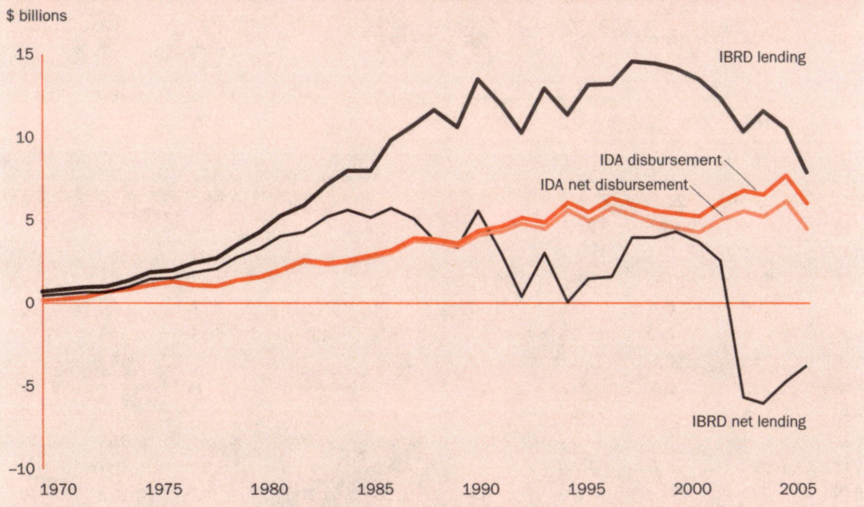

As the World Bank's nonconcessional lending portfolio matures, repayment of principal has begun to balance out new disbursements. IDA, as the World Bank's concessional financing arm, has maintained a steady flow of new funds to the world's poorest countries.

Source: World Bank Debtor Reporting System.

Definitions

• **Net financial flows** are disbursements of public or publicly guaranteed loans and credits, less repayments of principal. • **IDA** is the International Development Association, the concessional loan window of the World Bank. • **IBRD** is the International Bank for Reconstruction and Development, the founding and largest member of the World Bank Group. • **IMF** is the International Monetary Fund. Its nonconcessional lending consists of the credit it provides to its members, mainly to meet their balance of payments needs. It provides concessional assistance through the Poverty Reduction and Growth Facility and the IMF Trust Fund. • **Regional development banks** include the African Development Bank, in Tunis, Tunisia, which lends to all of Africa, including North Africa; the Asian Development Bank, in Manila, Philippines, which serves countries in South and Central Asia and East Asia and Pacific; the European Bank for Reconstruction and Development, in London, United Kingdom, which serves countries in Europe and Central Asia; the European Development Fund, in Brussels, Belgium, which serves countries in Africa, the Caribbean, and the Pacific; and the Inter-American Development Bank, in Washington, D.C., which is the principal development bank of the Americas. Concessional financial flows cover disbursements made through concessional lending facilities. Nonconcessional financial flows cover all other disbursements. • **Others** is a residual category in the World Bank's Debtor Reporting System. It includes such institutions as the Caribbean Development Bank and the European Investment Bank. • **United Nations** includes the United Nations Development Programme (UNDP), United Nations Population Fund (UNFPA), United Nations Children's Fund (UNICEF), World Food Programme (WFP), and other UN agencies, such as the United Nations High Commissioner for Refugees, United Nations Relief and Works Agency for Palestine Refugees in the Near East, and United Nations Regular Programme for Technical Assistance.

Data sources

Data on net financial flows from international financial institutions are from the World Bank's Debtor Reporting System. These data are published in the World Bank's *Global Development Finance 2006* and electronically as *GDF Online*. Data on aid from UN agencies are from the DAC annual *Development Cooperation Report*. Data are available in electronic format on the OECD's *International Development Statistics* CD-ROM and to registered users at www.oecd.org/dataoecd/50/17/5037721.htm.

6.14 Movement of people

	Net migration		Migration stock		Refugees				Workers' remittances and compensation of employees			
	thousands		thousands		thousands				$ millions			
					By country of origin		By country of asylum		Received		Paid	
	1990–95	1995–2000	1990	2005	1995	2004	1995	2004	1990	2004	1990	2004
Afghanistan	3,313	–397	29	43	2,679.1	2,085.5	19.6	0.0	..	..	..	..
Albania	–423	–267	66	83	5.8	10.5	4.7	0.1	0	889	..	4
Algeria	–58	–185	274	242	1.5	10.7	192.5	169.0	352	2,460	31	..
Angola	143	–120	34	56	246.7	228.8	10.9	14.0	..	..	150	296
Argentina	50	–100	1,650	1,500	0.3	0.8	10.3	2.9	15	288	21	151
Armenia	–500	–225	659	235	201.4	13.4	219.0	235.2	..	336	..	127
Australia	390	510	3,984	4,097	0.0	0.0	62.1	63.5	2,370	2,744	674	1,955
Austria	262	45	473	1,234	0.1	0.1	34.4	17.8	635	2,475	320	2,013
Azerbaijan	–116	–128	361	182	200.5	250.6	233.7	8.6	..	228	..	200
Bangladesh	–260	–300	882	1,032	57.0	5.7	51.1	20.4	779	3,584	..	8
Belarus	15	14	1,271	1,191	0.1	8.2	29.0	0.7	..	244	..	80
Belgium	85	99	899	719	0.0	0.0	31.7	13.5	3,583	6,840	2,310	2,623
Benin	105	–29	76	175	0.1	0.3	23.8	4.8	101	55	21	6
Bolivia	–100	–100	60	116	0.2	0.3	0.7	0.5	5	158	8	43
Bosnia and Herzegovina	–1,000	350	56	41	769.8	229.3	40.0	22.2	..	1,824	..	26
Botswana	–7	–7	27	80	0.0	0.0	0.3	2.8	86	39	119	206
Brazil	–184	–130	804	641	0.1	0.4	2.1	3.3	573	3,575	12	401
Bulgaria	–309	–50	22	104	4.2	2.6	1.3	4.7	..	103	..	11
Burkina Faso	–128	–121	345	773	0.1	0.9	29.8	0.5	140	50	81	44
Burundi	–250	–400	333	100	350.6	485.8	173.0	48.8	..	..	6	4
Cambodia	194	100	38	304	61.2	18.1	0.0	0.4	9	177	14	139
Cameroon	–5	0	171	137	2.0	7.6	45.8	58.9	23	11	111	..
Canada	643	733	4,319	6,106	0.0	0.1	152.1	141.4	..	..	..	..
Central African Republic	37	11	63	76	0.2	31.1	33.9	25.0	..	..	36	..
Chad	20	99	74	437	59.7	52.7	0.1	259.9	1	..	39	..
Chile	90	60	108	231	14.3	1.2	0.3	0.6	1	13	7	3
China	–1,281	–1,950	380	596	104.7	134.7	288.3	299.4	210	21,283	5	2,067
Hong Kong, China	300	300	2,218	2,999	0.2	0.0	1.5	1.9	..	240	..	319
Colombia	–200	–200	102	123	1.9	47.4	0.2	0.1	495	3,190	44	50
Congo, Dem. Rep.	1,208	–1,410	919	539	89.7	462.2	1,433.8	199.3	..	..	..	..
Congo, Rep.	14	42	130	288	0.2	28.2	19.4	68.5	4	1	55	24
Costa Rica	62	128	418	441	0.2	0.1	24.2	10.4	12	320	..	192
Côte d'Ivoire	200	150	1,953	2,371	0.2	23.7	297.9	72.1	44	148	471	635
Croatia	153	–150	475	661	245.6	215.5	198.6	3.7	..	1,222	..	69
Cuba	–100	–100	100	74	24.9	15.7	1.8	0.8	..	..	..	..
Czech Republic	38	52	424	453	2.0	4.5	2.7	1.1	..	454	..	1,337
Denmark	58	84	220	389	0.0	0.0	64.8	65.3	464	1,075	160	1,226
Dominican Republic	–220	–180	103	156	0.0	0.1	1.0	..	315	2,471	..	24
Ecuador	–50	–300	78	114	0.2	0.7	0.2	8.5	51	1,610	2	7
Egypt, Arab Rep.	–600	–500	176	166	0.9	5.4	5.4	90.3	4,284	3,341	27	13
El Salvador	–57	–38	47	24	23.5	4.5	0.2	0.2	366	2,564	3	33
Eritrea	–359	–9	12	15	286.7	131.1	1.1	4.2	..	..	..	..
Estonia	–117	–46	382	202	0.4	1.0	..	0.0	..	164	..	27
Ethiopia	888	–77	1,155	555	101.0	63.1	393.5	116.0	5	133	1	9
Finland	43	20	61	156	0.0	0.0	10.2	11.3	63	577	16	164
France	424	219	5,907	6,471	0.0	0.1	155.2	139.9	4,035	12,663	6,949	4,882
Gabon	20	14	128	245	0.0	0.0	0.8	13.8	..	6	147	115
Gambia, The	45	45	118	232	0.2	0.8	6.6	7.3	10	8	..	..
Georgia	–560	–350	338	191	0.3	6.6	0.1	2.6	..	303	..	26
Germany	2,688	1,134	5,936	10,144	0.4	0.7	1,267.9	876.6	4,876	6,497	6,856	10,442
Ghana	40	–51	717	1,669	13.6	14.8	83.2	42.1	6	82	4	6
Greece	470	300	412	974	0.2	0.3	4.4	2.5	1,817	1,242	122	497
Guatemala	–360	–390	264	53	42.9	4.4	1.5	0.7	119	2,591	14	36
Guinea	350	–227	402	406	0.4	3.9	672.3	139.3	27	42	20	48
Guinea-Bissau	20	–11	14	19	0.8	1.0	15.4	7.5	1	23	12	7
Haiti	–105	–105	19	30	13.9	9.2	..	..	61	876	63	..

Movement of people

	Net migration		Migration stock		Refugees				Workers' remittances and compensation of employees			
	thousands		thousands		thousands				$ millions			
					By country of origin		By country of asylum		Received		Paid	
	1990–95	1995–2000	1990	2005	1995	2004	1995	2004	1990	2004	1990	2004
Honduras	–40	–20	270	26	1.2	0.6	0.1	0.0	63	1,142	..	1
Hungary	101	100	348	316	2.4	3.4	11.4	7.7	..	307	..	128
India	–1,407	–1,400	7,493	5,700	5.0	13.3	227.5	162.7	2,384	21,727	106	1,008
Indonesia	–725	–900	466	160	9.8	27.9	0.0	0.2	166	1,866	..	913
Iran, Islamic Rep.	–1,512	–456	3,809	1,959	112.4	115.1	2,072.0	1,046.0	1,200	1,032	..	..
Iraq	170	139	84	28	718.7	311.9	116.7	46.1	..	..	..	..
Ireland	–1	89	230	585	0.0	0.0	0.4	7.2	286	358	165	856
Israel	484	276	1,633	2,661	0.9	0.6	..	0.6	812	398	850	2,116
Italy	573	600	1,346	2,519	0.1	0.2	74.3	15.7	5,075	2,172	3,764	4,745
Jamaica	–100	–100	21	18	0.0	0.3	0.0	..	229	1,623	27	425
Japan	248	280	877	2,048	0.0	0.0	5.4	2.0	508	931	290	1,411
Jordan[a]	495	35	1,146	2,225	0.5	1.2	0.7	1.1	499	2,287	71	272
Kazakhstan	–1,509	–1,320	3,619	2,502	0.1	6.1	15.6	15.8	..	167	..	1,353
Kenya	222	–21	146	345	9.3	3.8	234.7	239.8	139	494	7	34
Korea, Dem. Rep.	0	0	34	37	0.0	0.3	..	..	..	..	..	..
Korea, Rep.	–115	–80	572	551	0.0	0.2	0.0	0.0	1,037	832	364	2,545
Kuwait	–626	347	1,551	1,669	0.8	0.6	3.3	1.5	..	..	770	2,402
Kyrgyz Republic	–273	–27	623	288	0.0	3.3	13.4	3.8	..	189	..	73
Lao PDR	–10	–7	23	25	58.2	16.1	..	..	11	1	..	1
Latvia	–174	–56	805	449	0.2	3.2	..	0.0	..	230	..	13
Lebanon[a]	178	–30	520	657	13.5	19.9	1.9	1.8	1,818	2,700	..	..
Lesotho	–84	–36	7	6	0.0	0.0	0.1	..	428	355	..	29
Liberia	–283	555	81	50	744.6	335.5	120.1	15.2	..	..	..	..
Libya	10	10	457	618	0.6	1.6	4.0	12.2	..	10	446	790
Lithuania	–100	–109	349	165	0.1	1.5	0.0	0.5	..	325	..	28
Macedonia, FYR	–27	–5	95	121	12.9	5.1	9.0	1.0	..	213	..	16
Madagascar	–6	–3	58	63	0.1	0.1	0.1	..	8	16	18	7
Malawi	–835	–50	1,157	279	0.0	0.1	1.0	3.7	..	1	..	1
Malaysia	230	390	1,014	1,639	0.1	0.2	5.3	24.9	325	987	230	3,464
Mali	–260	–284	60	46	77.2	0.5	17.9	11.3	107	154	45	58
Mauritania	–15	10	94	66	84.3	31.1	34.4	0.5	14	2	31	..
Mauritius	–7	–2	9	21	0.0	0.1	..	..	..	215	1	11
Mexico	–1,800	–2,000	702	644	0.4	1.7	38.7	4.3	3,098	18,143	..	..
Moldova	–121	–70	579	440	0.5	11.9	..	0.1	..	703	..	52
Mongolia	–60	–90	7	9	0.0	0.3	..	..	..	203	..	49
Morocco	–300	–300	85	132	0.3	1.3	0.1	2.1	2,006	4,221	16	42
Mozambique	650	75	122	406	125.6	0.1	0.1	0.6	70	58	25	20
Myanmar	–126	60	101	117	152.3	161.0	..	..	6	118	..	25
Namibia	3	20	119	143	0.0	1.3	1.7	14.8	13	15	30	18
Nepal	–101	–99	413	819	0.0	1.2	124.8	124.9	0	823	..	64
Netherlands	190	161	1,192	1,638	0.1	0.3	80.0	126.8	709	2,164	1,393	5,153
New Zealand	79	20	529	642	..	0.0	3.8	5.4	762	1,132	367	911
Nicaragua	–110	–155	41	28	23.9	1.8	0.6	0.3	0	519	..	..
Niger	5	–6	115	124	10.3	0.7	27.6	0.3	14	26	66	9
Nigeria	–96	–95	447	971	1.9	23.9	8.1	8.4	10	2,273	9	21
Norway	42	67	185	344	0.0	0.0	47.6	44.0	158	392	295	916
Oman	25	–40	452	628	0.0	0.0	..	0.0	39	40	856	1,826
Pakistan	–2,611	–41	6,556	3,254	5.3	25.9	1,202.5	960.6	2,006	3,945	1	11
Panama	8	11	62	102	0.2	0.0	0.9	1.6	110	127	22	87
Papua New Guinea	0	0	33	25	2.0	0.0	9.6	7.6	5	6	43	17
Paraguay	–25	–25	183	168	0.1	0.0	0.1	0.0	34	260	..	..
Peru	–450	–350	56	42	5.9	4.8	0.6	0.8	87	1,123	75	123
Philippines	–900	–900	164	374	0.5	0.4	0.8	0.1	1,465	11,634	5	16
Poland	–77	–71	1,127	703	19.7	10.7	0.6	2.5	..	2,710	..	460
Portugal	–7	175	436	764	0.0	0.1	0.2	0.4	4,479	3,212	77	1,024
Puerto Rico	–4	–1	322	418	0.0	..	..	..	..	..	..	..

6.14 Movement of people

	Net migration		Migration stock		Refugees				Workers' remittances and compensation of employees			
	thousands		thousands		thousands				$ millions			
					By country of origin		By country of asylum		Received		Paid	
	1990–95	1995–2000	1990	2005	1995	2004	1995	2004	1990	2004	1990	2004
Romania	–529	–350	143	133	17.0	5.9	0.2	1.6	..	132	..	8
Russian Federation	1,858	2,300	11,525	12,080	207.0	108.0	*246.7*	1.9	..	2,668	..	5,534
Rwanda	–1,714	1,977	73	121	1,819.4	63.8	7.8	50.2	3	10	21	31
Saudi Arabia	–325	75	4,743	6,361	0.3	*0.2*	13.2	240.6	..	..	11,221	13,555
Senegal	–100	–100	293	326	17.6	8.3	66.8	20.8	142	511	79	57
Serbia and Montenegro	200	–100	130	512	86.1	237.0	650.7	276.7	..	4,129	..	..
Sierra Leone	–380	–110	112	119	379.5	41.8	4.7	65.4	..	25	..	3
Singapore	250	368	727	1,843	0.0	*0.0*	0.1	0.0	..	..	..	..
Slovak Republic	9	9	41	124	0.0	*0.7*	2.3	0.4	..	425	..	15
Slovenia	38	8	178	167	12.9	0.6	22.3	0.3	*38*	290	*2*	60
Somalia	–1,083	–214	633	282	638.7	389.3	0.6	0.4	..	..	..	..
South Africa	1,125	364	1,225	1,106	0.5	*0.3*	101.4	27.7	136	521	1,199	935
Spain	500	676	766	4,790	0.0	*0.1*	5.9	5.6	2,186	6,900	254	5,411
Sri Lanka	–182	–160	461	368	107.6	114.0	0.0	0.1	401	1,590	..	236
Sudan	–158	–207	1,273	639	445.3	730.7	674.1	141.6	62	1,403	2	2
Swaziland	–38	–12	73	45	0.0	*0.0*	0.7	0.7	113	89	4	131
Sweden	151	60	781	1,117	0.0	*0.0*	199.2	73.4	153	643	654	672
Switzerland	80	80	1,376	1,660	0.0	*0.0*	82.9	47.7	924	1,760	8,168	12,796
Syrian Arab Republic[a]	–30	–30	711	985	8.0	21.4	36.2	15.6	385	855	..	42
Tajikistan	–313	–345	426	306	59.0	56.8	0.6	3.3	..	252	..	119
Tanzania	591	–206	574	792	0.1	*0.7*	829.7	602.1	..	11	..	33
Thailand	–88	–88	391	1,050	0.2	*0.3*	106.6	121.1	973	1,622	199	..
Togo	–122	128	163	183	93.2	10.8	10.9	11.3	27	149	13	28
Trinidad and Tobago	–24	–20	51	38	0.0	*0.0*	..	..	3	87	22	..
Tunisia	–22	–20	38	38	0.3	*2.6*	0.2	0.1	551	1,432	13	19
Turkey	71	135	1,150	1,328	44.9	174.6	12.8	3.0	3,246	804	..	..
Turkmenistan	50	–50	307	224	0.1	*0.8*	23.3	13.3	..	..	..	..
Uganda	135	–66	550	518	24.2	32.0	229.4	250.5	..	306	..	231
Ukraine	598	–700	7,097	6,833	1.7	89.6	5.2	2.5	..	411	..	20
United Arab Emirates	340	567	1,330	3,212	*0.0*	*0.0*	0.4	0.1	..	..	..	..
United Kingdom	381	574	3,753	5,408	0.1	*0.2*	90.9	289.1	2,099	6,350	2,034	2,957
United States	5,200	6,200	23,251	38,355	0.3	*0.4*	623.3	420.9	1,170	3,038	11,850	38,751
Uruguay	–20	–16	98	84	0.3	*0.1*	0.1	0.1	..	57	..	1
Uzbekistan	–340	–400	1,653	1,268	0.1	7.3	2.6	44.5	..	..	..	..
Venezuela, RB	40	40	1,024	1,010	0.5	*0.6*	1.6	0.2	1	20	701	214
Vietnam	–270	–200	28	21	543.5	349.8	34.4	2.4	..	3,200	..	..
West Bank and Gaza[a]	–5	11	911	1,680	72.8	350.6	..	..	..	692	..	..
Yemen, Rep.	650	–50	107	265	0.4	*1.6*	53.5	66.4	1,498	1,283	106	108
Zambia	–7	86	280	275	0.0	*0.1*	130.0	173.9	..	..	17	24
Zimbabwe	–182	–125	804	511	0.0	9.6	0.5	6.9	1	..	16	..
World	..[b]	..[b]	154,688 s	190,206 s	12,518.5 s	8,650.0 s	14,896.1 s	9,236.8 s	68,584 s	227,579 s	66,295 s	154,070 s
Low income	–3,592	–4,422	32,672	28,018	9,143.2	5,854.5	7,369.9	4,054.4	8,115	43,967	1,471	3,049
Middle income	–9,367	–9,689	50,374	49,923	3,358.7	2,795.0	4,487.2	2,563.5	23,036	117,127	4,610	22,929
Lower middle income	–11,096	–10,646	25,684	24,234	2,804.9	2,260.7	4,060.2	2,438.6	13,919	84,060	793	7,284
Upper middle income	1,729	957	24,690	25,689	553.8	534.3	427.0	124.9	9,117	33,067	3,817	15,645
Low & middle income	–12,958	–14,111	83,047	77,942	12,501.9	8,649.4	11,857.0	6,617.8	31,151	161,094	6,081	25,978
East Asia & Pacific	–3,072	–3,859	2,748	4,432	932.9	708.3	447.0	456.1	3,263	41,250	527	6,770
Europe & Central Asia	–3,398	–1,858	34,071	31,137	1,881.8	1,454.9	1,436.9	657.3	3,246	19,431	..	9,725
Latin America & Carib.	–3,776	–4,156	6,355	5,795	155.7	88.9	93.9	36.2	5,776	41,051	1,002	1,895
Middle East & N. Africa	–1,030	–1,396	8,828	9,642	948.0	835.5	2,510.4	1,468.7	11,432	20,353	1,566	3,112
South Asia	–1,368	–2,401	15,845	11,229	2,958.7	2,349.9	1,625.5	1,268.8	5,572	31,671	115	1,388
Sub-Saharan Africa	–314	–439	15,200	15,706	5,624.8	3,211.9	5,743.4	2,730.8	1,862	7,339	2,871	3,089
High income	12,929	14,104	71,641	112,264	16.6	0.6	3,039.1	2,618.9	37,433	66,485	60,214	128,092
Europe EMU	5,247	3,538	17,772	30,167	1.0	*1.8*	1,665.3	1,218.9	27,744	46,269	22,226	43,819

a. Palestinian refugees under the mandate of the United Nations Relief and Works Agency for Palestine Refugees in the Near East are not included in statistics from the United Nations Office of the High Commissioner for Refugees. b. World totals computed by the United Nations sum to zero, but because the aggregates shown here refer to World Bank definitions, regional and income group totals do not equal zero.

About the data

Movement of people, most often through migration, is a significant part of integration. Migrants contribute to the economies of both their host country and their country of origin. Yet reliable statistics on migration are difficult to collect and are often incomplete, making international comparisons a challenge.

The United Nations Population Division provides data on net migration and migration stock. To derive estimates of net migration, the organization takes into account the past migration history of a country or area, the migration policy of a country, and the influx of refugees in recent periods. The data to calculate these official estimates come from a variety of sources, including border statistics, administrative records, surveys, and censuses. When no official estimates can be made due to insufficient data, net migration is derived through the balance equation, which is the difference between overall population growth and the natural increase during the 1990–2000 intercensal period.

The data used to estimate the international migrant stock at a particular point in time are obtained mainly from population censuses. The estimates are derived from the data on foreign-born population—those who have residence in one country but who were born in another country. When data on the foreign-born population are not available, data on foreign population are used as estimates.

After the breakup of the Soviet Union in 1991, people living in one of the newly independent countries who were born in another of the countries were classified as international migrants. Estimates of migration stock in the newly independent states from 1990 on are based on the 1989 census of the Soviet Union.

For countries with information on the international migration stock for at least two points in time, interpolation or extrapolation was used to estimate the international migrant stock on July 1 of the reference years. For countries with only one observation, estimates for the reference years were derived using rates of change in the migrant stock in the years preceding or following the single observation available. A model was used to estimate migration for countries that had no data.

Registration, together with other sources—including estimates and surveys—are the main sources of refugee data. Yet there are difficulties in collecting accurate statistics. Although refugees are often registered individually, the accuracy of registrations varies greatly. Many refugees may not be aware of the need to register or may choose not to do so. And administrative records tend to overestimate the number of refugees because it is easier to register than to de-register. Palestinian refugees under the mandate of the United Nations Relief and Works Agency for Palestinian Refugees in the Near East are not included in the statistics of the United Nations Office of the High Commissioner for Refugees (UNHCR).

Workers' remittances and compensation of employees are World Bank staff estimates based on data from the International Monetary Fund's (IMF) *Balance of Payments Yearbook*. The IMF data are supplemented by World Bank staff estimates for missing data for countries where workers' remittances are important. The data reported here are the sum of three items defined in the IMF *Balance of Payments Manual* (fifth edition). These are workers' remittances, compensation of employees, and migrants' transfers. Workers' remittances are classified as current private transfers from migrant workers who are residents of the host country to recipients in their country of origin. They include only transfers made by workers who have been living in the host country for more than a year, irrespective of their immigration status. Compensation of employees is the income of migrants who have lived in the host country for less than a year. Migrants' transfers are defined as the net worth of migrants who are expected to remain in the host country for more than one year that is transferred from one country to another at the time of migration.

The distinction between these three items is not always consistent in the data reported by countries to the IMF. In some cases, countries compile data on the basis of the citizenship of migrant workers rather than their residency status. Some countries also report remittances entirely as workers' remittances or compensation of employees. Following the fifth edition of the *Balance of Payments Manual* in 1993, migrants' transfers are considered a capital transaction but in previous editions they were regarded as current transfers. For these reasons the figures presented in the table take all three items into account.

6.14a

Officially recorded remittance flows are surging

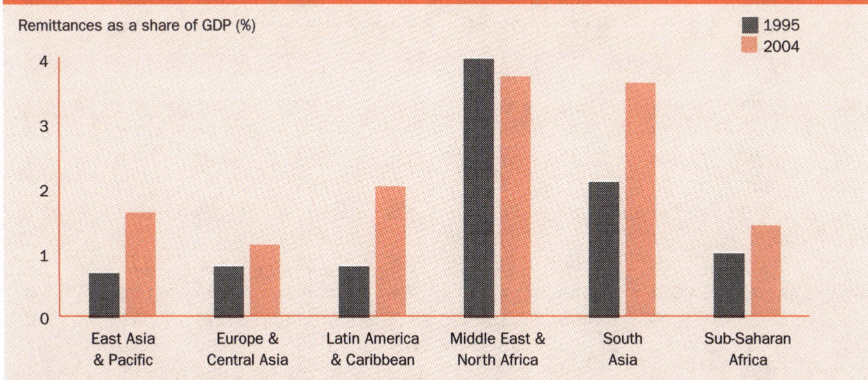

Officially recorded remittances have increased dramatically in all regions. As a share of GDP, remittances have more than doubled in East Asia and Pacific and Latin America and the Caribbean.

Source: International Monetary Fund Balance of Payments database.

Definitions

• **Net migration** is the net average annual number of migrants during the period, that is, the annual number of immigrants less the annual number of emigrants, including both citizens and noncitizens. Data are five-year estimates. • **Migration stock** is the number of people born in a country other than that in which they live. It includes refugees. • **Refugees** are people who are recognized as refugees under the 1951 Convention Relating to the Status of Refugees or its 1967 Protocol, the 1969 Organization of African Unity Convention Governing the Specific Aspects of Refugee Problems in Africa, people recognized as refugees in accordance with the UNHCR statute, people granted a refugee-like humanitarian status, and people provided with temporary protection. Asylum seekers are people who have applied for asylum or refugee status and who have not yet received a decision or who are otherwise registered as asylum seekers. • **Country of origin** generally refers to the nationality or country of citizenship of a claimant. • **Country of asylum** is the country where an asylum claim was filed. • **Workers' remittances and compensation of employees, received** and **paid** comprise current transfers by migrant workers and wages and salaries earned by nonresident workers.

Data sources

Data on net migration come from the United Nations Population Division's *World Population Prospects: The 2004 Revision*. Data on migration stock come from the United Nations Population Division's *Trends in Total Migrant Stock: The 2005 Revision*. Data on refugees are from the United Nations Office of the High Commissioner for Refugees' *Statistical Yearbook 2004*. Data on remittances are World Bank staff estimates based on IMF balance of payments data.

6.15 Travel and tourism

	International tourists (thousands)				Tourism expenditure in the country				Tourism expenditure in other countries			
	Inbound		Outbound		$ millions		% of exports		$ millions		% of imports	
	1995	2004	1995	2004	1995	2004	1995	2004	1995	2004	1995	2004
Afghanistan	..	..	..	..	..	..	..	..	1	..	..	..
Albania	40	42	12	..	70	756	23.2	*46.0*	19	668	2.3	*19.6*
Algeria	520	1,234	1,090	1,417	32	*112*	..	..	186	*255*	..	..
Angola	9	194	3	..	27	82	0.7	0.6	113	86	3.2	0.8
Argentina	2,289	3,353	3,815	3,385	2,550	2,990	10.2	7.5	4,013	3,561	15.4	12.6
Armenia	12	263	..	*169*	14	103	4.7	10.5	12	102	1.7	6.7
Australia	3,726	5,215	2,519	*3,388*	11,658	17,946	16.8	15.9	7,074	13,004	9.5	9.9
Austria	17,173	19,373	*3,713*	6,798	14,529	18,401	16.2	11.4	11,686	12,811	12.7	8.2
Azerbaijan	93	1,349	*432*	1,473	88	79	11.2	1.9	165	140	12.8	2.2
Bangladesh	156	271	830	*1,414*	..	*59*	..	*0.7*	*251*	*389*	*3.4*	*3.5*
Belarus	161	67	626	514	28	379	0.5	2.4	101	574	1.8	3.4
Belgium	5,560	*6,690*	*5,645*	*7,268*	..	10,044	..	..	..	15,295	..	..
Benin	138	*72*	*418*	..	*79*	*108*	*12.1*	*15.1*	48	*53*	5.4	*4.9*
Bolivia	284	405	249	281	92	265	7.5	10.4	72	219	4.6	9.4
Bosnia and Herzegovina	*115*	*165*	..	..	..	514	..	17.6	..	169	..	2.4
Botswana	521	*975*	*369*	..	176	*459*	7.3	*12.4*	153	*235*	7.5	*8.5*
Brazil	1,991	4,794	2,600	*2,293*	1,085	3,389	2.1	3.1	3,982	3,752	6.3	4.7
Bulgaria	3,466	4,630	3,524	3,882	662	2,718	9.8	19.4	312	1,356	4.8	8.2
Burkina Faso	124	*163*	..	..	..	..	..	..	..	..	..	..
Burundi	34	..	36	..	2	*1*	1.9	*2.8*	..	..	..	..
Cambodia	220	1,055	31	239	71	674	7.3	20.8	22	80	1.6	2.2
Cameroon	100	*226*	..	..	75	..	3.7	..	140	..	8.7	..
Canada	16,932	19,095	18,206	19,595	9,176	14,925	4.2	4.0	12,658	19,730	6.3	5.9
Central African Republic	26	..	..	..	4	*3*	..	..	43	*29*	..	..
Chad	19	*21*	..	..	43	*25*	..	..	38	*80*	..	..
Chile	1,540	1,785	1,070	2,343	1,186	1,554	6.1	4.1	934	1,196	5.1	4.0
China	20,034	41,761	4,520	*20,222*	*12,626*	27,755	*6.1*	4.2	*9,220*	21,360	*5.6*	3.5
Hong Kong, China	10,200	21,811	3,023	5,003	..	11,815	..	3.8	..	..	..	..
Colombia	1,433	791	1,057	1,405	887	1,340	7.2	6.9	1,162	1,644	7.3	8.2
Congo, Dem. Rep.	35	*35*	..	..	..	..	..	..	..	..	..	..
Congo, Rep.	37	*22*	..	..	15	*26*	1.1	*1.0*	69	*85*	5.1	*5.3*
Costa Rica	785	1,453	273	425	763	1,585	17.1	18.4	336	481	7.1	5.3
Côte d'Ivoire	188	..	..	..	103	*76*	2.4	*1.2*	312	*551*	8.2	*11.0*
Croatia	1,485	7,912	..	..	..	7,191	..	40.3	..	872	..	4.3
Cuba	742	2,017	72	115	963	1,915	..	..	..	..	..	..
Czech Republic	3,381	6,061	44,873	36,650	..	4,956	..	6.5	..	2,659	..	3.5
Denmark	2,124	3,358	*5,035*	4,630	..	..	..	..	..	..	..	..
Dominican Republic	1,776	3,450	168	368	..	..	..	..	267	448	4.4	5.0
Ecuador	440	793	271	605	315	369	6.1	4.2	331	577	5.8	6.2
Egypt, Arab Rep.	2,871	*5,746*	2,683	*3,644*	2,954	6,328	22.3	23.9	1,371	1,543	8.0	5.7
El Salvador	235	966	348	1,218	152	632	7.5	14.7	99	321	2.7	4.6
Eritrea	315	87	..	..	58	73	..	..	..	..	..	..
Estonia	530	1,750	1,764	*2,075*	452	1,102	17.6	12.5	121	481	4.2	5.0
Ethiopia	103	*180*	120	..	177	457	23.1	27.1	30	61	2.1	1.6
Finland	1,779	*2,047*	5,147	5,798	2,384	2,867	5.0	4.0	2,853	3,597	7.6	5.9
France	60,033	75,121	18,686	21,131	31,295	..	8.6	..	20,699	..	6.2	..
Gabon	125	*222*	..	*236*	94	*84*	3.2	*2.5*	183	*239*	10.3	*12.7*
Gambia, The	45	*73*	..	..	*67*	..	*30.5*	..	16	..	6.9	..
Georgia	85	368	228	*317*	*75*	209	*13.1*	12.8	*171*	196	*12.1*	7.9
Germany	14,847	*18,399*	*55,800*	*74,600*	24,052	35,589	4.0	3.4	66,981	78,553	11.3	8.6
Ghana	286	*483*	..	..	30	495	1.9	14.2	74	270	3.5	5.0
Greece	10,130	*13,969*	*1,738*	..	4,182	12,809	26.9	26.2	1,495	2,880	6.0	4.7
Guatemala	563	1,182	333	854	216	806	7.7	17.5	167	456	4.5	5.4
Guinea	*12*	45	..	..	1	*32*	0.1	*4.3*	29	29	2.9	3.0
Guinea-Bissau	..	..	..	..	..	*3*	..	*3.7*	6	*21*	6.7	*20.7*
Haiti	145	..	..	..	..	..	..	..	..	..	..	..

	International tourists				Tourism expenditure in the country				Tourism expenditure in other countries			
	thousands											
	Inbound		Outbound		$ millions		% of exports		$ millions		% of imports	
	1995	2004	1995	2004	1995	2004	1995	2004	1995	2004	1995	2004
Honduras	271	672	149	295	85	403	5.2	13.1	99	269	5.3	6.1
Hungary	2,878	3,270	13,083	17,558	2,938	4,084	14.9	6.2	1,501	2,908	7.5	4.2
India	2,124	*2,726*	3,056	*5,351*	..	*4,128*	..	*5.0*	..	*4,758*	..	*5.1*
Indonesia	4,324	5,321	1,782	..	..	5,226	..	5.8	..	4,570	..	5.8
Iran, Islamic Rep.	489	1,659	1,000	*2,921*	205	1,324	1.1	..	247	4,353	1.6	..
Iraq	61	..	*199*	..	..	..	..	..	..	..	..	..
Ireland	4,818	6,982	2,547	5,409	2,698	5,962	5.5	3.9	..	5,287	..	4.2
Israel	2,215	1,506	2,259	3,614	3,491	2,819	12.7	5.5	2,626	3,663	7.4	7.0
Italy	31,052	37,071	*18,173*	23,349	30,426	37,872	10.3	8.7	17,219	24,062	6.9	5.7
Jamaica	1,147	1,415	..	..	1,199	1,733	35.3	44.5	173	318	4.6	6.0
Japan	3,345	6,138	15,298	16,831	4,894	14,343	1.0	2.3	46,966	48,175	11.2	8.9
Jordan	1,074	2,013	1,128	*1,533*	973	1,621	28.0	27.1	719	585	14.7	6.2
Kazakhstan	..	3,073	*523*	3,915	155	793	2.6	3.5	296	917	4.9	4.9
Kenya	896	*927*	..	..	590	808	20.0	19.2	183	..	5.2	..
Korea, Dem. Rep.	..	..	..	..	..	..	..	..	..	..	..	..
Korea, Rep.	3,753	5,818	3,819	8,826	6,670	7,870	4.5	2.6	6,947	13,103	4.5	4.9
Kuwait	72	91	878	1,928	309	414	2.2	1.2	2,513	4,140	19.9	22.4
Kyrgyz Republic	36	*248*	42	*45*	..	97	..	10.3	*7*	63	*0.7*	5.5
Lao PDR	60	236	..	..	52	..	12.8	..	34	..	4.5	..
Latvia	539	1,079	1,812	2,457	37	343	1.8	5.7	62	429	2.8	5.2
Lebanon	450	1,278	..	..	710	5,931	..	..	..	3,719	..	..
Lesotho	87	..	..	..	29	..	14.6	..	17	37	1.6	2.6
Liberia	..	..	..	..	..	..	..	..	..	..	..	..
Libya	56	*142*	484	..	4	261	0.1	1.5	98	789	1.7	7.5
Lithuania	650	*1,491*	1,925	3,504	102	874	3.2	7.4	107	646	2.7	4.8
Macedonia, FYR	147	165	..	..	*35*	77	*2.7*	3.7	*30*	84	*1.7*	2.6
Madagascar	75	*139*	39	..	106	*118*	14.2	*10.5*	79	*67*	8.0	*4.1*
Malawi	192	*421*	..	..	22	*43*	4.7	*9.5*	53	*48*	8.0	*10.8*
Malaysia	7,469	15,703	20,642	30,761	5,044	*6,799*	6.1	*5.7*	2,722	*3,401*	3.1	*3.5*
Mali	42	*70*	..	..	26	*136*	4.9	*11.8*	74	*94*	7.5	*6.4*
Mauritania	..	..	..	..	..	..	..	..	30	..	5.9	..
Mauritius	422	719	107	180	616	1,156	26.2	33.4	184	277	7.5	7.7
Mexico	20,241	20,618	8,450	12,494	6,847	11,566	7.7	5.7	3,587	8,034	4.4	3.7
Moldova	32	24	71	68	71	119	8.0	8.9	73	157	7.3	7.4
Mongolia	108	301	..	..	33	205	6.5	16.9	22	207	4.2	14.7
Morocco	2,602	*4,552*	1,317	*1,694*	1,469	4,541	16.2	27.3	356	913	3.2	4.6
Mozambique	..	*441*	..	..	..	96	..	5.5	..	140	..	5.9
Myanmar	117	242	..	..	169	98	12.9	3.1	*38*	32	*1.5*	1.3
Namibia	399	*695*	..	..	..	426	..	18.4	..	..	..	..
Nepal	363	385	100	286	232	260	22.5	21.2	167	205	10.3	9.4
Netherlands	6,574	9,646	12,313	*16,463*	10,611	*11,745*	4.4	*4.4*	13,151	*14,201*	6.1	*5.7*
New Zealand	1,409	2,334	920	1,733	..	..	..	..	..	..	..	..
Nicaragua	281	615	255	701	51	191	7.7	11.6	56	158	4.9	5.5
Niger	35	*55*	10	..	*26*	*29*	*7.1*	*7.0*	26	*39*	5.7	*5.7*
Nigeria	656	*887*	..	..	54	*263*	0.4	*1.5*	939	..	7.3	..
Norway	2,880	3,600	590	*2,588*	2,730	3,400	4.9	3.1	4,481	8,788	9.6	11.9
Oman	279	*630*	..	*2,060*	..	708	..	5.0	..	795	..	7.5
Pakistan	378	648	..	..	582	763	5.7	4.7	654	1,590	4.6	7.2
Panama	345	621	185	256	372	903	4.9	10.2	181	344	2.3	3.8
Papua New Guinea	42	59	51	*92*	..	..	..	..	..	..	..	..
Paraguay	438	309	427	170	162	84	3.4	2.5	173	121	3.3	3.4
Peru	444	1,203	508	1,281	521	1,169	7.9	8.0	428	821	4.5	6.5
Philippines	1,760	2,291	1,615	*1,803*	1,141	2,412	4.3	5.6	551	1,558	1.7	3.1
Poland	19,215	14,290	36,387	27,226	6,927	6,499	19.4	6.8	5,865	4,157	17.3	4.2
Portugal	9,511	11,617	..	..	5,646	8,922	17.5	17.2	2,540	3,359	6.4	5.1
Puerto Rico	3,131	3,541	1,237	1,361	1,828	3,024	..	..	1,155	1,584	..	..

6.15 Travel and tourism

	International tourists (thousands)				Tourism expenditure in the country				Tourism expenditure in other countries			
	Inbound		Outbound		$ millions		% of exports		$ millions		% of imports	
	1995	2004	1995	2004	1995	2004	1995	2004	1995	2004	1995	2004
Romania	2,757	..	5,737	6,972	689	607	7.3	2.2	749	672	6.6	2.0
Russian Federation	10,290	22,051	21,329	24,410	..	6,958	..	3.4	..	16,527	..	12.7
Rwanda	..	..	..	..	4	..	5.4	..	13	..	3.5	..
Saudi Arabia	3,325	8,579	..	3,811	..	6,540	..	5.0	..	4,262	..	6.4
Senegal	280	363	..	..	168	*269*	11.2	*14.7*	154	*129*	8.5	*4.9*
Serbia and Montenegro	228	580	..	..	..	..	..	..	..	..	..	..
Sierra Leone	38	44	*6*	28	..	..	..	..	51	30	19.4	8.9
Singapore	6,422	*5,705*	2,867	*4,221*	..	..	..	..	..	..	..	..
Slovak Republic	903	1,401	218	457	630	932	5.7	*3.5*	338	903	3.2	*2.6*
Slovenia	732	1,499	..	2,800	1,128	1,726	10.9	8.8	606	940	5.6	4.7
Somalia	..	..	..	..	..	..	..	..	..	..	..	..
South Africa	4,488	6,678	2,520	*3,794*	2,655	6,729	7.7	11.9	2,414	3,661	7.2	6.3
Spain	34,920	53,599	3,648	5,121	27,510	51,125	20.5	19.0	5,768	13,337	4.3	4.3
Sri Lanka	403	566	504	680	367	808	7.9	11.1	279	499	4.7	5.5
Sudan	29	*51*	195	..	..	..	..	..	..	..	..	..
Swaziland	300	459	..	..	54	*16*	5.3	*0.9*	45	*34*	3.5	*3.0*
Sweden	2,310	*7,627*	10,127	13,977	4,390	*6,548*	4.6	*4.9*	6,816	*9,375*	8.4	*8.4*
Switzerland	6,946	*6,530*	11,148	*11,427*	11,354	12,208	9.2	6.7	9,478	10,599	8.7	7.2
Syrian Arab Republic	815	3,032	1,746	*3,997*	..	1,888	..	23.1	..	698	..	8.8
Tajikistan	..	..	..	..	..	9	..	0.7	..	..	..	..
Tanzania	285	566	157	..	*344*	610	*28.4*	28.0	*424*	446	*21.6*	14.0
Thailand	6,952	11,737	1,820	2,709	9,257	13,054	13.2	11.4	4,791	5,343	5.8	5.0
Togo	53	*61*	..	..	..	*26*	..	*3.8*	41	*37*	6.1	*3.9*
Trinidad and Tobago	260	443	261	..	232	*437*	8.3	*7.4*	91	*143*	4.3	*3.3*
Tunisia	4,120	5,998	1,778	*2,274*	1,838	2,432	23.0	18.3	294	427	3.3	3.0
Turkey	7,083	16,826	3,981	7,299	..	..	..	..	..	..	..	..
Turkmenistan	218	..	21	..	*13*	..	*0.7*	..	*74*	..	*4.1*	..
Uganda	160	512	*148*	231	..	306	..	26.5	..	..	..	..
Ukraine	3,716	*12,514*	6,552	*14,795*	*448*	1,512	*2.2*	3.8	*405*	1,193	*1.9*	3.4
United Arab Emirates	2,315	*5,871*	..	..	632	1,594	..	..	..	4,475	..	..
United Kingdom	23,537	27,755	41,345	64,194	27,624	37,193	8.6	7.0	30,749	68,778	9.4	11.4
United States	43,490	46,085	51,285	61,776	93,700	112,780	11.8	9.8	60,924	93,217	6.8	5.3
Uruguay	2,022	1,756	*562*	*495*	725	579	20.7	14.4	332	281	9.3	7.7
Uzbekistan	92	*231*	*246*	*400*	*15*	*48*	..	..	..	..	..	..
Venezuela, RB	700	492	534	816	995	531	4.8	1.3	1,852	1,603	11.0	7.3
Vietnam	1,351	2,928	..	..	..	..	..	..	..	..	..	..
West Bank and Gaza	..	*40*	..	..	*104*	*4*	..	..	..	..	..	..
Yemen, Rep.	61	*155*	..	..	..	..	..	..	..	183	..	3.7
Zambia	163	*578*	..	..	47	*149*	*6.1*	..	*83*	..	*6.2*	..
Zimbabwe	1,363	..	256	..	145	194	..	..	106	..	..	..
World	538,382 t	777,534 t	643,624 t	*813,857* t	497,366 t	743,043 t	8.0 w	6.7 w	481,338 t	704,549 t	7.9 w	6.7 w
Low income	11,676	*18,248*	..	..	..	*11,002*	..	*6.3*	..	*13,586*	..	*5.5*
Middle income	160,566	274,130	229,999	*288,152*	*109,238*	173,162	*8.2*	6.5	*72,853*	107,645	*5.6*	5.2
Lower middle income	69,138	138,963	48,397	*90,985*	*50,953*	92,627	*7.6*	6.4	*35,108*	56,308	*5.4*	4.2
Upper middle income	91,253	136,098	170,126	183,796	49,746	79,894	9.0	6.6	33,865	51,483	6.9	6.7
Low & middle income	175,026	*259,534*	276,829	*350,077*	*118,632*	189,112	*8.1*	6.6	*83,495*	123,650	*5.7*	5.2
East Asia & Pacific	44,247	84,175	36,006	*71,020*	*34,630*	60,901	*7.1*	5.4	*20,630*	35,398	*4.9*	3.9
Europe & Central Asia	59,537	106,564	152,343	164,140	..	..	..	6.3	..	..	..	6.9
Latin America & Carib.	39,852	51,220	21,948	*27,174*	20,622	34,115	7.1	5.8	18,987	25,624	6.5	5.3
Middle East & N. Africa	13,594	*25,048*	13,353	*20,255*	11,217	*19,489*	12.3	17.3	5,190	13,083	4.3	5.9
South Asia	3,819	*4,979*	5,151	*8,690*	..	*6,343*	..	7.4	..	*7,017*	..	6.9
Sub-Saharan Africa	12,536	*18,873*	..	..	6,345	*12,459*	6.9	12.5	7,078	*9,642*	7.0	*7.5*
High income	357,681	469,854	314,894	429,211	393,324	554,322	7.9	6.7	408,872	581,301	8.2	7.2
Europe EMU	197,165	*255,184*	*137,608*	*177,310*	175,494	262,294	8.2	7.8	175,352	228,047	8.2	7.0

About the data

Tourism is defined as the activities of people traveling to and staying in places outside their usual environment for no more than one year for leisure, business, and other purposes not related to an activity remunerated from within the place visited. The social and economic phenomenon of tourism has grown substantially over the past quarter century. Past descriptions of tourism focused on the characteristics of visitors, such as the purpose of their visit and the conditions in which they traveled and stayed. Now, there is a growing awareness of the direct, indirect, and induced effects of tourism on employment, value added, personal income, government income, and the like.

Statistical information on tourism is based mainly on data on arrivals and overnight stays along with balance of payments information. But these data do not completely capture the economic phenomenon of tourism or give governments, businesses, and citizens the information needed for effective public policies and efficient business operations. Credible data are needed on the scale and significance of tourism. Information on the role tourism plays in national economies throughout the world is particularly deficient. Although the World Tourism Organization reports that progress has been made in harmonizing definitions and measurement units, differences in national practices still prevent full international comparability.

The data in the table are from the World Tourism Organization, a specialized agency of the United Nations. The data on international inbound and outbound tourists refer to the number of arrivals and departures of visitors within the reference period, not to the number of people traveling. Thus a person who makes several trips to a country during a given period is counted each time as a new arrival. International visitors include tourists (overnight visitors), same-day visitors, cruise passengers, and crew members.

The World Tourism Organization is improving its coverage of tourism expenditure data. It is now using balance of payments data from the International Monetary Fund (IMF), supplemented by data received from individual countries. The new data, shown in the table, now include travel and passenger transport items as defined in the IMF's *Balance of Payments Manual*.

Aggregates are based on the World Bank's classification of countries and differ from those in the World Tourism Organization's publications. Countries not shown in the table but for which data are available are included in the regional and income group totals. The aggregates in the table are calculated using the World Bank's weighted aggregation methodology (see *Statistical methods*) and differ from aggregates provided by the World Tourism Organization.

6.15a

International tourist arrivals reached an all-time high in 2004

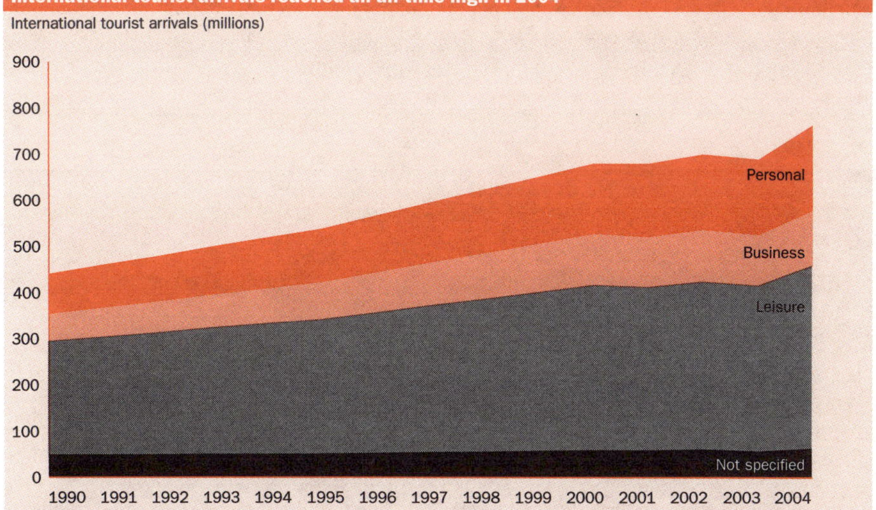

Since 1990 international tourist arrivals have been increasing steadily at 4 percent a year. In 2004 about half of international tourist arrivals were for leisure, recreation, and holidays; 16 percent for business; and another 24 percent for other personal motives such as visiting friends and relatives, religious purposes, and health treatment.

Source: World Tourism Organization.

Definitions

• **International inbound tourists** (overnight visitors) are the number of tourists who travel to a country other than that in which they have their usual residence, but outside their usual environment, for a period not exceeding 12 months and whose main purpose in visiting is other than an activity remunerated from within the country visited. • **International outbound tourists** are the number of departures that people make from their country of usual residence to any other country for any purpose other than a remunerated activity in the country visited. • **Tourism expenditure in the country** is expenditures by international inbound visitors, including payments to national carriers for international transport. These receipts include any other prepayment made for goods or services received in the destination country. They also may include receipts from same-day visitors, except in cases where these are important enough to justify separate classification. Their share in exports is calculated as a ratio to exports of goods and services (for definition of exports of goods and services see *Definitions* for table 4.8). • **Tourism expenditure in other countries** is expenditures of international outbound visitors in other countries, including payments to foreign carriers for international transport. These expenditures may include those by residents traveling abroad as same-day visitors, except in cases where these are important enough to justify separate classification. Their share in imports is calculated as a ratio to imports of goods and services (for definition of imports of goods and services see *Definitions* for table 4.8).

Data sources

Data on visitors and tourism expenditure are available in the World Tourism Organization's *Yearbook of Tourism Statistics* and *Compendium of Tourism Statistics 2006*. Data in the table are updated from electronic files provided by the World Tourism Organization. Data on exports and imports are from the IMF's *International Financial Statistics* and World Bank staff estimates.

PRIMARY DATA DOCUMENTATION

The World Bank is not a primary data collection agency for most areas other than business and investment climate surveys, living standards surveys, and external debt. As a major user of socioeconomic data, however, the World Bank places particular emphasis on data documentation to inform users of data in economic analysis and policymaking. Differences in the methods and conventions used by the primary data collectors—usually national statistical agencies, central banks, and customs services—may give rise to significant discrepancies over time both within countries and across them. Delays in reporting data and the use of old surveys as the base for current estimates may severely compromise the quality of national data.

The tables in this section provide information on sources, methods, and reporting standards of the principal demographic, economic, and environmental indicators in *World Development Indicators*. Additional documentation is available from the World Bank's Country Statistical Information Database at www.worldbank.org/data.

The demand for good quality statistical data is increasing. Timely and reliable statistics are key to the broad development strategy often referred to as "managing for results." Monitoring and reporting on publicly agreed indicators is central to implementing poverty reduction strategies and lies at the heart of the Millennium Development Goals and the new Results Measurement System adopted for the 14th replenishment of the International Development Association.

In October 2002 an information paper prepared for the World Bank's Board of Executive Directors, "Building Statistical Capacity to Monitor Development Progress," requested a briefing on the state of national statistics and statistical capacity. This briefing highlighted the increasing demand for better data, the need for action—particularly through a strategic approach to statistical capacity building at the country level—and the value of engagement in this area by the World Bank.

A global action plan to improve national and international statistics was agreed on during the Second Roundtable on Measuring for Results in February 2004 in Marrakech, Morocco. The plan, now referred to as the Marrakech Action Plan for Statistics, or MAPS, has been widely endorsed and forms the overarching framework for statistical capacity building.

PRIMARY DATA DOCUMENTATION

	National currency	Fiscal year end	National accounts					Balance of payments and trade			Government finance	IMF data dissemination standard
			Reporting period	Base year	SNA price valuation	Alternative conversion factor[a]	PPP survey year	Balance of Payments Manual in use	External debt	System of trade	Accounting concept	
Afghanistan	Afghan afghani	Mar. 20	FY	2002	VAB						B	
Albania	Albanian lek	Dec. 31	CY	1996[b,c]	VAB		1996	BPM5	Actual	G	C	G
Algeria	Algerian dinar	Dec. 31	CY	1980	VAB			BPM5	Actual	S	B	
Angola	Angolan kwanza	Dec. 31	CY	1997	VAP	1991–96		BPM4	Preliminary	S		G
Argentina	Argentine peso	Dec. 31	CY	1993	VAB	1971–84	1996	BPM5	Actual	S	C	S
Armenia	Armenian dram	Dec. 31	CY	1996[b,c]	VAB	1990–95	2000	BPM5	Actual	S	C	S
Australia	Australian dollar	Jun. 30	FY	2000[b,c]	VAB		2002	BPM5		G	C	S
Austria	Euro	Dec. 31	CY	2000[b]	VAB		2002	BPM5		S	C	S
Azerbaijan	Azeri manat	Dec. 31	CY	2003[b,c]	VAB	1992–95	2000	BPM5	Actual	G	C	G
Bangladesh	Bangladesh taka	Jun. 30	FY	1996[b]	VAB	1960–2004	1996	BPM5	Actual	G	C	G
Belarus	Belarusian rubel	Dec. 31	CY	2000[b]	VAB	1990–95	2000	BPM5	Actual	G	C	S
Belgium	Euro	Dec. 31	CY	2000[b]	VAB		2002	BPM5		S	C	S
Benin	CFA franc	Dec. 31	CY	1985	VAP	1992	1996	BPM5	Estimate	S		G
Bolivia	Boliviano	Dec. 31	CY	1990[b]	VAB	1960–85	1996	BPM5	Actual	S	C	G
Bosnia and Herzegovina	Konvertible mark	Dec. 31	CY	1996[c]	VAB			BPM5	Actual		C	
Botswana	Botswana pula	Jun. 30	FY	1994[b]	VAB		1996	BPM5	Actual	G	B	G
Brazil	Brazilian real	Dec. 31	CY	1995	VAB		1996	BPM5	Actual	S	C	S
Bulgaria	Bulgarian lev	Dec. 31	CY	2002[b,c]	VAB	1978–89, 1991–92	2002	BPM5	Actual	G	C	S
Burkina Faso	CFA franc	Dec. 31	CY	1990	VAP	1992–93		BPM4	Actual	G	C	G
Burundi	Burundi franc	Dec. 31	CY	1980	VAB			BPM5	Actual	S	C	
Cambodia	Cambodian riel	Dec. 31	CY	2000	VAB			BPM5	Actual	G	C	G
Cameroon	CFA franc	Dec. 31	CY	1980	VAB	1965–2001	1996	BPM5	Preliminary	S	B	G
Canada	Canadian dollar	Mar. 31	CY	2000[b]	VAB		2002	BPM5		G	C	S
Central African Republic	CFA franc	Dec. 31	CY	1987	VAB			BPM4	Preliminary	S		G
Chad	CFA franc	Dec. 31	CY	1995[b]	VAB			BPM5	Preliminary	S	C	G
Chile	Chilean peso	Dec. 31	CY	1986	VAB		1996	BPM5	Actual	S	C	S
China	Chinese yuan	Dec. 31	CY	1990	VAP	1978–93	1986	BPM5	Preliminary	S	B	G
Hong Kong, China	Hong Kong dollar	Dec. 31	CY	2000	VAB		1996	BPM5		G	C	S
Colombia	Colombian peso	Dec. 31	CY	1994	VAB	1992–94	1993	BPM5	Actual	S	B	S
Congo, Dem. Rep.	Congo franc	Dec. 31	CY	1987	VAB	1999–2001		BPM5	Preliminary	S	C	G
Congo, Rep.	CFA franc	Dec. 31	CY	1978	VAP		1996	BPM5	Preliminary	S	C	G
Costa Rica	Costa Rican colon	Dec. 31	CY	1991[b]	VAB			BPM5	Actual	S	C	S
Côte d'Ivoire	CFA franc	Dec. 31	CY	1996	VAP		1996	BPM5	Estimate	S	C	G
Croatia	Croatian kuna	Dec. 31	CY	1997[b]	VAB		2002	BPM5	Actual	G	C	S
Cuba	Cuban peso	Dec. 31	CY	1984	VAP					G		S
Czech Republic	Czech koruna	Dec. 31	CY	1995[b]	VAB		2002	BPM5	Preliminary	G	C	S
Denmark	Danish krone	Dec. 31	CY	2000[b]	VAB		2002	BPM5		G	C	S
Dominican Republic	Dominican peso	Dec. 31	CY	1990	VAP			BPM5	Estimate	G	C	G
Ecuador	U.S. dollar	Dec. 31	CY	2000	VAP		1996	BPM5	Preliminary	S	B	S
Egypt, Arab Rep.	Egyptian pound	Jun. 30	FY	1992	VAB	1965–91	1996	BPM5	Actual	S	C	S
El Salvador	Salvadoran colon	Dec. 31	CY	1990	VAP	1982–90		BPM5	Actual	S	C	S
Eritrea	Eritrean nakfa	Dec. 31	CY	1992	VAB			BPM4	Actual			
Estonia	Estonian kroon	Dec. 31	CY	2000[b]	VAB	1991–95	2002	BPM5	Actual	G	C	S
Ethiopia	Ethiopian birr	Jul. 7	FY	1981[b]	VAB	1965–2004		BPM5	Actual	G	C	G
Finland	Euro	Dec. 31	CY	2000[b]	VAB		2002	BPM5		G	C	S
France	Euro	Dec. 31	CY	2000[b,c]	VAB		2002	BPM5		S	C	S
Gabon	CFA franc	Dec. 31	CY	1991	VAP	1993	1996	BPM5	Estimate	S	B	G
Gambia, The	Gambian dalasi	Jun. 30	CY	1987	VAB			BPM5	Actual	G	B	G
Georgia	Georgian lari	Dec. 31	CY	1994[b,c]	VAB	1990–95	2000	BPM5	Actual	G	C	
Germany	Euro	Dec. 31	CY	2000[b]	VAB		2002	BPM5		S	C	S
Ghana	Ghanaian cedi	Dec. 31	CY	1975	VAP	1973–87		BPM5	Actual	G	B	
Greece	Euro	Dec. 31	CY	2000[b,c]	VAB		2002	BPM5		S	C	S
Guatemala	Guatemalan quetzal	Dec. 31	CY	1958	VAP		1980	BPM5	Actual	S	B	G
Guinea	Guinean franc	Dec. 31	CY	1994	VAB		1996	BPM5	Estimate	S	B	G
Guinea-Bissau	CFA franc	Dec. 31	CY	1986	VAB	1970–86		BPM5	Preliminary	G		G
Haiti	Haitian gourde	Sep. 30	FY	1976	VAB	1991		BPM5	Actual	G		

PRIMARY DATA DOCUMENTATION

	Latest population census (including registration-based censuses)	Latest demographic, education, or health household survey	Source of most recent income and expenditure data	Vital registration complete	Latest agricultural census	Latest industrial data	Latest trade data	Latest freshwater withdrawal data
Afghanistan	1979	MICS, 2003					1977	1987
Albania	2001	MICS, 2000	LSMS, 2002	Yes	1995	1990	2004	1995
Algeria	1998	MICS, 2000	HLSS, 1995		1973	2003	2004	1995
Angola	1970	MICS, 2000			1964–65		1991	1987
Argentina	2001		EPH, 2001	Yes	1988	1999	2004	1995
Armenia	2001	DHS, 2005	ILCS, 2003	Yes			2004	1994
Australia	2001		SIHC, 1994	Yes	1990	2003	2004	1985
Austria	2001		Microcensus 2000	Yes	1990	2003	2004	1991
Azerbaijan	1999	MICS, 2000	HBS, 2003	Yes			2004	1995
Bangladesh	2001	DHS, 2004	HES.2000		1976	2003	2004	1990
Belarus	1999		IES, 2002	Yes	1994		2004	1990
Belgium	2001		ECHP, 2000	Yes	1990	2003	2004	..
Benin	2002	DHS, 2001			1992–93	1999	2002	1994
Bolivia	2001	DHS, 2003	MECOVI, 2002			2000	2004	1987
Bosnia and Herzegovina	1991	MICS, 2000	LSMS, 2001	Yes		1991	2004	1995
Botswana	2001	MICS, 2000	HIES, 1993–94		1993	2002	2001	1992
Brazil	2000	DHS, 1996	PNAD, 2002		1996	1995	2004	1992
Bulgaria	2001		HBS, 2003	Yes		2002	2004	1988
Burkina Faso	1996	DHS, 2003	EVCBM, 2003		1993	2003	2004	1992
Burundi	1990	MICS, 2000	Priority survey, 1998			1991	2004	1987
Cambodia	1998	DHS, 2005	SES, 1997				2004	1987
Cameroon	1987	DHS, 2004	Priority survey, 2001		1972–73	1999	2004	1987
Canada	2001		SLID, 2000	Yes	1991	2003	2004	1991
Central African Republic	1988	MICS, 2000	EPI, 1993			1993	2003	1987
Chad	1993	DHS, 2004				1975	1995	1987
Chile	2002		CASEN, 2000	Yes	1997	2003	2004	1987
China	2000	Population, 1995	HHS (rural/urban), 2001		1996	2001	2004	1993
Hong Kong, China	2001			Yes		2002		
Colombia	1993	DHS, 2005	ECV, 2003		1988	2003	2004	1996
Congo, Dem. Rep.	1984	DHS, 2006			1990		1986	1990
Congo, Rep.	1996	DHS, 2005			1986	1988	1995	1987
Costa Rica	2000	CDC, 1993	EHPM, 2001	Yes	1973	2003	2004	1997
Côte d'Ivoire	1998	AIS, 2005	LSMS, 2002		1974–75	2003	2003	1987
Croatia	2001		HBS, 2001	Yes		1992	2004	1996
Cuba	2002	MICS, 2000		Yes		1989	2001	1995
Czech Republic	2001	CDC, 1993	Microcensus 1996/97	Yes	..	1998	2004	1991
Denmark	2001		Income Tax Register 1997	Yes	1989	2003	2004	1990
Dominican Republic	2002	DHS, 2002	ENFT, 2003		1971	2003	2001	1994
Ecuador	2001	CDC, 1999	LSMS, 1998		1997	2003	2004	1997
Egypt, Arab Rep.	1996	DHS, 2005	HECS, 2000	Yes	1989–90	2002	2004	1996
El Salvador	1992	CDC, 1994	EHPM, 2002	Yes	1970–71	2003	2004	1992
Eritrea	1984	DHS, 2002				2001	2003	
Estonia	2000		HBS, 2003	Yes	1994	2001	2004	1995
Ethiopia	1994	DHS, 2005	ICES, 2000		1988–89	2002	2003	1987
Finland	2000		IDS, 2000	Yes	1990	2003	2004	1991
France	1999		HBS, 1994/95	Yes	1988	2003	2004	1999
Gabon	1993	DHS, 2000			1974–75	2003	2004	1987
Gambia, The	2003	MICS, 2000	HHS, 1998			1982	2003	1982
Georgia	2002	MICS, 2000	SGH, 2003	Yes			2004	1990
Germany	1995		GSOEP, 2000	Yes	1993	2000	2004	1991
Ghana	2000	SPA, 2002, DHS, 2003	LSMS, 1998/99		1984	2003	2004	1997
Greece	2001		ECHP, 2000	Yes	1993	2003	2004	1980
Guatemala	2002	DHS, 1998–99	ENEI–2, 2002	Yes	1979	2003	2004	1992
Guinea	1996	DHS, 2005	LSMS, 1994		1996		2002	1987
Guinea-Bissau	1991	MICS, 2000	IES, 1993		1988		1995	1991
Haiti	2003	DHS, 2005	ECVH, 2001		1971	1996	1997	1991

PRIMARY DATA DOCUMENTATION

	National currency	Fiscal year end	National accounts					Balance of payments and trade			Government finance	IMF data dissemination standard
			Reporting period	Base year	SNA price valuation	Alternative conversion factor[a]	PPP survey year	Balance of Payments Manual in use	External debt	System of trade	Accounting concept	
Honduras	Honduran lempira	Dec. 31	CY	1978	VAB	1988–89		BPM5	Actual	S		G
Hungary	Hungarian forint	Dec. 31	CY	2000[b]	VAB		2002	BPM5	Actual	S	C	S
India	Indian rupee	Mar. 31	FY	1993	VAB	1960–2004		BPM5	Actual	G	C	S
Indonesia	Indonesian rupiah	Mar. 31	CY	1993	VAP		1996	BPM5	Preliminary	S	C	S
Iran, Islamic Rep.	Iranian rial	Mar. 20	FY	1982	VAB	1980–90	1996	BPM5	Actual	G	C	
Iraq	Iraqi dinar	Dec. 31	CY	1997	VAB					S		
Ireland	Euro	Dec. 31	CY	2000[b]	VAB		2000	BPM5		G	C	S
Israel	Israeli new shekel	Dec. 31	CY	2000[b]	VAP		2002	BPM5		S	C	S
Italy	Euro	Dec. 31	CY	2000[b]	VAB		2002	BPM5		S	C	S
Jamaica	Jamaica dollar	Dec. 31	CY	1996	VAP		1996	BPM5	Actual	G	C	G
Japan	Japanese yen	Mar. 31	CY	2000	VAB		2002	BPM5		G	C	S
Jordan	Jordan dinar	Dec. 31	CY	1994	VAB		1996	BPM5	Actual	G	B	G
Kazakhstan	Kazakh tenge	Dec. 31	CY	1995[b,c]	VAB	1987–95	2000	BPM5	Actual	G	C	S
Kenya	Kenya shilling	Jun. 30	CY	2001	VAB		1996	BPM5	Actual	G	B	G
Korea, Dem. Rep.	Democratic Republic of Korea won	Dec. 31	CY	..	..			BPM5				
Korea, Rep.	Korean won	Dec. 31	CY	2000[b]	VAP		2002	BPM5		S	C	S
Kuwait	Kuwaiti dinar	Jun. 30	CY	1995	VAP			BPM5		S	C	G
Kyrgyz Republic	Kyrgyz som	Dec. 31	CY	1995[b,c]	VAB	1990–95	2000	BPM5	Actual	G	B	S
Lao PDR	Lao kip	Dec. 31	CY	1990	VAB		1993	BPM5	Preliminary	G		
Latvia	Latvian lat	Dec. 31	CY	2000[b]	VAB	1991–95	2002	BPM5	Actual	S	C	S
Lebanon	Lebanese pound	Dec. 31	CY	2002	VAB			BPM4	Actual	G	B	G
Lesotho	Lesotho loti	Mar. 31	CY	1995[b]	VAB			BPM5	Actual	G	C	G
Libya	Libyan dinar	Dec. 31	CY	1975	VAB	1986		BPM5		G		
Liberia	Liberian dollar	Dec. 31	CY	1992	VAB				Estimate			G
Lithuania	Lithuanian litas	Dec. 31	CY	2000[b]	VAB	1990–95	2002	BPM5	Actual	G	C	S
Macedonia, FYR	Macedonian denar	Dec. 31	CY	1995[b]	VAB		2002	BPM5	Actual	G		G
Madagascar	Malagasy ariary	Dec. 31	CY	1984	VAB		1996	BPM5	Actual	S	C	G
Malawi	Malawi kwacha	Mar. 31	CY	1994	VAB		1996	BPM5	Actual	G	B	G
Malaysia	Malaysian ringgit	Dec. 31	CY	1987	VAP		1993	BPM5	Preliminary	G	C	S
Mali	CFA franc	Dec. 31	CY	1987	VAB		1996	BPM4	Actual	G		G
Mauritania	Mauritanian ouguiya	Dec. 31	CY	1985	VAB			BPM4	Actual	G		G
Mauritius	Mauritian rupee	Jun. 30	FY	1998	VAB		1996	BPM5	Actual	G	C	G
Mexico	Mexican new peso	Dec. 31	CY	1993[b]	VAB		2002	BPM5	Actual	G	C	S
Moldova	Moldovan leu	Dec. 31	CY	1996[b,c]	VAB	1987–95	2000	BPM5	Actual	G	C	G
Mongolia	Mongolian tugrik	Dec. 31	CY	1995	VAP		2000	BPM5	Actual	S	C	G
Morocco	Moroccan dirham	Dec. 31	CY	1980	VAP		1996	BPM5	Actual	S	C	S
Mozambique	Mozambican metical	Dec. 31	CY	1995	VAB	1992–95		BPM5	Preliminary	S		G
Myanmar	Myanmar kyat	Mar. 31	FY	1985	VAP			BPM5	Estimate	G	C	
Namibia	Namibia dollar	Mar. 31	CY	1995[b]	VAB			BPM5			B	G
Nepal	Nepalese rupee	Jul. 14	FY	1995	VAB	1966–2004	1996	BPM5	Actual	S	C	G
Netherlands	Euro	Dec. 31	CY	2000[b,c]	VAB		2002	BPM5		S	C	S
New Zealand	New Zealand dollar	Mar. 31	FY	2000	VAB		2002	BPM5		G	C	
Nicaragua	Nicaraguan gold cordoba	Dec. 31	CY	1998	VAP	1965–93		BPM5	Actual	S	C	G
Niger	CFA franc	Dec. 31	CY	1987	VAP	1993		BPM5	Preliminary	S		G
Nigeria	Nigerian naira	Dec. 31	CY	1987	VAB	1971–98	1996	BPM5	Preliminary	G		G
Norway	Norwegian krone	Dec. 31	CY	2000[b,c]	VAB		2002	BPM5		G	C	S
Oman	Rial Omani	Dec. 31	CY	1988	VAP		1996	BPM5	Actual	G	B	G
Pakistan	Pakistan rupee	Jun. 30	FY	2000	VAB	1972–2004	1996	BPM5	Preliminary	G	C	G
Panama	Panamanian balboa	Dec. 31	CY	1996[c]	VAP		1996	BPM5	Actual	S	C	G
Papua New Guinea	Papua New Guinea kina	Dec. 31	CY	1983	VAP	1989		BPM5	Actual	G	B	
Paraguay	Paraguayan guarani	Dec. 31	CY	1982	VAP	1982–88		BPM5	Actual	S	B	G
Peru	Peruvian new sol	Dec. 31	CY	1994	VAB	1985–91	1996	BPM5	Actual	S	C	S
Philippines	Philippine peso	Dec. 31	CY	1985	VAP		1996	BPM5	Actual	G	B	S
Poland	Polish zloty	Dec. 31	CY	2002[b,c]	VAB		2000	BPM5	Actual	S	C	S
Portugal	Euro	Dec. 31	CY	2000[b]	VAB		2002	BPM5		S	C	S
Puerto Rico	U.S. dollar	Jun. 30	FY	1954	VAP					G		

PRIMARY DATA DOCUMENTATION

	Latest population census (including registration-based censuses)	Latest demographic, education, or health household survey	Source of most recent income and expenditure data	Vital registration complete	Latest agricultural census	Latest industrial data	Latest trade data	Latest freshwater withdrawal data
Honduras	2001	DHS, 2005	EPHPM, 2003		1993	2003	2003	1992
Hungary	2001		FBS, 2002	Yes	1994	2003	2004	1991
India	2001	DHS, 2005	LSMS, 1999/2000		1986	2003	2004	1990
Indonesia	2000	DHS, 2002, Special, 2002	SUSENAS, 2002		1993	2002	2004	1990
Iran, Islamic Rep.	1996	Demographic, 1995	SECH, 1998	Yes	1988	2003	2003	1993
Iraq	1997	MICS, 2000			1981	2003	1976	1990
Ireland	2002		ECHP, 2000	Yes	1991	2003	2004	1980
Israel	1995		HES, 2001	Yes	1983	2003	2004	1997
Italy	2001		SHIW, 2000	Yes	1990	2000	2004	1998
Jamaica	2001	CDC, 1997, MICS, 2000	LSMS, 2000	Yes	1979	2003	2002	1993
Japan	2000			Yes	1990	2003	2004	1992
Jordan	1994	DHS, 2002	HIES, 1997		1997	2003	2004	1993
Kazakhstan	1999	DHS, 1999	HBS, 2003	Yes			2004	1993
Kenya	1999	DHS, 2004	WMS II, 1997		1981	2003	2004	1990
Korea, Dem. Rep.	1993	MICS, 2000						1987
Korea, Rep.	2000		NSFIE, 1998/99	Yes	1991	2003	2004	1994
Kuwait	1995	FHS, 1996		Yes	1970	2001	2001	1994
Kyrgyz Republic	1999	DHS, 1997	HBS, 2003	Yes			2004	1994
Lao PDR	1995	MICS, 2000	ECS I, 2000		1999		1974	1987
Latvia	2000		HBS, 2003	Yes	1994	2002	2004	1994
Lebanon	1970	MICS, 2000			1999		2003	1996
Lesotho	2001	MICS, 2004	HBS, 1995		1989–90	1985	2002	1987
Libya	1995	MICS, 2000			1987	2003	2004	1999
Liberia	1984						1984	1987
Lithuania	2001		HBS, 2003	Yes	1994		2004	1995
Macedonia, FYR	2002		HBS, 2003	Yes	1994	1996	2004	1996
Madagascar	1993	DHS, 2003/04	Priority survey, 2001		1984	2003	2004	1984
Malawi	1998	DHS, 2004	HHS, 1997/98		1992–93	2003	2004	1994
Malaysia	2000		HIBAS, 1997	Yes		2001	2004	1995
Mali	1998	DHS, 2006	EMCES, 1994		1978		2001	1987
Mauritania	2000	Special, 2003	LSMS, 2000		1985	1978	1996	1985
Mauritius	2000	CDC, 1991		Yes		1998	2004	..
Mexico	2000	Population, 1995	ENIGH, 2002	Yes	1991	2000	2004	1998
Moldova	1989	DHS, 2005	HBS, 2003	Yes		2002	2004	1992
Mongolia	2000	MICS, 2000	LSMS/Integrated Survey, 1998	Yes		1995	2003	1993
Morocco	1994	DHS, 2003/04	LSMS, 1998/99		1997	2001	2004	1998
Mozambique	1997	Interim, 2003	NHS, 1996/97			2003	2002	1992
Myanmar	1983	MICS, 2000			1993	2002	1992	1987
Namibia	2001	DHS, 2000	NHIES, 1993		1995	1994	2003	1991
Nepal	2001	DHS, 2006	LSMS, 2003/04		1992	2002	2003	1994
Netherlands	2002		ECHP, 1999	Yes	1989	2003	2004	1991
New Zealand	2001			Yes	1990	2003	2004	1991
Nicaragua	1995	DHS, 2001	LSMS, 2001		1963	2003	2004	1998
Niger	2001	DHS, 2006			1980	1998	2003	1988
Nigeria	1991	DHS, 2003	LSMS, 2003		1960	2003	2003	1987
Norway	2001		IF 2000	Yes	1989	2003	2004	1985
Oman	2003	FHS, 1995			1979	2003	2004	1991
Pakistan	1998	RHS, 2000–01	PIHS, 2002		1990	2003	2004	1991
Panama	2000	LSMS, 1997	EH, 2002		1990	2003	2004	1990
Papua New Guinea	2000	DHS, 1996	HGS, 1996			2003	2003	1987
Paraguay	2002	CDC, 1998	EIH, 2002		1991	2003	2004	1987
Peru	1993	DHS, 2000	ENAHO, 2002		1994	1996	2004	1992
Philippines	2000	DHS, 2003	FIES, 2000	Yes	1991	2003	2004	1995
Poland	2002		HBS, 2002	Yes	1990	2003	2004	1991
Portugal	2001			Yes	1989	2003	2004	1990
Puerto Rico	2000			Yes	1987	2001		

PRIMARY DATA DOCUMENTATION

	National currency	Fiscal year end	National accounts					Balance of payments and trade			Government finance	IMF data dissemination standard
			Reporting period	Base year	SNA price valuation	Alternative conversion factor[a]	PPP survey year	Balance of Payments Manual in use	External debt	System of trade	Accounting concept	
Romania	Romanian leu	Dec. 31	CY	1999[b,c]	VAB	1987–89, 1992	2002	BPM5	Actual	S	C	S
Russian Federation	Russian ruble	Dec. 31	CY	2000[b,c]	VAB	1987–95	2000	BPM5	Preliminary	G	C	S
Rwanda	Rwanda franc	Dec. 31	CY	1995	VAP			BPM5	Estimate	G	C	G
Saudi Arabia	Saudi Arabian riyal	Dec. 31	CY	1999	VAP			BPM4		G		
Senegal	CFA franc	Dec. 31	CY	1987[b]	VAP		1996	BPM5	Preliminary	S	B	G
Serbia and Montenegro	Yugoslav new dinar	Dec. 31	CY	1998	VAB				Actual		C	
Sierra Leone	Sierra Leonean leone	Jun. 30	CY	1990[b]	VAB	1971–79, 1987	1996	BPM5	Actual	G	B	G
Singapore	Singapore dollar	Mar. 31	CY	1995	VAB		1996	BPM5		G	B	S
Slovak Republic	Slovak koruna	Dec. 31	CY	1995[b]	VAP		2002	BPM5	Actual	G	C	S
Slovenia	Slovenian tolar	Dec. 31	CY	2000[b]	VAB		2002	BPM5		S	C	S
Somalia	Somali shilling	Dec. 31	CY	1985	VAB	1977–90			Estimate			
South Africa	South African rand	Mar. 31	CY	2000[b]	VAB			BPM5	Preliminary	S	C	S
Spain	Euro	Dec. 31	CY	2000[b]	VAB		2002	BPM5		S	C	S
Sri Lanka	Sri Lankan rupee	Dec. 31	CY	1996	VAB		1996	BPM5	Actual	G	B	G
Sudan	Sudanese dinar	Dec. 31	CY	1982	VAB	1970–95		BPM5	Actual	G	B	G
Swaziland	Lilangeni	Mar. 31	CY	1985	VAB				Preliminary		B	G
Sweden	Swedish krona	Jun. 30	CY	2000[c]	VAB		2002	BPM5		G	C	S
Switzerland	Swiss franc	Dec. 31	CY	2000	VAB		2002	BPM5		S	C	S
Syrian Arab Republic	Syrian pound	Dec. 31	CY	2000	VAP	1970–2004	1996	BPM5	Estimate	S	C	
Tajikistan	Tajik somoni	Dec. 31	CY	1997[b,c]	VAB	1990–95	2000	BPM5	Preliminary	G	C	G
Tanzania	Tanzania shilling	Dec. 31	CY	1992	VAB		1996	BPM5	Preliminary	S		G
Thailand	Thai baht	Sep. 30	CY	1988	VAP		1996	BPM5	Preliminary	G	C	S
Togo	CFA franc	Dec. 31	CY	1978	VAP		1993	BPM5	Actual	S		G
Trinidad and Tobago	Trinidad and Tobago dollar	Dec. 31	CY	2000	VAP		1996	BPM5	Actual	S	C	G
Tunisia	Tunisian dinar	Dec. 31	CY	1990	VAP		1996	BPM5	Actual	G	C	S
Turkey	Turkish lira	Dec. 31	CY	1987	VAB		2000	BPM5	Actual	S	B	S
Turkmenistan	Turkmen manat	Dec. 31	CY	1987[b,c]	VAB	1987–95, 1997–2004	2000	BPM5		G		
Uganda	Uganda shilling	Jun. 30	FY	1998	VAB	1980–99		BPM5	Actual	G	B	G
Ukraine	Ukrainian hryvnia	Dec. 31	CY	2003[b,c]	VAB	1990–95	2000	BPM5	Actual	G	C	S
United Arab Emirates	U.A.E. dirham	Dec. 31	CY	1995	VAB		1993	BPM4		G	C	
United Kingdom	Pound sterling	Dec. 31	CY	2000[b]	VAB		2002	BPM5		G	C	S
United States	U.S. dollar	Sep. 30	CY	2000[c]	VAB		2002	BPM5		G	C	S
Uruguay	Uruguayan peso	Dec. 31	CY	1983	VAP		1996	BPM5	Actual	S	C	S
Uzbekistan	Uzbek sum	Dec. 31	CY	1997[c]	VAB	1990–95	2000	BPM5	Actual	G		
Venezuela, R.B.	Venezuelan bolivar	Dec. 31	CY	1984	VAB		1996	BPM5	Actual	G	C	G
Vietnam	Vietnamese dong	Dec. 31	CY	1994	VAP	1991	1996	BPM4	Preliminary	G	C	G
West Bank and Gaza	Israeli new shekel	Dec. 31	CY	1998	VAB		1993					
Yemen, Rep.	Yemen rial	Dec. 31	CY	1990	VAP	1991–96	1996	BPM5	Actual	G	B	G
Zambia	Zambian kwacha	Dec. 31	CY	1994	VAB	1990–92	1996	BPM5	Estimate	G	B	G
Zimbabwe	Zimbabwe dollar	Jun. 30	CY	1990	VAB	1991, 1998	1996	BPM5	Actual	G	C	G

Note: For explanation of the abbreviations used in the table see notes following the table.

a. World Bank estimates including adjustments for fiscal year reporting. b. Country uses the 1993 System of National Accounts methodology. c. Original chained constant price data are rescaled.

PRIMARY DATA DOCUMENTATION

	Latest population census (including registration-based censuses)	Latest demographic, education, or health household survey	Source of most recent income and expenditure data	Vital registration complete	Latest agricultural census	Latest industrial data	Latest trade data	Latest freshwater withdrawal data
Romania	2002	CDC, 1999	LSMS, 2003	Yes		2000	2004	1994
Russian Federation	2002	LSMS, 1992	LMS, Round 9, 2002	Yes	1994–95	2002	2004	1994
Rwanda	2002	DHS, 20055	LSMS, 1999/2000		1984	1986	2003	1993
Saudi Arabia	2004	Demographic, 1999			1983	1989	2003	1992
Senegal	2002	DHS, 2005	ESASM, 1995		1960	2002	2004	1987
Serbia and Montenegro	2002	MICS, 2000		Yes		2002	1990	
Sierra Leone	2004	MICS, 2000	SHEHEA, 1989–90		1985	1993	2002	1987
Singapore	2000	General household, 1995		Yes		2003	2004	1975
Slovak Republic	2001		Microcensus, 1996	Yes		1999	2004	1991
Slovenia	2002		HBS, 1998	Yes	1991	2002	2004	1996
Somalia	1987	MICS, 2000				2003	1982	1987
South Africa	2001	DHS, 2004	IES, 2000			2003	2004	1990
Spain	2001		ECHP, 2000	Yes	1989	2003	2004	1997
Sri Lanka	2001	DHS, 1993	HIES, 2002	Yes	1982	2000	2004	1990
Sudan	1993	MICS, 2000				2003	2003	1995
Swaziland	1997	MICS, 2000	SHIES, 1994/95			2003	2002	..
Sweden	1990	DHS, 2006	HINK, 2000	Yes	1981	2003	2004	1991
Switzerland	2000		EVE, 2000	Yes	1990	1997	2004	1991
Syrian Arab Republic	1994	MICS, 2000			1981	2003	2004	1995
Tajikistan	2000	MICS, 2000	LSMS, 2003	Yes	1994		2000	1994
Tanzania	2002	SPA, 2006	HIES, 2000/01		1995	2003	2004	1994
Thailand	2000	DHS, 1987	SES, 2002		1993	2002	2003	1990
Togo	1981	MICS, 2000			1996	2003	2004	1987
Trinidad and Tobago	2000	MICS, 2000	LSMS, 1992	Yes	1982	2000	2003	1997
Tunisia	1994	MICS, 2000			1961	2003	2004	1996
Turkey	2000	DHS, 1998	LSMS, 2002		1991	2003	2004	1997
Turkmenistan	1995	DHS, 2000	LSMS, 1998	Yes			2000	1994
Uganda	2002	AIS, 2004	NIHS III, 2002		1991	2003	2004	1970
Ukraine	2001	MICS, 2000	HBS, 2003	Yes			2002	1992
United Arab Emirates	1995				1998	2001	2001	1995
United Kingdom	2001		FRS, 1999	Yes	1993	2001	2004	1991
United States	2000	Current population, 1997	CPS, 2000	Yes	1997	2003	2004	1990
Uruguay	1996		ECH, 2003	Yes	1990	2000	2004	1965
Uzbekistan	1989	Special, 2002	FBS, 2000	Yes				1994
Venezuela, R.B.	2001	MICS, 2000	EHM, 2000	Yes	1997–98	2003	2004	1970
Vietnam	1999	AIS, 2005	LSMS, 2002		1994	2000	2003	1990
West Bank and Gaza	1997	Demographic, 1995			1971			
Yemen, Rep.	1994	DHS, 1997	HBS, 1998		1982–85	2001	2004	1990
Zambia	2000	SPA, 2005	LCMS II, 1998		1990	2003	2004	1994
Zimbabwe	2002	DHS, 2005/06	LCMS III, 2002/03		1960	2003	2004	1987

Primary data documentation notes

• **Fiscal year end** is the date of the end of the fiscal year for the central government. Fiscal years for other levels of government and the reporting years for statistical surveys may differ, but if a country is designated as a fiscal year reporter in the following column, the date shown is the end of its national accounts reporting period.

• **Reporting period** for national accounts and balance of payments data is designated as either calendar year basis (CY) or fiscal year basis (FY). Most economies report their national accounts and balance of payments data using calendar years, but some use fiscal years that straddle two calendar years. In *World Development Indicators* fiscal year data are assigned to the calendar year that contains the larger share of the fiscal year. If a country's fiscal year ends before June 30, the data are shown in the first year of the fiscal period; if the fiscal year ends on or after June 30, the data are shown in the second year of the period. Balance of payments data are shown by calendar year and so are not comparable to the national accounts data of the countries that report their national accounts on a fiscal year basis.

• **Base year** is the year used as the base period for constant price calculations in the country's national accounts. Price indexes derived from national accounts aggregates, such as the gross domestic product (GDP) deflator, express the price level relative to prices in the base year. Constant price data reported in *World Development Indicators* are rescaled to a common 2000 reference year. See *About the data* for table 4.1 for further discussion of rescaling.

• **System of National Accounts (SNA) price valuation** shows whether value added in the national accounts is reported at basic prices (VAB) or at producer prices (VAP). Producer prices include the value of taxes paid by producers and thus tend to overstate the actual value added in production. See *About the data* for tables 4.1 and 4.2 for further discussion of national accounts valuation.

• **Alternative conversion factor** identifies the countries and years for which a World Bank–estimated conversion factor has been used in place of the official exchange rate (line rf in the International Monetary Fund's [IMF] *International Financial Statistics*). Estimates also include adjustments to correspond to the fiscal years in which national accounts data have been reported. See *Statistical methods* for further discussion of the use of alternative conversion factors.

• **Purchasing power parity (PPP) survey year** refers to the latest available survey year for the International Comparison Program's estimates of purchasing power parities (PPPs). For a more detailed description of PPP see *About the data* for table 1.1.

• **Balance of Payments Manual in use** refers to the classification system used for compiling and reporting data on balance of payments items in table 4.15. BPM4 refers to the fourth edition of the IMF's *Balance of Payments Manual* (1977), and BPM5 to the fifth edition (1993).

• **External debt** shows debt reporting status for 2004 data. *Actual* indicates that data are as reported, *preliminary* indicates that data are preliminary and include an element of staff estimation, and *estimate* indicates that data are World Bank staff estimates.

• **System of trade** refers to the United Nations general trade system (G) or the special trade system (S). For imports under the general trade system both goods entering directly for domestic consumption and goods entered into customs storage are recorded as imports at the time of arrival; under the special trade system goods are recorded as imports when they are declared for domestic consumption whether at the time of entry or on withdrawal from customs storage. Exports under the general system comprise outward-moving goods: (a) national goods wholly or partly produced in the country; (b) foreign goods, neither transformed nor declared for domestic consumption in the country, that move outward from customs storage; and (c) nationalized goods that have been declared from domestic consumption and move outward without having been transformed. Under the special system of trade, exports comprise categories (a) and (c). In some compilations categories (b) and (c) are classified as re-exports. Direct transit trade, consisting of goods entering or leaving for transport purposes only, is excluded from both import and export statistics. See *About the data* for tables 4.4, 4.5, and 6.2 for further discussion.

• **Government finance accounting concept** describes the accounting basis for reporting central government financial data. For most countries government finance data have been consolidated (C) into one set of accounts capturing all the central government's fiscal activities. Budgetary central government accounts (B) exclude some central government units. See *About the data* for tables 4.10, 4.11, and 4.12 for further details.

• **IMF data dissemination standard** shows the countries that subscribe to the IMF's Special Data Dissemination Standard (SDDS) or General Data Dissemination System (GDDS). *S* refers to countries that subscribe to the SDDS and have posted data on the Dissemination Standards Bulletin Board web site (posted data are at http://dsbb.imf.org). *G* refers to countries that subscribe to the GDDS. The SDDS was established by the IMF for member countries that have or that might seek access to international capital markets to guide them in providing their economic and financial data to the public. The GDDS helps countries disseminate comprehensive, timely, accessible, and reliable economic, financial, and sociodemographic statistics. IMF member countries voluntarily elect to participate in either the SDDS or the GDDS. Both the GDDS and the SDDS are expected to enhance the availability of timely and comprehensive data and therefore contribute to the pursuit of sound macroeconomic policies. The SDDS is also expected to improve the functioning of financial markets.

• **Latest population census** shows the most recent year in which a census was conducted and in which at least preliminary results have been released.

• **Latest demographic, education, or health household survey** gives information on the household surveys used in compiling the demographic, education, and health data in section 2. CDC is Centers for Disease Control and Prevention, DHS is Demographic and Health Survey, FHS is Family Health Survey, MICS is the Multiple Indicator Cluster Survey, and RHS is Reproductive Health Survey.

• **Source of most recent income and expenditure data** shows household surveys that collect income and expenditure data. HBS is Household Budget Survey; ICES is Income, Consumption, and Expenditure Survey; IES is Income and Expenditure Survey; LSMS is Living Standards Measurement Study; and SES is Socio-Economic Survey.

• **Vital registration complete** identifies countries judged to have complete registries of vital (birth and death) statistics by the United Nations Department of Economic and Social Information and Policy Analysis, Statistical Division, and reported in *Population and Vital Statistics Reports*. Countries with complete vital statistics registries may have more accurate and more timely demographic indicators than other countries.

• **Latest agricultural census** shows the most recent year in which an agricultural census was conducted and reported to the Food and Agriculture Organization of the United Nations.

Primary data documentation notes

• **Latest industrial data** refer to the most recent year for which manufacturing value added data at the three-digit level of the International Standard Industrial Classification (ISIC, revision 2 or revision 3) are available in the United Nations Industrial Development Organization database.

• **Latest trade data** show the most recent year for which structure of merchandise trade data from the United Nations Statistical Division's Commodity Trade (Comtrade) database are available.

• **Latest freshwater withdrawal data** refer to the most recent year for which data on freshwater withdrawals have been compiled from a variety of sources. See *About the data* for table 3.5 for more information.

STATISTICAL METHODS

This section describes some of the statistical procedures used in preparing the World Development Indicators. It covers the methods employed for calculating regional and income group aggregates and for calculating growth rates, and it describes the *World Bank Atlas* method for deriving the conversion factor used to estimate gross national income (GNI) and GNI per capita in U.S. dollars. Other statistical procedures and calculations are described in the *About the data* sections following each table.

Aggregation rules

Aggregates based on the World Bank's regional and income classifications of economies appear at the end of most tables. The countries included in these classifications are shown on the flaps on the front and back covers of the book. Most tables also include aggregates for the member countries of the European Monetary Union (EMU). Members of the EMU on 1 January 2004 were Austria, Belgium, Finland, France, Germany, Greece, Ireland, Italy, Luxembourg, the Netherlands, Portugal, and Spain. Other classifications, such as the European Union and regional trade blocs, are documented in *About the data* for the tables in which they appear.

Because of missing data, aggregates for groups of economies should be treated as approximations of unknown totals or average values. Regional and income group aggregates are based on the largest available set of data, including values for the 152 economies shown in the main tables, other economies shown in table 1.6, and Taiwan, China. The aggregation rules are intended to yield estimates for a consistent set of economies from one period to the next and for all indicators. Small differences between sums of subgroup aggregates and overall totals and averages may occur because of the approximations used. In addition, compilation errors and data reporting practices may cause discrepancies in theoretically identical aggregates such as world exports and world imports.

Five methods of aggregation are used in *World Development Indicators:*

- For group and world totals denoted in the tables by a *t*, missing data are imputed based on the relationship of the sum of available data to the total in the year of the previous estimate. The imputation process works forward and backward from 2000. Missing values in 2000 are imputed using one of several proxy variables for which complete data are available in that year. The imputed value is calculated so that it (or its proxy) bears the same relationship to the total of available data. Imputed values are usually not calculated if missing data account for more than a third of the total in the benchmark year. The variables used as proxies are GNI in U.S. dollars, total population, exports and imports of goods and services in U.S. dollars, and value added in agriculture, industry, manufacturing, and services in U.S. dollars.
- Aggregates marked by an *s* are sums of available data. Missing values are not imputed. Sums are not computed if more than a third of the observations in the series or a proxy for the series are missing in a given year.
- Aggregates of ratios are denoted by a *w* when calculated as weighted averages of the ratios (using the value of the denominator or, in some cases, another indicator as a weight) and denoted by a *u* when calculated as unweighted averages. The aggregate ratios are based on available data, including data for economies not shown in the main tables. Missing values are assumed to have the same average value as the available data. No aggregate is calculated if missing data account for more than a third of the value of weights in the benchmark year. In a few cases the aggregate ratio may be computed as the ratio of group totals after imputing values for missing data according to the above rules for computing totals.
- Aggregate growth rates are denoted by a *w* when calculated as a weighted average of growth rates. In a few cases growth rates may be computed from time series of group totals. Growth rates are not calculated if more than half the observations in a period are missing. For further discussion of methods of computing growth rates see below.
- Aggregates denoted by an *m* are medians of the values shown in the table. No value is shown if more than half the observations for countries with a population of more than 1 million are missing.

Exceptions to the rules occur throughout the book. Depending on the judgment of World Bank analysts, the aggregates may be based on as little as 50 percent of the available data. In other cases, where missing or excluded values are judged to be small or irrelevant, aggregates are based only on the data shown in the tables.

Growth rates

Growth rates are calculated as annual averages and represented as percentages. Except where noted, growth rates of values are computed from constant price series. Three principal methods are used to calculate growth rates: least squares, exponential endpoint, and geometric endpoint. Rates of change from one period to the next are calculated as proportional changes from the earlier period.

Least-squares growth rate. Least-squares growth rates are used wherever there is a sufficiently long time series to permit a reliable calculation. No growth rate is calculated if more than half the observations in a period are missing. The least-squares growth rate, *r*, is estimated by fitting a linear regression trend line to the logarithmic annual values of the variable in the relevant period. The regression equation takes the form

$$\ln X_t = a + bt$$

which is equivalent to the logarithmic transformation of the compound growth equation,

$$X_t = X_o (1 + r)^t.$$

In this equation X is the variable, t is time, and $a = \ln X_o$ and $b = \ln (1 + r)$ are parameters to be estimated. If b^* is the least-squares estimate of b, then the average annual growth rate, *r*, is obtained as [exp(b^*) – 1] and is multiplied by 100 for expression as a percentage. The calculated growth rate is an average rate that is representative of the available observations over the entire period. It does not necessarily match the actual growth rate between any two periods.

Exponential growth rate. The growth rate between two points in time for certain demographic indicators, notably labor force and population, is calculated from the equation

$$r = \ln(p_n/p_0)/n$$

where p_n and p_0 are the last and first observations in the period, *n* is the number of years in the period, and ln is the natural logarithm operator. This growth rate is based on a model of continuous, exponential growth between two points in time. It does not take into account the intermediate values of the series. Nor does it correspond to the annual rate of change measured at a one-year interval, which is given by $(p_n - p_{n-1})/p_{n-1}$.

Geometric growth rate. The geometric growth rate is applicable to compound growth over discrete periods, such as the payment and reinvestment of interest or dividends. Although continuous growth, as modeled by the exponential growth rate, may be more realistic, most economic phenomena are measured only at intervals, in which case the compound growth model is appropriate. The average growth rate over *n* periods is calculated as

$$r = \exp[\ln(p_n/p_0)/n] - 1.$$

Like the exponential growth rate, it does not take into account intermediate values of the series.

World Bank Atlas method

In calculating GNI and GNI per capita in U.S. dollars for certain operational purposes, the World Bank uses the *Atlas* conversion factor. The purpose of the *Atlas* conversion factor is to reduce the impact of exchange rate fluctuations in the cross-country comparison of national incomes.

The *Atlas* conversion factor for any year is the average of a country's exchange rate (or alternative conversion factor) for that year and its exchange rates for the two preceding years, adjusted for the difference between the rate of inflation in the country and that in Japan, the United Kingdom, the United States, and the Euro Zone. A country's inflation rate is measured by the change in its GDP deflator.

The inflation rate for Japan, the United Kingdom, the United States, and the Euro Zone, representing international inflation, is measured by the change in the SDR deflator. (Special drawing rights, or SDRs, are the International Monetary Fund's unit of account.) The SDR deflator is calculated as a weighted average of these countries' GDP deflators in SDR terms, the weights being the amount of each country's currency in one SDR unit. Weights vary over time because both the composition of the SDR and the relative exchange rates for each currency change. The SDR deflator is calculated in SDR terms first and then converted to U.S. dollars using the SDR to dollar *Atlas* conversion factor. The *Atlas* conversion factor is then applied to a country's GNI. The resulting GNI in U.S. dollars is divided by the midyear population to derive GNI per capita.

When official exchange rates are deemed to be unreliable or unrepresentative of the effective exchange rate during a period, an alternative estimate of the exchange rate is used in the *Atlas* formula (see below).

The following formulas describe the calculation of the *Atlas* conversion factor for year *t*:

$$e_t^* = \frac{1}{3}\left[e_{t-2}\left(\frac{p_t}{p_{t-2}} \Big/ \frac{p_t^{S\$}}{p_{t-2}^{S\$}}\right) + e_{t-1}\left(\frac{p_t}{p_{t-1}} \Big/ \frac{p_t^{S\$}}{p_{t-1}^{S\$}}\right) + e_t\right]$$

and the calculation of GNI per capita in U.S. dollars for year *t*:

$$Y_t^{\$} = (Y_t/N_t)/e_t^*$$

where e_t^* is the *Atlas* conversion factor (national currency to the U.S. dollar) for year *t*, e_t is the average annual exchange rate (national currency to the U.S. dollar) for year *t*, p_t is the GDP deflator for year *t*, $p_t^{S\$}$ is the SDR deflator in U.S. dollar terms for year *t*, $Y_t^{\$}$ is the *Atlas* GNI per capita in U.S. dollars in year *t*, Y_t is current GNI (local currency) for year *t*, and N_t is the midyear population for year *t*.

Alternative conversion factors

The World Bank systematically assesses the appropriateness of official exchange rates as conversion factors. An alternative conversion factor is used when the official exchange rate is judged to diverge by an exceptionally large margin from the rate effectively applied to domestic transactions of foreign currencies and traded products. This applies to only a small number of countries, as shown in *Primary data documentation*. Alternative conversion factors are used in the *Atlas* methodology and elsewhere in *World Development Indicators* as single-year conversion factors.

CREDITS

This book draws on a wide range of World Bank reports and numerous external sources, listed in the bibliography following this section. Many people inside and outside the World Bank helped in writing and producing *World Development Indicators*. The team would like to particularly acknowledge the help and encouragement of François Bourguignon, Senior Vice President and Chief Economist of the World Bank, and Shaida Badiee, Director, Development Data Group. The team is also grateful to those who provided valuable comments on the entire book. This note identifies many of those who made specific contributions. Numerous others, too many to acknowledge here, helped in many ways for which the team is extremely grateful.

1. World view

The introduction to section 1 was prepared by Eric Swanson and Sulekha Patel with help from K. M. Vijayalakshmi and M. H. Saeed Ordoubadi. Stimulating discussions with members of the UN Interagency and Expert Group on the MDGs are gratefully acknowledged. K. M. Vijayalakshmi prepared table 1.1. Yonas Biru prepared the estimates of gross national income in purchasing power parity terms. Tables 1.2, 1.3, and 1.5 were prepared by Masako Hiraga. The team is grateful to Rudy Petras and Yasmin Ahmad at the Organisation for Economic Co-operation and Development (OECD) for data and advice on official development assistance flows and agricultural support estimates; Peter Ghys and Elizabeth Zaniewski at the Joint United Nations Programme on HIV/AIDS for historical estimates of HIV/AIDS; and Joshua Solomon and his colleagues for projections of HIV prevalence rates.

2. People

Section 2 was prepared by Masako Hiraga in partnership with the World Bank's Human Development Network and the Development Research Group in the Development Economics Vice Presidency. Mehdi Akhlaghi provided invaluable assistance in data and table preparation, and Vivienne Wang prepared the demographic estimates and projections. Sulekha Patel wrote the introduction with input from John May and Sarwar Lateef. The poverty estimates were prepared by Shaohua Chen of the World Bank's Poverty Monitoring Group with help from Prem Sangraula and Johan Mistiaen. The table on child labor was prepared by Furio Rosati of the Understanding Children's Work project. Contributions were provided by Eduard Bos and Emi Suzuki (population, health, and nutrition); Montserrat Pallares-Miralles (vulnerability and security); Raymond Muhula and Lianqin Wang (education); and Lucia Fort and Juan Carlos Guzman Roa (gender). Comments and suggestions at various stages of production came from Eric Swanson.

3. Environment

Section 3 was prepared by M. H. Saeed Ordoubadi and Mayhar Eshragh-Tabary in partnership with the World Bank's Environmentally and Socially Sustainable Development Network and in collaboration with the World Bank's Development Research Group and Transportation, Water, and Urban Development Department. Important contributions were made by Edward Gillin and Carola Fabi of the Food and Agriculture Organization; Ricardo Quercioli of the International Energy Agency; Amay Cassara, Christian Layke, Daniel Prager, and Robin White of the World Resources Institute; Laura Battlebury of the World Conservation Monitoring Centre; and Gerhard Metchies of GTZ. Mehdi Akhlaghi made important contributions to the statistical methods and management of the databases for the section. The World Bank's Environment Department and Rural Development Department devoted substantial staff resources to the book, for which the team is very grateful. M. H. Saeed Ordoubadi wrote the introduction with valuable comments from Sarwar Lateef, Eric Swanson, and Bruce Ross-Larson and Meta de Coquereaumont, who also edited the text. Other contributions were made by Kiran Pandey (biodiversity); Susmita Dasgupta, Craig Meisner, Kiran Pandey, and David Wheeler (air and water pollution); Mahyar Eshragh-Tabary, Augusto Clavijo, Maria Emilia Ferire, Christine Kessides, Solly Angel, and Micah Perlin (urban housing conditions); and Kirk Hamilton, Giovanni Ruta, Beat Hintermann, and Suzette Galitano (adjusted savings). Valuable comments and contributions were also provided by Kyran O'Sullivan and Anton Dobronogov.

4. Economy

Section 4 was prepared by K. M. Vijayalakshmi in close collaboration with the Macroeconomic Data Team of the World Bank's Development Data Group, led by Soong Sup Lee. K. M. Vijayalakshmi and Eric Swanson wrote the introduction with valuable suggestions from Barbro Hexeberg, Sarwar Lateef, and W. Bill Shaw. Contributions to the section were provided by Azita Amjadi (trade) and Ibrahim Levent (external debt). The national accounts data for low- and middle-income economies were gathered by the World Bank's regional staff through the annual Unified Survey. Maja Bresslauer, Victor Gabor, Augusto Clavijo, and Soong Sup Lee worked on updating, estimating, and validating the databases for national accounts. The team is grateful to the World Trade Organization, the United Nations Industrial Development Organization, and the OECD for access to the databases.

5. States and markets

Section 5 was prepared by David Cieslikowski in partnership with the World Bank's Private Sector Department, the Infrastructure Network, its Poverty Reduction and Economic Management Network, the International Finance Corporation, and external partners. Raymond Muhula and Juan Carlos Rodriguez provided invaluable assistance in data and table preparation. David Cieslikowski wrote the introduction to the section with valuable comments from Sarwar Lateef, Eric Swanson, and Peter Roberts. Other contributors include Ada Karina Izaguirre and William Butterfield (privatization and infrastructure projects); Marta Kozak (micro, small, and medium-size enterprises); Mary Hallward-Driemeier (investment climate); Simeon Djankov and Caralee McLeish (business environment); Alka Banerjee and Isilay Cabuk (Standard & Poor's global stock market indexes); Stijn Claessens, Asli Demirgüç-Kunt, Margaret Miller, and Himmat Kalsi (financial); Peter Roberts, Tsukasa Hattori, and Henrich Bofinger (transport); Jane Degerlund of Containerisation International (ports); Esperanza Magpantay and Vanessa Grey of the International Telecommunication Union, and Christine Zhen-Wei Qiang (communications and information); Ernesto Fernandez Polcuch of the United Nations Educational, Scientific, and Cultural Organization Institute for Statistics (research and development, researchers, and technicians); Anders Halvorsen of the World Information Technology and Services Alliance (information and communication technology expenditures); Terrence Taylor of the International Institute for Strategic Studies (military personnel); and Bjorn Hagelin and Petter Stålenheim of the Stockholm International Peace Research Institute (military expenditures and arms transfers).

6. Global links

Section 6 was prepared by Amy Heyman, Changqing Sun, and Eric Swanson in partnership with the World Bank's Development Research Group (trade), the Prospects Group (commodity prices), and external partners. Many thanks to Sarwar Lateef, Neil Fantom, Ibrahim Levent, Azita Amjadi, Jean-Jacques Dethier, and Andrew Burns for initial comments and feedback about possible revisions to the section. Substantial input for the data came from Azita Amjadi, Jerzy Rozanski (tariffs), Gloria Moreno, Nevin Fahmy, and Ibrahim Levent (financial data). Other contributors include Francis Ng and Dominique van der Mensbrugghe (trade); Dilek Aykut (foreign direct investment flows); Betty Dow (commodity prices); Bela Hovy and Christian Oxenball of the United Nations Office of the High Commissioner for Refugees; Marta Roig, Hania Zlotnik, and Francois Pelletier of the United Nations Population Division (migration); Brian Hammond and Yasmin Ahmad of the OECD (aid); Antonio Massieu and Teresa Ciller of the World Tourism Organization (tourism); Henri Laurencin and David Cristallo of the United Nations Conference on Trade and Development (trade), and K. M. Vijayalatshmi (remittances). Mehdi Akhlaghi and Will Prince provided valuable technical assistance.

Other parts

Preparation of the maps on the inside covers was coordinated by Jeff Lecksell of the World Bank's Map Design Unit. *Users guide* was prepared by David Cieslikowski. *Statistical methods* was written by Eric Swanson. *Primary data documentation* was coordinated by K. M. Vijayalakshmi. Awatif Abuzeid assisted in updating the *Primary data documentation* table. *Partners* and *Index of indicators* were prepared by Richard Fix with assistance from Gonca Okur and Priya Pandya.

Database management

Database management was coordinated by Mehdi Akhlaghi with cross-team participation, including Deepa Ramachandran Pai for systems development, to create an integrated World Development Indicators database. This database was used to generate the tables for *World Development Indicators* and related products such as *WDI Online*, *Little Data Book*, *The Little Green Data Book*, and the *World Development Indicators* CD-ROM.

Design, production, and editing

Richard Fix, with the assistance of Gonca Okur, coordinated all stages of production with Communications Development Incorporated. Communications Development Incorporated provided overall design direction, editing, and layout, led by Meta de Coquereaumont and Bruce Ross-Larson with the assistance of Christopher Trott. The editing and production team consisted of Jodi Baxter, Brendon Boyle, Michael Diavolikis, Timothy Walker, and Elaine Wilson. Communications Development's London partner, Grundy & Northedge, provided art direction and design. Staff from External Affairs oversaw printing and dissemination of the book.

Client services

The Development Data Group's Client Services Team (Azita Amjadi, Richard Fix, Gonca Okur, Priya Pandya, and William Prince) contributed to the design and planning of *World Development Indicators* and helped coordinate work with the Office of the Publisher.

Administrative assistance and office technology support

Estela Zamora and Awatif Abuzeid provided administrative assistance. Jean-Pierre Djomalieu, Gytis Kanchas, Nacer Megherbi, and Shahin Outadi provided information technology support.

Publishing and dissemination

The Office of the Publisher, under the direction of Dirk Koehler, provided valuable assistance throughout the production process. Brenda Mejia and Stephen McGroarty coordinated printing and supervised marketing and distribution. Chris Neal of the Development Economics Vice President's managed the communications strategy.

World Development Indicators CD-ROM

Programming and testing were carried out by Reza Farivari and his team: Azita Amjadi, Ying Chi, Ramgopal Erabelly, Nacer Megherbi, Gonca Okur, Shahin Outadi, and William Prince. Masako Hiraga produced the social indicators tables. William Prince coordinated user interface design and overall production and provided quality assurance. Photo credits: Curt Carnemark, Francis Dobbs, Julio Etchart, Tran Thi Hoa, Edwin Hu man, Anvar Ilyasov, Michael Mertaugh, Shehzad Noorani, Tomas Sennett, and Ray Witlin (World Bank). The interactive text was produced by Intermax, Inc.

WDI Online

Design, programming, and testing were carried out by Reza Farivari and his team: Mehdi Akhlaghi, Azita Amjadi, Saurabh Gupta, Gonca Okur, and Shahin Outadi. William Prince coordinated production and provided quality assurance. Valentina Kalk and Triinu Tombak of the Office of the Publisher were responsible for implementation of *WDI Online* and management of the subscription service.

Client feedback

The team is grateful to the many people who have taken the time to provide comment on its publications. Their feedback and suggestions have helped improve this year's edition.

BIBLIOGRAPHY

AbouZahr, Carla, and Tessa Wardlaw. 2004. *Maternal Mortality in 2000: Estimates Developed by WHO, UNICEF, and UNFPA*. Geneva: World Health Organization.

African Union and UNECA (United Nations Economic Commission for Africa). 2005. "Transport and the Millennium Development Goals in Africa." Background working document prepared for the meeting of experts for the African Transport Ministers on the Role of Transport in Achieving the Millennium Development Goals, April 4–5, Addis Ababa. [www4.worldbank.org/afr/ssatp/Resources/PapersNotes/transport_mdg.pdf]

Ahmad, Sultan. 1992. "Regression Estimates of Per Capita GDP Based on Purchasing Power Parities." Policy Research Working Paper 956. World Bank, International Economics Department, Washington, D.C.

———. 1994. "Improving Inter-Spatial and Inter-Temporal Comparability of National Accounts." *Journal of Development Economics* 44 (1): 53–75.

Alderman, Harold, Peter F. Orazem, and Elizabeth Paterno. 2001. "School Quality, School Cost and the Public/Private School Choices of Low-Income Households in Pakistan." *Journal of Human Resources* 36 (2): 304–26.

Ball, Nicole. 1984. "Measuring Third World Security Expenditure: A Research Note." *World Development* 12 (2): 157–64.

Barro, Robert J. 1991. "Economic Growth in a Cross-Section of Countries." *Quarterly Journal of Economics* 106 (2): 407–43.

Beck, Thorsten, and Ross Levine. 2001. "Stock Markets, Banks, and Growth: Correlation or Causality?" Policy Research Working Paper 2670. World Bank, Development Research Group, Washington, D.C.

Beck, Thorsten, Asli Demirgüç-Kunt, and Maria Soledad Martizez Peria. 2005. "Reaching Out: Access to and Use of Banking Services across Countries." Policy Research Working Paper 3754. World Bank, Development Research Group, Washington, D.C.

Behrman, Jere R., and Mark R. Rosenzweig. 1994. "Caveat Emptor: Cross-Country Data on Education and the Labor Force." *Journal of Development Economics* 44 (1): 147–71.

Bhalla, Surjit. 2002. *Imagine There Is No Country: Poverty, Inequality, and Growth in the Era of Globalization.* Washington, D.C.: Institute for International Economics.

Bilsborrow, R. E., Graeme Hugo, A. S. Oberai, and Hania Zlotnik. 1997. *International Migration Statistics*. Geneva: International Labour Office.

Bloom, David E., and Jeffrey G. Williamson. 1998. "Demographic Transitions and Economic Miracles in Emerging Asia." *World Bank Economic Review* 12 (3): 419–55.

Bourguignon, François. 2006. "Dynamics of Institutions, Development, and the Elites." Presentation at the Annual World Bank Conference on Development Economics (ABCDE), January 18, St. Petersburg, Russia.

Brown, Lester R., Michael Renner, Christopher Flavin. 1998. *Vital Signs 1998: The Environmental Trends That Are Shaping Our Future*. New York: W.W. Norton.

Brown, Lester R., Michael Renner, and Brian Halweil. 1999. *Vital Signs 1999: The Environmental Trends That Are Shaping Our Future*. New York: W.W. Norton.

Brown, Lester R., Christopher Flavin, Hilary F. French, and others. 1998. *State of the World 1998: A Worldwatch Institute Report on Progress toward a Sustainable Society*. New York: W.W. Norton.

Caiola, Marcello. 1995. *A Manual for Country Economists*. Training Series 1. Vol. 1. Washington, D.C.: International Monetary Fund.

Carr, Dara. 2004. "Improving the Health of the World's Poorest People." Health Bulletin 1. Population Reference Bureau, Washington, D.C.

CELADE (Centro Latinoamericano de Demografia). Various issues. *Boletín Demografico*.

Chaudhury, Nazmul, Jeffrey S. Hammer, Michael Kremer, Karthik Muralidharan, and F. Halsey Rogers. 2004. "Teacher and Health Care Provider Absenteeism: A Multi-Country Study." World Bank, Washington, D.C.

Chen, Shaohua, and Martin Ravallion. 2004. "How Have the World's Poorest Fared since the 1980s?" *World Bank Research Observer* 19 (2): 141–69.

Claessens, Stijn. 2005. "Access to Financial Services: A Review of the Issues and Public Policy Objectives." Policy Research Working Paper 3589. World Bank, Operations and Policy Department, Washington, D.C.

Cleland, John, and Steven Sinding. 2005. "What Would Malthus Say about AIDS in Africa?" *The Lancet* 367 (9512): 730.

Collier, Paul, and David Dollar. 1999. "Aid Allocation and Poverty Reduction." Policy Research Working Paper 2041. World Bank, Development Research Group, Washington, D.C.

———. 2001. "Can the World Cut Poverty in Half? How Policy Reform and Effective Aid Can Meet the International Development Goals." Policy Research Working Paper 2403. World Bank, Development Research Group, Washington, D.C.

Commission for Africa. 2005. "Our Common Interest: Report of the Commission for Africa." Glasgow, UK. [www.commissionforafrica.org/english/report/thereport/english/11-03-05_cr_report.pdf]

Commission of the European Communities, IMF (International Monetary Fund), OECD (Organisation for Economic Co-operation and Development), United Nations, and World Bank. 2002. *System of Environmental and Economic Accounts: SEEA 2000.* New York.

Containerisation International. 2006. *Containerisation International Yearbook 2006.* London: Informa Maritime and Transport.

Corrao, Mario Ann, G. Emmanuel Guindon, Namita Sharma, and Donna Fakhrabadi Shokoohi, eds. 2000. *Tobacco Control Country Profiles*. Atlanta, Ga.: American Cancer Society.

CSD (Commission on Sustainable Development). 1997. *Comprehensive Assessment of the Freshwater Resources of the World.* Report of the Secretary-General. New York.

Deaton, Angus. 2002. "Counting the World's Poor: Problems and Possible Solutions." *World Bank Research Observer* 16 (2): 125–47.

Demirgüç-Kunt, Asli, and Ross Levine. 1996a. "Stock Market Development and Financial Intermediaries: Stylized Facts." *World Bank Economic Review* 10 (2): 291–321.

Demirgüç-Kunt, Asli, Baybars Karacaovali, and Luc Laeven. 2005. "Deposit Insurance around the World: A Comprehensive Database." Policy Research Working Paper 3628. World Bank, Washington, D.C.

De Onis, Mercedes, and Monika Blössner. 2000. "The WHO Global Database on Child Growth and Malnutrition: Methodology and Applications." *International Journal of Epidemiology* 32: 518–26.

De Onis, Mercedes, Monika Blössner, Elaine Borghi, Edward A. Frongillo, and Richard Morris. 2004. "Estimates of Global Prevalence of Childhood Underweight in 1990 and 2015." *Journal of the American Medical Association* 291 (21): 2600–06.

Development Committee. 2003. "Supporting Sound Policies with Adequate and Appropriate Financing: Implementing the Monterrey Consensus at the Country Level." SecM2003-0370. World Bank and International Monetary Fund. Washington, D.C.

———. 2005. "Infrastructure and the World Bank." DC2005-0015. World Bank and International Monetary Fund. Washington, D.C.

DKT International. 1998. "1997 Contraceptive Social Marketing Statistics." Washington, D.C.

Doyle, John J., and Gabrielle J. Persley, eds. 1996. *Enabling the Safe Use of Biotechnology: Principles and Practice.* Environmentally Sustainable Development Studies and Monographs Series 10. Washington, D.C.: World Bank.

Drucker, Peter F. 1994. "The Age of Social Transformation." *Atlantic Monthly,* November.

Easterly, William. 2000. "Growth Implosions, Debt Explosions, and My Aunt Marilyn: Do Growth Slowdowns Cause Public Debt Crises?" Policy Research Working Paper 2531. World Bank, Development Research Group, Washington, D.C.

Eurostat (Statistical Office of the European Communities). Various years. *Demographic Statistics.* Luxembourg.

———. Various years. *Statistical Yearbook.* Luxembourg.

Evenson, Robert E., and Carl E. Pray. 1994. "Measuring Food Production (with Reference to South Asia)." *Journal of Development Economics* 44 (1): 173–97.

Faiz, Asif, Christopher S. Weaver, and Michael P. Walsh. 1996. *Air Pollution from Motor Vehicles: Standards and Technologies for Controlling Emissions.* Washington, D.C.: World Bank.

Fankhauser, Samuel. 1995. *Valuing Climate Change: The Economics of the Greenhouse.* London: Earthscan.

FAO (Food and Agriculture Organization). 1986. "Inter-Country Comparisons of Agricultural Production Aggregates." Economic and Social Development Paper 61. Rome.

———. 1996. *Food Aid in Figures 1994.* Vol. 12. Rome.

———. 2001a. *Agriculture: Towards 2015/30.* Rome.

———. 2001b. *State of Food Insecurity in the World 2001.* Rome.

———. 2003. *State of the World's Forests 2003.* Rome.

———. Various years. Fertilizer Yearbook. FAO Statistics Series. Rome.

———. Various years. Production Yearbook. FAO Statistics Series. Rome.

———. Various years. The State of Food Insecurity in the World. Rome.

———. Various years. Trade *Yearbook.* FAO Statistics Series. Rome

Frankel, Jeffrey. 1993. "Quantifying International Capital Mobility in the 1990s." In *On Exchange Rates.* Cambridge, Mass.: MIT Press.

Frankhauser, Pierre. 1994. "Fractales, tissus urbains et reseaux de transport." *Revue d'economie politique* 104: 435–55.

Fredricksen, Birger. 1993. *Statistics of Education in Developing Countries: An Introduction to Their Collection and Analysis.* Paris: United Nations Educational, Scientific, and Cultural Organization.

Gallup, John L., and Je rey D. Sachs. 1998. "The Economic Burden of Malaria." Harvard Institute for International Development, Cambridge, Mass.

Gannon, Colin, and Zmarak Shalizi. 1995. "The Use of Sectoral and Project Performance Indicators in Bank-Financed Transport Operations." TWU Discussion Paper 21. World Bank, Transportation, Water, and Urban Development Department, Washington, D.C.

Gardner, Robert. 1998. "Education." Demographic and Health Surveys, Comparative Study 29. Macro International, Calverton, Md.

Gardner-Outlaw, Tom, and Robert Engelman. 1997. "Sustaining Water, Easing Scarcity: A Second Update." Population Action International, Washington, D.C.

Goldfinger, Charles. 1994. *L'utile et le futile: L'économie de l'immatériel.* Paris: Editions Odile Jacob.

GTZ (German Agency for Technical Cooperation). 2004. *Fuel Prices and Taxation.* Eschborn, Germany.

Gupta, Sanjeev, Hamid Davoodi, and Erwin Tiongson. 2000. "Corruption and the Provision of Health Care and Education Services." IMF Working Paper 00/116. International Monetary Fund, Washington, D.C.

Gupta, Sanjeev, Brian Hammond, and Eric Swanson. 2000. "Setting the Goals." *OECD Observer* 223: 15–17.

Gwatkin, Davidson, and Michel Guillot. 2000. "The Burden of Disease among the Global Poor." Health, Nutrition, and Population Series. World Bank, Washington, D.C.

Habyarimana, James, Jishnu Das, Stefan Dercon, and Pramila Krishnan. 2003. "Sense and Absence: Absenteeism and Learning in Zambian Schools." World Bank, Washington, D.C.

Hamilton, Kirk, and Michael Clemens. 1999. "Genuine Savings Rates in Developing Countries." *World Bank Economic Review* 13 (2): 333–56.

Hanushek, Eric. 2002. *The Long-Run Importance of School Quality.* NBER Working Paper 9071. Cambridge, Mass.: National Bureau of Economic Research.

Happe, Nancy, and John Wakeman-Linn. 1994. "Military Expenditures and Arms Trade: Alternative Data Sources." IMF Working Paper 94/69.

BIBLIOGRAPHY

International Monetary Fund, Policy Development and Review Department, Washington, D.C

Harrison, Ann. 1995. "Factor Markets and Trade Policy Reform." World Bank, Washington, D.C.

Hatzichronoglou, Thomas. 1997. "Revision of the High-Technology Sector and Product Classification." STI Working Paper 1997/2. Organisation for Economic Co-operation and Development, Directorate for Science, Technology, and Industry, Paris.

Heck, W. W. 1989. "Assessment of Crop Losses from Air Pollutants in the U.S." In J. J. McKenzie and M. T. El Ashry, eds., *Air Pollution's Toll on Forests and Crops*. New Haven, Conn.: Yale University Press.

Heston, Alan. 1994. "A Brief Review of Some Problems in Using National Accounts Data in Level of Output Comparisons and Growth Studies." *Journal of Development Economics* 44 (1): 29–52.

Hettige, Hemamala, Muthukumara Mani, and David Wheeler. 1998. "Industrial Pollution in Economic Development: Kuznets Revisited." Policy Research Working Paper 1876. World Bank, Development Research Group, Washington, D.C.

IEA (International Energy Agency). 2002. *World Energy Outlook: Energy and Poverty*. Paris.

———. Various years. *Energy Balances of OECD Countries*. Paris.

———. Various years. *Energy Statistics and Balances of Non-OECD Countries*. Paris.

———. Various years. *Energy Statistics of OECD Countries*. Paris.

IFPRI (International Food Policy Research Institute). 1999. *Soil Degradation: A Threat to Developing-Country Food Security by 2020*. Washington, D.C.

ILO (International Labour Organization). Various years. *Key Indicators of the Labour Market*. Geneva: International Labour Office.

———. Various years. Yearbook of Labour Statistics. Geneva: International Labour Office.

IMF (International Monetary Fund). 1977. *Balance of Payments Manual*. 4th ed. Washington, D.C.

———. 1993. *Balance of Payments Manual*. 5th ed. Washington, D.C.

———. 1995. *Balance of Payments Compilation Guide*. Washington, D.C.

———. 1996. *Balance of Payments Textbook*. Washington, D.C.

———. 2000. *Monetary and Financial Statistics Manual*. Washington, D.C.

———. 2001. *Government Finance Statistics Manual*. Washington, D.C.

———. 2004a. *Compilation Guide on Financial Soundness Indicators*. Washington, D.C.

———. 2004b. *World Economic Outlook*. Chapter 3. Washington, DC.

———. 2005. *Global Financial Stability Report*. Washington, D.C.

———. Various issues. *Direction of Trade Statistics*.

———. Various issues. *International Financial Statistics*.

———. Various years. *Balance of Payments Statistics Yearbook*. Parts 1 and 2. Washington, D.C.

———. Various years. *Direction of Trade Statistics Yearbook*. Washington, D.C.

———. Various years. *Government Finance Statistics Yearbook*. Washington, D.C.

———. Various years. *International Financial Statistics Yearbook*. Washington, D.C.

IMF (International Monetary Fund), OECD (Organisation for Economic Co-operation and Development), United Nations, and World Bank. 2000. *A Better World for All: Progress towards the International Development Goals*. Washington, D.C.

International Civil Aviation Organization. 2005. Civil Aviation Statistics of the World database. Montreal.

International Institute for Strategic Studies. 2005. *The Military Balance 2005–2006*. London: Oxford University Press.

International Road Federation. 2005. *World Road Statistics 2005*. Geneva.

International Working Group of External Debt Compilers (Bank for International Settlements, International Monetary Fund, Organisation for Economic Co-operation and Development, and World Bank). 1987. *External Debt Definitions*. Washington, D.C.

Inter-Secretariat Working Group on National Accounts (Commission of the European Communities, International Monetary Fund, Organisation for Economic Co-operation and Development, United Nations, and World Bank). 1993. *System of National Accounts*. Brussels, Luxembourg, New York, and Washington, D.C.

IPCC (Intergovernmental Panel on Climate Change). 2001a. *Climate Change 2001*. Cambridge: Cambridge University Press.

———. 2001b. *Climate Change 2001: The Scientific Basis; Contribution of Working Group I to the Third Assessment Report of the Intergovernmental Panel on Climate Change*. Cambridge: Cambridge University Press.

———. 2001c. *Climate Change 2001: Impacts, Adaptation, and Vulnerability; Contribution of Working Group II to the Third Assessment Report of the Intergovernmental Panel on Climate Change*. Cambridge: Cambridge University Press.

———. 2001d. *Climate Change 2001: Mitigation; Contribution of Working Group II to the Third Assessment Report of the Intergovernmental Panel on Climate Change*. Cambridge: Cambridge University Press.

ITU (International Telecommunication Union). 2005. World Telecommunication Indicators Database. Geneva.

IUCN (World Conservation Union). 1998. *1997 IUCN Red List of Threatened Plants*. Gland, Switzerland.

———. 2000. *2000 IUCN Red List of Threatened Animals*. Gland, Switzerland.

Izaguirre, Ada Karina. 2005. "Private Infrastructure: Emerging Market Sponsors Dominate Private Flows". Public Policy for the Private Sector Note 299. World Bank, Private Sector Development, Washington, D.C.

Joint Learning Initiative. 2004. *Human Resources for Health: Overcoming the Crisis*. Boston, Mass.

Kaufmann, Daniel. 2005. "Click Refresh Button: Investment Climate Reconsidered." *Development Outreach*, March.

Kaufmann, Daniel, Aart Kraay, and Massimo Mastruzzi. 2005. "Governance Matters IV: Governance Indicators for 1996–2004." Policy Research Working Paper 3630. World Bank, Washington, D.C.

Kozak, Marta. 2005. "Micro, Small, and Medium Enterprises: A Collection of Published Data." International Finance Corporation, Washington, D.C.

Kent, Mary M., and Carl Haub. 2005. "The Demographic Divide: What It Is and Why It Matters." Excerpted from the forthcoming Population Reference Bureau's Population Bulletin "The Demographic Divide." Washington, D.C.

Knetter, Michael. 1994. *Why Are Retail Prices in Japan So High? Evidence from German Export Prices.* NBER Working Paper 4894. Cambridge, Mass.: National Bureau of Economic Research.

Kunte, Arundhati, Kirk Hamilton, John Dixon, and Michael Clemens. 1998. "Estimating National Wealth: Methodology and Results." Environmental Economics Series 57. World Bank, Environment Department, Washington, D.C.

Lanjouw, Jean O., and Peter Lanjouw. 2001. "The Rural Non-Farm Sector: Issues and Evidence from Developing Countries." *Agricultural Economics* 26 (1): 1–23.

Lanjouw, Peter, and Gershon Feder. 2001. "Rural Nonfarm Activities and Rural Development: From Experience toward Strategy." Rural Strategy Discussion Paper 4. World Bank, Washington, D.C.

Lewis, Karen K. 1995. "Puzzles in International Financial Markets." In Gene Grossman and Kenneth Rogoff, eds., *Handbook of International Economics.* Vol. 3. Amsterdam: North Holland.

Lewis, Stephen R., Jr. 1989. "Primary Exporting Countries." In Hollis Chenery and T. N. Srinivasan, eds., *Handbook of Development Economics.* Vol. 2. Amsterdam: North Holland.

Lovei, Magdolna. 1997. "Toward Effective Pollution Management." *Environment Matters* (Fall): 52–53.

Lucas, R. E. 1988. "On the Mechanics of Economic Development." *Journal of Monetary Economics* 22: 3–42.

Mani, Muthukumara, and David Wheeler. 1997. "In Search of Pollution Havens? Dirty Industry in the World Economy, 1960–95." World Bank, Policy Research Department, Washington, D.C.

McCarthy, F. Desmond, and Holger Wolf. 2001. "Comparative Life Expectancy in Africa." Policy Research Working Paper 2668. World Bank, Development Research Group, Washington, D.C.

McCay, J., M. Erkson, and O. Shafey. 2006. *Tobacco Atlas.* 2nd ed. Atlanta, Ga.: American Cancer Society.

Midgley, Peter. 1994. "Urban Transport in Asia: An Operational Agenda for the 1990s." Technical Paper 224. World Bank, Washington, D.C.

Morgenstern, Oskar. 1963. *On the Accuracy of Economic Observations.* Princeton, N.J.: Princeton University Press.

Morisset, Jacques. 2000. "Foreign Direct Investment in Africa: Policies Also Matter" Policy Research Working Paper 2481. World Bank, Washington D.C.

National Science Board. 2004. *Science and Engineering Indicators 2004.* Arlington, Va.: National Science Foundation.

Netcraft. 2005. "Netcraft Secure Server Survey." [www.netcraft.com/].

Newfarmer, Richard, ed. 2006. *Trade, Doha, and Development: A Window into the Issues.* Washington, D.C.: World Bank.

NRI (National Research Institute) and World Bank. 2003. "Public Expenditure and Service Delivery in Papua New Guinea: Draft." Washington, D.C.

Obstfeldt, Maurice. 1995. "International Capital Mobility in the 1990s." In P. B. Kenen, ed., *Understanding Interdependence: The Macroeconomics of the Open Economy.* Princeton, N.J.: Princeton University Press.

Obstfeldt, Maurice, and Kenneth Rogoff 1996. *Foundations of International Macroeconomics.* Cambridge, Mass.: MIT Press.

OECD (Organisation for Economic Co-operation and Development). 1985. *Measuring Health Care 1960–1983: Expenditure, Costs, Performance.* Paris.

———. 1996. *Trade, Employment, and Labour Standards: A Study of Core Workers' Rights and International Trade.* Paris.

———. 1997. *Employment Outlook.* Paris.

———. 2003. *Agricultural Policies in OECD Countries: Monitoring and Evaluation 2003.* Paris

———. Various issues. *Main Economic Indicators.* Paris.

———. Various years. *International Development Statistics.* CD-ROM. Paris

———. Various years. *National Accounts.* Vol. 1, Main Aggregates. Paris

———. Various years. *National Accounts.* Vol. 2, Detailed Tables. Paris.

———. Various years. *Trends in International Migration: Continuous Reporting System on Migration.* Paris

OECD (Organisation for Economic Co-operation and Development) DAC (Development Assistance Committee). Various years. *Development Cooperation Report.* Paris

———. Various years. *Geographical Distribution of Financial Flows to Aid Recipients: Disbursements, Commitments, Country Indicators.* Paris

OECD Journal on Development. 2006. *Development Co-operation Report 2005: Efforts and Policies of the Members of the Development Assistance Committee.* Volume 7, issue 1.

O'Meara, Molly. 1999. "Reinventing Cities for People and the Planet." Worldwatch Paper 147. Worldwatch Institute, Washington, D.C.

Özden, Çaglar, and Maurice Schiff, eds. 2005. *International Migration, Remittances, and the Brain Drain.* New York: Palgrave Macmillan.

Palacios, Robert, and Montserrat Pallares-Miralles. 2000. "International Patterns of Pension Provision." Social Protection Discussion Paper 0009. World Bank, Human Development Network, Washington, D.C.

Pandey, Kiran Dev, Katharine Bolt, Uwe Deichmann, Kirk Hamilton, Bart Ostro, and David Wheeler. 2003. "The Human Cost of Air Pollution: New Estimates for Developing Countries." World Bank, Development Research Group and Environment Department, Washington, D.C.

BIBLIOGRAPHY

Pearce, David, and Giles Atkinson. 1993. "Capital Theory and the Measurement of Sustainable Development: An Indicator of Weak Sustainability." *Ecological Economics* 8 (2): 103–08.

Pilling, David. 1999. "In Sickness and in Wealth." *Financial Times*, October 22.

Plucknett, Donald L. 1991. "Saving Lives through Agricultural Research." Issues in Agriculture 16. World Bank, Consultative Group on International Agricultural Research, Washington, D.C.

PricewaterhouseCoopers. 2004a. *Corporate Taxes 2004–2005: Worldwide Summaries.* New York.

———. 2004b. *Individual Taxes 2004–2005: Worldwide Summaries.* New York.

Rama, Martin, and Raquel Artecona. 2002. "A Database of Labor Market Indicators across Countries." World Bank, Development Research Group, Washington, D.C.

Ravallion, Martin, and Shaohua Chen. 1996. "What Can New Survey Data Tell Us about the Recent Changes in Living Standards in Developing and Transitional Economies?" World Bank, Policy Research Department, Washington, D.C.

Rodrik, Dani. 1996. "Labor Standards in International Trade: Do They Matter and What Do We Do About Them?" Overseas Development Council, Washington, D.C.

Rodrik, Dani, and Arvind Subramanian. 2003. "The Primacy of Institutions (and What This Does and Does Not Mean)." *Finance & Development* 40 (2): 31–34.

Romer, P. M. 1986. "Increasing Returns and Long-Run Growth." *Journal of Political Economy* 94 (5): 1002–37.

Ruggles, Robert. 1994. "Issues Relating to the UN System of National Accounts and Developing Countries." *Journal of Development Economics* 44 (1): 77–85.

Ryten, Jacob. 1998. "Fifty Years of ISIC: Historical Origins and Future Perspectives." ECA/STAT.AC. 63/22. United Nations, Statistics Division, New York.

Saghir, Jamal. 2005. "Energy and Poverty: Myths, Links, and Policy Issues. Energy Working Notes 4. World Bank, Washington, D.C.

Sala-i-Martin, Xavier. 2002. *The Disturbing "Rise" in Global Income Inequality.* NBER Working Paper 8904. Cambridge, Mass.: National Bureau of Economic Research.

Salomon, Joshua A., Daniel R. Hogan, John Stover, Karen A. Stanecki, Neff Walker, Peter D. Ghys, and Bernhard Schwartländer. 2005. "Integrating HIV Prevention and Treatment: From Slogans to Impact." *PLoS Medicine* 2 (1): e16.

Shiklovanov, Igor. 1993. "World Fresh Water Resources." In Peter H. Gleick, ed., *Water in Crisis: A Guide to Fresh Water Resources.* New York: Oxford University Press.

SIPRI (Stockholm International Peace Research Institute). 2005. SIPRI Yearbook 2005: Armaments, Disarmament, and International Security. Oxford: Oxford University Press

Smith, Lisa, and Laurence Haddad. 2000. "Overcoming Child Malnutrition in Developing Countries: Past Achievements and Future Choices." 2020 Brief 64. International Food Policy Research Institute, Washington, D.C.

Srinivasan, T. N. 1994a. "Database for Development Analysis: An Overview." *Journal of Development Economics* 44 (1): 3–28.

———. ed. 1994b. Special Issue on Database for Development Analysis. *Journal of Development Economics* 44 (1).

Standard & Poor's. 2000. *The S&P Emerging Market Indices: Methodology, Definitions, and Practices.* New York.

———. 2005. *Global Stock Markets Factbook 2005.* New York.

Tarmann, Allison. 2002. Response to Hunger Tests New Priorities. *Population Today,* November/December 2001.

Taylor, Alan M. 1996a. *International Capital Mobility in History: Purchasing Power Parity in the Long Run.* NBER Working Paper 5742. Cambridge, Mass.: National Bureau of Economic Research.

———. 1996b. *International Capital Mobility in History: The Saving-Investment Relationship.* NBER Working Paper 5743. Cambridge, Mass.: National Bureau of Economic Research.

UNACC/SCN (United Nations Administrative Committee on Coordination, Subcommittee on Nutrition). Various years. *Update on the Nutrition Situation.* Geneva.

UNAIDS (Joint United Nations Programme on HIV/AIDS) and WHO (World Health Organization). 2005. *AIDS Epidemic Update: December 2005.* Geneva.

———. Various years. *Report on the Global AIDS Epidemic.* Geneva.

UNCTAD (United Nations Conference on Trade and Development). 2003. *The Least Developed Countries Report.* Geneva

———. Various years. *Handbook of Statistics.* Geneva.

UNEP (United Nations Environment Programme). 1991. *Urban Air Pollution.* Nairobi.

UNESCO (United Nations Educational, Scientific, and Cultural Organization). 1997. *International Standard Classification of Education.* Paris

———. 2005. *Literacy for Life.* Paris.

———. 2006. *EFA Global Monitoring Report.* Paris.

UNESCO (United Nations Educational, Scientific, and Cultural Organization) Institute for Statistics. Various Years. *Global Education Digest.* Paris.

UNESCWA (United Nations Economic and Social Commission for Western Asia). 1997. "Purchasing Power Parities: Volume and Price Level Comparisons for the Middle East, 1993." E/ESCWA/STAT/1997/2. Amman, Jordan.

UNFCCC (United Nations Framework Convention on Climate Change). 2005. "Kyoto Protocol to the United Nations Framework Convention on Climate Change." Bonn, Germany.

UNFPA (United Nations Population Fund). 2005. *State of World Population.* New York.

UN-HABITAT (United Nations Human Settlements Programme). 2003. *Global Report on Human Settlements.* Nairobi.

UNHCR (United Nations High Commissioner for Refugees). 2005. *Statistical Yearbook 2003.* Geneva.

UNICEF (United Nations Children's Fund). Various years. *The State of the World's Children*. New York: Oxford University Press.

UNIDO (United Nations Industrial Development Organization). Various years. *International Yearbook of Industrial Statistics*. Vienna.

United Nations. 1947. *Measurement of National Income and the Construction of Social Accounts*. New York.

———. 1968. "A System of National Accounts: Studies and Methods." Series F, no. 2, rev. 3. New York.

———. 1990. "International Standard Industrial Classification of All Economic Activities, Third Revision." Statistical Papers Series M, no. 4, rev. 3. New York.

———. 1992. "Handbook of the International Comparison Programme." Studies in Methods Series F, no. 62. New York.

———. 1993. "SNA Handbook on Integrated Environmental and Economic Accounting." Series F, no. 61. Statistical Office, New York.

———. 1999. "Integrated Environmental and Economic Accounting: An Operational Manual." Studies in Methods Series F, no. 78. New York.

———. 2000. *We the Peoples: The Role of the United Nations in the 21st Century*. New York.

———. 2004. "Trends in Total Migrant Stock: The 2003 Revision." POP/DB/MIG/Rev.2003. Department of Economic and Social Affairs, New York.

———. 2005a. "The Energy Challenge for Achieving the Millennium Development Goals." New York.

———. 2005b. *The Millennium Development Goals Report*. New York.

United Nations Millennium Project. 2005. *Taking Action: Achieving Gender Equality and Empowering Women*. Task Force on Education and Gender Equality. London: Earthscan.

United Nations Population Division. 2002. *International Migration Report 2002*. New York.

———. 2003. *World Population Prospects: The 2004 Revision*. POP/DB/WPP/Rev. 2004/1/F10. Department of Economic and Social Affairs, New York.

———. 2004. *World Urbanization Prospects: The 2003 Revision*. New York.

———. 2005. *World Population Prospects: The 2004 Revision Highlights*. ESA/P/WP.193. Department of Economic and Social Affairs, New York

———. Various years. *Levels and Trends of Contraceptive Use*. New York.

United Nations Statistics Division. 1985. *National Accounts Statistics: Compendium of Income Distribution Statistics*. New York.

———. Various issues. *Monthly Bulletin of Statistics*. New York.

———. Various years. *Energy Statistics Yearbook*. New York.

———. Various years. *International Trade Statistics Yearbook*. New York

———. Various years. *National Accounts Statistics: Main Aggregates and Detailed Tables*. Parts 1 and 2. New York.

———. Various years. *National Income Accounts*. New York.

———. Various years. *Population and Vital Statistics Report*. New York.

———. Various years. *Statistical Yearbook*. New York

U.S. Environmental Protection Agency. 1995. *National Air Quality and Emissions Trends Report 1995*. Washington, D.C.

Walsh, Michael P. 1994. "Motor Vehicle Pollution Control: An Increasingly Critical Issue for Developing Countries." World Bank, Washington, D.C.

Watson, Robert, John A. Dixon, Steven P. Hamburg, Anthony C. Janetos, and Richard H. Moss. 1998. *Protecting Our Planet, Securing Our Future: Linkages among Global Environmental Issues and Human Needs*. Nairobi and Washington, D.C.: United Nations Environment Programme, U.S. National Aeronautics and Space Administration, and World Bank.

WHO (World Health Organization). 1983. *International Classification of Diseases*. 10th rev. Geneva.

———. 1997. "Coverage of Maternity Care." Geneva.

———. 1999. *World Health Report 1999: Making a Difference*. Geneva

———. 2004a. *Beyond the Numbers: Reviewing Maternal Deaths and Complications to Make Pregnancy Safer*. Geneva.

———. 2004b. *Tobacco Control Country Profiles 2003*. Geneva.

———. 2004c. *World Report on Road Traffic Injury Prevention*. Geneva.

———. 2006. *Global Atlas of the Health Work Force*. Geneva.

———. Various years. *Global Tuberculosis Control Report*. Geneva.

———. Various years. *World Health Report*. Geneva.

WHO (World Health Organization) and UNICEF (United Nations Children's Fund). 2003. *The Africa Malaria Report 2003*. Geneva.

———. 2004. *Meeting the MDG Drinking Water and Sanitation Target: A Mid-term Assessment of Progress*. Geneva.

WIPO (World Intellectual Property Organization). 2004. *Industrial Property Statistics*. Geneva.

WITSA (World Information Technology and Services Alliance). 2004. "Digital Planet 2004: The Global Information Economy." Vienna, Va.

Wolf, Holger C. 1997. *Patterns of Intra- and Inter-State Trade*. NBER Working Paper 5939. Cambridge, Mass.: National Bureau of Economic Research.

World Bank. 1990. *World Development Report 1990: Poverty*. New York: Oxford University Pres

———. 1992. *World Development Report 1992: Development and the Environment*. New York: Oxford University Press.

———. 1995. "China's GDP in U.S. Dollars, Based on Purchasing Power Parity." Policy Research Working Paper 1415. Washington, D.C.

———. 1996a. *Environment Matters* (summer). Environment Department, Washington, D.C.

———. 1996b. "Livable Cities for the 21st Century: A Directions in Development book." Washington, D.C.

———. 1996c. "National Environmental Strategies: Learning from Experience." Environment Department, Washington, D.

———. 1997a. *Can the Environment Wait? Priorities for East Asia*. Washington, D.C.

BIBLIOGRAPHY

———. 1997b. "Expanding the Measure of Wealth: Indicators of Environmentally Sustainable Development." Environmentally Sustainable Development Studies and Monographs Series, no. 17. Washington, D.C.

———. 1997c. "Rural Development: From Vision to Action." Environmentally Sustainable Development Studies and Monographs Series, no. 12. Washington, D.C.

———. 1999a. "Fuel for Thought: Environmental Strategy for the Energy Sector." Environment Department, Energy, Mining, and Telecommunications Department and International Finance Corporation, Washington, D.C.

———. 1999b. *Greening Industry: New Roles for Communities, Markets, and Governments.* New York: Oxford University Press.

———. 2000a. *Trade Blocs.* New York: Oxford University Press.

———. 2000b. *World Development Report 2000/2001: Attacking Poverty.* New York: Oxford University Press.

———. 2001. *World Development Report 2002: Building Institutions for Markets.* New York: Oxford University Press.

———. 2002a. *A Case for Aid: Building a Consensus for Development Assistance.* Washington, D.C.

———. 2002b. "The Environment and the Millennium Development Goals." Washington, D.C.

———. 2002c. "Financial Impact of the HIPC Initiative: First 24 Country Cases." Washington, D.C.

———. 2002d. *Globalization, Growth, and Poverty: Building an Inclusive World Economy.* New York: Oxford University Press.

———. 2003a. "The Millennium Development Goals for Health: Rising to the Challenges." Washington, D.C.

———. 2003b. *World Bank Atlas.* Washington, D.C.

———. 2003c. *World Development Report 2004: Making Services Work for the Poor.* New York: Oxford University Press.

———. 2004a. "Competing in the Global Economy: An Investment Climate Assessment for Uganda." Investment Climate Assessment. Washington, D.C.

———. 2004b. "Measuring Results: Improving National Statistics in IDA Countries." International Development Association, Washington, D.C. [http://siteresources.worldbank.org/IDA/Resources/MeasuringResultsStatistics.pdf].

———. 2004c. *Partnerships in Development: Progress in the Fight against Poverty.* Washington, D.C.

———. 2004d. *Private Participation in Infrastructure Project Database.* [http://ppi.worldbank.org/].

———. 2004e. *Reforming Infrastructure: Privatization, Regulation, and Competition.* New York: Oxford University Press.

———. 2004f. *World Bank Atlas.* Washington, D.C.

———. 2004g. *World Development Report 2005: A Better Investment Climate for Everyone.* New York: Oxford University Press.

———. 2005a. *Building Effective States: Forging Engaged Societies; Report of the World Bank Task Force on Capacity Development in Africa.* Washington, D.C.

———. 2005b. "Financing Africa's Infrastructure Needs: Experts Tackle Challenge." 1818 Society News, June 9.

———. 2005c. "Meeting the Challenge of Africa's Development: A World Bank Group Action Plan." Africa Region, World Bank, Washington, D.C.

———. 2005d. *World Development Report 2006: Equity and Development.* New York: Oxford University Press.

———. 2005e. *Rolling Back Malaria: The World Bank Global Strategy and Booster Program.* Washington, D.C.

———. 2006a. *Doing Business in 2006: Creating Jobs.* Washington, D.C.

———. 2006b. "Investment Climate Surveys Online." [http://iresearch.worldbank.org/ics/jsp/index.jsp].

———. Various issues. *Global Commodity Markets.*

———. Various years. *Global Development Finance.* Washington, D.C.

———. Various years. *Global Economic Prospects and the Developing Countries.* Washington, D.C.

———. Various years. *World Development Indicators.* Washington, D.C.

World Bank and International Monetary Fund. 2005. *Global Monitoring Report 2005: Millennium Development Goals; From Consensus to Momentum.* Washington, D.C.

World Energy Council. 1995. *Global Energy Perspectives to 2050 and Beyond.* London.

World Resources Institute, UNEP (United Nations Environment Programme), UNDP (United Nations Development Programme), and World Bank. Various years. *World Resources: A Guide to the Global Environment.* New York: Oxford University Press.

World Tourism Organization. 2002a. *Compendium of Tourism Statistics 2002.* Madrid.

———. 2002b. *Yearbook of Tourism Statistics.* Vols. 1 and 2. Madrid.

WTO (World Trade Organization). Various years. *Annual Report.* Geneva.

INDEX OF INDICATORS

References are to table numbers.

INDEX OF INDICATORS

D

E

INDEX OF INDICATORS

G

INDEX OF INDICATORS

I

INDEX OF INDICATORS

N

INDEX OF INDICATORS

R

INDEX OF INDICATORS

S

T

INDEX OF INDICATORS